W9-CCH-026

THE

EPISTLE OF ST. JAMES

THE GREEK TEXT

WITH

INTRODUCTION NOTES AND COMMENTS

BY

JOSEPH B. MAYOR, M.A. Camb., Litt.D. Dubl.

SECOND EDITION

BAKER BOOK HOUSE
Grand Rapids, Michigan

Reprinted 1978 from the 1897 edition

ISBN: 0-8010-6073-7

PHOTOLITHOPRINTED BY CUSHING - MALLOY, INC.
ANN ARBOR, MICHIGAN, UNITED STATES OF AMERICA
1978

VIRO REVERENDO

F. J. A. HORT, S.T.P.

SACRI TEXTUS AD PRISTINAM FORMAM REVOCANDI

DILIGENTISSIMO PERITISSIMOQUE AUCTORI

HAEC QUALIACUMQUE STUDIA

QUAE UTINAM DIFFICILLIMAE EPISTULAE LECTORIBUS

SPLENDIDIOREM LUCEM EDITIONIS HORTIANAE IAM DUDUM DESIDERANTIBUS

ALIQUID SALTEM LUCIS AFFERRE POSSINT

A VETERE AMICO ET CONDISCIPULO

Dedicantur

PREFACE TO THE FIRST EDITION

In writing my Preface I bring to a close a work which has for some years been my chief occupation, and which has indeed been seldom out of my thoughts since the time when, as an undergraduate, I first made acquaintance with Coleridge's Aids to Reflection, *and was led in consequence to study with some care the Epistle of St. James, to which reference is made in the earlier Aphorisms of that book.*

In the Introduction I have stated my reasons for believing this Epistle to be the earliest of the books of the New Testament, written probably in the fifth decade of the Christian era by one who had been brought up with Jesus from his childhood and whose teaching is in many points identical with the actual words of our Lord as recorded in the Synoptic Gospels. If I am not mistaken, it presents to us a picture of pre-Pauline Christianity, which is not only interesting historically, but is likely to be of special value in an age of religious doubt and anxiety like the present. Amongst those to whom the formulas of later Christianity have lost or are losing their significance, there must be many who will find a message suited to them in the language of this, the least technical of all the Epistles, many who will appreciate the strong practical sense and earnest philanthropy of St. James, and take to heart his warnings against unreal professions of whatever kind. In its plain positive teaching his Epistle affords a common platform for Christians of every degree of attainment, from which they may advance again with new hope to such further developments of the faith, as it may be given to each from above to receive and to profit by.

The eighth and ninth Chapters of the Introduction deal with the Grammar and Style of the Epistle, and, in some degree, with those of the New Testament writers generally. As a corollary to these, I have, in the tenth Chapter, pointed out some objections to the hypothesis which has been lately revived amongst us, that the Greek is a translation from an Aramaic original.

As regards the Text I have been almost entirely dependent on the labours of others, especially those of Tischendorf, Bishop Westcott and Dr. Hort. In the very rare cases in which I have ventured to depart from a reading of WH., I have carefully explained my reasons for doing so in the Notes. The comparison of three Latin Versions of the Epistle, and the collations of the Codex Patiriensis and Codex Bobiensis will, I hope, be found useful by those who are interested in textual criticism.

In the Notes it has been my aim, treating the book like any other ancient writing, to ascertain the precise meaning of each sentence, phrase, and word, as it was intended by the writer, and understood by those to whom his Epistle was addressed. The names of previous annotators, to whom I am indebted, will be found in the eleventh Chapter of the Introduction. In the Comments which follow I have in the first place viewed the Epistle more as a whole, tracing the general connexion of ideas and illustrating and discussing the wider questions involved: and, in the second place, regarding it as an integral portion of the canonical Scriptures, which are recognised by all Christians as authoritative in matters of faith, I have to some small extent endeavoured to show in what sense its teaching is to be understood by us now, and how it is to be applied to the circumstances of modern life.

It only remains for me to acknowledge with hearty thanks the assistance I have received from friends who have looked through portions of the proof-sheets especially to Dr. E. A. Abbott (A), the Rev. G. H. Gwilliam (G.H.G.) Prof. Sanday (S) and Dr. Charles Taylor, Master of St. John's College, Cambridge (C.T.), whose initials are appended to notes communicated by them.

October 24, 1892.

PREFACE TO THE SECOND EDITION

The Second Edition has been revised throughout and enlarged by nearly fifty pages, the greater part of which (pp. cliv—clxxviii) is occupied with an examination of the theories of Harnack and Spitta as to the date of the Epistle. The substance of these pages is contained in two articles which appeared in the Expositor for May and July 1897.[1]

July 16, 1897.

[1] In an important work which has just appeared (*Einleitung in d. N. T.* pp. 52–108), Dr. Zahn upholds the early date and the genuineness of the Epistle, and criticizes the theories of Harnack and Spitta.

ADDENDA ET CORRIGENDA

P. vi.—A friend sends the following note. ‘Donne in his 2nd sermon on the Nativity, speaking of the heresies which had been put forward on the subject, refers to Helvidius in the words “and Helvidius said, she had children after.” Coleridge (*Notes on English Divines*, i. 74, ed. 1853) remarks on this “*Annon Scriptura ipsa*? And a *heresy* too”!’

P. xvii.—With this use of εἰ μή may be compared the use of ἀλλ’ ἤ in Deut. iv. 12 ὁμοίωμα οὐκ εἴδετε ἀλλ’ ἢ φωνήν, Arist. *Pax.* 475 οὐδ’ οἵδε δ’ εἷλκον οὐδὲν ἀργεῖοι πάλαι ἀλλ’ ἢ κατεγέλων τῶν ταλαιπωρουμένων.

P. xlix. l. 23.—For *Apocalypse* read *Apocalapse.*

P. lxiii.—After l. 6 insert the seeming references to our Epistle to be found in the Testament of Job (*Texts and Studies* v. 1), which Dr. James considers to be a Greek paraphrase of a Hebrew Midrash on Job, the paraphrase being the work of a Christian living in Egypt in the 2nd or 3rd century. It exists in two forms, one of which (M) was printed by Mai in 1833, probably from a Vatican MS., the other by Dr. James from a Paris MS. (P) in 1897. The following resemblances to our Epistle have been pointed out by the editor: c. iv. ἐὰν ὑπομείνῃς ποιήσω σου τὸ ὄνομα ὀνομαστόν...ἵνα γνῷς ὅτι ἀπροσωπόληπτός ἐστιν...καὶ ἐγερθήσῃ ἐν τῇ ἀναστάσει [M. adds εἰς ζῳὴν αἰώνιον·] ἔσῃ γὰρ ὡς ἀθλητὴς πυκτεύων καὶ καρτερῶν πόνους [M. reads πειρασμούς] καὶ ἐκδεχόμενος τὸν στέφανον: cf. James i. 2, 4, 12, ii. 1, v. 7, 11. c. xii. (M) οὐκ ὑστέρησά ποτε μισθὸν μισθωτοῦ ἢ ἄλλου τινὸς ἢ ἀφῆκα τὸν μισθὸν αὐτοῦ ἐσόμενον παρ’ ἐμοὶ μίαν ἑσπέραν ἐν τῇ οἰκίᾳ μου: cf. James v. 4. c. xv. (a quotation from Sirach x. 7) βδέλυγμα ἐστιν ἐναντίον τοῦ θεοῦ ἡ ὑπερηφανία: James iv. 6. c. xxvi. μακροθυμήσωμεν ἕως ἂν ὁ κύριος σπλαγχνισθεὶς ἐλεήσῃ ἡμᾶς, cf. also xxvii.: James v. 7. c. xxxiii. ὁ κόσμος ὅλος παρελεύσεται καὶ ἡ δόξα αὐτοῦ φθαρήσεται...ἐμοὶ δὲ ὁ θρόνος ὑπάρχει ἐν τῇ ἁγίᾳ γῇ καὶ ἡ δόξα αὐτοῦ ἐν τῷ αἰῶνί ἐστιν τοῦ ἀπαραλλάκτου [M. τῷ, -κτῳ]...οὗτοι οἱ βασιλεῖς παρελεύσονται...ἡ δὲ δὸξα καὶ τὸ καύχημα αὐτῶν ἔσονται ὡς ἔσοπτρον· ἐμοὶ δὲ ἡ βασιλεία εἰς αἰῶνας αἰώνων καὶ ἡ δόξα καὶ εὐπρέπεια αὐτῆς ἐν τοῖς ἅρμασιν τοῦ πατρὸς ὑπάρχει: James i. 10, 11, 9, 23, 12, ii. 5, iv. 14. c. xxxvi. ἐν τοῖς γηίνοις οὐ συνέστηκεν (ἡ καρδία μου) ἐπεὶ ἀκατάστατος ἡ γῆ...ἐν δὲ τοῖς ἐπουρανίοις συνέστηκεν: James i. 8.

P. 30, l. 22.—For ‘Hermes’ read Hermas.

P. 32, l. 8.—Read Acts v. 41. πειρασμοῖς, Spitta cites Judith viii. 25 παρὰ ταῦτα πάντα εὐχαριστήσωμεν Κυρίῳ τῷ Θεῷ ἡμῶν ὃς πειράζει ἡμᾶς καθὰ καὶ τοὺς πατέρας ἡμῶν, *Test. Jos.* 2 ἐν δέκα πειρασμοῖς δόκιμόν με ἀνέδειξεν καὶ ἐν πᾶσιν αὐτοῖς ἐμακροθύμησα, ὅτι...πολλὰ ἀγαθὰ δίδωσιν ἡ ὑπομονή, 1 Macc. ii. 52 ’Αβραὰμ οὐκ ἐν πειρασμῷ εὑρέθη πιστός;

P. 33.—For δοκίμιον, cf. Plato, *Tim.* 65 C ὅσα μὲν γὰρ εἰσίοντα περὶ τὰ φλέβια, οἱόνπερ δοκίμια τῆς γλώσσης τεταμένα ἐπὶ τὴν καρδίαν κ.τ.λ.

P. 35, last line but 7.—Read 1 Cor. i. 7. Spitta cites *Test. Abr.* p. 93 τί ἔτι λείπεται τῇ ψυχῇ εἰς τὸ σώζεσθαι;

P. 41, l. 15.—Add Orig. *Princip.* p. 162 διψυχίαν ἀποθέμενος.

P. 42.—ἀκατάστατος, see *Test. Jobi* c. xxxvi. cited in *Addenda* to p. lxiii.

P. 44.—παρελεύσεται, see *Test. Jobi* c. xxxiii. cited above on p. lxiii.

P. 45.—ἐξέπεσε, cf. Job. xv. 30 τὸν βλαστόν αὐτοῦ μαράναι ἄνεμος ἐκπέσοι δὲ αὐτοῦ τὸ ἄνθος. εὐπρέπεια, Herm. *Vis.* i. 3, 4

P. 46.—στέφανον, see above *Test. Jobi* iv.

P. 48.—ἀπὸ θεοῦ πειράζομαι, cf. Herm. *Sim.* vi. 3, 5.

P. 49.—Cf. *Acta Johannis* ed. James p. 6 σὸν λοιπὸν ἔστω μὴ πειράζειν τὸν ἀπείραστον.

P. 56.—Note on πατρὸς τῶν φώτων, for Wisdom vii. 16 read 'vii. 26.' Add *Test. Abr.* ed. James p. 37 (of the Archangel Michael) 'He is the father of all lights' (πατὴρ τοῦ φωτός in the Greek, *ib.* p. 111). Last line but 4, for Job. xxviii. read xxxviii.

P. 57.—παραλλαγή, cf. *Test. Jobi* xxxiii. cited above.

P. 60, last line.—Read νόμου.

P. 61, l. 4.—For Rom. i. 3 read i. 11. On the use of εἰς τό in Rom. i. 20, and vii. 4, 5, Burton (*Moods and Tenses*, § 411) agrees with the view given in the text, but Gifford and Sanday in their notes understand it of purpose.

P. 62.—βραδὺς εἰς ὀργήν, the opposite of ὀξυκολία in Herm. *Mand.* v. 1, 3, 6, x. 1.

P. 68.—ἐν ἐσόπτρῳ, cf. *Acta Johannis* ed. James p. 12 ἔσοπτρόν εἰμί σοι τῷ νοοῦντι με, and *Test. Jobi* xxxiii. cited above.

P. 73.—χαλιναγωγῶν, read for 'Philo M. 1, p. 6,' 'p. 680.'

P. 75.—Add *Test. Jobi* iv. cited above, and xliii. κύριος παρ' ᾧ οὐκ ἔστιν προσωποληψία, also *Const. Apost.* vii. 31.

P. 84, last line but 13.—For 'Matt. x. 7' read 'x. 17.'

P. 89.—πάντων ἔνοχος, cf. Clem. Hom. 13, 14 εἰ πάντα καλὰ διαπράξαιτό τις, μιᾷ τῇ πρὸς τὸ μοιχήσασθαι ἁμαρτίᾳ κολασθῆναι δεῖν ὁ προφήτης ἔφη.

P. 91.—ἀνέλεος is found in *Test. Abr.* § 16, as also ἀνιλέως and ἀνηλέης in § 12 (ed. James p. 91, 96).

P. 95.—On χορτάζεσθε *ad fin.* cf. Philo M. 1, p. 137 χόρτος ἀλόγου τροφή ἐστιν.

P. 104, *v.* 2.—πταίομεν, cf. *Test. Jobi* xxxviii. ὅλως ἂν πταίσῃ μου τὸ στόμα εἰς τὸν δεσπότην.

v. 3.—The suggestion that εἰ δέ is merely an itacistic corruption of ἴδε, receives strong confirmation from the fact that there are no less than three examples of similar corruption in the few lines of the newly discovered Logia, in a MS. considerably older than B, and therefore approaching more nearly to the date of its archetype.

P. 107.—ἐλαχίστου, cf. Blass *Gr.* p. 33 on the use of the superlative in later Greek.

P. 108, l. 15.—Read 'metonymy.'

P. 112.—τὸν τροχὸν τῆς γενέσεως. I am indebted to Dr. Gifford for the following illustrations of this strange phrase: Herod. i. 207 κύκλος τῶν ἀνθρωπηΐων ἐστὶ πρηγμάτων, Plat. *Politic.* 271 B ξυνανακυκλουμένης εἰς τἀναντία τῆς γενέσεως, Arist. *Probl.* xvii. καθάπερ καὶ φασὶ κύκλον εἶναι τὰ ἀνθρώπινα, Orphic. *Fr.* vi. 17 ἓν δὲ δέμας βασίλειον ἐν ᾧ τάδε πάντα τελεῖται.

P. 137, l. 20.—For 'Eccl. xii. 12' read 'xii. 7.' Dr. Gifford writes to me 'It seems more natural to understand as the subject ὁ Θεός (the *jealous* God being the dominant idea of the context both before and after), than to leave ἐπιποθεῖ without an object.' I think there is much force in this.

P. 146.—πρὸς ὀλίγον, cf. Plut. *Mor.* 116 A πρὸς ὀλίγον ἔχρησαν, Lucian *Nigr.* 23; so πρὸς ὥραν Joh. v. 35, 2 Cor. vii. 8, πρὸς καιρόν Luke viii. 13.

P. 152.—ὁ ἀφυστερημένος, cf. *Test. Jobi* xii. cited above.

P. 155.—μακροθυμήσατε, cf. *Test. Jobi* xxvi. cited above.

P. 180.—On v. 20 Harnack (*Text. u. Unters.* vii. 2 p. 22) cites *Pistis Sophia* p. 265 'Qui vivicaverit ψυχὴν unam et servaverit eam, χωρὶς gloriae quam habet in regno luminis, accipiet aliam gloriam loco ψυχῆς quam servavit.' B. Weiss reads with B σώσει ψυχὴν ἐκ θανάτου αὐτοῦ, but must we not then have had αὐτῆς to suit ψυχήν?

TABLE OF CONTENTS

INTRODUCTION

CHAPTER I

THE AUTHOR

CHAPTER II

EXTERNAL EVIDENCE FOR THE AUTHENTICITY OF THE EPISTLE

TABLE OF CONTENTS

CHAPTER III

RELATION OF THE EPISTLE TO EARLIER WRITINGS

CHAPTER IV

RELATION OF THE EPISTLE TO THE OTHER BOOKS OF THE NEW TESTAMENT

CHAPTER V

CHAPTER VI

PERSONS TO WHOM THE EPISTLE IS ADDRESSED AND PLACE FROM WHICH IT IS WRITTEN

CHAPTER VII. PART I

ON THE DATE OF THE EPISTLE

CHAPTER VII. PART II

HARNACK AND SPITTA ON THE DATE OF THE EPISTLE

CHAPTER VIII

ON THE GRAMMAR OF ST. JAMES

CHAPTER IX

ON THE STYLE OF ST. JAMES

CHAPTER X

DID ST. JAMES WRITE IN GREEK OR IN ARAMAIC?

TABLE OF CONTENTS

CHAPTER XI

CHAPTER XII

TEXT OF ST. JAMES

CHAPTER I

The Author

The writer calls himself 'Jacob' (from which our name 'James' is derived through the Italian 'Giacomo'), and describes himself as 'a servant of God and of the Lord Jesus Christ.' As the name was very common in the first century, and the description is one which is applicable to all Christians, it is evident that he must have been distinguished from other Jacobs by position or character, so as to justify him in addressing the 'Twelve Tribes in the Dispersion' with the tone of authority which is so marked a feature in the Epistle before us. This inference receives support from the Epistle of Jude, the writer of which styles himself 'servant of Jesus Christ and brother of Jacob,' evidently assuming that his brother's name would carry weight with those whom he addresses.

Internal Evidence. The writer speaks with authority,

The Epistle of Jacob, or James, is strongly contrasted not only with the Epistles to the Romans and Galatians, against which some have supposed it to be directed, but also with the First Epistle of St. Peter, which in some points it closely resembles. The general characteristic by which it is distinguished from these Epistles is its Jewish tone of thought, style and doctrine. In style it reminds one now of the Proverbs, now of the stern denunciations of the prophets, now of the parables in the Gospels. It has scarcely any direct reference to Christ, who is indeed only named twice.[1] In commending the duty of patience (v. 7–11), the writer refers, with the Psalmist (cxxvi. 6), to the example of the husbandman, and to Job and the prophets of the Old Testament: if he alludes to our Lord at all, he only does so obscurely in ver. 6 'ye killed the just; he doth not resist you';

and in the tone of the Old Testament rather than of the New.

[1] i. 1, ii. 1.

while St. Peter on the contrary dwells exclusively on the example of Christ (cf. 1 Pet. ii. 19–24, iv. 12–14). So in urging the duty of prayer reference is made, not (as in Heb. v. 7) to the promises or the prayers of Christ, but to the prayer of Elijah: the duty of kindness, and the warning against evil-speaking in ch. iii. are based not on the example of Christ and the thought of our common brotherhood in Him (as in 1 Pet. ii. 23, Rom. xii. 5, Eph. iv. 25), but on the parables of nature, on the fact that man was created in the image of God, and on general reasoning: and again (in iv. 11, 12) speaking evil of a brother is condemned as putting a slight on the Law, not as causing pain to Christ. No mention is made of the death or resurrection of Christ, or of the doctrines of the Incarnation and Atonement. To a careless reader the tone of the Epistle, as a whole, seems scarcely to rise above the level of the Old Testament; Christian ideas are still clothed in Jewish forms. Thus the Law, called for the sake of distinction 'the law of liberty' or 'the royal law,' seems to stand in place of the Gospel or even of Christ himself (ii. 8–13, iv. 11): the love of the world is condemned in the language of the Old Testament as adultery against God. This contrast rises to its highest point in treating of the relation between Faith and Works (ii. 14–26). While St. Paul writes (Rom. iii. 28) 'We reckon therefore that a man is justified by faith apart from the works of the law,' the language of St. James is (ii. 24) 'Ye see then how that by works a man is justified and not by faith only.' And while the case of Abraham is cited in Rom. iv. 3, 13, 16 in proof of the doctrine of justification by faith, and the case of Rahab is cited for the same purpose in Heb. xi. 31, St. James makes use of both to prove that man is justified by works (ii. 25). I shall have to go more fully into these questions hereafter, and shall then point out some considerations which will to a certain extent qualify the first impression left on the mind by a perusal of the Epistle; but speaking generally we may safely say that it has a more Jewish cast than any other writing of the New Testament, and that the author must have been one who would be more in sympathy with the Judaizing party and more likely to exercise an influence over them than any of the three great leaders Peter, Paul or John.

If we turn now to the Epistles of St. Paul and to the Acts of the Apostles we find mention there of a James who exactly fulfils the conditions required in the writer of our Epistle. In Gal. i. 18, 19 St. Paul says that three years after his conversion, probably about the year 38 A.D., he went from Damascus to Jerusalem and stayed with Peter fifteen days, seeing no other apostle but only James the Lord's brother. This is quite in accordance with what we read in the Acts xii. 17, where Peter, on his escape from prison (A.D. 44), is recorded to have gone to the house of Mary the mother of Mark, and desired that the news of his escape might be sent to James and the brethren. In Gal. ii. 1–10 St. Paul describes a later visit to Jerusalem after an interval of fourteen years, *i.e.* about A.D. 51. In this visit the leaders of the Church, James, Peter and John (*l.c.* ver. 9), after hearing his report of his first missionary journey, signified their approval of his work and 'gave right hands of fellowship,' agreeing that Paul and Barnabas should preach to the Gentiles and they themselves to the circumcision. In verses 11–14 of the same chapter Peter's inconsistency in regard to eating with the Gentiles at Antioch is explained by the arrival of certain from James, πρὸ τοῦ γὰρ ἐλθεῖν τινὰς ἀπὸ Ἰακώβου μετὰ τῶν ἐθνῶν συνήσθιεν· ὅτε δὲ ἦλθον, ὑπέστελλεν καὶ ἀφώριζεν ἑαυτὸν φοβούμενος τοὺς ἐκ περιτομῆς This second visit is more fully described in Acts xv. 4–29, where James appears as President of the Council held to consider how far the Gentile Christians should be required to conform to the customs of the Jews. It is James who sums up the discussion, and proposes the resolution which is carried, in the words ἐγὼ κρίνω μὴ παρενοχλεῖν τοῖς ἀπὸ τῶν ἐθνῶν ἐπιστρέφουσιν ἐπὶ τὸν Θεόν, κ.τ.λ.

This agrees with what is said in the Epistles and Acts of James, the President of the Church at Jerusalem.

It is important to notice that in his speech (ver. 14) Peter is called Symeon, a name never assigned to him elsewhere in the Acts or in any part of the N.T. except in 2 Pet. i. 1. From this we gather that the actual words of the speaker are recorded either in their original form or in a translation; and it becomes thus a matter of interest to learn whether there is any resemblance between the language of our Epistle and that of the speech said to have been uttered by James, and of the circular containing the decree, which was probably drawn up by him.[1] I cannot but think it a remarkable coincidence that, out of

Remarkable agreements between our Epistle and the speech of James in Acts xv.

[1] The similarity between the First Epistle of St. Peter and the speeches ascribed to him in the Acts is noticed in Alford's Greek Testament, vol. iv. *Prolegomena*, p. 137.

230 words contained in the speech and circular, so many should reappear in our Epistle, written on a totally different subject. They are as follows: (1) the epistolary salutation *χαίρειν* (Jas. i. 1, Acts xv. 23), found in only one other passage of the N.T., the letter of Lysias to Felix (Acts xxiii. 26): (2) the curious phrase borrowed from the LXX. which occurs in the N.T. only in Acts xv. 17 *ἐφ' οὓς ἐπικέκληται τὸ ὄνομά μου ἐπ' αὐτούς*, and James ii. 7 *τὸ καλὸν ὄνομα τὸ ἐπικληθὲν ἐφ' ὑμᾶς*: (3) *ἀκούσατε ἀδελφοί μου* found in James ii. 5 alone in the Epistles, compared with *ἄνδρες ἀδελφοὶ ἀκούσατέ μου* in Acts xv. 13: (4) *ἐπισκέπτεσθαι* James i. 27, Acts xv. 14: (5) *ἐπιστρέφειν* James v. 19, 20, Acts xv. 19: (6) *τηρεῖν* and *διατηρεῖν*, James i. 27 *ἄσπιλον ἑαυτὸν τηρεῖν ἀπὸ τοῦ κόσμου*, Acts xv. 29 *ἐξ ὧν διατηροῦντες ἑαυτοὺς εὖ πράξετε*: (7) *ἀγαπητός* occurs in the Acts only in xv. 25 *σὺν τοῖς ἀγαπητοῖς Βαρνάβᾳ καὶ Παύλῳ*, while *ἀδελφοί μου ἀγαπητοί* is found three times in our Epistle: (8) perhaps we may compare also the repetition of the word *ἀδελφός* in James iv. 11 *μὴ καταλαλεῖτε ἀλλήλων ἀδελφοί· ὁ καταλαλῶν ἀδελφοῦ ἢ κρίνων τὸν ἀδελφὸν αὐτοῦ κρίνει τὸν νόμον κ.τ.λ.* and Acts xv. 23 *οἱ πρεσβύτεροι ἀδελφοὶ τοῖς κατὰ τὴν Ἀντιόχειαν...ἀδελφοῖς χαίρειν*: and the pregnant use of the word *ὄνομα* in James v. 10 *ἐλάλησαν ἐν τῷ ὀνόματι Κυρίου*, ver. 14 *ἀλείψαντες ἐλαίῳ ἐν τῷ ὀνόματι*, ii. 7 *τὸ καλὸν ὄνομα* and in Acts xv. 14 *λαβεῖν ἐξ ἐθνῶν λαὸν τῷ ὀνόματι αὐτοῦ*, ver. 26 *ὑπὲρ τοῦ ὀνόματος τοῦ Κυρίου ἡμῶν Ἰησοῦ Χριστοῦ*.

Further agreements between what we are told of James in Acts xxi. and our Epistle.

To return to our immediate subject: James is seen in the same position of authority in Acts xxi. 18, when Paul presents himself before him on his return from his third missionary journey (A.D. 58). After joining in praise to God for the success which had attended his labours, James and the elders who are with him warn St. Paul of the strong feeling against him which had been excited among the 'myriads of Jewish believers who were all zealous for the law' (*ζηλωταὶ τοῦ νόμου*) by the report that he had taught the Jews of the Dispersion to abandon circumcision and their other customs. To counteract this impression, they recommended him to join in a Nazarite vow, which had been undertaken by four members of their community, as a proof that the report was unfounded and that he himself walked according to the law. The description here given of the state of feeling at Jerusalem and of St. James' anxiety to avoid causing any offence to it is quite in accordance with the tone of our Epistle and may help to explain the reserve with which distinctive Christian doctrines are treated in it. Is it going too far to compare the use of ἁγνίζω in Acts xxi. 24 and James iv. 8, and the construction of δαπανᾶν in the same verse (δαπάνησον ἐπ' αὐτοῖς) and in James iv. 3 ἵνα ἐν ταῖς ἡδοναῖς ὑμῶν δαπανήσητε?

This James is also known as the Lord's brother.

The only other passage in which James is mentioned by name in the Epistles is 1 Cor. xv. 7, where we are told that Jesus appeared to James after his Resurrection. Of this more will be said shortly. But we have seen that in Gal. i. 19 he receives the appellation of 'the Lord's brother,' and there are further allusions to the 'brethren of the Lord' in 1 Cor. ix. 5, which is generally taken to imply that they were all married, and in Acts i. 14, where we are told that after the Ascension 'the Eleven with the women and Mary the mother of Jesus and his brethren remained together at Jerusalem waiting for the promise of the Spirit.' These passages also will come in for further consideration immediately.

Reason why this title is not used in the Epistle.

An objection may be raised to the identification of the writer of the Epistle with the brother of the Lord, on the ground that no claim is made to this title in either of the Epistles which go by the names of the brothers James and Jude. If they were really brothers of the Lord, would they not have laid stress on the authority derived from this relationship, just as St. Paul lays stress on his apostleship? But what was Christ's own teaching on the matter? When his mother and brothers sought on one occasion to use the authority, which they assumed that their kinship gave them, they were met by the words 'Who is my mother, and who are my brethren?' And he stretched out his hand to his disciples and said 'Behold my mother and my brethren.' St. Paul expresses the same idea, of the disappearance of the earthly relationship in the higher spiritual union, by which all the members of the body are joined to the Head, in the words 'though we have known Christ after the flesh, yet now know we him so no more,' 2 Cor. v. 16. Surely it is only what we should have expected beforehand, that James and Jude would shrink from claiming another name than that of 'servant' to express the relation in which they stood to their risen Lord, after having failed (as I shall shortly endeavour to show) to acknowledge Him as their Master in the days of his humiliation.

So far we have arrived at the following conclusions: the writer

Three explanations of this title.

of the Epistle is or, to allow for a moment the possibility of its not being genuine, wishes to be understood as being, the President of the Church at Jerusalem, and the brother of the Lord.[1] We have now to investigate the meaning of this last expression.[2] Is it to be understood literally of half-brothers of the Lord, sons of Mary his mother and of Joseph his reputed father (the Helvidian view)? Or is it to be understood of foster-brothers, sons of his reputed father by a former wife (the Epiphanian view)? Or is it to be understood of the cousins of the Lord, sons of Clopas or Alphaeus, the husband of his mother's sister, who bore the same name as herself (the Hieronymian view)? It may be well first to bring together the passages bearing on this subject in the Gospels, and then to examine them more carefully in reference to the three theories above stated. I quote from the R.V.

Passages in the New Testament bearing upon the subject.

Matt. i. 25. Joseph . . . took unto him his wife and knew her not till she had brought forth a son.

Luke ii. 7. She brought forth her first-born son.

John ii. 12. After this he went down to Capernaum, he and his mother and his brethren and his disciples: and there they abode not many days.

Mark vi. 1–6. And he cometh into his own country; and his disciples follow him. And when the sabbath was come, he began to teach in the synagogue: and many hearing him were astonished, saying . . . Is not this the carpenter, the son of Mary, and brother of James, and Joses, and Judas, and Simon? and are not his sisters here with us? And they were offended in him. And

[1] I have made no reference to the Tübingen theory which supposes the Acts to be a *Tendenz-schrift* written with the view of minimizing the difference between St. Paul and St. James, (1) because I do not see that it in any way affects my argument, unless it should be maintained that the writer of the Acts had our Epistle before him and intentionally imitated its language, which would give an even stronger support to my argument from a different point of view; and (2) because the theory itself seems to me by this time exploded.

[2] In the discussion which follows I have had constantly before me Bp. Lightfoot's dissertation on the Brethren of the Lord, admirable alike for thoroughness, clearness, and fairness, which is contained in his *Galatians* (10th ed, pp. 252–291). I have also consulted Credner's *Einleitung in d. N. T.*, Laurent's *Neutest. Studien*, Mill's *Pantheistic Principles*, Part II. pp. 220–316, and the articles 'Maria' and 'Jakobus' in Herzog's *Encycl. f. prot. Theol.* I should have been glad to put the question aside with a simple reference, but I think there are some considerations which have not been sufficiently attended to, and that the Epistle gains an added interest from what I hold to be the right solution of the difficulty. [Since this was written I have read Canon Farrar's able discussion of the subject in his *Early Days of Christianity*, ch. xix., and Bungener's *Rome et la Bible*, both of whom take the same view as I have done.]

Jesus said unto them, A prophet is not without honour, save in his own country, and among his own kin, and in his own house. Cf. Matt. xiii. 54–56, Luke iv. 16–30, John vi. 42.

Mark iii. 20—22, 31—33. And the multitude cometh together again, so that they could not so much as eat bread. And when his friends (οἱ παρ' αὐτοῦ) heard it they went out to lay hold on him: for they said, He is beside himself. And the scribes which came down from Jerusalem said, He hath Beelzebub, and by the prince of the devils casteth he out the devils. . . . And there come his mother and his brethren; and standing without, they sent unto him, calling him. And a multitude was sitting about him; and they say unto him, Behold, thy mother and thy brethren without seek for thee. And he answered them and saith, Who is my mother and my brethren? And looking round on them that sat round about him he saith, Behold my mother and my brethren! For whosoever shall do the will of God, the same is my brother and sister and mother. Cf. Matt. xii. 46—50, Luke viii. 19—21.

John vii. 2—8. Now the feast of the Jews, the feast of tabernacles, was at hand. His brethren therefore said unto him, Depart hence and go into Judaea, that thy disciples also may behold thy works which thou doest. For no man doeth anything in secret and himself seeketh to be known openly. If thou doest these things manifest thyself to the world. For even (οὐδέ) his brethren did not believe on him. Jesus therefore saith unto them, My time is not yet come, but your time is alway ready. The world cannot hate you, but me it hateth, because I testify of it that its works are evil.

Matt. xxvii. 56. And many women were there beholding from afar, which had followed Jesus from Galilee, ministering unto him: among whom was Mary Magdalene, and Mary the mother of James and Joses, and the mother of the sons of Zebedee.

Mark xv. 40. And there were also women beholding from afar: among whom were both Mary Magdalene, and Mary the mother of James the less (τοῦ μικροῦ) and of Joses, and Salome. A little below (ver. 47) the second Mary is called 'Mary the mother of Joses,' and in xvi. 1 'the mother of James,' as in Luke xxiv. 10.

John xix. 25—27. There were standing by the cross his mother, and his mother's sister, Mary the *wife* of Clopas, and Mary Magdalene. When Jesus therefore saw his mother and the disciple standing by, whom he loved, he saith unto his mother, Woman, behold thy son! Then saith he to the disciple, Behold thy mother! And from that hour the disciple took her to his own home.

Acts i. 14 These all (that is, the eleven apostles) with one accord continued steadfastly in prayer, *σὺν γυναιξὶν καὶ Μαριὰμ τῇ μητρὶ τοῦ Ἰησοῦ καὶ τοῖς ἀδελφοῖς αὐτοῦ.*

Gal. i. 18, 19 After three years I went up to Jerusalem to visit Cephas, and tarried with him fifteen days. But others of the apostles saw I none, save (*εἰ μή*) James the Lord's brother.

1 Cor. ix. 5 Have we not a right to take about a wife that is a believer (*γυναίκα ἀδελφὴν*) *ὡς καὶ οἱ λοιποὶ ἀπόστολοι καὶ οἱ ἀδελφοὶ τοῦ Κυρίου καὶ Κηφᾶς; ἢ μόνος ἐγὼ καὶ Βαρνάβας οὐκ ἔχομεν ἐξουσιὰν μὴ ἐργάζεσθαι;*

Natural conclusion from the language of the New Testament confirmed by later writers.

A. I think that any one reading these passages, without any preconceived idea on the subject, would naturally draw the conclusion that Mary was the true wife of Joseph, and bore to him at least four sons (James, Joses, Judas, and Simon) and two daughters; that the sons were not included among the twelve apostles, but were, on the contrary, disbelievers in the Messiahship of Christ, and inclined at one time to entertain doubts as to His sanity, though after His death they threw in their lot with His disciples.

Hegesippus tells us that Clopas was brother of Joseph, and calls Symeon, son of Clopas, cousin of the Lord, reserving the term 'brother' for James and Jude.

Setting aside the apocryphal books of the N.T., the earliest reference to this subject in the post-apostolic writers is found in Hegesippus (about 160 A.D.). His testimony, preserved by Eusebius (*H.E.* iv. 22), while it is totally opposed to the Hieronymian view, is consistent either with the conclusion to which we are led by the language of Scripture, or with the view of Epiphanius. It is to the effect that 'after the martyrdom of James the Just on the same charge as the Lord, his paternal uncle's child, Symeon the son of Clopas, was next made Bishop of Jerusalem, being put forward by all as the second in succession, because he was a cousin of the Lord' (*μετὰ τὸ μαρτυρῆσαι Ἰάκωβον τὸν δίκαιον ὡς καὶ ὁ Κύριος ἐπὶ τῷ αὐτῷ λόγῳ, πάλιν ὁ ἐκ τοῦ θείου αὐτοῦ Συμεὼν ὁ τοῦ Κλωπᾶ καθίσταται ἐπίσκοπος, ὃν προέθεντο πάντες ὄντα ἀνεψιὸν τοῦ Κυρίου δεύτερον*). Some have understood this to mean that Symeon and James were both sons of the Lord's reputed uncle Clopas, and thus that Symeon was the second of His cousins who was Bishop of Jerusalem. But Bp. Lightfoot well remarks that, if this were meant, we must have had *ἕτερος τῶν ἐκ τοῦ θείου*, not *ὁ ἐκ τοῦ θείου*, and that it would have been far more natural simply to have said *ὁ ἀδελφὸς αὐτοῦ*. The meaning of *δεύτερον* is made clear from Euseb. *H.E.* iii. 22 *τῶν ἐπ' Ἀντιοχείας Εὐοδίου πρώτου καταστάντος, δεύτερος ἐν τοῖς δηλουμένοις Ἰγνάτιος ἐγνωρίζετο. Συμεὼν ὁμοίως δεύτερος μετὰ τὸν τοῦ Σωτῆρος ἡμῶν ἀ δ ε λ φ ὸ ν τῆς ἐν Ἱεροσολύμοις ἐκκλησίας κατὰ τούτους τὴν λειτουργίαν ἐγκεχειρισμένος ἦν*; *ib.* iii. 32 *ἐν ᾧ* (*διωγμῷ*) *Συμεῶνα τὸν τοῦ Κλωπᾶ, ὃν δεύτερον καταστῆναι τῆς ἐν Ἱεροσολύμοις ἐκκλησίας ἐπίσκοπον ἐδηλώσαμεν, μαρτυρίῳ τὸν βίον ἀναλῦσαι παρειλήφαμεν.* These passages are important as showing that, while the son of Clopas is described as the cousin of Jesus, James is still described as His brother: so too Jude (*ib.* iii. 20). The relationship is more exactly defined in the 11th ch. of the same book, where it is said that after the death of James, the surviving apostles and disciples of the Lord elected Symeon as his successor, *ἀνεψιόν, ὥς γε φασί, γεγονότα τοῦ Σωτῆρος· τὸν γὰρ οὖν Κλωπᾶν ἀδελφὸν τοῦ Ἰωσὴφ ὑπάρχειν Ἡγήσιππος ἱστορεῖ.*

Tertullian distinctly asserts that 'the brethren' were uterine brothers of Jesus.

Tertullian (*d.* 220 A.D.) is, however, the first extant writer who distinctly asserts that the 'brethren' were uterine brothers of Jesus. Arguing against Marcion, who had made use of the text, 'Who is My mother, and who My brother?' to prove that Christ was not really man, he says: *Nos contrario dicimus, primo, non potuisse illi annuntiari quod mater et fratres ejus foris starent . . . si nulla illi mater et fratres nulli fuissent. . . . At vere mater et fratres ejus foris stabant. . . . Tam proximas personas foris stare extraneis intus defixis ad sermones ejus . . . merito indignatus est. Transtulit sanguinis nomina in alios, quos magis proximos pro fide judicaret . . . in semet ipso docens, qui patrem aut matrem aut fratres præponeret verbo Dei, non esse dignum discipulum* (*Adv. Marc.* iv. 19). Similarly arguing from the same text against the Marcionite Apelles, he says 'the words are not inconsistent with the truth of his humanity. No one would have told him that his mother and his brethren stood without, *qui non certus esset habere illum matrem et fratres. . . . Omnes nascimur, et tamen non omnes aut fratres habemus aut matrem. Adhuc potest et patrem magis habere quam matrem, et avunculos magis quam fratres. . . . Fratres Domini non crediderunt in illum. . . . Mater aeque non demonstratur adhæsisse ei. . . . Hoc denique in loco apparet incredulitas eorum* (*De Carne Christi*, 7). As Tertullian in these passages gives no hint that the brothers of Jesus stood to him in any other relation than other men's brothers do to them, or that his relationship to them was not as real as that to his mother, so in other treatises he takes it for granted that Mary ceased to be a virgin after the birth of Christ (*De Monogamia* 8) *Duæ nobis antistites Christianæ sanctitatis occurrunt, monogamia et continentia. Et Christum quidem virgo enixa est, semel nuptura post partum* ('being about to defer her marriage union till after the birth of her son,' lit. 'being about to marry first after her delivery') *ut uterque titulus sanctitatis in Christi sensu dispungeretur per matrem et virginem et univiram;* and in even plainer words (*De Virg. Vel.* 6), where he discusses the meaning of the salutation *benedicta tu inter mulieres.* 'Was she called *mulier*, and not *virgo*, because she was espoused? We need not, at any rate, suppose a prophetic reference to her future state as a married woman': *non enim poterat posteriorem mulierem nominare, de qua Christus nasci non habebat, id est virum passam sed illa* (*illam ?*) *quæ erat præsens, quæ erat virgo* ('for the angel could not be referring to the wife that was to be, for Christ was not to be born of a wife, *i.e.* of one who had known a husband; but he referred to her who was before him, who was a virgin').

There is no primitive tradition in favour of the Perpetual Virginity. The Epiphanian view was first put forward in two apocryphal books of the second century, and accepted on the ground of sentiment by Origen and later writers.

These words of Tertullian, himself strongly ascetic, which were written about the end of the second century, do not betray any consciousness that he is controverting an established tradition in favour of the perpetual virginity. And Origen (*d.* 253 A.D.), though upholding the virginity, and objecting to the phrase used above by Tertullian (*quod asserunt eam nupsisse post partem, unde approbent non habent, Comm. in Luc.* 7), does not claim any authority for his own view, but only argues that it is admissible. Thus he says:[1] 'Some persons, on the ground of the tradition contained in the Gospel according to Peter or the Book of James, affirm that the brothers of Jesus were Joseph's sons by a former wife, to whom he was married before Mary. Those who hold this view wish to

[1] *Comm. in Matt.* xii. 55 (vol. iii. p. 45, Lomm.) τοὺς ἀδελφοὺς Ἰησοῦ φασί τινες εἶναι, ἐκ παραδόσεως ὁρμώμενοι τοῦ ἐπιγεγραμμένου κατὰ Πέτρον εὐαγγελίου ἢ τῆς βίβλου Ἰακώβου, υἱοὺς Ἰωσὴφ ἐκ προτέρας γυναικὸς συνωκηκυίας αὐτῷ πρὸ τῆς Μαρίας· οἱ δὲ ταῦτα λέγοντες τὸ ἀξίωμα τῆς Μαρίας ἐν παρθενίᾳ τηρεῖν μέχρι τέλους βούλονται, ἵνα μὴ τὸ κριθὲν ἐκεῖνο σῶμα . . . γνῷ κοιτὴν ἀνδρὸς μετὰ τὸ ἐπελθεῖν ἐν αὐτῇ πνεῦμα ἅγιον . . . Καὶ οἶμαι λόγον ἔχειν ἀνδρῶν μὲν καθαρότητος τῆς ἐν ἁγνείᾳ ἀπαρχὴν γεγονέναι τὸν Ἰησοῦν, γυναικῶν δὲ τὴν Μαριάμ.

preserve the honour of Mary in virginity to the end, in order that her body, once chosen for so high a purpose, might not be degraded to lower use, after the Holy Spirit had come upon her. . . . And I think it reasonable that, as Jesus was the first-fruit of purity and chastity among men, so Mary should be among women.' In accordance with this view we read in another passage,[1] 'Jesus had no natural brothers, seeing that neither was any other child born to the Virgin, nor was He Himself sprung from Joseph: wherefore (those mentioned) were His brothers only in a conventional sense, being sons of Joseph by a predeceased wife.'

The writings from which Origen borrowed his interpretation of the word 'brothers,' are two apocryphal books dating from about the middle of the second century. We learn from Eusebius, *H.E.* vi. 12, that Serapion, bishop of Antioch at the end of the second century, forbade the use of the Gospel of Peter to a Cilician Church, on the ground that it favoured the heretical views of the Docetæ. The latter portion of this Gospel (of course not containing the passage referred to by Origen) was discovered in a fragmentary condition in Egypt a few years ago, the *Editio Princeps* being published in 1892. The other book to which Origen refers, the *Protevangelium Jacobi*, is still extant. It contains the story of Anna and Joachim, the parents of Mary, of her miraculous birth and betrothal to Joseph to be her guardian, he having been designated for this honour, against his will, out of all the widowers of Israel, by the dove which issued from his rod. The names of Joseph's sons are variously given in the MSS. as Simon, Samuel, James. Subsequent apocryphal narratives relate the same story variously modified. As to the historical credibility of such stories it may suffice to quote Bp. Lightfoot's words (*Gal.* p. 275): 'These accounts, so far as they step beyond the incidents narrated in the canonical Gospels are pure fabrication.' Nor were they more highly esteemed by early orthodox writers; cf. *Const. Apost.* vi. 16, where we read of the 'poisonous apocryphal books in which the wicked heretics reproach the creation, marriage, the providential government of the world, the begetting of children,' etc.; and Jerome (*Comm. in Matt.* xii. 49), where he taunts those who con-

[1] *Catena Cord. in Johann.* ii. 12: ἀδελφοὺς μὲν οὐκ εἶχε φύσει οὔτε τῆς παρθένου τεκούσης ἕτερον οὐδὲ αὐτὸς ἐκ τοῦ Ἰωσὴφ τυγχάνων· νόμῳ τοιγαροῦν ἐχρημάτισαν αὐτοῦ ἀδελφοί, υἱοὶ Ἰωσὴφ ὄντες ἐκ προτεθνηκυίας γυναικός.

sidered the Lord's brethren to be sons of Joseph's by a former wife, as 'following the ravings of the apocryphal writings, and inventing a certain Melcha or Escha' (for Joseph's first wife).

I think that these facts prove that the belief in the Perpetual Virginity, which was growing up during the second century and established itself in the third century, was founded, not upon historic evidence, but simply on sentimental grounds, which may have gained additional strength from opposition to the Ebionites, who denied the miraculous birth of the Lord (Iren. iii. 21, Orig. *c. Cels.* v. 61). Even by Basil the Great, who died in 379 A.D., this belief is held, not as a necessary article of faith, but merely as a pious opinion,[1] 'since the lovers of Christ cannot endure to hear that the mother of God ceased to be a virgin.' Bp. Lightfoot (*l.c.* p. 285) adds that 'as immediately afterwards he refers, in support of his view, to some apocryphal work, which related that Zacharias was slain by the Jews for testifying to the virginity of the mother of Jesus (a story which closely resembles the narrative of His death in the *Protev.* §§ 23, 24), it may perhaps be inferred that he accepted that account of the Lord's brethren which ran through these apocryphal Gospels.' It is unnecessary to give the names of others who held that the 'brethren' were sons of Joseph by a former wife.[2] The chief supporter of this view is Epiphanius, who wrote against the Antidicomarianitæ about the year 370 A.D. The view of Tertullian was reasserted by Helvidius, Bonosus, and Jovinianus, about the year 380 A.D.

Jerome repudiates tradition and professes to derive his theory solely from Scripture.

B. Jerome's answer to Helvidius, which fastened on the Western Church the doctrine of the Perpetual Virginity and the interpretation of 'brethren' in the sense of 'cousins,' appeared about 383 A.D. Helvidius had attacked the prevailing view of the superiority

[1] *Hom. in Sanct. Christ. Gen.* ii. p. 600, ed. Garn. (Ἰωσὴφ) καὶ διαθέσει καὶ στοργῇ καὶ πάσῃ τῇ ἐπιβαλλούσῃ τοῖς συνοικοῦσιν ἐπιμελείᾳ γυναῖκα ἡγούμενος, τῶν γαμικῶν ἔργων ἀπείχετο· οὐκ ἐγίνωσκε γὰρ αὐτήν, φησίν, ἕως οὗ ἔτεκεν τὸν υἱὸν αὐτῆς τὸν πρωτότοκον. Τοῦτο δὲ ἤδη ὑπόνοιαν παρέχει ὥς, μετὰ τὸ καθαρῶς ὑπηρετήσασθαι τῇ γεννήσει τοῦ Κυρίου τῇ ἐπιτελεσθείσῃ διὰ τοῦ Πνεύματος τοῦ ἁγίου, τὰ νενομισμένα τοῦ γάμου ἔργα μὴ ἀπαρνησαμένης τῆς Μαρίας. Ἡμεῖς δέ, εἰ καὶ μηδὲν τῷ τῆς εὐσεβείας παραλυμαίνεται λόγῳ (μέχρι γὰρ τῆς κατὰ τὴν οἰκονομίαν ὑπηρεσίας ἀναγκαία ἡ παρθενία, τὸ δ' ἐφεξῆς ἀπολυπραγμονευτὸν τῷ λόγῳ τοῦ μυστηρίου), ὅμως διὰ τὸ μὴ καταδέχεσθαι τῶν φιλοχρίστων τὴν ἀκοὴν ὅτι ποτὲ ἐπαύσατο εἶναι παρθένος ἡ θεοτόκος, ἐκείνας ἡγούμεθα τὰς μαρτυρίας αὐταρκεῖς.

[2] They will be found in the catena of references contained in Lightfoor's essay (*Gal.* pp. 273–291).

of the unmarried to the married state by referring to the example of the Lord's mother, 'of whom we read in Scripture that she bore children to her husband Joseph.' Jerome does not attempt to answer this by appealing to tradition: on the contrary he altogether repudiates tradition, professing to derive his theory from a critical examination of Scripture. His argument briefly stated is, that James the brother of the Lord is called an Apostle by St. Paul, that he must therefore be identified with James the son of Alphaeus, since James the son of Zebedee was no longer living when Paul wrote; identified also with James the less in Mark xv, 40 (the comparative implying an opposition to James the greater,[1] viz. the son of Zebedee), this James being there stated to be brother of Joses. But in Mark vi. 3 we find a James and Joses among the brethren of Jesus, and this agrees with John xix. 25, where Mary the mother of James and wife of Alphaeus is called Mary of Clopas, sister of the Lord's mother; from whence it follows that the four brothers and two or more sisters mentioned in Mark vi. 3 and elsewhere are really first cousins of Jesus. Jerome himself had no information on the subject of Clopas, but suggests that he may possibly have been father of Mary. Later writers added further developments to this theory. Clopas was identified with Alphaeus, as another form of the common Aramaic original Chalphai; and 'Judas of James,' who occurs in St. Luke's list of the Apostles (Luke vi. 16, Acts i. 13), is identified with the writer of the Epistle, who calls himself 'brother of James' (Jude 1), and also with the brother of Joses, James and Simon in Mark vi. 3. Simon Zelotes, who is joined with James and Judas in the list of the Apostles, is supposed to be another of these brethren: and some held that Matthew, being identical with Levi the son of Alphaeus, must belong to the same family.

Bishop Lightfoot calls attention to the fact that not only does Jerome make no pretence to any traditional support for this view,[2]

[1] 'There is no scriptural or early sanction for speaking of the son of Zebedee as James the Great' (Lightfoot, *Gal.* p. 263).

[2] After disputing the value of the authorities appealed to by Helvidius, he sets aside the appeal to authority in the words *Verum nugas terimus et fonte veritatis omisso opinionum rivulos consectamur* (*Adv. Helv.* 17); and in another treatise (*De Viris Illustribus* 2) contrasts his own view with the Epiphanian in the words *Ut nonnulli existimant, Joseph ex alia uxore; ut autem mihi videtur, Mariae sororis matris Domini...filius* (Lightfoot, p. 259).

Jerome does not hold consistently to his own theory

but that he is himself by no means consistent in holding it. Thus in his comment on the Galatians written about 387 A.D. he says: 'James was called the Lord's brother on account of his high character, his incomparable faith, and his extraordinary wisdom; the other apostles are also called brothers (John xx. 17), but he pre-eminently so, to whom the Lord at his departure had committed the sons of his mother (*i.e.* the members of the Church at Jerusalem).' In a later work still, the epistle to Hedibia, written about 406, he speaks of Mary of Cleophas (Clopas), the aunt of our Lord, and Mary the mother of James and Josès, as distinct persons, 'although some contend that the mother of James and Joses was his aunt.'

I proceed now to examine the above argument:

Examination of his argument. The term ἀδελφός is never used for ἀνεψιός in the New Testament or in classical Greek.

(1) It is assumed that 'brother' (ἀδελφός) may be used in the sense of cousin (ἀνεψιός, found in Col. iv. 10). The supporters of this theory do not offer any parallel from the N.T., but they appeal to classical use both in Greek and Latin, and to the O.T. The examples cited from classical Greek are merely expressive of warm affection, or else metaphorical, as Plato, *Crito,* § 16, where the laws of Athens are made to speak of *οἱ ἡμέτεροι ἀδελφοὶ οἱ ἐν Ἅιδου νόμοι*. There is no instance in classical Greek, as far as I know, of ἀδελφός being used to denote a cousin. In Latin *frater* may stand for *frater patruelis,* where there is no danger of being misunderstood (cf. Cic. *ad Att.* i. 5. 1). The Hebrew word is used loosely to include cousin, as in Gen. xiv. 14—16 (of Abraham and Lot), where the LXX. has ἀδελφιδοῦς; in Levit. x. 4, where the first cousins of Aaron are called brethren (ἀδελφοί) of his sons, Nadab and Abihu; in 1 Chron. xxiii. 21, 22 ('The sons of Mahli, Eleazar and Kish. And Eleazar died, and had no sons, but daughters: and their brethren the sons of Kish took them'), where also the LXX. has ἀδελφοί. These passages seem to me to be hardly covered by the general rule laid down by Bishop Lightfoot (p. 261): "in an affectionate and earnest appeal intended to move the sympathies of the hearer, a speaker might not unnaturally address a relation or a friend or even a fellow-countryman as his 'brother': and even when speaking of such to a third person he might through warmth of feeling and under certain aspects so designate him." I think, however, the Bishop is entirely right when he goes on to say: "It is scarcely conceivable that the cousins of any one should

be commonly and indeed exclusively styled his 'brothers' by indifferent persons; still less, that one cousin in particular should be singled out and described in this loose way 'James, the Lord's brother.'" If we remark too the care with which Hegesippus (quoted above, pp. viii. ix.) employs the term ἀδελφός of James and Jude, the brothers of the Lord, while he keeps the term ἀνεψιός for Symeon, the cousin of the Lord and second bishop of Jerusalem, we shall feel that there is a strong probability against the use of ἀδελφοί in the N.T. to denote anything but brothers, *i.e.* in the case before us either half-brothers or foster-brothers, according to the evidence to be considered later on.

James, the brother of the Lord, was not one of the Twelve.

(2) Jerome's main argument is that James the Lord's brother was one of the Twelve, and therefore identical with James the son of Alphaeus. He grounds this assertion on a single passage in St. Paul, which I shall presently examine. Bishop Lightfoot and others have shown that it is not a necessary consequence of St. Paul's language, and that it is opposed to the distinction everywhere made in the N.T. between the Brethren of the Lord and the Twelve. Thus in Acts i. 14, after the list of the Eleven including James the son of Alphaeus, we read 'these all continued instant in prayer' σὺν γυναιξὶν καὶ Μαριὰμ τῇ μητρὶ τοῦ Ἰησοῦ καὶ τοῖς ἀδελφοῖς αὐτοῦ. It will hardly be said that they are included in the Twelve, as Mary among the women, and specially mentioned afterwards, as she is, only on account of their superior importance. If so, they would have been mentioned immediately after the Apostles; on the contrary they are placed after Mary, being joined with her, as in several other passages, because they, with her, constitute the family to which Jesus belonged. Again in John ii. 12 we read that Jesus went down to Capernaum αὐτὸς καὶ ἡ μήτηρ αὐτοῦ καὶ οἱ ἀδελφοὶ καὶ οἱ μαθηταὶ αὐτοῦ· καὶ ἐκεῖ ἔμειναν οὐ πολλὰς ἡμέρας; and in Matt. xii. 47 foll. 'One said to him' ἰδοὺ ἡ μήτηρ σου καὶ οἱ ἀδελφοί σου ἔξω ἑστήκασιν ζητοῦντές σοι λαλῆσαι . . . . 'and stretching forth his hand to his disciples he saith' ἰδοὺ ἡ μήτηρ μου καὶ οἱ ἀδελφοί μου· ὅστις γὰρ ἂν ποιήσῃ τὸ θέλημα τοῦ Πατρός μου, τοῦ ἐν οὐρανοῖς, αὐτός μου ἀδελφὸς καὶ ἀδελφὴ καὶ μήτηρ ἐστίν. In the last passage there is the same strong antithesis between natural earthly ties and his

duty to his Father in heaven, which we observe in the words spoken by him when found as a boy in the Temple.

On the contrary, we read that His brethren were not even believers

Notice also that there is in this passage not only a distinction made between the brethren of Jesus and his disciples, but a certain opposition is implied, which is brought out more clearly in St. Mark's narrative of the same event (iii. 21, 31–35). From the latter it appears that the reason why they of his family (*οἱ παρ' αὐτοῦ*) desired to speak with him was because the rumour which had reached them of his incessant labours led them to believe that his mind was overstrained. As St. Mark goes on to say (ver. 22) that the scribes accused Jesus of casting out devils through Beelzebub, and as we further read in John (x. 20, viii. 48) that many said 'He hath a devil and is mad'; it would seem, though it is not expressly stated, that these calumnious reports of his enemies had not been without effect on some members of his own family. At all events, they went out prepared *κρατεῖν αὐτόν*, *i.e.* to put him under some restraint. This narrative gives additional point to the words in Mark vi. 4, spoken with immediate reference to the unbelief of the people of Nazareth, *οὐκ ἔστιν προφήτης ἄτιμος εἰ μὴ ἐν τῇ πατρίδι αὐτοῦ καὶ ἐν τοῖς συγγενεῦσιν αὐτοῦ καὶ ἐν τῇ οἰκίᾳ αὐτοῦ*. If it were simply the disbelief of townspeople not immediately related to him, there seems no need for the addition 'in his own kinsfolk and in his own house.' This inference, which we naturally draw from the words of St. Mark, is confirmed by the express statement of St. John (vii. 3–5), *οὐδὲ γὰρ οἱ ἀδελφοὶ αὐτοῦ ἐπίστευον εἰς αὐτόν*, and by our Lord's words addressed to them (ver. 7), *οὐ δύναται ὁ κόσμος μισεῖν ὑμᾶς· ἐμὲ δὲ μισεῖ, ὅτι ἐγὼ μαρτυρῶ περὶ αὐτοῦ ὅτι τὰ ἔργα αὐτοῦ πονηρά ἐστιν*. Compare this with the words spoken shortly afterwards to the disciples (xv. 19), *εἰ ἐκ τοῦ κόσμου ἦτε, ὁ κόσμος ἂν τὸ ἴδιον ἐφίλει· ὅτι δὲ ἐκ τοῦ κόσμου οὐκ ἔστε, ἀλλ' ἐγὼ ἐξέλεξα ὑμᾶς ἐκ τοῦ κόσμου, διὰ τοῦτο μισεῖ ὑμᾶς ὁ κόσμος*. I defer the question as to the cause and nature of the unbelief imputed to the Lord's brothers, and the cause of their subsequent conversion. I simply note here that in vii. 3 they are represented as making a distinction between themselves and the disciples, and that in vv. 5–7 they are said to be on the side of the world against Christ. I think my readers will agree that the argument derived from St. Paul's words must be one of great force if it is to overthrow the combined evidence of so many passages, all showing that Christ's brothers were not included in the Twelve.

Examination of the text adduced on the other side. Meaning of *εἰ μὴ* in Gal. i. 19.

The words on which Jerome lays stress, as proving that James was one of the Twelve, are found in Gal. i. 18, 19, *ἀνῆλθον εἰς Ἱεροσόλυμα ἱστορῆσαι Κηφᾶν καὶ ἐπέμεινα πρὸς αὐτὸν ἡμέρας δεκάπεντε· ἕτερον δὲ τῶν ἀποστόλων οὐκ εἶδον, εἰ μὴ Ἰάκωβον τὸν ἀδελφὸν τοῦ Κυρίου.* Bishop Lightfoot in his note discusses whether this should be translated, 'I saw no other Apostle save James,' or 'I saw no other Apostle, but only James.' He gives instances to show that *εἰ μὴ* may have the latter force, *e.g.* Luke iv. 27, *πολλοὶ λεπροὶ ἦσαν ἐν τῷ Ἰσραὴλ ἐπὶ Ἐλισαίου τοῦ προφήτου, καὶ οὐδεὶς αὐτῶν ἐκαθαρίσθη εἰ μὴ Νααμὰν ὁ Σύρος*, Gal. ii. 16, *οὐ δικαιοῦται ἄνθρωπος ἐξ ἔργων νόμου ἐὰν μὴ διὰ πίστεως Ἰησοῦ Χριστοῦ*, Apoc. xxi. 27, *οὐ μὴ εἰσέλθῃ εἰς αὐτὴν πᾶν κοινὸν καὶ ὁ ποιῶν βδέλυγμα καὶ ψεῦδος, εἰ μὴ οἱ γεγραμμένοι ἐν τῷ βιβλίῳ τῆς ζωῆς*, *ib.* ix. 4. The peculiarity of these cases is that, whereas, according to the ordinary use, *εἰ μὴ* introduces an exception to a general statement applicable to the class to which the excepted case belongs, in the instances cited the excepted case is not included in the foregoing class. It appears to be originally a colloquial use, and is employed with comic effect in Arist. *Eq.* 185, &c. Thus here Naaman was not one of the many lepers in Israel; they who are written in the Book of Life are not included among those who are guilty of abomination and falsehood; faith is not included in the works of the law, but is contrasted with them as a different kind of justification. Accordingly, St. James need not be included in the preceding Apostles. Much in the same way we find *πλήν* used, where we should rather have expected *ἀλλά*, *e.g.* Acts xxvii. 22, *ἀποβολὴ γὰρ ψυχῆς οὐδεμία ἔσται ἐξ ὑμῶν πλὴν τοῦ πλοίου.* But even if we give its usual force to *εἰ μή*, it will not follow that St. James was included in the Twelve, for there can be no doubt that in Gal. i. 19 *ἕτερον* looks backward to *Κηφᾶν*, not forward to *Ἰάκωβον*. The sentence would have been complete at *εἶδον*, 'I saw Peter and none other of the Apostles.' Then it strikes St. Paul, as an afterthought, that the position of James, as President of the Church at Jerusalem, was not inferior to that of the Apostles, and he adds 'unless you reckon James among them.'

The term 'apostle' was not confined to the Twelve

That the term 'apostle' was not strictly confined to the Twelve appears from another passage in which James is mentioned, 1 Cor. xv. 4–7. Here it is said that Jesus after His resurrection 'appeared to Cephas, then to the Twelve, then to above 500 brethren at once, then to James, then to all the Apostles,' where we should perhaps consider the term to include the Seventy, according to the view of Irenaeus and other early writers. At any rate there can be no doubt as to St. Paul's apostleship. Barnabas also is called an apostle (Acts xiv. 4, 14), probably also Andronicus and Junias (Rom. xvi. 7), and Silvanus (1 Thess. ii. 6).[1]

It seems to me that the most natural interpretation of the two passages just dealt with is that which concedes the name 'apostle' in the wider sense to St. James, but makes a distinction between him and the Twelve. We should infer the same from 1 Cor. ix. 5, 6, 'have we not a right to take about a wife that is a believer' (*ἀδελφὴν γυναῖκα*) *ὡς καὶ οἱ λοιποὶ ἀπόστολοι και οἱ ἀδελφοὶ τοῦ Κυρίου καὶ Κηφᾶς; ἢ μόνος ἐγὼ καὶ Βαρνάβας οὐκ ἔχομεν ἐξόυσίαν μὴ ἐργάζεσθαι;* Here *οἱ λοιποὶ ἀπόστολοι* is contrasted with *ἐγὼ καὶ Βαρνάβας*: and apparently the 'brethren of the Lord' and 'Cephas' are particularized as being those who were known to make use of the liberty belonging of right to them all.

If it should be argued that, where the 'brethren of the Lord' are distinguished from the Twelve, this may be spoken loosely of the majority of them, and need not be understood to apply strictly to each separate brother; that it is consistent therefore with the supposition that James, for instance, was an Apostle, provided that Simon and Jude were not Apostles; the answer is that the theory derives part of its seeming strength from the coincidence of the names of three of the brethren of the Lord and three of the Twelve Apostles. But it is impossible to suppose repeated assertions to be made respecting the brethren of the Lord, which (on this supposition) are untrue of him who was by far the best known among them. Lastly it is to be noticed that neither James nor Jude claims the title of Apostle in his Epistle, and that Jude seems to disclaim the title for himself in ver. 17, *μνή-*

Neither James nor Jude call themselves Apostles.

[1] See Lightfoot, *l.c.*, pp. 92–101, and the *Didaché*, xi. 1. 5, with Funk's notes.

σθητε τῶν ῥημάτων τῶν προειρημένων ὑπὸ τῶν ἀποστόλων τοῦ Κυρίου.

The brothers of the Lord are always found in company with His mother.

(3) It has been shown that probability is strongly against a cousin of the Lord being habitually known as ἀδελφὸς Κυρίου, and that the evidence is overwhelming against the brothers of the Lord being included in the Twelve. Scarcely less strong is the argument against the Hieronymian view drawn from what we read of the relation of the brethren of the Lord to his mother. Though, according to this view, their own mother Mary was living at the time of the crucifixion, and though there is nothing to show that their father was not also living, yet they are never found in the company of their parents or parent, but always with the Virgin. They move with her and her divine Son to Capernaum and form one household there (John ii. 12); they take upon themselves to control and check the actions of Jesus; they go with Mary 'to take him,' when it is feared that his mind is becoming unhinged. They are referred to by the neighbours as members of his family in exactly the same terms as his mother and his reputed father; the neighbours, it is evident, have no more doubt as to the one relationship than they have as to the other; they have known the parents, they have known the children; there is in their eyes no mystery in the matter, nothing to suggest anything out of the common order of nature. It is suggested indeed that the Virgin and her sister were both widows at this time, and had agreed to form one household; but this is mere hypothesis, and is scarcely consistent with the remarks of the neighbours, who endeavour to satisfy themselves that Jesus was not entitled to speak as he had done, by calling to mind those nearest to him in blood. We read that Joseph was still alive at the time of the visit to the Temple in His twelfth year; the neighbours must surely have known whether these six or seven brothers and sisters were really Joseph's children or those of Joseph's sister-in-law. But we need not dwell further on this point, since the assumption on which the whole theory rests is untenable, as I now proceed to show.

The testimony of the neighbours goes to prove the reality of the fraternal, no less than of the maternal relation.

It is Salome, not Mary of Clopas, who is called by St. John the aunt of Jesus.

(4) That Mary of Clopas was the sister of Mary the mother of the Lord, is not only most improbable in itself (for where do we find two sisters with the same name ?), but is not the most natural interpretation of St. John xix. 25, *εἱστήκεισαν δὲ παρὰ τῷ σταυρῷ*

τοῦ Ἰησοῦ ἡ μήτηρ αὐτοῦ καὶ ἡ ἀδελφὴ τῆς μητρὸς αὐτοῦ, Μαρία ἡ τοῦ Κλωπᾶ καὶ Μαρία ἡ Μαγδαληνή (translated in the Peshitto, 'His mother and his mother's sister, *and* Mary of Cleopha and Mary Magdalene'). If we compare this verse with Mark xv. 40 and Matt. xxvii. 56, we find that, of the three women named as present in addition to the mother of Jesus, Mary Magdalene occurs in all three lists; 'Mary the mother of James and Joses' of the two synoptic Gospels is generally identified with 'Mary of Clopas'; and we then have left in Matthew 'the mother of the sons of Zebedee,' in Mark 'Salome,' and in John 'his mother's sister.' Salome is generally identified with 'the mother of the sons of Zebedee,' and there seems good reason also for identifying her with 'his mother's sister' in the Fourth Gospel. It does not seem likely that St. John would omit the name of his own mother; and the indirect way in which he describes her is very similar to the way in which he refers to himself as 'the disciple whom Jesus loved.' If we are right in this supposition, it is natural that the two sisters should be paired together, and then the two other Maries, just as we have the Apostles arranged in pairs without a connecting particle in Matt. x. 3, 4. If the sons of Zebedee were so nearly related to our Lord, it helps us to understand Salome's request that they might sit on His right hand and on His left hand in His glory, as well as the commendation by our Lord of his mother to one, who was not only his best-loved disciple, but her own nephew. If, however, this interpretation is correct, if the sister of the Lord's mother is not the mother of James and Joses, but the mother of the sons of Zebedee, then the foundation-stone of the Hieronymian theory is removed, and the whole fabric topples to the ground.

There is no ground for the identification either of James the Little with the brother of the Lord, or of Ἰούδας Ἰακώβου with the writer of the epistle of Jude.

(5) I take next two minor identifications, that of 'James the less' with the 'brother of the Lord,' and that of Ἰούδας Ἰακώβου, of Luke vi. 16 and Acts i. 13, with Jude the writer of the Epistle, who calls himself 'brother of James.' We have seen that Mary the mother of James τοῦ μικροῦ and of Joses, in Mark xv. 40, is probably the same as Mary of Clopas, and that we have no reason for inferring from the Gospels that she was related to Jesus. If so, there is an end to the supposition that James the less is James the brother of the Lord. But it is worth while to notice the mistranslation in which Jerome imagined that he found a further argument for the identification of our James with the son of

Alphaeus. The comparative *minor*, he says, suggests two persons, viz. the two Apostles of this name. But the Greek has no comparative, simply τοῦ μικροῦ, 'the little,' which no more implies a comparison with only one person, than any other descriptive epithet, such as εὐεργέτης or φιλάδελφος. As to Ἰούδας Ἰακώβου, no instance is cited for such an omission of the word ἀδελφός, and we must therefore translate 'Judas *son* of James' with the R.V. Independently of this, if James, Judas and Simon are all sons of Alphaeus, what a strange way is this of introducing their names in the list of the Apostles, 'James of Alphaeus, Simon Zelotes, Judas of James'! Why not speak of all as 'sons of Alphaeus,' or of the two latter as 'brothers of James'? Why not speak of all as 'brethren of the Lord'? It is especially strange that, if Judas were really known as such, he should have been distinguished in John (xiv. 22) merely by a negative, 'Judas not Iscariot,' and in the other Gospels by the appellation 'Lebbaeus' or 'Thaddaeus' (Matt. x. 3, Mark iii. 18).

There is no ground for identifying Clopas and Alphaeus.

(6) Much has been made of the identification of the names Alphaeus and Clopas, and of the duality of Clopas and Cleopas (Luke xxiv. 18). It seems doubtful whether the identification of the former and the separation of the latter pair can be maintained. Bp. Lightfoot considers that 'viewing the question as one of names only, it is quite as reasonable to identify Clopas with Cleopas as with Alphaeus' (*l.c.* pp. 256, 267). Supposing, however, our previous argument to be sound, the question is of no importance as to our main subject.

Extreme improbability of the Hieronymian view.

I have endeavoured to point out the difficulties which beset the Hieronymian theory and make it in my opinion less worthy of acceptance than either of the other theories. As it seems still to be the predominant theory in the Churches of Western Christendom, reformed[1] and unreformed, I have thought it might be well to show by a rough numerical estimate the force of the

[1] Even a commentator so little fettered by tradition as Dr. S. Cox writes thus in the *Expositor* for Jan. 1890, p. 68: 'James then (as I hold and shall assume, after a careful study of the various theories propounded about him...) was the son of Alphaeus, otherwise called Clopas, and of his wife, the sister of the Virgin Mary... Among his brothers were Simeon...Jude...Joses...and Levi the publican.' It is curious that the one authority to which Dr. Cox refers those who care to examine the controversy for themselves is 'the admirable summary in Dean Plumptre's commentary,' where, however, we read (p. 17) 'there is absolutely no ground for identifying the brother of the Lord with the son of Alphaeus.'

probabilities which are really arrayed against it. This will be found in the note below.[1]

C. I proceed now to examine the Epiphanian view, according to which the Lord's brothers were sons of Joseph by a former wife. This was the generally accepted view when Jerome put forward his new theory, and to a great extent it escapes the difficulties which, we have seen, attach to that theory.

There is no force in the objections made to the Epiphanian theory from the Hieronymian point of view.

Two unimportant objections made both to it and to the Helvidian theory from the Hieronymian point of view are: (1) that they assume the existence of two sets of cousins having two names in common, James and Joseph being found both among the sons of Alphaeus and among the Lord's brothers; and if we accept the statement of Hegesippus that Symeon was son of Clopas, and identify Clopas with Alphaeus, we then get a third name, Symeon, common to the families. This objection is based on several assumptions, one being that Mary the wife of Clopas was sister of the Virgin Mary, which has been shown to be all but incredible. But waiving this, why should it be thought improbable that three of the commonest Jewish names should be found in two sets of cousins? We have a greater variety of Christian names in ordinary use in England than there were then in Judea, but no one would think such a recurrence of names in any way remarkable or extraordinary; in fact, so far as my experience goes, the improbability is all the other way.

[1] Those who have followed the argument in the text will not, I think, regard the following estimates of the chances in favour of the several suppositions involved in the Hieronymian theory as giving an unfair representation of the case:

(*a*) for the use of ἀδελφός for cousin in the phrase ἀδελφὸς Κυρίου—one out of five ($\frac{1}{5}$), making 4 to 1 *against it.*

(*b*) for the brethren of the Lord being included in the Twelve—one out of ten ($\frac{1}{10}$), making 9 to 1 *against it.*

(*c*) for the supposed sons of Clopas-Alphaeus being always found in company—*not* with their own mother, who was certainly still living,—but with their aunt, residing with her and her Son, and taking on themselves to control the actions of the latter—one out of ten ($\frac{1}{10}$), making 9 to 1 *against it.*

(*d*) for two sisters having the same name—one out of ten ($\frac{1}{10}$), making 9 to 1 *against it.*

There are various other improbabilities, some of which have been already touched on, and others of even greater weight will appear in treating of the Epiphanian view, but I should be willing to rest the case on the four points here named, giving a resultant probability *in favour of* the simultaneous realisation of the four above-stated hypotheses of $\frac{1}{5 \times 10 \times 10 \times 10} = \frac{1}{5000}$, making 4999 probabilities to 1 *against it*, that is, against the truth of the Hieronymian theory.

(2) When a certain Mary is described as 'the mother of James' we naturally assume that the James intended is the most celebrated of the name, viz. the Lord's brother. But we elsewhere find the same Mary designated as mother of Joses (Mark xv. 47), or more generally of James and Joses (Matt. xxvii. 56, Mark xv. 40), so that no stress can be laid upon this.

Its real weakness lies in its forced interpretation of certain texts.

(3) It appears then that the Hieronymian theory is as weak in attack as it is in defence, and that if the Epiphanian theory is to be attacked with any prospect of success, it must be from the Helvidian side, on the ground that, no less than the Hieronymian, it gives an artificial and non-natural rendering of two passages of Scripture which we have still to consider; that it weakens the force of the narrative which we have already considered, telling how the mother of Jesus came with his brothers to take him; and gives a less natural meaning to the word 'brother.' The two passages yet to be considered are Matt. i. 24, Ἰωσὴφ . . . *παρέλαβεν τὴν γυναῖκα αὐτοῦ καὶ οὐκ ἐγίνωσκεν αὐτὴν ἕως οὗ ἔτεκεν υἱόν*, and Luke ii. 7, *καὶ ἔτεκεν τον υἱὸν αὐτῆς τὸν πρωτότοκον.* Reading these in connexion with those other passages which speak of the brothers and sisters of Jesus, it is hard to believe that the Evangelists meant us to understand, or indeed that it ever entered their heads that the words could be understood to mean, any thing else than that these brothers were sons of the mother and the reputed father of the Lord. It has been attempted however to prove that we need not take the passages referred to in their ordinary and natural sense. Thus Pearson, treating of the phrase *ἕως οὗ*, tells us that 'the manner of the Scripture language produceth no such inference,' as that, from a limit assigned to a negative, we may imply a subsequent affirmative: and he cites the following as instances in his favour. 'When God said to Jacob "I will not leave thee until I have done that which I have spoken to thee of" (Gen. xxviii. 15), it followeth not that, when that was done, the God of Jacob left him. When the conclusion of Deuteronomy was written it was said of Moses "No man knoweth of his sepulchre unto this day" (Deut. xxxiv. 6), but it were a weak argument to infer from thence, that the sepulchre of Moses has been known ever since. When Samuel had delivered a severe prediction unto Saul, he "came no more to see him unto the day of his death" (1 Sam. xv. 35); but it were a strange

Attempt to weaken the force of ἕως οὗ in Matt. i. 24.

collection to infer, that he therefore gave him a visit after he was dead. "Michal the daughter of Saul had no child unto the day of her death" (2 Sam. vi 23); and yet it were a ridiculous stupidity to dream of any midwifery in the grave. Christ promised his presence to the Apostles "until the end of the world" (Matt. xxviii. 20); who ever made so unhappy a construction, as to infer from thence that for ever after he would be absent from them?' (*Creed*, p. 174).

Importance of distinguishing between the limit which negatives, and the limit which suggests future action after the limit is attained.

It is difficult to believe that a man of Pearson's ability can have been blind to the difference between two kinds of limit, the mention of one of which suggests, while the mention of the other negatives, the future occurrence of the action spoken of. If we read 'the debate was adjourned till the papers should be in the hands of the members,' it as certainly implies the intention to resume the debate at a subsequent period, as the phrase 'the debate was adjourned till that day six months,' or 'till the Greek Kalends,' implies the contrary. So when it is said 'to the day of his death,' 'to the end of the world,' this is only a more vivid way of saying *in saecula saeculorum*. In like manner the phrase 'unto this day' implies that a certain state of things continued up to the very last moment known to the writer: the suggestion is of course that it will still continue. The remaining instance is that contained in Gen. xxviii. 15. This is a promise of continued help on the part of God until a certain end is secured. When that end is secured God is no further bound by his promise, however much the patriarch might be justified in looking for further help from his general knowledge of the character and goodness of God. To take now a case similar to that in hand: supposing we read 'Michal had no child till she left David and became the wife of Phaltiel,' we should naturally assume that after that she did have a child. So in Matt. i. 24 the limit is not one beyond which the action becomes naturally and palpably impossible: on the contrary it is just that point of time when under ordinary circumstances the action would become both possible and natural,[1] when therefore the reader, with-

[1] Compare Plut. *Qu. Conv.* viii. 1, Diog. L. iii. 2 (on the vision which appeared to Ariston warning him *μὴ συγγίνεσθαι τῇ γυναικί* till the birth of her son Plato: Origen *c. Cels.* i. 37 refers to this as an *arg. ad hom.*), Hygin. *F.* 29, quoted in Wetstein's note *in loco;* Athenag. *Apol.* 33 *ὡς γὰρ ὁ γεωργὸς καταβάλλων εἰς γῆν τὰ σπέρματα ἄμητον περιμένει, οὐκ ἐπισπείρων, καὶ ἡμῖν μέτρον ἐπιθυμίας ἡ παιδοποιΐα*, Const. Apost. vi. 28. 5 *μήτε μὴν ἐγκυμονούσαις ὁμιλείτωσαν* (*ταῖς γυναιξὶν οἱ ἄνδρες*), *οὐκ ἐπὶ παιδῶν γὰρ γενέσει τοῦτο ποιοῦσιν, ἀλλ' ἡδονῆς χάριν.* Clement of Alexandria *Strom.* iii. p. 543) calls this a law of nature.

out warning to the contrary, might naturally be expected to assume that it did actually occur. How far this assumption on the part of the reader, natural under ordinary circumstances, becomes unnatural under the very extraordinary circumstances of the case, will be discussed further on. I confine myself here to the argument from language.[1]

The use of πρωτότοκος in Luke ii. 7 implies that Jesus was not the only child of his mother.

The natural inference drawn from the use of the word πρωτότοκον in Luke ii. 7 is that other brothers or sisters were born subsequently; otherwise why should not the word μονογενής have been used as in Tobit iii. 15 μονογενής εἰμι τῷ πατρί μου, Luke vii. 12, viii. 42, &c.? In Rom. viii. 29 the word is used metaphorically, but retains its natural connotation, πρωτότοκον ἐν πολλοῖς ἀδελφοῖς, and so in every instance of its occurrence in the N.T. It occurs many times in its literal use in the LXX., e.g. Gen. xxvii. 19, 32, xliii. 33, Deut. xxi. 15, 1 Kings xvi. 34, 1 Chron. v. 1, xxvi. 10, but, so far as I have observed, never of an only son. It is said in answer to this by Bp. Lightfoot (p. 271) that "the prominent idea conveyed by the term first-born to a Jew would be not the birth of other children, but the special consecration of this one. The typical reference in fact is foremost in the mind of St. Luke, as he himself explains it, 'Every male that openeth the womb shall be called holy to the Lord' (ii. 23)." But need we ascribe to St. Luke any other purpose, in giving this quotation from the Mosaic law, beyond the simple desire to explain how it was that Simeon was enabled to see Him, who was not only 'the glory of his people Israel,' but also 'a light to lighten the Gentiles'? No doubt the law as to the first-born is equally valid whether there are other children or not; but St. Luke is not here concerned in stating the law, but in giving a narrative of domestic life, viewed retrospectively from the standpoint of accomplished facts: under these circumstances the use of the word πρωτότοκος is surely misleading, and therefore improbable, if there were no children born afterwards.[2]

[1] Laurent remarks on the use of the imperfect ἐγίνωσκε implying abstinence from a habit ('refrained from conjugal intercourse') as opposed to the far more usual ἔγνω denoting a single act.

[2] Suicer, ii. p. 877, quotes from Severianus, πρωτότοκος λέγεται ὁ ἀδελφοὺς ἔχων, and from Theodoret εἰ πρωτότοκος, πῶς μονογενής; the latter referring to a theological difficulty arising out of Col. i. 15 (where see Lightfoot), but the phrase naturally applies to the word taken in its simple meaning. In the Psalms of Solomon (xviii. 4) we have the two words combined so as to exclude the natural inference, ἡ παιδεία σου ἐφ' ἡμᾶς ὡς υἱὸν πρωτότοκον μονογενῆ. The latest editors suggest that these are duplicate renderings of the same Hebrew word (p. lxxx.). I may mention here Dr. Edersheim's remark, that, if the Epiphanian theory were true, our Lord would not have been the heir to David's throne according to the Genealogies, as his elder brother would have ranked before Him. (*Jesus the Messiah*, i. p. 364).

This is also suggested by the story of the visit to the Temple in His twelfth year.

I think also that there are circumstances connected with one remarkable episode in our Lord's childhood, which are more easily explicable if we suppose him not to have been his mother's only son. Is it likely that Mary and Joseph would have been so little solicitous about an only son, and that son the promised Messiah, as to begin their homeward journey after the feast of the Passover at Jerusalem, and to travel for a whole day without taking the pains to ascertain whether he was in their company or not? If they had several younger children to attend to, we can understand that their first thoughts would have been given to the latter; otherwise is it conceivable that Mary, however complete her confidence in her eldest Son, should first have lost him from her side, and then have allowed so long a time to elapse without an effort to find him?

Objections to the Helvidian view, that the brethren were sons of Joseph and Mary.

D. There are however some difficulties which must be grappled with before we can accept the Helvidian theory as satisfactory. (1) If the mother of Jesus had had other sons would He have commended her to the care of a disciple rather than to that of a brother? (2) Is not the behaviour of the brethren towards Jesus that of elders towards a younger? (3) The theory is opposed to the Church tradition. (4) It is abhorrent to Christian sentiment.

If Mary had had another son, she would not have been left to the care of a disciple.

(1) Bp. Lightfoot regards the first objection as fatal to the theory. 'Is it conceivable,' he says, 'that our Lord would thus have snapped asunder the most sacred ties of natural affection?' (p. 272). The usual answer to this is that the disbelief of the Lord's brothers would naturally separate them from his mother. But as this disbelief was even then on the point of being changed into undoubting faith; and as the separation, if it ever existed, of which there is no evidence, was at any rate to be changed in a day or two into the closest union with all true followers of the Lord; and as the preparation for this change must have been long perceptible to the eye of Jesus; it seems necessary to find another way of meeting the objection, if it is to be met at all. I think however that Bp. Lightfoot goes a little too far when he speaks just below of this hypothesis requiring us to believe that the mother, though 'living in the same city' with her sons 'and joining with them in a common worship (Acts i. 14), is consigned to the care of a stranger, of whose house she becomes henceforth the inmate.' We have seen that there is reason for believing Salome to have been the sister of Mary, and John therefore her nephew; but however

this may be, in any case, as her Son's dearest friend, he must have been well known to her. And if we try to picture to ourselves the circumstances of the case, it is not difficult to imagine contingencies which would make it a very natural arrangement. It is generally supposed (from 1 Cor. ix. 5) that the brothers of the Lord were married men: the usual age for marriage among the Jews was about eighteen: supposing them to have been born before the visit to the Temple of the child Jesus, they would probably have married before his Crucifixion. If then all her children were dispersed in their several homes, and if, as we naturally infer, her nephew John was unmarried and living in a house of his own, is there anything unaccountable in the Lord's mother finding a home with the beloved disciple? Could this be regarded in any way as a slight by her other sons? Must they not have felt that the busy life of a family was not suited for the quiet pondering which now more than ever would characterize their mother? and further that this communion between the Mother and the Disciple was likely to be not only a source of comfort to both, but also most profitable to the Church at large?

The brothers of the Lord act towards him as elders towards a younger.

(2) It depends more upon the positive age, than the relative age, of brothers, whether the interference of a younger with an elder is probable or improbable. When all have reached manhood and have settled in their different spheres, a few years' difference in age does not count for much. It might however be thought that those who had grown up with one like Jesus, must have felt such love and reverence for him, that they could never dream of blaming or criticizing what he thought best to do. Yet we know that his mother, to whom had been vouchsafed a much fuller revelation than was possible in their case, as to the true nature of her Son, did nevertheless on more than one occasion draw upon herself his reproof for ventured interference. If we remember how little even those whom he chose out as his Apostles were able to appreciate his aims and methods up to the very end of his life, how different was their idea of the Kingdom of Heaven and the office of the Messiah from His, we shall not wonder if his younger brothers, with all their admiration for his genius and goodness, were at times puzzled and bewildered at the words that fell from his lips; if they regarded him as a self-forgetting idealist and enthusiast, wanting in knowledge of the world as it was, and needing the constant care

of his more practical friends to provide him with the ordinary comforts and necessaries of life. Thus much, I think, is certain from the known facts of the case; and we need nothing more than this to explain their fear that his mind might be overstrained, and their attempt to dictate the measures he should adopt in going up to the Feast, just as his mother had attempted to dictate to him at the marriage of Cana.

The Helvidian theory is opposed to tradition.

(3) Dealing with the argument from tradition, we must bear in mind that what we are in search of is historical fact. The accepted historical belief at any given time depends, so far as the educated minority is concerned, partly upon the critical interpretation of supposed authentic documents by contemporary scholars, such as Jerome in the fourth century, who regarded it as mere waste of time to leave the Scriptures, the fountain of truth, and follow *opinionum rivulos*, the fancies of later writers who had no other ground for their guesses than the Scriptures themselves (Jer. *Adv. Helv.* 17). But even of the educated it is true to a certain extent, as it is entirely true of the uneducated, that they take their notions of history without inquiry either from the most popular epitome or from what may be loosely called tradition. And tradition as it exists in any age will probably have some nucleus of fact, but that nucleus is so transformed by the action of the imagination, and by the thoughts and feelings of the generations which have passed since the actual occurrences of which it embalms the memory, that we cannot trust it for details. Thus, while we may fully allow the interest and importance which attach to the thoughts and feelings of Christians in former ages, yet for our present purpose it seems desirable to separate our consideration of these from our consideration of tradition, as embodying an actual recollection of fact handed down orally from father to son, or crystallized in literature at a certain stage of its progress. There is also such a thing as manufactured tradition, like that of the Ciceroni, or merely literary tradition, like that which has grown up round the scenes of many of Scott's romances. In our investigation of any so-called tradition it is of the utmost importance to be on our guard against mistaking deliberate invention of this kind for natural growth.

What is meant by tradition?

We have seen already that neither from Tertullian writing in the second century, nor from Basil writing in the fourth, do we gather the existence of any established or authorized tradition in favour of the Epiphanian view. We have seen also that both Origen and Jerome trace back the origin of this view to the Apocryphal Gospels, and that Jerome puts forward his own view as an entirely novel hypothesis. I think therefore we may conclude that, setting aside these Gospels, there was no fixed recognized tradition on the subject before the end of the fourth century, though there was a growing feeling in favour of the perpetual virginity, which took definite shape in the title ἀειπαρθένος used of Mary by Athanasius; and the apocryphal fictions were eagerly embraced as affording a support for this belief. Jerome's view, being still more in accordance with the ascetic views of the time, was adopted by Augustine and the Latin Fathers generally; while in the Eastern Church, Chrysostom, who, in his earlier writings, favours the Epiphanian view, comes round to Jerome in the later. The subsequent Greek Fathers are, however, almost all on the side of Epiphanius; and the Greek, Syrian, and Coptic Calendars mark the distinction between James the brother of the Lord and James the son of Alphaeus by assigning a separate day to each. This distinction is also maintained, apart from any statement as to the exact relationship implied by the term 'brother,' in the *Clementine Homilies* and *Recognitions* of the second century, and the *Apostolic Constitutions* of the third.

Abstract of the argument of Epiphanias in favour of the perpetual virginity of Mary.

A short abstract of the argument of Epiphanius will show us the grounds on which he relied, and will also furnish an interesting specimen of tradition in the making. It is contained in the third book of his *Panarium*, *Haer*. lxxviii. (*Against the Adversaries of Mary*) p. 1037 foll.

In this age of heresy, he says, while some have ventured to propagate errors about the Trinity, others have turned their assaults against τῆς ἁγίας Μαρίας, τῆς ἀειπαρθένου. Surely her very name is enough to confute them. As Abraham is always the Friend of God, James and John always Sons of Thunder, so Mary always the Virgin. The assertion that she ever ceased to be a virgin shows a want of knowledge of Scripture and of history. For first of all it was determined by lot that she should be delivered to Joseph, a widower of eighty years, for the purpose of protection, not of marriage.[1] This Joseph was brother of Clopas and son of Jacob surnamed Panther. His first wife was of the tribe of Judah and by her he had six children, the eldest Jacob, surnamed Oblias and Just, the first to whom the Lord entrusted the episcopal throne, then Joses, Simeon, Judas, Mary, and Salome as we learn from Scripture (p. 1041). Epiphanius then lays stress on the use of the word

[1] See *Protevang.* 8, 9.

μνηστευθείσης not γαμηθείσης, and argues that a just man, such as Joseph is described to be, one too who is still honoured as a pattern of virginity, could never have regarded as his wife her who was the chosen vessel of the Holy Ghost. The Holy Family returned from Egypt when Jesus was four years old; and not long afterwards Joseph died. If he had been still alive or if Mary had had children of her own, would Jesus have entrusted her to John at the Crucifixion? And why is she called mother of John? Surely because she is μήτηρ ἀρχηγὸς τῆς παρθενίας. Nothing is said as to the Virgin's death, but it does not seem that she accompanied St. John to Ephesus. What does this silence intimate? I tremble almost to say it, but in the Apocalypse (xii. 13) I read 'the dragon persecuted the woman which brought forth the man child, and to the woman were given two wings of a great eagle, that she might fly into her place.' May not this have been fulfilled in the Holy Virgin, so that she never tasted of death? Again let us give heed to the lessons of Nature. Science tells us that the lioness can only bring forth once, and Christ is the lion of the tribe of Judah. James, the eldest son of Joseph, died in his ninety-sixth year, having preserved his virginity intact, having never cut his hair or used a bath, or tasted flesh, or worn more than one tunic. He alone was allowed to enter the Holy of Holies once a year and to wear the priestly petalum, because he was a Nazarite and of kin to the priests. After other particulars borrowed from Hegesippus (except that Epiphanius puts into the mouth of Symeon, son of Clopas, the words 'Why do you stone the Just? Behold he prayeth for you,' which Hegesippus ascribes to 'a priest of the sons of Rechab') he continues 'if then the sons of Joseph were virgins and Nazarites, how much more would their father have known how to respect the purity of the Virgin?' Can we conceive it possible that, after all the miracles which attended the birth of Jesus, this pious old man should have been guilty of impiety towards the sacred body ἐν ᾧ κατῳκίσθη Θεός? But why inquire into these things? Why not accept what is written and leave the rest to God. Surely you will not assert that our salvation depends on believing that Joseph did know his wife after the birth of her first-born. Had the Scripture asserted this we should have accepted it without scruple. We fully believe in the sanctity of marriage. But a prophet has no time for the cares and duties of marriage. Moses had no children after he entered on his prophetic office, and Mary was a prophet as is shown by Isa. viii. 3. Hence the daughters of Philip who prophesied were virgins, and Thecla broke off her engagement when converted by Paul.[1]

"But, it is said, how are we to explain such expressions as πρὶν ἢ συνελθεῖν αὐτοὺς, and οὐκ ἔγνω αὐτὴν ἕως ὅτου ἐγέννησε τὸν υἱὸν αὐτῆς τὸν πρωτότοκον. As to the latter it must be observed that it is not said τὸν πρωτότοκον αὐτῆς, not 'her first-born,' but 'her son, the first-born,' viz., the first-born of all creation. As to the former, what difficulty is there in the phrase οὐκ ᾔδει αὐτήν? [notice the tacit substitution of ᾔδει for ἔγνω]. How was Joseph to *know* the dignity conferred on her, until he had seen the miraculous birth? Then as to the phrase πρὶν ἢ συνελθεῖν, this might represent an expectation on the part of Joseph, but this, as we have seen, was precluded by his great age."

But while we do due honour to the Virgin, we must beware of deifying her, as some have done, οὔτε γὰρ θεὸς ἡ Μαρία, οὔτε ἀπ' οὐρανοῦ τὸ σῶμα, ἀλλ' ἐκ συλλήψεως ἀνδρὸς καὶ γυναικός, κατ' ἐπαγγελίαν δὲ, ὥσπερ ὁ Ἰσαάκ. Epiphanius then proceeds to deal with his seventy-ninth heresy 'Against the Collyridians who offer sacrifice to Mary'; where he refers to the history and traditions of Mary, as stating that it was revealed to Joachim in the desert that his wife Anna should bear a child.[2]

[1] Thecla also appears as a patroness of virginity in Methodius (*Banquet of the Ten Virgins*), written towards the close of the third century.

[2] Cf. *Protev.* c. 4, *Nativ. S. Mariae*, c. 3 (Thilo p. 321 foll.).

Growth of ascetic views of marriage.

I will make one or two remarks on this passage and then consider any further arguments advanced by later writers on the same side. The exaltation of virginity above marriage, of which we see traces in the New Testament itself, as in Apoc. xiv. 4, 1 Cor. vii. 1, as well as among the Essenes and Therapeutae (Josephus *B.J.* ii. 8. 2, Philo *Frag.* M. 2 p. 633, *Vit. Cont.* pp. 471 foll.), and against the exaggeration of which St. Paul warns Timothy (1 Ep. iv. 1), spread rapidly both amongst heretics and orthodox Christians. Of the former, Saturninus, Marcion, the Encratites and the Montanists in the second century are named as either depreciating or actually forbidding marriage among their adherents. Of the latter, evidence may be found in Athenagoras *Apol.* 28 εὕροις δ' ἂν πολλοὺς τῶν παρ' ἡμῖν καὶ ἄνδρας καὶ γυναῖκας καταγηράσκοντας ἀγάμους ἐλπίδι τοῦ μᾶλλον συνέσεσθαι τῷ Θεῷ; in such language as that of Cyprian (*Hab. Vir.* 3) *flos est ille ecclesiastici germinis . . . Dei imago respondens ad sanctimoniam Domini, illustrior portio gregis Christi;* ib. 22 *quod futuri sumus, vos jam esse coepistis...cum castae perseveratis et virgines, angelis Dei estis aequales*; and in the rash act by which Origen, at the beginning of the third century, believed himself to be carrying out the words of Christ (Matt. xix. 12). The same tendency is also noticeable in the neo-Pythagoreans and neo-Platonists. By the end of the third century it began to produce its natural consequence in the institution of celibate communities and the discouragement of marriage among the clergy. In the Council of Nicaea a determined attempt was made to compel married clergy to separate from their wives, and the hermit Paphnutius, who led the opposition, only pleaded in favour of what he calls the ancient custom, which, while it forbade marriage after a man had been ordained, did not require him to leave the wife whom he had married as a layman.[1] We cannot doubt that those who were agitating for a stricter rule would make use of the example of the Virgin, insisting on the name as implying a permanent state, and would endeavour to give an artificial strength to their cause by the addition of imaginary circumstances to the simple narrative of the Gospel.

The story of the Nativity gradually modified under the influence of the ascetic spirit.

Thus it was not enough to suppose the brethren of the Lord to be sons of Joseph by a former wife; Joseph's age must be increased so as to make it impossible for him to have had children by his

[1] See Stanley, *Eastern Church*, Lect. V.

second wife, though this supposition contradicts what the upholders of this view maintain to be the very purpose of Mary's marriage, viz. to screen her from all injurious imputations. How could the marriage effect this, if the husband were above eighty years of age, as Epiphanius says, following the Apocryphal Gospels? Again, if this were the case, why should not the Evangelist have stated it simply, instead of using the cautionary phrases *πρὶν ἢ συνελθεῖν* and *οὐκ ἐγίνωσκεν αὐτὴν ἕως οὗ ἔτεκεν*? But even this was not enough for the ascetic spirit. Further barriers must be raised between the contamination of matrimony and the virgin ideal. Joseph himself becomes a type of virginity: the 'brethren' are no longer his sons, but sons of Clopas, who was either his brother by one tradition, or his wife's sister's husband by another. Mary is made the child of promise and of miracle like Isaac, though not yet exalted to the honours of the Immaculate Conception; and we see Epiphanius already feeling his way to the doctrine of her Assumption, which was accepted by Gregory of Tours in the sixth century. One other development may be noticed, as it is found in the *Protevangelium*, c. 20, though not mentioned by Epiphanius, viz. that not only the Conception but the Birth of our Lord was miraculous; in the words of Jeremy Taylor 'He that came from his grave fast tied with a stone and signature, and into the college of the Apostles, the doors being shut . . . came also (as the Church piously believes) into the world so without doing violence to the virginal and pure body of his mother, that he did also leave her virginity entire.'[1]

Fantastic application of prophecy.

This miracle, superfluous as it is and directly opposed to the words of St. Luke (ii. 23), is yet accepted by Jerome and his followers; and it is in reference to it that Bp. Lightfoot (*l.c.* p. 371) thinks that too much stress has been laid by modern writers on the false asceticism of the early Church as the only cause of the dislike to the Helvidian view. He considers that this dislike is 'due quite as much to another sentiment which the Fathers fantastically expressed by a comparison between the conception and the burial of our Lord. As after death his body was placed in a sepulchre wherein never man before was laid, so it seemed fitting that the womb consecrated

[1] Chrys. *Hom.* cxlii. (ap. Suicer, ii. p. 306) *ὁ Χριστὸς προῆλθεν ἐκ μήτρας καὶ ἄλυτος ἔμεινεν ἡ μήτρα*, and it was affirmed in the 79th Canon of the Council *in Trullo* towards the end of the seventh century.

by His presence should not thenceforth have borne any offspring of man.' So we find Pearson (*Creed*, p. 326) citing in proof of the ἀειπαρθενία Ezek. xliv. 2 'This gate shall be shut, it shall not be opened, and no man shall enter in by it; because the Lord, the God of Israel, hath entered in by it, therefore it shall be shut.' It would surely have been more to the purpose to cite the words of the Messianic psalm (lxix. 8) 'I have become a stranger to my brethren and an alien to *my mother's children*,' this psalm being used to illustrate the earthly life of our Lord both by St. John, 'The zeal of thy house has eaten me up; they gave me also gall for my meat, and in my thirst they gave me vinegar to drink,' and by St. Luke, 'Let their habitation be desolate.' Whether these sentiments of the Fathers are to be regarded as something independent of the idea of the impurity of marriage or as a natural offshoot of it, which I should be rather inclined to believe, is not of much importance. The only question worth considering is: Are these sentiments so authoritative as to justify us in twisting the words of the Scripture narrative and giving to them a non-natural sense? This question I shall endeavour to answer in the next section.

The Helvidian view opposed to Christian sentiment.

(4) It is 'the tendency,' says Dr. Mill (*l.c.* p. 301), 'of the Christian mystery, God manifest in the flesh, when heartily received, to generate an unwillingness to believe that the womb thus divinely honoured should have given birth to other merely human progeny.' 'The sentiment of veneration for this august vessel of grace which has ever animated Christians . . . could not have been wanting to the highly-favoured Joseph.' 'On the impossibility of refuting these sentiments . . . the truly Catholic Christian will have pleasure in reposing.' So Epiphanius, Jerome, and other ancient writers speak of this as a 'pious belief,' and the same is reiterated by Hammond and Jeremy Taylor cited by Mill (p. 309). In answer to this I would say that unless we are prepared to admit all the beliefs of the mediaeval Church, we must beware of allowing too much authority to pious opinions. Is there any extreme of superstition which cannot plead a 'pious opinion' in its favour? Of course it is right in studying history, whether sacred or profane, to put ourselves in the position of the actors, to imagine how they must have felt and acted; but this is not quite the same thing as imagining how we ourselves should have felt and

Danger of imputing the sentiment of a later age to an earlier.

acted under their circumstances, until at least we have done our best to strip off all that differentiates the mind of one century from the mind of another. If we could arrive at the real feeling of Joseph in respect to his wife, and of Mary in respect to her Son before and after his birth, this would undoubtedly be an element of the highest importance for the determination of the question before us: but to assume that they must have felt as a monk, or nun, or celibate priest of the Middle Ages; to assume even, with Dr. Mill, that they fully understood the mystery 'God manifest in the flesh,' is not merely to make an unauthorized assumption, it is to assume what is palpably contrary to fact.

Jewish sentiment on the subject at the time of the Christian era.

Mary and Joseph were religious Jews, espoused to one another, as it is natural to suppose, in the belief prevalent among the Jews that marriage was a duty, and that a special blessing attached to a prolific union.[1] They looked forward, like Simeon and Anna, to the coming of the Messiah, the prophet like unto Moses who would speak the words of God to the people, the Prince of the house of David, who would not merely judge the heathen and restore again the glories of Solomon, but would sit as a refiner and purifier of silver and purify the sons of Levi themselves, and yet one who would bear the sins of many and make intercession for the transgressors.[2] To both it is revealed that the Messiah should be born

[1] Cf. the language of Mary's kinswoman Elizabeth in Luke i. 25, and Lightfoot, *Coloss.* p. 139, 'The Talmudic writings teem with passages implying not only the superior sanctity, but even the imperative duty of marriage. The words of Gen. i. 28 were regarded not merely as a promise, but as a command, which was binding upon all. It is a maxim of the Talmud that "Any Jew who has not a wife is no man" (*Yebamoth*, 63 *a*). The fact indeed is so patent, that any accumulation of examples would be superfluous, and I shall content myself with referring to *Pesachim*, 113 *a*, *b*, as fairly illustrating the doctrine of orthodox Judaism on this point'; *ib.* pp. 168, 9, 'The early disciples in the mother Church of Jerusalem show Pharisaic but not Essene sympathies. It was altogether within the sphere of orthodox Judaism that the Jewish element in the Christian brotherhood found its scope.' Cf. also C. Taylor, *Lectures on the Didaché*, pp. 86–88.

[2] See Ryle and James, *Psalms of Solomon*, p. lii. (speaking of the 17th Psalm): 'It may be taken, we believe, as presenting, more accurately than any other document, a statement of the popular Pharisaic expectation regarding the Messiah, shortly before the time when our Lord Jesus, the Christ, appeared.' Among the characteristics of the Messiah's rule there given, it is stated that 'He is to be a descendant of David,' that His Mission is of a twofold character, destructive towards Gentiles and sinners, restorative as regards Israel: His rule is spiritual, holy, wise, and just: 'all his subjects will be sons of God, all will be holy,' cf. Ps. xvii. 35 καὶ αὐτὸς βασιλεὺς δίκαιος καὶ διδακτὸς ὑπὸ Θεοῦ ἐπ' αὐτούς. καὶ οὐκ ἔστιν ἀδικία ἐν ταῖς ἡμέραις αὐτοῦ ἐν μέσῳ αὐτῶν, ὅτι πάντες ἅγιοι καὶ βασιλεὺς αὐτῶν Χριστὸς Κύριος (*al.* Κυρίου). But (p. lv.) 'though endowed with divine gifts, he is nothing more than man. Neither of supernatural birth, nor of pre-existence in the bosom of God, or among the angels of God, do we find any trace. He is an

of Mary by a miraculous conception. Joseph is told that 'his name is to be called Jesus, because he shall save his people from their sins.' Mary is told in addition that 'he shall be called the Son of the Highest, and that the Lord God shall give him the throne of his father David, and he shall reign over the house of Jacob for ever.' There is surely nothing in these words which would disclose the Christian mystery 'God manifest in the flesh.' They point to a greater Moses, or David, or Solomon, or Samuel. Mary's hymn of praise is founded on the recollection of Hannah's exultation at the fulfilment of prophecy in the birth of her son. Her mind would naturally turn to other miraculous births, to that of Isaac under the old dispensation, to that now impending in the case of her cousin Elizabeth. And as there was nothing in the announcement made to them which could enable them to realize the astounding truth that he who was to be born of Mary was VERY GOD OF VERY GOD, so there is nothing in the subsequent life of Mary which would lead us to believe that she, any more than his Apostles, had realized it before his Resurrection. On the contrary, it is plain that such a belief fully realized would have made it impossible for her to fulfil, I do not say her duties towards her husband, but her duties towards the Lord himself during his infancy and childhood. It is hard enough even now to hold together the ideas of the Humanity and Divinity of Christ without doing violence to either; but to those who knew him in the flesh we may safely say it was impossible until the Comforter had come and revealed it unto them. As to what should be the relations between the husband and wife after the birth of the promised Child there is one thing we may be sure of, viz. that these would be determined not by personal considerations, but either by immediate inspiration, as the journey to Egypt and other events had been, or, in the absence of this, by the one desire to do what they believed to be best for the bringing up of the Child entrusted to them. We can imagine their feeling it to be a duty to abstain from bringing other children into the world, in order that they might devote themselves more exclusively

What Scripture suggests as to the feelings of Mary and Joseph.

idealized Solomon. Again (p. lxii.) they remark, 'it is a matter not without interest and importance that our Psalms, which stand closest of all extant Jewish religious poetry to the Christian era, are so conspicuously similar to the songs contained in the opening chapters of St. Luke's Gospel.' The editors appear even to suggest the possibility that the so-called Psalms of Solomon may have been written by the author of the *Nunc dimittis* (p. lix. n.). In Justin's dialogue (§49) Trypho asserts that the general belief of the Jews is that Christ would be merely man.

to the nurture and training of Jesus. On the other hand, the greatest prophets and saints had not been brought up in solitude. Moses, Samuel and David had had brothers and sisters. It might be God's will that the Messiah should experience in this, as in other things, the common lot of man. Whichever way the Divine guidance might lead them, we may be sure that the response of Mary would be still as before, 'Behold the handmaid of the Lord, be it unto me according to thy word.'

There is no evidence of any sentiment on their part which would justify us in wresting the plain language of Scripture.

Even if the language of the Gospels had been entirely neutral on this matter, it would surely have been a piece of high presumption on our part to assume that God's Providence must always follow the lines suggested by our notions of what is seemly; but when every conceivable barrier has been placed in the way of this interpretation by the frequent mention of brothers of the Lord, living with his mother and in constant attendance upon her; when He is called her first-born son, and when St. Matthew goes into what we might have been inclined to think almost unnecessary detail in fixing a limit to the separation between husband and wife; can we characterize it otherwise than as a contumacious setting up of an artificial tradition above the written Word, if we insist upon it that 'brother' must mean, not brother, but either cousin or one who is no blood-relation at all; that 'first-born' does not imply other children subsequently born; that the limit fixed to separation does not imply subsequent union?

Result of the discussion.

The conclusion then, to which our discussion leads, is that James the Lord's brother was son of Joseph and Mary, brought up with Jesus until his eighteenth year at any rate, not one of the Twelve, not even a disciple till the very end of our Saviour's life, but convinced, as it would seem, by a special appearance to him of the risen Lord, and joining the company of the disciples before the day of Pentecost. After the martyrdom of Stephen, when the Apostles were scattered from Jerusalem, we find James holding a position of authority in the Church of Jerusalem (Gal. i. 18, 19, Acts xii. 17), which, as we may probably conjecture, had been conceded to him as brother of the Lord, and retaining this position till the end of his life.

Further particulars are supplied by Josephus, Hegesippus, the

Additional particulars of the life of James gathered from uninspired writings.

Gospel according to the Hebrews, and other Apocryphal books including in these the Clementine Homilies and Recognitions. We have to be on our guard against the Ebionite tendencies of some of these writers, and their delight in puerile marvels and ascetic practices, but we may perhaps accept the general outline as correct, since St. James occupied a prominent position, and the facts were for the most part patent to all the world, in marked contrast with the circumstances of the infancy and childhood of our Lord.

The appearance of the Lord to James after the resurrection as narrated in the Gospel according to the Hebrews.

The Gospel according to the Hebrews, which Bp. Lightfoot speaks of as 'one of the earliest and most respectable of the apocryphal narratives' (Gal. p. 274), is quoted by Jerome (*De Vir. Illustr.* 2) to the following effect: The gospel known as that according to the Hebrews, which I have translated into Greek and Latin, and which is often referred to by Origen, tells us that the Lord after his resurrection appeared to James, who had sworn that he would not eat bread from the hour in which he had drunk the cup of the Lord till he saw him risen from the dead. Jesus therefore 'took bread and blessed and brake it and gave it to James the Just, and said to him, My brother, eat thy bread, for the Son of Man has risen from the dead.' [1]

[1] The Latin is *Dominus autem cum dedisset sindonem servo sacerdotis* (apparently implying that Malchus was present at the resurrection and received from the Lord's hands the linen cloth in which his body had been wrapt), *ivit ad Jacobum et apparuit ei—juraverat enim Jacobus se non comesurum panem ab illa hora qua biberat calicem Domini, donec videret eum resurgentem a dormientibus;—rursusque post paululum 'afferte, ait Dominus, mensam et panem.' Statimque additur: Tulit panem et benedixit ac fregit et dedit Jacobo Justo et dixit ei, 'Frater mi, comede panem tuum, quia resurrexit Filius hominis a dormientibus.'* Bp. Lightfoot reads *calicem Dominus* for *calicem Domini*, 'as the point of time which we should naturally expect is not the institution of the eucharist, but the Lord's death,' to which He had Himself alluded under the phrase of 'drinking the cup' (Matt. xx. 22, 23, xxvi. 39, 42; cf. *Mart. Polyc.* 14, *ἐν τῷ ποτηρίῳ τοῦ Χριστοῦ σου*), and the Greek translation, which goes under the name of Sophronius, has Κύριος. There is however no various reading in Herding's edition of the *De Vir. Illustr.*, and Mr. Nicholson, in his edition of the fragments of the Gospel according to the Hebrews (pp. 62 foll.), gives instances of the untrustworthiness of the Greek translator. If *Domini* is the true reading, 'the writer represented James as present at the Last Supper, but it does not follow that he regarded him as one of the Twelve. He may have assigned to him...a position apart from, and in some respects superior to, the Twelve... It is characteristic of a Judaic writer that an appearance which seems in reality to have been vouchsafed to James to win him over from his unbelief, should be represented as a reward for his devotion' (Lightfoot, *l.c.*). The story appears in three other forms, given in Nicholson, none of which date the oath from the Last Supper. Thus Gregory of Tours, in the sixth century, (*Hist. Franc.* i. 21) writes: *Fertur Jacobus Apostolus, cum Dominum jam mortuum vidisset in cruce, detestatum esse atque jurasse numquam se comesturum panem nisi Dominum cerneret resurgentem. Tertia die rediens Dominus...Jacobo se ostendens ait 'surge Jacobe, comede, quia jam a mortuis resurrexi'*; his contemporary,

It will be seen from the note that there are other versions of the story, and that in these the vow is said to have been made after the death of Christ. It is easy to see how a confusion might have arisen if James, whether having heard from others or himself having witnessed the events of the Last Supper, had shaped his vow after the Lord's own words 'I will not drink henceforth of the fruit of the vine, till the kingdom of God shall come.' There is, I think, a ring of genuineness about the narrative. Whereas we usually find in the Apocryphal Gospels some real incident of our Lord's life smothered in a parasitic growth of puerilities and trivialities, here there is an originality and simplicity which is not unworthy of the genuine Gospels themselves.

Hegesippus on James.

I pass on now to Hegesippus, who is quoted to the following effect in Euseb. *H.E.* ii. 23:

The charge of the Church then (after the Ascension) devolved on James the brother of the Lord in concert with the Apostles. He is distinguished from the others of the same name by the title 'Just' (righteous) which has been applied to him from the first. He was holy from his mother's womb, drank no wine or strong drink, nor ate animal food; no razor came on his head, nor did he anoint himself with oil, or use the bath. To him alone was it permitted to enter into the Holy Place, for he wore no woollen, but only linen. And alone he would go into the temple, where he used to be found on his knees, asking forgiveness for the people, so that his knees became hard like a camel's because he was ever upon them worshipping God and asking forgiveness for the people. Accordingly through his exceeding righteousness he was called righteous ('Just') and 'Oblias' which being interpreted is 'the defence of the people' and 'righteousness,' as the prophets declared of him.[1] Some of the seven sects, which I have mentioned, inquired of him, 'What is the door of Jesus (τίς ἡ θύρα τοῦ Ἰησοῦ)?'[2] And he said that he was the Saviour, whereupon some believed that Jesus is the Christ. Now the forementioned sects did not believe in the resurrection or in the coming of one to recompense each man according to his works. But as many as did believe, believed through James.

---

the pseudo-Abdias (*Hist. Apost.* vi. 1), who refers to Hegesippus as his authority for part of his account of James, says that he was son of Joseph by a former wife, and so full of love to Jesus *ut crucifixo eo cibum capere noluerit, priusquam a mortuis resurgentem videret, quod meminerat sibi et fratribus a Christo agente in vivis fuisse praedictum. Quare ei primum omnium, ut et Mariae Magdalenae et Petro apparere voluit...et ne diutinum jejunium toleraret, favo mellis oblato ad comedendum insuper Jacobum invitavit.* Similarly in the thirteenth century Jac. de Voragine (*Legend. Aur.* lxvii.): *In Parasceue autem mortuo Domino, sicut dicit Josephus et Hieronymus in libro De Viris Illustribus, Jacobus votum vovit*, &c., mixing up in what follows the accounts of Jerome and Gregory. Mr. Nicholson thinks that Josephus here stands for Hegesippus, the names being often interchanged, and that the latter may be the original authority for the particulars in which the later writers differ from Jerome.

[1] Probably a reference to the verse cited below, Isa. iii. 10 (LXX. version).

[2] Mosheim, quoted in Routh, *Rel. Sacr.* i. 237, suggests that 'Jesus' here is a misreading of the original Aramaic word (*Jeschua*) denoting 'Salvation.'

So when many of the rulers believed, there was a disturbance among the Jews and the Scribes and the Pharisees, saying that there was a danger that all the people would look to Jesus as the Christ. They came together therefore and said to James 'We pray thee restrain the people, for they have gone astray in regard to Jesus thinking him to be the Christ. We pray thee to persuade all that have come to the passover about Jesus. For we all listen to thee. For we and all the people bear witness that thou art just, and hast no respect of persons. Do thou therefore stand on the pinnacle of the temple, so that thou mayest be conspicuous and thy words may be well heard by all the people, and persuade them not to go astray about Jesus. For all the tribes have come together with the Gentiles also on account of the Passover.' Then the forementioned Scribes and Pharisees set James on the pinnacle of the temple and cried to him 'O thou just one to whom we are all bound to listen, since the people are going astray after Jesus who was crucified, tell us what is the door of Jesus.' And he answered with a loud voice 'Why do you ask me concerning Jesus the Son of Man? He is both seated in Heaven on the right hand of Power, and will come on the clouds of heaven.' And when many were convinced and gave glory at the witness of James, and cried 'Hosanna to the Son of David,' the same Scribes and Pharisees said to each other 'We have done ill in bringing forward such a testimony to Jesus, but let us go up and cast him down that they may fear to believe him.' And they cried out saying 'Oh, oh, even the just has gone astray' and they fulfilled that which is written in Isaiah 'Let us take away the just, for he is not for our purpose; wherefore they shall eat the fruits of their deeds.' So they went up and they cast down James the Just, and said to one another 'let us stone James the Just.' And they began to stone him, since he was not killed by the fall; but he turned round and knelt down saying 'O Lord God my Father, I beseech thee, forgive them, for they know not what they do.' While they were thus stoning him one of the priests of the sons of Rechab, of whom Jeremiah the prophet testifies, cried out 'Stop! What do ye? The Just is praying for you.' And one of them who was a fuller smote the head of the Just one with his club. And so he bore his witness. And they buried him on the spot, and his pillar still remains by the side of the Temple (with the inscription),[1] 'He hath been a true witness both to Jews and Greeks that Jesus is the Christ.' And immediately Vespasian commenced the siege.

The brief account given by Josephus (*Ant. Jud.* xx. 9. 1) of the death of James exhibits some important divergences from that of Hegesippus.

Account of his death by Josephus.

During the interval between the death of Festus (probably in the year 62 A.D.) and the arrival of his successor Albinus, the high priest Ananus the younger, being of rash and daring spirit and inclined like the Sadducees in general to extreme severity in punishing, brought to trial James, the brother of Jesus who is called the Christ, and some others before the court of the Sanhedrin, and having charged them with breaking the laws, delivered them over to be stoned. Josephus adds that the better class of citizens and

---

[1] This seems the force of the Greek ἔτι αὐτοῦ ἡ στήλη μένει παρὰ τῷ ναῷ· μάρτυς οὗτος ἀληθὴς Ἰουδαίοις τε καὶ Ἕλλησιν γεγένηται κ.τ.λ. Wieseler in the *JB. f. deutsche Theologie* 1878, pp. 99 foll., understands στήλη of a cenotaph, consisting of a broken pillar with inscription, erected by later Christians close to the temple of Jupiter Capitolinus, which was built by Hadrian on the site of the Jewish Temple. Jerome (*De Vir. Ill.* 2) renders στήλη by *titulus*.

those who were versed in the laws were indignant at this and made complaints both to King Agrippa and to Albinus, on the ground that Ananus had no right to summon the Sanhedrin without the consent of the procurator; and that Agrippa in consequence removed him from the high priesthood.[1]

Origen (*Cels.* i. p. 35 Spencer) and Eusebius (*H.E.* ii. 23) also cite Josephus as ascribing the miseries of the siege to the divine vengeance for the murder of James the Just; but this does not occur in his extant writings.

Bp. Lightfoot's comments on these accounts

Bishop Lightfoot's comments on the preceding (*l.c.* pp. 366 and 330) are worth quoting.[2] Of the account given by Josephus he says: 'It is probable in itself, which the account in Hegesippus is not, and is such as Josephus might be expected to write, if he touched on the matter at all. His stolid silence about Christianity elsewhere cannot be owing to ignorance, for a sect which had been singled out for years before he wrote, as a mark for imperial vengeance at Rome, must have been only too well known in Judaea. On the other hand, if the passage had been a Christian interpolation, the notice of James would have been more laudatory, as is actually the case in the spurious addition read by Origen and Eusebius.' Of Hegesippus he says: 'His account presents some striking resemblances with the portion of the Clementine Recognitions conjectured to be taken from the Ebionite *'Αναβαθμοὶ Ἰακώβου* (so called as describing the ascents of James up the temple stairs, whence he harangued the people): and we may hazard the conjecture that the story of the martyrdom, to which Hegesippus is indebted, was the grand *finale* of these "Ascents." The Recognitions record how James refuted the Jewish sects; Hegesippus makes the conversion of certain of these sects the starting-point of the persecution which led to his martyrdom. In the Recognitions he is thrown down the flight of steps and left as dead by his persecutors, but is taken up alive by the brethren: in

[1] Schürer (*Jewish People*, vol. ii. p. 186 foll. Eng. Tr.) gives what to me appears a very singular reason for rejecting this date. The passage, he says, has probably suffered from Christian interpolation, since Origen read it differently from our text, as agreeing with Hegesippus in bringing the death of James into close relation with the fall of Jerusalem. But if there were such interpolation, its object must surely have been to magnify the importance of James' martyrdom and make it the immediate cause of God's anger shown in the destruction of the guilty city. It is plain therefore that the inconsistent date (62 A.D.) cannot have formed a part of the interpolation. Jerome *l.c.* says that Clem. Al., in his *Hypot.* bk. vii., gave the same date as Josephus. In *Ant.* xx. 9. 6 Josephus assigns a different cause for the fall of Jerusalem, viz. the presumption of the Levites in wearing the dress of the priests. Eusebius (*H. E.* ii. 23) says that the Jews made their attack on James after Paul had been rescued from their hands and sent to Rome. In Chron. Euseb. the date of his death is 63 A.D.

[2] I have given them in a slightly condensed form.

Hegesippus he is hurled from the still loftier station, and this time his death is made sure.' 'There is much in the account which cannot be true: the assigning to him a privilege which was confined to the high priest alone is plainly false; such an imagination could only have arisen in a generation which knew nothing of the temple services. Moreover the account of his testimony and death not only contradicts the brief contemporary notice of Josephus, but is so full of high improbabilities that it must throw discredit on the whole context. Still it is possible that James may have been a Nazarite, may have been a strict ascetic.' Perhaps it may seem even more incredible that the Jews could have been in doubt as to the belief of him who had been the most prominent member of the Church at Jerusalem for twenty years or more, or could have imagined that one of such firm, unbending character, the very opposite of a Cranmer, could be induced to deny his faith before the people.

Position assigned to James in the Clementine Homilies.

In the Clementine Homilies James stands at the head of the whole Church, as is shown by the commencement of the letter from Clement, Κλήμης Ἰακώβῳ τῷ κυρίῳ καὶ ἐπισκόπων ἐπισκόπῳ διέποντι δὲ τὴν <ἐν> Ἱερουσαλὴμ ἁγίαν Ἑβραίων ἐκκλησίαν καὶ τὰς πανταχῇ Θεοῦ προνοίᾳ ἱδρυθείσας καλῶς κ.τ.λ.

General conclusion as to the life and character of James.

What do we gather from all this with regard to the life and character of James the Just, the son of that Joseph of whom also it is recorded that he was 'a just man'? The word 'just' implies one who not only observes but loves the law, and we may be sure that the reverence for the Jewish law, which shows itself in our Epistle, was learnt in the well-ordered home of Nazareth. There, too, he may have acquired, with the full sanction of his parents, who would gladly devote the eldest-born of Joseph in such marked way to the future service of God and his Messiah, those strict ascetic habits which tradition ascribes to him. But the constant intercourse with Him who was full of grace and truth, in childhood as in manhood, must have prepared James to find in the Ten Commandments no mere outward regulations, but an inner law of liberty and love written in the heart. That deep interest in the mysteries of the kingdom, that earnest search after truth which led the child Jesus to remain behind in the temple, both listening to the doctors and asking them questions, must surely have had its effect upon his brother. Whatever means of instruction were within reach of the home at

His training and education.

Hellenism in Syria.

Nazareth would, we may feel certain, have been eagerly taken advantage of by all its inmates. While accepting, therefore, the view which seems to be best supported, that Jesus and his brothers usually spoke Aramaic, we are surely not bound to suppose that with towns like Sepphoris and Tiberias in their immediate vicinity, with Ptolemais, Scythopolis,[1] and Gadara at no great distance, they remained ignorant of Greek. In the eyes of the Scribes they might 'never have learnt letters,' since they had not attended the rabbinical schools at Jerusalem; but the ordinary education of Jewish children and the Sabbath readings in the synagogue would give sufficient start to enable any intelligent boy to carry on his studies for himself; while the example of Solomon and the teaching of the so-called 'sapiential' books, with which the writer of our Epistle was familiarly acquainted, held up the pursuit of knowledge and wisdom as the highest duty of man.[2] Not many years before, four of the most accomplished literary men of the time were natives of Gadara, Philodemus the Epicurean, a friend of Cicero and one of the poets of the Anthology, whose writings fill the larger part of the Herculanean scrolls; Theodorus the instructor of Tiberius in rhetoric; Meleager, the famous writer of epigrams and collector of the first Greek Anthology; and Menippus the Cynic, whose dialogues were imitated by Varro and Lucian.[3] The question whether our Epistle was originally written in Greek will be considered further on; but these considerations may perhaps lead us to the conclusion that it was not more impossible for a peasant of Galilee to learn to write good Greek, than for one who had been brought up as a Welsh peasant to learn to write good English, or for a Breton to write good French; far more likely, we might think, than that a clever Hindoo should, as so many have done, make himself familiar with the best English authors, and write a good English style. Connected with this is the question, as to which something will be said in a future chapter, whether there are any

[1] Neubauer (*Stud. Bibl.* i. p. 67) says, 'The inhabitants of Beth Shean or Scythopolis are mentioned as pronouncing Hebrew badly, and Scythopolis is considered an exclusively Greek town.' See T. K. Abbott, *Essays*, 1891, pp. 129–182.

[2] See Schürer, *Jewish People*, §§ 27 (on School and Synagogue) with the references to Philo and Josephus. The visit to Egypt (Matt. i. 13 foll.) suggests another channel for Hellenistic influences.

[3] Strabo says of Gadara (xvi. 29), ἐκ δὲ τῶν Γαδάρων Φιλόδημός τε ὁ Ἐπικούρειος καὶ Μελέαγρος καὶ Μένιππος ὁ σπουδογέλοιος καὶ Θεόδωρος ὁ καθ' ἡμᾶς ῥήτωρ. Meleager in his epitaph on himself (*Anth. Pal.* vii. 417) calls it the Syrian Athens, πάτρα δέ με τίκτει Ἀτθὶς ἐν Ἀσσυρίοις ναιομένη Γαδάροις.

indications of acquaintance with Greek poets and philosophers on the part of St. James, and possibly even of our Lord Himself.

Characteristics of the Epistle which accord with the supposition that the writer was son of Joseph and Mary.

There are other characteristics of our Epistle which find their best explanation in the supposition that James was the son of Joseph and Mary. The use of parables was common among Jewish teachers, and especially common in Galilee,[1] but it was carried to an unusual extent by our Lord, both in his preaching to the multitude, of which it is said 'without a parable spake he not unto them' (Matt. xiii. 34), and even in his ordinary conversation, which constantly ran into a parabolic or figurative form, to the great bewilderment of his disciples, as when he bid them 'beware of the leaven of the Pharisees' (Matt. xvi. 6, cf. John xvi, 29, Luke viii. 10). One distinctive feature of our Lord's use of parables is that there is nothing forced or artificial either in the figure or in the application: natural phenomena and the varied circumstances of human life are watched with an observant eye and a sympathetic and loving imagination, and the spiritual analogies which they suggest are seen to flow naturally from them. And we may be sure that the habit of mind which showed itself in the use of parables was not acquired after manhood. The love of nature, the sympathy in all human interests, the readiness to find 'sermons in stones and good in everything' must have characterized the child Jesus and coloured all his intercourse with his fellows from his earliest years. It is interesting, therefore, to find the same fondness for figurative speech in the Epistles of his brothers St. James and St. Jude. This will be fully treated of in the subsequent Essay on Style.

The use of figurative speech.

Close connexion between the Epistle and the Sermon on the Mount.

Another marked feature of our Epistle is the close connexion between it and the Sermon on the Mount, in which our Lord, at the commencement of his career, laid down the principles of the kingdom of God which he came to establish on earth. This will be shown in detail further on. It will suffice to refer here to the more general harmony between the two as to the spiritual view of the Law (James i. 25, ii. 8, 12, 13, Matt. v. 17–44), the blessings of adversity (James i. 2, 3, 12, ii. 5, v. 7, 8, 11, Matt. v. 3–12), the dangers and the uncertainty of wealth (James i. 10, 11, ii. 6, 7, iv. 4, 6, 13–16, v. 1–6, Matt. vi. 19–21, 24–34), the futility of a mere pro-

[1] Cf. Neubauer in *Studia Biblica*, i. p. 52, 'It is stated in the Talmud that Galileans were wandering preachers, and excelled especially in the aggadic or homiletic interpretation of the biblical texts, which was often expressed in the form of a parable.' He refers to his *Géographie du Talmud*, p. 185.

fession of religion (James i. 26, 27, Matt. vi. 1–7), the contrast between saying and doing (James i. 22–25, ii. 14–26, iii. 13, 18, Matt. vii. 15–27), the true nature of prayer (James i. 5–8, iv. 3, v. 13–18, Matt. vi. 6–13), the incompatibility between the love of the world and the love of God (James ii. 5, iii. 6, iv. 4–8, Matt. vi. 24), the need to forgive others if we would be forgiven ourselves (James ii. 12, 13, Matt. vi. 14, 15), the tree known by its fruits (James iii. 11, 12, Matt. vii. 16–20), the interdiction of oaths (James v. 12, Matt. v. 34–37), and of censoriousness (James iv. 11, 12, Matt. vii. 1–5), the praise of singleness of aim (James i. 8, iv. 8, Matt. vi. 22, 23). It is to be noticed that, close as is the connexion of sentiment and even of language in many of these passages, it never amounts to actual quotation. It is like the reminiscence of thoughts often uttered by the original speaker and sinking into the heart of the hearer, who reproduces them in his own manner. And the Sermon on the Mount is made up of what may be called the commonplaces of Christ's teaching, the fundamental ideas with which he commenced his ministry.

Reminiscences of other sayings recorded in the Gospels;

But these reminiscences are not confined to the Sermon on the Mount, or to our Lord's words as reported by St. Matthew. Thus the opposition between faith and wavering (*διακρίνεσθαι*) which appears in James i. 6, ii. 4 is found also in Matt. xxi. 21, Mark xi. 23, 24; the royal law of James ii. 8 is the same of which it is said in Matt. xxii. 39 that on it and its companion law, which enjoins love to God, 'hang all the law and the prophets'; the desire to be called Rabbi is condemned alike in James iii. and Matt. xxiii. 8–12; the dangers of hasty speaking are pointed out in James iii. 2 and in Matt. xii. 37; the Judge 'standeth before the door' in James v. 9, 'he is nigh even at the doors' in Matt. xxiv. 33, Mark xiii. 29; the woes denounced against the prosperous and self-confident in James iv. 9, v. 1 are also found in Luke vi. 24, 25; the light, and the truth, and the freedom inspired by the truth, of which so much is said in the discourses reported by St. John, are recalled to us in James i. 17, 18, 25; and there are many other similar parallels which will suggest themselves to the attentive reader.

also of unrecorded sayings.

The thought naturally suggests itself, If St. James in his short Epistle has preserved so much of the teaching of our Lord as recorded in the Gospels—more, it has been said, than is contained in all the other Epistles put together—is it not probable that he may have also preserved sayings of our Lord not recorded in the Gospels? Dr. A. Resch, in his collection of such unrecorded sayings,[1] includes several verses from our Epistle which are mentioned in my note on i. 12: 'Blessed is the man that endureth temptation: for when he hath been approved he shall receive the crown of life, which he promised to them that love him.' This is repeated in nearly the same words in ii. 5, 'Did not God choose them that are poor to the world to be rich in faith and heirs of the kingdom which he promised to them that love him?' and in 2 Tim. iv. 8, 1 Pet. v. 4, Apoc. ii. 10. Beyond this passage, however, I am not satisfied that any of those quoted by Resch are certainly to be included in the *Agrapha*, though it can hardly be doubted that there must be other echoes of Christ's words in the Epistle, which we are now unable to identify, as they do not occur in the Gospels and are not expressly ascribed to Him either by St. James or by any early writer. Dr. Resch seems to regard the frequency of quotation by subsequent writers as a proof that the passage was originally uttered by Christ, but is not this to assume that it was impossible for a text from St. James to get into general circulation?

Possible causes of the unbelief of James.

Leaving this subordinate point, the facts we have been considering are certainly confirmatory of the belief that St. James was really our Lord's brother, and not only so, but that he grew up under his Brother's influence, and that his mind was deeply imbued with his Brother's teaching. How then are we to explain the fact that at a later period 'he did not believe on him'?

I have given what seems to me the general explanation on p. xxvii. foll., but, after reviewing the particular points in which we have definite proof of agreement from the Epistle written by St. James long after he had enrolled himself among the disciples, we may perhaps gather from its silence a confirmation of what we might have suspected on general grounds, that one of his character of mind would find a difficulty in accepting some of the utterances of Christ. 'Before Abraham was, I am,' 'Except ye eat the flesh of the Son of Man and drink his blood, ye have no life in you,'—these must have been 'hard sayings' to the brother of Jesus even more than to strangers. It is highly probable that his faith may

[1] *Agrapha: Aussercanonische Evangelienfragmente* (Leipzig, 1889).

have been shaken by the absence of any sign from heaven to announce the inauguration of the temporal reign of the Messiah. We can imagine also that he may have found a stumbling-block in our Lord's severity towards the religious leaders of the time and his tenderness shown to publicans and sinners, so unlike the Psalmist's declaration 'I will not know a wicked person,' 'I hate them with a perfect hatred.'

His conversion.

This state of mind, while perhaps not incompatible with the belief in Christ's mission as a preacher of righteousness, and a willingness to accept him as the anointed King of the Jewish people, might easily lead to an anxious solicitude as to his sanity, and the prudence of the measures he took for extending the number of his adherents. Yet underneath this anxiety there must have always been on the part of the brothers an intense love and reverence for Jesus, a suspicion that, after all, if it were only practicable, His course was a nobler, simpler course than that which they themselves suggested; just as the friends of Socrates felt when he refused to follow their counsel and escape from prison. I do not quite understand Bp. Lightfoot's saying that the circumstances of the Crucifixion were such as 'to confirm rather than dissipate the former unbelief.' If Crito and the other friends of Socrates felt that his death had added a crown of glory to his life, and raised affection into all but worship; how much more must this have been the case with the friends of Jesus, when according to his word 'the corn of wheat had fallen into the ground and died,' and they could look back on that life of pure self-sacrifice, that high mysterious perfection of which they had all along been dimly conscious, and remember how its sorrows had been increased by the lack of sympathy on the part of those who should have been the nearest and the dearest. How natural that a brother standing beneath the Cross, having heard of the words spoken at the Last Supper, should then at last have thrown in his lot with Jesus and resolved, whether in despairing remorse or with some faint dawning of believing hope, 'I too will no more eat bread nor drink wine till the kingdom of God shall come!' How natural also that one of the earliest appearances of the Risen Lord should have been made to his repentant brother, and that that brother should from that day forth have united himself to the company of the Apostles, and been chosen by them to preside over the church in Jerusalem, while they proceeded to carry out their Master's last charge, to preach the Gospel to every nation![1]

[1] One or two points may be added here from Jerome's account given in *Vir. Ill.* 2, *Post passionem Domini statim ab apostolis Hierosolymarum episcopus ordinatus.* (This may be compared with Clem. Al. *Hypot.* vi. and vii. cited in Euseb. *H. E.* ii. 1 Πέτρον γάρ φησι καὶ Ἰάκωβον καὶ Ἰωάννην μετὰ τὴν ἀνάληψιν τοῦ Σωτῆρος μὴ ἐπιδικάζεσθαι δόξης, ἀλλ' Ἰάκωβον τὸν δίκαιον ἐπίσκοπον Ἱεροσολύμων ἑλέσθαι. . . Ἰακώβῳ τῷ δικαίῳ καὶ Ἰωάννῃ καὶ Πέτρῳ μετὰ τὴν ἀνάστασιν παρέδωκε τὴν γνῶσιν ὁ Κύριος. Οὗτοι τοῖς λοιποῖς ἀποστόλοις παρέδωκαν.) . . . *Triginta itaque annis Hierosolymae rexit ecclesiam, id est, usque ad septimum Neronis annum* (A.D. 60), *et juxta templum, ubi et praecipitatus fuerat, sepultus titulum usque ad obsidionem Titi et ultimam Adriani notissimum habuit. Quidam e nostris in monte Oliveti eum conditum putant, sed falsa eorum opinio est.*

CHAPTER II

On the External Evidence for the Authenticity of the Epistle

A. *Direct Evidence. Catalogues, &c.*[1]

I HAVE endeavoured to show that the general tone and character of the Epistle are just such as we should expect from James the Lord's brother, as he is described to us in the New Testament. It remains now to exhibit the external evidence for its authenticity. We will take, as our starting-point in the investigation, the well-known passage in which Eusebius distinguishes between the disputed (*ἀντιλεγόμενα*) and the undisputed (*ὁμολογούμενα*) books which made up 'the New Testament' and were publicly read in Church at the time when he wrote (Lightfoot, in *D. of Ch. Biog.* ii. p. 323, gives 314 A.D. as the date of the earlier books of the *H. E.*). Together they contain all the books included in our present Canon and no others, those which were 'disputed, though generally known,' being the Epistle which goes under the name of James (*τῶν δ' ἀντιλεγομένων, γνωρίμων δ' οὖν ὅμως τοῖς πολλοῖς, ἡ λεγομένη Ἰακώβου φέρεται*) and that of Jude as well as the second of Peter and the so-called second and third of John, 'whether they really belong to the Evangelist or possibly to another of the same name.' The Apocalypse of St. John he had before doubtfully classed among the undisputed, but questions whether it should not rather be classed with the spurious, like the Acts of Paul and the Revelation of Peter (*H. E.* iii. 25). Elsewhere, speaking more particularly of our Epistle, he says, 'The first of the

[1] This is taken chiefly from Westcott's *History of the Canon of the N.T.* and Zahn's *Gesch. d. Neutestamentlichen Kanons.*

Epistles styled Catholic is said to be by James the Lord's brother. But I must remark that it is held by some to be spurious. Certainly not many old writers have mentioned it, as neither have they the Epistle of Jude, which is also one of the seven so-called Catholic Epistles' (*ib.* ii. 23). His own practice, however, betrays no suspicion of its genuineness, as he not only recognizes it as an authority (*Eccl. Theol.* ii. 25 οὐκ εἰδὼς ὅτι καὶ τὰ δαιμόνια πιστεύουσι καὶ φρίττουσι, *ib.* iii. 2 καθ' ὃ λέλεκται ἐν ἑτέροις, ἐξομολογεῖσθε ἀλλήλοις τὰς ἁμαρτιάς) but in one passage quotes James iv. 11 as Scripture (*Comm. in Psalm.* p. 648 Montf.), in another quotes James v. 13 as spoken by the holy Apostle (*ib.* p. 247).

The doubt as to the canonicity of the Epistle in early times is sufficiently shown by its omission from some of the early versions and catalogues of Sacred Books. Thus it is omitted from the earliest extant catalogue, contained in what is known as the Muratorian Fragment, of which Bp. Westcott says that it may be regarded as 'a summary of the opinion of the Western Church on the Canon shortly after the middle of the second century.'[1] Of the disputed books this contains two Epistles of St. John, the Apocalypse, and Jude, omitting Hebrews, James, and Peter 1, 2. It has been suggested, however, that there is a corruption, in the text, where it now speaks of the Apocalypse of Peter (*Apocalypse etiam Johannis et Petri tantum recipimus quam quidam ex nostris legi in ecclesia nolunt*), and that the original Greek may have been something of this sort: καὶ ἡ ἀποκάλυψις δὲ Ἰωάννου καὶ Πέτρου [ἐπιστολὴ μία, ἣν] μόνην ἀποδεχόμεθα· [ἔστι δὲ καὶ ἑτέρα] ἣν τινες τῶν ἡμετέρων ἀναγινώσκεσθαι ἐν ἐκκλησίᾳ οὐ θέλουσιν. Bp. Westcott remarks that the canon of the old Latin version used by Tertullian corresponds with the Muratorian in omitting the Epistle of St. James, the second of St. Peter, and Hebrews.[2] The Canon Mommsenianus, first published by Th. Mommsen in 1886 from a MS. of the tenth century, containing the *Liber Generationis* attributed to Hippolytus, appears to belong to the year 359 A.D., and to have been written in Africa.[3] It contains all our canonical books with the exception of James, Jude, and Hebrews; but the mention

[1] Dr. Sanday places it at the end of the century (*Expositor*, 1891, p. 408).

[2] Tertullian, it is true, refers to the Hebrews (*De Pudic.* c. 20), but not as canonical or authoritative; just in the same way as he refers to St. James in the passages quoted below.

[3] See for this Dr. Sanday's article on the 'Cheltenham List of the Canonical Books' (*Studia Biblica*, iii. 217 foll.).

of the three Epistles of St. John and the two of Peter is followed by the words *una sola*, apparently a correction by an early reader.[1] On the other hand, the old Syriac version (Peshitto)[2] contains all the books of our present Canon excepting the Apocalypse, the second of Peter, and the second and third of John. Origen (*Hom. in Jos.* vii. 1) recognizes all our books, and the catalogue contained in the Catechism of Cyril of Jerusalem (348 A.D.) includes all but the Apocalypse, with an urgent warning against the use of any other books. With him agrees Gregory of Nazianzus writing about the same time, who ends his metrical catalogue with the words *πάσας ἔχεις. Εἴ τις δὲ τούτων ἐκτός, οὐκ ἐν γνησίοις.* Athanasius, in his 39th Festal Letter, dated 367 A.D., gives precisely our present Canon, concluding with the words *ἐν τούτοις μόνοις τὸ τῆς εὐσεβείας διδασκαλεῖον εὐαγγελίζεται. μηδεὶς τούτοις ἐπιβαλλέτω, μηδὲ τούτων ἀφαιρείσθω τι.* Amphilochius, bishop of Iconium, speaks less confidently in a metrical catalogue (about 380 A.D.), *τινὲς δὲ φασὶ τὴν πρὸς Ἑβραίους νόθον, οὐκ εὖ λέγοντες· γνησία γὰρ ἡ χάρις. εἶεν. τί λοιπόν; καθολικῶν ἐπιστολῶν τινὲς μὲν ἑπτὰ φασίν, οἱ δὲ τρεῖς μόνας χρῆναι δέχεσθαι, τὴν Ἰακώβου μίαν, μίαν δὲ Πέτρου, τὴν τ' Ἰωάννου μίαν, τινὲς δὲ τὰς τρεῖς καὶ πρὸς αὐταῖς τὰς δύο Πέτρου δέχονται τὴν Ἰουδᾶ δ' ἑβδόμην· τὴν δ' Ἀποκάλυψιν τὴν Ἰωάννου πάλιν τινὲς μὲν ἐγκρίνουσιν, οἱ πλείους δέ γε νόθον λέγουσιν.* Epiphanius, bishop of Salamis in Cyprus, who died about 403 A.D., gives 'a canon of the N.T. exactly coinciding with our own' (*adv. Haeres.* lxxvi. 5). On the other hand we are told that our Epistle was rejected by Theodore of Mopsuestia (d. 429).[3]

Towards the end of the fourth century Jerome (representing the views of the Church of Rome) and Augustine (representing the Church of Carthage) pronounced in favour of our present Canon. The judgment of the former is given in the Vulgate and in the catalogue contained in his epistle *Ad Paulinum* liii. 8; elsewhere speaking of James he says (*Vir. Ill.* 2) *Jacobus qui appellatur frater Domini...unam tantum scripsit epistulam, quae de*

[1] C. H. Turner (*Stud. Bibl.* iii. 308) suggests that the original list contained only 1 John and 1 Peter, and that this was corrected by a later scribe, who appended the note *una sola* implying that the MS. named only one Epistle in each case.

[2] This has usually been ascribed to the beginning of the second century, but from the absence of references to the Catholic Epistles in the *Doctrine of Addai* and the *Homilies* of Aphraates it has been argued that these Epistles were not included in the earliest Syrian Canon. See *Stud. Bibl.* iii. p. 245, *Class. Rev.* iii. 456 foll.

[3] *See* Leontius quoted by Westcott, *Can.* pp. 513 and 576.

septem Catholicis est, quae et ipsa ab alio quodam sub nomine ejus edita asseritur, licet paulatim tempore procedente obtinuerit auctoritatem. Augustine (*De Doctrina Christiana,* ii. 12), after giving a complete list of the sacred books, adds *in his omnibus libris timentes Deum et pietate mansueti quaerunt voluntatem Dei.* He took part in the third Council of Carthage (397 A.D.), where our present Canon of Scripture received its first undoubted synodical ratification; though this was not binding on the Eastern Church till it was sanctioned by the Trullan or Quinisext Council of 692 A.D. It will have been observed that, while the Churches of Rome and Carthage long doubted the canonicity of the Epistle of St. James, it was acknowledged from a very early period by the Churches of Jerusalem and (probably) of Syria, and is included in the catalogues of Sacred Books which have come down to us from the Churches of Egypt and Asia Minor. The difference is easily explained from the fact that the Epistle was probably written at Jerusalem and addressed to the Jews of the Eastern Dispersion; it did not profess to be written by an Apostle or to be addressed to Gentile churches, and it seemed to contradict the teaching of the great Apostle to the Gentiles.

B. *Indirect Evidence. Quotations and Allusions.*

Thus far I have confined myself to the evidence as to the canonicity of our Epistle, which is to be found in catalogues more or less formal; but the casual references which occur in early writers are of no less importance and interest as bearing on the question (1) of its date, and (2) of the authority attaching to it, as proceeding from an inspired writer, if not an Apostle, yet one whose words were no less weighty than those of an Apostle. Most of the references occur without any mark of citation; and in some cases it may be thought that the resemblance to St. James is merely accidental; but if I do not deceive myself, the general result is to show that our Epistle was more widely known during the first three centuries than has been commonly supposed. It is a remarkable fact that our earliest witnesses belong to the Church which was one of the latest to recognize the Epistle as canonical, viz. the Church of Rome. Zahn explains this from the preponderatingly Jewish character of that Church during the first century of its existence (*Neut. Kan.* I. p. 963). In proportion as the

Gentile element in the Church increased, the Judaistic epistle fell into the background. A parallel case is that of the Epistle to the Hebrews, which Clement seems to have known by heart, but which, like the Epistle of James, is omitted in the Muratorian Canon.

Clement of Rome, *Epistle to the Corinthians.* A.D. 95. The fact that Clement balances the teaching of St. Paul by that of St. James is sufficient proof of the authority he ascribed to the latter, see below on c. 33.[1] Cf. Spitta pp. 230–236.

c. 3 ἐκ τούτου (from prosperity) ζῆλος καὶ φθόνος καὶ ἔρις καὶ στάσις, διωγμὸς καὶ ἀκαταστασία, πόλεμος καὶ αἰχμαλωσία...διὰ τοῦτο πόρρω ἄπεστιν ἡ δικαιοσύνη καὶ εἰρήνη, ἐν τῷ ἀπολείπειν ἕκαστον τὸν φόβον τοῦ Θεοῦ...ἀλλὰ ἕκαστον βαδίζειν κατὰ τὰς ἐπιθυμίας αὐτοῦ τὰς πονηράς, c. 14 τοῖς ἐν ἀλαζονείᾳ καὶ ἀκαταστασίᾳ μυσεροῦ ζήλους ἀρχηγοῖς ἐξακολουθεῖν : James iv. 2 ἐπιθυμεῖτε καὶ οὐχ ἔχετε· φθονεῖτε (?) καὶ ζηλοῦτε καὶ οὐ δύνασθε ἐπιτυχεῖν· μάχεσθε καὶ πολεμεῖτε, iii. 16 ὅπου γὰρ ζῆλος καὶ ἐριθία, ἐκεῖ ἀκαταστασία καὶ πᾶν φαῦλον πρᾶγμα, *ib.* 18 καρπὸς δὲ δικαιοσύνης ἐν εἰρήνῃ σπείρεται τοῖς ποιοῦσιν εἰρήνην.

*c. 5 ἀλλ' ἵνα τῶν ἀρχαίων ὑποδειγμάτων παυσώμεθα...λάβωμεν τῆς γενεᾶς ἡμῶν τὰ γενναῖα ὑποδείγματα, shortly afterwards Paul is mentioned as a pattern ὑπομονῆς, c. 17 μιμηταὶ γενώμεθα of the prophets, of Abraham, the friend of God, . . . Ἰὼβ ἦν δίκαιος καὶ ἄμεμπτος κ.τ.λ. : James v. 10 ὑπόδειγμα λάβετε τῆς κακοπαθίας καὶ τῆς μακροθυμίας τοὺς προφήτας, ver. 11 τὴν ὑπομονὴν Ἰὼβ ἠκούσατε.

c. 13 ταπεινοφρονήσωμεν οὖν, ἀδελφοί, ἀποθέμενοι πᾶσαν ἀλαζονείαν καὶ...ὀργάς, καὶ ποιήσωμεν τὸ γεγραμμένον·...μὴ καυχάσθω ὁ σοφὸς ἐν τῇ σοφίᾳ αὐτοῦ...μηδὲ ὁ πλούσιος ἐν τῷ πλούτῳ αὐτοῦ, cf. 57. 2 : James i. 9, 10, 19, 20, 21, 22.

*c. 21 ἐγκαυχωμένοις ἐν ἀλαζονείᾳ τοῦ λόγου αὐτῶν : James iv. 16 καυχᾶσθε ἐν ταῖς ἀλαζονείαις ὑμῶν.

c. 21 μαθετωσαν τί ταπεινοφροσύνη παρὰ Θεῷ ἰσχύει : James v. 16, πολὺ ἰσχύει δέησις δικαίου.

*c. 23 ὁ οἰκτίρμων κατὰ πάντα καὶ εὐεργετικὸς πατὴρ ἔχει σπλάγχνα ἐπὶ πάντας τοὺς φοβουμένους αὐτόν...καὶ προσηνῶς τὰς χάριτας αὐτοῦ ἀποδιδοῖ τοῖς προσερχομένοις αὐτῷ ἁπλῇ διανοίᾳ· διὸ μὴ διψυχῶμεν, c. 19 ἴδωμεν αὐτὸν (Θεὸν) κατὰ διάνοιαν καὶ ἐμβλέψωμεν τοῖς ὄμμασι τῆς ψυχῆς εἰς τὸ μακρόθυμον αὐτοῦ βούλευμα : James v. 11 τὸ τέλος Κυρίου εἴδετε, ὅτι πολύσπλαγχνός ἐστιν ὁ Κύριος καὶ οἰκτίρμων, i. 5 αἰτείτω παρὰ τοῦ διδόντος Θεοῦ πᾶσιν ἁπλῶς καὶ μὴ ὀνειδίζοντος, αἰτείτω δὲ ἐν πίστει μηδὲν διακρινόμενος...μὴ γὰρ οἰέσθω ὅτι λήμψεταί τι παρὰ τοῦ Κυρίου ἀνὴρ δίψυχος.

*c. 23 (a quotation from an earlier treatise, perhaps *Eldad and Modat*, as Lightfoot suggests) πόρρω γενέσθω ἀφ' ἡμῶν ἡ γραφὴ αὕτη ὅπου λέγει Ταλαίπωροι εἰσιν οἱ δίψυχοι οἱ διστάζοντες τὴν ψυχήν, also quoted in Clem. R. ii. 11 λέγει γὰρ ὁ προφητικὸς λόγος Ταλαίπωροι κ.τ.λ. There is nothing to show whether this treatise was earlier or later than the Epistle of St. James.

*c. 30 ποιήσωμεν τὰ τοῦ ἁγιασμοῦ πάντα, φεύγοντες καταλαλιὰς...βδελυκτὴν ὑπερηφανίαν. Θεὸς γάρ, φησίν, ὑπερηφάνοις ἀντιτάσσεται, ταπεινοῖς δὲ δίδωσιν χάριν...ἐνδυσώμεθα τὴν ὁμόνοιαν ταπεινοφρονοῦντες...ἀπὸ παντὸς ψιθυρισμοῦ καὶ καταλαλιᾶς πόρρω ἑαυτοὺς ποιοῦντες, ἔργοις δικαιούμενοι καὶ μὴ λόγοις : the quotation from Prov. iii. 34 is given by James (iv. 6) and

[1] I have prefixed an asterisk to the more striking parallels.

Peter (1 Ep. v. 5) in the same form, reading Θεὸς for the Κύριος of the LXX.; in iv. 11 James condemns καταλαλιά; in ii. 25 he opposes justification by works to justification by faith, which latter, as explained in ver. 14 (ἐὰν πίστιν λέγῃ τις ἔχειν) and by the illustration from a mere profession of charity in ver. 16, is equivalent to Clement's μὴ λόγοις.

*c. 33 After speaking of the necessity of faith in ch. 32, Clement here urges the necessity of good works. In his note Bp. Lightfoot points out other instances of Clement's effort to reconcile and combine the teaching of the Apostles of the Circumcision and the Uncircumcision. Thus Abraham, whom Clement (c. 10 and 17) after St. James (ii. 23) speaks of as ὁ φίλος (τοῦ Θεοῦ) προσαγορευθείς, is rewarded neither for faith alone, nor works alone, but for faith combined with righteousness and truth (c. 31), with obedience and hospitality (c. 10). So too of Rahab it is said (c. 12) διὰ πίστιν καὶ φιλοξενίαν ἐσώθη Ῥαὰβ ἡ πόρνη.

*c. 35 ἀγωνισώμεθα εὑρεθῆναι ἐν τῷ ἀριθμῷ τῶν ὑπομενόντων αὐτόν, ὅπως μεταλάβωμεν τῶν ἐπηγγελμένων δωρεῶν: James i. 12, 17.

*c. 38 ὁ σοφὸς ἐνδεικνύσθω τὴν σοφίαν αὐτοῦ μὴ ἐν λόγοις ἀλλ' ἐν ἔργοις ἀγαθοῖς, see above on c. 30: James iii. 13 τίς σοφὸς...ἐν ὑμῖν; δειξάτω ἐκ τῆς καλῆς ἀναστροφῆς τὰ ἔργα αὐτοῦ ἐν πραΰτητι σοφίας.

c. 40 ἐγκεκυφότες εἰς τὰ βάθη τῆς θείας γνώσεως, c. 53 ἐγκεκύφατε εἰς τὰ λογία τοῦ θεοῦ: James i. 25 ὁ δὲ παρακύψας εἰς νόμον τέλειον τὸν τῆς ἐλευθερίας.

*c. 46 ἱνατί ἔρεις καὶ θυμοὶ καὶ διχοστασίαι καὶ σχίσματα πόλεμός τε ἐν ὑμῖν; James iv. 1 πόθεν πόλεμοι καὶ πόθεν μάχαι ἐν ὑμῖν;

Pseudo-Clement, *Homily to the Corinthians* (often called the Second Epistle to the Corinthians), written towards the middle of the second century.

c. 4 μὴ καταλαλεῖν ἀλλήλων: James iv. 11.

*c 15 μισθὸς γὰρ οὐκ ἔστιν μικρὸς πλανωμένην ψυχὴν καὶ ἀπολλυμένην ἀποστρέψαι εἰς τὸ σωθῆναι, c. 16 ἀγαπὴ δὲ καλύπτει πλῆθος ἁμαρτιῶν· προσευχὴ δὲ ἐκ καλῆς συνειδήσεως ἐκ θανάτου ῥύεται, c. 17 συλλάβωμεν ἑαυτοῖς καὶ τοὺς ἀσθενοῦντας ἀνάγειν περὶ τὸ ἀγαθὸν ὅπως σωθῶμεν ἅπαντες, καὶ ἐπιστρέψωμεν ἀλλήλους, the Jacobean terms διψυχία and κακοπαθεῖν occur immediately afterwards: James v. 16 εὔχεσθε ὑπὲρ ἀλλήλων ὅπως ἰαθῆτε. πολὺ ἰσχύει δέησις δικαίου ἐνεργουμένη, ver. 19 ἐάν τις ἐν ὑμῖν πλανηθῇ ἀπὸ τῆς ἀληθείας καὶ ἐπιστρέψῃ τις αὐτόν, γινώσκετε ὅτι ὁ ἐπιστρέψας ἁμαρτωλὸν ἐκ πλάνης ὁδοῦ αὐτοῦ σώσει ψυχὴν ἐκ θανάτου καὶ καλύψει πλῆθος ἁμαρτιῶν. Clement seems to combine this with 1 Pet. iv. 8.

*c. 20 Θεοῦ ζῶντος πεῖραν ἀθλοῦμεν καὶ γυμναζόμεθα τῷ νῦν βίῳ ἵνα τῷ μέλλοντι στεφανωθῶμεν...οὐδεὶς τῶν δικαίων ταχὺν καρπὸν ἔλαβεν, ἀλλ' ἐκδέχεται αὐτόν: James v. 7 ἰδοὺ ὁ γεωργὸς ἐκδέχεται τὸν τίμιον καρπὸν τῆς γῆς μακροθυμῶν ἐπ' αὐτῷ, cf. i. 2, 3, 12.

The *Didaché* is usually assigned in its present form to the end of the first century, but was probably founded on an earlier Jewish work: see C. Taylor, *Lectures on the Teaching of the Twelve Apostles*, pp. 8–48. It is difficult in these early writings to satisfy oneself in regard to resemblances to our canonical books, whether these arise from direct quotation or are merely allusions to the oral teaching which preceded the composition of the books. The following passages, however, seem to take a colouring from the Epistle of St. James.

ii. 4 οὐκ ἔσῃ διγνώμων οὐδὲ δίγλωσσος· παγὶς γὰρ θανάτου ἡ διγλωσσία: James iii. 6—8, 9, 10.

ii. 5 οὐκ ἔσται ὁ λόγος σου ψευδής, οὐ κενός, ἀλλὰ μεμεστωμένος πράξει: James iii. 14 μὴ ψεύδεσθε κατὰ τῆς ἀληθείας, ii. 20 θέλεις δὲ γνῶναι, ὦ ἄνθρωπε κενέ, ὅτι ἡ πίστις χωρὶς τῶν ἔργων ἀργή ἐστιν; *ib.* i. 21, 26, ii. 14—17, iii. 18 ἡ ἄνωθεν σοφία...μεστὴ ἐλέους καὶ καρπῶν ἀγαθῶν.

*iv. 3 οὐ διψυχήσεις πότερον ἔσται ἢ οὔ, see above ii. 4 διγνώμων and v. 1 διπλοκαρδία: James i. 8, iv. 8.

iv. 14 ἐν ἐκκλησίᾳ ἐξομολογήσῃ τὰ παραπτώματά σου, cf. xiv. 1 κατὰ κυριακὴν...εὐχαριστήσατε, προεξομολογησάμενοι τὰ παραπτώματα ὑμῶν, ὅπως καθαρὰ ἡ θυσία ᾖ: James v. 16 ἐξομολογεῖσθε οὖν ἀλλήλοις τὰ παραπτώματα (*al.* τὰς ἁμαρτίας)...ὅπως ἰαθῆτε.

v. 1 ἡ δὲ τοῦ θανάτου ὁδός ἐστιν αὕτη· πρῶτον πάντων πονηρά ἐστι καὶ κατάρας μεστή...φόνοι, μοιχεῖαι, ἐπιθυμίαι...διπλοκαρδία...ὑπερηφανία, κακία, αὐθάδεια, πλεονεξία...ζηλοτυπία...ἀλαζονεία...ὧν μακρὰν πραΰτης καὶ ὑπομονή...οὐκ ἐλεοῦντες πτωχόν...ἀποστρεφόμενοι τὸν ἐνδεόμενον, καταπονοῦντες τὸν θλιβόμενον, πλουσίων παράκλητοι, πενήτων ἄνομοι κριταί: James iii. 10, 13, 16, iv. 2, 6, 16, i. 3, 4, 14, 21, ii. 2, 3, 6, 16, v. 4, 6, 11.

The Epistle of Barnabas, which was written, according to Bishop Lightfoot (*Apostolic Fathers,* Part I. vol. ii. 503 foll. 1890) at Alexandria during the reign of Vespasian (A.D. 70–79),[1] according to Hilgenfeld in the reign of Nerva (A.D. 96–98), according to Volkmar during the reign of Hadrian (A.D. 119–138), contains references to the Gospels and to some of St. Paul's Epistles. The following appear to be allusions to St. James.

*I. 2 οὕτως ἔμφυτον τῆς δωρεᾶς <τῆς> πνευματικῆς χάριν εἰλήφατε, cf. ix. 9 οἶδεν ὁ τὴν ἔμφυτον δωρεὰν τῆς διδαχῆς αὐτοῦ θέμενος ἐν ὑμῖν: James i. 21 ἐν πραΰτητι δέξασθε τὸν ἔμφυτον λόγον, *ib.* ver. 17 πᾶν δώρημα τέλειον ἄνωθέν ἐστιν.

I. 8 ἐγὼ δέ, οὐχ ὡς διδάσκαλος ἀλλ' ὡς εἷς ἐξ ὑμῶν, ὑποδείξω ὀλίγα, cf. iv. 6 ἔτι δὲ καὶ τοῦτο ἐρωτῶ ὑμᾶς, ὡς εἷς ἐξ ὑμῶν ὤν, *ib.* 9 οὐχ ὡς διδάσκαλος, ἀλλ' ὡς πρέπει ἀγαπῶντι, ἀφ' ὧν ἔχομεν μὴ ἐλλιπεῖν, γράφειν ἐσπούδασα: James iii. 1 μὴ πολλοὶ διδάσκαλοι γίνεσθε ἀδελφοί μου, cf. Matt. xxiii. 8.

*II 6 ταῦτα οὖν κατήργησεν ἵνα ὁ καινὸς νόμος τοῦ Κυρίου ἡμῶν Ἰησοῦ Χριστοῦ ἄνευ ζυγοῦ ἀνάγκης ὢν κ.τ.λ.: James i. 21.

VI. 17 ἡμεῖς τῇ πίστει τῆς ἐπαγγελίας καὶ τῷ λόγῳ ζωοποιούμενοι ζήσομεν κατακυριεύοντες τῆς γῆς: James i. 18.

X. 3 ὅταν σπαταλῶσιν ἐπιλανθάνονται τοῦ Κυρίου ἑαυτῶν, ὅταν δὲ ὑστερηθῶσιν ἐπιγινώσκουσι τὸν Κύριον: James v. 5, ii. 6, 7.

[1] Bishop Lightfoot argues for this date on the strength of the prophecy contained in ch. 4; but it is difficult to reconcile it with the fact that the Epistle appears to contain references to St. John's Gospel, and is undoubtedly posterior to the *Didaché,* which itself contains quotations from the Gospels, as well as from some of the Pauline Epistles, and is usually assigned to the closing years of the first century. It is not, however, certain whether we have the original form either of the *Didaché* or of the Epistle of Barnabas. Harnack (*Chronologie,* p. 426) gives strong reasons for supposing it to have been written in the year 130.

XIX. 5 οὐ μὴ διψυχήσῃς πότερον ἔσται ἢ οὐ: taken straight from *Didaché* iv. 4, ultimately from James i. 8.

XIX. 8 οὐκ ἔσῃ πρόγλωσσος· παγὶς γὰρ τὸ στόμα θανάτου: altered from *Did.* apparently to bring it nearer to James i. 19. iii. 6, 8.

*XIX. 10 μνησθήσῃ ἡμέραν κρίσεως...μελετῶν εἰς τὸ σῶσαι ψυχὴν τῷ λόγῳ, ἢ διὰ τῶν χειρῶν σου ἐργάσῃ εἰς λύτρωσιν ἁμαρτιῶν σου (altered from *Did.* iv. 6 so as to bring it nearer to St. James): James v. 9, 12, i. 21, v. 20 ὁ ἐπιστρέψας ἁμαρτωλὸν...σώσει ψυχὴν ἐκ θανάτου καὶ καλύψει πλῆθος ἁμαρτιῶν.

XXI. 2 ἐρωτῶ τοὺς ὑπερέχοντας...ἐγγὺς ἡ ἡμέρα ἐν ᾗ συναπολεῖται πάντα τῷ πονηρῷ· ἐγγὺς ὁ Κύριος καὶ ὁ μισθὸς αὐτοῦ...5 ὁ δὲ Θεὸς...δῴη ὑμῖν σοφίαν, σύνεσιν, ἐπιστήμην, γνῶσιν τῶν δικαιωμάτων αὐτοῦ, ὑπομονήν: James v. 1—5, 8, i. 3—5.

XX. In the account of the Way of Death, borrowed, with variations, from the *Didaché* v., we find the insertion χήρᾳ καὶ ὀρφανῷ μὴ προσέχοντες: James i. 27.

Testamenta XII. Patriarcharum, written about the beginning of the second century by a Jewish Christian,[1] who seems to have been much influenced by the teaching and example of St. James. Thus Mr. Sinker, in his edition (1869), calls attention to the high estimate of poverty and of an ascetic life (p. 21 foll. p. 121), to the view of the Law 'as an eternal system of justice' which had been 'partially changed in its outward aspects and workings by the coming of Christ, who is called ἄνδρα ἀνακαινοποιοῦντα τὸν νόμον' (p. 26), to the commendation of wisdom, benevolence, compassion, peaceableness, above all of ἁπλότης, the opposite to διψυχία.[2]

**Reuben* 2 πνεῦμα συνουσίας μεθ' ἧς συνεισέρχεται διὰ τῆς φιληδονιας ἡ ἁμαρτία, 4 ὄλεθρος ψυχῆς ἐστὶν ἡ πορνεία χωρίζουσα Θεοῦ καὶ προσεγγίζουσα τοῖς εἰδώλοις...πλανῶσα τὸν νοῦν καὶ τὴν διάνοιαν καὶ κατάγει νεανίσκους εἰς ᾅδην...ἐὰν μὴ κατισχύσῃ ἡ πορνεία τὴν ἔννοιαν οὐδὲ Βελίαρ κατισχύσει ὑμῶν, *Reub.* 5 ἐγένοντο ἐν ἐπιθυμίᾳ ἀλλήλων καὶ συνέλαβον τῇ διανοίᾳ τὴν πρᾶξιν: James i. 14, 15, iv. 1, 4, 8.

Sym. 3 ὁ φθόνος κυριεύει πάσης τῆς διανοίας τοῦ ἀνθρώπου καὶ...πάντοτε ὑποβάλλει ἀνελεῖν τὸν φθονούμενον: James iv. 2.

Sym. 4 φυλάξασθε ἀπὸ παντὸς ζήλου καὶ φθόνου καὶ πορεύεσθε ἐν ἁπλότητι ψυχῆς...ἀποστήσατε ἀφ' ὑμῶν τὸ πνεῦμα τοῦ φθόνου, ὅτι ἀγριοῖ τὴν ψυχήν...ὀργὴν καὶ πόλεμον παρέχει τῷ διαβουλίῳ καὶ εἰς αἵματα παροξύνει: James iv. 1, 2.

Lev. 14 ὑμεῖς οἱ φωστῆρες τοῦ οὐρανοῦ ὡς ὁ ἥλιος καὶ ἡ σελήνη· τί ποιήσουσι πάντα τὰ ἔθνη ἐὰν ὑμεῖς σκοτισθῆτε ἐν ἀσεβείᾳ, cf. 18, *Jud.* 24: James i. 17.

Jud. 13 μὴ πορεύεσθε ὀπίσω τῶν ἐπιθυμιῶν ὑμῶν μηδὲ ἐνθυμήσεσι

---

[1] This is now much questioned in Germany, where the dominant view is that it is a Jewish writing interpolated: so Schnapp, *Die Test. der xii Patr.*, Halle, 1884; Schürer agrees in the main. (S.)

[2] Bishop Lightfoot (*Gal.* p. 319 foll.) says of the *Test. xii. Patr.* 'the language in the moral and didactic portions takes its colour from the Epistle of James,' and quotes Ewald to the same effect.

διαβουλίων ὑμῶν ἐν ὑπερηφανίᾳ καρδίας ὑμῶν, καὶ μὴ καυχᾶσθε ἐν ἔργοις ἰσχύος ὑμῶν: James i. 14, ii. 4, iv. 6, 16.

ib. 13 τὸ πνεῦμα τοῦ ζήλου καὶ τῆς πορνείας παρετάξατο ἐν ἐμοί: James iv. 1.

ib. 14 ἐν διαλογισμοῖς ῥυπαροῖς (οἶνος) συνταράσσει τὸν νοῦν εἰς πορνείαν...καί, εἰ πάρεστι τὸ τῆς ἐπιθυμίας αἴτιον, πράσσει τὴν ἁμαρτίαν: James i. 14, 15, 21.

ib. 18 (φιλαργυρία) ἀφιστᾷ νόμου Θεοῦ καὶ τυφλοῖ τὸ διαβούλιον τῆς ψυχῆς καὶ ὑπερηφανίαν ἐκδιδάσκει καὶ οὐκ ἀφίει ἄνδρα ἐλεῆσαι τὸν πλησίον αὐτοῦ: James iv. 4, 6, ii. 1—9.

ib. 19 ὁ Θεὸς ὁ οἰκτίρμων καὶ ἐλεήμων: James v. 11.

**ib.* 20. On man's responsibility. δύο πνεύματα σχολάζουσι τῷ ἀνθρώπῳ, τὸ τῆς ἀληθείας καὶ τὸ τῆς πλάνης, καὶ μέσον ἐστὶ τὸ τῆς συνέσεως τοῦ νοός, οὗ ἐὰν θέλῃ κλῖναι...καὶ ἐμπεπύρισται ὁ ἁμαρτήσας ἐκ τῆς ἰδίας καρδίας καὶ ἆραι πρόσωπον οὐ δύναται πρὸς τὸν κριτήν: James i. 13, 15, v. 19, 20.

ib. 21. The oppression of the poor by the rich: James ii. 6, 7, v. 1—6.

ib. 22 ἕως παρουσίας τοῦ Θεοῦ τῆς δικαιοσύνης: James v. 7.

ib. 25 οἱ ἐν λύπῃ τελευτήσαντες ἀναστήσονται ἐν χαρᾷ καὶ οἱ ἐν πτωχείᾳ διὰ Κύριον πλουτισθήσονται καὶ οἱ ἐν πενίᾳ χορτασθήσονται...οἱ δὲ ἀσεβεῖς πενθήσουσι καὶ ἁμαρτωλοὶ κλαύσονται: James ii. 5, iv. 9.

Isach. 3 ὁ Θεὸς συνεργεῖ τῇ ἁπλότητί μου· παντὶ γὰρ πένητι καὶ παντὶ θλιβομένῳ παρεῖχον τῆς γῆς τὰ ἀγαθὰ ἐν ἁπλότητι καρδίας: James ii. 22, 15, 16, i. 5.

ib. 4 ὁ ἁπλοῦς χρυσίου οὐκ ἐπιθυμεῖ, τὸν πλησίον οὐ πλεονεκτεῖ, βρωμάτων ποικίλων οὐκ ἐφίεται, ἐσθῆτα διάφορον οὐ θέλει, χρόνους μακροὺς οὐχ ὑπογράφει ζῆν, ἀλλὰ μόνον ἐκδέχεται τὸ θέλημα τοῦ Θεοῦ: James v. 2—5, ii. 2, iv. 13—15.

ib. 7 πᾶν πνεῦμα Βελίαρ φεύξεται ἀφ᾽ ὑμῶν καὶ...πάντα ἄγριον θῆρα καταδουλώσεσθε, *Nephth.* 8, *Benj.* 5: James iv. 7, iii. 7.

**Zab.* 7 εἶδον θλιβόμενον ἐν γυμνότητι χειμῶνος καὶ σπλαγχνισθεὶς ἐπ᾽ αὐτὸν...ἱμάτιον ἔδωκα...ἔχετε εὐσπλαγχνίαν κατὰ παντὸς ἀνθρώπου ἐν ἐλέει ἵνα καὶ ὁ Κύριος εἰς ὑμᾶς σπλαγχνισθεὶς ἐλεήσῃ ὑμᾶς... ὅσον γὰρ ἄνθρωπος σπλαγχνίζεται εἰς τὸν πλησίον, τοσοῦτον Κύριος εἰς αὐτόν: James i. 27, ii. 15, 16, 13.

Dan. 5 ἀπόστητε θυμοῦ καὶ μισήσατε τὸ ψεῦδος ἵνα Κύριος κατοικήσῃ ἐν ὑμῖν καὶ φύγῃ ἀφ᾽ ὑμῶν ὁ Βελίαρ: James iv. 4, 5, 7, iii. 14.

ib. ἅγιος Ἰσραὴλ βασιλεύων ἐπ᾽ αὐτοὺς ἐν ταπεινώσει καὶ ἐν πτωχείᾳ, καὶ ὁ πιστεύων ἐπ᾽ αὐτῷ βασιλεύσει ἐν ἀληθείᾳ ἐν τοῖς οὐρανοῖς: James i. 9, 10, ii. 5.

**ib.* 6 προσέχετε ἑαυτοῖς ἀπὸ τοῦ Σατανᾶ...ἐγγίζετε δὲ τῷ Θεῷ: James iv. 7, 8.

ib. διατηρήσατε ἑαυτοὺς ἀπὸ παντὸς ἔργου πονηροῦ καὶ ἀπορρίψατε τὸν θυμὸν καὶ πᾶν ψεῦδος καὶ ἀγαπήσατε τὴν μακροθυμίαν: James i. 27, 18—21, iii. 14, v. 7, 8, 10.

**Nephth.* 2 Κύριος πάντα ἄνθρωπον ἔκτισε κατ᾽ εἰκόνα ἑαυτοῦ ...ὡς ὁ νοῦς αὐτοῦ, οὕτω καὶ τὸ ἔργον αὐτοῦ...ὡς ἡ καρδία αὐτοῦ, οὕτω καὶ τὸ στόμα αὐτοῦ...ὡς ἡ ψυχὴ αὐτοῦ, οὕτω καὶ ὁ λόγος αὐτοῦ ἢ ἐν νόμῳ Κυρίου ἢ ἐν νόμῳ Βελίαρ: James iii. 9, ii. 14, 17, iii. 2, 11, 12, 15, 17.

**ib.* 3 μὴ σπουδάζετε...ἐν λόγοις κενοῖς ἀπατᾶν τὰς ψυχάς, ὅτι σιωπῶντες ἐν καθαρότητι καρδίας συνήσετε τὸ θέλημα τοῦ Θεοῦ κρατεῖν καὶ ἀπορρίπτειν τὸ θέλημα τοῦ διαβόλου. Ἥλιος καὶ σελήνη καὶ ἀστέρες οὐκ ἀλλοιοῦσι τάξιν αὐτῶν· οὕτως καὶ ὑμεῖς μὴ ἀλλοιώσητε νόμον Θεοῦ ἐν ἀταξίᾳ πράξεων ὑμῶν. ἔθνη πλανηθέντα...ἠλλοίωσαν τάξιν: James i. 19, 26, 27, iv. 7, i. 17.

Gad. 3 τὴν ἀλήθειαν ψέγει, τῷ κατορθοῦντι φθονεῖ, καταλαλιὰν ἀσπάζεται, ὑπερηφανίαν ἀγαπᾷ: James iii. 14, iv. 2, 6, 11.

ib. 4 ἐὰν πταίσῃ ὁ ἀδελφὸς...σπεύδει ἵνα κριθῇ: James ii. 10—12.

ib. 4 τὸ πνεῦμα τῆς ἀγάπης ἐν μακροθυμίᾳ συνεργεῖ τῷ νόμῳ τοῦ Θεοῦ εἰς σωτηρίαν ἀνθρώπων: James v. 7, 8, 20, ii. 22.

ib. 5 (τὸ μῖσος) ἰοῦ διαβολικοῦ τὴν καρδίαν πληροῖ, cf. 6 τὸν ἰὸν τοῦ μίσους, cf. *Sym.* 4 πνεῦμα ἰοβόλον: James iii. 6, 8.

ib. καταλαλεῖ: James iv. 11. ἀνηλεῶς: James ii. 13.

ib. 7 Κυρίῳ ὕμνον προσφέρετε...μὴ φθονεῖτε...μὴ ζηλώσητε: James v. 13, iv. 2.

ib. ὅρον Κυρίου ἐκδέξασθε: James v. 11.

Asher 1 δύο ὁδοὺς ἔδωκεν ὁ Θεὸς...καὶ δύο διαβούλια...καὶ δύο τέλη: James i. 12, 14, 15, v. 19, 20.

ib. ὁ θησαυρὸς τοῦ διαβόλου (*al.* διαβουλίου) ἰοῦ πονηροῦ πνεύματος πεπλήρωται, see above on Gad. 5.

ib. 2 πλεονεκτῶν τὸν πλησίον παροργίζει τὸν Θεὸν, καὶ τὸν ὕψιστον ἐπιορκεῖ καὶ τὸν πτωχὸν ἐλεᾷ, τὸν ἐντολέα τοῦ νόμου Κύριον ἀθετεῖ καὶ παροξύνει...τὴν ψυχὴν σπιλοῖ...καὶ τοῦτο μὲν διπρόσωπον: James v. 4, 12, ii. 15, 16, iv. 11, 12, i. 27, 8.

ib. 3 οἱ διπρόσωποι οὐ Θεῷ ἀλλὰ ταῖς ἐπιθυμίαις αὐτῶν δουλεύουσιν ἵνα τῷ Βελίαρ ἀρέσωσι: James iv. 1, 3, 7, 8.

**Jos.* 2 ἐν δέκα πειρασμοῖς δόκιμόν με ἀνέδειξεν (Κύριος) καὶ ἐν πᾶσιν αὐτοῖς ἐμακροθύμησα, ὅτι μέγα φάρμακόν ἐστιν ἡ μακροθυμία καὶ πολλὰ ἀγαθὰ δίδωσιν ἡ ὑπομονή: James i. 2, 3, 4, 12, v. 7, 10, 11.

**ib.* 10 ἐὰν τὴν ἁγνείαν μετέλθητε ἐν ὑπομονῇ καὶ ταπεινώσει καρδίας, Κύριος κατοικήσει ἐν ὑμῖν...ὅπου δὲ κατοικεῖ ὁ ὕψιστος κἂν τις περιπέσῃ φθόνῳ ἢ δουλείᾳ...Κύριος...οὐ μόνον ἐκ τῶν κακῶν ῥύεται ἀλλὰ καὶ ὑψοῖ: James i. 2, 3, 12, iv. 5, 10.

ib. ἐν ἐσχάταις ἡμέραις: James v. 3.

**Benj.* 4 εἴδετε τοῦ ἀγαθοῦ ἀνδρὸς τὸ τέλος· μιμήσασθε ἐν ἀγαθῇ διανοίᾳ τὴν εὐσπλαγχνίαν αὐτοῦ ἵνα καὶ ἡμεῖς στεφάνους δόξης φορέσητε: James v. 11, i. 12.

ib. τὸν Θεὸν ἀνυμνεῖ...τὸν ἀθετοῦντα τὸν ὕψιστον νουθετῶν ἐπιστρέφει: James v. 13, 19, 20.

**ib.* 6 ἡ ἀγαθὴ διάνοια οὐκ ἔχει δύο γλώσσας εὐλογίας καὶ κατάρας, ὕβρεως καὶ τιμῆς, λύπης καὶ χαρᾶς, ὑποκρίσεως καὶ ἀληθείας, πενίας καὶ πλούτου, ἀλλὰ μίαν ἔχει περὶ πάντων εἰλικρινῆ καὶ καθαρὰν διάθεσιν...πᾶν γὰρ ὃ ποιεῖ ἢ λαλεῖ...οἶδεν ὅτι Κύριος ἐπισκέπτει ψυχὴν αὐτοῦ καὶ καθαίρει τὴν διάνοιαν αὐτοῦ πρὸς τὸ μὴ καταγνωσθῆναι ὑπὸ Θεοῦ: James iii. 10, ii. 1—4, 13—17, i. 9, 10, iv. 8, ii. 12.

ib. 7 τοῦ Βελίαρ πᾶν ἔργον διπλοῦν ἐστὶ, καὶ οὐκ ἔχει ἁπλότητα: James i. 8, iv. 4, 8.

**ib.* πρῶτον συλλαμβάνει ἡ διάνοια διὰ τοῦ Βελίαρ, cf. Reub. 5: James i. 15.

Ignatius, d. about 115 A.D.

There is little general resemblance between the epistles of Ignatius and that of St. James, but the following phrases may be noted.

μὴ πλανᾶσθε, ἀδελφοί μου, *Eph.* 16, *Philad.* 3, cf. *Magn.* 8, *Eph.* 5, *Smyrn.* 6: James i. 16 (also found in St. Paul, whose writings were certainly well known to Ignatius).

*ἀδιάκριτος, used in the sense 'whole-hearted,' as by St. James (iii. 17), apparently by no previous writer, *Trall.* 1, *Magn.* 15, cf. *Rom. inscr.* and *Philad. inscr.* quoted *in loc.*

Smyrn. 11 ἵνα οὖν τέλειον ὑμῶν γένηται τὸ ἔργον, πρέπει κ.τ.λ....τέλειοι ὄντες τέλεια καὶ φρονεῖτε: James i. 4 ἡ δὲ ὑπομονὴ ἔργον τέλειον ἐχέτω, ἵνα ἦτε τέλειοι.

Polyc. 1 αἰτοῦ σύνεσιν πλείονα ἧς ἔχεις, *ib.* 2 τὰ δὲ ἀόρατα αἴτει ἵνα σοι φανερωθῇ, ὅπως μηδενὸς λείπῃ: James i. 5 εἰ δέ τις λείπεται σοφίας, αἰτείτω παρὰ τοῦ διδόντος Θεοῦ, ver. 4, ἵνα ἦτε τέλειοι...ἐν μηδενὶ λειπόμενοι.

[Pseudo-Ignatius, probably written in the 4th century.

Philipp. 11 πῶς πειράζεις τὸν ἀπείραστον, ἐπιλαθόμενος τοῦ νομοθέτου παρακελευομένου ὅτι οὐκ ἐκπειράσεις Κύριον τὸν Θεόν σου; James i. 12.

Smyrn. 6 τόπος καὶ ἀξίωμα καὶ πλοῦτος μηδένα φυσιούτω· ἀδοξία καὶ πενία μηδένα ταπεινούτω· τὸ γὰρ ὅλον πίστις ἡ εἰς Θεόν: James i. 9, 10.

Ephes. 17 διὰ τί ἔμφυτον τὸ περὶ Θεοῦ παρὰ Χριστοῦ λαβόντες κριτήριον εἰς ἄγνοιαν καταπίπτομεν; James i. 21.]

Polycarp, d. 155 A.D.

Ad Phil. 3 ἐδίδαξεν ἀκριβῶς τὸν περὶ τῆς ἀληθείας λόγον...ἔγραψεν ἐπιστολάς, εἰς ἃς ἐὰν ἐγκύπτητε, δυνηθήσεσθε οἰκοδομεῖσθαι: James i. 18, 25.

c. 5 χαλιναγωγοῦντες ἑαυτοὺς ἀπὸ παντὸς κακοῦ: James i. 26, iii. 2.

*c. 6 οἱ πρεσβύτεροι...εἰς πάντας εὔσπλαγχνοι, ἐπιστρέφοντες τὰ ἀποπεπλανημένα, ἐπισκεπτόμενοι πάντας ἀσθενεῖς, μὴ ἀμελοῦντες χήρας ἢ ὀρφανοῦ ἢ πένητος...ἀπεχόμενοι πάσης ὀργῆς, προσωποληψίας, κρίσεως ἀδίκου: James v. 20, i. 27, 19, ii. 1.

*c. 11 *sicut passibilia membra et errantia eos revocate; ut omnium vestrum corpus salvetis. Hoc enim agentes vos ipsos aedificatis:* James v. 20.

Our next witness, Hermas, who probably wrote before the middle of the second century, abounds in references to St. James, dwelling especially on the subject of διψυχία. His peculiar style of quotation is well described by Dr. Taylor, who has made a careful study of the manner in which he has used the *Didaché* and St. James in the *Journal of Philology*, vol. xviii. pp. 297 foll. He disguises the Scriptures from which he quotes, 'the form of his work, which claims to be the embodiment of a revelation, not allowing him to cite them openly.' 'He allegorizes, he disintegrates, he amalgamates. He plays upon the sense or varies the form of a saying, he repeats its words in fresh combinations or replaces them by synonyms, but he will not cite a passage simply and in its entirety' (*l.c.* pp. 324, 5). Spitta thinks that this is a Jewish writing of the time of Claudius with later Christian interpolations (pp. 243–437). On its relation to our Epistle see pp. 382–391. Apparently he is unacquainted with Dr. Taylor's paper.

*In *Mand.* ix. δίψυχος and its cognates occur fourteen times in forty lines, ἆρον ἀπὸ σεαυτοῦ τὴν διψυχίαν καὶ μηδὲν ὅλως διψυχήσῃς αἰτησασθαι παρὰ τοῦ Θεοῦ...αἰτοῦ παρ' αὐτοῦ ἀδιστάκτως καὶ γνώσῃ τὴν πολυσπλαγχνίαν αὐτοῦ...οὐκ ἔστι γὰρ ὁ Θεὸς ὡς οἱ ἄνθρωποι οἱ μνησικακοῦντες ἀλλ' αὐτὸς ἀμνησίκακός ἐστιν,[1] *ib.* § 5 οἱ γὰρ διστάζοντες εἰς τὸν Θεόν, οὗτοί εἰσιν οἱ δίψυχοι καὶ οὐδὲν ὅλως ἐπιτυγχάνουσι τῶν αἰτημάτων αὐτῶν...οἱ δὲ ὁλοτελεῖς ὄντες ἐν τῇ πίστει πάντα αἰτοῦνται πεποιθότες ἐπὶ τὸν Κύριον καὶ λαμβάνουσιν, *ib.* § 8 ἐὰν δὲ ἐκκακήσῃς καὶ διψυχήσῃς αἰτούμενος, σεαυτὸν αἰτιῶ καὶ μὴ τὸν διδόντα σοι [*Sim.* vi. 3. 5 οὐκ ἀναβαίνει αὐτῶν ἐπὶ τὴν καρδίαν ὅτι ἔπραξαν πονηρὰ ἔργα ἀλλ' αἰτιῶνται τὸν Κύριον] *Mand.* ix. § 11 βλέπεις ὅτι ἡ πίστις ἄνωθέν ἐστι παρὰ τοῦ Κυρίου καὶ ἔχει δύναμιν μεγάλην· ἡ δὲ διψυχία ἐπίγειον πνεῦμά ἐστι παρὰ τοῦ διαβόλου δύναμιν μὴ ἔχουσα: James i. 5—8 αἰτείτω παρὰ τοῦ διδόντος Θεοῦ πᾶσιν ἁπλῶς, καὶ μὴ ὀνειδίζοντος, καὶ δοθήσεται αὐτῷ· αἰτείτω δὲ ἐν πίστει μηδὲν διακρινόμενος...μὴ γὰρ οἰέσθω ὁ ἄνθρωπος ἐκεῖνος ὅτι λήμψεταί τι παρὰ τοῦ Κυρίου ἀνὴρ δίψυχος, ver. 13 μηδεὶς πειραζόμενος λεγέτω ὅτι ἀπὸ Θεοῦ πειράζομαι, ver. 17 πᾶν δώρημα τέλειον ἄνωθέν ἐστιν καταβαῖνον ἀπὸ τοῦ Πατρὸς τῶν φώτων, ii. 22 βλέπεις ὅτι ἡ πίστις συνήργει τοῖς ἔργοις, iii. 15 οὐκ ἔστιν αὕτη ἡ σοφία ἄνωθεν κατερχομένη, ἀλλὰ ἐπίγειος, ψυχική, δαιμονιώδης, iv. 7 ἀντίστητε τῷ διαβόλῳ καὶ φεύξεται ἀφ' ὑμῶν, v. 16 πολὺ ἰσχύει δέησις δικαίου ἐνεργουμένη, v. 11.

**Mand.* ii. 2 μηδενὸς καταλάλει, *ib.* § 3 πονηρὰ ἡ καταλαλιά, ἀκατάστατον δαιμόνιόν ἐστιν, v. 2. 7 πεπληρωμένος τοῖς πνεύμασι τοῖς πονηροῖς ἀκαταστατεῖ ἐν πάσῃ πράξει αὐτοῦ περισπώμενος ὧδε κἀκεῖσε ὑπὸ τῶν πνευμάτων τῶν πονηρῶν, *Sim.* vi. 3. 5 τιμωροῦνται οἱ μὲν ζημίαις...οἱ δὲ πάσῃ ἀκαταστασίᾳ... ἀκαταστατοῦντες ταῖς βουλαῖς: James i. 6 ὁ διακρινόμενος ἔοικε κλύδωνι θαλάσσης ἀνεμιζομένῳ καὶ ῥιπιζομένῳ, ver. 8, iv. 11 μὴ καταλαλεῖτε ἀλλήλων, iii. 6 ἡ γλῶσσα...φλογιζομένη ὑπὸ τῆς γεέννης, v. 8 (ἡ γλῶσσα) ἀκατάστατον κακόν, iii. 16 ὅπου ζῆλος...ἐκεῖ ἀκαταστασία.

**Mand.* ii. 4 πᾶσιν ὁ Θεὸς δίδοσθαι θέλει ἐκ τῶν ἰδίων δωρημάτων, *Sim.* ii. 7 τοῦτο ἔργον δεκτὸν παρὰ τῷ Θεῷ, ὅτι...εἰργάσατο εἰς τὸν πένητα ἐκ τῶν δωρημάτων τοῦ Κυρίου: James i. 17 πᾶν δώρημα τέλειον ἄνωθέν ἐστιν, i. 5 αἰτείτω παρὰ τοῦ διδόντος Θεοῦ ἁπλῶς, ver. 27, ii. 15, 16.

Mand. ii. 6 μηθὲν διακρίνων τίνι δῷ ἢ μὴ δῷ, *Sim.* ii. 1 κατανοοῦντος (μου) πτελέαν καὶ ἄμπελον καὶ διακρίνοντος περὶ αὐτῶν...ὁ ποιμὴν λέγει Τί συ ἐν ἑαυτῷ ζητεῖς περὶ τῆς πτελέας καὶ τῆς ἀμπέλου; (here διακρίνω seems to have much the same force as διακρίνομαι): James i. 6 αἰτείτω δὲ ἐν πίστει μηδὲν διακρινόμενος.

**Mand.* iii. 1 ἀλήθειαν ἀγάπα...ἵνα τὸ πνεῦμα ὃ ὁ θεὸς κατῴκισεν ἐν τῇ σαρκὶ ταύτῃ ἀληθὲς εὑρεθῇ...καὶ οὕτως δοξασθήσεται ὁ Κύριος ὁ ἐν σοὶ κατοικῶν, *Mand.* iv. 5 ἐὰν μακρόθυμος ἔσῃ, τὸ πνεῦμα τὸ ἅγιον τὸ κατοικοῦν ἐν σοὶ καθαρὸν ἔσται μὴ ἐπισκοτούμενον ὑπὸ ἑτέρου πονηροῦ πνεύματος, ἀλλ' ἐν εὐρυχώρῳ κατοικοῦν ἀγαλλιάσεται...ἐὰν δὲ ὀξυχολία τις προσέλθῃ, εὐθὺς τὸ πνεῦμα τὸ ἅγιον, τρυφερὸν ὄν (being sensitive and fastidious), στενοχωρεῖται...καὶ ζητεῖ ἀποστῆναι ἐκ τοῦ τόπου, cf. *Sim.* v. 5, *Mand.* v. 2. 6, vi. 2. 3, x. 2. 2: James iv. 5 πρὸς φθόνον ἐπιποθεῖ τὸ πνεῦμα ὃ κατῴκισεν ἐν ἡμῖν, cf. ver. 4 and i. 20.

**Mand.* iv. 1. 2 ἡ γὰρ ἐνθύμησις αὕτη Θεοῦ δούλῳ ἁμαρτία μεγάλη ἐστίν, ἐὰν δέ τις ἐργάσηται τὸ ἔργον τὸ πονηρὸν τοῦτο, θάνατον ἑαυτῷ κατεργάζεται, cf. *Vis.* i. 1. 8 below: James i. 14, 15.

**Mand.* viii. 9 (good works), πρῶτον πάντων πίστις...ἀγάπη, ὁμόνοια, ἀληθεία, ὑπομονή...χήραις ὑπηρετεῖν, ὀρφανοὺς καὶ ὑστερουμένους ἐπισκέπτεσθαι...ἐσκανδαλισμένους ἀπὸ τῆς πίστεως... ἐπιστρέφειν καὶ εὐθύμους ποιεῖν, ἁμαρτάνοντας νουθετεῖν: James i. 3, ii. 8, i. 27, v. 19, 20, 13.

**Mand.* x. 2 ὅταν ὁ δίψυχος ἐπιβάληται πρᾶξίν τινα καὶ ταύτης ἀποτύχῃ...ἡ λύπη αὕτη εἰσπορεύεται εἰς τὸν ἄνθρωπον, *ib.* 3 ἔνδυσαι οὖν τὴν ἱλαρότητα τὴν πάντοτε ἔχουσαν χάριν παρὰ τῷ Θεῷ: James iv. 2, i. 2.

---

[1] Cf. *Sim.* ix. 23, 24 πάντοτε ἁπλοῖ...παντὶ ἀνθρώπῳ ἐχορήγησαν ἀνονειδίστως.

**Mand.* xi. (on true and false teachers) § 5 πᾶν πνεῦμα ἀπὸ Θεοῦ δοθὲν...ἀφ' ἑαυτοῦ λαλεῖ πάντα, ὅτι ἄνωθέν ἐστιν...τὸ δὲ πνεῦμα τὸ λάλουν κατὰ τὰς ἐπιθυμίας τῶν ἀνθρώπων ἐπίγειόν ἐστι, cf. § 6 and § 11, § 8 ὁ ἔχων τὸ πνεῦμα τὸ θεῖον τὸ ἄνωθεν πραΰς ἐστι καὶ ἡσύχιος καὶ ταπεινόφρων καὶ ἀπεχόμενος ἀπὸ πάσης πονηρίας καὶ ἐπιθυμίας ματαίας τοῦ αἰῶνος τούτου...οὐδὲ ὅταν θέλῃ ἄνθρωπος λαλεῖν, λαλεῖ τὸ πνεῦμα τὸ ἅγιον, ἀλλὰ τότε λαλεῖ ὅταν θελήσῃ αὐτὸν ὁ Θεὸς λαλῆσαι, § 12 ὁ ἄνθρωπος ἐκεῖνος ὁ δοκῶν πνεῦμα ἔχειν ὑψοῖ ἑαυτὸν καὶ θέλει πρωτοκαθεδρίαν ἔχειν καὶ εὐθὺς ἰταμός ἐστι καὶ ἀναιδὴς καὶ πολύλαλος...τῶν τοιούτων ἐπίγειόν ἐστι τὸ πνεῦμα ... εἰς συναγωγὴν ἀνδρῶν δικαίων οὐκ ἐγγίζει ἀλλ' ἀποφεύγει αὐτούς: James iii. 1, 15—17.

Mand. xi. 9. ὅταν ἔλθῃ ὁ ἄνθρωπος ὁ ἔχων τὸ πνεῦμα τὸ θεῖον εἰς συναγωγὴν ἀνδρῶν δικαίων τῶν ἐχόντων πίστιν θείου πνεύματος, καὶ ἔντευξις γένηται πρὸς τὸν Θεὸν...τότε πληρωθεὶς ὁ ἄνθρωπος τῷ πνεύματι τῷ ἁγίῳ λαλεῖ εἰς τὸ πλῆθος καθὼς ὁ Κύριος βούλεται, *ib.* 17 σὺ δὲ πίστευε τῷ πνεύματι τῷ ἐξερχομένῳ ἀπὸ τοῦ Θεοῦ καὶ ἔχοντι δύναμιν, *ib.* 20 λάβε τὴν δύναμιν τὴν ἄνωθεν ἐρχομένην, *Vis.* iii. 1, 8, κάθισον ὧδε: James ii. 2, v. 16, iii. 15.

**Mand.* xii. 1 ἆρον ἀπὸ σαυτοῦ πᾶσαν ἐπιθυμίαν πονηράν, ἔνδυσαι δὲ τὴν ἐπιθυμίαν τὴν ἀγαθὴν...ἐνδεδυμένος γὰρ ταύτην μισήσεις τὴν πονηρὰν ἐπιθυμίαν καὶ χαλιναγωγήσεις αὐτὴν καθὼς βούλει. ἀγρία γὰρ ἡ ἐπιθυμία ἡ πονηρὰ καὶ δυσκόλως ἡμεροῦται: James iii. 2 (on the evil caused by the tongue) χαλιναγωγῆσαι, ver. 4 ὅπου ἡ ὁρμὴ βούλεται, ver. 8 τὴν δὲ γλῶσσαν οὐδεὶς δαμάσαι δύναται.

**Mand.* xii. 2 ἡ ἐπιθυμία ἡ πονηρά, ἐὰν ἴδῃ σε καθωπλισμένον τῷ φόβῳ τοῦ Θεοῦ καὶ ἀνθεστηκότα αὐτῇ, φεύξεται ἀπὸ σοῦ μακράν, § 4 ὁ διάβολος μόνον φόβον ἔχει, ὁ δὲ φόβος αὐτοῦ τόνον οὐκ ἔχει· μὴ φοβήθητε οὖν αὐτὸν καὶ φεύξεται ἀφ' ὑμῶν, § 5 δύναται ὁ διάβολος ἀντιπαλαῖσαι, καταπαλαῖσαι δὲ οὐ δύναται· ἐὰν οὖν ἀντισταθῆτε αὐτῷ νικηθεὶς φεύξεται ἀφ' ὑμῶν κατησχυμμένος, *ib.* vii. 2: James iv. 7 ἀντίστητε τῷ διαβόλῳ καὶ φεύξεται ἀφ' ὑμῶν.

Mand. xii. 4 (God gave man power over the four kinds of animals) εἰ οὖν ὁ ἄνθρωπος κύριός ἐστι τῶν κτισμάτων τοῦ Θεοῦ...οὐ δύναται καὶ τούτων τῶν ἐντολῶν κατακυριεῦσαι; James iii. 7.

Mand. xii. 6 ὅσοι ἂν καθαρίσωσιν ἑαυτῶν τὰς καρδίας ἀπὸ τῶν ματαίων ἐπιθυμιῶν τοῦ αἰῶνος τούτου...ζήσονται τῷ Θεῷ: James i. 27, iv. 8.

Sim. i. 8 χήρας καὶ ὀρφανοὺς ἐπισκέπτεσθε, *Mand.* viii. 10, *Vis.* iii. 9, 2: James i. 27.

**Sim.* ii. 5 ὁ πένης πλούσιός ἐστιν ἐν τῇ ἐντεύξει...καὶ δύναμιν μεγάλην ἔχει ἡ ἔντευξις αὐτοῦ παρὰ τῷ Θεῷ: James ii. 5 οὐχ ὁ Θεὸς ἐξελέξατο τοὺς πτωχοὺς τῷ κόσμῳ πλουσίους ἐν πίστει, v. 16.

**Sim.* v. 4 ὃς ἂν δοῦλος ᾖ τοῦ Θεοῦ καὶ ἔχῃ τὸν Κύριον ἑαυτοῦ ἐν τῇ καρδίᾳ αἰτεῖται παρ' αὐτοῦ σύνεσιν καὶ λαμβάνει...ὁ δὲ Κύριος πολυεύσπλαγχνός ἐστι καὶ πᾶσι τοῖς αἰτουμένοις παρ' αὐτοῦ ἀδιαλείπτως δίδωσι, σὺ δὲ ἐνδεδυναμωμένος ὑπὸ τοῦ ἁγίου ἀγγέλου καὶ εἰληφὼς παρ' αὐτοῦ τοιαύτην ἔντευξιν καὶ μὴ ὢν ἀργός, διατί οὐκ αἰτῇ παρὰ τοῦ Κυρίου σύνεσιν; James i. 1 Θεοῦ...δοῦλος, ver. 5 εἴ τις λείπεται σοφίας, αἰτείτω παρὰ τοῦ διδόντος Θεοῦ πᾶσιν ἁπλῶς, v. 11, ii. 20, v. 16 δέησις ἐνεργουμένη, on which see note.

Sim. v. 5. 1 παράμονος εἶ, vii. 6 παράμεινον ταπεινοφρονῶν: James i. 25.

Sim. vi. 1. 1 (ἐντολαὶ) δυνάμεναι σῶσαι ψυχὴν ἀνθρώπου: James i. 21 τον ἔμφυτον λόγον, τον δυνάμενον σῶσαι τὰς ψυχὰς ὑμῶν.

**Sim.* vi. 1. 2 μὴ διψυχήσῃς, ἀλλ' ἔνδυσαι τὴν πίστιν τοῦ Κυρίου, *Vis.* iv. 1. 8: James ii. 1 μὴ ἐν προσωποληψίαις ἔχετε τὴν πίστιν τοῦ Κυρίου Ιησοῦ Χριστοῦ, ver. 4 οὐ διεκρίθητε;

**Sim.* vi. 1. 6 τὰ πρόβατα...τρυφῶντα ἦν καὶ λίαν σπαταλῶντα, *ib.* § 2. 4 οὗτοί εἰσιν οἱ προδεδωκότες μὲν ἑαυτοὺς ταῖς τρυφαῖς καὶ ἀπάταις, εἰς δὲ τὸν Κύριον οὐδὲν ἐβλασφήμησαν: James v. 5 ἐτρυφήσατε ἐπὶ τῆς γῆς καὶ ἐσπαταλήσατε.

**Sim.* vii. 4 δεῖ τὸν μετανοοῦντα ... θλιβῆναι ἐν πάσαις θλίψεσι ποικίλαις, vi. 3 τιμωρεῖ αὐτοὺς ποικίλαις τιμωρίαις: James i. 2.

Sim. viii. 3 τὸ δένδρον τοῦτο τὸ μέγα...νόμος Θεοῦ ἐστιν, ὁ δὲ νόμος οὗτος υἱὸς Θεοῦ ἐστι κηρυχθεὶς εἰς τὰ πέρατα τῆς γῆς: James iv. 11.

**Sim.* viii. 6. 4 ὧν αἱ ῥάβδοι...βεβρωμέναι ὑπὸ σητὸς εὑρέθησαν, οὗτοί εἰσιν οἱ ἀποστάται καὶ προδόται τῆς ἐκκλησίας καὶ βλασφημήσαντες ἐν ταῖς ἁμαρτίαις αὐτῶν τὸν Κύριον, ἔτι δὲ καὶ ἐπαισχυνθέντες τὸ ὄνομα Κυρίου τὸ ἐπικληθὲν ἐπ' αὐτούς: James ii. 6 οὐκ αὐτοὶ βλασφημοῦσιν τὸ καλὸν ὄνομα τὸ ἐπικληθὲν ἐφ' ὑμᾶς, cf. v. 2 τὰ ἱμάτια ὑμῶν σητόβρωτα γέγονεν.

Sim. viii. 9. 1 οὗτοί εἰσι πιστοὶ μὲν γεγονότες, πλουτήσαντες δὲ καὶ γενόμενοι ἔνδοξοι παρὰ τοῖς ἔθνεσιν ὑπερηφανίαν μεγάλην ἐνεδύσαντο καὶ ὑψηλόφρονες ἐγένοντο καὶ κατέλιπον τὴν ἀλήθειαν...ἀλλ' ἐνέμειναν τῇ πίστει μὴ ἐργαζόμενοι τὰ ἔργα τῆς πίστεως, *ib.* 10. 3 οὗτοί εἰσιν οἱ πιστεύσαντες μόνον, τὰ δὲ ἔργα τῆς ἀνομίας ἐργαζόμενοι: James ii. 14, iv. 6.

Sim. ix. 16 πρὶν φορέσαι τὸν ἄνθρωπον τὸ ὄνομα τοῦ υἱοῦ τοῦ Θεοῦ νεκρὸς ἐστιν, ὅταν δὲ λάβῃ τὴν σφραγῖδα ἀποτίθεται τὴν νέκρωσιν καὶ ἀναλαμβάνει τὴν ζωήν, *ib.* 14, 5: James ii. 7, i. 21.

Sim. ix. 19 ὑποκριταὶ καὶ διδάσκαλοι πονηρίας, μὴ ἔχοντες καρπὸν δικαιοσύνης...οἱ τοιοῦτοι ὄνομα μὲν ἔχουσιν, ἀπὸ δὲ τῆς πίστεως κενοί εἰσιν, καὶ οὐδεὶς ἐν αὐτοῖς καρπὸς ἀληθείας: James iii. 1, 14, 18, ii. 14, 17.

**Sim.* ix. 21 ὥσπερ αἱ βοτάναι ἥλιον ἰδοῦσαι ἐξηράνθησαν, οὕτω καὶ οἱ δίψυχοι ὅταν θλίψιν ἀκούσωσι...τὸ ὄνομα ἐπαισχύνονται τοῦ Κυρίου αὐτῶν: James i. 11, 8, ii. 7.

Sim. ix. 21. 2 τὰ ῥήματα αὐτῶν μόνα ζῶσι, τὰ δὲ ἔργα αὐτῶν νεκρά ἐστίν, *Mand.* x. 1: James ii. 15—17, 26.

Sim. ix. 22 ἐπαινοῦσι δὲ ἑαυτοὺς ὡς σύνεσιν ἔχοντας καὶ θέλουσιν ἐθελοδιδάσκαλοι εἶναι...διὰ ταύτην τὴν ὑψηλοφροσύνην πολλοὶ ἐκενώθησαν ὑψοῦντες ἑαυτούς: James iii. 1, 15, ii. 20.

**Sim.* ix. 23 εἰ ὁ Θεὸς οὐ μνησικακεῖ τοῖς ἐξομολογουμένοις τὰς ἁμαρτίας, ἄνθρωπος...ἀνθρώπῳ μνησικακεῖ ὡς δυνάμενος ἀπολέσαι ἢ σῶσαι αὐτόν; *Mand.* xii. 6 φοβήθητε τὸν πάντα δυνάμενον σῶσαι καὶ ἀπολέσαι; James iv. 12 εἷς ἐστιν νομοθέτης καὶ κριτής, ὁ δυνάμενος σῶσαι καὶ ἀπολέσαι.

**Sim.* ix. 26 ὥσπερ τὰ θηρία διαφθείρει τῷ ἑαυτῶν ἰῷ τὸν ἄνθρωπον καὶ ἀπολλύει, οὕτω καὶ τῶν τοιούτων ἀνθρώπων (δολίων καὶ καταλάλων) τὰ ῥήματα: James iii. 8 γλῶσσα μεστὴ ἰοῦ θανατηφόρου.

**Sim.* ix. 31. 4 δεῖ ὑμᾶς...βοηθεῖν ἀλλήλοις...ἑκάστῳ τῆς τοῦ Κυρίου ὁδοῦ παρεκκλίνοντι πᾶσαν ἀφαιροῦντες ταῖς διδασκαλίαις πονηρίαν, ὥσπερ καὶ ἀφ' ὑμῶν αὐτῶν, ἵνα καὶ ὁ ποιμὴν χαρίσηται ὑμῖν εἰ ὑγιᾶ πάντα ταῦτα τὰ ἀπολωλότα δέξεται πρόβατα, x. 4. 3 *hujusmodi animam qui liberat magnum sibi gaudium adquiret*...qui novit angustiam ejus et non redimit eam, *magnum peccatum admittit* et fit reus sanguinis ejus: James v. 19, 20, iii. 1.

**Vis.* i. 1. 8 ἐπὶ τὴν καρδίαν σου ἀνέβη ἡ ἐπιθυμία τῆς πονηρίας...ἁμαρτία γέ ἐστι καὶ μεγάλη ... οἱ πονηρὰ βουλευόμενοι ἐν ταῖς καρδίαις θάνατον ἑαυτοῖς ἐπισπῶνται, § 2. 1 πῶς ἱλάσομαι τὸν Θεὸν περὶ τῶν ἁμαρτιῶν μου τῶν τελείων; see above *Mand.* iv. 1: James i. 14, 15.

Vis. i. 2 κἀγὼ λυπούμενος καὶ κλαίων εἶπον, Κυρία χαῖρε. καὶ εἶπέν μοι, Τί στυγνὸς Ἑρμᾶ, ὁ μακρόθυμος καὶ ἀστομάχητος, ὁ πάντοτε γελῶν, τί οὕτω κατηφὴς τῇ ἰδέᾳ καὶ οὐχ ἱλαρός; James iv. 9 ταλαιπωρήσατε καὶ πενθήσατε καὶ κλαύσατε· ὁ γέλως ὑμῶν εἰς πένθος μεταστραφήτω καὶ ἡ χαρὰ εἰς κατήφειαν.

Vis. ii. 2. 4 οὐκ ἀπέχεται τῆς γλώσσης ἐν ᾗ πονηρεύεται...ἀφίενται αὐτοῖς αἱ ἁμαρτίαι πᾶσαι ἐὰν ἄρωσιν ἀπὸ τῆς καρδίας αὐτῶν τὰς διψυχίας: James iii. 1. 8.

Vis. ii. 2. 7 μακάριοι ὑμεῖς ὅσοι ὑπομένετε τὴν θλῖψιν: James i. 12.
**Vis.* iii. 9. 5 βλέπετε τὴν κρίσιν τὴν ἐπερχομένην...βλέπετε οἱ γαυρούμενοι ἐν τῷ πλούτῳ ὑμῶν, μήποτε στενάξουσιν οἱ ὑστερούμενοι, καὶ ὁ στεναγμὸς αὐτῶν ἀναβήσεται πρὸς τὸν Κύριον: James v. 1 foll., esp. ver. 4 ὁ μισθὸς τῶν ἐργατῶν...ὁ ἀφυστερημένος ἀφ' ὑμῶν κράζει καὶ αἱ βοαὶ τῶν θερισάντων εἰς τὰ ὦτα Κυρίου Σαβαὼθ εἰσελήλυθαν, ver. 8, 9.
Vis. iii. 13 εὐθὺς ἐπελάθετο: James i. 24.
**Vis.* iv. 3 τὸ μὲν μέλαν οὗτος ὁ κόσμος ἐστὶν ἐν ᾧ κατοικεῖτε...τὸ δὲ λευκὸν μέρος ὁ αἰὼν ὁ ἐπερχόμενός ἐστιν, ἐν ᾧ κατοικήσουσιν οἱ ἐκλεκτοὶ τοῦ Θεοῦ· ὅτι ἄσπιλοι καὶ καθαροὶ ἔσονται οἱ ἐκλελεγμένοι εἰς ζωὴν αἰώνιον, *Mand.* ii. 4 πᾶσιν ὑστερουμένοις δίδου ἁπλῶς...φύλασσε τὰς ἐντολὰς ταύτας ἵνα ἡ μετάνοιά σου...ἐν ἁπλότητι εὑρεθῇ καὶ ἡ καρδία σου καθαρὰ καὶ ἀμίαντος *Sim.* v. 6 πᾶσα σὰρξ ἀπολήψεται μισθὸν ἡ εὑρεθεῖσα ἀμίαντος καὶ ἄσπιλος, *Sim.* ix. 26. 2 οἱ μὲν τοὺς σπίλους ἔχοντες διάκονοί εἰσι κακῶς διακονήσαντες καὶ διαρπάσαντες χηρῶν καὶ ὀρφανῶν τὴν ζωήν: James i. 27 θρησκεία καθαρὰ καὶ ἀμίαντος παρὰ τῷ Θεῷ και πατρὶ αὕτη ἐστὶν ἐπισκέπτεσθαι ὀρφανοὺς καὶ χήρας ἐν τῇ θλίψει αὐτῶν, ἄσπιλον ἑαυτὸν τηρεῖν ἀπὸ τοῦ κόσμου, i. 5.

Hermas also uses some rare words which are found in James, e.g. πολύσπλαγχνος (see n. on v. 11); καταδυναστεύω *Mand.* xii. 5, James ii. 6; δίψυχος, -ια and ἐπίγειος (of which exx. are given above).

Justin Martyr, d. about 165 A.D.

**Apol.* i. 16 μὴ ὀμόσητε ὅλως· ἔστω δὲ ὑμῶν τὸ ναὶ ναί, καὶ τὸ οὒ οὔ (prefixing the article with James v. 12).
c. 32 οἱ πιστεύοντες, ἐν οἷς οἰκεῖ τὸ παρὰ τοῦ Θεοῦ σπέρμα, ὁ λόγος: James i. 18, 21, iv. 5.
c. 61 ἐν τῷ ὕδατι ἐπονομάζεται τῷ ἑλομένῳ ἀναγεννηθῆναι τὸ τοῦ Θεοῦ ὄνομα: James i. 18, ii. 7.
c. 67 οἱ εὐποροῦντες...ἕκαστος ὃ βούλεται δίδωσι καὶ τὸ συλλεγόμενον παρὰ τῷ προεστῶτι ἀποτίθεται καὶ αὐτὸς ἐπικουρεῖ ὀρφανοῖς τε καὶ χήραις καὶ τοῖς...λειπομένοις: James i. 27, ii. 15.
**Tryph.* 49 (Χριστῷ) ὃν καὶ τὰ δαιμόνια φρίσσουσιν καὶ πᾶσαι ἁπλῶς αἱ ἀρχαί, c. 131, μέλλει ἐξολοθρευθήσεσθαι τὰ δαιμόνια καὶ δεδιέναι τὸ ὄνομα αὐτοῦ καὶ πάσας τὰς ἀρχὰς...ὁμοίως ὑφορᾶσθαι αὐτόν: James ii. 19.
**ib.* 100 (Εὔα) τὸν λόγον τὸν ἀπὸ τῆς ὄφεως συλλαβοῦσα παρακοὴν καὶ θάνατον ἔτεκε: James i. 15.

Justin frequently uses the word ἐνεργεῖν, ἐνεργεῖσθαι (James v. 16) and has also the rare πολυσπλαγχνία (*Tryph.* 55).

Ep. ad Diognetum, probably written about 150 A.D.

c. 7 οὐ γὰρ ἐπίγειον εὕρημα τοῦτ' αὐτοῖς παρεδόθη . . . ἀλλ' αὐτὸς ὁ παντοκράτωρ . . . ἀπ' οὐρανῶν τὴν ἀλήθειαν καὶ τὸν λόγον τὸν ἅγιον . . . ἀνθρώποις ἐνίδρυσε καὶ ἐγκατεστήριξε ταῖς καρδίαις: James iii. 15, i. 17, 18, 21.
ib. ταῦτα τῆς παρουσίας αὐτοῦ δείγματα: James v. 7.
*c. 9 (ὁ Θεὸς) οὐκ ἐμίσησεν ἡμᾶς...οὐδὲ ἐμνησικάκησεν ἀλλὰ ἐμακροθύμησεν...αὐτὸς τὸν ἴδιον υἱὸν ἀπέδοτο λύτρον ὑπὲρ ἡμῶν...τί γὰρ ἄλλο τὰς ἁμαρτίας ἡμῶν ἠδυνήθη καλύψαι ἢ ἐκείνου δικαιοσύνη; James i. 5, v. 20 (cf. Psa. lxxxv. 2).
*c. 10 ὁ Θεὸς τοὺς ἀνθρώπους ἠγάπησε...οἷς ὑπέταξε πάντα τὰ ἐν τῇ γῇ...οὓς ἐκ τῆς ἰδίας εἰκόνος ἔπλασε...οἷς τὴν ἐν οὐρανῷ βασιλείαν ἐπηγγείλατο καὶ δώσει τοῖς ἀγαπήσασιν αὐτόν: James iii. 7, 9, i. 12, ii. 5.

Marcus the Valentinian (fl. 150 A.D.), in a formulary cited by Irenaeus:

*Iren. *Haer.* i. 13. 6 ἰδοὺ ὁ κριτὴς ἐγγύς: James v. 9.

Athenagoras, flourished about A.D. 170.

Apol. c. 24 τῆς κοσμικῆς σοφίας καὶ <τῆς> θεολογικῆς...διαλλαττουσῶν, καὶ τῆς μὲν οὔσης ἐπουρανίου τῆς δὲ ἐπιγείου: James iii. 15.

Acta Johannis (Zahn's ed.) written by Prochorus in the fifth century, but incorporating materials of the second century.[1]

*p. 75. 13 foll. μακάριος ἄνθρωπος ὃς οὐκ ἐπείρασεν τὸν Θεὸν ἐν τῇ καρδίᾳ αὐτοῦ. ὅμως καὶ τοῖς Ἰσραηλίταις τότε πειράζουσιν τὸν Θεὸν ὁ ἀπείραστος τῇ πείρᾳ ἐκείνων τὴν εὐθύτητα ἐδίδου...καὶ σὺ μὴ πείραζε Θεὸν καὶ οὐ μὴ πειρασθῇς κακοῦ, p. 113. 5 μὴ πείραζε τὸν ἀπείραστον, p. 190. 18 μακάριος ὅστις οὐκ ἐπείρασεν ἐν σοὶ τὸν Θεὸν, ὁ γὰρ σὲ πειράζων τὸν ἀπείραστον πειράζει: James i. 13.

*p. 141. 14 ἐρρύσατο αὐτὸν ἀπὸ τοῦ ἰοῦ τοῦ θανατηφόρου: James iii. 8.

*p. 167. 10 εἰς τὸν τῆς διδασκαλίας ὅρον τοῦ θεολόγου παρακύψωμεν: James i. 25.

*p. 170. 20 ὁ πολυεύσπλαγχνος Θεός: James v. 11 (reading of Thl.).

*p. 244 n. ἐὰν περιπέσῃς πειρασμοῖς μὴ πτοηθήσῃ: James i. 2.

Irenaeus, d. about 200 A.D.

*iv. 16. 2 *credidit Deo et reputatum est illi ad justitiam et amicus Dei vocatus est*, cf. iv. 13. 4: James ii. 23.

*v. 1. 1 *factores sermonum ejus facti...facti autem initium facturae*: James i. 22, 18.

*iv. 34. 4 *libertatis lex*, id est verbum Dei ab apostolis annuntiatum, iv. 39. 4 τὰ οὖν ἀποστάντα τοῦ πατρικοῦ φωτὸς καὶ παραβάντα τὸν θεσμὸν τῆς ἐλευθερίας παρὰ τὴν αὐτῶν ἀπέστησαν αἰτίαν, cf. iii. 12. 14, iv. 9, 2, iv. 37. 1: James i. 25, ii. 12, i. 17.

Theophilus, d. about 185 A.D.

*i. 15 δεῖξόν μοι τὸν ἄνθρωπόν σου, κἀγώ σοι δείξω τὸν Θεόν μου James ii. 18.

ii. 15 οἱ ἐπιφανεῖς ἀστέρες καὶ λαμπροί εἰσιν εἰς μίμησιν τῶν προφητῶν · διὰ τοῦτο καὶ μένουσιν ἀκλινεῖς...οἱ δὲ ἑτέραν ἔχοντες τάξιν τῆς λαμπρότητος τύποι εἰσὶν τοῦ λαοῦ τῶν δικαίων. Οἱ δ' αὖ μεταβαίνοντες...οἱ καὶ πλάνητες καλούμενοι, καὶ αὐτοὶ τύπος τυγχάνουσιν τῶν ἀφισταμένων ἀνθρώπων ἀπὸ τοῦ Θεοῦ: James i. 17 (Jude 13).

Clement of Alexandria (d. about 220 A.D.) is said by Eusebius (*H. E.* vi. 14) to have included in his *Outlines* (ἐν ταῖς ὑποτυπώσεσι) short explanations of all the sacred books μηδὲ τὰς ἀντιλεγομένας παρελθών, τὴν Ἰούδα λέγω καὶ τὰς λοιπὰς καθολικὰς ἐπι-

[1] See Salmon, *Introduction to the N. T.*, pp. 378 foll.

στολάς, τήν τε Βαρνάβα καὶ τὴν Πέτρου λεγομένην ἀποκάλυψιν. Cassiodorius (*Inst. div. lit.* 8) on the other hand says that Clement commented 'on the Canonical Epistles, that is to say, on the first Epistle of St. Peter, the first and second of St. John, and the Epistle of St. James.' The notes on 1 Peter, Jude, 1 John, 2 John are still extant in a Latin translation, and some have doubted whether he really wrote on the other Catholic epistles, and would read *Jude* for *James* in Cassiodorius, see however Zahn, *N. K.* I. 322, *Forschungen* iii. 153, Sanday in *Stud. Bibl.* iii. 248.

**Protr.* c. 10, p. 86 ἡ δύναμις ἡ θεϊκὴ ἐπιλάμψασα τὴν γῆν σωτηρίου σπέρματος ἐνέπλησε τὸ πᾶν...(ὁ λόγος) ἐξ αὐτῆς ἀνατείλας τῆς πατρικῆς βουλήσεως ῥᾷστα ἡμῖν ἐπέλαμψε τὸν Θεόν, c. 11, p. 90, λόγος ἀληθείας, λόγος ἀφθαρσίας, ὁ ἀναγεννῶν τὸν ἄνθρωπον, c. 10, p. 83 ὁ τῶν ἀγαθῶν ἀΐδιος δοτήρ, cf. *Paed.* i. p. 125 τῷ γοῦν γάλακτι, τῇ κυριακῇ τροφῇ εὐθὺς μὲν ἀποκυηθέντες τιθηνούμεθα, *ib.* p. 123 ὁ λόγος τὰ πάντα τῷ νηπίῳ, καὶ πατὴρ καὶ μήτηρ καὶ παιδαγωγὸς καὶ τροφεύς: James i. 17, 18 πᾶν δώρημα τέλειον ἄνωθέν ἐστιν, καταβαῖνον ἀπὸ τοῦ πατρὸς τῶν φώτων...βουληθεὶς ἀπεκύησεν ἡμᾶς λόγῳ ἀληθείας, cf. ver. 5.

Strom. ii. p. 439, iv. 611, *Paed.* iii. p. 259 καὶ φίλον αὐτὸν (Ἀβραὰμ) ὠνόμασεν τῆς οἴκοι καταφρονήσαντα περιουσίας, *ib.* p. 279: James ii. 23.

**ib.* iv. p. 570 τέλειον ἔργον ἀγάπης ἐνεδείξατο: James i. 4, iii. 13.

**ib.* iv. p. 572 Ἰὼβ ἐγκρατείας ὑπερβολῇ καὶ πίστεως ὑπεροχῇ πένης μὲν ἐκ πλουσίου...γενόμενος ἡμῖν τέ ἐστι παράδειγμα ἀγαθὸν ἀναγεγραμμένος, δυσωπῶν τὸν πειράσαντα, εὐλογῶν τὸν πλάσαντα: James v. 10, 11, iv. 7.

**ib.* iv. p. 613 ὁ σοφὸς ἐνδεικνύσθω τὴν σοφίαν αὐτοῦ μὴ λόγοις μόνον ἀλλ' ἐν ἔργοις ἀγαθοῖς, see above on Clem. R. c. 38: James iii. 13.

**ib.* v. p. 707 τῷ τοῦ Κυρίου ῥητῷ Ἔστω ὑμῶν τὸ ναὶ ναί, καὶ τὸ οὒ οὔ (prefixing the article with James v. 12).

ib. vi. p. 778. ἀπαραβάτως τὰ κατὰ τὰς ἐντολὰς κατορθῶν· τὸ δ' ἐστι θρησκεύειν τὸ θεῖον διὰ τῆς ὄντως δικαιοσύνης ἔργων τε καὶ γνώσεως: James i. 27.

ib. vi. p. 825 ἐὰν μὴ πλεονάσῃ ὑμῶν ἡ δικαιοσύνη πλείων τῶν γραμματέων καὶ Φαρισαίων τῶν κατὰ ἀποχὴν κακῶν δικαιουμένων, σὺν τῷ μετὰ τῆς ἐν τούτοις τελειώσεως, καὶ [τῷ] τὸν πλησίον ἀγαπᾶν καὶ εὐεργετεῖν δύνασθαι, οὐκ ἔσεσθε βασιλικοί: *ib.* iv. p. 626 αἴτημα τὸ βασιλικώτατον διδάσκων αἰτεῖσθαι, τὴν τῶν ἀνθρώπων σωτηρίαν: James ii. 8.

Origen (d. 253 A.D.) is apparently the first who cites the Epistle as Scripture and as written by St. James.

**Comm. in Joh.* xix. 6 ἐὰν γὰρ λέγηται μὲν πίστις, χωρὶς δὲ ἔργων τυγχάνῃ, νεκρά ἐστιν ἡ τοιαύτη, ὡς ἐν τῇ φερομένῃ Ἰακώβου ἐπιστολῇ ἀνέγνωμεν, cf. *ib.* xix. 1, xx. 10, *ad Rom.* ii. 12, viii. 1, *in Josh.* x.: James ii. 20, 26.

**Sel. in Exod.* xv. 25 (Lomm. viii. p. 324) ὅτε Θεὸς πειράζει, ἐπ' ὠφελείᾳ πειράζει, οὐκ ἐπὶ τῷ κακοποιῆσαι. Διὸ καὶ ἐλέχθη ὅτι Ὁ Θεὸς ἀπείραστός ἐστι κακῶν...ὁ οὖν φέρων τοὺς πειρασμοὺς γενναίως στεφανοῦται. Ἄλλο δέ ἐστιν ἐπὶ τοῦ διαβόλου· ἐκεῖνος γὰρ πειράζει ἵνα τοὺς πειθομένους αὐτῷ θανατώσῃ cf. *Levit.* xii. 3: James i. 13—15.

Comm. in ep. ad Rom. ii. 13 (Lomm. vi. p. 134) *et fides sine operibus mortua* dicitur et ex operibus sine fide nemo apud Deum justificatur : James ii 17, 26.

**ib.* iv. 1 (Lomm. vi. p. 235) In alio Scripturae loco dicitur de Abraham quod *ex operibus fidei justificatus sit*, cf. *ib.* iv. 3 : James ii. 21, 22, 23.

**ib.* iv. 8 Nec solus haec Paulus scribit : audi et Jacobum fratrem Domini similia protestantem cum dicit *Qui voluerit amicus esse saeculi hujus, inimicus Dei constituetur :* James iv. 4.

**ib.* ix. 24 sicut et Jacobus apostolus dicit *Omne datum bonum et omne donum perfectum desursum est descendens a Patre luminum :* James i. 17.

**Hom. in Gen.* viii. 10 Generas autem gaudium *si omne gaudium existimaveris cum in tentationes varias incideris* et istud gaudium offeras in sacrificium Deo : James i. 2.

**ib.* ii. 6 Omnipotentis Dei misericordiam deprecemur, qui nos *non solum auditores verbi sui* faciat, *sed et factores :* James i. 22.

**ib.* i. 7 Ipse ait per prophetam *Appropinquate mihi et appropinquabo vobis, dicit Dominus*, cf. on *Exod.* iii. below : James iv. 8, cf. Zech. i. 3.

**Hom. in Exod.* viii. 4 Sed et apostolus Jacobus dicit *Vir duplex animo inconstans est in omnibus viis suis :* James i. 8.

**Hom. in Exod.* iii. 3 Hoc idem Jacobus Apostolus cohortatur, dicens *Resistite autem diabolo et fugiet a vobis*, cf. *Comm. in Rom.* iv. 8, which adds the words *appropinquate Deo et appropinquabit vobis :* James iv. 7, 8.

**Hom. in Lev.* ii. 4 Ita enim dicit scriptura divina *Qui converti fecerit peccatorem ab errore viae suae salvat animam a morte et cooperit multitudinem peccatorum :* James v. 20.

**ib.* Jacobus Apostolus dicit *Si quis autem infirmatur vocet presbyteros ecclesiae et imponant ei manus, ungentes eum oleo in nomine Domini. Et oratio fidei salvabit infirmum, et si in peccatis fuerit remittentur ei :* James v. 14—15.

**ib.* xiii. 3 Jacobus Apostolus dicit *Fructus autem justitiae in pace seminatur :* James iii. 18.

**Hom. in Num.* xviii. 1 Ille erat apud quem *non est transmutatio nec commutationis umbra :* James i. 17.

**Sel. in Psalm.* cxviii. 6 Εἰ ὁ π ά σ α ς π ο ι ή σ α ς τ ὰ ς ἐ ν τ ο λ ὰ ς π τ α ί σ α ς δ ὲ ἐ ν μ ι ᾷ γ ί ν ε τ α ι π ά ν τ ω ν ἔ ν ο χ ο ς, καλῶς γέγραπται Τότε οὐ μὴ αἰσχυνθῶ ἐν τῷ με ἐπιβλέπειν ἐπὶ πάσας τὰς ἐντολάς σου : James ii. 10.

**ib.* ver. 153 Μακάριον ἐνώπιον τοῦ Θεοῦ ταπεινοῦσθαι· φησὶ γὰρ Ἰάκωβος Τ α π ε ι ν ώ θ η τ ε ἐ ν ώ π ι ο ν Κ υ ρ ί ο υ κ α ὶ ὑ ψ ώ σ ε ι ὑ μ ᾶ ς : James iv. 10.

**ib.* ver. 171 ὥσπερ τῶν εὐθυμούντων ἐστὶ τὸ ψάλλειν—ε ὐ θ υ μ ε ῖ γ ά ρ τις, φησίν, ἐ ν ὑ μ ῖ ν, ψ α λ λ έ τ ω—οὕτω τὸ ὑμνεῖν τῶν θεωρούντων τοὺς λόγους τῶν δικαιωμάτων ἐστίν, cf. *Sel. in Psalm.* xii. 6, *ib.* xlvi. 7, lxv. 4 : James v. 13.

**ib.* xxxi. 5 πνεῦμα ἡ γραφὴ ποτὲ μὲν...τὴν ψυχὴν (καλεῖ), ὡς παρὰ Ἰακώβῳ Ὥ σ π ε ρ δ ὲ τ ὸ σ ῶ μ α χ ω ρ ὶ ς π ν ε ύ μ α τ ο ς ν ε κ ρ ό ν ἐ σ τ ι : James ii. 26.

**ib.* xxxvii. 24 Apostolus enim est qui dicit *In multis enim offendimus omnes*, et *si quis in verbo non offendit, hic perfectus est vir :* James iii. 1. 2.

**Sel. in Jerem.* xlviii. ὑ π ε ρ η φ ά ν ο ι ς γ ὰ ρ ὁ Θ ε ὸ ς ἀ ν τ ι τ ά σ σ ε τ α ι, cf. *Hom. in Ezek.* ix. 2 : James iv. 6.

**Princip.* i. 6 *scienti bonum et non facienti peccatum est illi :* James iv. 17.

**Comm. in Prov.* (Mai *Nov. Bibl.* vii. 51) ὁ Ἰάκωβός φησιν, ἀλλήλοις ἐξαγγέλλετε τὰ παραπτώματα ὑμῶν ὅπως ἰάθητε.

Tertullian, d. about 230 A.D.

Bapt. 20 Nam et praecesserat dictum, *Neminem intentatum regna caelestia consecuturum* (perhaps said with immediate reference to Matt. v. 10, but the form seems to be coloured by a reminiscence of James i. 12, 13.

**De Orat.* 8 ‘Ne nos inducas in tentationem,’ id est, ne nos patiaris induci ab eo utique qui tentat. ceterum *absit ut Dominus tentare videatur*...Diaboli est *et infirmitas et malitia* : James i. 13.

**De Orat.* 29 Sed et *retro oratio...imbrium utilia prohibebat.* Nunc vero *oratio justitiae* omnem iram Dei avertit, pro inimicis excubat...*Mirum si aquas caelestes extorquere novit*, quae potuit et ignes impetrare? *Sola est oratio quae Deum vincit.* Sed Christus eam nihil mali novit operari...Itaque nihil novit nisi defunctorum *animas de ipso mortis itinere vocare, debiles reformare, aegros remediare*...eadem *diluit delicta*, tentationes repellit...*peregrinantes reducit*... lapsos erigit : James v. 16—20.

**Adv. Jud.* 2 Unde *Abraham amicus Dei deputatus?* James ii. 23.

Dionysius of Alexandria, d. 265 A.D.—

**Comm. in Lucam* (Migne *Patr. Gr.* x. p. 1595), after distinguishing between the phrases ἐπειράσθη and εἰς πειρασμὸν εἰσῆλθεν proceeds ὁ μὲν πονηρὸς εἰς τοὺς πειρασμοὺς καθέλκει οἷα πειραστὴς (? πειραστὸς) κακῶν· ὁ δὲ Θεὸς πειράζων τοὺς πειρασμοὺς περιφέρει ὡς ἀπείραστος κακῶν. ὁ γὰρ Θεός, φησὶν, ἀπείραστός ἐστι κακῶν : James i. 13.

Gregory Thaumaturgus, d. about 270 A.D.—

**Fragment quoted in Catena* (Westcott *Can.* p. 437) δῆλον γὰρ ὡς πᾶν ἀγαθὸν τέλειον θεόθεν ἔρχεται : James i. 17.

Clementine Homilies, early in the third century.

*iii. 55 τοῖς δὲ οἰομένοις ὅτι ὁ Θεὸς πειράζει...ἔφη Ὁ πονηρός ἐστιν ὁ πειράζων, ὁ καὶ αὐτὸν πειράσας : James i. 13.

iii. 54 (ἡ ἀλήθεια ἡ σώζουσα) ἦν καὶ ἔστιν ἐν τῷ Ἰησοῦ ἡμῶν λόγῳ, cf. μεταλαβεῖν τὸν τῆς ἀληθείας λόγον i. 16, σώζειν δυνάμενοι λόγοι, *Ep. ad Jac.* 5, 6, λόγοι ζωοποιοί, *Ep. ad Jac.* 19 : James i. 18, 21.

*xi. 4 ὁ εἰς Θεὸν εὐσεβεῖν θέλων ἄνθρωπον εὐεργετεῖ ὅτι εἰκόνα Θεοῦ τὸ ἀνθρώπου βαστάζει σῶμα...τιμὴν οὖν τῇ τοῦ Θεοῦ εἰκόνι...προσφέρειν δεῖ οὕτως, πεινῶντι τροφήν, διψῶντι ποτόν κ.τ.λ., iii. 17 ὁ εἰκόνα καὶ ταῦτα αἰωνίου βασιλέως ὑβρίσας τὴν ἁμαρτίαν εἰς ἐκεῖνον ἀναφερομένην ἔχει οὗπερ καθ' ὁμοίωσιν ἡ εἰκὼν ἐτύγχανεν οὖσα, xvii. 7 ὁ αὐτὸν σέβειν θέλων τὴν ὁρατὴν αὐτοῦ τιμᾷ εἰκόνα, ὅπερ ἐστὶν ἄνθρωπος· ὅτι ἂν οὖν τις ποιήσει ἀνθρώπῳ, εἴτε ἀγαθὸν εἴτε κακόν, εἰς ἐκεῖνον ἀναφέρεται : James iii. 9.

*viii. 7 οὐ γὰρ ὠφελήσει τινὰ τὸ λέγειν ἀλλὰ το ποιεῖν· ἐκ παντὸς οὖν τρόπου καλῶν ἔργων χρεία : James ii. 14, i. 22.

*vii. 8 ἡ δὲ ὑπ' αὐτοῦ (τοῦ Θεοῦ) ὁρισθεῖσα θρησκεία ἐστὶν αὕτη· τὸ μόνον αὐτὸν σέβειν καὶ τῷ τῆς ἀληθείας μόνῳ πιστεύειν προφήτῃ...μὴ ἀκαθάρτως βιοῦν...πάντας δὲ σωφρονεῖν, εὐποιεῖν, μὴ ἀδικεῖν· παρὰ τοῦ πάντα δυναμένου Θεοῦ ζωὴν αἰώνιον προσδοκᾶν, εὐχαῖς καὶ δεήσεσιν συνεχέσιν αἰτουμένους αὐτὴν λαβεῖν : James i. 27, 5, 6, 12, 18.

viii. 6 μιᾶς δι' ἀμφοτέρων (Ἰησοῦ καὶ Μωυσέως) διδασκαλίας οὔσης τὸν τούτων τινὶ πεπιστευκότα ὁ Θεὸς ἀποδέχεται· ἀλλὰ τὸ πιστεύειν τῷ διδασκάλῳ ἕνεκα τοῦ ποιεῖν τὰ ὑπὸ τοῦ Θεοῦ λεγόμενα γίνεται : James i. 25, ii. 8, 10—12, iv. 11.

xi. 11 ἔχθρα τίς ἐστιν Θεῷ ἐν ὑμῖν ἄλογος ἐπιθυμία : James iv. 4, 1, i. 14.

*iii. 55 ἔστω ὑμῶν τὸ ναὶ ναί, καὶ τὸ οὔ οὔ : James v. 12.

*xiii. 16 καλῷ ἐσόπτρῳ ὁρᾷ εἰς τὸν Θεὸν ἐμβλέπουσα : James i. 23.

Ep. ad Jac. 11 διὸ προφήτου ἀληθῶς ὄντες μαθηταί, ἀποθέμενοι τὴν διχόνοιαν, ἐξ ἧς γίνεται ἡ κακοπραξία, προθύμως τὸ εὐποιεῖν ἀναδέξασθε : James i. 21—23, 8, iv. 8.

Constitutiones Apostolicae, a compilation of the fourth century, portions of which belong to a much earlier date.

*i. 23 μηδὲ ἐπιτετηδευμένῃ σὺ τῇ ἐσθῆτι χρήσῃ εἰς ἀπάτην...μηδὲ χρυσήλατον σφενδόνην τοῖς δακτύλοις σου περιθῇς· ὅτι ταῦτα πάντα ἑταιρισμοῦ τεκμήρια ὑπάρχει : James ii. 2.

*ii. 6 ἔστω δὲ ὁ ἐπίσκοπος...μὴ πλεονέκτης...μὴ φιλοπλούσιος, μὴ μισόπτωχος, μὴ κατάλαλος...μὴ θυμώδης...μὴ ταῖς τοῦ βίου πραγματείαις συμπεπλεγμένος...μὴ δίγνωμος, μὴ δίγλωσσος...ὅτι πάντα τὰ τοιαῦτα ἐχθρὰ τοῦ Θεοῦ ὑπάρχει καὶ δαιμόνων φίλα: James ii. 1—7, iv. 11, i. 20, 27, 8, iii. 9.

*ii. 36 μὴ κρῖναι τὸν ἐπίσκοπόν σου ἢ τὸν συλλαϊκόν· ἐὰν γὰρ κρίνῃς τὸν ἀδελφόν, κριτὴς ἐγένου, μηδενός σε προχειρισαμένου: James iv. 11, 12.

ii. 37 ὅπου δὲ ὀργή, ἐκεῖ ὁ Κύριος οὐκ ἔστιν: James i. 20.

*ii. 58 εἰ δὲ ἐν τῷ καθέζεσθαι ἕτερός τις ἐπέλθοι εὐσχήμων καὶ ἔνδοξος ἐν τῷ βίῳ, σὺ ὁ ἐπίσκοπος μὴ προσωποληπτῶν καταλίπῃς τὴν διακονίαν τοῦ λόγου ἵνα διατάξῃ αὐτῷ προεδρίαν, ἀλλὰ μένε ἡσύχιος...οἱ δὲ ἀδελφοὶ διὰ τῶν διακόνων παραδεχέσθωσαν αὐτόν...εἰ δὲ πτωχὸς ἢ ἀγενὴς ...ἐπέλθοι...καὶ τούτοις τόπον ποιήσει ἐξ ὅλης τῆς καρδίας ὁ διάκονος, ἵνα μὴ πρὸς ἄνθρωπον αὐτοῦ γένηται ἡ προσωπόληψις ἀλλὰ πρὸς Θεὸν ἡ διακονία εὐάρεστος. τὸ δὲ αὐτὸ ποιείτω καὶ ἡ διάκονος ταῖς ἐπερχομέναις γυναιξὶν πτωχαῖς ἤτοι πλουσίαις: James ii. 1—4, i. 27.

*ii. 8 ἀνὴρ ἀδόκιμος ἀπείραστος παρὰ Θεῷ: James i. 12, 13.

Lactantius, fl. 300 A.D.—

**Epitome* c. 65 *si enim ficti ab uno Deo* et orti ab uno homine, *consanguinitatis jure sociamur;* omnem igitur *hominem diligere debemus...Si quis victu indiget, impertiamus; si quis nudus occurrit vestiamus. Pupillis defensio, viduis tutela nostra non desit*...Magnum misericordiae opus est *aegros pauperes visere atque refovere.* Haec...si quis obierit, *verum et acceptum sacrificium Deo immolavit*...Deus quia justus est suamet ipsum lege, et sua condicione prosequitur : *miseretur ejus quem viderit misericordem; inexorabilis est ei quem precantibus cernit immitem...contemnenda est pecunia* et ad caelestes transferenda *thesauros ubi* nec fur effodiat *nec rubigo consumat:* James iii. 9, ii. 8, 15, 16, i. 27, ii. 13.

Instit. v. 1. 9 *si lucrari hos a morte*...non potuerimus, si ab illo *itinere devio ad vitam* lucemque *revocare,* quoniam ipsi *saluti suae repugnant;* nostros tamen confirmabimus : James v. 19, 20.

**Instit.* vii. 21 *daemones reformidant quia torquentur ab eo ac puniuntur* : James ii. 19.

Athanasius, d. 373 A.D.—

**De Decretis Nic. Syn.* 4 τὴν ἐλευθερίαν τῆς ἑαυτῶν ψυχῆς ἄλλοις προπίνοντες τούτους καὶ καθηγεμόνας τῆς αἱρέσεως ἔχειν ἐθέλουσιν, ἀνθρώπους, ὡς εἶπεν ὁ Ἰάκωβος διψύχους καὶ ἀκαταστάτους ὄντας ἐν πάσαις ταῖς ὁδοῖς αὐτῶν καὶ μὴ μίαν μὲν ἔχοντας γνώμην ἄλλοτε δὲ ἄλλως μεταβαλλομένους : James i. 8.

**Orat. tert. c. Arian* 6 καθὼς Ἰάκωβος ὁ ἀπόστολος διδάσκων ἔλεγε βουληθεὶς ἀπεκύησεν ἡμᾶς λόγῳ ἀληθείας: James i. 18.

**Ep. ad Afr.* 8 ἁπλῆ γάρ ἐστιν οὐσία ἐν ᾗ οὐκ ἔνι ποιότης οὐδέ, ὡς εἶπεν ὁ Ἰάκωβος, παραλλαγή τις ἢ τροπῆς ἀποσκίασμα: James i. 17.

And elsewhere. See above on his canon of the N. T.

Chrysostom, A.D. 347–407.

One quotation will be enough to show how highly he esteemed St. James. For his comments on our Epistle, see the *Fragmenta in Ep. Cath.* in Migne *Patr. Gr.* p. 64.

Orat. de Paenit. v. καὶ εἰ βούλεσθε παράξω ὑμῖν ἀξιόπιστον μάρτυρα, τὸν ἀδελφόθεον Ἰάκωβον φάσκοντα· ἡ πίστις χωρὶς τῶν ἔργων νεκρά ἐστι.

Lastly Didymus (d. 394), the head of the catechetical school at Alexandria, who taught Jerome and Rufinus, has left brief comments on all the Catholic Epistles. Within three years of his death the Western Church also, at the Council of Carthage (397), had formally pronounced on the Canonical character of the Epistle, which is quoted like the other Scriptures by Jerome and Augustine. See Bp. Wordsworth in *Stud. Bibl.* I. 128, 129.

CHAPTER III

The Relation of the Epistle to Earlier Writers

(1) *Canonical Books of the Old Testament.* (2) *Apocrypha.* (3) *Philo.* (4) *Greek Philosophers.*

(1) *Canonical Books of the Old Testament.*

Genesis—

Besides the general reference to the history of Abraham in James ii. 21—23, on which compare especially Gen. xxii. 1—18, we have in James ii. 23 a quotation from Gen. xv. 6 καὶ ἐπίστευσεν Ἀβραὰμ τῷ Θεῷ καὶ ἐλογίσθη αὐτῷ εἰς δικαιοσύνην, only reading, as in Rom. iv. 3, Philo, &c., ἐπίστευσεν δέ for καὶ ἐπ. [The Hebrew here has the active 'God counted it to him.'] It is probable also that φίλος Θεοῦ ἐκλήθη in the same verse of James is a quotation from Gen. xviii. 17 οὐ μὴ κρύψω ἀπὸ Ἀβραὰμ τοῦ παιδός μου, where Philo reads τοῦ φίλου μου: see the notes.

i. 26 καὶ εἶπεν ὁ Θεός Ποιήσωμεν ἄνθρωπον κατ' εἰκόνα ἡμετέραν καὶ καθ' ὁμοίωσιν, καὶ ἀρχέτωσαν τῶν ἰχθύων τῆς θαλάσσης καὶ τῶν πετεινῶν τοῦ οὐρανοῦ καὶ τῶν κτηνῶν καὶ πάσης τῆς γῆς καὶ πάντων τῶν ἑρπετῶν τῶν ἑρπόντων ἐπὶ τῆς γῆς. This is the source of two verses in James: iii. 9 ἐν αὐτῇ εὐλογοῦμεν τὸν Κύριον καὶ Πατέρα, καὶ ἐν αὐτῇ καταρώμεθα τοὺς ἀνθρώπους τοὺς καθ' ὁμοίωσιν Θεοῦ γεγονότας (which should also be compared with Gen. ix. 6, as tracing back our duty towards our fellow-men to our common participation in the divine image), and iii. 7 πᾶσα γὰρ φύσις θηρίων τε καὶ πετεινῶν, ἑρπετῶν τε καὶ ἐναλίων, δαμάζεται καὶ δεδάμασται τῇ φύσει τῇ ἀνθρωπίνῃ, for the classification of animals and their subjugation to man. With this should be compared Gen. ix. 2.

iv. 10 φωνὴ αἵματος τοῦ ἀδελφοῦ βοᾷ πρός με ἐκ τῆς γῆς, cf. below Deut. xxiv. 15.

Exodus—

ii. 23 see below on Deut. xxiv. 15.
xx. 5 Θεὸς ζηλωτής, see below on Deut. iv. 24.
xx. 13 The LXX. here puts the seventh commandment before the sixth, as

in James ii. 11 and Luke xviii. 20. The two latter, however, change the *ο ὐ μ ο ι χ ε ύ σ ε ι ς* of the former (which is preserved in Matt. v. 27) into *μὴ μοιχεύσῃς*.

xxii. 22 *πᾶσαν χήραν καὶ ὀρφανὸν οὐ κακώσετε*: James i. 27, cf. Deut. xxiv. 17.

Leviticus—

xix. 13 *οὐκ ἀδικήσεις τὸν πλησίον...καὶ οὐ μὴ κοιμηθήσεται ὁ μισθὸς τοῦ μισθωτοῦ σου παρὰ σοὶ ἕως πρωΐ*, cf. below Deut. xxiv. 15.

xix. 15 *οὐ λήψῃ πρόσωπον πτωχοῦ οὐδὲ μὴ θαυμάσῃς πρόσωπον δυναστοῦ· ἐν δικαιοσύνῃ κρινεῖς τὸν πλησίον σου*: apparently the earliest use of the phrase *λ α μ β ά ν ε ι ν π ρ ό σ ω π ο ν*, referred to in James ii. 1, 9.

xix. 18 *ἀ γ α π ή σ ε ι ς τ ὸ ν π λ η σ ί ο ν σ ο υ ὡ ς σ ε α υ τ ό ν*, quoted literally in James ii. 8, as in Matt. xxii. 39.

Numbers—

xv. 30 *καὶ ψυχὴ ἥτις ποιήσῃ ἐν χειρὶ ὑπερηφανιας, τὸν Θεὸν οὗτος παροξυνεῖ*, James iv. 6.

Deuteronomy—

iv. 7 *ποῖον ἔθνος μέγα ᾧ ἐστὶν αὐτῷ Θεὸς ἐ γ γ ί ζ ω ν*, and ver. 4 *ὑμεῖς οἱ προσκείμενοι Κυρίῳ τῷ Θεῷ ὑμῶν ζῆτε πάντες*: James iv. 8 *ἐ γ γ ί σ α τ ε τ ῷ Θεῷ καὶ ἐ γ γ ί σ ε ι ὑμῖν.*

iv. 24 *Κύριος ὁ Θεός σου πῦρ καταναλίσκον ἐστί, Θεὸς ζηλωτής*, Deut. xxxii. 11 foll. *ὡς ἀετὸς...ἐπὶ τοῖς νόσσοις αὐτοῦ ἐ π ε π ό θ η σ ε*, ver. 16 *παρώξυνάν με ἐπ' ἀλλοτρίοις*, ver. 19 *καὶ εἶδε Κύριος καὶ ἐζήλωσε*, ver. 21: James iv. 4, 5 *μοιχαλίδες οὐκ οἴδατε ὅτι ἡ φιλία τοῦ κόσμου ἔχθρα τοῦ Θεοῦ ἐστίν;...ἢ δοκεῖτε ὅτι κενῶς ἡ γραφὴ λέγει Πρὸς φθόνον ἐπιποθεῖ τὸ πνεῦμα ὃ κατῴκισεν ἐν ἡμῖν;*

vi. 4 *ἄκουε Ἰσραήλ, Κ ύ ρ ι ο ς ὁ Θ ε ὸ ς ἡ μ ῶ ν ε ἷ ς ἔ σ τ ι ν*, quoted exactly in Mark xii. 29, referred to in James ii. 19.

xi. 14 *δώσει τὸν ὑετὸν τῇ γῇ σου καθ' ὥραν πρώϊμον κ. ὄψιμον*, cf. Hos. vi. 4, Jer. v. 24, Joel ii. 23, Zech. x. 1: James v. 7.

xiv. 2 *καί σε ἐ ξ ε λ έ ξ α τ ο Κύριος ὁ Θεός σου γενέσθαι σε λαὸν αὐτῷ περιούσιον*: James ii. 5.

xxiv. 15 *αὐθημερὸν ἀποδώσεις τὸν μισθὸν αὐτοῦ...ὅτι πένης ἐστὶ καὶ...κ α τ α β ο- ή σ ε τ α ι κ α τ ὰ σ ο υ π ρ ὸ ς Κ ύ ρ ι ο ν καὶ ἔ σ τ α ι ἐ ν σ ο ὶ ἁ μ α ρ τ ί α*, Exod. ii. 23 *ἀ ν έ β η ἡ β ο ὴ α ὐ τ ῶ ν πρὸς τὸν Θεόν*, Jer. xxii. 13, Mal. iii. 5: James v. 4 *ἰδοὺ ὁ μισθὸς τῶν ἀμησάντων τὰς χώρας ὑμῶν, ὁ ἀφυστερημένος ἀφ' ὑμῶν, κράζει· καὶ αἱ βοαὶ τῶν θερισάντων εἰς τὰ ὦτα Κυρίου Σαβαὼθ εἰσελήλυθαν*, iv. 17 *ἁμαρτία αὐτῷ ἐστίν.*

xxviii. 58 *τὸ ὄνομα τὸ ἔντιμον, τὸ θαυμαστὸν τοῦτο, Κύριον τὸν Θεόν σου*: James ii. 7 *τὸ καλὸν ὄνομα.*

xxxii. 18 *Θεὸν τὸν γεννήσαντα σε ἐγκατέλιπες*: James i. 18.

xxxii. 36—39 *ἐγὼ ἀποκτείνω καὶ ζῆν ποιήσω*: James iv. 12, cf. ver. 6.

Joshua—

ii. esp. verses 5, 11, 12, 15, 16: referred to in James ii. 25 *ὁμοίως καὶ Ῥαὰβ ἡ πόρνη οὐκ ἐξ ἔργων ἐδικαιώθη ὑποδεξαμένη τοὺς ἀγγέλους καὶ ἑτέρᾳ ὁδῷ ἐκβαλοῦσα* and Heb. xi. 31.

I. Kings—

iii. 9—12 (prayer of Solomon): James i. 5 *εἴ τις λείπεται σοφίας αἰτείτω παρὰ τοῦ διδόντος Θεοῦ πᾶσιν ἁπλῶς.*

xviii. 1, 42 (prayer of Elijah): James v. 17, 18, and Luke iv. 25.

2 Chron. xx. 7 Art not thou our Father who gavest it (the land) to Abraham thy friend (Heb.): James ii. 23.

Job. The general moral of this book, that patient endurance of affliction leads to wisdom and to final happiness, is also that enforced in the Epistle of James: see especially xlii. 12 ὁ δὲ Κύριος εὐλόγησε τὰ ἔσχατα Ἰὼβ ἢ τὰ ἔμπροσθεν: James v. 11 τὴν ὑπομονὴν Ἰὼβ ἠκούσατε καὶ τὸ τέλος Κυρίου εἴδετε.

v. 17 μακάριος ἄνθρωπος ὃν ἤλεγξεν ὁ Κύριος: James i. 12.
vii. 9 ὥσπερ νέφος ἀποκαθαρθὲν ἀπ' οὐρανοῦ κ.τ.λ.: James iv. 14.
xiii. 28 παλαιοῦται...ὥσπερ ἱμάτιον σητόβρωτον: James v. 2 τὰ ἱμάτια ὑμῶν σητόβρωτα γέγονεν.
xxiv. 24 πολλοὺς γὰρ ἐκάκωσε τὸ ὕψωμα αὐτοῦ, ἐμαράνθη δὲ ὥσπερ μολόχη ἐν καύματι ἢ ὥσπερ στάχυς ἀπὸ καλάμης αὐτόματος ἀποπεσών; *ib.* xxvii. 21 ἀναλήψεται δὲ αὐτόν (τὸν πλούσιον) καύσων καὶ ἀπελεύσεται, cf. below, Jonah iv. 8: James i. 10, 11 (ὁ πλούσιος) ὡς ἄνθος χόρτου παρελεύσεται· ἀνέτειλεν γὰρ ὁ ἥλιος σὺν τῷ καύσωνι καὶ ἐξήρανεν τὸν χόρτον καὶ τὸ ἄνθος αὐτοῦ ἐξέπεσεν...οὕτως καὶ ὁ πλούσιος μαρανθήσεται.
xxxiii. 23 ἄγγελοι θανατηφόροι (not in the Heb.): James iii. 8 (γλῶσσα) μεστὴ ἰοῦ θανατηφόρου.

Psalms—

vii. 14 ὠδίνησεν ἀδικίαν, συνέλαβε πόνον, καὶ ἔτεκεν ἀνομίαν: James i. 15 ἡ ἐπιθυμία συλλαβοῦσα τίκτει ἁμαρτίαν.
xii. 2 ἐν καρδίᾳ καὶ ἐν καρδίᾳ ἐλάλησαν: James i. 8 δίψυχος.
xxiv. 4 ἀθῷος χερσὶ καὶ καθαρὸς τῇ καρδίᾳ, cf. lxxiii. 13: James iv. 8 καθαρίσατε χεῖρας, ἁμαρτωλοί, καὶ ἁγνίσατε καρδίας, δίψυχοι.
l. 20 κατὰ τοῦ ἀδελφοῦ σου κατελάλεις: James iv. 11 ὁ καταλαλῶν ἀδελφοῦ...καταλαλεῖ νόμου.
lxxxiii. 13, 14 ὁ Θεός μου θοῦ αὐτοὺς ὡς τροχὸν...ὡσεὶ πῦρ ὃ διαφλέξει δρυμόν, ὡσεὶ φλὸξ κατακαῦσαι ὄρη: James iii. 5 ἡλίκον πῦρ ἡλίκην ὕλην ἀνάπτει, ver. 6 φλογίζουσα τὸν τροχὸν τῆς γενέσεως.
lxxxv. 9 ἐγγὺς τῶν φοβουμένων αὐτὸν τὸ σωτήριον αὐτοῦ, τοῦ κατασκηνῶσαι δόξαν ἐν τῇ γῇ ἡμῶν: James ii. 1 τὴν πίστιν τοῦ Κυρίου ἡμῶν Ἰησοῦ Χριστοῦ, τῆς δόξης.
ciii. 8 οἰκτίρμων καὶ ἐλεήμων ὁ Κύριος, μακρόθυμος και πολυέλεος, cf. Joel ii. 13, Ps. lxxxvi. 15, Exod. xxxiv. 6: James v. 11 πολύσπλαγχνός ἐστιν ὁ Κύριος κ. οἰκτίρμων.
cxix. 45 'I will walk at liberty, for I seek thy precepts': James i. 25 νόμος ἐλευθερίας.
cxxvi. 6, 7 (sowing in tears, reaping in joy): James v. 7, see below on Hos. vi. 1—3.
cxl. 3 ἠκόνησαν γλῶσσαν αὐτῶν ὡσεὶ ὄφεως, ἰὸς ἀσπίδων ὑπὸ τὰ χείλη αὐτῶν: James iii. 8.

Proverbs—

ii. 6 Θεὸς δίδωσι σοφίαν: James i. 5 εἴ τις λείπεται σοφίας αἰτείτω παρὰ τοῦ διδόντος Θεοῦ πᾶσιν.
iii. 34 Κύριος ὑπερηφάνοις ἀντιτάσσεται ταπεινοῖς δὲ δίδωσι χάριν: quoted literally (except for the change of Κύριος into ὁ Θεός) in James iv. 6 and 1 Pet. v. 5.
x. 12 'Hatred stirreth up strife, but love covereth all sins' (LXX. μῖσος ἐγείρει νεῖκος, πάντας δὲ τοὺς μὴ φιλονεικοῦντας καλύπτει φιλία): James v. 20 ὁ ἐπιστρέψας ἁμαρτωλὸν...καλύψει πλῆθος ἁμαρτιῶν, cf. 1 Pet. iv. 8.

x. 19 ἐκ πολυλογίας οὐκ ἐκφεύξῃ ἁμαρτίαν, cf. xii. 13 δι' ἁμαρτίαν χειλέων ἐμπίπτει εἰς παγίδας ἁμαρτωλός, vi. 2: James iii. 2 εἴ τις ἐν λόγῳ οὐ πταίει, οὗτος τέλειος ἀνήρ.

xi. 30 ἐκ καρποῦ δικαιοσύνης φύεται δένδρον ζωῆς: James iii. 18 καρπὸς δὲ δικαιοσύνης ἐν εἰρήνῃ σπείρεται τοῖς ποιοῦσιν εἰρήνην.

xiv. 21 ὁ ἀτιμάζων πένητας ἁμαρτάνει: James ii. 6 ἠτιμάσατε τὸν πτωχόν. Cf. Sir. x. 22.

xvi. 27 ἀνὴρ ἄφρων...ἐπὶ τῶν ἑαυτοῦ χειλέων θησαυρίζει πῦρ: James iii. 6 καὶ ἡ γλῶσσα πῦρ...ἡ φλογιζομένη ὑπὸ τῆς γεέννης, cf. v. 3.

xix. 3 ἀφροσύνη ἀνδρὸς λυμαίνεται τὰς ὁδοὺς αὐτοῦ, τὸν δὲ Θεὸν αἰτιᾶται τῇ καρδίᾳ αὐτοῦ: James i. 13, 14.

xxvi. 28 γλῶσσα ψευδὴς μισεῖ ἀλήθειαν, στόμα δὲ ἄστεγον ποιεῖ ἀκαταστασίας: James iii. 16 ὅπου ζῆλος καὶ ἐριθία, ἐκεῖ ἀκαταστασία.

xxvii. i. μὴ καυχῶ τὰ εἰς αὔριον, οὐ γὰρ γινώσκεις τί τέξεται ἡ ἐπιοῦσα, *ib.* iii. 28: James iv. 13, 14, 16 ἄγε νῦν οἱ λέγοντες Σήμερον ἢ αὔριον πορευσόμεθα...οἵτινες οὐκ ἐπίστασθε τὸ τῆς αὔριον...νῦν δὲ καυχᾶσθε ἐν ταῖς ἀλαζονίαις.

xxvii. 21 δοκίμιον ἀργυρίῳ καὶ χρυσῷ πύρωσις, ἀνὴρ δὲ δοκιμάζεται διὰ στόματος ἐγκωμιαζόντων αὐτόν, cf. xvii. 3 ὥσπερ δοκιμάζεται ἐν καμίνῳ ἄργυρος καὶ χρυσός, οὕτως ἐκλεκταὶ καρδίαι παρὰ Κυρίῳ: James i. 3, iii. 2.

xxix. 11 ἐὰν ἴδῃς ἄνδρα ταχὺν ἐν λόγοις, γίνωσκε ὅτι ἐλπίδα ἔχει μᾶλλον ἄφρων αὐτοῦ, cf. xiii. 3: James i. 19.

Ecclesiastes—

vii. 9 μὴ σπεύσῃς ἐν πνεύματί σου τοῦ θυμοῦσθαι, ὅτι θυμὸς ἐν κόλπῳ ἀφρόνων ἀναπαύεται: James i. 19 βραδὺς εἰς ὀργήν.

Isaiah—

i. 11—17 τί μοι πλῆθος τῶν θυσιῶν ὑμων; λέγει Κύριος· πλήρης εἰμὶ ὁλοκαυμάτων κριῶν...λούσασθε, καθαροὶ γένεσθε...μάθετε καλὸν ποιεῖν...κρίνατε ὀρφανῷ καὶ δικαιώσατε χήραν, cf. Exod. ii. 23, xxii. 22: James i. 25, 26, 27, iv. 8

v. 7—9 'He looked for judgment, but behold oppression; for righteousness, but behold a cry (κραυγήν). Woe unto them that join house to house, that lay field to field'...ἠκούσθη γὰρ εἰς τὰ ὦτα Κυρίου Σαβαὼθ ταῦτα (the Heb. of the last clause is different), cf. Deut. xxiv. 15: James v. 1—4.

ix. 18, x. 17, 18, cf. on Psa. lxxxiii. 14.

xiii. 6 ὀλολύζετε, ἐγγὺς γὰρ ἡμέρα Κυρίου: James v. 1 quoted below under Jer. xxv. 34.

xxxii. 17 καὶ ἔσται τὰ ἔργα δικαιοσύνης εἰρήνη, cf. above Prov. xi. 30: James iii. 18 καρπὸς δὲ δικαιοσύνης ἐν εἰρήνῃ σπείρεται τοῖς ποιοῦσιν εἰρηνην.

xl. 6, 7 πᾶσα σὰρξ χόρτος καὶ πᾶσα δόξα ἀνθρώπου ὡς ἄνθος χόρτου. ἐξηράνθη ὁ χόρτος καὶ τὸ ἄνθος ἐξέπεσε, τὸ δὲ ῥῆμα τοῦ Θεοῦ ἡμῶν μένει εἰς τὸν αἰῶνα: James i. 10, 11 (ὁ πλούσιος) ὡς ἄνθος χόρτου παρελεύσεται· ἀνέτειλεν γὰρ ὁ ἥλιος...καὶ ἐξήρανεν τὸν χόρτον καὶ τὸ ἄνθος αὐτοῦ ἐξέπεσεν. Cf. below 1 Pet. i. 24, where the quotation is given almost verbatim.

xli. 8. The seed of Abraham my friend (Heb.): James ii. 23.

l. 9 σὴς καταφάγεται ὑμᾶς: James v. 2 τὰ ἱμάτια σητόβρωτα, ver. 3 (ὁ ἰὸς) φάγεται τὰς σάρκας ὑμῶν.

liv. 5—8. 'Thy Maker is thy husband (the LXX. is different)...the Lord hath called thee as a wife forsaken...even a wife of youth when she is cast off'...χρόνον μικρὸν κατέλιπόν σε καὶ μετ' ἐλέους μεγάλου ἐλεήσω σε· ἐν θυμῷ μικρῷ ἀπέστρεψα τὸ πρόσωπόν μου ἀπὸ σοῦ καὶ ἐν ἐλέει αἰωνίῳ ἐλεήσω σε, εἶπεν ὁ ῥυσάμενός σε Κύριος: James iv. 6, 7. Cf. above, Deut. iv. 24.

lxi. 1 τὸ πνεῦμα Κυρίου ἐπ' ἐμέ...εὐαγγελίσασθαι πτωχοῖς ἀπέσταλκέ με, cf. xxix. 19: James ii. 5 ὁ Θεὸς ἐξελέξατο τοὺς πτωχοὺς τῷ κόσμῳ κληρονόμους τῆς βασιλείας.

Jeremiah—

ix. 23 μὴ καυχάσθω ὁ σοφὸς ἐν τῇ σοφίᾳ αὐτοῦ καὶ μὴ καυχάσθω ὁ ἰσχυρὸς ἐν τῇ ἰσχύϊ αὐτοῦ καὶ μὴ καυχάσθω ὁ πλούσιος ἐν τῷ πλούτῳ αὐτοῦ, ἀλλ' ἢ ἐν τούτῳ καυχάσθω ὁ καυχώμενος, συνιεῖν καὶ γινώσκειν ὅτι ἐγὼ εἰμὶ Κύριος ὁ ποιῶν ἔλεος καὶ κρίμα καὶ δικαιοσύνην ἐπὶ τῆς γῆς, ὅτι ἐν τούτοις τὸ θέλημά μου, λέγει Κύριος: James i. 9, 10 καυχάσθω δὲ ὁ ἀδελφὸς ὁ ταπεινὸς ἐν τῷ ὕψει αὐτοῦ, ὁ δὲ πλούσιος ἐν τῇ ταπεινώσει αὐτοῦ, i. 18 βουληθεὶς κ.τ.λ., ii. 13, v. 11.

xii. 3 ἅγνισον αὐτοὺς εἰς ἡμέραν σφαγῆς: James v. 5.

xxv. (xxxii.) 34 ἀλαλάξατε...καὶ κεκράξατε καὶ κόπτεσθε...ὅτι ἐπληρώθησαν αἱ ἡμέραι ὑμῶν εἰς σφαγήν, xii. 3 ἅγνισον αὐτοὺς εἰς ἡμέραν σφαγῆς αὐτῶν: James v. 1 κλαύσατε ὀλολύζοντες ἐπὶ ταῖς ταλαιπωρίαις ὑμῶν ταῖς ἐπερχομέναις, *ib.* ver. 5 ἐθρέψατε τὰς καρδίας ἐν ἡμέρᾳ σφαγῆς, *ib.* iv. 9 ταλαιπωρήσατε καὶ πενθήσατε καὶ κλαύσατε.

Ezekiel—

xxxiii. 31, 32 ἀκούουσι τὰ ῥήματά σου καὶ αὐτὰ οὐ μὴ ποιήσουσιν: James i. 22 23 γίνεσθε δὲ ποιηταὶ λόγου καὶ μὴ ἀκροαταὶ μόνον.

Daniel—

xii. 12 μακάριος ὁ ὑπομένων: James v. 11 ἰδοὺ μακαρίζομεν τοὺς ὑπομένοντας, *ib.* i. 12.

Hosea—

i. 6. ἀντιτασσόμενος ἀντιτάξομαι αὐτοῖς, cf. Prov. iii. 34: James iv. 6.

vi. 1—4 'Come and let us return unto the Lord, for He hath torn and He will heal us'...καὶ ἥξει ὡς ὑετὸς ἡμῖν πρώϊμος καὶ ὄψιμος: James v. 7 μακροθυμήσατε οὖν ἀδελφοὶ ἕως τῆς παρουσίας τοῦ Κυρίου. Ἰδοὺ ὁ γεωργὸς ἐκδέχεται τὸν τίμιον καρπὸν τῆς γῆς μακροθυμῶν ἐπ' αὐτῷ ἕως λάβῃ πρόϊμον καὶ ὄψιμον.

vi. 6 ἔλεος θέλω ἢ θυσίαν: James ii. 13.

Joel—

ii. 1 κηρύξατε...διότι πάρεστιν ἡμέρα Κυρίου, ὅτι ἐγγύς: James v. 8 στηρίξατε τὰς καρδίας ὑμῶν ὅτι ἡ παρουσία τοῦ Κυρίου ἤγγικε.

Amos—

iii. 10 'They know not to do right who store up violence and robbery in their palaces' οἱ θησαυρίζοντες ἀδικίαν καὶ ταλαιπωρίαν ἐν ταῖς χώραις αὐτῶν: James v. 3, 4 ἐθησαυρίσατε ἐν ἐσχάταις ἡμέραις· ἰδοὺ ὁ μισθὸς...τῶν ἀμησάντων τὰς χώρας ὑμῶν...κράζει.

ix. 12 ὅπως ἐκζητήσωσιν οἱ κατάλοιποι τῶν ἀνθρώπων καὶ πάντα τὰ ἔθνη ἐφ' οὓς ἐπικέκληται τὸ ὄνομά μου ἐπ' αὐτούς, λέγει Κύριος: James ii. 7 τὸ καλὸν ὄνομα τὸ ἐπικληθὲν ἐφ' ὑμᾶς. The verse is quoted with slight varieties in the speech of St. James (Acts xv. 17).

Jonah—

iv. 8 καὶ ἐγένετο ἅμα τῷ ἀνατεῖλαι τὸν ἥλιον καὶ προσέταξεν ὁ Θεὸς πνεύματι καύσωνι συγκαίοντι, καὶ ἐπάταξεν ὁ ἥλιος ἐπὶ τὴν κεφαλὴν τοῦ Ἰωνᾶ, see above on Job xxiv. 24: James i. 11.

Micah—

vi. 5 ἡ δικαιοσύνη τοῦ Κυρίου is said to consist, not in ritual or offerings, but in doing justly and loving mercy: James i. 20 ὀργὴ γὰρ ἀνδρὸς δικαιοσύνην Θεοῦ οὐκ ἐργάζεται, cf. ver. 27.

Zechariah—

i. 3 ἐπιστρέψατε πρός μέ, λέγει Κύριος τῶν δυνάμεων καὶ ἐπιστραφήσομαι πρὸς ὑμᾶς: James iv. 8 cited above on Deut. iv. 7.

i. 14—16 τάδε λέγει Κύριος, Ἐζήλωκα τὴν Ἱερουσαλὴμ καὶ τὴν Σιὼν ζῆλον μέγαν ...διὰ τοῦτο λέγει Κύριος Ἐπιστρέψω ἐπὶ Ἱερουσαλὴμ ἐν οἰκτιρμῷ, καὶ ὁ οἶκός μου ἀνοικοδομηθήσεται ἐν αὐτῇ, *ib.* viii. 2, 3: James iv. 6 quoted above on Isa. liv. 5.

ii. 5 'I will be the glory in the midst of her' (LXX. εἰς δόξαν): James ii. 1 quoted on Psa. lxxxv. 9.

vi. 14 ὁ δὲ στέφανος ἔσται τοῖς ὑπομένουσι (Hebrew different): James i. 12 μακάριος ἀνὴρ ὃς ὑπομένει πειρασμὸν ὅτι δόκιμος γενόμενος λήμψεται τὸν στέφανον τῆς ζωῆς.

x. 1 αἰτεῖσθε παρὰ Κυρίου ὑετὸν καθ' ὥραν πρώϊμον καὶ ὄψιμον: James v. 7.

xiii. 9 δοκιμῶ αὐτοὺς ὡς δοκιμάζεται τὸ χρυσίον, cf. Mal. iii. 3: James i. 3, 12.

Malachi—

ii. 6 ἐν εἰρήνῃ κατευθύνων ἐπορεύθη μετ' ἐμοῦ καὶ πολλοὺς ἐπέστρεψεν ἀπὸ ἀδικίας: James iii. 18 quoted above on Prov. xi. 30.

iii. 5 ἔσομαι μάρτυς...ἐπὶ τοὺς ἀποστεροῦντας μισθὸν μισθωτοῦ καὶ τοὺς καταδυναστεύοντας χήραν καὶ τοὺς κονδυλίζοντας ὀρφανούς...καὶ τοὺς μὴ φοβουμένους με, λέγει Κύριος παντοκράτωρ: James v. 3, 4 quoted above on Amos iii. 10, Deut. xxiv. 15, also James i. 27, ii. 6, cf. above Exod. xxii. 22.

iii. 6 ἐγὼ Κύριος ὁ Θεὸς ὑμῶν καὶ οὐκ ἠλλοίωμαι: James i. 17, cf. Numb. xxiii. 19.

iv. 2 ἥλιος δικαιοσύνης: James i. 17.

(2) Apocrypha.

Wisdom of Jesus, Son of Sirach—

Beside the general resemblance between this book and the Epistle of St. James on the use of the Tongue, seen in Sir. xix. 6–12, xx. 4–7, 17–19, xxxv. 5–10, xxviii. 13–26 as compared with James iii., we may notice the following closer resemblances.

i. 19 οὐ δυνήσεται θυμώδης ἀνὴρ (al. θυμὸς ἄδικος) δικαιωθῆναι, ἡ γὰρ ῥοπὴ τοῦ θυμοῦ αὐτοῦ πτῶσις αὐτῷ: James i. 20.

i. 25 μὴ προσέλθῃς Κυρίῳ ἐν καρδίᾳ δίσσῃ, *ib.* ii. 12—14 οὐαὶ... ἁμαρτωλῷ ἐπιβαίνοντι ἐπὶ δύο τρίβους· οὐαὶ καρδίᾳ παρειμένῃ, ὅτι οὐ πιστεύει, οὐαὶ ὑμῖν τοῖς ἀπολωλεκόσι τὴν ὑπομονήν, *ib.* v. 9. 10 μὴ πορεύου ἐν πάσῃ ἀτραπῷ· οὕτως ὁ ἁμαρτωλὸς ὁ δίγλωσσος· ἴσθι ἐστηριγμένος ἐν συνέσει σου, καὶ εἷς ἔστω σου ὁ λόγος: James i. 8, v. 8.

ii. 1—6 εἰ προσέρχῃ δουλεύειν Κυρίῳ ἑτοίμασον τὴν ψυχήν σου...εἰς πειρασμόν...καὶ ἐν ἀλλάγμασι ταπεινώσεώς σου μακροθύμησον, ὅτι ἐν πυρὶ δοκιμάζεται χρυσός, *ib.* iv. 17, 18 (ἡ σοφία) βασανίσει αὐτὸν ἐν παιδείᾳ αὐτῆς ἕως οὗ ἐμπιστεύσῃ τῇ ψυχῇ αὐτοῦ, καὶ πειράσει αὐτὸν ἐν τοῖς δικαιώμασιν αὐτῆς, καὶ πάλιν...ἀποκαλύψει αὐτῷ τὰ κρυπτὰ αὐτῆς, xxxi. 9. 10 ὁ πολύπειρος ἐκδιηγήσεται σύνεσιν· ὃς οὐκ ἐπειράθη ὀλίγα οἶδεν: James i. 2.

iii. 17 ἐν πραΰτητι τὰ ἔργα σου διέξαγε: James iii. 13.

iii. 18 ὅσῳ μέγας εἶ, τοσούτῳ ταπεινοῦ σεαυτόν, καὶ ἔναντι Κυρίου εὑρήσεις χάριν, *ib.* x. 21 πλούσιος καὶ ἔνδοξος καὶ πτωχός, τὸ καύχημα αὐτῶν φόβος Κυρίου: James i. 9, 10.

iv. 1—6 τὴν ζωὴν τοῦ πτωχοῦ μὴ ἀποστερήσῃς...ἀπὸ δεομένου μὴ ἀποστρέψῃς ὀφθαλμὸν καὶ μὴ δῷς τόπον ἀνθρώπῳ καταράσασθαί σε· καταρωμένου γάρ σε ἐν πικρίᾳ ψυχῆς αὐτοῦ τῆς δεήσεως αὐτοῦ ἐπακούσεται ὁ ποιήσας αὐτόν, *ib.* xxxii. 13, 17: James v. 4, ii. 15, 16.

iv. 10 γίνου ὀρφανοῖς ὡς πατὴρ καὶ ἀντὶ ἀνδρὸς τῇ μητρὶ αὐτῶν, καὶ ἔσῃ ὡς υἱὸς Ὑψίστου: James i. 27.

iv. 29 μὴ γίνου τραχὺς (al. ταχὺς) ἐν γλώσσῃ σου καὶ νωθρὸς καὶ παρειμένος ἐν τοῖς ἔργοις σου, *ib.* v. 11 γίνου ταχὺς ἐν ἀκροάσει σου, καὶ ἐν μακροθυμίᾳ φθέγγου ἀπόκρισιν: James i. 19, ii. 14—26.

v. 13 δόξα καὶ ἀτιμία ἐν λαλιᾷ, καὶ γλῶσσα ἀνθρώπου πτῶσις αὐτῷ, *ib.* xix. 16 τίς οὐχ ἥμαρτησεν ἐν τῇ γλώσσῃ αὐτοῦ; *ib.* xiv. 1 μακάριος ἀνὴρ ὃς οὐκ ὠλίσθησεν ἐν στόματι αὐτοῦ, *ib.* xxii. 25 τίς δώσει ἐπὶ στόμα μου φυλακὴν...ἵνα μὴ πέσω ἀπ' αὐτῆς, καὶ ἡ γλῶσσά μου ἀπολέσῃ με, *ib.* xxv. 8, xxviii. 26: James iii. 2.

vi. 18 ὡς ὁ ἀροτριῶν καὶ ὁ σπείρων πρόσελθε αὐτῇ (σοφίᾳ), καὶ ἀνάμενε τοὺς ἀγαθοὺς καρποὺς αὐτῆς: James v. 7.

vii. 10 μὴ ὀλιγοψυχήσῃς ἐν τῇ προσευχῇ σου: James i. 6.

x. 7 μισητὴ ἔναντι Κυρίου καὶ ἀνθρώπων ὑπερηφανία, ver. 9 τί ὑπερηφανεύεται γῆ καὶ σποδός; ver. 12 ἀρχὴ ὑπερηφανίας ἀνθρώπου ἀποσταμένου ἀπὸ Κυρίου, καὶ ἀπὸ τοῦ ποιήσαντος αὐτὸν ἀπέστη ἡ καρδία αὐτοῦ, ver. 18 οὐκ ἔκτισται ἀνθρώποις ὑπερηφανία, *ib.* xiii. 19 βδέλυγμα ὑπερηφάνῳ ταπεινότης, *ib.* xv. 8 ἡ σοφία μακράν ἐστιν ὑπερηφανίας: James iv. 6.

x. 22 οὐ δίκαιον ἀτιμάσαι πτωχὸν συνετὸν καὶ οὐ καθήκει δοξάσαι ἄνδρα ἁμαρτωλόν: James ii. 2, 3, 6.

x. 10 βασιλεὺς σήμερον καὶ αὔριον τελευτήσει, *ib.* xi. 16, 17 (where the rich oppressor says) εὗρον ἀνάπαυσιν καὶ νῦν φάγομαι ἐκ τῶν ἀγαθῶν μου, καὶ οὐκ οἶδε τίς καιρὸς παρελεύσεται καὶ καταλείψει αὐτὰ ἑτέροις καὶ ἀποθανεῖται: James iv. 14.

xi. 25 κάκωσις ὥρας ἐπιλησμονὴν ποιεῖ τρυφῆς: James i. 25.

xii. 11 ἔσῃ αὐτῷ ὡς ἐκμεμαχὼς ἔσοπτρον: James i. 23.

xiv. 23 (μακάριος ἀνὴρ) ὁ παρακύπτων διὰ τῶν θυρίδων αὐτῆς (σοφίας): James i. 25.

xv. 6 (ὁ φοβούμενος Κύριον) εὐφροσύνην καὶ στέφανον ἀγαλλιάματος καὶ ὄνομα αἰῶνος κατακληρονομήσει: James i. 12.

xv. 11—20 μὴ εἴπῃς ὅτι διὰ Κύριον ἀπέστην· ἃ γὰρ ἐμίσησεν οὐ ποιήσεις· μὴ εἴπῃς ὅτι αὐτός με ἐπλάνησεν, οὐ γὰρ χρείαν ἔχει ἀνδρὸς ἁμαρτωλοῦ. πᾶν βδέλυγμα ἐμίσησεν ὁ Κύριος...αὐτὸς ἐξ ἀρχῆς ἐποίησεν ἄνθρωπον καὶ ἀφῆκεν αὐτὸν ἐν χειρὶ διαβουλίου αὐτοῦ...ἔναντι ἀνθρώπων ἡ ζωὴ καὶ ὁ θάνατος καὶ ὃ ἐὰν εὐδοκήσῃ δοθήσεται αὐτῷ: James i. 12—15.

xvii. 3, 4 κατ' εἰκόνα ἑαυτοῦ ἐποίησεν αὐτούς· ἔθηκε τὸν φόβον αὐτοῦ ἐπὶ πάσης σαρκὸς καὶ κατακυριεύειν θηρίων καὶ πετεινῶν: James iii. 9, 7.

xvii. 26 τί φωτεινότερον ἡλίου; καὶ τοῦτο ἐκλείπει, *ib.* xxvii. 11 ὁ δὲ ἄφρων ὡς σελήνη ἀλλοιοῦται: James i. 17.

xviii. 15, xxxi. 16, xliii. 22 καύσων: James i. 11.

xviii. 17 μωρὸς ἀχαρίστως ὀνειδιεῖ καὶ δόσις βασκάνου ἐκτήκει ὀφθαλμούς, xx. 14 (ἄφρων) ὀλίγα δώσει καὶ πολλὰ ὀνειδιεῖ, xli. 22 μετὰ τὸ δοῦναι μὴ ὀνείδιζε: James i. 5.

xix. 18—22 πᾶσα σοφία φόβος Κυρίου καὶ ἐν πάσῃ σοφίᾳ ποίησις νόμου...ἔστι πανουργία καὶ αὕτη βδέλυγμα, xxi. 12 οὐ παιδευθήσεται ὃς οὐκ ἔστι πανοῦργος, ἔστι δὲ πανουγία πληθύνουσα πικρίαν: James iii. 13—17.

xxi. 15 (λόγον σοφὸν) ἤκουσεν ὁ σπαταλῶν καὶ ἀπήρεσεν αὐτῷ, xxvii. 13 ὁ γέλως αὐτῶν ἐν σπατάλῃ ἁμαρτίας: James v. 5.

xxviii. 1, 2 ὁ ἐκδικῶν παρὰ Κυρίου εὑρήσει ἐκδίκησιν...ἄφες ἀδίκημα τῷ πλησίον σου, καὶ τότε δεηθέντος σου αἱ ἁμαρτίαι σου λυθήσονται: James ii. 13.

xxviii. 12 ἐὰν φυσήσῃς σπινθῆρα ἐκκαήσεται, καὶ ἐὰν πτύσῃς ἐπ' αὐτὸν σβεσθήσεται, καὶ ἀμφότερα ἐκ τοῦ στόματός σου ἐξελεύσεται. ψιθυρὸν καὶ δίγλωσσον καταρᾶσθαι, xxxi. 24 εἷς εὐχόμενος καὶ εἷς καταρώμενος, τίνος φωνῆς εἰσακούσεται ὁ δεσπότης; James iii. 10.

xxviii. 13—26, esp. ver. 14 γλῶσσα τρίτη πολλοὺς ἐσάλευσε, καὶ διέστησεν αὐτοὺς ἀπὸ ἔθνους εἰς ἔθνος καὶ πόλεις ὀχυρὰς καθεῖλε, ver. 18 πολλοὶ ἔπεσαν ἐν στόματι μαχαίρας, ἀλλ' οὐχ ὡς οἱ πεπτωκότες διὰ γλῶσσαν, ver. 21 θάνατος πονηρὸς ὁ θάνατος αὐτῆς, και λυσιτελὴς μᾶλλον ὁ ᾅδης αὐτῆς· οὐ μὴ κρατήσῃ εὐσεβῶν καὶ ἐν τῇ φλογὶ αὐτῆς οὐ καήσονται· οἱ καταλείποντες Κύριον ἐμπεσοῦνται εἰς αὐτήν, καὶ ἐν αὐτοῖς ἐκκαήσεται καὶ οὐ μὴ σβεσθῇ· ἐπαποσταλήσεται αὐτοῖς ὡς λέων, καὶ ὡς πάρδαλις λυμανεῖται αὐτούς: James iii. 5—8.

xxix. 10 ἀπόλεσον ἀργύριον δι' ἀδελφὸν καὶ φίλον καὶ μὴ ἰωθήτω ὑπὸ τὸν λίθον εἰς ἀπώλειαν· θὲς τὸν θησαυρόν σου κατ' ἐντολὰς Ὑψίστου, καὶ λυσιτελήσει σοι μᾶλλον ἢ τὸ χρυσίον, xii. 10 ὡς γὰρ ὁ χαλκὸς ἰοῦται, οὕτως ἡ πονηρία αὐτοῦ, xxxiv. 5 ὁ ἀγαπῶν χρυσίον οὐ δικαιωθήσεται, καὶ ὁ διώκων διαφθορὰν αὐτὸς πλησθήσεται: James v. 2, 3.

xxxi. 22 φονεύων τὸν πλησίον ὁ ἀφαιρούμενος συμβίωσιν καὶ ἐκχέων αἷμα ὁ ἀποστερῶν μισθὸν μισθίου: James v. 4.

xxxvi. 2 ὁ ὑποκρινόμενος ἐν νόμῳ ὡς ἐν καταιγίδι πλοῖον: James i. 6.

xxxviii. 9 ἐν ἀῤῥωστήματί σου μὴ παράβλεπε, ἀλλ' εὖξαι Κυρίῳ καὶ αὐτὸς ἰάσεταί σε: James v. 14.

Book of Wisdom—

i. 1, 2, 3 ἐν ἁπλότητι καρδίας ζητήσατε αὐτόν (τὸν Κύριον), ὅτι εὑρίσκεται τοῖς μὴ πειράζουσιν αὐτόν, ἐμφανίζεται δὲ τοῖς μὴ ἀπιστοῦσιν αὐτῷ. σκολιοὶ γὰρ λογισμοὶ χωρίζουσιν ἀπὸ Θεοῦ: James i. 6—8, ii. 4, iv. 3.

i. 11 φυλάξασθε γογγυσμὸν ἀνωφελῆ καὶ ἀπὸ καταλαλιᾶς φείσασθε γλώσσης: James iv. 11, v. 9.

ii. 4 παρελεύσεται ὁ βίος ἡμῶν ὡς ἴχνη νεφέλης, καὶ ὡς ὁμίχλη διασκεδασθήσεται διωχθεῖσα ὑπὸ ἀκτίνων ἡλίου: James iv. 14.

ii. 10 καταδυναστεύσωμεν πένητα δίκαιον, μὴ φεισώμεθα χήρας, 12—20, esp. ver. 20 θανάτῳ ἀσχήμονι καταδικάσωμεν αὐτόν, cf. xv. 14, xvii. 2: James ii. 6, v. 6.

ii. 23 ὁ Θεὸς ἔκτισε τὸν ἄνθρωπον ἐπ' ἀφθαρσίᾳ, καὶ εἰκόνα τῆς ἰδίας ἰδιότητος ἐποίησεν αὐτόν: James iii. 9.

iii. 4—6 ἐν ὄψει ἀνθρώπων ἐὰν κολασθῶσιν (οἱ δίκαιοι), ἡ ἐλπὶς αὐτῶν ἀθανασίας πλήρης, καὶ ὀλίγα παιδευθέντες μεγάλα εὐεργετηθήσονται, ὅτι ὁ Θεὸς ἐπείρασεν αὐτούς...ὡς χρυσὸν...ἐδοκίμασεν αὐτούς: James i. 2, 3, 12, 13.

v. 8 τί ὠφέλησεν ἡμᾶς ἡ ὑπερηφανία; καὶ τί πλοῦτος μετὰ ἀλαζονείας συμβέβληται ἡμῖν; παρῆλθεν ἐκεῖνα πάντα ὡς σκιά, ver. 15, 16 δίκαιοι δὲ ...λήψονται τὸ βασίλειον τῆς εὐπρεπείας καὶ τὸ διάδημα τοῦ κάλλους ἐκ χειρὸς Κυρίου: James iv. 6, 16, i. 10, 11, 12.

vii. 7 foll. viii. ix. x., wisdom given in answer to prayer: James i. 5.

vii. 18 τροπῶν ἀλλαγὰς καὶ μεταβολὰς καιρῶν, ver. 29 ἔστι γὰρ σοφία εὐπρεπεστέρα ἡλίου καὶ ὑπὲρ πᾶσαν ἄστρων θέσιν, φωτὶ συγκρινομένη εὑρίσκεται προτέρα· τοῦτο μὲν γὰρ διαδέχεται νύξ, σοφίας δὲ οὐκ ἀντισχύει κακία: James i. 17.

ix. 6 κἂν γάρ τις ᾖ τέλειος ἐν υἱοῖς ἀνθρώπων τῆς ἀπὸ σοῦ σοφίας ἀπούσης εἰς οὐδὲν λογισθήσεται; James i. 5.

ix. 17 βουλὴν δέ σου τίς ἔγνω, εἰ μὴ σὺ ἔδωκας σοφίαν, καὶ ἔπεμψας τὸ ἅγιόν σου πνεῦμα ἀπὸ ὑψίστων James i. 2—5, iii. 15, 17.

xi. 9 ὅτε γὰρ ἐπειράσθησαν, καίπερ ἐν ἐλέει παιδευόμενοι, ἔγνωσαν πῶς μετ' ὀργῆς κρινόμενοι ἀσεβεῖς ἐβασανίζοντο· τούτους μὲν γὰρ ὡς πατὴρ νουθετῶν ἐδοκίμασας, ἐκείνους δὲ ὡς βασιλεὺς καταδικάζων ἐξήτασας: James i. 2, 3, 12.

[For other quotations in illustration of our Epistle, taken from the Apocrypha and other Jewish writings, especially from Judith, 4 Maccabees, Psalms of Solomon, Jubilees, Enoch, 4 Esra, Apocalypsis Mosis, Testamentum Abrahae, Pirke Aboth, see Spitta's Briefe d. Jakobus.]

(3) Philo.[1]

Mund. Opif. M. i. p. 7 (τὸ νοητὸν φῶς) ἐστιν ὑπερουράνιος ἀστὴρ πηγὴ τῶν αἰσθητῶν ἀστέρων: James i. 17.

Leg. All. i. p. 50 M φιλόδωρος ὢν ὁ Θεὸς χαρίζεται τὰ ἀγαθὰ πᾶσι καὶ τοῖς μὴ τελείοις, *Plantat.* p. 342 τὴν ἐκ τοῦ προαιρετικῶς εἶναι φιλόδωρον...ἐλπίδα ζωπυρεῖν: James i. 17.

p. 52 contrasts τὴν ἐπίγειον σοφίαν with τὴν θείαν καὶ οὐράνιον: James iii. 15, 17.

ib. οὐ γὰρ δύεται καὶ σβέννυται ἀλλ' ἀεὶ πέφυκεν ἀνατέλλων ὁ ὀρθὸς λόγος: James i. 17.

p. 64 περίττου πανουργίας ἀπέχεσθαι: James i. 21 ἀποθέμενοι πᾶσαν... περισσείαν κακίας.

p. 72 πᾶν μὲν οὖν τὸ γεννητὸν ἀναγκαῖον τρέπεσθαι· ἴδιον γάρ ἐστι τοῦτο αὐτοῦ, ὥσπερ Θεοῦ τὸ ἄτρεπτον εἶναι, cf. p. 82: James i. 17.

p. 72 ὁ νοῦς σὺν πολλαῖς δυνάμεσι καὶ ἕξεσιν ἐγεννᾶτο, λογικῇ, ψυχικῇ, φυτικῇ, ὥστε καὶ αἰσθητικῇ: James iii. 15.

p. 80 ὅταν γὰρ ἁμαρτῇ...αἰτιᾶται τὰ θεῖα, τὴν ἰδίαν τροπὴν προσάπτων Θεῷ, cf. *De Prof.* p. 558: James i. 13, 14.

p. 86 κάλλιστον ἀγῶνα τοῦτον διάθλησον καὶ σπούδασον στεφανωθῆναι κατὰ τῆς τοὺς ἄλλους νικώσης ἡδονῆς καλὸν καὶ εὐκλεᾶ στέφανον: James i. 12.

p. 102 δωρεὰ καὶ εὐεργεσία καὶ χάρισμα Θεοῦ τὰ πάντα, 108 Θεοῦ ἴδιον τὰ μὲν ἀγαθὰ προτείνειν καὶ φθάνειν δωρούμενον, cf. i. p. 161, ii. p. 246: James i. 17.

p. 108 τὸν ἐγκύμονα θείων φώτων λόγον: James i. 17.

p. 131 Comparison of reason and passion to the ship and the chariot guided by the rudder and the reins, cf. *Agric.* i. 271: James iii. 3, 4.

p. 132 Folly of forming plans without reference to Providence: James iv. 13.

p. 135 οὗτοι ἐξέρχονται μὲν ἀπὸ τῶν ἁμαρτημάτων, εἰς ἕτερα δε εἰσέρχονται· τὸν δὲ τελείως ἐγκρατῆ δεῖ πάντα φεύγειν τὰ ἁμαρτήματα καὶ τὰ μείζω καὶ τὰ ἐλάττω: James ii. 14.

---

[1] Many of the quotations which follow will be found in Schneckenburger's commentary and in Siegfried's *Philo*, pp. 310 foll.

p. 141 ἀνάγκη ὅταν ἀπὸ τῆς τοῦ Θεοῦ φαντασίας ἐξέλθῃ διάνοια...νεὼς αὐτίκα θαλαττευούσης τρόπον, ἀντιστατούντων βιαίως πνευμάτων, ὧδε καὶ ἐκεῖσε φέρεσθαι: James i. 6.

Cherubim i. p. 142 M τὸ μὲν θεῖον ἄτρεπτον, τὸ δὲ γενόμενον φύσει μεταβλητόν: James i. 17.

p. 147 τίς ὁ σπείρων τὰ καλὰ πλὴν ὁ τῶν ὅλων πατήρ; σπείρει μὲν οὗτος, τὸ δὲ γέννημα τὸ ἴδιον ὃ ἔσπειρε δωρεῖται: James i. 18.

p. 149 ὅταν ὁ ἐν ἡμῖν νοῦς αἰσθήσει πλησιάσῃ, ἥδε συλλαμβάνει ...ἐγκύμων τε γίνεται καὶ εὐθὺς ὠδίνει καὶ τίκτει κακῶν ψυχῆς τὸ μέγιστον: James i. 15.

p. 161 ὁ Θεὸς δωρητικὸς τῶν ἁπάντων: James i. 17.

Sacr. Ab. et Caini p. 173 παντελεῖς αἱ τοῦ ἀγεννήτου δωρεαὶ πᾶσαι: James i. 17.

p. 177 γένεσιν μᾶλλον Θεοῦ προτετιμήκασι: James i. 23, iii. 6.

p. 181 οὐχ ἵνα σάλον καὶ τροπὴν καὶ κλύδωνα ὧδε καὶ ἐκεῖσε φορούμενος ἀστάτως ὑπομένῃς, ἀλλ' ἵνα, ὥσπερ εἰς...λιμένα τὴν ἀρετὴν ἀφικόμενος, βεβαίως ἱδρυνθῇς: James i. 6.

Deterius potiori insidiari p. 195 πεπλάνηται τῆς πρὸς εὐσέβειαν ὁδοῦ θρησκείαν ἀντὶ ὁσιότητος ἡγούμενος: James i. 27.

p. 196 ἐπιστομίζων ταῖς τοῦ συνειδότος ἡνίαις τὸν αὐθάδη δρόμον γλώττης, cf. *Mut. Nom.* p. 615, *Sacr. Ab. et C.* 171: James iii. 2.

p. 199 πηγὴ λόγων διάνοια καὶ στόμιον αὐτῆς λόγος, ὅτι τὰ ἐνθυμήματα διὰ τούτου καθάπερ νάματα ἀναχεῖται: James iii. 10.

p. 200 ἀχαλίνῳ κεχρημένους γλώττῃ, cf. *Somn.* M. i. p. 695 τὸ στόμα ἐάσαντες ἀχαλίνωτον, *Monarch.* ii. p. 219: James i. 26.

Poster. Caini 230 and 231, a description of the δίψυχος, esp. ὄντως γὰρ ἀτρέπτῳ ψυχῇ πρὸς τὸν ἄτρεπτον Θεὸν μόνη πρόσοδός ἐστιν: James i. 7, 8.

ib. Θεοῦ μὲν ἴδιον στάσις, γενέσεως δὲ μετάβασις: James i. 17, iii. 6.

p. 244 ἡ πρὸς Θεὸν ὁδὸς, ἅτε βασιλέως οὖσα, εἰκότως ὠνόμασται βασιλική... ἣν ὁ νόμος καλεῖ Θεοῦ ῥῆμα: James ii. 8.

p. 261 τὴν μισάρετον καὶ φιλήδονον γένεσιν, cf. above p. 177: James iii. 6.

Deus immut. p. 284 οὐ μόνον δικάσας ἐλεεῖ, ἀλλ' ἐλεήσας δικάζει· πρεσβύτερος γὰρ δίκης ὁ ἔλεος παρ' αὐτῷ ἐστιν: James ii. 13.

Agricultura p. 316 οὐδὲν ἔστιν ὃ μὴ πρὸς ἡδονῆς δελεασθὲν εἵλκυσται, cf. p. 512, 568, ii. p. 470, 474: James i. 14.

p. 322 ὅταν ὁ πόλεμος ἐγγὺς καὶ ἐπὶ θύρας ὢν ἤδη τυγχάνῃ: James v. 8, 9.

De Plantatione p. 335 καθάπερ ἀνίσχων ἥλιος ὅλον τὸν οὐρανοῦ κύκλον φέγγους ἀναπληροῖ, τὸν αὐτὸν τρόπον αἱ ἀρετῆς ἀκτῖνες ἀναλάμψασαι τὸ διανοίας χωρίον μεστὸν αὐγῆς καθαρᾶς ἀπεργάζονται, cf. p. 566, 631, ii. p. 254: James i. 17.

De Ebrietate p. 368 τὸν ἐν ψυχῇ τῶν ἐπιθυμιῶν ἐμφύλιον πόλεμον, cf. *Victim.* ii. 253 ὅτῳ ἐγκάθηνται καὶ ἐλλοχῶσιν ἐπιθυμίαι, also p. 445, 678, ii. 205: James iv. 1.

De Conf. Linguae p. 412 βραδὺς ὠφελῆσαι, ταχὺς βλάψαι: James i. 19.

De Migr. Abr. p. 445 εἰ γάρ τις βουληθείη τὸν ὄχλον μιᾶς ψυχῆς διανεῖμαι πολλὰς ἂν εὕροι τάξεις ἀκοσμούσας, ὧν ἡδοναὶ ἢ ἐπιθυμίαι ...καὶ αἱ τούτων συγγενεῖς ταξιαρχοῦσι: James iv. 1.

ib. οὗτος ὁ ὅρος ἐστὶ τοῦ μεγάλου, τὸ τῷ Θεῷ συνεγγίζειν ἢ ᾧ ὁ Θεὸς συνεγγίζει: James iv. 8.

p. 454 μηδὲν οὖν μήτε τῶν εἰς εὐλογίας καὶ εὐχάς, μήτε τῶν εἰς βλασφημίας καὶ κατάρας ἐπὶ ταῖς ἐν προφορᾷ διεξόδοις ἀναφερέσθω μᾶλλον ἢ διανοίᾳ, ἀφ' ἧς ὥσπερ ἀπὸ πηγῆς ἑκάτερον εἶδος τῶν λεχθέντων δοκιμάζεται, cf. p. 199: James iii. 10, 11.

p. 455 ὅσα δ' ἂν μὴ εὑρίσκῃ παρ' ἑαυτῷ (ὁ δίκαιος) τὸν μόνον πάμπλουτον αἰτεῖται

Θεόν· ὁ δὲ τὸν οὐράνιον ἀνοίξας θησαυρὸν ὀμβρεῖ καὶ ἐπινίφει τὰ ἀγαθὰ ἀθρόα: James i. 5, 17, v. 16.

p. 459 εἰσί τινες ἐνδοιασταὶ καὶ ἐπαμφοτερισταὶ πρὸς ἑκάτερον τοῖχον ὥσπερ σκάφος ὑπ' ἐναντίων πνευμάτων διαφερόμενον ἀποκλίνοντες...ἐφ' ἑνὸς στηριχθῆναι βεβαίως ἀδυνατοῦντες: James i. 6, v. 8.

p. 466 ὁ νοῦς...ὡς πρὸς κάτοπτρον ἀφορῶν ἀλήθειαν: James i. 23.

Quis Rer. Div. Haer. p. 512 ἐπιθυμία ὁλκὸν ἔχουσα δύναμιν τὸ ποθούμενον διώκειν ἀναγκάζει: James i. 14.

Cong. Erud. Grat. p. 524 ὑπομονή the queen of virtues: James i. 3, 4, v. 11.

p. 526 ἡ ἄνευ πράξεως θεωρία ψιλὴ πρὸς οὐδὲν ὄφελος τοῖς ἐπιστήμοσιν: James ii. 14.

p. 529 τοῦ βίου μιμητὴν ἔδει τὸν ἀσκητὴν οὐκ ἀκροατὴν λόγων εἶναι: James i. 23.

De Profugis p. 558 τίς ἂν γένοιτο αἰσχίων κατηγορία ἢ τὸ φάσκειν μὴ περὶ ἡμᾶς ἀλλὰ περὶ Θεὸν γένεσιν εἶναι τῶν κακῶν; James i. 13.

p. 563 (ὁ λόγος) ἀμέτοχος καὶ ἀπαράδεκτος παντὸς εἶναι πέφυκεν ἁμαρτήματος, cf. ii. 280 (Θεὸς) μόνος εὐδαίμων, πάντων μὲν ἀμέτοχος κακῶν, πλήρης δὲ ἀγαθῶν τελείων, μᾶλλον δὲ αὐτὸς ὢν τὸ ἀγαθὸν ὃς τὰ κατὰ μέρος ὤμβρισεν ἀγαθά: James i. 13, 17.

p. 566 ὁ Θεὸς λαμπροτάτῳ φωτὶ ἑαυτῷ τὰ ὅλα αὐγάζει...τὴν αἰθέριον σοφίαν ὁ Θεὸς ἄνωθεν ἐπιψεκάζει, cf. 571, 579: James i. 17.

p. 568 δέλεαρ ὁλκῷ κεχρημένον δυνάμει, cf. 569: James i. 14.

p. 577 καλὴν ταπείνωσιν, φρονήματος ἀλόγου καθαίρεσιν περιέχουσαν: James i. 10, iv. 6, 10.

De Somniis p. 631 μὴ θαυμάσῃς εἰ ὁ ἥλιος ἐξομοιοῦται τῷ πατρὶ τῶν συμπάντων, 632 Κύριος γὰρ οὐ μόνον φῶς ἀλλὰ καὶ παντὸς ἑτέρου φωτὸς ἀρχέτυπον, 637 τὰς Θεοῦ αὐγὰς ἃς δι' ἔλεον τοῦ γένους ἡμῶν εἰς νοῦν τὸν ἀνθρώπινον οὐρανόθεν ἀποστέλλει: James i. 17.

p. 664 τροχὸν ἀνάγκης ἀτελευτήτου: James iii. 6.

p. 678 βαθείας εἰρήνης ἀναπλησθέντας τῆς ἐν ἑαυτοῖς, ἢ πρὸς ἀλήθειαν ἐστὶν εἰρήνη, καὶ διὰ τοῦτ' εὐδαίμονας νομισθέντας, ὅτι τὸν ἀπὸ τῶν παθῶν ἀναρριπιζόμενον ἐμφύλιον πόλεμον οὐδ' ὄναρ ἐπήσθοντο κ.τ.λ., cf. above p. 368: James iii. 17, 18, iv. 1.

De Abrahamo M ii. p. 8 ὁ τέλειος ὁλόκληρος ἐξ ἀρχῆς: James i. 4.

De Josepho p. 61 εὐδοξεῖς καὶ τετίμησαι; μὴ καταλαζονεύου· ταπεινὸς εἶ ταῖς τύχαις; ἀλλά τὸ φρόνημα μὴ καταπιπτέτω: James i. 9. 10.

p. 62 εὑρήσει τὸν οὐρανὸν ἡμέραν αἰώνιον νυκτὸς καὶ πάσης σκιᾶς ἀμέτοχον: James i. 17.

De Decalogo p. 192 τὸ κάλλιστον ἔρεισμα τῆς ψυχῆς ἐξέκοψαν τὴν περὶ τοῦ ζῶντος ἀεὶ Θεοῦ ὑπόληψιν, ὥσπερ τε ἀνερμάτιστα σκάφη ὧδε καὶ ἐκεῖσε σαλεύουσι διαφερόμενοι τὸν αἰῶνα: James i. 6.

p. 194 κάλλιστον καὶ βιωφελέστατον τὸ ἀνώμοτον: James v. 12.

p. 196 οὐ γὰρ ὅσιον δι' οὗ στόματος τὸ ἱερώτατον ὄνομα προφέρεταί τις, διὰ τούτου φθέγγεσθαί τι τῶν αἰσχρῶν: James iii. 9, 10.

p. 204 μόνη ἐπιθυμία τὴν ἀρχὴν ἐξ ἡμῶν λαμβάνει καὶ ἔστιν ἑκούσιος: James i. 14.

p. 205 οἱ γὰρ Ἑλλήνων καὶ βαρβάρων πόλεμοι πάντες ἀπὸ μιᾶς πηγῆς ἐρρύησαν ἐπιθυμίας: James iv. 1.

p. 208 (ἐπιθυμία) οἷα φλὸξ ἐν ὕλῃ νέμεται δαπανῶσα πάντα: James iii. 5.

De Victimis p. 246 τὸν Θεὸν ἀμιγῆ κακῶν τὰ ἀγαθὰ δωρούμενον: James i. 17.

p. 250 ὁλόκληρον καὶ παντελῆ διάθεσιν ἧς ἡ ὁλόκαυτος θυσία σύμβολον, cf. *Merc. Mer.* p. 265 δεῖ τὸν μέλλοντα θύειν σκέπτεσθαι μὴ εἰ τὸ ἱερεῖον ἄμωμον, ἀλλ' εἰ ἡ διάνοια ὁλόκληρος αὐτῷ καὶ παντελὴς καθέστηκε: James i. 4.

p. 254 ὁ Θεός ἐστιν ἡλίου ἥλιος παρέχων ἐκ τῶν ἀοράτων πηγῶν ὁρατὰ φέγγη: James i. 17.

De Spec. Leg. p. 331 λυπουμένων ὀφθαλμοὶ συννοίας γέμουσι καὶ κατηφείας James iv. 9.

De Creatione Principum, p. 366 (τὸ Ἰουδαίων ἔθνος) τοῦ σύμπαντος ἀνθρώπων γένους ἀπενεμήθη οἷά τις ἀπαρχὴ τῷ ποιητῇ καὶ πατρί: James i. 18.

De Nobilitate p. 442 τοῦ θείου πνεύματος, ὅπερ ἄνωθεν καταπνευσθὲν εἰσῳκήσατο τῇ ψυχῇ, περιτιθέντος τῷ μὲν σώματι κάλλος, τοῖς δὲ λόγοις πειθῶ: James iv. 5.

Omnis Probus Liber p. 452 ὅσοι μετὰ νόμου ζῶσιν ἐλεύθεροι· νόμος δὲ ἀψευδὴς ὁ ὀρθὸς λόγος, οὐκ ἐν χαρτιδίοις ἢ στήλαις ἀλλ' ὑπ' ἀθανάτου φύσεως ἐν ἀθανάτῳ διανοίᾳ τυπωθείς: James i. 18, 21, 25.

p. 470 πρὸς ἐπιθυμίας ἐλαύνεται ἢ ὑφ' ἡδονῆς δελεάζεται: James i. 14.

Vita Contempl. p. 474 τὸ συνηθὲς ὁλκὸν καὶ δελεάσαι δυνατώτατον: James i. 14.

De Incorr. Mundi p. 521 εἰ μὴ πρὸς ἀνέμων ῥιπίζοιτο τὸ ὕδωρ: James i. 6.

De Praem. et Poen. p. 421 τίς γὰρ οὐκ ἂν εἴποι ὅτι σοφὸν ἄρα γένος τοῦτ' ἔστιν, ᾧ τὰς θείας παραινέσεις ἐξεγένετο μὴ κενὰς ἀπολιπεῖν τῶν οἰκείων πράξεων ἀλλὰ πληρῶσαι τοὺς λόγους ἔργοις ἐπαινετοῖς; James ii. 14—26.

(4) Greek Philosophers.

While the more general resemblances between the philosophers and the Bible are no doubt to be explained on St. Paul's principle of the law written in the heart (Rom. ii. 15), yet there is probably more to be said on behalf of the view that the former may have been influenced, directly or indirectly, by Jewish teaching, than is generally recognized in the present day. I think there can be no doubt that some of the touches in Virgil's fourth Eclogue are derived from Isaiah through the Sibylline forgeries; and Sir A. Grant and Bishop Lightfoot have both called attention to the fact that several of the Stoics came from the East. On the other hand it is certain that the Jews after the time of Alexander were much influenced by Greek thought, as we see in the Book of Wisdom, the 4th Book of Maccabees, and above all in Philo. Possibly the parallels that follow are to be explained as reminiscences of Greek Philosophy filtered down through the writings of some Hellenistic Jew; but I would not exclude the possibility that Stoic parallels in St. James may have been taken directly from such a writer as Posidonius. I have given occasional references to post-Augustan authors, because the later Stoics borrow so much from their predecessors. Perhaps the parallels from Lucian and Porphyry should rather be regarded as taken directly from Christian sources.

Plato, *Phaedo*, 66 C καὶ γὰρ πολέμους καὶ στάσεις καὶ μάχας οὐδὲν ἄλλο παρέχει ἢ τὸ σῶμα καὶ αἱ τούτου ἐπιθυμίαι, cf. Cic. *Fin.* i. 43 *ex cupiditatibus odia*, discidia, discordiae, seditiones, *bella nascuntur...intus etiam in animis inclusae inter se dissident et discordant* : James iv. 1.

Minos 317 C τὸ μὲν ὀρθὸν νόμος ἐστὶ βασιλικός, τὸ δὲ μὴ ὀρθὸν οὔ : James ii. 8.

Arist. *Mechan.* 5 τὸ πηδάλιον, μικρὸν ὂν καὶ ἐπ' ἐσχάτῳ τῷ πλοίῳ, τοσαύτην δύναμιν ἔχει ὥστε ὑπὸ μικροῦ οἴακος καὶ ἑνὸς ἀνθρώπου δυνάμεως, καὶ ταύτης ἠρεμαίας, μεγάλα κινεῖσθαι μεγέθη πλοίων : James iii. iv.

Stoic Maxims—

Sapiens liber, dives, rex.

μόνος ὁ σοφὸς ἐλεύθερος. Cic. *Parad.* 34 *quid est libertas? potestas vivendi ut velis: quis igitur vivit ut vult, nisi qui recta sequitur, qui gaudet officio, qui ne legibus quidem propter metum paret, sed eas sequitur et colit, quod id salutare maxime esse judicat: Fin.* iii. 75 *solus liber nec dominationi cujusquam parens nec oboediens cupiditati:* Sen. *V. B.* 15. 5 *Deo parere libertas est:* Epict. *Diss.* iv. 1. 13 αὕτη ἡ ὁδὸς (submission) ἐπ' ἐλευθερίαν ἄγει, αὕτη μόνη ἀπαλλαγὴ δουλείας τὸ δυνηθῆναί ποτ' εἰπεῖν ἐξ ὅλης ψυχῆς τὸ Ἄγου δέ μ' ὦ Ζεῦ κ.τ.λ., cf. iv. 3, quoted below under 'Friend of God': James i. 25, ii. 8.

μόνος ὁ σοφὸς πλούσιος, Cic. *Parad.* 42 foll.: Plato, *Phaedr.* p. 279 πλούσιον νομίζοιμι τὸν σοφόν: James ii. 5 οὐχ ὁ Θεὸς ἐξελέξατο τοὺς πτωχοὺς τῷ κόσμῳ πλουσίους ἐν πίστει; cf. i. 9, 10.

Cic. *Fin.* iii. 75 (*sapiens*) *rectius appellabitur rex quam Tarquinius qui nec se nec suos regere potuit:* Hor. *Od.* ii. 2. 21 *regnum et diadema tutum deferens uni, &c.:* Philo ii. p. 39 τῷ γὰρ ὄντι πρῶτος ὁ σοφὸς τοῦ ἀνθρώπων γένους ὡς κυβερνήτης μὲν ἐν νηΐ, ἄρχων δε ἐν πόλει : James ii. 8 νόμον βασιλικόν, ver. 5.

True joy.—James i. 2.

Sen. *Ep.* 23. 2 ad summa pervenit qui *scit quo gaudeat...disce gaudere...nolo tibi umquam deesse laetitiam; volo illam tibi domi nasci...verum gaudium res severa est*, Philo *Det. Pot. Ins.* M. i. p. 217 ἐπεὶ ἐν τοῖς τῆς ψυχῆς μόνοις ἀγαθοῖς ἡ ἀνόθευτος χαρὰ εὑρίσκεται, ἐν ἑαυτῷ πᾶς σοφὸς χαίρει.

Solidarity of virtues.—James ii. 10, 11.

Chrysippus ap. Plut. ii. p. 1046 F τὰς ἀρετὰς ἀντακολουθεῖν ἀλλήλαις, οὐ μόνον τῷ τὴν μίαν ἔχοντα πάσας ἔχειν, ἀλλὰ καὶ τῷ κατὰ μίαν ὁτιοῦν ἐνεργοῦντα κατὰ πάσας ἐνεργεῖν· οὔτ' ἄνδρα τέλειον εἶναι τὸν μὴ πάσας ἔχοντα τὰς ἀρετὰς, οὔτε πρᾶξιν τελείαν ἥτις οὐ κατὰ πάσας πράττεται τὰς ἀρετάς, Stob. *Ecl.* ii. 198 πάντα τὸν καλὸν καὶ ἀγαθὸν ἄνδρα τέλειον εἶναι λέγουσι διὰ τὸ μηδεμίας ἀπολείπεσθαι ἀρετῆς.

The friend of God.—James ii. 24.

Plato, *Leg.* iv. 716 D ὁ μὲν σώφρων Θεῷ φίλος, ὅμοιος γάρ, Epict. iv. 3. 9 ἐλεύθερος γάρ εἰμι καὶ φίλος τοῦ Θεοῦ ἵν' ἑκὼν πείθωμαι αὐτῷ.

The indwelling Spirit.—James iv. 5.

Sen. *Ep.* 41. 2 *sacer intra nos spiritus sedet malorum bonorumque nostrorum observator et custos: hic prout a nobis tractatus est, ita nos ipse tractat, Ep.* 73. 15 *Deus in homines venit: nulla sine Deo mens bona est, semina in corporibus humanis divina dispersa sunt, quae, si bonus cultor excipit, similia origini prodeunt*, Posid. ap. Gal. *Hipp. et Plat.* v. p. 469 τὸ δὲ τῶν παθῶν αἴτιον τὸ μὴ κατὰ πᾶν ἕπεσθαι τῷ ἐν αὐτῷ δαίμονι.

Trial and Temptation.—James i. 2, 12–15.

Sen. *Prov.* ii. 2 *omnia adversa exercitationes putet vir fortis*, ib. 6 *doloribus, damnis exagitentur ut verum colligant robur*, Epict. *fr.* 112 πάσης κακίας οἷόν τι δέλεαρ ἡδονὴ προβληθεῖσα τὰς λιχνοτέρας ψυχὰς ἐπὶ τὸ ἄγκιστρον τῆς ἀπωλείας ἐφέλκεται, Lucian. *Tyrann.* 4 τὰς ἡδονῶν ὀρέξεις χαλιναγωγεῖν.

ὁ Θεὸς ἀπείραστος κακῶν.—James i. 13.

Plut. ii. 1102 F. πάντων πατὴρ καλῶν ὁ Θεός ἐστι καὶ φαῦλον οὐδὲν ποιεῖν αὐτῷ θέμις, ὥσπερ οὐδὲ πάσχειν, Anton. vi. 1 οὐδεμίαν ἐν ἑαυτῷ αἰτίαν ἔχει τοῦ κακοποιεῖν, κακίαν γὰρ οὐκ ἔχει, Sext. Emp. *Matt.* ix. 91 τὸ τέλειον καὶ ἄριστον παντὸς κακοῦ ἀναπόδεκτον, cf. Epic. ap. Diog. L. x. 138 τὸ μακάριον καὶ ἄφθαρτον οὔτε αὐτὸ πράγματα ἔχει οὔτε ἄλλῳ παρέχει.

Desire and Aversion.—James i. 2, iv. 12.

Epict. *Ench.* i. 2 μέμνησο ὅτι ὀρέξεως ἐπαγγελία ἐπιτυχία οὗ ὀρέγῃ· ἐκκλίσεως ἐπαγγελία τὸ μὴ περιπεσεῖν ἐκείνῳ ὃ ἐκκλίνεται· καὶ ὁ μὲν ἐν ὀρέξει ἀποτυγχάνων ἀτυχής· ὁ δὲ ἐν ἐκκλίσει περιπίπτων δυστυχής, *Diss.* iii. 2, 3 πάθος ἄλλως οὐ γίνεται εἰ μὴ ὀρέξεως ἀποτυγχανούσης ἢ ἐκκλίσεως περιπιπτούσης· οὗτός (ὁ τόπος) ἐστιν ὁ ταραχὰς, θορύβους, ἀτυχίας ἐπιφέρων . . . ὁ φθονεροὺς, ὁ ζηλοτύπους ποιῶν, *ib.* iv. 10 εἰ μὴ θέλεις ὀρέγεσθαι ἀποτευκτικῶς μηδ' ἐκκλίνειν περιπτωτικῶς, μηδενὸς ὀρέγου τῶν ἀλλοτρίων ἔτι, μηδὲν ἔκκλινε τῶν μὴ ἐπί σοι.

Man made in the image of God has authority over the lower animals. James iii. 7–9.

Cic. *N. D.* i. 90 *nec vero intellego cur maluerit Epicurus deos hominum similes dicere quam homines deorum*, *Leg.* i. 25 *virtus eadem in homine ac Deo est...est igitur homini cum Deo similitudo*, *N. D.* ii. 161 *jam vero immanes et feras beluas nanciscimur venando ut...utamur domitis et condocefactis*, Sen. *Benef.* ii. 29.

Simile of the mirror.—James i. 23.

Epict. *Diss.* ii. 14 τί σοι κακὸν πεποίηκα; εἰ μὴ καὶ τὸ ἔσοπτρον τῷ αἰσχρῷ ὅτι δεικνύει αὐτὸν αὐτῷ οἷός ἐστιν; Bias ap. Stob. *Flor.* 21. 11 θεώρει ὥσπερ ἐν κατόπτρῳ τὰς σαυτοῦ πράξεις ἵνα τὰς μὲν καλὰς ἐπικοσμῇς τὰς δὲ αἰσχρὰς καλύπτῃς.

Simile of the fig-tree and its fruit.—James iii. 12.

Sen. *Ep.* 87 § 25 *non nascitur ex malo bonum, non magis quam ficus ex olea*, Plut. ii. 472 F. τὴν ἄμπελον σῦκα φέρειν οὐκ ἀξιοῦμεν οὐδὲ τὴν ἐλαίαν βότρυς.

The venom of the tongue.—James iii. 8.

Lucian, *Fug.* 19 ἰοῦ μεστὸν τὸ στόμα.

The rust of unused wealth.—James v. 3.

Plut. ii. 164 F. ὑπολαμβάνει τὸν πλοῦτον ἀγαθὸν εἶναι μέγιστον· τοῦτο τὸ ψεῦδος ἰὸν ἔχει, νέμεται τὴν ψυχήν, ib. 819 E. φιλοχρηματία ὥσπερ μεστὸν ἰοῦ νόσημα τῆς ψυχῆς, Epict. *Diss.* iv. 6. 14 (principles unused) ὡς ὁπλάρια ἀποκείμενα κατίωται.

Hearing and doing.—James i. 22.

Porphyr. *Abstin.* i. 57 δι' ἔργων ἡμῖν τῆς σωτηρίας, οὐ δι' ἀκροάσεως λόγων ψιλῆς γινομένης.

CHAPTER IV

On the Relation of the Epistle to the other Books of the New Testament.

(1) *Synoptic Gospels.* (2) *Gospel and Epistles of St. John.* (3) *Acts of the Apostles.* (4) *Epistles of St. Paul.* (5) *Epistles of St. Peter and St. Jude.* (6) *Epistle to the Hebrews.* (7) *Apocalypse.*

[The parallels which seem of most importance have an asterisk prefixed.]

(1) Synoptic Gospels.

Matthew—

iii. 2 *ἤγγικεν ἡ βασιλεία τῶν οὐρανῶν*: James v. 8.

*v. 3 *μακάριοι οἱ πτωχοὶ (τῷ πνεύματι) ὅτι αὐτῶν ἐστιν ἡ βασιλεία τῶν οὐρανῶν* (the words in brackets are omitted in the parallel passage, Luke vi. 20), Matt. xix. 28 *καθήσεσθε καὶ ὑμεῖς ἐπὶ θρόνους*: James ii. 5.

*v 7 *μακάριοι οἱ ἐλεήμονες ὅτι αὐτοὶ ἐλεηθήσονται*, *ib.* vi. 14, 15, xviii. 21—35: James ii. 13.

v. 8 *μακ. οἱ καθαροὶ τῇ καρδίᾳ*: James iv. 8.

v. 9 *μακ. οἱ εἰρηνοποιοί*: James iii. 18.

*v. 11, 12 *μακ. ἐστε ὅταν ὀνειδίσωσιν ὑμᾶς...χαίρετε καὶ ἀγαλλιᾶσθε ...οὕτως γὰρ ἐδίωξαν τοὺς προφήτας*, Luke vi. 22: James i. 2, v. 10, 11.

v. 16 *οὕτως λαμψάτω τὸ φῶς ὑμῶν ὅπως...δοξάζωσιν τὸν πατέρα ὑμῶν*: James i. 17.

v. 17 *μὴ νομίσητε ὅτι ἦλθον καταλῦσαι τὸν νόμον...οὐκ ἦλθον καταλῦσαι ἀλλὰ πληρῶσαι*: James i. 25 (a law, but a perfect law of liberty).

v. 19 *ὃς ἐὰν λύσῃ μίαν τῶν ἐντολῶν τούτων τῶν ἐλαχίστων καὶ διδάξῃ οὕτως τοὺς ἀνθρώπους, ἐλάχιστος κληθήσεται ἐν τῇ βασιλείᾳ τῶν οὐρανῶν· ὃς δ' ἂν ποιήσῃ καὶ διδάξῃ οὗτος μέγας κληθήσεται*: James ii. 10, i. 22.

*v. 34—37 *ἐγὼ δὲ λέγω ὑμῖν μὴ ὀμόσαι ὅλως, μήτε ἐν τῷ οὐρανῷ... μήτε ἐν τῇ γῇ...μήτε εἰς Ἱεροσόλυμα...μήτε ἐν τῇ κεφαλῇ σου...ἔστω δὲ ὁ λόγος ὑμῶν ναὶ ναί, οὒ οὔ· τὸ δὲ περισσὸν τούτων ἐκ τοῦ πονηροῦ ἐστίν*: James v. 12.[1]

---

[1] Spitta, who explains away every other resemblance between St. James and the Synoptic Gospels, is compelled to allow that there is here a tangible literary connexion. He will not hear however of a reminiscence of Christ's teaching by the author of our epistle. On the contrary this is not the teaching of Christ, as is shown by his own behaviour when adjured by the high priest: it is an interpolated saying borrowed by the Evangelist from the same unknown Jewish source from which St. James took it.

v. 48 ἔσεσθε οὖν ὑμεῖς τέλειοι, xix. 21 εἰ θέλεις τέλειος εἶναι : James i. 4, iii. 2.

*vi. 16 τὸν ἄρτον ἡμῶν τὸν ἐπιούσιον δὸς ἡμῖν σήμερον : James ii. 15, 16.[1]

*vi. 19 μὴ θησαυρίζετε ὑμῖν θησαυροὺς ἐπὶ τῆς γῆς ὅπου σὴς καὶ βρῶσις ἀφανίζει, Luke xii. 21 : James v. 2, 3.

*vi. 22 ἐὰν ᾖ ὁ ὀφθαλμός σου ἁπλοῦς, ὅλον τὸ σῶμά σου φωτινὸν ἔσται, ver. 24 οὐδεὶς δύναται δυσὶ κυρίοις δουλεύειν...τὸν ἕνα μισήσει καὶ τὸν ἕτερον ἀγαπήσει...οὐ δύνασθε Θεῷ δουλεύειν καὶ μαμωνᾷ, Luke xvi. 13 : James iv. 4, 8 δίψυχοι.

vi. 29 οὐδὲ Σολόμων ἐν πάσῃ τῇ δόξῃ περιεβάλετο ὡς ἓν τούτων, Luke xii. 27, 28 : James i. 11.

vi. 33 ζητεῖτε πρῶτον τὴν βασιλείαν τοῦ Θεοῦ καὶ τὴν δικαιοσύνην αὐτοῦ : James i. 20.

*vi. 34 μὴ μεριμνήσητε εἰς τὴν αὔριον : James iv. 13, 14.

*vii. 1 μὴ κρίνετε ἵνα μὴ κριθῆτε, Luke vi. 37 καὶ μὴ καταδικάζετε : James iv. 11, 12, v. 9.

*vii. 7, 8 αἰτεῖτε καὶ δοθήσεται ὑμῖν...πᾶς γὰρ ὁ αἰτῶν λαμβάνει, Luke xi. 9, 10 : James i. 5, iv. 3.

vii. 11 ὁ πατὴρ ὑμῶν ὁ ἐν τοῖς οὐρανοῖς δώσει ἀγαθὰ τοῖς αἰτοῦσιν αὐτόν : James i. 17.

vii. 13 ἡ ὁδὸς ἡ ἀπάγουσα εἰς τὴν ἀπώλειαν...ἡ ἀπάγουσα εἰς τὴν ζωήν : James v. 19, 20.

*vii. 16 ἀπὸ τῶν καρπῶν αὐτῶν ἐπιγνώσεσθε αὐτούς· μήτι συλλέγουσιν ἀπὸ ἀκανθῶν σταφυλὰς ἢ ἀπὸ τριβόλων σῦκα; οὕτω πᾶν δένδρον ἀγαθὸν καρποὺς καλοὺς ποιεῖ, Luke vi. 44, 45 ἕκαστον δένδρον ἐκ τοῦ ἰδίου καρποῦ γινώσκεται, οὐ γὰρ ἐξ ἀκανθῶν συλλέγουσιν σῦκα οὐδὲ ἐκ βάτου σταφυλὴν τρυγῶσιν. ὁ ἀγαθὸς ἄνθρωπος ἐκ τοῦ ἀγαθοῦ θησαυροῦ τῆς καρδίας προφέρει τὸ ἀγαθόν, καὶ ὁ πονηρὸς ἐκ τοῦ πονηροῦ προφέρει τὸ πονηρόν· ἐκ γὰρ περισσεύματος καρδίας λαλεῖ τὸ στόμα αὐτοῦ, Matt. xii. 33, cf. Isa. v. 2 ἔμεινα τοῦ ποιῆσαι σταφυλὴν καὶ ἐποίησεν ἀκάνθας : James iii. 10—13, 18, i. 21.

*vii. 21—23 of religion professed with the lips but not exhibited in the life : James i. 26, 27, ii. 14—26, iii. 13, 14.

*vii. 24 πᾶς ὅστις ἀκούει μου τοὺς λόγους καὶ ποιεῖ αὐτοὺς ὁμοιωθήσεται ἀνδρὶ φρονίμῳ...καὶ πᾶς ὁ ἀκούων καὶ μὴ ποιῶν ὁμοιωθήσεται ἀνδρὶ μωρῷ, Luke viii. 21 ἀδελφοί μου οὗτοί εἰσιν οἱ τὸν λόγον τοῦ Θεοῦ ἀκούοντες καὶ ποιοῦντες, Luke xi. 28 μακάριοι οἱ ἀκούοντες τὸν λόγον τοῦ Θεοῦ καὶ φυλάσσοντες : James i. 22—25.

*viii. 29 ἔκραξαν λέγοντες τί ἡμῖν καὶ σοί, υἱὲ τοῦ Θεοῦ ; ἦλθες ὧδε πρὸ καιροῦ βασανίσαι ἡμᾶς ; Luke iv. 34, 41, viii. 27—29, x. 17 : James ii. 19.

*x. 22 ὁ δὲ ὑπομείνας εἰς τέλος οὗτος σωθήσεται, xxiv. 13 : James i. 12.

x. 28 τὸν δυνάμενον καὶ ψυχὴν καὶ σῶμα ἀπολέσαι : James iv. 12.

xi. 2 πτωχοὶ εὐαγγελίζονται, Luke vii. 22, cf. Isa. lxi. 1 : James ii. 5.

xi. 19 ἐδικαιώθη ἡ σοφία ἀπὸ τῶν ἔργων αὐτῆς : James iii. 13.

xi. 29 πραΰς εἰμι καὶ ταπεινὸς τῇ καρδίᾳ καὶ εὑρήσετε ἀνάπαυσιν : James iii. 13, 17.

xii. 7 εἰ ἐγνώκειτε τί ἐστιν Ἔλεος θέλω καὶ οὐ θυσίαν, οὐκ ἂν κατεδικάσατε τοὺς ἀναιτίους, Luke vi. 37 : James ii. 13, v. 6.

*xii. 32 ἀφεθήσεται αὐτῷ : James v. 15.

xii. 34 πῶς δύνασθε ἀγαθὰ λαλεῖν πονηροὶ ὄντες; see above on vii. 16 : James iii. 10.

---

[1] See Chase (*The Lord's Prayer in the Early Church,* p. 48), who gives reasons for believing that ἐπιούσιος is a second liturgical rendering of the original Aramaic, represented in Matt. by σήμερον, in Luke xi. 3 by τὸ καθ' ἡμέραν, in James ii. 15 by τῆς ἐφημέρου τροφῆς.

*xii. 36 πᾶν ῥῆμα ἀργόν...ἀποδώσουσιν περὶ αὐτοῦ λόγον...ἐκ γὰρ τῶν λόγων σου δικαιωθήσῃ καὶ ἐκ τῶν λόγων σου καταδικασθήσῃ, xv. 11 τὸ ἐκπορευόμενον ἐκ τοῦ στόματος τοῦτο κοινοῖ τὸν ἄνθρωπον: James iii. 1, 2, i. 19.

xii. 39 γενεὰ μοιχαλίς, xvi. 4, Mark viii. 38 : James iv. 3.

xiii. 3—23, Parable of the Sower, see Luke viii. below.

xiii. 6 ἡλίου ἀνατείλαντος ἐκαυματίσθη καὶ......ἐξηράνθη: James i. 11.

xiv. 30 ὀλιγόπιστε εἰς τί ἐδίστασας; xvii. 20: James i. 6—8.

xv. 13 πᾶσα φυτεία ἣν οὐκ ἐφύτευσεν ὁ πατήρ μου...ἐκριζωθήσεται: James i. 21.

*xviii. 4 ὅστις ταπεινώσει ἑαυτὸν ὡς τὸ παιδίον τοῦτο οὗτός ἐστιν ὁ μείζων ἐν τῇ βασιλείᾳ, xx. 25—27, xxiii. 12 ὅστις ὑψώσει ἑαυτὸν ταπεινωθήσεται καὶ ὅστις ταπεινώσει ἑαυτὸν ὑψωθήσεται, Mark ix. 35, Luke xiv. 11, ix. 48, xxii. 26 ὁ μείζων ἐν ὑμῖν γινέσθω ὡς ὁ νεώτερος καὶ ὁ ἡγούμενος ὡς ὁ διακονῶν: James i. 9, 10, iv. 10.

xxi. 21 ἐὰν ἔχητε πίστιν καὶ μὴ διακρίθητε, cf. Mark xi. 23 : James i. 6, ii. 4.

xxiv. 3, 27, 37, 39 ἡ παρουσία: James v. 8.

*xxiv. 33 ἐγγύς ἐστιν ἐπὶ θύραις : James v. 8, 9.

*xxv. 34—46 the sheep and the goats : James ii. 13.

Mark—

vi. 13 ἤλειφον ἐλαίῳ πολλοὺς ἀρρώστους καὶ ἐθεράπευον, xvi. 18 ἐπὶ ἀρρώστους χεῖρας ἐπιθήσουσιν καὶ καλῶς ἕξουσιν: James v. 14.

*vii. 1—23 condemnation of ceremonialism : James i. 26, 27.

*xii. 28—31 ποία ἐστὶν ἐντολὴ πρώτη πάντων; ἀπεκρίθη ὁ Ἰησοῦς ὅτι πρώτη ἐστίν Ἄκουε, Ἰσραήλ, Κύριος ὁ Θεὸς ἡμῶν Κύριος εἷς ἐστίν, ...δευτέρα αὕτη Ἀγαπήσεις τὸν πλησίον σου ὡς σεαυτόν· μείζων τούτων ἄλλη ἐντολὴ οὐκ ἔστιν, cf. Matt. xxii. 36 : James ii. 8—10, 19.

Luke—

iv. 25 ἐκλείσθη ὁ οὐρανὸς ἔτη τρία καὶ μῆνας ἕξ: James v. 17.

v. 22 διαλογισμοί in bad sense, cf. vi. 8, ix. 46, 47, xxiv. 38: James ii. 4.

*vi. 24 οὐαὶ ὑμῖν τοῖς πλουσίοις...οὐαὶ...οἱ ἐμπεπλησμένοι νῦν, οὐαὶ οἱ γελῶντες νῦν, ὅτι πενθήσετε καὶ κλαύσετε: James ii. 6, iv. 9, v. 1—5.

*viii. The parable of the Sower, ver. 8 ἔπεσεν εἰς τὴν γῆν τὴν ἀγαθὴν καὶ φυὲν ἐποίησεν καρπόν, ver. 11 ὁ σπόρος ἐστὶν ὁ λόγος τοῦ Θεοῦ, ver. 13 μετὰ χαρᾶς δέχονται τὸν λόγον καὶ...ἐν καιρῷ πειρασμοῦ ἀφίστανται, ver. 15 τὸ δὲ ἐν τῇ καλῇ γῇ οὗτοί εἰσιν οἵτινες ἐν καρδίᾳ καλῇ καὶ ἀγαθῇ ἀκούσαντες τὸν λόγον κατέχουσιν καὶ καρποφοροῦσιν ἐν ὑπομονῇ, ver. 18 βλέπετε οὖν πῶς ἀκούετε: James i. 18, 19, 21, 25.

viii. 24, 25 ἐπετίμησεν τῷ ἀνέμῳ καὶ τῷ κλύδωνι...καὶ ἐγένετο γαλήνη. εἶπεν δὲ αὐτοῖς Ποῦ ἡ πίστις ὑμῶν; James i. 6.

*xii. 16—21. Parable of the Rich Fool : James iv. 13—15.

*xii. 47 ὁ γνοὺς τὸ θέλημα τοῦ κυρίου αὐτοῦ καὶ μὴ.. ποιήσας πρὸς τὸ θέλημα αὐτοῦ δαρήσεται πολλάς: James iv. 17.

*xvi. 8 τὸν οἰκονόμον τῆς ἀδικίας, ver 9 τοῦ μαμωνᾶ τῆς ἀδικίας: James iii. 6.

xvi. 19 foll. Dives and Lazarus: James ii. 2—7.

xx. 46, 47 προσέχετε ἀπὸ τῶν γραμματέων τῶν θελόντων περιπατεῖν ἐν στολαῖς καὶ φιλούντων...πρωτοκαθεδρίας ἐν ταῖς συναγωγαῖς...οἳ ἐσθίουσιν τὰς οἰκίας τῶν χηρῶν καὶ προφάσει μακρὰ προσεύχονται· οὗτοι λήμψονται περισσότερον κρίμα: James i. 27, ii. 2, iii. 1.

xxi. 19 ἐν τῇ ὑπομονῇ κτήσεσθε τὰς ψυχὰς ὑμῶν: James i. 3, 4.

(2) *Gospel and Epistles of St. John.*[1]—Though our Epistle does not generally show such a close verbal agreement with the Gospel of St. John as it does with the Synoptic Gospels, yet there is considerable resemblance in respect to such general ideas as the World, the Truth, the Light, the Glory, the New Birth, the Liberty of Christ. No doubt the writings of St. John exhibit, as we should expect, a far greater depth of thought and a more advanced Christianity than are to be found in our Epistle; but, along with this, there is a general harmony and community of ideas, such as might naturally result from remembrances of a common teaching, or from continued association on the part of the two writers. If we come to the conclusion that in some cases this similarity is more easily explained by direct borrowing, it seems to me that the borrower is in all probability St. John. The richness and fulness of expression in such passages as 1 John ii. 15, iii. 9, iii. 17, 21, might easily grow out of the brief hints given in the parallels of St. James, but it is scarcely conceivable that the latter should have deliberately discarded thoughts of such interest and value, if he had had them in writing before him. The same considerations will apply to the parallels to our Epistle which are to be found in the writings of St. Peter and St. Paul. It was easy for the latter, writing from a more advanced standing-point, to bring out and to emphasize the more distinctively Christian doctrines which were still undeveloped and to some extent latent in St. James. That St. James should deliberately have gone backwards, when those doctrines had once received definite expression, is at any rate less probable. A further consideration is that, if we allow a connexion between our Epistle and those of the other Apostles, it is easier to explain this on the supposition that the latter were acquainted with the manifesto of the President of the Church at Jerusalem, rather than on the supposition that he was acquainted with a variety of writings addressed to distant Churches. It is to be remembered also that these parallels are not confined to the earlier or the more important Epistles of St. Paul, and that some of the most striking parallels appear in what are thought to be the latest writings in the N. T., viz. the

[1] On the resemblances between the writings of St. James and St. John see P. Ewald *Das Hauptproblem der Evangelienfrage*, Leipzig, 1890, pp. 58 foll. His aim being to prove that the Gospel of St. John is a faithful record of the teaching of Christ, he endeavours to show that it is in harmony with our Epistle, which he regards as the oldest document of the N.T.

Epistles of St. John, probably composed after the death of St. James, and long after the probable date of his Epistle, as deduced from other considerations.

* i. 4 ἐν αὐτῷ ζωὴ ἦν καὶ ἡ ζωὴ ἦν τὸ φῶς τῶν ἀνθρώπων, ver. 9 ἦν τὸ φῶς τὸ ἀληθινὸν ὃ φωτίζει πάντα ἄνθρωπον ἐρχόμενον εἰς τὸν κόσμον, cf. iii. 19—21, viii. 12, etc. : James i. 17, 18.

i. 14 ὁ λόγος ἐσκήνωσεν ἐν ἡμῖν καὶ ἐθεασάμεθα τὴν δόξαν αὐτοῦ : James ii. 1.

*iii. 3 ἐὰν μή τις γεννηθῇ ἄνωθεν, οὐ δύναται ἰδεῖν τὴν βασιλείαν τοῦ Θεοῦ, ver. 8 το πνεῦμα ὅπου θέλει πνεῖ, ver. 13 ὁ ἐκ τοῦ οὐρανου καταβάς, i. 13 : James i. 17, 18 (P. Ewald considers γεννάω and ἀποκυέω to be different renderings of the original Aramaic word used by our Lord).

iii. 31 ὁ ἄνωθεν ἐρχόμενος ἐπάνω πάντων ἐστίν· ὁ ὢν ἐκ τῆς γῆς ἐκ τῆς γῆς ἐστιν καὶ ἐκ τῆς γῆς λαλεῖ: James iii. 15, 17.

iv. 23 ὁ πατὴρ τοιούτους ζητεῖ τοὺς προσκυνοῦντας : James i. 27.

vi. 33 ὁ ἄρτος τοῦ Θεοῦ ἐστιν ὁ καταβαίνων ἐκ τοῦ οὐρανοῦ καὶ ζωὴν διδοὺς τῷ κόσμῳ : James i. 17 πᾶν δώρημα τέλειον ἄνωθέν ἐστι καταβαῖνον ἀπὸ τοῦ πατρὸς τῶν φώτων.

*vi. 39 τοῦτό ἐστι τὸ θέλημα τοῦ πέμψαντός με ἵνα πᾶς ὁ θεωρῶν τὸν υἱὸν καὶ πιστεύων εἰς αὐτὸν ἔχῃ ζωὴν αἰώνιον, cf. i. 13, iii. 3 foll. : James i. 18 βουληθεὶς ἀπεκύησεν ἡμᾶς, ver. 12.

*vi. 63 τὰ ῥήματα ἃ ἐγὼ λελάληκα ὑμῖν πνεῦμά ἐστιν καὶ ζωή ἐστιν, ver. 68 ῥήματα ζωῆς αἰωνίου ἔχεις : James i. 21 δέξασθε τὸν ἔμφυτον λόγον τὸν δυνάμενον σῶσαι τὰς ψυχὰς ὑμῶν.

vii. 19 οὐδεὶς ἐξ ὑμῶν ποιεῖ τὸν νόμον : James iv. 11 ποιητὴς νόμου, cf. i. 22, 25.

*viii. 31, 32 ἐὰν μείνητε ἐν τῷ λόγῳ τῷ ἐμῷ...γνώσεσθε τὴν ἀλήθειαν καὶ ἡ ἀλήθεια ἐλευθερώσει ὑμᾶς, cf. xiv. 17, xvii. 17, xviii. 37 : James i. 18 ἀπεκύησεν ἡμᾶς λόγῳ ἀληθείας, ver. 25 ὁ παρακύψας εἰς νόμον τέλειον τὸν τῆς ἐλευθερίας καὶ παραμείνας κ.τ.λ. ii. 12.

ix. 41 εἰ τυφλοὶ ἦτε, οὐκ ἂν εἴχετε ἁμαρτίαν· νῦν δὲ λέγετε ὅτι βλέπομεν· ἡ οὖν ἁμαρτία ὑμῶν μένει : James iv. 17.

*xiii. 17 εἰ ταῦτα οἴδατε, μακάριοί ἐστε ἐὰν ποιῆτε αὐτά : James i. 25, iv. 17.

*xiv. 14 ἐάν τι αἰτήσητε ἐν τῷ ὀνόματί μου, ἐγὼ ποιήσω, cf. xv. 7 ἐὰν μείνητε ἐν ἐμοὶ καὶ τὰ ῥήματά μου ἐν ὑμῖν μένῃ, ὃ ἐὰν θέλητε αἰτήσεσθε καὶ γενήσεται ὑμῖν, xvi. 23 foll. : James i. 5, iv. 3.

xiv. 17 τὸ πνεῦμα τῆς ἀληθείας ὃ ὁ κόσμος οὐ δύναται λαβεῖν : James iv. 4, iii. 14.

xiv. 27 εἰρήνην τὴν ἐμὴν δίδωμι ὑμῖν, οὐ καθὼς ὁ κόσμος δίδωσιν ἐγὼ δίδωμι ὑμῖν : James iii. 13—17, iv. 1 foll.

xv. 14, 15 ὑμεῖς φίλοι μου ἐστὲ ἐὰν ποιῆτε ὅσα ἐγὼ ἐντέλλομαι κ.τ.λ. : James ii. 23.

xv. 18, 19 εἰ ἐκ τοῦ κόσμου ἦτε ὁ κόσμος ἂν τὸ ἴδιον ἐφίλει· ὅτι δὲ ἐκ τοῦ κόσμου οὐκ ἐστὲ, ἀλλ' ἐγὼ ἐξελεξάμην ὑμᾶς ἐκ τοῦ κόσμου, διὰ τοῦτο μισεῖ ὑμᾶς ὁ κόσμος : James iv. 4, ii. 4.

1 *Ep. John*—

*i. 5 ὁ Θεὸς φῶς ἐστὶν καὶ σκοτία οὐκ ἔστιν ἐν αὐτῷ οὐδεμία : James i. 17.

i. 6 ψευδόμεθα καὶ οὐ ποιοῦμεν τὴν ἀλήθειαν : James iii. 6 ψεύδεσθε κατὰ τῆς ἀληθείας.

*i. 8—10 ἐὰν εἴπωμεν ὅτι ἁμαρτίαν οὐκ ἔχομεν, ἑαυτοὺς πλανῶμεν κ.τ.λ. : James iii. 2 πολλὰ γὰρ πταίομεν ἅπαντες, i. 16, 22, 26.

*ii. 3—6 ὁ λέγων ὅτι ἔγνωκα αὐτὸν καὶ τὰς ἐντολὰς αὐτοῦ μὴ τηρῶν ψεύστης ἐστιν κ.τ.λ. cf. iii. 7 μηδεὶς πλανάτω ὑμᾶς· ὁ ποιῶν τὴν δικαιοσύνην δίκαιός ἐστιν: James iii. 13, i. 16. ii. 14—26.

ii. 9—11 ὁ λέγων ἐν τῷ φωτὶ εἶναι καὶ τὸν ἀδελφὸν αὐτοῦ μισῶν ἐν τῇ σκοτίᾳ ἐστιν κ.τ.λ.: James iii. 13—18 (true and false wisdom), ii. 1—4, 15, 16.

*ii. 15 ἐάν τις ἀγαπᾷ τὸν κόσμον, οὐκ ἔστιν ἡ ἀγάπη τοῦ πατρὸς ἐν αὐτῷ· ὅτι πᾶν τὸ ἐν τῷ κόσμῳ, ἡ ἐπιθυμία τῆς σαρκὸς καὶ ἡ ἐπιθυμία τῶν ὀφθαλμῶν καὶ ἡ ἀλαζονία τοῦ βίου οὐκ ἔστιν ἐκ τοῦ πατρός: James iv. 4—6, iv. 1, i. 14, 15, iv. 16.

ii. 18 ἐσχάτη ὥρα ἐστίν: James v. 3.

ii. 24 ὃ ἠκούσατε ἀπ' ἀρχῆς ἐν ὑμῖν μενέτω: James i. 25.

*ii. 25 αὕτη ἐστὶν ἡ ἐπαγγελία ἣν αὐτὸς ἐπηγγείλατο ἡμῖν, τὴν ζωὴν τὴν αἰώνιον: James i. 12 λήμψεται τὸν στέφανον τῆς ζωῆς ἣν ἐπηγγείλατο τοῖς ἀγαπῶσιν αὐτόν.

iii. 8 ὁ ποιῶν τὴν ἁμαρτίαν ἐκ τοῦ διαβόλου ἐστίν, cf. ver. 10: James iv. 7, iii. 6.

*iii. 9 ὁ γεγεννημένος ἐκ τοῦ Θεοῦ ἁμαρτίαν οὐ ποιεῖ, ὅτι σπέρμα αὐτοῦ ἐν αὐτῷ μένει, cf. ii. 29, iv. 7 πᾶς ὁ ἀγαπῶν ἐκ Θεοῦ γεγέννηται, v. 1, 4, 18: James i. 18, 21.

*iii. 17 ὃς δ' ἂν ἔχῃ τὸν βίον τοῦ κόσμου καὶ θεωρῇ τὸν ἀδελφὸν αὐτοῦ χρείαν ἔχοντα καὶ κλείσῃ τὰ σπλάγχνα ἀπ' αὐτοῦ πῶς ἡ ἀγάπη τοῦ Θεοῦ μένει ἐν αὐτῷ; τεκνία μὴ αγαπῶμεν λόγῳ ἀλλὰ ἐν ἔργῳ καὶ ἀληθείᾳ: James ii. 5, ver. 15, 16, i. 22, 25.

*iii. 21, 22 ἐὰν ἡ καρδία μὴ καταγινώσκῃ, παρρησίαν ἔχομεν πρὸς τὸν Θεόν, καὶ ὃ ἐὰν αἰτῶμεν λαμβάνομεν ὅτι τὰς ἐντολὰς αὐτοῦ τηροῦμεν, v. 14 ἐάν τι αἰτώμεθα κατὰ τὸ θέλημα αὐτοῦ ἀκούει ἡμῶν: James i. 6, 7, iv, 3, v. 16.

iv. 12 ἐὰν ἀγαπῶμεν ἀλλήλους ὁ Θεὸς ἐν ἡμῖν μένει: James ii. 8, iv. 5.

iv. 20 ἐάν τις εἴπῃ ὅτι ἀγαπῶ τὸν Θεὸν, καὶ τὸν ἀδελφὸν αὐτοῦ μισῇ, ψεύστης ἐστίν, cf. ii. 9 above: James ii. 16, iii. 9, 10, ii. 1—4.

v. 16 ἐάν τις ἴδῃ τὸν ἀδελφὸν αὐτοῦ ἁμαρτάνοντα ἁμαρτίαν μὴ πρὸς θάνατον, αἰτήσει, καὶ δώσει αὐτῷ ζωήν: James v. 15, 19, 20.

v. 19 ὁ κόσμος ὅλος ἐν τῷ πονηρῷ κεῖται: James iv. 4—7 κόσμος... διάβολος.

3 *Ep. John*—

ver. 12 Δημητρίῳ μεμαρτύρηται...ὑπὸ αὐτῆς τῆς ἀληθείας: James iii. 14 μὴ ψεύδεσθε κατὰ τῆς ἀληθείας.

(3) *Acts of the Apostles*—

ii. 17 ἐν ταῖς ἐσχάταις ἡμέραις: James v. 3.

*x. 20 πορεύου σὺν αὐτοῖς μηδὲν διακρινόμενος, cf. xi. 12, μηδὲν διακρίναντα: James i. 6 αἰτείτω ἐν πίστει μηδὲν διακρινόμενος.

xv. 5. τηρεῖν τὸν νόμον: only found elsewhere in N. T. in James ii. 10, though φυλάσσειν νόμον and τηρεῖν λόγον or ἐντολάς are common enough.

xv. 13—29, xxi. 20—25, speeches and letter of James. For resemblances between these and our Epistle see above, pp. iii.–v.

(4) *Epistles of St. Paul*—

Beside the general considerations mentioned under (2), there are special reasons which make it more probable that St. Paul was acquainted with the Epistle of St. James than St. James with those of St. Paul. We know both from the Epistle to the Galatians (ii. 12) and from the Acts (xv. 1, 5, 24) that the Judaizing opposition to St. Paul at Antioch was encouraged by persons who professed to represent the views of the Church of Jerusalem and of its President in particular. If there were any epistle known to the Syrian Church bearing the name of James, it may be taken for granted that this would have been eagerly read by Paul when he was about to plead in behalf of the freedom of his Gentile converts before the Church of Jerusalem. More particularly would this be so, if any phrases in the epistle could be turned against his own doctrine of justification by faith, by those who maintained that Jew and Gentile alike could only be justified by the works of the law. It has been justly remarked that the words 'whoever shall keep the whole law and yet offend in one point, he is guilty of all' (James ii. 10) might easily be twisted by the Judaizers so as to represent St. James as insisting on the observance of the whole Mosaic code; and that it is perhaps this misinterpretation which is referred to in the words 'we have heard that certain which went out from us troubled you saying, Ye must be circumcised and keep the law, to whom we gave no such commandment' (Acts xv. 24).[1] On the other hand there is much less likelihood of St. Paul's Epistles, addressed to distant churches and dealing so much with personal questions, being brought under the notice of St. James. That there is a connexion between the epistles of the two men, has been the general belief in the Church from the time of Augustine downwards; but this connexion has been usually explained on the supposition that James meant either directly to controvert Paul's own teaching, or at any rate to put forward considerations which might serve to restrain the extravagances of his followers. It has been pointed out however by the more careful students of our Epistle, such as Neander and Bp. Lightfoot, that the argument therein contained on Faith and Works has no bearing on St. Paul's doctrine, its purport being, in the words of John Bunyan, to insist that 'at the Day of Doom, men shall be judged according to their fruit. It will not be said then *Did you believe?* but, *Were you doers or talkers only?*' 'For as the body without the soul is but a dead carcase, so *saying*, if it be alone, is but a dead carcase also'—a doctrine which of course is common to St. Paul, as to every other writer in the N.T.

[1] Plumptre, p. 40 foll.

But it does not follow, as some have maintained, that because our Epistle gives no answer to St. Paul's argument addressed to the Romans, there is therefore no connexion between them. I think it is impossible to read carefully the passages given below, without feeling that the one writer copied from the other; and that, while St. James has no reference to St. Paul, St. Paul on the contrary writes with constant reference to St. James, sometimes borrowing phrases or ideas, sometimes introducing a distinction for the purpose of avoiding ambiguity, at other times distinctly controverting his arguments as liable to be misapplied, though conscious all the while of a general agreement in his conclusions. As examples of borrowing, sometimes with additions and improvements, I will only refer here to Rom. ii. 13, 25, v. 3, vii. 23, xiv. 4, 22. As examples of new distinctions introduced compare James ii. 24 *ἐξ ἔργων δικαιοῦται ἄνθρωπος καὶ οὐκ ἐκ πίστεως μόνον*, with Gal. ii. 16 *οὐ δικαιοῦται ἄνθρωπος ἐξ ἔργων νόμου, ἐὰν μὴ διὰ πίστεως Ἰησοῦ Χριστοῦ.*

The controversial matter must be dealt with at greater length. The two main points at issue are (1) the necessity of works, (2) Abraham's justification by faith. James had said over and over again 'Faith without works is dead' (ii. 17, 20, 24, 26); his meaning being (as is plain from ver. 14, and the illustration of a philanthropy which is limited to words (vv. 15, 16), as well as from the whole tone and argument of the Epistle), not to depreciate faith, which is with him not less than with St. Paul the very foundation of the Christian life. (cf. i. 3, 6, ii. 1, v. 15), but to insist that faith, like love, is valueless, if it has no effect on the life, but expends itself in words. St. Paul himself does the same in 1 Thess. i. 3, Gal. v. 6, 1 Cor. xiii. 2, Rom. ii. 6—20, and indeed throughout his Epistles; but in arguing against his Judaizing antagonists, who denied salvation to the Gentiles unless they were circumcised and in all other respects performed 'the works of the law,' he had maintained that it was impossible for men to be justified by these works, and that it was by faith alone that even the Jews and Abraham himself, no less than Gentiles, must be justified. He therefore challenges the phrase of St. James *ἡ πίστις χωρὶς τῶν ἔργων ἀργή ἐστιν, νεκρά ἐστιν* by a direct contradiction, *λογιζόμεθα γὰρ δικαιοῦσθαι πίστει ἄνθρωπον χωρὶς ἔργων νόμου*, in support of which he appeals (1) to Deut. xxvii. 26 'Cursed is every one that continueth not in all things which are written in the book of the law to do them,' as proving the absolute obedience required by the law, Gal. iii. 10, (2) to the confession of the Psalmist (xiv. cxliii. 2, cf. Rom. iii. 20, Gal. ii. 16) that 'by the works of the law shall no flesh be justified,' and to that of the Preacher (vii. 20, cf. Rom. iii. 23) 'there is not a just man upon earth that doeth good and sinneth not.' If the contrary supposition were true; if St. James wrote after St. Paul, must he not, with these passages before him, have either attempted to meet the arguments, if he dissented; or if he agreed with them (as he certainly does in ii. 10, 11 and in iii. 2), would he not have avoided the use of phrases such as *χωρὶς τῶν ἔργων*, which were liable to be misunderstood alike by the followers and the opponents of the Apostle to the Gentiles?

St. Paul goes on to argue that the blessings promised to Abraham and all the families of the earth in him, and the covenant made with Abraham and his seed, are anterior to and irrespective of the law; that the Scripture expressly attributes to Abraham a righteousness, not of works, but of faith, and states generally that 'the just shall live by faith.' To these arguments again no reference is made by St. James, except to the familiar quotation *ἐπίστευσεν Ἀβραὰμ τῷ θεῷ καὶ ἐλογίσθη αὐτῷ εἰς δικαιοσύνην* (James ii. 21, 22), which was probably in common use among the Jews to prove that orthodoxy of doctrine sufficed for salvation. Such an application of the text St. James meets by pointing out that Abraham's faith proved itself by action, when he offered Isaac on the altar: if he had not acted thus, he would not have been accounted righteous, or called the Friend of God. It is interesting to observe how St. Paul deals with this statement, to which he distinctly refers in Rom. iv. 2. St. James had said *Ἀβραὰμ ὁ πατὴρ ἡμῶν οὐκ ἐξ ἔργων ἐδικαιώθη*; St. Paul replies *εἰ γὰρ Ἀβαὰμ ἐξ ἔργων ἐδικαιώθη, ἔχει καύχημα*, but this, as he shows, is inconsistent with the phrase 'reckoned for righteousness,' which, like the similar phrase in Ps. xxxii. 1, 2, implies an act of free grace on the part of God, not a strict legal obligation of wages earned for work done. His second answer is to replace the quotation in its original context (Rom. iv. 16—22), as spoken of the birth, not of the sacrifice of Isaac. Abraham's faith in the promised birth was a settled trust in God, a long-continued hoping against hope: it was this posture of mind, not any immediate action consequent upon it, which was reckoned to him for righteousness (ἐνεδυναμώθη τῇ πίστει δοὺς δόξαν τῷ Θεῷ καὶ πληροφορηθεὶς ὅτι ὃ ἐπήγγελται δυνατός ἐστιν καὶ ποιῆσαι. διὸ ἐλογίσθη αὐτῷ εἰς δικαιοσύνην). Nor is he content to leave to the Jews the exclusive boast in the fatherhood of Abraham (James ii. 21): all who inherit Abraham's faith are sons of Abraham (Gal. iii. 7, Rom. iv. 12). All this is most apposite in reference to the argument of St. James and the use which might be made of it by Judaizers; but put the case the other way, suppose St. James to have written after St. Paul; and how inconceivable is it that he should have made no attempt to guard his position against such an extremely formidable attack! Again if St. James was really opposed to St. Paul and desired to maintain that man was saved, not by grace, but by obedience to the law of Moses, which was incumbent alike on Gentile and on Jew, why has he never uttered a syllable on the subject, but confined himself to the task of proving that a faith which bears no fruits is a dead faith?

As I am on the subject of faith it may be convenient to mention here that the treatment of this subject in the Epistle to the Hebrews is such as to suggest that the writer was acquainted with our Epistle, as well as with the Epistle to the Romans. The language of St. James was liable to be misunderstood because he does not state distinctly what he means by 'faith.' In the eleventh chapter of the Hebrews the author begins with a definition of faith and illustrates its power by a long series of examples. In ver. 6 he explains why it is impossible to please God without faith. In vi. 15 Abraham is said to have obtained the promise through his patience (μακροθυμήσας): in xi. 8 his faith is evinced by his obedience to the call to leave his own country and go he knew not where; in ver. 9 by his living as a stranger in the land of promise awaiting the establishment of the City of God. In ver. 11 faith is said to have enabled Sarah to conceive when she was past age. In ver. 17 it is pointed out that the offering up of Isaac by Abraham flowed naturally from his faith, that He who had given the promise 'In Isaac shall thy seed be called' was able even to raise him from the dead. In vv. 13–16 it is said of the patriarchs collectively, that they died in faith not having received the promises but having saluted them afar off, desiring a better country, that is an heavenly. Faith is exhibited throughout the chapter not as in rivalry with works, as might seem to be the case in the writings of St. Paul and St. James, but as the cause and ground of all the noble deeds of the ancient worthies. Thus, though it may be true to say with St. James 'that Rahab was justified by works,' yet it is a higher and deeper truth to say that she was saved by faith, since her works were only the natural outcome and fruit of her faith. Compare Spitta pp. 202–225.

1 *Thessalonians* (A.D. 52)[1]—

v. 23 ὁ Θεὸς...ἁγιάσαι ὑμᾶς ὁλοτελεῖς, καὶ ὁλόκληρον ὑμῶν τὸ πνεῦμα καὶ ἡ ψυχὴ καὶ τὸ σῶμα ἀμέμπτως ἐν τῇ παρουσίᾳ τοῦ Κυρίου ἡμῶν Ἰησοῦ Χριστοῦ τηρηθείη: James i. 4 ἡ δὲ ὑπομονὴ ἔργον τέλειον ἐχέτω ἵνα ἦτε τέλειοι καὶ ὁλόκληροι, cf. iii. 15, v. 8, ii. 1, i. 27.

1 *Corinthians* (Spring of A.D. 57)[2]—

*i. 27 τὰ μωρὰ τοῦ κόσμου ἐξελέξατο ὁ Θεὸς ἵνα καταισχύνῃ τοὺς σοφούς, καὶ τὰ ἀσθενῆ τοῦ κόσμου ἵνα καταισχύνῃ τὰ ἰσχυρά...ὅπως μὴ καυχήσηται πᾶσα σὰρξ ἐνώπιον τοῦ Θεοῦ: James ii. 5 οὐχ ὁ Θεὸς ἐξελέξατο τοὺς πτωχοὺς τῷ κόσμῳ πλουσίους ἐν πίστει, i. 9, 10 καυχάσθω δὲ ὁ ἀδελφὸς ὁ ταπεινὸς ἐν τῷ ὕψει αὐτοῦ, ὁ δὲ πλούσιος ἐν τῇ ταπεινώσει αὐτοῦ.

ii. 9 ἃ ὀφθαλμὸς οὐκ εἶδεν...ὅσα ἡτοίμασεν ὁ Θεὸς τοῖς ἀγαπῶσιν αὐτόν: James i. 12, ii. 5.

*ii. 14 ψυχικὸς δὲ ἄνθρωπος οὐ δέχεται τὰ τοῦ πνεύματος τοῦ Θεοῦ, μωρία γὰρ αὐτῷ ἐστίν: James iii. 15 οὐκ ἔστιν αὕτη ἡ σοφία ἄνωθεν κατερχομένη ἀλλὰ ἐπίγειος, ψυχική, δαιμονιώδης.

*iii. 18 μηδεὶς ἑαυτὸν ἐξαπατάτω· εἴ τις δοκεῖ σοφὸς εἶναι ἐν ὑμῖν, μωρὸς γενέσθω, cf. Gal. vi. 3 εἰ γὰρ δοκεῖ τις εἶναί τι, μηδὲν ὤν, ἑαυτὸν φρεναπατᾷ: James i. 26 εἴ τις δοκεῖ θρησκὸς εἶναι μὴ χαλιναγωγῶν γλῶσσαν ἀλλ' ἀπατῶν καρδίαν ἑαυτοῦ κ.τ.λ.

vi. 9, xv. 33, cf. Gal. vi. 7, μὴ πλανᾶσθε: James i. 16 μὴ πλανᾶσθε (nowhere else in N. T.).

xiii. 12 βλέπομεν δι' ἐσόπτρου, cf. Cor. iii. 18 τὴν δόξαν Κυρίου κατοπτριζόμενοι: James i. 23 ἐν ἐσόπτρῳ.

xiv. 33 (in reference to disorderly meetings) οὐ γάρ ἐστιν ἀκαταστασίας ὁ θεός, ἀλλὰ εἰρήνης: James iii. 16, 17 ὅπου ζῆλος καὶ ἐριθία, ἐκεῖ ἀκαταστασία...ἡ δὲ ἄνωθεν σοφία εἰρηνική.

xv. 35 ἀλλ' ἐρεῖ τις Πῶς ἐγείρονται οἱ νεκροί; James ii. 8 ἀλλ' ἐρεῖ τις Σὺ πίστιν ἔχεις (the phrase is not uncommon, and is apparently used in different senses by St. Paul and by St. James).

2 *Corinthians* (Autumn of A.D. 57)—

iv. 6 ὁ Θεὸς ὁ εἰπὼν Ἐκ σκότους φῶς λάμψει, ὃς ἔλαμψεν ἐν ταῖς καρδίαις ἡμῶν πρὸς φωτισμὸν τῆς γνώσεως: James i. 17 δώρημα τέλειον... καταβαῖνον ἀπὸ τοῦ πατρὸς τῶν φώτων.

*vi. 7 ἐν λόγῳ ἀληθείας, ἐν δυνάμει Θεοῦ, cf. Col. i. 5 ἐλπίδα ἣν προηκούσατε ἐν τῷ λόγῳ τῆς ἀληθείας τοῦ εὐαγγελίου, Eph. i. 13 ἀκούσαντες τὸν λόγον τῆς ἀληθείας, τὸ εὐαγγέλιον τῆς σωτηρίας, 2 Tim. ii. 15 ὀρθοτομοῦντα τὸν λόγον τῆς ἀληθείας: James i. 18 βουληθεὶς ἀπεκύησεν ἡμᾶς λόγῳ ἀληθείας (the

---

[1] I take the dates from Lewin's *Fasti Sacri* except in the case of the Epistles to the Galatians and Philippians, where I follow Bp. Lightfoot (*Gal.* pp. 36—56 and *Phil.* pp. 30—46).

[2] Ramsay gives 55 as the date of 1 Cor., 56 as the date of 2 Cor., and 53 as the date of Galatians (*St. Paul the Traveller*, pp. 189, 275, 286).

phrase occurs nowhere else in N. T. but is found in LXX. Psa. cxix. 43 μὴ περιελῇς ἐκ τοῦ στόματός μου λόγον ἀληθείας, ὅτι ἐπὶ τοῖς κρίμασί σου ἐπήλπισα, καὶ φυλάξω τὸν νόμον σου διὰ παντός.

*viii. 2 ἐν πολλῇ δοκιμῇ θλίψεως ἡ περισσεία τῆς χαρᾶς αὐτῶν: James i. 2, 21.

*xii. 20 ἔρις ζῆλος θυμοὶ ἐριθίαι καταλαλιαὶ...ἀκαταστασίαι: James iii. 14, 16, iv. 11.

Galatians (Close of A.D. 57)—

On the relation between St. Paul and St. James in regard of Justification and the example of Abraham, see ii. 15, 16, iii. 6, and compare the remarks at the head of this section (4).

iii. 26 πάντες γὰρ υἱοὶ Θεοῦ ἐστὲ διὰ τῆς πίστεως ἐν Χ. Ἰ., iv. 6 ὅτι δὲ ἐστὲ υἱοί, ἐξαπέστειλεν ὁ Θεὸς τὸ πνεῦμα τοῦ Υἱοῦ αὐτοῦ εἰς τὰς καρδίας ὑμῶν κρᾶζον Ἀββᾶ ὁ Πατήρ: James i. 18, iv. 5.

iv. 22—31 the son of the bondwoman and the son of the free, Mount Sinai and Jerusalem which is above, v. 13 ἐπ' ἐλευθερίᾳ ἐκλήθητε, ver. 18 εἰ πνεύματι ἄγεσθε οὐκ ἐστὲ ὑπὸ νόμον: James i. 25, ii. 12.

v. 3 ὀφειλέτης ἐστὶν ὅλον τὸν νόμον ποιῆσαι: James ii. 10 ὅστις ὅλον τὸν νόμον τηρήσῃ πταίσῃ δὲ ἐν ἑνί, γέγονεν πάντων ἔνοχος.

v. 17 ἡ σὰρξ ἐπιθυμεῖ κατὰ τοῦ πνεύματος, τὸ δὲ πνεῦμα κατὰ τῆς σαρκός, ταῦτα γὰρ ἀλλήλοις ἀντίκειται: James iv. 4, 5.

vi. 9 τὸ καλὸν ποιοῦντες μὴ ἐγκακῶμεν· καιρῷ γὰρ ἰδίῳ θερίσομεν μὴ ἐκλυόμενοι James v. 7.

Romans (A.D. 58)—

*i. 16, 17 (τὸ εὐαγγέλιον) δύναμις Θεοῦ ἐστιν εἰς σωτηρίαν παντὶ τῷ πιστεύοντι...δικαιοσύνη γὰρ Θεοῦ ἐν αὐτῷ ἀποκαλύπτεται, cf. iii. 21, 25: James i. 21 δέξασθε τὸν ἔμφυτον λόγον τὸν δυνάμενον σῶσαι τὰς ψυχὰς ὑμῶν, ver. 20 ὀργὴ ἀνδρὸς Θεοῦ δικαιοσύνην οὐκ ἐργάζεται. The phrase δικ. Θ. is taken from Micah vi. 5.

ii. 1 ὦ ἄνθρωπε πᾶς ὁ κρίνων...τὰ γὰρ αὐτὰ πράσσεις ὁ κρίνων, cf. ix. 20: James ii. 20 ὦ ἄνθρωπε κενέ, iv. 11 quoted below on xiv. 4.

*ii. 5 θησαυρίζεις σεαυτῷ ὀργὴν ἐν ἡμέρᾳ ὀργῆς: James v. 3 ἐθησαυρίσατε ἐν ἐσχάταις ἡμέραις, ver. 5 ἐθρέψατε τὰς καρδίας ἐν ἡμέρᾳ σφαγῆς. Both founded on precedents in O.T.

*ii. 13 οὐ γὰρ οἱ ἀκροαταὶ νόμου δίκαιοι παρὰ τῷ Θεῷ, ἀλλ' οἱ ποιηταὶ νόμου δικαιωθήσονται: James i. 22 γίνεσθε ποιηταὶ λόγου καὶ μὴ ἀκροαταὶ μόνον, 25 ὁ δὲ παρακύψας εἰς νόμον τέλειον τὸν τῆς ἐλευθερίας... οὐκ ἀκροατὴς...γενόμενος ἀλλὰ ποιητὴς ἔργου, οὗτος μακάριος, cf. ii. 24, iv. 11 ποιητὴς νόμου.

*ii. 17—24 on teachers who do not practise what they teach: James iii. 1, 13 foll., i. 26, ii. 8 foll., on over-eagerness to teach and the dangers of teaching.

*ii. 25 ἐὰν παραβάτης νόμου ᾖς ἡ περιτομή σου ἀκροβυστία γέγονεν, ver. 27: James ii. 11 εἰ δὲ οὐ μοιχεύεις φονεύεις δέ, γέγονας παραβάτης νόμου.

iii. 28 λογιζόμεθα δικαιοῦσθαι πίστει ἄνθρωπον χωρὶς ἔργων νόμου: James ii. 24, compare remarks at the head of this section (4).

*iv. 1—5, 16—22. Paul here betrays a consciousness that Abraham had been cited as an example of works, and endeavours to show that the word λογίζομαι is inconsistent with this: James ii. 21—23.

iv. 20 εἰς τὴν ἐπαγγελίαν τοῦ Θεοῦ οὐ διεκρίθη τῇ ἀπιστίᾳ ἀλλ' ἐδυναμώθη τῇ πίστει, cf. xiv. 23: James i. 6, ii. 4.

*v. 3—5 καυχώμεθα ἐν ταῖς θλίψεσιν, εἰδότες ὅτι ἡ θλίψις ὑπομονὴν κατεργάζεται, ἡ δὲ ὑπομονὴ δοκιμήν, ἡ δὲ δοκιμὴ ἐλπίδα, ἡ δὲ ἐλπὶς οὐ καταισχύνει, ὅτι ἡ ἀγάπη τοῦ Θεοῦ ἐκκέχυται, cf. 1 Cor. 27-29:

James i. 2—4 πᾶσαν χαρὰν ἡγήσασθε ὅταν πειρασμοῖς περιπέσητε...γινώσκοντες ὅτι τὸ δοκίμιον ὑμῶν τῆς πίστεως κατεργάζεται ὑπομονὴν, ἡ δὲ ὑπομονὴ ἔργον τέλειον ἐχέτω ἵνα ἦτε τέλειοι. (Here it is more probable that Paul is working up a hint received from James, than that the less complete analysis should have been borrowed from the more complete.) Cf. also James i. 9 καυχάσθω ὁ ἀδελφὸς ἐν τῷ ὕψει, ver. 5, 9—12, 17.

vi. 23 τὰ γὰρ ὀψώνια τῆς ἁμαρτίας θάνατος, τὸ δὲ χάρισμα τοῦ Θεοῦ ζωὴ αἰώνιος: James i. 15.

*vii. 23 βλέπω ἕτερον νόμον ἐν τοῖς μέλεσίν μου ἀντιστρατευόμενον τῷ νόμῳ τοῦ νοός μου καὶ αἰχμαλωτίζοντά με τῷ νόμῳ τῆς ἁμαρτίας τῷ ὄντι ἐν τοῖς μέλεσίν μου, cf. vi. 13. xiii. 12: James iv. 1 πόθεν πόλεμοι; οὐκ ἐντεῦθεν ἐκ τῶν ἡδονῶν ὑμῶν τῶν στρατευομένων ἐν τοῖς μέλεσιν ὑμῶν; (Here too James is simpler, Paul more developed.)

*viii. 7 τὸ φρόνημα τῆς σαρκὸς ἔχθρα εἰς Θεόν, τῷ γὰρ νόμῳ τοῦ Θεοῦ οὐχ ὑποτάσσεται: James iv. 4 ἡ φιλία τοῦ κόσμου ἔχθρα τοῦ Θεοῦ ἐστίν, ver. 7 ὑποτάγητε τῷ Θεῷ, ἀντίστητε δὲ τῷ διαβόλῳ.

*viii. 21 αὐτὴ ἡ κτίσις ἐλευθερωθήσεται...εἰς τὴν ἐλευθερίαν τῆς δόξης τῶν τέκνων τοῦ Θεοῦ, ver. 23 ἀλλὰ καὶ αὐτοὶ τὴν ἀπαρχὴν τοῦ πνεύματος ἔχοντες... στενάζομεν υἱοθεσίαν ἀπεκδεχόμενοι, xi. 16 εἰ ἡ ἀπαρχὴ ἁγία καὶ τὸ φύραμα: James i. 18 ἀπεκύησεν ἡμᾶς...εἰς τὸ εἶναι ἡμᾶς ἀπαρχήν τινα τῶν αὐτοῦ κτισμάτων, ver. 25 νόμος ἐλευθερίας. (Paul works up the hint of St. James into a far more elaborate conception.)

x. 3 ἀγνοοῦντες τὴν τοῦ Θεοῦ δικαιοσύνην καὶ τὴν ἰδίαν ζητοῦντες στῆσαι: see above on i. 16, 17.

xi. 17, 18 κατακαυχᾶσθαι: James ii. 13, iii. 14.

xii. 14 εὐλογεῖτε καὶ μὴ καταρᾶσθε: James iii. 10.

*xiii. 3 θέλεις δὲ μὴ φοβεῖσθαι; τὸ ἀγαθὸν ποίει: James ii. 20 θέλεις δὲ γνῶναι; Ἀβραὰμ οὐκ ἐξ ἔργων ἐδικαιώθη;

xiii. 12 ἀποθώμεθα τὰ ἔργα τοῦ σκότους, ἐνδυσώμεθα τὰ ὅπλα τοῦ φωτός: James i. 21 ἀποθέμενοι πᾶσαν ῥυπαρίαν καὶ περισσείαν κακίας...δέξασθε τὸν ἔμφυτον λόγον τὸν δυνάμενον σῶσαι τὰς ψυχὰς ὑμῶν.

*xiv. 4 σὺ τίς εἶ ὁ κρίνων ἀλλότριον οἰκέτην; τῷ ἰδίῳ κυρίῳ στήκει ἢ πίπτει, cf. ii. 1 and 1 Cor. iv. 3—5 ὁ ἀνακρίνων με Κύριός ἐστιν, ὥστε μὴ πρὸ καιροῦ τι κρίνετε: James iv. 11 εἷς ἔστιν νομοθέτης καὶ κριτής, σὺ δὲ τίς εἶ, ὁ κρίνων τὸν πλησίον; (It is hardly conceivable that a later writer could lose the point of ἀλλότριον οἰκέτην and τῷ ἰδίῳ κυρίῳ, though these are natural improvements to make, if the simpler form is the older.)

*xiv. 22, 23 σὺ πίστιν ἔχεις; κατὰ σαυτὸν ἔχε...ὁ δὲ διακρινόμενος, ἐὰν φαγῇ, κατακέκριται, ὅτι οὐκ ἐκ πίστεως: James ii. 18 σὺ πίστιν ἔχεις κἀγὼ ἔργα ἔχω, i. 16 αἰτείτω ἐν πίστει μηδὲν διακρινόμενος, ὁ γὰρ διακρινόμενος ἔοικε κλύδωνι θαλάσσης.

Philippians (A.D. 62)—

i. 11 πεπληρωμένοι καρπὸν δικαιοσύνης: see on Heb. xii. 11.

iii. 9 τὴν ἐκ Θεοῦ δικαιοσύνην: see on Rom. i. 16.

iv. 6 ὁ Κύριος ἐγγύς: James v. 8.

Colossians (A.D. 63)—

ii. 4 ἵνα μή τις παραλογίσηται ὑμᾶς ἐν πιθανολογίᾳ: James i. 22 παραλογισάμενοι ἑαυτούς.

iii. 8 νυνὶ δὲ ἀπόθεσθε καὶ ὑμεῖς τὰ πάντα, ὀργὴν, θυμὸν, κακίαν, βλασφημίαν: see on Eph. iv. 22.

iii. 12 ἐνδύσασθε...ταπεινοφροσύνην, πραΰτητα, μακροθυμίαν: James i .21, iv. 10, v. 7.

Ephesians (A.D 63)—

i. 5 προορίσας ἡμᾶς εἰς υἱοθεσίαν...κατὰ τὴν εὐδοκίαν τοῦ θελήματος αὐτοῦ: James i. 18 βουληθεὶς ἀπεκύησεν ἡμᾶς.

i. 13 τὸν λόγον τῆς ἀληθείας, see on 2 Cor. vi. 7.

*iv. 13, 14 μέχρι καταντήσωμεν οἱ πάντες...εἰς ἄνδρα τέλειον...ἵνα μηκέτι ὦμεν νήπιοι, κλυδωνιζόμενοι καὶ περιφερόμενοι παντὶ ἀνέμῳ τῆς διδασκαλίας: James i. 4 ἵνα ἦτε τέλειοι καὶ ὁλόκληροι ἐν μηδενὶ λειπόμενοι, ver. 6 ὁ διακρινόμενος ἔοικεν κλύδωνι θαλάσσης ἀνεμιζομένῳ καὶ ῥιπιζομένῳ. (St. Paul's is the more finished: his metaphor seems built upon the simile in St. James.)

*iv. 22—25 ἀποθέσθαι ὑμᾶς κατὰ τὴν προτέραν ἀναστροφὴν τὸν παλαιὸν ἄνθρωπον τὸν φθειρόμενον κατὰ τὰς ἐπιθυμίας τῆς ἀπάτης, ἀνανεοῦσθαι δὲ τῷ πνεύματι τοῦ νόος ὑμῶν καὶ ἐνδύσασθαι τὸν καινὸν ἄνθρωπον τὸν κατὰ Θεὸν κτισθέντα...ἐν ὁσιότητι τῆς ἀληθείας. Διὸ ἀποθέμενοι τὸ ψεῦδος κ.τ.λ. cf. 1 Pet. ii. 1: James i. 21, 15, 26, 18.

iv. 30, 31 μὴ λυπεῖτε τὸ πνεῦμα τὸ ἅγιον τοῦ Θεοῦ, ἐν ᾧ ἐσφραγίσθητε...πᾶσα πικρία καὶ θυμὸς καὶ ὀργὴ καὶ κραυγὴ καὶ βλασφημία ἀρθήτω ἀφ' ὑμῶν σὺν πάσῃ κακίᾳ: James iv. 5, iii. 14, i. 20, ii. 7.

Epistle to Titus (A.D. 64)—

iii. 2 μηδένα βλασφημεῖν, ἀμάχους εἶναι, ἐπιεικεῖς, πᾶσαν ἐνδεικνυμένους πραΰτητα, ver. 3 ἦμεν γάρ ποτε...ἀπειθεῖς, πλανώμενοι, δουλεύοντες ἐπιθυμίαις καὶ ἡδοναῖς ποικίλαις ἐν κακίᾳ καὶ φθόνῳ διάγοντες, ver. 8 ἵνα φροντίζωσιν καλῶν ἔργων προΐστασθαι οἱ πεπιστευκότες Θεῷ: James iii. 13 δειξάτω ἐκ τῆς καλῆς ἀναστροφῆς τὰ ἔργα αὐτοῦ ἐν πραΰτητι σοφίας, ver. 17 ἡ δὲ ἄνωθεν σοφία...ἁγνή, εἰρηνική, ἐπιεικής, εὐπειθής, cf. i. 21, iv. 1.

First Epistle to Timothy (A.D. 64)—

*i. 7 θέλοντες εἶναι νομοδιδάσκαλοι: James iii. 1 μὴ πολλοὶ διδάσκαλοι γίνεσθε.

*v. 22 σεαυτὸν ἁγνὸν τήρει, vi. 14 τηρῆσαί σε τὴν ἐντολὴν ἄσπιλον: James i. 27 ἄσπιλον ἑαυτὸν τηρεῖν ἀπὸ τοῦ κόσμου.

*vi. 17 τοῖς πλουσίοις ἐν τῷ νῦν αἰῶνι παράγγελλε μὴ ὑψηλοφρονεῖν μηδὲ ἠλπικέναι ἐπὶ πλούτου ἀδηλότητι...πλουτεῖν ἐν ἔργοις καλοῖς: James i. 10, ii. 5, iii. 13.

Second Epistle to Timothy (A.D. 66)—

ii. 9 ἐν ᾧ κακοπαθῶ μέχρι δεσμῶν ὡς κακοῦργος, ver. 3 συγκακοπάθησον ὡς καλὸς στρατιώτης Ἰησοῦ Χριστοῦ, iv. 5 σὺ δὲ νῆφε ἐν πᾶσιν, κακοπάθησον: James v. 13 κακοπαθεῖ τις ἐν ὑμῖν; προσευχέσθω, ver. 10 ὑπόδειγμα λάβετε τῆς κακοπαθίας τοὺς προφήτας.

ii. 12 πιστὸς ὁ λόγος...εἰ ὑπομένομεν, καὶ συμβασιλεύσομεν, cf. iv. 7: James i. 12 μακάριος ὃς ὑπομένει πειρασμὸν ὅτι δόκιμος γενόμενος λήμψεται τὸν στέφανον τῆς ζωῆς ὃν ἐπηγγείλατο τοῖς ἀγαπῶσιν αὐτόν. (Probably St. Paul quotes from an early hymn founded on the same original ἄγραφον as the verse of St. James.)

ii. 15 σπούδασον σεαυτὸν δόκιμον παραστῆσαι τῷ Θεῷ...ὀρθοτομοῦντα τὸν λόγον τῆς ἀληθείας: James i. 12, 18.

iii. 1 ἐν ἐσχάταις ἡμέραις ἐνστήσονται καιροὶ χαλεποί: James v. 1—5, esp. 3 ἐθησαυρίσατε ἐν ἐσχάταις ἡμέραις.

*iv. 7, 8 τὸν ἀγῶνα ἠγώνισμαι...λοιπὸν ἀπόκειταί μοι ὁ τῆς δικαιοσύνης στέφανος ὃν ἀποδώσει μοι ὁ Κύριος...ὁ δίκαιος κριτής, οὐ μόνον δὲ ἐμοὶ ἀλλὰ καὶ πᾶσιν τοῖς ἠγαπηκόσι τὴν ἐπιφάνειαν αὐτοῦ: James i. 12, see above on ii. 12 πιστὸς ὁ λόγος.

(5) *Epistles of St. Peter and St. Jude*—

I think no unprejudiced reader can doubt that the resemblances between the Epistle of St. James and the First Epistle of St. Peter, the recurrence in them of the same words and phrases, and their common quotations from the O.T., are such as to prove conclusively that the one borrowed from the other. Nor can there be much doubt as to which of the two was the borrower, if we observe how, in almost every case, the common thought finds fuller expression in St. Peter. Thus both Epistles are addressed to the Diaspora, but in St. Peter we have the distinctive touch ἐκλεκτοῖς παρεπιδήμοις διασπορᾶς. St. James addresses the Twelve Tribes of the Diaspora without limitation; but his letter, as I have argued in the chapter on the *Persons Addressed*, would probably be circulated mainly among the Jews of the Eastern Dispersion; while St. Peter, writing, as I imagine, during the imprisonment of St. Paul at Rome to the Jews of Asia Minor, with the view of removing their prejudices against his teaching, took the Epistle of St. James as his model, but ingrafted upon it the more advanced Christian doctrine which he shared with St. Paul. If we accept the genuineness of the Second Epistle, we shall find an interesting parallel in the close relation between it and the Epistle of St. Jude. These however are of course matters of more or less uncertainty. But the close connexion between James i. 2 and 1 Pet. i. 6, 7 is proved beyond all doubt by the recurrence in both of the phrases ποικίλοις πειρασμοῖς and τὸ δοκίμιον ὑμῶν τῆς πίστεως with its unusual order of words. Assuming then, as we must, that one copied from the other, we find the trial of faith illustrated in St. Peter (as in Psa. lxvi. 10, Prov. xvii. 3, Job xxiii. 10, Zech. xiii. 9, Mal. iii. 3) by the trying of the precious metals in the fire: we find also the addition, ὀλίγον ἄρτι, εἰ δέον, λυπηθέντες, which looks as if it were intended to soften down the uncompromising Stoicism of St. James' πᾶσαν χαρὰν ἡγήσασθε. Again comparing James i. 18 and 1 Pet. i. 23, we find the bare 'begat he us with the word of truth' of the former expanded into 'having been begotten again not of corruptible seed, but of incorruptible, through the word of God which liveth and abideth.' So in 1 Pet. ii, 1, 2, the simpler expression of James (i. 21) 'Wherefore putting away all filthiness and overflowing of malice, receive with meekness the implanted word which is able to save your souls' is elaborated into 'Putting away therefore all malice and all guile and hypocrisies and envies and all evil speakings, as newborn babes long for the spiritual (λογικόν) milk which is without guile, that ye may grow thereby unto salvation.' Compare also James i. 12 with 1 Pet. v. 4 where 'the crown of life' becomes 'the crown of glory which fadeth not away'; James iv. 10 with 1. Pet. v. 6, where 'Humble yourselves in the sight of God and he shall exalt you' becomes 'Humble yourselves under the mighty hand of God that he may exalt you in due time.' In the immediate context the simple 'Resist the devil' of James, becomes 'Your adversary the devil as a roaring lion walketh about seeking whom he may devour; whom resist stedfast in the faith' in Peter. The most important changes are those in which the tone of the New Testament is substituted for that of the Old, as in 1 Pet. ii. 21, where Christ is set before us as our example of patient suffering, in contrast with James v. 10, where the example of the prophets is appealed to. Perhaps under this head may be mentioned the change from *στηρίξατε τὰς καρδίας*, in James v. 9, to *ὁ Θεὸς αὐτὸς στηρίξει* in 1 Pet. v. 10; and the employment of the emphatic *πρὸ πάντων* to enforce the exhortation to brotherly love in 1 Pet. iv. 8, instead of the exhortation to abstain from swearing in James v. 12.

There is a curious difference between the use made of quotations from the Old Testament in the two Epistles. St. James seldom quotes exactly. We can see by his phraseology that he has some passage of the Old Testament in his mind, but he uses it freely to colour his language, applying it to his own immediate purpose without any scrupulous reference to its original context. It is this laxity of quotation which causes the difficulty in James iv. 4–6 and presents what is probably an 'unwritten word' of Christ under two forms in i. 12 and ii. 5. If we turn to the quotations which are common to him and to St. Peter, we often find the inexact and careless reminiscences of the former corrected and supplemented in the latter. Thus there can be little doubt that when St. James used the phrase *δοκίμιον πίστεως* he had in his mind Prov. xxvii. 21 *δοκίμιον ἀργυρίῳ καὶ χρυσῷ πύρωσις, ἀνὴρ δὲ δοκιμάζεται διὰ στόματος ἐγκωμιαζόντων αὐτόν*, and Prov. xvii. 3, which is nearer in meaning though less closely allied in expression, *ὥσπερ* δοκιμάζεται ἐν καμίνῳ ἄργυρος καὶ χρυσός, οὕτως ἐκλεκταὶ καρδίαι παρὰ Κυρίῳ, and accordingly we find St. Peter supplying these words (δοκίμιον) πολυτιμότερον χρυσίου τοῦ ἀπολλυμένου διὰ πυρὸς δὲ δοκιμαζομένου. Another quotation appears in James i. 10, 11 (let the rich man boast in his humiliation) ὅτι ὡς ἄνθος χόρτου παρελεύσεται· ἀνέτειλεν γὰρ ὁ ἥλιος σὺν τῷ καύσωνι καὶ ἐξήρανεν τὸν χόρτον καὶ τὸ ἄνθος αὐτοῦ ἐξέπεσεν καὶ ἡ εὐπρέπεια τοῦ προσώπου αὐτοῦ ἀπώλετο· οὕτως καὶ ὁ πλούσιος ἐν ταῖς πορείαις αὐτοῦ μαρανθήσεται. This is evidently taken mainly from Isa. xl. 6, 7, where the perishing nature of man is contrasted with the imperishableness of God's Word. St. James, it will be seen, confines himself to the former branch of the comparison, limiting it indeed to the case of the rich man, and makes no mention here of the Word. But in 1 Pet. i. 23 the new life communicated by the living and abiding Word of God, which St. James treats of in another part of his Epistle, is the subject of the discourse (ἀναγεγεννημένοι...διὰ λόγου ζῶντος Θεοῦ καὶ μένοντος); this is then proved by the quotation, given almost literally from Isaiah, as follows: διότι πᾶσα σὰρξ ὡς χόρτος καὶ πᾶσα δόξα αὐτῆς ὡς ἄνθος χόρτου· ἐξηράνθη ὁ χόρτος καὶ τὸ ἄνθος ἐξέπεσεν· τὸ δὲ ῥῆμα Κυρίου μένει εἰς τὸν αἰῶνα, the only changes being the insertion of the first ὡς, the substitution of αὐτῆς for ἀνθρώπου and of Κυρίου for τοῦ Θεοῦ ἡμῶν. In the passage of St. James we observe the intermingling of another quotation from the Book of Jonah iv. 8 ἐγένετο ἅμα τῷ ἀνατεῖλαι τὸν ἥλιον καὶ προσέταξεν ὁ Θεὸς πνεύματι καύσωνι.

In the difficult passage James iv. 4–6 ('whosoever would be a friend of the world becomes thereby an enemy of God. Or think ye that the Scripture saith without meaning, Jealously yearneth the Spirit which he hath implanted in you? But he giveth more grace: wherefore he saith') ὁ Θεὸς ὑπερηφάνοις ἀντιτάσσεται ταπεινοῖς δὲ δίδωσιν χάριν, the concluding Greek words are exactly the same as in 1 Pet. v. 5, being taken literally from the LXX. of Prov. iii. 34, except that this latter has Κύριος for ὁ Θεός. The context however in which they occur differs much in the two Epistles. St. Peter uses them to enforce the duty of humility in our intercourse with our fellow-men, 'Ye younger be subject unto the elder: yea all of you gird yourselves with humility for *God resisteth the proud, but giveth grace to the humble,*' which is probably the original application in the Proverbs; but St. James, as we have seen, seems to make 'the proud' equivalent to 'the friends of the world,' and the 'humble' to be those who submit themselves to God.

The last quotation is that from the Hebrew (not the LXX.) of Prov. x. 12, 'Hatred stirreth up strife, but *love covereth all sins,*' which we find in James v. 20 and 1 Pet. iv. 8; but here again the former simply makes use of a familiar phrase without regard to the bearing of the context, applying it to the conversion of the erring ὁ ἐπιστρέψας ἁμαρτωλὸν ἐκ πλάνης ὁδοῦ αὐτοῦ . . . καλύψει πλῆθος ἁμαρτιῶν, while St. Peter keeps to the original application, πρὸ πάντων τὴν εἰς ἑαυτοὺς ἀγάπην ἐκτενῆ ἔχοντες, ὅτι ἀγάπη καλύπτει πλῆθος ἁμαρτιῶν.

It is scarcely necessary to point out how these facts confirm the general evidence as to the priority of our Epistle to that of St. Peter. The language of a Christian writer, in the first century even more than in the nineteenth, was inevitably coloured by his study of the O.T. This fully accounts for the Scriptural quotations and allusions in St. James. It is again perfectly natural that a contemporary of St. James, reviewing his Epistle in order to adapt it for a special class of readers, should, it may be even unconsciously, correct the references to the O.T., sometimes by supplying points which had been overlooked, as in speaking of the trial of faith, sometimes by applying them with more exactness, as in regard to the simile of the fading flower. But surely the converse supposition is most improbable, that the later writer should deliberately misquote and misapply passages which were correctly given in his authority! [Compare what is said in answer to Brückner on this point in ch. vii., and Spitta pp. 183–202.]

*i. 1 ἐκλεκτοῖς παρεπιδήμοις διασπορᾶς: James i. 1 ταῖς δώδεκα φυλαῖς ταῖς ἐν τῇ διασπορᾷ.

*i. 3 ὁ κατὰ τὸ πολὺ αὐτοῦ ἔλεος ἀναγεννήσας ἡμᾶς εἰς ἐλπίδα ζῶσαν... εἰς κληρονομίαν ἄφθαρτον καὶ ἀμίαντον: James i. 18 βουληθεὶς ἀπεκύησεν ἡμᾶς λόγῳ ἀληθείας, ver. 27 θρησκεία καθαρὰ καὶ ἀμίαντος, ii. 5 κληρονόμους τῆς βασιλείας.

*i. 6 ἐν ᾧ ἀγαλλιᾶσθε, ὀλίγον ἄρτι...λυπηθέντες ἐν ποικίλοις πειρασμοῖς ἵνα τὸ δοκίμιον ὑμῶν τῆς πίστεως...εὑρεθῇ εἰς ἔπαινον, ver. 8, 9 ἀγαλλιᾶτε χαρᾷ ἀνεκλαλήτῳ...κομιζόμενοι τὸ τέλος τῆς πίστεως, σωτηρίαν ψυχῶν, iv. 13 καθὸ κοινωνεῖτε τοῖς τοῦ Χριστοῦ παθήμασι χαίρετε, ἵνα καὶ ἐν τῇ ἀποκαλύψει τῆς δόξης αὐτοῦ χαρῆτε ἀγαλλιώμενοι: James i. 2 πᾶσαν χαρὰν ἡγήσασθε...ὅταν πειρασμοῖς περιπέσητε ποικίλοις, γινώσκοντες ὅτι τὸ δοκίμιον ὑμῶν τῆς πίστεως κατεργάζεται ὑπομονήν, ἡ δὲ ὑπομονὴ ἔργον τέλειον ἔχετω ἵνα ἦτε τέλειοι, v. 11 τὸ τέλος τοῦ Κυρίου εἴδετε, i. 21 δέξασθε τὸν λόγον τὸν δυνάμενον σῶσαι τὰς ψυχὰς ὑμῶν.

*i. 12 εἰς ἃ ἐπιθυμοῦσιν παρακύψαι: James i. 25 ὁ παρακύψας εἰς νόμον.

i. 13 διὸ ἀναζωσάμενοι τὰς ὀσφύας, see below ii. 1: James i. 21 διὸ ἀποθέμενοι (both follow a reference to the preaching of the Gospel).

i. 17 τὸν ἀπροσωπολήμπτως κρίνοντα: James ii. 1 μὴ ἐν προσωποληµψίαις ἔχετε τὴν πίστιν τοῦ Κυρίου ἡμῶν.

i. 19 τιμίῳ αἵματι ὡς ἀμνοῦ...ἀσπίλου: James i. 27 ἄσπιλον ἑαυτὸν τηρεῖν, v. 7 τίμιον καρπόν.

i. 22 τὰς ψυχὰς ἡγνικότες ἐν τῇ ὑπακοῇ τῆς ἀληθείας εἰς φιλαδελφίαν ἀνυπόκριτον: James iv. 8 ἁγνίσατε καρδίας, i. 18 λόγῳ ἀληθείας, iii. 17 ἡ ἄνωθεν σοφία...μεστὴ ἐλέους...ἀνυπόκριτος.

*i. 23 ἀναγεγεννημένοι οὐκ ἐκ σπορᾶς φθαρτῆς ἀλλ' ἀφθάρτου διὰ λόγου ζῶντος Θεοῦ καὶ μενόντος, διότι πᾶσα σὰρξ ὡς χόρτος καὶ πᾶσα δόξα αὐτῆς ὡς ἄνθος χόρτου· ἐξηράνθη ὁ χόρτος καὶ τὸ ἄνθος ἐξέπεσεν, τὸ δὲ ῥῆμα Κυρίου μένει: James i. 18 (cf. above on ver. 3), i. 10 (ὁ πλούσιος) ὡς ἄνθος χόρτου παρελεύσεται, ἀνέτειλεν γὰρ ὁ ἥλιος καὶ ἐξήρανεν τὸν χόρτον καὶ τὸ ἄνθος αὐτοῦ ἐξέπεσεν.

*ii. 1 ἀποθέμενοι οὖν πᾶσαν κακίαν καὶ πάντα δόλον καὶ ὑπόκρισιν καὶ φθόνους καὶ πάσας καταλαλιὰς ὡς ἀρτιγέννητα βρέφη τὸ λογικὸν...γάλα ἐπιποθήσατε ἵνα ἐν αὐτῷ αὐξήθητε εἰς σωτηρίαν (resumes i. 13), cf. iii. 21 σαρκὸς ἀπόθεσις ῥύπου: James i. 18 ἀπεκύησεν ἡμᾶς, 21 διὸ ἀποθέμενοι πᾶσαν ῥυπαρίαν καὶ περισσείαν κακίας ἐν πραΰτητι δέξασθε τὸν ἔμφυτον λόγον τὸν δυνάμενον σῶσαι τὰς ψυχάς, iii. 14. 17, iv. 11.

*ii. 11 παρακαλῶ...ἀπέχεσθαι τῶν σαρκικῶν ἐπιθυμιῶν αἵτινες στρατεύονται κατὰ τῆς ψυχῆς: James iv. 1 πόθεν πόλεμοι;...οὐκ ἐντεῦθεν ἐκ τῶν ἡδονῶν ὑμῶν τῶν στρατευομένων ἐν τοῖς μέλεσιν ὑμῶν;

*ii. 12 τὴν ἀναστροφὴν ὑμῶν ἔχοντες καλὴν ἵνα...ἐκ τῶν καλῶν ἔργων ἐποπτεύοντες δοξάσωσι τὸν Θεὸν, cf. iii. 2 τὴν ἐν φόβῳ ἁγνὴν ἀναστροφήν, 16 τὴν ἀγαθὴν ἐν Χριστῷ ἀναστροφήν: James iii. 13 δειξάτω ἐκ τῆς καλῆς ἀναστροφῆς τὰ ἔργα αὐτοῦ ἐν πραΰτητι σοφίας.

ii. 15 ὡς ἐλεύθεροι...ἀλλ' ὡς Θεοῦ δοῦλοι: James i. 25, ii. 12 νόμος ἐλευθερίας, i. 1 Θεοῦ δοῦλος.

ii. 18 ὑποτασσόμενοι τοῖς δεσπόταις, iii. 1 ὑποτασσόμεναι τοῖς ἀνδράσιν, see below v. 5: James iv. 7 ὑποτάγητε τῷ Θεῷ.

ii. 20, 21 εἰ ἀγαθοποιοῦντες καὶ πάσχοντες ὑπομενεῖτε, τοῦτο χάρις παρὰ Θεῷ· εἰς τοῦτο γὰρ ἐκλήθητε, ὅτι καὶ Χριστὸς ἔπαθεν ὑπὲρ ὑμῶν, ὑμῖν ὑπολιμπάνων ὑπογραμμόν: James v. 10, 11 ὑπόδειγμα λάβετε τῆς κακοπαθίας καὶ τῆς μακροθυμίας τοὺς προφήτας...ἰδοὺ μακαρίζομεν τοὺς ὑπομείναντας, cf. i. 12.

ii. 25 πλανώμενοι ἐπεστράφητε: James v. 19 ἐάν τις ἐν ὑμῖν πλανηθῇ ...καὶ ἐπιστρέψῃ τις αὐτόν.

iii. 15 μετὰ πραΰτητος, cf. ver. 4: James i. 21 ἐν πραΰτητι.

iv. 7 πάντων τὸ τέλος ἤγγικεν· σωφρονήσατε οὖν: James v. 8 στηρίξατε τὰς καρδίας, ὅτι ἡ παρουσία τοῦ Κυρίου ἤγγικεν, ver. 3 ἐν ἐσχάταις ἡμέραις.

*iv. 8 πρὸ πάντων τὴν εἰς ἑαυτοὺς ἀγάπην ἐκτενῆ ἔχοντες, ὅτι ἀγάπη καλύπτει πλῆθος ἁμαρτιῶν: James v. 12 πρὸ πάντων μὴ ὀμνύετε, ver. 20 γινωσκέτε ὅτι ὁ ἐπιστρέψας ἁμαρτωλὸν...καλύψει πλῆθος ἁμαρτιῶν. Cf. the original Prov. x. 12 'love covereth all sins,' where the LXX. has πάντας τοὺς μὴ φιλονεικοῦντας καλύπτει.

iv. 14 τὸ τῆς δόξης καὶ τὸ τοῦ Θεοῦ πνεῦμα: James ii. 1 τὴν πίστιν Ἰησοῦ Χριστοῦ τοῦ Κυρίου ἡμῶν, τῆς δόξης.

iv. 12, 13 μὴ ξενίζεσθε τῇ...πυρώσει πρὸς πειρασμὸν ὑμῖν γινομένῃ...ἀλλὰ χαίρετε ἵνα καὶ ἐν τῇ ἀποκαλύψει τῆς δόξης αὐτοῦ χαρῆτε ἀγαλλιώμενοι: see above on i. 6.

iv. 16 εἰ ὡς Χριστιανὸς (πάσχει)...δοξαζέτω τὸν Θεὸν ἐν τῷ ὀνόματι τούτῳ: James ii. 7 τὸ καλὸν ὄνομα τὸ ἐπικληθὲν ἐφ' ὑμᾶς.

*v. 4 κομιεῖσθε τὸν ἀμαράντινον τῆς δόξης στέφανον, cf. i. 3: James i. 12 λήμψεται τὸν στέφανον τῆς ζωῆς.

*v. 5, 6 νεώτεροι ὑποτάγητε πρεσβυτέροις· πάντες δὲ ἀλλήλοις τὴν ταπεινοφροσύνην ἐγκομβώσασθε, ὅτι ὁ Θεὸς ὑπερηφάνοις ἀντιτάσσεται ταπεινοῖς δὲ δίδωσιν χάριν. ταπεινώθητε οὖν ὑπὸ τὴν κραταιὰν χεῖρα τοῦ Θεοῦ ἵνα ὑμᾶς ὑψώσῃ ἐν καιρῷ, ver. 8 γρηγορήσατε· ὁ ἀντίδικος ὑμῶν διάβολος...περιπατεῖ ζητῶν καταπιεῖν· ᾧ ἀντίστητε στερεοὶ ἐν τῇ πίστει: James iv. 6, 7 διὸ λέγει Ὁ Θεὸς ὑπερηφάνοις ἀντιτάσσεται, ταπεινοῖς δὲ δίδωσιν χάριν· ὑποτάγητε οὖν τῷ Θεῷ, ἀντίστητε δὲ τῷ διαβόλῳ, ver. 10 ταπεινώθητε ἐνώπιον Κυρίου καὶ ὑψώσει ὑμᾶς, v. 16 ἐξομολογεῖσθε οὖν ἀλλήλοις τὰς ἁμαρτίας καὶ εὔχεσθε ὑπὲρ ἀλλήλων, after bidding the sick to send for the elders to pray over them in ver. 14. I cannot but think that there is remarkable similarity in the extension of the injunction, that the elders should pray for the people and hear their confession (as is implied in ver. 14), to the mutual prayer and confession of ver. 16, and the extension in St. Peter from submission of the younger to the elder to mutual submission.

v. 10 ὁ Θεὸς...ὀλίγον παθόντας αὐτὸς...στηρίξει: James v. 9 μακροθυμήσατε καὶ ὑμεῖς, στηρίξατε τὰς καρδίας.

2 *Peter*—

i. 1 πίστιν ἐν δικαιοσύνῃ τοῦ Θεοῦ ἡμῶν: James i. 20 δικαιοσύνην Θεοῦ.

i. 12 ἐστηριγμένους ἐν τῇ παρούσῃ ἀληθείᾳ: James v. 10.

i. 16 παρουσίαν, cf. iii. 4, 12: James v. 8.

i. 17 ὑπὸ τῆς μεγαλοπρεποῦς δόξης: James ii. 1.

ii. 2 δι' οὓς ἡ ὁδὸς τῆς ἀληθείας βλασφημηθήσεται, ver. 15 καταλείποντες εὐθεῖαν ὁδὸν ἐπλανήθησαν: James v. 19, 20.

ii. 7 ὑπόδειγμα μελλόντων: James v. 10.

*ii. 13, 14 ἡδονὴν ἡγουμένοι τὴν ἐν ἡμέρᾳ τρυφήν, σπίλοι καὶ μῶμοι ἐντρυφῶντες ἐν ταῖς ἀπάταις...ὀφθαλμοὺς ἔχοντες μεστοὺς μοιχαλίδος...δελεάζοντες ψυχὰς ἀστηρίκτους: James v. 5, i. 14. 27, iv. 4, iii. 17.

iii. 3 ἐπ' ἐσχάτων τῶν ἡμερῶν...κατὰ τὰς ἰδίας ἐπιθυμίας αὐτῶν πορευόμενοι: James v. 3, i. 14.

iii. 14 σπουδάσατε ἄσπιλοι...εὑρεθῆναι ἐν εἰρήνῃ: James i. 27, iii. 18.

Jude—

1 Ἰησοῦ Χριστοῦ δοῦλος: James i. 1.

9 διακρινόμενος, cf. ver. 22: James i. 6.

19 ψυχικοί: James iii. 15.

(6) *Epistle to the Hebrews*—

I have given reasons above (4) for supposing that the eleventh chapter of this Epistle was written with a knowledge of St. James' argument on Faith. If I am not mistaken there is a further allusion to St. James in ch. xii. 11, where (as in 1 Pet. i. 6) there seems to be a kind of concession to those who felt themselves unequal to the high-strained appeal πᾶσαν χαρὰν ἡγήσασθε. 'Chastisement,' the writer allows, 'does not seem for the moment to be a ground for rejoicing but for grief, nevertheless afterwards' —it has the effect St. James ascribes to it—'it produces the peaceable fruit of righteousness.' It may be added that the evils of the Jewish Church are more developed, and the threatened judgments more imminent, in this Epistle than in St. James; that persecutions are referred to as matters of the past (x. 32–34), and that in xiii. 7 many have seen an allusion to the martyrdom of St. James himself. Cf. Spitta 226–228.

i. 3 *ὢν ἀπαύγασμα τῆς δόξης*: James ii. 1.

ii. 4 *κατὰ τὴν αὐτοῦ θέλησιν*, x. 10 *ἐν ᾧ θελήματι ἡγιασμένοι ἐσμέν*: James i. 18 *βουληθεὶς ἀπεκύησεν ἡμᾶς.*

ii. 10 *διὰ παθημάτων τελειῶσαι*, cf. v. 8, 13, 14, vi. 1: James i. 4 *ἡ δὲ ὑπομονὴ ἔργον τέλειον ἐχέτω ἵνα ἦτε τέλειοι.*

iii. 6 *ἐὰν τὸ καύχημα τῆς ἐλπίδος κατάσχωμεν*: James i. 9 *καυχάσθω δὲ ὁ ἀδελφὸς...ἐν τῷ ὕψει αὐτοῦ.*

iv. 11 *ἐν τῷ αὐτῷ ὑποδείγματι τῆς ἀπειθείας*, viii. 5 *ὑπόδειγμα τῶν ἐπουρανίων*: James v. 10 *ὑπόδειγμα κακοπαθίας.*

v. 7 *τὸν δυνάμενον σώζειν αὐτὸν ἐκ θανάτου*: James iv. 12 *ὁ δυνάμενος σῶσαι καὶ ἀπολέσαι.*

vi. 1 *θεμέλιον καταβαλλόμενοι μετανοίας ἀπὸ νεκρῶν ἔργων καί πίστεως ἐπὶ Θεόν*, cf. ix. 14 *καθαριεῖ τὴν συνείδησιν ὑμῶν ἀπὸ νεκρῶν ἔργων εἰς τὸ λατρεύειν Θεῷ ζῶντι*: James ii. 26 *ἡ πίστις χωρὶς ἔργων νεκρά ἐστιν*, i. 26, 27.

vii. 19 *οὐδὲν ἐτελείωσεν ὁ νόμος, ἐπεισαγωγὴ δὲ κρείττονος ἐλπίδος δι' ἧς ἐγγίζομεν τῷ Θεῷ*, vii. 16, ix. 11, x. 1 *σκιὰν ἔχων ὁ νόμος τῶν μελλόντων ἀγαθῶν...οὐδέποτε δύναται τοὺς προσερχομένους τελειῶσαι*: James i. 4, 25, ii. 12, iv. 8.

x. 24 *κατανοῶμεν ἀλλήλους εἰς παροξυσμὸν...καλῶν ἔργων, μὴ ἐγκαταλείποντες τὴν ἐπισυναγωγὴν ἑαυτῶν*, cf. Tit. iii. 8: James iii. 13, ii. 2.

*x. 36 *ὑπομονῆς ἔχετε χρείαν ἵνα τὸ θέλημα τοῦ Θεοῦ ποιήσαντες κομίσησθε τὴν ἐπαγγελίαν*: James i. 4, 12.

xi. While James uses the word *πίστις* loosely and inconsistently, in *Heb.* we have a definition of faith followed by a host of examples which exhibit it as the root of action. In all probability it was written after the Romans and James; compare ver. 8—10, 17—19, on Abraham, ver. 31 on Rahab: James ii. 21—23, 25: see remarks under section (4) above.

xii. 1 *ἀποθέμενοι τὴν εὐπερίστατον ἁμαρτίαν δι' ὑπομονῆς τρέχωμεν τὸν προκείμενον ἀγῶνα*, ver. 7 *εἰς παιδείαν ὑπομένετε*: James i. 21, ver. 4.

*xii. 11 *πᾶσα μὲν παιδεία πρὸς μὲν τὸ παρὸν οὐ δοκεῖ χαρᾶς εἶναι ἀλλὰ λύπης, ὕστερον δὲ καρπὸν εἰρηνικὸν τοῖς δι' αὐτῆς γεγυμνασμένοις ἀποδίδωσιν δικαιοσύνης*, ver. 14, 15 *εἰρήνην διώκετε...ἐπισκοποῦντες μή τις ῥίζα πικρίας ἐνοχλῇ*: seems to explain James i. 2—4 *πᾶσαν χαρὰν ἡγήσασθε ...ἵνα ἦτε τέλειοι*, iii. 18 *καρπὸς δὲ δικαιοσύνης ἐν εἰρήνῃ σπείρεται τοῖς ποιοῦσιν εἰρήνην.*

xiii. 4 *τίμιος ὁ γάμος καὶ ἡ κοίτη ἀμίαντος*, cf. vii. 26: James v. 7, i. 27.

xiii. 18 *καλῶς ἀναστρέφεσθαι*: James iii. 13 *δειξάτω ἐκ τῆς καλῆς ἀναστροφῆς τὰ ἔργα αὐτοῦ.*

(7) *Apocalypse*—

i. 3 *μακάριος ὁ ἀναγινώσκων καὶ οἱ ἀκούοντες τοὺς λόγους τῆς προφητείας καὶ τηροῦντες τὰ ἐν αὐτῇ γεγραμμένα· ὁ γὰρ καιρὸς ἐγγύς*, cf. xxii. 10: James i. 25, v. 8.

i. 9 ἐν τῇ βασιλείᾳ καὶ ὑπομονῇ Ἰησοῦ Χριστοῦ, cf. ii. 2, 3, 19, iii. 10 ἐτηρήσας τὸν λόγον τῆς ὑπομονῆς μου κἀγώ σε τηρήσω ἐκ τῆς ὥρας τοῦ πειρασμοῦ, xiii. 10, xiv. 12 : James i. 2—4, 12, ii. 5, 10.

*ii. 9 οἶδά σου τὴν θλίψιν καὶ τὴν πτωχείαν, ἀλλὰ πλούσιος εἶ: James ii. 5.

*ii. 10 ἵνα πειρασθῆτε...γίνου πιστὸς ἄχρι θανάτου, καὶ δώσω σοι τὸν στέφανον τῆς ζωῆς : James i. 12.

*iii. 1 οἶδά σου τὰ ἔργα, ὅτι ὄνομα ἔχεις ὅτι ζῇς, καὶ νεκρὸς εἶ: James ii. 17, 26, i. 26.

*iii. 17 λέγεις ὅτι Πλούσιός εἰμι...καὶ οὐκ οἶδας ὅτι σὺ εἶ...ὁ πτωχός, cf. above ii. 9 : James i. 10, ii. 6, 7, v. 1—5.

*iii. 20 ἰδοὺ ἕστηκα ἐπὶ τὴν θύραν καὶ κρούω : James v. 9.

xi. 6 οὗτοι ἔχουσιν τὴν ἐξουσίαν κλεῖσαι τὸν οὐρανὸν ἵνα μὴ ὑετὸς βρέχῃ (μῆνας τεσσαράκοντα καὶ δύο) : James v. 17.

xiv. 1 ἔχουσαι τὸ ὄνομα αὐτοῦ γεγραμμένον ἐπὶ τῶν μετώπων αὐτῶν, cf. iii. 12 : James ii. 7.

xiv. 4 οὗτοι ἠγοράσθησαν ἀπὸ τῶν ἀνθρώπων ἀπαρχὴ τῷ Θεῷ : James i. 18.

xiv. 12 ὧδε ἡ ὑπομονὴ τῶν ἁγίων ἐστίν, οἱ τηροῦντες τὰς ἐντολὰς τοῦ Θεοῦ καὶ τὴν πίστιν Ἰησοῦ (combining faith and works) : cf. above i. 9 : James ii. 1, 10.

CHAPTER V

The Contents of the Epistle

The design of the Epistle is on the one hand to encourage those to whom it is addressed to bear their trials patiently, and on the other hand to warn them against certain errors of doctrine and practice.

I. *Of Trial.*—i. 1–18.

(1) Trial is sent in order to perfect the Christian character. That it may have this effect wisdom is needed; and this wisdom is given in answer to believing prayer.—i. 2–6.

A warning against double-mindedness. The believer should recognize the greatness of his calling, and not allow himself to be either elated or depressed by outward circumstances.—i. 7–11.

(2) Patient endurance of trial leads to the crown of life promised to all that love God.—i. 12.

(3) Though outward trial is appointed by God for our good, we must not imagine that the inner weakness which shows itself under trial is from God. God is perfect goodness, and only sends what is good. The disposition to misuse God's appointments comes from man's own lusts, which, if yielded to, lead to death as their natural consequence.—i. 13–15.

(4) So far from God's tempting man to evil, it is only by His will, through the regenerating power of His word, that we have been raised to that new and higher life which shall eventually penetrate and renew the whole creation.—i. 16–18.

II. *How we should receive the Word.*—i. 19–27.

(1) As humble listeners, not as excited speakers.—i. 19–21.

(2) Nor is it enough to listen to the word; we must carry it out in action.—i. 22–24.

(*a*) Blessing comes to him alone who patiently studies the word, and frames his life in accordance with the law of liberty embodied therein.—i. 25.

(*b*) Ritual observance is of no avail unless it helps us to rule the tongue, and practise brotherly kindness and unworldliness.—i. 26, 27.

III. *Warning against respect of persons.*—ii. 1–13.

(1) Courtesy to the rich, if combined with discourtesy to the poor, is a sign of weakness of faith, and proves that we are not whole-hearted in the service of Him who is the only glory of believers.—ii. 1–4.

(2) The poor have more title to our respect than the rich, since they are often rich in faith and heirs of the kingdom; while it is the rich who maltreat the brethren and blaspheme the name of Christ.—ii. 5–7.

(3) If it is from obedience to the royal law of love that we show courtesy to the rich, it is well: but if we do this only from respect of persons, it is a breach of the law and a defiance of the lawgiver, no less than murder or adultery.—ii. 8–11.

(4) Remember that we shall all be tried by the law of liberty, which looks to the heart, and not to the outward action only. It is the merciful who obtain mercy.—ii. 12, 13.

IV. *Belief and Practice.*—ii. 14–26.

(1) A mere profession of faith without corresponding action is of no avail.—ii. 14.

(*a*) As may be seen in the parallel case of benevolence when it does not go beyond words.—ii. 15–17.

(*b*) Without action we have no evidence of the existence of faith.—ii. 18.

(*c*) The orthodox belief of the Jew is shared by the demons, and only serves to increase their misery.—ii. 19.

(2) True faith, such as that of Abraham and Rahab, necessarily embodies itself in action.—ii. 20–26.

V. *Warnings with regard to the use of the tongue.*—iii. 1–12.

(1) Great responsibility of the office of teacher.—iii. 1.

(2) Difficulty and importance of controlling the tongue.—iii. 2–8

(*a*) In our human microcosm the tongue plays the part of the world, and it is used by the powers of evil for our ruin.—iii. 6.

(*b*) Its malign and devastating influence.—iii. 5–8.

(*c*) It is like the rudder of a ship: he who can rule it rules the whole life and activity.—iii. 2–4.

(3) Inconsistency of supposing that we can offer acceptable praise to God as long as we speak evil of man who is made in the image of God.—iii. 9–12.

VI. *True and false Wisdom.*—iii. 13–18.

(1) The wisdom which comes from God is simple and straightforward, full of kindness and all good fruits.—iii. 13, 17, 18.

(2) If there is a wisdom which does not conduce to peace, but is accompanied by bitterness and jealousy, it is not from above, but is earthly, carnal, devilish.—iii. 14–16.

VII. *Warning against quarrelsomeness and worldliness.*—iv. 1–17.

(1) The cause of quarrelling is that each man seeks to gratify his own selfish impulses, and to snatch his neighbour's portion of worldly good.—iv. 1, 2.

(2) No satisfaction can be thus obtained. Even our prayers can give us no satisfaction if they are infected with this worldly spirit.—iv. 3.

(3) God demands the service of the whole heart, and will reveal Himself to none but those who yield up their wills to His.—iv. 4–6.

(4) Therefore resist the devil, who is the prince of this world, and turn to God in humble repentance.—iv. 7–10.

(5) Cease to find fault with others. Those who condemn their neighbours condemn the law itself, and usurp the office of Him, the Lord of life and death, who alone has the power and right to judge.—iv. 11, 12.

(6) Worldliness is also shown in the confident laying-out of plans of life without reference to God.—iv. 13–17.

VIII. *Denunciations and Encouragements.*—v. 1–11.

(1) Woe to those who have been heaping up money and living in luxury on the very eve of judgment. Woe especially to those who have ground down the poor and murdered the innocent.—v. 1–6.

(2) Let the brethren bear their sufferings patiently, knowing that the Lord is at hand, and that He will make all things turn out for their good. Let them imitate Job and the prophets, and so inherit the blessings pronounced on those that endure.—v. 6–11.

IX. *Miscellaneous precepts.*—v. 12–20.

(1) Swear not.—v. 12.

(2) Let all your feelings of joy and sorrow be sanctified and controlled by religion.—v. 13.

(3) In sickness let the elders be called in to pray and anoint the sick with a view to his recovery.—v. 14, 15.

(4) Confess your faults to one another, and pray for one another with all earnestness.—v. 16–18.

(5) The blessing on one who wins back a sinner from the error of his ways.—v. 19, 20.

Though the letter flows on from point to point without pretending to strict logical sequence, yet it is easy to distinguish certain leading principles on which the whole depends. Thus, in regard to practice, the leading principle is the necessity of whole-heartedness in religion. A man may think to serve God and Mammon at once (*διψυχία*, i. 8, iv. 8), but God insists on the surrender of the whole heart to Him: the love of the world is incompatible with the love of God (iv. 4–7). Most men seek to compromise matters, and their religion thus becomes a *ὑπόκρισις*. They flatter themselves that they are religious, because they are fluent in speaking on religious subjects (i. 19, iii. 1); or because they find 'the words of the preacher as a lovely song of one that has a pleasant voice' (i. 19, 22–25); or because they are conscious of genuine indignation at the sight of error in others (i. 19, 20, iii. 14, iv. 11, 12); or because of their punctuality in religious observances (i. 26, 27); or because of a partial obedience to this or that law (ii. 10–12); or because of their orthodoxy of belief (ii. 14–26); but all this is mere self-deception (i. 22, 26, ii. 14, 17, 19, 26, iii. 15). Knowledge not used only entails a heavier punishment (iii. 1, iv. 17). The only religion which is of value in the sight of God is that which influences the whole life and activity (i. 27, 4, 22–25, ii. 12–26, iii. 13, 17, iv. 11, 17). Faith, love, wisdom, religion—all alike are spurious if they fail to produce the fruit of good works.

We will next consider the doctrinal basis of St. James' practical teaching. Man was created in the image of God (iii. 9), the All-Good (i. 13, 17); but he has fallen into sin by yielding to his lower impulses against his sense of right (i. 14, 15, iv. 1–3, 17); and the natural consequence of sin is death, bodily and spiritual (i. 15, v. 3, 5, 20). Not only is man liable to sin; but as a matter of fact we all sin, and that frequently (iii. 2). God of His free bounty has provided a means by which we might conquer sin and rise to a new life, in His word sown in our hearts (i. 18 *βουληθεὶς ἀπεκύησεν ἡμᾶς λόγῳ ἀληθείας*, i. 21 *δέξασθε τὸν ἔμφυτον λόγον τὸν δυνάμενον σῶσαι τὰς ψυχὰς ὑμῶν*). Our salvation depends on the way in which we receive the word (i. 21). If we have a stedfast faith in God's goodness as revealed to us through our Lord Jesus Christ (i. 13, ii. 1, i. 5–7); if we read, mark, learn, and inwardly digest the word, so as to make it the guiding principle of our life, the law of liberty by which all our words and actions are regulated (i. 25, ii. 12), then our souls are saved from death, we are made inheritors of the kingdom promised to those that love God (i. 12, 25, ii. 5).

But the training by which we are prepared for this crown of life is not pleasant to the natural man. It involves trial and endurance (i. 2–4, 12): it involves constant watchfulness and self-control, and prayer for heavenly wisdom, in order that we may resist the temptations of the world, the flesh and the devil (i. 26, iii. 2–8, 15, iv. 1–5). Thus faith is exercised; we are enabled to see things as God sees them (ii. 1, 5); to rise above the temporal to the eternal (i. 9–11); to be not simply patient, but to rejoice in affliction (i. 2, v. 7, 8, 10, 11), and exult in the hope set before us (i. 9–12); until at last we grow up to the full stature of a Christian (i. 4, iii. 2), wise with that wisdom which comes from above, the wisdom which is stedfast, unpretending, gentle, considerate, affectionate, full of mercy and good fruits, the parent of righteousness and peace (iii. 17, 18).

But there are many who choose the friendship of the world instead of the friendship of God, so vexing His Holy Spirit, and yielding themselves to the power of the devil; yet even then He does not leave them to themselves, but gives more grace. He hedges in their way in the present, and warns them of further judgment to come (iv. 4–6, v. 1–8). If they humble themselves under His hand and repent truly of their sins, He will lift them up; if they draw nigh to Him, He will draw nigh to them (iv. 7–10). Here, too, we may be helpful to one another by mutual confession, and by prayer for one another. Great is the power of prayer prompted by the Spirit of God (v. 15–20).

It is characteristic of the austere tone of the Epistle that it, alone of the Epistles of the New Testament, contains no attempt to conciliate the favour of the readers by direct words of praise. In it we hear the bracing call of duty uttered by one who speaks with earnest sympathy indeed and without a particle of Pharisaic assumption, but who feels that he has the right to speak and expects to be obeyed.[1]

[1] Zahn (*Skizzen* p. 50) remarks on the fact that St. James does not suggest any legislative or social change. He does not tell the rich to restore the early communism of the Church and share their wealth with the poor. In describing Christian perfection he does not recall the words of Christ, 'If thou wilt be perfect, sell what thou hast and give to the poor.' He insists only on change of heart and motive, on learning to estimate aright the value of life and of its accessories, and to look forward to the future judgment. He teaches both rich and poor what really constitutes the title to honour and respect. It is not left to the community or to officials to alleviate the distress of others, whether bodily or mental. All Christians are exhorted to visit the sick, feed the hungry, convert the erring, pray for all. The Word of Truth lays down no precise rule as to social organization.

CHAPTER VI

PERSONS TO WHOM THE EPISTLE IS ADDRESSED, AND PLACE FROM WHICH IT IS WRITTEN.

ST. JAMES addresses the Twelve Tribes in the Dispersion. For the meaning of this phrase see the note on i. 1. I propose here to sum up briefly the historical facts which it represents.

If we view the history of Israel from the outside, one of its most remarkable characteristics is the long series of compulsory transplantations undergone by this people from the time of Tiglath-Pileser up to the present day. The Assyrian transplantation took place in the latter half of the eighth century B.C. In it, we are told that the tribes of Reuben and Gad and the half-tribe of Manasseh, together with the bulk of the Samaritans and some of the tribe of Judah, were removed to upper Mesopotamia (1 Chron. v. 26, 2 Kings xvii. 4–6, and xviii. 13). In the second transplantation the tribes of Judah and Benjamin were removed to Babylon about the year 600 B.C. (Dan. i. 1, 2, 2 Kings xxiv. 14–16, xxv., Jer. lii.). The extent and importance of the Eastern Dispersion is shown in the Books of Esther and Tobit: Philo, writing shortly after the Christian era, says that Babylonia and the most fertile satrapies beyond the Euphrates were inhabited by Jews (*ad Caium*, M. 2, p. 587); and we learn from Josephus that early in the first century after Christ, Mesopotamia was for some fifteen years under the rule of the Jewish leaders Asidaeus and Anilaeus,[1] and that, after the death of the latter, more than 50,000 Jews were massacred in the city of Seleucia (*Ant.* xviii. 9, 4–9). A third transplantation was that to Egypt, which commenced as a voluntary emigration in the time of Nebuchadnezzar (2 Kings xxv. 26), but received a great development in the foundation of Alexandria under Alexander and

[1] Lewin, *Fasti Sacri*, gives A.D. 18 to 33 as the period of their rule.

Ptolemy I. (Jos. *B.J.* ii. 18. 7, *Ant.* xii. 1). Ptolemy also planted colonies of Jews in Cyrene and the neighbourhood (Jos. *c. Ap.* ii. 4, *Ant.* xiv. 7. 2). In the reign of Ptolemy Philometor (B.C. 180—145) a temple modelled after that at Jerusalem was built at Leontopolis for the Egyptian Jews, whose number is estimated at not less than one million by Philo (*in Flacc.* M. 2 p. 523). The same reasons which led to the Jews being established by their Macedonian conquerors in Egypt, led to their being established also in the Greek towns founded in the East by the Seleucid dynasty. 'The Jews,' says Mommsen, 'had a conspicuous share in the Hellenizing of the East': they were chosen for this purpose 'from their pliancy and serviceableness on the one hand and from their unyielding tenacity on the other.' 'The Jews of the Greek towns became Greek-speaking Orientals,' 'the use of the Greek language was compulsory,' but, to compensate for this, 'they were allowed up to a certain degree to govern themselves.' 'Mesopotamia was covered with Greek commonwealths,' 'the inhabitants of Palestine were only a portion, and not the most important portion, of the Jews: the Jewish communities of Babylonia, Syria, Asia Minor, and Egypt were far superior to those of Palestine. (*The Provinces,* vol. ii. pp. 8, 162—167 Eng. tr.) The most important of the Seleucid cities were the Babylonian Seleucia and the Syrian Antioch, in the latter of which special privileges were granted to the Jews by its founder Seleucus Nicator (Jos. *Ant.* xii. 3. 1). At a later period Antiochus the Great transported 2,000 Jewish families from Babylonia to Phrygia and Lydia (Jos. *Ant.* xii. 3. 4).

The capture of Jerusalem by Pompeius in B.C. 63 led to the transplantation of Jews to Rome, where they were settled in the Trans-Tiberine quarter. As early as B.C. 59 Cicero defending L. Flaccus (§ 66) speaks of their numbers and audacity in endeavouring to influence the judges: *scis quanta sit manus, quanta concordia, quantum valeat in contionibus.*[1] In the same passage he commends Flaccus for having stopped the exportation of the sacred tribute from the Jews in Asia to Jerusalem.

Beside these more or less compulsory transplantations, the pursuit of commerce led many Jews to find a home in foreign lands. There is scarcely a place mentioned in the Acts which is without its synagogue or *proseucha;* and Strabo (*ap.* Jos. *Ant.* xiv.

[1] See Hausrath *Neut. Zeitg.* Part ii. c. 2 and references in Mayor's *Juvenal,* xiv. 96, above all Schürer, *Hist. of the Jewish People,* Eng. tr. vol. iv. 232 foll.

7. 2) says that 'it is hard to find a spot in the whole world which is not occupied and dominated by Jews,' the privileges they had enjoyed under their Greek rulers being confirmed and extended by the Roman emperors from the same motives of policy. So Josephus says (*c. Ap.* ii. 39) 'there is no city, no tribe, whether Greek or barbarian, in which Jewish law and Jewish custom have not taken root.'

It was expected of the members of the Diaspora that they should not only send to the temple their yearly didrachmon, but that they should at least once in their life go up to offer their sacrifice there in person. Among those who listened to Peter's address on the day of Pentecost there were inhabitants of Parthia, Media, Elam, Mesopotamia, Cappadocia, Pontus, Asia, Phrygia, Pamphylia, Egypt, the parts of Libya about Cyrene, Rome, Crete, Arabia. Those who disputed with Stephen are said to have belonged to the synagogues of the freedmen of Rome, of Cyrene and Alexandria, and of Cilicia and Asia (Acts vi. 9). Philo enumerates the following provinces as inhabited by Jews: Egypt, Phoenicia, Syria, Pamphylia, Cilicia, the greater part of Asia as far as Bithynia and Pontus, Thessalia, Boeotia, Macedonia, Aetolia, Attica, Argos, Corinth, the fairest districts of the Peloponnese, Euboea, Cyprus, Crete, not to mention the settlements beyond the Euphrates (*Leg. ad Caium* M. 2 p. 587). The proselytes who attached themselves to the worship of the synagogues, the εὐσεβεῖς and σεβόμενοι of the Acts, as they shared in the persecutions of the Jews (Tac. *Ann.* ii. 85, Suet. *Dom.* 12), would doubtless be generally reckoned as belonging to the Diaspora. It was as occasional visitors to Jerusalem that the Jews and Proselytes of the Dispersion would come under the cognizance of the President of the Christian community at Jerusalem. The instructions and warnings contained in his Epistle would naturally be founded on his observation of their special needs and dangers, as well as on his intimate acquaintance with the national character and the general conditions of the time. On this something will be said presently.

It may be asked however whether we are to understand St. James as using the word Diaspora here in its widest sense, or whether he had any special portion of the Diaspora in his eye when he wrote. St. Peter (i. 1) confines himself to the Diaspora of Asia Minor. His Epistle, as we have seen, was drawn up with a distinct reference to that of St. James, which in some respects served as a model for his own. It seems natural therefore to suppose that one reason why it was addressed to these particular provinces of the Diaspora was that they were less likely to be acquainted with the Epistle of St. James than the provinces omitted. It is also probable that the name Diaspora would be understood to refer, in the first instance, to the original Eastern Diaspora, settled in Babylon and Mesopotamia, and extending as far as the eastern and northern borders of Palestine. Josephus tells us that his *History of the Jewish War* was first written in Aramaic and addressed τοῖς ἄνω βαρβάροις, whom he afterwards explains to be the dwellers in Parthia, Babylonia, Arabia, Adiabene, and the countries on the other side of the Euphrates (*B. J. Prooem.* i. 2), but that subsequently he translated it into Greek for the benefit of the Romans (*Ap.* i. 9). It is also noticeable that these eastern provinces are the ones first named in the list given of the foreign Jews who were present at the feast of Pentecost (Acts ii. 9—11). We know that there were Christians in Damascus and Antioch at a very early period (Acts ix. 2, 10, 14, 19, 25, xi. 19—21), as well as in Cyprus and Phoenicia (Acts iv. 36, xi. 19, 20). St. Peter writes from Babylon (v. 13), which should perhaps be understood literally of the city on the Euphrates and the surrounding district. An early legend represents a King of Edessa corresponding with our Lord and welcoming the mission of the apostle Thaddaeus (Euseb. *H. E.* i. 13).

We will now see what more is to be learnt in regard to the readers of the Epistle from the Epistle itself. James writes to them as being himself a servant of Jesus Christ (i. 1), and he assumes that they hold the faith of Christ (ii. 1) and recognize that they are no longer under a yoke of bondage but under the perfect law of liberty (i. 25, ii. 12). They are mixed up however with men who are not only unbelievers but who blaspheme the name of Christ and persecute the believers (ii. 6, 7). The believers themselves are mostly poor (ii. 5); the few rich belonging to their body (i. 10) are in danger of falling away through covetousness, worldliness and pride (iv. 3—6, 13—16). The rich generally appear as persecutors and oppressors, keeping back the hire of their labourers, killing innocent men, themselves the slaves of lust and luxury, fattening themselves in the day of slaughter (ii. 6, 7, v. 3—6). The Church is under the superintendence of Elders, who, or some of whom, are possessed of miraculous gifts of healing; St. James gives instructions as to the use of this gift (v. 14, 15). Their place of meeting is the synagogue, to which strangers are admitted (ii. 2—4). They are exposed to trials of many kinds, especially from their rich oppressors, and it is one main object of the Epistle to encourage them to patient endurance (i. 2, 12, ii. 6, v. 7, 8, 10, 11). There is much however to blame in themselves: their faith is very weak; they are inclined to murmur and complain both against God and against man (i. 6—8, 13, iv. 11, v. 9); their religion and their philanthropy alike are a matter of words and forms, without corresponding feelings and actions (i. 22, 25—27, ii. 14—26); they are deficient in genuine love of man as man; they are haughty to the poor, obsequious to the rich (ii. 1—9, 15, 16). They are censorious, quarrelsome, given to oaths, ambitious, self-confident, eager to set themselves up as teachers, greedy of pleasure, forgetful of God (iii. 1, 6, 9, 14, iv. 1—8, 13, 16, v. 12).

How far do these characteristics agree with what we read elsewhere? First, as to the rich oppressors: I have pointed out, in my note on ii. 6, that these were in all probability Jews. The Gentiles for a long time took no interest in the internal disputes of Jewish sects: they might punish the Christian missionaries as disturbers of the public peace, but they were very unlikely 'to blaspheme Christ' themselves (James ii. 7). Again, if they were Gentiles, why should the rich, rather than the poor, take the trouble to persecute such an insignificant body? In Ephesus and Philippi, it is the rabble who make the loudest outcry against the Christians. On the other hand, if we turn to the Jews, we find that the rich were as a fact the leaders in the persecutions. It was the party of the high priest, the wealthy Sadducees (Jos. *Ant.* xviii. 1.4), who laid hold of the Apostles, as recorded in Acts iv. 1—3); it was with their sanction and that of the Sanhedrin in general, including the Pharisaic section (Acts xxii. 5, xxvi. 10, 12), both being combined against the disciples, as they had been against their Master (Joh. xi. 47, 57, xviii. 3, Matt. xxvi. 3), that Saul, the Pharisee, took the lead in the stoning of Stephen and the ensuing raid on the Church (Acts viii. 1, ix. 1, 2, 21); [1] at

[1] 'The members of the new sect being strict observers of the law and agreeing with the Pharisees in their opposition to the Sadducees, appeared in a favorable light to at least the more moderate of the former,' until the opposition of the Gospel to

Antioch in Pisidia it was the higher class of proselytes who were stirred up by the Jews to expel Paul out of their coasts (Acts xiii. 50). So in the Book of Enoch the Sadducees are referred to as wealthy oppressors, xciv. 6 foll., xcvii. 8–10.

It is easy to understand this hostility of the richer and more powerful Jews to the Christians. The prosperous and well-to-do are naturally suspicious of reformers: and Christ and His disciples were reformers of a very thorough-going kind. They preached that the kingdom of heaven was for the poor, that it was easier for a camel to go through the eye of a needle than for a rich man to enter the kingdom of heaven. The rich man who would enter therein must no longer count his riches his own; he must sell all that he had and give to the poor; he must glory no longer in wealth and station, but in having learnt that his superiority only marked him out as intended by God to be the minister and servant of all (James i. 10, Mark x. 43, 44). But there were other and more special grounds for the hatred entertained by the chief priests and Pharisees for the name of Christ. On two separate occasions Christ had openly denounced the buying and selling which was carried on in the Temple under the sanction and for the profit of the worldly-minded and avaricious priests and their partisans: in his parable of the Vineyard and the Husbandmen he had prophesied their speedy overthrow; and St. Luke concludes his narratives of the two incidents in much the same words, 'the chief priests and the scribes and the chief of the people sought to destroy him' (Luke xix. 47, xx. 19, 20). Even more scathing was his denunciation of the intellectual aristocracy, 'Woe unto you, scribes and Pharisees, hypocrites.' As he had weighed humble poverty in the balance against self-satisfied wealth, so he weighed modest ignorance against self-satisfied learning in the words 'I thank thee, O Father, because thou hast hid these things from the wise and prudent and hast revealed them unto babes'; and even went so far as to declare that the publican and harlot were nearer to the kingdom of God than the self-righteous Pharisee. Yet again, the Sadducees' disbelief in the resurrection was directly challenged by the declaration of the Apostles that they were themselves eye-witnesses of the resurrection of Christ.

Pharisaic Judaism found definite expression in the teaching of the Hellenistic Stephen (Neander, *History of the Planting of the Christian Church*, Eng. tr. I. 56 foll.).

If further proof were needed to show that the persecutors referred to by St. James were wealthy Jews and not Gentiles, it might be found in the absence of all allusion to Gentiles in our Epistle. Nothing is said as to hardships suffered from them, nothing as to the duty of evangelizing them, or as to the conditions under which they should be received into the Church, nothing as to difficulties of social intercourse, e.g. as regards eating or marriage. There is no reference to that which was the burning question at the Council of Jerusalem (A.D. 51) and on the occasion of St. Paul's later visit to Jerusalem (A.D. 58), viz. the necessity of the rite of circumcision (Acts xv., xxi. 21—25), a question which occupies such an important place in the Epistles to the Galatians and the Romans. It is inconceivable that, if the question were one about which difficulties were generally felt or which was giving rise to practical complications at the time, it could have been passed over in a circular letter addressed to Jewish residents in Gentile lands, especially as the writer inadvertently uses language which, though not itself bearing on this subject, might seem at first sight to have a reference to St. Paul's argument, that circumcision is unnecessary because faith in Christ is the sole means of justification. We may therefore conclude with considerable probability that it had not yet become a matter of pressing importance. If we compare the First Epistle of St. Peter we find a different state of things; the Gentiles are there distinctly alluded to, as making false charges against the Christians (ii. 12), who are exhorted to submit to the constituted civil authorities and silence their gainsayers by their good behaviour (ii. 13—15). It is further stated that some of the Christians had joined in the immoralities of the Gentiles in their unconverted days, and had subsequently incurred their displeasure by the change in their way of life (iv. 3, 4).

As to the faults of the Christians, the tone of St. James is much more severe than that of St. Peter in his First Epistle, but so far as the latter does specify any charge, it is that of impatience, murmuring, evil-speaking, to which we find many parallels in the plainer spoken Epistle of St. James. St. Paul, as we have seen, in his Epistles to the Galatians and Romans lays stress mainly on the temptation which beset the Jews to substitute legal righteousness, the performance of the works of the law with all its slavish scrupulosity, for the righteousness which is by faith in Christ; but he also takes occasion to warn them against another and no less dangerous error, that an orthodox profession of faith, unaccompanied by the fruits of good living, could suffice for salvation. While the former error forms the subject of the first four chapters of the Galatians, the second is dealt with in the two later chapters. It is not abstract faith which avails, but faith working by love: those who fulfil the works of the flesh shall not inherit the kingdom of God: whatever a man soweth that shall he reap (Gal. v. 14—26). So he insists in his Epistle to the Romans that it is not the hearer but the doer of the law that is justified (ii. 13); that it is vain to profess a knowledge of God and claim to be a guide to the blind, an instructor of the foolish, unless we practise what we preach (ii. 17—23). He warns his readers against laying the blame of their own sins on God (ix. 10 foll.); he urges them to patience in tribulation, to perseverance in prayer, to bless and curse not, to condescend to things that are lowly, to give place to wrath (xii. 12—19), not to judge others, since we shall all stand at the judgment-seat of God, to follow after things which make for peace, and things whereby we may edify one another (xiv. 3, 4, 10—13, 19); and to turn away from those which cause divisions (xvi. 17). The parallels from St. James will be found in a previous chapter (p. xciv foll.).

It has been pointed out above that there is no allusion in this Epistle to the controversy between the Judaizers and the upholders of Gospel freedom, nay, that this controversy is so entirely ignored that the writer is able to use the technical terms of the controversy with a totally different reference. In like manner other controversies or topics which are handled elsewhere by his contemporaries are left unnoticed by him. There is no direct reference to the atoning sacrifice of Christ; none to the Sacraments; none to the details of the Second Coming; none to Church organization, as in the Pastoral Epistles. There is no allusion to incipient gnosticism, as in the Epistle to the Colossians and those to Timothy and Titus and in the writings of St. John. It is assumed that those addressed accept Jesus as the Messiah, that the new law of liberty has been written in their hearts by the indwelling Spirit: but they are still 'zealous for the law,' as St. James describes them in the Acts; they still seem to form one body with their unbelieving compatriots; still, as St. James says again, 'hear Moses read to them every sabbath in the synagogues.'

In fact they exhibit an immature stage of Christianity, such as must have continually been found among those who had become believers on the day of Pentecost or through the preaching of some passing evangelist, but were without any regularly organised system of Christian teaching (James iii. 1 foll.).

The arguments of the Tübingen school, in opposition to the Jewish nationality of those addressed, will be considered in the chapter which follows, on the Date of the Epistle. Various incidental expressions have been noticed by editors[1] as bearing on this point. Abraham is called 'our father' in ii. 21, which in this straightforward matter-of-fact Epistle must, by all rules of interpretation, be taken, like the 'Twelve Tribes of the Dispersion,' in its literal sense, unless reason can be shown to the contrary. The readers are supposed to be acquainted with the story of Job, Elijah and the prophets (v. 11, 17). The phrase 'Lord of Sabaoth' (v. 4), the reference to Jewish oaths and to the Jewish propensity to curse and swear (iii. 9, v. 12), the term 'synagogue' used for their place of meeting (ii. 1), the high value attributed to the Law and to the confession of the Unity of God—all mark the Jewish nationality of the readers, and would be unmeaning or inappropriate if the Epistle were addressed to Gentiles. The same thing appears from the reference to their avarice and their restless pursuit of wealth (iv. 13—16, v. 1—4).

As regards the place from which the Epistle was written, if we are right in supposing that it was written by the Brother of the Lord, there can be little doubt that it was dated from Jerusalem. This supposition is confirmed by incidental allusions to the early and latter rains (v. 7), to the effect on vegetation of the burning wind (i. 11), to the existence of salt and bitter springs (iii. 11), to the cultivation of figs and olives (iii. 12), and to the neighbourhood of the sea (i. 6, iii. 4).

[1] See Beyschlag, p. 8.

CHAPTER VII

On the Date of the Epistle[1]

Part I

The general result of the external and internal evidence points to the fifth decade after Christ as the time of the composition of our Epistle.

We have seen in Chapter II. that the Epistle was recognized as canonical at the third Council of Carthage (A.D. 397), that it was included in their lists of Sacred Writings by Athanasius in 367 and by Cyril of Jerusalem in 348, that it is quoted by name as authoritative by Eusebius in his *Commentary on the Psalms* (*c.* 330) and by Origen (*c.* 230) and is by both attributed, though with a certain degree of hesitation, to James, the brother of the Lord; that it was apparently commented on, along with the other Catholic Epistles, by Clement of Alexandria, and is referred to anonymously by Irenaeus, Theophilus, Justin Martyr, the writers of the Epistle to Diognetus and the so-called second epistle of Clement, by Ignatius, Polycarp, above all by Hermas during the second century; by Clement of Rome, and the author of the Didaché during the 1st century, also by Barnabas, and the author of the Testaments of the Twelve Patriarchs, who are commonly assigned to the same century. We have seen in Chapter I. that the contents of the Epistle are entirely in harmony with the supposition that it was written by James the brother of the Lord, who was martyred in the year 63 according to Josephus, in 68 according to Hegesippus. It agrees in character with all that we read of James in the Epistles of St. Paul and in the Acts of the Apostles; it agrees in style and diction with the speeches and letter of James literally recorded in the latter book. In Chapter IV. we have seen that it is quoted by several of the writers of the N. T.,

[1] It is not my aim here, any more than in other chapters, to put forward an independent scheme of chronology of my own; but, assuming the general correctness of the usually accepted chronology, I have endeavoured to determine, with reference to it, the date of the Epistle, supposed to be previously unknown.

notably by St. Peter and by St. Paul; by the latter certainly in his Epistles to the Romans and Galatians written in 58 and 57, probably in his two Epistles to the Corinthians (57) and possibly in his first Epistle to the Thessalonians (52).

This date is confirmed by the absence of any reference either to the fall of Jerusalem,

The results thus obtained are confirmed by a comparison of the Epistle with contemporary history. If it had been written between the fall of Jerusalem (A.D. 70) and the death of Clement (usually dated about A.D. 95) it must inevitably have had some reference to the preceding calamity in which so many Jews of the Dispersion had been involved. In our Epistle there is a reference to tribulation, but this arises from the oppression and persecution of the Christians by rich and prosperous Jews, who are compared to beasts fattened for slaughter, and over whom it is said that judgment is already impending: the writer is looking forward, not backward. I need not say how utterly inappropriate such language would be, if addressed to the crushed and broken remnant of the Jews in the years immediately following the utter ruin of their city and temple and nation under Titus. The leaders of the persecution, the Sadducean hierarchy, had been exterminated. The wealthier Jews in general, partly from the hatred of their Gentile neighbours, partly from internal animosities, from desire of revenge for past ill-treatment, or from mere greed and envy of the rich on the part of the poor, had been plundered of everything in the reign of terror which prevailed, alike in Jerusalem itself and generally throughout the East, wherever Jews were to be found. If here and there a solitary individual had succeeded in saving some fraction of his former possessions, certainly he had no longer the power to persecute others.

or to the admission of Gentiles into the Church.

A second mark of time in the Epistle is its silence as to the existence of Gentile Christians and the conditions on which Gentiles should be admitted into the Church. If it was written after the violent agitation caused by St. Paul's preaching to the Gentiles and after the decision of the Council of Jerusalem (51)[1], it must surely have contained some reference to these events. It is impossible to suppose that St. James, who was responsible for the compromise agreed to at the Council, and who refers to it subse-

[1] Harnack in his recently published *Chronologie d. Altchristlichen Litteratur* (1897) throws back the dates of Paul's life generally, putting his conversion in the year following the Crucifixion, and his martyrdom in 64, the Apostolic Council being assigned to the year 47. Prof. Ramsay thinks it took place in the end of 49 (*Paul the Traveller*, p. 153.)

quently on a later visit of St. Paul to Jerusalem (Acts xxi. 26), would have failed to make use of the opportunity to urge the Jews of the Dispersion to observe the terms of the compact and deal fairly by their Gentile neighbours. Nor does it seem possible to accept Dr. Plummer's suggestion that it may have been written between 53 and 62 (*St. James,* p. 61), after the controversy on the subject had cooled down; because we have no evidence that the controversy did cool down during that period. On the contrary, the furious assault of the Jews on St. Paul at Jerusalem (A.D. 58) turned on this very question. When he began to speak of his commission to the Gentiles, they burst out, 'Away with such a fellow from the earth' (Acts xxii. 22); and St. James had previously warned him that, among the believing Jews, there were many thousands zealous for the law, who had been informed that he taught the Jews among the Gentiles to forsake Moses and not to circumcise their children (Acts xxi. 20, 21). This was at Jerusalem: how far the excitement was from having cooled down in the provinces, is evident from the Epistle to the Galatians (57). It does not seem that the baptism of Cornelius had aroused anything like the same exasperation, partly no doubt because St. Peter was not suspected as St. Paul was, partly because Cornelius was already a 'proselyte of the gate,' and did not pass at once from heathenism to Christianity like St. Paul's converts. On hearing the explanation of the former 'they of the circumcision held their peace and glorified God' (Acts xi. 18). There is no reason therefore for throwing back the date of the Epistle to the period before the conversion of Cornelius. But it probably was not much later, for we read shortly afterwards (Acts xi. 20) that the Greeks in Antioch received the word from some of those who had been scattered in the persecution of Stephen, and that Barnabas was sent from Jerusalem to inquire into the circumstances.

The allusions to Church order and discipline contained in the Epistle are in accordance with an early date.

Another evidence of the early date of the Epistle may be found in the hints which it lets fall as to Church discipline and order. The synagogue is their place of meeting, though it is a synagogue of which Christians have the control.[1] No mention is made of 'bishops' or 'deacons,' but only of teachers and elders (iii. 1, v. 14). Teaching seems to be still quite unorganized, as in the Church of Corinth (1 Cor. xiv. 26 foll.): it is not confined to regularly ordained church officers: there is no

[1] See note on ii. 2.

warning (as in 1 Tim. v. 22), to 'lay hands suddenly on no man': all we find is a deprecation of the eagerness on the part of individual members of the congregation to come forward as instructors. The elders, called 'elders of the Church' to distinguish them from the elders of the Jewish community, are supposed either themselves to possess miraculous powers of healing or to control the exercise of such powers on the part of others: they are to pray for the sick and apparently to hear their confession (v. 14, 15); but this does not imply any distinctive spiritual authority, for in the next verse the injunction is made general, 'Confess your sins to one another and pray for one another.' It is interesting to compare the parallel passage in 1 Pet. v. 1–5. There the elders hold a much more important position: they are fellow elders of the Apostle himself, shepherds of the flock of God, who shall receive their reward from the chief Shepherd on his appearance: the younger are to be subject to them. But then follows, as in St. James, the extension of this injunction to all, including the elders themselves; *πάντες δὲ ἀλλήλοις τὴν ταπεινοφροσύνην ἐγκομβώσασθε*, 'yea, all of you gird yourselves (cf. Joh. xiii. 4) with humility towards one another.' Further the means enjoined by St. James for the miraculous healing take us back to the earliest age of the Church. The only other reference in the New Testament to the use of oil for the sick, is in St. Mark's account of the mission of the Twelve, 'They anointed with oil many that were sick and healed them' (vi. 13).

So too is its Judaic tone. No less confirmatory of an early date is the Judaic tone of the Epistle. The change from a narrow national and ceremonial religion to the universal and spiritual religion promulgated by Christ cannot be made in a moment, even where the old religion is as corrupt and irrational as modern Hinduism; far less where there is so much to satisfy the claims of the reason and conscience, as in the law of Moses. That law was intended as a schoolmaster to bring men to Christ. Those who had been duly prepared by it and 'were waiting for the consolation of Israel' were able at once to welcome Jesus as the expected Messiah, to accept his spiritualization of the Law given on Sinai, and acknowledge their own inability to fulfil the new law of liberty except through the promised help of the Holy Spirit. The sermons reported in the Acts scarcely go beyond this. A few perhaps would be able to make a further advance, and confess the Divinity of Christ and the atonement wrought by Him for the sins of the whole world, but the majority of Jewish Christians between the day of Pentecost and the fall of Jerusalem were probably even less advanced. They did not understand that the former things had passed away, and that from henceforth neither Jews nor Gentiles were bound by the Mosaic Law. The work of James was to lead on men, who were in this stage of religious belief, to higher views, as they were able to bear it. He was especially fitted for this work because he was so much in sympathy with those whom he addressed. By nature slow to move, he had from his childhood loved the Law, as the old psalmists did; the Gospel itself was in his view still the ancient law, revealed at length in its perfect form, and written in the mind and heart of the believer, as Jeremiah had prophesied. We are not of course justified in assuming that his own belief was limited to what is set down in the Epistle. He wrote doubtless what he believed would be most useful for the majority of those whom he addressed. He could only appeal to motives which would have force with them, and build up his arguments on premisses which they would concede. This perhaps may account for his referring to the example of Job and the prophets rather than of Christ. Supposing, as was probably the case, that our Gospels were not yet in existence, and that the Christian teaching of these Jews of the Dispersion was founded on short collections of *logia,* containing parables and aphorisms of Christ, it is quite possible that the details of his life may have been less familiar to them than the lessons from the Old Testament read to them in the synagogue every Sabbath day. Still each year must have seen more of the life and teaching of Christ set down in writing; each year must have left its impress on the mind of St. James. One who so strenuously did the Father's will must have learnt more and more of the doctrine, and received ever fuller revelation from the Spirit of truth. So far as this consideration goes, we should be led to assign the Epistle to the earliest possible date after the day of Pentecost.

On the other hand it was written after a persecution; St. James had attained a position of authority, and the persons

The considerations on the other side are (1) the position evidently held by the writer; (2) the absence of any reference to an immediately preceding conversion of those to whom he writes; (3) the reference to persecutions endured by them. The third consideration would forbid us to assign an earlier date than A.D. 37, the martyrdom of Stephen, which gave the signal for a great

addressed were no longer recent converts. persecution against the Church at Jerusalem, and which was followed by the mission of Saul to Damascus (and doubtless by that of other emissaries to other parts of the Diaspora), bearing letters from the high priest to excite the authorities of the synagogues against the Christians. The tone used by St. James in reference to the trials of the Christians does not imply, as the tone of St. Peter would seem to do, that the persecution was then either at its height or immediately impending (1 Pet. iv. 12), but rather to the sequel of a persecution with its πειρασμοὶ ποικίλοι of animosities excited and losses endured, of liability to insults and to interference with their religious services, as in Heb. x. 32. If those addressed were still suffering under severe persecutions we should have heard less of their petty rivalries and worldly scheming. As to the position of St. James in the Church of Jerusalem, the first intimation we have of it is in Gal. i. 18, where St. Paul mentions that he saw him and St. Peter on his visit to Jerusalem three years after his conversion. A more certain proof of it may be found in Peter's message, sent to him on the occasion of his escape from prison in 44 A.D. (Acts xii. 17). Lastly the picture given of the Church is not that of one just founded. A circular letter cannot of course take note of the special circumstances of each individual congregation, and it is quite possible and even probable that some of those addressed may have only lately received the Gospel, but it is evident that the majority must have been Christians of some years' standing. Taking into account these various considerations we may perhaps name the year 40 A.D., as the earliest, and 50 A.D.[1] as the latest, at which the Epistle could have been written.

The prevailing view at the present time is in favour of an early date. This is pretty much the conclusion which has been arrived at by the majority of recent editors and others who have treated of the date of the Epistle; so that we may say that it is now generally recognized as being the earliest portion of the New Testament. This is the view of Schneckenburger (*Annot.* p. 138, *Beiträge* 200 ff.), Neander (*Planting of the Christian Church*, Eng. tr. 1842), Von Hofmann, Huther, Beyschlag (*Comm.* and *Theol. Stud. u. Krit.* for 1874), Erdmann, Schegg, Alford, Plumptre, Ritschl (*Altkatholische Kirche* ed. 2), Weiss (*Einleitung*, 1886, p. 706 foll.), P. Ewald (*Hauptproblem*, 1890), Mangold's edition of Bleek's *Einleitung*, 1886, pp. 706, 713, Lechler, *Apostolic and Post-Apostolic Times* (Eng. tr. 1886, vol. i. 290). I venture to

[1] Or 46, if we accept Harnack's chronology.

think that the grounds for this conclusion have been considerably strengthened by the minute comparison made in a previous Chapter, between the parallel passages in St. James and in the Epistle to the Romans and the First Epistle of St. Peter. If I am not greatly mistaken, that comparison has proved not only that St. James has not copied from the other Epistles, but that these show distinct traces of having been written with reference to his Epistle. The strength however of the general argument is not to be measured by the strength of any one line of proof, however irrefragable we may deem it, but by the cumulative force of many converging probabilities. After having given many years' study to the subject, I am convinced that the more closely it is examined, the more will this hypothesis of the priority of our Epistle be found to meet all difficulties, and explain all the facts of the case.

Examination of the grounds on which it has been assigned to the close of St. James's life.

Those who take a different view suppose that it was either written by St. James towards the close of his life, or that it is a forgery from the hand either of an Ebionite or of a Christian Essene, whether in the first or second century. The former view is maintained by Kern (ed. 2), Wiesinger, Woldemar Schmidt, Bruno Brückner, Wordsworth, and Farrar (*Early Days of Christianity*, p. 310 foll.).

(1) 'Use of the name "Christ" without the article.'

The reasons assigned by the last-mentioned writer are (1) 'the prevalence of the name of Christ, instead of the title the Christ.' But the name Christ never occurs by itself in this Epistle, but only in the phrase Ἰησοῦς Χριστός, which is found without the article in every book of the New Testament, except the Gospel of St. Luke and the Third Epistle of St. John; whereas the phrase Ἰησοῦς ὁ Χριστός or ὁ Χριστὸς Ἰησοῦς occurs nowhere, except in the Acts (four times) and once in Coloss. ii. 6.

(2) 'Condition of the churches addressed.'

A second argument is 'the condition and wide dissemination of the churches to which it is addressed,' which make it necessary to assume that 'many years had elapsed since the day of Pentecost.' As to this, there is nothing to suggest the wide dissemination of the churches to which it is addressed, beyond the phrase 'The Twelve Tribes of the Diaspora,' which is no doubt wide enough in conception, but defines nothing as to the actual extent of country occupied. It is consistent with two copies sent, say, to Antioch and to Damascus, or with one hundred copies distributed throughout the East. All that it implies is that the advice contained in the letter is in the opinion of the writer suitable for all or any Jews of the Dispersion. The argument derived from the 'condition of the churches' is more fully stated in Davidson's *Introduction* (1894) I. 279, 'Distinctions of places in Christian churches, an ambitious love of preeminence, an unworthy partiality for the rich, are inconsistent with an early period.' 'Amid the worldly views and arrangements which prevailed in these Christian assemblies early Christian love had grown cold.'

There is no ground for attributing an ideal perfection to the primitive Christians.

I have only two faults to find with this argument. It is contradicted, first, by all we know of the facts of the case, and, secondly, by general experience. All the evidence we have as to the state of the early Church from the baptism of Christ to the last record in the Acts is opposed to these dreams of an ideal perfection. It is unnecessary to refer to 'the ambitious love of preeminence,' the faithlessness, the narrowness, which marked even the greatest of the Apostles during our Lord's lifetime. Let us start with the day of Pentecost. Take the early chapters of the Acts; how long did the state of things described in the fourth chapter continue? How long could it be said that the multitude of them that believed were of one heart and one soul and had all things in common? In the very next chapter we find Ananias and Sapphira lying to the Holy Ghost: in the sixth chapter the Grecian Jews murmur against the Hebrews because their widows were neglected in the daily visitation: in the eighth chapter Simon wishes to purchase spiritual gifts with money: in the fifteenth chapter we read of the jealousy of the Jews towards the Gentiles, which almost proved fatal to the infant Church: in the nineteenth Paul meets with disciples who had not so much as heard 'whether there be any Holy Ghost': in the twentieth he warns the elders of the Church at Ephesus that after his departure 'grievous wolves shall enter in, yea, from among your own selves shall men arise speaking perverse things to draw away the disciples after them': in the twenty-first it seems that Christian Jews joined with others who were zealous for the law, in the attempt to kill Paul. If we turn to the Epistles, we find in Rom. ii. and xiv. many of the faults condemned by St. James. The Corinthians within five years of their conversion are broken up by schisms: they are as much given to vainglory and jealousy and strife and censorious judgments as the churches to which St. James writes. They are more addicted to sins of the flesh; they indulge to excess even when they meet together for the Lord's Supper; they go to law one with another in the courts of the heathen; their religious meetings are a scene of confusion and disorder from each man's eagerness to get a hearing; they are falling back into idolatry; they even dispute the authority of their spiritual father and deny his apostleship. So the Galatians within ten years of their conversion have departed from the Gospel which Paul preached, and have to be sternly warned against the works of the flesh. Even in his earliest Epistle written to the Thessalonians shortly after their conversion, he bids them be at peace among themselves, admonish the disorderly, encourage the faint-hearted, quench not the Spirit, despise not prophesyings. The Epistles to the Seven Churches in the Apocalypse, the first of St. John, the second of St. Peter, that of St. Jude and that to the Hebrews, give an even less satisfactory picture of the Christian Church than the Epistle of St. James does.

So far as St. Paul himself is concerned, his later Epistles, such as those to the Philippians and Ephesians, describe a nearer approach to a perfect state of things in the churches addressed than is to be found in his earlier Epistles. And this, of course, is what we should naturally expect. A church just converted from Judaism or heathenism will not at once lose the traces of its former condition. The Pharisee, who loved the chief seat in the synagogue and to be called of men Rabbi, will not on the moment of conversion lose his liking for these things, any more than the Corinthian will at once learn reverence and purity. Christian perfection is a plant of slow growth. I have already alluded to the way in which the Jews of the Diaspora would probably have received the Gospel. Some would have been powerfully affected by hearing St. Peter preach on the day of Pentecost; others might have been baptized by a passing evangelist. To judge of the probable effect, let us take a similar case in the present day. Place before your mind the most successful of modern missions to the heathen, or of revivals at home. Is any one so sanguine as to imagine that congregations thus founded will be at once freed from the dangers of ambition and worldliness for years to come? If there is such a person, let me recommend to him a study of the life of Fox or Wesley, or of any honest missionary journal.

(3) 'Waning belief in the nearness of the Second Coming.'

A third argument is 'the sense of delay in the Second Coming,' for which reference is made to ch. v. 7, 8: 'Be patient, therefore, brethren,...for the Coming of the Lord is at hand.' I have myself referred to the same passage, as proving that the writer shared the belief expressed by St. Paul in his earlier Epistles as to the immediate Coming of the Lord. It is in strong contrast with the language used in 2 Peter iii. 3, 8: 'Knowing this, that in the last times mockers shall come...saying Where is the promise of his coming? for from the days that the fathers fell asleep all things continue as they were from the beginning of the creation': 'But forget not this one thing, beloved, that one day is with the Lord as a thousand years, and a thousand years as one day.' It seems to me that the words of St. James, while they prove his own expectation of the speedy appearance of the Lord, do not at all disprove the same expectation on the part of those whom he addresses. A man might easily be impatient under continued ill-treatment, even though he believed, as an abstract dogma, that the Judge was soon to appear. St. James urges him to make it a living truth, affecting his daily practice. A fourth argument is that founded on the discussion about faith and works, which, in Dean Farrar's opinion, 'finds its most reasonable explanation in the supposition that he is striving to remove the dangerous inferences to which St. Paul's doctrine of justification by faith was liable.' The difficulty as to the absence of any reference to the subject debated in the Council of Jerusalem is got over by the assumption that 'the circumcision question was speedily forgotten.' On these points I have already said all that I think necessary.[1]

Arguments of Dr. Davidson to prove that it was written by an anonymous Ebionite shortly before the fall of Jerusalem.

I turn now to other arguments adduced by Dr. Davidson. He is of opinion that 'the direction to send for the elders of the Church, and their use of oil with the prayer of faith, savours of a post-apostolic time.' Why? The Apostles made use of oil in healing the sick (Mark vi. 13), and any Jewish community would be under the direction of elders. But 'the office of elder was originally confined to the Church's outer guidance,' and here 'the office of eldership is separated from the members of the Church, a thing which did not exist in primitive Christianity.' The meaning is not very clearly expressed. If certain members of the Church were chosen to hold the office of elder, they were *ipso facto* separated from the other members of the Church; and spiritual functions are certainly implied in 1 Thess. v. 12-14, 1 Pet. v. 2, and in Acts xx. 17 and 28. The passage in St. James seems to imply an earlier condition of things, for he there enjoins *mutual* confession and prayer.

[1] Compare the earlier paragraphs of this chapter and pp. lxxxix to xciii.

Dr. Davidson goes on to deny the authenticity of the Epistle on the ground (1) that the acquaintance which it shows with St. Paul's Epistles, especially those to the Romans and Galatians, and, above all, its polemic aspect towards the doctrine of justification by faith alone, assign it to a post-apostolic period. [This argument has, of course, no weight with those who consider that this Epistle was written before those of St. Paul, and who do not therefore recognize any polemic aspect towards St. Paul's doctrine. I have shown, in ch. iv., that St. James is attacking that most ancient of all religious heresies, which puts words and professions in the place of deeds and conduct.] (2) 'The style of writing is too good for James.' Something has been said on this point already in pp. xli. and xlii., and more will be said shortly in the chapter on the Language of the Epistle. (3) 'It is not likely that James, the Lord's brother, would have directly opposed Paul's doctrine...That he should have written against it argues a want of respect for the Apostle of the Gentiles incompatible with James's position.' Quite true; but of no force against those who deny the polemic aspect. (4)[1] 'The essential doctrines of Christianity are wanting in the Epistle...Had James written it, we should naturally expect some mention of Christ's resurrection at least...On the other hand, the Mosaic law, circumcision, &c., are passed over, and the royal law of liberty is exalted...The writer had therefore attained to a subjective standpoint beyond James; to ideas of Christian liberty like the Pauline...Although the statement of Christian doctrines is incomplete as well as imperfect, and the writer's point of view more Jewish than Christian, he occupies a spiritual stage in Jewish Christianity which James the Just scarcely reached.' It might be well if the writer of these confused and self-contradictory sentences would take the trouble carefully to compare the teaching of the Sermon on the Mount with that of St. James, and consider how far his remarks are applicable to the former. (5) 'The letter is professedly addressed to all Jewish-Christians out of Palestine. But were there churches composed of such members?...Churches were of a mixed character except in Palestine. Wiesinger therefore may well ask, Where shall we look for the Jewish-Christians out of Palestine which will satisfy the requirements of the Epistle?—a question not answered by reference to Acts ii. 5-11, xi. 91, &c.,

[1] This argument has disappeared from the last edition (1894), but I have allowed my remarks to stand, as the general thread of the discussion seems to me to be still marked by the same inconsistency as that on which I have commented above.

because the passages are far from implying the extensive establishment of Jewish-Christian churches immediately after Pentecost. The earliest history contains no clear trace of such churches widely scattered through the lands.' In answer we may say that undoubtedly there must have been such churches previously to the admission of Gentiles into the Church, otherwise than as proselytes. It was to persecute such a church that Saul went to Damascus with authority from the high priest. Such were all churches founded before the conversion of Cornelius, and the great majority of churches founded before 51, except those founded by St. Paul. There is just as little point in Dr. Davidson's further remark that 'the writer does not convey the impression that his knowledge of their condition was minute or specific, for his language is general, such as a later author, writing in his name, would employ.' Of course a circular letter cannot deal with personal relations. Dr. Davidson then states his own conclusion that it was written after James's death, in his name, by a moderate Ebionite, shortly before the destruction of Jerusalem.[1] One does not quite see why the moderate Ebionite should have been capable of writing in 68 the letter which we have been just told it was impossible for St. James to have written six years before. If the moderate Ebionite 'occupied a spiritual stage which James the Just hardly reached,' should we not 'naturally expect some mention of Christ's resurrection at least'? But these men in buckram, who are always at the disposal of our modern critics, are wonderfully Protean in their characteristics as in their powers.

Von Soden's arguments against the genuineness of the Epistle are opposed to facts.

Let us turn, however, from the halting and hesitating disciple to the uncompromising idealism and superiority to fact of the German masters, to whose guidance he has surrendered himself. We may take Von Soden as one of the latest representatives of the school. Here is a summary of his Introduction to our Epistle, so far as it relates to its date and authenticity, which is contained in the *Hand-Kommentar zum N.T.*, brought out under the direction of Professors Holtzmann, Lipsius, and others, in 1890:—

In thought and expression there is considerable resemblance between our epistle and the writings of Clement of Rome, and especially of Hermas. There is however no reason to suppose any literary connexion between them. They resemble one another, simply because they were produced under the same con-

---

[1] In his last edition Dr. Davidson holds that it was written about A.D. 90.

ditions. This view is confirmed by the fact that no trace of our epistle is to be found throughout the 2nd century. Hegesippus knows nothing of an epistle of James. The supposed reminiscences in Clement of Alexandria are just as likely to be reminiscences of Philo or Peter or Clement of Rome. Origen is the first to mention the epistle, without however accepting its genuineness, as is evident from his comment on Matthew xiii. 55, in which he gives some account of the Lord's brothers and refers to the epistle of Jude, but not to that of James.

What is to be said when people, who ought to know better, make statements of this sort? I can only refer my readers to my chapter on the External Evidence for the Authenticity of the Epistle, and ask whether the quotations there given from Clement of Rome and others are not sufficient evidence that our Epistle was known in the first century; whether the quotations from Ignatius, Polycarp, Justin Martyr, the Ep. ad Diognetum, Irenaeus, above all Hermas, are not such as to prove that our Epistle was studied by these writers in the second century; whether any one with the smallest particle of historical sense or literary feeling could for a moment dream that the author of the Shepherd was prior to, or contemporary with, the writer of our Epistle; whether the fact that Origen, having other things of more interest to tell about St. James, omits to mention that he wrote this Epistle (as he also omits to mention that he presided over the Council at Jerusalem), while he mentions the Epistle of St. Jude, because about St. Jude he has nothing else to tell—whether, I say, this fact gives the slightest ground for supposing that Origen doubted the authority of an Epistle, which he over and over again cites as Scripture, and as written by James, the brother of the Lord.

The Epistle was well known to many writers of the second century;

Let us hear next what Von Soden has to say on the relation of our Epistle to other books of the New Testament.

The writer is acquainted with the epistle to the Romans and the first epistle to the Corinthians. The tone is similar to that in the Hebrews, though there is no literary connexion between them. On the other hand it is partly copied from the 1st of Peter. The isolated resemblances to the Apocalypse prove nothing. It is closely connected with the Gospel and Acts of Luke, having the same Ebionite leaning, and giving the words of Christ in the same form, while there seems no trace of the special tradition of Matthew, such as we find in section v. 17–vi. 13 of his Gospel (except for the injunction as to swearing). There is however no direct copying from the Gospels. With the writings of John there is no kind of connexion. The writer is acquainted with the LXX., but betrays no knowledge of the Hebrew text of the Old Testament. He is well acquainted with the sapiential books of the Apocrypha and with Philo. There are also signs of his having some knowledge of Greek literature.

and it is not copied from other books of the N.T.

Here too the conclusions arrived at seem to me entirely at variance with the facts, as I think will be apparent to any one who will ponder what has been said in my chapter on the relation of the Epistle to Contemporary Writings. Some may be surprised to hear that Marcion's favourite gospel is distinguished by Ebionite leanings.[1] It is true however that in some cases, not by any means the majority, the references to the words of Christ which occur in our Epistle approach more nearly to the form in which they are given by St. Luke, than to the form in which they are given by St. Matthew. The quotations in my fourth chapter will show that it is quite a mistake to speak of section v. 17—vi. 13 in the latter, or of the Gospel and Epistles of St. John, as affording no parallels to St. James. Nor is it true that the Epistle betrays no knowledge of the Hebrew. Compare my note on v. 20, where the quotation from Prov. x. 12 has no resemblance to the rendering of the LXX.

The next paragraph of Von Soden treats of the Readers for whom the Epistle was intended. He argues that the address to the Twelve Tribes of the Dispersion is entirely misleading, and possibly a later insertion, as Harnack has suggested. His reasons are as follows:

Von Soden finds nothing Judaic in the Epistle.

Nothing in the letter suggests Jewish readers. No reference is made to the Temple, the Worship, the Law. Instead of this, the one supreme rule of life, by obedience to which man receives the blessing of salvation, is the implanted word, which is styled the perfect law of liberty. But there is no attempt to connect this law with the teaching of the Old Testament; and the prescribed Jewish ritual is not argued against, but simply ignored. It is impossible that monotheism could have been the distinctive article of faith with Jewish Christians: impossible that they could have magnified this faith to the depreciation of works. Nor could works with them ever mean works of love as distinguished from works of the law. [Then follows the argument, already noticed, as to the impossibility of discovering any purely Jewish church in the Diaspora. I have shown above that, previous to the Council of Jerusalem, the great majority of churches must have been of this type.] Von Soden well draws out the impossibility of the burning question, of the admission of Gen-

---

[1] Apparently the only ground for this strange assumption is that on two occasions St. Luke records our Lord's teaching in its strong paradoxical form, without the explanatory additions by which it is qualified elsewhere. Thus in Luke vi. 20 we read *μακάριοι οἱ πτωχοί*, but in Matt. v. 3 we have the addition *τῷ πνεύματι*; in Luke xviii. 25 we have nothing to soften the statement 'It is easier for a camel to go through the eye of a needle than for a rich man to enter into the kingdom of God,' but in Mark x. 24 the word 'rich' is explained by 'them that trust in riches.' But it is a mere misuse of words to characterize as Ebionism even an ascetic admiration of poverty. The essence of Ebionism is of course the rejection of the divinity of Christ, and the belief in the permanent obligation of the Jewish ceremonial, with which was connected a high esteem for the Gospel of St. Matthew, and a strong aversion to St. Paul's writings.

tiles into the Church, being ignored in an epistle addressed to the Diaspora (*if written after this date*). He gives us again the old argument, answered above, that we cannot conceive first love cooling down, say, in a period of ten years. He considers that it was written at a time of degeneracy, when the Jewish element in the Church had lost all significance; that perhaps the title may be after all genuine, because Christians had then learnt to regard themselves as the true Israel, strangers and pilgrims in the world, waiting for the hour of their Lord's appearing. If it had been really intended for Jews, there must have been more of local colouring. The instances alleged for this local colouring are not exclusively applicable to Jews.

Its teaching as to the value of ritual and orthodox belief is just what might be expected from St. James writing to Jews;

The only argument here which seems to call for examination is founded on the fact that the Jewish Christians are charged with laying too much stress, not on their ritual (the works of the law), but on their orthodox belief in one God. No doubt there is a striking difference between the language of St. James and the language of St. Paul on this point; a difference entirely in accordance with all we know of the two men. St. James, living among Jews, himself practising the Jewish ritual, saw no objection to Jewish Christians continuing their ritual observances, as long as they ascribed no merit to them. He warns his readers, however, not to suppose that the outward rite could commend them to God (i. 27): the religious service which God approved consisted in charity and unworldliness. Is not this perfectly natural teaching from a Jewish apostle to Jewish believers, who would at once recognize it as a re-publication of the teaching of Isaiah and Micah on the same subject? Does then the improbability consist in the assumption that Jewish Christians were in danger of trusting in their orthodox monotheism to the neglect of the perfect law of love? It is plain at any rate that if there were any people who were likely to pride themselves on this belief, they must have been Jews by birth, not Gentiles. Moreover we know as a matter of fact that Jews did pride themselves just on this point, did believe that their orthodoxy placed them on a pinnacle above all other people, and was of itself efficient to salvation; compare the words of Justin spoken to a Jew (*Tryph.* p. 370 D), 'You and others like you (*i.e.* Judaizing Christians) deceive yourselves with words, saying that, though you should be sinners, yet because you know God, the Lord will not impute sin to you,' and see Lightfoot, *Gal.* pp. 154–164, and the quotations in my note on ii. 19. In the same way they are rebuked by John the Baptist and by our Lord for priding themselves on their descent from Abraham (Matt. iii. 8, 9, vii. 21–23, Luke xiii. 24–30). It would be just as rational to deny that the sapiential books of the Bible and Apocrypha were written for Jews by Jews, as to deny this of the Epistle of St. James.

so too its teaching as to the Law.

To go now a little more into detail, Von Soden tells us that nothing is said of the Temple, the Worship, the Law. We have seen that with regard to worship, a most important rule is laid down, which implies the insignificance of the Mosaic ritual no less than our Lord's words 'neither in this mountain nor yet at Jerusalem.' As to the Temple, one does not quite see how it could be introduced in a letter to Jews residing abroad, unless it were to urge them to send contributions more regularly or to come up more frequently to Jerusalem. But trivial details of this sort would be entirely out of place in the exhortations of one who may be best described as the living embodiment of the Sermon on the Mount. As to the Law, how can it be said to be ignored, when there is a distinct reference to the common Jewish error, that you might pick and choose your favourite commandment and confine your attention to that: 'Whoever offends in a single point is guilty of the whole law; for he that said Thou shalt not commit adultery, said also Thou shalt not kill'? and when in iv. 11 the Law appears as the representative of the Lawgiver and Judge? This conception of the Law, as the expression of the mind and will of God, leads at once to its being regarded as a Law of Liberty, the guiding principle of life, not the mere written statute. Von Soden asks why St. James does not point out that such a Law of Liberty was already recognized in the Old Testament. The answer is that it was unnecessary, because the very phrase would naturally recall to the minds of his Jewish readers similar expressions in the Old Testament (see note on i. 25), and would also be felt to be in entire accordance with the ethical teaching of Christ, as contained in what we know as the Sermon on the Mount, and probably in the earliest summaries provided for the use of believers.

Meaning of the term 'works' in the Epistle.

Lastly Von Soden asserts that Jewish Christians would never limit the sense of *ἔργα* to 'works of love' but would necessarily include in it St. Paul's 'works of the law.' In the actual passage in question (ii. 14–26) we need not limit *ἔργα* to works of love, strictly speaking: the sacrifice of Isaac (ii. 21) could hardly be described as such. They are *ἔργα καλά* in the widest sense; though they exhibit no doubt the joint action of faith and love, if there is any meaning in the illustration from almsgiving contained in vv. 15, 16, and any reference to the royal law of ver. 8, or to the pattern of pure religion depicted in i. 27. Is this then an unusual sense of the word *ἔργον* in the New Testament? Does it usually include a reference to strict ceremonial observance? Would it be naturally understood by Jews to include this? In John viii. 39 the works of Abraham (*i.e.* his hospitality &c., Gen. xviii.) are contrasted with the murderous intentions of the Jews; in Apoc. xx. 12 we read that the dead will be judged *κατὰ τὰ ἔργα αὐτῶν*, meaning of course the same as *κατὰ τὴν πρᾶξιν αὐτοῦ* in Matt. xvi. 27, which is explained of works of love in Matt. xxv. 34-46. So over and over again we find in the Apocalypse *οἶδα τὰ ἔργα σου*, referring, as the context shows, to moral conduct. St. Paul, writing after St. James, finds it necessary to distinguish the *ἔργα πίστεως* and the *ἔργα ἀγάπης*, the natural fruits of faith and love, from the *ἔργα νόμου*, dead works done from slavish obedience to an external law.

Does St. James ignore the Resurrection?

Again Von Soden, like his school in general, exaggerates the negative side of the Epistle: the writer, he says, ignores the Resurrection. What does he make of the phrase *τῆς δόξης* in ii. 1? This surely involves the belief in the Resurrection and Ascension and even in the Divinity of Christ.

Von Soden's theory that it was written in the time of Domitian is inconsistent with the modest heading.

The final result of his investigation is that the Epistle was written at Rome during the reign of Domitian to Christians generally. Beyschlag well asks, If so, what possible inducement was there for the forger, who was certainly no sectarian, like the author of the Clementines, but an orthodox believer, to inscribe his letter with the name of James, rather than of Peter? and if he was determined to choose James, what possible motive could he have for using the modest description 'servant' instead of 'brother' of the Lord Jesus Christ?

W. Brückner's theory, that it was copied from 1 Peter and therefore cannot have been written before Hadrian.

I will now take the most recent statement of the theory that the Epistle was written in the second century. This is contained in W. Brückner's *Die chronologische Reihenfolge der Neutestamentlichen Briefe*, Haarlem, 1890.

According to his view the only epistles written during the first century were those to the Romans, Corinthians, Galatians, Philemon, Philippians, Hebrews, and the 1st to the Thessalonians. The first epistle of Peter was written during the persecution under Trajan. As our epistle borrows from it and shows no traces of being written under stress of persecution, the latter cannot be assigned to an earlier period than the reign of Hadrian. The priority of Peter to James is proved as follows. The topics common to both epistles are better expressed and more logically handled, the phrases used are more exact and appropriate in the former than in the latter. For instance the exhortation to rejoice in tribulation is common to both; but in Peter we see that there is real occasion for it; those whom he addresses are actually in the midst of a fiery trial, suffering for righteousness' sake (iii. 14, iv. 12); this persecution is the work of the devil whom they resist by their patient endurance (v. 8, 9); they are bidden to exult, not in their trial itself, but in the glory which is to follow, the salvation ready to be revealed in the last time (i. 5, iv. 13); they are encouraged by the reminder of their high calling (i. 3, ii. 9, 20, 21, iii. 14, &c.), by the example of Christ whose sufferings they share (ii. 21, iii. 18, iv. 13), and by the hope of the promised reward (i. 4, 7). The tone of the epistle is throughout that of hopefulness, and the exultant joy in tribulation is only the issue and climax of this hopefulness. In James it is just the reverse: he borrows the phrase 'manifold temptation,' but there is no special appropriateness in it; those whom he addresses are not suffering persecution from the heathen: so too he borrows the phrase 'resist the devil,' but this is not connected with the general thought of trial; he bids them rejoice in tribulation, but he gives no reason for their doing so; he has not prepared the way for it by the spirit-stirring appeals and encouragements of Peter; if he refers to the future it is only to remind them of the terrible coming of the Judge.

is founded on a superficial and misleading comparison between the two Epistles, in regard (1) to the exhortation to rejoice in trials,

Now to examine this: could any one imagine from Brückner's description that St. James grounds his exhortation to rejoice, on the fact that trial works endurance, and endurance Christian perfection (i. 2—4)? could he imagine that it is James who says, he who endures trial will receive the crown of life, the kingdom promised to all that love God (i. 12, ii. 5)? that it is James who speaks of the profession of Christianity as in itself a patent of nobility (i. 9), and refers to the fact of Christ's being the glory of Christians as annihilating all earthly distinctions (ii. 1)? It is no doubt true that he puts in the fore-front of his Epistle the high-toned, uncompromising summons to rise superior to human weakness, and rejoice in what the world thinks misery. I have elsewhere spoken of this as an instance of the stoicism of St. James, and pointed out how the same demand is softened down by the gentler and more sympathetic Apostle. But it is not more stoical than it is Christ-like: it is a reminiscence, like so much besides, of the actual words of his divine Brother, 'Blessed are ye that weep now; blessed are ye when men shall hate you, and separate you from their company, and cast out your name as evil for the Son of man's sake; rejoice ye in that day and leap for joy.' If Christ did not shrink from this sublime paradox, if paradox was one of the most efficient weapons used by Him as well as by older reformers, by Socrates and the Stoics, to shake men out of their slumbers and rouse them to aim at a new and higher ideal, why are we to dispute St. James's right to use it, as if it could only be ascribed to an unintelligent repetition of St. Peter's language? If Brückner had paid a little more attention to our Epistle he would have seen that one of its most marked characteristics is the commencement of each paragraph by a statement of the practical maxim, usually a precept or an interrogation, which it is intended to enforce; e.g. i. 19 contains the maxim, 'Let each be swift to hear, slow to speak, and slow to wrath,' which is explained and illustrated in vv. 20—27; the injunction against respect of persons in ii. 1 is explained and illustrated in vv. 2—10; the maxim that faith without works is valueless in ii. 14 is explained and illustrated in vv. 15—26, &c. Again, it is true that there is no reference in our Epistle to persecutions from the heathen; but, if the readers are liable to be dragged before the Jewish courts on a charge of Christianity by their unbelieving countrymen (ii. 6, 7); if they are oppressed by their rich neighbours, who withhold their wages and threaten their life (v. 4—6); it is surely a little absurd to deny that they are *ἐν ποικίλοις πειρασμοῖς*. It is true again that the devil is not referred to as the cause of these outward *πειρασμοί*, but rather as the god of this world, the inspirer of a false wisdom, the instigator of all the evil wrought by means of the tongue (iv. 4—7, iii. 6, 15); which some may perhaps consider to be both a deeper and a wider conception of diabolic activity than that in the parallel passage of St. Peter.

Brückner next compares James i. 18, 21 with 1 Pet. i. 23, ii. 1. The general conception in both is the same, that Christians are born again through the instrumentality of the Word of God; and the practical inference the same, to cast away all that might hinder the reception of the Word; but while all is natural and straightforward in Peter, James shows that he copies without understanding, by his use of the term *ἔμφυτον*. In ver. 18 he had said that God *ἀπεκύησεν ἡμᾶς λόγῳ ἀληθείας*, in ver. 21 he says *δέξασθε τὸν ἔμφυτον λόγον*, but how can we receive what has been already engrafted? (2) the doctrine of regeneration,

This is a criticism founded simply on a misapprehension of the meaning of a term, as to which see my note *in loco* and also (for the force of these verbals in -*τος*) on *ἀπείραστος* i. 13.

The next point raised is, that in 1 Pet. v. 1–11 there is a better logical connexion than in the parallel passage James iv. 6–10, and that the former is therefore the original. The general drift in Peter is as follows:—(vv. 1–4) the elders are admonished to take charge of the flock of Christ, not as having dominion over them, but as setting them an example: by so doing they will receive from the chief Shepherd, on his appearing, the crown of glory which fadeth not away: (vv. 5–7) the admonition is extended to others, 'Likewise ye younger be subject unto the elder; yea, all of you gird yourselves with humility to serve one another, for God resisteth the proud, but (3) the admonition to resist the devil, giveth grace to the humble: humble yourselves therefore under the mighty hand of God, that he may exalt you in due time, casting all your care upon him because he careth for you. (vv. 8–10) Be sober, be watchful; your adversary, the devil, as a roaring lion, walketh about, seeking whom he may devour; whom withstand, steadfast in the faith, knowing that the same sufferings are accomplished in your brethren who are in the world; and the God of all grace who called you unto His eternal glory in Christ, after that ye have suffered a little while, shall Himself perfect, stablish, strengthen you.'

The order of thought here is the following: the elder are not to lord it over the younger; the younger are to be subject to the elder, or rather all are to serve one another, girding themselves with humility. [So far humility is an attitude of man towards man: in what follows it is the attitude of man towards God.] God resists the proud, but gives grace to the humble: if we humble ourselves before him, he will exalt us in due time. It would seem from the following clause that this exaltation refers, in the first place, to the deliverance from temporal anxieties. The devil appears in ver. 8 as the cause of these anxieties: he seeks to terrify the Christians into apostasy; but God will stablish and strengthen them after a short period of suffering. It can hardly be said that the logical connexion is very strict in these verses. The admonition to the elders has little to do with withstanding the devil, as the cause of their present anxieties; and humility towards man does not seem quite the same thing as humility towards God.

Now take the parallel passage in James: (iv. 1-3) quarrels come from unsatisfied lusts; you are unsatisfied, because you either do not ask of God, or you ask in a worldly spirit; (ver. 4) the friendship of the world is enmity with God; whoever seeks the world's friendship, thereby becomes the enemy of God; (vv. 5-10) the Spirit of God within us jealously demands the possession of our whole heart, but gives all the more grace (in consequence of that jealousy). Hence the Scripture says, 'God resists the proud (i.e. the worldly), but gives grace to the humble.' Be subject therefore to God, and withstand the devil (the prince of this world), and he will flee from you. Draw nigh to God and he will draw nigh to you. Repent, and humble yourselves in the sight of God, and he will exalt you.

I think no careful reader can fail to see that Brückner has exactly reversed the truth, and that the order of thought is much more logical here than in St. Peter. All falls naturally under the heading 'loyalty to God.' The word 'humility' is used throughout in reference to our attitude towards God. Quarrels arise from an unchastened desire for worldly good. We cannot have peace either in ourselves or with our neighbours until we submit ourselves unreservedly to God, who resists those that aim at worldly success and make a god of self, but gives grace to those that surrender up their wills to His. He who tempted Eve tempts us also to set up our will against God's will; but, if we refuse to listen, the tempter flies; while any attempt on our part to draw near to God brings Him near to us. The meaning of 'exaltation,' *ὑψώσει*, in the 10th verse is explained by *τῷ ὕψει* in i. 9. It refers to no outward prosperity, but to the moral dignity which belongs to him who has made God his portion.

(4) the common quotations,

Brückner refers, as I have done, to the common quotations contained in the two Epistles. I pointed out that it was characteristic of St. James to quote carelessly, of St. Peter to quote accurately; that the former uses a biblical phrase without reference to its original context, while the latter holds fast to the original context. To me this seemed to favour the supposition that St. Peter was the copyist. Brückner takes the reverse view. I leave it to each man's common-sense to say which is right, after he has compared the contexts of the quotations in the two Epistles.

(5) the use of two phrases in St. James which have to be explained from St. Peter.

His next point is that *τὸ καλὸν ὄνομα* in James ii. 7 has to be explained from 1 Pet. iv. 14–16 *εἰ ὀνειδίζεσθε ἐν ὀνόματι Χριστοῦ μακάριοι...εἰ δὲ ὡς Χριστιανὸς (πάσχει), μὴ αἰσχυνέσθω, δοξαζέτω δὲ τὸν Θεὸν ἐν τῷ ὀνόματι τούτῳ*. This is a similar case to the preceding. In my view it exhibits St. Peter, as usual, filling up the bare outline of St. James. That the phrase needs no explanation is plain from the parallel passages quoted in my notes *in loco* and on v. 14 *ἐν τῷ ὀνόματι*.

Lastly he thinks that the *πρὸ πάντων* of James v. 12 has been transferred from its more appropriate context in 1 Pet. iv. 8. In my note on v. 12 I have pointed out that *πρὸ πάντων* must be understood in reference to other manifestations of an impatient spirit, and not as exalting the abstaining from oaths above all other Christian duties. Probably it was a common phrase with the writer. If it was suggested, as I believe, to St. Peter by his acquaintance with our Epistle, he would naturally employ it of a matter of more general importance.

Brückner's conclusion is that the Epistle was forged by an Essene living at Rome in the latter half of the second century.

In a later chapter of the same volume Brückner deals with the Epistles which he assigns to the second century as having been written after the 1st epistle of Peter. These are the second to the Thessalonians, and those to the Colossians and Ephesians, belonging to the earlier half of the century; and secondly, the Pastoral Epistles, James, Jude, the second of Peter, and those of John, which he considers to have been written subsequently to 150 A.D. With regard to our Epistle he refers to what he has said before, as to its being copied from 1 Pet. and cites parallels from Romans, Corinthians, Hebrews, Apocalypse and the Gospel of St. Matthew to show that it was written after these. In reply to Beyschlag he asserts that the Judaizing tone of the Epistle is not the naïve Judaism of an early Jewish Christian writer, but that it implies a late stage of the doctrinal development, inasmuch as it attacks Paulinism as the seed of an existing Gnosticism. The writer betrays his Essene tendency by his prohibition of swearing, his contempt for riches, his dislike of trade, warning against sins of the tongue, high esteem of poverty, &c. He takes the pseudonym of James, as a contemporary had taken that of Peter; because the traditional reputation of the ascetic president of the Church of Jerusalem seemed likely to give most authority to his teaching. Partly in order to mark his own opposition to all that was characteristic of Paul, partly to imitate the style of James, he makes use of the simple salutation χαίρειν, which he found in a circular ascribed to him in the Acts. The address to the Twelve Tribes of the Diaspora cannot be taken literally. The true address reveals itself in the phrase 'your synagogue' (ii. 2), by which we are in all probability to understand a little conventicle of Essene Christians at Rome. The phrase 'Diaspora' denotes similar scattered conventicles, in which alone 'the true Israel,' 'the poor,' are to be found. By 'the rich,' who occasionally drop into their conventicles and so cruelly oppress and persecute the brethren, is meant Christians outside of the conventicle. All the warnings of the epistle are meant to preserve this little flock from the snares of Paulinism.

Pfleiderer's general view of the development of post-Pauline Christianity.

It is difficult for Englishmen to treat these baseless vagaries with becoming seriousness. To us they at once suggest the great Shakespearian Cryptogram, or somebody's attempt to prove that the *Annals* of Tacitus were written by a monk of the Middle Ages. But that we may not be too hasty in assuming that the new criticism has nothing more solid to offer us, we will turn now to a better known name, and examine what Pfleiderer has to tell us in his *Urchristenthum*, which is an expansion of the Hibbert Lectures delivered by him in 1885.

He distinguishes two lines of development in post-Pauline Christianity. The one, which he calls Christian Hellenism, is represented by the epistle to the Hebrews, which he assigns to the end of the 1st century, the first epistle of Clement (between 100 and 120 A.D.), the first of Peter (not earlier than Trajan), that of Barnabas (between 120 and 125 A.D.), the epistle to the Colossians and Ephesians and the Gospel of John (about 140 A.D.). The other, which he ealls Antignostic Hellenism, marks the period of the Antonines. It is again subdivided into Catholicized Hellenism and Catholicized Paulinism (p. 845). The former branch is represented by the Johannean and the Pastoral epistles, the epistle of Polycarp to the Philippians, which with Volkmar's expurgations may be regarded as a fairly genuine piece, the Ignatian epistles, together with that of Jude and the second of Peter. The latter branch is represented by the second epistle of Clement, the Shepherd of Hermas, written about the same time as the Gospel of Matthew (that is, towards the middle of the 2nd century), the epistle of James and the Didaché, which last Pfleiderer considers to be later than Hermas and possibly later than Clemens Alexandrinus. This Catholicized Paulinism is characterized by a practical undogmatic tone, reminding one of the Synoptic Gospels.

This brief sketch of Pfleiderer's view of the general development of Christianity was needed in order to enable the reader to appreciate his remarks on James in particular (pp. 865–880).

He considers that the author of our Epistle was a contemporary of Hermas and borrowed from him.

Pfleiderer agrees with Schwegler that our epistle is just the Shepherd stripped of its Apocalyptical imagery. In both writings we have a protest on behalf of the practical piety of the common people against the increasing secularization of religion in the wealthy and intellectual circles, which we may compare with similar protests made by the Waldensians or Minorites in later times. Our epistle must evidently belong to the post-Pauline period; otherwise it must have contained some reference to the controversial topics of which St. Paul treats, such as the abrogation of the Mosaic law, circumcision, sabbaths and festivals, the position of Israel as the chosen people, the relation of the Old to the New Covenant, &c. The question then arises, How long after the death of St. Paul must it be placed? We are enabled to answer this partly from the lateness of patristic evidence as to the existence of the epistle, and partly from its dependence on other Christian writings. (1) As to the former our epistle is in a worse position than any other of the books of the N. T. Origen is the first to quote it directly, and he expressly says that it was not generally recognized as canonical. There is no reference to it in Clemens Alexandrinus or Irenaeus or Tertullian, not even in the Clementines. Moreover it is omitted in the Muratorian canon, which recognizes the Shepherd. This silence of the oldest witnesses is inexplicable if it belonged to the Apostolic age. (2) The writer was acquainted with the epistles to the Romans and Galatians, as is apparent from his use of the Pauline formula of 'justification by faith'; also with the epistle to the Hebrews, the Apocalypse (including the most recent portion of the latter, which dates from the time of Hadrian), the 1st epistle of Peter, above all with Hermas, whom Pfleiderer regards as the older writer, because the aphorisms of St. James are there found embedded in a suitable context. In any case the two writings were composed under similar circumstances and without doubt nearly at the same time. These facts prove that the address to the Twelve Tribes of the Diaspora is not to be understood literally. If there were then any pure Jewish churches it could only have been in Judea, which is excluded by the term Diaspora. Besides what reason could there be for confining the exhortation of the epistle to the Jewish Christians? It was not they but the Gentiles who were in danger of trusting in faith without works. We must therefore understand the phrase in reference to the true Israel scattered throughout the world. It is a mistake to lay any stress on the term 'synagogue,' which is freely used of Christian churches by Hermas and Ignatius.

The aim of the writer is a restoration of a retiring unworldly Christianity of self-renunciation and brotherly kindness: what he especially attacks is the worldliness of the upper classes. His condemnation of a wisdom which he characterizes as earthly, psychical, devilish, reminds us of the words in which Hermas describes the Gnostic teachers and prophets who were to be found at Rome in the middle of the second century, and must probably be understood of these. Jude, too, speaks of the Gnostics as ψυχικοί, and charges them with complaining of destiny (v. 16 μεμψίμοιροι), which we may compare with James i. 13, where we read of some who complain of God as tempting them to evil. So we are told of a treatise addressed to the Gnostic Florinus by Irenaeus, in proof that God was not the author of evil. The reference in iv. 11 to those who 'judge the law,' would apply to the attacks of such Gnostics as Cerdon and Marcion on the O. T. Lastly, the degradation of Paul's justifying faith into an unfruitful assent of the intellect was nowhere so likely to be found as among the Gnostics. To this ultra-Pauline Gnosticism James opposes no Judaizing theology, but the simple rules of practical Christianity as understood by the Catholic Church. His polemic does not touch Paul's own doctrine: Paul would never have given the name of faith to this dead intellectual assent; but it does touch the Gnostics who claimed the authority of Paul, and James fails to distinguish between the two views. This is easily explicable from the fact that James himself, like his contemporaries (compare the Ignatian and the Pastoral Epistles), no longer uses faith in its old sense of absolute trust, forming the only foundation of Christian piety, but makes it coordinate with love, patience, obedience, works, &c.

The Soteriology of the Epistle approaches so nearly to that of the Gospels, that it is no wonder some have been tempted to assign it to a very early period. This however has been shown to be impossible by a comparison with other Christian writings; and it is also inconsistent with the absence of all allusion to the apologetic and eschatological topics which so much occupied the attention of the early Church. We find here no attempt to prove that Jesus was the Messiah, and that he would shortly return to reveal the promised salvation. The undogmatic character of the epistle is to be explained, like the dogmatic simplicity of John, not on the supposition that it was written before Christianity had become dogmatic, but that dogma was already securely settled. The Church of Rome, however, with its predominantly practical tendency, rejected those speculative and mystical elements of Paulinism, which were retained and developed by the churches of Asia Minor. And thus it is that the Catholicized Paulinism of the second century approaches so nearly to pre-Christian Hellenism. Monotheism, the Moral Law, Future Retribution, these are the prominent doctrines in both; the only difference being that, in the former, these doctrines are based upon Revelation and propagated by an organized institution.

Pfleiderer abandons some of the positions of his predecessors.

It will be seen that on several points Pfleiderer recedes from the ground occupied by his predecessors of the negative school. He allows that our Epistle could not have been written whilst the admission of Gentiles into the Church was still a burning question: he allows that it is not intended as an answer to the Epistle to the Romans, and that in fact St. Paul would have assented to all that is said in it as to the futility of an unfruitful faith. He does not regard the author as an Ebionite or Essene, or suppose him to be addressing some small dissenting body: on the contrary, James is a typical Catholic of the latter half of the second century, and gives expression to the ethical undogmatic Christianity of the time: further, he is addressing the Church of Rome, which he rightly assumes to be representative, in its defects, of the degeneracy of the Church at large. Pfleiderer ridicules Schwegler's identification of the rich with Gentile, and the poor with Jewish Christians (p. 872): he explains *ἔμφυτον* correctly, in opposition to both

Schwegler and Brückner (p. 877). On the main point, however, he holds to the Tübingen view, that the Epistle was written in the latter half of the second century, his chief argument being that it bears traces of being written after the Epistle to the Romans, the 1st of St. Peter, and Hermas.

Principles for determining the relative priority of two writers, when the resemblance is so great as to make it probable that one borrowed from the other.

I will not here repeat what I have said before as to the mutual relations of the above-named Epistles, but will simply state the general principles which I think ought to determine our judgment in this and similar cases. Where it is agreed that there is a direct literary connexion between two writers, A and B, treating of the same subject from apparently opposite points of view, and using the same illustrations, if it shall appear that the argument of B meets in all respects the argument of A, while the argument of A has no direct reference to that of B, the priority lies with A. Again where it is agreed that there is a connexion between two writers, treating of the same subject, on the same scale, from the same point of view, and using the same quotations, it is probable that the writer who gives the thought in its most terse and rugged form, and takes least trouble to be precise in the wording of his quotations is the earlier writer. Using these tests, I venture to think that it has been proved conclusively, that the Epistle of St. James is prior to the first Epistle of St. Peter and to that of St. Paul to the Romans; and this one fact is sufficient to upset the whole house of cards erected by Pfleiderer. Supposing however that the priority of James to Paul were still a matter of doubt, I should not be at all more inclined to admit the possibility of our Epistle having been written at the late date assigned to it by Pfleiderer. None of his arguments seems to me to be of such a nature as we should rely on, if it were a question about secular writers. Take for instance his assertion that Hermas was prior to James. From a literary point of view, this seems to me on a par with saying that Quintus Smyrnaeus is prior to Homer, or Apuleius to Cicero. But on what does he ground the assertion? 'That which occurs in an aphoristic form in James, is found in its natural context in Hermas' (p. 868). As examples he gives James iv. 7, 'Resist the devil and he will flee from you,' compared with *Mand.* xii. 5 (abridged), where Hermas says, 'Man desires to keep the commands of God, but the devil is strong and overcomes him.' The angel answers, 'The devil cannot overcome the servants of God who place

The supposition that our Epistle was copied from Hermas is inadmissible.

their hope entirely in Him. If you resist him he will be vanquished and flee away.' On this it may be observed (1) that the saying occurs in three other passages of Hermas (*Mand.* vii. 2, xii. 2, 4), and that it also occurs thrice in what is probably a much earlier treatise, the *Testaments of the Twelve Patriarchs;* (2) that every text quoted by a preacher is naturally imbedded in a suitable context, if the preacher knows his business; (3) that St. James's style is confessedly condensed and aphoristic, but this is no evidence of lateness, rather the contrary; (4), that, as has been shown above in answer to Brückner, the saying is quite in its place in our Epistle. His other examples are James iii. 15 (the contrast of earthly and heavenly wisdom) compared with *Mand.* xi., James i. 27 (on true religion) compared with *Mand.* viii., James i. 20 ('the wrath of man worketh not the righteousness of God') compared with *Mand.* v., a passage which would have been more appropriately compared with James iv. 5. As to all these examples I am confident that every unprejudiced reader who takes the trouble to examine them, will agree with me, that it would be as reasonable to say that any modern sermon is older than its text, as to say that these comments are older than the parallels in St. James. There is not even any marked abruptness in the original context to excuse such extraordinary perversity of judgment. And then the fatuity of imagining that a man of such strong individuality, whose every words attests his profound and unshakable convictions, could condescend to borrow from one so immeasurably his inferior, whose thoughts show about an equal mixture of cleverness and silliness, and whose language, as Dr. Taylor has proved, is little more than a patchwork of old materials, new furbished to avoid detection!

Origen's witness in favour of the canonicity of our Epistle.

As regards Pfleiderer's attempt to prove the lateness of our Epistle from the absence of patristic evidence in its favour, I must refer the reader to my second chapter, where he will find quotations enough to enable him to decide the matter for himself. But as he has made the assertion that Origen expressly says that it was not recognized as canonical (*aber ausdrücklich als angezweifelte Schrift*), I will here briefly sum up the evidence of Origen on this point: (1) he never denies the genuineness of the Epistle; (2) he simply uses in one passage (*Comm. in Joh.* xix. 6, L. ii. 190) the ambiguous phrase ἡ φερομένη Ἰακώβου ἐπιστολή, which at the outside means that, though the Epistle was in general circulation under that name, yet he did not take upon himself to assert its authenticity; (3) in Rufinus' Latin translation of Origen's writings we find our Epistle referred to as follows: *Comm. in ep. ad Rom.* iv. 1, *in alio Scripturae loco,* ib. iv. 8 *audi et Jacobum fratrem Domini,* ib. ix. 24 *Jacobus Apostolus dicit,* and frequently; cf. *Hom. in Ex.* iii. 3, viii. 4, *Lev.* ii. 4, where it is also called *Scriptura divina;* (4) these expressions of the Latin, which some have without ground suspected, are borne out by similar expressions in the original Greek; thus in *Sel. in Psalm.* xxxi. 5 (Lomm. xii. p. 129) the Epistle (ὡς παρὰ Ἰακώβῳ) is referred to as ἡ γραφή, and it is quoted as authoritative in *Sel. in Exod.* xv. 25, *Comm. in Joh.* xx. 10 and elsewhere (see above, pp. lxiv. foll.); (5) in two distinct passages Origen gives a list of the Sacred Books, and in both of these the Epistle of St. James is included (*Hom. in Gen.* xxvi. 18, *Hom. in Jos.* vii. 1; see Westcott, *Canon,* pp. 406 foll.).

It is not true that the phenomena of our Epistle are inconsistent with an early date.

I next take the assertion that, if our Epistle had been written before the Council of Jerusalem, it must have contained arguments to prove that Jesus was the Messiah, such as those we find ascribed to St. Peter in the Acts, and must also have dwelt more upon the Second Coming. If the writer were addressing unconverted Jews, as St. Peter does in Acts ii., or were endeavouring to recall Jews who were in danger of falling away, as the author of the Epistle to the Hebrews does, such arguments would no doubt be in place; but as he is writing to believers, who accept Christ as the Lord of Glory and future Judge (James ii. 1, v. 9), such arguments would be out of place in a short letter, directed to the special object of inculcating a practical morality on those who were already believers. Nor can I see why we should expect more to be said about the Second Coming. Is it not enough that we are told 'the Judge stands before the door,' and 'he that endureth temptation shall receive the crown of life'? Another point is that James has lost the old meaning of faith, and makes it, not the foundation of the Christian life, but merely one among a number of co-ordinate virtues. I do not deny that he at times uses πίστις in the sense of a mere intellectual belief; but when he describes the Christian religion as 'the faith of our Lord Jesus Christ' (ii. 1), when he makes faith the essential condition of all prevailing prayer (i. 6, v. 15), when he ascribes the beginning of spiritual life to our regeneration by the word of truth (i. 18)—and how can we receive that word except through the instrumentality of faith?—he seems to me to rate faith as highly as St. Paul himself. Yet even St. Paul sets faith below love, and goes so far as to say, 'Though I have all faith so as to remove mountains, but have not charity, I am nothing.'

I really cannot see that Pfleiderer has anything else in the way of argument to offer for his view. All that he tells us is that towards the middle of the second century the Catholic Church had very much lost its hold of distinctive doctrine, that it was secular in tone, and was occupied in controversy with the Gnostics, to whom he considers that allusion is made by James, where he condemns a psychical and diabolical wisdom, and speaks against those who judge the law, and who impute to God the blame for their wrong-doing. If it were certain that the epistle dated from this time, we might be justified in supposing such allusions, but as all probability is against it, we have no reason to go so far to explain references which would be applicable in any age. The only difficulty would be in the term ψυχικός, but this is already used in the first Epistle to the Corinthians.

On the other hand it has some characteristics which are inexplicable on Pfleiderer's hypothesis.

Without entering into any discussion as to the correctness of Pfleiderer's estimate of the state of Christianity under the Antonines, and without repeating the positive argument for the early date of James, I will simply mention here some characteristics of the Epistle which seem to me inexplicable on the hypothesis of the date given by Pfleiderer. The first, already noticed by Beyschlag, relates to the heading, 'James the servant of God.' It is quite consistent with the modesty which marks the Epistle throughout, that James himself should adopt this humble title; but is it conceivable that a late writer, wishing to secure a hearing by the adoption of a famous name, should throw away all the distinguishing adjuncts, Apostle, Bishop of Jerusalem, Bishop of Bishops, Brother of the Lord, and call himself plain James, a name which could attract no attention and excite no interest? Would the Church of Rome have submitted patiently to the extremely severe reproofs of this unknown James? Would there be any appropriateness in speaking of *the rich*, as dragging the believers before the law-courts and blaspheming the noble name by which they were called? Would the thoroughly Hebraic tone of the Epistle, the appeal to the example of Elijah, Job and the prophets instead of Christ, the phrase 'Lord of Sabaoth,' the warning against the use of Jewish oaths, the stern censure of landowners who withheld the wages of the reapers, suit the circumstances of the Christians of Rome in that age? Where were the free labourers referred to? The latifundia of Italy were worked by slaves. Lastly, the writer looks for the immediate coming of the Lord to judgment (v. 7–9). Do we find any instance of a like confident expectation in any writer of the latter half of the second century?

The question of the genuineness of our Epistle must be considered in connexion with that of the genuineness of the other books of the N. T.

Some of my readers may wonder at my spending so much time on the examination of what will strike them as mere arbitrary hypothesis. My reason for doing so is (1) that we English are so conscious of what we owe to German industry and research, that we are sometimes tempted to accept without inquiry the latest theory that hails from Germany. This danger is perhaps less threatening at present in regard to the criticism of the New Testament, than in regard to some other departments of study, partly from our sense of the seriousness of the practical issues involved, and partly from our trust in the perfect fairness, the exhaustive learning and the sound historical and literary judgment of the great scholar and theologian whom we have recently lost. What Bishop Lightfoot has tested and approved, we believe we may accept as proven, so far as present lights go. But (2) fanciful and one-sided as German criticism often is, it is constantly stimulating and suggestive, bringing to light new facts or putting old facts in a new light. And therefore on both grounds, for the sake of what we may learn from it, as well as to point out its shortcomings and exaggerations, I have thought it worth while to lay its last word before English readers. I have done my best to examine fairly point by point the argument in favour of the late origin of our Epistle; but it is impossible to estimate fully its strength or its weakness, unless we view it in connexion with the general theory, first put forward by F. C. Baur, of which it forms a part. According to that theory the larger portion of the writings of the New Testament are forgeries of the second century. I have endeavoured to show the improbability of this theory in the case of one small Epistle. Others have done the same for other books of the New Testament. But the improbability attaching to the theory as affecting one or another separate book of the New

Large demands on the credulity of their readers made by the advanced critics.

Testament is as nothing in comparison with the combined improbability of one half of the books having been forged in the second century. For consider the demand thus made upon us. We have on the one side a century which beyond all question witnessed the greatest advance in morality and religion which has ever taken place on our earth. If this advance is to be explained by natural causes we must assume the existence of extraordinary powers, spiritual, moral and intellectual, in the men by whom it was brought about. The histories of the time, written by contemporaries, as we believe—at any rate written, as even our opponents admit, within a hundred years, more or less, of the events which they record—tell us that there were such men then living, and depict them so clearly and vividly that we seem to be personally acquainted with them. Again we have letters purporting to be written by some of these men, which so fully answer the expectations excited by the histories and soar so high above the ordinary level of human thought, that they have for some eighteen centuries been regarded by the most enlightened of mankind as containing, along with the histories, a divine ideal and an inspired rule of conduct for the whole human race. On the other hand we have in the second century an age in which the Christian Church, as far as we can judge from its history and from the undisputed writings of the time, was decidedly wanting in power and ability, not merely in comparison with the first, but in comparison with most of the later centuries. Yet it is in this feeble age that Baur and his followers have sought to find the authors of the books which bear, and in the judgment of united Christendom worthily bear, the great names of James, Peter, Paul, and John. It is not one author of this inspired stamp they are in search of, but four at least; for there is no pretence that any one individual could have produced works so diverse in doctrine, thought and style; nay, their separatist hypotheses make it necessary for them to assume a fifth, a sixth, and even a seventh author. And yet not a trace of one of them is to be found in the history or literature of the second century. No one is bold enough to name a man whom he considers capable of having written even the least of these works. Would it be at all a wilder hypothesis if one were to assume that half the plays of Shakspeare were written by an anonymous author or authors of the time of Charles the Second?

Their axioms and their method.

How are we to account for such extraordinary aberration on the part of able and honest men? It seems to me that it is due partly to prejudice and partly to an error of method. First, as to prejudice: they start with two assumptions, (1) that the presumption is always against the truth of tradition; (2) that miracles are impossible. The former prejudice is a natural reaction from the opposite extreme, that tradition is always right; and it falls in with the natural delight in novelty, and the temptation to take the side which affords most scope for new and startling combinations. There is also a natural impatience at the tone of virtuous orthodoxy often assumed by the defenders of tradition, and a generous eagerness to take the side which has suffered most from misrepresentation in the past, and which still finds it necessary at times to resist attempts on the part of the champions of authority to intimidate opponents and stifle discussion; a feeling too that, in order to the final ascertainment of truth, the negative argument is as needful as the positive, and that up to the present century the former has scarcely had justice done to it among Christian writers. The second prejudice naturally leads to the attempt to weaken the force of the evidence adduced in favour of miracles. If the accounts of miracles proceed from eye-witnesses, it is difficult, on this hypothesis, not to condemn them of deliberate falsehood, which our opponents are unwilling to do, not merely because they do not wish to give unnecessary offence, but because they are themselves convinced of the honesty and high tone of the writers. If, however, it can be proved that these writers lived a hundred years after the events they record, then they are simply the mouthpiece of tradition, which, without any deliberate falsification, would spontaneously clothe the bare nucleus of fact with the garment of the supernatural.

Next, as to the error of method. Men assume *a priori* that the Christian Church and Christian theology must have had such and such a development; that if we find one doctrine especially prominent in a particular writer, he must have been the author of that doctrine, which must therefore have been unknown before him and denied by all but his immediate school; and again, that if we meet with any teaching which seems inconsistent with such a doctrine, it must have proceeded from a controversialist of the opposite school: so that we are guilty, for instance, of an anachronism in assigning to Christ the words, 'Think not that I am come to destroy the law and the prophets,' 'One jot or one tittle shall not pass from the law' (Pfleiderer, page 492 foll.), since they involve the principles of Paulinism and anti-Paulinism. But why cannot we act here as we do in the parallel case of the disciples of Socrates? We do not dispute the genuineness of a Cynic or Cyrenaic or Academic phrase attributed to Socrates, because he did not carry out these different lines of thought to the full extent to which each was carried by his disciples. Yet it is assumed *a priori* that James, Peter, and John being typical of particular aspects of Christianity, anything in their writings which appears to be inconsistent with that special aspect must be pronounced spurious; that even a man so many-sided and so full of growth as St. Paul must be tied down to the ideas which occupied him during a certain critical period of the Church's development. If we were to impose the same rule on Mr. Gladstone, how little we should leave him of all the books and speeches which now bear witness to his incessant activity and versatility of mind.

But perhaps the most mischievous manifestation of the *a priori* method is when it seizes on some small side-incident, and makes it the corner-stone of a huge theory, by which all the phenomena are to be explained, or, in the event of a too stubborn resistance, to be exploded. Such an incident is the difference between St. Peter and St. Paul, of which passing mention is made in Galatians ii. 11, 12, and in which Baur finds the key to the whole of the early history of the Church as well as to the Christian literature of the first two centuries. It might really seem as if to some of his followers the main article of the Creed was 'I believe in the quarrel between Peter and Paul, and in the well-meaning but unsuccessful attempts of Luke and others to smooth it over and keep it in the background.'

Result of similar criticism in the case of classical authors.

It may encourage those who are fearful as to the results of the present attack on the integrity of the books of the New Testament, to call to mind the history of the same struggle in regard to the writings of classical authors. There too a narrow *a priori* dogmatism has in times past attempted to deprive us of half the dialogues of Plato and some of the noblest satires of Juvenal; but in the great majority of instances the result of the close examination to which the classical writings have been subjected has only served to establish more firmly the genuineness of the disputed books and passages, and so we cannot doubt it will be with the New Testament[1] Experience proves the truth of the maxim—*Opinionum commenta delet dies, naturae judicia confirmat.*

[1] It is especially interesting to note how in both spheres we find the first thoughts of youth corrected by the second thoughts of maturer age. Thus Zeller, who in his *Platonische Studien*, 1839, had argued against the genuineness of Plato's *De Legibus*, in his *History of Greek Philosophy* treats it as the undoubted work of Plato. In like manner Kern, who in an article in the *Tüb. Theolog. Zeitschr.* for 1835, part 2, had ascribed our epistle to an unknown writer of the 2nd century, argues in his commentary, 1838, in favour of its genuineness; De Wette, who in the earlier editions of his commentary had denied the authenticity of the epistle, in his 5th edition (1848) regards it as probably authentic; Lechler, who in the 1st and 2nd editions of his book on the Apostolic and Post-Apostolic Times had made it a post-Pauline production, treats it as pre-Pauline in his last edition of 1885 (Eng. tr. 1886); and from the preface to the 2nd edition of Ritschl's *Altkatholische Kirche*, 1857, it would seem that Ritschl's views had developed in a similar direction.

CHAPTER VII

Part II

Harnack and Spitta on the Date of the Epistle

Two important works have recently appeared, in which very opposite views are taken as to the date of the Epistle of St. James. One is *Die Chronologie des altchristlichen Litteratur bis Eusebius*, brought out this year (1897) by the distinguished theologian, Adolf Harnack; the other, F. Spitta's learned and acute contribution, *Zur Geschichte und Litteratur des Urchristenthums*, vol. ii., 1896, of which 239 pages are occupied with a very careful study of the Epistle. I take them in this order because Harnack on this particular book still adheres to the old Tübingen tradition, from which he has receded in regard to many of the other documents of the New Testament, while Spitta occupies an entirely independent position. As Harnack only devotes six pages to the subject, and refers to Jülicher's *Einleitung*, 1894, as supplementing his argument, I have joined them together in the discussion which follows.

Jülicher begins (p. 129) with a general attack upon the authenticity of the Catholic Epistles. They are not really epistles at all; there is nothing personal about them; the epistolary form was simply adopted, by a stranger writing to strangers, in imitation of the widely-circulated epistles of St. Paul. This is enough to prove that they are post-Pauline, and therefore not written by any of the Apostles ('damit ist schon gesagt dass sie erst aus nachpaulinischen Zeit, also nicht wohl von Uraposteln herrühren können'). Harnack also remarks on the fact that St. James reads more like a homily than a letter, as casting doubt on its genuineness.

Are we to understand then that an epistle must be judged spurious, if it is occupied with impersonal matter, or if it is a sermon or treatise masking under this form? If so, we must deny the genuineness of Seneca's letters to Lucilius, of the *De Arte Poetica* of Horace, of the letters to Herodotus and Menœceus, in which Epicurus summed up his philosophy. But if all these are allowed to be genuine, St. Paul was not the first person to make use of the epistolary form for didactic purposes; and if we further accept the account given of the Apostolic Council[1] in the Acts, he was not even the first Jew to indite a circular letter; he was only following the example already set by the President of the Council in his circular to the Churches; as to which it has been already pointed out that the resemblances between it and the Epistle of St. James lead to the conclusion that they proceed from the same hand.[2] Jülicher, however—I am not certain about Harnack—would probably deny that the account of the Council given in the Acts is historical. Let us assume then that St. Paul was the first Jew to write a didactic letter for general circulation, why is his example to remain unfruitful, not only till after his own death, but till the death of the last of the Apostles, say thirty years later? For this is what is required by his argument. Otherwise all the Catholic Epistles might still have been written as early as 60 A.D. by those whose names they bear.

I proceed now to consider the arguments offered in favour of the date 120–150 favoured by Jülicher and Harnack. Both lay stress on the low moral and religious tone implied by the language of the writer. Worldliness had reached such a pitch as can only be paralleled in the Shepherd of Hermas, with which indeed our Epistle has so much in common that both must be ascribed to the same age. Instances of this deplorable degeneracy are i. 13, in which the readers are warned against making God the Author of temptation; ii. 14, where orthodox belief is put forward as excusing lukewarmness or sin; ii. 6, where it is stated that the rich members of the Church drag their poorer brethren before the law courts and blaspheme the Holy Name by which they are called, a picture of the time which is in entire agreement with what we read in Hermas (*Sim.* viii. 4, ix. 19, etc.) of the apostates and informers within the Church (*ἀποστάται καὶ βλάσφημοι εἰς τὸν κύριον καὶ προδόται τῶν δούλων τοῦ θεοῦ*). Such a state of things, implying that Christianity was a crime punishable in the Roman courts, and

[1] Harnack places the Council in the year 47, and considers that St. Paul's earliest epistle was not written before 48–49.
[2] P. iii. foll.

that the Christian body included a number of rich men, who were so indifferent to their religion as to purchase safety for themselves by informing against their brethren and even dragging them before the tribunals, is not conceivable before the year 120 (Harnack, p. 485 f).

Taking the last argument first, I observe that one trait in St. James's description, *αὐτοὶ ἕλκουσιν ὑμᾶς εἰς κριτήρια*, is not to be found in Hermas, and it seems very improbable that actual members of the Church, though from cowardice (*Sim.* ix. 21. 3) they might apostatize and give information against their brethren, would themselves take the lead in dragging them before the magistrate. I observe also that there is nothing in our epistle to suggest that the court was Roman rather than Jewish; nor again that the rich persecutors were Christians. As Dr. Plummer has pointed out, the Holy Name was not called over *them*, but (*ἐφ' ὑμᾶς*) over those whom they arrested. The whole passage (ii. 2–7) is directed against the respect of persons shown in favouring the rich at the expense of the poor; this is illustrated by the supposition of two strangers visiting the synagogue, of whom nothing is known, except that one is well dressed, the other in shabby clothes. St. James says their hearts should have been drawn rather to the poor than to the rich, because the poor made up the bulk of the Christian community, while the rich were their persecutors. If we want a parallel to the 'dragging before the tribunals,' we find one ready to our hand in Acts viii. 3, where Saul, *σύρων ἄνδρας καὶ γυναῖκας*, committed them to prison. So far, I see no reason why we should not understand the words of St. James with reference to the persecution of the first Christians by Jews, especially by the rich Sadducees, as in Acts iv. 1, xiii. 50, in accordance with the warning of our Lord (Matt. x. 17).

I take now the other instances of degeneracy, which, it is said, could not have been paralleled in the Church before the time of Hermas. The first is the warning against making God accountable for temptation. I must say I am surprised at this being instanced as an extraordinary example of depravity. From the time when Adam threw the blame of his eating of the forbidden tree on 'the woman whom *Thou gavest to be with me*' down to the present moment, I should have thought this the natural and almost inevitable excuse by which man, conscious of wrong-doing, endeavours to palliate his fault to himself. Whether he pleads hereditary bias, or overwhelming passion, or the force of circumstances or of companionship, all these are in the end ordained or permitted by Divine Providence. In my note on the passage I have quoted from Homer, from the Proverbs, from Philo, from St. Paul, as bearing witness to this universal tendency of fallen humanity.

Nor can I see that there is anything unprecedented or abnormal in the idea that orthodox belief is sufficient for justification. Justin tells us (*Dial.*, 370 D) this was the idea of the Jews in his day, who believed that, 'though they were sinners, yet, if they knew God, the Lord would not impute sin to them.' Is this at all more heinous than the belief with which John the Baptist charged the Jews, that, as Abraham's children, they stood in no need of repentance? Is it more heinous than the belief of the Pharisee that he should be justified because, unlike the publican, he fasted twice in the week, and gave tithes of all that he possessed? Is it not in fact Paul's own description of a Jewish Christian (Rom. ii. 17–25): 'Thou art called a Jew and restest in the law and makest thy boast of God, and art confident that thou thyself art a guide of the blind, a light of them that sit in darkness . . . thou that makest thy boast of the law, through breaking the law dishonourest thou God'? I will venture to say that the history of the Church in every age, as well as the experience of every individual Christian, attests the need of this warning of St. James against confounding orthodoxy of belief with true religion? At any rate it was so with the many thousands of Pharisaic zealots belonging to the Church over which St. James presided.

Another ground on which Jülicher denies the genuineness of the Epistle is that the Greek is too good for James. This objection has been already answered in p. xli.

The view of the Mosaic law contained in the Epistle is regarded as proof that it could not have had James for its author. Thus Jülicher asks, How could the strict legalist against whom Peter did not venture to maintain his right to eat with Gentiles ('vor dem Petrus eine Tischgemeinschaft mit Heidenchristen nicht zu vertheidigen gewagt hätte'), have written a letter in which no mention is made of the ceremonial law, in which worship is made to consist in morality, and in which the perfect law of liberty, culminating in the royal law of love, is spoken of with enthusiasm? One who could write thus must have looked on the old law as a law of bondage. So, too, Harnack, 'Law with this writer is not the Mosaic law in its concrete character, but a sort of essence of law which he has distilled for himself' (p. 486).

The incident referred to is not quite correctly stated. It is not James himself, but 'certain from James' (Gal. ii. 12), whose presence had this baneful effect on Peter and the other Jews. That they did not represent the real feeling of St. James is not only probable from the fact that the responsible leaders of a party are usually less extreme than their followers, but it is also expressly stated, if we accept the account given in Acts xv. 24; for there we read that James had previously had to complain of unauthorized persons speaking in his name (*τινὲς ἐξ ἡμῶν ἐξελθόντες ἐτάραξαν ὑμᾶς λόγοις . . . λέγοντες περιτέμνεσθαι καὶ τηρεῖν τὸν νόμον, οἷς οὐ διεστειλάμεθα*). James was certainly included in the number of those who sanctioned the conduct of St. Peter in eating with Cornelius (Acts xi. 1–3, 18), and later on (xxi. 20) we find him explaining to Paul the difficulty he had in controlling the zealots of his party, the converted Pharisees of xv. 5. There is nothing in the New Testament to suggest that he was an extreme legalist. Even tradition goes no further than to show that his own practice was ascetic: it does not state that he enforced this practice on others. When Harnack says he invented a law of his own ('ein Gesetz welches er sich destillirt hat'), he seems to me to shut his eyes to the main factor in the history. If the author was really the brother of Jesus, brought up with Him from infancy, and acknowledging Him as Messiah before His departure from earth, he must have been greatly influenced by His teaching, as indeed is abundantly shown in the Epistle. What then was Christ's teaching as to the law? I make no reference to the Fourth Gospel, as the discourses there may be supposed to be coloured by the reporter, but in the Sermon on the Mount we see the law of the letter changed to a law of the spirit. The law of love to God and love to man is described as the great commandment on which hang all the law and the prophets. Men are called to bear Christ's easy yoke and light burden, as opposed to those heavy burdens which the scribes, sitting in Moses' seat, lay upon men's shoulders, and of which Peter afterwards declared that 'neither our fathers nor we were able to bear them.' How was it possible that the brother of the Lord should seek to reimpose such a yoke? Harnack and Jülicher write as if Christianity began with Paul. Yet even in the Old Testament the law is called perfect (Ps. xix. 7, and liberty is associated with the law (Ps. cxix. 45), 'I will walk at liberty, for I seek Thy precepts'; *ib.* 32, 'I will run the way of Thy commandments when Thou shalt enlarge my heart'); so, when St. Paul contrasts the fleshy tables of the heart with tables of stone, he only reproduces the words of the prophet, 'I will put my law in their inward parts.' Nor was the idea of a law of liberty strange to the rabbinical writers or to Philo. Spitta quotes from Pirke Aboth vi. 2 (a comment on Exodus xxxii. 6), 'None is free but the child of the law,' and from Philo ii. 452, '*ὅσοι μετὰ νόμου ζῶσιν ἐλεύθεροι.*'

I now proceed to the consideration of the section on Faith and Works, which is put forward as a crucial instance in favour of the late date of the Epistle. To narrow the field of discussion as much as possible, I will say at once that I agree with my opponents in holding that the resemblance between this portion of the Epistle and St. Paul's Epistle to the Romans is too great to be accidental. One of the two must have been written with reference to the other. I agree also in considering that the argument of St. James entirely fails to meet the argument of St. Paul. It is in fact quite beside it, and, if intended to meet it, rests upon a pure misconception of St. Paul's meaning. From this my opponents infer that it could not have been written by James the Just, or indeed by any contemporary of St. Paul. The identification of Paul's faith in Christ, which works by love, with the barren belief in the existence of one God, which is shared even by devils; the confusion between the works of the law, which Paul condemns, with the fruits of faith, which he demands of every Christian—this was not possible till lapse of time had brought forgetfulness of the tyranny of the old Mosaic law, and made it possible to understand 'the works of the law' to mean moral conduct. If James had written this section, he would have been rudely and ignorantly attacking Paul as guilty of heresy, but if it was written in the year 130, the author might well imagine that he was only expressing St. Paul's own meaning in other words. Feeling sure that the great Apostle would never have encouraged the idea that a mere profession of orthodoxy could win heaven, he might naturally seek to follow his language as closely as possible in giving their due weight to faith and works respectively ('deshalb stellte er mit möglichst nahem Anschluss an Paulus' Worte fest, wie beide Glaube und Werke zu ihrem Recht gelangen'). The 'vain man' of *v.* 20 is not Paul (as Schwegler supposed, and as he must have been if James were the author), but some one who claimed St. Paul's sanction for a religion of barren orthodoxy.

I pause here for a moment to consider the very extraordinary proceeding of the author whom Jülicher has conjured up for us. We are to suppose that he wishes to disabuse his neighbours of the notion that St. Paul would have condoned their idle and vicious lives on the ground that they were sound in their belief. If this was the author's intention, surely he would have quoted such passages as the chapter in praise of charity, or the list of the fruits of the Spirit, or the moral precepts which abound in the Epistles, rather than flatly contradict St. Paul's language as to the justifying power of faith. One can imagine with what just scorn Jülicher himself would have treated a makeshift theory of the kind, if it had been put forward in defence of Catholic, instead of Tübingen, tradition. But this is far from exhausting the self-contradictions involved in the supposition. Though the reason for postponing the date of the Epistle is that the misunderstanding shown in it of St. Paul's doctrine of faith and works is inconceivable at an earlier period, yet we are now told that there was no real misunderstanding in the mind of this late author: he did not identify St. Paul's faith with the belief of devils, or his works of the law with the fruits of faith. The only person who labours under the misunderstanding is the 'vain man' of *v.* 20.

The attempt to explain the section as a production of the 2nd century having failed, as I have tried to show, is it not better to look at the matter from the other side, and see whether it may not be more in accordance with the facts of the case to suppose James to have written before Paul? Neither Jülicher nor Harnack will listen to such a suggestion for a moment. The latter tells us that, with the exception of a few critics whose assertions are every day losing ground ('mehr und mehr in Vergessenheit gerathen'), all are now agreed that the Epistle does not belong to the Apostolic age. The former calls it ridiculous ('komisch') to dream of its being written in 30 or 40 A.D. Such flowers of speech need not detain us: like the anathemas of earlier times, they are the natural weapons of those who wish to strengthen a weak cause by the intimidation of adversaries. I must, however, express my regret that Harnack should have spoken in such slighting terms of men like Mangold, Spitta, Lechler, Weiss, Beyschlag, Schneckenburger, above all, of the great Neander, all of whom have given their opinion in favour of the priority of James. If Neander's great name is 'passing into oblivion,' I venture to think it argurs ill for the future of theological study in Germany. But let us see what further arguments are alleged against the early date of the Epistle. 'A discussion on Faith and Works as the ground of Justification could not have arisen before the question had been brought into prominence by St. Paul's writings. The attempt to assign the priority to St. James springs from the wish to leave no room for opposition between the two' (Jülicher). 'The misuse of the Pauline formula is presupposed in the Epistle.' 'The doctrine of justification by faith and works combined belongs to the time of Clement, Hermas, and Justin; we cannot conceive that it was a mere repetition of what had existed ninety years before; diese Annahme, die uns an die seltsamste Dublette zu glauben nöthigen würde, unhaltbar ist' (Harnack). To this we may add the more general statement of Jülicher quoted with approval by Harnack, that when we compare this Epistle with what we know of the prevailing views and interests of Apostolic Christianity, we find ourselves in an altogether different world, the world of the two Roman Clements, of Hermas and of Justin. The specific Christian doctrines are conspicuous by their absence; Christ is hardly mentioned, and only as the coming Judge. Moreover, its late date is shown by plain allusions to the Gospels, the Hebrews, the Epistles of Paul and 1 Peter, and it is closely connected with Hermas, though it cannot be absolutely decided which of the two borrowed from the other.

I take first Jülicher's assertion that it was the wish to get rid of the controversy between Paul and James which was father to the thought that James was the first to open the debate. This, of course, will not apply to those who hold, as I do, that we have Paul's answer to James in the Epistle to the Romans. For others the easiest way of getting rid of the controversy would have been to accept the Tübingen view, that James had nothing to do with the Epistle, which was forged in his name by a late writer. (2) The impossibility of a historical 'Dublette' is a bold *a priori* assumption, to which I think few Englishmen will give their assent. We are not prepared to admit principles which would lead us to deny the existence of Elizabethan Puritanism, of the High Churchism of

Andrews and Laud, of the 'Latitude men' of the same century, on the ground that we find history repeating itself in the Low Churchmen, the Tractarians and the Broad Churchmen of the 19th century. How far more philosophical was the view of Thucydides when he magnified the importance of the lessons of history, because 'the future will surely, after the course of human things, reproduce, if not the very image, yet the near resemblance of the past!' There is nothing against which the historical inquirer should be more on his guard than any *a priori* assumption in determining such a question as this: Is the character, are the contents, of the Epistle of St. James consistent with what we know of the pre-Pauline Church, of the teaching of Christ, and of contemporary Jewish opinion? I venture to think there is a correspondence so exact that, given the one side, it would have been possible to infer the other side. We will test this in the case of Faith and Works. Faith is with St. James the essential condition of effectual prayer (i. 6, v. 15), it is the essence of religion itself, so that Christianity is described as 'the faith of our Lord Jesus Christ' (ii. 1); the trials of life are to prove faith (i. 3); those who are rich in faith are heirs of the kingdom (ii. 5). Just so in the Gospels: Christians are those who believe in Christ (Matt. xviii. 6; Mark ix. 42); faith in God is the condition of prayer; 'all things are possible to him that believeth' (Mark ix. 23); 'whatsoever things ye desire when ye pray, believe that ye have received them, and ye shall have them' (Mark xi. 24); 'He did not many mighty works there because of their unbelief' (Matt. xiii. 58); 'thy faith hath saved thee' (Mark v. 34). But faith, which comes from hearing, must be proved, not by words, but by deeds, if it is to produce its effect (Jas. i. 22, 25, 26; ii. 14–26). So in the Gospels: 'By their fruits ye shall know them,' 'Whosoever heareth these sayings of Mine and doeth them, I will liken him to a wise man' (Matt. vii. 20, 24), 'The Son of Man shall come in the glory of His Father, and then He shall reward every man according to his works' (Matt. xvi. 27). The relation of faith and works as shown in James ii. 22, 'Faith wrought with his works, and by works was his faith made perfect,' agrees with the image of 'fruits' used in Matthew vii. 20, xii. 33, and with the language of 4 Ezra, 'one of the very few Jewish writings which can be attributed with any confidence to the Apostolic age,'[1] cf. vii. 34:

[1] Lightfoot, *Galatians*, p. 161.

veritas stabit et fides convalescet et opus subsequetur et merces ostendetur; xiii. 23: *Ipse custodibit qui in periculo inciderint, qui habent operas et fidem ad fortissimum*; ix. 7: *omnis qui salvus factus fuerit et qui poterit effugere per opera sua vel per fidem in qua credidit, is relinquetur de prædictis periculis et videbit salutare meum.* In the last passage faith and works are mentioned as alternative grounds of salvation, not, as in the two other passages, as constituting together the necessary qualification; but they all show that the question of salvation by faith or works had been in debate before St. Paul wrote; cf. also vii. 24, 76–98, viii. 32–36. It is worth noting that the 7th and the 9th chapters are included in that portion of the book which Kabisch considers to have been written at Jerusalem B.C. 31.[1]

It was indeed impossible that, with such texts before them as Proverbs xxiv. 12 and Jeremiah xxxii. 19, in which God's judgment is declared to be according to man's works, and, on the other hand, Genesis xv. 6 and Habakkuk ii. 4, in which it is said that faith is counted for righteousness, the question of how to reconcile the opposing claims of faith and works should not be frequently discussed among the Jews. Lightfoot, *l.c.*, quotes many examples from Philo and the rabbinical writers in which the case of Abraham is cited and the saving power of faith is magnified. On the other hand the doctrine of justification by works is put forward in the most definite form in some of the passages cited above from 4 Ezra or again in the Psalms of Solomon ix. 7 *f.* 'O God, our works are in the choice and power of our soul, that we should execute righteousness and unrighteousness in the works of our hands...He that doeth righteousness treasureth up life for himself with the Lord, and he that doeth unrighteousness causeth the destruction of his own soul.'[2]

The only question that can arise is as to the first use of the phrase 'justified by faith.' The word *δικαιόω* is often used, *e.g.*, in 1 Kings, viii. 32 *δικαιῶσαι δίκαιον, δοῦναι αὐτῷ κατὰ τὴν δικαιοσύνην αὐτοῦ*, Ps. cxliii. 2 *οὐ δικαιωθήσεται ἐνώπιον σου πᾶς ζῶν*, Isa. xlv. 26 *ἀπὸ κυρίου δικαιωθήσονται . . . πᾶν τὸ σπέρμα τῶν υἱῶν Ἰσραήλ*, Matt. xii. 37 *ἐκ τῶν λόγων σου δικαιωθήσῃ*; but I am not aware of any instance of the use of *δικαιοῦσθαι ἐκ πίστεως* or *ἐξ ἔργων* prior to Paul and James. It does not follow that it

[1] James, *Texts and Studies*, vol. iii. 2, p. 89.
[2] Cp. Spitta p. 73.

was therefore introduced by one of them for the first time. Both seem to use it as a familiar phrase. In any case we have no right to assume that it was borrowed by James from Paul; for, as I have shown above,[1] while the argument of James on justification bears no relation to that of Paul, the argument of Paul exactly meets that of James. It is just like the pieces of a dissected puzzle: put Paul above, and no amount of squeezing will bring them together; put Paul below and James above, and they fit into one another at once. If this is so, it is unnecessary to spend time in showing that James does not quote from Hebrews and 1 Peter and other epistles of Paul, far less from Clement or Hermas, but all these from him. For proofs that this is so in each case, and for the principles which should determine our judgment of priority, I must refer to pp. lxxxix foll., xcviii, ciii, cxlv.

To my mind there is only one real difficulty in the supposition that the Epistle was written by James the Just, say, in the year 45, and this difficulty consists in the scanty reference to our Lord. It is not easy to explain why James should have been content to refer to Job and the prophets, as examples of patience, where Peter refers to Christ. It may have been, as I have elsewhere suggested, that the facts of our Lord's life were less familiar to these early Jewish converts of the Diaspora than the Old Testament narratives, which were read to them every Sabbath day. Perhaps, too, the Epistle may have been intended to influence unconverted as well as converted Jews. In any case, I do not see that the difficulty becomes easier if we transfer the writing to a time when the Gospels were universally read. On the other hand Spitta's hypothesis, to which I shall turn immediately, has undoubtedly the merit of removing it.

I have endeavoured to show that the Epistle is a natural product of pre-Pauline Christianity. I now turn to the other side of Harnack's 'Dublette,' and venture with all diffidence to ask whether the half-century or so which embraces the names of Clement, Hermas and Justin was really characterised by such a monotonous uniformity of system and doctrine as is supposed, and whether it is true that the Epistle of James is of the same colour or want of colour? It would take too long to compare together the several writings which are assigned to this period. A mere recapitulation of names taken from Harnack's Chronological Table

[1] P. xci foll.

will, I think, suffice to throw grave suspicion upon the correctness of such sweeping generalizations.[1]

A.D. 90–110, *Pastoral Epistles;* 93–96, *Apocalypse of John;* 93–97, First Epistle of Clement; 80–110, *Gospel and Epistles of John, Aristion's Appendix to Mark;* 110–117, Letters of Ignatius and Polycarp; 100–130, *Jude,* Preaching of Peter, Gospel of Peter; 120–140, *James,* Apocalypse of Peter; 125 (?), Apology of Quadratus; 130, Epistle of Barnabas; 133–140, Appearance of the Gnostics, Basilides in Alexandria, Satornilus in Antioch, Valentinus and Cerdo in Rome; 131–160, Revised form of the Didaché; 138, Marcion in Rome; 140, Shepherd of Hermas in its present form; 138–147, Apology of Aristides; 145–160, Logia of Papias; 150–175, *Second of Peter* (Harn. p. 470); 152, Justin's Apology; 155, Death of Polycarp, Epistle of the Church at Smyrna; 155–160, Justin's Dialogue with Trypho, Carpocratian heresy; 157, Appearance of Montanus; 165, Martyrdom of Justin.

A resultant photograph intended to give the form and body of a time illustrated by such incongruous names would, I fear, leave only an undistinguishable blot. It may be worth while, however, to devote a little space to the consideration of the Shepherd of Hermas, which is generally allowed to approach more nearly than any of those mentioned above to the Epistle of James. The resemblances have been pointed out in chap. ii. p. lviii foll., and the reasons for regarding them as proving the priority of James are given there and in Dr. C. Taylor's article in the *Journal of Philology,* xviii. 297 foll. I shall endeavour here to exhibit the main differences, and shall then consider what they suggest as to the relative priority of the two books.

Hermas distinctly says that he wrote after the death of the Apostles (*Vis.* iii. 5; *Sim.* ix. 15. 6), and that the gospel had been already preached in all the world (*Sim.* viii. 3. 2; ix. 17. 4, 25. 2); he distinguishes between confessors (*Vis.* iii. 2. 5; *Sim.* viii. 3) and martyrs 'who had endured scourging, crucifixion, and wild beasts for the sake of the Name' (*Vis.* iii. 2); the ransom of the servants of God from prison is mentioned among good works (*Mand.* viii. 10); fasting is insisted on (*Vis.* iii. 10. 6), it is referred to as 'keeping a station' (*Sim.* v. 1), nothing should be taken on a fast day but bread and water, and what is saved is to be given to those who are in need (*Sim.* v. 3); through cowardice some Christians are ashamed of the

[1] Canonical books are marked by italics.

name of the Lord and offer sacrifice to idols (*Sim.* ix. 21); baptism being essential to salvation (*Vis.* iii. 3. 5), even the saints of the old dispensation had to be baptized before they could enter the kingdom of God, and this baptism they received from the hands of the Apostles when they visited the other world after death (*Sim.* ix. 16); it is rightly said that there is no other repentance except that remission of sins which we obtain in baptism (*Mand.* iv. 3); by special indulgence one more opportunity only is granted to the Church (*Vis.* ii. 2), but to the Gentiles repentance is possible till the last day;[1] special favour and honour are bestowed on him who does more than is commanded in works of supererogation (*Sim.* v. 2, 3: *Mand.* iv. 4); martyrs and confessors should not glory in their sufferings, but rather thank God, who has allowed them to expiate their sins by their sufferings (*δοξάζειν ὀφείλετε τὸν θεόν, ὅτι ἀξίους ὑμᾶς ἡγήσατο ὁ θεὸς ἵνα πᾶσαι ὑμῶν αἱ ἁμαρτίαι ἰαθῶσιν . . . αἱ γὰρ ἁμαρτίαι ὑμῶν κατεβάρησαν, καὶ εἰ μὴ πεπόνθατε ἕνεκεν τοῦ ὀνόματος κυρίου, διὰ τὰς ἁμαρτίας ὑμῶν τεθνήκειτε ἂν τῷ θεῷ* (*Sim.* ix. 28. 5, 6). [This seems to have been the opinion of the Gnostic Basilides, see Clem. Alex., *Str.*, iv. p. 600: *προαμαρτήσασάν φησι τὴν ψυχὴν ἐν ἑτέρῳ βίῳ τὴν κόλασιν ὑπομένειν ἐνταῦθα, τὴν μὲν ἐκλεκτὴν ἐπιτίμως διὰ μαρτυρίου, τὴν ἄλλην δὲ καθαιρομένην οἰκείᾳ κολάσει.*] The name of Christ is not mentioned, but we read that the 'Son of God,' who is the cornerstone and foundation of the Church, the door through which all men and angels must enter to be saved, who existed before all worlds as the Holy Spirit, became incarnate in human flesh, *τὸ πνεῦμα τὸ ἅγιον, τὸ προόν, τὸ κτίσαν πᾶσαν τὴν κτίσιν κατῴκισεν ὁ θεὸς εἰς σάρκα ἣν ἠβούλετο* (*Sim.* v. 5, 6, ix. 1, 12, 14). Harnack thinks that the Son of God is identified with Michael, the first of the angels, see his notes on *Vis.* iii. 4. 1, v. 2, *Sim.* viii. 3. 3, ix. 6. Believers who have persevered to the end become angels after death (*Sim.* ix. 24, 25, cf. Clem. Al., *Ecl. Pr.*, p. 1004, *οἱ γὰρ ἐξ ἀνθρώπων εἰς ἀγγέλους μεταστάντες χίλια ἔτη μαθητεύονται ὑπὸ τῶν ἀγγέλων εἰς τελειότητα ἀποκαθιστάμενοι, εἶτα οἱ μὲν διδάξαντες μετατίθενται εἰς ἀρχαγγελικὴν ἐξουσίαν*). Mention is made of false prophets who give responses for money and lead astray the double-minded (*Mand.* xi.), and also of false teachers (Gnostics) who profess to know everything and really know nothing (*Sim.* ix.

[1] This strict Montanistic view is not consistently adhered to (cf. *Mand.* xii. 6; *Sim.* viii. 8).

22): some of the deacons are charged with defrauding orphans and widows (*Sim.* ix. 26. 2).

Surely no unprejudiced person who will weigh these passages can help seeing that it must have taken many years to change the Church and the teaching of St. James into the Church and the teaching of Hermas. A long process of development must have been passed through before the simple, practical religion of the one could have been transformed into the fanciful schematism[1] and formalism of the other. Still more striking is the contrast of the two men: the latter the Bunyan, as he has been called, of the Church's silver age, but a Bunyan who has lost his genius, and exchanged simplicity for *naïveté* and his serious heavenward gaze for a perpetual smirk of sex-consciousness[2] and self-consciousness; the former a greater Ambrose of the heroic age, his countenance still lit up with the glory of one who had been brought up in the same household with the Lord, and who kept and pondered the words which had fallen from His lips.

It only remains to give Harnack's views as to the integrity of the Epistle. Place it in what year he will, he finds it impossible to be satisfied. It is paradox from beginning to end. There is no system, no connexion. The use of the word πειρασμός in chap. i. is inconsistent with the use of πειράζομαι a few lines below. A portion of the Epistle reads like a true reproduction of the words of the Lord, plain, energetic, profound; another portion resembles the Hebrew prophets; another is in the best style of Greek rhetoric; another exhibits the theological controversialist. But the most paradoxical thing of all is that, in spite of this diversity, there is still perceptible an inner unity both of thought and expression. The only explanation seems to be that it is an amalgamation of homiletical fragments originally written by a Christian teacher about 125 A.D., and put together and edited after the death of the writer, probably without any name or address. Then, at the end of the century, it occurred to some one to publish it, under the name of St. James, as an epistle addressed to the Twelve Tribes, *i.e.*, to the Church at large.

This account of the Epistle seems to me worth notice as showing that the Tübingen solution of the problem of authorship is found to be inadequate even by the ablest supporter of the Tübingen

[1] Cp. the simile of the Rods in *Sim.* viii.

[2] See especially *Vis.* i. 1–8, γελάσασά μοι λέγει, κ.τ.λ., *Sim.* ix. 11.

theory. It is unnecessary here to examine it in detail, but I may remark that it is vitiated by the same *a priori* method to which I called attention before. A letter is not necessarily bound together by strict logic, like a philosophical treatise. More commonly it is a loose jotting down of facts, thoughts, or feelings, which the writer thinks likely to be either interesting or useful to his correspondent. If slowly written, as this undoubtedly was, it naturally reflects the varying moods of the writer's mind. Even the Hebrew prophets are not always denunciatory; even St. Paul is not always argumentative.

I am far however from admitting the alleged want of connexion in our Epistle; nor do I think it will be admitted by any careful reader, or by any one who will take the trouble to read my fifth chapter (on the Contents of the Epistle) or the analysis given in Massebieau, pp. 2–5. As to the objection founded on the use of the same word in different senses, this might easily arise from a limited vocabulary or a defect in subtilty of discrimination. In the particular instance cited, objective temptation is naturally and properly expressed by the noun, subjective temptation by the verb. But the same mental characteristic is seen in the double uses of *πίστις* and *σοφία*, and in my edition (p. 202) I illustrated this by the double use of *ἔρις* in Hesiod, and of *πανουργία* in Sirac. xxi. 12. The peculiarity is imitated by Hermas in his use of the word *τρυφή* (*Sim.* vi. 5).

Having thus pointed out what appear to me the overwhelming objections to the Tübingen theory, that the Epistle was written in the middle of the second century after Christ, I have now to examine the opposite theory which makes it a product of the first century before Christ. As I joined Jülicher with Harnack in considering the former theory, so I propose to supplement Spitta's *Zur Geschichte des Urchristenthums* by Massebieau's very interesting paper, *L'Épître de Jacques, est-elle l'Œuvre d'un Chrétien?* pp. 1–35, reprinted from the *Revue de l'Histoire des Religions* for 1895, in which he arrives independently at the same conclusion as Spitta.

The arguments adduced in favour of the pre-Christian authorship of the Epistle seem to me to be of far greater weight than those which we have previously considered, and I am willing to admit that a strong case is made out for the supposition of interpolation in chap. ii. 1; still my opinion as to the genuineness of the Epistle, as a whole, remains unshaken. The main point of attack is of course the universally acknowledged reticence as to higher Christian doctrines and to the life and work of our Lord. What is new is (1) the careful examination of the two passages in which the name of Christ occurs, and (2) the attempt to show that there is nothing in the Epistle which may not be paralleled from Jewish writings. As regards (1) it is pointed out that in both passages the sentence would read as well or better if the name of Christ were omitted. To take first the case which offers most difficulties from the conservative point of view (ii. 1), *μὴ ἐν προσωπολημψίαις ἔχετε τὴν πίστιν τοῦ κυρίου [ἡμῶν Ἰησοῦ Χριστοῦ] τῆς δόξης*, it is pointed out that the construction of *τῆς δόξης* has been felt as a great difficulty by all the interpreters, and that this difficulty disappears if we omit the words in brackets. We then have the perfectly simple phrase 'the faith of the Lord of glory,' the latter words, or words equivalent to them, being frequently used of God in Jewish writings, as in Ps. xxix. 3 *ὁ θεὸς τῆς δόξης*, Ps. xxiv. 7–10 *ὁ βασιλεὺς τῆς δόξης*, and especially in the Book of Enoch, *e.g.* xxii. 14 *ηὐλόγησα τὸν κύριον τῆς δόξης*, xxv. 3 *ὁ μέγας κύριος τῆς δόξης*, *ib.* ver. 7, xxvii. 5 *ηὐλόγησα τὸν κύριον τῆς δόξης καὶ τὴν δόξαν αὐτοῦ ἐδήλωσα καὶ ὕμνησα*, *ib.* ver. 3.[1] It is next pointed out that there are undoubted examples of the interpolation of the name of Christ in the N. T., *e.g.* Col. i. 2, 2 Thess. i. 1, James v. 14, and that the use of the phrase *κύριος τῆς δόξης* of Christ in 1 Cor. ii. 8 may have led to the insertion of the gloss here. In the preceding verse (i. 27), which is closely connected with this, *ὁ θεὸς καὶ πατήρ* is represented as watching over the orphan and widow; the only true service in His sight is to visit them in their affliction, and keep oneself unspotted from the world. The second chapter is still occupied with our treatment of the poor. We are warned not to let our faith in the Lord be mixed up with respect of persons (v. 1) and worldly motives (v. 4), and (in v. 5) we are reminded that it is the poor whom God has chosen to be rich in faith. Must not the 'Lord' of the intermediate verse be the same as the 'God' of i. 27 and ii. 5? The same conclusion is suggested by a comparison with the 1st Epistle of Peter, which may be regarded as in some respects a Christianized version of our Epistle. There are many resemblances between 1 Pet. i. 17–21

[1] Cited by Spitta, pp. iv. and 4.

and Jas. i. 26–ii. 2. Thus *μάταιος* of Jas. i. 26 recurs in Pet. i. 18; *πατρί, ἄσπιλον, κόσμου* of Jas. i. 27 recur in Pet. i. 17, 19, 20; *προσωποληµψίαις, πίστιν, δόξης* of Jas. ii. 1 are found in Pet. i. 17, 21; *χρυσοδακτύλιος* of Jas. ii. 2 and *ὁ χρυσὸς καὶ ὁ ἄργυρος κατίωται* of Jas. v. 3 are represented in Pet. i. 18 by the words *φθαρτοῖς, ἀργυρίῳ ἢ χρυσίῳ.* What do we find then in Pet. to correspond to *μὴ ἐν προσωποληµψίαις ἔχετε τὴν πίστιν τοῦ κυρίου ἡμῶν Ἰησοῦ Χριστοῦ τῆς δόξης?* The words of Pet. i. 17 are *εἰ πατέρα ἐπικαλεῖσθε τὸν ἀπροσωλήμπτως κρίνοντα,* and we may gather his interpretation of *πίστιν* and *δόξης* from ver. 21 *τοὺς δἰ αὐτοῦ πιστοὺς εἰς θεὸν τὸν ἐγείραντα αὐτὸν ἐκ νεκρῶν καὶ δόξαν αὐτῷ δόντα, ὥστε τὴν πίστιν ὑμῶν . . . εἶναι εἰς θεόν.* Here it is the Father, not Christ, who judges without respect of persons; faith is in God, not in Christ; the glory is resident in God and bestowed by Him on Christ. Would St. Peter have written thus, if he had had the present text of our Epistle before his eyes?

The same method of treatment is applied in i. 1 *Ἰάκωβος θεοῦ καὶ κυρίου Ἰησοῦ Χριστοῦ δοῦλος*, but while Massebieau would bracket only the name *Ἰησοῦ Χριστοῦ*, Spitta omits the four words between *θεοῦ* and *δοῦλος*, giving the phrase *θεοῦ δοῦλος* which we find in Tit. i. 1. Massebieau's excision would give *θεοῦ καὶ κυρίου δοῦλος*, which he thinks is supported by the other compound phrases (*ὁ θεὸς καὶ πατήρ*, i. 27; *ὁ κύριος καὶ πατήρ*, iii. 9) used of God in the Epistle. I do not however remember any example of the phrase *θεὸς καὶ κύριος*. Philo has *κύριος καὶ θεός* in this order (M., p. 581), and *κύριος ὁ θεός* occurs frequently, even where the Hebrew has the inverted order, as Ps. lxxxv. 8, 'I will hearken what God the Lord will say.' Of the two suggestions I prefer Spitta's, but it has nothing special to recommend it, as we found to be the case in the previous verse. If the Epistle is proved on other grounds to be pre-Christian, we should then be compelled to admit interpolation here, but not otherwise. We cannot, of course, deny that interpolation is a *vera causa*. We have examples of Hebrew books which have undergone Christian revision in the Fourth Book of Ezra, the Testaments of the Twelve Patriarchs, the Didaché, the Sibylline Books, &c. A natural objection however to the alleged interpolation in this case is that, if it were desired to give a Christian colour to a Hebrew treatise, the interpolator would not have confined himself to inserting the name of Christ in two passages only; he would at any rate have introduced some further reference to the life and work of Christ, where it seemed called for. Spitta answers this by citing the case of 4 Ezra vii. 28, where 'Jesus' is read in the Latin, instead of 'Messiah' read in the Syriac and other versions, also the Testament of Abraham, which closes with the Christian doxology. But if we turn to Dr. James' edition of these apocryphal books, we shall find that interpolation is by no means limited to these passages; see his remarks on Test. Abr., p. 50 foll. and 4 Ezra, p. xxxix. I think therefore that the balance of probability is greatly against the idea that a Christian wishing to adapt for Church use the Hebrew treatise which now goes under the name of James, would have been contented with these two alterations.

I turn next to the more general proofs adduced by Spitta to show that the Epistle, setting aside the two verses in question, does not rise above the level of pre-Christian Hebrew literature, and that its apparent connexion with other books of the New Testament is to be explained either by a common indebtedness to earlier Hebrew writings, or by the dependence of the other books on our Epistle.[1] In like manner Massebieau, after giving an excellent analysis of the argument, urges that not only does it make no distinct reference to the Christian scheme of salvation, but that it absolutely excludes it. Salvation is wrought by the Word or the Truth, the Law of Liberty progressively realized by human effort aided by Divine Wisdom. If this Word, or this Wisdom, has descended to earth, it is not in the form of a distinct person, but as an influence, an indwelling spirit, animating and guiding those who are begotten from above, the elect heirs of the kingdom. If belief in Christ is compatible with such a system of doctrine, it can only be belief in Him as a Messiah preparing the way for the kingdom of God. He is no longer essential to salvation. And if not recognised as Saviour, neither is He recognised as Teacher. It is true there is much in the Epistle which is also alleged to have been spoken by Jesus, but there is nothing to mark this as of special importance or authority, like the citations from the Old Testament. The words of our Lord seem to stand on the same level with the writer's own words. At times there appears even to be a contradiction between the teaching of Jesus and that of James, as when the latter tries to excite the anger of his readers against the rich, who had maltreated them, instead of reminding them that their duty was to love their

[1] Spitta, pp. 10–13.

enemies and to do good to them that hated them. In like manner whereas Jesus had foretold that the Son of Man should come in the glory of His Father to reward every man according to his works, James evidently regards God as the final Judge, for the Judge and the Lawgiver are one (iv. 12), and the cry of the injured husbandmen goes up to the Lord of Sabaoth, whose coming the brethren are to await in patience, for He is near, even at the doors (v. 4, 7, 8, 9).[1]

I cannot help thinking that much of the difficulty which is found in the Epistle, arises from our bringing to its study the idea of Christianity which we have derived from the writings of St. Paul. If we compare its doctrine with that of the first two Gospels, I think that in some respects it shows a distinct advance on these. *There*, as *here*, and also in Romans x. 17, faith cometh by hearing, and hearing by the word of God; it is the word sown in the heart and carried out in the life which is the appointed means of salvation; but it is not so distinctly stated there, as it is here, that it is God, the sole Author of all good, who of His own will makes use of the word to quicken us to a new life. St. John alone of the Evangelists has risen to the same height in the words 'As many as received Him, to them gave He power to become the sons of God; which were born not of blood, nor of the will of the flesh, nor of the will of man, but of God.' If it be said that the Pentecostal gift of the Spirit forms the dividing line between fully developed and rudimentary Christianity, and that we have no right to compare what professes to be a product of the one with what professes to belong to the other; it may be answered (1) that the Evangelists themselves wrote with a full knowledge of the later development of Christianity, so far as it is shown in the Acts, and (2) that a comparison with this later Christianity confirms our previous result. St. James would have agreed not only with the words ascribed to St. Peter, 'In every action he that feareth Him and worketh righteousness is acceptable to Him,' 'Repent and be baptized every one of you, in the name of Jesus Christ for the remission of sins, and ye shall receive the gift of the Holy Ghost'; but also with the words ascribed to St. Paul, 'By Him all that believe are justified from all things, from which ye could not be justified by the law of Moses,' 'I commend you to God and to the word of His grace, which is able to build you up and to give

[1] Massebieau, pp. 2–9.

you an inheritance among all them that are sanctified.' Compare with these verses the universalist tone of St. James, his reference to the Name by which we are called, to the Spirit implanted in us, the distinctive epithets attached to the royal law of liberty, the promise of the kingdom to those that love God and are begotten again through the word of truth to be a kind of firstfruits of His creatures. Even St. Paul's own Epistles, so far as the earliest group, consisting of the two addressed to the Thessalonians, is concerned, do not go much beyond St. James. The main subject of this group in contrast with the subject of the second group, consisting of the Epistles to the Corinthians, Galatians and Romans, is defined by Bp. Lightfoot[1] to be Christ the Judge, as opposed to Christ the Redeemer. One topic indeed is absent from our Epistle, viz., the reference to the Resurrection as proving that Jesus is the Messiah; but if this is a letter addressed, as it purports to be, to believers by a believer, there was no reason to insist on what was already acknowledged by both parties.

So much in answer to the charge that it falls below the standard of early Christianity. The next thing is to show that it rises above the standard of contemporary Hebrew writings. Spitta seems to think that, if, taking the whole range of pre-Christian Jewish literature, inspired and uninspired, he can here and there discover a parallel for a precept or a maxim of St. James, this is enough to prove that the Epistle is itself pre-Christian; but surely this is to forget that the New Testament has its roots in the Old Testament, and that Christ came not to destroy but to fulfil. The right course, as it seems to me, is to take an undoubted product of the first century B.C. and compare it with our Epistle. I have chosen for this purpose the Psalms of Solomon, a treatise which is considered by its latest editors to approach so nearly to Christian thought and sentiment, that they have hazarded the conjecture that it might have been written by the author of the *Nunc Dimittis* included in St. Luke's Gospel. The first difference which strikes me is the narrow patriotism of the one, contrasted with the universalism of the other. In the Psalms of Solomon everything centres in Israel and Jerusalem. The past history of Israel is referred to as showing that it was under the special protection and government of God (ix., xvii.). God punished the sins of Israel in times past by the captivity in Babylon, He punishes them now by the

[1] *Biblical Essays*, p. 224.

desecration of their Temple by the Romans (ii. 2, 20–24, viii. 12 foll.). But the impiety of the foes of Israel is not unavenged; Pompeius, the great Roman conqueror, has died a shameful death in Egypt (ii. 30–33). Chapter iv. is thoroughly Jewish in its imprecations. The future glories of Israel are celebrated in chapters x. and xi. The coming of the Messiah as the king of Israel forms the subject of xvii. 23 foll. and xviii. In chapter xvi. the Psalmist prays that he may be strengthened to resist the seductions of the 'strange woman.' In iii. 9 the just man makes atonement for his sins by fasting (ἐξιλάσατο περὶ ἀγνοίας ἐν νηστείᾳ). The reader will at once see how different the whole atmosphere is from that of our Epistle.

It may be said, however, that we must seek our parallel not in the narrow-minded Hebraism of Palestine, but in the enlightened Hellenism of Philo. Let us take then any treatise of Philo's which touches on the same subjects as our Epistle, say that on the *Decalogue* or the *Heir of the Divine Blessing*; do we find ourselves brought at all nearer to the mind of our author? The great object of Philo is to mediate between the Jew and the Gentile, to interpret Gentile philosophy to the one, and Jewish religion to the other. And his chief instrument in this work is one which had been already applied by the Stoics to the mythology of Greece, the principle of allegorization. He endeavours to commend the Jewish sacred books to the educated Gentile world by explaining them as an allegory in which their own moral and physical ideas are inculcated. To do this he is obliged to neglect altogether the literal meaning; the lessons which spring naturally from the incidents described are often entirely inverted (*e.g.* the story of Tamar) in order to extract by any torture some reference to some fashionable thesis of the day, say the dogma of the interchange of the four elements. The same frivolity is shown in the mystical interpretation of numbers, such as 7 and 10. It is true there is combined with this an earnest protest against polytheism, together with a more practical morality, and a loftier religious philosophy, than is to be met with in Gentile writers; but the tone is far removed from that of St. James. The former is very much at ease in Zion, the latter has the severity and intensity of one of the old Hebrew prophets; the former is a well-instructed scribe, the latter speaks with authority; the former is a practised writer of high aim and great ability, gifted with imagination, feeling, eloquence, the latter speaks as he is moved by the Spirit of God. That, after all, is the broad distinction between our Epistle and all uninspired writing: it carries with it the impress of one who had passed through the greatest of all experiences, who had seen with his eyes that Eternal Life which was with the Father and was manifested to the Apostles.

I proceed now to consider the remaining arguments adduced by Massebieau, after which I shall mention some points in the Epistle which seem to be irreconcilable with Jewish authorship, and shall then go on to examine some of the parallels offered by Spitta.

Massebieau thinks that, if St. James were a Christian, he could not have failed to make a more marked distinction between what he speaks from himself and what he takes from the Gospels. I think the reason why he has not done so is that, while, like a good steward, he brings out things new and old from his treasury, he feels that all is given to him from above: the new, as well as the old, is the teaching of Christ. As to the supposed contradiction between the language of St. James and that of Christ in regard to loving our enemies, it is enough to refer to the many warnings against anger (i. 19), quarrelling (iii. 9, iv. 1, 2), and murmuring (v. 8, 9), and to the praise of gentleness, humility, and a peaceable spirit (i. 21, iii. 17, iv. 6). Even where he reminds his readers that the rich deserve no favour at their hands, he is careful to add at once, 'If you show favour to them because you remember the royal law, which bids us love our neighbour as ourselves, then you are right; but if it is mere respect of persons, you transgress the law.' As to the coming Judge, any apparent contradiction is explained by St. Paul's language (Acts xvii. 31), 'God hath appointed a day in which He will judge the world in righteousness by the Man whom He hath ordained.'

Among things which seem to be incompatible with Jewish authorship may be mentioned the use of the phrase *ἀδελφοί μου ἀγαπητοί* which occurs three times (i. 16, 19, ii. 5) and is very natural as an expression of the strong *φιλαδελφία* which united the early disciples. Spitta only cites examples of the formal *ἀδελφοί*. His attempt to explain away the Christian motive of i. 18 seems to me equally unsuccessful. We read there *βουληθεὶς ἀπεκύησεν ἡμᾶς λόγῳ ἀληθείας εἰς τὸ εἶναι ἡμᾶς ἀπαρχήν τινα τῶν αὐτοῦ κτισμάτων*, which Spitta understands of the first creation of man. He defends this on the ground (1) that the preceding verse reminds one of the words 'God saw that it was good' (Gen. i.); (2) that there is a reference to the creation in two parallel passages of the Apocrypha (Sir. xv. 11–20, Wisdom i. 13 f., ii. 23 f.). He interprets λόγῳ ἀληθείας of the creative word, comparing Psalm xxxii. 6, 'By the word of the Lord were the heavens made,' Aseneth 12 σύ κύριε, εἶπας καὶ πάντα γεγόνασι, καὶ ὁ λόγος ὁ σὸς ζωή ἐστιν πάντων σου τῶν κτισμάτων, and thinks that ἀπαρχή refers to man's pre-eminence over the rest of the creation. The answer to this is that the whole object of the passage is to show the impossibility of temptation proceeding from God, because He is all-good and of His own will infused into us new life by the Gospel, in order that we might be the firstfruits of a regenerated world. The meaning of λόγῳ ἀληθείας is proved from its constant use in the New Testament, especially from Ephesians i. 13 ἀκούσαντες τὸν λόγον τῆς ἀληθείας, τὸ εὐαγγέλιον τῆς σωτηρίας, and the parallel in 1 Peter i. 23–25, where the phrase ἀναγεγεννημένοι . . . διὰ λόγου ζῶντος θεοῦ is explained by the words τὸ δὲ ῥῆμα κυρίου μένει εἰς τὸν αἰῶνα· τοῦτο δέ ἐστι τὸ ῥῆμα τὸ εὐαγγελισθὲν εἰς ὑμᾶς. It is plain too from the 21st and following verses, where it is called 'the engrafted word which is able to save your souls,' and where we are warned to be 'doers of the word and not hearers only.' Yet even here Spitta (θέσιν διαφυλάττων) sticks to it that we are to think only of the creative word. How are we to *do* the creative word? How is it to save our souls? How is it to be to us 'the perfect law of liberty' of v. 25? All these phrases have a distinctively Christian meaning shown in the parallels I have cited from St. Peter and St. Paul. To understand them in any other sense makes nonsense of the whole passage. The word ἀπαρχή also is mistranslated by Spitta. It denotes not a climax, but a prophecy.

I will notice only one more passage out of many that I had marked, viz. v. 14, 15 προσευξάσθωσαν ἐπ' αὐτὸν ἀλείψαντες ἐλαίῳ ἐν τῷ ὀνόματι· καὶ ἡ εὐχὴ τῆς πίστεως σώσει τὸν κάμνοντα, καὶ ἐγερεῖ αὐτὸν ὁ κύριος. This simple regulation as to the method to be pursued in working a miracle of healing, seems to me not less strong a proof that the Epistle was written at a time when such miracles were expected to be wrought, and were regarded as customary incidents—a state of mind of which I do not think any example is to be found either in the century preceding the preaching of the Baptist, or in the post-apostolic age—I say, this is not less strong a proof of a contemporary belief in such miracles, than are St. Paul's directions about the gift of tongues and prophecy, as to the existence of those phenomena in his day.

I have argued above, p. iii. foll., that the Epistle must have been written by St. James, (1) because of the resemblance which it bears to the speeches and circular of St. James recorded in the Acts; (2) because it exactly suits all that we know of him. It was his office to interpret Christianity to the Jews. He is the authority whom St. Paul's opponents profess to follow. Tradition even goes so far as to represent the unbelieving Jews as still doubting, at the end of his life, whether they might not look to him for a declaration against Christianity.[1] (3) The extraordinary resemblance between our Epistle and the Sermon on the Mount and other discourses of Jesus is most easily accounted for, if we suppose it to have been written by the brother of the Lord (above, p. xli. foll.). Spitta labours to show that this resemblance is due to the fact that both borrow from older Jewish writings. Even if this were so, it would be far more probable that one of the two borrowed indirectly through the other, than that they should both have chanced to collect, each for himself, the same sayings from a variety of obscure sources. But it is mere perversity to put forward such vague parallels as are adduced from rabbinical writings on the subject of oaths, for instance, or the perishable treasures of earth, by way of accounting for the exact resemblance existing between James v. 12 and Matthew v. 34–37, James v. 2, 3 and Matthew vi. 19.

As to the warning against oaths, Spitta has nothing to appeal to beyond the very general language of Ecclesiastes ix. 2, Sirac. xxiii. 9–11, Philo M. 2, p. 194, in contrast to the literal agreement of James, 'Above all things swear not, neither by the heaven, neither by the earth, neither by any other oath; but let your yea be yea, and your nay nay, lest ye fall into condemnation,' and Matthew, 'Swear not at all; neither by heaven, for it is God's throne; nor by the earth, for it is his footstool; neither by Jerusalem, for it is the city of the great king: neither shalt thou swear by thy head, because thou canst not make one hair white or black. But let your communication be Yea, yea; Nay, nay; for whatsoever is more than these cometh of evil.' He suggests, however, that possibly the latter passage was not really spoken by Christ at all, since He did not act upon it when adjured by the chief priest: it

[1] Hegesippus in Eus., *H. E.*, ii. 23.

may have been a Jewish maxim in vogue at the time, which was incorporated in the Sermon on the Mount at a later period. Even if it were spoken by Christ, He may possibly have taken it from some Jewish source of which we have no record.

On the perishableness of earthly riches the agreement is not quite so close; still there is much more similarity between James' 'Go to now, ye rich, weep and howl for your miseries which are coming upon you: your riches are corrupted and your garments are moth-eaten; your silver and your gold are rusted, and their rust shall be for a testimony against you, and shall eat your flesh as fire: ye have laid up your treasure in the last days'—there is, I say, much more similarity between this and Matthew's 'Lay not up for yourselves treasures upon earth, where moth and rust doth corrupt,' than there is between either of these and the passage from Enoch xcvii. 8–10 referred to by Spitta: 'Woe to you who acquire silver and gold in unrighteousness, yet say, *We have increased in riches; we have possessions, and we have acquired everything we desire. And now let us do that which we purpose; for we have gathered silver, and our granaries are full, and plentiful as water are the husbandmen in our houses.* And like water your lies will flow away; for riches will not abide with you, but will ascend suddenly from you; for ye have acquired it all in unrighteousness, and ye will be given over to a great condemnation.'

It is, I think, unnecessary to go further. In almost every instance in which Spitta attempts to explain away parallels between our Epistle and the Gospels, which have been pointed out by commentators, his efforts seem to me to be scarcely less abortive than in the cases I have examined. The authenticity of the Epistle remains in my judgment alike impregnable to assault, whether it be urged from the pre-Christian or from the post-Apostolic side.

CHAPTER VIII

ON THE GRAMMAR OF ST. JAMES

ORTHOGRAPHY

Instead of the more usual forms we meet with the following:

Consonants.

σσ for ττ is the ordinary use in the Greek Testament, as in πράσσω, φυλάσσω, ταράσσω, and in our Epistle φρίσσουσιν ii. 19, ἀντιτάσσεται iv. 6: see Hort *G.T.* App. pp. 148, 149, W. Schmid *Der Atticismus* ii. p. 82, *s.v.* ἁρμόττειν, Blass (*N.T.Gr.* p. 23 foll.)

We find however the following exceptions, according to the readings of the best MSS.:

τὸ ἔλαττον Heb. vii. 7, ἔλαττον *adv.* 1 Tim. v. 9, ἐλαττοῦσθαι John iii. 30, ἠλάττωσας Heb. ii. 7 (from LXX.), ἠλαττωμένον Heb. ii. 9, ἠλαττόνησε 2 Cor. viii. 15 (from LXX.); but ἐλάσσω John ii. 10, ἐλάσσονι Rom. ix. 12 (from LXX.).

ἥττημα 1 Cor. vi. 7, Rom. xi. 12, ἥττηται 2 Pet. ii. 19, ἥττωνται *ib.* ver. 20; but ἡσσώθητε 2 Cor. xii. 13, ἥσσων 1 Cor. xi. 17, ἧσσον *adv.* 2 Cor. xii. 15.

κρεῖττον 1 Cor. vii. 9, 1 Pet. iii. 17, 2 Pet. ii. 21 and often in Hebrews; but κρεῖσσον 1 Cor. vii. 38, *ib.* ix. 17, Phil. i. 23, Heb. vi. 9, x. 34.

[The usage of Josephus varies like that of the N.T. Thus in *Ant.* xix. (ed. Niese) we find ἔτασσον § 99, but διετάττετο § 325; κρείσσων § 112, but κρειττόνων § 211; ἥσσων § 173, ἡσσώμενοι § 181, but ἔλαττον § 291; ἀπαλλάσσων § 213, but ἐξαλλάττων xvi. 12. The double sigma seems however to be constant in πράσσω.]

In some words the σσ is preserved in the later Attic also, as in ἄβυσσος, βασίλισσα, πτήσσω, πτώσσω, ἐρέσσω.

ν for γν is constant in the N. T. in γίνομαι and γινώσκω. According to Meisterhans, *Gr. d. Att. Inschr.* p. 141, γίγνομαι is the reading of the Attic inscriptions without exception up to 292 B.C., and γίνομαι, equally without exception, between 290 and 30 B.C.

Vowels.

ι for ει in abstract substantives: see Hort *l.c.* p. 153, and compare ἐριθία(?) James iii. 16, ἀλαζονίαις iv. 16, κακοπαθίας v. 10; but περισσείαν i. 21, θρησκεία i. 27 (ἐθελοθρησκία Col. ii. 23).

πρόϊμος for πρώιμος (v. 7), for which Hort compares χρεοφειλέτης, Στοϊκός.

πραΰτης for the classical πραότης i. 21; the forms πραΰς and πρᾶος are both classical, the former being preferred in the feminine and generally in the oblique cases.

Hiatus.

Hiatus is not shunned by the Hellenistic, as it is by the later Attic writers. Thus in i. 4 it occurs six times; and elision is proportionably rare, the only words elided in our Epistle being ἀλλά in ii. 18 ἀλλ᾽ ἐρεῖ τις (but ἀλλὰ ἀπατῶν i. 26, ἀλλὰ ἐπίγειος iii. 15), ἐπί in ii. 7 ἐφ᾽ ὑμᾶς, *v.* 7 ἐπ᾽ αὐτῷ, and v. 14 ἐπ᾽ αὐτόν; ἀπό in ἀφ᾽ ὑμῶν iv. 7, v. 5; παρά in παρ᾽ ᾧ i. 17; κατά in καθ᾽ ἑαυτήν ii. 17, καθ᾽ ὁμοίωσιν iii. 9, κατ᾽ ἀλλήλων v. 9. On the other hand we have ὑπό unelided in iii. 4 ὑπὸ ἐλαχίστου: in fact the only word which is uniformly elided in the *G.T.* is παρά, but the word is comparatively rare, and does not occur before a proper name beginning with a vowel. Of unelided κατά we find instances in Acts iii. 17 κατὰ ἄγνοιαν, *ib.* xxii. 3 κατὰ ἀκρίβειαν, Rom. ii. 2 κατὰ ἀλήθειαν, *ib.* iii. 5, 1 Cor. iii. 3, ix. 8, xv. 32 κατὰ ἄνθρωπον, Rom. xiv. 15 κατὰ ἀγάπην &c. Unelided ἐπί is found in Luke iii. 2 ἐπὶ Ἰωάννην, *ib.* v. 36 ἐπὶ ἱμάτιον, *ib.* xi. 17 ἐπὶ οἶκον, *ib.* xxi. 10 ἐπὶ ἔθνος &c.; unelided ἀπό in Luke viii. 43 ἀπὸ ἐτῶν, *ib.* xiii. 21 ἀπὸ ἀνατολῶν, *ib.* xvi. 18 ἀπὸ ἀνδρός; unelided ὑπό in Luke vii. 27 ὑπὸ ἀνέμου, *ib.* xxi. 24 ὑπὸ ἐθνῶν &c. Unelided διά is found in Heb. v. 14 διὰ ἕξιν, 2 Cor. v. 7 διὰ εἴδους and before proper names. In general we may say that elision takes place before a pronoun, or a word with which the preposition is habitually joined, but not before a proper name, or a word which it is important to make distinct.

Other modes of avoiding hiatus are crasis, ν ἐφελκυστικόν, and final ς in such words as οὕτως.

Of crasis we have two examples, κἀγώ ii. 18, where see note, and κἄν for καὶ ἄν (=ἐάν) v. 15. For this use of ἄν see John xii. 32, xiii. 20, xvi. 23, xx. 23; and for the crasis Mark xvi. 18, Luke xiii. 9, also Winer p. 51.

ν ἐφελκυστικόν and the final ς in οὕτως are constant in St. James as in the rest of the N.T.:[1] cf. i. 6 ἔοικεν κλύδωνι, ii. 12 οὕτως λαλεῖτε.

Inflexions.

(*A*) *Nouns*, (*B*) *Verbs*.

A. (*a*) *Indeclinable Hebrew names*, Ἀβραάμ ii. 21, Ῥαάβ ii. 25, Σαβαώθ v. 4, Ἰώβ v. 11.

(*b*) *Irregular*, Ἰησοῦς i. 1, ii. 1.

(*c*) *Neuter nouns of third declension taking the place of masculine nouns of second declension, e.g.* τὸ ἔλεος James. ii. 13 and always in N.T.; also in Test. Zab. 5, 8, Clem. R. 9, 28, &c. ὁ ἔλεος always in classical writers, Philo M. ii. 44 ἐλέῳ, 52 ἔλεον: so τὸ σκότος is regularly used in N.T. while it is rare in classical writers: ζῆλος and πλοῦτος, always masculine in classical writers, as in James and the rest of the N.T., are sometimes used by St. Paul as neuters in the nom. and acc., see Eph. i. 7 (but ὁ πλοῦτος in Eph. i. 18), 2 Cor. ix. 2 τὸ ζῆλος (but τὸν ζῆλον in 2 Cor. vii. 7). (Cf. Blass § 9).

(*d*) *Adjectives with two instead of three terminations*, μάταιος i. 26, as in Tit. iii. 9, cf. Winer p. 80.

(*e*) *The dual is not used in the N.T.*

B. (*a*) *Indicative Mood of Verbs*.

a. *Future:*

(1) Of verbs in -ιζω (see Hort *l.c.* p. 163, Meisterhans *l.c.* p. 143).

-ίσω for -ιῶ usually, except in 2nd and 3rd pl., cf. ἐγγίσει iv. 8 (?), γνωρίσει Eph. vi. 21, γνωρίσουσιν Col. iv. 9 (?), βαπτίσει Matt. iii. 11 and elsewhere, χωρίσει Rom. viii. 35, θερίσει 2 Cor. ix. 6 (*bis*), Gal. vi. 7, 8 (*bis*), θερίσομεν 1 Cor. ix. 11, Gal. vi. 9,

[1] The best editors however have ἔδοξε κἀμοί Luke i. 2, ἔλαχε τοῦ *ib.* i. 9. See Winer p. 44, Schmid ii. p. 250, Meisterhans, *Gramm. d. Att. Inschr.* pp. 88, 89, Blass. § 5. 3.

χαρίσεται Rom. viii. 32, φωτίσει Apoc. xxii. 5 (?), 1 Cor. iv. 5, μετασχηματίσει Phil. iii. 21, χρηματίσει Rom. vii. 3, χρονίσει Heb. x. 37 (?), ἀφορίσει Matt. xxv. 32 (but ἀφοριοῦσιν *ib.* xiii. 49), κομίσεται Eph. vi. 8, Col. iii. 25 (?) (but κομιεῖσθε 1 Pet. v. 4). The following are examples of the Attic form, παροργιῶ Rom. x. 19, μετοικιῶ Acts vii. 43, καθαριεῖ Heb. ix. 14, διακαθαριεῖ Matt. iii. 12, χρονιεῖ Sirac. vi. 20, ἐλπιοῦμεν Sirac, ix. 19, φωτιοῦσιν Ep. Jerem. 67, στηριεῖ Sirac. vi. 36 (but στηρίξει, 1 Pet. v. 10 and aor. στηρίξατε James v. 8; on the other hand we find στήρισον Luke xxii. 32), καθιεῖ Job xxxvi. 7, καθιοῦνται Ps. cxxxii. 12, σκορπιεῖ Job. xxxiv. 15 (but διασκορπίσει xxxvii. 11), ἀφανιεῖ Job xxxix. 24, θεριοῦσιν Ps. cxxvi. 2, μακαριοῦσιν Luke i. 48, ἐλπιοῦσιν Matt. xii. 21, μετοικιῶ Acts vii. 43.

(2) κερδαίνω, κερδήσομεν iv. 13 (of which Veitch cites examples from the fragments of Euripides and from an epigram of Menecrates Smyrnaeus) instead of the classical κερδανοῦμεν. The form κερδήσω is related to κερδήσομαι (found in Herodotus and Josephus) as the forms ἀκούσω Matt. xii. 19, ἁμαρτήσω Matt. xviii. 21, ἀπαντήσω Mark xiv. 13, γελάσω Luke vi. 21, διώξω Matt. xxiii. 34, ἐπαινέσω 1 Cor. xi. 21, ἐπιορκήσω Matt. v. 33, κλαύσω Luke vi. 35, κράξω Luke xix. 40, ῥεύσω John vii. 38, σπουδάσω 2 Pet. i. 15, to the middle forms in ordinary use.

(3) λαμβάνω, λήμψομαι i. 12 (cf. προσωπολημψία ii. 1, προσωπολημπτεῖτε ii. 9), so Herod. λάμψομαι, ἐλάμφθην.

(4) ἐσθίω, φάγεται for ἔδεται v. 3, cf. Luke xiv. 15, xvii. 8 φάγεσαι καὶ πίεσαι, Gen. iii. 3 οὐ φάγεσθε, ver. 14, xliii. 16, Exod. xii. 8, Ezek. xxv. 4, Ps. cxxviii. 2, Eccl. iii. 13, Sir. vi. 2, 18, xliii. 21. It seems to be used as a present in Sirac. xxxvi. 23. See below p. ccxii.

β. *Aorist.*

First aorist used where the 2nd aor. was used by classical writers, *e.g.* βλαστάνω, ἐβλάστησα (v. 18) instead of ἔβλαστον; so κατέλειψα (Acts vi. 2) for κατέλιπον. We might be tempted to suppose that the 1st aor. was here preferred by St. James, as more suited to the transitive force which he gives to the word; but ἐβλάστησα is intransitive in Matt. xiii. 26, Heb. ix. 4, and ἔβλαστον is transitive in Eurip. *fr. inc.* 269 Wagner, cited by

Veitch, who also gives examples of the use of the 1st aor. from Empedocles, Theophrastus, &c.

γ. *Perfect.*

(1) 3rd pl. *-αν* for *-ασι*: *εἰσελήλυθαν* v. 4, see examples cited in note, and Hort *Notes on Orthography* (*G.T.* app. p. 166), also Blass § 21.

(2) *οἶδα, οἶδας* for *οἶσθα* John xxi. 15, 1 Cor. vii. 16 and always in N.T., also found in classical authors, *e.g.* Xen. *Mem.* iv. 6. 6, Eur. *Alc.* 780. *οἴδαμεν* Matt. xxii. 16 and always in N.T., also in classical authors, *e.g.* Xen. *Anab.* ii. 4. 6. *οἴδατε* James iv. 4 and usually in N.T., also in classical writers: *ἴστε* is however found in i. 19, Heb. xii. 17, perhaps in Eph. v. 5. *οἴδασιν* Luke xi. 44 and usually in N.T., also in Xen. *Oec.* xx. 14; but *ἴσασιν* in Acts xxvi. 4. Cf. Schmid i. pp. 85, 232.

(*b*) *Imperative Mood.*

(1) *ἤτω* for *ἔστω* v. 12, where see note. Veitch cites Hippocr. viii. 340, Aretaeus i. 2. 79.

(2) *κάθου* for *κάθησο* ii. 3, see note.

Syntax.

The Article.

The simplest use of the article when coupled with a singular noun is to single out, as concerned in the assertion made, one particular member of the class denoted by the noun, which member is supposed to be at once recognized by the reader either from his general knowledge, as *ὁ Θεός*, or from information supplied in the context, as *τὴν ἐσθῆτα, τῷ πτωχῷ* in ii. 3, after previous mention. Thus in ii. 14 *μὴ δύναται ἡ πίστις σῶσαι αὐτόν;* the article marks that the faith spoken of has been already described in the previous words; in ii. 25 *ἡ πόρνη* refers to one particular harlot, Rahab, of whom alone the assertion made holds good; in iii. 5 and the following verses *ἡ γλῶσσα* refers to the human tongue exclusively; in v. 9 *ὁ κριτής* is the Lord who is shortly to appear in judgment. Sometimes the class may consist, in the mind of the speaker, of one member only: *e.g.* i. 7 *παρὰ τοῦ Κυρίου* of the one God, i. 11 *ὁ ἥλιος...τῷ καύσωνι*, i. 27 *τοῦ κόσμου*, v. 18 *ὁ οὐρανός*. On the other hand the absence of the article implies that the assertion made about the noun is not more true of one member of the class than of another. This is naturally expressed by the English indefinite article in such passages as i. 6 *ἔοικεν κλύδωνι*, where the comparison is to a wave generally, not to any particular wave; so in iii. 12 *μὴ δύναται συκῆ ἐλαίας ποιῆσαι;* and ii. 18 *ἐὰν ἀδελφὸς ἢ ἀδελφὴ γυμνοὶ ὑπάρχωσιν*, ii. 24 *ἐξ ἔργων δικαιοῦται ἄνθρωπος*, i. 23 *ἐν ἐσόπτρῳ*.

When the class as a whole is spoken of, the article is used either with the collective noun, as *ἡ ἐκκλησία* v. 14; or with the plural of the persons or things composing the class, as *οἱ πλούσιοι* ii. 6, *τῶν ἵππων* iii. 3, *τοὺς ἀνθρώπους* iii. 9; or with one such person or thing, considered as typical or representative of the class (the 'generic' article), *e.g.* *ὁ πλούσιος* i. 11, *ἡ πηγή* iii. 11, *ὁ γεωργός* v. 7. If the article is omitted, the plural denotes that some of the class are concerned in the assertion, without saying anything as to the rest of the class, as *κἂν ἁμαρτίας ᾖ πεποιηκώς* v. 15, *πλῆθος ἁμαρτιῶν* v. 20, *ἐξ ἔργων δικαιοῦται ἄνθρωπος* ii. 24, *ἕλκουσιν ὑμᾶς εἰς κριτήρια* ii. 6.

If two or more nouns denoting different persons or things are joined by *καί*, the article is regularly repeated with each, as in iii. 11 *τὸ γλυκὺ καὶ τὸ πικρόν*; but if the nouns taken together are regarded as denoting or constituting one person or thing, the article is only used with the first, as in iii. 9 *εὐλογοῦμεν τὸν Θεὸν καὶ Πατέρα*.

One case in which the Greek use of the article agrees with French and German in opposition to the English is that of abstractions such as *ἡ δόξα*, *ἡ πίστις*, which are thus, as it were, personified and looked at as something existing apart from the person or action with which they are concerned, cf. ii. 17 *ἡ πίστις, ἐὰν μὴ ἔχῃ ἔργα, νεκρά ἐστιν*, ii. 20, 22 *ἡ πίστις συνήργει τοῖς ἔργοις αὐτοῦ καὶ ἐκ τῶν ἔργων ἡ πίστις ἐτελειώθη*, where R. V. has 'Faith wrought with his works and by works was faith made perfect.' In the oblique cases the article is generally omitted unless (as in i. 2 *τὸ δοκίμιον ὑμῶν τῆς πίστεως*, ii. 1 *τὴν πίστιν τοῦ Κυρίου ἡμῶν*) the noun is defined by the context. Thus we have ii. 14 *ἐὰν πίστιν λέγῃ τις ἔχειν* and i. 6 *αἰτείτω ἐν πίστει*, because it is not faith absolute, faith as a self-existent idea, which is spoken of, but merely faith relative, a quality attributed to an act or an individual. So ii. 24 *ἐξ ἔργων δικαιοῦται ἄνθρωπος καὶ οὐκ ἐκ πίστεως μόνον* 'from actions, not from believing.' In v. 15 ἡ εὐχὴ τῆς πίστεως σώσει τὸν κάμνοντα, the article is used with εὐχή because of the preceding προσευξάσθωσαν, and πίστεως has the article by sympathy, unless we prefer to translate 'Faith's prayer,' giving its full personifying force to the article. It is not necessary however, either in classical or Hellenistic Greek, for the abstract noun always to take the article even in the nominative: thus we have ii. 13 κατακαυχᾶται ἔλεος κρίσεως, where we might have expected τὸ ἔλεος τῆς κρίσεως κατακαυχᾶται, but the absence of the article gives a further point to the antithesis, first by bringing together the contrasted words, and second by calling attention to the connotation of the words. So iii. 10 ἐκ τοῦ αὐτοῦ στόματος ἐξέρχεται εὐλογία καὶ κατάρα 'out of the same mouth proceedeth blessing and cursing,' which might of course also be translated 'a blessing and a curse.' Such omission of the article is especially common in proverbs or other familiar and sententious phrases.

We will now consider the case in which the Greek anarthrous noun is represented in English by the noun with definite article. A well-known instance is that of βασιλεύς standing for the king of Persia. Here the intermediate stage would be ὁ βασιλεύς 'the king *par excellence*,' as Englishmen were accustomed to speak of 'the Duke' meaning 'the Duke of Wellington'; then after a time βασιλεύς by itself gets to be regarded as a proper name. In our Epistle, we find the article regularly used with Κύριος and Θεός in the nominative (*e.g.* i. 13, ii. 5, 19, iv. 6, 15, v. 11, 15); but the oblique cases sometimes take the article (*e.g.* iv. 4 ἔχθρα τοῦ Θεοῦ...ἐχθρὸς τοῦ Θεοῦ, ii. 1 τὴν πίστιν τοῦ Κυρίου, v. 7, 8 ἡ παρουσία τοῦ Κυρίου *bis*, iv. 7 ὑποτάγητε τῷ Θεῷ, iv. 8 ἐγγίσατε τῷ Θεῷ, ii. 23 ἐπίστευσεν τῷ Θεῷ, iii. 9 εὐλογοῦμεν τὸν Κύριον, i. 27 παρὰ τῷ Θεῷ, i. 7 παρὰ τοῦ Κυρίου) and sometimes omit it (*e.g.* i. 1 Θεοῦ καὶ Κυρίου δοῦλος, i. 20 ὀργὴ ἀνδρὸς δικαιοσύνην Θεοῦ οὐκ ἐργάζεται, iii. 9 καθ' ὁμοίωσιν Θεοῦ, ii, 23 φίλος Θεοῦ, v. 4 τὰ ὦτα Κυρίου, v. 10 ἐν τῷ ὀνόματι Κυρίου, v. 11 τὸ τέλος Κυρίου, i. 13 ἀπὸ Θεοῦ πειράζομαι, iv. 10 ἐνώπιον Κυρίου). The practice of St. James in this respect is that of the other writers of the N.T. The nominative Θεός, when it stands as the subject of the sentence, is rarely found without the article: St. Paul uses the anarthrous form twice in Gal. ii. 6 πρόσωπον Θεὸς ἀνθρώπου οὐ λαμβάνει, where the absence of the articles gives a sharper point to the antithesis, and vi. 7 Θεὸς οὐ μυκτηρίζεται: in both cases the absence of the article brings into greater prominence the characteristic quality and connotation of the noun, not so much 'God' simply, but 'He who is God.' The rule is less strict in regard to Κύριος, because this was freely used without the article in the LXX. for the Sacred Name: so we find it in quotations (Rom. iv. 8, ix. 28, 29, 1 Cor. iii. 20), especially in the phrase λέγει Κύριος (Acts vii. 49, xv. 17), but also in other passages, as Mark xiii. 20, Acts xii. 11. A similar word is Χριστός, which in the Gospels usually has the article, meaning 'the Anointed One,' but in the Epistles has become a proper name and drops the article. It has been often debated whether νόμος is used in a similar way without the article to denote the Mosaic law. It is used of this with the article ii. 10 ὅλον τὸν νόμον τηρήσῃ, ii. 9 ἐλεγχόμενοι ὑπὸ τοῦ νόμου, but without the article in ii. 11 γέγονας παραβάτης νόμου, iv. 11 οὐκ εἶ ποιητὴς νόμου, in both which cases the R. V. has 'the law,' but perhaps the Greek would be more exactly given by a compound, 'law-breaker,' 'law-observer.' So iv. 11 ὁ καταλαλῶν ἀδελφοῦ...καταλαλεῖ νόμου καὶ κρίνει νόμον, where also R. V. has 'the law,' but perhaps a more correct rendering would be 'speaks against law and judges law,' the absence of the article serving, as in the case of Θεός above, to give prominence to the connotation of the noun. A similar word is λόγος, which is found with the article in i. 21 τὸν ἔμφυτον λόγον; without it in i. 22 ποιηταὶ λόγου, 23 ἀκροατὴς λόγου, in both of which the R. V. has 'the word,' but the more strict interpretation would be 'word-doers,' 'word-hearer.'

A noun may be qualified by the addition of an adjective or participle, or of a genitive, or an adverb or adverbial phrase. If the article is used, a noun thus qualified may take one of three forms, either (1) ὁ καλὸς παῖς, ὁ τοῦ ἀνδρὸς πατήρ, or (2) ὁ παῖς ὁ καλός, τὴν δικαιοσύνην τὴν ἐκ τοῦ νόμου Rom. x. 5, or (3) the less common παῖς ὁ καλός, ἐν πίστει τῇ τοῦ Υἱοῦ τοῦ Θεοῦ Gal. ii. 20. With the genitive or adverbial phrase we find also, instead of the more idiomatic (1) or (2), the loose collocation (4) τὴν πίστιν τοῦ Κυρίου, where the article is attached to the governing substantive, which is either followed or preceded by the genitive or adverbial phrase. Of (1) we have the following examples: τὸν τίμιον καρπόν v. 7, τῆς καλῆς ἀναστροφῆς iii. 13, τὸν ἔμφυτον λόγον i. 21; of (2) τὴν ἐσθῆτα τὴν λαμπράν ii. 3, τῇ φύσει τῇ ἀνθρωπίνῃ iii. 7, ὁ νομοθέτης ὁ δυνάμενος iv. 12, ταῖς ταλαιπωρίαις ὑμῶν ταῖς ἐπερχομέναις v. 1, ὁ μισθὸς τῶν ἐργατῶν τῶν ἀμησάντων τὰς χώρας, ὁ ἀφυστερημένος v. 4; of (3) ἀδελφὸς ὁ ταπεινός (so *B*) i. 9, νόμον τέλειον τὸν τῆς ἐλευθερίας i. 25, ἀτμίς ἐστε ἡ πρὸς ὀλίγον φαινομένη iv. 14, where the article makes the tendency to appear and disappear a quality of the vapour, and not a mere accidental circumstance; so in Heb. vi. 7 γῆ γὰρ ἡ πιοῦσα, ix. 2 σκηνὴ κατεσκευάσθη ἡ πρώτη; of (4) we have τὰ ἐπιτήδεια τοῦ σώματος ii. 16, τὸν τροχὸν τῆς γενέσεως iii. 6, ἡ φιλία τοῦ κόσμου iv. 4, ἡ ὁρμὴ τοῦ εὐθύνοντος iii. 4. The loose construction (4) is more usual than the compact (1) in St. James and the N.T. generally, especially where a pronoun is concerned, as τὸ ἄνθος αὐτοῦ, ἐν τῷ ὕψει αὐτοῦ (very rarely the compact, as in i. 18 τῶν αὐτοῦ κτισμάτων,[1] Phil. ii. 30 τὸ ὑμῶν ὑστέρημα): sometimes the gen. precedes, as in iii. 3 τῶν ἵππων τοὺς χαλινούς, v. 12 ἤτω ὑμῶν τὸ ναὶ ναί, 1 Tim. iv. 14 ἵνα σου ἡ προκοπὴ φανερὰ ᾖ. The loose construction also prevails in long or complex phrases, cf. iv. 1 τῶν ἡδονῶν τῶν στρατευομένων ἐν τοῖς μέλεσιν, where the more idiomatic form would have been τῶν ἐν τοῖς μέλεσιν στρατευομένων ἡδονῶν, and i. 5 παρὰ τοῦ διδόντος Θεοῦ πᾶσιν ἁπλῶς, where we might have expected either π. τοῦ Θεοῦ τοῦ πᾶσιν ἁπλῶς διδόντος, or π. τοῦ πᾶσιν ἁπλῶς διδόντος Θεοῦ: so i. 3 τὸ δοκίμιον ὑμῶν τῆς πίστεως might have been more compactly expressed τὸ τῆς πίστεως ὑμῶν δοκίμιον. Classical parallels will be found in the note on i. 5. We find the compact construction however in iii. 9 τοὺς καθ' ὁμοίωσιν Θεοῦ γεγονότας and frequently in both Epistles of Peter, as in the First i. 14 ταῖς πρότερον ἐν τῇ ἀγνοίᾳ ὑμῶν ἐπιθυμίαις, ii. 9 τοῦ ἐκ σκότους ὑμᾶς καλέσαντος, ii. 15 τὴν τῶν ἀφρόνων ἀνθρώπων ἀγνωσίαν, iii. 2 τὴν ἐν φόβῳ ἁγίαν ἀναστροφὴν ὑμῶν, v. 1 ὁ καὶ τῆς μελλούσης ἀποκαλύπτεσθαι δόξης κοινωνός: in the Second i. 4 τῆς ἐν τῷ κόσμῳ ἐν τῇ ἐπιθυμίᾳ φθορᾶς, ii. 7 τῆς τῶν ἀθέσμων ἐν ἀσελγείᾳ ἀναστροφῆς, ii. 10 τοὺς ὀπίσω σαρκὸς ἐν ἐπιθυμίᾳ μιασμοῦ πορευομένους.

If we wish to distinguish the shades of meaning attaching to these different modes of qualifying the noun, (1) denotes the final stage of thought by which the subject is combined with its qualification so as to form one new complex subject; (2) gives the

[1] This shows that A. Buttmann, p. 102 (cited in Winer p. 193 n.), is wrong in his limitation, 'The insertion of the personal pronoun occurs in Paul only, and with no other pronoun than ὑμῶν.' Cf. also 1 Joh. ii. 27 τὸ αὐτοῦ χρίσμα, 1 Th. ii. 19, Rom. iii. 24.

definite subject first, and then adds its qualification as a second thought; (3) gives an indefinite subject first, and afterwards defines it by its qualification: this has still more the air of a second thought. Both (2) and (3) may serve a rhetorical purpose by giving prominence to the qualification, which is to some extent merged and lost in (1). The last (4) is the least artistic form, and gives the mental impression in its first rough shape, unmodified by the secondary action of the mind.

In these compound phrases the use of the article is also affected by what may be called the Law of Correlation or Sympathy. If one noun is dependent on another, the article is, in general, used either with both or with neither; and thus, if the one noun can dispense with the article, it is sometimes omitted with the other also, even when, if it stood alone, the latter would naturally have taken the article. Thus we have *ἄνθος χόρτου* i. 10, not *ἄνθος τοῦ χόρτου, δοῦλος Θεοῦ* i. 1, not *δοῦλος τοῦ Θεοῦ, ἀκροατὴς λόγου* i. 23, not *ἀκροατὴς τοῦ λόγου, ἡμέρᾳ σφαγῆς*, not *τῇ ἡμέρᾳ σφαγῆς* or *ἡμέρᾳ τῆς σφαγῆς, νόμον τὸν τῆς ἐλευθερίας* i. 25, *διὰ νόμου ἐλευθερίας* ii. 12; so *ἔργα νόμου* or *τὰ ἔργα τοῦ νόμου*, not *ἔργα τοῦ νόμου* or *τὰ ἔργα νόμου*. Apparent exceptions may sometimes be explained (as v. 10 *ἐν τῷ ὀνόματι Κυρίου*, v. 11 *τὸ τέλος Κυρίου*) by the fact that *Κύριος* is a proper name, the construction being the same as in *τὴν ὑπομονὴν Ἰώβ*.

From the above uses of the article in an attributive phrase we must carefully distinguish its use in predication, of which the type is *ἀγαθὸς ὁ ἀνήρ*, the subject being known by the presence of the article, the predicate by its absence, as in i. 26 *τούτου μάταιος ἡ θρησκεία*, iv. 4 *ἡ φιλία τοῦ κόσμου ἔχθρα τοῦ Θεοῦ ἐστίν*. Hence we characterize *μακάριος ἀνήρ* in i. 12 as a predicate (like *τέλειος ἀνήρ* in iii. 2), 'He is a blessed man who,' instead of dividing them with the English Version and making *ἀνήρ* subject, 'Blessed is the man.' The same phrase is shown to be predicative in Rom. iv. 8 (*μακάριος ἀνὴρ οὗ οὐ μὴ λογίσηται ἁμαρτίαν*) by the preceding *μακάριοι ὧν ἀφέθησαν αἱ ἀνομίαι*. In James ii. 19 *εἷς ἐστὶν ὁ θεός* the presence of the article shows that *εἷς* is predicative; in iv. 12, if we read *εἷς ἐστὶν νομοθέτης*, the absence of the article shows that *εἷς* is subject; but if we read *εἷς ἔστιν νομοθέτης*, making *ἔστιν* not the copula, but the substantive verb, *εἷς* becomes an epithet of *νομ.* 'there is one lawgiver.' And so *θρησκεία καθαρά* in i. 27 'this, viz. visiting widows and orphans,

&c., is pure religion,' cf. Acts ix. 15 σκεῦος ἐκλογῆς ἐστί μοι οὗτος, John i. 19 αὕτη ἐστὶν ἡ μαρτυρία Ἰωάννου. We have examples of oblique predication in i. 27 ἄσπιλον ἑαυτὸν τηρεῖν, v. 10 ὑπόδειγμα λάβετε τῆς κακοπαθίας τοὺς προφήτας, and ii. 5 οὐχ ὁ Θεὸς ἐξελέξατο τοὺς πτωχοὺς τῷ κόσμῳ πλουσίους ἐν πίστει; 'has not God chosen the poor to the world (to be) rich in faith?' The article however may be used with the predicative noun when it does not denote a class in which the subject is included, but a concept of equal extension with which it is declared to be identical, as iii. 6 ὁ κόσμος τῆς ἀδικίας ἡ γλῶσσα καθίσταται 'the tongue is (represents) the unrighteous world.'

The English possessive pronoun is expressed in classical Greek by the article alone, except for the sake of clearness or emphasis. So too occasionally in the N.T. *e.g.* Matt. xxvii. 24 ἀπενίψατο τάς χεῖρας, Luke v. 13 ἐκτείνας τὴν χεῖρα, James ii. 15 λειπόμενοι τῆς ἐφημέρου τροφῆς 'in lack of their daily food' [or perhaps 'the day's food'], ii. 14 ἐὰν πίστιν λέγῃ τις ἔχειν, ἔργα δὲ μὴ ἔχῃ, μὴ δύναται ἡ πίστις σῶσαι αὐτόν; 'can his faith save him?' [But perhaps it is better to take the article simply as referring to the previous πίστις, 'can the faith (spoken of) save him'?], v. 16 ἐξομολογεῖσθε ἀλλήλοις τὰς ἁμαρτίας 'confess your sins to each other,' or perhaps 'confess the sins (spoken of in v. 15)'. The latter however seems here less appropriate, as the sins spoken of in v. 15 were those of the sick man alone.

Generally however in the N.T. the genitive of the demonstrative or personal pronoun is added, *e.g.* i. 21 τὰς ψυχὰς ὑμῶν, ii. 8 τὸν πλησίον σου, ii. 18 τὴν πίστιν σου...τῶν ἔργων μου, iii. 16 τοῖς μέλεσιν ὑμῶν, i. 8 ταῖς ὁδοῖς αὐτοῦ, i. 10 τῷ ὕψει αὐτοῦ...τῇ ταπεινώσει αὐτοῦ, i. 11 τὸ ἄνθος αὐτοῦ...τοῦ προσώπου αὐτοῦ...ἐν ταῖς πορείαις αὐτοῦ. Where the genitive of the pronoun belongs to more than one noun, it may be stated only once, *e.g.* iii. 13 δειξάτω ἐκ τῆς καλῆς ἀναστροφῆς (αὐτοῦ) τὰ ἔργα αὐτοῦ, iv. 9 ὁ γέλως ὑμῶν εἰς πένθος μεταστραφήτω καὶ ἡ χαρὰ (ὑμῶν) εἰς κατήφειαν, ii. 18 δείξω ἐκ τῶν ἔργων μου τὴν πίστιν (μου).

Occasionally the article is omitted, and the pronoun alone employed, as in i. 26 μὴ χαλιναγωγῶν γλῶσσαν ἑαυτοῦ ἀλλ' ἀπατῶν καρδίαν ἑαυτοῦ, ii. 2 εἰς συναγωγὴν ὑμῶν (if we translate 'into your synagogue' instead of 'into a synagogue,' or 'meeting, of yours'), v. 20 ὁ ἐπιστρέψας ἁμαρτωλὸν ἐκ πλάνης ὁδοῦ αὐτοῦ σώσει ψυχὴν αὐτοῦ. This is very common in the LXX., and especially in the

Apocrypha, *e.g.* ἐπὶ καρδίαν ἡμῶν Baruch iii. 7, cf. Sir. ii. 17, v. 2! xiii. 19, Psalm. Sal. vi. 7, μὴ μνησθῇς ἀδικιῶν πατέρων ἡμῶν, ἀλλὰ μνήσθητι χειρός σου Baruch iii. 5, δικαιώματα αὐτοῦ οὐκ ἔγνωσαν οὐδὲ ἐπορεύθησαν ὁδοῖς ἐντολῶν Θεοῦ *ib.* iv. 13, ἐπὶ τραχήλους αὐτῶν ἐπιβήσῃ, v. 25, 1 Macc. ii. 10 ποῖον ἔθνος οὐκ ἐκληρονόμησε βασιλείαν αὐτῆς; ('her kingdom'), v. 44 ἐν ὀργῇ αὐτῶν 'in their wrath,' v. 70 ἔθαψαν αὐτὸν ἐν τάφοις πατέρων αὐτῶν 'in the sepulchre of their fathers,' Sir. i. 11 ἐν ἡμέρᾳ τελευτῆς αὐτοῦ εὐλογηθήσεται 'in the day of his end,' iii. 5 ἐν ἡμέρᾳ προσευχῆς αὐτοῦ, iii. 10 ἐν ἀτιμίᾳ πατρός σου, Psalm. Sal. iv. 18 ἀπὸ κροτάφων αὐτοῦ 'from his temples,' viii. 5 παρελύθη γόνατά μου coming between συνετρίβη ἡ ὀσφύς μου and ἐφοβήθη ἡ καρδία μου. In like manner the article is omitted with the possessive pronoun, *e.g.* Prov. iii. 5 ἐπὶ σῇ σοφίᾳ μὴ ἐπαίρου, v. 21 τήρησον ἐμὴν βουλήν.

Sometimes both article and genitive are omitted, as in iv. 8 καθαρίσατε χεῖρας ἁμαρτωλοὶ καὶ ἁγνίσατε καρδίας δίψυχοι 'cleanse your hands ye sinners, and purify your hearts ye double-minded.' Probably this is to be explained as a proverbial phrase approaching to a compound, like our 'shake-hands,' 'up-stairs.' We may compare Sir. xxxviii. 10 εὔθυνον χεῖρας καὶ ἀπὸ πάσης ἁμαρτίας καθάρισον καρδίαν, 1 Macc. xii. 39 ἐζήτησε Τρύφων ἐκτεῖναι χεῖρα ἐπὶ 'Αντίοχον.

I will now take in order, with one or two exceptions which will be noted later, the remaining instances in which an anarthrous Greek noun takes the definite article in the R.V. These are i. 10 ὡς ἄνθος χόρτου παρελεύσεται 'as the flower of the grass he shall pass away.' I see no objection here to a more literal rendering 'as a flower of grass,' *i.e.* 'as a wild flower'; in ver. 11 we have the article τὸν χόρτον, τὸ ἄνθος because they have been already referred to: i. 20 ὀργὴ ἀνδρὸς δικαιοσύνην Θεοῦ οὐκ ἐργάζεται 'the wrath of man worketh not the righteousness of God' might perhaps be rendered 'a man's wrath worketh not God's righteousness,' but I am disposed to think that the absence of the article (which is facilitated here by the law of correlation, δικαιοσύνην dropping its article in order to conform with the naturally anarthrous Θεοῦ, and the phrase ὀργὴ ἀνδρός being in like manner made conformable to the phrase δ. Θ.) is intended to emphasize the contrast by bringing together the contrasted nouns, as in ii. 13, of which I have spoken above: v. 16 πολὺ ἰσχύει δέησις δικαίου ἐνεργουμένη 'the supplication of a righteous man availeth much in its working' might perhaps be better translated 'a righteous man's supplication availeth much when actuated by the Spirit.' iii. 18 *καρπὸς δὲ δικαιοσύνης ἐν εἰρήνῃ σπείρεται*, here it is to be noted that *καρπ. δικ.* is a phrase found in Phil. i. 11, Heb. xii. 11, as well as in Amos vi. 12, Prov. xi. 30, and is therefore liable to the abbreviation which naturally attaches to all proverbial expressions. Possibly also the writer may have felt that the proleptic use of *καρπός* would have acquired additional harshness if the article were prefixed. It would have been natural to say *τὸ σπέρμα σπείρεται*, but *καρπός* is not that which is sown, but that which it is hoped will spring up. Peaceful sowing results in righteousness as its fruit.

I proceed to the case of anarthrous epithets where the English has the definite article. Such are v. 3 *ἐν ἐσχάταις ἡμέραις* 'in the last days,' which occurs also in 2 Tim. iii. 1: it may be compared with 1 John ii. 18 *ἐσχάτη ὥρα ἐστίν*, 1 Pet. i. 5 *ἐν καιρῷ ἐσχάτῳ*, Sir. i. 11 *εὖ ἔσται ἐπ' ἐσχάτων*, and even ii. 3 *ἐπ' ἐσχάτων σου*. On the other hand we find *ἐν ταῖς ἐσχάταις ἡμέραις* Acts ii. 17, and *τῇ ἐσχάτῃ ἡμέρᾳ* seven times in St. John's Gospel. In James v. 7 the R.V. 'until it receive the early and the latter rain' stands for the Greek *ἕως λάβῃ πρόϊμον καὶ ὄψιμον*. In this last case both article and substantive are dropped by colloquial abbreviation, as we have 'Paul's' in old writers for 'St. Paul's church.'

In English we join the article with the superlative, even when it forms part of the predicate; whereas the Greeks always omitted it in such cases (*e.g.* *πάντων φιλομαθέστατος Κῦρος ἦν*), and also where the superlative denotes a high degree of any quality, as James iii. 4 *ὑπὸ ἐλαχίστου πηδαλίου*. Similarly the classical writers omit the article with the ordinal numeral, as Thuc. v. 81 *τέταρτον καὶ δέκατον ἔτος τῷ πολέμῳ ἐτελεύτα*, and so, in Matt. xx. 3 and elsewhere, we find expressions like *περὶ τρίτην ὥραν*. The omission is probably to be accounted for by the wish to shorten familiar expressions where there is no danger of misunderstanding being caused by it, just as we might say '7th Victoria,' or 'Acts seven two.'

I come now to the phrases which I had reserved before: i. 18 *ἀπεκύησεν ἡμᾶς λόγῳ ἀληθείας*, with which may be compared 2 Cor. vi. 7 *ἐν λόγῳ ἀληθείας, ἐν δυνάμει Θεοῦ*, and Col. i. 5 *ἐν τῷ λόγῳ τῆς ἀληθείας τοῦ εὐαγγελίου*. The meaning in the two latter expressions is the same, but in Colossians it is stated at length, whereas in Corinthians the Apostle just touches it in his rapid enumeration of the different ways in which he showed himself a minister of God. Similarly we have *λόγον ζωῆς* Phil. ii. 16. Both *λόγος* and *ἀλήθεια* belong to the class of abstract words which may either take the article or not, according to the pleasure of the speaker; and if one is made anarthrous, the other will usually be so too by the rule of sympathy or correlation. A precisely similar case is ii. 12 *διὰ νόμου ἐλευθερίας μέλλοντες κρίνεσθαι.* In both cases I think the qualifying noun gains additional importance by the omission of the article. In ii. 8 we have the anarthrous adjective *νόμον τελεῖτε βασιλικόν,* where the adjective comes in rather as an after-thought to complete the phrase *νόμον τελεῖτε.* In my note I have compared *πνεῦμα ἅγιον, διαθήκη ἁγία* Luke i. 72, 1 Macc. i. 15, 73.

The remaining case (i. 25) combines the adjective and the genitive *νόμον τέλειον τὸν τῆς ἐλευθερίας.* Here the addition would be quite regular if *τέλειον* were absent. It is best, I think, to regard *νόμον τέλειον* as parallel to *νόμον βασιλικόν* above, being equivalent to *τὸν τέλειον νόμον.*

It must indeed be confessed that the Hellenistic writers are very lax in their use of the article with a noun qualified by an attributive adjective or genitive. They may be said to have introduced into Greek prose the freedom of Greek poetry, itself a tradition handed down from the Homeric ages, before the use of the article had been developed out of the demonstrative pronoun. This freedom would naturally commend itself to foreigners learning Greek, to whom Greek gender would be as great a stumbling-block as German or French gender is to Englishmen now, and who, as a matter of fact, did often confuse the masculine and neuter gender, see above p. clxxxi. We find examples in Baruch i. 3 *ἐν ὦσι παντὸς τοῦ λαοῦ,* where *ἐν ὦσι* may be regarded as a prepositional phrase (like *ἐκ στόματος λεόντων* 1 Macc. ii. 60), Bar. i. 8 *τὰ σκεύη οἴκου Κυρίου,* where the omission of the article before *οἴκου* is probably to be explained by its forming a phrase with *Κυρίου,* Sir. i. 5 *ῥίζα σοφίας τίνι ἀπεκαλύφθη;* ('the root of wisdom'), ver. 9 *φόβος Κυρίου καύχημα* 'the fear of the Lord is glory,' ver. 16 *στέφανος σοφίας φόβος Κυρίου* 'the fear of the Lord is the crown of wisdom,' vii. 9 *Θεῷ ὑψίστῳ* 'to the most high God,' xxxi. 13 *πνεῦμα φοβουμένων*

Κύριον ζήσεται, Psalm. Sal. iii. 7 *ἀλήθεια τῶν δικαίων παρὰ Θεοῦ* 'the truth of the just comes from God,' iii. 16 *ἡ ζωὴ αὐτῶν ἐν φωτὶ Κυρίου*, xiii. 1 *δεξιὰ Κυρίου ἐσκέπασέν με* followed by *ὁ βραχίων Κυρίου ἔσωσέν με*, Job xxxi. 18 *διὰ ἀσέβειαν δώρων ὧν ἐδέχοντο*, xxxviii. 17 *ἀνοίγονται πύλαι θανάτου*, v. 31 *δεσμὸν Πλειάδος ἔγνως ;* xxxix. 1 *ἔγνως καιρὸν τοκετοῦ τραγελάφων πέτρας ;* Prov. ii. 17 *ἡ ἀπολιποῦσα διδασκαλίαν νεότητος καὶ διαθήκην θείαν ἐπιλελησμένη*, ver. 22 *ὁδοὶ ἀσεβῶν ἐκ γῆς ὀλοῦνται*, iii. 33 *κατάρα Θεοῦ ἐν οἴκοις ἀσεβῶν*, 'the curse of God is on the houses of the impious,' 2 Sam. xxiv. 10 *ἐπάταξε καρδία Δαβὶδ αὐτόν*, Jonah ii. 4 *ἀπέρριψάς με εἰς βάθη καρδίας θαλάσσης*. We also find the article omitted with the participle when used as a substantive, as in Prov. v. 13 *οὐκ ἤκουον φωνὴν παιδεύοντός με*. For similar omissions in N.T. cf. Luke i. 15 *ἐκ κοιλίας μητρὸς αὐτοῦ*, ver. 17 *ἐν πνεύματι καὶ δυνάμει Ἠλία, ἐπιστρέψαι καρδίας πατέρων ἐπὶ τέκνα καὶ ἀπειθεῖς ἐν φρονήσει δικαίων*, ver. 35 *δύναμις Ὑψίστου ἐπισκιάσει σε*, ver. 51 *διεσκόρπισεν ὑπερηφάνους διανοίᾳ καρδίας αὐτῶν*, ver. 78 *διὰ σπλάγχνα ἐλέους Θεοῦ ἡμῶν*, ii. 9 *δόξα Κυρίου*, ver. 13 *πλῆθος στρατιᾶς οὐρανίου*, ver. 25 *προσδεχόμενος παράκλησιν τοῦ Ἰσραήλ*, Heb. iv. 3 *ἀπὸ καταβολῆς κόσμου*, ver. 13 *λόγον δικαιοσύνης*, 1 Pet. i. 1 *ἐκλεκτοῖς παρεπιδήμοις διασπορᾶς*, ver. 23 *διὰ λόγου ζῶντος Θεοῦ καὶ μένοντος* 'by the word of God which liveth and abideth,' iii. 12 *ὀφθαλμοὶ Κυρίου ἐπὶ δικαίους καὶ ὦτα αὐτοῦ εἰς δέησιν αὐτῶν, πρόσωπον δὲ Κυρίου ἐπὶ ποιοῦντας κακά*, 2 Pet. ii. 5 *ἀρχαίου κόσμου οὐκ ἐφείσατο...κατακλυσμὸν κόσμῳ ἀσεβῶν ἐπάξας*. It is curious that the Apocalypse in spite of its startling solecisms of construction approaches more nearly to the classical usage as regards the article than many other parts of the N.T.

The use of the article with *πᾶς* and *ὅλος* is the same in the N.T. as in ordinary Greek. When *πᾶς* is anarthrous, it is equivalent to the Eng. 'every,' if joined to a common singular noun, as in i. 17 *πᾶν δώρημα τέλειον*, i. 19 *πᾶς ἄνθρωπος*, iii. 7 *πᾶσα φύσις θηρίων*, iii. 16 *πᾶν φαῦλον πρᾶγμα* : if joined to a plural, or to an abstract noun which properly denotes only a single subject, it is equivalent to 'all,' as in i. 21 *πᾶσαν ῥυπαρίαν* 'all filthiness,' i. 2 *πᾶσαν χαρὰν ἡγήσασθε* 'think it entire joy'; so perhaps *πᾶσα δόσις ἀγαθή* 'all good giving' in i. 17; in the phrase *πᾶσα καύχησις τοιαύτη* iv. 16 it may be better to translate 'every such boasting,' because the addition of *τοιαύτη* splits up the idea of *καύχησις*, while the absence of the article forbids us to make a new unit, such as would be implied by ἡ τοιαύτη καύχησις. We find the article in i. 8 ἐν πάσαις ταῖς ὁδοῖς αὐτοῦ 'in all his ways,' and with ὅλος in ii. 10 ὅλον τὸν νόμον, iii. 2 ὅλον τὸ σῶμα. More rarely we find ὅλος placed after the article and substantive, as in τὸν κόσμον ὅλον Mark viii. 36. In both these cases ὅλος is properly in apposition, and is thus more forcible than when it is placed between the article and substantive, as it sometimes is in classical writings, but never in the N.T. Πᾶς however occurs in this order in Acts xx. 18 τὸν πάντα χρόνον, Gal. v. 14 ὁ πᾶς νόμος, &c.

An adjective or participle may stand by itself as a substantive, if its omitted subject is made sufficiently clear by gender, number, and context, e.g. Θεὸς ὑπερηφάνοις ἀντιτάσσεται iv. 6, εἰδότι καλὸν ποιεῖν.. ἁμαρτία ἐστίν iv. 17; and such a substantive may be defined by the article like a proper substantive, e.g. i. 6 ὁ διακρινόμενος, i. 11 ὁ πλούσιος, ii. 16 τὰ ἐπιτήδεια, iii. 11 τὸ γλυκύ, τὸ πικρόν. In like manner the infinitive, which is used by itself as a substantive in apposition in i. 27 θρησκεία καθαρὰ αὕτη ἐστίν, ἐπισκέπτεσθαι ὀρφανούς, may be defined by the article and thus become capable of inflexion, as in τοῦ μὴ βρέξαι, v. 17. The same holds good of adverbs or any other indeclinable word or phrase, as in v. 12 ἤτω ὑμῶν τὸ ναὶ ναί, where the article serves to distinguish the first ναί, which is subject, from the second ναί, which is predicate. It has been stated above that a substantive may be qualified by an adverb interposed between it and the article, as ἡ ἄνωθεν σοφία in iii. 17. If the noun is such as can be easily supplied in thought, from its being part of a common phrase or any other reason, it is often omitted, as in ἡ αὔριον (ἡμέρα) iv. 13. Again the neuter article is often used with the genitive to express generally what belongs to the person or thing denoted, and thus we get the phrase τὸ τῆς αὔριον in the verse referred to.

Pronouns.

Demonstrative.

οὗτος used to emphasize the apodosis in i. 23 εἴ τις ἀκροατὴς... οὗτος ἔοικεν ἀνδρί κ.τ.λ, i. 25 ὁ παρακύψας εἰς νόμον τέλειον... οὗτος μακάριος. See Winer, p. 199. As subject, attracted to the gender of the predicative noun, i. 27 θρησκεία καθαρὰ αὕτη ἐστίν, ἐπισκέπτεσθαι ὀρφανούς.

ὅδε, supposed to be used for ὁ δεῖνα, see n. on iv. 13, εἰς τήνδε τὴν πόλιν.

αὐτός = Lat. *ipse*, emphatic, (*a*) ordinary use i. 12 ὁ Θεὸς ἀπείραστός ἐστιν, πειράζει δὲ αὐτὸς οὐδένα, ii. 6 (οἱ πλούσιοι) αὐτοὶ ἕλκουσιν ὑμᾶς: (*b*) special Hellenistic use ii. 7 οὐκ αὐτοὶ βλασφημοῦσιν, see notes on the two verses: (*c*) the nom. is not used pleonastically by St. James, as by St. Luke in xxiv. 13, 14 δύο ἐξ αὐτῶν ἦσαν πορευόμενοι...καὶ αὐτοὶ ὡμίλουν πρὸς ἀλλήλους.

ὁ αὐτός iii. 10 ἐκ τοῦ αὐτοῦ στόματος, ver. 11 ἐκ τῆς αὐτῆς ὀπῆς. St. James does not use αὐτὸς ὁ in this sense, as St. Luke does in the phrase αὐτῇ τῇ ὥρᾳ (lit. 'at the very hour'), which occurs in ii. 38, vii. 21, Acts xvi. 18 and elsewhere.

αὐτός = Lat. *is*, unemphatic in the oblique cases; but gaining a certain emphasis by repetition, as in iii. 9 ἐν αὐτῇ εὐλογοῦμεν καὶ ἐν αὐτῇ καταρώμεθα: or by position, as in St. Luke xxiv. 24 αὐτὸν δὲ οὐκ εἶδον, ver. 31 αὐτῶν δὲ διηνοίχθησαν οἱ ὀφθαλμοί. It is also used pleonastically, not only in the genitive with the article, as in the cases mentioned above; but when occurring in apposition to the noun, or participle equivalent to noun, as in iv. 17 εἰδότι καὶ μὴ ποιοῦντι ἁμαρτία αὐτῷ ἐστιν.

αὐτοῦ instead of ἑαυτοῦ,[1] in i. 18 ἀπεκύησεν ἡμᾶς εἰς τὸ εἶναι ἡμᾶς ἀπαρχὴν τῶν αὐτοῦ κτισμάτων (ACP have ἑαυτοῦ); i. 26 Tregelles and Tischendorf read (with Sin, AKL &c.) μὴ χαλιναγωγῶν γλῶσσαν αὐτοῦ ἀλλὰ ἀπατῶν καρδίαν αὐτοῦ, where I have followed WH. in reading (with B+) ἑαυτοῦ. See also note on v. 20, where some of the latest editors read ψυχὴν αὐτοῦ.

ἑαυτοῦ is used for σεαυτοῦ in i. 22 γίνεσθε ποιηταὶ καὶ μὴ ἀκροαταὶ μόνον παραλογιζόμενοι ἑαυτούς, ii. 4 διεκρίθητε ἐν ἑαυτοῖς. We find however σεαυτόν in ii. 8.

The use of the article with the demonstrative pronoun is the same as in classical writers, cf. i. 7 ὁ ἄνθρωπος ἐκεῖνος, iii. 15 αὕτη ἡ σοφία, iv. 13 τήνδε τὴν πόλιν.

Relative.

Attracted ii. 5 κληρονόμους τῆς βασιλείας ἧς ἐπηγγείλατο. Indefinite (with ἐάν for ἄν) iv. 4 ὃς ἐὰν βουληθῇ φίλος εἶναι τοῦ κόσμου; ii. 10 ὅστις ὅλον τὸν νόμον τηρήσῃ, iv. 13 (οἱ λέγον-

[1] See Lightfoot on Col. i. 20, Hort *App.* 144 and examples in Schweighäuser's *Lex. Polyb.* s.v.

τες...κερδήσομεν) οἵτινες οὐκ ἐπίστασθε τὸ τῆς αὔριον, 'whereas ye know not,' see note.

Interrogative.

τίς introducing hypothetical clause iii. 13 τίς σοφὸς ἐν ὑμῖν; δειξάτω: with pregnant force iv. 12 σὺ τίς εἶ; 'how weak and ignorant?'

ποία ἡ ζωή; iv. 14: dependent i. 24 ἐπελάθετο ὁποῖος ἦν. Double question iii. 5 ἡλίκον πῦρ ἡλίκην ὕλην ἀνάπτει.

Indefinite with idiomatic force i. 18 εἰς τὸ εἶναι ἡμᾶς ἀπαρχήν τινα τῶν αὐτοῦ κτισμάτων.

Number and Gender.

A singular noun is used for a plural in iii. 14 εἰ ἐριθίαν ἔχετε ἐν τῇ καρδίᾳ ὑμῶν, in contrast with v. 5 ἐθρέψατε τὰς καρδίας ὑμῶν, and v. 8 στηρίξατε τὰς καρδίας ὑμῶν.

A singular verb precedes two subjects joined by καί: iii. 10 ἐκ τοῦ αὐτοῦ στόματος ἐξέρχεται εὐλογία καὶ κατάρα.

First plural of verb used in courtesy: iii. 1 μεῖζον κρίμα λημψόμεθα, iii. 9 ἐν αὐτῇ εὐλογοῦμεν καὶ ἐν αὐτῇ καταρῶμεν.

A plural verb and adjective follow a subject consisting of two nouns joined by a disjunctive conjunction in ii. 15 ἐὰν ἀδελφὸς ἢ ἀδελφὴ γυμνοὶ ὑπάρχωσιν.

A plural verb follows a singular indefinite pronoun: ii. 16 ἐάν τις ἐξ ὑμῶν εἴπῃ...μὴ δῶτε δέ.

The imperative ἄγε is used as an exclamation with a plural in iv. 13 ἄγε νῦν οἱ λέγοντες, and v. 1 ἄγε νῦν οἱ πλούσιοι.

The neuter plural referring to persons is used with a plural verb in ii. 10 τὰ δαιμόνια πιστεύουσιν.

The plural of abstract nouns is used to express the various manifestations of the abstract idea, e.g. ii. 1 μὴ ἐν προσωπολημψίαις ἔχετε τὴν πίστιν.

Cases.

(1) *Nominative.*

There is a tendency in the Hellenistic writings, notably in the Apocalypse, to put the noun of apposition into the nominative, even where the original noun is oblique; thus we have in iii. 8 τὴν γλῶσσαν οὐδεὶς δαμάσαι δύναται followed by ἀκατάστατον κακόν, μεστὴ ἰοῦ, which we can here explain as a new sentence with the subject ἡ γλῶσσά ἐστιν understood; but such an explanation fails in Apoc. iii. 12 γράψω ἐπ' αὐτὸν τὸ ὄνομα τῆς καινῆς Ἱερουσαλήμ, ἡ καταβαίνουσα ἀπὸ τοῦ Θεοῦ μου, καὶ τὸ ὄνομά μου τὸ καινόν, and in other passages referred to in my note. We have however many examples of the ordinary apposition, as in the nom. i. 1 Ἰάκωβος δοῦλος, ver. 8 ὁ ἄνθρωπος ἐκεῖνος...ἀνὴρ δίψυχος, ii. 21 Ἀβραὰμ ὁ πατὴρ ἡμῶν, ii. 25 Ῥαὰβ ἡ πόρνη, i. 27 θρησκεία καθαρὰ αὕτη ἐστίν, ἐπισκέπτεσθαι ὀρφανούς, where αὕτη is in apposition to the following infinitive; in the gen. i. 1 Κυρίου Ἰησοῦ Χριστοῦ, and the harsh use in ii. 2 τὴν πίστιν τοῦ Κυρίου ἡμῶν Ἰησοῦ Χριστοῦ, τῆς δόξης, where see note; in the acc. ii. 21 Ἰσαὰκ τὸν υἱὸν αὐτοῦ; not to mention such cases as i. 1 ταῖς δώδεκα φυλαῖς ταῖς ἐν τῇ διασπορᾷ, iii. 6 ἡ γλῶσσα ἡ σπιλοῦσα, v. 4 ὁ μισθὸς ὁ ἀφυστερημένος, which are treated of under the article.

(2) *Accusative.* See *Prepositions.*

Of the Object, ii. 7 βλασφημοῦσιν τὸ ὄνομα (for εἰς, περί or κατά cl.), iii. 9 καταρώμεθα τοὺς ἀνθρώπους (for cl. dat.), v. 6 κατεδικάσατε τὸν δίκαιον (for cl. gen.), v. 12 μὴ ὀμνύετε τὸν οὐρανόν (so in classical writers, who also use κατά *c. gen.* as in Heb. vi. 13, but never εἰς or ἐν, as in Matt. v. 34, 35).

Of Duration, v. 17 οὐκ ἔβρεξεν ἐνιαυτοὺς τρεῖς.

Adverbial (defining the extent of the action), i. 6 μηδὲν διακρινόμενος, iii. 2 πολλὰ πταίειν.

Subject of Infinitive: see below, under *Pleonasm.*

(3) *Genitive.* See *Prepositions* and *Infinitive.*

With substantives, (*a*) possessive, (a_1) objective, (a_2) subjective, (*b*) of quality, (*c*) of material.

(a_1) i. 22 ποιητὴς λόγου, iv. 11 ποιητὴς νόμου, i. 25 ποιητὴς ἔργου, iv. 4 φίλος τοῦ κόσμου, ii. 1 τὴν πίστιν τοῦ Κυρίου (representing the verbal phrase πιστεύω Κυρίῳ or εἰς Κ.).

(a_2) i. 20 ὀργὴ ἀνδρός, δικαιοσύνη Θεοῦ, v. 11 τὸ τέλος Κυρίου, v. 15 ἡ εὐχὴ τῆς πίστεως.

(*b*) i. 25 and ii. 12 νόμος ἐλευθερίας, i. 25 ἀκροατὴς ἐπιλησμονῆς, ii. 4 κριταὶ διαλογίσμων πονηρῶν, iii. 6 ὁ κόσμος τῆς ἀδικίας, and (unless these two had better be classed as 'possessive,' γένεσις and τροπή being personified) i. 23 τὸ πρόσωπον τῆς γενέσεως αὐτοῦ, i. 17 τροπῆς ἀποσκίασμα.

(c) i. 12 τὸν στέφανον τῆς ζωῆς 'the crown which consists in life eternal,' iii. 18 καρπὸς δικαιοσύνης 'the fruit which consists in justice.'

With adjectives, (a) of possession and privation, (b) defining the sphere.

(a) iii. 8 μεστὴ ἰοῦ, iii. 17 μεστὴ ἐλέους.

(b) i. 13 ἀπείραστος κακῶν, ii. 10 πάντων ἔνοχος (the latter would come under the smaller category of judicial words).

With verbs, (a) of attainment or its opposite, (b) of aim with infinitive, (c) compounded with κατά.

(a) i. 5 λείπεται σοφίας, ii. 15 λειπόμενοι τροφῆς.

(b) v. 17 προσηύξατο τοῦ μὴ βρέξαι.

(c) ii. 6 καταδυναστεύουσιν ὑμῶν, ii. 13 κατακαυχᾶται κρίσεως, iv. 11 καταλαλεῖ νόμου, ἀλλήλων, but καταδικάζω and καταρῶμαι take an accusative in St. James.

The *Genitive Absolute* does not occur in this epistle.

(4) *Dative.* See *Prepositions.*

General, of Indirect Object, with transitive verbs (a), with intransitive or passive verbs or adjectives (b).

(a) ii. 5 ἐπηγγείλατο, iv. 6 δίδωσιν.

(b) i. 6 ἔοικεν κλύδωνι, i. 23 ἔοικεν ἀνδρί, iv. 6 ὑπερηφάνοις ἀντιτάσσεται, iii. 3 εἰς τὸ πείθεσθαι αὐτοὺς ἡμῖν, iv. 7 ὑποτάγητε τῷ Θεῷ, ἀντίστητε τῷ διαβόλῳ, iv. 8 ἐγγίσατε τῷ Θεῷ, v. 17 ὁμοιοπαθὴς ἡμῖν.

Special Uses, expressing (a) contact, (b) person possessing, (c) person to whose judgment or estimate reference is made, (d) *Dat. Commodi,* (e) agent.

(a) i. 2 περιπίπτειν πειρασμοῖς.

(b) v. 3 ὁ ἰὸς εἰς μαρτύριον ὑμῖν ἔσται, iv. 17 ἁμαρτία αὐτῷ ἐστίν.

(c) ii. 5 τοὺς πτωχοὺς τῷ κόσμῳ.

(*d*) iii. 18 καρπὸς σπείρεται τοῖς ποιοῦσιν εἰρήνην, see notes.
(*e*) iii. 7 πᾶσα φύσις δαμάζεται τῇ φύσει.

Instrumental.

i. 18 ἀπεκύησεν λόγῳ, ii. 25 ἑτέρᾳ ὁδῷ ἐκβαλοῦσα, (cf. Xen. *Hell.* iv. 5. 13 πορεύεσθαι τῇ ὁδῷ, Thuc. ii. 98) v. 14 ἀλείψαντες ἐλαίῳ, v. 17 προσευχῇ προσηύξατο with intensive force, see note.

PREPOSITIONS.

With accusative.

διά. *expressing the ground,* iv. 2 οὐκ ἔχετε διὰ τὸ μὴ αἰτεῖσθαι.

εἰς. *of place,* i. 25 παρακύψας εἰς νόμον, ii. 6 εἰς κριτήρια ἕλκειν iv. 13 πορευσόμεθα εἰς τὴν πόλιν: *of reference,* i. 19 βραδὺς εἰς ὀργήν, ταχὺς εἰς τὸ ἀκοῦσαι: *of result and purpose,* iv. 9 ὁ γέλως εἰς πένθος μεταστραφήτω, i. 18 ἀπεκύησεν ἡμᾶς εἰς τὸ εἶναι ἡμᾶς ἀπαρχήν, iii. 3 βάλλομεν εἰς τὸ πείθεσθαι ἡμῖν, v. 3 ὁ ἰὸς εἰς μαρτύριον ἔσται, cf. Mark xiv. 55 ἐζήτουν μαρτυρίαν εἰς τὸ θανατῶσαι, Acts vii. 19 ποιεῖν τὰ βρέφη ἔκθετα εἰς τὸ μὴ ζωογονεῖσθαι, found especially in St. Paul's Epistles, but also, though rarely, in classical authors, *e.g.* Xen. *Mem.* iii. 6. 2 εἰς τὸ ἐθελῆσαι ἀκούειν, and Kühner's n. on *Anab.* viii. 8. 20. The use in ii. 23 ἐλογίσθη εἰς δικαιοσύνην is unclassical.

ἐπί. *of place,* ii. 21 ἀνενέγκας Ἰσαὰκ ἐπὶ τὸ θυσιαστήριον, ii. 3 ἐπιβλέπειν ἐπὶ τὸν φοροῦντα, v. 14 προσευξάσθωσαν ἐπ' αὐτόν, iii. 7 τὸ ὄνομα τὸ ἐπικληθὲν ἐφ' ὑμᾶς.

κατά. 'according to,' iii. 9 καθ' ὁμοίωσιν Θεοῦ γεγονότας, ii. 8 κατὰ τὴν γραφήν, ii. 17 νεκρά ἐστιν καθ' ἑαυτήν ('taken by itself').

πρός. *of time,* iv. 14 πρὸς ὀλίγον φαινομένη (unclassical): 'in accordance with,' iv. 5 πρὸς φθόνον ἐπιποθεῖ ('jealously'), see examples of adverbial use in Schmid *Atticismus* ii. p. 242.

ὑπό. 'below' (*i.e.* 'on a lower level than'), ii. 3 ὑπὸ τὸ ὑποπόδιον: 'under' (tropical), v. 12 ὑπὸ κρίσιν πεσεῖν, cf. Aesch. 56. 29 τὰ μέγιστα ὑπὸ τὴν τῶν δικαστηρίων ἔρχεται ψῆφον.

With genitive.

ἀντί. 'instead of,' iv. 15 οἱ λέγοντες Σήμερον πορευσόμεθα... ἀντὶ τοῦ λέγειν ὑμᾶς Ἐὰν κ.τ.λ., cf. Xen. *Hier.* v. 1 ἀντὶ τοῦ ἄγασθαι φοβοῦνται, *Mem.* I. 2. 64 ἀντὶ τοῦ μὴ νομίζειν θεούς, φανερὸς ἦν θεραπεύων.

ἀπό. (*a*) *motion from,* (*b*) *separation,* (*c*) *origin and cause.*

(*a*) i. 17 καταβαῖνον ἀπὸ τοῦ Πατρός, iv. 7 φεύξεται ἀφ' ὑμῶν, v. 19 πλανᾶσθαι ἀπὸ τῆς ἀληθείας.

(*b*) i. 27 ἄσπιλον ἑαυτὸν τηρεῖν ἀπὸ τοῦ κόσμου, where ἀπό belongs to both τηρεῖν and ἄσπιλον, or rather to their joint effect (cf. Luke xii. 15 φυλάσσεσθε ἀπὸ πλεονεξίας, Acts xx. 26 καθαρὸς ἀπὸ τοῦ αἵματος).

(*c*) i. 13 ἀπὸ Θεοῦ πειράζομαι, v. 4 ὁ μισθὸς ὁ ἀφυστερημένος ἀφ' ὑμῶν.

διά. = instrumental dative, ii. 12 διὰ νόμου ἐλευθερίας κρίνεσθαι (cf. Rom. ii. 12 διὰ νόμου κριθήσονται).

ἐνώπιον (Hellenistic). iv. 10 ταπεινώθητε ἐνώπιον Κυρίου.

ἐκ or ἐξ. *local*, iii. 10 ἐκ στόματος ἐξέρχεται εὐλογία, iii. 11 ἐκ τῆς ὀπῆς βρύει τὸ γλυκύ, v. 20 ἐπιστρέψας ἁμαρτωλὸν ἐκ πλάνης: *partitive*, ii. 16 τίς ἐξ ὑμῶν; *causal*, ii. 21, 24, 25 ἐξ ἔργων ἐδικαιώθη, iv. i. ἐκ τῶν ἡδονῶν μάχαι, ii. 22 ἐκ τῶν ἔργων ἡ πίστις ἐτελειώθη, ii. 18 δείξω ἐκ τῶν ἔργων μου τὴν πίστιν, iii. 13 δειξάτω ἐκ τῆς καλῆς ἀναστροφῆς τὰ ἔργα. (In the last three examples the force is nearly that of the instrumental dative.)

ἐπί. *local*, v. 17 οὐκ ἔβρεξεν ἐπὶ τῆς γῆς.

ἕως (not used as a preposition before Aristotle). v. 7 μακροθυμήσατε ἕως τῆς παρουσίας.

κατά. 'against,' v. 9 στενάζετε κατ' ἀλλήλων, iii. 14 ψεύδεσθε κατὰ τῆς ἀληθείας.

παρά. i. 5 αἰτεῖν παρὰ Θεοῦ, i. 7 λήμψεται παρὰ τοῦ Κυρίου.

πρό. *local*, v. 9 πρὸ τῶν θυρῶν ἕστηκεν: *tropical*, v. 12 πρὸ πάντων μὴ ὀμνύετε.

ὑπέρ. v. 16 εὔχεσθε ὑπὲρ ἀλλήλων.

ὑπό. *expressing the agent* (used of inanimate things and abstractions), i. 14 ὑπὸ τῆς ἐπιθυμίας πειράζεται, iii. 4 ὑπὸ ἀνέμων ἐλαυνόμενα, ὑπὸ πηδαλίου μετάγεται, iii. 6 φλογιζομένη ὑπὸ γεέννης, ii. 9 ἐλεγχόμενοι ὑπὸ τοῦ νόμου.

χωρίς. ii. 18 χωρὶς τῶν ἔργων, *ib.* 20, 26.

With Dative.

ἐν. (*a*) *of place*, 'in,' 'among,' hence of clothing, (*b*) *of circumstances and accompaniments of action*, (*c*) *of time*, (*d*) *of the sphere*, (*e*) *of mental state*, (*f*) *of ground or cause*, (*g*) *of instrument:*

(*a*) iii. 6 ἡ γλῶσσα καθίσταται ἐν τοῖς μέλεσιν, i. 23 κατανοεῖν τὸ πρόσωπον ἐν ἐσόπτρῳ (here it approximates to use *g*), iii. 14 ἐριθίαν ἔχετε ἐν τῇ καρδίᾳ, iv. 1 πόθεν μάχαι ἐν ὑμῖν; v. 13 τίς ἐν ὑμῖν; v. 14 ἀσθενεῖ τις ἐν ὑμῖν; ii. 4 διεκρίθητε ἐν ἑαυτοῖς, ii. 2 πτωχὸς ἐν ἐσθῆτι ῥυπαρᾷ.

(*b*) i. 8 ἀκατάστατος ἐν ταῖς ὁδοῖς, i. 11 ἐν ταῖς πορείαις μαρανθήσεται, i. 27 ἐπισκέπτεσθαι χήρας ἐν τῇ θλίψει αὐτῶν, v. 10 ἐλάλησαν ἐν τῷ ὀνόματι Κυρίου, v. 14 ἀλείψαντες ἐν τῷ ὀνόματι (the action is accompanied by the use of the Name).

(*c*) v. 4 ἐν ἐσχάταις ἡμέραις.

(*d*) i. 4 ἐν μηδενὶ λειπόμενοι, i. 25 μακάριος ἐν τῇ ποιήσει, ii. 5 πλούσιος ἐν πίστει, ii. 10, iii. 2 ἐν ἑνί, ἐν λόγῳ πταίειν.

(*e*) i. 21 ἐν πραΰτητι δέξασθε τὸν λόγον, iii. 13 δειξάτω τὰ ἔργα αὐτοῦ ἐν πραΰτητι σοφίας, ii. 1 ἐν προσωπολημψίαις τὴν πίστιν ἔχετε, ii. 16 ὑπάγετε ἐν εἰρήνῃ, iii. 18 ἐν εἰρήνῃ σπείρεται, i. 6 αἰτεῖν ἐν πίστει, iv. 16 καυχάσθω ἐν ταῖς ἀλαζονίαις αὐτοῦ.

(*f*) i. 9 καυχάσθω ἐν τῷ ὕψει, i. 10 κ. ἐν τῇ ταπεινώσει, iv. 3 ἐν ταῖς ἡδόναις δαπανᾶν.

(*g*) iii. 9 ἐν τῇ γλώσσῃ εὐλογοῦμεν τὸν Κύριον, cf. i. 23.

In i. 17 we find ἔνι used for ἔνεστι, παρ' ᾧ οὐκ ἔνι παραλλαγή, see note.

ἐπί. (*a*) *ground*, (*b*) *the object of any emotion*.

(*a*) v. 1 ὀλολύζοντες ἐπὶ ταῖς ταλαιπωρίαις.

(*b*) v. 7 μακροθυμῶν ἐπ' αὐτῷ (*i.e.* the crop).

παρά. *expressive of* (*a*) *an attribute*, (*b*) *a judgment*.

(*a*) i. 17 παρ' ᾧ οὐκ ἔνι παραλλαγή.

(*b*) i. 27 θρησκεία καθαρὰ παρὰ τῷ Θεῷ αὕτη ἐστίν.

σύν. i. 11 ἀνέτειλεν σὺν τῷ καύσωνι.

VERB.

Voices.

Active and Middle combined iii. 3, 4, 5 ἴδε τῶν ἵππων τοὺς χαλινοὺς εἰς τὰ στόματα βάλλομεν,...ἰδοὺ καὶ τὰ πλοῖα μετάγεται ὑπὸ πηδαλίου...ἰδοὺ ἡλίκον πῦρ ἡλίκην ὕλην ἀνάπτει, iv. 2, 3 οὐκ ἔχετε διὰ τὸ μὴ αἰτεῖσθαι ὑμᾶς· αἰτεῖτε καὶ οὐ λαμβάνετε διότι κακῶς αἰτεῖσθε.

Passive used impersonally, iv. 15 κἂν ἁμαρτίας ᾖ πεποιηκὼς ἀφεθήσεται αὐτῷ.

Aor. Pass. with Middle use, iv. 10 ταπεινώθητε, v. 19 πλανηθῇ.

Doubt whether Passive or *Middle*, i. 6 διακρινόμενος, iii. 6 and iv. 4 καθίσταται, ii. 16 θερμαίνεσθε καὶ χορτάζεσθε, v. 16 ἐνεργουμένη.

Under this head we may place the use of Intransitive Verbs in a Transitive sense, *e.g.* βρύω iii. 11 where see note, βλαστάνω aor. ἐβλάστησα v. 18, but intr. in Matt., Mark, Heb.

Tenses.

Present (*a*) *praesens historicum* in connexion with aorist to express a continued state, v. 6 ἐφονεύσατε τὸν δίκαιον· οὐκ ἀντιτάσσεται ὑμῖν (=οὐκ ἀντιτασσόμενον).

(*b*) in connexion with perfect to strengthen an assertion, iii. 17 πᾶσα φύσις δαμάζεται καὶ δεδάμασται. Compare examples in Schmid *Atticismus* ii. p. 276, J. E. B. Mayor in *J. of Phil.* vol. xx. p. 265.

Future, for imperative, ii. 8 ἀγαπήσεις τὸν πλησίον σοῦ: for opt. with ἄν, ii. 18 ἀλλ' ἐρεῖ τις.

Aorist (*a*) gnomic, i. 11 ἀνέτειλεν, ἐξήρανεν, ἐξέπεσεν, ἀπώλετο, i. 24 κατενόησεν, ἐπελάθετο.

(*b*) referring to a point of time implied but not stated, i. 12 ἐπηγγείλατο, ii. 6 ἠτιμάσατε.

(*c*) answering to Eng. perfect and so translated in R.V., v. 11 ὑπομονὴν Ἰὼβ ἠκούσατε καὶ εἴδετε, v. 3 ἐθησαυρίσατε, v. 5 ἐτρυφήσατε, ἐσπαταλήσατε, ἐθρέψατε, v. 6 κατεδικάσατε, ἐφονεύσατε. See Dr. Weymouth in *Classical Review* v. 267 foll.

Perfect (*a*) denoting immediate sequence, i. 24 κατενόησε καὶ ἀπελήλυθεν, ii. 10 ὅστις πταίσῃ γέγονεν ἔνοχος, ii. 11 εἰ φονεύεις γέγονας παραβάτης.

(*b*) prophetic, v. 2, 3 σέσηπεν, γέγονεν, κατίωται.

The periphrastic tense so common in St. Luke (cf. xxiv. 13 ἦσαν πορευόμενοι εἰς κώμην, ver. 32 ἡ καρδία καιομένη ἦν) is found by some in James i. 17, iii. 15 where see notes.

Moods.

Imperative present used thirty-one times, aorist twenty-eight times; the latter used to express urgency without implying a mere momentary action, i. 2 πᾶσαν χαρὰν ἡγήσασθε, v. 7 μακροθυμήσατε ἕως τῆς παρουσίας τοῦ Κυρίου (cf. Winer p. 395).

Subjunctive (*a*) hypothetical after ἐάν ii. 2, 14, 15, 16, 17, iv. 15, v. 19, after κἄν v. 16; (*b*) of time after ὅταν i. 2, ἕως v. 7; (*c*) of purpose after ἵνα i. 4, v. 9, 13, after ὅπως v. 16; (*d*) indefinite after ὃς ἐάν iv. 4, after ὅστις ii. 10; (*e*) of aorist with prohibitive force ii. 11 μὴ μοιχεύσῃς.

Optative not used.

Infinitive.

(*a*) *Without article.* Besides the ordinary use after δύναμαι, δυνατός, θέλω, χρή, μέλλω, we find the infinitive after εἰδότι iv. 17, the epistolary χαίρειν depending on λέγω understood i. 1, and ἐπισκέπτεσθαι used in apposition to the subject of the sentence in i. 27.

(*b*) *With article* (1) after preposition i. 18 ἀπεκύησεν ἡμᾶς εἰς τὸ εἶναι ἡμᾶς ἀπαρχήν, i. 19 ταχὺς εἰς τὸ ἀκοῦσαι, βραδὺς εἰς τὸ λαλῆσαι, iii. 3 χαλινοὺς εἰς τὰ στόματα βάλλομεν εἰς τὸ πείθεσθαι, iv. 3 οὐκ ἔχετε διὰ τὸ μὴ αἰτεῖσθαι, iv. 15 ἄγε νῦν οἱ λέγοντες Κερδήσομεν...ἀντὶ τοῦ λέγειν κ.τ.λ.; (2) in the genitive expressive of aim, v. 17 προσηύξατο τοῦ μὴ βρέξαι: not used for simple infin. as in Luke xxiv. 25 βραδεῖς τοῦ πιστεύειν.

Participle.

(*a*) *Without article.*

Present, (1) describing a noun, either as attribute, e.g. i. 7 ἔοικεν κλύδωνι ἀνεμιζομένῳ καὶ ῥιπιζομένῳ, i. 23 ἔοικεν ἀνδρὶ κατανοοῦντι τὸ πρόσωπον, v. 16 ἰσχύει δέησις ἐνεργουμένη (that is, if we take this to mean 'an inspired prayer'; if we translate 'prayer is of might, if urgent,' it will come under a different head); or as predicate, e.g. ii. 15 ἐὰν ὑπάρχωσιν λειπόμενοι, iii. 15 ἔστιν αὕτη ἡ σοφία ἄνωθεν κατερχομένη: (2) standing for a noun iv. 17 εἰδότι καλὸν ποιεῖν καὶ μὴ ποιοῦντι ἁμαρτία ἐστίν 'to one knowing how to do right and not doing it there is sin,' where in classical Greek we should at least have had τῷ εἰδότι κ.τ.λ., if not τὸ μὴ ποιεῖν: (3) explaining a preceding adjective i. 4 ὁλόκληρος, ἐν μηδενὶ λειπόμενος: (4) explaining a preceding adverb or adverbial phrase i. 17 πᾶν δώρημα ἄνωθέν ἐστιν, καταβαῖνον ἀπὸ τοῦ Πατρός, i. 6 ἐν πίστει, μηδὲν διακρινόμενος, ii. 12 οὕτως λαλεῖτε ὡς μέλλοντες κρίνεσθαι: (5) qualifying a verb, either by describing its mode of action, as i. 14 *πειράζεται ὑπὸ τῆς ἐπιθυμίας ἐξελκόμενος καὶ δελεαζόμενος*, v. 1 *κλαύσατε ὀλολύζοντες*, v. 7 *ἐκδέχεται τὸν καρπὸν μακροθυμῶν*; or by introducing some new consideration, which may be causal, as i. 2 *πᾶσαν χαρὰν ἡγήσασθε γινώσκοντες κ.τ.λ.*, iii. 1 *μὴ γίνεσθε διδάσκαλοι εἰδότες κ.τ.λ.*; or concessive, as iii. 3 *τὰ πλοῖα τηλικαῦτα ὄντα καὶ ὑπὸ ἀνέμων σκληρῶν ἐλαυνόμενα μετάγεται* ('though so great'); or may describe the circumstances under which the action takes place, as i. 13 *μηδεὶς πειραζόμενος λεγέτω*, i. 26 *εἴ τις δοκεῖ θρησκὸς εἶναι μὴ χαλιναγωγῶν γλῶσσαν ἀλλ' ἀπατῶν καρδίαν*; or the accompaniments, sometimes including the consequence, as ii. 9 *ἁμαρτίαν ἐργάζεσθε ἐλεγχόμενοι ὑπὸ τοῦ νόμου*, i. 22 *μὴ γίνεσθε ἀκροαταὶ μόνον παραλογιζόμενοι ἑαυτούς* ('ye commit sin *and* are convicted,' 'be not hearers only *and thus* deceive yourselves').

Aorist expresses priority of time, e.g. i. 12 *δόκιμος γενόμενος λήμψεται τὸν στέφανον* ('after being tried'), i. 15 *ἡ ἐπιθυμία συλλαβοῦσα τίκτει ἁμαρτίαν, ἡ δὲ ἁμαρτία ἀποτελεσθεῖσα ἀποκυεῖ θάνατον* ('when it has conceived,' 'when it has come to maturity'); when joined with an imperative the aorist denotes that the action expressed by it must be done before the action expressed by the imperative, e.g. i. 21 *ἀποθέμενοι ῥυπαρίαν δέξασθε τὸν λόγον* ('lay aside filthiness and receive the word'), v. 14 *προσευξάσθωσαν ἀλείψαντες* ('let them anoint and pray'). The prior action may be the cause of what follows, e.g. i. 18 *βουληθεὶς ἀπεκύησεν ἡμᾶς*. It may also explain a preceding adverbial phrase, e.g. ii. 21 *ἐξ ἔργων ἐδικαιώθη ἀνενέγκας Ἰσαάκ*, ii. 25 *ἐξ ἔργων ἐδικαιώθη ὑποδεξαμένη τοὺς ἀγγέλους*.

Perfect only found in the periphrastic subjunctive v. 15 *ᾖ πεποιηκώς*.

Future does not occur. Instead we have the periphrastic *μέλλων κρίνεσθαι* ii. 12.

(*b*) *With article.*

Present as attributive adjective i. 5 *παρὰ τοῦ διδόντος Θεοῦ πᾶσιν ἁπλῶς*, i. 21, ii. 3, iii. 6, iv. 1, v. 1; as substantive iii. 4 *ὅπου ἡ ὁρμὴ τοῦ εὐθύνοντος βούλεται*, v. 15 *ἡ εὐχὴ σώσει τὸν κάμνοντα*, i. 6, 12, ii. 3, 5, iii. 18, iv. 11, 12. Often the reference is not confined to present time, but is equally applicable to past and future, as in the examples quoted.

Aorist. Always used of something which precedes the main action: as attribute in ii. 7 τὸ ὄνομα τὸ ἐπικληθέν, v. 4 τῶν ἐργατῶν τῶν ἀμησάντων; as subject i. 25 ὁ παρακύψας εἰς νόμον, ii. 13, v. 11, v. 20.

Perfect as attribute iii. 9 τοὺς ἀνθρώπους τοὺς γεγονότας, v. 4 ὁ μισθὸς ὁ ἀφυστερημένος.

Compound Sentence.

(1) *Substantival Clauses.*

(*a*) *Indirect statement.* This is never expressed in this Epistle by the infinitive, but only by ὅτι with indicative.

ὅτι follows γινώσκω i. 3, ii. 20, v. 20; οἶδα iii. 1, iv. 1; ὁράω ii. 24, v. 11; βλέπω ii. 22; δοκέω iv. 5; οἴομαι i. 7; πιστεύω ii. 19.

(*b*) *Indirect question.* i. 24 ἐπελάθετο ὁποῖος ἦν.

[*The direct statement* is frequently used in quotations by St. James, being introduced once by a pleonastic ὅτι in i. 13 λεγέτω ὅτι πειράζομαι; but generally appended immediately to the verb of saying, as in ii. 3, 11, 23, 18, iv. 5, 13, 15, or to the noun γραφή, as in ii. 8.]

(2) *Adjectival clauses introduced by relative pronouns.*

i. 12 *bis*, i. 17, ii. 5, iv. 5, 13, v. 10.

(3) *Adverbial clauses.*

(*a*) *Causal clause.*

i. 10 καυχάσθω...ὅτι παρελεύσεται, i. 12 μακάριος...ὅτι λήμψεται, i. 22, 23 γίνεσθε ποιηταὶ...ὅτι ἔοικεν, v. 8 στηρίξατε καρδίας ὅτι ἤγγικεν, iv. 3 οὐ λαμβάνετε διότι κακῶς αἰτεῖσθε.

(*b*) *Temporal* (α), *Local* (β), and *Modal* (γ) *clauses.*

(α) i. 2 χαρὰν ἡγήσασθε ὅταν περιπέσητε, v. 7, μακροθυμῶν ἕως λάβῃ. (β) iii. 4 μετάγεται ὅπου ἡ ὁρμὴ βούλεται, iii. 16 ὅπου ζῆλος, ἐκεῖ ἀκαταστασία. (γ) ii. 26 ὥσπερ τὸ σῶμα νεκρόν, οὕτως καὶ ἡ πίστις.

(*c*) *Final clause.*

i. 4 ἡ ὑπομονὴ ἔργον τέλειον ἐχέτω, ἵνα ἦτε τέλειοι, iv. 3 αἰτεῖσθε, ἵνα δαπανήσητε, v. 9 μὴ στενάζετε, ἵνα μὴ κριθῆτε,

v. 12 ἤτω τὸ ναὶ ναί, ἵνα μὴ πέσητε, v. 16 εὔχεσθε ὅπως ἰαθῆτε.

(*d*) *Conditional clause.*

εἰ *with pres. ind. in both protasis and apodosis* ii. 8 εἰ νόμον τελεῖτε καλῶς ποιεῖτε, i. 23, i. 26, ii. 9, iii. 2, iv. 11; *with pres. ind. in protasis and perf. ind. in apodosis* ii. 11 εἰ φονεύεις, γέγονας παραβάτης; *with pres. ind. in protasis and pres. imperat. in apodosis* cf. i. 5 εἴ τις λείπεται, αἰτείτω, iii. 14.

ἐάν *with pres. subj. in protasis and pres. ind. in apodosis* ii. 17 ἡ πίστις, ἐὰν μὴ ἔχῃ ἔργα, νεκρά ἐστιν, ii. 14 τί ὄφελος (ἐστὶν) ἐὰν πίστιν λέγῃ τις ἔχειν, ii. 15; *with fut. ind. in apodosis* iv. 15 ἐὰν Κύριος θέλῃ (*al.* θελήσῃ) ζήσομεν; *with aor. subj. in protasis and aor. ind. in apodosis* ii. 2 ἐὰν εἰσέλθῃ, οὐ διεκρίθητε; *with pres. imperat. in apodosis* v. 19 ἐὰν τις πλανηθῇ, γινωσκέτω (*al.* pres. ind. γινώσκετε); *with perf. subj. in protasis and fut. ind. in apodosis* v. 15 κἂν ἁμαρτίας ᾖ πεποιηκὼς ἀφεθήσεται.

ὅστις *with aor. subj. in protasis and perf. ind. in apodosis* ii. 10 ὅστις τὸν νόμον τηρήσῃ πταίσῃ δὲ ἐν ἑνὶ, γέγονεν ἔνοχος. Other examples both from classical and Hellenistic writers are given in my note.

ὃς ἐάν *with aor. subj. in protasis and pres. ind. in apodosis* iv. 4 ὃς ἐὰν βουληθῇ φίλος εἶναι, ἐχθρὸς καθίσταται. Other examples both from classical and Hellenistic writings given in note.

Without conditional particle.

Imperative in protasis followed by καί *and future indicative* i. 5 αἰτείτω καὶ δοθήσεται.

Interrogative in protasis followed by imperative in apodosis iii. 13 τίς σοφὸς ἐν ὑμῖν; δειξάτω τὰ ἔργα, v. 13 κακοπαθεῖ τις; προσευχέσθω.

NEGATIVES.[1]

οὐ after εἰ i. 23 εἴ τις ἀκροατὴς λόγου ἐστὶν καὶ οὐ ποιητής, see note.

ii. 11 εἰ δὲ οὐ μοιχεύεις φονεύεις δέ, see note.

iii. 2 εἴ τις ἐν λόγῳ οὐ πταίει after πολλὰ πταίομεν.

μή after εἰ i. 25 εἴ τις δοκεῖ θρησκὸς εἶναι μὴ χαλιναγωγῶν γλῶσσαν.

[1] Cf. W. Schmid *Atticismus* i. p. 50, 99 foll., 243 foll., 260 foll.

μή *with imperative* i. 22 γίνεσθε ποιηταὶ καὶ μὴ ἀκροαταί.

μή *with participle in imperative clause* i. 5 αἰτείτω μηδὲν διακρινόμενος.

μή *with participle implying condition* iv. 17 εἰδότι καλὸν ποιεῖν καὶ μὴ ποιοῦντι ἁμαρτία ἐστίν.

μή *with participle in subjunctive clause* depending on ἵνα i. 4 ἵνα ἦτε τέλειοι ἐν μηδενὶ λειπόμενοι.

μή *with participle preceded by article* ii. 13 ἡ κρίσις ἀνέλεος τῷ μὴ ποιήσαντι ἔλεος, where the reference is not to a particular person but to a class, see Winer p. 606.

i. 5 αἰτείτω παρὰ τοῦ διδόντος Θεοῦ πᾶσιν καὶ μὴ ὀνειδίζοντος. Here we might suppose μή to be used with the participle because the principal verb is imperative, as in Luke iii. 11 ὁ ἔχων δυὸ χιτῶνας μεταδότω τῷ μὴ ἔχοντι (but this too is better explained as generic, not *huic qui non habet*, but *ei qui non habeat*), *ib.* xix. 27 τοὺς ἐχθρούς μου τούτους τοὺς μὴ θελήσαντάς με βασιλεῦσαι ἀγάγετε ὧδε (but here too I should rather take it as a clause in apposition, referring τούτους to a certain type of men, 'the fellows that would not have me reign over them,' not simply 'these men who would not'); but I think it is better explained as in 2 Cor. v. 21 τὸν μὴ γνόντα ἁμαρτίαν ὑπὲρ ἡμῶν ἁμαρτίαν ἐποίησεν *eum qui non nosset peccatum pro nobis peccatum fecit*, 'one whose characteristic was sinlessness he made sin'; so here, 'let him ask of God whose characteristic it is to give to all without upbraiding.'

μή *interrogative expecting negative answer* ii. 14 μὴ δύναται ἡ πίστις σῶσαι αὐτόν; iii. 11 μήτι ἡ πηγὴ...βρύει τὸ γλυκύ; iii. 12 μὴ δύναται συκῆ ἐλαίας ποιῆσαι;

οὔτε *used for* οὐδέ iii. 12 οὔτε ἁλυκὸν γλυκὺ ποιῆσαι ὕδωρ.

Other Adverbs and Particles.

ἄγε interjectional, not found elsewhere in N.T., occurs in the LXX. and classical authors, see note on iv. 13.

ἀλλά. In four passages it has its ordinary force of contrasting a positive with a negative conception, as in i. 25 οὐκ ἀκροατὴς... ἀλλὰ ποιητής, i. 26, iii. 15, iv. 11. In the remaining passage, ii. 18 ἀλλ' ἐρεῖ τις, it appears to have the unusual force of the Latin *immo*, adding emphasis to what has been already said; cf 1 Pet. iii. 14 ἀλλ' εἰ καὶ πάσχοιτε διὰ δικαιοσύνην, μακάριοι, and see note *in loco*.

ἄ ν (see above under subjunctive and compound sentences) is not used by our author with the past indicative, though this is common enough in other books of the N.T. e.g. Heb. xi. 2, 9, Gal. iv. 15, Matt. xi. 21, or with the optative, a construction which is found only in Luke and Acts. It is omitted with ὅστις before a subjunctive in ii. 10, and likewise with ἕως in v. 7. The former construction is very rare in the N.T. but is found occasionally in classical Greek, both verse and prose: the latter is not uncommon in the N.T. and is found in classical poetry and in Aristotle. Instead of ἄν we find ἐάν used with the relative in classical Greek as well as in the N.T., see note on ὃς ἐάν iv. 4.

ἐ ν τ ε ῦ θ ε ν, pleonastic use before ἐκ τῶν ἡδονῶν iv. 1.

ἔ π ε ι τ α used, as in classical authors, after πρῶτον μέν without an accompanying δέ in iii. 17.

ὅ π ο υ, used for ὅπῃ or ὅποι iii. 4.

ο ὕ τ ω ς, generally used with reference to a preceding comparison, as in i. 11, ii. 17, but in ii. 12 explained by what follows, οὕτως λαλεῖτε ὡς μέλλοντες κρίνεσθαι, seemingly pleonastic in iii. 10, where see note.

ὧ δ ε is used, as in the N.T. generally and in Theocritus and the post-classical writers, of place,[1] for the classical ἐνταῦθα or ἐνθάδε, of which the former is not found in the N.T. and the latter only in Luke (including Acts) and John.

ἤ interrogative, = Latin *an*, implying a negative answer, iv. 5.

For γάρ, δέ, καί, οὖν, τε, see Index.

Ellipsis.

Of substantive in agreement with adjective or adjectival phrase: v. 7 ἕως λάβῃ πρόϊμον καὶ ὄψιμον (ὑετόν), iii. 12 οὔτε ἁλυκὸν (ὕδωρ) γλυκὺ ποιῆσαι ὕδωρ, iv. 14 τὸ τῆς αὔριον (ἡμέρας).

Of substantive depending on previous substantive: v. 14 ἐν τῷ ὀνόματι (τοῦ Κυρίου), see note.

Of subject to verb: i. 12 ὃν ἐπηγγείλατο (ὁ Κύριος) τοῖς ἀγαπῶσιν αὐτόν, iv. 6 διὸ λέγει (ὁ Θεός), ii. 23 ἐλογίσθη αὐτῷ εἰς δικαιοσύνην (τὸ πιστεύειν understood from previous clause), iii. 8 quoted below

[1] It is denied by most grammarians following Aristarchus that the local sense is found in Homer and the earlier authors, but in many passages its use seems to approach very near to that of our 'hither,' e.g. *Il.* xviii. 392 Ἥφαιστε πρόμολ' ὧδε, Soph. *O. T.* 7. ὧδ' ἐλήλυθα, and other passages quoted in Ellendt's Lex., Plato *Prot.* 328 ὧδε ἀφικέσθαι.

under *Substantive Verb*, i. 5 εἴ τις λείπεται σοφίας αἰτείτω...καὶ δοθήσεται αὐτῷ (σοφία), (cf. the use of the impersonal in v. 15 κἂν ἁμαρτίας ᾖ πεποιηκὼς ἀφεθήσεται αὐτῷ), iv. 10 ταπεινώθητε ἐνώπιον Κυρίου καὶ (Κύριος) ὑψώσει ὑμᾶς, v. 17 οὐκ ἔβρεξεν ἐπὶ τῆς γῆς (ὁ Θεός).

Of object or adverbial clause: i. 19 ἴστε (τοῦτο) ἀδελφοί, i. 25 ὁ παρακύψας εἰς νόμον καὶ παραμείνας (ἐν αὐτῷ), cf. John viii. 31 ἐὰν μείνητε ἐν τῷ λόγῳ τῷ ἐμῷ ἀληθῶς μαθηταί μου ἐστέ, 2 John 9 μὴ μένων ἐν τῇ διδαχῇ τοῦ Χριστοῦ.

Of substantive verb: i. 12 μακάριος ἀνὴρ (ἐστιν) ὃς ὑπομένει, ii. 14 and 16 τί ὄφελος (ἐστιν); iii. 2 οὗτος τέλειος ἀνήρ, iii. 6 ἡ γλῶσσα πῦρ, iii. 8 ἀκατάστατον κακὸν (ἡ γλῶσσά ἐστιν) μεστὴ ἰοῦ, iii. 13 τίς σοφὸς ἐν ὑμῖν; iii. 16 ὅπου ζῆλος, ἐκεῖ ἀκαταστασία, iv. 1 πόθεν μάχαι;

Of verb governing infinitive: iii. 12 μὴ δύναται συκῆ ἐλαίας ποιῆσαι; οὔτε ἁλυκὸν γλυκὺ (δύναται) ποιῆσαι [or is ποιήσει the right reading here?]

Pleonasm.

Of ἀνήρ, with δίψυχος i. 8 (as in Herm. *Mand.* ix. 6), μακάριος i. 12, κατανοοῦντι i. 23, χρυσοδακτύλιος ii. 2, cf. Luke xxiv. 19 (Ἰησοῦς) ἐγένετο ἀνὴρ προφήτης.

Of ἄνθρωπος, with ἐκεῖνος i. 7, with πᾶς i. 19.

Of the subject of the infinitive: iii. 3 τῶν ἵππων τοὺς χαλινοὺς εἰς τὰ στόματα βάλλομεν εἰς τὸ πείθεσθαι αὐτοὺς ἡμῖν, iv. 4 οὐκ ἔχετε διὰ τὸ μὴ αἰτεῖσθαι ὑμᾶς, iv. 13–15 ἄγε νῦν οἱ λέγοντες...ἀντὶ τοῦ λέγειν ὑμᾶς.

Of the possessive pronoun or its equivalents: iv. 1 ἐκ τῶν ἡδονῶν ὑμῶν τῶν στρατευομένων ἐν τοῖς μέλεσιν ὑμῶν, see above, under *Article.*

Of the demonstrative pronoun, added immediately before or after the verb, in apposition with a remote noun, for the sake of clearness or emphasis: i. 23 εἴ τις ἀκροατής ἐστιν...οὗτος ἔοικεν: or introducing an explanatory phrase or noun in apposition: i. 27 θρησκεία καθαρά ἐστιν αὕτη ἐπισκέπτεσθαι ὀρφανούς.

Of αὐτός *in other cases beside the genitive:* iii. 17 εἰδότι καὶ μὴ ποιοῦντι ἁμαρτία αὐτῷ ἐστίν.

Of φύσις *with gen.:* iii. 7 πᾶσα φύσις θηρίων δαμάζεται, common in the Stoic writings, see note *in loco.*

Of καρδία *with gen.:* i. 26 ἀπατῶν καρδίαν ἑαυτοῦ.

Order of Words.

(1) of substantive and attribute; (2) of governing and governed nouns; (3) of subject and predicate; (4) of governing verb and case; (5) of interrogative particle.

(1) The adjective generally follows immediately on its substantive, as in i. 4 *ἔργον τέλειον*, i. 8 *ἀνὴρ δίψυχος*, ii. 2 *ἀνὴρ χρυσοδακτύλιος*, ii. 2 *ἐσθῆτι λαμπρᾷ*, but we find also the adjective preceding in i. 12 *μακάριος ἀνήρ*, iii. 2 *τέλειος ἀνήρ*, ii. 2 *ῥυπαρᾷ ἐσθῆτι*, &c., and always in the case of *πᾶς*. It is unusual for the substantive to be separated from the adjective by an intervening verb, (except in the case of the substantive verb) as in i. 2 *ὅταν πειρασμοῖς περιπέσητε ποικίλοις*, iv. 6 *μείζονα δίδωσιν χάριν*, iii. 13 *γλυκὺ ποιῆσαι ὕδωρ*, iv. 12 *εἷς ἔστιν νομοθέτης*, v. 17 *Ἠλείας ἄνθρωπος ἦν ὁμοιοπαθὴς ἡμῖν*. In these cases the adjective is made more prominent by separation, though it is probable that a feeling of rhythm had a good deal to do with the departure from the usual order.

(2) Omitting the genitive of the pronoun, which has been already dealt with, we find the genitive placed immediately after the governing noun in 50 cases as compared with three in which it precedes, the latter being i. 1 *Θεοῦ δοῦλος*, iii. 3 *τῶν ἵππων τοὺς χαλινούς*, i. 17 *τροπῆς ἀποσκίασμα*. In one instance the governing noun is separated by an intervening verb from the governed, *τὴν γλῶσσαν οὐδεὶς δαμάσαι δύναται ἀνθρώπων*, where greater emphasis is given to *ἀνθρώπων* by its position.

(3) Where the subject (not being a relative pronoun) is expressed, it precedes the predicative verb in about 55 cases, and follows it in about 20. When the predicate is expressed by the substantive verb and complement, the subject precedes the verb in about 16 cases and follows in about 8. I do not here take note of cases in which the verb is omitted, for which see *Ellipsis* above. As a rule the subject precedes the complement (predicative substantive or adjective), but we have the following exceptions: i. 26 *μάταιος ἡ θρησκεία*, i. 27 *θρησκεία καθαρὰ αὕτη ἐστίν*, ii. 19 *εἷς ἐστὶν ὁ Θεός*, iii. 6 *ὁ κόσμος τῆς ἀδικίας ἡ γλῶσσα καθίσταται*, v. 11 *πολύσπλαγχνός ἐστιν ὁ Κύριος*. In oblique predication, where subject and complement come under the government of a causative verb, we find the predicative noun preceding in i. 27 *ἄσπιλον ἑαυτὸν τηρεῖν*, v. 10 *ὑπόδειγμα λάβετε τῆς κακοπαθίας*

τοὺς προφήτας: the subject precedes in ii. 5 ὁ Θεὸς ἐξελέξατο τοὺς πτωχοὺς τῷ κόσμῳ πλουσίους ἐν πίστει, and in i. 18 ἀπεκύησεν ἡμᾶς εἰς τὸ εἶναι ἡμᾶς ἀπαρχήν. Sometimes an adverbial phrase supplies the place of an oblique subject, as in i. 2 χαρὰν ἡγήσασθε ὅταν πειρασμοῖς περιπέσητε, which might have been expressed by χ. ἡγ. πειρασμούς or τὸ πειρασμοῖς περιπεσεῖν: sometimes of an oblique predicate, as in ii. 1 μὴ ἐν προσωποληψίαις ἔχετε τὴν πίστιν, which might have been expressed μὴ προσωποληπτοῦσαν ἔχ. τ. π.

(4) The verb usually precedes the case it governs unless the speaker intends the substantive to be emphatic, as in ii. 14 τι ὄφελος ἐὰν πίστιν λέγῃ τις ἔχειν, ἔργα δὲ μὴ ἔχῃ, where λέγῃ τις intervening between πίστιν and its verb gives additional force to the former. In this Epistle the verb precedes in 88 cases and follows in 32, omitting relative clauses.

(5) In interrogative sentences the word which contains the interrogation usually comes first, but is sometimes postponed for emphasis, as in iv. 12 σὺ δὲ τίς εἶ; ii. 21 Ἀβραὰμ...οὐκ ἐξ ἔργων ἐδικαιώθη; ver. 21 Ῥαὰβ...οὐκ ἐξ ἔργων ἐδικαιώθη;

CHAPTER IX

On the Style of St. James

The last chapter contained a survey of the grammatical usages of our Epistle. In the present chapter I propose to consider what conclusions may be drawn from that survey, as well as from an examination of the vocabulary of the Epistle, from the use of rhetorical figures, the rhythm and arrangement of words, in reference to the Author's command over the resources of the Greek language and the distinctive qualities of his style.

To deal first with any peculiarities of *Inflexion*, he adheres to classical usage, with the majority of the writers of the N.T., as regards the gender of πλοῦτος and ζῆλος, which are sometimes made neuter by St. Paul.

As regards the Future, the reading κερδήσομεν is not quite certain in iv. 13. It is not found elsewhere in the Bible, but the only trace of the Attic κερδανῶ is the doubtful reading in 1 Cor. ix. 21, while the aor. ἐκέρδησα is common. Again, φάγομαι in v. 3 is the only future of ἐσθίω employed in the N.T. In the LXX. ἔδομαι and φάγομαι are both common, and are sometimes used in the same passage without any difference of meaning, e g. Numb. xviii. 10 φάγομαι, ver. 11 ἔδομαι, Deut. xii. 20 and 24 φάγομαι, ver. 22 ἔδεται, so too καταφάγομαι and κατέδομαι.

As to the Perfect, we find parallels to εἰσελήλυθαν in John, Luke, Paul, and Laconian inscriptions. As there is no instance of the 3rd pl. either of the imperfect or 2nd aor. in our Epistle, there is no evidence to show whether James would have used such barbarous forms as εἴχοσαν with John, or παρελάβοσαν with Paul, see Hort *Appendix,* p. 165.

As to the Imperative, ἤτω occurs twice in the LXX. and only in one other place of the N.T. (1 Cor. xvi. 22). It is also found in inscriptions from Asia Minor. κάθου occurs elsewhere in the N.T.

only in quotations from the LXX.: it is said to have been used by Aristophanes and Menander, but does not occur in their existing remains. See below, notes on ii. 3, v. 12.

I go on now to *Syntactical Uses.*

The Article. We found James omitting this, contrary to classical usage, where the noun was defined by a pronominal genitive, as in i. 26 *χαλιναγωγῶν γλῶσσαν ἑαυτοῦ, ἀπατῶν καρδίαν ἑαυτοῦ*, v. 20 *σώσει ψυχὴν αὐτοῦ.* This license, common in LXX., is very rare in the other books of the N.T. except in the first two chapters of St. Luke and in quotations from the LXX., cf. Matt. xix. 28 *ἐπὶ θρόνου δόξης αὐτοῦ*, Luke i. 15 *ἐκ κοιλίας μητρὸς αὐτοῦ*, ver. 25 *ἀφελεῖν ὄνειδός μου*, ver. 51 *ἐν βραχίονι αὐτοῦ...διανοίᾳ καρδίας αὐτῶν*, Heb. x. 16 *ἐπὶ καρδίας αὐτῶν* (fr. LXX.), Jude 14 *ἐν ἁγίαις μυριάσιν αὐτοῦ.* See above, p. clxxxix. foll.

A similar license found in our Epistle is the omission of the article when the noun is defined by a genitive other than a pronoun, as in i. 18 *ἀπεκύησεν ἡμᾶς λόγῳ ἀληθείας*, ii. 12 *διὰ νόμου ἐλευθερίας κρίνεσθαι*, i. 20 *ὀργὴ ἀνδρὸς δικαιοσύνην Θεοῦ οὐκ ἐργάζεται.* This is very common in the LXX. and occurs, I think, in all the books of the N.T., especially after a preposition, e.g. 1 Cor. i. 1 *διὰ θελήματος Θεοῦ*, *ib.* ii. 15 *τίς ἔγνω νοῦν Κυρίου* vi. 9 *Θεοῦ βασιλείαν*, x. 21 *ποτήριον Κυρίου*, Heb. x. 39 *εἰς περιποίησιν ψυχῆς*, x. 28 *ἀθετήσας νόμον Μωυσέως*, xii. 22 *πόλει Θεοῦ ζῶντος, ἐκκλησίᾳ πρωτοτόκων ἀπογεγραμμένων ἐν οὐρανοῖς.* The omission of the article with the attribute, as in ii. 8 *νόμον βασιλικόν*, is less frequent except in the combination *πνεῦμα ἅγιον*: we find it however in 1 Pet. i. 23 *διὰ λόγου ζῶντος*, 2 Pet. ii. 5 *ἀρχαίου κόσμου οὐκ ἐφείσατο*, ver. 8 *ψυχὴν δικαίαν ἐβασάνιζεν*, ver. 15 *καταλείποντες εὐθεῖαν ὁδόν.* See above, p. cxcii. foll.

St. James' use of the *Pronoun* is more idiomatic than is usual in the N.T. I cannot call to mind any other example of *τις* used, like *quidam*, to soften what might seem a harsh or exaggerated expression, as in i. 18 *ἀπαρχήν τινα.* We have also the double interrogative *ἡλίκον πῦρ ἡλίκην ὕλην ἀνάπτει;* and the pregnant use of *ὅστις* = 'whereas' in iv. 13, for which compare Acts xvii. 11 *οὗτοι ἦσαν εὐγενέστεροι τῶν ἐν Θεσσαλονίκῃ, οἵτινες ἐδέξαντο τὸν λόγον κ.τ.λ.* 'in that they received the word,' *ib.* vii. 53, Rom. i. 25, Phil. iv. 3 with Lightfoot's note, Winer p. 209 n. and for examples from classical writers, Isaeus vi. 43 εἰς τοῦτο ἀναιδείας ἥκουσιν ὥστε διεμαρτύρουν τἀναντία οἷς αὐτοὶ ἔπραξαν, οἵτινες ἀπέγραψαν αὐτοὺς κ.τ.λ., Xen. *Ages.* i. 36 ἄξιον ἄγασθαι αὐτοῦ, ὅστις ὑπ' οὐδενὸς ἐκρατήθη, Ellendt, *Lex. Soph.* s.v. ii. 3. The only unclassical use is the modified Hellenistic emphasis on αὐτοὶ in ii. 7 = 'is it not they who'? We do not find St. Luke's αὐτὸς ὁ for ὁ αὐτός, nor ὅς nor ποῖος for τίς, as seems to be the case in Matt. xxvi. 50, xxiv. 43, Acts xxiii. 34.

None of the examples mentioned under *Number and Gender* are contrary to classical usages, while some are idiomatic, e.g. ἄγε νῦν with plural verb, a use of ἄγε which is not found elsewhere in the N.T.

Cases.—The use of the Nom. in apposition to an oblique case (iii. 8 τὴν γλῶσσαν...μεστὴ ἰοῦ) is certainly harsh, but admits of some explanation, which distinguishes it from the solecisms quoted in the note from St. Mark and the Apocalypse.

Perhaps the point in which our Epistle departs most from classical usage is in regard to the Genitive of Quality, such as ἀκροατὴς ἐπιλησμονῆς i. 25, κριταὶ διαλογισμῶν πονηρῶν ii. 4, ὁ κόσμος τῆς ἀδικίας iii. 6. Vorst explains this by the comparative paucity of adjectives in the Hebrew language (*Hebr.* pp. 244 foll.), comparing Acts ix. 15 σκεῦος ἐκλογῆς, Heb. i. 9 ἡ ῥάβδος τῆς εὐθύτητος, Hosea xii. 7 where the Heb. 'balance of deceit' is expressed by ζυγὸς ἀδικίας of the LXX., but in Prov. xx. 23 by ζυγὸς δόλιος.

The only use of the Dative which seems to call for notice here is the Hebraistic use of the cognate with intensive force in v. 17 προσευχῇ προσηύξατο. This is found in several books of the N.T. but apparently not in St. Paul's writings.

Prepositions.—The constructions ὁ ἰὸς εἰς μαρτύριον ἔσται, and ἐλογίσθη εἰς δικαιοσύνην are Hebraistic and not found in classical authors, though common in the N.T., see notes on ii. 23, v. 3. The distinction between εἰς and ἐν is never lost in St. James, as it is in some of the writers of the N.T.

ἐπί: used with acc. where we might have expected either the simple dat. or dat. with ἐπί, e.g. ii. 7 after ἐπικαλεῖν (cf. 2 Chron. vii. 14 ἐφ' οὓς ἐπικέκληται τὸ ὄνομά μου, Acts xix. 13 ὀνομάζειν ἐπὶ τοὺς ἔχοντας τὰ πνεύματα τὸ ὄνομα τοῦ Κυρίου, but Plato *Tim.* 60 ᾧ γένει κέραμον ἐπωνομάκαμεν, *Rep.* vi. 493 ὀνομάζειν *ταῦτα πάντα ἐπὶ ταῖς τοῦ μεγάλου ζῴου δόξαις*, Stallb. on *Rep.* v. 470); v. 14 after *προσεύχομαι* (cf. Mark xvi. 18 *ἐπὶ ἀρρώστους χεῖρας ἐπιθήσουσιν*, Acts viii. 17, Acts ix. 17, but more usually with dat. as in Mark v. 23, vii. 30).

πρός: for the post-classical phrase *πρός ὀλίγον* iv. 14, cf. Plut. *Mor.* 116 A, Justin M. *Apol.* i. 12 *οὐκ ἄν τις τὴν κακίαν πρὸς ὀλίγον ἡρεῖτο.* There is only one instance of *πρός* with gen. in N.T. (Acts xxviii. 34), and six with the dat.; but the acc. is sometimes used where we might have expected *παρά* with dat., as in Matt. xiii. 56 *αἱ ἀδελφαὶ πρὸς ἡμᾶς εἰσίν.*

ἐν: the following are unclassical, *λαλεῖν* and *ἀλείφειν ἐν τῷ ὀνόματι* v. 10, 14, *πλούσιος ἐν πίστει* i. 6 (where a classical writer would rather have used the simple gen. or dat.), *καυχάσθω ἐν τῷ ὕψει* i. 9 (where a classical writer would rather have used *ἐπί*), *ἐν τῇ γλώσσῃ εὐλογεῖν* iii. 9 (instead of the simple dat.). These uses are shared by the other writers of the N.T.

Tenses and Moods.—We have examples of the idiomatic use of tenses in the gnomic aorist, i. 11, 24, and the juxtaposition of aor. and perf. in i. 24 *κατενόησε καὶ ἀπελήλυθεν* and of the pres. and perf. in iii. 17 *δαμάζεται καὶ δεδάμασται.* The use of the moods also conforms to the classical standard except that the optative is absent, as it is also in Matthew, the Gospel and Epistles of John, and the Epistle to the Hebrews and the Apocalypse. We have no instance in our Epistle of such constructions as *ἵνα* followed by a fut. ind., which we find in John xvii. 2 *ἵνα δώσει*, 1 Pet. iii. 1 *ἵνα κερδηθήσονται*, and frequently in the Apocalypse; still less of *ἵνα* with pres. ind. as in 1 Cor. iv. 6 *ἵνα φυσιοῦσθε*, Gal. iv. 17 *ἵνα ζηλοῦτε*, though it is possible that these forms may be used by mistake either for pres. subj. or fut. ind. (Winer p. 363). A similar license is the use of *ἐάν* with indic. in 1 Thess. iii. 8 *ἐὰν ὑμεῖς στήκετε*, Acts viii. 31 *ἐὰν μή τις ὁδηγήσει*, Luke xix. 40 *ἐὰν οὗτοι σιωπήσουσιν*, 1 John v. 15 *ἐὰν οἴδαμεν*; of *ὅταν* with indic. Apoc. iv. 9 *ὅταν δώσουσιν*, Mark xi. 19 *ὅταν ἐγένετο*, ver. 25 *ὅταν στήκετε*, Mark iii. 11 *ὅταν ἐθεώρουν.* Again, St. James affords no instance of unclassical uses of the infinitive, such as *ἐγένετο... ἐλθεῖν*, so common in Luke; nor of the gen. of the article with inf. instead of the simple inf. as in Luke xvii. 1 *ἀνένδεκτόν ἐστιν τοῦ τὰ σκάνδαλα μὴ ἐλθεῖν*, Acts iii. 11 *πεποιηκόσι τοῦ περιπατεῖν*; nor of *ἵνα* with subj. instead of simple inf. as in Matt. xviii. 6

συμφέρει αὐτῷ ἵνα κρεμασθῇ λίθος, John iv. 34 *ἐμὸν βρῶμά ἐστιν ἵνα ποιῶ τὸ θέλημα*, Luke i. 43 *πόθεν μοι τοῦτο ἵνα ἔλθῃ ἡ μήτηρ*, 1 Cor. iv. 3 *ἐμοὶ εἰς ἐλάχιστόν ἐστιν ἵνα ὑφ' ὑμῶν ἀνακριθῶ*, or instead of the inf. with art. explaining the purport of what precedes, as in Phil. i. 9 *τοῦτο προσεύχομαι, ἵνα ἡ ἀγάπη περισσεύσῃ*, 1 John iv. 17 *ἐν τούτῳ τετελείωται ἡ ἀγάπη, ἵνα παρρησίαν ἔχωμεν*, or where we should have expected the inf. with *ὥστε*, e.g. Gal. v. 17 *ταῦτα ἀλλήλοις ἀντίκειται, ἵνα μὴ ἃ ἐὰν θέλητε ποιῆτε*, 1 Th. v. 4 *οὐκ ἐστὲ ἐν σκότει, ἵνα ἡ ἡμέρα ὑμᾶς ὡς κλέπτας καταλάβῃ*.

On the whole I should be inclined to rate the Greek of this Epistle as approaching more nearly to the standard of classical purity than that of any other book of the N.T. with the exception perhaps of the Epistle to the Hebrews. The author of the latter has no doubt greater copiousness, and more variety of constructions; he is also occasionally very idiomatic, as in the phrase *ἔμαθεν ἀφ' ὧν ἔπαθεν* v. 8; but while the distinction between *μή* and *οὐ* is carefully preserved in our Epistle, we find in the Hebrews *μή* used incorrectly after *ἐπεί*, ix. 17 *ἐπεὶ μὴ τότε* (*al.* *μήποτε*) *ἰσχύει, ὅτε ζῇ ὁ διαθέμενος*, and with the participle, xi. 8 *ἐξῆλθεν μὴ ἐπιστάμενος*, ver. 13 *κατὰ πίστιν ἀπέθανον μὴ κομίσαντες*, ver. 27 *πίστει κατέλιπεν Αἴγυπτον μὴ φοβηθεὶς τὸν θυμὸν τοῦ βασιλέως* (in contrast with James i. 25). Again, the latter writer is less accurate in his use of the moods and tenses than our author. Thus we find the aor. with *οὔπω* in xii. 4, where a classical writer would have used the perfect, *οὔπω μέχρις αἵματος ἀντικατέστητε...καὶ ἐκλέλησθε τῆς παρακλήσεως*: we find *ὅταν* with the aor. subj. followed by pres. ind. in i. 6 *ὅταν πάλιν εἰσαγάγῃ τὸν πρωτότοκον εἰς τὴν οἰκουμένην λέγει*, where *ὅταν εἰσαγάγῃ* seems to be equivalent to *εἰσάγων*: we find irregular uses of the inf. in ii. 3 *ἀρχὴν λαβοῦσα λαλεῖσθαι*, ii. 15 *διὰ παντὸς τοῦ ζῆν*, ix. 24 *εἰς οὐρανὸν εἰσῆλθεν νῦν ἐμφανισθῆναι τῷ προσώπῳ τοῦ Θεοῦ*, vi. 10 *οὐ γὰρ ἄδικος ὁ Θεὸς ἐπιλαθέσθαι τοῦ ἔργου*: we find post-classical uses of the prepositions, e.g. *παρὰ* after the comparative in i. 4, iii. 3 and elsewhere; *εἰς* used with persons, ii. 3 *εἰς ἡμᾶς ἐβεβαιώθη*; *εἰς τὸ* used of the consequence, xi. 3 *πίστει νοοῦμεν κατηρτίσθαι τοὺς αἰῶνας ῥήματι Θεοῦ εἰς τὸ μὴ 'κ φαινομένων γεγονέναι*; *ἀπό* used where a classical writer would have written *διά* with acc. v. 7 *εἰσακουσθεὶς ἀπὸ τῆς εὐλαβείας*; not to mention the use of such a Pauline anacoluthon as xiii. 5 *ἀφιλάργυρος ὁ τρόπος, ἀρκούμενοι τοῖς παροῦσιν*.

I do not of course assert that St. James writes with the same facility as St. Paul. The former was evidently a slow and careful writer, while the latter speaks as he is moved, without regard to accuracy or ornament, in the provincial Greek which was familiar to him from childhood. Nor again is it meant that the Greek of our Epistle is such as could be mistaken for that of a classical writer. There are undoubtedly harsh phrases, such as i. 17 *τροπῆς ἀποσκίασμα*, i. 23 *τὸ πρόσωπον τῆς γενέσεως*, ii. 4 *κριταὶ διαλογισμῶν πονηρῶν*, and awkward and obscure sentences, such as ii. 1 *μὴ ἐν προσωποληψίαις ἔχετε τὴν πίστιν τοῦ Κυρίου ἡμῶν Ἰησοῦ Χριστοῦ τῆς δόξης*, iii. 6 *ὁ κόσμος τῆς ἀδικίας ἡ γλῶσσα καθίσταται ἐν τοῖς μέλεσιν ἡμῶν ἡ . . . φλογίζουσα τὸν τροχὸν τῆς γενέσεως*, iii. 12 *μὴ δύναται συκῆ ἐλαίας ποιῆσαι; οὔτε ἁλυκὸν γλυκὺ ποιῆσαι ὕδωρ*, also iv. 5, 6, 17. But Schleiermacher and Dr. S. Davidson are entirely mistaken when they allege as proofs that 'the author was not accustomed to write Greek' such thoroughly idiomatic phrases as i. 2 *ὅταν πειρασμοῖς περιπέσητε ποικίλοις*, and the admirably energetic *βουληθεὶς* in i. 18 (*βουληθεὶς ἀπεκύησεν ἡμᾶς λόγῳ ἀληθείας*). Nor can I see that there is any ground for stumbling in the use of *πορείαις* in i. 11 or of *ἀπεκύησεν* in i. 18. The latter, it is true, is not a classical word, but the question is not, of course, about classical, but about post-classical Greek, in which this word was of general use. If it is objected that St. James uses, in the sense of 'begetting,' a word which properly means 'to bring forth,' the answer is that both here and in i. 15 the word is used metaphorically, and that in the Hebrew Scriptures terms properly employed of the mother are used to denote God's relation towards mankind.

Vocabulary.[1]

I proceed now to examine the vocabulary of St. James, giving lists (1) of the words which are apparently used for the first time by him, (2) of words used by him alone among biblical writers, (3) of LXX. words employed by him alone among the writers of the N.T. It is stated in each case whether the word is classical or post-classical, taking the year 300 B.C. as a rough dividing line.

[1] In making this list I have been materially assisted by the lists given in Thayer's *Lexicon* and in *Studia Biblica*, i. p. 149.

Thirteen words are apparently used for the first time by St. James: see notes *in loco.* ἀνέλεος ii. 13 only in *Test. Abr.* 16; ἀνεμιζόμενος i. 6 only in Hesychius, Schol. to Homer and Joannes Moschus, 620 A.D.; ἀπείραστος i. 13 used by Clem. Al. and other fathers in the same sense, probably with reference to St. James, by Josephus in a different sense; ἀποσκίασμα i. 17 used by Basil (vol. i. p. 17 in Migne *P. G.*), where he speaks of the world as ἀποσκίασμα τῆς δυνάμεως τοῦ Θεοῦ, and Cyril Alex. i. 189 πτηνῶν ἀποσκίασμα *volucrum adumbratam formam;* δαιμονιώδης iii. 15 only found in Schol. to Arist. *Ranae* and Symmachus' version of the Psalms; δίψυχος i. 8 and iv. 8, found in the *Didaché*, and quoted from an unknown apocryphal writing by Clem. Rom., used by the latter and by Hermas and subsequent writers with evident reference to St. James; θρησκός i. 26 only found in Theognostus *Can.* (fl. 820); πολύσπλαγχνος v. 11 only found elsewhere in Hermas; προσωπολημπτεῖν ii. 9 only found elsewhere in Orig. *Proverb.* c. 19; προσωπολημψία ii. 1 used also by St. Paul and by Polycarp; ῥυπαρία i. 21 found also in Plutarch, &c.; χαλιναγωγεῖν i. 27, iii. 2, used also by Polycarp, Hermas, and Lucian; χρυσοδακτύλιος ii. 2, not found elsewhere.

Besides these there are six words used by St. James which do not occur either in the LXX. (including the Apocrypha) or in the N.T.: βρύω iii. 11 used intransitively by classical writers, transitively, as here, by some of the Fathers; ἐνάλιος, iii. 7 classical; εὐπειθής iii. 17, cl. and Philo, (εὐπειθέω and εὐπείθεια occur in 4 Macc.); ἐφήμερος ii. 15 classical; κατήφεια iv. 9 classical and Philo.

One word σητόβρωτος (v. 2) is found elsewhere only in LXX., Job. xiii. 28, and in *Sibyll. Orac.* quoted in note.

The following occur in the LXX. but not in the rest of the N.T.: ἀδιάκριτος[1] iii. 17, post-classical and rare in this sense, has a different sense in Prov. xxv. 1; ἀκατάστατος i. 8, iii. 8, classical, Isa. liv. 11; ἁλυκός iii. 12 cl. and in Numb. iii. 12, Deut. iii. 17; ἀμάω v. 4 cl. and in Lev. xxv. 11, Deut. xxiv. 19, Isa. xvii. 5; ἁπλῶς i. 5, cl., Prov. x. 10; ἀποκυέω[1] post-cl. used by Philo and 4 Macc. xv. 14; ἀφυστερέω v. 4, post-cl., Polyb., Diod., Neh. ix. 10, Sir. xiv. 14; βοή v. 4, cl., Ex. ii. 23; γέλως iv. 9 cl., Gen. xxi. 6; ἔοικε i. 6, 23, cl., Job. vi. 25; ἔμφυτος i. 21 cl., Wisdom xii. 10; ἐξέλκω i. 14, cl. Gen. xxxvii. 28; ἐπιτήδειος ii. 16 cl. and in 1 Macc. iv. 46, Wisdom iv. 5; ἐπιλησμονή i. 25, only found besides

[1] Each of these words occurs once in Aristotle.

in Sir. xi. 25; ἐπιστήμων iii. 13, cl., Deut. i. 13, &c.; εὐπρέπεια i. 11, cl., Ps. l. 2; θανατήφορος iii. 8, cl., Numb. xviii. 22; κακοπαθία v. 10, cl., Mal. i. 13; κατιόω v. 3, post-cl., Lam. iv. 1; κατοικίζω iv. 5, cl., Exod. ii. 21 +; κενῶς iv. 5, cl., Isa. xlix. 4; μαραίνω i. 11, cl., Job xv. 30; μετάγω iii. 3, 4, cl., 1 Kings viii. 48 +; μεγαλαυχέω (or μεγάλα αὐχέω) iii. 5, cl., Ezek. xvi. 50 + (the simple αὐχέω is class., but does not occur in LXX.); νομοθέτης iv. 12, cl., Ps. ix. 20; ὀλολύζω v. 1, cl., Joel i. 5 +; ὁμοίωσις iii. 9, cl., Gen. i 26 +; ὄψιμος v. 7, cl., Deut. xi. 14 +; παραλλαγή i. 17, cl., 2 K. ix. 20; πικρός iii. 11, 14, cl., Gen. xxvii. 34 +; ποίησις i. 25, cl., Sir. xix. 18; πρόϊμος v. 7, cl., Deut. xi. 14; ῥιπίζω i. 6 cl., Dan. ii. 35 ἐρρίπισεν ὁ ἄνεμος (where Theodotion has ἐξῆρεν), and Philo; σήπω v. 2, cl., Job. xl. 7; ταλαιπωρέω iv. 9, cl., Mic. ii. 4 +; ταχύς i. 19, cl., Prov. xxix. 20 +; τροπή i. 17, cl., Deut. xxxiii. 14 +; τροχός iii. 6, cl., Ps. lxxxiii. 13 +; τρυφάω v. 5, cl., Neh. ix. 25 +; ὕλη iii. 5, cl., Isa. x. 17 +; φιλία iv. 4, cl., Prov. xix. 7 +; φλογίζω, iii. 6, cl., Ps. xcvi. 3; φρίσσω ii. 19, cl., Job iv. 14 +; χρή iii. 10, cl., Prov. xxv. 27 τιμᾶν δὲ χρὴ λόγους ἐνδόξους.[1]

Of the unusual words mentioned above it is to be noted that some are of a technical nature, connected with fishing, as ἀνεμίζω, ῥιπίζω, ἐνάλιος, ἐξέλκω, ἁλυκόν. Possibly the last may have been a local expression for a salt spring. Others are connected with husbandry, as ἀμάω, βρύω, ἐπιτήδεια, κατιόω, μαραίνω ὄψιμος, πρόϊμος, σέσηπε, σητόβρωτος. Others however are perfectly general, as ἀνέλεος, πολύσπλαγχνος, ἀπείραστος, θρησκός, εὐπειθής. Then there are others, very common in classical writers, which we wonder not to find used in the other parts of the N.T., such as χρή, γέλως, ἔοικε, ὕλη, ἁπλῶς, πικρός, ταχύς, λείπεσθαι 'to be wanting in.' In some cases this absence may be due to accident, since we find other forms of the same stem commonly used. Thus we have many instances of ἐν τάχει, and we find also ταχινός, ταχέως, ταχύ, τάχιον, τάχιστα. In like manner we find πικρία, πικραίνω, πικρῶς, γελᾶν and καταγελᾶν, ἁπλοῦς and ἁπλότης. There is no mention of forests in the N.T. except in St. James, which accounts for ὕλη not being found: but χρή and ἔοικε stand on another footing. For the latter we always have ὅμοιός ἐστι in the other books; and for the former either δεῖ (used sometimes where a classical writer would certainly have preferred χρή) or ὀφείλω. It appears then that, so far as the use of these two

[1] χρή is omitted in the Concordances to the LXX.

words is concerned, St. James is more idiomatic than the other canonical writers, and for the rest that he uses with freedom rare words and compounds, all of them correctly formed and some of them possibly formed by himself. He is however a purist in regard to those combinations of prepositions and adverbs which are so marked a feature of late Greek, e.g. ὑπερλίαν 2 Cor. xi. 5, ἐφάπαξ Heb. vii. 27, ἐκπάλαι 2 Pet. ii. 3, ἀπὸ τότε Matt. iv. 17, ἀπὸ πέρυσι 2 Cor. viii. 10, cf. Winer, p. 525.

Another point deserving notice in St. James, which might seem to denote limited acquaintance with the language, is his use of general instead of special terms; though, as regards ποιεῖν and διδόναι, Vorst (*Hebr.* pp. 158—163, 167, 59) considers that this extended use is derived from the corresponding Hebrew words.

ποιεῖν. ἔλεος ii. 13, εἰρήνην iii. 18, ἁμαρτίαν v. 15, συκῆ ἐλαίας οὐ ποιεῖ iii. 12, ἁλυκὸν οὐ δύναται γλυκὺ ποιῆσαι ὕδωρ iii. 12, ποιήσομεν ἐκεῖ ἐνιαυτόν iv. 13, ποιεῖν καλόν iv. 17, π. καλῶς ii. 8, 19, cf. ποιητὴς λόγου i. 22 ποιητὴς νόμου iv. 11, ποιητὴς ἔργου i. 25.

ἐργάζεσθαι. ἁμαρτίαν ii. 9, δικαιοσύνην i. 20, τὸ δοκίμιον ὑμῶν τῆς πίστεως κατεργάζεται ὑπομονήν i. 3.

λαμβάνειν. τι παρὰ τοῦ Κυρίου i. 7, τὸν στέφανον τῆς ζωῆς i. 12, κρίμα λήμψεσθε iii. 1, αἰτεῖτε καὶ οὐ λαμβάνετε iv. 3, ἕως ἂν (ὁ καρπὸς) λάβῃ πρόϊμον v. 7, ὑπόδειγμα λάβετε τοὺς προφήτας v. 10.

ἔχειν. ἡ ὑπομονὴ ἔργον τέλειον ἐχέτω i. 4, μὴ ἐν προσωπολημψίαις ἔχετε τὴν πίστιν ii. 1, πίστιν, ἔργα ἔχει τις ii. 14, 18, πίστις ἔχει ἔργα ii. 17 (cf. Clem. R. ii. 6, 9 ἔργα ἔχοντες), ζῆλον ἔχετε ἐν τῇ καρδίᾳ iii. 14, ἐπιθυμεῖτε καὶ οὐκ ἔχετε iv. 2.

διδόναι. ὁ οὐρανὸς ὑετὸν ἔδωκεν v. 18.

I go on now to speak of the style of the Epistle, as exhibited in the writer's use of rhetorical figures and of rhythm. Though we do not find here the oratorical power of the Epistle to the Hebrews or the rapid and impassioned eloquence of St. Paul; though there is no attempt to build up a number of subordinate clauses into elaborate periods; yet there is something too of rhetorical skill, and at times of idiomatic phraseology which is very telling. The sentences are short, simple, direct, conveying weighty thoughts in weighty words, and giving the impression of a strong and serious individuality as well as of a poetic imagination.

Use of metaphor and simile:

(1) *derived from rural life*, i. 10 the transitory nature of earthly prosperity is illustrated by the flower which withers away and loses all its beauty under the burning sun and wind; iii. 11 the right use of speech is illustrated by the spring which only gives forth sweet water, by the tree which produces only its own proper fruit; iii. 18 righteousness is a fruit whose seed is sown in peace; iv. 14 man's life is like a shifting mist; v. 7 patience under persecution is inculcated by the example of the husbandman who waits patiently for the rains which shall bring the crop to perfection; iii. 5 a careless word is compared to the spark which sets on fire a forest; iii. 3 as the horse is turned by the bridle, so man's activity is controlled by putting a check on the tongue; iii. 8 the tongue is like the deaf adder which refuses to hear the voice of the charmer.

(2) *derived from sea and stars*, i. 6 a man who cannot make up his mind is compared to a wave driven by the wind and tossed; iii. 4 the control which a man is enabled to exert over his actions by learning to bridle his tongue is compared to the steering of a ship by the rudder; i. 17 God the source of all light is compared to a sun which never suffers obscuration or change.

(3) *derived from domestic life*, i. 15 the development of sin is compared to conception, birth, growth and death; i. 18 the renewal of man's nature by the reception of the Divine Word is compared to conception and birth; i. 23 a careless listener is compared to one who gives a hasty glance at a mirror; ii. 26 the relation between the acceptance of a dogma and practical goodness is compared to that between the body and the animating spirit of life; iv. 4 unfaithfulness to God is compared to adultery; v. 2 the decay and rust to which stored up wealth is liable is a symbol of the disease which eats away the unjust and covetous soul.

(4) *derived from public life*, i. 12 the future happiness of the righteous is described as 'the crown of life,' iv. 1 pleasures are like a hostile army encamped in our body, v. 4 wages which are kept back cry to God for justice.

Paronomasia :[1]

(1) It is a marked feature of the writer's style to link together clauses and sentences by the repetition of the leading word or some of its cognates: compare i. 3–6 τὸ δοκίμιον τῆς πίστεως κατεργάζεται ὑπομονήν· ἡ δὲ ὑπομονὴ ἔργον τέλειον ἐχέτω, ἵνα ἦτε τέλειοι ἐν μηδενὶ λειπόμενοι· εἰ δέ τις λείπεται σοφίας, αἰτείτω . . . αἰτείτω δὲ ἐν πίστει μηδὲν διακρινόμενος· ὁ γὰρ διακρινόμενος κ.τ.λ.; i. 13–15 μηδεὶς πειραζόμενος λεγέτω ὅτι ἀπὸ Θεοῦ πειράζομαι· ὁ γὰρ Θεὸς ἀπείραστός ἐστιν κακῶν, πειράζει δὲ αὐτὸς οὐδένα· ἕκαστος δὲ πειράζεται ὑπὸ τῆς ἰδίας ἐπιθυμίας· εἶτα ἡ ἐπιθυμία τίκτει ἁμαρτίαν, ἡ δὲ ἁμαρτία ἀποκυεῖ θάνατον; i. 19, 20 βραδὺς εἰς τὸ ἀκοῦσαι, βραδὺς εἰς ὀργήν· ὀργὴ γὰρ ἀνδρὸς Θεοῦ δικαιοσύνην οὐκ ἐργάζεται; i. 21–25 δέξασθε τὸν ἔμφυτον λόγον...γίνεσθε δὲ ποιηταὶ λόγου καὶ μὴ ἀκροαταὶ μόνον...ὅτι εἴ τις ἀκροατὴς λόγου ἐστὶν καὶ οὐ ποιητής...οὐκ ἀκροατὴς ἐπιλησμονῆς γενόμενος ἀλλὰ ποιητὴς ἔργου, οὗτος μακάριος ἐν τῇ ποιήσει αὐτοῦ ἔσται; i. 26, 27 εἴ τις δοκεῖ θρησκὸς εἶναι...τούτου μάταιος ἡ θρησκεία· θρησκεία καθαρὰ αὕτη ἐστίν κ.τ.λ.; ii. 2–7 ἐὰν εἰσέλθῃ ἀνὴρ χρυσοδακτύλιος ἐν ἐσθῆτι λαμπρᾷ, εἰσέλθῃ δὲ καὶ πτωχὸς ἐν ῥυπαρᾷ ἐσθῆτι, ἐπιβλέψητε δὲ ἐπὶ τὸν φοροῦντα τὴν ἐσθῆτα τὴν λαμπρὰν...καὶ τῷ πτωχῷ εἴπητε κ.τ.λ. ... οὐχ ὁ Θεὸς ἐξελέξατο τοὺς πτωχούς ...ὑμεῖς δὲ ἠτιμάσατε τὸν πτωχόν...οἱ πλούσιοι αὐτοὶ ἕλκουσιν ...αὐτοὶ βλασφημοῦσιν; ii. 8–12 the word νόμος occurs in each of these verses; ii, 12 οὕτως λαλεῖτε καὶ οὕτως ποιεῖτε; ii. 13 ἡ κρίσις ἀνέλεος τῷ μὴ ποιήσαντι ἔλεος, κατακαυχᾶται ἔλεος κρίσεως; in ii. 14–26 τί ὄφελος begins 14 and ends 16, the phrase πίστιν ἔχειν occurs twice, ἔργα ἔχειν thrice, ἐξ ἔργων δικαιοῦσθαι occurs thrice and ἐκ πίστεως δικαιοῦσθαι once, πίστις is found eight times, and ἔργα five times in other collocations, πιστεύω thrice, χωρὶς ἔργων twice, (ἡ πίστις) νεκρά ἐστιν twice, we have also τὸ σῶμα χωρὶς πνεύματος νεκρόν and δεῖξόν μοι τὴν πίστιν σου...κἀγώ σοι δείξω κ.τ.λ.; iii. 2–4 πολλὰ πταίομεν

[1] I use this term in the loose sense in which it is employed by Schmid in his *Atticismus*, to express the repetition of the same word or root.

ἅπαντες· εἴ τις ἐν λόγῳ οὐ πταίει, οὗτος δυνατὸς χαλιναγωγῆσαι καὶ ὅλον τὸ σῶμα· ἴδε τῶν ἵππων τοὺς χαλινοὺς εἰς τὰ στόματα βάλλομεν καὶ ὅλον τὸ σῶμα μετάγομεν· ἰδοὺ καὶ τὰ πλοῖα μετάγεται; iii. 5–8 ἡ γλῶσσα μικρὸν μέλος ἐστίν· ἰδοὺ ἡλίκον πῦρ ἡλίκην ὕλην ἀνάπτει· καὶ ἡ γλῶσσα πῦρ, ὁ κόσμος τῆς ἀδικίας ἡ γλῶσσα καθίσταται ἐν τοῖς μέλεσιν ἡμῶν...ἡ φλογίζουσα τὸν τροχὸν τῆς γενέσεως καὶ φλογιζομένη ὑπὸ τῆς γεέννης. πᾶσα φύσις θηρίων τε καὶ πετεινῶν ἑρπετῶν τε τε καὶ ἐναλίων δαμάζεται καὶ δεδάμασται τῇ φύσει τῇ ἀνθρωπίνῃ· τὴν δέ γλῶσσαν οὐδεὶς δαμάσαι δύναται ἀνθρώπων; iii. 9 ἐν αὐτῇ εὐλογοῦμεν καὶ ἐν αὐτῇ καταρώμεθα...ἐκ τοῦ αὐτοῦ στόματος ἐξέρχεται εὐλογία καὶ κατάρα; iii. 11–18 τὸ γλυκὺ καὶ τὸ πικρόν...συκῆ ἐλαίας, ἄμπελος σῦκα...ἁλυκὸν γλυκύ...εἰ ζῆλον πικρὸν ἔχετε καὶ ἐριθίαν...οὐκ ἔστιν αὕτη ἡ σοφία ἄνωθεν κατερχομένη...ὅπου γὰρ ζῆλος καὶ ἐριθία, ἀκαταστασία... ἡ δὲ ἄνωθεν σοφία πρῶτον μὲν ἁγνή ἐστιν, ἔπειτα εἰρηνική, μεστὴ καρπῶν ἀγαθῶν...καρπὸς δὲ δικαιοσύνης ἐν εἰρήνῃ σπείρεται τοῖς ποιοῦσιν εἰρήνην; iv. 1–3 πόθεν πόλεμοι καὶ πόθεν μάχαι; οὐκ ἐντεῦθεν ἐκ τῶν ἡδονῶν ...μάχεσθε καὶ πολεμεῖτε. οὐκ ἔχετε διὰ τὸ μὴ αἰτεῖσθαι· αἰτεῖτε καὶ οὐ λαμβάνετε διότι κακῶς αἰτεῖσθε, ἵνα ἐν ταῖς ἡδοναῖς δαπανήσητε; iv. 4–10 ἡ φιλία τοῦ κόσμου ἔχθρα τοῦ Θεοῦ· ὃς ἐὰν οὖν βουληθῇ φίλος εἶναι τοῦ κόσμου ἐχθρὸς τοῦ Θεοῦ καθίσταται...ὁ Θεὸς ὑπερηφάνοις ἀντιτάσσεται, ταπεινοῖς δὲ δίδωσιν χάριν· ὑποτάγητε οὖν τῷ Θεῷ...ἐγγίσατε τῷ Θεῷ καὶ ἐγγίσει ὑμῖν...ταπεινώθητε ἐνώπιον Κυρίου; iv. 11, 12 μὴ καταλαλεῖτε ἀλλήλων ἀδελφοί· ὁ καταλαλῶν ἀδελφοῦ ἢ κρίνων τὸν ἀδελφὸν αὐτοῦ καταλαλεῖ νόμου καὶ κρίνει νόμον· εἰ δὲ νόμον κρίνεις οὐκ εἶ ποιητὴς νόμου ἀλλὰ κριτής. εἷς ἔστιν νομοθέτης καὶ κριτής· σὺ δὲ τίς εἶ, ὁ κρίνων τὸν πλησίον; iv. 13–17 αὔριον ...τὸ τῆς αὔριον, ποιήσομεν...ποιήσομεν, φαινομένη...ἀφανιζομένη, καυχᾶσθε...καύχησις, καλὸν ποιεῖν...ποιοῦντι; v. 3–11 ὁ ἄργυρος κατίωται καὶ ὁ ἰὸς φάγεται τὰς σάρκας...μακροθυμήσατε ἕως τῆς παρουσίας τοῦ Κυρίου...μακροθυμῶν...μακροθυμήσατε καὶ ὑμεῖς, ὅτι ἡ παρουσία τοῦ Κυρίου ἤγγικεν. μὴ στενάζετε ἵνα μὴ κ ρ ι θ ῆ τ ε· ἰδοὺ ὁ κ ρ ι τ ὴ ς πρὸ τῶν θυρῶν ἕστηκεν· ὑπόδειγμα λάβετε τῆς μ α κ ρ ο θ υ μ ί α ς τοὺς προφήτας· μακαρίζομεν τοὺς ὑ π ο μ ε ί ν α ν τ α ς· τὴν ὑ π ο μ ο ν ὴ ν Ἰὼβ ἠκούσατε; v. 17–20 π ρ ο σ ε υ χ ῇ π ρ ο σ η ύ ξ α τ ο τοῦ μὴ β ρ έ ξ α ι, καὶ οὐκ ἔ β ρ ε ξ ε ν...καὶ πάλιν π ρ ο σ η ύ ξ α τ ο...ἐάν τις π λ α ν η θ ῇ καὶ ἐ π ι σ τ ρ έ ψ ῃ τις αὐτόν, γινώσκετε ὅ τ ι ὁ ἐ π ι σ τ ρ έ ψ α ς ἁμαρτωλὸν ἐκ π λ ά ν η ς ὁδοῦ αὐτοῦ σώσει ψυχήν.

I have quoted all the examples of the recurrence of a word or stem under one head for convenience sake; but it will be easily seen that the recurrence is not always due to the same cause. It is partly owing to the preference for short sentences, which require the noun to be repeated for the sake of clearness; whereas in a complex sentence the relative pronoun or some connecting particle might have answered the purpose. But it is plain that the repetition is often intended to give emphasis, as in i. 19 *βραδύς*, ii. 6, 7 *αὐτοί*, iii. 6 *φλογίζουσα—φλογιζομένη*, iii. 7 *δαμάζεται καὶ δεδάμασται*, iii. 9 *ἐν αὐτῇ*, iv. 1 *πόθεν*, iv. 12 *ἀδελφός* and *νόμος*, v. 17 *προσευχῇ προσηύξατο*. It is probable however, as we may judge from the following section, that the recurrence of the same sound was in itself pleasing to the writer and contributed, along with his love of definiteness, to produce repetition, where there is no special reason to be found in the circumstances of the case.

Alliteration and Homoeoteleuta:

With the letter *d*:

i. 1 δοῦλος ταῖς δώδεκα φυλαῖς ταῖς ἐν τῇ διασπορᾷ.

i. 6 αἰτείτω δὲ μηδὲν διακρινόμενος, ὁ γὰρ διακρινόμενος ἔοικε κλύδωνι.

ii. 16 μὴ δῶτε δὲ τὰ ἐπιτήδεια.

iii. 8 τὴν δὲ γλῶσσαν οὐδεὶς δαμάσαι δύναται.

d and *p*: i. 21 διὸ ἀποθέμενοι πᾶσαν ῥυπαρίαν καὶ περισσείαν κακίας ἐν πραΰτητι δέξασθε τὸν ἔμφυτον λόγον τὸν δυνάμενον κ.τ.λ.

p: i. 2 πᾶσαν χαρὰν ἡγήσασθε ὅταν πειρασμοῖς περιπέσητε ποικίλοις.

i. 17 πᾶσα δόσις ἀγαθὴ καὶ πᾶν δώρημα τέλειον...ἀπὸ τοῦ πατρὸς τῶν φώτων, παρ' ᾧ οὐκ ἔνι παραλλαγὴ ἢ τροπῆς ἀποσκίασμα, cf. also i. 3, 11, 22, iii. 2.

p, l, th: i. 24 ἀπελήλυθεν καὶ ἐπελάθετο.

l: i. 4 τέλειον, τέλειοι, ὁλόκληροι, λειπόμενοι.
iii. 4 πλοῖα τηλικαῦτα...ὑπὸ ἀνέμων σκληρῶν ἐλαυνόμενα μετάγεται ὑπὸ ἐλαχίστου πηδαλίου ὅπου... βούλεται.

m: iii. 5 μικρὸν μέλος ἐστὶν καὶ μεγάλα αὐχεῖ.

k: i. 26, 27 δοκεῖ θρησκὸς εἶναι, χαλιναγωγῶν γλῶσσαν ...καρδίαν. ... θρησκεία καθαρὰ ...ἐπισκέπτεσθαι χήρας...ἄσπιλον ἑαυτὸν τηρεῖν ἀπὸ τοῦ κόσμου.
ii. 3 κάθου ὧδε καλῶς.
iv. 8 καθαρίσατε χεῖρας...ἁγνίσατε καρδίας.

n, t, o: ii. 10 ὅστις γὰρ ὅλον τὸν νόμον τηρήσῃ, πταίσῃ δὲ ἐν ἑνὶ γέγονεν πάντων ἔνοχος.

Alliteration is the more marked when it affects the prominent words as in i. 21 διὸ...δέξασθε...δυνάμενον.

Sometimes we have the recurrence not of one letter only but of a syllable, as in v. 2 ὁ πλοῦτος σέσηπεν, τὰ ἱμάτια σητόβρωτα γέγονεν, ii. 4 οὐ διε κ ρ ί θητε καὶ ἐγένεσθε κ ρ ι ταὶ διαλογισμῶν, i. 24 cited above; or of several syllables (ὁμοιοτέλευτα) as i. 7 ἀνεμιζομένῳ καὶ ῥιπιζομένῳ, i. 14 ἐξελκόμενος καὶ δελεαζόμενος, ii. 16 θερμαίνεσθε καὶ χορτάζεσθε, ii. 19 πιστεύουσιν καὶ φρίσσουσιν, iv. 9 ταλαιπωρήσατε καὶ πενθήσατε καὶ κλαύσατε, v. 5 ἐτρυφήσατε καὶ ἐσπαταλήσατε, v. 6 κατεδικάσατε, ἐφονεύσατε, iii. 17 ἀδιάκριτος, ἀνυπόκριτος, v. 4 τῶν ἀμησάντων...τῶν θερισάντων, ii. 12 οὕτως λαλεῖτε καὶ οὕτως ποιεῖτε. Sometimes there is a recurrence of the same preposition in compounds, as ἀπὸ in i. 15, and i. 18 ἀπεκύησεν...ἀπαρχήν, παρά in i. 25 ὁ δὲ π α ρ α κ ύ ψ α ς εἰς νόμον καὶ π α ρ α μ ε ί ν α ς, and i. 17 παρ' ᾧ...παραλλαγή. This similarity of sound is often used to mark a correspondence or give point to an antithesis, as in i. 10, 11 where the former sentence ends with παρελεύσεται, the latter with μαρανθήσεται, v. 2, 3 ὁ πλοῦτος ὑμῶν...ὁ χρυσὸς ὑμῶν. Often this is combined with balancing of clauses (ἰσόκωλα) as in i. 19 τ α χ ὺ ς ε ἰ ς τ ὸ ἀ κ ο ῦ σ α ι, β ρ α δ ὺ ς ε ἰ ς τ ὸ λ α λ ῆ σ α ι, iv. 7 ὑ π ο τ ά γ η τ ε τ ῷ Θ ε ῷ, ἀ ν τ ί σ τ η τ ε δ ὲ τ ῷ δ ι α β ό λ ῳ, iv. 8 κ α θ α ρ ί σ α τ ε χ ε ῖ ρ α ς ἁ μ α ρ τ ω λ ο ὶ κ α ὶ ἁ γ ν ί σ α τ ε κ α ρ δ ί α ς δίψυχοι, i. 15 ἡ ἐ π ι θ υ μ ί α σ υ λ λ α β ο ῦ σ α τ ί κ τ ε ι ἁ μ α ρ τ ί α ν, ἡ δ ὲ ἁ μ α ρ τ ί α ἀ π ο τ ε λ ε σ θ ε ῖ σ α ἀ π ο κ υ ε ῖ θ ά ν α τ ο ν, iv. 13 π ο ρ ε υ σ ό μ ε θ α ε ἰ ς τήνδε τὴν πόλιν καὶ π ο ι ή σ ο μ ε ν ἐκεῖ ἐνιαυτὸν καὶ ἐ μ π ο ρ ε υ σ ό μ ε θ α καὶ κ ε ρ δ ή σ ο μ ε ν. The frequency of these parallels in St. James does not require us to suppose that he had been trained in the use of their figures of speech by the Greek rhetoricians, but is probably to be traced to his familiarity with Hebrew poetry, which is founded on the principle of parallelism.[1]

Asyndeton:

This figure is most commonly used in enumeration (1) and antithesis (2). Of the former we have examples in iii. 15 οὐκ ἔστιν αὕτη ἡ σοφία ἄνωθεν κατερχομένη, ἀλλὰ ἐπίγειος, ψυχική, δαιμονιώδης, and 17 ἡ ἄνωθεν σοφία πρῶτον μὲν ἁγνή ἐστιν, ἔπειτα εἰρηνική, ἐπιεικής, εὐπειθής, μεστὴ ἐλέους καὶ καρπῶν ἀγαθῶν, ἀδιάκριτος, ἀνυπόκριτος, i. 19 βραδὺς εἰς τὸ λαλῆσαι, βραδὺς εἰς ὀργὴν, v. 6 κατεδικάσατε, ἐφονεύσατε τὸν δίκαιον. Of the latter we have an example in the verse last quoted, ἐφονεύσατε τὸν δίκαιον being followed by οὐκ ἀντιτάσσεται ὑμῖν, where it would have been more usual to insert ὁ δέ before οὐκ; also in i. 19 ταχὺς εἰς τὸ ἀκοῦσαι, βραδὺς εἰς τὸ λαλῆσαι, i. 27 ἐπισκέπτεσθαι ὀρφανοὺς καὶ χήρας, ἄσπιλον ἑαυτὸν τηρεῖν, ii. 13 ἡ γὰρ κρίσις ἀνέλεος τῷ μὴ ποιήσαντι ἔλεος· κατακαυχᾶται ἔλεος κρίσεως, where again we might have expected τὸ δὲ ἔλεος κατακαυχᾶται. But the writer also uses *asyndeton* to express a result, iv. 2 οὐκ ἔχετε· φονεύετε (or φθονεῖτε if that is the true reading)...οὐ δύνασθε ἐπιτυχεῖν· μάχεσθε.

Rhythm:

I have mentioned that St. James makes no attempt at elaborate periods. There are I think only two sentences in his Epistle which exceed four lines: one is ii. 2–4, where the construction is clearly defined, ἐὰν εἰσέλθῃ ἀνὴρ χρυσοδακτύλιος...εἰσέλθῃ δὲ καὶ πτωχός...ἐπιβλέψητε δὲ ἐπὶ τὸν φοροῦντα...καὶ εἴπητε...καὶ τῷ πτωχῷ εἴπητε...οὐ διεκρίθητε ἐν ἑαυτοῖς; the other (iv. 13–15) ἄγε νῦν οἱ λέγοντες Σήμερον πορευσόμεθα...οἵτινες οὐκ ἐπίστασθε...ἀντὶ τοῦ λέγειν Ἐὰν ὁ Κύριος θέλῃ, ζήσομεν κ.τ.λ. contains, it is true, an anacoluthon, but the mind is not kept in suspense; each clause is intelligible in itself. On the other hand, we find sentences of ten lines in the 1st epistle of Peter, of

[1] See Jebb's *Sacred Literature*, Lond. 1820, in which James i. 9, 10, 15, 17, 22, 25, iii. 1–12, iv. 6–10, v. 1–6, are analysed as specimens of parallelism.

twelve lines in the epistle to the Hebrews, and of more than twenty in the epistle to the Ephesians. The complexity of the sentences in these epistles and in St. Paul's writings generally arises from the accumulation (1) of relative clauses, one depending on another, as in Col. i. 24–29 ὑπὲρ τοῦ σώματος αὐτοῦ, ὅ ἐστιν ἡ ἐκκλησία, ἧς ἐγενόμην διάκονος...τοῖς ἁγίοις αὐτοῦ, οἷς ἠθέλησεν ὁ Κύριος γνωρίσαι τί τὸ πλοῦτος τῆς δόξης...ὅ ἐστιν Χριστὸς...ὃν ἡμεῖς καταγγέλλομεν...εἰς ὃ καὶ κοπιῶ, (2) of participles, including genitives absolute, as in Heb. ix. 6–10 τούτων δὲ οὕτως κατεσκευασμένων...εἰσίασιν οἱ ἱερεῖς τὰς λατρείας ἐπιτελοῦντες.. τοῦτο δηλοῦντος τοῦ πνεύματος...ἔτι τῆς πρώτης σκηνῆς ἐχούσης τάξιν...καθ' ἣν θυσίαι προσφέρονται μὴ δυνάμεναι τελειῶσαι τὸν λατρεύοντα, Col. ii. 13–15 συνεζωοποίησεν ἡμᾶς αὐτῷ, χαρισάμενος τὰ παραπτώματα, ἐξαλείψας τὸ καθ' ἡμῶν χειρόγραφον...καὶ αὐτὸ ἦρκεν ἐκ τοῦ μέσου προσηλώσας... ἀπεκδυσάμενος...καὶ ἐδειγμάτισεν...θριαμβεύσας αὐτούς, (3) of prepositional phrases, as in Eph. i. 3 εὐλογητὸς ὁ Θεὸς ... ὁ εὐλογήσας ἡμᾶς ἐν πάσῃ εὐλογίᾳ ἐν τοῖς ἐπουρανίοις ἐν Χριστῷ, καθὼς ἐξελέξατο ἡμᾶς ἐν αὐτῷ πρὸ καταβολῆς κόσμου, εἶναι ἡμᾶς ἀμώμους κατενώπιον αὐτοῦ ἐν ἀγάπῃ προορίσας ἡμᾶς εἰς υἱοθεσίαν διὰ Ἰησοῦ εἰς αὐτόν, κατὰ τὴν εὐδοκίαν...εἰς ἔπαινον τῆς χάριτος ἧς ἐχαρίτωσεν ἡμᾶς ἐν τῷ ἠγαπημένῳ, ἐν ᾧ ἔχομεν τὴν ἀπολύτρωσιν διὰ τοῦ αἵματος αὐτοῦ, τὴν ἄφεσιν τῶν παραπτωμάτων, κατὰ τὸ πλοῦτος τῆς χάριτος αὐτοῦ, ἧς ἐπερίσσευσεν εἰς ἡμᾶς ἐν πάσῃ σοφίᾳ...γνωρίσας τὸ μυστήριον ...κατὰ τὴν εὐδοκίαν αὐτοῦ ἣν προέθετο ἐν αὐτῷ εἰς οἰκονομίαν ...ἀνακεφαλαιώσασθαι τὰ πάντα ἐν τῷ Χριστῷ, τὰ ἐπὶ τοῖς οὐρανοῖς καὶ τὰ ἐπὶ τῆς γῆς ἐν αὐτῷ, ἐν ᾧ κ.τ.λ. This sentence may stand as an epitome of the other ways in which St. Paul fills out his sentences : e.g. (4) with nouns in apposition, as τὴν ἄφεσιν; (5) with epexegetic infinitive, as εἶναι ἡμᾶς, ἀνακεφαλαιώσασθαι. St. James, on the other hand, never doubles the relative, never uses genitive absolute, does not accumulate prepositions, or use the epexegetic infinitive—in a word, never allows his principal sentence to be lost in the rank luxuriance of the subordinate clauses. This appears plainly from the following statistics. The number of simple sentences, i.e. sentences having no subordinate finite verb, in the Epistle is 140 according to my reckoning. I include in this all co-ordinate clauses. The number of sentences with a single subordinate clause is 42. I include here subordinate clauses of direct narration; but, where a subordinate clause contains two or more verbs under the same government, as ii. 10 ὅστις τηρήσῃ ...πταίσῃ δέ, I only reckon one clause. The number of sentences with two subordinate clauses is 7. They are the following: i. 2, 3 χαρὰν ἡγήσασθε, ὅταν περιπέσητε...γινώσκοντες ὅτι τὸ δοκίμιον κατεργάζεται ὑπομονήν, ii. 2–4 ἐὰν εἰσέλθῃ...καὶ εἴπητε Σὺ κάθου...οὐ διεκρίθητε; ii. 8 εἰ νόμον τελεῖτε κατὰ τὴν γραφὴν Ἀγαπήσεις...καλῶς ποιεῖτε, ii. 15, 16 ἐὰν...εἴπῃ τις Ὑπάγετε... τί ὄφελος; iv. 3 οὐ λαμβάνετε διότι κακῶς αἰτεῖσθε, ἵνα... δαπανήσητε, v. 19 ἐάν τις πλανηθῇ...γινώσκετε ὅτι σώσει ψυχήν. The following three sentences have three or more subordinate clauses: i. 12 μακάριος ὃς ὑπομένει...ὅτι λήμψεται τὸν στέφανον ὃν ἐπηγγείλατο, iv. 5, 6 δοκεῖτε ὅτι κενῶς λέγει Πρὸς φθόνον ἐπιποθεῖ τὸ πνεῦμα ὃ κατῴκισεν ἐν ἡμῖν; iv. 13–15 ἄγε νῦν οἱ λέγοντες Σήμερον πορευσόμεθα...οἵτινες οὐκ ἐπίστασθε τὰ τῆς αὔριον...ἀντὶ τοῦ λέγειν Ἐὰν ὁ Κύριος θέλῃ ζήσομεν.

Short however as are the sentences of St. James, they are, I think, better formed and more rhythmical than are to be found elsewhere in the N.T. except in the 15th chapter of the 1st epistle to the Corinthians. To my ear there is something of the Miltonic 'organ-voice' in sentences such as[1] i. 11 ἀνέτειλεν γὰρ ὁ ἥλιος σὺν τῷ καύσωνι | καὶ ἐξήρανεν τὸν χόρτον | καὶ τὸ ἄνθος αὐτοῦ ἐξέπεσεν | καὶ ἡ εὐπρέπεια τοῦ προσώπου αὐτοῦ ἀπώλετο || οὕτως καὶ ὁ πλούσιος | ἐν ταῖς πορείαις αὐτοῦ | μαρανθήσεται |, i. 13 μηδεὶς | πειραζόμενος | λεγέτω | (ὅτι) ἀπὸ Θεοῦ | πειράζομαι || ὁ γὰρ Θεὸς | ἀπείραστός ἐστιν κακῶν | πειράζει δὲ αὐτὸς | οὐδένα |, iii. 17 ἡ δὲ ἄνωθεν σοφία | πρῶτον μὲν ἁγνή ἐστιν | ἔπειτα εἰρηνική | ἐπιεικής | εὐπειθής | μεστὴ ἐλέους καὶ καρπῶν ἀγαθῶν || ἀδιάκριτος | ἀνυπόκριτος |, i. 21, 25–27, iii. 6–9, 15, 17, 18, iv. 13, 14, v. 1–6. The weight and harmony of the rhythm seem to depend partly on the balance of clauses, partly on the recurrence of sounds, partly on the length of syllables, as in καύσωνι, ἐξήρανεν, προσώπου, ἀπείραστος, and partly on the careful selection of the closing words, cf. μαρανθήσεται, πειράζομαι above, δελεαζόμενος i. 14, ἀποσκίασμα i. 17, μάταιος ἡ θρησκεία i. 26, ἐπηγγείλατο τοῖς ἀγαπῶσιν αὐτόν (where observe the alliteration in *g* and *p*) ii. 5, μεστὴ ἰοῦ θανατηφόρου iii. 8, ἐπίγειος, ψυχική, δαιμονιώδης iii. 15, ἀφανιζομένη iv. 14, Κυρίου Σαβαὼθ εἰσελήλυθαν v. 4.

[1] I have divided the sentences so as to show what seem to me the natural pauses in reading.

St. James employs this strong weighty rhythm in poetical and prophetical passages, such as we find chiefly in the 1st and 3rd chapters and the beginning of ch. v. In argumentative or colloquial passages, such as we find in chapters ii. and iv. and the latter part of chapter v. the rhythm employed is very different, generally plain and unlaboured, and often crisp, sharp, abrupt, running much into interrogations, as in ii. 14 *τί ὄφελος ἀδελφοί μου ἐὰν πίστιν λέγῃ τις ἔχειν, ἔργα δὲ μὴ ἔχῃ; μὴ δύναται ἡ πίστις σῶσαι αὐτόν;* v. 13 *κακοπαθεῖ τις ἐν ὑμῖν; προσευχέσθω· εὐθυμεῖ τις; ψαλλέτω.*

If we are asked to characterize in a few words the more general qualities of St. James' style, as they impress themselves on the attentive reader, perhaps these would be best summed up in the terms, energy, vivacity, and, as conducive to both, vividness of representation. By the last I mean that dislike of mere abstractions, that delight in throwing everything into picturesque and dramatic forms, which is so marked a feature in our Epistle. This is seen partly in the use of metaphorical expressions of which I have spoken above. Thus the thought of an undecided character calls up the image of some light object tossing on the surface of the wave; the development of sin in the heart and life takes the form of the birth and growth of a living creature; the conviction produced by the Word is figured by the reflexion of the face in the mirror and so on. And often the figure becomes more realistic by the way in which it is introduced, as an actual narrative of a past event: so in i. 11 of the withering of the flower, in i. 24 of the man looking into the mirror, 'he beheld himself, and is gone, and straightway forgot what manner of man he was.' In like manner, abstract qualities are exhibited in concrete shape. Is it respect of persons, or an unreal profession of philanthropy which calls for rebuke? St. James at once dramatizes the scene; particularizing the place—the synagogue; the persons—the rich with his fine clothes and gold ring, the poor in his shabby attire; the opposite treatment of the two—the fawning on the rich *σὺ κάθου ὧδε καλῶς*, the supercilious neglect of the poor *σὺ στῆθι ἐκεῖ ἢ κάθου ὑπὸ τὸ ὑποπόδιόν μου.* With a similar fine irony he paints the behaviour of the *soi-disant* philanthropist, 'If a brother or sister be naked and in lack of daily food, and one of you say to them, Go in peace, be ye warmed and filled, and yet ye give them not the things needful to the body; what does it profit?' Even error of doctrine receives the same dramatic treatment, e.g. i. 13 'Let no man say when he is tempted ὅτι ἀπὸ Θεοῦ πειράζομαι'; and so in ii. 18 foll. where the vanity of faith without works is exposed; and iv. 13 foll. where the worldly feeling on one side, and the religious feeling on the other, are embodied in the contrasted speeches, 'To-day or to-morrow we will go to this city, and spend a year there, and trade and get gain,' and again 'If the Lord will, we shall live and do this or that.' In further illustration of what I understand by the quality of vividness I will only instance the frequent reference to examples, such as Abraham, Rahab, Job, Elijah; and the personification of the Law in iv. 11, of the Tongue in iii. 1—8. Suffice it to say that it pervades the whole of the Epistle, and is markedly seen in the detailed particularity of the descriptions, such as that of the oppression of the rich in v. 1—6. All this tends to give vivacity and energy to the style. Other causes of vivacity are the appealing ἀδελφοί μου, and the very frequent use of interrogation and of the imperative mood. It is scarcely worth while to quote, but I will just refer to v. 13 'Is any among you suffering? let him pray. Is any cheerful? let him sing praise. Is any among you sick? let him call for the elders of the Church': for the imperative, compare i. 2 and following verses, πᾶσαν χαρὰν ἡγήσασθε—ἡ δὲ ὑπομονὴ ἔργον τέλειον ἐχέτω—αἰτείτω—μὴ οἰέσθω—καυχάσθω. Compare too the sudden apostrophes, μὴ πλανᾶσθε—ἴστε—ἀκούσατε—θέλεις δὲ γνῶναι—βλέπεις—ὁρᾶτε—ἴδε—ἰδού—ἄγε νυν.

In specifying energy as the prominent feature of St. James' style, I mean that, whatever he says, he says forcibly, with the tone of one who is entirely convinced both of the truth and of the importance of the message which he has to deliver. He wastes no words; he uses no circumlocution; at times, as in ii. 1, he even becomes obscure from over-condensation; he pays no more regard to the persons of men that did Elijah or John the Baptist. We feel, as we read, that we are in the presence of a strong, stern, immovable personality, a true pillar[1] and bulwark[2] of the Church, one in whom an originally proud and passionate nature, richly endowed with a high poetical imagination and all a prophet's indignation against wrong-doing and hypocrisy, is now softened and controlled by the gentler influences of the wisdom

[1] Στῦλος, Gal. ii. 9.
[2] 'Oblias' in Hegesippus *ap.* Eus. *H.E.* ii. 23.

which cometh from above. Still in its rugged abruptness, in the pregnant brevity of its phrases, in the austerity of its demand upon the reader, in concentrated irony and scorn, this Epistle stands alone among the Epistles of the New Testament. Take for instance the language used of those who place their reliance in the holding of an orthodox creed, *σὺ πιστεύεις ὅτι εἷς ἐστὶν ὁ Θεός· καλῶς ποιεῖς· καὶ τὰ δαιμόνια πιστεύουσιν καὶ φρίσσουσιν*: compare this, not with the writings of a weakling like Hermas, whom some have ventured to name in the same breath with St. James, but with the writings of St. Paul himself. The flashes of irony, which break through St. Paul's splendid vindication of his apostolic authority in the Second Epistle to the Corinthians, seem passionless and pale, contrasted with the volcanic energy which glows beneath the denunciations of St. James. Or take the woes pronounced on the rich in the fifth chapter of our Epistle: would it be possible to find anywhere a nobler example—I will not say of Demosthenic, but of Hebraic *δεινότης*, than where the rust of the unused coin is first made to witness to the defrauding of the labourer, and then avenges his ill usage by eating away the heart of his oppressor? And what energy there is in the pathetic close, *κατεδικάσατε, ἐφονεύσατε τὸν δίκαιον· οὐκ ἀντιτάσσεται ὑμῖν*!

CHAPTER X

DID ST. JAMES WRITE IN GREEK OR IN ARAMAIC?

IN the First Series of *Studia Biblica*, p. 144 foll., Bishop John Wordsworth adduces the following arguments to show that our Epistle was probably written in Aramaic:[1]—(1) This was the language usually spoken by our Lord. (2) It was used by St. Paul in his address to the mob of Jerusalem. (3) We are told by Papias that the Gospel of St. Matthew was originally written in Hebrew (i.e. Aramaic) and interpreted by each as he was able.[2] (4) Papias also states that St. Mark acted as interpreter to St. Peter, and Glaucias, claimed by the Gnostics as the teacher of Basilides, is named as another interpreter of the same Apostle.[3] Jerome takes it for granted that the Epistles of St. Peter were not originally written in Greek, and thinks that the difference between them was due to the employment of different men as interpreters.[4] (5) Some of the Fathers supposed the Epistle to the Hebrews to have been written in Hebrew.[5] Josephus wrote his book on the Wars of the Jews in 'his national language' and

[1] According to Wold. Schmidt (*Lehrgehalt d. Jakobus-Briefes*, p. 10) the Aramaic origin of the Epistle had been previously maintained by Faber (*Obs. in epist. Jacobi ex Syro*, Coburg, 1770), Schmidt (*Historisch-Kritische Einleitung in N. T.*, Giessen, 1818), Bertholdt (*Einleitung*, Erlangen, 1819).

[2] Eus. *H.E.* iii. 39 Ματθαῖος μὲν οὖν Ἑβραΐδι διαλέκτῳ τὰ λόγια συνεγράψατο, ἡρμήνευσε δ' αὐτὰ ὡς ἦν δυνατὸς ἕκαστος, κ.τ.λ.

[3] Eus. *ib.* Μάρκος ἑρμηνευτὴς Πέτρου γενόμενος ὅσα ἐμνημόνευσεν ἀκριβῶς ἔγραψεν, Clem. Al. *Strom.* vii. 17, p. 898 ὁ Βασιλείδης κἂν Γλαυκίαν ἐπιγράφηται διδάσκαλον, ὡς αὐχοῦσιν αὐτοί, τὸν Πέτρου ἑρμηνέα, κ.τ.λ.

[4] Hieron. *Ad Hedibiam ep.* 120, 12 *Denique et duo epistolae quae feruntur Petri stilo inter se et charactere discrepant structuraque verborum. Ex quo intelligimus pro necessitate rerum diversis eum usum interpretibus.* Bp. W. suggests that, if Glaucias was the translator of the Second Epistle, this might account for the doubt as to its canonicity.

[5] See Clem. Al. *ap.* Eus. *H.E.* vi. 14 τὴν πρὸς Ἑβραίους ἐπιστολὴν Παύλου μὲν εἶναι φησί, γεγράφθαι δὲ Ἑβραίοις Ἑβραικῇ φωνῇ, Λουκᾶν δὲ φιλοτίμως αὐτὴν μεθερμηνεύσαντα ἐκδοῦναι τοῖς Ἕλλησιν, also Jerome and others cited in Alford's *Prolegomena*, vol. iv. 1. p. 76.

sent it to the 'upper barbarians,' whom he explains to be the Jews beyond the Euphrates, &c.; he afterwards made a translation into Greek, *χρησάμενός τισι πρὸς τὴν Ἑλληνίδα φωνὴν συνέργοις.*[1]

The Bishop considers that these parallels make it probable *a priori* that the Epistle was written in Aramaic. He supports this conclusion by the assumption that St. James could not have written such Greek as that in which the Epistle has come down to us, containing, as it does, many words with classical rather than biblical associations, and implying a wide range of classical reading.[2]

'This rich vocabulary is not unlike that which may have been possessed by a professional interpreter, but is very remarkable if we attribute it to an unlearned Jew writing perhaps the earliest book of the N.T.'

Lastly the hypothesis of an Aramaic original is supported by a comparison between our present Greek text and that which must have been the parent of the Corbey version (pp. 136–144). The most remarkable of these divergences are the omission of *τῆς πίστεως* in i. 3; the translation of *τροπῆς ἀποσκίασμα* by '*modicum obumbrationis*' (=*ῥοπὴ ἀποσκιάσματος*) in i. 17; *blasphemant in bono nomine* for *βλασφημοῦσι τὸ καλὸν ὄνομα* ii. 7, which Bp. W. compares with v. 10 and v. 15, where the genitives *τῆς κακοπαθίας* and *τῆς πίστεως* are also expressed by prepositional phrases, *de malis passionibus, in fide*, such as might be used in Hebrew or Syriac; *exploratores* for *τοὺς ἀγγέλους* ii. 25 as in the Syriac and other versions; *et lingua ignis seculi iniquitatis* for *καὶ ἡ γλῶσσα πῦρ ὁ κόσμος τῆς ἀδικίας* iii. 6, where the Peshitto has 'the tongue is a fire; the world of iniquity is as it were a wood'; *fornicatores* for *μοιχαλίδες* iv. 4 agrees with the Peshitto; *inconstans* for *ἀκαταστασία* iii. 16, and *frater* for *ἀδελφοί* iv. 11, are said to be easily explicable as renderings of the same Hebrew word. *Qui araverunt* for *τῶν ἀμησάντων* v. 4, *frequens* for *ἐνεργουμένη* v. 16, the omission of *κενῶς*, and the translation

[1] *c. Ap.* i. 9, *B. J. Prooem.* 1.

[2] This argument is founded on certain lists of words, which I found very helpful in drawing up my own lists in Ch. IX. They contain however some inaccuracies: e.g. among 'classical non-Septuagint words' we find ἀλυκός, ἀμάω, ἀποκυέω, which occur either in the O.T. or Apocrypha in the passages indicated in my list; we find also δίψυχος, which, as far as I know, is never used in profane Greek of any epoch, and ῥυπαρία, for which the earliest authority is post-classical. To the 'very rare words' should be added ἐπιλησμονή, πολύσπλαγχνος, προσωποληmπτεῖν, χαλιναγωγεῖν.

of ἐπιποθεῖ by *convalescit* in iv. 5, are also cited as evidences of a different original.[1]

Before dealing with these arguments it may be well to turn to the Greek text itself and see whether it reads like an original or a translation. It must be granted that this is not altogether an easy matter to decide. There are no doubt many translations which tell their character at once; translations from Oriental languages, which seem to make it their aim to exhibit in the crudest colours the contrast of eastern and western thought and speech; translations from the German, which faithfully preserve the heavy prolixity of the original; or translations which betray a different origin by their affectation of French elegance and lightness. The case however even here would be complicated, if it were a question whether a particular book were an original, written, say, by an Anglicized German, or a translation from the German by an Englishman; and this is really the question before us; for all that could be claimed for our Epistle, supposing it not to be a translation from the Aramaic, is that it was written by a Greek-speaking Jew. So much is plain from the style and vocabulary, even if we were entirely in the dark as to the writer. There is however nothing in it of the scrupulous anxiety of a translator cautiously treading in the footsteps of his author. On the contrary, it is written in strong, simple Greek, used with no slight rhetorical skill by one who has something of his own to say, and says it with perfect freedom. If a translation, it is a translation of the stamp of our authorized English version, or of Luther's German version, which have become the recognized standards and models of excellence in their respective languages. But the frequent use of the different figures of speech, alliteration, homoeoteleuton, &c., to which attention has been called in a previous chapter, is an ornament which a translator is hardly likely to venture upon for himself, and which it will often be impossible to reproduce in a different language. If we compare χαίρειν and χαράν[2] in i. 1, 2,

[1] Bp. W. also quotes the Corbey version, *res vestrae* for ἱμάτια in v. 2, as pointing to 'the double sense of the Syriac and Chaldee *mân*,' which stands here in the Peshitto for 'garment,' but is commonly used for 'goods' of any kind. In the *Classical Review* v. 68 I have adduced a parallel from Rufinus' version of Euseb. *H.E.* ii. 23 (a fuller) λαβὼν τὸ ξύλον ἐν ᾧ ἀπεπίεζε τὰ ἱμάτια *fullo arrepto fuste in quo res exprimere solent*, which may suggest that this use of *res* was not more uncommon in the later Latin than the colloquial use of 'things' for 'clothes' in English.

[2] The use of χαίρειν in itself is strongly opposed to the idea of an Aramaic original, which would naturally have used the word meaning 'Peace,' as the Peshitto does; and this would have rendered impossible the play on words contained in χαράν.

with the Vulgate *salutem* and *gaudium*, or πειρασμοῖς περιπέσητε ποικίλοις with the Vulgate *in tentationes varias incideritis*, none could doubt that the former in each case was the original. A still stronger argument will be supplied if we hold with Ewald that i. 17 πᾶσα δόσις ἀγαθὴ καὶ πᾶν δώρημα τέλειον is a quotation from a hexameter poem. Another test of a translation is the obscurity arising from a misapprehension of the meaning of the original. Examples of this may be found even where the translator has a consummate mastery of his own language, e.g. Ps. xlix. 5 (P.B.) 'Wherefore should I fear when the wickedness of my heels compasseth me about,' *ib.* lix. 8 'Or ever your pots be made hot with thorns, so let indignation vex him even as a thing which is raw,' which have at last been made intelligible to English readers in the R.V. Compare also 1 Tim. vi. 5, 'supposing that gain is godliness' where the R.V. has 'supposing that godliness is a way of gain,' or in our Epistle i. 21 'superfluity of naughtiness' where the R.V. has 'overflowing of wickedness.' When we meet with an unmeaning or difficult expression of this kind in a translation, we naturally turn to the original to see how it arose. The question is then: Do we meet with any difficulty in our Epistle such as might suggest that it is due to the misunderstanding of an assumed original? Perhaps there are two passages as to which if they occurred in an undoubted translation, we should be curious to know what was the original intended by them. The first is the phrase φλογίζουσα τὸν τροχὸν τῆς γενέσεως in iii. 6, and the second πρὸς φθόνον ἐπιποθεῖ τὸ πνεῦμα ὃ κατῴκισεν ἐν ὑμῖν. It hardly seems likely that St. James would have used the obscure phrase 'wheel of existence' if it sounded as strange to those whom he was addressing as it sounds to us now. The more probable supposition is that it had got into familiar use among Greek-speaking Jews. And this is confirmed by the parallel passages quoted in my note. The second difficulty turns simply on the use of the phrase πρὸς φθόνον for 'jealously,' to which no precise parallel has been adduced; but φθόνος and φθονέω being sometimes used of jealousy rather than envy, there seems no insuperable objection to a similar use of the adverbial phrase. In any case the difficulty would not be lessened by the supposition of its being a translation from Aramaic. On the whole we may safely say that the general impression produced by a study of the Greek is much in favour of its being an original.

But can we suppose that the son of a Galilean carpenter would have been capable of writing such idiomatic Greek? We have seen above (p. xli.) that Galilee was studded with Greek towns, and that it was certainly in the power of any Galilean to gain a knowledge of Greek; even if he were, as Prof. Neubauer holds, brought up in ignorance of any language but Aramaic, and not, as Prof. T. K. Abbott is inclined to believe, speaking Greek as freely as Aramaic.[1] We know also that the neighbouring town of Gadara was celebrated as an important seat of Greek learning and literature, and that the Author of our Epistle shows an acquaintance with ideas and phrases which were probably derived, mediately or immediately, from the Stoic philosophers.[2] If we call to mind further that he seems to have paid particular attention to the sapiential books, both canonical and apocryphal, and that a main point in these is to encourage the study of 'the dark sayings of the wise'; that the wisdom of Edom and Teman is noted as famous by some of the prophets,[3] and that the interlocutors in the book of Job are assigned with probability to this and neighbouring regions;—taking into account all these considerations, we may reasonably suppose that our author would not have scrupled to avail himself of the opportunities within his reach, so as to master the Greek language, and learn something of Greek philosophy. This would be natural, even if we think of James as impelled only by a desire to gain wisdom and knowledge for himself, but if we think of him also as the principle teacher of the Jewish believers, many

[1] See Neubauer in *Studia Biblica* i. pp. 39–74, Abbott *Essays on the Original Texts of the Old and New Testaments*, p. 162, where he argues that the inhabitants of Palestine at the time of the Christian era were bilingual, and illustrates the occasional use of Aramaic by our Lord from the parallel case of Irish phrases in the mouth of Irishmen who habitually speak English. The Rev. G. H. Gwilliam, whom I had consulted as to the relation of the language of the Peshitto to Aramaic, writes that 'he prefers to speak of the vernacular of Palestine, rather than to use the term Aramaic,' because the vernacular of Palestine in the first century of the Christian era 'included many dialects, some of which were extremely corrupt. In centres of Jewish life and influence, I believe a knowledge of Hebrew was cultivated: in Samaria we know from the literary remains that a form of Chaldee was spoken: in Galilee, it appears that the common tongue was a very mixed dialect, and according to Deutsch (*Remains*, *The Talmud*, p. 42) Palestinian patois was a mere jargon. Amongst these many forms of speech I find no place for Syriac properly so called. The language of the Peshitto was the language of Edessa. It was closely related to Chaldee and Samaritan, and indeed not very far removed, after all, from Hebrew. It is a curious question, which I am not prepared to answer, whether one who habitually spoke one of these dialects, could easily understand a speaker in another of them. I suspect there were considerable differences of pronunciation which are now lost for ever.'

[2] See above pp. lxxx. foll.

[3] Obad. 8, Jer. xlix. 7.

of whom were Hellenists, instructed in the wisdom of Alexandria, then the natural bent would take the shape of duty: he would be a student of Greek in order that he might be a more effective instructor to his own people.[1] The use of rare compounds, to which the Bishop calls attention, is certainly remarkable; but I am not sure that it is most easily explained by his supposition of the employment of a professional interpreter. A man of ability, who has to express himself in a foreign tongue, which he has learnt partly from books, is not unlikely to be insensible to the distinction between the language of poetry and prose, and to eke out his limited resources by combining familiar roots. I think this might be illustrated from the style of the book of Wisdom, and from the English writings of foreigners, e.g. Kossuth's *Speeches*.

It appears to me then (1) that the phenomena of the Greek epistle, which goes under the name of St. James, are strongly against its being a translation; (2) that the writer was acquainted with the Greek books of the Apocrypha and with the principles of the Stoic philosophy; (3) that the balance of probability is in favour of St. James having been able to write Greek, but that this need not preclude us from supposing that he may have availed himself of the assistance of a Hellenist 'brother' in revising his Epistle. A fourth reason which indisposes me to accept the hypothesis of an Aramaic original is the fact of its disappearance without leaving any trace behind. The existing Syriac version of St. James is generally supposed to be a translation from the Greek; and 'it is significant that the Edessene scribes do not seem to recognize any tradition that the Epistle was written in any language but Greek. As far as I know, they content themselves with the title "Epistle of James the Apostle." One ancient MS. however in the Brit. Mus. adds to the subscription "which he wrote from Jerusalem"' (G. H. Gwilliam).

With regard to the inferences drawn from the peculiarities of the Corbey version, it may be worth while to compare the variations in the Peshitto, whether regarded as witnessing to the

[1] It may be worth while to note that James is mentioned by an ancient writer as the translator of the original Hebrew of St. Matthew's Gospel into Greek, see the *Synopsis Scripturae Sacrae* included in the writings of Athanasius (Migne, vol. iv. p. 432) *τὸ μὲν οὖν κατὰ Ματθαῖον εὐαγγέλιον ἐγράφη ὑπ' αὐτοῦ τοῦ Ματθαίου τῇ Ἑβραΐδι διαλέκτῳ...ἡρμηνεύθη δὲ ὑπὸ Ἰακώβου τοῦ ἀδελφοῦ τοῦ Κυρίου τὸ κατὰ σάρκα, ὃς καὶ πρῶτος ἐχειροτονήθη ἐπίσκοπος ὑπὸ τῶν ἁγίων ἀποστόλων ἐν Ἱεροσολύμοις.* Probably this was only a guess suggested by the resemblance between our Epistle and St. Matthew's Gospel.

contents of an original Greek or an original Aramaic text. I quote the Latin translation given in Leusden and Schaaf's *Nov. Test. Syr.* 1717.

i. 3 *κατεργάζεται ὑπομονήν*, *facit vos possidere patientiam.*

i. 4 *ἡ δὲ ὑπομονὴ ἔργον τέλειον ἐχέτω*, *ipsi autem patientiae erit opus perfectum.*

i. 6 *ἔοικεν κλύδωνι θαλάσσης ἀνεμιζομένῳ καὶ ῥιπιζομένῳ*, *similis est fluctibus maris quos commovet ventus.*

i. 7 *γάρ* omitted.

i. 11 *σὺν τῷ καύσωνι*, *in calore suo.*

i. 14 *ἐξελκόμενος καὶ δελεαζόμενος*, *et cupit et attrahitur.*

i. 17 *πᾶσα δόσις ἀγαθὴ καὶ πᾶν δώρημα τέλειον*, *omnis donatio bona et completa.*

i. 18 *εἰς τὸ εἶναι ἡμᾶς ἀπαρχήν τινα*, *ut essemus primitiae.*

i. 19 *ἴστε ἀδελφοί μου ἀγαπητοί· ἔστω δὲ πᾶς ἄνθρωπος ταχύς*, *et vos fratres mei dilecti, quisque ex vobis sit velox.*

i. 21 *περισσείαν κακίας*, *multitudinem malitiae.*

i. 25 *ἀκροατὴς ἐπιλησμονῆς* *auditor auditionis quae oblivioni traditur.* [Here the Peshitto gives a more exact parallel to the corresponding clause (implying, as the Greek original, *ἀκροατὴς ἀκοῆς* in contrast with *ποιητὴς ἔργου*). Is this to be regarded as an explanatory addition ?]

ii. 4 *κριταὶ διαλογισμῶν πονηρῶν*, *interpretes cogitationum malarum.*

ii. 8 *μέντοι*, *et.*

ii. 13 *κατακαυχᾶται ἔλεος κρίσεως*, *exultabimini supra judicium.*[1]

iii. 2 *χαλιναγωγῆσαι*, *in servitute continere* [destroying the connexion with the *χαλινούς* of the following verse].[2]

iii. 4 *ὑπὸ ἐλαχίστου πηδαλίου*, *a ligno exiguo.*

iii. 5 *ἰδού*, *etiam.*

iii. 6 *καὶ ἡ γλῶσσα πῦρ, ὁ κόσμος τῆς ἀδικίας ἡ γλῶσσα καθίσταται ἐν τοῖς μέλεσιν ἡμῶν, ἡ σπιλοῦσα ὅλον τὸ σῶμα καὶ φλογίζουσα τὸν τροχὸν τῆς γενέσεως, καὶ φλογιζομένη ὑπὸ τῆς γεέννης*, *et lingua ignis est, et mundus peccati veluti silva est, et ipsa lingua, cum sit inter membra nostra, maculat totum corpus nostrum*

[1] 'The Syriac is a little vague perhaps, but I have no doubt that the *present* is the tense intended.'—G. H. G.

[2] 'The connexion of the verses is however maintained by the use of the same verb in different conjugations: ver. 2 "who is able to subjugate all his body"; ver. 3 "that the horses may subjugate themselves to us." The metaphor is also lost in i. 26, where the Peshitto has "hold" (not "bridle") "his tongue."'—G. H. G.

et incendit series generationum nostrarum quae currunt veluti rotae, ac incenditur ipsa igne.[1] [On the interpolation *veluti silva* I have said something in my note. The interpretation of the phrase φλογίζουσα...τῆς γενέσεως seems to be an explanatory paraphrase, like that in i. 25.]

iii. 17 ἀνυπόκριτος, *vultum non accipit.*[2]

iv. 9 ταλαιπωρήσατε καὶ πενθήσατε καὶ κλαύσατε, *humiliate vos et lugete.*

iv. 16 πᾶσα καύχησις τοιαύτη πονηρά ἐστιν, *omnis gloriatio quae est ejus modi a malo est.*

v. 2 σέσηπεν, *corrupta sunt et fetuerunt.*

v. 6 οὐκ ἀντιτάσσεται, *et non restitit.*

In these variations I do not see that there is anything to suggest that the Peshitto represents more truly than the Greek the thought of the original author. On the contrary we find that the force of the Greek is often lost or blurred by the disappearance of a metaphor, as in i. 14, i. 26, iii. 2, or by the substitution of a weaker for a more vigorous phrase, as in i. 6, i. 17, i. 21, ii. 8, iii. 6, v. 6. The variations of the Corbey Latin seem to me to belong generally to the same category; and to be due either to want of ability or want of conscientiousness on the part of the translator. Where they appear to be confirmed by the variations of the Peshitto, it is possible, as Prof. Rendel Harris has shown in his brilliant study on the Codex Bezae, that the Latin was directly influenced by the Syriac. 'The Syriasms found in the Latin text of several ancient MSS. exceed in harshness the Syriasms of the Greek text.' He considers that the Latin text of the Codex Bezae dates from the second century and arranges its constituents (prior to the end of that century) in the following order:

(1) Original Greek Text.
(2) Original Latin Text.
(3) Poetical Glosses interpolated from the popular Homeric centos which had been used to dress up the Gospel narrative.
(4) Primitive Syriac version.
(5) Montanist Glosses.

[1] 'The relative *quae* here refers to *series*.'—G. H. G.
[2] 'This is the regular Syriac rendering of ὑποκριτής and its cognates.'—G. H. G.

If this at all represents the true state of the case, it is evident that these early possibilities of corruption make it extremely precarious to argue from the minute particularities of any existing form of the Latin text to the actual original of the Epistle as it left the hands of the author.

CHAPTER XI[1]

Bibliography

(See the following chapter on the *Apparatus Criticus*)

I. *Text.*

Tischendorf, N.T. ed. 8 (Ti.) with Gregory's Prolegomena, 3 vols. 1869—1894.

Tregelles, N.T. (Tr.). 1887.

Westcott and Hort, N.T. (WH.). Camb. 1881.

Weiss, Bernhard, *Die Katholische Briefe, Textkritische Untersuchungen.* 1892.

Sabatier, *Bibliorum Sacrorum Latinae Versiones.* 1749.

Speculum ed. Weihrich. 1887.

Priscillian, ed. Schepss. 1889.

Codex Corbeiensis in *Studia Biblica* i. 115 foll.

Codex Amiatinus, ed. Tischendorf. 1873.

Codex Fuldensis, ed. Ranke. 1868.

Codex Vaticanus, photographed by Cozza-Luzi. 1889.

Leusden and Schaaf, *Nov. Test. Syr.* 1717.

Norton, *Translation of the Peshitto text of Hebrews, James, 1 Pet., 1 Joh.* 1889.

II. *Commentaries.*

A. Ancient.

Didymus Alex. *In Epistolas Catholicas Enarratio,* Migne *Patr. Gr.* vol. 39, p. 1750 foll.

Chrysostom, *Fragm. in Epist. Cathol.,* Migne *P.G.* vol. 64, pp. 1039—1052.

Cramer, J. A., *Catena in Ep. Cath.,* pp. 1—40. Oxf. 1840.

[1] The list in large print contains the books which I have myself consulted. I have not seen the books contained in the subsequent list. An asterisk is prefixed to those editions of St. James which, from one cause or other, I thought most useful.

Matthaei, C. F., *Scholia in Ep. Jacobi*, pp. 183—195. Riga, 1782.

Oecumenius, Migne *P.G.* vol. 119, pp. 455—510.

Theophylact, Migne *P.G.* vol. 125, pp. 1134—1190.

Euthymius Zigabenus. Athens, 1887.

Bede, Migne *Pat. Lat.* vol. 93, pp. 10—41.

B. Modern.

a. Special on St. James.

*Bassett, F. T., *Catholic Epistle of St. James.* 1876.

Benson and Michaelis, *Paraphrasis et Notae.* 1756.

*Beyschlag, W., pp. 239. Göttingen, 1888. [A much improved revision of Huther. Take it all in all, the most useful edition for students.]

Bouman, H., pp. 273. Utrecht, 1865.

Brückner, Br., and de Wette, pp. 192—270. Leipzig, 1865

Burger, K., in Strack and Zöckler's *Kurzgefasster Kommentar* 1888.

Carr, A., in *Cambridge Greek Testament.* 1896.

*Cellerier, J. E., *Étude et Commentaire*, pp. xxv., 200. Geneva. 1850.

*Dale, R. W., *Discourses on the Epistle of James.* 1895.

Erdmann, D., 383 pp. Berlin, 1881.

Ewald, H., pp. 176—230. Göttingen, 1870.

Feine, *D. Jakobusbriefe nach Lehranschauungen u. Enstehungsverhältnissen untersucht.* Eisenach, 1893.

*Gebser, A. R. pp. xiii., 418. Berlin, 1828. [Gives full extracts from the patristic commentaries.]

Gloag, *Popular Commentary.* 1883.

*Heisen, *Novae Hypotheses interpretandae Epistolae Jacobi*, pp. 951. 4to. Bremen, 1739. [Notes on the more difficult verses in ch. i.—iv. 5, a monument of learning and industry.]

von Hofmann, G. Ch. K., pp. 179. Nördlingen, 1876.

Herder, *Briefe zweener Brüder Jesu.* Stuttgart, 1852.

Huther in Meyer's *Critical and Exegetical Handbook*, Eng. tr. Edinb. 1882.

Johnstone, R., *Lectures Exegetical and Practical*, ed. 2. Edinb. 1889.

*Kern, F. H., 242 pp. Tübingen, 1838. [An able and original writer. Introduction very interesting.]

Neander, Eng. tr. 1851.

Peile, T. W. 1852.

*Plummer, A., (*Expositor's Bible.*) 1891.

*Plumptre, E. H. (*Cambridge Series.*) 1878.

Pott, D. J., Latin Notes. Göttingen, 1816.

*Price, J. (Pricaeus) in *Critici Sacri.* [Learned.]

Punchard, in *Ellicott's N. T. Commentary for English Readers.* 1884.

*Schegg, P., pp. 279. München, 1883. [Roman Catholic.]

*Schneckenburger (Lat. Notes). Stuttgardt, 1832. [Sensible and independent; illustrates freely from Philo.]

*Scott (Dean), in *Speaker's Commentary.*

Semler, *Paraphrasis cum Notis.* 1781.

von Soden, H., *Hand-Commentar.* Freiburg, 1890.

*Spitta, F., *Zur Geschichte u. Litteratur des Urchristentums,* vol. ii. 1896.

*Stier, R., Eng. tr. 1859. [Homiletic.]

*Theile, C. G. G., Comm. in Epistolam Jacobi. 1833. [A condensed variorum edition.]

Trenkle. Freiburg. 1894. (R. C. with full bibliography of older commentaries.)

de Wette, see Brückner.

*Wiesinger, Aug., pp. 211. Königsberg, 1854.

b. General, in which St. James is included.

Alford's *Greek Testament,* vol. iv. 1864.

Bengel's *Gnomon.* 1850.

Bloomfield, S. T., *Gr. Test.* 1855.

Cajetan, *Notae in Epistolam S. Jacobi* (contained in his *Epistolae S. Pauli,* vol. ii. pp. ccvii. foll.).

Calvin, ed. Tholuck, vol. vii. Berlin, 1834.

Cornelius a Lapide. Paris, 1648.

Erasmus, in Poole's *Synopsis.*

Estius, pp. 1095—1148. Paris, 1661.

Grinfield, *Nov. Test. Editio Hellenistica.* 1843. *Scholia Hellenistica.* 1848.

Grotius, in Poole's *Synopsis.*

Hammond, *Paraphrase and Annotations on the N.T.*

Lange, *Theologisch-homiletisches Bibelwerk,* 1862, Eng. tr. Edinb. 1870.

Macknight, *A New Translation of the Apostolical Epistles, with a Commentary and Notes.* 1809.

Poole (Poli), *Synopsis.* 1669.

Wetstein, *Gr. Test.* with Latin notes. Amst 1751.

Wordsworth, Chr., *Gr. T.* with Eng. notes. 1870.

c. *Of other books of the New Testament.*

Blass, F., *Acta Apostolorum.* 1895.

Ellicott, 1st *Ep. to the Corinthians.* 1887.

—— *Ep. to the Ephesians.* 1884.

—— *Ep. to Thessalonians.* 1880.

—— *Pastoral Epistles.* 1883.

Gifford, *Ep. to the Romans.* 1886.

Lightfoot, J. B., *Ep. to the Galatians.* 1890.

—— *Ep. to the Colossians.* 1875.

—— *Ep. to the Philippians.* 1879.

Sanday and Headlam, *Ep. to the Romans* (*International Critical Commentary*). 1895.

Westcott, B. F., *Ep. to the Hebrews.* 1892.

—— *Gospel of St. John.* 1884.

—— *Epistles of St. John.* 1889.

III. *Illustrative Works.*

A. Grammars and Dictionaries.

Blass, F., *Grammar to the N. T.* (German). 1896.

Bruder, *Concordance,* rev. ed. Lips. 1888.

Burton, *Syntax of Moods and Tenses in G. T.* ed. 2. 1893.

Buttmann, A., *Grammar on the N. T.* (German). 1859, tr. by Thayer. 1876.

Cremer, *Biblico-theological Lexicon,* Eng. tr. Edinb. 1878–1886.

Goodwin, *Moods and Tenses.* 1889.

Green, *Gr. of the New Testament Dialect.* 1842.

Hatch and Redpath, *Concordance to the LXX.* 6 vols. 1897.

Herzog, *Real-Encyklopädie f. protest. Theologie.*

Kennedy, H. A. A., *Sources of N. T. Greek.* Edinburgh, 1895.

Kuehner, *Gr. Sprachlehre,* ed. 3 by Blass, 1890 foll.

Meisterhans, *Grammatik der Attischen Inschriften,* ed. 2. 1888.

Middleton, *On the Article,* ed. Rose. 1841.

Moulton and Geden, *Concordance to G. T. according to the best Texts.* Edinburgh, 1897.
Schleusner, *Lexicon in LXX.* Lips. 1820.
Schmid, W., *Der Atticismus von Dionysius Halik. bis auf den zweiten Philostratus.* 4 vols. 1887—1896.
Smith, *Dictionary of the Bible.*
—— *Dictionary of Christian Biography.*
—— *Dictionary of Christian Antiquities.*
Sophocles, *Greek Lexicon of the Roman and Byzantine Periods.* New York, 1888.
Stephani Thesaurus, ed. Hase. 1831—1865.
Suicer, *Thesaurus.* Utrecht. 1746.
Thayer-Grimm, *Greek-English Lexicon to the N. T.* 1888.
Trench, *Synonyms of the N. T.* 1855.
Trommius, *Concordance to the LXX.*
Veitch, *Irregular Greek Verbs.* Oxf. 1888.
Viteau, *Étude sur le Grec du N. T.* 2 vols. 1893–7.
Winer, *Grammar of the N. T.*, Eng. tr. by Moulton. 1870.
———— ed. Schmiedel, vol. i. 1894.

B. Editions of Ancient Writers.[1]

Apocrypha—

Acta Apostolorum Apocrypha, Tischendorf, 1851, ed. 2 by Lipsius and Bonnet. 1891.
Acta Johannis, Zahn. 1880.
Apocalypses Apocryphae, Tischendorf. 1866.
Apocryphal Gospels ed. Thilo (*Cod. Apocr. N. T.*) Lips. 1832.
Evangelia Apocrypha, Tischendorf. 1876.
Gospels, Acts and Revelations, Eng. tr. (in Ante-Nicene Libr.). Edinb. 1870.
Codex Apocryphus Nov. Test. ed. Fabricius. 1703.
Codex Pseudepigraphus Vet. Test. ed. Fabricius. 1722.
Gospel according to the Hebrews, Nicholson. Lond. 1879.
Libri Apocryphi Vet. Test. ed. Fritzsche. Lips. 1871.
Nov. Test. extra Canonem receptum, ed. Hilgenfeld. 1866.
Ante-Nicene Libr. Additional vol., containing recently discovered works. Edinb. 1897.

[1] Patristic references are generally to the pages in Migne's *Patrologia* except in the case of the editions specified in the text.

Psalms of Solomon, ed. Ryle and James. Camb. 1891.

Apostolicae Constitutiones. Ueltzen, 1853.

Barnabas, ed. Hilgenfeld. 1877.

Clemens Alexandrinus, Dindorf, 4 vols. Oxf. 1869.

Clemens Romanus, Lightfoot. Camb. 1877.

Clementina, Dressel. 1853.

—— Eng. tr. in the Ante-Nicene Library. Edinb. 1870.

Didaché (*Doctrina Duodecim Apostolorum*), F. X. Funk. 1887.

—— R. Schaff. 1885.

—— C. Taylor, *Lectures on*. 1886.

Enoch, book of, ed. Charles. 1893.

Epiphanius, ed. Oehler. Berlin, 1856.

Eusebius, *H. E.* and *Praep. Evang.* Heinichen. Lips. 1827, 1842.

Hermas, ed. Gebhardt and Harnack. Lips. 1877.

Jewish Fathers (J. F.), (new ed. preparing), C. Taylor. Camb. 1877.

Josephus, ed. Niese, 7 vols. 1887—1895.

Ignatius, ed. Lightfoot. Camb. 1885.

Irenaeus, ed. Stieren. Lips. 1853.

Justin Martyr, ed. Otto. Jena. 1847.

Oracula Sibyllina, ed. *Rzack*. 1891.

Patres Apostolici, Jacobson. 1847. Lightfoot and Harmer. 1891.

Philo, ed. Richter. Lips. 1828. (New ed. by Cohn and Wendland in progress.)

Pirke Aboth, ed. Taylor. See *Jewish Fathers*.

Septuagint, ed. Swete, 3 vols. 1887—96.

Testamenta XII Patriarcharum, ed. Sinker, 1869; also in Fabricius' *Cod. Pseud. V. T.* (sometimes referred to under the name of the particular patriarch).

Testament of Abraham, ed. James in *Texts and Studies* ii. 2. 1892.

—— *of Job*, ed. James in *Texts and Studies* v. 1, p. 104 foll. 1897.

C. Miscellaneous.

Abbott, T. K., *Essays on the Original Text of the Old and New Testaments*. 1891.

Beyschlag, *Neutestamentliche Theologie*, ed. 2. 1896.

Bigg, C., *Christian Platonists of Alexandria*. Oxf. 1886.

Bingham, *Antiquities of the Christian Church.* 1852.

Brückner, W., *Die Chronologische Reihenfolge in welche die Briefe d. N. T. verfasst sind.* Haarlem, 1890.

Butler's *Analogy*, ed. Fitzgerald. 1849.

Chase, *The Lord's Prayer in the Early Church.* Camb. 1891.

Credner, *Einleitung.* Halle, 1836.

Daillé, *De Sacramentali sive Auriculari Confessione.* Geneva, 1661.

Davidson, Sam., *Introduction to the N. T.* 3rd ed. 2 vols. 1894.

Ewald, Paul, *Das Hauptproblem d. Evangelienfrage.* Leipzig, 1890.

Farrar, *Early Days of Christianity.* 1882.

Field, *Otium Norvicense.* Oxf. 1886.

Gfrörer, A., *Urchristenthum.* Stuttgardt, 1831.

Gloag, *Introduction to the Catholic Epistles.* Edinb. 1887.

Gregory, C. R., *Prolegomena to Tischendorf's N. T.* Lips. 1894.

Harnack, *Chronologie des altchristlichen Litteratur bis Eusebius.* 1897.

—— *Lehrbuch der Dogmengeschichte,* 3 vols. ed. 2. 1892. Eng. tr. in progress. 1894.

Harris, Rendel, *A Study of Codex Bezae.* Camb. 1892.

Hatch, *Essays in Biblical Greek.* Oxf. 1889.

Hausrath, *Neutestamentliche Zeitgeschichte.* Heidelberg, 1873.

Holtzmann, *Einleitung*, ed. 3. 1892.

Jebb, J., *Sacred Literature.* Lond. 1820.

Jülicher, *Einleitung.* 1894.

Kenyon, *Our Bible and the Ancient MSS.* 1895.

Lardner's *Credibility of the Gospel History.* 1788.

Laurent, *Neutestamentliche Studien.* Gotha, 1866.

Lechler, *Apostolic and post-Apostolic Times,* Eng. tr. 1886.

Lewin, *Fasti Sacri.* Lond. 1865.

Lightfoot's *Horae Hebraicae.*

Lightfoot, J. B., *Biblical Essays.* 1893.

Loesner, *Adnotationes ad N. T. e Philone.* 1777.

Mangold's ed. of Bleek's *Einleitung in das N. T.* 1886.

Martène, *De Antiquis Ecclesiae Ritibus.* Antw. 1736.

Meuschen, *Nov. Test. et Talmude illustratum.* 1736.

Mill, W. H., *Pantheistic Principles.* 1861.

Mommsen, *History of Rome, The Provinces,* Eng. tr. 1886.

Neander, *History of the Planting of the Christian Church*, Eng. tr. 1842.
Pearson, *On the Creed*, ed. Chevallier. Camb. 1849.
Pfleiderer, *Urchristenthum.* 1887.
Ramsay, W. M., *St. Paul the Traveller and the Roman Citizen.* 1896.
—— *The Church in the Roman Empire before* A.D. 170. ed. 4.
—— *Cities and Bishoprics of Phrygia.* 1895.
—— *Historical Geography of Asia Minor.* 1890.
Resch, *Agrapha.* Leipz. 1889. (Criticized in Ropes' *Die Sprüche Jesu*, Leipzig, 1896.)
Reuss, *Hist. of the Sacred Scriptures*, Eng. tr. Edinb. 1884.
Ritschl, A., *Altkatholische Kirche*, ed. 2. Bonn, 1857.
Rüegg, Arnold, *Die Neutestamentliche Kritik seit Lachmann.* 1892.
Salmon, G., *Introduction to the N. T.* ed. 4. 1889.
—— *Thoughts on the Textual Criticism of the N. T.* 1897.
Schmid, C. F., *Biblical Theology*, Eng. tr. Edinb. 1870.
Schmidt, Wold., *Lehrgehalt d. Jakobus-Briefes.* Leipz. 1869.
Schöttgen, *Horae Hebraicae.* 1733.
Schürer, *Jewish People in the time of Christ*, Eng. tr. Edinb. ed. 2, 5 vols. 1891.
Scrivener, *Introduction to the Criticism of the N. T.*, ed. 4, by E. Miller. 1894.
Siegfried, *Philo als Ausleger d. Alten Testaments.* Jena, 1875.
Schneckenburger, *Beiträge zur Einleitung ins N.T.* Stuttg. 1832.
Stanley, A. P., *Sermons and Essays on the Apostolic Age.* 1874.
Studia Biblica, Oxf. 1885 foll.
Texts and Studies, ed. by J. Armitage Robinson. Camb. 1891 foll.
Vorst, *de Hebraismis N. T.* Lips. 1778.
Weiss, B., *Einleitung.* Berlin, 1886. Eng. tr., 1888.
Westcott and Hort, *N. T. Introduction and Appendix.* Camb. 1881.
Westcott, *On the Canon of the N. T.* 1866.
Wilke, Ch. G., *Neutestamentliche Rhetorik.* Dresden, 1843.
Wolf, *Curae Philologicae.* Basil, 1741.
Zahn, *Forschungen.* 1881—84.
—— *Geschichte d. Neutestamentlichen Kanons*, 1888 foll.
—— *Einleitung in d. N. T.* vol. I. 1897.

[Unless otherwise stated, the books which follow are commentaries on the Epistle of St. James.]

Alexander Natalis, *In Epist. Cathol.* Lyon, 1621.
Alsted, J. H., *Pleias Apost. c. notationibus.* 1640.
Althamer, *In Epist. Jacobi.* 1527.
Aretius, B., *Comm. in Epp. Cath.* 1589.
Augusti, *Catholic Epistles.* With German notes. 1801, 1808.
Bengel, *Erklärende Umschreibung der Briefe Jac. Pet. &c.* Göttingen 1776.
Blom, A. H., *Der Brief van Jakobus.* 1869.
Boon, A., *De Epistolae Jacobi cum lib. Sirac. convenientia.* Gron. 1866.
Brochmand. 1706.
Baumgarten. (Germ. notes.) Halle, 1750.
Carpzof, *Epistolae Catholicae c. scholiis.* Hal. 1790.
Damm. (Germ. notes.) Berlin, 1747.
Faber, *Observ. in Ep. J. ex Syro.* Cob. 1774.
Flachs, S. A., *Τὰ ἅπαξ λεγόμενα Epistolae Jacobi.* Lips. 1730.
Gans, E. A., *Über Gedankengang im Br. d. Jakobus.* 1874.
Göpfert. (Germ. notes.) 1791.
Grashof. (Germ. notes.) 1830.
Grynaeus, *Epistolae Catholicae.* Basil, 1543.
Hensler. (Germ. notes.) 1801.
Horneius, *In Catholicas Epistolas Expositio.* Brunsv. 1652.
Hottinger. (Lat. notes.) Lips. 1815.
Jachmann. (Germ. notes.) Leipz. 1838.
Justiniani, *Explanationes in Epist. Catholicas.* Lyon, 1621.
Kaiser, C. F., *De nonnullis epist. Jac. virtutibus.* Halle, 1797.
Küchler, C. G., *De Rhetorica Epist. Jac. indole.* 1818.
Lisco, *N. T.* Berlin, 1840.
Messmer, Al., *Erklärung d. Cathol. Briefe.* Brixen, 1863.
Morus. (Lat. notes.) Lips. 1794.
Rosenmüller. (Germ. notes.) Leipz. 1787.
Scharling. (Lat. notes.) Copenhagen, 1841.
Scherer, J. L. W. (Germ. notes.) 1799.
Schirmer. (Germ. notes.) Bresl. 1778.
Schultess. (Lat. notes.) Zurich, 1824.
Schulze, D., *D. schriftst. Char. u. Werth des Petr. Jud. u. Jac.* Lips. 1802.
Seemiller. (Lat. notes.) Nuremb. 1783.
Storr, *Diss. Exeget. in. ep. Jac.* 1784.
Weber, M., *De Ep. Jac. cum. ep. atque oratione Act. xv inserta utiliter comparanda.* Vitb. 1795.
Winer, *Observ. in epist. Jac. e Versione Syriaca.* 1827.
Zachariae, *Erklärung der Briefe Jacobi, Petri, &c.* Göttingen, 1776.

CHAPTER XII

APPARATUS CRITICUS[1]

Greek Manuscripts

I. *Manuscripts written in large capitals* (*Uncials*)

Fourth Century

B. Codex Vaticanus. No. 1209 in the Vatican Library at Rome. Written continuously without breathings or accents. Stops are rare, but a full stop is sometimes represented by a vacant space. Probably contained all the canonical books of the Old and New Testament; but almost the whole of Genesis, part of the Psalms, the later chapters of Hebrews, the Pastoral Epistles, Philemon and the Apocalypse are now wanting. It is generally regarded as the most valuable of all the MSS. containing a pure Pre-Syrian text (WH. *Intr.* p. 150) and is not unfrequently followed by Westcott and Hort against the other chief MSS., compare i. 9, 22, ii. 3, 19, 26, iv. 8, 9, 14, v. 7, 14, 20. Errors from itacism are frequent, especially the confusion of *αι* and *ε* (as in ii. 14 *κατακαυχατε,* 24 *ὁραται* B^1, iv. 6 *ἀντιτασσετε*, iv. 8 *φευξετε* B^1, v. 7 *ἐκδεχετε* B^1, v. 16 *ἐξομολογεισθαι* B^1, *προσευχεσθαι* B^1) and the writing of *ει* for *ι* (as in i. 6 *διακρεινομενος*, *ῥειπιζομενῳ*, ii. 6 *ἠτειμασατε*, iii. 7 *ἀνθρωπεινῃ*, iv. 8 *ὑμειν*, iv. 14 *ἀτμεις*, v. 3 *εἰος*

[1] The materials for my Apparatus Criticus have been found mainly in Westcott and Hort's *Introduction and Text*, the Greek Testaments of Alford and Tregelles, the articles by Bishop Wordsworth and Professor Sanday contained in *Studia Biblica* for 1885, the *Introduction to Textual Criticism* by Horne and Tregelles, Scrivener's *Plain Introduction to the Criticism of the New Testament*, 1883 ; above all, in Tischendorf, eighth edition, published 1869 and 1872, together with the *Prolegomena* by C. R. Gregory. I have also compared, throughout, the photograph of *Codex B*, Sabatier's *Latin Versions*, the *Codex Amiatinus* by Tischendorf, the *Codex Fuldensis* by Ranke, together with Weihrich's edition of the *Speculum*, and Schepss' edition of *Priscillian*.

B^1, v. 7 *τειμιον*). The codex has at length been made accessible to all by the beautiful photographic reproduction brought out under the direction of Signor Cozza-Luzi, the Librarian of the Vatican.

SIN. (or א). CODEX SINAITICUS, discovered by Tischendorf in the convent at Mount Sinai on Feb. 4, 1859, and published by him in 1862. It is now in the library at St. Petersburg. It is written continuously without stops or breathings. Contained originally the whole of the Old Testament, including the Apocrypha (of this a large portion is now wanting); the New Testament (still entire); the Epistle of Barnabas and the Shepherd of Hermas (of this last a large part is lost). Errors from itacism, such as the confusion of *αι* and *ε*, *ει* and *ι*, are frequent. Westcott and Hort consider it the most valuable MS. after B, giving in the main a Pre-Syrian text but to a certain extent corrupted by Western and Alexandrian readings. Tischendorf, as was natural, *codicem suum re vera praestantissimum fortasse plus aequo miratus est* (C. R. Gregory *Prol.* to Tischendorf's N.T. p. 353), and has in some instances been thus induced to prefer what seems to me an inferior reading. See especially iii. 5, 6, where his text is *ἰδοῦ ἡλίκον· πῦρ ἡλίκην ὕλην ἀνάπτει ἡ γλῶσσα. πῦρ, ὁ κόσμος τῆς ἀδικίας, ἡ γλῶσσα καθίσταται ἐν τοῖς μέλεσιν ἡμῶν, καὶ σπιλοῦσα ὅλον τὸ σῶμα καὶ φλογίζουσα κ.τ.λ.*, iv. 2 *μάχεσθε καὶ πολεμεῖτε. καὶ οὐκ ἔχετε διὰ τὸ μὴ αἰτεῖσθαι ὑμᾶς· αἰτεῖτε κ.τ.λ.*

Fifth Century.

A. CODEX ALEXANDRINUS in the British Museum. Contains the old and New Testaments, together with two epistles of Clement. It is written continuously with occasional stops and, very rarely, a breathing or accent. A photographic facsimile of the N.T. was brought out by the authorities of the British Museum in 1879.

C. CODEX EPHRAEMI. No. 9 in the Library at Paris. This is a palimpsest containing fragments of the Old and New Testaments, over which were written in the 12th century some treatises of Ephraem the Syrian. About three-fifths of the N.T. are preserved. The writing is continuous, with occasional stops, and spaces left at the end of a paragraph. It was printed by Tischendorf in 1843. The end of St. James (iv. 3 to v. 20) is wanting.

Ninth Century.

K. (also marked K_2, to distinguish it from Codex Cyprius the K of the Gospels). CODEX MOSQUENSIS in the Library of the Holy Synod at Moscow. Contains the Catholic Epistles with a catena and St. Paul's Epistles with the scholia of Damascenus. The text is written in square uncials with breathings, accents and stops, the comment in round letters. Collated by Matthaei for his edition of the Catholic Epistles published in 1782.

L. (L_2). CODEX ANGELICUS ROMANUS in the Angelican Library of the Augustinian monks at Rome. Contains part of the Acts, the Epistles of St. Paul, and the whole of the Catholic Epistles. Collated by Tregelles and Tischendorf.

P. (P_2). CODEX PORFIRIANUS, a palimpsest belonging to Bishop Porfirius, of St. Petersburg: first printed by Tischendorf in *Mon. Sacr. Ined.* vol. 5, 1865, written in a slovenly hand with accents, breathings and stops. Contains the Acts, Catholic Epistles, Epistles of St. Paul, the Apocalypse. Wanting in St. James ii. 13—21.

Besides the above uncial MSS., C. R. Gregory describes three, two of which have not yet been collated (Tischendorf's N.T. vol. iii. p. 445 foll.).

ב *Vatic. Gr.* 2061 (=Cod. Patiriensis), of the 5th century, containing James iv. 14—v. 20. Shortly to be published by Batiffol. See the collation below on p. cclv.

Ψ. *Athous Laurae*, of the 8th or 9th century, containing James i. ii. iii.

S. *Athous Laurae*, of the 8th or 9th century, contains all the Catholic Epistles.

II. *Manuscripts written in cursive letters* (*Minuscules*).

C. R. Gregory (Tisch. N.T. *Proleg.* p. 617—652) gives a list of 416 MSS. of the Acts and Catholic Epistles belonging to this class, the greater part being still uncollated. They range from the 9th to the 16th century. They are usually referred to by their number, but Scrivener, in the appendix to his edition of the Codex Augiensis denoted a certain number by the use of small letters *a*, *b*, *c*, to *p*,[1]

[1] These have now had numbers assigned to them by Gregory, pp. 638, foll., 795 foll.; and by Scrivener himself, p. 259 f., ed. 3.

and has been followed in this by Tischendorf. Those of most value appear to be 13 (see WH. *Intr.* p. 192), 9, 29, 36, 40, 46, 61, 66, 69, 73, 78, 133, 137.

III. *Lectionaries.*

These are books containing the lessons read in church, mostly from the Gospels. C. R. Gregory (Tisch. *Proleg.* pp. 778—791) gives a list of 265 *Lectionarii Apostoli* containing lessons from the Acts and Epistles, some in uncials, some in cursives, ranging from the 9th to the 17th century. They are referred to as lect. 1 &c.

Ancient Versions.

[As may be seen from the Latin versions which follow, the resemblance between the ancient versions and the original is often so close as to represent not simply the words, but even the order in which the words occur; they are therefore of the greatest value in determining the readings of the Greek text.[1]]

A. Latin.

I. Pre-Hieronymian, or Old Latin.

1. *Corb.* (*ff*). The Corbey MS. of the Old Latin Version of St. James now in the Imperial Library at St. Petersburg, collated by Prof. V. Jernstedt in 1884 and printed with the original spelling and punctuation, accompanied by the valuable notes of Bishop John Wordsworth, in pp. 115—123 of *Studia Biblica*, 1885. Compare, too, the paper by Professor Sanday in the same volume, pp. 233—263. The transcript given below is from Sabatier's *Bibliorum Sacrorum Latinae Versiones Antiquae*, 1749. I have not thought it necessary to adhere strictly to his spelling or punctuation, but any other divergence is mentioned in the notes. I have also stated where Sabatier's reading is unsupported by the MS., and on one or two occasions have noticed the punctuation of the MS., which is however in general too capricious to build upon.[2]

[1] On the use of versions and early quotations see an essay in *Stud. Bibl.* ii. p. 195 foll.

[2] Tischendorf mentions the Vienna *Codex Bobiensis* of the fifth century, as containing the following fragments of St. James: i. 1-5, iii. 13-18, iv. 1, 2, v. 19, 20. This must be distinguished from *k*, the Cod. Bob. at Turin, which contains the Gospels of

2. *Speculum* (*m*). This is a common-place book of texts arranged under different heads, wrongly ascribed to St. Augustine. First printed by Cardinal Mai in the *Nova Patrum Bibliotheca* vol. i. pt. 2. The latest edition is that by Weihrich in the *Corp. Scr. Eccl. Lat.* Vienna, 1887, from which the transcript below is taken. Prof. Sanday in his review of Weihrich (*Class. Rev.* iv. 414 foll.) notices the close resemblance between the readings in the *Speculum* and those in the writings of Priscillian edited in the same series by Schepss in 1889 from a MS. of the 6th century. I have therefore placed in the same column with the quotations from the *Speculum* those from

3. *Priscillian* (died 385 A.D.). Dr. Sanday is of opinion that the *Speculum* 'was put together somewhere in the circle in which Priscillian moved, and from a copy of the Bible, which, if not exactly his, was yet closely related to it.' I have distinguished the quotations from those in the *Speculum* by inclosing them in square brackets. Dr. Schepss (p. 17) had already compared Priscillian's version of James v. 1 foll. with that given in the *Speculum*.

II. Vulgate (Vulg.).

1 *Codex Amiatinus.* Written probably at Jarrow about the end of the seventh century,[1] and sent as a present to Rome by Ceolfrid in 716 A.D.; printed by Tischendorf in 1850 and 1854. Contains the whole Latin Bible with the exception of the book of Baruch. In the notes I have mentioned where it differs from the *Codex Fuldensis,* written in the same century, and from the genuine *Speculum* of St. Augustine, edited with the other *Speculum* by Weihrich.

Latt. denotes the consensus of the Latin versions.

B. *Syriac.*

1. *Pesh. The Peshitto* (i.e. 'simple') version contains the whole Bible with the exception of the 2nd epistle of Peter, 2nd and 3rd

St. Matthew and St. Mark, and is transcribed by Tischendorf in the 'Anzeige-Blatt' to the *Wiener Jahrbücher* of 1847, 8, 9. I have not been able to see any transcript of the fragments from St. James, which Tischendorf denotes by the letter (*s*); but it would seem from his critical notes that it is generally in agreement with the Vulgate against Corb. and Spec. [Since the above was written, I have been enabled, through the kindness of Prof. Sanday, to make a copy of Belsheim's transcript of this Codex. See postscript below.]

[1] See *Studia Biblica* ii. p. 273 foll.

of John, Jude and the Apocalypse. It is ascribed to the 2nd century, but was probably revised in the 4th century. A new edition is preparing by the Rev. G. H. Gwilliam, see his article on the *Materials for the Criticism of the Peshitto N.T.* in *Stud. Bibl.* iii. p. 47 foll.

2 *Syr.* The recension by Thomas of Harkel in the 7th century of the version made by Polycarp, a Chorepiscopus, in 508 A.D., for Philoxenus, bishop of Hierapolis.

Syrr. denotes the consensus of the Syriac versions.

C. *Egyptian Versions.*

1. *Copt.* Coptic, Bohairic, or Memphitic, the version of Lower Egypt, made probably not later than the 2nd century,[1] contains the whole of the N.T.

2. *Sah.* The Sahidic or Thebaic, the version of Upper Egypt, of about the same antiquity, also contained the entire N.T., but has come down to us in a fragmentary condition.

D. *Aethiopic Version.* Assigned to the 4th century.

Aeth^{rom} denotes the text as given in the Roman edition of 1548.
Aeth^{pp} the text in Pell Platt's edition 1826—30.

E. *Armenian Version.*

Arm. made early in the 5th century.

[P.S.—I print below a copy of Batiffol's collation of the Codex Patiriensis, and of Belsheim's Codex Bobiensis, for both of which I am indebted to Prof. Sanday.]

LECTIONES COD. PATIRIENSIS

(=ב, Vat. 2061, Gregory *Proleg.* p. 447 *f.*) ad Ep. Jac. iv. 14—v. 17.

iv. 14. ἔπειτα δὲ.
iv. 15. ζήσω[μεν] . . . ποιήσωμεν.
v. 3. κατίωται καὶ ὁ ἄργυρος.
v. 3. ὁ ἰὸς ὡς πῦρ.
v. 4. εἰσεληλύθεισαν.

---

[1] So Lightfoot in Scrivener's *Introd.*, p. 371. Some Coptic scholars would assign a later date, at all events to the version of the Catholic Epistles.

v. 5. ως ἐν ἡμέρᾳ.
v. 7. ἕως ἂν λάβῃ.
v. 7. πρόϊμον *tantum cum* B.
v. 8. μακροθυμήσατε (*sine* οὖν).
v. 9. ἀδελφοί μου κατ᾽ ἀλλήλων.
v. 9. κατακριθῆτε.
v. 10. ὑπόδειγμα δὲ.
v. 10. λάβετε . . . καὶ τῆς μακροθυμίας ἔχετε (*lectio ex duabus confusa*).
v. 10. τῷ ὀνόματι (*sine* ἐν).
v. 10. τοῦ Κυρίου.
v. 11. ὑπομένοντας.
v. 12. ἀδελφοί (*om.* μου).
v. 12. εἰς ὑπόκρισιν.
v. 14. τοῦ Κυρίου.
v. 15. ἦν *pro* ᾖ.

CODEX BOBIENSIS.

In the Imperial Library of Vienna there is a MS. volume, numbered 16 in the Catalogue, which contains, among a variety of other treatises, fragments of a pre-Hieronymian Latin version of the Acts, the Epistle of St. James, and the First Epistle of St. Peter written on palimpsest. The volume originally belonged to the Monastery of Bobbio, founded by Columban, and was brought from Naples to Vienna in 1717. The fragments were partially published by Tischendorf in the *Anzeigeblatt* to the *Wiener Jahrbücher der Literatur* of 1847, and more completely by J. Belsheim, Christiania, 1886.[1] The text of the Epistles, not of the Acts, approaches very nearly to the Vulgate. It is difficult to read, and in some passages (here printed in italics) could not be determined with certainty. I have preserved the capitals and punctuation of the original.

I. (1) Jacobus dī et dn̄ī ihū xpi servus duodecim tr...sunt in dispersione salutem. (2) omne gaudium existimate fratres mei. cum in temtationibus variis incideritis. (3) scientes quod probatio fidei vestrae patientiam operatur. (4) patientia autem opus perfectum habeat ut sitis perfecti et integri in nullo deficientes. (5) Si quis enim vestrum indiget sapientia petat hic a dō qui dat omnibus affluenter et non improperat et dabitur ei. (6) postulet autem fide nihil dubitans quoniam qui *dubitat similis est fluctui maris qui a vento fertur ac defertur* (7) *ne speret homo ille quid accipit a dō.* (8) *homo duplici corde inconstans in omnibus viis suis.* (9) glorietur autem frater humilis in altitudine sua (10) et dives autem in humilitate sua quoniam sicut flos faeni transibit (11) exortus est enim sol cum ardore arescit faenum et flos ejus decidit et decor vultus ejus deperdit ita et dives in itineribus suis marescit. (12) beatus vir qui suffert temptationem quia cum probatus fuerit accipiet coronam vitae quam repromisit ds̄ diligentibus se (13) nemo cum temptatur dicat quia a dō temptatur. ds̄ enim non temptator malorum est. ipse autem neminem temptat. (14) unusquisque vero temptatur a concupiscentia *abstractus et illectus.* (15) *deinde concupiscentia cum conceperit parit peccatum vero cum consummatum est generat mortem.* (16) *nolite errare fratres mei dilectissime* (17) *omne donum bonum et omne donum perfectum* descendens desursum a patre luminum apud quem non est transmutatio......(18) voluntarie generavit nos verbo veritatis ut simus initium aliquid creaturae ejus. (19) scite fratres mei

---

[1] The above particulars are taken from Belsheim's volume.

dilectissime. si autem omnis homo velox ad audiendum tardus autem ad loquendum et tardus ad iram (20) quod iracundia enim viri justitiam dī non operatur (21) propter quod abicientes omnem inmunditiam et abundantiam malitiae in mansuetudine suscipite insitum verbum quod potest salvare animas vestras. (22) Estote autem factores verbi et non auditores tantum fallentes vosmet ipsos. (23) quia si quis auditor est verbi et non factor hic aestimabitur viro consideranti vultum nativitatis suae in speculo. (24) consideravit enim se et abiit statim et oblitus est qualis fuerat. (25) qui autem perspexit in legem perfectum libertatis et permanserit in ea non auditor obliviosus factus sed factor operis hic salvatur opere suo.

II. (14) ...cordia judicium. quid proderit fratres si fidem quis se dicat... non habet. numquid fides...eum. (15) si autem frater et soror...et indigeant victum quo...(16) dicat autem aliquis...calefacimini et saturamini non dederitis autem ei quae necessaria sunt corpori quid proderit. (17) sic et fides si non habet opera mortua est in semetipso (18) sed dicet quis tu fidem habes et ego opera habeo ostende mihi fidem tuam sine operibus. et ego ostendam tibi ex operibus meis fidem meam. (19) tu credes quia unus est ds̄ bene facis et daemonia credunt et contremiscunt. (20) Vis autem scire o homo inanis quoniam fides sine operibus otiosa est (21) abraham pater noster non ex operibus justificatus est offerens isac filium (super) altare. (22) videte quoniam fides (coope)ratur operibus illius et ex (oper)ibus fide consummata est. (23) (sup)pleta est scriptura dicens (cre)didit autem abraham dō reputatum est illi ad justitiam (ami)cus dī. (24) videtis autem (ex op)ere justificatus est. Videtis quoniam ex operibus justificatur homo et non ex fide tantum (25) similiter et raab meretrix nonne ex operibus justificata est suscipiens nuntios et alia via eiciens (26) sicut enim corpus sine spiritu mortuum est ita et fides sine operibus mortua est. (III. 1) nolite multi magistri fieri fratres mei scientes quoniam majus judicium sumitis. (2) in multis enim *erramus* omnes. si quis in verbo non offendit hic perfectus est vir etiam postens se infrenare corpus totum. (3) si autem equis freno in ora mittimus ad consentiendum nobis et omne corpus illorum circumferimus. (4) ecce naves quam magnae sint et a ventis validis feruntur circumferuntur a modico gubernaculo ubi impetus dirigentis voluerit. (5) ita et lingua modicum quidem membrum et magna exaltat. ecce quantus ignis quam magnam silvam incendit ...inter vos (13) ostendat ex bona conversatione operationem suam in mansuetudine sapientiae (14) quod si zelum amarum habent et contentiones in cordibus vestris nolite gloriari et mendaces esse adversum veritatem. (15) non est ista sapientia desursum descendens sed terrena animalis diabolica (16) ubi enim zelus et contentio ibi inconstantia et omne opus pravum (17) quae autem desursum est sapientia primum quidem pudica est deinde pacifica modeste suadibilis plena misericordia et fructibus bonis non judicans sine simulatione. (18) fructus autem justitiae in pace seminatur facientibus pacem. (IV. 1) Et unde bella et lites in vobis. nonne hinc ex concupiscentiis vestris quae militant in membris vestris (2) concupiscentes et non habetis...

V. 19. Fratres mei si quis ex vo...a veritate et convertit quisquis eum (20) scire debet quoniam qui converti fecerit peccatorem ab errore viae suae solvat animam ejus a morte et cooperit multitudinem peccatorum.]

Quotations in Early Writers.

On the importance of these quotations compare especially Westcott and Hort, *Intr.*, pp. 83, 87-89, 112-115, 159-162, Resch's *Agrapha* § 3. Bishop Wordsworth states that the Epistle of St.

James is not cited at all by Tertullian [1] or Cyprian, and rarely cited by Latin writers before the time of Jerome and Augustine, the former of whom has 133 quotations, the latter 389 (*Stud. Bibl.*, pp. 128, 129).

The following writers are referred to in the critical notes. The exact references will be found in Tischendorf:—

Aug.	Augustine, 4th century.	Epiph.	Epiphanius, 4th century.
Cass.	Cassiodorius, 6th.	Jer.	Jerome, 4th.
Cyr.	Cyril of Alexandria, 5th.	Oec.	Oecumenius, 11th.
Dam.	Joannes Damascenus, 8th.	Orig.	Origen, 3rd.
Did.	Didymus of Alexandria, 4th.	Thl.	Theophylact, 11th.
Eph.	Ephraem Syrus, 4th.	Zig.	Euthymius Zigabenus, 12th.

Other Abbreviations.

ins. = insert.
om. = omit.
rec. = textus receptus.
m. appended to the sign of a MS. implies a marginal reading.
Ti. = Tischendorf, ed. 8.
Tr. = Tregelles.
W. = Bernhard Weiss, 1892.
WH. = Westcott and Hort, 1881.
R. & P. = Rost and Palm's Gr. Lex.
L. & S. = Liddell and Scott.
+ means that the preceding reading is found in other MSS. besides those particularized.
&c. means that the preceding reading is found in the majority of MSS.

[1] Rönsch (*Das Neue Testament Tertullians*, 1871) agrees with this statement. In my note on ch. v. 16, πολὺ ἰσχύει, I have quoted a passage from Tert. *De Oratione* which seems to me a reminiscence of St. James, but it must be allowed that neither Tertullian nor Cyprian cites him as an authority where they might well have done so.

THE CATHOLIC EPISTLES.

THOUGH the word καθολική does not form part of the Title of the Epistle of St. James in any of the older MSS., yet the fact that this Epistle was included from an early period in the collection known as the Catholic Epistles, which followed the Acts and preceded the Epistles of St. Paul, seems to call for a short note on the history and meaning of the term.

Eusebius is the first to mention the fact in the words τοιαῦτα τὰ κατὰ τὸν Ἰάκωβον, οὗ ἡ πρώτη τῶν ὀνομαζομένων καθολικῶν ἐπιστολῶν εἶναι λέγεται (*H.E.* ii. 23), and we find the same asserted in the Catalogues of the Canonical Books ratified by the Councils of Laodicea and of Carthage, as well as in the lists given by Cyril of Jerusalem, Athanasius, Gregory Nazianzen, and Amphilochius before the end of the fourth century.[1] Earlier uses of the term may be found in Clement of Alexandria (*Strom.* iv. 15, p. 605 P), where, in speaking of the Epistle put forth by the Apostolic Council recorded in Acts xv., he says κατὰ τὴν ἐπιστολὴν τὴν καθολικὴν τῶν ἀποστόλων ἁπάντων; and in Origen, with reference to the Epistle of Barnabas (*c. Cels.* i. 63) γέγραπται ἐν τῇ Βαρνάβα καθολικῇ ἐπιστολῇ, as well as to the Epistles of St. John, St. Peter, and St. Jude.[2] Apollonius (*c.* 210 A.D.) reproached Themison the Montanist with writing a catholic epistle in imitation of the Apostle (St. John).[3]

The meaning of the term is thus stated by Oecumenius in his Preface to our Epistle: καθολικαὶ λέγονται αὗται οἱονεὶ ἐγκύκλιοι· οὐ γὰρ ἀφωρισμένως ἔθνει ἑνὶ ἢ πόλει, ὡς ὁ θεῖος Παῦλος τοῖς Ῥωμαίοις ἢ Κορινθίοις προσφωνεῖ ταύτας τὰς ἐπιστολὰς ὁ τῶν τοιούτων τοῦ Κυρίου μαθητῶν θίασος, ἀλλὰ καθόλου τοῖς πιστοῖς ἤτοι Ἰουδαίοις τοῖς ἐν τῇ διασπορᾷ, ὡς καὶ ὁ Πέτρος, ἢ καὶ πᾶσι τοῖς ὑπὸ τὴν αὐτὴν πίστιν Χριστιανοῖς τελοῦσιν. Thus understood, the term is not properly applicable to the 2nd and

[1] See the quotations in Westcott's *History of the Canon*, App. D

[2] For the references see Pott's *Commentary*, p. 3.

[3] See Eus. *H.E.* v. 21. On the supposed mention of Catholic Epistles in the Muratorian Fragment, see Zahn *N.K.* II. i. p. 93.

3rd Epistles of St. John, which would, however, naturally be regarded as appendages to the First Epistle.

A secondary and later meaning of the term is derived from its use in reference to the Church. An epistle came to be called catholic as being catholic in spirit and accepted by the Catholic Church: hence it is sometimes equivalent to 'canonical.'[1]

[1] See *Dict. of Ch. Ant. s.v.*, Westcott, *Canon*, p. 477 *n.*

THE EPISTLE OF ST. JAMES

ΙΑΚΩΒΟΥ ΕΠΙΣΤΟΛΗ.

ΚΕΦ. α΄.

1 Ἰάκωβος, Θεοῦ καὶ Κυρίου Ἰησοῦ Χριστοῦ δοῦλος,
ταῖς δώδεκα φυλαῖς ταῖς ἐν τῇ διασπορᾷ χαίρειν.
2 Πᾶσαν χαρὰν ἡγήσασθε, ἀδελφοί μου, ὅταν πειρασμοῖς περιπέσητε ποικίλοις,
3 γινώσκοντες ὅτι τὸ δοκίμιον ὑμῶν τῆς πίστεως
κατεργάζεται ὑπομονήν·
4 ἡ δὲ ὑπομονὴ ἔργον τέλειον ἐχέτω, ἵνα ἦτε τέλειοι
καὶ ὁλόκληροι, ἐν μηδενὶ λειπόμενοι.
5 Εἰ δέ τις ὑμῶν λείπεται σοφίας, αἰτείτω παρὰ τοῦ
διδόντος Θεοῦ πᾶσιν ἁπλῶς καὶ μὴ ὀνειδίζοντος, καὶ
δοθήσεται αὐτῷ.
6 Αἰτείτω δὲ ἐν πίστει, μηδὲν διακρινόμενος· ὁ γὰρ
διακρινόμενος ἔοικεν κλύδωνι θαλάσσης ἀνεμιζομένῳ καὶ
ῥιπιζομένῳ.
7 Μὴ γὰρ οἰέσθω ὁ ἄνθρωπος ἐκεῖνος ὅτι λήμψεταί τι
παρὰ τοῦ Κυρίου,
8 ἀνὴρ δίψυχος, ἀκατάστατος ἐν πάσαις ταῖς ὁδοῖς
αὐτοῦ.
9 Καυχάσθω δὲ [ὁ] ἀδελφὸς ὁ ταπεινὸς ἐν τῷ ὕψει
αὐτοῦ,

I.—3. *της πιστεως* Sin. AB^1CKLP &c. pesh., om. $B^3$81 corb. syr.

5. *του διδοντος θεου*: A *του θεου του διδοντος*.

7 (and ver. 12). *λημψεται* Sin. AB, *ληψεται* KLP &c. | *τι*: om. Sin. + | *κυριου*, Ti. W. *κυριου*. Treg. *κυριου* WH.

9. *ὁ* bef. *αδελφος* Sin. &c. Ti. Treg. W., om. B arm. (WH. bracket).

VULGATE.

CODEX AMIATINUS (α).

I—1 Iacobus dei et domini
nostri Iesu Christi seruus
duodecim tribubus (β) quae
sunt in dispersione salutem.
2 Omne gaudium existimate,
fratres mei, cum in tempta-
tionibus uariis incideritis,
3 scientes quod probatio fidei
uestrae patientiam operatur.
4 Patientia (γ) opus perfectum habeat, ut sitis perfecti et
integri, in nullo deficientes.
5 Si quis autem uestrum indiget sapientiam (δ), postulet
a deo qui dat omnibus affluenter et non inproperat, et
dabitur ei. 6 Postulet autem
in fide, nihil haesitans : qui
enim (ε) haesitat, similis est
fluctui maris, qui a vento
mouetur et circumfertur. 7
Non ergo (ζ) aestimet homo
ille quod accipiat aliquid a
domino, 8 uir duplex (η)
animo, inconstans in omnibus
uiis suis. 9 Glorietur autem
frater humilis in exaltatione
sua ;

(α) I have taken this from Tischendorf's edition of 1854, but have not thought it necessary to preserve such spellings as *mechaberis, merorem, praetiosum.* I have compared the readings of the Codex Fuldensis (Ranke's ed. 1868) and also those of the genuine *Speculum Augustini* (edited by Weihrich, along with the spurious Speculum, which follows in the 3rd col.). The genuine *Speculum* is usually so close to the Vulgate that it has been thought that Augustine himself only gave the references, and that the passages were copied from the Vulgate by a later scribe.

(β) F. *tribus.*
(γ) F. ins. *autem.*
(δ) F. *sapientia.*
(ε) F. *autem.*
(ζ) Spec. Aug. *enim.*
(η) F. *duplici.*

CORBEY MS.

I—1 Iacobus dei et domini
Iesu Christi seruus xii tribubus[a] quae sunt in dispersione
salutem. 2 Omne gaudium
existimate fratres mei quando
in uarias temptationes incur-
ritis, 3 scientes quod probatio uestra operatur sufferentiam. 4 Sufferentia autem
opus consummatum habeat,
ut sitis consummati et integri
in nullo deficientes. 5 Et si
cui uestrum deest sapientia,
petat a deo, quia dat omnibus
simpliciter et non inproperat,
et dabitur illi. 6 Petat autem
in fide nihil dubitans : qui
autem dubitat similis est
fluctui maris, qui a uento
fertur et defertur : 7 nec
speret se homo ille quoniam
accipiet aliquid a domino.[b]
8 Homo duplici corde inconstans in omnibus uiis suis.
9 Glorietur autem frater humilis in altitudine sua ;

[a] MS *tribus.*
[b] Full stop in MS.

Quotations from the SPECULUM and PRISCILLIAN.[1]

[1] The oldest MSS. of the former are (F) Floriacensis, assigned to the end of the 7th century (*Palaeogr. Soc.* Ser. II. p. 34), (S) Sessorianus, (M) Michaelinus, (α and μ) Breviata Theodulphi, all belonging to the 8th or 9th century. The quotations from Priscillian are inclosed in square brackets The figures denote the pages in Weihrich's and Schepss' editions.

10 ὁ δὲ πλούσιος ἐν τῇ ταπεινώσει αὐτοῦ, ὅτι ὡς
ἄνθος χόρτου παρελεύσεται.
11 Ἀνέτειλεν γὰρ ὁ ἥλιος σὺν τῷ καύσωνι καὶ ἐξήρανεν
τὸν χόρτον, καὶ τὸ ἄνθος αὐτοῦ ἐξέπεσεν, καὶ ἡ εὐπρέπεια
τοῦ προσώπου αὐτοῦ ἀπώλετο· οὕτως καὶ ὁ πλούσιος ἐν
ταῖς πορείαις αὐτοῦ μαρανθήσεται.
12 Μακάριος ἀνὴρ ὃς ὑπομένει πειρασμόν, ὅτι δόκιμος
γενόμενος λήμψεται τὸν στέφανον τῆς ζωῆς, ὃν ἐπηγγείλατο τοῖς ἀγαπῶσιν αὐτόν.
13 Μηδεὶς πειραζόμενος λεγέτω ὅτι Ἀπὸ Θεοῦ πειρά-
ζομαι· ὁ γὰρ Θεὸς ἀπείραστός ἐστιν κακῶν, πειράζει δὲ
αὐτὸς οὐδένα.
14 Ἕκαστος δὲ πειράζεται ὑπὸ τῆς ἰδίας ἐπιθυμίας
ἐξελκόμενος καὶ δελεαζόμενος·
15 εἶτα ἡ ἐπιθυμία συλλαβοῦσα τίκτει ἁμαρτίαν, ἡ δὲ
ἁμαρτία ἀποτελεσθεῖσα ἀποκυεῖ θάνατον.
16 Μὴ πλανᾶσθε, ἀδελφοί μου ἀγαπητοί·
17 πᾶσα δόσις ἀγαθὴ καὶ πᾶν δώρημα τέλειον ἄνωθέν
ἐστιν, καταβαῖνον ἀπὸ τοῦ πατρὸς τῶν φώτων, παρ᾽ ᾧ οὐκ
ἔνι παραλλαγὴ ἢ τροπῆς ἀποσκίασμα.
18 Βουληθεὶς ἀπεκύησεν ἡμᾶς λόγῳ ἀληθείας, εἰς τὸ
εἶναι ἡμᾶς ἀπαρχήν τινα τῶν αὐτοῦ κτισμάτων.
19 Ἴστε, ἀδελφοί μου ἀγαπητοί· ἔστω δὲ πᾶς ἄνθρωπος

11. om. *αυτου* after *προσωπου* B | *πὸρειαις* BCLP &c. *ποριαις* Sin. A + Thl.

12. *ανηρ* : A *ανθρωπος* | *ὑπομενεῖ* KLP, *ὑπομεινῃ* 13, *sustinuerit* corb. + | *επηγγειλατο* Sin. AB corb. +, *επ. ὁ κυριος* KLP syr. Thl. Oec. &c., *επ. κυριος* C, *επ. ὁ θεος* vulg. copt. aeth. pesh. +

13. *απο* ABCKLP &c., *ὑπο* Sin. 69.

15. om. *ἡ* before *επιθυμια* C. | *ἀποκύει* Ti. Treg.

17. *εστιν,* WH., *εστιν* Ti. Treg. | *καταβαινων* A 13 | *απο* : K + *παρα* | *ενι* : Sin. P + *εστιν* | *τροπης αποσκιασμα* Sin.[3] ACKLP vulg. &c., *τροπης αποσκιασματος* Sin. B (Dr. Hort suggests that *ἀποσκιάσματος* may be caused either by *ἀπό* being regarded as a separate word, or by the incorporation of an original *αὐτός*, which precedes *βουληθείς* 'in a good cursive (40) and two Syric texts.' *Intr.* p. 218. In a private letter to Dr. Westcott dated Feb. 3, 1861, he suggests that the archetype may have had *ἀποσκιασμός*. Bp. Wordsworth would prefer to read either *ῥοπὴ ἀποσκιάσματος* implied in *modicum obumbrationis* corb., or *ῥοπῆς ἀποσκίασμα* implied in *momenti obumbratio* Aug.).

18. *βουληθεις* : vulg. + *βουληθεις γαρ*, 40 *αυτος γαρ βουληθεις* | *αὐτου* Sin.[1] BKL &c., Treg. Ti. WH., *ἑαυτου* Sin.[3] ACP. WH.[m] See below ver. 26.

19. *ιστε* Sin.[3] ABC 73 83 (*scitote* corb. copt. syr.[m] arm., *scitis* vulg.), *ὥστε* KLP syr. Thl. Oec. &c., *ιστω* Sin.[1] [*και νυν αδελφοι ἡμων εστω* aeth.[pp] *εστε αδελ. ἡμ. και εστω* aeth.[ro] *et vos fratres mei dilecti quisque ex vobis sit* pesh.], after *ιστε* ins.

VULGATE.

10 diues autem in humilitate
sua, quoniam sicut flos faeni
transibit (α). 11 Exortus est
enim sol cum ardore et arefe-
cit faenum et flos eius decidit
et decor uultus eius deperiit :
ita et diues in itineribus suis
marcescet (β). 12 Beatus uir
qui suffert temptationem,
quia (γ) cum probatus fuerit
accipiet coronam uitae, quam
repromisit deus diligentibus
se. 13 Nemo cum temptatur
dicat quoniam (δ) a deo temptatur. Deus enim intempta-
tor malorum est, ipse autem
neminem temptat. 14 Unus-
quisque uero temptatur a
concupiscentia sua abstractus
et inlectus ; 15 dehinc (ε)
concupiscentia cum conce-
perit parit peccatum, peccatum uero cum consummatum
fuerit generat mortem. 16
Nolite itaque errare, fratres
mei dilectissimi. 17 Omne
datum optimum et omne
donum perfectum de sursum
est descendens a patre luminum, apud quem non est
transmutatio nec uicissitu-
dinis obumbratio. 18 Uolun-
tarie (ζ) enim (η) genuit nos
uerbo ueritatis, ut simus
aliquod initium (θ) creaturae
eius. 19 Scitis, fratres mei
dilecti. Sit autem omnis homo
uelox ad audiendum, tardus

(α) Spec. Aug. *transiet.*
(β) F. *marcescit.*
(γ) F. *quoniam.*
(δ) F. *quia.*
(ε) F. *dein.*
(ζ) MS. *voluntariae.*
(η) F. om. *enim.*
(θ) F. *init. aliq.*

CORBEY MS.

10 locuples autem in humilitate sua, quoniam sicut flos
feni transiet. 11 Orietur enim
sol cum aestu suo et siccat
fenum et flos eius cadit et
dignitas facie*i*[a] ipsius perit :
sic et locuples in actu suo
marcescit. 12 Beatus vir
qui[b] sustinuerit temptationem : quoniam probatus factus accipiet coronam uitae
quam promitt*it*[c] eis qui eum
diligunt.[d] 13 Nemo qui temptatur dicat quoniam a deo
temptatur : deus autem malorum temptator non est : temptat ipse neminem. 14 Unusquisque autem temptatur a
sua concupiscentia, abducitur
et eliditur.[e] 15 Deinde concupiscentia concipit et parit
peccatum : peccatum autem
consummatum adquirit mor-
tem.[f] 16 Nolite errare fratres
mei dilecti. 17 Omnis datio
bona et omne donum perfectum desursum descendit a
patre luminum apud quem
non est permutatio uel modicum obumbrationis. 18
Uolens peperit nos uerbo
ueritatis ut simus primitiae
conditionum eius. 19 Scitote
fratres mei dilecti. Sit autem

[a] MS. *facie.*
[b] MS. *quia* as in ver. 5.
[c] MS. *promittet.*
[d] This verse is quoted almost in the same words by Chromatius (a contemporary of Jerome), *Tract. in S. Matt.* xiv. 7. See *Stud. Bibl.* p. 135.
[e] Probably a misreading for *elicitur* or *eluditur*. Bp. Wordsworth however suggests that it may represent a Greek reading ἐκκρουόμενος or παρακρουόμενος. Cf. Cassian. *Coll.* xii. 7, *primus pudicitiae gradus est ne uigilans impugnatione carnali monachus elidatur.*
[f] The remarkable rendering *adquirit mortem* is also found in Chrom. *l.c.* ix. 1.

SPECULUM AND PRISCILLIAN.

I—19 (W. pp.
603 and 524) Sit
uero omnis homo
citatus audire et

ταχὺς εἰς τὸ ἀκοῦσαι, βραδὺς εἰς τὸ λαλῆσαι, βραδὺς εἰς ὀργήν·

20 ὀργὴ γὰρ ἀνδρὸς δικαιοσύνην Θεοῦ οὐκ ἐργάζεται.

21 Διὸ ἀποθέμενοι πᾶσαν ῥυπαρίαν καὶ περισσείαν κακίας ἐν πραΰτητι δέξασθε τὸν ἔμφυτον λόγον τὸν δυνάμενον σῶσαι τὰς ψυχὰς ὑμῶν.

22 Γίνεσθε δὲ ποιηταὶ λόγου καὶ μὴ ἀκροαταὶ μόνον παραλογιζόμενοι ἑαυτούς·

23 ὅτι εἴ τις ἀκροατὴς λόγου ἐστὶν καὶ οὐ ποιητής, οὗτος ἔοικεν ἀνδρὶ κατανοοῦντι τὸ πρόσωπον τῆς γενέσεως αὐτοῦ ἐν ἐσόπτρῳ·

24 κατενόησεν γὰρ ἑαυτὸν καὶ ἀπελήλυθεν καὶ εὐθέως ἐπελάθετο ὁποῖος ἦν.

25 Ὁ δὲ παρακύψας εἰς νόμον τέλειον τὸν τῆς ἐλευθερίας καὶ παραμείνας, οὐκ ἀκροατὴς ἐπιλησμονῆς γενόμενος ἀλλὰ ποιητὴς ἔργου, οὗτος μακάριος ἐν τῇ ποιήσει αὐτοῦ ἔσται.

26 Εἴ τις δοκεῖ θρησκὸς εἶναι, μὴ χαλιναγωγῶν γλῶσσαν ἑαυτοῦ ἀλλὰ ἀπατῶν καρδίαν ἑαυτοῦ, τούτου μάταιος ἡ θρησκεία.

27 Θρησκεία καθαρὰ καὶ ἀμίαντος παρὰ τῷ Θεῷ καὶ Πατρὶ αὕτη ἐστίν, ἐπισκέπτεσθαι ὀρφανοὺς καὶ χήρας ἐν τῇ θλίψει αὐτῶν, ἄσπιλον ἑαυτὸν τηρεῖν ἀπὸ τοῦ κόσμου.

δε A | *εστω δε* Sin. BCP[1] latt. copt., *και εστω* A 13, *εστω* KLP[2] syr. arm. Thl. Oec. &c.

20. *ουκ εργαζεται* Sin. ABC[3] +, *ου κατεργαζεται* C[1]KLP &c.

21. *περισσευμα* A 13. 68. | *πραυτητι*, W., *πρ. σοφιας* P, *πρ. καρδιας* Thl. | *ὑμων* Sin. ABCKP &c. *ἡμων* L+.

22. *λογου* : C[2] 38. 73. 83. + aeth. Thl. *νομου* | *ακροαται μονον* B latt. syrr. copt. arm. aeth. Thl. Treg. WH., *μονον ακροαται* Sin. ACKLP Oec. &c. Ti.

23. om. *ὁτι* A 13 | *της γενεσεως* : om. pesh. +

25. *παραμεινας* : vulg. syrr. arm. + add *εν αυτω* | *ουκ ακροατης* Sin. ABC + latt. pesh. copt. Aug. Cass. Bede, *οὑτος ουκ ακρ.* KLP &c. syr. arm. Thl. Oec.

26. *ει* Sin. ABKL &c. syr. arm. Thl. Oec., *ει δε* CP 13 + latt. pesh. copt. Bede Tr.[m] | *θρῆσκος* Treg. | *ειναι* Sin. ABCP 13 latt. syrr. copt. Bede, *ειναι εν υμιν* KL &c. Thl. Oec. | *χαλινών* B. | *γλ. ἑαυτου* BPc 101. latt. Thl. WH., *γλ. αυτου* Sin. ACKL Oec. &c. Ti. Treg. WH.[m] | *καρδ. ἑαυτου* BC latt. Thl. WH., *καρδ. αυτου* Sin. AKLP Oec. &c. Treg. Ti. WH.[m] | *θρησκεια* ABCKLP &c. Treg. WH., *θρησκια* Sin. Ti.

27. *θρησκεια* as in preceding verse : A 70. 83. 123 pesh. add *γαρ*, syr. latt. copt. *δε* | *παρα τῳ θεῳ* Sin.[3] ABC[1]P 13 + Treg. WH., *παρα θεῳ* Sin.[1] C[2]KL 40. 73. &c. Ti. | ins. *τῳ* bef. *πατρι* A. | om. *και* bef. *πατρι* 99, 126. pesh. aeth. +, cf. corb. | *ἑαυτον* : A. aeth. *σεαυτον* | *απο* : CP *εκ*.

Vulgate.

autem ad loquendum et tardus
ad iram (α): 20 ira (α) enim
uiri iustitiam dei non operatur. 21 Propter quod abicientes omnem inmunditiam et
abundantiam malitiae in mansuetudine suscipite insitum
uerbum dei (β), quod potest
saluare animas uestras. 22
Estote autem factores uerbi,
et non auditores tantum fallentes uosmet ipsos. 23 Quia si
quis auditor est uerbi et non
factor, hic conparabitur uiro
consideranti uultum natiuitatis suae in speculo : 24 con-
siderauit enim (γ) se et abiit
et statim oblitus est qualis
fuerit. 25 Qui autem per-
spexerit in lege perfecta (δ)
libertatis et permanserit in
ea (ε) non auditor obliuiosus
factus sed factor operis, hic
beatus in facto suo erit. 26
Si quis autem putat se religiosum esse, non refrenans
linguam suam sed seducens
cor suum, huius uana est religio. 27 Religio autem (ζ)
munda et inmaculata apud
deum et patrem haec est, uisitare pupillos et uiduas in tribulatione eorum, et (η) in-
maculatum se custodire ab
hoc saeculo.

(α) Spec. Aug. *iracundiam* and *-dia* for *iram* and *ira*.
(β) F. om. *dei*.
(γ) F. *autem*.
(δ) Spec. Aug. *legem perfectam*.
(ε) Spec. Aug. and F. om. *in ea*.
(ζ) F. om. *autem*.
(η) F. om. *et*.

Corbey MS.

omnis homo uelox ad audi-
endum, tardus autem ad
loquendum, tardus autem ad
iracundiam. 20 Iracundia
enim uiri iustitiam dei non
operatur. 21 Et ideo ex-
ponentes omnes sordes et
abundantiam malitiae, per
clementiam excipite genitum
uerbum, qui potest [a] saluare
animas uestras. 22 Estote
autem factores uerbi et non
auditores tantum, aliter con-
siliantes. 23 Quia si quis
auditor uerbi est et non factor,
hic est similis homini respi-
cienti faciem natalis [b] sui in
speculo : 24 aspexit se et
recessit et in continenti oblitus est qualis erat. 25 Qui
autem respexit in legem con-
summatam libertatis et per-
seuerans, non audiens ob-
liuionis factus, sed factor
operum, hic beatus erit in
operibus suis. 26 Si quis
autem putat se religiosum
esse, non infrenans linguam
suam, sed fallens cor suum,
huius uana est religio. 27
Religio autem munda et inmaculata apud dominum haec
est : uisitare orfanos et
uiduas in tribulatione eorum,
seruare se sine macula a saeculo.

[a] MS. *potestis*.
[b] MS. *natali*.

Speculum and Priscillian.

tardus loqui piger
in iracundia.

20 Iracundia
enim uiri iustiti-
am Dei non ope
ratur.

26 (W. p. 524)
Si quis putat su-
perstitiosum [1] se
esse, non refre-
nans linguam su-
am, sed fallens
cor suum,[2] huius
uana religio est.
27 (W. p. 411)
Sanctitas autem
pura et incontam-
inata haec est apud
Deum patrem, ui-
sitare orfanos et
uiduas in angustia
ipsorum et inma-
culatum se seruare
a mundo.

[1] So S; *religiosum* M +.
[2] Om. *sed—suum* M +.

ΚΕΦ. β΄.

1 Ἀδελφοί μου, μὴ ἐν προσωποληψίαις ἔχετε τὴν
πίστιν τοῦ Κυρίου ἡμῶν Ἰησοῦ Χριστοῦ, τῆς δόξης.
2 Ἐὰν γὰρ εἰσέλθῃ εἰς συναγωγὴν ὑμῶν ἀνὴρ
χρυσοδακτύλιος ἐν ἐσθῆτι λαμπρᾷ, εἰσέλθῃ δὲ καὶ
πτωχὸς ἐν ῥυπαρᾷ ἐσθῆτι,
3 ἐπιβλέψητε δὲ ἐπὶ τὸν φοροῦντα τὴν ἐσθῆτα τὴν
λαμπρὰν καὶ εἴπητε Σὺ κάθου ὧδε καλῶς· καὶ τῷ πτωχῷ
εἴπητε Σὺ στῆθι ἐκεῖ ἢ κάθου ὑπὸ τὸ ὑποπόδιόν μου,
4 οὐ διεκρίθητε ἐν ἑαυτοῖς καὶ ἐγένεσθε κριταὶ διαλογισμῶν πονηρῶν;
5 Ἀκούσατε, ἀδελφοί μου ἀγαπητοί· οὐχ ὁ Θεὸς
ἐξελέξατο τοὺς πτωχοὺς τῷ κόσμῳ πλουσίους ἐν πίστει
καὶ κληρονόμους τῆς βασιλείας ἧς ἐπηγγείλατο τοῖς
ἀγαπῶσιν αὐτόν;
6 Ὑμεῖς δὲ ἠτιμάσατε τὸν πτωχόν. Οὐχ οἱ πλούσιοι
καταδυναστεύουσιν ὑμῶν καὶ αὐτοὶ ἕλκουσιν ὑμᾶς εἰς
κριτήρια;
7 **Οὐκ** αὐτοὶ βλασφημοῦσιν τὸ καλὸν ὄνομα τὸ
ἐπικληθὲν ἐφ᾽ ὑμᾶς;
8 **Εἰ** μέντοι νόμον τελεῖτε βασιλικὸν κατὰ τὴν
γραφήν Ἀγαπήσεις τὸν πλησίον σου ὡς σεαυτόν, καλῶς
ποιεῖτε·

II.—1. *προσωπολημψιαις* Sin. ABC, *προσωποληψιαις* KLP &c. | *χριστου,* WH.^{m} *χριστου* WH. Treg. Ti. | *της δοξης* bef. *του κυριου* 69. 73. a c, om. 13. sah. Cass. (*τ. δοξης.* Treg. Ti. *τ. δοξης;* WH.).

2. *εις συναγωγην* Sin.^{1}BC, *εις την σ.* Sin.^{3}AKLP &c. Thl. Oec.

3. *επιβλεψητε δε* BCP + corb. syr. Thl. Treg.^{m} WH., *και επιβλεψητε* Sin. AKL &c. Oec. Ti. Treg. | *ειπητε* (1st) Sin. ABC + corb. syr. Thl., *ειπ. αυτῳ* KLP vulg. &c. Oec. | *εκει η καθου* Sin. ACKLP &c. Treg. Ti. WH.^{m}, *η καθου εκει* B corb. WH. | *ὡδε* ins. (after 2nd *καθου*) Sin. C^{2}KLP &c. Thl. Oec., om. ABC^{1} 13. 65. 69 a c latt. pesh. WH. Ti. Treg. | *ὑπο* Sin. AB^{1}CKL &c., *επι* B^{2}P a c d 13. 29. 69 + pesh. arm. | aft. *ὑποποδιον* ins. *των ποδων* A 13 vulg. syrr. aeth. Aug.

4. *ου διεκριθητε* Sin. AB^{2}C 13. 14. 36. 69. 73 + syrr. vulg. copt. Treg. Ti. WH., *και ου διεκ.* KLP &c. Thl. Oec., *διεκ.* B^{1} corb. WH.^{m} (without interrogation).

5. *τῳ κοσμῳ* Sin A^{1}BC^{1} syr., *εν τῳ κοσμῳ* 27. 43. 64, *ε. τ. κ. τουτῳ* 29 vulg., *του κοσμου* A^{2}C^{2}KLP &c. pesh., *του κοσμου τουτου* aeth. Oec.$^{txt.}$, om. 113. | *βασιλειας* : Sin.^{1} A *επαγγελιας* cf. Heb. vi. 17.

6. *ουχ* : AC^{1} a c 69. 180 *ουχι* | *καταδυναστευουσιν ὑμων* Sin.^{3}BCKLP &c. Thl. Oec. Treg. WH., *κ. ὑμας* Sin.^{1} A 19. 20. 65 Ti.

7. *ουκ* : A c 13 syr. aeth. *και.*

8. *τον βασιλικον* P, *βασιλικον* bef. *τελειτε* C syr. | *ὡς σεαυτον* : B *ὡς σαυτον,* 4. 25. 28. 31 + Thl. *ὡς ἑαυτον,* a *ὡς ἑαυτους.*

Vulgate.

II—1 Fratres mei, nolite in personarum acceptione (*a*) habere fidem domini nostri Jesu Christi gloriae. 2 Etenim si introierit in conuentu uestro uir aureum [anulum habens in ueste candida, introierit autem et pauper in sordido habitu, 3 et intendatis in (*β*) eum qui indutus est ueste praeclara et dixeritis ei (*γ*) Tu sede hic bene, pauperi autem dicatis Tu sta illic aut sede sub scabillo pedum meorum, nonne iudicatis apud uosmet ipsos et facti estis iudices cogitationum iniquarum? 5 Audite, fratres mei dilectissimi; nonne deus elegit pauperes in hoc mundo diuites in fide et heredes regni quod promisit (*δ*) deus diligentibus se? 6 Uos autem exhonorastis pauperem. Nonne diuites per potentiam opprimunt uos, et ipsi adtrahunt (*ε*) uos ad iudicia? 7 Nonne ipsi blasphemant bonum nomen quod inuocatum est super uos? 8 Si tamen legem perficitis regalem secundum scripturas Diliges proximum tuum sicut te ipsum, bene facitis (*ζ*):

(*α*) F. *-tionem.*
(*β*) F. om. *in.*
(*γ*) F. om. *ei.*
(*δ*) Spec. Aug and F. *repromisit.*
(*ε*) F. *trahunt.*
(*ζ*) F. *facis.*

Corbey MS.

II—1 Fratres mei, nolite in acceptione personarum habere fidem domini nostri Iesu Christi hon*o*ris.[a] 2. Si autem intrauerit in synagogam uestram homo anulos aureos in digitos habens in ueste splendida, intret autem pauper in sordida ueste; 3 respiciatis autem qui uestitus est ueste candida et dicatis, Tu hic sede bene, et pauperi dicatis, Tu sta, aut sede illo sub scamello meo; 4 diiudicati estis inter uos, facti estis iudices cogitationum malarum. 5 Audite fratres mei dilecti, nonne deus elegit pauperes saeculi locupletes in fide et heredes regni quod expromisit diligentibus eum? 6 Uos autem frustratis pauperem. Nonne diuites potentantur in uobis, et ipsi uos tradunt ad iudicia? 7 Nonne ipsi blasphemant in bono nomine quod uocitum est in uobis? 8 Si tamen lege consummamini regale[b] secundum scripturam, Diliges proximum tuum tanquam te; bene facitis.

[a] MS. *honeris.*
[b] So MS.; Sab. *regali.*

Speculum and Priscillian.

[II—5 (Sch. p. 17) deus elegit pauperes mundi diuites fidei, heredes regni.]

9 εἰ δὲ προσωπολημπτεῖτε, ἁμαρτίαν ἐργάζεσθε,
ἐλεγχόμενοι ὑπὸ τοῦ νόμου ὡς παραβάται.
10 Ὅστις γὰρ ὅλον τὸν νόμον τηρήσῃ, πταίσῃ δὲ ἐν
ἑνί, γέγονεν πάντων ἔνοχος.
11 Ὁ γὰρ εἰπών Μὴ μοιχεύσῃς, εἶπεν καί Μὴ
φονεύσῃς· εἰ δὲ οὐ μοιχεύεις, φονεύεις δέ, γέγονας
παραβάτης νόμου.
12 Οὕτως λαλεῖτε καὶ οὕτως ποιεῖτε ὡς διὰ νόμου ἐλευθερίας μέλλοντες κρίνεσθαι.
13 Ἡ γὰρ κρίσις ἀνέλεος τῷ μὴ ποιήσαντι ἔλεος·
κατακαυχᾶται ἔλεος κρίσεως.
14 Τί ὄφελος, ἀδελφοί μου, ἐὰν πίστιν λέγῃ τις ἔχειν,
ἔργα δὲ μὴ ἔχῃ ; μὴ δύναται ἡ πίστις σῶσαι αὐτόν;
15 Ἐὰν ἀδελφὸς ἢ ἀδελφὴ γυμνοὶ ὑπάρχωσιν καὶ
λειπόμενοι τῆς ἐφημέρου τροφῆς,
16 εἴπῃ δέ τις αὐτοῖς ἐξ ὑμῶν Ὑπάγετε ἐν εἰρήνῃ,
θερμαίνεσθε καὶ χορτάζεσθε, μὴ δῶτε δὲ αὐτοῖς τὰ
'πιτήδεια τοῦ σώματος, τί ὄφελος ;
17 Οὕτως καὶ ἡ πίστις, ἐὰν μὴ ἔχῃ ἔργα, νεκρά ἐστι
καθ' ἑαυτήν.
18 Ἀλλ' ἐρεῖ τις Σὺ πίστιν ἔχεις κἀγὼ ἔργα ἔχω·

9. προσωπολημπτειτε Sin. ABC (as in ver. 1).

10. τηρηση Sin. BC+latt. Thl. Oec., τηρησει KLP &c., πληρωσει A a c 63. 69 syr., πληρωσας τηρησει 13, τελεσει 66. 73 | πταιση Sin. ABC latt. Thl. Oec., πταισει KLP &c.

11. ειπας A | μη μοιχευσῃς : Sin. L+ μη -σεις | φονευσῃς—μοιχευσῃς (transp.) C 69+syr. arm. Thl. | μοιχευεις φονευεις Sin. ABC. φονευεις μοιχευεις (transp.) 15. 70. arm., μοιχευσεις φονευσεις K &c. Thl., μοιχευσῃς φονευσῃς LP+ | παραβατης : A αποστατης.

13. ανελεος Sin. ABCKP &c., ανηλεος 13. 38+, ανιλεως L + Chrys. Thl. | ελεον K. +Chr. | κατακαυχαται Sin.[1] KL &c., και κατακ. aeth. Thl. +, κατακ. δε Sin.[3] 40 +corb. vulg. syr. Oec., κατακαυχασθω 27 +copt., κατακαυχασθω δε A 13, κατακαυχατε B (cf. αντιτασσετε iv. 6, φευξετε iv. 8), κατακαυχασθε C[2] (in eras.) pesh. | ελεος (2nd) Sin. AB+Thl., ελεον CKL+ Oec. (Ti. compares τὸ ἔλεον ap. Herodian *Epim.* p. 235).

14. τι οφελος BC[1] arm. (as in ver. 16) Treg.[m] WH., τι το οφελος Sin. AC[2]KL &c. Treg. Ti. W. | τις bef. λεγῃ AC Treg.[m] | ἡ πιστις : corb. spec. *fides sola*, sah. adds *sine operibus*.

15. εαν Sin. B+corb. spec. copt. arm., εαν δε ACKL vulg. &c. | λειπομενοι Sin. BCK syrr. arm., λειπ. ωσιν ALP &c. Oec. Thl.

16. ειπῃ δε : A+και ειπῃ | οφελος BC[1] (as in ver. 14).

17. εχῃ εργα : L arm. Thl. Oec. &c. εργα εχῃ.

18. πιστιν εχεις, Treg. Ti. W. π. εχεις WH. π. εχεις ; WH.[m] | εργα εχω· Treg. Ti. ε. εχω, W. ε. εχω. WH. | χωρις των Sin. ABCP+latt. syrr. copt. arm. aeth., εκ των KL &c. Thl. | εργων (1st) Sin. ABP+latt. syrr., εργων σου CKL &c. aeth. Thl. | σοι δειξω Sin. B+ WH. Treg. Ti., δειξω σοι ACKL syrr. &c.

VULGATE.

9 si autem personas accipitis,
peccatum operamini, redar-
guti a lege quasi transgres-
sores. 10 Quicumque autem
totam legem seruauerit, of-
fendat autem in uno, factus
est omnium reus. 11 Qui
enim dixit Non moechaberis,
dixit et Non occides : quod
si non moechaberis, occides
autem, factus es transgressor
legis. 12 Sic loquimini et
sic facite, sicut per legem
libertatis incipientes iudicari :
13 iudicium enim sine misericordia illi qui non fecerit (α)
misericordiam, superexal-
tat (β) autem misericordia iudicio. 14 Quid proderit,
fratres mei, si fidem quis dicat
se habere, opera autem non
habeat? numquid poterit fides
saluare eum ? 15 Si autem
frater aut soror nudi sint (γ)
et indigeant (γ) uictu coti-
diano, 16 dicat autem aliquis de uobis illis Ite in
pace, caleficamini (δ) et saturamini, non dederitis autem
eis quae necessaria sunt corporis (ε), quid proderit? 17
Sic et fides, si non habeat (ζ)
opera, mortua est in semet
ipsa (η). 18 Sed dicet aliquis (θ) Tu fidem habes, et

(α) F. *fecit.*
(β) F. *-exultat.*
(γ) F. *sunt...indigent.*
(δ) F. *-ficiemini.*
(ε) F. *corpori.*
(ζ) F. *habet.*
(η) F. *ipsam.*
(θ) F. *quis.*

CORBEY MS.

9 Si autem personas acci-
pitis, peccatum operamini, a
lege traducti tanquam trans-
gressores. 10 Qui enim totam
legem seruauerit, peccauerit
autem in uno, factus est omnium reus. 11 Nam qui
dixit, Non moechaberis, dixit
et, Non occides. Si autem
non moechaberis, occideris
autem, factus es[a] transgressor
legis. 12 Sic loquimini et
sic facite quasi a lege libera-
litatis iudicium sperantes.
13 Iudicium autem non
miserebitur ei qui non
fecit misericordiam, super-
gloriatur autem misericordia iudicium. 14 Quid
prodest fratres mei si quis
dicat se fidem habere, opera
autem non habeat? numquid
potest fides eum sola saluare?
15 Siue frater siue soror nudi
sint, et desit eis uictus coti-
dianus, 16 dicat autem illis
ex uestris aliquis, Uadite in
pace, calidi estote et satulli ;
non dederit autem illis ali-
mentum corporis; quid et
prodest? 17 Sic et fides, si
non habeat opera, mortua est
sola. 18 Sed dicet aliquis
Tu operam[b] habes, ego fidem

[a] MS. *est.*
[b] Sab. *opera.*

SPECULUM AND PRISCILLIAN.

II—13 (W. p.
411) Iudicium e-
nim sine miseri-
cordia ei[1] qui non
fecit misericordi-
am ; quoniam mi-
sericordia praefer-
tur iudicio. 14
Quid prode est
fratres, si fidem
quis dicat in semet
ipso manere, opera
autem non habe-
at? Numquid po-
test fides sola sal-
uare eum? 15 Si
frater aut soror
nudi fuerint et
defuerit eis coti-
dianus cibus ; 16
dicat autem eis
aliquis uestrum :
Ite in pace et ca-
lefacimini et satie-
mini, et non det
eis necessaria cor-
poris, quid prode
est haec dixisse
eis? 17 Sic et
fides quae non ha-
bet opera, mortua
est circa se.

[1] S. *his.*

δεῖξόν μοι τὴν πίστιν σου χωρὶς τῶν ἔργων, κἀγώ σοι
δείξω ἐκ τῶν ἔργων μου τὴν πίστιν.
19 Σὺ πιστεύεις ὅτι εἷς ἐστὶν ὁ Θεός· καλῶς ποιεῖς·
καὶ τὰ δαιμόνια πιστεύουσιν καὶ φρίσσουσιν.
20 Θέλεις δὲ γνῶναι, ὦ ἄνθρωπε κενέ, ὅτι ἡ πίστις
χωρὶς τῶν ἔργων ἀργή ἐστιν;
21 Ἀβραὰμ ὁ πατὴρ ἡμῶν οὐκ ἐξ ἔργων ἐδικαιώθη,
ἀνενέγκας Ἰσαὰκ τὸν υἱὸν αὐτοῦ ἐπὶ τὸ θυσιαστήριον;
22 Βλέπεις ὅτι ἡ πίστις συνήργει τοῖς ἔργοις αὐτοῦ
καὶ ἐκ τῶν ἔργων ἡ πιστις ἐτελειώθη,
23 καὶ ἐπληρώθη ἡ γραφὴ ἡ λέγουσα Ἐπίστευσεν
δὲ Ἀβραὰμ τῷ Θεῷ, καὶ ἐλογίσθη αὐτῷ εἰς δικαιοσύνην,
καὶ φίλος Θεοῦ ἐκλήθη.
24 Ὁρᾶτε ὅτι ἐξ ἔργων δικαιοῦται ἄνθρωπος καὶ οὐκ
ἐκ πίστεως μόνον.
25 Ὁμοίως δὲ καὶ Ῥαὰβ ἡ πόρνη οὐκ ἐξ ἔργων
ἐδικαιώθη, ὑποδεξαμένη τοὺς ἀγγέλους καὶ ἑτέρᾳ ὁδῷ
ἐκβαλοῦσα;
26 Ὥσπερ γὰρ τὸ σῶμα χωρὶς πνεύματος νεκρόν ἐστιν,
οὕτως καὶ ἡ πίστις χωρὶς ἔργων νεκρά ἐστιν.

ΚΕΦ. γ΄.

1 Μὴ πολλοὶ διδάσκαλοι γίνεσθε, ἀδελφοί μου, εἰδότες
ὅτι μεῖζον κρίμα λημψόμεθα·

Thl. Oec. Treg.^{m}, *σοι* corb. aeth. | om. *μου* after *εργων* (2) latt. syr. | *πιστιν* (3rd) Sin. BC. + corb. arm., *πιστιν μου* AKLP vulg. syrr. copt. aeth. &c. Thl. Oec.

19. *είς εστιν ὁ θεος* Sin. A. 68. vulg. pesh. copt. arm. aeth.^{pp} Cyr. Ti. Treg., *είς ὁ θεος εστιν* C syr. WH.^{m} W., *είς θεος εστιν* B 69 a c Thl. WH. Treg.^{m}, *είς ὁ θεος* corb. aeth.^{ro} Cyr., *ὁ θεος είς εστιν* K^{2}L &c. Did. Oec. (with interrog. Ti. WH.). —*και τα δαιμ. πιστ. και φρισσουσιν*—, W.

20. *αργη* BC^{1} + corb. fuld. sah., *νεκρα* Sin. AC^{2}KLP &c. vulg. syrr. copt. arm. aeth. Oec.

22. *συνηργει* Sin.^{3} BCKLP &c. vulg. syrr. Thl. Oec. WH. Treg.^{m}, *συνεργει* Sin.^{1} A corb. Ti. Treg. | *ετελειωθη;* Treg.

23. *επιστευσεν δε*: L + latt. om. *δε*.

24. *ὁρατε* Sin. AB^{2} (by corr. fr. *-ται*) CP latt. syrr. copt. arm. aeth. Thl., *ὁρατε τοινυν* KL &c. Oec. | *μονον;* Treg.

25. *ὁμοιως*: C pesh. copt. arm. aeth. *οὕτως* | *δε και*: C pesh. copt. arm. *και* | *αγγελους*: CLK^{m} + pesh. corb. arm. *κατασκοπους*.

26. *ὥσπερ γαρ* Sin. ACKLP &c. Ti. Treg. WH.^{m}, *ὥσπερ δε* corb. Orig., *ὥσπερ* B pesh. arm. aeth. WH. | *εργων* Sin. B 69 a Orig. Treg. Ti. WH., *των εργων* ACKLP &c. Thl. Oec. Treg.^{m}

III.—1. *λημψομεθα* Sin. ABC as above.

VULGATE.

ego opera habeo: ostende mihi fidem tuam sine operibus, et ego ostendam tibi ex operibus fidem meam. 19 Tu credis quoniam unus est deus. Bene facis: et daemones credunt et contremiscunt. 20 Uis autem scire, o homo inanis, quoniam fides sine operibus mortua (*a*) est? 21 Abraham pater noster nonne ex operibus iustificatus est offerens Isaac filium suum super altare? 22 Uides quoniam fides cooperabatur operibus illius, et ex operibus fides consummata est. 23 Et suppleta est scriptura dicens Credidit Abraham deo, et reputatum est ei (β) ad iustitiam, et amicus dei appellatus est. 24 Uidetis quoniam ex operibus iustificatur homo et non ex fide tantum? 25 Similiter autem et Raab meretrix nonne ex operibus iustificata est, suscipiens nuntios et alia uia eiciens? 26 Sicut enim corpus sine spiritu mortuum (γ) est, ita et fides sine operibus mortua est.

III—1 Nolite plures magistri fieri (δ), fratres mei, scientes quoniam maius iudicium sumitis.

(α) By correction *otiosa* as in F.
(β) F. *illi*.
(γ) F. *emortuum*.
(δ) Spec. Aug. *effici*.

CORBEY MS.

habeo: ostende mihi fidem sine operibus: et ego tibi de operibus fidem. 19 Tu credis quia unus deus: bene facis: et daemonia credunt et contremiscunt. 20 Uis autem scire o homo uacue, quoniam fides sine operibus uacua est? 21 Abraham pater noster, nonne ex operibus iustificatus est, offerens Isaac filium suum super aram? 22 Uides quoniam fides communicat cum operibus suis, et ex operibus fides confirmatur, 23 et impleta est scriptura dicens, Credidit Abraham domino et aestimatum est ei ad iustitiam, et amicus dei uocatus est. 24 Uidetis quoniam ex operibus iustificatur homo et non ex fide tantum. 25 Similiter et Raab fornicaria, nonne ex operibus iustificat*a*[a] est, cum suscepisset exploratores ex xii tribu*bus*[b] filiorum Israel et per aliam uiam eos eiecisset? 26 Sicut autem corpus sine spiritu mortuum est, sic fides sine opera mortua est. III—1 Nolite multi magistri esse fratres mei, scientes quoniam maius iudicium accipiemus.

[a] MS. *iustificatus*.
[b] MS. and Sab. *tribus*, as in I. 1.

SPECULUM AND PRISCILLIAN.

[II—19 (Sch. p. 27) credes quia unus deus est: hoc et daemonia faciunt et perhorrescunt.]

26 (W. p. 411) Sicut enim corpus sine spiritu mortuum est, sic et fides sine operibus mortua est.

III—1 (W. p. 524) Nolite multiloqui esse fratres mei; scientes [1] quia maius iudicium accipietis:

[1] S. om. *scientes*.

2 πολλὰ γὰρ πταίομεν ἅπαντες. Εἴ τις ἐν λόγῳ οὐ πταίει, οὗτος τέλειος ἀνήρ, δυνατὸς χαλιναγωγῆσαι καὶ ὅλον τὸ σῶμα.

3 Ἴδε γὰρ τῶν ἵππων τοὺς χαλινοὺς εἰς τὰ στόματα βάλλομεν εἰς τὸ πείθεσθαι αὐτοὺς ἡμῖν, καὶ ὅλον τὸ σῶμα αὐτῶν μετάγομεν.

4 Ἰδοὺ καὶ τὰ πλοῖα, τηλικαῦτα ὄντα καὶ ὑπὸ ἀνέμων σκληρῶν ἐλαυνόμενα, μετάγεται ὑπὸ ἐλαχίστου πηδαλίου ὅπου ἡ ὁρμὴ τοῦ εὐθύνοντος βούλεται.

5 Οὕτως καὶ ἡ γλῶσσα μικρὸν μέλος ἐστὶν καὶ μεγάλα αὐχεῖ. Ἰδοὺ ἡλίκον πῦρ ἡλίκην ὕλην ἀνάπτει.

6 Καὶ ἡ γλῶσσα πῦρ, ὁ κόσμος τῆς ἀδικίας ἡ γλῶσσα καθίσταται ἐν τοῖς μέλεσιν ἡμῶν, ἡ σπιλοῦσα ὅλον τὸ σῶμα καὶ φλογίζουσα τὸν τροχὸν τῆς γενέσεως καὶ φλογιζομένη ὑπὸ τῆς γεέννης.

7 Πᾶσα γὰρ φύσις θηρίων τε καὶ πετεινῶν, ἑρπετῶν τε καὶ ἐναλίων, δαμάζεται καὶ δεδάμασται τῇ φύσει τῇ ἀνθρωπίνῃ·

8 τὴν δὲ γλῶσσαν οὐδεὶς δαμάσαι δύναται ἀνθρώπων· ἀκατάστατον κακόν, μεστὴ ἰοῦ θανατηφόρου.

2. *δυνατος*: Sin. + Cyr. Thl. *δυναμενος*.

3. *ιδε γαρ*: *ειδε γαρ* Sin.^{1} *ecce enim* pesh., *ιδε* CP 'al. plus 40' arm. syr. sah. (*et ecce* aeth.^{pp}) Zig. Thl. (see Notes), *ει δε* Sin.^{3} ABKL 'al. 25' latt. copt. Oec. Dam. Treg. W. Ti. WH., *quare ergo* spec., *et insuper* aeth.^{ro}, *sicut autem* Bede | *εις τα στοματα*: A + arm. syrr. *εις το στομα* | *εις το πειθεσθαι* Sin. BC, *προς τ. π.* AKLP &c. Oec. Thl. | *αυτους ἡμιν* Sin. BKLP &c., *ἡμιν αυτους* AC + Treg.^{m} | *μεταγομεν αυτων* A 13.

4. *ιδου*: 24 *ειδε* | ins. *τα* bef. *τηλικαυτα* B | *σκληρων ανεμων* AL &c. | *ὁπου* Sin. B sah., *ὁπου αν* ACKLP &c. Treg.^{m} | *βουλεται* Sin. BL, *βουληται* ACKP &c. Thl. Oec.

5. *οὑτως*: *ὡσαυτως* A + | *μεγαλα αυχει* ABC^{1}P latt. Eph., *μεγαλαυχει* Sin. C^{2}KL &c. Thl. Oec. | *ιδου*: spec. *et sicut* cf. Bede on ver. 3. | *ἡλικον* Sin. A^{2}BC^{1}P vulg. Oec., *ολιγον* A^{1}C^{2}KL &c. corb. syrr. sah. copt. arm. aeth.

6. *και ἡ γλωσσα* Sin.^{3} ABCKLP &c. WH. Treg., *ἡ γλωσσα* Sin.^{1} Ti. (punctuating ἀνάπτει ἡ γλῶσσα.) | *πυρ.* W. | *αδικιας* WH., *αδικιας.* Treg., *αδικιας,* Ti. (*et mundus iniquitatis sicut silva est* pesh.) | *οὑτως* ins. bef. 2nd *ἡ γλῶσσα* P &c. Thl. Oec., *οὑτως και* L 106, om. Sin. ABCK + latt. syrr. sah. copt. arm. Dam. | *ἡ σπιλουσα*: *και σπ.* Sin.^{1} Ti. | *τον τροχον της γενεσεως*: after *γενεσεως* ins. *ἡμων* Sin. 7. 25. 68 vulg. pesh. (*series generationum nostrarum quae currunt veluti rotae*). aeth. (for *γενεσεως*, *γεεννης* Thl. Oec.).

7. om. 2nd *τε* A + arm. | *δαμαζεται και δεδαμασται*: om. *καὶ δεδαμασται* pesh.

8. *δαμασαι δυναται ανθρωπων* BC syr. WH. Treg., *δυναται δαμασαι ανθρ.* Sin. AKP a c 69. 133 + Treg.^{m} Ti., *δυναται ανθρ. δαμασαι* L &c. arm. Cyr. Thl. Oec. | *ακαταστατον* Sin. ABP latt. +, *ακατασχετον* CKL &c. Epiph. Cyr. Dam. Thl. Oec.

Vulgate.

2 In multis enim offend-
imus omnes: si quis in
uerbo non offendit, hic perfectus est uir: potest etiam
circumducere freno (*a*) totum
corpus. 3 Si autem equis (*β*)
frenos in ora mittimus ad consentiendum nobis, et omne corpus illorum circumferimus.
4 Ecce et naues, cum magnae
sint et a uentis ualidis minen-
tur (*γ*), circumferuntur (*δ*) a
modico gubernaculo ubi impetus dirigentis uoluerit. 5
Ita et lingua modicum quidem
membrum est et magna exaltat (*ε*). Ecce quantus ignis
quam magnam siluam in-
cendit. 6 Et lingua ignis est,
uniuersitas iniquitatis lingua constituitur in membris
nostris, quae maculat totum
corpus et inflammat rotam
natiuitatis nostrae, inflam-
mata a gehenna. 7 Omnis
enim natura bestiarum et
uolucrum et serpentium cete-
rorumque (*ζ*) domantur et
domata (*η*) sunt a natura
humana: 8 linguam autem
nullus hominum domare
potest: inquietum malum,
plena ueneno mortifero.

(*a*) F. *fr. cir.*
(*β*) F. *equorum.*
(*γ*) Passive from *mino*, 'are driven.'
(*δ*) F. adds *autem.*
(*ε*) F. *exultat.*
(*ζ*) Possibly a corruption of *cetorum*, or it may represent a Greek misreading αλλων or εναλλων for εναλιων. F. reads *et uolucrum et repentium etiam ceterorum.*
(*η*) F. *domita.*

Corbey MS.

2 Multa autem erramus om-
nes. Si quis in uerbo non
errat, hic erit consummatus
uir: potens est se infrenare,
et totum corpus. 3 Si autem
equorum frenos in ora mittimus ut possint consentire, et
totum corpus ipsorum conuer-
timus. 4 Ecce et naues tam
magnae sunt et a uentis tam
ualidis feruntur, reguntur
autem paruulo gubernaculo
et ubicumque diriguntur uo-
luntate[a] eorum qui eas guber-
nant. 5 Sic et lingua paruu-
lum membrum est et magna
gloriatur.[b] Ecce pusillum
ignis in quam magna[c] silua
incendium facit! 6 Et lingua ignis saeculi iniquitatis:
lingua posita est in membris
nostris, quae maculat totum
corpus et inflammat rotam
natiuitatis et incenditur a
gehenna. 7 Omnis autem
natura bestiarum siue uolati-
lium, repentium et natantium
domatur et domita est: 8
naturae autem humanae linguam nemo hominum domare
potest: inconstans malum
plena ueneno mortifero.[d]

[a] By corr. from *uolumptate.*
[b] MS. *gloriantur.*
[c] So MS.; *magnam siluam* Sab. See below, ver. 13.
[d] MS. *mortifera.*

Speculum and Priscillian.

2 multa enim om-
nes delinquimus.
Si quis in uerbo
non delinquit, hic
perfectus uir est;
potest[1] frenare to-
tum corpus et di-
rigere. 3 Quare
ergo[2] equis frena
in ora[3] mittuntur,
nisi in eo ut sua-
deantur a nobis et
totum corpus cir-
cumducamus? 4
Ecce et[4] naues
quae tam[5] inmen-
sae sunt sub uen-
tis duris feruntur
et circumducun-
tur a paruissimo
gubernaculo ubi
impetus dirigentis
uoluerit. 5 Sic
et lingua pars
membri[6] est, sed
est magniloqua.
Et sicut paruus
ignis magnam sil-
uam incendit, 6
ita et lingua ignis
est: et mundus
iniquitatis per lin-
guam constat in
membris nostris,
quae maculat to-
tum corpus et in-
flammat rotam
geniturae[7] et in-
flammatur a geni-
tura. 7 Omnis
enim natura bes-
tiarum et auium
et serpentium et
beluarum mariti-
marum domatur
et subiecta est
naturae humanae:
8 linguam autem

[1] M + ins. *etiam.*
[2] M + *uero.*
[3] M + *ore.*
[4] M + om. *et.*
[5] For *quae tam* S has *quiaetam.*
[6] M + ins. *parua.*
[7] The words *rot. gen.* are found in Prisc. p. 26.

9 Ἐν αὐτῇ εὐλογοῦμεν τὸν Κύριον καὶ Πατέρα, καὶ ἐν
αὐτῇ καταρώμεθα τοὺς ἀνθρώπους τοὺς καθ' ὁμοίωσιν
Θεοῦ γεγονότας·

10 ἐκ τοῦ αὐτοῦ στόματος ἐξέρχεται εὐλογία καὶ
κατάρα. Οὐ χρή, ἀδελφοί μου, ταῦτα οὕτως γίνεσθαι.

11 Μήτι ἡ πηγὴ ἐκ τῆς αὐτῆς ὀπῆς βρύει τὸ γλυκὺ καὶ
τὸ πικρόν;

12 Μὴ δύναται, ἀδελφοί μου, συκῆ ἐλαίας ποιῆσαι, ἢ
ἄμπελος σῦκα; Οὔτε ἁλυκὸν γλυκὺ ποιῆσαι ὕδωρ.

13 Τίς σοφὸς καὶ ἐπιστήμων ἐν ὑμῖν; δειξάτω ἐκ τῆς
καλῆς ἀναστροφῆς τὰ ἔργα αὐτοῦ ἐν πραΰτητι σοφίας.

14 Εἰ δὲ ζῆλον πικρὸν ἔχετε καὶ ἐριθίαν ἐν τῇ καρδίᾳ
ὑμῶν, μὴ κατακαυχᾶσθε καὶ ψεύδεσθε κατὰ τῆς ἀληθείας.

15 Οὐκ ἔστιν αὕτη ἡ σοφία ἄνωθεν κατερχομένη, ἀλλὰ
ἐπίγειος, ψυχική, δαιμονιώδης.

16 Ὅπου γὰρ ζῆλος καὶ ἐριθία, ἐκεῖ ἀκαταστασία καὶ
πᾶν φαῦλον πρᾶγμα.

17 Ἡ δὲ ἄνωθεν σοφία πρῶτον μὲν ἁγνή ἐστιν, ἔπειτα
εἰρηνική, ἐπιεικής, εὐπειθής, μεστὴ ἐλέους καὶ καρπῶν
ἀγαθῶν, ἀδιάκριτος, ἀνυπόκριτος.

18 Καρπὸς δὲ δικαιοσύνης ἐν εἰρήνῃ σπείρεται τοῖς
ποιοῦσιν εἰρήνην.

9. *τον κυριον* Sin.ABCP corb. pesh. copt. arm. + Cyr., *τον θεον* KL vulg. syr. &c. Epiph. Thl. Oec.

12. *ελαιας* : Vulg. *ficus* | *ουτε ἁλυκον γλυκυ* ABC^1+arm. (*neque salinus locus aquam dulcem facere*), *οὕτως ουτε ἁλυκ. γλ.* C^2 latt. pesh. (and reading *ουδε* for *ουτε*) Sin. 13, *οὕτως ουδεμια* (*ουτε μια* Pc) *φηγη ἁλυκον και γλυκυ* KLP &c. Thl. Oec.

14. *ει δε* : AP+add *αρα.* | *εριθιαν* 101. 13.^{lect} Dam. WH., *ερειθιαν* B^1, *ερειθειαν* A, *εριθειαν* Sin. B^{3}CKLP &c. Ti. Treg. | *τῃ καρδιᾳ* : *ταις καρδιαις* Sin. + latt. syrr. copt. arm. | *καυχασθε* A+ | *και ψευδεσθε κατα της αληθειας* ABCKLP &c. Treg. WH., *της αληθειας και ψευδεσθε* Sin.^{1} Ti., *κατα τ. α. κ. ψ* Sin.^{3} pesh. *ne inflemini adversus veritatem nec mentiamini.*

15. *αλλα* Sin. B, *αλλ'* ACKLP.

16. *εριθια* 101. 13.^{lect}, *εριθεια* B^1, *ερειθεια* B^2, *ερεις* C, *ερις* P. | *εκει* BCKLP &c., *εκει και* Sin. A+.

17. *ανυποκριτος* Sin. ABCP+latt. syr. copt. arm. Did. Ephr., *και ανυπ.* KL &c. Thl. Oec.

18. *ὁ καρπος* Sin. | *της δικαιοσυνης* K Oec. +.

VULGATE.

9. In ipsa benedicimus deum
et patrem, et in ipsa maledicimus homines qui ad similitudinem dei facti sunt: 10
ex ipso ore procedit benedictio
et maledictio. Non oportet,
fratres mei, haec ita fieri.
11 Numquid fons de eodem
foramine emanat dulcem
et amaram aquam? 12 Num-
quid potest, fratres mei,
ficus uuas facere aut uitis
ficus? Sic neque salsa dulcem potest facere aquam.
13 Quis sapiens et discipli-
natus inter uos? ostendat ex
bona conuersatione operationem suam (α) in mansuetudi-
nem (β) sapientiae. 14 Quod
si zelum amarum habetis et
contentiones (γ) in cordibus
uestris, nolite gloriari et mendaces esse aduersus ueritatem.
15 Non est (δ) ista sapientia
de sursum descendens, sed
terrena animalis diabolica.
16 Ubi enim zelus et con-
tentio, ibi inconstantia et
omne opus prauum. 17 Quae
autem de sursum est sapientia,
primum quidem pudica est,
deinde pacifica, modesta, suadibilis (ε), plena misericordia
et fructibus bonis, non iu-
dicans (ζ), sine simulatione.
18 Fructus autem iustitiae
in pace seminatur facientibus
pacem.

(α) F. *opera sua*.
(β) F. *-tudine*.
(γ) F. adds *sunt*.
(δ) F. adds *enim*.
(ε) Spec. Aug. and F. add *bonis consentiens*, doubtless a gloss on *suadibilis*.
(ζ) Spec. Aug. *diiudicans*; F. joins with the following words, omitting *non*; Augustine *inaestimabilis*.

CORBEY MS.

9 In ipsa benedicimus dominum et patrem, et per ipsam
maledicimus homines qui ad
similitudinem dei facti sunt.
10 ex ipso ore exit benedictio
et maledictio. Non decet fratres mei haec sic fieri. 11
Numquid fons ex uno fora-
mine bullit dulcem et salmaci-
dum? 12 Numquid potest, fratres mei, ficus oliuas facere, aut
uitis ficus? Sic nec salmaci-
dum dulcem facere aquam.
13 Quis sapiens et discipli-
nosus in uobis demonstrat de
bona conuersatione opera sua
in sapientiae clementia[a]? 14
Si autem zelum amarum ha-
betis et contentionem in prae-
cordiis uestris, quid alapa-
mini[b] mentientes contra ueritatem? 15 Non est sapientia
quae descendit desursum,
sed terrestris, animalis, dae-
monetica. 16 Ubi autem
zelus et contentio, inconstans ibi et omne prauum
negotium. 17 Dei autem
sapientia primum sancta est,
deinde pacifica et uerecun-
diae consentiens, plena misericordiae et fructuum bon-
orum, sine diiudicatione, ir-
reprehensibilis,[c] sine hypo-
crisi. 18 Fructus autem iustitiae in pace seminatur qui
faciunt pacem.

[a] So MS.; *clementiam*, Sab. and W. final *m* being often omitted in MS.
[b] Martianay suggested *eleuamini*, but Bp. Wordsworth refers to Ducange for the gloss *alapator*=καυχητής.
[c] Probably a gloss on *s. di.* which has got into the text.

SPECULUM AND PRISCILLIAN.

hominum domare nemo potest nec retinere a malo, quia plena est mortali veneno.

13 (W. p. 463) Quis prudens et sciens uestrum! Monstret de bona conuersatione opera sua in mansuetudine et prudentia.

ΚΕΦ. δ´.

1 Πόθεν πόλεμοι καὶ πόθεν μάχαι ἐν ὑμῖν; οὐκ ἐντεῦθεν, ἐκ τῶν ἡδονῶν ὑμῶν τῶν στρατευομένων ἐν τοῖς
μέλεσιν ὑμῶν;
2 Ἐπιθυμεῖτε, καὶ οὐκ ἔχετε· φονεύετε. Καὶ ζηλοῦτε,
καὶ οὐ δύνασθε ἐπιτυχεῖν· μάχεσθε καὶ πολεμεῖτε. Οὐκ
ἔχετε διὰ τὸ μὴ αἰτεῖσθαι ὑμᾶς·
3 αἰτεῖτε καὶ οὐ λαμβάνετε, διότι κακῶς αἰτεῖσθε, ἵνα
ἐν ταῖς ἡδοναῖς ὑμῶν δαπανήσητε.
4 Μοιχαλίδες, οὐκ οἴδατε ὅτι ἡ φιλία τοῦ κόσμου
ἔχθρα τοῦ Θεοῦ ἐστίν; ὃς ἐὰν οὖν βουληθῇ φίλος εἶναι
τοῦ κόσμου, ἐχθρὸς τοῦ Θεοῦ καθίσταται.
5 Ἢ δοκεῖτε ὅτι κενῶς ἡ γραφὴ λέγει Πρὸς φθόνον
ἐπιποθεῖ τὸ πνεῦμα ὃ κατῴκισεν ἐν ἡμῖν;
6 Μείζονα δὲ δίδωσιν χάριν· διὸ λέγει Ὁ Θεὸς
ὑπερηφάνοις ἀντιτάσσεται, ταπεινοῖς δὲ δίδωσιν χάριν.
7 Ὑποτάγητε οὖν τῷ Θεῷ· ἀντίστητε δὲ τῷ διαβόλῳ,
καὶ φεύξεται ἀφ᾽ ὑμῶν·
8 ἐγγίσατε τῷ Θεῷ, καὶ ἐγγίσει ὑμῖν. Καθαρίσατε
χεῖρας, ἁμαρτωλοί, καὶ ἁγνίσατε καρδίας, δίψυχοι

IV.—1. *ποθεν* (2nd) Sin. ABCP corb. spec. +, om. KL vulg. &c.

2. *φονευετε και* MSS. edd. and vv., *φονευετε. και* WH.^{m} *φονειτε και* Oec.$^{txt.}$, *φθονειτε και* Eras. Calv. Bez. Ewald | *ουκ εχετε* ABKL + WH. Treg., *και ουκ εχετε* Sin. P + latt. syrr. copt. arm. aeth. Thl. Oec. Ti., *ουκ εχετε δε* rec. Here C comes to an end.

3. *δαπανησητε* Sin.^{3} AKLP (with full stop Treg. WH. with comma Ti.), *καταδαπανησητε* Sin.^{1}, *δαπανησετε* B (without following stop).

4. *μοιχαλιδες* Sin.^{1} AB 13 (joined with what precedes in Sin. B Ti.), *μοιχοι και μοιχαλιδες* Sin.^{3}KPL &c., *μοιχοι* latt. pesh. copt. aeth. arm. | after 1st *κοσμου* Sin. vulg. arm. aeth. pesh. add *τουτου* | *ἔχθρα* LP &c. syrr., *ἐχθρά* latt. aeth. | *του θεου εστιν* ABKLP &c. WH. Treg., *εστιν τῳ θεῳ* Sin. copt. Ti. | *ὅς εαν* BP + WH. Ti., *εαν* Sin.^{1}, *ὅς αν* Sin.^{3} AKL &c. Thl. Oec. Treg. | *ουν* om. L + | *εχθρος, εχθρα* Sin.^{1}

5. *κενως* om. corb. | *λεγει* joined with *προς φθονον* in A 4. 10. 11. 14. 15. 16. 21. 38. + arm. (question after *ἡμιν* WH. Treg. after *λεγει* with comma after *ἡμιν* Ti.),—*προς φθ. επ. τ. πν. ὁ κατ. εν ημιν, μ. δ. διδωσιν χαριν*—W. | *κατωκισεν* Sin. AB 101. 104, *κατωκησεν* KLP &c. latt. syrr. copt. Thl. Oec.

6. *διο λεγει—διδωσιν χαριν* om. LP + | *ὁ θεος* : 5. 16 + *κυριος* | *αντιτασσετε* B cf. ver. 7.

7. *αντιστητε δε* Sin. AB a b 13 + latt. copt., *αντιστητε* KLP &c. Th. Oec. | *φευξετε* B^{1}, *φευξεται* B.^{2}

8. *εγγισει* B WH., *εγγιει* Alf. Treg. Ti (without specifying MSS.).

Vulgate.

IV—1 Unde bella et lites inter uos (α)? nonne (β) ex concupiscentiis uestris quae militant in membris uestris? 2 Concupiscitis, et non habetis: occiditis et zelatis, et non potestis adipisci: litigatis et belligeratis, et (γ) non habetis propter quod non postulatis: 3 petitis et non accipietis (δ), eo quod male petatis, ut in concupiscentiis uestris insumatis. 4 Adulteri, nescitis quia amicitia huius mundi inimica est dei (ε)? Quicumque ergo uoluerit amicus esse saeculi huius, inimicus dei constituitur. 5 An (ζ) putatis quia inaniter scriptura dicat Ad inuidiam concupiscit spiritus qui habitat (η) in uobis? 6 Maiorem autem dat gratiam: propter quod dicit, Deus superbis resistit, humilibus autem dat gratiam. 7 Subditi igitur estote deo: resistite autem diabolo, et fugiet a uobis: 8 adpropinquate (θ) deo (ι). et adpropinquabit (κ) uobis, Emundate manus, peccatores, et purificate corda, duplices animo.

(α) F. *in uobis.*
(β) Spec. Aug. and F. insert *hinc.*
(γ) F. om *et.*
(δ) F. *accipitis.*
(ε) F. *deo.*
(ζ) F. *aut.*
(η) F. *inhabitat.*
(θ) Spec. Aug. *adpropriate*
(ι) F. *domino.*
(κ) MS. and F. *-uit.*

Corbey MS.

IV—1[a] Unde pugnae et unde rixae in uobis? Nonne hinc? ex uoluptatibus uestris quae militant in membris uestris? 2 Concupiscitis et non habetis[b]: occiditis: et zelatis, et non potestis impetrare: rixatis et pugnatis et non habetis, propter quod non petitis. 3 Petitis et non accipitis, propter hoc quod male petitis, ut in libidines uestras erogetis. 4 Fornicatores, nescitis quoniam amicitia saeculi inimica dei est? Quicumque ergo uoluerit amicus saeculi esse inimicus dei perseuerat. 5 Aut putatis quoniam dicit scriptura, Ad inuidiam conualescit spiritus qui habitat in uobis? 6 Maiorem autem dat gratiam. Propter quod dicit, Deus superbis resistit, humilibus[c] autem dat gratiam. 7 Subditi estote deo: resistite autem zabolo, et fugiet a uobis. 8 Accedite ad dominum, et ipse ad uos accedet.[d] Mundate manus peccatores, et sanctificate corda uestra duplices corde.

[a] In verses 1—5 the only stops in MS. are after *impetrare*, *fornicatores*, and *dei est*.
[b] MS. *habebitis.*
[c] MS. *humilis.*
[d] MS. *accedit.*

Speculum and Priscillian.

IV—1 (W. p. 525) Unde bella, unde rixae in uobis? nonne de uoluntatibus[1] uestris quae militant in membris uestris[2] et sunt uobis suauissima?

[IV—4 (Sch. pp. 57, 90, 94) omnis amicitia mundi inimica est dei.]

7 (W. p. 465) Humiliate uos Deo et resistite diabulo et fugiet[3] a uobis: 8 proximate Deo et proximabit uobis.[4]

[1] This word being sometimes spelt *uolumptas*, as in Corb. iii. 4, was easily confused with *uoluptas.*
[2] The words from *unde* to *uestris* are found in Prisc. pp. 63, 96.
[3] *Fugiet* omitted by all the MSS.
[4] *Adpropiate domino et adpropinquabit uobis* μ.

9 Ταλαιπωρήσατε καὶ πενθήσατε καὶ κλαύσατε· ὁ γέλως ὑμῶν εἰς πένθος μετατραπήτω καὶ ἡ χαρὰ εἰς κατήφειαν.

10 Ταπεινώθητε ἐνώπιον Κυρίου, καὶ ὑψώσει ὑμᾶς.

11 Μὴ καταλαλεῖτε ἀλλήλων, ἀδελφοί· ὁ καταλαλῶν ἀδελφοῦ ἢ κρίνων τὸν ἀδελφὸν αὐτοῦ καταλαλεῖ νόμου καὶ κρίνει νόμον· εἰ δὲ νόμον κρίνεις, οὐκ εἶ ποιητὴς νόμου ἀλλὰ κριτής.

12 Εἷς ἔστιν νομοθέτης καὶ κριτής, ὁ δυνάμενος σῶσαι καὶ ἀπολέσαι· σὺ δὲ τίς εἶ, ὁ κρίνων τὸν πλησίον;

13 Ἄγε νῦν οἱ λέγοντες Σήμερον ἢ αὔριον πορευσόμεθα εἰς τήνδε τὴν πόλιν καὶ ποιήσομεν ἐκεῖ ἐνιαυτὸν καὶ ἐμπορευσόμεθα καὶ κερδήσομεν·

14 (οἵτινες οὐκ ἐπίστασθε τὸ τῆς αὔριον· ποία γὰρ ἡ ζωὴ ὑμῶν; ἀτμὶς γάρ ἐστε ἡ πρὸς ὀλίγον φαινομένη, ἔπειτα καὶ ἀφανιζομένη·)

15 ἀντὶ τοῦ λέγειν ὑμᾶς Ἐὰν ὁ Κύριος θελήσῃ, καὶ ζήσομεν καὶ ποιήσομεν τοῦτο ἢ ἐκεῖνο.

9. *και κλαυσατε* BKLP &c. Treg. WH., *κλαυσατε* Sin. A Ti., om. pesh. + Aug. | *μετατραπητω* BP 69. a c Thl. WH. W., *μεταστραφητω* Sin. AKL &c. Oec. Ti. Treg. WH.[m]

10. *ταπεινωθητε* : Sin. adds *ουν* | *του* bef. *κυριου* D + | .

11. *αλληλων αδελφοι* : *αδελφοι μου αλληλων* A + | *η κρινων* Sin. ABP syrr. sah. copt. arm. +, *και κρ.* KL &c. | *ουκ ει ποιητης* : P + *ουκετι ει π.*, K + *ουκετι π. ει.*

12. *νομοθετης* BP WH. W., *ὁ νομ.* Sin. AKL &c. Ti. Treg. WH.[m] (*εἷς ἔστιν* WH., *εἷς ἐστιν ὁ* WH.[m]) | *και κριτης* Sin. ABP &c., om. KL + | *συ δε* : om. *δε* sah. syr. arm. + Oec. | *ὁ κρινων* Sin. ABP +, *ὃς κρινεις* KL &c. | *τον πλησιον* Sin. ABP latt. syrr. copt. arm., *τον ἑτερον* KL &c. [K + add *ὁτι ουκ εν ανθρωπῳ αλλ εν θεῳ τα διαβηματα ανθρωπου κατευθυνεται*].

13. *η αυριον* Sin. B 13. 27. 29. 40. 69 + latt. pesh. sah. copt. aeth. Jer., *και αυριον* AKLP &c. Cyr. Thl. Oec. | *πορευσομεθα* Sin. BP + latt. Cyr. Oec., *πορευσωμεθα* AKL + Thl. | *ποιησομεν* BP + WH. Ti., *-σωμεν* Sin. AKL + Treg | *εκει* om. A 13 Cyr. | *ενιαυτον* Sin. BP 36. latt. copt. Jer., *ενιαυτον ἑνα* AKL &c. syrr. arm. Cyr. Thl. Oec | *εμπορευσομεθα* Sin. ABP +, *-σωμεθα* KL + | *κερδησομεν* Sin. ABP, *-σωμεν* KL +.

14. *επιστασθε* : P. 68 *επιστανται* | *το της αυριον* Sin. KL &c. latt. pesh. sah. copt. Thl. Oec. Treg. Ti., *τα της αυριον* AP 7. 13. 69. 106 a c syr. Treg.[m] WH.[m], *της αυριον* B WH. W. | *ποια γαρ ἡ ζωη* Sin.[3] AKLP &c. Treg.[m] WH.[m], *ποια ἡ ζωη* Sin.[1] c syr. arm. aeth.[ro] (aeth.[pp] corb. *quae autem*) WH. W., *ποια ζωη* B | *ὑμων* : *ἡμων* 13. 69. + syr. Thl. | *ατμις γαρ εστε* B + syr. arm. aeth. Oec., *ατμις γαρ εστιν* L (L *ατμη*) corb. + Jer. Dam. Thl., *ατμις γαρ εσται* KP +, *ατμις εστιν* vulg. copt., *ατμις εσται* A (*ατμις εστε* WH.[m]), om. Sin. | *ἡ προς* Sin. AKL &c. Ti. WH.[m], *προς* BP WH. | *επειτα και* Sin. ABK corb., *επειτα δε* sah. Thl. Oec., *επειτα δε και* LP &c., *επειτα* 36. 38. 69 + copt. syr. [—*ατμις γαρ εστε...αφανιζομενη*—W.]

15. *θελησῃ* Sin. AKL latt. Cyr. &c. Treg. Ti. WH.[m] W., *θελῃ* BP a d 69 Treg.[m] WH. | *ζησομεν* Sin. ABP + (Ti. makes it a part of the protasis), *ζησωμεν* KL &c. Cyr. Thl. Oec. | *και ποιησομεν* Sin. ABP +, *ποιησομεν* vulg. sah. copt. pesh. arm. aeth. Cyr., *και ποιησωμεν* KL &c. Thl. Oec.

Vulgate.

9 Miseri estote et lugete et
plorate : risus uester in luctum
conuertatur et gaudium in
maerorem. 10 Humiliamini
in conspectu domini et exalt-
a*bi*t (*a*) uos. 11 Nolite detra-
here alterutrum (*β*), fratres
mei (*γ*). Qui detrahit fratri
aut qui iudicat fratrem suum,
detrahit legi et iudicat legem :
si autem iudicas legem, non
es (*δ*) factor legis sed iudex.
12 Unus est legislator et
iudex, qui potest perdere et
liberare : tu autem quis es
qui iudicas proximum ? 13
Ecce nunc qui dicitis Hodie
aut crastino ibimus in illam
ciuitatem et faciemus quidem
ibi annum et mercabimur et
lucrum faciemus, 14 qui
ignoratis quid sit (*ε*) in crastinum : quae enim est uita
uestra ? uapor est ad modicum parens et (*ζ*) deinceps
exterminabitur (*η*) : 15 pro eo
ut dicatis Si dominus uoluerit
et (*θ*) uixerimus, faciemus
hoc aut illud.

(*α*) MS. *-uit.* F. *-bit.*
(*β*) Spec. Aug. *de alterutro.*
(*γ*) F. om. *mei.*
(*δ*) F. *est.*
(*ε*) Spec. Aug. and F. *erit.*
(*ζ*) F. om. *et.*
(*η*) F. *exterminatur.*
(*θ*) Spec. Aug. and F. add *si.*

Corbey MS.

9 Lugete miseri et plorate :
risus uester in luctum conuertatur et gaudium in tris-
titiam. 10 Humiliate uos
ante dominum et exaltabit
uos. 11 Nolite retractare
de alterutro, fratres.[a] Qui
retractat de fratre, et iudicat fratrem suum, retractat
de lege et iudicat legem. Si
autem iudicas legem, non es
factor legis sed iudex. 12
Unus est legum positor et
iudex, qui potest saluare et
perdere : tu autem quis es
qui iudicas proximum ? 13
Iam nunc qui dicunt ; hodie
aut cras ibimus in illam ciuitatem et faciemus ibi annum
et negotia*bi*mur[b] et lucrum
faciemus : 14 qui ignoratis
crastinum. Quae autem uita
uestra ? momentum[c] enim
est, per modica uisibilis, deinde et exterminata. 15 Propter quod dicere uos oportet :
Si dominus uoluerit et uiue-
mus et faciemus hoc aut[d]
illud.

[a] MS. *frater.*
[b] MS. *negotiamur.*
[c] So MS. ; Dr. Hort suggests *flamentum* ; Dr. Sanday thinks the translator mistook ἀτμός for ἄτομος (*Stud. Bibl.* pp. 137, 140).
[d] So MS. ; *et* Sab.

Speculum and Priscillian.

10 (W. p. 448)
Humiliamini ante
conspectum Do-
mini et exaltabit
uos. 11 Fratres
nolite uobis[1] de-
trahere. Qui
enim[2] uituperat
fratrem suum et
iudicat, legem ui-
tuperat et iudicat.
Si legem iudicas,
iam non factor
legis sed iudex es.
12 Unus est enim
legum dator et iu-
dex qui potest sa-
luare et perdere.[3]
Tu autem quis es
qui iudicas proxi-
mum ?

[1] F. *uobis*, S. *uos*.
[2] S. *enim*, F. *autem*.
[3] Prisc. p. 66 (*deus*) *solus potens saluare perdere*.

16 Νῦν δὲ καυχᾶσθε ἐν ταῖς ἀλαζονίαις ὑμῶν· πᾶσα
καύχησις τοιαύτη πονηρά ἐστιν.
17 Εἰδότι οὖν καλὸν ποιεῖν καὶ μὴ ποιοῦντι ἁμαρτία
αὐτῷ ἐστίν.

ΚΕΦ. ε΄.

1 Ἄγε νῦν οἱ πλούσιοι, κλαύσατε ὀλολύζοντες ἐπὶ ταῖς
ταλαιπωρίαις ὑμῶν ταῖς ἐπερχομέναις.
2 Ὁ πλοῦτος ὑμῶν σέσηπεν, καὶ τὰ ἱμάτια ὑμῶν σητόβρωτα γέγονεν·
3 ὁ χρυσὸς ὑμῶν καὶ ὁ ἄργυρος κατίωται, καὶ ὁ ἰὸς
αὐτῶν εἰς μαρτύριον ὑμῖν ἔσται καὶ φάγεται τὰς σάρκας
ὑμῶν ὡς πῦρ· ἐθησαυρίσατε ἐν ἐσχάταις ἡμέραις.
4 Ἰδοὺ ὁ μισθὸς τῶν ἐργατῶν τῶν ἀμησάντων τὰς
χώρας ὑμῶν, ὁ ἀφυστερημένος ἀφ᾽ ὑμῶν, κράζει· καὶ αἱ
βοαὶ τῶν θερισάντων εἰς τὰ ὦτα Κυρίου Σαβαὼθ εἰσελήλυθαν.
5 Ἐτρυφήσατε ἐπὶ τῆς γῆς καὶ ἐσπαταλήσατε·
ἐθρέψατε τὰς καρδίας ὑμῶν ἐν ἡμέρᾳ σφαγῆς.
6 Κατεδικάσατε, ἐφονεύσατε τὸν δίκαιον· οὐκ ἀντιτάσσεται ὑμῖν.
7 Μακροθυμήσατε οὖν, ἀδελφοί, ἕως τῆς παρουσίας
τοῦ Κυρίου. Ἰδοὺ ὁ γεωργὸς ἐκδέχεται τὸν τίμιον
καρπὸν τῆς γῆς, μακροθυμῶν ἐπ᾽ αὐτῷ ἕως λάβῃ
πρόϊμον καὶ ὄψιμον.

16. καυχασθε: Sin. + κατακαυχ. | αλαζονιαις Sin. AB^{1}LP + WH. Ti., αλαζονειαις B^{3}K &c. Treg. W. | πασα: ἁπασα Sin.

V.—1. επερχομεναις ABKLP &c., επ. ὑμιν Sin. 5. 8. 25 vulg. pesh. copt. arm. aeth.

3. κατιωται bef. και ὁ αργυρος A 13 | φαγεται: φαινετε Sin.^{1} | ὡς πυρ Sin.^{1} BKL &c., ὁ ιος· ὡς πυρ Sin.^{3} AP+(full stop after ὡς πυρ Ti. Treg. WH.^{m}, bef. ὡς πυρ AL+pesh. Treg.^{m} WH.), aeth. spec. Thl. add ὅ after πυρ | εσχαταις ἡμεραις: A ἡμερ. εσχ.

4. αφυττερημενος Sin. B^1, απεστερημενος AB^{3}P &c., αποστερημενος KL | εισεληλυθαν BP, -λυθεν A+, εισεληλυθασιν Sin. KL &c.

5. om. και A 73. copt. | εν ἡμερᾳ Sin.^{1} BP 13. latt. +, εν ἡμεραις A, ὡς εν ἡμερᾳ Sin.^{3} KL &c.

6. δίκαιον· Ti., δίκαιον. WH. | ὑμιν. Ti. Treg., ὑμιν; WH.

7. επ αυτω: επ αυτον KL &c. Thl., om. vulg. arm. | ἑως λαβῃ ABKL+, ἑως αν λ. Sin. P. 13 &c. | προιμον Sin. AB^{1}P, πρωιμον B^{3}KL &c. | ὑετον bef. προιμον AKLP &c. pesh., om. B 31. vulg. sah. arm. WH. Treg. Ti., καρπον bef. προιμον Sin.^{3} (καρπον τον Sin.^{1}) corb. copt. +

VULGATE.

16 Nunc autem exultatis in superbiis uestris. Omnis exultatio talis maligna est. 17 Scienti igitur bonum facere et non facienti, peccatum est illi.

V—1 Agite (*a*) nunc, diuites, plorate ululantes in miseriis quae aduenient uobis. 2 Divitiae uestrae putrefactae sunt, et uestimenta uestra a tineis comesta sunt: 3 aurum et argentum vestrum aeruginavit, et aerugo eorum in testimonium uobis erit et manducabit carnes uestras sicut ignis. Thesaurizastis iram (*β*) in nouissimis diebus. 4 Ecce merces operariorum qui messuerunt regiones uestras, qui fraudatus est a uobis, clamat (*γ*), et clamor ipsorum in aures domini sabaoth introiuit. 5 Epulati estis super terram et in luxuriis enutristis corda uestra in diem (*δ*) occisionis. 6 Adduxistis (*ε*), occidistis iustum, et (*ζ*) non resistit (*η*) uobis. 7 Patientes igitur estote, fratres, usque ad aduentum domini. Ecce agricola expectat pretiosum fructum terrae, patienter ferens donec accipiat temporaneum (*θ*) et serotinum:

(*a*) Corrected in MS. fr. ***age***, which is read by Spec. Aug. and F.
(*β*) Spec. Aug. and F. omit ***iram***.
(*γ*) Spec. Aug. ***fraudati sunt... clamant.***
(*δ*) F. ***die.***
(*ε*) F. ***addixistis.***
(*ζ*) Spec. Aug. and F. om. *et*.
(*η*) F. ***restitit.***
(*θ*) F. ***temporiuum.***

CORBEY MS.

16 Nunc autem gloriamini in superbia uestra. Omnis gloria talis mala est. 17 Scientibus autem bonum facere et non facientibus, peccatum illis est. V—1 Iam nunc locupletes plorate ululantes in miseriis uestris aduenientibus. 2 Diuitiae uestrae putrierunt, res uestrae tiniauer*unt*.[a] 3 Aurum uestrum et argentum aeruginauit, et aerugo ipsorum erit uobis in testimonium et manducabit carnes uestras tanquam ignis. Thesaurizastis et in nouissimis diebus. 4 et ecce mercedes operariorum, qui arauerunt[b] in agris uestris, quod abnegastis, clamabunt, et uoces qui messi sunt ad aures domini sabaoth introiverunt. 5 Fruiti estis super terram et abusi estis: cibastis corda uestra in die occisionis. 6 Damnastis et occidistis iustum: non resistit uobis. 7 Patientes ergo estote fratres usque ad aduentum domini. Ecce agricola expectat honoratum fructum terrae, patiens in ipso usquequo accipiat matutinum et serotinum fructum.

[a] MS. ***tiniauer***, Sab. ***tinea uero.***
[b] 'The contrast between ploughmen and reapers makes the picture more complete...but no extant Greek MS. or other authority has ***ploughed.***'—Bp. Wordsworth, ***in loc.***

SPECULUM AND PRISCILLIAN.

V — 1 (W. p. 395) Age[1] nunc diuites plangite uos ululantes[2] super miserias uestras quae superueniunt 2 diuitiis uestris. Putruerunt et tiniauerunt uestes[3] uestrae. 3 Aurum et argentum vestrum quod reposuistis in nouissimis diebus aeruginauit et aerugo eorum in testimonium uobis erit et comedit[4] carnes uestras sicut ignis.

[V—1 (Sch. p. 17) age nunc diuites plangite ululantes super miserias uestras quae superueniunt diuitiis uestris; putruerunt et tiniauerunt uestes uestrae; aurum uestrum et argentum uestrum quod reposuistis in nouissimis diebus aeruginabit et aerugo eorum in testimonium uobis erit et comedet carnes uestras sicut ignis.]

5 (W. p. 639) Et uos deliciati estis super terram et luxoriati estis: creastis autem corda uestra in die[5] occisionis.

[1] ***age*** M. ***agite*** S.
[2] M + om. ***ululantes.***
[3] M + ***uestimenta uestra.***
[4] ***comedit*** S, ***comedet*** M +.
[5] M ***diem.***

8 Μακροθυμήσατε καὶ ὑμεῖς, στηρίξατε τὰς καρδίας
ὑμῶν, ὅτι ἡ παρουσία τοῦ Κυρίου ἤγγικεν.
9 Μὴ στενάζετε, ἀδελφοί, κατ' ἀλλήλων, ἵνα μὴ
κριθῆτε· ἰδοὺ ὁ κριτὴς πρὸ τῶν θυρῶν ἕστηκεν.
10 Ὑπόδειγμα λάβετε, ἀδελφοί, τῆς κακοπαθίας καὶ
τῆς μακροθυμίας τοὺς προφήτας οἳ ἐλάλησαν ἐν τῷ
ὀνόματι Κυρίου.
11 Ἰδοὺ μακαρίζομεν τοὺς ὑπομείναντας· τὴν ὑπομονὴν Ἰὼβ ἠκούσατε, καὶ τὸ τέλος Κυρίου εἴδετε, ὅτι
πολύσπλαγχνός ἐστιν ὁ Κύριος καὶ οἰκτίρμων.
12 Πρὸ πάντων δὲ, ἀδελφοί μου, μὴ ὀμνύετε, μήτε τὸν
οὐρανὸν μήτε τὴν γῆν μήτε ἄλλον τινὰ ὅρκον· ἤτω δὲ
ὑμῶν τὸ ναὶ ναί, καὶ τὸ οὒ οὔ· ἵνα μὴ ὑπὸ κρίσιν πέσητε.
13 Κακοπαθεῖ τις ἐν ὑμῖν; προσευχέσθω· εὐθυμεῖ τις;
ψαλλέτω.
14 Ἀσθενεῖ τις ἐν ὑμῖν; προσκαλεσάσθω τοὺς πρεσβυτέρους τῆς ἐκκλησίας, καὶ προσευξάσθωσαν ἐπ' αὐτὸν
ἀλείψαντες ἐλαίῳ ἐν τῷ ὀνόματι·
15 καὶ ἡ εὐχὴ τῆς πίστεως σώσει τὸν κάμνοντα, καὶ
ἐγερεῖ αὐτὸν ὁ Κύριος· κἂν ἁμαρτίας ᾖ πεποιηκώς,
ἀφεθήσεται αὐτῷ.
16 Ἐξομολογεῖσθε οὖν ἀλλήλοις τὰς ἁμαρτίας, καὶ

8. *μακροθυμησατε* ABKP &c., *μακρ. ουν* Sin. L+.

9. *αδελφοι*: (A 13+add *μου*) bef. *κατ αλληλων* ABP 5. 13. 69. + Treg. WH., after *κατ αλλ.* Sin. L. syrr. &c. Thl. Oec. Ti., om. K 15. 16 + | *κριθητε*: Oec. + *κατακριθητε*.

10. *λαβετε*: om. A 13 aeth. (adding *εχετε* after *μακροθυμιας* with Sin.[3] +) | *αδελφοι* ABP+, *αδ. μου* Sin. KL &c. | *κακοπαθιας* B[1]P WH., *κακοπαθειας* AB[3]L &c. Treg. Ti., *καλοκαγαθιας* Sin. | *εν τῳ ονοματι* BP+, *εν ονοματι* Sin. Chr., *τῳ ονοματι* AKL &c.

11. *ὑπομειναντας* Sin. ABP latt. syrr. +, *υπομενοντας* KL copt. arm. aeth. Thl. Oec. &c. | *ειδετε* Sin. B[1]K &c., *ιδετε* AB[3] LP + | *πολυσπλαγχνος*: Thl. + *πολυευσπλαγχνος* | *ὁ κυριος* Sin. AP+Treg. Ti. WH. *κυριος* B WH.[m] W., om. KL+.

12. *προ παντων δε* Sin.[3] ABLP &c., *π. παντων ουν* Sin.[1], *π. παντων* K + | ins. *ὁ λογος* bef. *ὑμων* (from Matt. v. 37) Sin.[1] copt. aeth + | *και*: om. latt. copt. | *τὸ Ναί ναὶ καὶ τὸ Οὔ οὔ*, WH. *τὸ ναὶ ναὶ, καὶ τὸ οὒ οὔ*, Ti. | *ὑπο κρισιν* Sin. AB 8. 13. 25. 27. 29. 36. latt. syrr. copt. aeth., *εις ὑποκρισιν* KLP &c.

14. *επ αυτον*: Sin.[1] *επ αυτους* | *αλειψαντες* BP a corb. Dam. WH. Ti., *αλ. αυτον* Sin. AKL &c. Treg. | *ονοματι του κυριου* Sin. KLP &c. Treg. Ti. W., *ον. κυριου* A+Orig. Treg.[m], *ον. ιῡ χῡ* 6, *ον. τ. κυριου ιῡ* 7[lect], *ονοματι* B (WH. bracket *του κυριου*).

15. *αφεθησεται*: P + *αφεθησονται*.

16. *ουν* Sin. ABKP + vulg. copt. syr., *δε* 107 pesh., om. L &c. corb. arm. aeth. | *τας ἁμαρτιας* Sin. ABP 5. 6. 13. 43. 65. 73. a c d syr. latt. Eus. Ephr. Dam.

VULGATE.

8 patientes estote et uos (*a*),
confirmate corda uestra, quoniam aduentus domini adpro-
pinqua*u*it (β). 9 Nolite in-
gemiscere, fratres, in alterutrum, ut non iudicemini : ecce
iudex ad (γ) ianuam adsistit.
10 Exemplum accipite, fratres, laboris et patientiae
per (δ) prophetas qui locuti
sunt in nomine domini. 11
Ecce beatificamus qui sustinuerunt : sufferentiam Iob audistis, et finem domini vidistis,
quoniam misericors est dominus et miserator. 12 Ante
omnia autem, fratres mei,
nolite iurare, neque per caelum neque per terram neque
aliud quodcumque iuramen-
tum. Sit autem sermo
uester (ε) Est est, Non non,
ut non sub iudicio decidatis.
13 Tristatur aliquis uestrum ?
oret aequo animo et psallat.
14 Infirmatur quis in (ζ)
uobis ? inducat presbyteros
ecclesiae, et orent super eum,
ungentes eum oleo in nomine
domini. 15 Et oratio fidei
saluabit infirmum, et alle-
uabit eum dominus ; et si in
peccatis sit, dimittentur (η)
ei. 16 Confitemini ergo alterutrum peccata uestra, et

(α) F. adds *et*.
(β) MS. *adpropinquabit* with F.
(γ) F. *ante*.
(δ) F. om. *per*.
(ε) Spec. Aug. *uestrum*, omitting *sermo*.
(ζ) F. *aliquis ex*.
(η) F. *remittetur*.

CORBEY MS.

8 Et uos patientes estote,
confortate praecordia uestra,
quoniam aduentus domini
adpropiauit. 9 Nolite in-
gemiscere fratres in alterutrum, ne in iudicium in-
cidatis. Ecce iudex ante
ianuam stat. 10 Accipite
experimentum fratres de
malis passionibus et de patientia prophetas qui locuti sunt in nomine domini.
11 Ecce beatos dicimus qui
sustinuerunt. Sufferentiam
Iob audistis et finem domini
uidistis, quoniam uisceraliter
dominus misericors est. 12
Ante omnia autem, fratres
mei, nolite iurare neque per
caelum neque per terram, nec
alterutrum iuramentum. Sit
autem apud uos, Est est, Non
est non est ; ne in iudicium
incidatis. 13 Anxiat aliquis
ex uobis [a] ? oret : hilaris
est ? psalmum dicat. 14 Et in-
firm*us* [b] est aliquis in uobis ?
uocet presbyteros, et orent
super ipsum ungentes oleo in
nomine domini : 15 et oratio
in fide saluabit laborantem,
et suscitabit [c] illum dominus,
et si peccata fecit, remittun-
tur ei. 16 Confitemini alterutrum peccata uestra et

[a] So MS. ; *ex uobis aliquis*, Sab.
[b] MS. *infirmis*.
[c] MS. *-uit*.

SPECULUM AND PRISCILLIAN.

εὔχεσθε ὑπὲρ ἀλλήλων, ὅπως ἰαθῆτε. Πολὺ ἰσχύει δέησις
δικαίου ἐνεργουμένη.
17 Ἠλείας ἄνθρωπος ἦν ὁμοιοπαθὴς ἡμῖν, καὶ προσευχῇ προσηύξατο τοῦ μὴ βρέξαι, καὶ οὐκ ἔβρεξεν ἐπὶ
τῆς γῆς ἐνιαυτοὺς τρεῖς καὶ μῆνας ἕξ·
18 καὶ πάλιν προσηύξατο, καὶ ὁ οὐρανὸς ὑετὸν
ἔδωκεν καὶ ἡ γῆ ἐβλάστησεν τὸν καρπὸν αὐτῆς.
19 Ἀδελφοί μου, ἐάν τις ἐν ὑμῖν πλανηθῇ ἀπὸ τῆς
ἀληθείας καὶ ἐπιστρέψῃ τις αὐτόν,
20 γινωσκέτε ὅτι ὁ ἐπιστρέψας ἁμαρτωλὸν ἐκ πλάνης
ὁδοῦ αὐτοῦ σώσει ψυχὴν ἐκ θανάτου καὶ καλύψει
πλῆθος ἁμαρτιῶν.

WH. Treg. Ti. W., *τα παραπτωματα* KL &c. pesh. Orig. Aug. Thl. Oec., add *ὑμων* L. 69. a c latt. syrr. copt. aeth. | *ευχεσθε* Sin. KLP &c. Thl. Oec, Treg. Ti. WH.^{m}, *προσευχεσθε* AB 73 Ephr. Treg.^{m} WH. (altered to suit *προσευχ.* in ver. 17 ?).

17. *ηλειας* B^1 (and Sin. B in Matt. xvii. 3, 4, 10, 11, 12, Luke iv. 26, ix. 8. Mk. viii. 28), *ηλιας* Sin. AB^3KLP &c.

18. *ὑετον εδωκεν* BKLP &c. Treg.^{m} WH., *εδωκεν ὑετον* A 13. 73. latt. + Treg. Ti. WH.^{m}, *εδ. τον ὑετον* Sin.

19. *αδελφοι μου* Sin. ABKP syrr. latt. +, *αδελφοι* L &c. Did. Oec. | *απο της αληθειας* ABKLP &c. latt. syr. aeth., *απο της ὁδου της αληθειας* Sin. pesh. copt. +.

20. *γινωσκετε ὁτι* B 31 c syr. aeth. Treg.^{m} WH., *γινωσκετω ὁτι* Sin. AKLP &c. Treg. Ti.. WH.^{m} om. corb. sah. | *σωσει* : corb. Orig. *σωζει*, fuld. *saluauit* | *ψυχην αυτου εκ θανατου* Sin. P. 5. 7. 8. 13. 15. 36 syrr. copt. aeth. Ti. WH. W., *την ψ. α. ε. θ.* A 73. arm., *ψυχην εκ θανατου* KL &c. sah. Orig. Thl. Oec. Treg., *ψ. εκ θανατου αυτου* B corb. aeth. W. WH.^{m} | *καλυψει* : vulg. Orig. Dam. *καλυπτει*.

Subscription.—K with most MSS. has none, B *ιακωβου*, Sin. *επιστολη ιακωβου*, A 40. 67. 177 *ιακωβου επιστολη*, P 63 *ιακωβου αποστολου επιστολη καθολικη*, L *τελος του ἁγιου αποστολου ιακωβου επιστολη καθολικη*, 38 *τελος της επιστολης του ἁγιου αποστολου ιακωβου του αδελφοθεου*.

VULGATE.

orate pro inuicem, ut salue-
mini : multum enim ualet
deprecatio iusti adsidua. 17
Helias homo erat similis
nobis passibilis, et oratione
orauit ut non plueret super
terram, et non pluit annos
tres et menses sex ; 18 et
rursus orauit, et caelum dedit
pluuiam et terra dedit fructum suum. 19 Fratres mei,
si quis ex uobis errauerit
a ueritate et conuerterit quis
eum, 20 scire debet quo-
niam qui conuerti fecerit
peccatorem ab errore uiae (*a*)
suae, saluabit (*β*) animam
eius a morte et cooperit (*γ*)
multitudinem peccatorum.—
EXPLICIT EPISTULA JACOBI
APOSTOLI.

(*a*) MS. *uitae.*
(*β*) F. *saluauit.*
(*γ*) Spec. Aug. and F. *operit.*

CORBEY MS.

orate pro alterutro ut remit-
tatur uobis : multum potest
petitio iusti frequens. 17
Helias homo erat similis nobis, et oratione orauit ut non
plueret et non pluit in terra
annis tribus et mensibus sex.
18 Sed iterum orauit, et caelum dedit pluui*am*,[a] et terra
germinauit fructum suum. 19
Fratres mei si quis ex uobis
errauerit a ueritate et aliquis
eum reuocauerit ; 20 qui
reuocauerit peccatorem de erroris uia, saluat animam de
morte sua et operiet multitudinem peccati. — EXPLICIT
EPISTOLA JACOBI FILII ZAE-
BEDEI.

[a] MS. *pluuium.*

SPECULUM AND PRISCILLIAN.

NOTES

Ver. 1. **Ἰάκωβος.**] See Introduction, ch. I.

Θεοῦ καὶ Κυρίου Ἰησοῦ Χριστοῦ δοῦλος.] This epistle and that of St. Jude are the only ones in which we find the writer announcing himself as simply δοῦλος. St. Paul joins ἀπόστολος with δοῦλος in Rom. i. 1, Tit. i. 1; more commonly he styles himself simply ἀπόστολος Ἰ. Χ., as in 1 Cor. i. 1, 2 Cor. i. 1, Gal. i. 1 (here διὰ Ἰ. Χ.), Eph. i. 1, Col. i. 1, and in both epistles to Timothy; in Philemon i. 1 he is δέσμιος Χ. Ἰ.; in his earliest epistles (1 Th. i. 1, 2 Th. i. 1), where he joins Silvanus and Timothy with himself, he makes use of no distinctive title; in Phil. i. 1 he speaks of himself and Timothy as δοῦλοι Χ. Ἰ. St. Peter styles himself ἀπόστολος Ἰ. Χ. in his 1st, δοῦλος καὶ ἀπ. Ἰ. Χ. in his 2nd epistle. St. John's 1st epistle is anonymous; in the 2nd and 3rd he calls himself ὁ πρεσβύτερος. So far as it goes, this peculiarity of the epistles of the two brothers, James and Jude, is (1) in favour of the view that neither of them was included in the number of the Twelve; (2) it shows that the writer of this epistle was so well known that it was unnecessary alike for him and for his brother to add any special title to distinguish him from others who bore the same name; (3) if we hold, as there seems every reason for doing, that the writer is the James whom St. Paul speaks of as the brother of the Lord, we find here an example of the refusal 'to know Christ after the flesh' which appears in ii. 1; the same willingness to put himself on a level with others which appears in iii. 1, 2. The phrase δοῦλος Θεοῦ is used of Moses (Dan. ix. 11, Mal. iv. 4), who is also called θεράπων (Ex. xiv. 31, Numb. xii. 7, Jos. i. 2) and παῖς (Jos. xi. 12, xii. 6). Δοῦλος is also used generally of the prophets (Jer. vii. 25, Dan. ix. 10, Apoc. x. 7, &c.).

The combination Θ. κ. Κ. Ἰ. Χ. is found in almost every epistle. That Θεοῦ is used here for the Father is evident from 2 Pet. i. 2 ἐν ἐπιγνώσει τοῦ Θεοῦ καὶ Ἰησοῦ τοῦ Κυρίου ἡμῶν. For the absence of the article see Essay on Grammar.

ταῖς δώδεκα φυλαῖς.] The chosen people are still regarded as constituting twelve tribes by the writers of the N.T. So St. Paul (Acts xxvi. 7) speaks of τὸ δωδεκάφυλον ἡμῶν waiting for the promised kingdom; and in Matt. xix. 28 it is said that the twelve apostles shall hereafter 'sit on twelve thrones judging the twelve tribes of Israel': comp. also Rev. vii. 4 foll. The prophets looked forward to the reunion of Israel and Judah (Isa. xi. 12, 13, Jerem. iii. 18), and under Hezekiah and Josiah many of the remnant of the Ten Tribes came up to worship at Jerusalem (2 Chr. xxix. 24, xxx. 1, xxxiv. 9). So twelve goats were offered as a sin-offering for the twelve tribes at the dedication of the second Temple (Ezra vi. 17, 1 Esdras vii. 8, Spitta compares Sibyll. ii. 170 ἡνίκα δωδεκάφυλος ἀπ' ἀντολίης λαὸς ἥξει). There would be no reason for keeping up the old feud between the tribes in the captivity; and while it is probable that some of those who were carried away by Shalmanezer may have adopted the manners and religion of the neighbouring heathen, many would no doubt attach themselves to the later captives from Judah, and either return with the minority of these to Judaea, or continue to live in Assyria with the majority. The book Tobit professes to give the story of a religious captive of the tribe of Naphtali; and Anna (Luke ii. 36) is an instance of a resident in Judah belonging to the tribe of Asher. See *D. of B.* under *Captivities.* This form of address is one among many indications of an early date for the epistle, the Christian Jews not being yet definitely marked off from their unbelieving countrymen. [Hermes (*Sim.* ix. 17) however includes all the nations under heaven in his Twelve Tribes. C.T.]

ἐν τῇ διασπορᾷ.] See Introduction on the readers to whom the epistle is addressed, and cf. 1 Pet. i. 1 ἐκλεκτοῖς παρεπιδήμοις διασπορᾶς Πόντου, Γαλατίας, Καππαδοκίας, Ἀσίας καὶ Βιθυνίας (if St. James, as is probable, is here addressing the Jews of the eastern dispersion, this may have suggested to St. Peter his letter to the western dispersion), John vii. 35 εἰς τὴν διασπορὰν τῶν Ἑλλήνων, Deut. xxviii. 25 ἔσῃ διασπορὰ ἐν πάσαις βασιλείαις τῆς γῆς, *ib.* xxx. 4, Ps. cxlvii. 2 τὰς διασπορὰς τοῦ Ἰσραὴλ ἐπισυνάξει, Isa. xlix. 6, Jer. xv. 7, Neh. i. 9, Tobit xiii. 3, Judith v. 19 ἐπιστρέψαντες ἐπὶ τὸν Θεὸν αὐτῶν ἀνέβησαν ἐκ τῆς διασπορᾶς οὗ διεσπάρησαν, 2 Macc. i. 27; and Westcott, art. on *Dispersion* in *D of B.*

χαίρειν.] χαῖρε is the regular form of Greek salutation, as in Luke i. 28, 2 John 10; like *salve* in Latin. In letters it takes the form χαίρειν (λέγει), like *salutem* (*dicit*). Horace (*Ep.* i. 8. 1 and 15) uses the more literal translation *gaudere et bene rem gerere* (χαίρειν καὶ εὖ πράττειν). It is said to have been first used by Cleon in sending news of the capture of Pylos (Luc. *Laps. inter Salut.* 3, Suidas *s.v.*). Aristophanes in his latest play speaks of it as already old-fashioned, *Plut.* 322 χαίρειν μὲν ὑμᾶς ἐστιν, ἄνδρες δημόται, ἀρχαῖον ἤδη προσαγορεύειν καὶ σαπρόν· ἀσπάζομαι δ'. Plato is said to have preferred the phrase εὖ πράττειν in writing to his intimates (Pl. *Ep.* 3, p. 315). The Pythagoreans used ὑγιαίνειν (see Menage on Diog. L. iii. 61). In the N.T. the epistolary χαίρειν is only found here and in Acts xxiii. 26 (the letter of Lysias to Felix) and xv. 23 (the letter, probably drawn up by St. James, from the Church at Jerusalem to the brethren in Antioch, Syria and Cilicia). It occurs also in the letters of Alexander and Demetrius cited in 1 Macc. x. 18, 25. In 2 Macc. ix. 19 we find the above forms of salutation combined, τοῖς χρηστοῖς Ἰουδαίοις τοῖς πολίταις πολλὰ χαίρειν καὶ ὑγιαίνειν καὶ εὖ πράττειν βασιλεὺς καὶ στρατηγὸς Ἀντίοχος. The ancient Hebrew salutation was 'Peace' (which the Peshitto gives here), as in Gen. xliii. 23, and (epistolary) in Ezra iv. 17, v. 7. In 2 Macc. i. 1 we have the Greek and Hebrew joined, χαίρειν, καὶ εἰρήνην ἀγαθήν. As a spoken salutation we have examples of εἰρήνη in Luke x. 5, xxiv. 36 (cf. Jas. ii. 16): the epistolary use is found in 3 John 15 εἰρήνη σοι, 1 Pet. v. 14. In the other epistles these simple greetings are further developed, as χάρις καὶ εἰρήνη (Rom. i. 7, 1 Cor. i. 3, 2 Cor. i. 2, Gal. i. 3, Eph. i. 2, Phil. i. 2, Col. i. 2, 1 and 2 Thess., Philemon 3, Apoc. i. 4, 1 Pet. i. 2, 2 Pet. i. 2); in the pastoral epistles and in 2 John we have the fuller form χάρις ἔλεος εἰρήνη; Jude has ἔλεος καὶ εἰρήνη καὶ ἀγάπη. There is no preliminary salutation in Hebrews, 1 John, 3 John. We meet with the final salutation ἡ χάρις τοῦ Κυρίου Ἰ. Χ. μεθ' ὑμῶν in many of the epistles. Another final salutation is ἔρρωσθε = Lat. *valete* (Acts xv. 29): see Heisen *Nov. Hyp.* pp. 95–144, The use of the form χαίρειν naturally suggests the identity of the writer of this epistle with the writer of the circular in the Acts, and is at any rate a strong argument against the view that our epistle was written towards the close of the first century. Is it conceivable that, after the introduction of the fuller Christian salutation, any one professing to write in the name of the most honoured member of the church at Jerusalem would have fallen back on the comparatively cold and formal χαίρειν?

2. **πᾶσαν.**] This does not mean strictly totality of joy, as though there were no joy besides, but merely denotes a superior degree to μεγάλην or πολλήν. Possibly the expression originated in an attraction from πᾶν εἶναι χαράν, and is thus equivalent to 'entire, unmixed joy.' Cf. Phil. ii. 29 μετὰ πάσης χαρᾶς. 1 Pet. ii. 18 ἐν παντὶ φόβῳ, 1 Tim. ii. 2 ἐν πάσῃ εὐσεβείᾳ, *ib.* ii. 11 ἐν πάσῃ ὑποταγῇ, Tit. ii. 10, 15, iii. 2, Acts xvii. 11 ἐδέξαντο τὸν λόγον μετὰ πάσης προθυμίας, *ib.* xxiii. 1 πάσῃ συνειδήσει ἀγαθῇ. The same use is found in classical authors, e.g. Soph. *Phil.* 618 ὦ πῦρ σὺ καὶ πᾶν δεῖμα, *ib. El.* 293, Eur. *Med.* 453 πᾶν κέρδος ἡγοῦ ζημιουμένη φυγῇ, Epict. 3. 5 χάριν σοι ἔχω πᾶσαν, and in Latin, e.g. Cic. *N.D.* ii. 56 *omnis ordo*, where other instances are quoted in my note. The language is more measured in 1 Pet. i. 6, and Heb. xii. 11, πᾶσα μὲν παιδεία πρὸς μὲν τὸ παρὸν οὐ δοκεῖ χαρᾶς εἶναι ἀλλὰ λύπης, ὕστερον δὲ καρπὸν εἰρηνικὸν τοῖς δι' αὐτῆς γεγυμνασμένοις ἀποδίδωσιν δικαιοσύνης. But neither does St. James say that trial *is* all joy; he bids us *count* it joy, that is, look at it from the bright side, as capable of being turned to our highest good.

χαρὰν ἡγήσασθε.] The word χαρά echoes the preceding χαίρειν according to the wont of the writer. See ὑπομονή, τέλειον, λειπόμενοι just below, and the Essay on Grammar and Style. Χαρά is here ground of rejoicing, as in Luke ii. 10. The salutation might sound like a mockery to those who were suffering under various trials, but St. James proceeds to show that these very trials are a ground for joy. For the same realization of what was often a mere phrase of courtesy cf. Eur.

Hec. 426 ΠΟΛ. χαῖρ' ὦ τεκοῦσα, χαῖρε Κασσάνδρα τέ μοι. ʽΕΚ. χαίρουσιν ἄλλοι, μητρὶ δ' οὐκ ἔστιν τόδε, Tobit. v. 9 (*varia lectio*) ἐχαιρέτισεν αὐτὸν πρῶτος καὶ εἶπεν αὐτῷ, χαίρειν σοὶ καὶ πολλὰ γένοιτο· καὶ ἀποκριθεὶς Τ. εἶπεν αὐτῷ, τί μοι ἔτι ὑπάρχει χαίρειν; Plato *Ep.* 8 beginning. For the thought cf. Matt. v. 10–15, 1 Pet. iv. 12–14 μὴ ξενίζεσθε (at your trials) ὡς ξένου ὑμῖν συμβαίνοντος, it is not strange or foreign to your Christian life, but a part of your training for glory, therefore χαίρετε, so 1 Thess. iii. 3 οἴδατε ὅτι εἰς τοῦτο κείμεθα, Acts v. 4, Judith viii. 25.

ἡγήσασθε.] We might have expected the present tense, like ἡγεῖσθε in 2 Pet. iii. 15 and below λαλεῖτε ii. 12, as the aorist is used rather of a single act than of a continuous state; but it is here employed in reference to each separate temptation as it occurs, perhaps also as more urgent, like μακροθυμήσατε in v. 7. [The aorist is used as the authoritative imperative in 2 Tim. i. 8, 14, ii. 3, 15, &c. A.]: cf. Winer tr. p. 393 foll.

ἀδελφοί μου.] In the O.T. the word is used of Israelites generally (Lev. xxv. 46, Deut. xv. 3), denoting, as Philo says (*Carit.* M.2 p. 388), οὐ μόνον τὸν ἐκ τῶν αὐτῶν φύντα γονέων ἀλλὰ καὶ ὃς ἂν ἀστὸς ἢ ὁμόφυλος ᾖ: so also in N.T. (Acts ii. 29, Rom. ix. 3); but here it is more commonly used of the spiritual Israel (Matt. xxiii. 8, xxv. 40, Acts ix. 30, 1 Cor. v. 11), equivalent to the later 'Christians' (see below v. 9 and ii. 15). St. James frequently makes use of this appealing address (ii. 1, 14, iii. 1, 10, 12, v. 12, 19), sometimes without μου (iv. 11, v. 7, 9, 10), sometimes with the addition of ἀγαπητοί (i. 16, 19, ii. 5). The simple ἀδελφοί is the most frequent in St. Paul's epistles. In the two epistles of St. Peter and the other catholic epistles ἀγαπητοί is often used by itself.

πειρασμοῖς.] Here used of outward trial, as in the parallel passage in 1 Pet. i. 6 ἐν ᾧ ἀγαλλιᾶσθε, ὀλίγον ἄρτι εἰ δέον λυπηθέντες ἐν ποικίλοις πειρασμοῖς, ἵνα τὸ δοκίμιον ὑμῶν τῆς πίστεως...εὑρεθῇ εἰς ἔπαινον κ.τ.λ. We have examples of such trials in the persecutions which followed the martyrdom of Stephen and of James, and in St. Paul's description of his own sufferings (1 Cor. iv. 9 foll., 2 Cor. xi. 23 foll.). There may also be an allusion to the massacre of the Jews of the eastern Diaspora some ten years before the writing of the Epistle. The inner trial (temptation) is expressed below (v. 13) by the verb πειράζω. Dr. Hatch (*Essays in Biblical Greek*, p. 71 foll.) seems to me to restrict the sense too much to one kind of trial, viz. affliction. Riches, as we see from ver. 10 and 1 Tim. vi. 9, are as much a πειρασμός as poverty; and the temptation of Christ in the wilderness (Luke iv. 13) was not an appeal to fear but rather to hope and desire. See Comment on Temptation.

περιπέσητε.] The word brings out the externality of the temptation in opposition to the internal temptation arising from ἰδία ἐπιθυμία (v. 14). Cf. Luke x. 30 λησταῖς περιέπεσεν, 2 Macc. x. περιπεσεῖν κακοῖς, Plato *Legg.* ix. 877 C. π. συμφοραῖς, M. Ant. ii. 11 τοῖς μὲν κατ' ἀλήθειαν κακοῖς ἵνα μὴ περιπίπτῃ ὁ ἄνθρωπος, ἐπ' αὐτῷ τὸ πᾶν ἔθεντο, *Acta Johannis* Zahn p. 244 n. ἐὰν περιπέσῃς πειρασμοῖς μὴ πτοηθήσῃ. Heisen gives many examples.

ποικίλοις.] Also used of diseases and lusts (2 Tim. iii. 6, Matt. iv. 24), to which answers ποικίλη χάρις Θεοῦ (1 Pet. iv. 10). It is a common word in Philo. For examples of various trials see 2 Cor. vi. 4, 5, xi. 23 foll. Spitta cites 3 Macc. ii. 6 ποικίλαις καὶ πολλαῖς δοκιμάσας τιμωρίαις, 4 Macc. xv. 8, 21, xvi. 3, xvii. 7, xviii. 21.

3. **γινώσκοντες.**] In iii. 1, as in Rom. v. 3, we have the more usual εἰδότες, but γιν. is found Rom. vi. 6, Heb. x. 34, 2 Pet. i. 20, *ib.* iii. 3. Bishop Lightfoot thus distinguishes them (Gal. iv. 9): "whilst οἶδα, 'I know,' refers to the knowledge of facts absolutely, γινώσκω, 'I recognize,' being relative, gives prominence either to the attainment or the manifestation of knowledge." It may be questioned however whether fine distinctions of this sort were always observed in the Hellenistic use.

τὸ δοκίμιον ὑμῶν τῆς πίστεως.] On the order of the words, which is the same in 1 Pet. i. 6 quoted above, see below ver. 5 and the Essay on Grammar.[1] Δοκίμιον is here the instrument or means by which a man is tested (δοκιμάζεται) and proved (δόκιμος), as in Prov. xxvii. 21 δοκίμιον ἀργυρίῳ καὶ χρυσῷ πύρωσις, ἀνὴρ δὲ δοκιμάζεται διὰ στόματος ἐγκωμιαζόντων αὐτόν, Herodian ii. 10. 12 δοκίμιον στρατιωτῶν κάματος (Wetst.), Plut. *Mor.* p. 230 ἠρώτησεν εἰ δοκίμιον ἔχει τίνι τρόπῳ πειράζεται ὁ πολύφιλος...ἀτυχίᾳ, εἶπεν. The word δοκιμή is used in the same sense by St. Paul 2 Cor. viii. 2 ἐν πολλῇ δοκιμῇ θλίψεως ἡ περισσεία τῆς χαρᾶς αὐτῶν κ.τ.λ., *ib.* xiii. 3, but in Rom. v. 4 it is used of the result of endurance, tried and proved virtue, much as δοκίμιον in 1 Pet. i. 6. It is assumed here that πειρασμός is the δοκίμιον πίστεως. Compare with the whole passage Sir. ii. 1 foll, εἰ προσέρχῃ δουλεύειν Κυρίῳ ἑτοίμασον τὴν ψυχήν σου εἰς πειρασμόν· εὔθυνον τὴν καρδίαν σου καὶ καρτέρησον...πᾶν ὃ ἐὰν ἐπαχθῇ σοι δέξαι καὶ ἐν ἀλλάγμασι ταπεινώσεώς σου μακροθύμησον· ὅτι ἐν πυρὶ δοκιμάζεται χρυσὸς καὶ ἄνθρωποι δεκτοὶ ἐν καμίνῳ ταπεινώσεως. πίστευσον αὐτῷ καὶ ἀντιλήψεταί σου, Luke viii, 13 οὗτοι ῥίζαν οὐκ ἔχουσιν οἳ πρὸς καιρὸν πιστεύουσιν καὶ ἐν καιρῷ πειρασμοῦ ἀφίστανται...τὸ δὲ ἐν τῇ καλῇ γῇ οὗτοι, οἵτινες...τὸν λόγον κατέχουσιν καὶ καρποφοροῦσιν ἐν ὑπομονῇ. Seneca insists much on the use of adversity, *Prov.* 2. 2 *omnia adversa exercitationes putet vir fortis*; ib. 6 *patrium deus habet adversus bonos viros animum et illos fortiter amat; 'operibus,' inquit, 'doloribus, damnis exagitentur, ut verum colligant robur.'* Just below (3. 3) he quotes from Demetrius *nihil mihi videtur infelicius eo cui nihil umquam evenit adversi, non licuit enim se experiri.* There is a reminiscence of the text in Hermas *Vis.* iv. 3 ὥσπερ τὸ χρυσίον δοκιμάζεται...οὕτως καὶ ὑμεῖς δοκιμάζεσθε οἱ κατοικοῦντες ἐν αὐτῷ (τῷ κόσμῳ). οἱ οὖν μείναντες καὶ πυρωθέντες ὑπ' αὐτοῦ καθαρισθήσεσθε.

τῆς πίστεως.] That St. James no less than St. Paul regarded faith as the very foundation of religion is evident from this verse as well as from verse 6, ii. 1, v. 15. See Comment on Faith below.

κατεργάζεται.] An emphatic form of ἐργάζεται, 'works out,' often found in the epistle to the Romans; cf. especially v. 3 ἡ θλίψις ὑπομονὴν

[1] Bp. J. Wordsworth (*Stud. Bibl.* p. 137) thinks τῆς πίστεως may possibly be a gloss from St. Peter, rightly omitted by Corb.

κατεργάζεται, and see below on κατακαυχᾶσθε iii. 14. The simple verb is similarly used below i. 20, ii. 9 ἁμαρτίαν ἐργάζεσθε.[1]

ὑπομονήν.] Used (1) for the act of endurance (2 Cor. i. 6, vi. 4), and (2) for the temper of endurance, as here and in the parallel passages Rom. v. 3 and 2 Thess. i. 4. The verb is found below, ver. 12, Matt. xxiv. 13 ὁ ὑπομείνας εἰς τέλος σωθήσεται, Rom. xii. 12 τῇ ἐλπίδι χαίροντες, τῇ θλίψει ὑπομένοντες, τῇ προσευχῇ προσκαρτεροῦντες (where we find joy, endurance and prayer joined as in the text), Didaché xvi. 5 οἱ ὑπομείναντες ἐν τῇ πίστει αὐτῶν σωθήσονται. It corresponds generally to the Aristotelian καρτερία (cf. Heb. xi. 27 τὸν γὰρ ἀόρατον ὡς ὁρῶν ἐκαρτέρησεν) and to the Latin *patientia*, thus defined by Cic. *Invent.* ii. 54. 163 *patientia est honestatis aut utilitatis causa rerum arduarum ac difficilium voluntaria ac diuturna perpessio*; but its distinctively Christian quality is shown in Didymus' comment on Job vi. 5 quoted by Suicer οὐκ ἀναίσθητον εἶναι δεῖ τὸν δίκαιον κἂν καρτερῶς φέρῃ τὰ θλίβοντα· αὕτη γὰρ ἀρετή ἐστιν, ὅταν αἴσθησιν τῶν ἐπιπόνων δεχόμενός τις ὑπερφρονῇ τῶν ἀλγηδόνων διὰ τὸν Θεόν. Plut. (*Cons. ad Apoll.* 117) quotes from Eurip. τὰ προσπεσόντα δ' ὅστις εὖ φέρει βροτῶν, ἄριστος εἶναι σωφρονεῖν τέ μοι δοκεῖ. Philo (*Cong. Erud. Grat.* M. 1. 524), followed by Chrysostom (*ap.* Suic. *s.v.*), calls ὑπομονή the queen of virtues, and says it is typified by Rebecca. Bp. Lightfoot distinguishes it from μακροθυμία (Col. i. 12): see below on v. 7. Spitta cites Test. Jos. 2 ἐν δέκα πειρασμοῖς δόκιμόν με ἀνέδειξε καὶ ἐν πᾶσιν αὐτοῖς ἐμακροθύμησα· ὅτι μέγα φάρμακον ἡ μακροθυμία καὶ πολλὰ ἀγαθὰ δίδωσιν ἡ ὑπομονή, and refers to Jubilees ch. 17 and 18 and the Fourth book of Maccabees as showing that the Jews regarded Abraham as a pattern of faith and endurance tested by trial.

4. **ἡ δὲ ὑπομονή.**] See note on χαρά, ver. 2.

ἔργον τέλειον ἐχέτω.] 'Let it have its full effect,' 'attain its end.' Alf. translates 'let it have *a* perfect work,' but this does not quite represent the force of the original, which in colloquial English would be rather 'make a complete job of it' = τελέως ἐνεργείτω. In classical Greek we should probably have had τὸ ἔργον, but the omission of the article emphasizes the first point, that endurance shall be active not passive, as well as the second, that its activity shall not cease till it has accomplished its end. Cf. for the thought παραμείνας below ver. 25, Heb. x. 36, xii. 1 foll. δι' ὑπομονῆς τρέχωμεν τὸν προκείμενον ἡμῖν ἀγῶνα, v. 5 ἵνα μὴ κάμητε ταῖς ψυχαῖς ὑμῶν ἐκλυόμενοι κ.τ.λ., Clem. Al. *Str.* 4. p. 570 P. τελείωσιν τὸ μαρτύριον καλοῦμεν ὅτι τέλειον ἔργον ἀγάπης ἐνεδείξατο.

τέλειοι.] Not 'perfect' in the strict sense of the term, since πολλὰ πταίομεν ἅπαντες (below iii. 2), though all are bidden to aim at perfection, (Matt. v. 48, Eph. iii. 19). The word occurs again below iii. 2. It is used of animals which are full grown (cf. Herod. i. 83, where τὰ τέλεα τῶν προβάτων are opposed to γαλαθηνά, Thuc. v. 47), and hence, in this and other passages, of Christians who have attained maturity of character and understanding (Phil. iii. 15, where see Lightfoot's note, Col. i. 28, iv. 12, esp. 1 Cor. xiv. 20, Heb. v. 12–14). Thus it be-

[1] [The simple and compound forms are used together in Rom. ii. 9, 16, and 2 Cor. vii. 10. A.]

comes almost synonymous with πνευματικός and γνωστικός.[1] Philo contrasts it with ἀσκητικός and προκόπτων M. 1. p. 551 τοιαῦτα ὑφηγεῖται τῷ ἀσκητικῷ ἡ ὑπομονή, 552 τὸν ἀσκητικὸν τρόπον, καὶ νέον παρὰ τὸν τέλειον, καὶ φιλίας ἄξιον εἶναι τίθεμεν, 169 αἱ τέλειαι ἀρεταὶ μόνου τοῦ τελείου κτήματα, 582, 689: cf. the Stoic use (Stob. *Ecl.* ii. 198) πάντα δὲ τὸν καλὸν καὶ ἀγαθὸν ἄνδρα τέλειον εἶναι λέγουσι διὰ τὸ μηδεμιᾶς ἀπολείπεσθαι ἀρετῆς. The word ἄρτιος is used in the same sense in 2 Tim. iii. 17 ἵνα ἄρτιος ᾖ ὁ τοῦ Θεοῦ ἄνθρωπος πρὸς πᾶν ἔργον ἀγαθὸν ἐξηρτισμένος, cf. 1 Pet. v. 10 ὁ δὲ Θεὸς...ὀλίγον παθόντας αὐτὸς καταρτίσαι ὑμᾶς. In Heb. ii. 10 Christ himself is said to have been made perfect through sufferings. The word τέλειος is often used by later writers of the baptized, as by Clem. Al. *Paed.* i. 6. p. 113 P. ἀναγεννηθέντες εὐθέως τὸ τέλειον ἀπειλήφαμεν· ἐφωτίσθημεν γάρ· τὸ δὲ ἔστιν ἐπιγνῶναι Θεόν. οὔκουν ἀτελὴς ὁ ἐγνωκὼς τὸ τέλειον.

ὁλόκληροι.] *Omnibus numeris absoluti.* Used of a victim which is without blemish, complete in all its parts (*integer*), Jos. *Ant. Jud.* iii. 12. 2 τὰ ἱερεῖα θύουσιν ὁλόκληρα καὶ κατὰ μηδὲν λελωβημένα, also of the priest Philo M. 2. p. 225 παντελῆ καὶ ὁλόκληρον εἶναι τὸν ἱερέα προστέτακται, of the initiated Plato *Phaedr.* 250. Ὁλοκληρία is used of the lame man who was healed, Acts iii. 16. Hence, metaphorically, Philo M. 1. 190 τὰ δ' ἄλλα, ὅσα ψυχὴν ὁλόκληρον κατὰ πάντα τὰ μέλη παρέχεται, ὁλοκαυτοῦν Θεῷ, *ib.* M. 2. p. 265 δεῖ τὸν μέλλοντα θύειν σκέπτεσθαι, μὴ εἰ τὸ ἱερεῖον ἄμωμον, ἀλλ' εἰ ἡ διάνοια ὁλόκληρος αὐτῷ καὶ παντελὴς καθέστηκε, Herm. *Mand.* v. 2. 3 πίστις ὁλόκληρος, Polyb. 18. 28. 9 εὔκλεια ὁλόκληρος, Wisd. xv. 3 τὸ γὰρ ἐπίστασθαί σε ὁλόκληρος δικαιοσύνη, 1 Thess. v. 23. It is often joined with τέλειος, as in Plut. *Mor.* p. 1066 F. τέλειον ἐκ τούτων καὶ ὁλόκληρον ᾤοντο συμπληροῦν βίον, and in Philo. See on both words Heisen pp. 299–371. In this passage it would be contrasted with a partial keeping of the law such as we read of in ii. 9, 10.

ἐν μηδενὶ λειπόμενοι.] The preceding positive expression (ὁλόκληρος) is supported by the corresponding negative, as in ver. 6 ἐν πίστει μηδὲν διακρινόμενος. The only passages in the N.T. where the passive is used (as in Plato *Legg.* 9. 881 B δεῖ τὰς ἐνθάδε κολάσεις μηδὲν τῶν ἐν Αἴδου λείπεσθαι) are this and the following verse and ii. 15. Strictly it means 'being left behind by another.' It is used with the gen. both of person and thing, rarely of both together. More usually the thing is expressed by the dat. or acc., or with a preposition, εἴς τι, κατά τι, πρός τι, ἔν τινι. The active occurs with much the same sense in classical Greek, Arist. *Gen. An.* iv. 1. 36 οἱ εὐνοῦχοι μικρὸν λείπουσι τοῦ θήλεος τὴν ἰδέαν ('fall short of'), and is also used of the thing with dat. of the person, Luke xviii. 22 ἔν σοι λείπει ('is lacking'). We may compare 1 Cor. 7 μὴ ὑστερεῖσθαι ἐν μηδενὶ χαρίσματι. Μηδενί is required as it is a negative in a final clause, cf. Phil. iii. 9 ἵνα Χριστὸν κερδήσω...μὴ ἔχων ἐμὴν δικαιοσύνην, and Winer, p. 598.

There is a close resemblance between the scale here given of Christian growth and that in Rom. v. 4. After speaking of the Christian exulting (καυχώμεθα ver. 9 below) in the hope of the glory of God,

[1] [See 1 Chron. xxv. 8 τελείων καὶ μανθανόντων, where it means 'teachers.' A.]

nay even ἐν ταῖς θλίψεσιν, St. Paul continues εἰδότες ὅτι ἡ θλίψις (= τὸ δοκίμιον τῆς πίστεως or πειρασμός here) ὑπομονὴν κατεργάζεται. These two stages may be considered the same as those given here: but the third seems inconsistent. Here endurance leads to the perfection of the Christian character; there the words ἡ δὲ ὑπομονὴ δοκιμήν apparently reverse the first step of St. James. The word δοκιμή however is not there used in the same sense as our δοκίμιον, of which it is rather the result; and this, the tried and tested character, is not very different from St. James' 'perfection,' of which we may consider the two following stages in St. Paul (ἡ δὲ δοκιμὴ ἐλπίδα, ἡ δὲ ἐλπὶς οὐ καταισχύνει, ὅτι ἡ ἀγάπη τοῦ Θεοῦ ἐκκέχυται) to be marks or elements. There is a similar chain, including ὑπομονή, in 2 Pet. i. 5 foll., where however there seems no attempt to give a natural or chronological order.

5. **εἰ δέ τις λείπεται σοφίας.**] The preceding λειπόμενοι is caught up like τέλειος and ὑπομονή before. The thought omitted is thus supplied by Bede: *si quis vestrum non potest intellegere utilitatem tentationum quae fidelibus probandi causa eveniunt, postulet a Deo tribui sibi sensum quo dignoscere valeat quanta pietate Pater castigat filios* ('how am I to see trial in this light, and make this use of it? it needs a higher wisdom'). The ideas of wisdom and perfection are often joined, as in 1 Cor. ii. 7 σοφίαν λαλοῦμεν ἐν τοῖς τελείοις, Col. i. 28 διδάσκοντες πάντα ἄνθρωπον ἐν πάσῃ σοφίᾳ ἵνα παραστήσωμεν πάντα ἄνθρωπον τέλειον ἐν Χριστῷ, Wisd. ix. 6 κἂν γάρ τις ᾖ τέλειος ἐν υἱοῖς ἀνθρώπων τῆς ἀπό σου σοφίας ἀπούσης εἰς οὐδὲν λογισθήσεται. Hence Eulogius (*fl.* 590 A.D.), quoted by Heisen p. 377, speaks of ἡ τελειόποιος σοφία θεοῦ. On the true nature of wisdom see below iii. 13. To St. James, as to the writer of the book of Job (where the necessity of wisdom to understand the use of trial is much insisted on) and of the other sapiential books, wisdom is 'the principal thing,' to which he gives the same prominence as St. Paul to faith, St. John to love, St. Peter to hope. Not that wisdom is neglected in the other books of the N.T.: cf. Luke ii. 40, vii. 35, xi. 49, 1 Cor. i. 17 foll. (where true and false wisdom are contrasted), Col. i. 9 αἰτούμενοι ἵνα πληρώθητε τὴν ἐπίγνωσιν τοῦ θελήματος αὐτοῦ ἐν πάσῃ σοφίᾳ καὶ συνέσει πνευματικῇ, where see Lightfoot's note, Eph. i. 17 ἵνα ὁ Θεὸς δῴη ὑμῖν πνεῦμα σοφίας καὶ ἀποκαλύψεως ἐν ἐπιγνώσει αὐτοῦ, πεφωτισμένους τοὺς ὀφθαλμοὺς τῆς καρδίας εἰς τὸ εἰδέναι ὑμᾶς τίς ἐστιν ἡ ἐλπὶς τῆς κλήσεως αὐτοῦ, τίς ὁ πλοῦτος τῆς δόξης τῆς κληρονομίας κ.τ.λ., which may serve as a commentary on the whole of this passage, esp. on verses 10 and 12. The prayer for wisdom takes a more definitely Christian form in St. Paul's prayer for the Spirit. Compare Plut. *Mor.* 351 C. πάντα μὲν δεῖ τἀγαθὰ τοὺς νοῦν ἔχοντας αἰτεῖσθαι παρὰ τῶν θεῶν· μάλιστα δὲ τῆς περὶ αὐτῶν ἐπιστήμης, ὅσον ἐφικτόν ἐστιν ἀνθρώποις, μετιόντες εὐχόμεθα τυγχάνειν παρ' αὐτῶν ἐκείνων, ὡς οὐδὲν ἀνθρώπῳ λαβεῖν μεῖζον, οὐ χαρίσασθαι Θεῷ σεμνότερον ἀληθείας.

αἰτείτω παρὰ τοῦ διδόντος Θεοῦ πᾶσιν ἁπλῶς.] The great example is Solomon: cf. 1 Kings iii. 9–12, Prov. ii. 3, Wisdom vii. 7 foll., ix. 4 foll., Sir. i. 1 foll., li. 13 foll., Barnabas xxi. 5 ὁ Θεὸς δῴη ὑμῖν σοφίαν ἐν ὑπομονῇ, below iii. 17 ἡ ἄνωθεν σοφία. The more natural order of the words would have been παρὰ τοῦ πᾶσιν ἁπλῶς δ. Θ., or with article repeated π. τοῦ Θεοῦ, τοῦ π. ἁ. διδόντος: cf. for the hyperbaton 2 Pet. iii. 2 μνησθῆναι τῶν προειρημένων ῥημάτων ὑπὸ τῶν ἁγίων προφητῶν, Acts. xxvi. 6 ἐπ' ἐλπίδι τῆς εἰς τοὺς πατέρας ἡμῶν ἐπαγγελίας γενομένης ὑπὸ τοῦ Θεοῦ, Rom. viii. 18 τὴν μέλλουσαν δόξαν ἀποκαλυφθῆναι εἰς ἡμᾶς, Matt. xxv. 34 τὴν ἡτοιμασμένην ὑμῖν βασιλείαν ἀπὸ καταβολῆς κόσμου. We occasionally find the same thing in classical authors, when the qualifying clause between the article and substantive is itself further qualified or supplemented, as by a prepositional phrase (Xen. *Anab.* vi. 6. 19 ὁ ἀφαιρεθεὶς ἀνὴρ ὑπὸ Ἀγασίου, Thuc. i. 18 μετὰ τὴν τῶν τυράννων κατάλυσιν ἐκ τῆς Ἑλλάδος, see Krueger 50. 9, n. 8, 9; 10. 1, 2, 3), or by the object (Dem. *Cor.* 301 ὁ κατειληφὼς κίνδυνος τὴν πόλιν, Epict. *Diss.* i. 1 χρηστικὴ δύναμις ταῖς φαντασίαις), see Sandys *Lept.* p. 35 §§ 31. Here the unusual position gives a special prominence to πᾶσιν ἁπλῶς.

There are two ways in which ἁπλῶς (only here in N.T.) is taken, (1) in a logical sense, 'simply,' 'unconditionally,' 'without bargaining,' which may be said most truly of Him who makes his sun to rise on the evil and the good (Matt. v. 45): cf. Herm. *Mand.* ii. 4 πᾶσιν ὑστερουμένοις δίδου ἁπλῶς, μὴ διστάζων τίνι δῷς ἢ τίνι μὴ δῷς, πᾶσιν δίδου, and again immediately below ἁπλῶς is explained by μηδὲν διακρίνων: (2) in a moral sense, 'generously.' The latter is more in accordance with the use of ἁπλότης = 'liberality,' which is common in the N.T., cf. 2 Cor. viii. 2 ἐν πολλῇ δοκιμῇ θλίψεως ἡ περισσεία τῆς χαρᾶς αὐτῶν ἐπερίσσευσεν εἰς τὸ πλοῦτος τῆς ἁπλότητος αὐτῶν, ix. 11 ἐν παντὶ πλουτιζόμενοι εἰς πᾶσαν ἁπλότητα, ver. 13, Rom. xii. 8 ὁ μεταδιδοὺς ἐν ἁπλότητι. This use of ἁπλότης seems to come from the idea of frankness and openheartedness belonging to ἁπλοῦς. There is however no example of the adverb being thus used, and it seems on all accounts better to keep the ordinary sense 'unconditionally,' which also contrasts better with the following μὴ ὀνειδίζοντος. Cf. Philo *Cher.* M. 1 p. 161 ὁ Θεὸς οὐ πωλητὴρ ἐπευωνίζων τὰ ἑαυτοῦ κτήματα, δωρητικὸς δὲ τῶν ἁπάντων, ἀεννάους χαρίτων πηγὰς ἀναχέων, ἀμοιβῆς οὐκ ἐφιέμενος, *Alleg.* M. 1 p. 50 φιλόδωρος ὢν ὁ Θεὸς χαρίζεται τὰ ἀγαθὰ πᾶσι καὶ τοῖς μὴ τελείοις foll., *ib.* p. 251 πόθεν τὴν φρονήσεως διψῶσαν διάνοιαν εἰκός ἐστι πληροῦσθαι πλὴν ἀπὸ σοφίας Θεοῦ; Herm. *Mand.* ii. 4 πᾶσιν ὁ Θεὸς δίδοσθαι θέλει ἐκ τῶν ἰδίων δωρημάτων, where the context is full of reminiscences of St. James; *id. Sim.* v. 4. 3 ὃς ἂν δοῦλος ᾖ τοῦ Θεοῦ καὶ ἔχῃ τὸν Κύριον ἑαυτοῦ ἐν τῇ καρδίᾳ αἰτεῖται παρ' αὐτοῦ σύνεσιν καὶ λαμβάνει...ὅσοι δὲ ἀργοὶ (εἰσὶν) πρὸς τὴν ἔντευξιν ἐκεῖνοι διστάζουσιν αἰτεῖσθαι παρὰ τοῦ Κυρίου, *ib.* ix. 2. 6., Sen. *Ben.* 4. 25 *di quodcumque faciunt, in eo quid praeter ipsam faciendi rationem sequuntur?* Plut. *Mor.* 63. F, below ver. 17 πᾶσα δόσις ἀγαθή.

μὴ ὀνειδίζοντος.] Sir. 41. 22 μετὰ τὸ δοῦναι μὴ ὀνείδιζε, 18. 17 μωρὸς ἀχαρίστως ὀνειδιεῖ, καὶ δόσις βασκάνου ἐκτήκει ὀφθαλμούς, 20. 13 foll. δόσις ἄφρονος οὐ λυσιτελήσει σε· ὀλίγα δώσει καὶ πολλὰ ὀνειδίσει...μωρὸς ἐρεῖ... οὐκ ἔστι χάρις τοῖς ἀγαθοῖς μου, Herm. *Mand.* 9. 3 (after speaking of διψυχία) οὐκ ἔστι γὰρ ὁ Θεὸς ὡς οἱ ἄνθρωποι οἱ μνησικακοῦντες, ἀλλ' αὐτὸς ἀμνησίκακός ἐστι, *Sim.* 9. 23 ὁ Θεὸς οὐ μνησικακεῖ τοῖς ἐξομολογουμένοις τὰς ἁμαρτίας, ἀλλ' ἵλεως γίνεται, *Sim.* 9. 24 παντὶ ἀνθρώπῳ ἐχορήγησαν ἀνονειδίστως καὶ ἀδιστάκτως. So Philemon (Mein. *fr. inc.* 18. p. 401) καλῶς ποιήσας οὐ καλῶς ὠνείδισας· ἔργον καθεῖλες πλούσιον πτωχῷ λόγῳ, καυχώμενος τὸ δῶρον ὃ δέδωκας φίλῳ, Dem. *Cor.* 316 τὸ τὰς ἰδίας εὐεργεσίας ὑπομιμνήσκειν...μικροῦ δεῖν ὅμοιον ἐστι τῷ ὀνειδίζειν, Polyb. ix. 31.4, xxxviii. 4. 11 ὀνειδίσας εἰς ἀχαριστίαν, Plaut. *Amph* prol. 41 *nam quid ego memorem, ut alios in tragoediis vidi, Neptunum, Virtutem, Victoriam, Martem, Bellonam, commemorxre quae bona nobis fecissent...sed mos nunquam illi fuit patri meo optumo ut exprobraret quod bonis faceret boni*, Ter. *Andr.* i. 1. 17 *istaec commemoratio quasi exprobratio est immemori benefici*, Cic. *Lael.* 71, Sen. *Ben.* ii. 11, Plut. *Adul.* ii. 64. A. πᾶσα ὀνειδιζομένη χάρις ἐπαχθὴς καὶ ἄχαρις. The thought expressed is similar to that in Matt. xii. 20 (Isa. xlii. 1), and is intended to encourage those who were tempted to regard their trials as a sign of God's displeasure for their sin. It is not meant that God never upbraids (see Mark xvi. 14 ὠνείδισεν τὴν ἀπιστίαν αὐτῶν, Const. Apost. vii. 24 'prepare yourselves for worship' ἵνα μὴ ἀναξίως ὑμῶν τὸν Πατέρα καλούντων ὀνειδισθῆτε ὑπ' αὐτοῦ), but that where there is sincere repentance He freely gives and forgives whatever may have been the past sin.

δοθήσεται.] *Sc.* τὸ αἰτούμενον. The same words in Matt. vii. 7 αἰτεῖτε καὶ δοθήσεται ὑμῖν: cf. below ver. 17, also Clem. R. 13 and Polyc. *Phil.* 2.

6. **αἰτείτω δὲ ἐν πίστει.**] Again catching up the preceding verb. Cf. εὐχὴ τῆς πίστεως below v. 15, and for αἰτ. iv. 3, where also there is a limitation on the prayer which is sure of an answer. For the meaning of πίστις see Comment and Gfrörer *Philo*, p. 452 foll.

[The ἁπλότης of the Giver must be met by a corresponding ἁπλότης of the suppliant, as in the case of Solomon, who asked simply for wisdom, without a thought of material good things, cf. the words put into his mouth in Wisdom viii. 21 ἐνέτυχον τῷ Κυρίῳ καὶ εἶπον ἐξ ὅλης τῆς καρδίας μου. Spitta.]

μηδὲν διακρινόμενος.] The simple sense of the active is to 'divide,' often contrasted, as in Plato and Aristotle, with συγκρίνειν: so in the system of Empedocles (Diels p. 478) τὰ στοιχεῖα ποτὲ μὲν ὑπὸ τῆς φιλίας συγκρινόμενα, ποτὲ δὲ ὑπὸ τοῦ νείκους διακρινόμενα κ.τ.λ. In 1 Cor. iv. 7 (τίς σε διακρίνει;) it means to separate from others as superior. Similarly in the passive, as Philo M. I. p. 584 (a veil is interposed) ὅπως διακρίνηται τῶν εἴσω τὰ ἔξω. Hence it is used of quarrelling, Herod. 9. 58 μαχῇ διακριθῆναι πρός τινα, Acts xi. 2 διεκρίνοντο πρὸς αὐτὸν λέγοντες ('disputed'), Jude 9 τῷ διαβόλῳ διακρινόμενος, and in ver. 23 ἐλέγχετε διακρινομένους (Alf.), Jerem. xv. 10 δικαζόμενον καὶ διακρινόμενον πάσῃ τῇ γῇ, Ezek. xx. 35, 36 διακριθήσομαι πρὸς ('I will plead, contend, with you') ὃν τρόπον διεκρίθην πρὸς τοὺς πατέρας ὑμῶν. In the N.T. it is frequently used of internal division, like διαμερίζομαι (Luke xi. 18 ἐφ' ἑαυτὸν διεμερίσθη, cf. Virg. *Aen.* iv. 285 *animum nunc huc celerem nunc dividit illuc*); and contrasted with faith, Matt. xxi. 21 ἐὰν ἔχητε πίστιν καὶ μὴ διακριθῆτε, Mark xi. 23 ὅς ἂν εἴπῃ...καὶ μὴ διακριθῇ ἐν τῇ καρδίᾳ ἀλλὰ πιστεύσῃ ...ἔσται αὐτῷ ὃ ἐὰν εἴπῃ, Rom. iv. 20 εἰς τὴν ἐπαγγελίαν τοῦ Θεοῦ οὐ διεκρίθη τῇ ἀπιστίᾳ ἀλλ' ἐνεδυναμώθη τῇ πίστει, below ii. 4 οὐ διεκρίθητε ἐν ἑαυτοῖς; Acts x. 20 πορεύου μηδὲν διακρινόμενος, Rom. xiv. 23 ὁ διακρινόμενος ἐὰν φαγῇ κατακέκριται ὅτι οὐκ ἐκ πίστεως. This use is apparently confined to the N.T. and later Christian writings, e.g. Protev. Jac. 11 p. 216 T. ἀκούσασα δὲ Μαριὰμ διεκρίθη ἐν ἑαυτῇ λέγουσα· εἰ ἐγὼ συλλήψομαι, ὡς πᾶσα γυνὴ γεννᾷ; Clem. Hom. ii. 40 περὶ τοῦ μόνου Θεοῦ διακριθῆναι οὐκ ὀφείλεις, Socr. *H.E.* iii. 9 διεκρίνετο κοινωνεῖν Εὐσεβίῳ. The act. is also used in the sense of distinguishing, *discerno*, Matt. xvi. 3, Acts xv. 9 οὐδὲν διέκρινεν μεταξὺ ἡμῶν τε καὶ αὐτῶν, xi. 12 μηδὲν διακρίναντα (making no distinction), 1 Cor. xi. 29 μὴ διακρίνων τὸ σῶμα (not distinguishing the body of Christ from common food), xvi. 29 (discerning of spirits), so Herm. *Mand.* ii. 6 quoted on ἁπλῶς: also of deciding (judging) I Cor. vi. 5 ἀνὰ μέσον τοῦ ἀδελφοῦ, Ez. xxxiv. 17 προβάτου καὶ προβάτου, and with acc. of person 1 Cor. xi. 31, as in Psa. xlix. 4 διακρῖναι τὸν λαὸν αὐτοῦ, Prov. xxxi. 9, Zach. iii. 7.[1] The force of the word here may be illustrated by iv. 4 below and by Matt. vi. 24. Hermas paraphrases it by αἰτοῦ ἀδιστάκτως *Mand.* ix., a passage full of reminiscences of St. James. Μηδέν is required by the imperative, see Winer, p. 598.

ἔοικεν κλύδωνι.] Like a cork floating on the wave, now carried towards the shore, now away from it; opposite to those who have 'hope as an anchor of the soul, sure and steadfast, and which entereth within the veil,' Heb. vi. 19. For the figure cf. Eph. iv. 14, where we have opposed to the ἀνὴρ τέλειος of v. 13 νήπιοι κλυδωνιζόμενοι καὶ περιφερόμενοι παντὶ ἀνέμῳ τῆς διδασκαλίας, Sir. xxxiii. 2 ὁ ὑποκρινόμενος ἐν νόμῳ ὡς ἐν καταιγίδι πλοῖον. In Isa. lvii. 20 the sea is used as a type of restlessness, cf. Jude 13. For a similar figurative use of the name 'Euripus' see my note on Cic. *N.D.* iii. 24. So Matt. xi. 7 κάλαμον ὑπὸ ἀνέμου σαλευόμενον, Virg. *Aen.* xii. 487 *vario nequiquam fluctuat aestu*, Hor. *Ep.* i. 1. 99 *aestuat et vitae disconvenit ordine toto*, Seneca *Ep.* 95. 57 *non contingit tranquillitas nisi immutabile certumque judicium adeptis: ceteri decidunt subinde et reponuntur et inter intermissa appetitaque alternis fluctuantur*, *ib.* 52 *fluctuamus inter varia consilia, nihil libere volumus, nihil absolute, nihil semper.* Κλύδων is only found in the sing., cf. Luke viii. 24 ἐπετίμησεν τῷ ἀνέμῳ καὶ τῷ κλύδωνι τοῦ ὕδατος, and see Essay on Style. The word ἔοικε only here and below ver. 23 in the N.T.

ἀνεμιζομένῳ.] = classical ἀνεμόω. Perhaps coined by the writer. The only other examples quoted in Thayer are Schol. on *Od.* xii. 336, Hesych. s.v. ἀναψύξαι, Joan. Moschus ἀνεμίζοντος τοῦ πλοίου. Heisen notices (p. 441) that St. James has a fondness for verbs in -ιζω, e.g. ὀνειδίζω, ῥιπίζω, παραλογίζομαι, φλογίζω, ἐγγίζω, καθαρίζω, ἁγνίζω, ἀφανίζω, θησαυρίζω, θερίζω, στηρίζω, μακαρίζω.

ῥιπιζομένῳ.] From ῥιπίς, 'a fan'; most often used of fanning a flame.

[1] Hofmann, followed by Erdmann, explains διακρινόμενος here as middle, 'sich bei sich selbst in Bezug auf etwas fraglich stellen,' and supports this by a reference to 4 Macc. 2 (it should be i. 14) διακρίνωμεν δὲ τί ἐστιν λογισμὸς καὶ τί πάθος, where however διακ. has nothing to do with questioning, but means simply 'let us distinguish.' Dr. Abbott also would prefer to take it as a middle, comparing such cases as Eur. *Med.* 609 ὡς οὐ κρινοῦμαι τῶνδέ σοι τὰ πλείονα 'I will debate the matter no further,' Arist. *Nub.* 66 τέως μὲν οὖν ἐκρινόμεθ' (cf. the Latin *cernere bello*); and he thinks διεκρίθη may be used with a middle force, like ἀπεκρίθη for ἀπεκρίνατο. The idea of self-debate is much the same as that of self-division, and it may well be that the sense here takes a colour from the secondary, as well as from the primitive force of the verb κρίνω, but the connexion with the primitive notion 'division' is, I think, the more important, and harmonizes better with the word δίψυχος, which appears as a synonym just below.

Only found here in N.T. Cf. Philo *Incorr. Mund.* M. ii. p. 511 εἰ μὴ πρὸς ἀνέμων ῥιπίζοιτο τὸ ὕδωρ...ὑφ' ἡσυχίας νεκροῦται, and a comic fragment in Dio Chr. 32. p. 368 δῆμος ἄστατον κακόν, | καὶ θαλάσσῃ πάνθ' ὅμοιον ὑπ' ἀνέμου ῥιπίζεται, Aristoph. *Ran.* 360, Philo *Gig.* M. 1. p. 269 ἰδών τις τὸν ἐν ταῖς ψυχαῖς ἄλεκτον καὶ βαρὺν χειμῶνα, ὃς ὑπὸ βιαιοτάτης φορᾶς τῶν κατὰ βίον πραγμάτων ἀναῤῥιπίζεται, τεθαύμακεν εἰκότως εἴ τις ἐν κλύδωνι κυμαινούσης θαλάσσης γαλήνην ἄγειν δύναται: Epictetus i. 4. 19 has a similar use of μεταῤῥιπίζεσθαι.

7. **μὴ γὰρ οἰέσθω.**] This is the only passage in N.T. where the verb occurs, except οἶμαι John xxi. 25, οἰόμενοι Phil. i. 17. Οἴησις is often used in Philo in a bad sense = δόξα, as opposed to ἐπιστήμη. *Fides non opinatur* says Bengel on this passage, echoing the Stoic μὴ δοξάσειν τὸν σοφόν. Γάρ here, like the preceding, gives the reason for αἰτείτω ἐν πίστει.

ὁ ἄνθρωπος ἐκεῖνος.] For ἐκεῖνος simply, as in Mark xiv. 21, Matt. xxvi. 24, and *passim.*

τοῦ Κυρίου.] Here and below iv. 15, v. 10, 11 used of God: of Christ in i. 1, ii. 1 certainly, and v. 8, 14, 15 probably.

8. **ἀνὴρ δίψυχος.**] St. James commonly uses ἀνήρ with some characteristic word, as μακάριος i. 12, κατανοῶν i. 23, χρυσοδακτύλιος ii. 2, τέλειος iii. 2, keeping ἄνθρωπος for more general expressions, ἐκεῖνος, πᾶς, οὐδείς, &c. This agrees fairly with the use in the LXX. and Gospels: in the other epistles ἀνήρ is almost exclusively used in opposition to γυνή. This is the first appearance in literature of the word δίψ. (only found here and below iv. 8 in N.T.), unless we give an earlier date to the apocryphal saying quoted below from Clem. Rom.; the thought is found in Psa. xii. 2 'with a double heart (ἐν καρδίᾳ καὶ ἐν καρδίᾳ) do they speak[1],' 1 Chron. xii. 33, 1 Kings xviii. 21, Sirac. i. 25 μὴ ἀπειθήσῃς φόβῳ Κυρίου καὶ μὴ προσέλθῃς αὐτῷ ἐν καρδίᾳ δισσῇ, *ib.* ii. 12 οὐαὶ ἁμαρτωλῷ ἐπιβαίνοντι ἐπὶ δύο τρίβους...οὐαὶ ὑμῖν τοῖς ἀπολωλεκόσι τὴν ὑπομονήν. It is the opposite to Deut. iv. 29 ζητήσετε ἐκεῖ Κύριον τὸν Θεὸν ὑμῶν καὶ εὑρήσετε αὐτὸν ὅταν ἐκζητήσετε αὐτὸν ἐξ ὅλης τῆς καρδίας σου καὶ ἐξ ὅλης τῆς ψυχῆς σου ἐν τῇ θλίψει σου, and to Wisd. i. 1 ἐν ἁπλότητι καρδίας[2] ζητήσατε (τὸν Κύριον) ὅτι εὑρίσκεται τοῖς μὴ πειράζουσιν αὐτόν, ἐμφανίζεται δὲ τοῖς μὴ ἀπιστοῦσιν αὐτῷ. St. Paul describes a διψυχία in Rom. vii.: cf. below iv. 4, Philo M. 1. p. 230 πέφυκε γὰρ ὁ ἄφρων, ἀεὶ περὶ τὸν ὀρθὸν λόγον κινούμενος, ἠρεμίᾳ καὶ ἀναπαύσει δυσμενὴς εἶναι καὶ ἐπὶ μηδενὸς ἑστάναι παγίως καὶ ἐρηρεῖσθαι δόγματος, κ.τ.λ. Though seemingly introduced by St. James, the word was quickly taken up by subsequent writers: it occurs about forty times in Hermas, e.g. *Mand.* ix. 4. 5 foll. αἰτοῦ παρὰ τοῦ Κυρίου καὶ ἀπολήψῃ πάντα...ἐὰν δὲ διστάσῃς ἐν τῇ καρδίᾳ σου, οὐδὲν οὐ μὴ λήψῃ τῶν αἰτημάτων σου· οἱ γὰρ διστάζοντες, οὗτοί εἰσιν οἱ δίψυχοι...πᾶς γὰρ δίψυχος ἀνὴρ ἐὰν μὴ μετανοήσῃ δυσκόλως σωθήσεται: the whole chapter is a comment on our text, and full of reminiscences of this epistle; thus ἡ πίστις ἄνωθέν ἐστι παρὰ τοῦ Κυρίου καὶ ἔχει δύναμιν μεγάλην· ἡ δὲ διψυχία ἐπίγειον πνεῦμά ἐστι παρὰ τοῦ διαβόλου, δύναμιν μὴ ἔχουσα is an

[1] See Taylor's *Gospel in the Law*, p. 336 foll.; he considers that St. James here quotes from Prov. xxi. 8.

[2] The phrase occurs also Eph. vi. 5, Col. iii. 22.

echo of James iii. 15; οὐκ ἔστι γὰρ ὁ Θεὸς ὡς οἱ ἄνθρωποι οἱ μνησικακοῦντες reminds one of μὴ ὀνειδίζοντος just above. In the space of thirty lines we find fifteen instances of the use of δίψυχος and its derivatives. So Clem. Rom. i. c. 11 (Lot's wife is a warning) ὅτι οἱ δίψυχοι καὶ οἱ διστάζοντες περὶ τῆς τοῦ Θεοῦ δυνάμεως εἰς κρίμα...γίνονται, 23 (the Father bestows his favour on all that come to him) ἁπλῇ διανοίᾳ· διὸ μὴ διψυχῶμεν...πόῤῥω γενέσθω ἀφ' ἡμῶν ἡ γραφὴ αὕτη ὅπου λέγει Ταλαίπωροί[1] εἰσιν οἱ δίψυχοι, οἱ διστάζοντες τὴν ψυχὴν κ.τ.λ., Clem. Rom. ii. 11 μὴ διψυχῶμεν ἀλλὰ ἐλπίσαντες ὑπομείνωμεν, *ib.* 19 μὴ ἀγανακτῶμεν οἱ ἄσοφοι (cf. λείπεται σοφίας above) ὅταν τις ἡμᾶς νουθετῇ...ἐνίοτε γὰρ πονηρὰ πράσσοντες οὐ γινώσκομεν διὰ τὴν διψυχίαν καὶ ἀπιστίαν, Clem. Al. *Strom.* i. 29 § 181 (quoting Hermas), Didaché iv. 4 οὐ διψυχήσεις πότερον ἔσται ἢ οὔ, repeated by Barnabas xix. 5, and in Const. Apost. vii. 11, with the addition ἐν τῇ προσευχῇ σου...λέγει γὰρ ὁ Κύριος ἐμοὶ Πέτρῳ ἐπὶ τῆς θαλάσσης Ὀλιγόπιστε εἰς τί ἐδίστασας; Can. Eccl. 13, Act. Philip. in Hell. p. 99 Tisch. οἱ ὑπὸ τῆς πίστεως ἐστηριγμένοι οὐκ ἐδιψύχησαν, Enoch xci. 4 (Dillmann tr. p. 65) 'be not companions of those who are of a double heart.' Similar phrases are διχόνοια Clem. Hom. i. 11, διπλοκαρδία Didaché x. 1, Barn. xx. 1, διγνώμων Barn. xix. 7, δίγνωμος Const. Ap. ii. 6, 21, διπρόσωπος Test. Ash. iii. p. 691, διχόνους ἐπαμφοτεριστὴς ὁ ἄφρων Philo frag. M. 2. p. 663, δίλογος 1 Tim. iii. 8, δίγλωσσος, Sir. v. 9. For classical parallels cf. Xen. *Cyr.* vi. 1. 41 δύο γὰρ, ἔφη, σαφῶς ἔχω ψυχάς...οὐ γὰρ δὴ μία γε οὖσα ἅμα ἀγαθή τέ ἐστι καὶ κακή, οὐδ' ἅμα καλῶν τε καὶ αἰσχρῶν ἔργων ἐρᾷ καὶ ταὐτὰ ἅμα βούλεταί τε καὶ οὐ βούλεται πράττειν, Plato *Rep.* 8. 554 D (of the oligarchical man) οὐκ ἄρ' ἂν εἴη ἀστασίαστος ὁ τοιοῦτος ἐν ἑαυτῷ οὐδὲ εἷς ἀλλὰ διπλοῦς τις, and still more the tyrannical man 588 foll., Epict. *Ench.* 29. 7 ἕνα σε δεῖ ἄνθρωπον ἢ ἀγαθὸν ἢ κακὸν εἶναι. De Wette quotes Tanchuma on Deut. xxvi. 16 'with all thy heart,' *Ne habeant* (*qui preces ad deum facere velint*) *duo corda, unum ad deum, alterum vero ad aliam rem directum.*

WH. make ἀν. δίψ. subject of λήμψεται, but I prefer to take it with B (which puts a stop before ἀνήρ), the Peshitto, Wiesinger, Huther, &c., in apposition to the subject of οἰέσθω, like iii. 2 δυνατὸς χαλιναγωγῆσαι after τέλειος ἀνήρ, ver. 6 ὁ κόσμος τῆς ἀδικίας after πῦρ, ver. 8 ἀκατάστατον κακόν after γλῶσσαν (though here the apposition is irregular, see note), iv. 12 ὁ δυνάμενος after κριτής. The other way of taking it seems to me to lack the energy of St. James, appealing less directly to the person addressed and weakening the force and rhythm of the following clause. The Vulg., followed by Schneck., Hofmann, Schegg, &c., makes ver. 8 an entire sentence, *vir duplex inconstans est*; but, as Alford says, it is hardly possible that the writer could have introduced a hitherto unknown, or at any rate a very unusual word in this casual way; Alford himself makes it a new predicate to ὁ ἄνθρ. ἐκ. 'he is a man with two minds,' but the construction is certainly easier if we take it in apposition to the subject: it will then sum up in one pregnant word the substance of the two preceding verses.

[1] The quotation is from an apocryphal writing supposed by Lightfoot to be 'Eldad and Modad,' by Hilgenfeld to be the 'Assumption of Moses.'

ἀκατάστατος. Only here and below iii. 8 in N.T.: 'unsettled,' 'unstable' (cf. οὐκ ἔχουσι ῥίζαν Mark iv. 17); once in LXX. Isa. liv. 11 ταπεινὴ καὶ ἀκατάστατος ('tossed with tempest,' A.V. and R.V.); Herm. *Mand.* 2 ἀκατάστατον δαιμόνιον: it is used by classical writers, e.g. Dem. *F.L.* 383 ὁ μὲν δῆμός ἐστιν ἀσταθμητότατον πρᾶγμα τῶν πάντων καὶ ἀσυνθετώτατον, ὥσπερ ἐν θαλάσσῃ κῦμα ἀκατάστατον, ὡς ἂν τύχῃ κινούμενον, where see Shilleto; the verb occurs Tob. i. 15 αἱ ὁδοὶ ἠκαταστάτησαν ('were disturbed') καὶ οὐκέτι ἠδυνάσθην πορευθῆναι εἰς τὴν Μηδίαν, Herm. *Mand.* 5. 2. 7 ἀκαταστατεῖ ἐν πάσῃ πράξει αὐτοῦ, *id. Sim.* 6. 3. 5 ἀκαταστατοῦντες ταῖς βουλαῖς...λέγουσιν ἑαυτοὺς μὴ εὐοδοῦσθαι ἐν ταῖς πράξεσιν αὐτῶν καὶ...αἰτιῶνται τὸν Κύριον. Ἀκαταστασία, 'unsettlement,' 'restlessness,' occurs iii. 16 (where A.V. and R.V. have 'confusion'). It is found also in 1 Cor. xiv. 33 opposed to εἰρήνη, and in pl. Luke xxi. 9, 2 Cor. vi. 5, xii. 20 (where A.V. and R.V. have 'tumults'), Herm. *Mand.* 6. 3. 4: Polybius uses it both of political disturbance and of individual character, see iv. 5. 8 τὴν ἀκαταστασίαν καὶ μανίαν τοῦ μειρακίου.

ἐν πάσαις ταῖς ὁδοῖς.] 'In the whole course of his life': cf. below v. 20, Rom. iii. 16. It is a Hebraism for ἐν πᾶσι or ἅπαντα. The same comparison of life to a journey is implied in the words πορεύομαι, περιπατεῖν: see Vorst *Hebr.* p. 194 foll.

9. **καυχάσθω.**] Repeats the note of πᾶσαν χαράν ver. 2: it stands first in order to emphasize the opposition to διψυχία. Far from being thus undecided and unsettled, the Christian should exult in his profession. If in low estate, he should glory in the church, where all are brothers and there is no respect of persons; he should realize his own dignity as a member of Christ, a child of God, an heir of heaven: if rich, he should cease to pride himself on wealth or rank, and rejoice that he has learnt the emptiness of all worldly distinctions and been taught that they are only valuable when they are regarded as a trust to be used for the service of God and good of man. Cf. Sirac. 10. 21 πλούσιος καὶ ἔνδοξος καὶ πτωχός, τὸ καύχημα αὐτῶν φόβος Κυρίου, Jer. ix. 23 μὴ καυχάσθω ὁ σοφὸς ἐν τῇ σοφίᾳ αὐτοῦ...καὶ μὴ καυχάσθω ὁ πλούσιος ἐν τῷ πλούτῳ αὐτοῦ, 'but let him that glorieth glory in this, that he understandeth and knoweth me...saith the Lord,' Philo *Jos.* M. 2. 61 ταπεινὸς εἶ ταῖς τύχαις; ἀλλὰ τὸ φρόνημα μὴ καταπιπτέτω. πάντα σοι κατὰ νοῦν χωρεῖ; μεταβολὴν εὐλαβοῦ, Rom. i. 16, 1 Pet. iv. 16, 1 Cor. vii. 22 ὁ ἐν Κυρίῳ κληθεὶς δοῦλος, ἀπελεύθερος Κυρίου ἐστίν· ὁμοίως καὶ ὁ ἐλεύθερος κληθεὶς, δοῦλός ἐστι Χριστοῦ, *ib.* vii. 29, Phil. iv. 12 οἶδα ταπεινοῦσθαι, οἶδα καὶ περισσεύειν· ἐν παντὶ καὶ ἐν πᾶσιν μεμύημαι καὶ χορτάζεσθαι καὶ πεινᾶν, καὶ περισσεύειν καὶ ὑστερεῖσθαι, also a saying of Hillel quoted in Vajjik R. (Edersheim I. p. 532) 'My humility is my greatness and my greatness is my humility.' The word καυχ. is much used by St. Paul, generally in a good sense: the Christian's boast is in God (Rom. v. 11), in Christ (Rom. xv. 17, 1 Cor. i. 31, 2 Cor. x. 17, Gal. vi. 14, Phil. iii. 3 καυχώμενοι ἐν Χριστῷ Ἰησοῦ καὶ οὐκ ἐν σαρκὶ πεποιθότες), in the hope of salvation (Rom. v. 2): St. Paul glories in his converts (2 Cor. vii. 14, ix. 2, 3, 2 Thess. i. 4, Phil. ii. 16), in afflictions (Rom. v. 3), in infirmities (2 Cor. xii. 9): he apologises for boasting in self-justification (2 Cor. xi., xii.). There may be a wrong boasting in God and

in the law (Rom. ii. 17, 23), a boasting of self-righteousness towards God (Rom. iii. 27, iv. 2, 1 Cor. i. 29, iv. 7), an actual boasting in sin (1 Cor. v. 6), or on the ground of mere carnal advantages (2 Cor. xi. 18, Gal. vi. 13). It is used below of blamable self-confidence (iv. 16).

ὁ ἀδελφὸς ὁ ταπεινός.] WH. bracket the former ὁ, which is omitted in B. This would leave no doubt that ἀδελφός was a general term applying to both πλούσιος and ταπεινός. Even with the article this is the natural way of taking it. The objections will be considered below. Ταπ. here refers to outward condition as in Luke i. 52 καθεῖλε δυναστάς ...ὕψωσε ταπεινούς, Rom. xii. 16 μὴ τὰ ὑψηλὰ φρονοῦντες ἀλλὰ τοῖς ταπεινοῖς συναπαγόμενοι, cf. below ii. 5; in iv. 6 ταπ. refers to the character. Spitta quotes Sir. xi. 1, σοφία ταπεινοῦ ἀνυψώσει κεφαλὴν αὐτοῦ καὶ ἐν μέσῳ μεγιστάνων καθίσει αὐτόν.

10. **ὁ δε πλούσιος ἐν τῇ ταπεινώσει αὐτοῦ.**] 'Let the rich brother glory in his humiliation as a Christian': cf. Sir. 3. 18 ὅσῳ μέγας εἶ τοσούτῳ ταπεινοῦ σεαυτὸν καὶ ἔναντι Κυρίου εὑρήσει χάριν, 1 Tim. vi. 17 charge them who are rich in this world μὴ ὑψηλοφρονεῖν μηδὲ ἠλπικέναι ἐπὶ πλούτου ἀδηλότητι, Luke xvi. 15 τὸ ἐν ἀνθρώποις ὑψηλὸν βδέλυγμα ἐνώπιον τοῦ Θεοῦ, Matt. xviii. 4 ὅστις ταπεινώσει ἑαυτὸν...οὗτος ἔσται ὁ μείζων ἐν τῇ βασιλείᾳ τῶν οὐρανῶν, *ib.* xxiii. 12, 2 Cor. xi. 7 ἐμαυτὸν ταπεινῶν ἵνα ὑμεῖς ὑψώθητε, also below iv. 10, Philo M. 1. p. 577 ταπεινώθητι ὑπὸ τὰς χεῖρας αὐτῆς (*sc.* of Sarah = virtue) καλὴν ταπείνωσιν, φρονήματος ἀλόγου καθαίρεσιν ἔχουσαν, Xen. *R. Lac.* 8. 2 ἐν τῇ Σπάρτῃ οἱ κράτιστοι...τῷ ταπεινοὶ εἶναι μεγαλύνονται. We might understand ταπ. with reference to the loss of position, the scorn which one who became a Christian would have to suffer from his unbelieving fellow-countrymen (1 Cor. iv. 10–13); but it seems better to refer it, like ὕψος above, to the intrinsic effect of Christianity in changing our view of life. As the despised poor learns self-respect, so the proud rich learns self-abasement, cf. Luke xxii. 26 ὁ ἡγούμενος ὡς ὁ διακονῶν, Phil. iii. 3–8. Alf., after Bede, Pott, Huther and others, distinguishes ὁ πλούσιος from ὁ ἀδελφός on the ground (1) that the rich in this epistle are always spoken of in terms of great severity (ii. 6, v. 1 foll.); (2) that παρελεύσεται and μαρανθήσεται are not appropriate if spoken of a brother. He therefore supplies καυχᾶται, not καυχάσθω, after ὁ πλούσιος, with the sense 'whereas the rich man glories in his debasement,' and illustrates it from Phil. iii. 19 ὧν ἡ δόξα ἐν τῇ αἰσχύνῃ αὐτῶν. But ταπείνωσις never bears this sense in the Hellenistic writers. It and its cognates are used either in a good sense morally (as below iv. 6, 10), or of mere outward humiliation (as in Luke i. 48) ἐπέβλεψεν ἐπὶ τὴν ταπείνωσιν τῆς δούλης αὐτού, Sir. 2. 5 ἄνθρωποι λεκτοὶ δοκιμάζονται ἐν καμίνῳ ταπεινώσεως, *ib.* xi. 13, xx. 10, Psa. cxix. 50, 67, 71, 1 Macc. iii. 51, 2 Sam. xvi. 12, Neh. ix. 9). In the next place such a change of mood in the verb to be supplied is extremely harsh, and I think Alf. stands alone in supposing it possible. Equally impossible is the supposition of Oecumenius, Grotius and others that some such word as αἰσχυνέσθω or ταπεινούσθω should be supplied. However we understand πλούσιος, no interpretation is admissible which does not supply the imperative καυχάσθω. Bede, followed by Huther and Beyschlag, has attempted to reconcile this with the idea of πλούσιος,

as an unbeliever, by giving it a sarcastic force, 'let the rich man, if he will, glory in his degradation.' So too B. Weiss, who however explains ταπείνωσις of the speedy ruin which awaits him. It must be allowed that such bitterness of sarcasm is not impossible in the writer of ii. 19, iv. 4, v. 1–6; but could he so early in his letter, in cold blood so to speak, have thus anathematized the rich as a class, when we know from iv. 13–16 that some of those to whom he writes were wealthy traders? How could one who had known Nicodemus and Mary of Bethany, Joseph of Arimathaea and Barnabas, have thus denied to the rich the privilege of Christian membership? According to the correct interpretation all that he does is to repeat his master's warning in Matt. vi. 19 foll., xvi. 26, Mark x. 24, Luke xii. 15–21, xvi. 9–31; so St. Paul 1 Cor. vii. 29–31, cf. Herm. *Sim.* ii. 4 foll. and Zahn *Skizzen* p. 53.

ὅτι ὡς ἄνθος χόρτου παρελεύσεται.] A quotation (given more fully in Pet. i. 24) from Isa. xl. 6 πᾶσα σὰρξ χόρτος καὶ πᾶσα δόξα ἀνθρώπου ὡς ἄνθος χόρτου· ἐξηράνθη ὁ χόρτος καὶ τὸ ἄνθος ἐξέπεσεν: cf. Psa. lxxxix. 6. ciii. 15. It is evident that this is not a special threat intended only for the rich, but a general truth applicable to all, though more likely to be kept out of sight by the rich than by others. 'Let him glory in that which the world holds to be humiliation, but which is indeed the commencement of everlasting glory, because he must soon pass away from earth and leave behind the riches in which he is now tempted to glory.' Pliny *N.H.* 21. 1 has the same comparison, *Flores odoresque in diem gignit (natura) magna admonitione hominum, quae spectatissime floreant celerrime marcescere.*

παρελεύσεται.] Used in this sense, as well in common, as in Hellenistic Greek: cf. Mark xiii. 31 ὁ οὐρανὸς καὶ ἡ γῆ παρελεύσεται. It is not necessary to understand a new subject πλοῦτος from πλούσιος, though it is possible that the equivalent phrase in the LXX. δόξα ἀνθρώπου may have been in the writer's mind; but the rich man as such, whether believer or unbeliever, must quickly disappear, and, like the flower, lose τὴν εὐπρέπειαν τοῦ προσώπου.

11. **ἀνέτειλεν γὰρ ὁ ἥλιος.**] Gnomic aorist, as in the original Isa. xl. 7, and below ver. 24, cf. Winer, p. 347 note, Krueger, *Gr.* § 53. 10.

σὺν τῷ καύσωνι.] It is questioned whether κ. here means 'heat' simply, or a special burning wind blowing from the eastern desert over Palestine and from the south over Egypt. It is used of wind in the following: Jonah iv. 8 ἐγένετο ἅμα τῷ ἀνατεῖλαι τὸν ἥλιον καὶ προσέταξεν ὁ Θεὸς πνεύματι καύσωνι, Ezek. xvii. 10 (of a vine) οὐχὶ ἅμα τῷ ἅψασθαι αὐτῆς ἄνεμον τὸν καύσωνα ξηρανθήσεται, on which Jerome says *Austro flante qui Graece* καύσων *interpretatur*, Ez. xix. 10, Hos. xii. 1, Jer. xviii. 17, Hos. xiii. 15 ἐπάξει καύσωνα ἄνεμον Κύριος ἐκ τῆς ἐρήμου ἐπ' αὐτόν: and the destructive effect of the wind generally on vegetation is referred to in Psa. ciii. 16, Gen xli. 6, Virg. *Ecl.* ii. 58 *floribus Austrum immisi*, Prop. iv. 5. 59 *vidi ego odorati victura rosaria Paesti sub matutino cocta jacere noto.* There are however passages in which κ. seems more naturally understood of heat, e.g. Luke. xii. 55 (when ye see) νότον πνέοντα λέγετε ὅτι καύσων ἔσται, Matt. xx. 12 ἴσους τοῖς βαστάσασι τὸ βάρος τῆς ἡμέρας καὶ τὸν καύσωνα, Sirac. 18. 15 οὐχὶ καύσωνα ἀναπαύσει δρόσος, and Schegg is disposed to take κ. always in this sense, except where it is occompanied by ἄνεμος or πνεῦμα. I think that the addition of the article (Corbey '*cum aestu suo*,' Schegg '*its* heat,' but in Hellenistic Greek we should have expected τῷ κ. αὐτοῦ) and the resemblance to Jonah iv. 8 are in favour of the interpretation 'wind' here; so Bp. Middleton *On the Article* p. 422. Compare also Wetzstein's note on Job xxvii. 21 in Delitzsch's ed.: 'The name Sirocco, by which the E. wind is known, means literally *der von Sonnenaufgang herwehende*: it is not uncommon in spring, when it withers up all the young vegetation.' Other passages where the meaning of the word is doubtful are Sir. xxxi. 16, xliii. 22, Isa. xlix. 10, Judith viii. 3, Athenaeus iii. 2 καύσωνος ὥρᾳ ψυκτικώτατοι μελιλώτινοι στέφανοι. For the metaphor cf, Job xxvii. 21 ἀναλήψεται δὲ αὐτὸν (the rich) καύσων καὶ ἀπελεύσεται, *ib.* xxiv. 24 πολλοὺς ἐκάκωσε τὸ ὕψωμα αὐτοῦ, ἐμαράνθη δὲ ὥσπερ μολόχη ἐν καύματι ἢ ὥσπερ στάχυς ἀπὸ καλάμης αὐτόματος ἀποπεσών, Psa. xxxvii. 2, xcii. 7.

χόρτον.] Properly = *hortus* 'inclosure,' then used for a paddock, then for grass and fodder, from whence comes the use of χορτάζομαι = *edo* ii. 16. Here we may understand it loosely of wild flowers mixed with grass: cf. Matt. vi. 30.

ἐξέπεσε.] Used of flowers falling from the calyx in Isa. xl. 6, xxviii. 1, 4, Job xiv. 2, xv. 30: not found in this sense in classical writers.

εὐπρέπεια τοῦ προσώπου αὐτοῦ.] 'Grace of its countenance.' εὐπ. only here in N.T. In Sir. 24. 14 we have εὐπρεπὴς ἐλαία, Psa. 1. 2 ἐκ Σιὼν ἡ εὐπρέπεια τῆς ὡραιότητος αὐτοῦ, Psa. xcii. 1 εὐπρέπειαν ἐνεδύσατο, Aeschin. p. 18 τὴν τοῦ σώματος εὐπρέπειαν, Ps. Demosth. 1402, 1404. For thought cf. Matt. vi. 28 foll. Vorst *Hell. Lex.* p. 342 foll. regards προσ. as a Hebraistic pleonasm: others more correctly take it in the general sense of outward appearance, like *facies*.

ὁ πλούσιος.] The rich man *qua* rich, with no special reference to the rich brother.

ἐν ταῖς πορείαις.] It seems best to take this here in the literal sense, as in the only other passage in which it occurs in the N.T. (Luke xiii. 22), referring to the journeyings and voyages of the merchants: cf below iv. 13 foll. For the redundant αὐτοῦ cf. Winer, p. 179.

μαρανθήσεται.] Used on account of preceding simile (here only in N.T.): cf. Philo M. 2. p. 258 μήτ' ἐπὶ πλούτῳ, μήτ' ἐπὶ δόξῃ, μήθ' ἡγεμονίᾳ...σεμνυνθῇς, λογισάμενος ὅτι...ὀξεῖαν ἔχει τὴν μεταβολὴν μαραινόμενα τρόπον τινὰ πρὶν ἀνθῆσαι βεβαίως, Plut. *Qu. Conv.* 674 A ἀνθρώπου ἐκλιπόντος καὶ μαραινομένου, Herm. *Vis.* iii. 11. 2, *Sim.* ix. 23. 2.

12. **μακάριος ἀνήρ.**] See n. on v. 8. The same phrase occurs in Rom iv. 8 (a quotation from Psa. xxxii. 2); Psa. i. 1, xxxiv. 8, xl. 4, lxxxiv. 5; Prov. xxviii. 14, &c. See below v. 11. The absence of the article shows that ἀνήρ is part of the predicate. In Psa. xciv. 12 and Jer. xvii. 7 we have the more natural construction μακάριος (εὐλογημένος) ὁ ἄνθρωπος. For the classical way of expressing a similar sentiment cf. Pind. *Ol.* v. 61 μακάριος ὃς ἔχεις λόγων φερτάτον μναμῆιον, Soph. *Ant.* 578 εὐδαίμονες οἷσι κακῶν ἄγευστος αἰών. The pleonastic ἀνήρ is often found, as below iii. 2 τέλειος ἀνήρ, with ἁμαρτωλός Luke v. 8, προφήτης *ib.* xxiv. 19, φονεύς Acts iii. 14. This blessing is referred to below v. 11,

which seems to show, as Spitta says, that there is an allusion here to the rich man of ver. 10, cf. Sirac. xxxiv. (xxx.) 8 foll. *μακάριος πλούσιος ὃς εὑρέθη ἄμωμος καὶ ὃς ὀπίσω χρυσίου οὐκ ἐπορεύθη. τίς ἐστι; καὶ μακαριοῦμεν αὐτόν. τίς ἐδοκιμάσθη ἐν αὐτῷ καὶ ἐτελειώθη; καὶ ἔστω εἰς καύχησιν. τίς ἐδύνατο παραβῆναι καὶ οὐ παρέβη;* Job v. 17 *μακάριος ἄνθρωπος ὃν ἤλεγξεν ὁ Κύριος.*

ὃς ὑπομένει πειρασμόν.] So we have *μακ. ὃς φάγεται* Luke xiv. 15, but more commonly the subject is expressed by the participle, as Apoc. i. 3 *μακάριος ὁ ἀναγινώσκων.* This verse limits the general exhortation of ver. 2 to rejoice in trial. It is only he who endures that is blessed. There may be another result of trial, as is shown in the following verses. Cf. Herm. *Vis.* ii. 2, 7 *μακάριοι ὑμεῖς ὅσοι ὑπομένετε τὴν θλίψιν κ.τ.λ.*

δόκιμος.] See above on *δοκίμιον*, ver. 3.

τὸν στέφανον.] The word is used (1) for the wreath of victory in the games (1 Cor. ix. 25, 2 Tim. ii. 5); (2) as a festal ornament (Prov. i. 9, iv. 9, Cant. iii. 11, Herm. *Sim.* viii. 2, Isa. xxviii. 1, Wisd. ii. 8 *στεψώμεθα ῥόδων κάλυξι πρὶν ἢ μαρανθῆναι*, Judith xv. 13 *ἐστεφανώσαντο τὴν ἐλαίαν*): (3) as a public honour granted for distinguished service or private worth, as a golden crown was granted to Demosthenes (see his speech on the subject) and Zeno (Diog. L. vii. 10 *στεφανῶσαι χρυσῷ στεφάνῳ ἀρετῆς ἕνεκα καὶ σωφροσύνης*): references to these are very common in inscriptions; (4) as a symbol of royal or priestly dignity. The last is denied by Trench (*N.T. Syn.* p. 90, *στεφανος* 'is never, any more than *corona* in Latin, the emblem of royalty,'[1] but see 2 Sam. xii. 30 'David took their king's crown (*στέφανον*) from off his head, the weight of which was a talent of gold with the precious stones,' Psa. xxi. 1 foll. 'the king shall joy in thy strength...thou settest a crown (*στέφανον*) of pure gold on his head,' Zech. vi. 11 *λήψῃ ἀργύριον καὶ χρυσίον καὶ ποιήσεις στεφάνους καὶ ἐπιθήσεις ἐπὶ τὴν κεφαλὴν Ἰησοῦ τοῦ ἱερέως τοῦ μεγάλου*, Apoc. iv. 4 *ἐπὶ τοὺς θρόνους εἶδον εἴκοσι τέσσαρας πρεσβυτέρους καθημένους...καὶ ἐπὶ τὰς κεφαλὰς αὐτῶν στεφάνους χρυσοῦς*: in ch. v. 10 the same elders praise the Lamb for making kings and priests to God out of every nation: *ib.* xiv. 14 one like the Son of Man sat on the cloud *ἔχων ἐπὶ τῆς κεφαλῆς αὐτοῦ στέφανον χρυσοῦν*: lastly, in the mocking of our Lord (Matt xxvii. 29) there surely can be no doubt that the *στέφανος* and *κάλαμος* stand for the crown and sceptre. Virgil speaks of *regni coronam Aen.* 8, 505. Trench however is right in saying that *διάδημα* is more commonly used in this sense, e.g. Isa. lxii. 3 *ἔσῃ στέφανος κάλλους ἐν χειρὶ Κυρίου καὶ διάδημα βασιλείας ἐν χειρὶ Θεοῦ σου.* The question then is, from which of these uses is the metaphor here derived. Comparing ii. 5, where what is here said of the crown is repeated of the kingdom, it would seem natural to take the word as implying sovereignty, and this would agree with Wisd. v. 16 *δίκαιοι λήψονται τὸ βασίλειον τῆς εὐπρεπείας καὶ τὸ διάδημα τοῦ κάλλους ἐκ χειρὸς Κυρίου*, *ib.* iii. 8, Dan. vii. 27 'the kingdom was given to the saints of the Most High,' Apoc. i. 6, 1 Pet. ii. 9 *ὑμεῖς βασίλειον ἱεράτευμα*, Rom. v. 17 *οἱ τὴν περισσείαν τῆς χάριτος λαμβάνοντες*

[[1] Trench allows this use in his *Epistles to the Seven Churches*, p. 111. H. H. M.]

ἐν ζωῇ βασιλεύσουσιν, Luke xii. 32 'it is my Father's good pleasure to give you the kingdom,' *ib.* xxii. 28 'I appoint unto you a kingdom, and ye shall sit on thrones judging the twelve tribes of Israel,' 2 Tim. ii. 12 εἰ ὑπομένομεν καὶ συμβασιλεύσομεν, which reminds one of Zech. vi. 14 ὁ στέφανος ἔσται τοῖς ὑπομένουσι, following immediately after κατάρξει ἐπὶ τοῦ θρόνου αὐτοῦ; so the Stoic paradox *sapiens rex*. The nearest parallels to our passage are Apoc. ii. 10 γίνου πιστὸς ἄχρι θανάτου καὶ δώσω σοι τὸν στέφανον τῆς ζωῆς, 2 Tim. iv. 8 ἀποκεῖταί μοι ὁ τῆς δικαιοσύνης στέφανος ὃν ἀποδώσει μοι ὁ Κύριος ἐν ἐκείνῃ τῇ ἡμέρᾳ...καὶ πᾶσι τοῖς ἠγαπηκόσι τὴν ἐπιφάνειαν αὐτοῦ, 1 Pet. v. 4 φανερωθέντος τοῦ ἀρχιποιμένος κομιεῖσθε τὸν ἀμαράντινον τῆς δόξης στέφανον. The use of the article in all these seems to imply some well-known saying or a very definite expectation. On the other hand, the idea of a kingly crown seems less appropriate in them than that of a crown of merit or victory. The Rabbins talk of three crowns (Pirke Aboth iv. 19). Probably the metaphorical use would be coloured by all the literal uses. Other instances are Sir. 1. 16, vi. 30, xv. 6, Acta Matt. Tisch. p. 169 ἐγγύς ἐστιν τῆς ὑπομονῆς σου ὁ στέφανος, Philo *Legg. All.* M. p. 86 σπούδασον στεφανωθῆναι κατὰ τῆς τοὺς ἄλλους ἅπαντας νικώσης ἡδονῆς καλὸν καὶ εὐκλεᾶ στέφανον ὃν οὐδεμία πανήγυρις ἀνθρώπων ἐχώρησε.

τῆς ζωῆς.] Gen. of definition, as in the parallels quoted in the last n.: 'the crown which consists in life eternal.' Cf. 1 John ii. 25 αὕτη ἐστὶν ἡ ἐπαγγελία ἣν αὐτὸς ἐπηγγείλατο ὑμῖν, τὴν ζωὴν τὴν αἰώνιον, 1 Pet. iii. 7. This is contrasted with the fading away of earthly prosperity. Zeller and Hilgenfeld (*Ztschr. f. wiss. Theol.* 1873, p. 93 and p. 10) consider that the expression is borrowed from Apoc. ii. 10, this being the promise referred to below. [Wisdom promises a crown and life, Prov. iv. 9, iii. 18, Aboth vi. C.T.]

ὃν ἐπηγγείλατο τοῖς ἀγαπῶσιν αὐτόν.] Κύριος or Θεός is inserted in some MSS. but in AB Sin. &c. the subject is omitted, as in Heb. iv. 3 καθὼς εἴρηκεν, and often in introducing a quotation: cf. iv. 6, Eph. iv. 8, Gal. iii. 16, 1 Cor. vi. 16, Heb. x. 5, and Winer p. 735; also without a quotation in 1 Joh. v. 16 αἰτήσει, καὶ δώσει αὐτῷ ζωήν. Putting on one side Apoc. ii. 10, which was probably written subsequently to this epistle, we do not find the precise words τὸν στέφανον τῆς ζωῆς in any particular passage of the Bible. It is a question therefore whether they constitute an unwritten word, a record of oral teaching, such as we have in Acts xx. 35, and of which others have been preserved by early Christian writers;[1] or whether it is an instance of loose quotation, representing some of the verses cited above on στέφανος. For the latter view it may be said that it is apparently the same quotation which is repeated in different words below (ii. 5). For the former, that the undoubted references to the Sermon on the Mount

[1] They are collected in Resch's *Agrapha*. Leipzig. 1889. Besides this verse (on which he compares Isa. xxii. 17–21 and Acta Philippi, p. 147 T.) he includes i. 17 πᾶσα δόσις ἀγαθή, iv. 5 πρὸς φθόνον ἐπιποθεῖ, iv. 17 εἰδότι οὖν καλὸν ποιεῖν, v. 20 καλύψει πλῆθος among the number of sayings of Jesus unreported in our Gospels. I have long held that we have in this verse an 'unwritten word,' but I do not think there is much force in the arguments adduced by Resch as regards the other verses.

which occur in this epistle are in all probability actual reminiscences of spoken words, not copied from the written Gospel; and secondly, that it seems easier to explain the coincidence between St. James and the writer of the Apocalypse on this than on any other supposition. Promises to those that love God are found in Exod. xx. 6, Deut. vii. 9, *ib.* xxx. 16, 20, Jud. v. 30, Psa. v. 11, 2 Tim. iv. 8, 1 Cor. ii. 9 (a quotation from Isa. lxiv. 4, where however the LXX. has τοῖς ὑπομένουσιν ἔλεον for St. Paul's τοῖς ἀγαπῶσιν αὐτόν)..

13. **μηδεὶς πειραζόμενος λεγέτω ὅτι.**] *Hactenus de tentationibus quas permittente Domino exterius probandi gratia perpetimur disputavit: nunc incipit agere de illis quas interius instigante diabolo vel etiam naturae nostrae fragilitate suadente toleramus* (Bede). Through trial in itself is ordered by God for our good, yet the inner solicitation to evil which is aroused by the outer trial is from ourselves. The subst. πειρασμός denotes the objective trial, the v. πειράζομαι subjective temptation. Ὅτι introduces the direct oration as in Matt. vii. 23, John ix. 9, and often both in Hellenistic and classical Greek.

ἀπὸ Θεοῦ πειράζομαι.] Ἀπό expresses the remoter, as contrasted with the nearer cause expressed by ὑπό (Winer, p. 463 foll). Eve was the immediate cause of Adam's transgression, but Adam tried to make God the ultimate cause in the words 'whom thou gavest to be with me.' So the fault is often laid on hereditary disposition, on unfavourable circumstances, on sudden and overpowering πειρασμός. The same plea is noticed in both Jewish and heathen writers: cf. Prov. xix. 3 ἀφροσύνη ἀνδρὸς λυμαίνεται τὰς ὁδοὺς αὐτοῦ, τὸν δὲ Θεὸν αἰτιᾶται τῇ καρδίᾳ αὐτοῦ, Sir. xv. 11–20 μὴ εἴπῃς ὅτι διὰ Κύριον ἀπέστην· ἃ γὰρ ἐμίσησεν οὐ ποιήσεις· μὴ εἴπῃς ὅτι αὐτός με ἐπλάνησεν...πᾶν βδέλυγμα ἐμίσησεν ὁ Κύριος, καὶ οὐκ ἔστιν ἀγαπητὸν τοῖς φοβουμένοις αὐτόν· αὐτὸς ἐξ ἀρχῆς ἐποίησεν ἄνθρωπον καὶ ἀφῆκεν αὐτὸν ἐν χειρὶ διαβουλίου αὐτοῦ...ἔναντι ἀνθρώπων ἡ ζωὴ καὶ ὁ θάνατος κ.τ.λ., Rom. ix. 19 τί ἔτι μέμφεται; τῷ γὰρ βουλήματι αὐτοῦ τίς ἀνθέστηκε; Clem. *Hom.* iii. 55 τοῖς δὲ οἰομένοις ὅτι ὁ Θεὸς πειράζει...ἔφη· ὁ πονηρός ἐστιν ὁ πειράζων, ὁ καὶ αὐτὸν πειράσας, Herm. *Mand.* ix. 8 ἐὰν διψυχήσῃς αἰτούμενος σεαυτὸν αἰτιῶ καὶ μὴ τὸν διδόντα σοι, Tert. *Orat.* 8 (commenting on the Lord's Prayer) *absit ut Dominus tentare videatur*, Philo M. 1. p. 558 τίς ἂν γένοιτο αἰσχίων κακηγορία ἢ τὸ φάσκειν μὴ περὶ ἡμᾶς ἀλλὰ περὶ Θεὸν γένεσιν εἶναι τῶν κακῶν; *ib.* p. 214 οὐ γὰρ, ὥς ἔνιοι τῶν ἀσεβῶν, τὸν Θεὸν αἴτιον κακων φησὶ Μωϋσῆς, ἀλλὰ τὰς ἡμετέρας χεῖρας...καὶ τὰς ἑκουσίους τῆς διανοίας πρὸς τὸ χεῖρον τροπάς, Hom. *Il.* 19. 85 (Agamemnon excuses himself for his injustice towards Achilles) ἐγὼ δ' οὐκ αἴτιός εἰμι, ἀλλὰ Ζεὺς καὶ μοῖρα καὶ ἠεροφοῖτις ἐρινύς, οἵ τέ μοι εἰν ἀγορῇ φρεσὶν ἔμβαλον ἄγριον ἄτην, *Od.* i. 32 ὢ πόποι οἷον δή νυ θεοὺς βροτοὶ αἰτιόωνται· ἐξ ἡμῶν γάρ φασι κάκ' ἔμμεναι· οἱ δὲ καὶ αὐτοὶ σφῇσιν ἀτασθαλίῃσιν ὑπὲρ μόρον ἄλγε' ἔχουσιν, Aeschin. *Tim.* p. 27. 5. Nägelsb. *Hom. Theol.* p. 343 foll., *Nachhom. Theol.* 319 foll., and my note on Cic. *N.D.* iii. 76.

ἀπείραστός ἐστι κακῶν.] 'Untemptable of evil': not found elsewhere in N.T. or LXX.[1] The verb πειράζω, from which it is formed, is not

[1] This and the two following verses are quoted by Epiph. *Panar.* 1066.

used by the Attic writers. It could not be formed from πειράω, as the perf. and aor. passive are without the σ (πεπείραμαι, ἐπειράθην), but πειράζω being sometimes used in the sense 'to attempt' (e.g. Acts xvi. 7 ἐπείραζον κατὰ τὴν Βιθυνίαν πορεύεσθαι), ἀπείραστος might be equivalent to ἀπείρατος from πειράω. The usual force of the verbal in -τος is seen in ἀδέκαστος 'unbribable,' ἀνήκεστος 'incurable,' ἀβίωτος (βίος) 'intolerable,' ἀμετάβλητος 'unchangeable,' ἄῤῥηκτος 'infrangible.' Many of these verbals have the force of a perfect part. pass. (*intentatus* as well as *intentabilis*), and even an active force, like ἄπταιστος, ἀφύλακτος: cf. Lat. *penetrabilis* and Winer, p. 120. Hence a wide difference between commentators as to the force of ἀπείραστος here. Beyschlag says 'bei den Kirchenvätern wird Gott öfters einfach der Unversuchbare genannt,' but the only instances cited are Pseudo-Ignatius *De Baptismo ad Philipp.*[1] § 11 (Lightfoot vol. 3 p. 783) πῶς πειράζεις τὸν ἀπείραστον; and Photius *c. Manichaeos* iv. p. 25 (Migne *Patrol. Gr.* cii. col. 234) τοῖς Σαδδουκαίοις πειράζειν ἐπιχειρήσασι τὸν ἀπείραστον (written in the 9th cent.). The former is quoted in connexion with Matt. iv. 7, which leaves no doubt as to the sense in which ἀπείραστος is used. It is used in the same sense by Clem. Al. *Strom.* vii. p. 858 P. αὐστηρὸς οὐκ εἰς τὸ ἀδιάφθορον μόνον, ἀλλὰ καὶ εἰς τὸ ἀπείραστον· οὐδαμῇ γὰρ ἐνδόσιμον οὐδὲ ἁλώσιμον ἡδονῇ τε καὶ λύπῃ τὴν ψυχὴν παρίστησιν, *ib.* p. 874 P. ἐκεῖνος ἄνδρας νικᾷ ὁ γάμῳ καὶ παιδοποιίᾳ... ἐγγυμνησάμενος...πάσης κατεξανιστάμενος πείρας τῆς διὰ τέκνων καὶ γυναικὸς ...τῷ δὲ ἀοίκῳ τὰ πολλὰ εἶναι συμβέβηκεν ἀπειράστῳ. I have also found it in the *Acta Johannis* (Zahn p. 75, l. 15) τοῖς τότε πειράζουσιν τὸν Θεὸν ὁ ἀπείραστος τῇ πείρᾳ ἐκείνων τὴν εὐθύτητα ἐδίδου, p. 113. 5 μὴ πείραζε τὸν ἀπείραστον, p. 190. 18 μακάριος ὅστις οὐκ ἐπείρασεν ἐν σοὶ τὸν Θεὸν, ὁ γὰρ σὲ πειράζων τὸν ἀπείραστον πειράζει. In Const. Apost. ii. 8 λέγει ἡ γραφή· ἀνὴρ ἀδόκιμος ἀπείραστος παρὰ Θεῷ (which must apparently mean 'one who is without trial is unapproved in the sight of God'[2]) there is probably an allusion to our ver. 12 and to Heb. xii. 8. It is used in a different sense in Jos. *B.J.* vii. 8 οἱ σικάριοι τῆς παρανομίας ἤρξαντο μήτε λόγον ἄῤῥητον εἰς ὕβριν μήτ' ἔργον ἀπείραστον (*facinus intentatum*) εἰς ὄλεθρον παραλείποντες. In this sense the form ἀπείρατος (from πειράω) is more common, e.g. Demosth. 310, οὔτ' ἀπόνοια Σωσικλέους οὔτε συκοφαντία Φιλοκράτους...οὔτ' ἄλλο οὐδὲν ἀπείρατον ἦν τούτοις κατ' ἐμοῦ, Demad. p. 180 πρότερον ἀπείρατος ὢν πολεμίας σάλπιγγος ('having had no experience of'), Diod. i. 1 ἡ διὰ τῆς ἱστορίας περιγινομένη σύνεσις τῶν ἀλλοτρίων ἀποτευγμάτων...ἀπείρατον κακῶν ἔχει διδασκαλίαν, Plut. *Mor.* p. 119 F (of early death) εὐποτμότερος διὰ τοῦτο καὶ κακῶν ἀπείρατός ἐστιν, and in Jos. *J.B.* iii. 7. 32 ἔμειναν δὲ οὐδὲ Σαμαρεῖς ἀπείρατοι συμφορῶν, *ib.* v. 9. 3 γινώσκειν τὴν Ῥωμαίων ἰσχὺν ἀνυπόστατον, καὶ τὸ δουλεύειν τούτοις οὐκ ἀπείρατον αὐτοῖς, Pind. *Ol.* viii. 60 κουφότεραι γὰρ ἀπειράτων φρένες: the Ionic form occurs Hom. *Od.* ii. 170, Herod. vii. 9. 3

[1] This treatise was probably written towards the end of the 4th century (Lightfoot vol. i. p. 260).

[2] Cf. Tert. *Bapt.* c. 20 *neminem intentatum regna caelestia consecuturum* with reference to Luke xxii. 28, 29; Cassian. *Coll.* ix. 23 *omnis vir qui non est temptatus non est probatus*, 1 Cor. xi. 19.

ἔστω μηδὲν ἀπείρητον· αὐτόματον γὰρ οὐδέν, ἀλλ' ἀπὸ πείρης πάντα ἀνθρώποισι.

In accordance with the use of ἀπείρατος Alford translates 'unversed in things evil'; so Hofmann ('*Bösem fremd* oder *vom Uebeln unbetroffen*, auf keinem Fall aber *von Bösem oder zu Bösem unversucht oder unversuchbar*'), Brückner, Erdmann. Others (Vulg. Aeth. Luther) give it an active sense, 'God is not one who tempts to evil.' The latter interpretation would make the next clause (πειράζει δέ) mere tautology, and it has now no defenders. It seems to me that the case is equally strong against the former interpretation. The meaning of the rare word ἀπείραστος must be determined from the general force of πειράζω in the N.T., and especially from the following clause, which is evidently intended to be its exact correlative in the active voice (ἀπείραστος : πειράζει δὲ αὐτός). The relation of the two clauses would have been more clearly marked if μὲν had been added after ἀπ.: compare for its omission Jelf § 797, and below ii. 2, 11. Further it is impossible to read this sentence without being reminded of very similar phrases used about God by Philo and other post-Aristotelian philosophers, cf. Philo M. 1. p. 154 God is ἀκοινώνητος κακῶν, *ib.* 563 (ὁ λόγος) ἀμέτοχος καὶ ἀπαράδεκτος παντὸς εἶναι πέφυκεν ἁμαρτήματος, *ib.* M. 2. p. 280 God is μόνος εὐδαίμων καὶ μακάριος, πάντων μὲν ἀμέτοχος κακῶν, πλήρης δὲ ἀγαθῶν τελείων, μᾶλλον δὲ αὐτὸς ὢν τὸ ἀγαθόν, ὃς οὐρανῷ καὶ γῇ τὰ κατὰ μέρος ὤμβρισεν ἀγαθά, Plut. Mor. 1102 F πάντων πατὴρ καλῶν ὁ Θεός ἐστιν καὶ φαῦλον οὐδὲν ποιεῖν αὐτῷ θέμις, ὥσπερ οὐδὲ πάσχειν κ.τ.λ., M. Ant. 6. 1 οὐδεμίαν ἐν ἑαυτῷ αἰτίαν ἔχει τοῦ κακοποιεῖν· κακίαν γὰρ οὐκ ἔχει, οὐδέ τι κακῶς ποιεῖ, see Gataker's note there and on ii. 11, Sext. Emp. *Math.* ix. 91 τὸ τέλειον καὶ ἄριστον...παντὸς κακοῦ ἀναπόδεκτον, Seneca *Ira* 2. 27 *di nec volunt obesse nec possunt. Natura enim mitis et placida est, tam remota ab aliena injuria quam a sua*; ib. *Epist.* 95. 49 *nec accipere injuriam queunt nec facere; laedere enim laedique conjunctum est: summa illa ac pulcherrima omnium natura quos periculo exemit ne periculosos quidem fecit.* The original source seems to be the maxim of Epicurus, Diog. L. x. 138 τὸ μακάριον καὶ ἄφθαρτον οὔτε αὐτὸ πράγματα ἔχει οὔτε ἄλλῳ παρέχει, which is compared here by Oecumenius; see my note on Cic. *N.D.* i. 45. For the gen. κακῶν, which is perhaps more easily explained as meaning '*to* evil' than '*by* evil,' see Xen. *Cyrop.* iii. 3. 55 ἀπαίδευτος ἀρετῆς, Winer, p. 242, who compares 2 Pet. ii. 14 καρδίαν γεγυμνασμένην πλεονεξίας, Soph. *Ant.* 848 ἄκλαυτος φίλων. I think these are best classed under the head of 'Genitive of the Sphere,' an extension of the Inclusive ('Partitive') genitive, 'untemptable in regard of evil things,' just as it might be said of one who was wholly evil that he was ἀπείραστος ἀγαθῶν.[1] We have still to consider an objection drawn from the context: 'there is no question here of God being tempted, but of God tempting,' Alf. This is sufficiently met by the passages cited above from Philo, Plutarch, and Antoninus: God is incapable of tempting others to evil, because He is Himself absolutely insusceptible to evil; *i.e.* our belief in God's own character, His perfect purity and

[1] Von Soden destroys the sense of the passage by taking κακῶν of afflictions. It is of course used of moral evil, as in Rom. i. 30, 1 Cor. x. 6.

holiness, makes it impossible for us to suppose that it is from Him that our temptations proceed: so far from himself tempting others to evil, which would imply a delight in evil, he is by his own nature incapable of being even solicited to evil. For the difficulties connected with this subject see comment on Temptation below. Spitta gives up the passage as hopeless from a misapprehension of the meaning of δέ, which he confounds with ἀλλά.

14. **ἕκαστος δὲ πειράζεται ὑπὸ τῆς ἰδίας ἐπιθυμίας.**] Wetst. quotes Menachoth. f. 99. b (slightly shortened) *caro et sanguis seducit a viis vitae ad vias mortis: Deus a viis mortis ad vias vitae.* We may compare the famous words of Plato αἰτία ἑλομένου· Θεὸς ἀναίτιος *Rep.* x. 617, Cleanthes *ap.* Stob. *Ecl.* i. 2. 12 οὐδέ τι γίγνεται ἔργον ἐπὶ χθονὶ σοῦ δίχα, δαῖμον, πλὴν ὁπόσα ῥέζουσι κακοὶ σφετέρῃσιν ἀνοίαις...αὐτοὶ δ' αὖθ' ὁρμῶσιν ἄνευ καλοῦ ἄλλος ἐπ' ἄλλα κ.τ.λ., Chrysippus *ap.* Gell. 6. 2. 12; above all the discussion on the voluntary nature of virtue and vice in Arist. *Eth.* iii. 5. See also *Phaedr.* 238 ἐπιθυμίας ἀλόγως ἑλκούσης ἐπὶ ἡδονὰς καὶ ἀρξάσης (this tyranny of lust was called ὕβρις), Seneca *Ira* ii. 3 *affectus est non ad oblatas rerum species moveri, sed permittere se illis et hunc fortuitum motum prosequi*, Philo M. 2. p. 349 τὸ ἀψευδῶς ἂν λεχθὲν ἀρχέκακον πάθος ἐστὶν ἐπιθυμία, *ib.* 208 ἀδικημάτων πηγὴ ἐπιθυμία ἀφ' ἧς ῥέουσιν αἱ παρανομώταται πράξεις, *ib.* M. 2. p. 204 (in contrast with other affections which may be deemed involuntary) μόνη ἐπιθυμία τὴν ἀρχὴν ἐξ ἡμῶν λαμβάνει καὶ ἐστὶν ἑκούσιος. It is these ἐπιθυμίαι σαρκός, as they are frequently called, which constitute 'the law in our members' (Rom. vii. 23). St. James describes them below (iv. 1) as ἡδοναὶ 'warring in our members.' As ἐπιθυμία is here personified, there is no question about the use of ὑπό, on which see below iii. 4 n. For ἰδίας cf. 2 Tim. iv. 3, 2 Pet. iii. 2, Jude 18, 19.

ἐξελκόμενος καὶ δελεαζόμενος.] *Abstractus a recto itinere et illectus in malum*, Bede. Δέλεαρ and its cognates (used first of the arts of the hunter and then of those of the harlot) are often found in this connexion, see 2 Pet. ii. 14, 18, Philo M. 1, p. 604 ἐπιθυμιῶν δελέασιν ἀγκιστρεύσασθαι, pp. 265–267, *ib.* M. 2, p. 216 (on the attractions of idolatry) ἵνα ὄψιν καὶ ἀκοὴν δελεάσαντες συναρπάσωσι τὴν ψυχήν, *ib.* M. 1, p. 569 ἐγὼ μέν, ὅπερ εἰκὸς ἦν ἐργάσασθαι τὸν βουλόμενον τρόπου βάσανον καὶ δοκιμασίαν λάβεῖν, πεποίηκα δέλεαρ καθείς, ὁ δὲ ἐπεδείξατο τὴν ἑαυτοῦ φύσιν οὐκ εὐάλωτον, Plato *Tim.* 69 ἡδονὴν, μέγιστον κακοῦ δέλεαρ, Isocr. *Pax* 166 ὁρῶ τοὺς τὴν ἀδικίαν προτιμῶντας ὅμοια πάσχοντας τοῖς δελεαζομένοις τῶν ζώων, Anton. ii. 12 τὰ ἡδονῇ δελεάζοντα, Cic. *Cato* § 44. It is often found combined with ἕλκω or its cognates: Philo M. 2. p. 474 τὸ σύνηθες ὁλκὸν καὶ δελεάσαι δυνατώτατον, *ib.* M. 1. p. 316 ἓν γὰρ οὐδὲν ἔστιν ὃ μὴ πρὸς ἡδονῆς δελεασθὲν εἵλκυσται, *ib.* M. 2. p. 61 αἴσθησις δελεαζομένη θεάμασι...συνεφέλκεται καὶ τὴν ὅλην ψυχήν, *ib.* M. 1. p. 512 ἐπιθυμία ὁλκὸν ἔχουσα δύναμιν τὸ ποθούμενον διώκειν ἀναγκάζει, *ib.* p. 238 ἡδονῆς ὁλκοῦ δελέαστρα, Epict. *frag.* 112 πάσης κακίας οἷόν τι δέλεαρ ἡδονὴ προβληθεῖσα εὐκόλως τὰς λιχνοτέρας ψυχὰς ἐπὶ τὸ ἄγκιστρον τῆς ἀπωλείας ἐφέλκεται, Plut. *Mor.* 1093 C (the pleasures of geometry) δριμὺ καὶ ποικίλον ἔχουσαι τὸ δέλεαρ οὐδενὸς τῶν ἀγωγίμων ἀποδέουσιν, ἕλκουσαι καθάπερ ἴυγξι τοῖς διαγράμμασιν, *ib.* 547 C. The relation between the two words has been wrongly illustrated from Herod. ii. 70 ἐπεὰν νῶτον ὑὸς δελεάσῃ περὶ ἄγκιστρον...ὁ κροκόδειλος ἐντυχὼν τῷ νώτῳ καταπίνει, οἱ δὲ ἕλκουσιν· ἐπεὰν δὲ ἐξελκυσθῇ ἐς γῆν κ.τ.λ. This would make a ὕστερον πρότερον in our text, where the drawing is previous to the actual catching at the particular bait. Heisen cites a number of lines of Oppian in which ἕλκω and its compounds are used, as here, of the first drawing of the fish out from its original retreat, e.g. iii. 316 the bait ἐφέλκεται ἰχθύας εἴσω, iv. 359; cf. Xen. *Cyrop.* viii. 1. 22 ἐγκράτειαν οὕτω μάλιστ' ἂν ᾤετο ἀσκεῖσθαι εἰ αὐτὸς ἐπιδεικνύοι ἑαυτὸν μὴ ὑπὸ τῶν παραυτίκα ἡδονῶν ἑλκόμενον ἀπὸ τῶν ἀγαθῶν, *ib. Mem.* iii. 11. 18. In like manner the first effect of ἐπιθυμία is to draw the man out of his original repose, the second to allure him to a definite bait. Heisen illustrates this from the temptation of Eve, first moved from her secure trust in God by the words of the tempter (Gen. iii. 1–5), then attracted by the fruit itself (v. 6).[1] Another way of distinguishing between the two words is to suppose that ἐξέλκω implies the violence, δελ. the charm of passion, as in Philo M. 2, p. 470 πρὸς ἐπιθυμίας ἐλαύνεται ἢ ὑφ' ἡδονῆς δελεάζεται, 'driven by passion or solicited by pleasure,' but I prefer the former explanation. Spitta, comparing iv. 7, makes ὁ διάβολος the subject of ἐξέλκειν and thinks this word contains an allusion to Gen. iv. 7 'if thou doest not well, sin coucheth at the door,' where however the Greek has no resemblance to the Hebrew. It is much simpler to understand the participles as describing the manner of temptation by the ἐπιθυμία.

15. **συλλαβοῦσα τίκτει ἁμαρτίαν.**] For the metaphor cf. Psa. vii. 14 ὠδίνησεν ἀδικίαν, συνέλαβε πόνον καὶ ἔτεκεν ἀνομίαν, Philo M. 1. 40 οἷα ἑταιρὶς καὶ μάχλος οὖσα ἡδονὴ γλίχεται τυχεῖν ἐραστοῦ, *ib.* 149 ὅταν ὁ ἐν ἡμῖν νοῦς—κεκλήσθω δὲ 'Αδάμ—ἐντυχὼν αἰσθήσει—καλεῖται δὲ Εὔα—συνουσίας ὀρεχθεὶς πλησιάσῃ, ἥδε συλλαμβάνει...ἐγκύμων τε γίνεται καὶ εὐθυς ὠδίνει καὶ τίκτει κακῶν ψυχῆς τὸ μέγιστον, οἴησιν, *ib.* 183 ὥσπερ ταῖς γυναιξὶ πρὸς ζώων γένεσιν οἰκειότατον μέρος ἡ φύσις ἔδωκε μήτραν, οὕτω πρὸς γένεσιν πραγμάτων ὥρισεν ἐν ψυχῇ δύναμιν, δι' ἧς κυοφορεῖ καὶ ὠδίνει καὶ ἀποτίκτει πολλὰ διάνοια· τῶν δὲ ἀποκυομένων νοημάτων τὰ μὲν ἄῤῥενα, τὰ δὲ θηλέα, Justin M. *Trypho* 327 C παρθένος οὖσα Εὔα τὸν λόγον τὸν ἀπὸ τοῦ ὄφεος συλλαβοῦσα παρακοὴν καὶ θάνατον ἔτεκε, and in classical writers Theognis 153 τίκτει γὰρ κόρος ὕβριν, and Aesch. *Ag.* 727 foll. Sin is the result of the surrender of the will to the soliciting of ἐπιθυμία instead of the guidance of reason. In itself, ἐπιθυμία may be natural and innocent: it is when the man resolves to gratify it against what he feels to be the higher law of duty, that he becomes guilty of sin even before he carries out his resolve in act. Spitta thinks that here, as in the

[1] The two examples cited for this use of ἐξέλκειν by one commentator after another are somewhat doubtful. Arist. *Pol.* v. 10. 1311, b. 30 παρὰ τῆς γυναικὸς ἐξελκυσθείς might mean 'lured away from the side of his wife,' but hardly *ab uxore sollicitatus* (Alf.); and that which Alford calls 'the nearest correspondence of all, Plut. *de sera numinis vindicta* τὸ γλυκὺ τῆς ἐπιθυμίας ὥσπερ δέλεαρ ἐξέλκειν,' I have searched for in vain in the treatise referred to, and it is not to be found in Wyttenbach's Index. It is, I presume, a misquotation for the words which do occur in that treatise (p. 554 E) ἔχεται ἕκαστος ἀδικήσας τῇ δίκῃ, καὶ τὸ γλυκὺ τῆς ἀδικίας ὥσπερ δέλεαρ εὐθὺς ἐξεδήδοκε, τὸ δὲ συνειδὸς ἐγκείμενον ἔχων κ.τ.λ.

Miltonic allegory, Satan is regarded as the father of sin, and he refers in proof to Test. Benj. 7 πρῶτον συλλαμβάνει ἡ διάνοια διὰ τοῦ Βελίαρ, to Test. Reub. 3, where the seven spirits of the senses are said to be impregnated by the seven spirits of Belial, and to the rabbinical comments on Gen. vi. 2 foll. While fully allowing that Satan is represented in iii. 6 and iv. 7 as using man's lusts to destroy him, I cannot see that St. James here carries back the genealogy of sin beyond the ἐπιθυμία of the person tempted.

ἡ δὲ ἁμαρτία ἀποτελεσθεῖσα ἀποκυεῖ θάνατον.] ἡ δὲ ἁμαρτία takes up the preceding ἁμαρτίαν as ἡ δὲ ὑπομονή takes up ὑπομονήν in v. 4. Sin when full-grown, when it has become a fixed habit determining the character of the man, brings forth death. Cf. below ii. 22 ἐκ τῶν ἔργων ἡ πίστις ἐτελειώθη, and τέλειος above v. 4, Arist. *Hist. Anim.* ix. 1 (the distinctive characteristics of the sexes are shown at their fullest development in the human species) τοῦτο γὰρ ἔχει τὴν φύσιν ἀποτετελεσμένην ὥστε καὶ ταύτας τὰς ἕξεις εἶναι φανερωτέρας ἐν αὐτοῖς, Philo M. 1. p. 94 τῆς κακίας ἡ μὲν ἐν σχέσει ἡ δὲ ἐν κινήσει θεωρεῖται· νεύει δὲ πρὸς τὰς τῶν ἀποτελεσμάτων ἐκπληρώσεις ἡ ἐν τῷ κινεῖσθαι· διὸ καὶ χείρων, *ib.* 74 sensation (αἴσθησις) itself is passive, it becomes active when the reason (νοῦς) attaches itself to it, then you may see its old potential existence (δύναμιν καθ' ἕξιν ἠρεμοῦσαν) changed into an ἀποτέλεσμα and ἐνέργειαν, Philo M. 1. p. 211 (the thought of murder constitutes guilt) τῆς γνώμης ἴσον τῷ τελείῳ δυναμένης. ἕως μὲν γὰρ τὰ αἰσχρὰ μόνον ἐννοοῦμεν κατὰ ψιλὴν τοῦ νοῦ φαντασίαν, τότε τῆς διανοίας ἐσμὲν ὕποχοι· δύναται γὰρ καὶ ἀκουσίως ἡ ψυχὴ τρέπεσθαι· ὅταν δὲ προσγένηται τοῖς βουλευθεῖσιν ἡ πρᾶξις, ὑπαίτιον γίνεται καὶ τὸ βουλεύσασθαι· τὸ γὰρ ἑκουσίως διαμαρτάνειν ταύτῃ μάλιστα διαγνωρίζεται, Hermas *Mand.* iv. 2 ἡ ἐνθύμησις αὕτη Θεοῦ δούλῳ ἁμαρτία μεγάλη· ἐὰν δέ τις ἐργάσηται τὸ ἔργον τὸ πονηρὸν τοῦτο, θάνατον ἑαυτῷ κατεργάζεται.

The verb κύω or κυέω, in the sense of to be or to become pregnant, is common in older Greek, e.g. Il. ψ. 266 κυέουσαν, Plato *Theaet.* 151 B (in reference to the Socratic μαιευτική) ὑποπτεύων σε ὠδίνειν τι κυοῦντα ἔνδον. The aorist of the shorter form is used transitively (meaning 'to impregnate') in Aesch. *fr.* 38 ὄμβρος ἔκυσε γαῖαν, and in the middle (meaning 'to conceive') Hes. *Theog.* 405. Hence Hermann wished to limit the use of κύω to the male, κυέω to the female, but Lobeck (*Aj.* p. 102 foll., *Paral.* p. 556) shows that this distinction is not borne out by MSS. or grammarians. Eustathius even states the opposite, κύειν τὸ κατὰ γαστρὸς ἔχειν, κυῶ δὲ τὸ γεννῶ, ὅθεν οἱ κυήτορες, καὶ ἐκύει ἤγουν ἐγέννησε (p. 1548. 20, cited by Lob. *Aj.* 182). The compound is only found here and below, ver. 18, in N.T. It is used metaphorically in 4 Macc. 15. 14 ὦ μόνη γυνὴ τὴν εὐσέβειαν ὁλόκληρον ἀποκυήσασα, 'having given birth to piety in perfection.' It is common in Philo, Plutarch and the later authors generally. For the force of ἀπό (denoting cessation) cf. ἀπαλγέω, ἀπελπίζω, ἀποπονέω. For the thought cf. Rom. vi. 21–23, viii. 6, Matt. vii. 13–14, where the parallel between the two ways leading to death and life (the δύο ὁδοί of the Didaché and of Barnabas, 18. 1) is similarly brought out. The issue of sin is seen most plainly in sins of the body leading to bodily disease, but also in the deterioration of mind and character which accompanies every kind of sin, till the man is said to be νεκρὸς τοῖς παραπτώμασιν (Eph. ii. 1).

16. **μὴ πλανᾶσθε ἀδελφοί μου.**] 'Be not mistaken: not temptation but all that is good comes from God.' Cf. Matt. xxii. 29 πλανᾶσθε μὴ εἰδότες τὰς γραφάς, Luke xxi. 8 βλέπετε μὴ πλανηθῆτε. St. Paul uses the phrase μὴ πλανᾶσθε, 1 Cor. vi. 9, xv. 33, Gal. vi. 7. Here its earnestness is softened by the addition ἀδελφοί as in Ignat. *Philad*, 3, *Eph.* 16.

17. **πᾶσα δόσις ἀγαθὴ καὶ πᾶν δώρημα τέλειον.**] 'All good giving and every perfect gift' (descend from Him who gives to all liberally). The stress is laid on ἀγαθή and τέλειον. Beyschlag and Erdmann with others have assigned to πᾶσα the same meaning as it bore in v. 2, but this use is rarely found except in reference to abstract qualities, not to acts or things. No doubt such a rendering would give a more exact logical contradiction. 'All good comes from God' does not necessarily exclude the possibility of evil also coming from Him. But practically the opposition is sufficient, 'God does not tempt to evil: it is good, good of every kind, which comes from Him'; and if we are right in supposing the verse to be a quotation, there is the less reason to ask for an exact logical antithesis (cf. below, ii. 5). For the thought see Plato *Rep.* ii. 379 οὐδ' ἄρα ὁ Θεὸς πάντων ἂν εἴη αἴτιος...ἀλλ' ὀλίγων μὲν τοῖς ἀνθρώποις αἴτιος πολλῶν δὲ ἀναίτιος· πολὺ γὰρ ἐλάττω τἀγαθὰ τῶν κακῶν ἡμῖν· καὶ τῶν μὲν ἀγαθῶν οὐδένα ἄλλον αἰτιατέον, τῶν δὲ κακῶν ἄλλ' ἄττα δεῖ ζητεῖν τὰ αἴτια, ἀλλ' οὐ τὸν Θεόν, Dio Chr. *Or.* 32, p. 365 M. τοῦτο πείσθητε βεβαίως ὅτι τὰ συμβαίνοντα τοῖς ἀνθρώποις ἐπ' ἀγαθῷ πάνθ' ὁμοίως ἐστὶ δαιμόνια κ.τ.λ., Tobit iv. 14 αὐτὸς ὁ Κύριος δίδωσι πάντα τὰ ἀγαθά, Wisdom ii. 23 ὁ Θεὸς ἔκτισε τὸν ἄνθρωπον ἐπ' ἀφθαρσίᾳ ..φθόνῳ δὲ διαβόλου θάνατος εἰσῆλθεν. Philo M. 1, p. 53 Θεοῦ σπείροντος καὶ φυτεύοντος ἐν ψυχῇ τὰ καλὰ ὁ λέγων νοῦς ὅτι, ἐγὼ φυτεύω, ἀσεβεῖ, M. 2. p. 208 Θεὸς μόνων ἀγαθῶν αἴτιος κακοῦ δὲ οὐδενός, *ib.* M. 1. p. 432, 174 οὐδέν ἐστι τῶν καλῶν ὃ μὴ Θεοῦ τε καὶ θεῖον, *ib.* M. 2. p. 245 God is spoken of as ἀμιγῆ κακῶν τὰ ἀγαθὰ δωρούμενον, and above on ver 5.

It will be observed that the words make a hexameter line, with a short syllable lengthened by the metrical stress. I think Ewald is right in considering it to be a quotation from some Hellenistic poem. Spitta suggests that it may be taken from the Sibylline books, see below on iii. 8. The authority of a familiar line would add persuasion to the writer's words, and account for the somewhat subtle distinction between δοσ. ἀγ. and δω. τελ. Other examples of verse quotations in the N.T. are Tit. i. 12 Κρῆτες ἀεὶ ψεῦσται κακὰ θηρία γαστέρες ἀργαί, 1 Cor. xv. 33 φθείρουσιν ἤθη χρῆσθ' ὁμιλίαι κακαί, which follows a μὴ πλανᾶσθε, as here, without any mark of quotation, Acts xvii. 28 τοῦ γὰρ καὶ γένος ἐσμέν. More doubtful examples are John iv. 35 οὐχ ὑμεῖς λέγετε ὅτι ἔτι 'τετράμηνός ἐστι καὶ ὁ (χὠ) θερισμὸς ἔρχεται,' Heb. xii. 13 καὶ τροχιὰς ὀρθὰς ποιήσατε (al. ποιεῖτε) τοῖς ποσὶν ὑμῶν, where the source of the quotation (Prov. iv. 26 ὀρθὰς τροχιὰς ποίει τοῖς ποσίν) seems to have been altered for the purpose of versification. Dr. E. L. Hicks considers that traces of verse may be found in the second epistle of St. Peter (*Class. Rev.* iv. 49).

The distinction between δόσις and δώρημα is illustrated in Heisen 541–592 from Philo *Cher.* M. 1. p. 154 (a comment on Numbers xxviii. 2 τὰ δῶρά μου, δόματά μου) τῶν ὄντων τὰ μὲν χάριτος μέσης ἠξίωται, ἣ καλεῖται δόσις, τὰ δὲ ἀμείνονος, ἧς ὄνομα οἰκεῖον δωρεά, *id. Leg. All.* M. 1. p. 126 δῶρα δομάτων διαφέρουσι· τὰ μὲν γὰρ ἔμφασιν μεγέθους τελείων ἀγαθῶν δηλοῦσιν, ἃ τοῖς τελείοις χαρίζεται ὁ Θεός, τὰ δὲ εἰς βραχύτατον ἔσταλται, ὧν μετέχουσιν οἱ εὐφυεῖς ἀσκηταί, οἱ προκόπτοντες, *id.* M. 1. 240 δωρεαὶ αἱ τοῦ Θεοῦ καλαὶ πᾶσαι, *id.* M. 1. p. 102 δωρεὰ καὶ εὐεργεσία καὶ χάρισμα Θεοῦ τὰ πάντα ὅσα ἐν κόσμῳ καὶ αὐτὸς ὁ κόσμος ἐστί. The two words are found together in Dan. ii. 6 δόματα καὶ δωρεὰς καὶ τιμὴν πολλὴν λήψεσθε παρ᾽ ἐμοῦ, *ib.* v. 17 τὰ δόματά σου σοὶ ἔστω, καὶ τὴν δωρεὰν τῆς οἰκίας σου ἑτέρῳ δός, where there is the same difference between the corresponding words in the Hebrew; also in 2 Chron. xxxii. 23 ἔφερον δῶρα τῷ Κυρίῳ εἰς Ἱερουσαλὴμ καὶ δόματα τῷ Ἐζεκίᾳ βασιλεῖ. There is a similar peculiarity about the use of the verbs δίδωμι and δωρέομαι, e.g. in Philo M. 2. p. 183 ὁ γὰρ πρὸς τὸ ζῆν ἀφθονίαν δοὺς καὶ τὰς πρὸς τὸ εὖ ζῆν ἀφορμὰς ἐδωρεῖτο, the former expresses the simple act, the latter implies the accompanying generosity of spirit. Dr. Taylor notes (*J. of Philology*, vol. xviii. p. 299 foll.) that Hermas has borrowed the word δώρημα (*Mand.* 2 and *Sim.* ii. 7). Philo's distinction is further borne out by the fact that δώρημα in the only other passage in which it occurs in N.T. (Rom. v. 16) is used of a gift of God, and so δωρεά, wherever it occurs (John iv. 10, Acts ii. 13, viii. 20, x. 45, xi. 17, Rom. v. 15, 17, 2 Cor. ix. 11, Eph. iii. 7, iv. 7, Heb. vi. 4); δῶρον is mostly used of offerings to God. Again δόμα is always used of human gifts except in a quotation from LXX. ἔδωκε δόματα τοῖς ἀνθρώποις (Eph. iv. 8); but δόσις, which, like ποίησις below, v. 25, strictly means the act (as in Phil. iv. 15, the only other passage in N.T. εἰς λόγον δόσεως καὶ λήμψεως, Sirac. 32. 9 ἐν πάσῃ δόσει ἱλάρωσον τὸ πρόσωπόν σου, *ib.* 20. 9), is used equally of God in Sir. 1. 8 Κύριος ἐξέχεεν σοφίαν κατὰ τὴν δόσιν αὐτοῦ, *ib.* v. 15 δόσις Κυρίου παραμένει εὐσεβέσι, *ib.* 32. 10 δὸς Ὑψίστῳ κατά τὴν δόσιν αὐτοῦ. Thus δωρεά and δώρημα are always used in the higher sense, δόμα (with one exception) in the lower, while δόσις may have either sense. We might take as examples of δόσις here, the gradual instilling of wisdom, of δώρημα, the final crown of life. The choice of the epithets ἀγαθή and τέλειον is also in agreement with Philo's distinction; compare for the latter Clem. Al. *Paed.* 1. 6, p. 113 τέλειος ὢν τέλεια χαριεῖται δήπουθεν, Philo M. 1, p. 173 ὁλόκληροι καὶ παντελεῖς αἱ τοῦ ἀγεννήτου δωρεαὶ πᾶσαι,

ἄνωθέν ἐστιν.] WH., Ewald, Bouman, Hofmann, agree with the Vulg. *desursum est, descendens a patre luminum* in separating ἐστίν from καταβαῖνον. Alf., with the majority of commentators, takes them together (= καταβαίνει), referring to iii. 15 οὐκ ἔστιν αὕτη ἡ σοφία ἄνωθεν κατερχομένη, on which see n. There is no doubt that the Hellenistic usage admits of their being taken together, cf. Mark xiii. 25, where οἱ ἀστέρες ἔσονται πίπτοντες = πεσοῦνται Matt. xxiv. 29; Luke ix. 14, where ἐν τῷ εἶναι προσευχόμενον = ἐν τῷ προσεύχεσθαι v. 27; *ib.* v. 16 αὐτὸς ἦν ὑποχωρῶν ἐν τοῖς ἐρήμοις, v. 17, ἦν διδάσκων. For this extension of the periphrastic tense, itself merely an instance of the analytic tendency which marks the later stage of language, see Winer, p. 437, A. Buttmann, p. 264 foll., where many cases are given; Arist. *Met.* iv. 7 οὐδὲν διαφέρει τὸ ἄνθρωπος βαδίζων ἐστὶν τοῦ ἄνθρωπος βαδίζει. On the whole I think the rhythm and balance of the sentence is better preserved by separating ἐστι from καταβαῖνον. The construction will then be the same as is found in John viii. 23 ὑμεῖς ἐκ τῶν κάτω ἐστέ· ἐγὼ δὲ ἐκ τῶν ἄνω εἰμί, and implied below iii. 17 ἡ δὲ ἄνωθεν σοφία ἁγνή ἐστιν. For ἄνωθεν cf. John 3. 31, where it is equivalent to ἐκ τοῦ οὐρανοῦ immediately afterwards, Xen. *Symp.* vi. 7 (οἱ θεοὶ) ἄνωθεν μὲν ὕοντες ὠφελοῦσιν, ἄνωθεν δὲ φῶς παρέχουσιν, Philo M. 1, p. 645 Ἰσαὰκ διὰ τὰς ὀμβρηθείσας ἄνωθεν δωρεὰς ἀγαθὸς καὶ τέλειος ἐξ ἀρχῆς ἐγένετο.

καταβαῖνον ἀπὸ τοῦ πατρὸς τῶν φώτων.] Explains ἄνωθεν, just as ἐκ τῶν ἡδονῶν explains ἐντεῦθεν in iv. 1 below. The comparison of God to the sun, and of his influence to light, is found both in Jewish and in classical writers: for (1) see Malachi iv. 2 ἀνατελεῖ ὑμῖν τοῖς φοβουμένοις τὸ ὄνομά μου ἥλιος δικαιοσύνης, Psa. xxxv. 9, Isa, lx. 1, 19, 20, 1 John i. 5, Apoc. xxi. 23, Wisd. vii. 16 (σοφία) ἀπαύγασμά ἐστι φωτὸς ἀϊδίου, *ib.* v. 29 ἐστὶν γὰρ αὕτη εὐπρεπεστέρα ἡλίου καὶ ὑπὲρ πᾶσαν ἄστρων θέσιν, φωτὶ συγκρινομένη εὑρίσκεται προτέρα· τοῦτο μὲν γὰρ διαδέχεται νύξ, σοφίας δὲ οὐκ ἀντισχύει κακία, Philo M. 1. p. 637 πρὶν τὰς τοῦ μεγίστου καὶ ἐπιφανεστάτου Θεοῦ καταδῦναι περιλαμπεστάτας αὐγάς, ἃς δι' ἔλεον τοῦ γένους ἡμῶν εἰς νοῦν τὸν ἀνθρώπινον οὐρανόθεν ἀποστέλλει κ.τ.λ., *ib.* M. 1, p. 579 πηγὴ τῆς καθαρωτάτης αὐγῆς Θεός ἐστιν, ὥστε ὅταν ἐπιφαίνηται ψυχῇ, τὰς ἀσκίους καὶ περιφανεστάτας ἀκτῖνας ἀνίσχει, *ib.* p. 7 ἔστιν (ὁ θεῖος λόγος) ὑπερουράνιος ἀστὴρ, πηγὴ τῶν αἰσθητῶν ἀστέρων. (2) The chief passage in a classical author is the elaborate comparison between the sun and the ἰδέα τοῦ ἀγαθοῦ in Plato *Rep.* vi· 505 foll., and especially vii. 517 πᾶσι πάντων αὕτη ὀρθῶν τε καὶ καλῶν αἰτία.

For the word πατήρ compare Eph. i. 17 ὁ πατὴρ τῆς δόξης, 2 Cor. i. 3 ὁ πατὴρ τῶν οἰκτιρμῶν, Job xxxviii. 28 πατὴρ ὑετοῦ, John viii. 44, Philo M. 1. p. 631 μὴ θαυμάσῃς εἰ ὁ ἥλιος κατὰ τοὺς ἀλληγορίας κανόνας ἐξομοιοῦται τῷ πατρὶ καὶ ἡγεμόνι τῶν συμπάντων κ.τ.λ., and a little below (after citing Psa. xxvii. 1 Κύριος φῶς μου) οὐ μόνον φῶς ἀλλὰ καὶ παντὸς ἑτέρου φωτὸς ἀρχέτυπον, μᾶλλον δὲ ἀρχετύπου πρεσβύτερον καὶ ἀνώτερον, *ib.* M, 2. p. 254 ὁ Θεὸς καὶ νόμων ἐστὶ παράδειγμα ἀρχέτυπον καὶ ἡλίου ἥλιος, νοητὸς αἰσθητοῦ, παρέχων ἐκ τῶν ἀοράτων πηγῶν ὁρατὰ φέγγη τῷ βλεπομένῳ. Philo constantly uses the phrase ὁ πατὴρ τῶν ὅλων for the Creator.

τῶν φώτων.] Refers in the first place to the heavenly bodies (Gen. i. 3, 14—18, Psa. cxxxv. 7, Jer. xxxi 35, Sir. xliii. 1–12); which were by the Jews identified with the angels or hosts of God (cf. Job xxviii. 7, where they are expressly called 'sons of God,' Is. xiv. 12. foll. of Lucifer, and the benediction before Shema, 'Blessed be the Lord our God who hath formed the lights,' quoted by Edersheim *Sketches of Jewish Life* p. 269);[1] but secondly to intellectual and spiritual light, which is

[1] Philo speaks of the stars as ζῷα νοερά M. 1. p. 17. It is perhaps a slight confirmation of the idea that St. James had at one time been influenced by the Essenes, that the latter are said to have paid special reverence to the sun; compare Philo *Vit.*

more connected with the general meaning of the passage, though the remainder of this verse continues the metaphor drawn from light in the literal sense. Compare Matt. v. 14 ὑμεῖς ἐστὲ τὸ φῶς τοῦ κόσμου, Luke xvi. 8 υἱοὶ τοῦ φωτός, John v. 35 (John was) ὁ λύχνος ὁ καιόμενος καὶ φαίνων, and you were willing for a time to rejoice ἐν τῷ φωτὶ αὐτοῦ, Psa. cxix. 105 λύχνος τοῖς ποσί μου ὁ νόμος σου, καὶ φῶς τοῖς τρίβοις μου, and for plural Psa. cxxxvi. 7 τῷ ποιήσαντι φῶτα μεγάλα, Jer. iv. 23 ἐπέβλεψα εἰς τὸν οὐρανόν, καὶ οὐκ ἦν τὰ φῶτα αὐτοῦ, Philipp. ii. 16, Philo M. i. 108 τὸν ἐγκύμονα θείων φώτων λόγον. See Spitta's n.

παρ' ᾧ οὐκ ἔνι παραλλαγή.] For this somewhat rare use of παρά denoting an attribute or quality cf. Eph. vi. 9 προσωποληψία οὐκ ἔστιν παρ' αὐτῷ, Rom. ii. 11, *ib.* ix. 14 μὴ ἀδικία παρὰ τῷ Θεῷ; Job. xii. 13 παρ' αὐτῷ σοφία καὶ δύναμις, Dem. *Coron.* p. 318 εἰ δ' οὖν ἐστὶ καὶ παρ' ἐμοί τις ἐμπειρία, Winer p. 492. For οὐκ ἔνι cf. Gal. iii. 28 ὅσοι εἰς Χριστὸν ἐβαπτίσθητε...οὐκ ἔνι Ἰουδαῖος οὐδὲ Ἕλλην, where Lightfoot translates 'there is no place for,' and notes that 'not the fact only, but the possibility' is negatived. He approves Buttman's view (given by Winer, p. 96) that ἔνι 'is not a contraction from ἔνεστι, but the preposition ἐν, ἐνί, strengthened by a more vigorous accent, like ἔπι, πάρα, and used with an ellipsis of the substantive verb.' In 1 Cor. vi. 5 οὐκ ἔνι ἐν ὑμῖν οὐδεὶς σοφός the word has a weaker force, as often in Plato, Xen., &c.

παραλλαγή.] Only here in N.T.; used of mental aberration in LXX. ἐν παραλλαγῇ 'furiously' 2 Kings ix. 20; of the succession of beacon-lights, *Agam.* 490. Its general sense is the same as that of the v. παραλλάσσω, denoting variation from a set course, rule or pattern, as in Plut. *Mor.* 1039 B, Epict. *Diss.* i. 14 (referring to the changes of the seasons) πόθεν πρὸς τὴν αὔξησιν καὶ μείωσιν τῆς σελήνης καὶ τὴν τοῦ ἡλίου πρόσοδον καὶ ἄφοδον τοσαύτη παραλλαγὴ καὶ ἐπὶ τὰ ἐναντία μεταβολὴ τῶν ἐπιγείων θεωρεῖται; hence it is used for difference, as *ib.* ii. 23. 32 μηδεμίαν εἶναι παραλλαγὴν κάλλους πρὸς αἶσχος. Some commentators have thought it to be a *vox technica* of astronomy = παράλλαξις, our 'parallax,' but no instance of such a use is quoted. It is true it is a favourite word with the astronomer Geminus (contained in Petavius' *Uranologion*), but he uses it quite generally of the varying length of the day &c.; cf. p. 26 B ἀκολουθεῖ δὲ τούτῳ καὶ παραλλαγὴν τῶν ἡμερῶν μεγάλην γίνεσθαι διὰ τὴν τῶν τμημάτων ὑπεροχὴν ὧν φέρεται ὁ ἥλιος ὑπὲρ γῆν (*i.e.* the length of the day varies according to the sun's elevation). Other instances are cited by Gebser p. 83. We may therefore take the word to express the contrast between the natural sun, which varies its position in the sky from hour to hour and month to month, and the eternal Source of all light. A similar contrast is found in Epict. *Diss.* i. 14. 10 ἀλλὰ φωτίζειν μὲν οἷός τε ἐστὶν ὁ ἥλιος τηλικοῦτον μέρος τοῦ παντὸς, ὀλίγον δὲ τὸ ἀφώτιστον ἀπολιπεῖν, ὅσον οἷόν τ' ἐπέχεσθαι ὑπὸ σκιᾶς ἣν ἡ γῆ ποιεῖ· ὁ δὲ καὶ τὸν ἥλιον αὐτὸν πεποιηκὼς καὶ περιάγων, μέρος ὄντ' αὐτοῦ μικρὸν, ὡς πρὸς τὸ ὅλον, οὗτος δ' οὐ δύναται πάντων αἰσθάνεσθαι; cf. Wisdom vii. 29, Sir. xvii. 26, xxvii. 11, quoted in Introd. ch. 3.

Cont. M. 2. p. 485 ἐπὰν θεάσωνται τὸν ἥλιον ἀνίσχοντα...εὐημερίαν καὶ ἀλήθειαν ἐπεύχονται καὶ ὀξυωπίαν λογισμοῦ, Joseph. *B.J.* ii. 8. 5.

τροπῆς ἀποσκίασμα.] The A.V. 'shadow of turning,' though supported by the Old Latin *modicum obumbrationis* and by the Greek commentators and lexicographers and by Ewald in modern times, is undoubtedly wrong. The simple word σκιά may take this colloquial sense, as in Philo M. 1. p. 606 πεπιστευκὼς ἴχνος ἢ σκιὰν ἢ ὥραν ἀπιστίας δέχεται, Demosth. 552. 7 εἴ γε εἶχε στιγμὴν ἢ σκιὰν τούτων, but it is impossible that this should be the case with a ἅπ. λεγ. like ἀποσκίασμα. The cognate ἀποσκιασμός occurs Plut. *Pericl.* 6 γνωμόνων ἀποσκιασμούς of shadows thrown on the dial, and ἀποσκιάζω Plato *Rep.* vii. 532 C. Taking the word by itself we naturally think of the moon losing its borrowed light as it passes under the shadow of the earth. But the sun, the source of light, though it may be hidden from us by the interposition of some other body, cannot itself be overshadowed. So St. John tells us (1 *ep.* i. 5) ὁ Θεὸς φῶς ἐστὶ καὶ σκοτία ἐν αὐτῷ οὐκ ἔστιν οὐδεμία.

The word τροπή is only found here in N.T.; it is used of the heavenly movements in LXX. Deut. xxxiii. 14 καθ' ὥραν γεννημάτων ἡλίου τροπῶν, Job. xxxviii. 33 ἐπίστασαι τροπὰς οὐρανοῦ, also in Wisd. vii. 18 (God gave me to know) σύστασιν κόσμου καὶ ἐνέργειαν στοιχείων, τροπῶν ἀλλαγὰς καὶ μεταβολὰς καιρῶν, ἐνιαυτοῦ κύκλους καὶ ἀστέρων θέσεις, where it has its usual technical meaning 'solstices.' The R.V., in agreement with Gebser, Wiesinger, Alf., Beyschlag, Erdmann, translates 'shadow that is cast by turning,' which Alf. explains as referring to 'the revolution in which the heavens are ever found, by means of which the moon turns her dark side to us . . . . is eclipsed by the shadow of the earth, and the sun by the body of the moon.' But what a singular way of describing this to say that it is an overshadowing which comes from turning or change of position! 'Overshadowing of one another,' ἀλλήλων ἀποσκίασμα, would have been what we should have expected. Accordingly Schneckenburger and De Wette (Brückner) have rightly felt that τροπή must be taken here in another and far more usual sense, that of 'change in general' (like τύχης τροπαί Plut. *Mor.* p. 611, γνώμης τροπή ib. *Vit.* 410 F), since, as the latter says, 'schwierig ist damit (i.e. with the idea of revolution) ἀποσκίασμα in Verbindung zu bringen.' The liability of all that is created to change (Anton. vi. 23 τὰ ὄντα ἐν μυρίαις τροπαῖς, καὶ σχεδὸν οὐδὲν ἑστός, *ib.* viii. 6 πάντα τροπαί) is continually contrasted in Philo with the immutability of the Creator: cf. M. 1. p. 72 πᾶν τὸ γεννητὸν ἀναγκαῖον τρέπεσθαι· ἴδιον γάρ ἐστι τοῦτο, ὥσπερ Θεοῦ τὸ ἄτρεπτον εἶναι, *ib.* 82 πῶς ἄν τις πιστεύσαι Θεῷ; ἐὰν μαθῇ ὅτι πάντα τὰ ἄλλα τρέπεται, μόνος δὲ αὐτὸς ἄτρεπτός ἐστι, and (with a still closer resemblance to our text) *ib.* p. 80 ὅταν ἁμάρτῃ καὶ ἁμαρτηθῇ ὁ νοῦς ἀρετῆς, αἰτιᾶται τὰ θεῖα, τὴν ἰδίαν τροπὴν προσάπτων Θεῷ. Many similar passages will be found in the treatises *Leg. Alleg.* and *Cherub.* Cf. too Clem. Al. *Strom.* i. 418 P. τὸ ἑστὼς καὶ μόνιμον τοῦ Θεοῦ καὶ τὸ ἄτρεπτον αὐτοῦ φῶς. From this opposition to the Divine nature the word τροπή gets a second connotation implying moral frailty, as in Philo p. 72 ἀντιφιλονεικεῖ μοι ἡ τροπή, καὶ πολλάκις βουλόμενος καθῆκόν τι νοῆσαι ἐπαντλοῦμαι ταῖς παρὰ τὸ καθῆκον ἐπιῤῥοίαις, *ib.* 188 ὁ Θεοῦ θεραπευτὴς αἰώνιον ἐλευθερίαν κεκάρπωται, κατὰ τὰς συνεχεῖς τροπὰς τῆς ἀεικινήτου ψυχῆς ἰάσεις δεχόμενος ἐπαλλήλους...τῆς μὲν τροπῆς διὰ τὸ φύσει θνητὸν ἐγγινομένης, τῆς δὲ ἐλευθερίας διὰ τὴν τοῦ Θεοῦ θεραπείαν ἐπιγινομένης. Schneckenburger takes τροπή here in Philo's sense, and translates *obumbratio quae oritur ex inconstantia naturae.* This gives a very good sense, 'overshadowing of mutability,' as one might speak of 'an overshadowing of disgrace': no changes in this lower world can cast a shadow on the unchanging Fount of light. Or we may take τροπῆς as a qualitative genitive, and interpret as Stolz does, after Luther, 'keine abwechselnde Verdunkelung.' Beyschlag maintains that this would require τροπὴ ἀποσκιάσματος,[1] but why may not 'overshadowing of change' serve to express 'changing shadow' (i.e. an overshadowing which changes the face of the sun), just as well as 'a hearer of forgetfulness' in ver. 25 to express 'a forgetful hearer' or 'the world of wickedness' in iii. 6 to express 'the wicked world'? The meaning of the passage will then be 'God is alike incapable of change in his own nature (παραλλαγή) and incapable of being changed by the action of others (ἀποσκίασμα).' On the unchangeableness of God compare Mal. iii. 6, Heb. xiii. 8. It is on this doctrine that Plato founds his argument against the possibility of a Divine Incarnation (*Rep.* ii. 380 foll.). See comment. Spitta takes τροπή of the sun's invisible return from west to east and ἀποσκίασμα of the darkness of night.

18. **βουληθεὶς ἀπεκύησεν ἡμᾶς.**] So far from God tempting us to evil, His will is the cause of our regeneration. It is the doctrine expressed by St. Paul (Eph. i. 5) προορίσας ἡμᾶς εἰς υἱοθεσίαν διὰ Ἰ.Χ. εἰς αὐτόν, κατὰ τὴν εὐδοκίαν τοῦ θελήματος αὐτοῦ, Rom. xii. 2; by St. Peter (i. l. 3) ὁ κατὰ τὸ πολὺ αὐτοῦ ἔλεος ἀναγεννήσας ἡμᾶς εἰς ἐλπίδα ζῶσαν and ver. 23; by St. John (i. 13) οἳ οὐκ ἐξ αἱμάτων οὐδὲ ἐκ θελήματος σαρκὸς οὐδὲ ἐκ θελήματος ἀνδρὸς ἀλλ' ἐκ Θεοῦ ἐγεννήθησαν, and iii. 3–8, 1 ep. iv. 10. As the seed of sin and death is contained in the unrestrained indulgence of man's ἐπιθυμία, so the seed of righteousness and life in the word of God. For the general metaphor compare 1 John iii. 9 πᾶς ὁ γεγεννημένος ἐκ τοῦ Θεοῦ ἁμαρτίαν οὐ ποιεῖ, ὅτι σπέρμα αὐτοῦ ἐν αὐτῷ μένει, καὶ οὐ δύναται ἁμαρτάνειν ὅτι ἐκ τοῦ Θεοῦ γεγέννηται, Psa. lxxxvii. 4–6, lxxx. 18, cxix. 25 (quicken Thou me according to Thy word), Deut. xxxii. 18, Clem. Al. *Strom.* v. 2, p. 653 P. καὶ παρὰ τοῖς βαρβάροις φιλοσόφοις τὸ κατηχῆσαι καὶ φωτίσαι ἀναγεννῆσαι λέγεται, 1 Cor. iv. 15, and a Jewish saying in Schürer *Hist. of Jewish People*, i. p. 317, Eng. tr., 'A man's father only brought him into this world: his teacher, who taught him wisdom, brings him into the life of the world to come,'[2] also Philo M. 1. p. 147 (αἱ ἀρεταὶ) μὴ δεξάμεναι παρά τινος ἑτέρου ἐπιγονὴν ἐξ ἑαυτῶν μὲν μόνων οὐδέποτε κυήσουσι· τίς οὖν ὁ σπείρων ἐν αὐταῖς τὰ καλὰ πλὴν ὁ τῶν ὅλων πατήρ, *ib.* 108 τὸν ἐγκύμονα θείων φώτων λόγον, *ib.* 123, where the text Κύριος ἤνοιξε τὴν μήτραν Λείας is explained ὁ Θεὸς τὰς μήτρας ἀνοίγει σπείρων ἐν αὐταῖς τὰς καλὰς πράξεις, *ib.* 273. The choice of a word properly used of the mother is explained here by the reference to v. 15, but it may be compared with Deut. xxxii. 18 (R.V.),

[1] B reads τροπῆς ἀποσκιάσματος.

[2] Mishnah, Surenh. iv. 116 (*Jewish Fathers*, p. 85), cf. Juv. vii. 209 with Mayor's note.

Psa. vii. 14 quoted on v. 15 above, and with the use of ὠδίνειν Gal. iv. 19; also with Psa. xc. 2 (where the Heb. word translated 'thou hadst formed' means primarily 'to be in pangs with child,' 'to bear a child,' Jennings *in loc.*) and Psa. xxii. 9, Clem. Hom. ii. 52 Ἀδὰμ ὁ ὑπὸ τῶν τοῦ Θεοῦ χειρῶν κυοφορηθείς. On the word ἀπεκύησεν see v. 15. On the beneficence of the Divine Will cf. Philo M. 1. p. 342 καθ' ὃ μὲν οὖν ἄρχων ἐστίν, ἄμφω δύναται καὶ εὖ καὶ κακῶς ποιεῖν...καθ' ὃ δὲ εὐεργέτης, θάτερον μόνον βούλεται, τὸ εὐεργετεῖν, man's greatest blessing is to have the firm hope which springs from the consciousness of the loving will of God (ἐκ τοῦ προαιρετικῶς εἶναι φιλόδωρον), *ib.* M. 2. p. 367, 437 βουληθεὶς ὁ Θεὸς διὰ ἡμερότητα καὶ φιλανθρωπίαν παρ' ἡμῖν τοῦθ' ἱδρύσασθαι κ.τ.λ., Clem. Al. *Paed.* i. 6. p. 114 P ὡς γὰρ τὸ θέλημα αὐτοῦ (his absolute will)[1] ἔργον ἐστί, καὶ τοῦτο κόσμος ὀνομάζεται, οὕτως καὶ τὸ βούλημα αὐτοῦ (his desire) ἀνθρώπων ἐστὶ σωτηρία, καὶ τοῦτο ἐκκλησία καλεῖται, *ib. Strom.* vii p. 855 P. οὔτε γὰρ ὁ Θεὸς ἄκων ἀγαθός, ὃν τρόπον τὸ πῦρ θερμαντικόν, ἑκούσιος δὲ ἡ τῶν ἀγαθῶν μετάδοσις αὐτῷ, Plato *Tim.* 29 (on the cause of creation) λέγωμεν δι' ἥντινα αἰτίαν γένεσιν καὶ τὸ πᾶν τόδε ὁ ξυνιστὰς ξυνέστησεν. ἀγαθὸς ἦν, ἀγαθῷ δὲ οὐδεὶς περὶ οὐδενὸς οὐδέποτε ἐγγίγνεται φθόνος.

λόγῳ ἀληθείας.] The word (explained in the parallel passage, 1 Pet. i. 25, to be τὸ ῥῆμα τὸ εὐαγγελισθὲν εἰς ὑμᾶς, as in Rom. x. 8, 17) is God's instrument for communicating the new life: see below v. 21 λόγος ἔμφυτος, Matt. iv. 4, John vi. 63 τὰ ῥήματα ἃ ἐγὼ λελάληκα ὑμῖν πνεῦμά ἐστιν καὶ ζωή ἐστιν, xvii. 7, 8, Rom. x. 17, 1 Pet. i. 23. The phrase occurs Psa. cxix. 43 (cf. Eccl. xii. 10), Eph. i. 13 ἀκούσαντες τὸν λόγον τῆς ἀληθείας, τὸ εὐαγγέλιον τῆς σωτηρίας ὑμῶν...ἐσφραγίσθητε τῷ πνεύματι, 2 Cor. vi. 7 (approving ourselves as ministers of God) ἐν λόγῳ ἀληθείας, ἐν δυνάμει θεοῦ, 2 Tim. ii. 15 (Timothy is urged to show himself a workman rightly dividing) τὸν λόγον τῆς ἀληθείας, Col. i. 5 (the hope which you had) ἐν τῷ λόγῳ τῆς ἀληθείας τοῦ εὐαγγελίου, cf. Westcott on 1 Joh. i. 1. περὶ τοῦ λόγου τῆς ζωῆς. Alf., following Wiesinger, calls ἀληθείας a gen. of apposition, comparing Joh. xvii. 17 'thy word is truth'; why not objective, 'the declaration of the truth, viz. of God's love revealed in the life, death, and resurrection of Jesus Christ'? cf. below v. 19, and Westcott on Heb. x. 26,[2] see also John viii. 31, 32 'if ye continue in my word ye shall know the truth, and the truth shall make you free.' For the omission of the article with abstract words cf. Phil. ii. 16 λόγον ζωῆς ἐπέχοντες, Gal. v. 5 ἡμεῖς γὰρ πνεύματι ἐκ πίστεως ἐλπίδα δικαιοσύνης ἀπεκδεχόμεθα, below ver. 22 ποιηταὶ λόγου, iv. 11 νόμον, and see Essay on Grammar and Winer p. 198 foll. It is

[1] Bp. Westcott (Heb. vi. 17) says that 'as distinguished from θέλειν, βούλεσθαι regards a purpose with regard to something else, while θέλειν regards the feeling in respect to the person himself.' I should rather be disposed to say that the element of thought and desire is more prominent in βούλεσθαι, the element of pure volition (determination) in θέλειν, cf. below ἐὰν ὁ Κύριος θελήσῃ with the quotation from Plato *Alcib.* i. The distinction is of course liable to get blurred by such figurative uses as we have in iii. 4 ὅπου ἡ ὁρμὴ βούλεται.

[2] [I should prefer to take it as a possessive genitive 'words belonging to truth,' as (in 1 Cor. ii. 4, 18) σοφίας λόγοι 'words belonging to wisdom' or 'uttered by wisdom.' A.]

quite unnecessary to explain, as Hofmann, '*ein* Wort, nicht *das* Wort.'

εἰς τὸ εἶναι.] Most often used to express the end or aim, as here and below, iii. 3, Heb. vii. 25, Acts vii. 19, Rom. i. 4 (see Westcott *Heb.* p. 342); sometimes the result as in Rom. i. 20 *τὰ ἀόρατα αὐτοῦ τοῖς ποιήμασιν νοούμενα καθορᾶται...εἰς τὸ εἶναι αὐτοὺς ἀναπολογήτους*, *ib.* vii. 4, 5, 2 Cor. vii. 3, viii. 6, Gal. iii. 17, Heb. xi. 3; sometimes merely reference, as below ver. 29 *βραδὺς εἰς τὸ λαλῆσαι*[1]: see Winer p. 413 foll.

ἀπαρχήν τινα τῶν αὐτοῦ κτισμάτων.] The gifts of God were consecrated by devotion of the First-Fruits; see *D. of B.* s.v., where six kinds, private or public, are specified, and cf. Exod. xxii. 29 foll., Deut. xviii. 3, xxvi. 2 foll., Neh. x. 35, Ezek. xx. 40. Similar offerings were made among the Greeks and Romans, cf. Homeric *ἐπάρχομαι*, and *ἄργματα*, *Od.* xiv. 446, Herod. i. 92 (of the offerings of Croesus), Thuc. iii. 58 *ὅσα τε ἡ γῆ ἡμῶν ἀνεδίδου ὡραῖα, πάντων ἀπαρχὰς ἐπιφέροντες*, Isaeus *Dicaeog.* 42, Lat. *primitiae.* We find the word used metaphorically, Plato *Legg.* 767 C., Plutarch *Mor.* p. 40, where see Wytt.; so Philo M. 2. p. 366 (Israel) *τοῦ σύμπαντος ἀνθρώπων γένους ἀπενεμήθη οἷά τις ἀπαρχὴ τῷ ποιητῇ καὶ πατρί*, with ref. to Jer. ii. 3. St. Paul uses it of the first converts, Rom. xvi. 5 *ὅς ἐστιν ἀπαρχὴ τῆς Ἀσίας εἰς Χριστόν*, 1 Cor. xvi. 15 *ἀπ. τῆς Ἀχαίας* (speaking of the house of Stephanas). The faith of the patriarchs, sanctifying their posterity, is typified by the heave-offering of the dough (Numb. xv. 21) *εἰ ἡ ἀπαρχὴ ἁγία καὶ τὸ φύραμα* Rom. xi. 16. In 1 Cor. xv. 20 Christ Himself is called *ἀπ. τῶν κεκοιμημένων.* The nearest approach to St. James is found in 2 Thess. ii. 13 God has chosen you *ἀπαρχὴν εἰς σωτηρίαν*: in Rom. viii. 23 the existing manifestation of the Spirit is described as a mere *ἀπαρχή* in comparison with what shall be hereafter, 'the glorious liberty of the children of God,' which shall be extended to the whole creation: in Apoc. xiv. 4 the 144,000 are called *ἀπαρχὴ τῷ Θεῷ καὶ τῷ Ἀρνίῳ*, cf. the *ἐκκλησία πρωτοτόκων* of Heb. xii. 23. In the Clementine Homilies (i. 3) Peter speaks of Clement as *τῶν σωζομένων ἐθνῶν ἀπαρχή.* Τινά = Lat. *quemdam*, 'as it were,' marks that the word is used not strictly, but metaphorically. Κτισμάτων: cf. Wisd. xiii. 4 *ἐκ καλλονῆς κτισμάτων ἀναλόγως ὁ γενεσιουργὸς θεωρεῖται.* The writer uses the widest possible word, embracing not only Christians, but mankind in general, who were blessed in Abraham and still more in Christ; not only men, but all created things: cf. Rom. viii. 19–22, the *παλιγγενεσία* of Matt. xix. 28, the prophecies of Isa. xi. 6 foll., lxv. 13. The position of *αὐτοῦ* is unusual: cf. Joh. v. 47 *τοῖς ἐκείνου γράμμασιν*, 2 Cor. viii. 9 *τῇ ἐκείνου πτωχείᾳ*, *ib.* v. 14 *τὸ ἐκείνων ὑστέρημα*, 2 Tim. ii. 26 *τὸ ἐκείνου θέλημα*, Tit. iii. 5 *τὸ αὐτοῦ ἔλεος*, ver. 7 *τῇ ἐκείνου χάριτι*, 1 Pet. i. 3 *ὁ κατὰ τὸ πολὺ αὐτοῦ ἔλεος ἀναγεννήσας ἡμᾶς*, 1 John ii. 5 *ὃς δ' ἂν τηρῇ αὐτοῦ τὸν λόγον*, ver. 27 *τὸ αὐτοῦ χρίσμα διδάσκει ἡμᾶς*, 2 Pet. i. 9 *τῶν πάλαι αὐτοῦ ἁμαρτιῶν*, ver 16. *τῆς ἐκείνου μεγαλειότητος*, in all of

[1] [Out of forty-two Pauline passages I find only one (2 Cor. viii. 6) in which *εἰς τὸ* may not be translated 'in order that'; but often an action is said to have been done for a purpose contemplated not by the doer but by God, *e.g.* 1 Thess. ii. 16, Rom. i. 20, iv. 11, &c. A]

which there is an emphasis on the pronoun. Spitta's attempt to prove that ἀπεκύησεν refers to the creation, and that there is no allusion to Christian doctrine in this verse, seems to me an entire failure. Λόγος ἀληθείας is a *vox technica* of early Christianity, as may be seen from the N.T. quotations, and it would be a most unsuitable phrase for the creative word; not to mention that immediately below it is called 'the perfect law of liberty,' 'the ingrafted word which saves the soul,' of which we are to be 'doers not hearers.'

19. **ἴστε.**] 'All this you know: act upon your knowledge. Since it is through the word we are begotten anew, let us listen to it in meekness, instead of being so eager to give utterance to our own opinions. Do not think that overbearing fanaticism is in accordance with the will of God, or that fierce argumentation is the way to recommend God's truth.' Cf. below iii. 1 foll. with notes. We find the same appeal to the knowledge of the reader in i. 3, iii. 1. The form ἴστε is found elsewhere in N.T. only in Eph. v. 5 and Heb. xii. 17, οἴδατε being ordinarily used, as below iv. 4. It might be taken as an imperative 'be sure of this,' but I prefer to take it as indicative, as in Eph. v. 5 and Heb. xii. 17; cf. γινώσκετε below, v. 20, 1 John. ii. 20, iii. 5, 15.

πᾶς ἄνθρωπος.] This individualizing phrase is often found instead of πάντες in N.T., cf. John i. 9, ii. 10 πᾶς ἄνθρωπος πρῶτον τὸν καλὸν οἶνον τίθησι, Gal. v. 3, Col. i. 28 (thrice).

ταχὺς εἰς τὸ ἀκοῦσαι.] For this use of εἰς τό cf. 1 Thess. iv. 9 θεοδίδακτοί ἐστε εἰς τὸ ἀγαπᾶν ἀλλήλους, and such instances of the simple acc. after εἰς as Luke xii. 21 εἰς τὸν Θεὸν πλουτῶν, Rom. xvi. 19 σοφοὺς μὲν εἰς τὸ ἀγαθόν, ἀκεραίους δὲ εἰς τὸ κακόν. For the thought cf. Sir. ii. 29 μὴ γίνου ταχὺς (al. τραχὺς) ἐν γλώσσῃ σου, καὶ νωθρὸς ἐν τοῖς ἔργοις σου, *ib.* v. 11 γίνου ταχὺς ἐν ἀκροάσει σου καὶ ἐν μακροθυμίᾳ φθέγγου ἀπόκρισιν, *ib.* xx. 4, Prov. x. 19, xiii. 3, xxix. 11, Eccl. v. 1, 2, Taylor *Jewish Fathers*, p. 104, Zeno *ap.* Diog. L. vii. 23 διὰ ταῦτα δύο ὦτα ἔχομεν στόμα δὲ ἕν, ἵνα πλείω μὲν ἀκούωμεν ἧττονα δὲ λαλῶμεν, Demonax *ap.* Luc. § 51 (asked how one would best rule, he said) ἀόργητος καὶ ὀλίγα μὲν λαλῶν πολλὰ δὲ ἀκούων, Bias μίσει τὸ ταχὺ λαλεῖν, μὴ ἁμάρτῃς, (quoted with other maxims of the kind in Mullach's *Frag. Phil.* i. p. 212 foll.).

βραδὺς εἰς ὀργήν.] Ov. *Ex Ponto* i. 2. 121 *piger ad poenas, ad praemia velox*, Philo M. 1. p. 412 βραδὺς ὠφελῆσαι, ταχὺς βλάψαι, *ib.* ii. p. 522 βραδεῖς μὲν ὄντες τὰ καλὰ παιδεύεσθαι, τὰ δ' ἐναντία μανθάνειν ὀξύτατοι. For thought cf. iii. 9, 14–16, iv. 1, 2, 11, Prov. xvi. 32, Eccles. vii. 9 μὴ σπεύσῃς ἐν πνεύματί σου τοῦ θυμεῖσθαι.

20. **ὀργὴ γὰρ—ἐργάζεται.**] Sir. i. 19 οὐ δυνήσεται θυμώδης ἀνὴρ (al. θυμὸς ἄδικος) δικαιωθῆναι, Psa. cvi. 32, 33 (of Moses at Meribah). For the omission of the article see above v. 18 and Essay on Grammar; so θέλημα ἀνδρός John i. 13 οὐ γὰρ θελήματι ἀνθρώπου ἠνέχθη προφητεία 1 Pet. i. 21. The choice of ἀνήρ here, instead of ἄνθρωπος, was probably determined by the facts of the case; the speakers would be men, and they might perhaps imagine that there was something manly in violence as opposed to the feminine quality of πραΰτης, cf. Longin. *Sublim.* 32 τὴν μὲν τῶν ἐπιθυμιῶν οἴκησιν προσεῖπεν ὡς γυναικωνῖτιν, τὴν τοῦ θυμοῦ δὲ ὥσπερ ἀνδρωνῖτιν, Clem. Al. *Strom.* iii. p. 553 P. θυμὸν μὲν ἄρρενα ὁρμήν,

θήλειαν δὲ τὴν ἐπιθυμίαν. The word ἀνήρ is used of men in contrast to gods in Homer's phrase πατὴρ ἀνδρῶν τε θεῶν τε. Here the thought that it is God's righteousness brings out the absurdity of man's hoping to effect it by mere passion. Spitta destroys the force of the verse by understanding ὀργή of anger against God, felt by one who imputes to Him the temptations by which he is assailed.

δικαιοσύνην Θεοῦ.] Already in the O.T. we find righteousness described as the attribute and gift of God; Isa. xlv. 24, liv. 17, lxi. 10, 11, Jer. xxiii. 6, xxxiii. 15, 16, Dan. ix. 7, Hos. x. 12; and in Micah vi. 5 ἡ δικαιοσύνη τοῦ Κυρίου is declared not to consist in sacrifices but in doing justice and loving mercy. This is more clearly expressed in Matt. v. 20, vi. 33, Rom. i. 17 δικαιοσύνη Θεοῦ ἐν αὐτῷ (the Gospel) ἀποκαλύπτεται ἐκ πίστεως εἰς πίστιν, *ib.* iii. 5, 21 foll., x. 3 ἀγνοοῦντες τὴν τοῦ Θεοῦ δικαιοσύνην καὶ τὴν ἰδίαν δικαιοσύνην ζητοῦντες στῆσαι, τῇ δικαιοσύνῃ τοῦ Θεοῦ οὐχ ὑπετάγησαν. What St. James understood by the phrase was no doubt (1) the perfect obedience to the law of liberty contained in the Sermon on the Mount (see below ver. 25, ii. 8, 12) as distinguished from that outward observance which constitutes righteousness in the eye of man, and (2) the acknowledgment that such righteousness was the gift of God, wrought in us by His word received into our hearts (above ver. 5, 18, iii. 17). We may compare the phrase δίκαιοι ἐνώπιον τοῦ Θεοῦ Luke i. 6 (of Zechariah and his wife), Acts iv. 19, viii. 21, 1 Pet. iii. 4, &c. See Vorst *Hellen.* p. 399 foll., 649 foll.

ἐργάζεται.] So κατεργάζεται ὑπομονήν ver. 3, τῷ ποιήσαντι ἔλεος ii. 13, ἐργαζόμενος δικαιοσύνην Acts x. 35, Heb. xi. 33.

21. **διὸ ἀποθέμενοι πᾶσαν ῥυπαρίαν.**] 'Wherefore,' in order that we may yield ourselves to the divine influence, let us prepare our hearts. Cf. Eph. iv. 25 διὸ ἀποθέμενοι τὸ ψεῦδος λαλεῖτε ἀλήθειαν, 1 Pet. ii. 1 ἀποθέμενοι οὖν πᾶσαν κακίαν...τὸ λογικὸν ἄδολον γάλα ἐπιποθήσατε. It is a metaphor from the putting off of clothes, as in Heb. xii. 1 (stripping for the race), Rom. xiii. 12 where ἀποθώμεθα τὰ ἔργα τοῦ σκότους is opposed to ἐνδύσασθαι τὰ ὅπλα τοῦ φωτός, Eph. iv. 22 where ἀποθέσθαι τὸν παλαιὸν ἄνθρωπον is opposed to ἐνδύσασθαι τὸν καινὸν ἄνθρωπον, Col. iii. 8 foll. ἀπόθεσθε ὀργήν, θυμόν, κακίαν, βλασφημίαν, αἰσχρολογίαν... ἐνδύσασθε...ταπεινοφροσύνην, πραΰτητα κ.τ.λ., Clem. Rom. i. 13 ἀποθέμενοι πᾶσαν ἀλαζόνειαν...καὶ ὀργάς, Acta Matt. Tisch. p. 171 κακίαν ἀποθέμενοι... ἀγαπὴν ἐνδυσάμενοι, Justin. *Tryph.* p. 343 οἵτινες ἐν πορνείαις καὶ ἁπλῶς πάσῃ ῥυπαρᾷ πράξει ὑπάρχοντες, διὰ τῆς παρὰ τοῦ ἡμετέρου Ἰησοῦ κατὰ τὸ θέλημα τοῦ Πατρὸς χάριτος, τὰ ῥυπαρὰ ταῦτα, ἃ ἠμφιέσμεθα, κακὰ ἀπεδυσάμεθα, Clem. *Hom.* viii. 23 ἔνδυμα οὖν εἰ βούλεσθε γίνεσθαι θείου πνεύματος, σπουδάσατε πρῶτον ἐκδύσασθαι τὸ ῥυπαρὸν ὑμῶν πρόλημμα, ὅπερ ἐστὶν ἀκάθαρτον πνεῦμα. For the comparison between dress and character see Matt. xxii. 11 (the wedding garment), Apoc. iii. 4, 18 (white garment the symbol of purity), *ib.* vii. 14, xix. 8, Isa. lxi. 10, &c. The metaphor is continued in the word ῥυπαρία (ἅπ. λεγ. in N.T.): see below ii. 3, Isa. lxiv. 6 'our righteousness is as filthy rags,' Zech. iii. 4 ἀφέλετε τὰ ἱμάτια τὰ ῥυπαρὰ ἀπ' αὐτοῦ καὶ εἶπε πρὸς αὐτόν· Ἰδοὺ ἀφῄρηκα τὰς ἀνομίας σου, καὶ ἐνδύσατε αὐτὸν ποδήρη, Job. xiv. 4, Apoc. xxii. 11 ὁ ῥυπαρὸς ῥυπανθήτω. St. Paul uses the synonym μολυσμός 2 Cor. vii. 1 (filthi-

ness of the flesh and spirit). Strictly speaking the word ῥύπος is used of the wax of the ear, as in Hippocrates and Clem. Al. *Paed.* ii. p. 222 P. quoted by Heisen, who suggests that there may be an allusion to the purged ear, *aurium removendae sordes sunt quae audiendi celeritatem impedire queunt;* but it cannot be assumed without evidence that the derivative retained the original force of the simple word. The phrase σαρκὸς ἀπόθεσις ῥύπου is used of baptism in 1 Pet. iii. 21 ; and so Schegg would explain here ; but there is no reference here to a past event. The aorist participle is part and parcel of the command contained in the imperative δέξασθε, as in the quotations from St. Paul. Other examples of the metaphorical use are Philo M. 1. p. 597 (through repentance the soul washes away) τὰ καταῤῥυπαίνοντα, *ib.* 585, 273, Dion. Hal. *A.R.* xi. 5 ῥυπαίνοντες αἰσχρῷ βίῳ τὰς ἑαυτῶν τε καὶ τῶν προγόνων ἀρετάς, Epict. *Diss.* 2. 5 recommends the expulsion of a ῥυπαρὰ φαντασία by one which is καλὴ καὶ γενναία, Luc. *V. Auct.* 3 καθαρὰν τὴν ψυχὴν ἐργασάμενος καὶ τὸν ἐπ' αὐτῇ ῥύπον ἐκκλύσας, Acta Thomae, Tisch. p. 200 ῥυπαρὰ κοινωνία, ῥυπαρὰ ἐπιθυμία, Ignat. *Eph.* 16 ἐάν τις πίστιν θεοῦ ἐν κακῇ διδασκαλίᾳ φθείρῃ...ῥυπαρὸς γινόμενος εἰς τὸ πῦρ τὸ ἄσβεστον χωρήσει. Plutarch uses ῥυπαρία (like our 'shabbiness') of avarice (*Mor.* p. 60 D) : the compounds ῥυπαρόψυχος, ῥυπαρογνώμων are found in Byzantine writers. Its precise force in our text will be considered in the following note.

περισσείαν κακίας.] 'Overflowing (ebullition) of malice.' The meaning is best shown in the cognate phrase in Luke vi. 45 ('the evil man out of the evil treasure in his heart bringeth forth that which is evil') ἐκ γὰρ τοῦ περισσεύματος τῆς καρδίας λαλεῖ τὸ στόμα αὐτοῦ. The only other passages in which περισσεία occurs in N.T. are Rom. v. 17 τὴν περισσείαν τῆς χάριτος 'the superabundance of grace,' 2 Cor. viii. 2 ἡ περισσεία τῆς χαρᾶς...ἐπερίσσευσεν εἰς τὸ πλοῦτος τῆς ἁπλότητος αὐτῶν 'the overflowing of their joy overflowed to (so as to make up) the wealth of their generosity,' 2 Cor. x. 15 εἰς περισσείαν 'to overflowing' (abundantly). The writer warns his readers against hasty and passionate words, against the outbreak of evil temper. We may compare ζύμῃ κακίας in 1 Cor. v. 8, and the phrase ἀποτίθεσθαι τὰ πέριττα τῆς ψυχῆς quoted from Plut. *Mor.* p. 42 B in the n. on ἐσόπτρῳ ver. 23. Then comes the question whether ῥυπαρίαν is to be taken separately (Calvin, Bouman, Lange), or as governing κακίας along with περισσείαν. The fact that πᾶσαν is not repeated is in favour of the latter construction, which is supported by Matthaei's *Schol.* τὴν ἁμαρτίαν τὴν ῥυπαίνουσαν τὸν ἄνθρωπον φησί, τὴν ὡς περιττὴν οὖσαν ἐν ἡμῖν. Perhaps however it is better to give καί an epexegetic force, 'all defilement and effervescence of malice' being equivalent to 'all defilement caused by the overflowing malice of the heart': so Wiesinger 'allen Schmutz der reichlich bei ihnen sich findenden Bosheit.' Other explanations of περισσεία are (1) 'superfluity' A.V. (*malitiam majorem quam in Christianis expectaveris,* Theile). This would seem to make the writer guilty of the absurdity of supposing a certain amount of malice to be proper for a Christian. It might be said the same objection applies to the rendering *abundantia* 'overflowing', because it is the seat of the disease in the heart, not its manifestation in the words which the Christian should seek to get rid of. But St. James here speaks as below in ch. iii. and as our Lord in Matt. xv. 18, 19 of defilement arising from words: before we can receive the word of God into our hearts we must prepare the way by laying aside this open outward sin. (2) 'rank growth,' 'Auswuchs,' with reference to the ground which has to be prepared for sowing the seed of the word: so Alf., Bassett (who translates, clearing away every kind of 'rubbish, ῥυπαρία, and overgrowth'), Heisen, Loesner, Pott, comparing Philo M. 2. p. 258 περιτέμνεσθε τὰς σκληροκαρδίας, τὸ δέ ἐστι, τὰς περιττὰς φύσεις τοῦ ἡγεμονικοῦ, ἃς αἱ ἄμετροι τῶν παθῶν ἔσπειράν τε καὶ συνηύξησαν ὁρμαὶ καὶ ὁ κακὸς ψυχῆς γεωργὸς ἐφύτευσεν, ἀφροσύνη, μετὰ σπουδῆς ἀποκείρασθε. It does not however appear to be proved that either περισσεία or (still less) ῥυπαρία would bear the meaning suggested. (3) Hofmann, after Gebser and others, takes it in the sense of 'residuum,' 'what is left over and above': the Christians addressed have already renounced sin, but still sin is not entirely vanquished in them. It is true that περισσεία is not found in this sense, which would rather require περίσσευμα but we have περισσός Exod. x. 5 (the locust) κατέδεται πᾶν τὸ περισσὸν τῆς γῆς, τὸ καταλειφθὲν, ὃ κατέλιπεν ἡ χάλαζα, Joseph. *B.J.* ii. 6. 2 (they begged the Romans to pity) τὰ τῆς Ιουδαίας λείψανα καὶ μὴ τὸ περισσὸν αὐτῆς ἀποῤῥίψαι τοῖς ὠμῶς σπαράσσουσι, and so περίσσευμα Mark viii. 8 of the fragments of the loaves. (4) Nothing need be said of the strange interpretation *praeputium* adopted by Grotius, Hammond and Clericus, nor of Beza's *excrementum* = περίττωσις or περίττωμα. Heisen indeed cites a similar use of περιττεία from Clem. Rom. p. 183 (which I am unable to verify); but what meaning could κακίας have in connexion with the word thus understood? (5) Spitta, who refers to Ez. xxi. 26, xxviii. 11–19, thinks it means the finery in which sin dresses itself up. Those who take ῥυπαρία with an independent force understand it of the special sin of uncleanness, but there does not seem to be any special reference to that sin here, though there possibly may be in iv. 4, 8 below. Κακία seems best understood here of malice: cf. Lightfoot on Col. iii. 8 (ἀπόθεσθε ὀργήν, θυμόν, κακίαν): 'It is not, at least in the N.T., vice generally, but the vicious nature which is bent on doing harm to others, and is well described by Calvin (on Eph. iv. 31) *animi pravitas quae humanitati et aequitati est opposita.*' He refers to Trench *N.T. Synon*, § xi. p. 35 *seq.* It is not quite correct to say that it always bears this force in the N.T. (cf. Acts viii. 22, Matt. vi. 34), but here the preceding ὀργή and the following πραΰτης leave little doubt as to the meaning. [Is it possible that ῥυπαρία may be used to denote the passively mean and base, in opposition to κακία, an active form of vice, which leads περισσὰ πράσσειν?—C. T.]

ἐν πραΰτητι.] Cf. below iii. 13, 1 Pet. iii. 15, 2 Tim. ii. 25.

δέξασθε τὸν ἔμφυτον λόγον.] Cf. Acts xvii. 11 ἐδέξαντο τὸν λόγον μετὰ πάσης προθυμίας, 1 Thess. i. 6, ii. 13. Ἔμφυτος only here in N.T. Its common meaning is 'innate,' as in Wisd. xii. 10 ἔμφυτος ἡ κακία αὐτῶν, Plato *Eryx.* 398 C πότερον δοκεῖ εἶναι διδακτὸν ἡ ἀρετὴ ἢ ἔμφυτον, Justin M. *Apol.* ii. 8 (the Stoics and others have spoken well on moral questions) διὰ τὸ ἔμφυτον παντὶ γένει ἀνθρώπων σπέρμα τοῦ λόγου, *ib.* 13, and so Oecumenius here; but the word δέξασθε forbids this. We must therefore take it as the 'rooted word,' i.e. a word whose property it is to root itself like a seed in the heart: cf. Matt. xiii. 3–23 esp. ver. 21 οὐκ ἔχει ῥίζαν ἐν ἑαυτῷ, xv. 13 πᾶσα φυτεία ἣν οὐκ ἐφύτευσεν ὁ Πατήρ μου ὁ οὐράνιος ἐκριζωθήσεται, 1 Cor. iii. 6; Spitta refers to Esdras ix. 31 foll. The cognate words are used with a similar meaning, as Plut. *Mor.* p. 125 E διὰ τρυφὴν τὰς στάσεις ἐμφύεσθαι ταῖς πόλεσι, Xen. *R. Lac.* 3 τὸ αἰδεῖσθαι ἐμφυσιῶσαι βουλόμενος αὐτοῖς, so ἐμφυτεύω, ἐμφυτεία of grafting. The A.V. seems to identify our word with ἐμφύτευτον, which however would be out of place here, since the word is sown, not grafted, in the heart. Other examples occur in which it cannot mean 'innate,' e.g. Herod. ix. 94 of Euenius, to whom the gods granted the gift of prophesy as a solace after he had lost the sight of his eyes, μετὰ ταῦτα ἔμφυτον μαντικὴν εἶχεν, Barnab. i. 2, and ix. 9 τὴν ἔμφυτον δωρεὰν τῆς διδαχῆς αὐτοῦ θέμενος ἐν ὑμῖν, where Harnack quotes Ignat. *Eph.* 17 (*rec. maj.*) ἔμφυτον τὸ περὶ Θεοῦ παρὰ Χριστοῦ λαβόντες κριτήριον. In like manner σύμφυτος, which literally means 'congenital,' as in Jos. *Ant.* vi. 3. 3, is also used of that which has coalesced or grown into one since birth, as in Rom. vi. 5 σύμφυτοι γεγόναμεν τῷ ὁμοιώματι τοῦ θανάτου αὐτοῦ. The Latin *insitus* has the same two meanings, 'innate,' and 'ingrafted' or 'incorporated.' The verb is found in the same application, though with a different meaning, in Plut. *Mor.* 47. A τὸν ἐκ φιλοσοφίας ἐμφυόμενον εὐφυέσι νέοις δηγμὸν αὐτὸς ὁ τρώσας λόγος ἰᾶται. For the injunction cf. Job. xi. 13, 14, Deut xi. 18, and esp. xxx. 14 as explained in Rom x. 8, Jer. xxxi. 33, Acts xx. 32, 2 Cor. iii. 3, 1 Thess. ii. 13.

τὸν δυνάμενον σῶσαι τὰς ψυχὰς ὑμῶν.] Cf. below ii. 14, iv. 12, v. 20, 1 Pet. i. 9 τὸ τέλος τῆς πίστεως σωτηρίαν ψυχῶν, John v. 24 ὁ τὸν λόγον μου ἀκούων καὶ πιστεύων τῷ πέμψαντί με ἔχει ζωὴν αἰώνιον, Rom. i. 16 οὐκ ἐπαισχύνομαι τὸ εὐαγγέλιον, δύναμις γὰρ Θεοῦ ἐστὶν εἰς σωτηρίαν παντὶ τῷ πιστεύοντι, 2 Tim. iii. 15, Heb. x. 39 πίστεως ἐσμὲν εἰς περιποίησιν ψυχῆς, Barnab. xix. 8 μελετῶν εἰς τὸ σῶσαι ψυχὴν τῷ λόγῳ, Clem. *Hom.* iii. 54 ἡ ἀλήθεια ἡ σώζουσα ἦν καὶ ἔστιν ἐν τῷ Ἰησοῦ ἡμῶν λόγῳ, so we read of σώζειν δυνάμενοι λόγοι, ζωοποιοὶ λόγοι, *ib.* i. 5, 6, 19. Below v. 15 the phrase is used of bodily life: see Vorst, p. 123, Hatch, p. 101.

22. **γίνεσθε.**] The imperative ἔστε does not seem to be used in N.T., though ἴσθι and ἔστω are not uncommon. We may take γ. to mean not simply 'be,' but 'show yourselves more and more': see below iii. 1, Matt. x. 16 γίνεσθε οὖν φρόνιμοι, *ib.* xxiv. 44 γ. ἕτοιμοι, 1 Cor. xiv. 20, xv. 28, Eph. v. 1.

ποιηταὶ λόγου.] Cf. iv. 11 π. νόμου, Rom. ii. 13, where π. νόμου is opposed to ἀκροατὴς ν. as being justified before God, Matt. vii. 24 πᾶς ὅστις ἀκούει μου τοὺς λόγους τούτους καὶ ποιεῖ αὐτούς, Luke vi. 46, xi. 28, John xiii. 17, Ezek. xxxiii. 32, Sen. *Ep.* 108. 35 *sic ista ediscamus ut quae fuerint verba, sint opera*, Porphyr. *Abstin.* i. 57 δι' ἔργων ἡμῖν τῆς σωτηρίας, οὐ δι' ἀκροάσεως λόγων ψιλῆς γιγνομένης. The word ποιητής is only found six times in N.T., of which four are in St. James. Grotius quotes a rabbinical saying to the effect that there are two crowns, one of hearing, the other of doing.[1] Cf. also Taylor's *Jewish Fathers*, p. 63 'R. Chananiah used to say whosesoever works are in excess of his wisdom, his wisdom stands; and whosesoever wisdom is in excess of his works, his wisdom stands not'; *ib.* p. 75.

ἀκροαταί.] Regularly used of an attendant at a lecture, but distinguished from *μαθητής* by Isocr. *ad Nic.* 17 *ποιητῶν ἀκροατὴς, σοφιστῶν μαθητὴς γίγνου, ib.* p. 405 B.: similarly *ἀκουστής* and *auditor*. As Dr. Plummer observes, we naturally think of the reading of the Scriptures in the synagogue, on which the Jews laid such stress. The word is used three times by St. James, only once besides in N.T. (Rom. ii. 16).

παραλογιζόμενοι.] The only other passage in which it occurs in N.T. is Col. ii. 4 *ἵνα μηδεὶς ὑμᾶς παραλογίζηται ἐν πιθανολογίᾳ*, which Lightfoot explains 'lead you away by false reasoning.' In LXX. it is more loosely used, as 1 Sam. xxviii. 12 where the witch of Endor says to Saul *ἵνα τί παρελογίσω με;*

ἑαυτούς.] Regularly used in N.T., and often by classical authors, for the plural reflexive of the 1st and 2nd persons: cf. Winer, p. 187 foll., Vorst. p. 68.

23. **ὅτι.**] Here = *γὰρ*, giving the reason for the injunction 'do not be mere hearers,' because on such the word has no abiding influence. The causal connection denoted by *ὅτι*, which is sometimes so close as to make even a comma unnecessary (e.g. Matt. xx. 15 *ὁ ὀφθαλμός σου πονηρός ἐστιν ὅτι ἐγὼ ἀγαθός εἰμι;*), is sometimes so loose as to allow of its being separated from what precedes by a full stop, as in Mark iii. 30 *ἀμὴν λέγω ὑμῖν...ἁμαρτήματος. ὅτι ἔλεγον πνεῦμα ἀκάθαρτον ἔχει*, Luke xi. 18, *ib.* xiv. 11, Heb. viii. 10.

οὐ ποιητής.] *Οὐ* is used even in classical Greek after *εἰ*, when, as here, it may be considered to coalesce with the particular word or phrase to which it is joined, and not to affect the condition generally (this takes place most easily with such words as *θέλω* or *ἐάω*), or when the negative conception is immediately contrasted with its positive, as below iii. 2 *πολλὰ πταίομεν ἅπαντες. εἴ τις οὐ πταίει*, or when it may be regarded as parenthetical, being most exactly represented by the insertion of such a phrase as 'I do not say.' The same rule applies where the condition is assumed to be the fact, *εἰ* being equivalent to *ἐπεί* or *ὅτι*. But beside these cases, in which *οὐ* was admissible in classical Greek, the later Greek employs *εἰ οὐ* instead of *εἰ μή* as more emphatic, the latter being generally used without a verb (out of ninety-three examples cited by Bruder only fourteen are followed by a verb) in the sense of 'but' or 'except.' Of *εἰ οὐ* Bruder cites thirty-one examples, omitting however this verse and iii. 2. On the other hand, *μή* is always used with *ἐάν* (sixty-two instances in Bruder), never *οὐ*. See Winer, 599 foll., A. Buttmann, 296 foll.

[1] [On Exod. xxiv. 7, which ends (lit.) 'we will do and we will hear,' it is written (T. B. Shabbath 88*a*) that "when Israel put 'we will do' before 'we will hear,' there came 60 myriads of ministering angels, and attached to each Israelite two crowns, one corresponding to 'we will do' and the other to 'we will hear,' and when they sinned there came down 120 myriads of destroying angels and tore them off." —C. T.]

οὗτος.] The use of the pronoun to emphasize the apodosis after a relative, a condition or a participle, is a characteristic of the writer's style, cf. below 25, iii. 2.

ἔοικεν.] Only here and in ver. 6 in N.T.

ἀνδρὶ κατανοοῦντι ἑαυτόν.] For *ἀνδρί* see above ver. 8. Καταν. properly 'to take note of,' as in Xen. *Cyrop.* ii. 2. 28 *κατανοήσας τινὰ τῶν λοχαγῶν σύνδειπνον πεποιημένον ἄνδρα ὑπέραισχρον*, hence, on the one hand 'observe,' 'look at,' as here and Acts vii. 31, 32, and more generally 'see,' as in Psa. xciii. 9 *ὁ πλάσας τὸν ὀφθαλμόν, οὐχὶ κατανοεῖ;* on the other hand 'consider,' as in Heb. x. 24, Herm. *Sim.* viii. 2. 5, ix. 6. 3.

τὸ πρόσωπον τῆς γενέσεως αὐτοῦ.] On the difficult word *γένεσις* = 'fleeting earthly existence,' as in Judith xii. 18 *πάσας τὰς ἡμέρας τῆς γενέσεως* 'all the days of my life,' see below iii. 6. It is used here to contrast the reflexion in the mirror of the face which belongs to this transitory life, with the reflexion, as seen in the Word, of the character which is being here moulded for eternity.

ἐν ἐσόπτρῳ.] The figure of the mirror is also found 1 Cor. xiii. 12, contrasting the imperfect knowledge gained through the reflexion with the perfect knowledge of the reality (as in Plato's cave, *Rep.* vii.), 2 Cor. iii. 18 *ἡμεῖς ἀνακεκαλυμμένῳ προσώπῳ τὴν δόξαν Κυρίου κατοπτριζόμενοι* (reflecting as in a mirror) *τὴν αὐτὴν εἰκόνα μεταμορφούμεθα ἀπὸ δόξης εἰς δόξαν* with allusion to the glory which shone in the face of Moses, Sir. xii. 11, where the feigning of the hypocrite is compared to the rust on the face of the mirror which has to be rubbed off in order to see his real character, Wisd. vii. 26 *σοφία* is *ἔσοπτρον ἀκηλίδωτον τῆς τοῦ Θεοῦ ἐνεργείας*. It is often used by the poets (*e.g.* Eur. *Hipp.* 427–430, Ter. *Ad*, 415), and philosophers, as Seneca *N.Q.* i. 17 *inventa sunt specula ut homo ipse se nosset. Multa ex hoc consequuntur, primum sui notitiam deinde ad quaedam consilium, formosus ut vitaret infamiam, deformis ut sciret redimendum esse virtutibus quicquid corpori deesset; Ira* ii. 36 *quibusdam, ut ait Sextius, profuit iratis adspexisse speculum. Perturbavit illos tanta mutatio sui...et quantulum ex vera deformitate imago illa reddebat? Animus si ostendi posset intuentes nos confunderet; Clem.* i. 1 *scribere de clementia institui ut quodam modo speculi vice fungerer;* (Epict. *Diss.* ii. 14) the Stoic asks *τί σοι κακὸν πεποίηκα; εἰ μὴ καὶ τὸ ἔσοπτρον τῷ αἰσχρῷ ὅτι δεικνύει αὐτὸν αὐτῷ οἷός ἐστιν;* Plut. *Mor.* p. 42 B *οὐ γὰρ ἐκ κουρείου μὲν ἀναστάντα δεῖ τῷ κατόπτρῳ παραστῆναι καὶ τῆς κεφαλῆς ἅψασθαι τὴν περικοπὴν τῶν τριχῶν ἐπισκοποῦντα καὶ τῆς κουρᾶς τὴν διαφοράν· ἐκ δὲ ἀκροάσεως ἀπιόντα καὶ σχολῆς οὐκ εὐθὺς ἀφορᾶν χρὴ πρὸς ἑαυτόν, καταμανθάνοντα τὴν ψυχὴν, εἴ τι τῶν ὀχληρῶν ἀποτεθειμένη καὶ περίττων ἐλαφροτέρα γέγονε καὶ ἡδίων*, Bias *ap.* Stob. *Flor.* 21. 11 *θεώρει ὥσπερ ἐν κατόπτρῳ τὰς σαυτοῦ πράξεις ἵνα τὰς μὲν καλὰς ἐπικοσμῇς τὰς δὲ αἰσχρὰς καλύπτῃς*, often by Philo, cf. Gfrörer, p. 439, who cites M. 2. p. 483 (the law is compared by the Therapeutae to a living creature, of which the letter is the body and the spirit or intention the soul) *ἐν ᾧ ἤρξατο ἡ λογικὴ ψυχὴ διαφερόντως τὰ οἰκεῖα θεωρεῖν, ὥσπερ διὰ κατόπτρου τῶν ὀνομάτων ἐξαίσια κάλλη νοημάτων κατιδοῦσα, ib.* 197 (through the number seven) *ὡς διὰ κατόπτρου φαντασιοῦται ὁ νοῦς Θεὸν δρῶντα καὶ κοσμοποιοῦντα, ib.* 156 the priest should remember, as he bathes, that the laver was made out of the brazen mirror (Exod. xxxviii. 8), ἵνα καὶ αὐτὸς οἷα πρὸς κάτοπτρον αὐγάζῃ τὸν ἴδιον νοῦν, Clem. Hom. xiii. 16 καλῷ ἐσόπτρῳ ὁρᾷ εἰς τὸν Θεὸν ἐμβλέπουσα, Clem. Al. *Paed.* i. 9. p. 150 P. ὡς γὰρ τὸ ἔσοπτρον τῷ αἰσχρῷ οὐ κακόν, ὅτι δεικνύει αὐτὸν οἷός ἐστιν, καὶ ὡς ὁ ἰατρὸς τῷ νοσοῦντι οὐ κακός, ὁ τὸν πυρετόν ἀναγγέλλων αὐτοῦ...οὕτως οὐδὲ ὁ ἐλέγχων δύσνους τῷ κάμνοντι τὴν ψυχήν, Pseudo-Cypr. *De duobus Montibus* c. 13 *ita me in vobis videte, quomodo quis vestrum se videt in aquam aut in speculum.* The mirror, usually carried in the hand, was sometimes made of silver, but more frequently of a mixture of copper and tin (*D. of B.* s. v.). The point of comparison here is that the Word will show us what needs to be cleansed and amended in our lives, as the mirror in regard to our bodies. It shows us what we actually are in contrast with what our deceitful heart paints us (ver. 26): it shows us also what is the true ideal of humanity which we are called upon to realize in our lives.

24. **κατενόησε καὶ ἀπελήλυθεν.**] 'Just a glance and he is off.' For the gnomic aorist often used in comparisons see ver. 11 ἀνέτειλεν, A. Buttmann, p. 174, Goodwin, *M. and T.* § 30. The proleptic perf. (on which see Buttmann, p. 172) expresses the suddenness and completeness of the action, as in Xen. *Cyr.* iv. 2. 26 ὁ γὰρ κρατῶν ἅμα πάντα συνήρπακεν, Rom. xiv. 23 ὁ διακρινόμενος ἐὰν φαγῇ κατακέκριται, *ib.* vii. 2. On the combination of aorist and perfect see below ii. 10 ὅστις πταίσῃ γέγονεν, Winer, p. 339. Both he and Buttmann (p. 171) ignore the special force of the perfect here, and compare it with such barbarous uses as Apoc. v. 7 ἦλθε καὶ εἴληφε τὸ βιβλίον, where, as often in the arguments to the speeches of Demosthenes, the perfect cannot be distinguished from the aorist, cf. εἴληχε and πεποίηκεν for ἔλαχε and ἐποίησεν in *Pro Phorm. hyp.* p. 944. [γάρ, as in ver. 11, justifies the comparison: it is to such a hasty inspection that careless hearing is likened. B. Weiss.]

εὐθέως ἐπελάθετο.] Dr. Taylor (*J. of Phil.* vol. xviii. p. 317) has pointed out that the phrase is borrowed by Hermas in the remarkable passage *Vis.* iii. 13 2.

ὁποῖος ἦν.] The direct form ποῖος is always used in N.T. for indirect interrogation except in this verse and in Gal. ii. 6, 1 Thess. i. 9, 1 Corr. iii. 13. So always τίς, πόσος, πότε, πόθεν for ὅστις, ὁπόσος, ὁπότε, ὁπόθεν. Ὅπου and ὅπως are frequent, but the former is never, the latter only rarely, used in an interrogative sense.

25. **παρακύψας.**] 'bending over the mirror in order to examine it more minutely,' 'peering into it': so 1 Pet. i. 12 εἰς ἃ ἐπιθυμοῦσιν ἄγγελοι παρακύψαι. It is used of John and of Mary looking into the sepulchre (John xx. 5, 11), also in Sir. xiv. 23 (blessed is) ὁ παρακύπτων διὰ τῶν θυρίδων σοφίας, (and so, of spying through a window or door, Gen. xxvi. 8, 1 Chron. xvi. 29, Prov. vii. 6, Cant. ii. 9, Sir. xxi. 23), Philo M. 2. p. 554 ποῦ γὰρ τοῖς ἰδιώταις θέμις εἰς ἡγεμονικῆς ψυχῆς παρακύψαι βουλεύματα, in Act. Thom. (Tisch. p. 230) εἰς χάσμα παρακύψαι, Epict. *Diss.* i. 1, 16 παρακύπτομεν συνεχῶς τίς ἄνεμος πνεῖ. L. and S. translate 'stoop sideways,' but this does not seem a suitable attitude for close inspection or meditation, cf. Pers. iii. 80 *obstipo capite.*

'Looking sideways' would do to express 'peeping out of a window': by one who wished not to be seen; but in our text παρά seems to imply the bending of the upper part of the body horizontally, cf. παρατείνω, παραστορέννυμι. In classical writers we find it sometimes used with the opposite sense of a careless glance. e.g. Dem. 1 *Phil.* p. 46 τὰ ξενικὰ παρακύψαντα ἐπὶ τὸν τῆς πόλεως πόλεμον πρὸς Ἀρτάβαζον οἴχεται πλέοντα. Clement of Rome uses ἐγκύπτω in the sense of St. James' παρακ. as in i. 40 ἐγκεκυφότες εἰς τὰ βάθη τῆς θείας γνώσεως, where Lightfoot refers to other passages, esp. 45 ἐγκύπτετε εἰς τὰς γραφάς. So also M. Anton. iv. 3 εἰς ἃ ἐγκύψας, 'contemplating which things.'

νόμον τέλειον τὸν τῆς ἐλευθερίας.] The careful hearer feels that the λόγος ἀληθείας is, and must be, the law of his life, though a law of freedom: it is the ideal on which his eye is to be fixed, not a yoke too heavy for his shoulders to bear. Even of the Mosaic law the psalmist says (xix. 7) 'the law of the Lord is perfect,' but this is merely rudimentary when compared with the law of Christ (Gal. vi. 2), as is shown in detail in the Sermon on the Mount, and in the Epistle to the Hebrews. St. Paul speaks of himself as ἔννομος Χριστοῦ (1 Cor. ix. 21), and further describes the new law as νόμος πίστεως (Rom. iii. 27). It is of this he says in language which may serve as a comment on St. James, ὁ νόμος τοῦ πνεύματος τῆς ζωῆς ἐν Χριστῷ Ἰησοῦ ἐλευθέρωσέν με ἀπὸ τοῦ νόμου τῆς ἁμαρτίας καὶ τοῦ θανάτου. Jeremiah prophesied of this law (xxxi. 33) as a new covenant which should be written on the heart. What led St. James to call the Gospel a law of liberty here and in ii. 12? Clearly he must mean by it a law not enforced by compulsion from without, but freely accepted as expressing the desire and aim of the subject of it. Such free obedience is recognized even in the O.T., Exod. xxxv. 5, Deut. xxviii. 47, Psa. i. 2, xl. 8, liv. 6 'with a free heart will I sacrifice unto thee,' cxix. 32 'I will run the way of thy commandments when thou hast set my heart at liberty, *ib.* 45 'I will walk at liberty for I seek thy commandments,'[1] cxix. 97 'O how I love thy law.' This freedom is declared to be the gift of God, Psa. li. 12 'stablish me with thy free Spirit,' corresponding to the words of St. Paul (2 Cor. iii. 16) οὗ τὸ πνεῦμα Κυρίου ἐκεῖ ἐλευθερία. But probably the source of the phrase used by St. James is his recollection of the words recorded Matt. v. 17 οὐκ ἦλθον καταλῦσαι τὸν νόμον ἀλλὰ πληρῶσαι, and John viii. 32 γνώσεσθε τὴν ἀλήθειαν καὶ ἡ ἀλήθεια ἐλευθερώσει ὑμᾶς. It is another point in which St. James reminds us of the Stoics, cf. their paradox, ὅτι μόνος ὁ σοφὸς ἐλεύθερος καὶ πᾶς ἄφρων δοῦλος, on which Cicero (*Parad.* 34) comments *Quid est libertas? potestas vivendi ut velis: quis igitur vivit ut vult, nisi qui recta sequitur, qui gaudet officio, qui legibus quidem non propter metum paret sed eas sequitur atque colit quia id salutare maxime esse iudicat?* So Ov. *Met.* i. 90 *sponte sua sine lege fidem rectumque colebat,* of the golden age, and Plut. *Mor.* 780 τίς οὖν ἄρξει τοῦ ἄρχοντος; ὁ νόμος, ὁ πάντων βασιλεὺς θνητῶν τε καὶ ἀθανάτων, ὥς ἔφη Πίνδαρος, οὐκ ἐν βιβλίοις ἔξω γεγραμμένος, ἀλλ' ἔμψυχος ὢν ἐν αὐτῷ (the

[1] Cf. Taylor, *J.F.* p. 43 'R. Gamliel used to say Do His will as if it were thy will.'

ruler) λόγος, ἀεὶ συνοικῶν καὶ παραφυλάττων καὶ μηδέποτε τὴν ψυχὴν ἐῶν ἔρημον ἡγεμονίας, Philo M. 1 p. 120 νόμος γὰρ θεῖος οὗτος τὴν ἀρετὴν δι' ἑαυτὴν τιμᾶν, M. 2, p. 452 ὥσπερ τῶν πόλεων αἱ τυραννούμεναι δουλείαν ὑπομένουσι, αἱ δὲ νόμοις χρώμεναι εἰσὶν ἐλεύθεραι, οὕτω καὶ τῶν ἀνθρώπων παρ' οἷς μὲν ἂν ὀργὴ ἢ ἐπιθυμία...δυναστεύει πάντως εἰσὶ δοῦλοι, ὅσοι δὲ μετὰ νόμον ζῶσιν ἐλεύθεροι, Seneca *Vit. Beat.* 15 *in regno nati sumus: Deo parere libertas est;* cf. the Collect 'Whose service is perfect freedom.' The law of liberty is called τέλειος, as the heavenly Tabernacle in Heb. ix. 11, because it carries out, completes, realizes, the object and meaning of the Mosaic law which it replaces (Matt. v. 17). From ii. 8 and 12 we learn something of the contents of St. James' law of liberty; he agrees with St. Paul (Gal. v. 1 and xiii. 14, Rom. xiii. 10) in identifying it with the law of love. Possibly he may not have contrasted it so strongly as St. Paul and St. Peter with the bondage of the Mosaic law (cf. Acts xv. 10, Rom. viii. 2 foll., Gal. iv. 9 foll., 21 foll.), but his view naturally leads on to theirs. Cf. Iren. iv. 39 τὰ ἀποστάντα τοῦ πατρικοῦ φωτὸς καὶ παραβάντα τὸν θεσμὸν τῆς ἐλευθερίας παρὰ τὴν αὐτῶν ἀπέστησαν αἰτίαν, *ib.* iv. 34. 4 *libertatis lex id est verbum Dei ab apostolis annuntiatum*, iv. 37. 1, iv. 13. 2. For the position of the article see Essay on Grammar, and on the 'Torah' Cheyne's *Isaiah* i. 10.

παραμείνας.] Contrasted with the previous ἀπελήλυθε, as παρακύψας with κατενόησε. Cf. John viii. 31 ἐὰν μείνητε ἐν τῷ λόγῳ τῷ ἐμῷ...γνώσεσθε τὴν ἀλήθειαν κ.τ.λ., Luke ii. 19, 51, *ib.* viii. 15, Deut. xxvii. 26 ἐπικατάρατος πᾶς ἄνθρωπος ὃς οὐκ ἐμμένει ἐν πᾶσι τοῖς λόγοις τοῦ νόμου τούτου ποιῆσαι αὐτούς, Philo M. 1. p. 180 τό γε ἀψαμένους τῆς ἐπιστήμης μὴ ἐπιμεῖναι ὅμοιόν ἐστι τῷ γεύσασθαι σιτίων, Diod. ii. 29 ὀλίγοι παραμένουσιν ἐν τῷ μαθήματι (he is contrasting the superficial study and the absence of fixed principles among the Greeks with the opposite among the Chaldeans). The parable, as Oecumenius remarks, is incomplete, omitting to give the case of one who makes full use of the mirror, or rather blending the figure with the interpretation in the word παρακύψας.

ἀκροατὴς ἐπιλησμονῆς.] For the gen. of quality see below ii. 4 κριταὶ διαλογισμῶν πονηρῶν, iii. 6 ὁ κόσμος τῆς ἀδικίας (where see note), also Essay on Grammar, and Winer, p. 297. The only other passage in which ἐπιλ. occurs in all Greek literature is Sir. xi. 25 κάκωσις ὥρας ἐπιλησμονὴν ποιεῖ τρυφῆς. According to Meineke's correction of a scholium to Aristophanes (*Fr. Com.* ii. p. 223) the form was also used by Cratinus. The usual form is ἐπιλησμοσύνη. Other examples of such double forms will be found in *Class. Rev.* ii. 243.

ποιητὴς ἔργου.] This does not correspond exactly to the preceding phrase, as the genitive here is objective. A more exact opposite would have been π. φιλεργίας or ἐπιμελείας. The present phrase suggests such an opposite as ἀκροατὴς φωνῆς. It acquires however a qualitative force by dwelling upon and intensifying the meaning of the word ποιητής. We have above π. λόγου v. 22 and below π. νόμου iv. 11.

οὗτος.] See above v. 23.

μακάριος.] Cf. v. 12 above, and John xiii. 17 εἰ ταῦτα οἴδατε μακάριοί ἐστε ἐὰν ποιῆτε αὐτά, Seneca *Ep.* lxxv. 7 *non est beatus qui scit illa sed qui facit.*

ἐν τῇ ποιήσει.] Only here in N.T. It occurs in Sir. xix. 18 ἐν πάσῃ σοφίᾳ ποίησις νόμου, li. 19 ἐν ποιήσει νόμου διηκριβωσάμην.

26. **δοκεῖ θρησκὸς εἶναι.**] Here we have another source of self-deception, not in hearing, but in saying and doing. Cf. Erasmus: *Qui Judaismum sapiunt religionis laudem constituunt in palliis ac phylacteriis, in delectu ciborum, in lotionibus, in prolixis precibus ceterisque ceremoniis.* Δοκεῖ is used in N.T. either impersonally = (1) 'seems' as Acts xxv. 27 ἄλογόν μοι δοκεῖ, (2) 'seems good' as Luke i. 3 ἔδοξε κἀμοί: or personally (1) of others, Acts xvii. 18 ξένων δαιμονίων δοκεῖ καταγγελεὺς εἶναι, (2) of a man's self, 'think' as here. In this last meaning the word is used absolutely (*a*) Matt. xxiv. 44 ᾗ ὥρᾳ οὐ δοκεῖτε: or (*b*) with ὅτι Matt. vi. 7 δοκοῦσιν ὅτι εἰσακουσθήσονται: or (*c*), as here, with infinitive relating to same subject, cf. John v. 39 δοκεῖτε ἐν αὐταῖς ζωὴν ἔχειν, 1 Cor. iii. 18 εἴ τις δοκεῖ σοφὸς εἶναι, *ib.* viii. 2, x. 12, xiv. 37, Gal. vi. 3. In some cases (e.g. Gal. ii. 6, Phil. iii. 4) it is disputed whether 'seem' or 'think' is the right rendering. Here the question is decided by the following ἀπατῶν καρδίαν ἑαυτοῦ.

θρησκός.] ἅπ. λεγ. The word θρησκεία occurs Acts xxvi. 5 κατὰ τὴν ἀκριβεστάτην αἵρεσιν τῆς ἡμετέρας θρησκείας ἔζησα Φαρισαῖος, Col. ii. 18 θρησκείᾳ τῶν ἀγγέλων, and the compound ἐθελοθρησκεία (self-imposed worship) Col. ii. 23, where see Lightfoot: also in Wisd. xiv. 18 and 27 ἡ τῶν εἰδώλων θρησκεία, in 4 Macc. v. 6 τῇ Ἰουδαίων χρώμενος θρησκείᾳ, *ib.* v. 12, and in Josephus[1] *Ant.* iv. 4. 4 τοῖς κατ' οἶκον θύουσιν εὐωχίας ἕνεκα τῆς αὑτῶν ἀλλὰ μὴ θρησκείας, *ib.* v. 10. 1 γυναῖκας τὰς ἐπὶ θρησκείᾳ παραγινομένας, *ib.* ix. 13. 3 (of the priests) ἵνα ἀεὶ τῇ θρησκείᾳ παραμένωσι 'that they may always remain in attendance on public worship,' *ib.* xii. 5. 4 and xii. 6. 2. Philo carefully distinguishes the term from εὐσέβεια and ὁσιότης (M. 1. 195) πεπλάνηται τῆς πρὸς εὐσέβειαν ὁδοῦ, θρησκείαν ἀντὶ ὁσιότητος ἡγούμενος καὶ δῶρα τῷ ἀδεκάστῳ διδούς, and so Plut. *V. Alex.* 2 (where he gives the derivation from Θρῆσσα, which seems to have suggested to Dr. Hilgenfeld his strange idea that θρησκός is an Orphic word borrowed by St. James) δοκεῖ τὸ θρησκεύειν ὄνομα ταῖς κατακόροις γενέσθαι καὶ περιέργοις ἱερουργίαις. Dr. Hatch sums up the result of his investigation (*l.c.* p. 57) in the words 'religion in its external aspect, as worship or as one mode of worship contrasted with another, must be held to be its meaning in the N.T. as in contemporary writers.' I subjoin some examples from later writers, Justin. M. *Coh. ad Gent.* § 38 τὴν τῶν προγόνων θεοσέβειαν καταλιπόντες διδασκαλίᾳ βασκάνου δαίμονος ἐπὶ τὴν τῶν μὴ θεῶν ἐτράπησαν θρησκείαν, *ib.* 9, *id. Monarch.* 1 ἄτρεπτον ἔχειν τὴν εἰς τὸν πάντων γνώστην θρησκείαν, *ib.* τῶν εἰδώλων θρ. [in *Coh. ad Gent.* 10 it is identified with θεοσέβεια, the prophets being spoken of as teachers first of one, then of the other], Clem. Rom. i. 45 Ἀνανίας καὶ Ἀζαρίας καὶ Μισαὴλ ὑπὸ τῶν θρησκευόντων τὴν μεγαλοπρεπῆ καὶ ἔνδοξον θρησκείαν τοῦ ὑψίστου κατείρχθησαν εἰς κάμινον πυρός; μηδαμῶς τοῦτο γένοιτο, Clem. Al. *Strom.* vi. p. 795 P ἔδωκεν τὸν ἥλιον καὶ τὴν σελήνην καὶ τὰ ἄστρα εἰς θρησκείαν. It is of frequent

[1] The quotations from Josephus *Antiq.* are borrowed from Hatch *Bibl. Gr.* p. 56: add from *B.J.* vii. 3, 3 προσαγόμενοι ταῖς θρησκείαις πολὺ πλῆθος Ἑλλήνων, 'bringing over to their rites a multitude of Greeks.'

occurrence in Clem. Hom.; see the account there given (vii. 8) of the θρησκεία required by God. The verb θρησκεύω occurs in Wisd. xi. 15 with an object ἐθρήσκευον ἄλογα ἑρπετά, and xiv. 16 (in the passive) τυράννων ἐπιταγαῖς ἐθρησκεύετο τὰ γλυπτά, Josephus *B.J.* ii. 9, 2 ἦν παρ' αὐτοῖς θρησκευόμενον σάββατον, so Euseb. *H.E.* ii. 13 τούτους θρησκεύειν ἐπιχειροῦντες, Clem. Al. *Strom.* vi. § 77, p. 778 P τὸ δὲ (keeping the commandments) ἐστὶ θρησκεύειν τὸ θεῖον διὰ τῆς ὄντως δικαιοσύνης ἔργων τε καὶ γνώσεως, a passage much resembling the text, *ib.* iv. § 160, p. 636 P τῇ ἑβδόμῃ ἡ ἀνάπαυσις θρησκεύεται, 'is observed.' On the whole the words seem to answer to the Lat. *colo, cultus.* See Trench *Synonyms of N.T.* and Coleridge there cited.

χαλιναγωγῶν.] This seems to be the first use of the word. It occurs again below iii. 2 and in Herm. *Mand.* xii. 1 ἐνδεδυμένος τὴν ἐπιθυμίαν τὴν ἀγαθὴν μισήσεις τὴν πονηρὰν ἐπιθυμίαν καὶ χαλιναγωγήσεις αὐτήν, Polycarp *ad Phil.* v. 3 νεώτεροι χαλιναγωγοῦντες ἑαυτοὺς ἀπὸ παντὸς κακοῦ, also in Lucian *Tyrannicida* 4 τὰς ἡδονῶν ὀρέξεις χαλιναγωγεῖν, *De Saltat.* 70: Plutarch uses χαλινόω (read here by B.) in the same sense (*Mor.* p. 967). We find ἀχάλινον στόμα in Aristoph. *Ran.* 862, Eur. *Bacch.* 385 and often in Philo, e.g. M. 2. p. 5, 75, 219, M. 1. p. 6 ἀχαλίνωτον στόμα. Compare for metaphor Diog. L. v. 39 (of Theophrastus) θᾶττον ἔφη πιστεύειν δεῖν ἵππῳ ἀχαλίνῳ ἢ λόγῳ ἀσυντάκτῳ, Psa. xxxii. 9, xxxix. 1, cxli. 3. For thought see ver. 19, and below iii. 1–10.

ἀπατῶν καρδίαν ἑαυτοῦ.] We should rather have expected this to come in the apodosis: 'if any one thinks himself religious and yet does not bridle his tongue, he deceives himself and his religion is vain.' If included in the protasis it would have been more logically expressed by εἴ τις δοκεῖ θρῆσκος εἶναι, μὴ ὤν, ἀλλ' ἀπατῶν κ.τ.λ. For the general μὴ ὤν the writer substitutes that positive failing which he took to be the cause of this unreality. The phrase ἀπ. καρδ. is equivalent to παραλογιζόμενοι ἑαυτούς above ver. 22, cf. Rom. xvi. 18 διὰ τῆς εὐλογίας ἐξαπατῶσι τὰς καρδίας τῶν ἀκάκων, Gal. vi. 3 εἰ γὰρ δοκεῖ τις εἶναί τι, μηδὲν ὤν, ἑαυτὸν φρεναπατᾷ, 1 Cor. iii. 18 μηδεὶς ἑαυτὸν ἐξαπατάτω· εἴ τις δοκεῖ σοφὸς εἶναι ἐν ὑμῖν μωρὸς γενέσθω κ.τ.λ., Test. Nephth. p. 668 Fabr. μὴ σπουδάζετε ἐν λόγοις κενοῖς ἀπατᾶν τὰς ψυχὰς ὑμῶν, ὅτι σιωπῶντες ἐν καθαρότητι καρδίας δυνήσεσθε τὸ θέλημα τοῦ θεοῦ κρατεῖν, Hatch. p. 98.

μάταιος.] Cf, τί ὄφελος below ii. 14. Here with two terminations, as in Tit. iii. 9, but with three in 1 Cor. xv. 17, 1 Pet. i. 18, see Winer, p. 80: for thought cf. Isa. i. 10–17, Isocr. *ad Nicoc.* p. 18 E ἡγοῦ θῦμα τοῦτο κάλλιστον εἶναι καὶ θεραπείαν μεγίστην ἐὰν ὡς βέλτιστον καὶ δικαιότατον σαυτὸν παρέχῃς.

27. **καθαρὰ καὶ ἀμίαντος.**] Often found together, as in Herm. *Sim.* v. 7 τὴν σάρκα φύλασσε κ. καὶ ἀμ., Philo 2 M. p. 249, Dion. Hal. *A.R.* viii. 43, 52 κ. καὶ ἀμ. ἔχειν συμβήσεται τὴν ψυχὴν ἀπὸ παντὸς χόλου. Erasmus: *Purus est apud Judaeos qui morticinum non contigerit, qui lotus sit vivo flumine...impurus est qui carnem suillam ederit.*

παρὰ τῷ Θεῷ καὶ Πατρί.] The heavenly standard is appealed to here as above ver. 20 δικαιοσύνην Θεοῦ, 1 Pet. ii. 20 τοῦτο χάρις παρὰ Θεῷ, and below ἐνώπιον Θεοῦ iv. 10. The phrase ὁ Θεὸς καὶ Πατήρ is used below iii. 9 according to some MSS., and by St. Paul 1 Cor. xv. 24, Eph. v.

20, also with ἡμῶν added 1 Thess. i. 3, iii. 11, 13, Gal. i. 3, Phil. iv. 20. Θεὸς πατήρ is found Rom. i. 7, 1 Cor. i. 3, Eph. i. 2, &c., ὁ Θεὸς πατήρ Col. i. 3, iii. 17, where see Lightfoot, 1 Pet. i. 2 ὁ Θεὸς καὶ Πατὴρ τοῦ Κυρίου ἡμῶν Ἰ.Χ., Rom. xv. 16, 2 Cor. i. 3 &c.

αὕτη ἐστίν, ἐπισκέπτεσθαι.] For the attraction of τοῦτο to αὕτη see Madv. *Gr.* § 98 'a demonstrative pronoun to which a substantive is attached as predicate-noun by εἰμί &c. is apt to assume the gender and number of the substantive, Xen. *Oecon.* 8. 2 αὕτη πενία ἐστὶ σαφής, τὸ δεόμενόν τινος μὴ ἔχειν χρῆσθαι.' For the explanatory infinitive in apposition to αὕτη cf. Winer, p. 663 foll. The verb is used of visiting the sick in Matt. xxv. 36, 43, Sirac. vii. 35, and in classical Greek, as Xen. *Cyr.* v. 4. 10, viii. 3. 25.

ὀρφανοὺς καὶ χήρας.] God is called the father of the fatherless and judge of the widow Psa. lxviii. 5; there is a special curse on those who afflict the fatherless and widow Deut. xxvi. 19; the Pharisees are charged with devouring widows' houses (Luke xx. 47); cf. Exod. xxii. 22, Job. xxxi. 16, 17, Sirac. iv. 10 γίνου ὀρφανοῖς ὡς πατὴρ καὶ ἀντὶ ἀνδρὸς τῇ μητρὶ αὐτῶν. We find descriptions which recall many of the features of this passage in Barnab. xx. 2 χήρᾳ καὶ ὀρφανῷ οὐ προσέχοντες...ὧν μακρὰν καὶ πόρρω πραΰτης καὶ ὑπομονή...οὐκ ἐλεῶντες πτωχόν, εὐχερεῖς ἐν καταλαλίᾳ ..πλουσίων παράκλητοι, πενήτων ἄνομοι κριταί [this is partly borrowed from Didaché v.], Polycarp *Philipp.* 6 describes the πρεσβύτεροι as ἐπισκεπτόμενοι πάντας ἀσθενεῖς, μὴ ἀμελοῦντες χήρας ἢ ὀρφανοῦ ἢ πένητος... ἀπεχόμενοι πάσης ὀργῆς, προσωποληψίας, κρίσεως ἀδίκου; so in Clem. Hom. i. 8 Peter charges the presbyters, to act the part of parents to the orphans, of husbands to the widows, cf. Herm. *Mand.* 8. 10, where Harnack cites many illustrative passages, Ignat. *ad. Pol.* 4 χῆραι μὴ ἀμελείσθωσαν· μετὰ τὸν Κύριον σὺ αὐτῶν φροντιστὴς ἔσο.

ἄσπιλον ἑαυτὸν τηρεῖν.] For asyndeton see Essay on Grammar, cf. 1 Tim. vi. 14 τηρῆσαι τὴν ἐντολὴν ἄσπιλον, 1 Pet. i. 19, 2 Pet. iii. 14, Herm. *Vis.* iii. 4. 5 ἄσπιλοι καὶ καθαροὶ ἔσονται οἱ ἐκλελεγμένοι εἰς ζωὴν αἰώνιον, *Sim.* v. 6. 7, Lact. *Inst.* v. 9 (*Christianorum*) *omnis religio est sine scelere ac sine macula vivere*, above ver. 21 ῥυπαρίαν, below iii. 6 ἡ γλῶσσα ἡ σπιλοῦσα ὅλον τὸ σῶμα. For τηρεῖν 1 Tim. v. 22 σεαυτὸν ἁγνὸν τήρει, 2 Cor. xi. 9 ἐν παντὶ ἀβαρῆ ἐμαυτὸν ὑμῖν ἐτήρησα.

ἀπὸ τοῦ κόσμου.] See below iv. 4 with the comment, 2 Pet. ii. 20 ἀποφυγόντες τὰ μιάσματα τοῦ κόσμου. For ἀπό Acts xx. 26 καθαρὸς ἐγὼ ἀπὸ τοῦ αἵματος πάντων, Matt. xxvii. 24 ἀθῷος ἀπὸ, 2 Sam. iii. 28, Mark v. 34 ἴσθι ὑγιὴς ἀπὸ τῆς μάστιγός σου, Rom. vii. 3 ἐλευθέρα ἐστὶν ἀπὸ τοῦ νόμου. The classical writers use the simple genitive with καθαρός and ἀθῷος; ἐλεύθερος is found with ἀπὸ in Xen. and Plato; Hermas *Mand.* xi. 4 has κενὸς ἀπὸ τῆς ἀληθείας. See Ryle, *Psalms of Sol.* p. lxxxiii.

II. 1.—**ἀδελφοί μου.**] See n. on i. 2. There is special propriety in its use here, where he is urging them to brotherly kindness.

ἐν προσωποληψίαις.] Cf. Rom. ii. 11, Eph. vi. 9, Col. iii. 25, in all of which προσωποληψία is denied of God, Polycarp *ad Phil.* 6 ἀπεχόμενοι πάσης ὀργῆς, προσωποληψίας. The *v.* προσωποληπτεῖν occurs below v. 9., the *s.* προσωπολήπτης Acts x. 34 οὐκ ἔστι προσωπολήπτης ὁ Θεός, and the *adv.* ἀπροσωπολήμπτως 1 Pet. i. 17 also of God (of man Clem. Rom. i. 1). Barn. 4. 12 ὁ κύριος ἀπροσωπολήμπτως κρινεῖ τὸν κόσμον, Ps. Hippol. p. 117 Lagarde κριτὴς ἀπροσωπόληπτος. These, so far as I know are the only instances of the use of these compounds. The uncompounded λαμβάνειν πρόσωπον occurs in Luke xx. 21, Gal. ii. 6, and in LXX., Lev. xix. 15 οὐ λήμψῃ πρόσωπον πτωχοῦ οὐδὲ μὴ θαυμάσῃς πρόσωπον δυναστοῦ, Psa. lxxxiii. 2 ἕως πότε κρίνετε ἀδικίαν καὶ πρόσωπα ἁμαρτωλῶν λαμβάνετε; Malachi i. 8, 9, ii. 9, Sirac. iv. 21 (of false shame) μὴ λάβῃς πρόσωπον κατὰ τῆς ψυχῆς σου, *ib.* 27, xxxii. 12 f. κύριος κριτής ἐστι, καὶ οὐκ ἔστι παρ' αὐτῷ δόξα προσώπου· οὐ λήψεται πρόσωπον ἐπὶ πτωχοῦ...οὐ μὴ ὑπερίδῃ ἱκετείαν ὀρφανοῦ, καὶ χήραν ἐὰν ἐκχέῃ λαλίαν, 2 Kings iii. 14 πρόσωπον Ἰωσαφὰτ λαμβάνω, Didaché 4, 3, Can. Eccl. 20. In all these passages there is signified a bias of judgment owing to the position, rank, circumstances, popularity, and externals generally of the person judged. A just judge must not be influenced by personal prejudices, hopes or fears, but by the single desire to do justice. Other verbs used with πρόσωπον in much the same sense are θαυμάζειν, Jude 16 θαυμάζοντες πρόσωπον ὠφελείας χάριν, 2 Chron. xix. 7, Job xiii. 10, Prov. xviii. 5, Psalm. Sol. ii. 191 [used in good sense Gen. xix. 21 ἐθαύμασά[1] σου τὸ πρόσωπον, 'I have accepted thee']; ἐπιγινώσκειν, Deut. i. 17 οὐκ ἐπιγνώσῃ πρόσωπον ἐν κρίσει, *ib.* xvi. 19; ὑποστέλλεσθαι, Deut. i. 17 οὐ μὴ ὑποστείλῃ πρόσωπον ἀνθρώπου, Wisdom vi. 8; αἰδεῖσθαι, &c., Prov. xxiv. 23, ὃς οὐκ ἐπαισχυνθῇ πρόσωπον ἐντίμου Job xxxiv. 19; αἱρετίζειν, 1 Sam. xxv. 35 ᾑρέτισα τὸ πρόσωπόν σου (good sense); κρίνειν, Phocyl. 10 μὴ κρῖνε πρόσωπον. Equivalent phrases are βλέπειν or ὁρᾶν εἰς πρόσωπον Mark xii. 14, 1 Sam. xvi. 7 ἄνθρωπος ὄψεται εἰς πρόσωπον, ὁ δὲ θεὸς ὄψεται εἰς καρδίαν, 2 Cor. x. 7 τὰ κατά πρόσωπον βλέπετε; also κρίνειν κατ' ὄψιν John vii. 24, κατὰ τὴν δόξαν κρ. Isa. xi. 3, κατὰ τὴν σάρκα John viii. 15. In its strict sense the Greek would mean to accept the outside surface for the inner reality, the mask for the person,[2] cf. Epict. *Ench.* 17 μέμνησο ὅτι ὑποκριτὴς εἶ δράματος οἵου ἂν θέλῃ ὁ διδάσκαλος...σὸν τοῦτ' ἔστιν τὸ δοθὲν ὑποκρίνασθαι πρόσωπον καλῶς. The plural of the abstract refers to the many ways in which partiality may show itself, cf. below iv. 16 ἐν ἀλαζονίαις, 2 Pet. iii. 11 ἐν εὐσεβείαις, Col. iii. 22 ἐν ὀφθαλμοδουλείαις, Jude 18 ἐπιθυμίαι ἀσεβειῶν, Winer, p. 220, and for the similiar use in Latin my note on Cic. *N.D.* ii. 98.

ἔχετε τὴν πίστιν.] 'Do not have your faith in personal respects,' 'Do not you, who call yourselves believers in Christ, disgrace your faith by exhibitions of partiality.' WH. with marg. in R.V. take ἔχετε as indicative with a remark of interrogation, 'Do ye, in accepting persons,

[1] Aq. ᾖρα.

[2] Mr. Jennings on Psa. lxxxii. 2 says the Hebrew '*nâsâ pânîm* primarily involves the act of raising the face of another with the view of comforting him.' If this is so, the meaning is entirely lost in the Greek translations and a much more striking idea substituted in its place; see Lightfoot, *Gal.* ii. 6 "in the O. T. it is a neutral expression involving no subsidiary idea of partiality, and is much oftener found in a good than in a bad sense. When it becomes an independent Greek phrase, however, the bad sense attaches to it owing to the secondary meaning of πρόσωπον as 'a mask.'"

hold the faith?' &c· The interrogative rendering is also preferred by Stier, Schneckenburger, Kern, Gebser, Pott, and other commentators. I think it is simpler and more natural to take ἔχετε as imperative, especially as it is the commencement of a new section of the epistle, and it is the manner of the writer to begin by putting each topic forward clearly and explicitly, usually in the shape of a precept, and afterwards to enforce and illustrate it in a variety of forms. It certainly cannot be said that, taken interrogatively, the sentence gives a clear, unmistakable meaning. At first sight it would seem to suggest that those addressed are not guilty of respect of persons. And the following γάρ, which, if we take ἔχετε as imperative, gives a warning against respect of persons, because it is shown by an example to involve worldly-mindedness and unrighteous judgment, is hard to explain if we take ἔχετε as a question: ('Can it be that you are guilty of partiality? *For* if you make distinctions in your religious meetings you are not whole-hearted, but led away by worldly considerations.') The imperative also suits better the seriousness of the writer and the opening words ἀδελφοί μου. For ἐν expressing the sphere of manifestation cf. above i. 21 ἐν πραΰτητι, 1 Tim. i. 18 ἵνα στρατεύῃ ἐν αὐταῖς τὴν καλὴν στρατείαν. Μὴ ἔχετε is a more personal way of putting μὴ ἔστω ἡ πίστις, implying free-will and responsibility, cf. Mark ix. 50 ἔχετε ἐν ἑαυτοῖς ἅλας, Rom. x. 2 ζῆλον Θεοῦ ἔχουσιν ἀλλ' οὐ κατὰ ἐπίγνωσιν, below ii. 18 σὺ πίστιν ἔχεις κἀγὼ ἔργα ἔχω.

πίστιν τοῦ Κυρίου ἡμῶν.] For this objective genitive cf. Mark xi. 22 ἔχετε πίστιν Θεοῦ, Acts iii. 6 π. τοῦ ὀνόματος, Rom. iii. 22 δικαιοσύνη Θεοῦ διὰ πίστεως Ἰησοῦ Χριστοῦ, Gal. ii. 16, Apoc. xiv. 12. The same relation may be expressed by εἰς Acts xx. 21, ἐν Gal. iii. 26, πρός 1 Thes. 1–8, ἐπί Heb. vi. 1.

τῆς δόξης.] This genitive has been variously interpreted as having an objective, a subjective, or a qualitative force, and been connected in turn by different commentators with every substantive in the sentence: with προσπολημψίαις (1) by Erasmus, Calvin, Heisen, Michaelis; with πίστιν (2) by the Peshitto, Grotius, Cornelius à Lapide, Hammond and Hofmann; with the whole or a portion of the phrase τοῦ Κυρίου ...Χριστοῦ (3) by the majority of commentators. 1. Erasmus translates '*Cum partium studio quo ex sua quisque opinione quemlibet aestimat*'; Calvin, '*Ne in acceptionibus personarum fidem habeatis...ex opinione,*' which he explains '*Nam dum opum vel honorum opinio nostros oculos perstringit, veritas supprimitur.*' Both interpretations would make δόξης a subjective genitive, denoting the cause or source of προσωπολημψία. Michaelis, on the other hand, gives it an objective force, translating '*Admiratio hominum secundum externum splendorem*'; and much in the same way, Heisen. It is now generally recognised that the order of the words renders this explanation of the construction impossible. 2. The Peshitto, followed by Grotius, Hammond, Hofmann, &c., translates 'faith of (in) the glory of Christ' (objective genitive). Huther, 'Christ-given faith in the glory to be revealed'; Gataker, followed by Hottoman, 'the glorious faith in

Christ' (qualitative genitive). Though the interval between the two words πίστιν and δόξης in my opinion entirely precludes any qualitative connexion, it is perhaps not so decisive against Grotius' interpretation. To a certain extent we may find a parallel in i. 2: τὸ δοκίμιον ὑμῶν τῆς πίστεως, 'the proof of your faith,' is not unlike τὴν πίστιν...'Ιησοῦ Χριστοῦ τῆς δόξης 'the faith in Christ's glory'; but of course the harshness becomes greater with every additional word which separates them, and with the greater importance of those words. 3. It remains to consider the interpretations which make τῆς δόξης depend upon the whole, or a part, of the phrase preceding. These may be classified as follows (*a*) δόξης depending on Χριστοῦ only; (*b*) depending on 'Ιησοῦ Χριστοῦ (*c*) on τοῦ Κυρίου ἡμῶν; (*d*) on τοῦ Κυρίου understood; (*e*) on the whole phrase τ. Κ. ἡ. 'Ι. Χ. (*a*) 'The Messiah of glory': so Laurentius, Schulthess, Lange, Bouman. The objection to this is, that it is impossible thus to separate 'Ιησοῦ Χριστοῦ, and that in any case it would require the article before Χριστοῦ. (*b*) So Ewald: 'Den Glauben unsers Herrn, Jesus Christus der Herrlichkeit.' This seems to make an arbitrary division of the words, and is also liable to the same objections as (*e*). Moreover, do we ever find a proper name used with the genitive of quality? (*c*) 'Our Lord of glory, Jesus Christ.' So Schneckenburger De Wette, Wiesinger. If this were the writer's meaning, why did he not place the words τῆς δόξης after ἡμῶν? (*d*) 'Our Lord Jesus Christ (the Lord) of glory.' So Baumgarten, Semler and others; but it is without parallel, and is not supported by any of the latter commentators. (*e*) 'Of our glorious Lord Jesus Christ.' So Kern, Alford, Beyschlag, Erdmann, Schegg, and the great majority of modern commentators. We may allow that St. James makes frequent use of the genitive of quality, as in i. 25 ἀκροατὴς ἐπιλησμονῆς, ii. 4 κριταὶ διαλογισμῶν πονηρῶν, &c.: but it is very improbable that such a genitive would be appended to a phrase which is already complete in itself; and we may safely say that no one would have thought of such a construction for this passage if the other suggested interpretations had not involved equal or even greater harshness.

There is however a perfectly natural and easy construction suggested by Bengel, which has been set aside by later commentators on what seem to me very inadequate grounds. His note is, 'τῆς δόξης; *est appositio, ut ipse Christus dicatur ἡ δόξα...Christus gloria; hinc fideles gloriosi. Hanc fidelium gloriam nullus mundi honos aequat, nemo personarum acceptor agnoscit.*'[1] The objection made to it is that the abstract term δόξα, by itself, is too indefinite to bear this weight of meaning. But other abstractions are used of Christ. He calls himself the Truth, the Life; He is called the Word, why not the Glory? If we had before us such a sentence as μὴ ἔχετε ἐν ἀφροσύνῃ τὴν πίστιν τοῦ Κυρίου ἡμῶν 'Ιησοῦ Χριστοῦ, τοῦ λόγου, we should have no scruple in translating it 'Do not hold in folly the faith of our Lord Jesus Christ, who is the Word,' any more than we have in translating 1 Tim. i. 1 κατ' ἐπιταγὴν Κυρίου Χριστοῦ 'Ιησοῦ τῆς

[1] W. H. in their marginal reading imply this construction by placing a comma after Χριστοῦ. Cf. Ign. *Eph.* 3 'Ιησοῦς Χριστὸς τὸ ἀδιάκριτον ὑμῶν ζῆν.

ἐλπίδος ἡμῶν, 'According to the command of Christ Jesus, who is our hope.' Why should we object to the similar translation here, 'the faith of our Lord Jesus Christ, who is the glory'? The only question is whether the abstract δόξα is thus used of a person. Bengel cites Luke ii. 31 τὸ σωτήριον ὃ ἡτοίμασας...δόξαν λαοῦ σου Ἰσραήλ, Eph. i. 17 ὁ Θεὸς τοῦ Κυρίου ἡμῶν Ἰησοῦ Χριστοῦ, ὁ Πατὴρ τῆς δόξης, 1 Pet. iv. 14 εἰ ὀνειδίζεσθε ἐν ὀνόματι Χριστοῦ, μακάριοι, ὅτι τὸ τῆς δόξης καὶ τὸ τοῦ Θεοῦ Πνεῦμα ἐφ' ὑμᾶς ἀναπαύεται (where he takes δόξης as an appellation of Christ). Perhaps more striking parallels are 2 Pet. i. 17 φωνῆς ἐνεχθείσης τοιᾶσδε ὑπὸ τῆς μεγαλοπρεποῦς δόξης ('The words seem a periphrasis for God Himself,' Alf.), Col. i. 27 τί τὸ πλοῦτος τῆς δόξης τοῦ μυστηρίου τούτου, ὅ ἐστιν Χριστὸς ἐν ἡμῖν, ἡ ἐλπις τῆς δόξης, Rom. ix. 4, where it stands for the Shekinah (cf. 1 Sam. iv. 22, Psa. lxxviii. 61, *ib.* cvi. 20, Isa. iv. 5), John xvii. 22 ἐγὼ τὴν δόξαν ἣν δέδωκάς μοι δέδωκα αὐτοῖς, *ib.* i. 14 ἐθεασάμεθα τὴν δόξαν αὐτοῦ, δόξαν ὡς μονογενοῦς παρὰ Πατρὸς (of which Westcott says (p. xlvii.) 'Christ the Light of the world is seen by the believer to be the manifested Glory of God'), Heb. i. 3 ἀπαύγασμα δόξης, cf. Justin *Tryph.* 61 ὁ Θεὸς γεγέννηκε δύναμίν τινα ἐξ ἑαυτοῦ λογικὴν, ἥτις καὶ δόξα Κυρίου καλεῖται, ποτὲ δὲ υἱὸς, ποτὲ δὲ σοφία. Similarly μεγαλωσύνη is used Heb. i. 3, and δύναμις Matt. xxvi. 64, cf. Clem. Rom. i. 16 τὸ σκῆπτρον τῆς μεγαλωσύνης τοῦ Θεοῦ, ὁ Κύριος ἡμῶν Χριστὸς Ἰησοῦς. We may suppose that the reason why the word δόξα stands here alone, without ἡμῶν or τοῦ Πατρός, is in order that it may be understood in its fullest and widest sense of Him who alone comprises all glory in Himself. This interpretation is confirmed by the rhythm which makes a natural pause before τῆς δόξης.

Since the above note was written I find that Mr. Bassett in his commentary takes τῆς δόξης, as I have done, in apposition to τοῦ Κυρίου. In an appendix on this verse, to show that the name Shekinah was used by the Jews of God or of the Messiah, he cites Psa. lxxxv. 9 ἐγγὺς τῶν φοβουμένων αὐτὸν τὸ σωτήριον αὐτοῦ, τοῦ κατασκηνῶσαι δόξαν ἐν τῇ γῇ ἡμῶν, on which Jennings notes 'the glory is certainly as in Psa. lxiii. 2, Zech. vi. 12, 13, that of the Divine Presence which now again dawns on the restored people...St. John's description of the Advent of Christ offers an approximate parallel..."the Word was made flesh and dwelt (ἐσκήνωσε) among us and we beheld his glory...full of grace and truth": so here ver. 10 tells of a concurrence of Divine goodness and truth.' Bassett refers also to Hagg. ii. 7, 9, Zech. ii. 5 'I, saith the Lord, will be [the] glory in the midst of her,' *ib.* v. 8, 10, and to the book Sohar,[1] where the Son of God is spoken of as the Shekinah. Thus δόξα would appear to be equivalent to Emmanuel, cf. Apoc. xxi. 3 ἡ σκηνὴ (=Shekinah) τοῦ Θεοῦ μετὰ τῶν ἀνθρώπων, Lev. xxvi. 11, 12 θήσω τὴν σκηνήν μου ἐν ὑμῖν καὶ...ἐμπεριπατήσω ἐν ὑμῖν, καὶ ἔσομαι ὑμῶν Θεὸς καὶ ὑμεῖς ἔσεσθε μοι λαός, and Pirke Aboth iii. 3 'two that sit together and are occupied in words of Thorah have the Shekinah among them,' where Taylor com-

[1] 'Commenting on Psa. ii., Simeon ben Jochai speaks of "the Lord of the serving angels, the son of the Highest, yea, the Shekinah," and again, "God said Faithful Shepherd! verily thou art my Son, yea, the Shekinah."' Bassett, p. 101.

pares Matt. xviii. 20 'there am *I* in the midst of them.'[1] [Spitta thinks the difficulty of construction betrays the interpolation of ἡμῶν 'I.X. by the Christian editor (see above *Introd.* ch. vii.) and cites the following exx. of the use of ὁ Κύριος τῆς δόξης for Jehovah from Enoch: xxii. 14 ηὐλόγησα τ. Κύριον τῆς δόξης, xxv. 3 ὁ μέγας Κύριος τῆς δόξης, ὁ βασιλεὺς τοῦ αἰῶνος, also xxv. 7, xxvii. 3, 5.]

2. **εἰς συναγωγὴν ὑμῶν.**] Either 'to a meeting of yours,' or 'into your synagogue,' the article being omitted according to Hellenistic use, as in v. 20 ἐκ πλάνης αὐτοῦ. The word is used of a distinctively Christian assembly by Hermas *Mand.* xi. 9 (when a man having the Spirit of God comes) εἰς συναγωγὴν ἀνδρῶν δικαίων...καὶ ἔντευξις γένηται πρὸς τὸν Θεὸν τῆς συναγωγῆς τῶν ἀνδρῶν ἐκείνων (there the power of the Spirit is manifested). In the note Harnack says that the word is used in the earlier Greek only in active sense of 'bringing together,' but by Jewish writers of the apostolic age (1) of the religious community, (2) of the religious assembly, (3) of the place of assembly. It alternates with ἐκκλησία in the LXX., but the latter soon became the predominant and distinctive term among the Christians, συναγωγή being contrasted with it, as denoting an assembly of Jews or heretics, cf. Apoc. ii. 9, iii. 9 συναγωγὴ τοῦ Σατανᾶ, and many passages cited by Harnack from Tertullian, Irenaeus, Clem. Al., Apost. Constitt. It seems however that the Christians of Judaea retained the wider use, after it had been abandoned elsewhere, as Epiphanius xxx. 18 says of the Ebionites συναγωγὴν οὗτοι καλοῦσι τὴν ἑαυτῶν ἐκκλησίαν καὶ οὐχὶ ἐκκλησίαν (Lightfoot *Philipp.* p. 190). It is also found loosely used by other Christian writers in the sense of 'gathering' (ἐπισυναγωγή Heb. x. 25), as Ignat. *Polyc.* iv. 2 πυκνότερον συναγωγαὶ γινέσθωσαν (=Didaché xvi. 2 πυκνῶς συναχθήσεσθε), Theoph. *ad Autol.* ii. 14 δέδωκεν ὁ Θεὸς τῷ κόσμῳ...τὰς συναγωγὰς, λεγομένας δὲ ἐκκλησίας ἁγίας, Clem. Al. *Strom.* vi. 4, p. 756 ἀλήθεια οὐρανόθεν ἄνωθεν ἐπὶ τὴν συναγωγὴν τῆς ἐκκλησίας ἀφιγμένη, Const. Apostol. iii. 6, οὐ γὰρ ἐπὶ τὸ κοινὸν τῆς συναγωγῆς ἀνάπαυμα ἐν τῇ κυριακῇ καταντῶσιν. Some have supposed that συναγωγή should be taken in its ordinary sense of a Jewish synagogue, the epistle having been written at a time when the separation of Christians from Jews was not completely effected. Compare Westcott *Heb.* p. xxxviii. 'For a time the fellowship of the church and synagogue was allowed on both sides. Little by little the growth of the Gentile element in the church excited the active hostility of the Jews against the whole body of Christians, as it troubled the Jewish converts themselves. This hostility could not fail to be intensified in Palestine by the spread of aggressive nationalism there shortly before the outbreak of the Jewish war. . . . When as yet the national unbelief of the Jews was undeclared it was not possible to foresee that the coming of Christ would bring the overthrow of the old order. The approaching catastrophe was not realized in the earlier apostolic writings. In the

[1] Delitzsch, in his story on Jerusalem in the time of the Herods, says with reference to this verse of Aboth, 'they had often felt in past days that the Shekinah was in their midst, but now this gracious Presence assumed bodily form in the person of Jesus, as the Messiah of Israel'—(shortened from English tr. p. 121).

epistle to the Hebrews it is shown to be imminent.' So we read in Acts vi. 19 of Christians belonging to the synagogue of the Libertines; in Acts xv. 21 it seems to be implied that the Jewish Christians still heard Moses read in the synagogue every sabbath-day; *ib.* ix. 4 Saul takes letters to the synagogues in Damascus bidding them to purge themselves of Christian members, cf. xxii. 19 *ἐγὼ ἤμην φυλακίζων καὶ δέρων κατὰ τὰς συναγωγὰς τοὺς πιστεύοντας ἐπὶ σέ.* Afterwards in his missionary journeys St. Paul regularly begins by preaching in the synagogues (Acts xiii. 14, 43; xiv. 1; xvii. 1, 2, 10, 17; xviii. 4, 26; xix. 8); in Corinth we hear of his leaving the synagogue in consequence of the violent opposition of the Jews and making use of an adjoining house (Acts xviii. 7); at Ephesus he preached in the synagogue for three months before he withdrew to the school of Tyrannus (*ib.* xix. 9). In our text it is plain that the writer supposes the meeting-place mentioned to be open to non-Christians: strangers might enter it either from curiosity, or from sympathy, or from malice to spy out what was going on. St. Paul refers to such visits from strangers in 1 Cor. xiv. 23. But as it is called *συναγωγὴν ὑ μ ῶ ν*, it is evidently assumed that it was mainly under Christian direction. The precise circumstances would of course vary from town to town.

χρυσοδακτύλιος.] *ἅπ. λεγ.* Lucian (*Tim.* 20) uses *χρυσόχειρ* in the same sense, and Epict. *Diss.* i. 22 speaks of *γέρων χρυσοῦς δακτυλίους ἔχων πολλούς*, so Seneca *N.Q.* vii. 31 *omni articulo gemma exponitur*, Plin. *N.H.* xxxiii. ch. 6, Juv. i. 28: that the wearing of rings was customary among the Jews appears from Luke xv. 22. Clem. Al. *Paed.* iii. p. 288 says that a man should only wear a ring on the little finger, and that it should bear some religious emblem, dove, or fish, or anchor. In Const. Apost. i. 3 Christians are warned against fine clothing and wearing of rings (*μηδὲ χρυσήλατον σφενδόνην τοῖς δακτύλοις σου περιθῇς*), for these are all marks of wantonness. For *ἀνήρ* see above i. 8 n.

ἐν ἐσθῆτι λαμπρᾷ.] *ἐν* is classical in this use, like *in* in Latin. The same epithet is used (Luke xxiii. 11) of the robe in which Herod clothed Jesus [should this be identified with the *πορφυροῦν ἱμάτιον* put on him by the soldiers John xix. 2?], and of the angel (Acts x. 30), cf. Posidonius *ap.* Athen. v. p. 212 *d.* of the upstart Athenio, who *ἐξῄει χλαμύδα λαμπρὰν ἐκσύρων καὶ περικείμενος δακτύλιον χρυσίου*, Philo M. 2. p. 56 (of Joseph) *ἀντὶ ῥυπώσης λαμπρὰν ἐσθῆτα ἀντιδόντες*, Artemid. ii. 3 fin. *ἀεὶ δὲ ἄμεινον καθαρὰ καὶ λαμπρὰ ἱμάτια ἔχειν καὶ πεπλυμένα καλῶς ἢ ῥυπαρὰ καὶ ἄπλυτα.* There does not seem any reason to confine the meaning to white colour as Thomas Magister and Casaubon on Theophr. *Char.* 21. According to Wolf, the latter allows (in his *Exercitt. c. Bar.* xvi. 73, p. 532) that it may refer to any brilliant colour, and so Salmas. on Tertull. *Pall.* p. 182. In Euseb. *H.E.* ii. 10 a robe called *λαμπρὰ καὶ βασιλική* is afterwards described as *στολὴ ἐξ ἀργύρου πεποιημένη.* Here the contrast with *ῥυπαρά* 'soiled,' 'shabby,' (see above i. 21 n.) would perhaps be most marked in the case of white, which was also the usual colour worn by the Jews. Similar expressions are *ἱματισμὸς ἔνδοξος* Luke vii. 25, or *πολυτελής* 1 Tim. ii. 9.

εἰσέλθῃ δὲ καί.] 'And there come in also on the other hand.' For omission of the correlative μέν cf. above i. 13 πειράζει δέ, below v. 10 πταίσῃ δέ, iv. 6 ταπεινοῖς δέ, Matt. xxiii. 24, 25, Buttm. p. 312 foll. For the repetition of the verb see Essay on Grammar. For construction see below ver. 15 foll. ἐὰν γυμνοὶ ὑπάρχωσιν...εἴπῃ δέ τις...μὴ δῶτε δέ. We must suppose that in each case the man is unknown, and that each has his place assigned to him only on the ground of his appearance.

3. **ἐπιβλέψητε.**] 'Look with favour,' as in Luke i. 48, ix. 38, 1 Kings vii. 28, Psa. xxiv. 16. This meaning is not found in classical writers.

φοροῦντα.] So Matt. xi. 8 οἱ τὰ μαλακὰ φοροῦντες, and in classical writers.

κάθου ὧδε καλῶς.] The form κάθου for κάθησο occurs in Psa. cx. 1 κάθου ἐκ δεξιῶν μου (five times quoted in N.T.), and in Sir. ix. 9 μετὰ ὑπάνδρου γυναικὸς μὴ κάθου. It is attributed by the grammarians to Aristophanes and Menander, but it is not found in their extant remains. The corresponding indicative σὺ κάθῃ is found Acts xxiii. 3, see Winer p. 98. For καλῶς = *laute, pulchre*, i.e. 'in a good seat,' Field compares Alciph. *Ep.* iii. 20 ἄγει μέ τις λαβὼν εἰς τὸ θέατρον καθίσας ἐν καλῷ, Aelian *V.H.* ii. 13 ἐν καλῷ τοῦ θέατρου καθῆσθαι, see too Arist. *Eq.* 785 καθίζου μαλακῶς, Epict. *Diss.* i. 25, 27 πῶς οὖν θεωρήσω καλῶς ἐν τῷ ἀμφιθεάτρῳ; Theile quotes 'Ptolemy καλῶς ἐκάθισε a bust of Homer,' for which he gives the erroneous reference Socr. xiii, 22. On the distinctions in the synagogue see *D. of B.* s.v. and Matt. xxiii. 6; and, as to the duties of the deacons in finding seats for strangers in the congregation, Apost. Const. ii. 58 (where there may perhaps be an allusion to this passage in the words εἰ δὲ πτωχὸς ἢ ἀγενὴς ἢ ξένος ἐπέλθοι . . . καὶ τόπος οὐχ ὑπάρχει, καὶ τούτοις τόπον ποιήσει ἐξ ὅλης τῆς καρδίας ὁ διάκονος ἵνα μὴ πρὸς ἄνθρωπον γένηται ἡ προσωπόληψις, ἀλλὰ πρὸς Θεὸν ἡ διακονία εὐάρεστος κ.τ.λ.), Plut. *Mor.* 58 C.

καὶ τῷ πτωχῷ εἴπητε.] We should rather have expected δέ instead of καί to point the contrast to the case of the rich man; but the writer regards each action by itself, irrespective of the contrast, as constituting an instance of προσωποληψία.

ὑπὸ τὸ ὑποπόδιον.] i.e. 'on the floor close to my footstool,' cf. Exod. xix. 17 παρέστησαν ὑπὸ τὸ ὄρος, and such phrases as ὑπὸ τεῖχος, and see Luke x. 39 παρακαθίσασα παρὰ τοὺς πόδας τοῦ Κυρίου, *ib.* viii. 35 and Acts xxii. 3. The addition of τῶν ποδῶν in A and other MSS. is borrowed from Ps. cx. 1, which is quoted repeatedly in the N.T.

4. **οὐ διεκρίθητε ἐν ἑαυτοῖς.**]. 'Are you not divided in yourselves,' i.e. guilty of διψυχία, as in i. 8? You have not a single eye, but you are influenced by worldly considerations: you look to the world and not to Christ only. For διεκ. see on i. 6, and ἀδιάκριτος, iii. 17. For ἐν ἑαυτοῖς instead of ἐν ὑμῖν αὐτοῖς see i. 22 n. and cf. Mark xi. 23 διακριθῇ ἐν τῇ καρδίᾳ αὐτοῦ. For construction ἐὰν εἴπητε...οὐ διεκρίθητε, aor. instead of future or present, cf. 1 Cor. vii. 28 ἐὰν γαμήσῃς οὐχ ἥμαρτες, John xv. 6 ἐὰν μή τις μένῃ ἐν ἐμοὶ ἐβλήθη ἔξω καὶ ἐξηράνθη, Dem. *F.L.* p. 411 κἂν ἀναγκασθῇ που συντυχεῖν ἀπεπήδησεν εὐθέως. I think the aorist in such passages commonly expresses the immediateness of the consequence 'if

ye speak thus, ye are thereby shown to be,' cf. n. on i. 24 on a similar use of the perfect. In 1 Cor. vii. 28 it seems to show a wish on the part of the apostle to repudiate at once any idea of blaming a man for marrying; 'if you should marry, I don't mean to say it was wrong in you to get married,' see Winer p. 366 and Devarius ii. 451, there referred to; Goodwin § 155. Others take it as the gnomic aorist expressing a general fact, on which see i. 11, 24.

κριταὶ διαλογισμῶν πονηρῶν.] 'Wrong-considering judges,' gen. of quality like *ἀκροατὴς ἐπιλησμονῆς* above i. 25, *ὁ κόσμος τῆς ἀδικίας* below iii. 6, *κρίσιν βλασφημίας* Jude 9. Peile compares Soph. *Aj.* 888 *μακρᾶν ἀλατᾶν πόνων.* Any one who speaks against his neighbour becomes a *κριτής*, as we read below iv. 11. The reference here is to the worldly considerations of expediency which made them pay court to the rich and slight the poor. The phrase occurs also in Matt. xv. 19 *ἐκ τῆς καρδίας ἔρχονται διαλογισμοὶ πονηροί*, an example of such *διαλογισμοί* is given Luke v. 21, 22, Rom. i. 21, see Hatch p. 8.

5. **ἀκούσατε.**] One of the rousing words employed by St. James, like *μὴ πλανᾶσθε* i. 16, *ἄγε νῦν* iv. 13. It is not used in the other epistles. In the Gospels and Apocalypse we find the still more urgent *ὁ ἔχων οὖς ἀκουσάτω.* The simple *ἀδελφοί* of verse i. is here repeated in a more affectionate form, as i. 16, 19 repeat i. 2.

ἐξελέξατο.] Used (in middle voice only) of the choosing of Israel Deut. xiv. 1, 2, and of the 'elect' Eph. i. 4; St. Paul speaks in much the same way 1 Cor. i. 27 *τὰ μωρὰ τοῦ κόσμου ἐξελέξατο ὁ Θεός κ.τ.λ.*, and our Lord, Luke xviii. 25, Matt. xi. 5, 25.

τοὺς πτωχοὺς τῷ κόσμῳ.] 'Poor to the world' i.e. in the world's judgment, 'outwardly poor,' see below iv. 4 and Luke xii. 21 *ὁ θησαυρίζων ἑαυτῷ καὶ μὴ εἰς Θεὸν πλουτῶν.* For a similar antithesis of the outwardly poor and inwardly rich cf. above i. 9 *ὁ ταπεινὸς ἐν τῷ ὕψει*, 1 Tim. vi. 17, 18 *τοῖς πλουσίοις ἐν τῷ νῦν αἰῶνι*)(*πλουσίοις ἐν ἔργοις καλοῖς.*[1] So of the two kinds of wisdom below iii. 15 and 1 Cor. iii. 19 *ἡ σοφία τοῦ κόσμου μωρία παρὰ τῷ Θεῷ ἐστίν.* For dative cf. Acts vii. 20 *ἀστεῖος τῷ Θεῷ*, 2 Cor. x. 4 *δυνατὰ τῷ Θεῷ*, 1 Cor. ix. 2 *ἄλλοις οὐκ εἰμὶ ἀπόστολος*, Winer, p. 265. On *πτωχός* see Hatch p. 73. It is the regular word for 'poor' in N.T.

πλουσίους ἐν πίστει.] Oblique predicate, after *ἐξελέξατο.* This verb is sometimes used absolutely, as in Mark xiii. 20, 1 Cor. i. 27; sometimes with infinitive as in Acts i. 25 *ἀνάδειξον ὃν ἐξελέξω...λαβεῖν τὸν τόπον τῆς διακονίας ταύτης*, Eph. i. 4 *ἐξελέξατο ἡμᾶς ἐν αὐτῷ...εἶναι ἡμᾶς ἁγίους*, where *εἶναι ἡμᾶς* might be omitted, giving rise to the construction in the text, cf. Rom. viii. 29 *οὓς προέγνω καὶ προώρισεν συμμόρφους τῆς εἰκόνος*, Phil. iii. 21 *ὃς μετασχηματίσει τὸ σῶμα τῆς ταπεινώσεως ἡμῶν σύμμορφον τῷ σώματι τῆς δόξης αὐτοῦ*, 2 Cor. iii. 6 *ἱκάνωσεν ἡμᾶς διακόνους καινῆς διαθήκης*, Acts v. 31 *τοῦτον ὁ Θεὸς σωτῆρα ὕψωσεν*, Rom. iii. 25 *ὃν προέθετο ἱλαστηριον*, 1 John iv. 14 *ἀπέσταλκεν τὸν υἱὸν σωτῆρα τοῦ κόσμου*, also in classical. Greek as Plato *Meno* 94 *τούτους ἱππέας ἐδίδαξεν οὐδενὸς χείρους Ἀθηναίων*, especially with verbs of choosing and with the so-called 'factitive verbs' generally. Some

[1] [Compare Herm. *Sim.* ii.—C. T.]

take ἐν here with an instrumental sense, but this seems unnecessary. We find ἐν, expressing the sphere, used with πλούσιος and the cognate verbs in 1 Cor. i. 5 ἐν παντὶ λόγῳ ἐπλουτίσθητε, 2 Cor. ix. 11, 1 Tim. vi. 18 πλουτεῖν ἐν ἔργοις, so Eph. ii. 4 Θεὸς πλούσιος ὢν ἐν ἐλέει. Wetst. cites the rabbinical phrase 'rich in the law' = learned. The antithesis is not logically exact (cf. above i. 17 πᾶσα, and 25 ποιητὴς ἔργου): either the latter member should have been 'rich towards God,' or the former 'poor in worldly wealth' as opposed to those who are rich in the inner treasure of faith. Cf. Philo M 2. p. 425 οἷς μὲν γὰρ ἀληθινὸς πλοῦτος ἐν οὐρανῷ κατακεῖται διὰ σοφίας καὶ ὁσιότητος ἀσκηθεὶς, τούτοις καὶ ὁ τῶν χρημάτων τῆς γῆς περιουσιάζει, Test. Gad. 7 ὁ γὰρ πένης καὶ ἄφθονος ἐπὶ πᾶσι Κυρίῳ εὐχαριστῶν αὐτὸς παρὰ πᾶσι πλουτεῖ, Plato *Phaedr.* p. 279 πλούσιον νομίζοιμι τὸν σοφόν, Philo M 2. p. 5 ὁ μὴ τυφλὸς ἀλλ' ὀξὺ βλέπων πλοῦτος ἡ τῶν ἀρετῶν ἐστὶ περιουσία.

κληρονόμους τῆς βασιλείας.] Matt. v. 3 μακάριοι οἱ πτωχοὶ τῷ πνεύματι ὅτι αὐτῶν ἐστιν ἡ βασιλεία τῶν οὐρανῶν (τῷ πνεύματι is omitted in Luke xvi. 20), Matt. xxv. 35 δεῦτε οἱ εὐλογημένοι τοῦ πατρός μου κληρονομήσατε τὴν ἡτοιμασμένην ὑμῖν βασιλείαν ἀπὸ καταβολῆς κόσμου, 1 Pet. i. 4 εἰς κληρονομίαν ἄφθαρτον καὶ ἀμίαντον, Justin. M. *Diogn.* 10 οἷς τὴν ἐν οὐρανῷ βασιλείαν ἐπηγγείλατο καὶ δώσει τοῖς ἀγαπήσασιν αὐτόν, borrowed, as the final words show, from this passage. See Westcott's excellent note on Heb. vi. 12, pp. 167ff., where after tracing the use of the word κληρόνομος in the O.T. he says that in 'the N.T. the word is commonly used in connexion with the blessing (1 Pet. iii. 9) which belongs to divine sonship, the spiritual correlative to the promise to Abraham (Rom. iv. 13f.; viii. 17; Gal. iii. 18, 29; iv. 1, 7; Heb. vi. 12, 17; xi. 8). The son of God, as son, enjoys that which answers to his new birth (cf. Matt. v. 5; Eph. i. 14, 18; Col. iii. 24). This is described as "eternal life" (Matt. xix. 29; Tit. iii. 17; comp. Mark x. 17; Luke x. 25, xviii. 18), or "the kingdom of God" (1 Cor. vi. 9f.; xv. 50; Gal. v. 21; comp. Matt. xxv. 34; Eph. v. 5), or "salvation" (Heb. i. 14), an "inheritance incorruptible," "the eternal inheritance" (Heb. ix. 15).' Also p. 483, 'the heirship of man to the Divine blessing answering to his nature is founded on God's purpose in creation, on the gift of His image with the power of attaining to His likeness.'

ἧς ἐπηγγείλατο τοῖς ἀγαπῶσιν αὐτόν.] See above i. 12, where the same words are used of the crown. For attraction cf. 1 John iii. 24 ἐκ τοῦ πνεύματος οὗ ἔδωκεν, Winer p. 203. In the Psalms 'the poor' is almost equivalent to 'the godly'; with the same feeling the Jewish Christians took the name 'Ebionites.'

In this and the following verses their προσωποληψία is condemned (1) as impiety, contravening the purpose of God, who has selected the poor as special objects of His love; (2) as injustice and want of common sense, since it was the rich who oppressed them.

6. **ἠτιμάσατε.**] In the case supposed you slighted him by putting him into an inferior position, cf. Prov. xiv. 21 ὁ ἀτιμάζων πένητας ἁμαρτάνει, ἐλεῶν δὲ πτωχοὺς μακαριστός, *ib.* xxii. 22, Sir. x. 22 οὐ δίκαιον ἀτιμάσαι πτωχὸν συνετὸν καὶ οὐ καθήκει δοξάσαι ἄνδρα ἁμαρτωλόν, the word is also used Luke xx. 11, Acts v. 41. For a similar instance of unfair dis-

tinctions among Christians see 1 Cor. xi. 22. St. Peter in his 1st epistle ii. 17 lays down the rule πάντας τιμήσατε.

οἱ πλούσιοι καταδυναστεύουσιν ὑμῶν.] In the supposed case the sole ground of preference between the two strangers was that the one seemed rich, the other poor; but you have certainly no reason for favouring the rich as a class. The verb only occurs elsewhere in Acts x, 38 καταδυναστευομένους ὑπὸ τοῦ διαβόλου, in N.T. but we find the similar forms κατακυριεύειν and κατεξουσιάζειν Matt. xx. 25. It is not uncommon in LXX. with acc., cf. Micah ii. 2 οἴκους κατεδυνάστευον, Amos viii. 4, Wisd. ii. 10 καταδυναστεύσωμεν πένητα δίκαιον κ.τ.λ., *ib.* xv. 14. It is used with a gen. in Diod. 13. 73, and in Aristeas (cited by Spitta) xl. 4 μηδὲ τῇ περὶ ἑαυτοὺς ἰσχύι πεποιθότας ἑτέρων καταδυναστεύειν, also in Herm. *Mand.* xii. 5 καταδ. τῶν δούλων τ. Θεοῦ. For warnings against wealth cf. below v. 1 foll., 1 Tim. vi. 9, 10, Matt. xiii. 22, xix. 23 foll., Sir. xiii. 3, 18.

αὐτοὶ ἕλκουσιν ὑμᾶς εἰς κριτήρια;] 'With their own hands drag you to the tribunals.' The pronoun αὐτὸς is used in the nominative, not only with the meaning 'self' when attached to a subject, as in classical Greek, but also when itself standing for the subject, with a less amount of emphasis, which we might render 'he for his part' or 'it was he who,' as in the next clause; it is disputed whether it does not in some cases lose its emphatic force altogether, as in Luke xix. 2 καὶ ἰδοὺ ἀνὴρ ὀνόματι καλούμενος Ζακχαῖος, καὶ αὐτὸς ἦν ἀρχιτελώνης καὶ αὐτὸς πλούσιος, where it seems pleonastic, so xxiv. 31 αὐτῶν δὲ διηνοίχθησαν οἱ ὀφθαλμοὶ καὶ ἐπέγνωσαν αὐτόν· καὶ αὐτὸς ἄφαντος ἐγένετο ἀπ' αὐτῶν, see Winer, p. 186 foll.; A. Buttmann, p. 93 foll. I have not noticed the fem. and neut. used in this laxer signification. St. Paul condemns Christians for going to law with one another (1 Cor. vi. where see Wetst.): here St. James is speaking of the persecution of Christians by Jews, especially by the rich Sadducees, cf. Acts iv. 1, xiii. 50. Paul and Silas were dragged before the judgment-seat (called κριτήριον 1 Cor. vi. 2, 4, Exod. xxi. 6, Dan. vii. 9, Polyb. ix. 33; the classical word is δικαστήριον) at Philippi, ἐπιλαβόμενοι εἵλκυσαν εἰς τὴν ἀγορὰν ἐπὶ τοὺς ἄρχοντας (Acts xvi. 19); and of Saul before his conversion we read σύρων ἄνδρας καὶ γυναῖκας παρεδίδου εἰς φυλακήν. Our Lord foretold that his disciples would be cited before the law courts both of Jews and Gentiles (Matt. x. 7, 18), be expelled from the synagogues and put to death (John xvi. 2).

7. **οὐκ αὐτοὶ βλασφημοῦσιν τὸ καλὸν ὄνομα.**] 'Is it not they who blaspheme the noble name?' Βλάσφημος and its cognates are used generally of slander and evil-speaking, as in 2 Pet. ii. 11, Tit. iii. 2, Col. iii. 8: in the N.T. they have also the special meaning of impiety towards God and Christ (= λέγει ἀνάθεμα Ἰησοῦν): so St. Paul (Acts xxvi. 11) κατὰ πάσας τὰς συναγωγὰς πολλάκις τιμωρῶν αὐτοὺς ἠνάγκαζον βλασφημεῖν, and 1 Tim. i. 13 τὸ πρότερον ὄντα με βλάσφημον καὶ διώκτην καὶ ὑβριστήν. Cf. Justin. M. *Trypho* § 117 (Χριστοῦ) ὄνομα βεβηλωθῆναι κατὰ πᾶσαν τὴν γῆν καὶ βλασφημεῖσθαι οἱ ἀρχιερεῖς τοῦ λαοῦ ὑμῶν καὶ διδάσκαλοι εἰργάσαντο, *ib.* § 16 with Otto's note. We first read of the sin of blasphemy and its punishment in Lev. xxiv. 10–16.

If this is understood of wealthy members of the Church, we

must explain it, either by supposing that the rich were more readily induced to apostatize and blaspheme Christ (cf. Acts xxvi. 11, Plin. *Ep.* x. 97. 5, Polyc. *Mart.* 9) than the poor, which may be illustrated from Herm. *Sim.* viii. 6. 4 οὗτοί εἰσιν οἱ ἀποστάται καὶ προδόται τῆς ἐκκλησίας καὶ βλασφημήσαντες ἐν ταῖς ἁμαρτίαις αὐτῶν τὸν Κύριον (called βλάσφημοι εἰς τὸν Κύριον *ib.* ix. 19. 1) ἔτι δὲ καὶ ἐπαισχυνθέντες τὸ ὄνομα Κυρίου τὸ ἐπικληθὲν ἐπ' αὐτούς, where see Harnack's note; or, in accordance with Rom. ii. 24 τὸ ὄνομα τοῦ Θεοῦ δι' ὑμᾶς βλασφημεῖται ἐν τοῖς ἔθνεσιν (a quotation from Isa. lii. 5), 2 Pet. ii. 2 δι' οὓς ἡ ὁδὸς τῆς ἀληθείας βλασφημηθήσεται, 1 Tim. vi. 1 ἵνα μὴ τὸ ὄνομα τοῦ Θεοῦ βλασφημῆται, Tit. ii. 5, we may understand it of those who profess to know God but by their works deny him, Tit. i. 16, cf. Clem. Rom. ii. 13. The use of the active voice seems less suited to this interpretation, though Theile cites from Euseb. *H.E.* v. 1 διὰ τῆς ἀναστροφῆς αὐτῶν βλασφημοῦντες τὴν ὁδόν. On the whole I think the general sense of the passage suits better with the idea that the blasphemers are unbelieving Jews, as in Acts xiii. 45 ἀντέλεγον βλασφημοῦντες, and this is suggested, as Dr. Plummer remarks, by the following ἐφ' ὑμᾶς, not ἐπ' αὐτούς.

τὸ καλὸν ὄνομα.] Cf. below v. 14, Acts v. 41 ὑπὲρ τοῦ ὀνόματος ἀτιμασθῆναι, Phil. ii. 9, 10 τὸ ὄνομα τὸ ὑπὲρ πᾶν ὄνομα, Acts iv. 12 οὔτε ὄνομά ἐστιν ἕτερον ὑπὸ τὸν οὐρανὸν τὸ δεδομένον ἐν ἀνθρώποις ἐν ᾧ δεῖ σωθῆναι ἡμᾶς. Matt. i. 21, Deut. xxviii. 58 τὸ ὄνομα τὸ ἔντιμον τὸ θαυμαστὸν τοῦτο, Κύριον τὸν Θεόν σου, 2 Macc. viii. 15 ἕνεκεν τῆς ἐπ' αὐτοὺς ἐπικλήσεως τοῦ σεμνοῦ καὶ μεγαλοπρεποῦς ὀνόματος αὐτοῦ, Hermas *Vis.* iii. 3 τοῦ παντοκράτορος καὶ ἐνδόξου ὀνόματος, *ib.* iv. 1 τὸ ὄνομα αὐτοῦ (τοῦ Κυρίου) τὸ μέγα καὶ ἔνδοξον, *Sim.* ix. 18. 5, Taylor's *Jewish Fathers*, p. 80 foll. So Clem. Rom. i. 1 ὥστε τὸ σεμνὸν ὄνομα βλασφημηθῆναι, *ib.* 58.

τὸ ἐπικληθὲν ἐφ' ὑμᾶς.] This Hebraism comes from the LXX. (Amos ix. 12) πάντα τὰ ἔθνη ἐφ' οὓς ἐπικέκληται τὸ ὄνομά μου ἐπ' αὐτούς, also quoted by the writer of this epistle in his address to the Council at Jerusalem (Acts xv. 17). The phrase is common in the O.T., see Deut. xxviii. 10 ὄψονται πάντα τὰ ἔθνη ὅτι τὸ ὄνομα Κυρίου ἐπικέκληταί σοι, Numb. vi. 27, 2 Chron. vii. 14, Isa. lxii. 2, lxiii. 19, Jer. xxv. 29, 2 Macc. viii. 15. It is used not only of Israel, as the people of Jehovah, but also of the wife taking the husband's name (Isa. iv. 1), of children named after their father (Gen. xlviii. 16). It is questioned whether the reference here is to the name Χριστιανός, which came into use at Antioch apparently before St. Paul's first missionary journey (Acts xi. 26), and which is found Acts xxvi. 28, 1 Pet. iv. 16 (see Lightfoot's *Ignatius* vol. i. pp. 400–404); or to baptism, cf. Acts ii. 38 βαπτισθήτω ἕκαστος ὑμῶν ἐν τῷ ὀνόματι Ἰησοῦ Χριστοῦ, *ib.* viii. 16, x. 48, Hermas *Sim.* 9. 16 πρὶν φορέσαι τὸν ἄνθρωπον τὸ ὄνομα τοῦ Υἱοῦ τοῦ Θεοῦ νεκρός ἐστιν· ὅταν δὲ λάβῃ τὴν σφραγῖδα (baptism) ἀποτίθεται τὴν νέκρωσιν καὶ ἀναλαμβάνει τὴν ζωήν, Justin. M. *Apol.* i. p. 94 (in baptism) ἐπονομάζεται τῷ ἑλομένῳ ἀναγεννηθῆναι...τὸ τοῦ Πατρὸς τῶν ὅλων ὄνομα. The latter explanation seems the better, both as more suited to the phrase, which seems to imply an actual invocation of the name of Christ over each individual believer; and also because Christians were known to each other by such names as ἀδελφοί and πιστοί, while Χριστιανοί, like Ναζωραῖοι and Γαλιλαῖοι, was at first used by outsiders as a name of reproach.

8. This respect for the rich may *however* (μέντοι in its ordinary sense) proceed from a good motive; it may be you are filled with the spirit of love, ready to forgive injury and to do to others as you would have them do to you. If so, well and good. But if your conduct is really determined by worldly motives, if you treat the rich well simply because he is rich and you wish to gain favour with him, and treat the poor harshly because he cannot advance your interests, then you break the law which forbids respect of persons and enjoins special consideration for the poor. It will not do for you to plead that you are scrupulous in other duties. The law is a whole; it is the revelation of God's will: disregard to a single point is disregard to the Lawgiver; it is disobedience to God, and the spirit of disobedience breaks the law as a whole. Do not entertain any idea of keeping this or that particular precept and obtaining credit by that means. Such views belong to the slavish conception of law as a collection of unconnected rules bearing on outward conduct alone. The Christian law is a law of liberty; it is the free manifestation in outward act of the loving spirit within. We shall be judged not by the observance or neglect of this or that external rule, but by the degree in which our heart and life have been penetrated by the spirit of love. If we show kindness, consideration, compassion in our behaviour to other men, we shall meet the same in God's judgment of us.

νόμον τελεῖτε βασιλικόν.] Middleton (p. 423) thinks the absence of the article forbids the translation 'the royal law.' I do not understand what he means by the words, 'βασιλικός I interpret *excellent*, in which case the article is unnecessary.' We have no right to tone down the remarkable word βασιλικός, and even if we were at liberty to do so it makes very poor sense to say 'ye fulfil an excellent law.' Hofmann and Schegg however agree with M.: the latter says 'νόμον ohne Artikel, weil Jakobus nicht das Gesetz der Nächstenliebe meint, sondern ein spezielles Gebot das aus dem Nächstenliebe hervorgeht (viz. "Seeleneifer," the Jewish love of proselytizing, as he explains above) und so erhaben ist dass es ein königliches genannt zu werden verdient.' Such an interpretation needs no refutation, but it is strange that neither Winer nor Buttmann has referred to this passage in discussing the use of the article in the N.T. There is no difficulty in the anarthrous νόμος being used (as below iv. 11) for the law of Christ or of Moses on the same principle that βασιλεύς could be used for the king of Persia, but the addition of an anarthrous epithet should not have been passed over without comment, as it has been by the editors generally. The only other instances named by Winer are 1 Thess. i. 9 δουλεύειν Θεῷ ζῶντι καὶ ἀληθινῷ (which might there be indefinite, 'to serve a living and true God,' in contrast with the preceding ἐπεστρέψατε ἀπὸ τῶν εἰδώλων: see however Westcott on Heb. iii. 12 ἀποστῆναι ἀπὸ Θεοῦ ζῶντος 'the anarthrous title, which is far more common than ὁ Θ. ὁ ζῶν, always fixes attention upon the *character* as distinguished from the

"Person" of God. In every case it suggests a ground for corresponding thought or action'), and the constantly recurring Πνεῦμα ἅγιον, which is used not only after a preposition, as in Matt. i. 18 εὑρέθη ἐν γαστρὶ ἔχουσα ἐκ Πνεύματος ἁγίου, but also without a preposition and even in the nominative, e.g. Luke i. 15 Πνεύματος ἁγίου πλησθήσεται, 35 Πνεῦμα ἅγιον ἐπελεύσεται ἐπὶ σέ, *ib.* ii. 25 Πνεῦμα ἦν ἅγιον ἐπ' αὐτόν. It is noticeable that, when there is no article, the words are always in this order, but, with the article, τὸ ἅγιον Πν. is not much less common than τὸ Πν. τὸ ἅγ.[1] We may compare also Luke i. 72 μνησθῆναι διαθήκης ἁγίας αὐτοῦ and other exx. given in the Essay on Grammar. The phrase νόμον τελεῖτε is only found here and in Rom. ii. 27. The commandment of love on which all others hang (Rom. xiii. 8, Gal. v. 14) is rightly called 'supreme' βασιλικός: so Philo M. ii. 459 οἱ σοφοὶ βασιλικώτερον οὐδὲν ἀρετῆς νομίζοντες, *ib.* p. 364 βασιλικὴν εἴωθεν ὀνομάζειν Μωϋσῆς ὁδὸν τὴν μέσην ὑπερβολῆς καὶ ἐλλείψεως οὖσαν μεθόριον, *ib.* M. i. 526 astronomy is βασιλὶς τῶν ἐπιστημῶν, Justin. *Apol.* i. 12 ὁ λόγος οὗ βασιλικώτατον (superl. for comp.) ἄρχοντα οὐδένα οἴδαμεν. Spitta cites 4 Macc. xiv. 2 ὦ βασιλέων λογισμοὶ βασιλικώτεροι: Zahn (*Gesch. Neut. Kan.* i. 323) compares Clem. Al. *Strom.* vi. p. 164, the Scripture says 'if your righteousness do not exceed that of the scribes and Pharisees' (whose righteousness consisted only in abstaining from evil σὺν τῷ μετὰ τῆς ἐν τούτοις τελειώσεως) καὶ τῷ τὸν πλησίον ἀγαπᾶν καὶ εὐεργετεῖν δύνασθαι, οὐκ ἔσεσθε βασιλικοί, *ib.* vii. 73 ὅταν μὴ κατ' ἀνάγκην ἢ φόβον ἢ ἐλπίδα δίκαιός τις ᾖ ἀλλ' ἐκ προαιρέσεως, αὕτη ἡ ὁδὸς λέγεται βασιλικὴ ἣν τὸ βασιλικὸν ὁδεύει γένος. Clement's use reminds one of βασίλειον ἱεράτευμα (Ex. xix. 6. 1 Pet. ii. 9). And this would make excellent sense: Christ's law is not addressed to slaves, who must obey whether they will or not, but to kings who voluntarily embrace the law as their guide: cf. the Stoic paradox in Hor. *Ep.* i. 1. 106. A curiously close verbal resemblance is found in pseudo-Plato *Minos* 317 C τὸ μὲν ὀρθὸν νόμος ἐστὶ βασιλικός, τὸ δὲ μὴ ὀρθὸν οὔ, where βασιλικός apparently means 'worthy of a statesman,' it having been stated just before that laws are the compositions of those who know how to rule states, viz. οἱ πολιτικοί τε καὶ οἱ βασιλικοί: cf. id. *Ep.* 8, p. 354 C.

κατὰ τὴν γραφήν.] Of course the O.T. viz. Lev. xix. 18, of which the text is an exact quotation, cf. 1 Cor. xv. 3 κατὰ τὰς γραφάς.

ἀγαπήσεις τὸν πλησίον σου ὡς σεαυτόν.] In Hellenistic Greek, as in Hebrew, the fut. is often used for imperat. e.g. Matt. v. 48 ἔσεσθε ὑμεῖς τέλειοι, *ib.* vi. 5 οὐκ ἔσεσθε ὡς οἱ ὑποκριταί, Rom. vii. 7 οὐκ ἐπιθυμήσεις: this is very rarely the case in classical Greek, see Winer, p. 396. The law, which is limited in Leviticus by the context οὐ μηνιεῖς τοῖς υἱοῖς τοῦ λαοῦ σου, receives the widest significance as re-uttered by Christ Luke x. 27 foll., John xv. 2. Hillel is said to have told a proselyte that the essence of the law was contained in the saying 'what is hateful to thyself, do not to thy fellow,' and that the rest was only commentary.[2] The phrase ὁ πλησίον is classical (as also ὁ πέλας). We

[1] Bruder has 10 examples of the former and 26 of the latter.
[2] Taylor's *Jewish Fathers,* p. 37 n.

find it without a following gen. in Rom. xiii. 10, xv. 2; τὸν ἕτερον is used as its equivalent in Rom. xiii. 8, see Vorst, pp. 67, 562.

καλῶς ποιεῖτε.] Used ironically below ver. 19, but here simply as in 2 Pet. i. 19 (τὸν λόγον) ᾧ καλῶς ποιεῖτε προσέχοντες, Acts x. 33, 1 Cor. vii. 37, Phil. iv. 14. There is a similar phrase in the circular letter written from the Council of Jerusalem, probably by St. James, in Acts xv. 29 ἐξ ὧν διατηροῦντες ἑαυτοὺς εὖ πράξετε.

9. **προσωπολημπτεῖτε.**] ἅπ. λεγ. see above ver. 1 on προσωπολημψία.

ἁμαρτίαν ἐργάζεσθε.] See on i. 3 and 20, Matt. vii. 23 ἐργαζόμενοι ἀνομίαν.

ἐλεγχόμενοι ὑπὸ τοῦ νόμου.] 'Being convicted by the law,' personified as witness, so 4 Macc. 5. 33 ὦ παιδευτὰ νόμε, cf. Rom. vii. 7, Gal. iii. 24. So we have ὑπὸ τῆς συνειδήσεως ἐλεγχόμενοι in the disputed passage John viii. 9. The reference is to the law contained in Lev. xix. 15 μὴ θαυμάσῃς πρόσωπον δυναστοῦ, which immediately precedes the 'royal law' just cited.

ὡς παραβάται.] Similarly Homer uses ὑπερβαίνω and ὑπερβασίη *Il.* i. 497. Παραβαίνω with an object, such as νόμους, and even θεούς (see Herod. vi. 12), or absolutely (Aesch. *Ag.* 59), is quite classical; but the only certain example of this use of παραβάτης in a classical author is from the treatise περὶ τῶν ἐν Σικελίᾳ θαυμαζομένων ποταμῶν of Polemo (*fl.* about 180 B.C.) παραβάτης γενόμενος τῶν θεῶν *ap.* Macrob. *Sat.* v. 19; Epictetus (*Diss.* ii. 20. 14) uses τοὺς παραβατικῶς αὐτῆς ἔχοντας in the same sense. In Euseb. *H. E.* v. 18 ὢν ἤδη παραβάτης, it is equivalent to ἀποστάτης, and so in later writers. The metaphor is adapted to the idea of righteousness as the way in which a man should walk. It occurs absolutely Gal. ii. 18, with νόμου below ver. 11 and in Rom. ii. 25, 27 [1]; παράβασις is used by St. Paul and in Heb. ii. 2, ix. 15, and παραβαίνω in this sense Matt. xv. 2, 3.

10. **ὅστις ὅλον τὸν νόμον τηρήσῃ.**] 'Whoever keeps the law as a whole,' cf. Gal. v. 3. When ὅστις takes the subj. it is usually joined with ἄν, as in Matt. x. 33, xii. 50, Luke x. 35, John ii. 5, xiv. 13, Acts iii. 23, Gal. v. 10; when ἄν is omitted, the constant confusion of -ει and -ῃ in the MSS. makes it difficult to know whether the fut. or aor. subj. is the true reading. Beside this verse WH. give ὅστις ἀρνήσηται Matt. x. 33. In classical Greek ἄν is occasionally omitted, both in poetry, as Eur. *Ion.* 856 ὅστις ἐσθλὸς ᾖ, *Medea* 516, and in prose, as Thuc. iv. 18. 4 οἵτινες νομίσωσι, *ib.* 17. 2 οὗ ἀρκῶσι, see Kühner on Xen. *Mem.* i. 6. 13 ὅστις ποιῆται, Winer, p. 386, A. Buttmann, 197. We find ἕως λάβῃ without ἄν below v. 7, where see n. On the Hellenistic use of τηρεῖν with such words as νόμον see Vorst, p. 191 foll.

πταίσῃ δὲ ἐν ἑνί.] For πτ. see below iii. 2, Rom. xi. 11, Deut. vii. 25. It is a question whether ἑνί and the following πάντων should be regarded as masculine (agreeing with νόμῳ, νόμων) or neuter. It does not seem

[1] Dr. Plummer (p. 56) thinks the phrase may have been borrowed from the 'unwritten word' contained in the remarkable addition to St. Luke vi. 4, which we find in Cod. D, τῇ αὐτῇ ἡμέρᾳ θεασάμενός τινα ἐργαζόμενον τῷ σαββάτῳ εἶπεν αὐτῷ, Ἄνθρωπε εἰ μὲν οἶδας τί ποιεῖς μακάριος εἶ, εἰ δὲ μὴ οἶδας ἐπικατάρατος καὶ παραβάτης εἶ τοῦ νόμου.

that νόμος is ever used in the Bible of a particular precept = ἐντολή. The ten commandments are never called οἱ δέκα νόμοι. But might not St. James unconsciously pass from the collective sense of νόμος to the particular precepts of which it consisted, without reflecting that, strictly speaking, such a use of the term was illegitimate? The other explanation is not without difficulty. We have plenty of examples of the substantival use of the neuter ἕν in the nominative and accusative, but not often in the other cases. See however i. 4 ἐν μηδενὶ λειπόμενοι.

γέγονεν πάντων ἔνοχος.] For perfect following aorist see above i. 24. Ἔνοχος (lit. 'in the power of') is used with a genitive of the offence ('guilty of theft'), of the punishment (ἐν. θανάτου Matt. xxvi. 66), of the law sinned against, as here. It takes a dative of the tribunal. Πάντων is equivalent to ὅλου τοῦ νόμου.

The first reference here seems to be to those who fail in the one point of προσωπολημψία, though they may claim to keep the rest of the law; but there is a more general reference to the man who, thinking himself to be religious (i. 26), assumes that all is right with him, like the Pharisee in the parable (Luke xviii. 11). Some of the Rabbis actually laid it down that obedience to certain laws, e.g. the law about fringes and phylacteries, was as good as obedience to the whole.[1] Cf. Midrash Mishle on Prov. i. 10 *qui unum praeceptum servat est ac si totam legem servasset.* On the other hand, the principle here affirmed by St. James is also to be found in the sayings of the Rabbis: thus Schegg gives a story from a Midrash on Numbers:[2] 'R. Hunna having taught his disciples that he who committed adultery broke all the commandments, was asked by them to explain how this could be true of the fourth commandment'; and Wetstein to the same effect quotes two sayings of R. Jochanan from Sabb. f. 70. 2 *si faciat omnia, unum vero omittat, omnium et singulorum reus est;* and Pesikta f. 50. 1 *omnis qui dicit, totam legem ego in me recipio praeter verbum unum, hic sermonem Domini sprevit et praecepta ejus irrita fecit,* Horaioth 8 b: (Levit. v. 6) *R. Jose Galilaeus dixit: 'qui reus est unius, reus est omnium,'* cf. 4 Macc. 5. 18 μὴ μικρὰν εἶναι νομίσῃς ταύτην, εἰ μιαροφαγήσαιμεν, ἁμαρτίαν· τὸ γὰρ ἐπὶ μικροῖς καὶ μεγάλοις παρανομεῖν ἰσοδύναμόν ἐστιν, δι' ἑκατέρου γὰρ ὁμοίως ὑπερηφανεῖται, and Test. xii. Patr. 689 ἄλλος κλέπτει, ἀδικεῖ, ἁρπάζει, πλεονεκτεῖ, καὶ ἐλεεῖ τοὺς πτωχούς. διπρόσωπον μὲν τοῦτο, τὸ δὲ ὅλον πονηρόν ἐστιν. Cellerier cites Basil. *Bapt.* ii. 9 παράνομός ἐστιν ὁ μίαν ἐντολὴν παραβάς.

This passage of St. James is discussed at length by Augustine in a letter to Jerome (*Ep.* 167). He compares the teaching of St. James with the Stoic doctrine on the 'solidarity' of the virtues and vices, as to which see Stob. *Ecl.* ii. p. 112 τὸν μίαν ἔχοντα ἀρετὴν πάσας ἔχειν, καὶ τὸν κατὰ μίαν πράττοντα κατὰ πάσας πράττειν, *ib.* 116 φασὶ δὲ καὶ πάντα ποιεῖν τὸν σοφὸν κατὰ πάσας τὰς ἀρετάς· πᾶσαν γὰρ πρᾶξιν τελείαν αὐτοῦ

[1] [See Shemoth Rabb. xxv. end: 'the Sabbath weighs against all the precepts'; if they kept it, they were to be reckoned as having done all: if they profaned it, as having broken all. Rashi on Numbers xv. 38–40 says the same of the law of Fringes, but an integral part of this is to remember all the commandments.—C. T.]

[2] [Bemidkar Rabb. ix. on Numb. v. 14.—C. T.]

εἶναι, διὸ καὶ μηδεμίας ἀπολελεῖφθαι ἀρετῆς, *ib.* 120 κατὰ τὸ ἀνάλογον δὲ καὶ τὸν φαῦλον πάντα ὅσα ποιεῖ κακῶς ποιεῖν καὶ κατὰ πάσας τὰς κακίας, both doctrines flowing from their conception of virtue as the art of life. In the same way the Stoics asserted the equality of all virtues, Diog. L. vii. 101. We may compare St. Paul (Rom. xiv. 23) πᾶν ὃ οὐκ ἐκ πίστεως ἁμαρτία ἐστίν, and 1 Cor. x. 31 εἴτε οὖν ἐσθίετε εἴτε πίνετε εἴτε τι ποιεῖτε πάντα εἰς δόξαν Θεοῦ ποιεῖτε.[1]

11. **ὁ γὰρ εἰπών.**] The unity of the law flows from the unity of the law-giver (below iv. 12); it is the expression of one will. The essence of sin lies in disobedience to that Will however shown. It was by an appeal to the same principle that our Lord answered the question of the lawyer ποία ἐστὶ πρώτη πασῶν ἐντολή; 'The first of all the commandments is, Hear, O Israel; the Lord our God is one Lord; and thou shalt love the Lord thy God' Mark xii. 29. This spiritual view of the law rendered impossible the comparisons of which the Jews were so fond.

μὴ μοιχεύσῃς.] Here the seventh commandment precedes the sixth, as in Luke xviii. 20, Rom. xiii. 9, and (LXX.) Ex. xx. where the order is οὐ μοιχεύσεις, οὐ κλέψεις, οὐ φονεύσεις: cf. Philo M. 2, p. 189 ἡ δὲ ἑτέρα πεντὰς τὰς πάσας ἀπαγορεύσεις περιέχει μοιχειῶν, φόνου, κλοπῆς, ψευδομαρτυριῶν, ἐπιθυμιῶν, *ib.* p. 201 ἀπὸ μοιχείας ἄρχεται, *ib.* 207, 300 ἐν τῇ δευτέρᾳ δέλτῳ πρῶτον γράμμα τοῦτ' ἐστίν, οὐ μοιχεύσεις, Clem. Al. *Strom.* vi. 816. We have the usual order in Deut. v. 17, Matt. v. 21, 27, xix. 18; the order in Mark x. 19 varies in different MSS. The future οὐ μοιχεύσεις is used by St. Matthew, as in the LXX.; μή with the subjunctive by the other Evangelists, as here.

εἰ δὲ, οὐ μοιχεύεις, φονεύεις δέ.] For οὐ after εἰ see i. 23 οὐ ποιητής n. Here the more exact way of expression would be μοιχεύεις μὲν οὐ, φονεύεις δέ, the single word μοιχεύεις being negatived, 'if you commit *not* adultery, but murder.' For the omission of μέν in such antitheses see above v. 2 εἰσέλθῃ δέ and i. 13 πειράζει δέ, also 1 Pet. i. 8 ἄρτι μὴ ὁρῶντες πιστεύοντες δέ, v. 12 οὐχ ἑαυτοῖς ἡμῖν δέ.

γέγονας παραβάτης νόμου.] For perf. see i. 24; for παραβάτης above ver. 9. On omission of article see Essay on Grammar.

12. Let your words and acts, e.g. your behaviour to the poor, be regulated by the thought that you will be judged by a law of freedom (see i. 25), that is, by a law of the spirit, not of the letter. It will be a deeper-going judgment than that of man, for it will not stop short at particular precepts or even at the outward act, whatever it may be, but will penetrate to the temper and motive. On the other hand it sweeps away all anxious questioning as to the exact performance of each separate precept. If there has been in you the true spirit of love to God and love to man, that is accepted as the real fulfilment of the law. The same love which actuates the true Christian here actuates the Judge both here and hereafter, or rather He who is already dwelling in our hearts by faith assures us of that forgiveness in our own case which He enables us to show to others.

[1] Gebser cites Clem. Al. 2. 798 (it should be Orig. *Sel. in Psalm.* cxix. 6, Lomm. vol. xiii. p. 70) ὁ πάσας ποιήσας ἐντολάς, πταίσας δὲ ἐν μιᾷ γίνεται πάντων ἔνοχος.

οὕτως λαλεῖτε καὶ οὕτως ποιεῖτε.] The repetition of *οὕτως* is in accordance with the earnest weighty style of the writer: see i. 19 on *βραδύς*, and cf. Buttm. p. 341. It insists on the importance of a right regulation of speech (on which see ch. iii. below), as well as of action (on which see vv. 14—26 of this chapter). The reference in *οὕτως* is to the following *ὡς*, as in 1 Cor. ix. 26 *οὕτω πυκτεύω ὡς οὐκ ἀέρα δέρων*, *ib.* iii. 15 *σωθήσεται οὕτως ὡς διὰ πυρός*.

ὡς διὰ νόμου ἐλευθερίας μέλλοντες κρίνεσθαι.] The absence of the article, which was used in i. 25, serves to give prominence to the qualifying genitive. For other instances in N. T. of the classical use of *ὡς* with part. cf. 1 Cor. iv. 18, 2 Cor. v. 20, Heb. xiii. 17, and Winer p. 770*f.*

13. **ἡ γὰρ κρίσις ἀνέλεος τῷ μὴ ποιήσαντι ἔλεος.**] The reading *ἀνέλεος* is found in all the best MSS. instead of *ἀνίλεως*. Neither form occurs elsewhere, but we find *ἀνελεής* (in scholiasts and Philo M. ii. 53) and the more classical *ἀνηλεής* (Plato and Philo M. ii. 65), *ἀνελεήμων* (Wisd. xii. 5, Rom. i. 31). As to the formation, *ἀνέλεος* is regular from the classical *ὁ ἔλεος* (like *ἄλογος*, *ἄθεος*), but *τὸ ἔλεος* is the form used in N.T.,[1] from which would regularly be formed *ἀνελεής* (like *εὐγενής* from *γένος*) or *ἀνηλεής* (like *ἀνηρεφής* from *ἐρέφω*). We have another reference to *κρίσις* below v. 12. With *ποιεῖν ἔλεος* cf. Josh. ii. 12 *ὀμόσατέ μοι ὅτι ποιῶ ὑμῖν ἔλεος καὶ ποιήσατε καὶ ὑμεῖς ἔλεος*, Matt. vi. 2 *ὅταν ποιῇς ἐλεημοσύνην*, Tobit. xii. 9 *ἐλεημοσύνη ἐκ θανάτου ῥύεται καὶ αὕτη ἀποκαθαριεῖ πᾶσαν ἁμαρτίαν· οἱ ποιοῦντες ἐλεημοσύνας καὶ δικαιοσύνας πλησθήσονται ζωῆς*. For the thought cf. Matt. v. 7, vi. 14, vii. 1, xviii. 28-35 the parable of the debtor, xxv. 41-46 the description of the judgment, Tit. iii. 5, below v. 20, Psa. xviii. 25, 26, Prov. xvii. 5, Sirac. xxviii. 2*ff.* *ἄφες ἀδίκημα τῷ πλησίον σου καὶ τότε δεηθέντος σου αἱ ἁμαρτίαι σου λυθήσονται*, Tobit. iv. 7-12, Test. xii. Patr. p. 641 *ἔχετε εὐσπλαγχνίαν κατὰ παντὸς ἀνθρώπου ἐν ἐλέει ἵνα καὶ ὁ Κύριος εἰς ὑμᾶς σπλαγχνισθεὶς ἐλεήσῃ ὑμᾶς, ὅτι καί γε ἐπ' ἐσχάτων ἡμερῶν ὁ Θεὸς ἀποστέλλει τὸ σπλάγχνον αὐτοῦ ἐπὶ τῆς γῆς καὶ ὅπου εὑρῇ σπλάγχνα ἐλέους, ἐν αὐτῷ κατοικεῖ*, Sibyll. ii. 224 *ῥύεται ἐκ θανάτου ἔλεος, κρίσις ὁππότ' ἂν ἔλθῃ*, Dem. *Mid.* 547 *οὐδείς ἐστι δίκαιος τυγχάνειν ἐλέου τῶν μηδένα ἐλεούντων*. The reference to mercy looks backward to i. 27 and forward to ver. 15 foll.

κατακαυχᾶται ἔλεος κρίσεως.] 'Mercy triumphs over judgment.' The compound verb is found also below iii. 14 and Rom. xi. 18; the simple verb above i. 9. For the thought see Hosea vi. 6 *ἔλεος θέλω ἢ θυσίαν*, quoted in Matt. ix. 13, where the Pharisees complain of Jesus eating with publicans and sinners, and again Matt. xii. 7 when they find fault with the disciples for eating the ears of corn; Luke vii. 47, 1 Pet. iv. 8, Matt. xxiii. 23. The absence of a connecting particle is a feature in the vigorous style of the writer, cf. below v. 6 *κατεδικάσατε, ἐφονεύσατε τὸν δικαιον· οὐκ ἀντιτάσσεται ὑμῖν*, and above i. 19 *ταχὺς εἰς τὸ ἀκοῦσαι, βραδὺς εἰς τὸ λαλῆσαι*. Some MSS. insert *δέ*, as in ver. 15 below,

[1] Similar instances of change in gender in Hellenistic Greek are *τὸ πλοῦτος, τὸ ζῆλος, τὸ σκότος*, on which see Winer p. 76.

which would limit the scope of the words by presenting them as an antithesis to the preceding clause. It is such of course in the first instance: as the failure to show mercy or consideration for others forbids us to expect mercy ourselves, so by the exercise of mercy man gathers to himself 'a good reward against the day of necessity' (Tobit iv. 9), since 'God is not unrighteous to forget the labour that proceedeth of love' (Heb. vi. 10). But the asyndeton allows the words to be taken in their widest generality, as embodying the very essence of the Christian law of liberty, affirming the universal principle of God's judgment, even when it seems to be ἀνέλεος, and supplying the rule for the believer's daily life, cf. Philo M. 1. p. 284 commenting on Ps. 101. 1 'I will sing of mercy and judgment) οὐ μόνον δικάσας ἐλεεῖ ἀλλὰ ἐλεήσας δικάζει· πρεσβύτερος γὰρ δίκης ὁ ἔλεος παρ' αὐτῷ ἐστίν, ἅτε τὸν κολάσεως ἄξιον οὐ μετὰ τὴν δίκην ἀλλὰ πρὸ δίκης εἰδότι.

14—26. In this section St. James proceeds to enlarge on the meaning and nature of that faith in Jesus Christ which was spoken of in ver. 1 as inconsistent with προσωποληψία. He dwells on the contrast, noted in i. 26, between mere outward religion and the consecration of the life to God. If a man πίστιν ἔχει ἐν προσωποληψίαις, is not this the same as having a profession of faith which is not evidenced by deeds? But it is not such faith as this that can ever triumph over judgment. Compare the words of St. John (1 ep. ii. 4) ὁ λέγων ὅτι Ἔγνωκα αὐτὸν, καὶ τὰς ἐντολὰς μὴ τηρῶν, ψεύστης ἐστίν. The apocryphal fourth book of Esdras shows that the question of faith and works was at that time agitated among the Jews, see ix. 7, 8 'whoever shall be able to escape either by his works or by his faith shall see my salvation,' also viii. 33–36, xiii. 23 The following rabbinical quotations are cited from Gfrörer by Bishop Lightfoot *Gal.* p. 154 fol.: (*Mechilta* on Exod. xiv. 31) 'Abraham our father inherited this world and the world to come solely by the merit of the faith whereby he believed in God'; (*Siphre* on Deut. xi. 13) 'The sacred text[1] means to show that practice depends on doctrine and not doctrine on practice: and so we find God punishes more severely for doctrine than for practice, as it is said (Hosea iv. 1) *Hear the word of the Lord, &c.*: [2] 'As soon as a man has mastered the thirteen heads of the faith, firmly believing therein...though he may have sinned in every possible way...still he inherits eternal life.' It is to such views Justin refers (*Tryph.* 370 D) οὐχ ὡς ὑμεῖς ἀπατᾶτε ἑαυτοὺς καὶ ἄλλοι τινές...οἵ λέγουσιν ὅτι κἂν ἁμαρτωλοὶ ὦσι, Θεὸν δὲ γινώσκωσιν, οὐ μὴ λογίσηται αὐτοῖς Κύριος ἁμαρτίαν. For the relation of St. James' view of faith to that of St. Paul and the other apostles see Comment.

14. **τί ὄφελος.**] The omission of the article ('what good is it,' 'what boots it,' instead of 'what is the good'), especially when the verb is understood, is somewhat colloquial and has a sharp abruptness which suits the passage. It is omitted also by Philo M. 1. p. 241 τί γὰρ ὄφελος λέγειν μὲν τὰ βέλτιστα, διανοεῖσθαι δὲ καὶ πράττειν τὰ αἴσχιστα...τί δὲ ὄφελος

[1] The immediate reference is to Deut. v. 1 'and ye shall learn them and observe to do them,' which is cited on Deut. xi. See *Jewish Fathers*, p. 64.

[2] [This is a free rendering of Maimon. on Mishnah, Sanhedrin xi. 1. See however Surenh. iv. 264. C. T.]

ἃ μὲν χρὴ διανοεῖσθαι ἔργοις δὲ ἀτόποις καὶ λόγοις χρῆσθαι; and p. 295, 320, M 2. p. 333, also by Plato and Xen. The only other place in which the word occurs in N.T. is 1 Cor. xv. 32 εἰ κατ' ἄνθρωπον ἐθηριομάχησα, τί μοι τὸ ὄφελος;

ἔργα.] The ἔλεος of ver. 13. Cf. Clem. Hom. viii. 7 οὐ γὰρ ὠφελήσει τινὰ τὸ λέγειν ἀλλὰ τὸ ποιεῖν· ἐκ παντὸς οὖν τρόπου καλῶν ἔργων χρεία, Pirke Aboth 'say little, do much' (Taylor *J. F.* p. 38), Philo M. 1. p. 525 ἡ ἄνευ πράξεως θεωρία ψιλὴ πρὸς οὐδὲν ὄφελος τοῖς ἐπιστήμοσιν.

μὴ δύναται ἡ πίστις σῶσαι αὐτόν;] The interrogative μή, expecting of course a negative answer, occurs again below iii. 12, and is very frequent in the 1st epistle to the Corinthians and the Gospel of St. John. For σῶσαι cf. i. 21: it is the triumph of mercy over judgment of ver. 13. ἡ πίστις not faith absolutely, but such faith as this, *fides illa quam vos habere dicitis* (Bede).

15. **ἐὰν ἀδελφός.**] See n. on i. 2. If δέ is inserted after ἐάν we should have to consider this a second parallel case, in which profession is opposed to reality; but it makes better sense to omit it with B. and Sin. and take this as a concrete illustration of the abstract principle stated in ver. 14. Compare 1 John iii. 17, 18 (where the empty profession of love is contrasted with the living reality), Philo M. 1. p. 527 ὥσπερ ἐν ἰατροῖς ἡ λεγομένη λογοϊατρεία πολὺ τῆς τῶν καμνόντων ὠφελείας ἀποστατεῖ, φαρμάκοις γὰρ καὶ χειρουργίαις καὶ διαίταις ἀλλ' οὐ λόγοις αἱ νόσοι θεραπεύονται κ.τ.λ. For construction of ἐὰν γυμνοὶ ὑπάρχωσιν...εἴπῃ δέ τις...μὴ δῶτε δέ compare ver. 2 above ἐὰν εἰσέλθῃ...εἰσέλθῃ δέ... ἐπιβλέψητε δέ.

γυμνοί.] He still has before him the case of the poor who were slighted in the congregation. The word does not necessarily imply absolute nakedness: a person wearing only the *cetoneth*, or under-tunic (χιτωνίσκος or ὑποδύτης), was described as naked: thus it is used of Saul after having taken off his upper garments (1 Sam. xix. 24), of a warrior who has cast off his military cloak (Amos ii. 16), of Peter without his fisher's coat (ἐπενδύτης); cf. too Hesiod *Op.* 391 γυμνὸν σπείρειν imitated in *Georg.* i. 299. The same expression is applied to the poorly clad in Job xxii. 6, Isa. lviii. 7, Matt. xxv. 36, see *D. of B.* s.v. 'Dress' p. 454.

λειπόμενοι.] See on i. 4. As the best MSS. omit ὦσιν, this must be taken with ὑπάρχωσιν, cf. Acts viii. 16 βεβαπτισμένοι ὑπῆρχον. The plural is of course not strictly grammatical after the disjunctive conjunction, but it is a very natural irregularity; cf. Plato *Leg.* 8. 838 ὅταν ἀδελφὸς ἢ ἀδελφή τῳ γένωνται καλοί, Krueg. *Gr.* § 63. 3. 2. So a singular subject followed by μετά with gen. is sometimes joined with a plural verb: see below on δῶτε.

ἐφημέρου.] Only here in N.T.; not in LXX. Diod. iii. 31, Dion. H. viii. 41 and Aristides xlix. 537, 631, use the phrase ἐφήμερος τροφή, Philo M. 2, p. 538 has τὸ ἐφήμερον, probably quoted from a comic poet (πένητές ἐσμεν καὶ μόλις τοὐφήμερον εἰς αὐτὰ τἀναγκαῖα πορίζειν δυνάμεθα). Field cites Ael. *V.H.* iii. 29 Diogenes said he was πτωχὸς δυσείμων, βίον ἔχων τὸν ἐφήμερον, Menander p. 134 M. στρατεία δ' οὐ φέρει περιουσίαν ἐφήμερον δὲ καὶ προπετῆ βίον. It is defined by

Pollux as τὸ εἰς τὴν ἐπιοῦσαν μὴ μένον, cf. Herod. i. 32 οὐ γάρ τοι ὁ μέγα πλούσιος μᾶλλον τοῦ ἐπ' ἡμέρην ἔχοντος ὀλβιώτερός ἐστι.

16. **τις ἐξ ὑμῶν.**] Tit. i. 13 εἶπέ τις ἐξ αὐτῶν, and frequently. Sometimes τις is omitted both in the accusative as Matt. xxiii. 34 ἀποστέλλω προφήτας...καὶ ἐξ αὐτῶν ἀποκτενεῖτε, and in the nominative as John xvi. 17 εἶπον ἐκ τῶν μαθητῶν αὐτοῦ.

ὑπάγετε ἐν εἰρήνῃ.] Cf. the words of the jailor at Philippi to Paul πορεύεσθε ἐν εἰρήνῃ Acts xvi. 36, Jud. xviii. 6; but more commonly we find εἰς used, implying a future result, as in Mark v. 34 with ὕπαγε, Luke vii. 50 with πορεύου, also ch. viii. 48, 1 Sam. i. 17, xx. 42, with βάδιζε 2 Sam xv. 9, ἀπελύθησαν μετ' εἰρήνης Acts xv. 33. In Tobit xii. 5 we have ὕπαγε ὑγιαίνων in much the same sense. It is a formula of comfort ('be at ease,' 'have no anxiety') usually grounded upon some act or assurance, as 1 Sam. xx. 42 the oath of friendship between David and Jonathan, Acts xvi. 36 the order of the magistrates. Here it should have been followed or preceded by the gift of food and clothing instead of the mocking words.

θερμαίνεσθε καὶ χορτάζεσθε.] Beyschlag and others take these verbs in the middle sense 'warm yourselves and feed yourselves.' The Revisers retain the old version 'be ye warmed and fed,' which certainly gives a better sense and one more suited to the caustic irony of which St. James is a master. The sight of distress is unpleasant to these dainty Christians. They bustle out the wretched-looking brother or sister with seeming kindness and what sounds like an order to others to provide for their immediate relief, but without taking any step to carry out the order. Compare Hor. 2 *Sat.* 8. 25 *tibi di quaecunque preceris commoda dent.* To have said directly 'go and get warm, go and eat,' would have been giving an order which it was plainly not in their own power to obey: the other mode of address (like the barren fig-tree) excites a momentary delusive hope analogous to the impression produced by faith without deeds. It could only be rightly used where miraculous power accompanied the word, as in Mark v. 34 ὕπαγε εἰς εἰρήνην καὶ ἴσθι ὑγιὴς ἀπὸ τῆς μάστιγός σου. Otherwise it is only a specimen of that hypocrisy of saying without doing (λέγῃ ἔχειν ver. 14) which called forth the severest reproof of St. James as of his Master. The active of θερμ. is common in classical writers and is found once in LXX. (Sirac. 38. 17) θέρμανον κοπετόν, 'make hot the wailing,' never in N.T.: θερμαίνεσθαι occurs elsewhere in N.T. only in Mark xiv. 54, 67, John xviii. 18, 25 of Peter warming himself at the fire: in LXX. we find it with passive sense Hos. vii. 7 ἐθερμάνθησαν ὡς κλίβανος and in Hagg. i. 6 used, as here, with reference to clothing, ἐφάγετε καὶ οὐκ εἰς πλησμονήν...περιεβάλεσθε καὶ οὐκ ἐθερμάνθητε (where it must mean, not 'did not warm yourselves,' but 'were not warmed'), so Job xxxi. 20 ἀπὸ κουρᾶς ἀμνῶν μου ἐθερμάνθησαν οἱ ὦμοι αὐτῶν, 1 Kings i. 1 (of David) περιέβαλλον αὐτὸν ἱματίοις καὶ οὐκ ἐθερμαίνετο, tropically Psa. xxxviii. 3 ἐθερμάνθη ἡ καρδία μου ('my heart was heated') καὶ ἐν τῇ μελέτῃ μου ἐκκαυθήσεται πῦρ. The passive is also common in classical writers, as Eur. *El.* 402 χαρᾷ θερμαινόμεσθα καρδίαν. There is just as little objection to taking χορτάζεσθαι as passive. The noun χόρτος 'fodder,' on which see above i. 11, is used of human food by Hipponax the satirist *fr.* 34 B. δούλιος χόρτος. The verb, which is only used by classical writers of beasts or men like beasts (Plato *Rep.* ix. 586 βοσκημάτων δίκην βόσκονται χορταζόμενοι), or as a piece of slang (Eubulus 350 B.C. βόλβοις ἐμαυτὸν χορτάσων ἐλήλυθα), gets the general meaning of satisfying hunger in later Greek. Lobeck (*Phryn.* p. 64) compares it with ἐρεύγεσθαι as having lost its original specific meaning: see Matt. xiv. 20 ἔφαγον καὶ ἐχορτάσθησαν (were filled), Phil. iv. 12 μεμύημαι καὶ χορτάζεσθαι καὶ πεινᾶν, Psa. xxxvi. 19, lviii. 15, lxxx. 16, cvi. 9, cxxxi. 15 τοὺς πτωχοὺς χορτάσω ἄρτων, Acts vii. 11 οὐχ εὕρισκον χορτάσματα (sustenance). But the remembrance of the original sense was not quite lost for scholars: see Clem. Al. *Paed.* i. 155 P 'χορτασθέντες' φησίν, τὸ ἄλογον τῆς τροφῆς πλήρωμα χόρτασμα, οὐ βρῶμα εἰπών: cf. Sturz *Dial. Mac.* p. 200 foll.

μὴ δῶτε δέ.] The plural is often used after an indefinite singular, such as ἕκαστος, τις, ὅστις, see Krueg. *Gr.* § 58. 4. 5. To avoid separating words which are closely connected, δέ sometimes takes the third sometimes the fourth place in the sentence, e.g. with the preposition (below v. 12 πρὸ πάντων δέ), with the article (John x. 12 ὁ μισθωτὸς δέ), even the relative (2 Tim. iii. 8 ὃν τρόπον δέ), and with the negative, as here and Matt. xviii. 25 μὴ ἔχοντος δέ, Acts xvii. 6 μὴ εὑρόντες δέ, Acts xxi. 34 μὴ δυνάμενος δὲ γνῶναι, xxi. 14 μὴ πειθομένου δὲ αὐτοῦ, so οὐκ ἐγράφη δέ, οὐκ ἔγραψα δέ, οὐ θέλομεν δέ. Examples of the fourth place are John viii. 16 καὶ ἐὰν κρίνω δέ, vii. 13 ἐκ τοῦ ὄχλου δέ, xvii. 20 οὐ περὶ τούτων δέ, Acts iii. 1 ἐπὶ τὸ αὐτὸ δέ, xxvii. 14 μετ' οὐ πολὺ δέ, 1 Cor. iv. 18 ὡς μὴ ἐρχομένου δέ μου, even the fifth occurs in 1 John ii. 2 οὐ περὶ τῶν ὑμετέρων δὲ μόνον. In Justin M. *Apol.* ii. 8 we find an example of the sixth place, καὶ τοὺς ἀπὸ τῶν Στωικῶν δὲ δογμάτων.

τὰ ἐπιτήδεια τοῦ σώματος.] Only here in N.T., frequent in classical authors, e.g. Thuc. viii. 74 ὅσα περὶ τὸ σῶμα εἰς δίαιταν ὑπῆρχεν ἐπιτήδεια, Theophr. *Char.* xi. 5 φειδωνίῳ μέτρῳ μετρεῖν αὐτὸς τοῖς ἔνδον τὰ ἐπιτήδεια (their portions or rations).

17. **ἡ πίστις...νεκρά ἐστιν.**] The absence of works, the natural fruit of faith, proves that the faith is in itself lifeless, just as a compassion which expends itself in words only is counterfeit. Life cannot remain latent. Cf. Plaut. *Epid.* i. 2. 18 *quid te retulit beneficum esse oratione si ad rem auxilium emortuum est?* For metaphorical use of νεκρός, nearly = μάταιος i. 2. 6, or ἀργός below ver. 20, cf. below ver. 26, Heb. vi. 1 and ix. 14 ἔργα νεκρά, that is, 'works done apart from the vivifying influence of faith and love, with a view to earn salvation,' see above i. 26 n. and John xv. 4; Rom. vii. 8 χωρὶς νόμου ἁμαρτία νεκρά, 'sin is dormant till roused into activity by antagonism to law'; Epict. *Diss.* iii. 23. 28 ἂν μὴ ταῦτα ἐμποιῇ (viz. produce conviction of error) ὁ τοῦ φιλοσόφου λόγος, νεκρός ἐστι καὶ αὐτὸς καὶ ὁ λέγων.

καθ' ἑαυτήν.] Not a mere repetition of ἐὰν μὴ ἔχῃ ἔργα: the absence of fruit shows that it is not merely outwardly inoperative but inwardly dead.

18. **ἀλλ' ἐρεῖ τις.**] 'Nay, one may say, Thou hast faith and I works; do thou, if thou canst, prove thy faith without works and I will prove mine by my works.' It has been shown that faith without works is

of no value: one may go further and say that its existence is incapable of proof. The writer, with his usual modesty, puts himself in the background, does not claim to be the representative of perfect working faith, but supposes another to speak. Usually the phrase ἀλλ' ἐρεῖ τις is used of an objection, like νὴ Δία, *at enim*, as 1 Cor. xv. 35 ἀ.ἐ.τ. πῶς ἐγείρονται οἱ νεκροί; and in classical Greek, Xen. *Cyr*. iv. 3. 10 ἀλλ' ἐρεῖ τις ἴσως...ἀλλ' εἴποι ἄν τις, and so some would take it here: 'It may be objected that works and faith are different forms of genuine religion: your form may be faith, mine works, both equally acceptable in the sight of God.' The explanation is untenable, because it makes the imaginary objector treat the writer as though it was the latter who was exalting faith above works, instead of the opposite. Some commentators have had recourse to conjecture, as Pfleiderer (cited by Spitta) who thinks πίστιν and ἔργα should be transposed, and Spitta himself, who thinks that a reply of the solifidian (to the effect that there may be a genuine latent faith) must have been lost after ἐρεῖ τις, and that such a reply is implied in the words ὦ ἄνθρωπε κενέ of vers. 20. I prefer to give to ἀλλά a strengthening force = *immo*, like πλήν in Matt. xxvi. 64, cf. John xvi. 2 ἀποσυναγώγους ποιήσουσιν ὑμᾶς· ἀλλ' ἔρχεται ὥρα ἵνα πᾶς ὁ ἀποκτείνων ὑμᾶς δόξῃ λατρείαν προσφέρειν τῷ Θεῷ, Luke xvii. 8, ἀλλ' οὐχὶ ἐρεῖ αὐτῷ; (which I think should be translated 'nay! will he not rather say unto him?') 2 Cor. vii. 11 πόσην κατειργάσατο ὑμῖν σπουδήν, ἀλλὰ ἀπολογίαν, ἀλλὰ ἀγανάκτησιν, ἀλλὰ φόβον, κ.τ.λ., Phil. i. 18 ἐν τούτῳ χαίρω· ἀλλὰ καὶ χαιρήσομαι, Heb. iii. 16 τίνες παρεπίκραναν; ἀλλ' οὐ πάντες; with Alf.'s n., 1 Pet. iii. 14 ἀλλ' εἰ καὶ πάσχοιτε ...μακάριοι. Instead of the future the optative with ἄν would be more common in classical Greek, but the latter form is rather avoided by the Hellenistic writers, occuring only eight times in N.T. (thrice in Luke, five times in Acts), see A. Buttmann, p. 188, who cites Rom. v. 7 μόλις γὰρ ὑπὲρ δικαίου τις ἀποθανεῖται, &c. In Latin the future *dicet aliquis* is far more common than the present subjunctive, see Roby, vol. ii. pref. p. 101 foll.

κἀγὼ.] In the N.T. the contracted is more usual than the uncontracted form, see WH. *app*. p. 145, Winer p. 51. We also find κἀμοί, κἀμέ, κἀκεῖ, κἀκεῖνος. A close parallel to the form of this sentence is found in Theoph, *Autol*. i. 2 δεῖξόν μοι τὸν ἄνθρωπόν σου, κἀγώ σοι δείξω τὸν Θεόν μου.

χωρὶς τῶν ἔργων.] We must supply σου just as we supply μου after τὴν πίστιν. Cf. Rom. iii. 28 λογιζόμεθα δικαιοῦσθαι πίστει ἄνθρωπον χωρὶς ἔργων νόμου, *ib*. iv. 6 ὁ Θεὸς λογίζεται δικαιοσύνην χωρὶς ἔργων.

ἐκ τῶν ἔργων.] So v. 21 below and iii. 13 ἐκ τῆς καλῆς ἀναστροφῆς.

19. **σὺ πιστεύεις ὅτι εἷς ἐστιν ὁ Θεός.**] This reading supported by A. Sin. Pesh. &c. seems preferable to that of B (accepted by WH.) εἷς Θεός ἐστιν, as it expresses a more definite belief in the actual formula of Jewish orthodoxy given in Deut. vi. 4 ἄκουε Ἰσραήλ, Κύριος ὁ Θεὸς ἡμῶν Κύριος εἷς ἐστιν, Mark xii. 29, 1 Cor. viii. 4, 6, Hermas *Mand*. i. πρῶτον πάντων πίστευε ὅτι εἷς ἐστιν ὁ Θεός, Philo *Leg. ad C*. M. 2. p. 562 Ἰουδαίους δεδιδαγμένους ἐξ αὐτῶν σπαργάνων ἕνα νομίζειν τὸν πατέρα καὶ ποιητὴν τοῦ κόσμου Θεόν. Much is said of the excellence of the μοναρχικὴ

θρησκεία in the Clementine Homilies. This verse from Deuteronomy is the commencement of the Shema, that portion of the law which was appointed to be read or recited both morning and evening by every Jew. 'For him who reads the Shema with scrupulous precision as regards its several letters, they cool Gehinnom' (Berakoth 156, quoted in Taylor, *Jewish Fathers*, p. 52, and exc. iv.). St. Paul depicts the reliance placed by the Jews on their orthodoxy, Rom. ii. 17—22. The phrase πιστ. ὅτι denotes intellectual belief, as contrasted with πιστ. εἰς or ἐν denoting moral faith or trust; so Bede: *aliud est credere illi, aliud credere illum, aliud credere in illum. Credere illi, est credere vera esse quae loquitur; credere illum, credere quod ipse sit Deus; credere in illum est diligere illum. Credere vera esse quae loquitur multi et mali possunt; credunt enim esse vera et nolunt ea facere, quia ad operandum pigri sunt. Credere autem ipsum esse Deum, hoc et demones potuerunt. Credere vero in Deum soli novere qui diligunt Deum, qui non solo nomine sunt Christiani, sed et factis et vita; quia sine dilectione fides inanis.* WH. take the clause interrogatively: it seems to me more impressive to regard it as stating a simple matter of fact, like σὺ πίστιν ἔχεις before. There is no need to suppose with Winer (p. 678) that it expresses a condition, to which καλῶς ποιεῖς supplies the apodosis; what is prepared for is the following phrase καὶ τὰ δαιμόνια κ.τ.λ., not the merely parenthetic καλῶς ποιεῖς. Another question is whether St. James must be supposed to speak here in his own person, or whether this verse also must be assigned to the interlocutor introduced in v. 18. The repetition of σὺ πιστεύεις after σὺ πίστιν ἔχεις and the decided break before v. 20 seem to favour the latter view. We must suppose him thus to put forward the two arguments (1) belief without works (may possibly be a real belief, but) can never prove its existence; (2) it may exist, and yet be consistent with diabolic malignity.

καλῶς ποιεῖς.] The phrase is not necessarily ironical, see above v. 8 and Mark xii. 32 καλῶς εἶπες ὅτι εἷς ἐστιν, but is made ironical by the context, as in Mark vii. 9 καλῶς ἀθετεῖτε τὴν ἐντολήν, 2 Cor. xi. 4 εἰ ὁ ἐρχόμενος ἄλλον Ἰησοῦν κηρύσσει...καλῶς ἀνέχεσθε, John iv. 17 καλῶς εἶπας ὅτι ἄνδρα οὐκ ἔχω. It is often used in a colloquial sense by classical writers, e.g. Demosth. p. 141, 14 μετὰ ταῦτα ἡ τύχη καλῶς ποιοῦσα ('many thanks to her') πολλὰ πεποίηκε τὰ κοινά, id. *Mid.* p. 582 εἰσὶ μὲν εἰς τὰ μάλιστα αὐτοὶ πλούσιοι καὶ καλῶς ποιοῦσι, where Reiske translates *id vero laudo congratulorque*, id. *Coron.* p. 304, 26 (Philip's cruelty others have experienced) τῆς δὲ φιλανθρωπίας...ὑμεῖς καλῶς ποιοῦντες ('by good luck') τοὺς καρποὺς κεκόμισθε, Arist. *Plut.* 863 καλῶς τοίνυν ποιῶν ἀπόλλυται ('a good job too'): see Hermann's Viger, p. 362. [Diod. v. p. 442 R. καλῶς διεφθάρθαι 'a pretty clean sweep' A.]

τὰ δαιμόνια πιστεύουσιν.] This is the term regularly used in the Gospels for the evil spirits, also called πνεύματα ἀκάθαρτα or πονηρά, by whom men are possessed and who are themselves said to be subject to Beelzebub. We have instances both of their belief and their terror in Matt. viii. 29 (of Legion) ἔκραξαν λέγοντες τί ἡμῖν καὶ σοί, υἱὲ τοῦ Θεοῦ; ἦλθες ὧδε πρὸ καιροῦ βασανίσαι ἡμᾶς; of their belief, Luke iv. 41 'He suffered them not to speak because they knew he was the Christ,'

Acts xix. 15 'Jesus I know and Paul I know.' They suggest evil thoughts to men: hence σοφία δαιμονιώδης below iii. 15, διδασκαλίαις δαιμονίων 1 Tim. iv. 1. The same term is applied to heathen deities 1 Cor. x. 20 foll.

καὶ φρίσσουσιν.] The word, which properly means 'to bristle,' is used like the Lat. *horreo* of the physical signs of terror, especially of the hair standing on end, as in Job. iv. 14, 15. But the R.V. translation 'shudder,' seems too bold a metaphor to apply in English to spirits. It comes to express only a high degree of awe or terror, as Daniel, after the vision of the four beasts and their disappearance before the coming of the Son of Man, says ἔφριξε τὸ πνεῦμά μου (vii. 15), Prayer of Manasses 4 Κύριε ...ὃν πάντα φρίσσει καὶ τρέμει ἀπὸ προσώπου δυνάμεώς σου, hence τὸ φρικτὸν ὄνομα, φρικτὰ μυστήρια or ὄργια, μαρμαίρων τι φρικῶδες of the dazzling splendour of the robes of Herod (Euseb. *H.E.* ii. 10); it is even used of the effect on the mind of a favourable omen Xen. *Cyr.* iv. 2, 15 ὥστε πᾶσι μὲν φρίκην ἐγγίγνεσθαι πρὸς τὸ θεῖον, θάρρος δὲ πρὸς τοὺς πολεμίους. The occasion of this terror is mentioned in Matt. viii. 29 quoted above, cf. Heb. x. 27 (for those who sin after receiving knowledge of the truth there remains) φοβερά τις ἐκδοχὴ κρίσεως, Philo M. 1 p. 218 ἐπὶ τοῖς προσδοκωμένοις φοβεροῖς τρέμοντές τε καὶ φρίττοντες. We find many reminiscences of this saying of St. James, e.g. Justin *Trypho* 49 (Χριστὸν) καὶ τὰ δαιμόνια φρίσσει καὶ πᾶσαι ἁπλῶς αἱ ἀρχαὶ καὶ ἐξουσίαι τῆς γῆς, Acta Philippi T. p. 86 Θεὲ ὃν φρίττουσιν πάντες αἰῶνες...ὃν τρέμουσιν ἀρχαὶ τῶν ἐπουρανίων, Lactant. *de Ira* c. 23 *Apollo Milesius de Judaeorum religione consultus responso hoc indidit*...ὃν τρέμεται καὶ γαῖα καὶ οὐρανὸς ἠδὲ θάλασσα, ταρτάρεοί τε μυχοὶ καὶ δαίμονες ἐκφρίττουσιν, Orphica *ap.* Clem. Al. *Strom.* v. p. 724 P. δαίμονες ὃν φρίσσουσι (Herm. Orph. p. 454), Ignat. *Philip.* p. 175 (ὁ σταυρὸς) ἐστὶ τὸ τροπαῖον κατὰ τῆς αὐτοῦ (τοῦ διαβόλου) δυνάμεως, ὅπερ ὁρῶν φρίττει.

20. **θέλεις δὲ γνῶναι.**] Cf. Rom. xiii. 3 θέλεις δὲ μὴ φοβεῖσθαι; τὸ ἀγαθὸν ποίει. The question is equivalent to a condition 'if you wish for a conclusive proof that faith by itself cannot save, take the case of Abraham.' It would seem that from this point St. James speaks again in his own name.

ὦ ἄνθρωπε κενέ.] Cf. Rom. ii. 1 ὦ ἄνθρωπε πᾶς ὁ κρίνων, ix. 20 ὦ ἄνθρωπε, μενοῦνγε σὺ τίς εἶ; 1 Tim. vi. 11 ὦ ἄνθρωπε Θεοῦ. Κενός (= *Raca*) is defined (Epict. *Diss.* iv. 4. 25) as one ἐφ' οἷς οὐ δεῖ ἐπαιρόμενος: like *vanus* it is used of a man who cannot be depended on, whose deeds do not correspond to his words, hence of boasters (Soph. *Ant.* 703 οὗτοι διαπτυχθέντες ὤφθησαν κενοι) and impostors, joined with ἀλαζων Plut. *Vit.* p. 581 F. Perhaps the words in Hermas *Mand.* xi. 3 αὐτὸς κενὸς ὢν κενῶς ἀποκρίνεται κενοῖς· ὃ γὰρ ἂν ἐπερωτηθῇ πρὸς τὸ κένωμα τοῦ ἀνθρώπου ἀποκρίνεται, and *ib.* 13 (τὸ ἐπίγειον πνεῦμα) κολλᾶται τοῖς διψύχοις καὶ κενοῖς, 15 οἱ προφῆται οἱ κενοί, may refer to our text: cf. *Didaché* 2. 5 οὐκ ἔσται ὁ λόγος σου ψευδής, οὐ κενός, ἀλλὰ μεμεστωμένος πράξει. Hilgenfield and others who suppose this argument on faith and works to be directed against St. Paul imagine that St. Paul himself is here addressed. See Introduction.

ἀργή.] Nearly = νεκρά, which is read here by some MSS., cf. 2 Pet.

i. 8 ταῦτα (love, brotherly-kindness, &c.) οὐκ ἀργοὺς οὐδὲ ἀκάρπους καθίστησιν, Matt. xii. 36 πᾶν ῥῆμα ἀργόν.

21. **Ἀβραὰμ ὁ πατὴρ ὑμῶν.**] This was the constant title of Abraham, as is shown in Matt. iii. 8, John viii. 33 foll., Luke xvi. 24, Rom. iv. 1, 16. Its use favours the supposition that the epistle is addressed principally to Jews.

οὐκ ἐξ ἔργων ἐδικαιώθη;] The case of Abraham was naturally appealed to as the pattern of faith not by St. Paul only (in Rom. iv. and Gal. iii. 7, where we find the same quotation as in our next verse), but in Heb. xi. 8 and 1 Macc. ii. 52 Ἀβραὰμ οὐχὶ ἐν πειρασμῷ εὑρέθη πιστὸς καὶ ἐλογίσθη αὐτῷ εἰς δικαιοσύνην, *ib.* xliv. 20 foll., Wisd. x. 5, see Lightfoot *Galatians*, p. 151 foll. When the example of Abraham was abused as assuring justification to all who professed an orthodox belief, it was equally natural to show, as St. James has done, that Abraham's faith was not a mere profession but an extremely active principle, cf. Gen. xxii. 16 foll. οὗ εἵνεκεν ἐ π ο ί η σ α ς τ ὸ ῥ ῆ μ α τ ο ῦ τ ο καὶ οὐκ ἐφείσω τοῦ υἱοῦ σου...ἦ μὴν εὐλογῶν εὐλογήσω σε. Clement of Rome combines the views of St. James and St. Paul: see i. 10, 31, τίνος χάριν ηὐλογήθη Ἀβ.; οὐχὶ δικαιοσύνην καὶ ἀλήθειαν διὰ πίστεως ποιήσας; *ib.* 33 with Lightfoot's notes, and above ver. 14 n. For ἐξ ἔργων see ver. 18 and Matt. xii. 37 ἐκ τῶν λόγων δικαιωθήσῃ. Δικαιόω is strictly to make *i.e.* pronounce just, like ἀξιόω to pronounce or deem worthy or fitting, cf. Exod. xxiii. 7 οὐ δικαιώσεις τὸν ἀσεβῆ, 1 Kings viii. 32 δικαιῶσαι δίκαιον, δοῦναι αὐτῷ κατὰ τὴν δικαιοσύνην αὐτοῦ, Psa. cxliii. 2 οὐ δικαιωθήσεται ἐνώπιόν σου πᾶς ζῶν, Isa. xlv. 26 ἀπὸ Κυρίου δικαιωθήσονται...πᾶν τὸ σπέρμα τῶν υἱῶν Ἰσραήλ, Acts xiii. 39, Rom. iii. 28 λογιζόμεθα δικαιοῦσθαι πίστει ἄνθρωπον χωρὶς ἔργων νόμου, *ib.* iv. 1 εἰ Ἀβραὰμ ἐξ ἔργων ἐδικαιώθη ἔχει καύχημα, Habak. ii. 4 quoted in Rom. i. 17. See T. S. Evans on 1 Cor. vi. 11.

ἀνενέγκας Ἰσαάκ.] Cf. Gen. viii. 20 ἀπὸ πάντων τῶν κτηνῶν τῶν καθαρῶν ...ἀνήνεγκεν εἰς ὁλοκάρπωσιν ἐπὶ τὸ θυσιαστήριον, 1 Pet. ii. 5, 24 τὰς ἁμαρτιάς ἡμῶν ἀνήνεγκεν ἐπὶ τὸ ξύλον, Heb. vii. 27 ἀναφ. θυσίας, where Westcott distinguishes it from the classical term προσφέρω as properly describing the ministerial action of the priest, while the latter describes the action of the offerer. In the other passages of the N.T. in which Abraham's faith is mentioned it is differently proved: thus in Rom. iv. 1, 17–21 it is the faith in the promise of a son; in Heb. xi. 8–12 it is the departure from his own land to an unknown country; *ib.* 17–19 it is the sacrifice of Isaac in the faith that God would raise him up again from the dead. The much-quoted verse of Genesis (xv. 6) follows the promise of a son, but a special blessing follows the sacrifice of Isaac (*ib.* xxii. 12, 16–18). Philo has not less than twelve references to Gen. xv. 6 (see Lightfoot *Gal. l.c.*), the most striking passage being M. 1. p. 486 δίκαιον γὰρ οὕτως οὐδὲν ὡς ἀκράτῳ καὶ ἀμιγεῖ τῇ πρὸς Θεὸν μόνον πίστει κεχρῆσθαι...τὸ ἐπὶ μόνῳ τῷ ὄντι βεβαίως καὶ ἀκλινῶς ὁρμεῖν... δικαιοσύνης μόνον ἔργον. While St. Paul makes no reference to Gen. xvii. 17, in which Abraham is said to have laughed at the idea that he should have a son by Sarah (the earlier promise having been made when he was at least twelve years younger, and having no express reference to Sarah), Philo endeavours to show that this is no discredit to Abraham's faith (M. 1. p. 605).

ἐπὶ τὸ θυσιαστήριον.] Gen. xxii. 9 *ἐπέθηκεν αὐτὸν ἐπὶ τὸ θυσ.* The word, which is not found in classical writers, is used of the Jewish material altar or the Christian spiritual altar in the N.T., LXX., Philo, Josephus, and later writers. See Westcott, *Hebrews*, p. 453*ff.*

22. **βλέπεις.**] I prefer, with WH., to take this and *ὁρᾶτε* below v. 24 as a statement, not a question, both explaining *γνῶναι* in v. 20. It is used with *ὅτι* in Heb. iii. 19, 2 Cor. vii. 8.

συνήργει τοῖς ἔργοις.] 'Faith cooperated with his actions and was perfected by them': cf. Mark xvi. 20 *τοῦ Κυρίου συνεργοῦντος* (*sc. τοῖς ἀποστόλοις*), Rom. viii. 28, 1 Macc. xii. 1, Test. Issach. 3, Plut. *Mor.* p. 138 A. *τῇ ψυχῇ συνεργεῖ τὸ σῶμα καὶ συγκάμνει*, Philo M. 2, p. 616 *αὐγὴ τὸ ἀποστελλόμενον ἐκ φλογός, συνεργὸν ὀφθαλμοῖς εἰς τὴν τῶν ὁρατῶν ἀντίληψιν.* Here we have the opposite to *χωρὶς ἔργων.*

23. **ἐτελειώθη.**] As the tree is perfected by its fruits, so faith by its works. In like manner sin is spoken of (i. 15) as *ἀποτελεσθεῖσα* when transformed into act and habit and so producing its natural result; and *ὑπομονή* is exercised and made perfect by practice (i. 4). Wherever there are good works, it is due to the faith which inspires them, wherever there is genuine faith it must blossom into works, see 1 John ii. 5.

ἐπληρώθη.] So Matt. ii. 17 *ἐπληρώθη τὸ ῥηθὲν κ.τ.λ.* 'the word of prophecy about Rachel then received its true fulfilment.' In the sacrifice of Isaac was shown the full meaning of the word (Gen. xv. 6) spoken thirty or (as the Rabbis say) fifty years before in commendation of Abraham's belief in the promise of a child. When they were first spoken Abraham's faith was imperfect, as is shown by the question (Gen. xv. 8) 'Lord, whereby shall I know that I shall inherit it?' It was the willing surrender of the child of promise, 'accounting that God was able to raise him up from the dead,' which fully proved his faith. The Rabbis distinguish ten instances of faith in Abraham;[1] his faith was perfected in the sacrifice of Isaac, his justification was proved by his being acknowledged as friend of God. The Jews implore the mercy of God by the sacrifice of Isaac, as Christians by the sacrifice of Christ.[2]

ἡ γραφή.] The singular is used of a particular passage, as in Mark xv. 28 *ἐπληρώθη ἡ γραφὴ ἡ λέγουσα καὶ μετὰ τῶν ἀνόμων ἐλογίσθη.*

ἐπίστευσεν δέ.] The MSS. of the LXX., with the exception of 19 and 108, have *καὶ ἐπίστευσεν*, but *δέ* is found, instead of *καί*, in Philo M. 1. p. 605, Rom. iv. 3, Clem. Rom. i. 10. 6, Justin M. *Dial.* 92, showing that *δέ* was the then accepted reading (Hatch, p. 156).

ἐλογίσθη αὐτῷ εἰς δικαιοσύνην.] The original Hebrew (Gen. xv. 6) has the active, 'God counted it to him': the quotations in the N.T. (Rom. iv. 3 foll., Gal. iii. 6) have the passive with the LXX. Similar phrases occur Gen. vii. 1 (of Noah) *σὲ εἶδον δίκαιον ἐναντίον μοῦ*, Deut. vi. 25 'it shall be our righteousness (LXX. *ἐλεημοσύνη*) if we observe to do all

[1] See Taylor's *J.F.* p. 94.

[2] See Schegg here, and Delitzsch on Gen. p. 418 (ed. 1860). [Targum on Micah vii 20 adds *Remember for us the binding of Isaac.* C. T.]

these commandments before the Lord our God,' ch. xxiv. 12 foll. 'if he be a poor man thou shalt deliver him the pledge again when the sun goeth down...and it shall be righteousness (ἐλεημοσύνη) unto thee before the Lord thy God,' Ps. cvi. 30, 31 (then stood up Phinehas and executed judgment) καὶ ἐλογίσθη αὐτῷ εἰς δικαιοσύνην εἰς γενεὰν καὶ γενεάν. Compare also Levit. xxv. 31 αἱ δὲ οἰκίαι πρὸς τὸν ἀγρὸν λογισθήσονται 'shall be reckoned as,' Ps. xxxii. 2 (quoted in Rom. iv. 6, 8) μακάριος ἀνὴρ ᾧ οὐ μὴ λογίσηται Κύριος ἁμαρτίαν, Wisd. ix. 6 κἂν γάρ τις ᾖ τέλειος ἐν υἱοῖς ἀνθρώπων τῆς ἀπὸ σοῦ σοφίας ἀπούσης εἰς οὐδὲν λογισθήσεται. Δικαιοσύνη in the Bible is taken in even a wider sense than that noted by Aristotle *Eth.* v. 1. 15 αὕτη μὲν οὖν ἡ δικαιοσύνη ἀρετὴ μέν ἐστι τελεία, ἀλλ' οὐχ ἁπλῶς ἀλλὰ πρὸς ἕτερον, who quotes Theognis 147 ἐν δὲ δικαιοσύνῃ συλλήβδην πᾶσ' ἀρετή 'στιν. In the Bible it is the character of the man who fulfils his duty in all respects towards God, as well as towards his neighbour. The great importance of the text in Gen. xv. is that it is the first passage in which the 'law of liberty' is laid down. Definite set tasks irrespective of motives are exacted from slaves: in the family of God the motives of the children are the main thing in the eyes of the Father. Here the right state of mind is declared to be in God's sight equivalent to the right action; though, as St. James says, right action is the necessary result of the right feeling and it is only through right action that the right state of mind can be evidenced to others, so that the absence of right action (unless precluded by special circumstances) is a proof that the state of mind is not right. The faith of Abraham is the same as the trust which is so often declared blessed in the Psalms, e.g. Ps. ii. 12, xxxiv. 8.

φίλος Θεοῦ ἐκλήθη.] The precise words are not found in the LXX. In Gen. xviii. 17, where our version simply has 'Shall I hide from Abraham that thing which I do?' the LXX. has οὐ μὴ κρύψω ἀπὸ 'Αβ. τοῦ παιδός μου ἃ ἐγὼ ποιῶ, which is quoted by Philo (*Sobr.* M. 1, p. 401) with the words τοῦ φίλου μου, though elsewhere (*Leg. All.* M. 1, p. 93) he cites it without alteration. In 2 Chron. xx. 7 'Art thou not our God who...gavest it (the land) to the seed of Abraham, thy friend, for ever?', the LXX. has ἔδωκας αὐτὴν σπέρματι 'Αβραὰμ τῷ ἠγαπημένῳ σου εἰς τὸν αἰῶνα, Vulg. *semini Abraham amici tui;* Isa. xli. 8 'the seed of Abraham my friend' is in LXX. σπέρμα 'Αβραὰμ ὃν ἠγάπησα.[1] The appellation is still in use among the Arabs, 'with whom the name of Khalil Allah (the friend of God), or more briefly El Khalil, has practically superseded that of Abraham. Even Hebron, as the city of Abraham, has become El Khalil' (Plumptre *in loc.*). Clem. Rom. has the phrase twice, probably copying from St. James (i. 10 ὁ φίλος προσαγορευθείς with Lightfoot's n. and 17), and so Irenaeus iv. 16, 2 *Abraham credidit Deo et reputatum est illi ad justitiam et amicus Dei vocatus est.* Compare John xv. 14, 15, Wisd. vii. 27 (σοφία) εἰς ψυχὰς ὁσίας μεταβαίνουσα φίλους Θεοῦ καὶ προφήτας παρασκευάζει, Taylor's *J.F.* p. 113, and for the same sentiment in Greek philosophers see Xen. *Mem.* ii. 1. 33 (Virtue speaks in the allegory of Prodicus) δι' ἐμὲ φίλοι μὲν θεοῖς

[1] Other readings have φίλον, see Field, *Hexapla*, pp. 744 and 513.

ὄντες, ἀγαπητοὶ δὲ φίλοις, Plato *Leg.* iv. 716 D ὁ μὲν σώφρων Θεῷ φίλος, ὅμοιος γάρ, *Rep.* x. 613 'the righteous man is θεοφιλής and therefore all must turn out well with him', Epict. *Diss.* iv. 3. 9 ἐλεύθερος γάρ εἰμι καὶ φίλος τοῦ Θεοῦ, Cic. *N.D.* I. 121, II. 165.

25. **Ῥαὰβ ἡ πόρνη.**] Selected as an example the furthest removed from Abraham: so Erasmus '*tantum valet apud Deum misericordia ac beneficentia in proximum, ut mulier, ut meretrix, ut alienigena hospitalitatis officio commendata meruerit in catalogo piorum adnumerari.*' Probably it was on this account that her name was famous among the Jews. She was counted as one of the four chief beauties, the others being Sarah, Abigail, Esther; and was said to have been the ancestress of eight prophets (Meuschen, p. 40). She is also cited as an example of faith, Heb. xi. 31, and is mentioned in the genealogy in Matthew. Her faith is shown both by her actions here referred to and her words recorded in Josh. ii. 9, 11 'I know that the Lord God hath given you the land...the Lord your God, He is God in heaven above and in earth beneath.' Clement of Rome (i. 12) connects the two aspects, to which St. James and the writer of the epistle to the Hebrews direct attention, by his phrase διὰ πίστιν καὶ φιλοξενίαν ἐσώθη Ῥαάβ, see Lightfoot on this passage and also his appendix (pp. 413 and 470) on the attempt made both by Jewish and Christian writers (Josephus, Chrysostom, &c.) to weaken the force of the word πόρνη.

ὑποδεξαμένη τοὺς ἀγγέλους.] Heb. xi. 31 δεξαμένη τοὺς κατασκόπους. Both renderings are independent of the LXX. which says ἀπέστειλεν Ἰησοῦς δύο νεανίσκους κατασκοπεῦσαι. The word ὑποδ. occurs elsewhere in N.T. only in the writings of St. Luke.

ἑτέρᾳ ὁδῷ.] By a window instead of by the door, and to the mountain instead of straight back to the camp of the Israelites, Josh. ii. 15, 16. For this pregnant use of ἕτερος cf. Mark xvi. 12 ἐν ἑτέρᾳ μορφῇ, Acts ii. 4 ἑτέραις γλώσσαις.

ἐκβαλοῦσα.] In mild sense, as Matt. ix. 38 ὅπως ἐκβάλῃ ἐργάτας εἰς τὸν θερισμὸν αὐτοῦ, Mark i. 12 τὸ πνεῦμα ἐκβάλλει αὐτὸν εἰς τὴν ἔρημον (= ἄγει Luke, ἀνάγει Matt.), John x. 4 ὅταν τὰ ἴδια (πρόβατα) πάντα ἐκβάλῃ (= ἐξάγει, v. 3).

26. **τὸ σῶμα χωρὶς πνεύματος νεκρόν ἐστιν.**] It seems at first strange that the outward visible part of man should be compared to the invisible principle of faith, and the invisible spirit be compared to works which are the outward fruits of faith; but we must always keep in mind that St. James is speaking here not of faith of the heart, but of a mere lifeless profession of orthodoxy, 'professing to know God but in deeds denying Him' (2 Tim. iii. 5), 'having the form of godliness without the power' (Tit. i. 16).[1] And as 'faith' thus becomes a mere externality, so 'works' become identified with the working principle of love. It thus becomes easy to understand how a mere shell of profession void of the animating principle of love can be compared to a corpse. Or we might understand πνεῦμα of 'breath' as in Ps. cxlvi. 4, Isa. xi. 4, Apoc. xi. 11, xiii. 15 (so Peile and Bassett), which would give a simpler illustration: as a body

[1] The Hebrew word for 'body' is used for the essence of a thing, see *J.F.* p. 76.

which does not breathe is dead, so faith which does not act.[1] A similar metaphor is found in Curtius x. 6 (19) *militaris sine duce turba corpus sine spiritu est.* Spitta cuts the knot by reading κινήματος, (used in LXX. for all bodily motion) in place of πνεύματος.

III.—1. The writer goes back to the subject of i. 19 βραδὺς εἰς τὸ λαλῆσαι, and i. 26 μὴ χαλιναγωγῶν γλῶσσαν, which suggests the figure of vv. 2 and 3. It is also connected with that overvaluation of theory as compared with practice which formed the subject of the last chapter.

μὴ πολλοὶ διδάσκαλοι γίνεσθε.] In his circular letter (Acts xv. 24) St. James condemns unauthorised teachers, cf. Matt. xxiii. 7, 8, *ib.* xv. 14, Rom. ii. 17 foll., 1 Tim. i. 6, 7 θέλοντες εἶναι νομοδιδάσκαλοι κ.τ.λ., Heb. v. 12 ὀφείλοντες εἶναι διδάσκαλοι διὰ τὸν χρόνον πάλιν χρείαν ἔχετε τοῦ διδάσκειν ὑμᾶς τινὰ τὰ στοιχεῖα τῆς ἀρχῆς τῶν λογίων τοῦ Θεοῦ, Pirke Aboth i. 11 *dilige laborem et Rabbinatum odio habe* with Taylor's n., Herm. *Sim.* ix. 22 θέλουσιν ἐθελοδιδάσκαλοι εἶναι ἄφρονες ὄντες. The phrase means 'do not be too eager to teach,' 'do not press into the work of teaching,' lit. 'do not many of you become teachers.' For the use of πολλοί cf. Heb. vii. 23 καὶ οἱ μὲν, πλείονές εἰσι γεγονότες ἱερεῖς διὰ τὸ θανάτῳ κωλύεσθαι παραμένειν, ὁ δὲ...ἀπαράβατον ἔχει τὴν ἱερωσύνην. We read of διδάσκαλοι at Antioch (Acts xiii. 1): they are included in St. Paul's two lists of church officers, 1 Cor. xii. 28, where they come next after apostles and prophets, and Eph. iv. 11 where the order is apostles, prophets, evangelists, pastors and teachers. In 2 Tim. iv. 3 a time is foretold when the people will become impatient of sound doctrine and κατὰ τὰς ἰδίας ἐπιθυμίας ἑαυτοῖς ἐπισωρεύσουσιν διδασκάλους. In the only passages in which they are mentioned in the Didaché (xiii. 2, xv. 1, 2) they are joined with prophets and appear to stand on a higher level than the ἐπίσκοποι and διάκονοι, though these latter also should be carefully chosen for their office, ὑμῖν γὰρ λειτουργοῦσι καὶ αὐτοὶ τὴν λειτουργίαν τῶν προφητῶν καὶ διδασκάλων; see Hermas *Vis.* iii. 5 οἱ μὲν λίθοι οἱ τετράγωνοι...εἰσὶν οἱ ἀπόστολοι καὶ ἐπίσκοποι καὶ διδάσκαλοι καὶ διάκονοι, where Harnack says in *Sim.* ix. 15, 16 *episcopi et diaconi negliguntur quia ibi munus praedicandi evangelium solum respicitur. Doctores sunt omnes praedicatores Christianae veritatis, etsi neque apostoli neque presbyteri fuere. Certum est etiam saeculo secundo laicos in ecclesia publice docuisse,* and adds many references.

εἰδότες.] See on i. 3 γινώσκοντες, and i. 19 ἴστε.

μεῖζον κρίμα λημψόμεθα.] Greater than other Christians who do not set up to teach, compare (for the pregnant use of μείζων) iv. 6 below; and for thought, Matt. vii. 15 foll., xxiii. 14 foll. on false prophets, scribes and Pharisees, blind leaders of the blind, Mark xii. 38–40 βλέπετε ἀπὸ τῶν γραμματέων...προφάσει μακρὰ προσευχόμενοι, οὗτοι λήμψονται περισσότερον κρίμα, Luke xii. 47 δαρήσεται πολλάς, 2 Clem. R. 10 ἐπιμένουσι κακοδιδασκαλοῦντες τὰς ἀναιτίους ψυχάς, οὐκ εἰδότες ὅτι δίσσην ἕξουσι τὴν κρίσιν, Pirke Aboth, i. 18 'not learning but doing is the groundwork, and whoso multiplies words occasions sin.' For the phrase κρ. λ. 'to be condemned' see Rom. xiii. 2, Luke xx. 47. Other

[1] Origen however (*Sel. in Psalm* xxx.) says πνεῦμα here is equivalent to ψυχή.

references to judgment in this epistle are ii. 12, 13, v. 9, 12. By the use of the first person (corrected to the second in the Vulgate), St. James includes himself among the teachers whom he warns, as in v. 9, ii. 18, cf. 1 John i. 6, ii. 18 with Westcott's notes; so St. Paul 1 Cor. x. 6 foll., Heb. ii. 3, xii. 25, Ignat. *Eph.* 3 οὐ διατάσσομαι ὑμῖν ὡς ὤν τις...νῦν γὰρ ἀρχὴν ἔχω τοῦ μαθητεύεσθαι καὶ προσλαλῶ ὑμῖν ὡς συνδιδασκαλίταις μου.

2. **πολλὰ πταίομεν ἅπαντες.**] 1 John i. 8: Wetstein cites many similar sayings from heathen writers, e.g. Thuc. iii. 45 πεφύκασιν ἅπαντες καὶ ἰδίᾳ καὶ δημοσίᾳ ἁμαρτάνειν, Seneca *Clem.* i. 6 *peccamus omnes, alii gravia, alii leviora.* For πολλὰ see Mark ix. 26 πολλὰ σπαράξας ἐξῆλθεν, for πταίειν above ii. 10, 2 Pet. i. 10, Jude 24 τῷ δυναμένῳ φυλάξαι ὑμᾶς ἀπταίστους.

εἴ τις ἐν λόγῳ οὐ πταίει.] For εἰ οὐ see above i. 23, ii. 11: for the thought Matt. xii. 37 ἐκ τῶν λόγων σου δικαιωθήσῃ καὶ ἐκ τῶν λόγων σου καταδικασθήσῃ, *ib.* xv. 11 τὸ ἐκπορευόμενον ἐκ τοῦ στόματος, τοῦτο κοινοῖ τὸν ἄνθρωπον, 1 Pet. iii. 10, Prov. vi. 2 παγὶς ἰσχυρὰ ἀνδρὶ τὰ ἴδια χείλη, xv. 4, ἴασις γλώσσης δένδρον ζωῆς, Sirac. xiv. 1 μακάριος ἀνὴρ ὃς οὐκ ὠλίσθησεν ἐν στόματι αὐτοῦ, *ib.* xix. 16, xxv. 8, xxviii. 12–26, Philo M. 1. 615 τὸ μὲν οὖν ἄριστον καὶ τελεώτατον τοῦτ' ἔστιν, μηδὲ ἐνθυμοῦσθαί τι τῶν ἀτοπωτάτων κ.τ.λ., *ib.* 695 τοῦ δὲ σοφοῦ ἴδιον τοῖς ὑπὲρ ἡδονῆς καὶ ἐπιθυμίας λόγοις ὑπαντιάσαι ἐπὶ τοῦ στόματος καὶ τῆς γλώσσης, ἅπερ ἦν ὄργανα λόγου. παγίως γὰρ ἐπιβὰς αὐτοῖς δυνήσεται τὰς συνηγορούσας τῷ πάθει πιθανότητας ἀνατρέψαι.

οὗτος τέλειος ἀνήρ.] οὗτος marks the apodosis as in i. 23. For ἀνήρ see above i. 8; for τέλειος i. 4.

χαλιναγωγῆσαι.] See on i. 26, and cf. Philo M. 1. p. 196 (the true man within each) ἐπιστομίζων ταῖς τοῦ συνειδότος ἡνίαις τὸν αὐθάδη καὶ μετὰ ἀφηνιασμοῦ δρόμον γλώττης ἐπέσχεν, *ib.* p. 314.

καὶ ὅλον τὸ σῶμα.] Repeated in vv. 3 and 6. The figure of χαλ. is further carried out: by the bridle in the mouth we turn the horse as we will, so by controlling our words we can regulate our whole activity. We find the opposition of one member to the whole body, Matt. v. 29

3. **ἴδε γάρ.**] WH. with R.V. and all the recent editors (except Hofmann and Bassett, who keep ἴδε) read εἰ δέ. The evidence is as follows: AB with some inferior MSS. read ΕΙΔΕ, Vulg. and Corb. *si autem;* Sin. ΕΙΔΕ ΓΑΡ, (Sin.[3] omits γάρ), Pesh. *ecce enim;* Cod. Ephr. with many inferior MSS. and Theophyl. and Euth. Zig. in comment ΙΔΕ, Egyptian, Ethiopian and later Syriac versions *ecce.* The confusion between ει and ι being extremely common,[1] it is important to observe (1) that the insertion of γὰρ in Sin. seems to show that the preceding ειδε must be taken as an imperative (so B. Weiss, p. 34 'das eingeschaltete γαρ zeigt dass ιδε gemeint ist'); (2) that this view is

[1] Field compares Rom. ii. 17, where the old reading ἴδε σὺ Ἰουδαῖος has been changed to εἰ δέ by late editors, misled by the spelling of the majority of the uncial MSS., as in our text, and with equally disastrous effect on the construction. He points out that Sin. has εἴδου for ἴδου in Luke xxiii. 15, εἴδετε for ἴδετε Luke xxiv. 39, 1 John iii. 1. Below v. 11 the MSS. are nearly equally divided between ἴδετε and εἴδετε. In Luke vi. 3 Cod. D has εἴδε for ἴδε. These variations not being given in Bruder can only be ascertained by examining the MSS. In Epictetus, where ἴδε

supported by some of the oldest versions; (3) that as regards B in particular, since it 'shows a remarkable inclination to change ι into ει' (WH. *Introduction*, p. 306), its evidence here is of little weight.[1] We have therefore to fall back on other considerations: and it is plain that εἰ δὲ is not suited to the context. 'If a man does not stumble in word he is able to bridle his whole body. And if we put the bits into the horses' mouths that they may obey us,—we turn about their whole body also.' The natural apodosis to such a protasis would be 'let us also for the same purpose put a bridle in our own lips.' The present apodosis adds nothing to the clause εἰς τὸ πείθεσθαι, and it is difficult to find any natural meaning for δέ at the beginning of the verse: even the καί in apodosis is out of place; it would have been natural if the protasis had run εἰ τὸ στόμα μετάγομεν. Lastly, the καί after ἰδού in ver. 4 seems to look back to the preceding ἴδε. De Wette and Beyschlag felt these difficulties so strongly that they included the whole verse in the protasis and explained the construction as an aposiopesis. Thus the latter translates 'Wenn wir aber den Pferden die Zügel in die Mäuler legen um sie gehorsam zu machen, und so ihren ganzen Leib regieren, so sollten wir es doch auch uns selbst thun, d.h. auch unserer Zunge einen Zügel anlegen und so unseres ganzen Leibes sittlich mächtig werden'; and refers, for examples of aposiopesis after εἰ, to Luke xix. 42, Acts xxiii. 9, Mark vii. 11, which however are very unlike the present. In fact such an aposiopesis is simply impossible here, and in any case is opposed to the style of the writer: it is only suggested as a last resource by editors who felt themselves bound to this reading on the mistaken view of the overwhelming evidence in its favour, and in obedience to the hazardous maxim that the more difficult reading is always to be preferred. No doubt a copyist will avoid, if he can, a difficulty which stares him in the face; but as long as a protasis has an apodosis of any sort to follow, it is a matter of indifference to the copyist whether it adds anything new or merely repeats what is already included in the protasis. Spitta, recognising the confusion of thought and construction, explains this to his own satisfaction, by supposing that the writer was tempted to borrow the second comparison of the ship, and was in too great a hurry to adapt it to the context. Lachmann proposed to read οὐδέ with a question instead of εἰ δέ.

Hi motus animorum atque haec certamina tanta are set at rest by the application of a little common sense to the study of the MSS., if we will but make due allowance for the principle of *itacism*. Ἴδε γὰρ having been written ειδεγαρ (Sin.) and ειδε being read as two words, it was inevitable that the superfluous γὰρ should be dropped (as in B).[2] With ἴδε γὰρ we get exactly the right meaning expressed with

occurs only four times, in two instances the MS. has εἴδε (*Diss.* ii. 11. 13, iii. 16. 11). The Gizeh fragment of Enoch has ειδετε for ἴδετε ii. 2, iii. 3, ειδητε for ἴδητε xiv. 6, ε:δειν for ἰδεῖν xiv. 21.

[1] In this epistle B gives ει not only for long ι, as γεινώσκοντες, θλείψει, ῥειπιζομένῳ, εἰδός, but occasionally for short ι, as ἀνθρωπείνῃ, ἀτμείς. So C has σοφείας i. 5.

[2] In my former edition I read ἴδε simply with C, but this does not account for the insertion of γὰρ in Sin., and I now think that C emends the text of B.

the writer's usual animation. The casual use of the word χαλ. suggests the image to which he calls his readers' attention (so ἰδού introduces a simile in ver. 7). 'Lo! in horses we use the bit for the purpose of making them obey and thus control their whole body.' The less common active imperative is found along with the middle in Eccles. ii. 1 δεῦρο δὴ πειράσω σε ἐν εὐφροσύνῃ καὶ ἴδε ἐν ἀγαθῷ· καὶ ἰδοὺ καί γε τοῦτο ματαιότης, Mark iii. 32 and 34, ἰδοὺ ἡ μήτηρ σου...ἴδε ἡ μήτηρ μου, Matt. xxv. 6 and 22, xxvi. 51 and 66, John xvi. 29 and 32, Gal. ἴδε v. 2, ἰδού i. 20: St. Luke always uses ἰδού. The difference between them is well given by Donaldson (in Winer, p. 319): 'the middle often exhibits a signification which might be called *intensive*, but which really implies an immediate reference to some result in which the agent is interested. One of the commonest cases is that of the aorists ἰδεῖν and ἰδέσθαι, of which the former means simply "to see," the latter "to behold, to look with interest" . . . for this reason ἰδού is more frequently used than ἴδε in calling attention to something worth seeing.' So here ἴδε is 'lo!' ἰδού 'behold,' the latter calling attention to various particulars about the ship. Cf. a similar change below iv. 3 from αἰτεῖσθαι to αἰτεῖν.

τῶν ἵππων.] The gen. is here put in an emphatic place to mark the comparison. It belongs both to χαλινούς and to στόματα, probably more to the former as distinguishing it from the human bridle, so we have ἄχρι τῶν χαλινῶν τῶν ἵππων Apoc. xiv. 20, ἐπὶ τὸν χαλινὸν τοῦ ἵππου Zech. xiv. 20. Compare Psa. xxxii. 9.

βάλλομεν.] Mild force, as in ἐκβάλλω above ii. 25, cf. Ael. *V.H.* ix. 16 ἵππῳ ἐμβάλλειν χ., Xen. *De re equest.* vi. 7, ix. 9.

εἰς τὸ πείθεσθαι αὐτοὺς ἡμῖν.] Cf. Xen. *Cyr.* iv. 3. 9 πείθεται ὁ ἵππος χαλινῷ, Soph. *Ant.* 483, Philo M. 1. p. 21. The subject of the infinitive is specified, as in i. 18 εἰς τὸ εἶναι ἡμᾶς ἀπαρχήν, iv. 2 διὰ τὸ μὴ αἰτεῖσθαι ὑμᾶς, iv. 15 ἀντὶ τοῦ λέγειν ὑμᾶς.

4. **ἰδού.**] Never followed by accusative in N.T. See below ver. 5, v. 4, 7, 9, 11, and compare ἄγε νῦν, ἴστε, ἀκούσατε.

καὶ τὰ πλοῖα.] For this comparison see Arist. *Mechan.* 5 τὸ πηδάλιον μικρὸν ὂν καὶ ἐπ' ἐσχάτῳ τῷ πλοίῳ τοσαύτην δύναμιν ἔχει ὥστε ὑπὸ μικροῦ οἴακος καὶ ἑνὸς ἀνθρώπου δυνάμεως καὶ ταύτης ἠρεμαίας μεγάλα κινεῖσθαι μεγέθη πλοίων, Lucr. iv. 900, 4 Macc. vii. 1–3. The two figures are united Plut. *Mor.* p. 33 F, Philo M. 1, p. 131 ἐπειδὰν ὁ τῆς ψυχῆς ἡνίοχος ἢ κυβερνήτης ὁ νοῦς ἄρχῃ τοῦ ζώου ὅλου...εὐθύνεται ὁ βίος, *ib.* p. 311 ὁ ἱππεὺς φέρεσθαι δοκῶν αὐτὸς ἄγει τὸ κομίζον τρόπον κυβερνήτου, *ib.* 2. p. 521, Stob. *Flor.* p. 280 Mein. (a saying of Aristippus) κρατεῖ ἡδονῆς... ὥσπερ καὶ νεὼς καὶ ἵππου οὐχ ὁ μὴ χρώμενος, ἀλλ' ὁ μετάγων ὅποι βούλεται, Theoph. Simoc. *Ep.* 70 (Didot's *Epistolographi*, p. 783) ἡνίαις καὶ μάστιξι τοὺς ἵππους ἰθύνομεν, καὶ ναυτιλλόμεθα πῇ μὲν τοῖς ἱστίοις τὴν ναῦν ἐκπετάσαντες, πῇ δὲ ταῖς ἀγκύραις ταύτην χαλινώσαντες καθορμίζομεν· οὕτω κυβερνητέον καὶ τὴν γλῶτταν, Ἀξίοχε.

τηλικαῦτα.] Used elsewhere in N.T. only in 2 Cor. i. 10, Heb. ii. 3, Apoc. xvi. 18.

ὑπὸ ἀνέμων σκληρῶν ἐλαυνόμενα.] Cf. Matt. xi. 7 (Luke vii. 24) κάλαμον ὑπὸ ἀνέμου σαλευόμενον, *ib.* xiv. 24 πλοῖον βασανιζόμενον ὑπὸ τῶν κυμάτων, 2 Pet. ii. 17 ὁμίχλαι ὑπὸ λαίλαπος ἐλαυνόμεναι, Jude 12 νεφέλαι ὑπὸ ἀνέμων παραφερόμεναι, Apoc. vi. 13 συκῆ ὑπὸ ἀνέμου σειομένη, Dio. Chr. iii. p. 44 C κλύδωνος ὑπὸ ἀνέμων σκληρῶν μεταβαλλομένου, Ael. *V.H.* ix. 14 μὴ ἀνατρέπηται ὑπὸ τῶν ἀνέμων εἴ ποτε σκληροὶ κατέπνεον, Plato *Phaedo* 84 B ὑπὸ τῶν ἀνέμων διαφυσηθεῖσα ἡ ψυχή, Arist. *Anima* i. 5, 15 ψυχὴ φερομένη ὑπὸ τῶν ἀνέμων. The very frequent use of ὑπὸ before ἀνέμου and similar words suggests that here it retains something of its local force, not simply 'by,' but 'under.' Otherwise it is rarely used in the sense of 'by' with things, as below ὑπὸ πηδαλίου and v. 7, Luke viii. 14 ὑπὸ μεριμνῶν καὶ πλούτου...συμπνίγονται, 2 Pet. ii. 7 Λὼτ καταπονούμενον ὑπὸ τῆς τῶν ἀθέσμων διαστροφῆς. In i. 14 ὑπὸ τῆς ἐπιθυμίας, and ii. 9 ὑπὸ τοῦ νόμου, it is probably due to personification, as also in Col. ii. 18 φυσιούμενος ὑπὸ τοῦ νοὸς τῆς σαρκὸς αὐτοῦ. On its use in the Attic orators see Marchant in *Classical Review*, vol. iii. pp. 250, 438. For σκληρός contrasted with μαλακός compare our 'stiff breeze,' and see Prov. xxvii. 16 Βορέας σκληρὸς ἄνεμος, and passages cited above from Aelian and Dio Chrys.

πηδαλίου.] Only used elsewhere in N.T. in Acts xxvii. 40. For ἐλαχίστου (= very small) cf. Wisd. xiv. 5 ἐλαχίστῳ ξύλῳ πιστεύουσιν ἄνθρωποι ψυχὰς καὶ διελθόντες κλύδωνα σχεδίᾳ διεσώθησαν, Herm. *Mand.* xi. 20 ἡ χάλαζα ἐλάχιστόν ἐστι κοκκάριον, *Sim.* viii. 10 ἐλάχιστον ἥμαρτον, 1 Cor. iv. 3 εἰς ἐλάχιστόν ἐστι.

ὅπου.] Here for ὅπῃ 'in whichever direction,' as often for ὅποι (cf. John viii. 22 ὅπου ἐγὼ ὑπάγω), neither of these latter forms being found in N.T. or LXX. Similarly ἐκεῖ and ποῦ are found for ἐκεῖσε and ποῖ, like the English 'where' and 'here' for 'whither' and 'hither.' Even in classical writers we find ὅπου for ὅποι, as in Xen. *Mem.* i. 6. 6 βαδίζοντα ὅπου ἂν βούλωμαι. Cf. Winer, p. 592.

ἡ ὁρμὴ τοῦ εὐθύνοντος βούλεται.] 'The pressure (touch) of the steersman decides.' The word ὁρμή is used of the origin of motion either moral or physical. In N.T. it only occurs here and Acts xiv. 5 (of a rush or onset of the people); so LXX. Prov. iii. 25 οὐ φοβηθήσῃ ὁρμὰς ἀσεβῶν ἐπερχομένας, *ib.* xxi. 1 ὁρμὴ ὕδατος 'the rush of water': cf. the erroneous comment on this passage in Euth. Zig. and the Catena, πηδαλίῳ μικρῷ ὁρμὴν πλοίου μεταφέρομεν. It appears here to mean the slight pressure of the hand on the tiller, what Apuleius, speaking (*Flor.* 1. 2) of the eagle's flight, calls *nutus clemens laevorsum vel dextrorsum.* So Schegg, Erdmann, Theile, Wiesinger, Hofmann: on the other hand Calvin, Gebser, Beyschlag, Brückner, Alford understand ὁρμή metaphorically of an inclination of the mind (R.V. 'whither the impulse of the steersman willeth,' as in 1 Pet. iii. 17, 'if the will of God should so will' εἰ θέλοι τὸ θέλημα τοῦ θεοῦ). As βούλομαι cannot be used properly of a mere irrational impulse or whim any more than of muscular pressure, it seems to me less confusing to understand it of the latter: see above n. on i. 18, and (for the tropical use of βούλομαι) compare Plato *Symp.* 184 A τούτους βούλεται ὁ ἡμέτερος νόμος βασανίζειν, and its technical meaning in Arist. *Eth.* iii. 2 τὸ ἀκούσιον βούλεται λέγεσθαι οὐκ εἴ τις ἀγνοεῖ κ.τ.λ., *Top.* i. 7. p. 103 ταῦτα γὰρ πάντα τὸ ἓν βούλεται σημαίνειν. Similarly θέλω John ii. 8 τὸ πνεῦμα ὅπου θέλει πνεῖ,

Plato *Phaedr.* 230 D τὰ μὲν οὖν χωρία καὶ τὰ δένδρα οὐδέν με θέλει διδάσκειν, *Rep.* ii. 370 οὐκ ἐθέλει τὸ πραττόμενον τὴν τοῦ πράττοντος σχολὴν περιμένειν. For εὐθύν. cf. Philo M. 1. p. 422 φιλεῖ γὰρ ἔστιν ὅτε χωρὶς ἡνιόχων τε καὶ κυβερνητῶν ὅ τε πλοῦς καὶ ὁ δρόμος εὐθύνεσθαι, Eurip. *Cycl.* 15 ἐν πρύμνῃ δ' ἄκρᾳ αὐτὸς λαβὼν ηὔθυνον ἀμφῆρες δόρυ, Aesch. *Suppl.* 717 οἴαξ εὐθυντήρ.

5. **ἡ γλῶσσα μικρὸν μέλος.**] This comparison is quite in the Jewish proverbial style. The horse's mouth is small in comparison to the body, yet through it the whole body is directed; the rudder is small in comparison to the ship; the tongue small in comparison to the man; yet control this small member and you control the whole nature. This however is only the allegorical outside; by the smallness of the tongue is meant the insignificance, as we deem it, of speech in comparison with action; yet by controlling speech we acquire the power of controlling action. For the metonomy by which an independent personality seems to be attributed to the tongue, so that it stands for the temptations or sins which are concerned with the use of the tongue, though, as Augustine says (*Serm.* 17 cited by Corn. a Lapide), *ream linguam non facit nisi mens rea*, compare Matt. v. 29, 30 'if thine eye...thy right hand, cause thee to stumble'; Matt. xv. 19 'the things that come out of the mouth defile a man'; 1 John ii. 16 'the lust of the eyes.'

μεγάλα αὐχεῖ.] 'Vaunts great things.' There is no idea of vain boasting: the whole argument turns upon the reality of the power which the tongue possesses. Whether written as two words with AB, or as one (μεγαλαυχεῖ) with Sin. K L, &c., the phrase occurs nowhere else in N.T., but is found in Ezek. xvi. 50, Zeph. iii. 12 (A.V. 'to be haughty'), Sir. xlviii. 18, 2 Macc. xv. 32, cf. Ps. xii. 3 γλῶσσα μεγαλορρήμων. It may be compared with the Homeric εὔχομαι εἶναι and with Philo M. 1. p. 338 μεγάλης ψυχῆς τὸ αὔχημα γένεσιν ὑπερκύπτειν, *ib.* 158 τὸ δουλεύειν Θεῷ μέγιστον αὔχημα, *ib.* M. 2. 235 ἐγκράτεια δὲ καθαρὰ καὶ ἀκηλίδωτος ἀρετὴ, πάντων ὅσα πρὸς βρῶσιν καὶ πόσιν ἀλογοῦσα, καὶ ἐπάνω τῶν γαστρὸς ἡδονῶν αὐχοῦσα ἵστασθαι, βωμῶν ψανέτω. Observe the use of alliteration in μ to point the contrast of μικρὸν μέλος μεγάλα αὐχεῖ, and compare that in δ below ver. 8.

ἡλίκον πῦρ ἡλίκην ὕλην ἀνάπτει.] 'How small a fire kindles how large a forest,' cf. Philo M. 1. p. 455 σπινθὴρ καὶ ὁ βραχύτατος ὅταν καταπνευσθεὶς ζωπυρηθῇ μεγάλην ἐξάπτει πυράν, Phocyl. 144 ἐξ ὀλίγου σπινθῆρος ἀθέσφατος αἴθεται ὕλη. For the double question compare Mark xv. 24 βάλλοντες κλῆρον τίς τί ἄρῃ, and Luke xix. 15, Isocr. p. 240 οὐκ ἀγνοῶ ἡλίκος ὢν ('how old,' viz. 94) ὅσον ἔργον ἐνίσταμαι, Plato *Rep.* 4, p. 423 B ἡλίκῃ οὔσῃ (πόλει) ὅσην χώραν ἀφορισαμένους ἐᾶν (δεῖ), Soph. *Ant.* 933 οἷα πρὸς οἵων ἀνδρῶν πάσχω, Krueger *Gr.* 51. 14. 1, *ib.* § 17. 10, Seneca *Controv. Exc.* v. 5 *nesciebas quam levibus ignibus quanta incendia oriantur*, and Milton *P.L.* i. 91 'Into what pit thou seest from what height fallen.' There is no force in the objection that this interpretation gives opposite senses to the same word in the same sentence. Literally it is 'what (what-sized) a fire kindles what a forest,' but the context interprets the meaning of 'what' in either case. In Lucian *Hermot.*

5 ἡλίκους ἡμᾶς ἀποφαίνεις, οὐδὲ κατὰ τοὺς πυγμαίους ἐκείνους ἀλλὰ χαμαιπετεῖς παντάπασιν, the context shows the meaning to be 'how small': so in Epict. *Diss.* I. 12. 26 ἡλίκον μέρος πρὸς τὰ ὅλα. The reference to a burning forest is common both in the Bible, as Ps. lxxxiii. 14 ὡσεὶ πῦρ ὃ διαφλέξει δρυμόν, ὡσεὶ φλὸξ κατακαῦσαι ὄρη, Isa. ix. 18, x. 17, 18, Zech. xii. 6; and elsewhere, as Hom. *Il.* 455 πῦρ ἀΐδηλον ἐπιφλέγει ἄσπετον ὕλην οὔρεος ἐκ κορυφῆς, Thuc. ii. 77, Pind. *Pyth.* iii. 66, Eur. *Ino* fr. 415 D. μικροῦ γὰρ ἐκ λαμπτῆρος Ἰδαῖον λέπας πρήσειεν ἄν τις, †καὶ πρὸς ἄνδρ' εἰπὼν ἕνα† πύθοιντ' ἂν ἀστοὶ πάντες ἃ κρύπτειν χρεών, Philo M. 2. p. 208 ἡ ἐπιθυμία οἷα φλὸξ ἐν ὕλῃ νέμεται δαπανῶσα πάντα καὶ φθείρουσα, *ib.* 143, 349, M. 1. p. 671. The only other place in which ἀνάπτει occurs in N.T. is Luke xii. 49.[1]

6. **ἡ γλῶσσα πῦρ.**] Prov. xvi. 27 (ἀνὴρ ἄφρων) ἐπὶ τῶν ἑαυτοῦ χειλέων θησαυρίζει πῦρ, *ib.* xxvi. 18–22, Sir. xxviii. 11 ἔρις κατασπευδομένη ἐκκαίει πῦρ, *ib.* v. 22 οὐ μὴ κρατήσῃ εὐσεβῶν (ἡ γλῶσσα) καὶ ἐν τῇ φλογὶ αὐτῆς οὐ καήσονται, so some explain Psa. cxx. 4. On the other hand inspiration from above is also symbolized by fire Acts ii. 3, Isa. vi. 6, Jer. v. 14. I cannot see why Spitta objects to the καὶ before ἡ γλῶσσα. Just before, the writer had illustrated the thought of the great effect produced by the tongue, though itself so small, by the comparison of a forest kindled by a chance spark. This suggests another aspect of the tongue. It resembles fire in the points which he proceeds to mention. S. would also omit ἡ γλῶσσα πῦρ and ὁ κόσμος τῆς ἀδικίας as marginal summaries, the former of vv. 6–12, the latter of vv. 13–iv. 3. Nor is even this enough to satisfy his rage for expurgation. The clause ἡ (or καὶ) σπιλοῦσα ὅλον τὸ σῶμα is due to the same copyist who added to the text the marginal summaries.

ὁ κόσμος τῆς ἀδικίας ἡ γλῶσσα καθίσταται ἐν τοῖς μέλεσιν ἡμῶν.] The first point to be determined in this difficult verse is whether we should put our stop after πῦρ with the R.V., WH., Neander, Lange, Hofmann, Erdmann, Beyschlag; or after ἀδικίας with the margin, Alf., Huther, Schegg and the generality of editors. It seems to me that the former gives the only tenable construction. The sense may be difficult, but the grammar is clear, if we take ἡ γλῶσσα as subject to καθίσταται, with the attributive clause ἡ σπιλοῦσα—γεέννης, and make ὁ κόσμος τῆς ἀδικίας the predicate or complement. With the other punctuation ἡ σπιλοῦσα becomes the predicate, but there is no justification for the article: either we should have καθίσταται σπιλοῦσα or καθίσταται τὸ σπιλοῦν (μέλος): and in either case καθίσταται loses its proper force. The predicate is put first for emphasis, as in John i. 1 Θεὸς ἦν ὁ Λόγος, *ib.* iv. 24 πνεῦμα ὁ Θεός, 2 Pet. ii. 17 ὁ υἱός μου ὁ ἀγαπητός μου οὗτός ἐστιν, Luke iv. 41 τὸν Χριστὸν αὐτὸν εἶναι, see Winer, p. 689 *f.* As κόσμος is defined by the genitive τῆς ἀδικίας, it necessarily keeps the article in the predicate, cf. Apoc. xix. 13 κέκληται τὸ ὄνομα αὐτοῦ ὁ Λόγος τοῦ Θεοῦ, 1 Cor. xi. 3 παντὸς ἀνδρὸς ἡ κεφαλὴ ὁ Χριστός ἐστιν, Winer, p. 141. The fact that the subject ἡ γλῶσσα is repeated from the preceding clause of course

[1] [On fires kindled by the tongue see Midr. Rabb. on Levit. (xiv. 2) xvi. where the words are almost the same as those in St. James, *quanta incendia lingua excitat!* and Schoettgen p. 1021. C.T.]

facilitates the transposition of the predicate. We may suppose that the form of the sentence as it first occurred to the writer was ἡ γλῶσσα πῦρ, ὁ κόσμος τῆς ἀδικίας: and that for the sake of clearness he added the remaining words.

The next difficulty is the meaning of κόσμος here. Isidore of Pelusium (*fl.* 400 A.D.), followed by the Greek commentators, mentions two meanings (1) 'ornament,' ἐγκαλλώπισμα δοκεῖ τῆς ἀδικίας, because the tongue κοσμεῖ τὴν ἀδικίαν διὰ τῆς τῶν ῥητόρων εὐγλώττου δεινότητος: so Elsner, Wetstein, Semler, Storr, Ewald, and others; (2) 'the wicked world': at least this seems to be intended by the somewhat obscure expressions πῦρ ἐστι, πλῆθος ἀδίκως κατακαίουσα, and κόσμος ἐστὶ τῆς ἀδικίας, οἱονεὶ πρὸς τὸν συρφετώδη ὄχλον καὶ δημώδη ἐκφερομένη καὶ βλέπουσα, with which apparently should be connected the sentence just below, ταύτῃ γὰρ ἀλλήλοις κοινωνοῦμεν τῶν ἑαυτῶν νοημάτων. The majority however of modern commentators follow the Vulgate '*universitas iniquitatis*' (3), thus explained by Bede, '*Quia cuncta fere facinora per eam aut concinnantur . . . aut patrantur . . . aut defenduntur.*' So Erasmus, Calvin, Corn. à Lapide, Schneckenburger, Kern, De Wette, Wiesinger, Alford, Beyschlag, Erdmann. The objection to (3) is, that St. James elsewhere only uses the word κόσμος in a bad sense (i. 27 ἄσπιλον ἑαυτὸν τηρεῖν ἀπὸ τοῦ κόσμου, ii. 5, iv. 4 ἡ φιλία τοῦ κόσμου ἔχθρα τοῦ Θεοῦ ἐστίν); that only one example in all Greek literature is adduced for the meaning 'totality,' viz. Prov. xvii. 6 τοῦ πιστοῦ ὅλος ὁ κόσμος τῶν χρημάτων, τοῦ δὲ ἀπίστου οὐδὲ ὀβολός, if indeed this should not be rather understood literally of the inanimate world, as consisting of things which can be used and enjoyed. Lastly, the article seems scarcely consistent with this interpretation. 'A world of cares' is a natural expression for many cares; but if we say 'the world of care,' we are understood to predicate something about the world itself. Schegg's interpretation, 'the sphere or domain of iniquity,' is, I think, an improvement on (3) as far as sense goes, but it is not the natural meaning of κόσμος. The objections stated above are also applicable in part to (1). It is moreover a very harsh expression to call the tongue 'the ornament of injustice' because it is capable of being used to give a colour to injustice; and it falls flatly after the stronger word 'fire.'

Putting aside the commentators, if we read the words simply we can hardly fail to be reminded of the similar expressions in Luke xvi. 8, 9 τὸν οἰκονόμον τῆς ἀδικίας, τοῦ μαμωνᾶ τῆς ἀδικίας, where τῆς ἀδικίας is qualitative, as is shown by the parallel expression in ver. 11, τῷ ἀδίκῳ μαμωνᾷ (cf. i. 17 above). So Enoch 48. 7 'He preserveth the lot of the righteous, because they have hated this *world of unrighteousness.*' C.T. compares Jerome *Pelag.* II. 6 *seculum illud iniquitatis.* The meaning of the phrase will then be 'in our microcosm the tongue represents or constitutes the unrighteous world' which is probably the meaning of the version in the Speculum, *mundus iniquitatis per linguam constat in membris vestris:* cf. 1 John v. 19 ὁ κόσμος ὅλος ἐν τῷ πονηρῷ κεῖται, and below iv. 4.[1] In the same way it might be said

[1] [I think the force of the expression is better brought out if we explain τ. ἀδικίας as a possessive genitive, 'the world which is under the dominion of unrighteousness,'

ἡ ἐπιθυμία τῆς σαρκὸς ὁ γαστὴρ καθίσταται ἐν τοῖς μέλεσιν. The tongue represents the world, because it is that member by which we are brought into communication with other men; it is the organ of society, the chief channel of temptation from man to man. Here it is described as ἡ σπιλοῦσα τὸ σῶμα, but in i. 27 this is said to be the effect of the world; true religion is shown by keeping oneself ἄσπιλον ἀπὸ τοῦ κόσμου. Olshausen, Stier, and Lange give this meaning to the passage, and I think it is hinted at by the Greek commentators. Dr. Taylor has pointed out (*J. of Phil.* xviii. p. 320) that, in place of the phrase ἡ γλῶσσα, ὁ κόσμος τῆς ἀδικίας, Hermas uses ἡ πονηρὰ ἐπιθυμία in *Mand.* xii. 1 μισήσεις τὴν πονηρὰν ἐπιθυμίαν καὶ χαλιναγωγήσεις αὐτὴν καθὼς βούλει (cf. above ver. 4, ὅπου ἡ ὁρμὴ τοῦ εὐθύνοντος βούλεται), ἀγρία γάρ ἐστιν ἡ ἐπιθυμία ἡ πονηρὰ καὶ δυσκόλως ἡμεροῦται (cf. below ver. 8, οὐδεὶς δαμάσαι δύναται). Again, *Vis.* ii. 2, he uses the phrase οὐκ ἀπέχεται τῆς γλώσσης ἐν ᾗ πονηρεύεται.

Dr. Taylor further illustrates the text, if understood in the sense *universitas inquitatis*, from T. B. Berachoth 15b, 'Life and death are in the hand of the tongue. Has the tongue a hand? No, but as the hand kills, so the tongue. The hand kills only at close quarters: the tongue is called an arrow as killing at a distance. An arrow kills at forty or fifty paces: but of the tongue it is said (Psa. lxiii. 9) "they have set their mouth in heaven and their tongue goeth through the earth." It ranges over the whole earth and reaches to heaven.'

It may be worth while to mention that the Peshitto, followed by Morus, Bassett and others, takes κόσμος τῆς ἀδικίας independently of ἡ γλῶσσα, and supplies ὕλη as subject: 'the tongue is the fire, the world of wickedness the forest' (which it consumes). It is possible that there was an old gloss ὕλη intended to explain a difficulty; but it is inconsistent with the general thought: the tongue sets on fire the τροχὸς γενέσεως not the κόσμος τῆς ἀδικίας, and it has been already shown that to put the stop after ἀδικίας gives an impossible construction for the following clause.

The word καθίσταται literally means 'is set,' 'is constituted.'[1] It is opposed to ὑπάρχω, because it implies a sort of adaptation or development as contrasted with the natural or original state; to γίνομαι, because it implies something of fixity. So in iv. 4 ὃς ἐὰν βουληθῇ φίλος εἶναι τοῦ κόσμου, ἐχθρὸς τοῦ Θεοῦ καθίσταται, 'Whoever will be a friend of the world thereby becomes (is constituted) an enemy of God.' Cf. Thuc. iv. 92 πρὸς τοὺς ἀστυγείτονας πᾶσι τὸ ἀντίπαλον κα.

i.e. the world as converted by our diseased imaginations into an opaque looking-glass for selfishness, instead of a window for the view of God. Compare Rom. vi. 16 τὸ σῶμα τῆς ἀδικίας.—A.]

[1] That it is passive and not middle may be inferred from the fact that out of the twenty-two instances in Bruder, while sixteen belong to the active voice and two are 1st aor. pass., there are only four examples of the ambiguous form καθίσταται, two of which are those cited above from this epistle, and the other two (Heb. v. 1 πᾶς ἀρχιερεὺς ἐξ ἀνθρώπων λαμβανόμενος ὑπὲρ ἀνθρώπων καθίσταται, 'is ordained for men' [A. V.], and viii. 3) are undoubtedly passive. Westcott compares Philo M. 2, p. 151, τῷ μέλλοντι ἱερεῖ καθίστασθαι. In this passage the Vulgate has *constituitur*, Corbey *posita est*.

ἐλεύθερον καθίσταται 'equality constitutes freedom,' Isocr. p. 37 οἱ μεγίστας ἐπ' ἀρετῇ δόχας ἔχοντες πλείστων δεσπόται καθίστανται. For ἐν τοῖς μέλεσιν cf. iv. 1 below.

ἡ σπιλοῦσα ὅλον τὸ σῶμα.] Of course an attribute of ἡ γλῶσσα. See above i. 27, Jude 23 μισοῦντες τὸν ἀπὸ τῆς σαρκὸς ἐσπιλωμένον χιτῶνα, 2 Pet. ii. 13 σπῖλοι καὶ μῶμοι, Test. Aser. p. 690 Fabr. ὁ πλεονεκτῶν τὴν ψυχὴν σπιλοῖ. For the thought cf. Matt. xv. 11 τὸ ἐκπορευόμενον ἐκ τοῦ στόματος τοῦτο κοινοῖ τὸν ἄνθρωπον. The phrase ὅλ. τ. σῶμα occurs above vers. 2 and 3.

φλογίζουσα.] Here only in N.T. Psa. xcvi. 3 πῦρ φλογιεῖ τοὺς ἐχθρούς, Wisd. iii. 28 πῦρ φλογιζόμενον ἀποσβέσει ὕδωρ, Exod. ix. 24.

τὸν τροχὸν τῆς γενέσεως.] In this extremely difficult expression it seems better to read τροχόν 'wheel' than τρόχον 'course' (for which δρόμος is the word used in the N.T. and LXX.), as the former alone supplies a natural figure in the wheel which, catching fire from the glowing axle, is compared to the wide-spreading mischief done by the tongue. Heisen cites Achmet *Oneirocritica* 160 (8th cent. A.D.) εἰ δὲ ἴδῃ ὅτι ἤλαυνεν ἐν τῷ διφρῷ καὶ οἱ τροχοὶ ἐφλογίσθησαν ἐκ τῆς ἐλάσεως, εὑρήσει νόσον ἀναλόγως τῆς φλογώσεως.[1] A consideration of the context will exclude some of the explanations which have been offered. The clause is evidently meant to be distinct from and stronger than that which precedes: it cannot therefore be anything confined to the individual. This forbids any reference to Eccles. xii. 6 συντροχάσῃ ὁ τροχὸς ἐπὶ τὸν λάκκον, or to physiological phrases, such as we find in Galen *Hipp. et Platt.* 711 borrowed from Plat. *Tim.* 79 (the whole

[1] It may be worth while to compare other instances of the metaphorical use of τροχός. In Sibyl. ii. 87 (Phocyl. 27) we find κοινὰ πάθη πάντων· βίοτος τροχός· ἄστατος ὄλβος, Anacr. iv. 7 τροχὸς ἅρματος γὰρ οἷα, βίοτος τρέχει κυλισθείς. In both of these the point of the comparison seems that of fortune's wheel; that which is highest soon changes to lowest, and *vice versa;* so in Sil. Ital. vi. 120 *per varios praeceps casus rota volvitur aevi* and Boeth. *Cons.* 2. 2 *haec nostra vis est, hunc continuum ludum ludimus; rotam volubili orbe versamus, infima summis, summa infimis mutare gaudemus*, cf. Plut. *Numa* p. 69 *fin.*, Clem. Al. *Strom.* v. p. 672 P. on the emblematic wheel of the Egyptians. In Psa. lxxxiii. 13 ὁ Θεός μου θοῦ αὐτοὺς ὡς τροχόν, Isa. xvii. 13, *ib.* xxix. 5, it is used as an emblem of destruction 'make them as a wheel, a whirling thing': cf. Psa. lxxvii. 11 φωνὴ τῆς βροντῆς σου ἐν τῷ τροχῷ 'in the heaven' A.V. but Hitzig and others 'with a whirlwind.' In Sirac. xxxvi. 5 τροχὸς ἁμάξης σπλάγχνα μωροῦ καὶ ὡς ἄξων στρεφόμενος ὁ διαλογισμὸς αὐτοῦ Fritzsche understands the phrase of a constant going round and round in the same rut, making no advance. Hilgenfeld (*Zeitschr. f. wissensch. Theol.* 1873 p. 1 foll.) quotes from Lob. *Agl.* p. 799 passages from Orphic writers in which metempsychosis is styled κύκλος or τροχὸς γενέσεως, as Simplic. *de Caelo* ii. p. 91 (I have been unable to find this in the Berlin ed. of the Scholia), speaking of Ixion as a symbol of the soul, προσδέδεται ὑπὸ τοῦ Θεοῦ τῷ τῆς μοίρας τροχῷ καὶ τῆς γενέσεως, ὃν ἀδύνατον μεταλλάξαι κατ' Ὀρφέα κ.τ.λ., Proclus *in Tim.* v. 330 μία σωτηρία ψυχῆς τοῦ κύκλου τῆς γενέσεως ἀπαλλάττουσα καὶ τῆς πολλῆς πλάνης καὶ τῆς ἀνηνύτου ζωῆς ἡ πρὸς τὸ νοερὸν εἶδος ἀναδρομή, where also there is a reference to the Orphic poems. [The word τροχὸς in Psa. lxxvii. is the rendering of 'galgal', the rabbinic word for the celestial sphere, the plural of which is used for the several spheres concentric with the earth, in which the planets were supposed to be set. Thus τροχ. τ. γεν. might stand for 'the whole sphere of man's nature.' Then φλογίζω might be used with allusion to lightning as an all-pervading fire, see Psa. xxix. 7, xcvii. 4 Matt. xxiv. 27. We find τροχοί and πῦρ brought together in Dan. vii. 9. cf. Sib. Orac. II. 296 ἐκ ποταμοῦ μεγάλου πύρινος τροχὸς αὐτούς (ἀμφικαθέξει) 'an encircling fire.'—C.T.]

process of respiration) οἷον τροχοῦ περιαγομένου γίγνεται, which is afterwards alluded to as ἡ τοῦ τροχοῦ περιαγωγή. On the other hand it cannot be referred to the material world, of which Simplicius speaks (*Comm. in Epict. Ench.* p. 94 *b*) as τῷ ἀπεραντῷ τῆς γενέσεως κύκλῳ, διὰ τοῦτο ἐπ' ἄπειρον προϊόντι, διὰ τὸ τὴν ἄλλου φθορὰν ἄλλου γένεσιν εἶναι, which is merely another way of expressing the Heraclitean flux, ὁ τῆς γενέσεως ποταμὸς ἐνδελεχῶς ῥέων (Plut. *Mor.* p. 406). St. James speaking here of the tongue's power of mischief in its widest extent can only refer to the world of human life, the sphere of the worldly spirit, ὁ κόσμος, of which the tongue is the organ and representative in our body, and which is always at enmity with God (below iv. 4).

Turning now to the word γένεσις, the consideration of which was deferred on its first occurrence i. 23, it is used (1) of *birth* Matt. i. 18, Luke i. 14, so Gen. xl. 20 ἡμέρα γενέσεως 'birth-day,' *ib.* xxxi. 13 γῆ τῆς γενέσεως 'native land,' (2) of *creation* Gen. ii. 4 βίβλος γενέσεως οὐρανοῦ καὶ γῆς, Wisd. i. 14 σωτήριοι αἱ γενέσεις τοῦ κόσμου 'all God's creations are wholesome' refering to the absence of poisons in Paradise (see Grimm *in. loc.*). But it is in Philo we find the fully developed meaning (3) in which it stands for the seen and temporal as opposed to the unseen and eternal, e.g. M. 1. p. 569 τὰ πρὸς γένεσιν τῶν πρὸς Θεὸν μακρὰν ἀπέζευκται· τῇ μὲν γὰρ τὰ φανερὰ μόνα, τῷ δὲ καὶ ἀφανῆ γνώριμα, and a little below θεώμενος ὅσα ἐν γενέσει φθειρόμενα καὶ γεννώμενα, *ib.* 231 Θεοῦ μὲν ἴδιον ἠρεμία καὶ στάσις, γενέσεως δὲ μετάβασίς τε καὶ μεταβατικὴ πᾶσα κίνησις *ib.* 697 (those who claim for man the attributes of God) τὸ ἀκαθαίρετον τοῦ Θεοῦ κράτος γενέσει τῇ ἀκαταστάτως ἀπολλυμένῃ καὶ φθειρομένῃ περιάπτοντες, *ib.* 177 (as there are some who prefer the body to the soul, so there are some who) γένεσιν μᾶλλον Θεοῦ προτετιμήκασι, *ib.* 219 (unless God chastens us, we shall not be servants of Him who is merciful) γενέσεως δὲ τῆς ἀνηλεοῦς, *ib.* 261 τὴν μισάρετον καὶ φιλήδονον γένεσιν, *ib.* 608 Moses rebuked those who gave the first place γενέσει and only the second to God, *ib.* 538 μεγάλης ψυχῆς τὸ αὔχημα, γένεσιν ὑπερκύπτειν καὶ μόνου τοῦ ἀγεννήτου περιέχεσθαι, *ib.* 668 εὐσέβεια γενέσεως μέν ἐστιν ἀλλοτρία, Θεοῦ δὲ οἰκεία, *ib.* 251 ἡ ἀρετῆς φύσις μόνη τῶν ἐν γενέσει καλή τε καὶ ἀγαθή, *ib.* 486 τὸ ἀπιστῆσαι γενέσει τῇ πάντα ἐξ ἑαυτῆς ἀπίστῳ, μόνῳ δὲ πιστεῦσαι Θεῷ...μεγάλης καὶ Ὀλυμπίου διανοίας ἔργον ἐστίν (cf. p. 486), *ib.* 502 the Logos is the Mediator between γένεσις and God, *ib.* 497 the fourth commandment was given ἵνα τὴν ἀπραξίαν αὐτῆς (τῆς ἑβδομάδος) μελετῶσα γένεσις εἰς μνήμην τοῦ ἀοράτως πάντα δρῶντος ἔρχηται, *ib.* 477 τότε καιρὸς ἐντυγχάνειν γένεσιν τῷ πεποιηκότι ὅτε τὴν ἑαυτῆς οὐθένειαν ἔγνωκεν. I need not quote further to show that γένεσις is used not only of the inanimate creation but of the whole life of man upon earth. The idea is partly Jewish and partly Platonic, see Plat. *Rep.* viii. p. 525 B (Mathematics are useful to the philosopher) διὰ τὸ τῆς οὐσίας ἁπτέον εἶναι, γενέσεως ἐξαναδύντι, *Tim.* 29 λέγωμεν δι' ἥντινα αἰτίαν γένεσιν καὶ τὸ πᾶν τόδε ὁ ξυνιστὰς ξυνέστησεν, Plut. *Mor.* p. 593 D αἱ ἀπηλλαγμέναι γενέσεως ψυχαὶ δαίμονές εἰσιν, Philolaus *ap.* Stob. *Ecl.* 1. c. 22 φιλομετάβολος γένεσις, *ib.* c. 20.

How are we then to understand τροχός? We may keep close to the original meaning and suppose it to denote the incessant change of life 'which never continues in one stay,' though this is perhaps sufficiently implied by the word γένεσις; or we may suppose the metaphor borrowed not from the wheel in motion, but from the shape of the wheel at rest, the circle or sphere of this earthly life, meaning all that is contained in our life[1]; the tongue being the axle, the central fire from which the whole is kindled. This seems to make the better sense, though the other meaning gives more precise point to φλογίζουσα. Lucian's treatise *De Calumnia* will illustrate how it is that the tongue sets on fire 'the round of life,' cf. 1 (through calumny) καὶ οἶκοι ἀνάστατοι γεγόνασι καὶ πόλεις ἄρδην ἀπολώλασι, cf. Sirac. xxviii. 14 foll.[2] For other interpretations see Pott pp. 317–329, Heisen pp. 819–880.[3]

φλογιζομένη ὑπὸ τῆς γεέννης.] For the repetition of different parts of the same verb see above i. 13 ἀπείραστος—πειράζει, and below ver. 7 δαμάζεται—δεδάμασται. The name Gehenna (Γαιέννα) occurs only once in LXX. (Josh. xviii. 16), more commonly it is denoted as φάραγξ Ἐννόμ, see Wetstein i. p. 299, *D. of B.* under 'Gehenna' and 'Tophet.' It is found in Matt. v. 22 τὴν γεένναν τοῦ πυρός (where see Rabbinical quotations in Wetstein), *ib.* v. 29, x. 28, xviii. 9, xxiii. 15 υἱὸν γεέννης, ver. 33 κρίσις γεέννης, often in Orac. Sibyl. as i. 103, ii. 292, Acta Johannis T. p. 276, Pirke Aboth. i. 6 'the wicked inherit Gehenna,' *ib.* v. 29, 31. As οὐρανός stands for Θεός, so γεέννα for διάβολος, see below ver. 15 σοφία δαιμονιώδης, iv. 7, John viii. 44, 1 John iii. 8–10 ὁ ποιῶν τὴν ἁμαρτίαν ἐκ τοῦ διαβόλου ἐστίν, κ.τ.λ. Here we have the origin of sin carried back beyond the ἐπιθυμία of the individual man as shown above i. 14. Thus we have combined in this passage the three hostile principles, the world embodied in the tongue, the flesh in the members (iv. 1 as well as here) and Satan using both for his own purpose. Wetst. quotes from the Targum on Ps. cxx. (*lingua dolosa cum carbonibus juniperi*) *qui incensi sunt in Gehenna*, and other passages to the same effect. See Sir. li. 4–6 and below on ἀκατάστατον a quotation from Hermas.

7. **πᾶσα γάρ.**] Introduces the proof of the preceding statement by reverting to the original figure contained in the word χαλιναγωγεῖν. The fact that the tongue is the one thing which defies man's power to control it is a sign that there is something satanic in its bitterness.

φύσις.] Here used with a pleonastic force, like *natura* in Latin; see Plut. *Mor.* 1112 F, where κενοῦ φύσις is said to be the same as αὐτὸ

[1] This use of τροχός is illustrated by the Homeric phrases κηροῖο μέγαν τροχόν, *Od.* xii. 173, στέατος τροχόν, *ib.* xxi. 178, and by the concentric circles of land and water described in Plato's *Critias*, p. 113 foll. It agrees too, as appears from Dr. Taylor's note above, with the Rabbinical terminology.

[2] Mr. W. F. R. Shilleto compares Eur. *Andr.* 642, σμικρᾶς ἀπ' ἀρχῆς νεῖκος ἀνθρώποις μέγα γλῶσσ' ἐκπορίζει.

[3] It may be interesting to some readers if I give here the earliest extant commentary on this difficult phrase (Isid. Pel. ii. 158). The text is cited, probably from memory, in the form φλογίζουσα ὅλον τὸ σῶμα καὶ σπιλοῦσα τὸν τροχὸν τῆς ζωῆς and explained as follows: ὅτι τὸν τροχὸν τὸν χρόνον ἐκάλεσε διὰ τὸ τροχοειδὲς καὶ κυκλικὸν σχῆμα, εἰς ἑαυτὸν γὰρ ἀνελίττεται, is vouched for by the words of the psalmist, εὐλογήσεις τὸν στέφανον τοῦ ἐνιαυτοῦ τῆς χρηστότητός σου· κἀνταῦθα γὰρ ἀπὸ τοῦ κυκλικοῦ σχήματος στέφανος εἰκότως ὁ χρόνος ὠνόμασται.

τὸ κενὸν, and my n. on Cic. *N.D.* II. 136 *alvi natura.* If we are to translate it, it is best done by an adverb 'every kind of animal is *naturally* subject to man.' Brute nature under all its forms is under the control of human nature. It is also vaguer than πάντα τὰ θηρία and may be supposed to admit of individual exceptions.

θηρίων τε καὶ πετεινῶν ἑρπετῶν τε καὶ ἐναλίων.] The classification resembles that in Gen. i. 26, ix. 2 ὁ φόβος ὑμῶν ἔσται ἐπὶ πᾶσι τοῖς θηρίοις τῆς γῆς, ἐπὶ πάντα τὰ πετεινὰ τοῦ οὐρανοῦ καὶ ἐπὶ πάντα τὰ κινούμενα ἐπὶ τῆς γῆς καὶ ἐπὶ πάντας τοὺς ἰχθύας τῆς θαλάσσης, Deut. iv. 17, 18, Acts x. 12 τὰ τετράποδα τῆς γῆς καὶ τὰ ἑρπετὰ καὶ τὰ πετεινὰ τοῦ οὐρανοῦ, 1 Kings iv. 33 (Solomon) ἐλάλησε περὶ τῶν κτηνῶν καὶ περὶ τῶν πετεινῶν καὶ περὶ τῶν ἑρπετῶν καὶ περὶ τῶν ἰχθύων. So Philo M. 2. p. 352 foll. divides ζῷα into τετράποδα, ἔνυδρα, ἑρπετὰ, πτηνά. The word θηρία has a wider or narrower meaning: it may even include bees, fishes, and worms (see exx. in lex.), or may be confined to quadrupeds or more strictly to wild beasts, which is of course the prominent idea here, as there is no need to insist on the fact that domestic beasts are tamed. In like manner ἑρπετά is used in a wider sense for animals which walk on four or more legs, in contradistinction to man who walks on two, as in Xen. *Mem.* i. 4. 11 and the poets; but also for the very unscientific class of reptiles, including the weasel, the mouse, the lizard, the grasshopper (Lev. xi. 21, 29). The word ἐνάλιος is not found elsewhere in the Bible, but it is quite classical (cf. Soph. *Ant.* 345 πόντου τ' εἰναλίαν φύσιν), and is used, as here, with substantival force by Plut. *Mor.* 669 τὸ τῶν ἐναλίων γένος, *ib.* 729, cf. ps. Arist. *Mund.* 5 ἐναλίων ζώων καὶ πεζῶν καὶ ἀερίων φύσεις ἐχώρισε. For the coupling of the words in the list by τε and καὶ compare Rom. i. 14 Ἕλλησί τε καὶ βαρβάροις, σοφοῖς τε καὶ ἀνοήτοις. Probably beasts and birds are coupled as the nobler orders, and the other two because some of the ἑρπετὰ are amphibious, and others, as snakes, closely resemble some fishes.

δαμάζεται καὶ δεδάμασται.] Elsewhere in N.T. only in Mark v. 4 of the untamable demoniac; in LXX. Dan. ii. 40 used of iron which subdues all things; in classical writers both literally and metaphorically. For the writer's love of *paronomasia* see Essay on Grammar, and Winer p. 793 foll. Here of course emphasis is gained by the combination of the present and perfect: the art of taming is no new thing, but has belonged to the human race from the first, cf. Juv. iii. 190 *quis timet aut timuit*, viii. 70 *damus ac dedimus* with Mayor's n. in *J. of Phil.* xx. p. 265, John x. 38, Heb. vi. 10.

τῇ φύσει.] *Dat. of the agent*, an extension of the *dat. commodi* used most frequently with the perfect tense; see Madvig's *Gr. Synt.* 38*g*, Winer p. 274 (where this passage is however wrongly explained as *dat. instr.*), Marchant in *Class. Rev.* vol. iii. pp. 250, 437, and for the similar use in Latin, passages cited *s.v.* 'dative' in the Index to my Cic. *N.D.*

On the thought cf. Isoc. *Nic.* p. 17 μὴ καταγνῶς ἀνθρώπων τοσαύτην δυστυχίαν, ὡς περὶ μὲν τὰ θηρία τέχνας εὑρήκαμεν αἷς αὐτῶν τὰς ψυχὰς ἡμεροῦμεν...ἡμᾶς δ' αὐτοὺς οὐδὲν ἂν πρὸς ἀρετὴν ὠφελήσαιμεν (No! believe that our nature can be amended by training), Soph. *Antig.* 332 foll. Philo M. 1. p. 20 foll. 2. p. 200 πολλάκις ἔγνων ἡμερωθέντας λέοντας ἄρκτους παρδάλεις κ.τ.λ. Field cites Eur. *Aeol.* (*ap.* Plut. *Mor.* p. 954) ἦ βραχύ τοι σθένος ἀνέρος· ἀλλὰ ποικιλίᾳ πραπίδων δαμᾷ φῦλα πόντου χθονίων τ' ἀερίων τε παιδεύματα. It was a common-place of the Stoics, see Cic. *N.D.* II. 151, 158 foll., Senec. *Benef.* ii. 29 *cogita quanta nobis tribuerit Parens noster, quanto valentiora animalia sub iugum miserimus, quanto velociora consequamur, quam nihil sit mortale non sub ictu nostro positum.* Erasmus in his Paraphrase illustrates as follows: *cicurantur leones, mansuescunt tigrides, serviunt etiam elephanti, subiguntur et crocodili, mitescunt aspides, redduntur familiares aquilae et vultures, ad amicitiam alliciuntur delphini.* The writer here follows Gen. i. 28, ix. 2, Ps. viii. 6–8.

8. **οὐδεὶς δαμάσαι δύναται ἀνθρώπων.**] But if so, how can the Psalmist say παῦσον τὴν γλῶσσάν σου ἀπὸ κακοῦ (xxxiv. 13), and vow not to sin with the tongue (xvii. 3, xxxix. 1)? So Prov. xiii. 3. This may be partly explained by the emphatic position of ἀνθρώπων. Man cannot do it by himself, but he who is τέλειος may do it (ver. 2), and such perfection is attainable through the help of God given in answer to prayer; see above i. 5 and compare the Psalmist's prayer, cxli. 3. So Aug. *de nat. et grat.* c. 15 *non enim ait, linguam nullus domare potest, sed nullus hominum; ut cum domatur, Dei misericordia, Dei adjutorio, Dei gratia fieri fateamur.* The Pelagians, followed here by Oecumenius, read this verse as a question (Schegg). In the next place ἡ γλῶσσα, when regarded as setting on fire the whole round of life, is not simply the speech of the individual, but that multiplied and re-echoed a thousand-fold by the voices of others and by the power of the press; *parva metu primo mox sese attollit in auras.* However a man may learn to control his own tongue, these echoes are beyond all human power.

ἀκατάστατον κακόν.] Cf. above i. 8, also Herm. *Mand.* ii. 3 πονηρὰ ἡ καταλαλιά, ἀκατάστατον δαιμόνιόν ἐστιν, μηδέποτε εἰρηνεῦον, where Harn. cites Orig. *in Joann.* (Opp. iv. p. 355) οὐκ ὤκνησαν καὶ τὰ νομισθέντα ἂν ἐλάχιστα εἶναι τῶν ἁμαρτημάτων δαιμονίοις προσάψαι οἱ φήσαντες τὴν ὀξυχολίαν δαιμόνιον εἶναι, ὁμοίως δὲ καὶ τὴν καταλαλιάν, and below ver. 16 ἀκαταστασία. Erdmann and Hofmann read ἀκατάσχετον with Cod. Ephr., the Peshitto, and some other versions, and we find the word similarly used by Philo M. 1. p. 695 τὸ στόμα διανοίξαντες καὶ ἐάσαντες ἀχαλίνωτον, καθάπερ ῥεῦμα ἀκατάσχετον, φέρεσθαι τὸν ἀκριτόμυθον λόγον ἐῶσι. This would suit the passage very well, agreeing with Ps. xii. 4; but the other reading is generally accepted and gives a good sense 'restless,' 'unquiet,' like the least tameable beasts; others translate as in i. 8 'unstable,' 'inconsistent,' which they think agrees better with v. 9 foll., but it is a somewhat incongruous epithet for κακόν. See above i. 8. We should naturally take the words ἀκ. κ. as acc. in apposition to τὴν γλῶσσαν, like i. 8 ἀνὴρ δίψυχος, but the following nom. makes it more probable that there is a sudden change of construction, ἀκ. κ. being the predicate of an independent sentence with ἡ γλῶσσα understood as subject; cf. Mark xii. 38 foll. βλέπετε ἀπὸ τῶν θελόντων ἐν στολαῖς περιπατεῖν...οἱ κατεσθίοντες τὰς οἰκίας τῶν χηρῶν· οὗτοι λήμψονται περισσότερον κρίμα. In the Apocalypse we meet with many of these irregular appositions, e.g. i. 5 ἀπὸ Ἰησοῦ Χριστοῦ, ὁ μάρτυς ὁ πιστός, *ib.* xx. 2 ἐκράτησεν τὸν δράκοντα, ὁ ὄφις ὁ ἀρχαῖος, ὅς ἐστιν διάβολος, Winer, p. 668 foll., A. Buttmann, p. 68 foll. So even in Homer, *Il.* vi. 395, x. 437.

μεστὴ ἰοῦ θανατηφόρου.] For μεστή see below ver. 17, 2 Pet. ii. 14, Rom. i. 29 μεστοὺς φθόνου. The metaphor here is taken from Ps. lviii. 4, and cxl. 3 ἰὸς ἀσπίδων ὑπὸ τὰ χείλη αὐτῶν quoted in Rom. iii. 13, Eccles. x. 11 foll., cf. Lucian *Fugit.* 19 ἰοῦ μεστὸν αὐτοῖς τὸ στόμα (speaking of pseudo-philosophers), Test. Gad. p. 680 F τὸ μῖσος ἰοῦ διαβολικοῦ τὴν καρδίαν πληροῖ, Acta Philippi T. p. 76 ἔστιν δὲ τὸ κατοικητήριον αὐτοῦ (i.e. of the Serpent) Τάρταρος...φεύγετε οὖν ἀπ' αὐτοῦ ἵνα μὴ ὁ ἰὸς αὐτοῦ ἐκχυθῇ ἐπὶ τὸ στόμα ὑμῶν...ἡ τῶν κακῶν ἐπιθυμία πᾶσα ἐξ αὐτοῦ προελήλυθεν, Didaché ii. 4 οὐκ ἔσῃ διγνώμων οὐδὲ δίγλωσσος· παγὶς γὰρ θανάτου ἡ διγλωσσία, Barn. 19, Clem. Al. *Paed.* 301 P. For θαν., which occurs here only in N.T., cf. Job. xxxiii. 23 ἐὰν ὦσι χίλιοι ἄγγελοι θανατηφόροι, 4 Macc. viii. 17 θανατηφόρος ἀπείθεια: it is used by Xen., Plato, &c. Spitta refers to Sibyl. *fr.* iii. 32 (*Prooem.* 71) for the phrase θανατηφόρος ἰός.

9. **ἐν αὐτῇ εὐλογοῦμεν.**] What makes the tongue more mischievous is that it serves the purpose of the δίγλωσσος, hiding evil under the mask of good. For instrumental use of ἐν see Winer p. 485. Here it might be possible to give it a stricter sense, 'in this part we bless God,' did we not also meet with such unmitigated Hebraisms as πατάσσειν or ἀποκτείνειν ἐν μαχαίρᾳ Luke xxii. 49, Apoc. xiii. 10, Psal. Sol. ii. 1 ἐν κριῷ κατέβαλε τείχη ὀχυρά. It was customary with the Jews, whenever they uttered the name of God, to add 'Blessed (be) He.' Hence we find ὁ εὐλογητός used as a name for God in Mark xiv. 61. This sense of εὐλ. is peculiar to Hellenistic writers, see Westcott, *Heb.* p. 203 foll.

τὸν Κύριον καὶ Πατέρα.] This phrase does not occur elsewhere in the Bible: the nearest approach to it is in 1 Chron. xxix. 10 εὐλογητὸς εἶ, Κύριε, ὁ Θεὸς Ἰσραήλ, ὁ Πατὴρ ἡμῶν, Isa. lxiii. 16 σὺ Κύριε πατὴρ ἡμῶν, Matt. xi. 25 ἐξομολογοῦμαι σοι Πάτερ, Κύριε τοῦ οὐρανοῦ καὶ τῆς γῆς. We may compare Philo on the name Κύριος καὶ Θεὸς (M. 1. p. 581), δικαιοῖ τῶν μὲν φαύλων λέγεσθαι κύριος καὶ δεσπότης, τῶν δ' ἐν προκοπαῖς καὶ βελτιώσεσι θεός, τῶν δ' ἀρίστων καὶ τελειοτάτων ἀμφότερον (being governed as he adds below, by Him as κύριος, and benefited by Him as θεός). The name πατήρ is used with reference to man's being made in the image of God.

καὶ ἐν αὐτῇ.] Emphatic repetition. 'It is through it we bless God, through it we curse men.' Compare Philo M. 2. p. 196 οὐ γὰρ ὅσιον δι' οὗ στόματος τὸ ἱερώτατον ὄνομα προφέρεταί τις, διὰ τούτου φθέγγεσθαί τι τῶν αἰσχρῶν, Sir. xxviii. 12, Erasm. *Adag.* under the heading *ex eodem ore calidum et frigidum efflare*, Diog. L. i. 105 (Anacharsis) ἐρωτηθεὶς τι ἐστιν ἐν ἀνθρώποις ἀγαθόν τε καὶ φαῦλον, ἔφη 'γλῶσσα.' Similar stories are told of Pittacus and Bias as to that part of the sacrifice which is at once most useful and most harmful (Plut. *Mor.* p. 506. *ib.* 38 and 146, *Fragm.* xi. 41, p. 30, Didot).

καταρώμεθα.] Ps. lxii. 4 ἐν στόματι αὐτῶν εὐλόγουν καὶ τῇ καρδίᾳ αὐτῶν κατηρῶντο, Rom. xii. 13 εὐλογεῖτε καὶ μὴ καταρᾶσθε, Sirac. xxxi. 24 εἷς εὐχόμενος καὶ εἷς καταρώμενος· τίνος φωνῆς εἰσακούσεται ὁ δεσπότης; Test.

Patr. p. 734 F ἡ ἀγαθὴ διάνοια οὐκ ἔχει δύο γλώσσας εὐλογίας καὶ κατάρας. An example of such cursing is in John vii. 49 ὁ ὄχλος οὗτος...ἐπάρατοί εἰσιν, Shimei's of David 2 Sam. xvi. 5. St. James uses the first person as in ver. 1.

τοὺς καθ' ὁμοίωσιν Θεοῦ γεγονότας.] Gen. i. 26 ποιήσωμεν ἄνθρωπον κατ' εἰκόνα ἡμετέραν καὶ καθ' ὁμοίωσιν, *ib.* v. 27, ix. 6, Sirac. xvii. 3, Wisd. ii. 23 ὁ Θεὸς ἔκτισε τὸν ἄνθρωπον ἐπ' ἀφθαρσίᾳ καὶ εἰκόνα τῆς ἰδίας ἰδιότητος ἐποίησεν αὐτόν, 4 Esdr. viii. 44, 1 Cor. xi. 7 (on the question of covering the head) ἀνὴρ εἰκὼν καὶ δόξα Θεοῦ ὑπάρχων, Philo M. 1. p. 16 ἡ δὲ εἰκὼν λέλεκται κατὰ τὸν τῆς ψυχῆς ἡγεμόνα νοῦν, *ib.* 35 πᾶς ἄνθρωπος κατὰ μὲν τὴν διάνοιαν ᾠκειοῦται θείῳ λόγῳ, τῆς μακαρίας φύσεως ἐκμαγεῖον ἢ ἀπόσπασμα ἢ ἀπαύγασμα γεγονώς, κατὰ δὲ τὴν τοῦ σώματος κατασκευὴν ἅπαντι τῷ κόσμῳ, Clem. Rec. v. 23 *si vere velitis Dei imaginem colere, homini benefacientes veram in eo Dei imaginem coleretis* foll., Clem. Hom. iii. 17 ὁ εἰκόνα καὶ ταῦτα αἰωνίου βασιλέως ὑβρίσας τὴν ἁμαρτίαν εἰς ἐκεῖνον ἀναφερομένην ἔχει οὗπερ καθ' ὁμοίωσιν ἡ εἰκὼν ἐτύγχανεν οὖσα, *ib.* xi. 4, Clem. Al. *Str.* vi. 9, p. 776, Taylor, *J.F.* p. 70, where R. Aqiba is quoted to the effect 'whosoever sheddeth blood, they reckon it to him as if he diminished *the likeness.*' A distinction is drawn by Irenaeus *Haer.* v. 16, 2 and others of the Fathers between εἰκών, the common image belonging to the whole human race in virtue of their being all partakers in reason and conscience, and ὁμοίωσις the potentiality of moral assimilation to the Divine goodness, cf. Philo *Opif.* M. p. 16 ἐπεὶ οὐ σύμπασα εἰκὼν ἀρχετύπῳ παραδείγματι ἐμφερής, πολλαὶ δὲ εἰσὶν ἀνόμοιοι, προσεπεσημήνατο εἰπὼν τῷ κατ' εἰκόνα τὸ καθ' ὁμοίωσιν εἰς ἔμφασιν ἀκριβοῦς ἐκμαγείου and Hagenbach *Hist. of Doctr.* § 56, vol. i. p. 214 tr., also n. on ἐπίγειος ver. 15 below. On the pagan view see Acts xvii. 38 and my nn. on Cic. *N.D.* I. 1 *ad agnitionem animi* and I. 90 *nec vero intellego cur maluerit Epicurus deos hominum similes dicere quam homines deorum.* Though the Divine image is traceable in every child of man (as Bengel says, *remanet nobilitas indelebilis*), yet it is only perfect in the Second Adam (Heb. i. 3, Col. i. 15, 2 Cor. iv. 4), into whose image the believer is being gradually transformed (Col. iii. 10, Eph. iv. 24, 2 Cor. iii. 18). For the argument here cf. Gen. ix. 6, Prov. xiv. 31, Matt. xxv. 35 foll., below iv. 11, 12, 1 John iv. 20.

10. **ἐκ τοῦ αὐτοῦ στόματος.**] This seems to imply that it is the combination of blessing and cursing which is condemned, and that either may be allowable by itself. Can this be the meaning of St. James? What was the general feeling of the Jews about cursing? The old law required the Israelite to curse on Mont Ebal and bless on Mount Gerizim. The fact too that cursing was forbidden in special cases, as against parents (Exod. xxi. 17), the king (*ib.* xxii. 28), the deaf (Lev. xix. 14), seems to show that it was not generally condemned under the old dispensation. It is referred to without implying blame, Prov. xi. 26, xxiv. 24, xxvi. 2, xxx. 10, Eccles. vii. 21, x. 90. Compare also the curse of Canaan by Noah (Gen. ix. 25), that of Simeon and Levi by their father (Gen. xlix. 7), of the builder of Jericho by Joshua (Josh. vi. 26), Abimelech by Jotham (Jud. ix. 20, 57), Meroz by Deborah (*ib.* v. 23), the children by Elisha (2 K. ii. 24), apostate Jews by Nehemiah

(Neh. xiii. 25), and the imprecations in the Psalms. Are we then to suppose that St. James here attaches a special force to the words *καθ' ὁμοίωσιν Θεοῦ γεγονότας*? Does he mean by this, 'men transformed into the divine image'? This seems precluded by a comparison of the passages cited at the end of the preceding note, in which a similar inference is drawn from man's general relation to the Creator. Must we then conclude that cursing in itself is here condemned as a form, and that the worst form, of *καταλαλιὰ* and *κρίσις* (below iv. 11)? So St. Paul, Rom. xii. 14 *εὐλογεῖτε καὶ μὴ καταρᾶσθε*, cf. Luke vi. 28. Cursing will then be the overflow of the bitter water spoken of in ver. 11, 'the water which causeth the curse' (Numbers v. 18); a sign of the *ζῆλος πικρός* which characterizes the wisdom of this world (below ver. 14). Nor is this view of the wrongfulness of cursing unknown in the O.T.: cf. Job xxxi. 29, 30 ('neither have I suffered my mouth to sin by wishing a curse to his, i.e. my enemy's, soul'); it is the mark of the wicked that *ἀρᾶς τὸ στόμα αὐτοῦ γέμει καὶ πικρίας*, Ps. x. 7. But then, why is not St. James content to condemn cursing in itself? Why does he only condemn it when combined with what is good, blessing? It is because 'the wrath of man worketh not the righteousness of God' (above i. 20), because 'bitterness proves that we are lying against the truth' (below v. 14); in the words of St. John (1 ep. iv. 20) because 'he that loveth not his brother cannot love God,' so that the mixture of cursing proves the unreality of the blessing, cf. Matt. xii. 34, *ib.* v. 23, 24.

ἐξέρχεται εὐλογία καὶ κατάρα.] Where there is one predicate to several connected subjects, of which the nearest to the verb is in the singular number, the predicate, if it precedes the subjects, may itself be in the singular, as though it referred only to the nearest subject: cf. 1 Tim. vi. 4 *ἐξ ὧν γίνεται φθόνος, ἔρις, βλασφημίαι*, Apoc. ix. 17, *ἐκ τῶν στομάτων αὐτῶν ἐκπορεύεται πῦρ καὶ καπνὸς καὶ θεῖον*, Winer, p. 651, Madv. § 2 *b.*, Krueg. 63. 4.

οὐ χρὴ ταῦτα οὕτως γίνεσθαι.] *χρή* not found elsewhere in N.T., occurs in Prov. xxv. 27 *τιμᾶν χρὴ λόγους ἐνδόξους*. It is about equivalent to *ὀφείλομεν*, weaker than *δεῖ*, which properly implies not merely what ought to be, but what must be, though at times it comes very near to *χρή*, as in Mark xiii. 14 *ἑστὼς ὅπου οὐ δεῖ*, 2 Tim. ii. 24 *δοῦλον Κυρίου οὐ δεῖ μάχεσθαι*. Some hold that *οὕτως* is pleonastic with *ταῦτα*, merely adding emphasis, as where it marks the apodosis (Winer, p. 678): should it not rather be taken as summing up what was said before of the manner in which the blessings and curses are uttered with an unbridled tongue under the violence of passion? I think we cannot assume that St. James would have condemned such anathemas as we find in 1 Cor. xvi. 22, Gal. i. 8. Dr. Plummer compares Numb. xxiii. 8 'How shall I curse whom God hath not cursed?

11. **μήτι ἡ πηγὴ ἐκ τῆς αὐτῆς ὀπῆς βρύει τὸ γλυκὺ καὶ τὸ πικρόν.**] For the interrogative *μή* compare ver. 12; the softened form *μήτι* is common in N.T., cf. the parallel in Matt. vii. 16 *μήτι συλλέγουσιν ἀπὸ ἀκανθῶν σταφυλήν*; *ib.* xxvi. 22, but comparatively rare in classical writers. For figure cf. Isa. lv. 1, Joh. iv. 14, Philo M. 1. p. 199 *πηγὴ λόγων διάνοια καὶ στόμιον αὐτῆς λόγος, ὅτι τὰ ἐνθυμήματα πάντα διὰ τούτου καθάπερ*

νάματα ἀπὸ γῆς εἰς τοὐμφανὲς ἐπιρρέοντα ἀναχεῖται, *ib.* 447. Βρύει is not found elsewhere in N.T. or LXX.: in classical Greek it is used intransitively with the dative, as in Arist. *Nub.* 45 (βίος) βρύων μελίτταις, Hom. *Il.* xvii. 56 ἔρνος βρύει ἄνθεϊ λευκῷ also with gen. (Soph. *O.C.* 17 χῶρος...βρύων δάφνης, ἐλαίας), properly in reference to plants bursting into bud and flower, or of the land in spring (Xen. *Cyneg.* v. 12), then metaphorically ἄχη βρύει Aesch. *Choeph.* 62, θράσει βρύων *Ag.* 177, λόγοι μεστοὶ πνεύματος θείου καὶ βρύοντες δυνάμει Justin M. *Tryph.* 9. The only instance cited from a classical author for the transitive use is Anacr. (44, 1. 2 Bergk) χάριτες βρύουσι ῥόδα, where however Hermann reads ῥόδου βρύουσιν: Justin M. (*Tryph.* 114) has τῆς πέτρας ζῶν ὕδωρ βρυούσης, cf. Chrysostom (*hom. in mart.*, Migne *Patrol.* vol. 50, p. 664) οἱ τάφοι τῶν μαρτύρων βρύουσιν εὐλογίαν, Clem. Hom. ii. 45 πηγὰς γῇ βρύσας Θεός. Eustath. in Il. ρ, p. 1126, 42 (*ap.* Wetst.) says it is properly used of olive blossoms and, later, of springs, as in Acta Johannis p. 276 T. βρύουσαν τὴν πηγὴν εὗρον, Acta Thomae p. 22, Clem. Hom. iii. 36. Ὀπή 'a cleft in a rock,' elsewhere in N.T. only in Heb. xi. 38, also in LXX., Exod xxxiii. 22, Obad. 3. Πικρόν only used here and below in N.T. Its use here in preference to ἁλυκόν or ἁλμυρόν is doubtless owing to its often being found in a figurative sense, e.g. ver. 14, Ps. lxiv. 3, Sirac. iv. 6 καταρᾶσθαι ἐν πικρίᾳ ψυχῆς. It is descriptive of sea-water, like *amarus*, our 'brackish.' The Dead Sea however, to which St. James is probably alluding, was really bitter and had both salt and fresh springs on its shores. Other examples of bitter waters are Marah (Exod. xv. 23), 'the water that causeth the curse' (Numb. v. 18–27), Apoc. viii. 11. Pliny *N.H.* ii. 103 has a fable of a fountain of the Sun which was sweet and cold at noon and bitter and hot at midnight. Antigonus (*Mirab.* 148 *ap.* Wetst.) gives an account of such a spring τὸν δὲ Ἱμέραν ἐκ μιᾶς πηγῆς σχιζόμενον τὸ μὲν ἁλυκὸν τῶν ῥείθρων ἔχειν, τὸ δὲ πότιμον: in 4 Esdras v. 9 one of the prodigies which announce Messiah's coming is *in dulcibus aquis salsae invenientur.*

12. **μὴ δύναται.**] See on ii. 14.

συκῆ ἐλαίας ποιῆσαι.] Cf. for the use of ποιεῖν Matt. iii. 10 πᾶν δένδρον μὴ ποιοῦν καρπόν, Gen. i. 11, Vorst, p. 162 and 830; and for the proverbial figure Matt. vii. 16, *ib.* xii. 33, Isa. v. 2, Seneca *Ep.* 87 *non nascitur ex malo bonum, non magis quam ficus ex olea*, Epict. *Diss.* ii. 20 πῶς γὰρ δύναται ἄμπελος μὴ ἀμπελικῶς κινεῖσθαι ἀλλ' ἐλαικῶς; ἢ ἐλαία πάλιν μὴ ἐλαικῶς ἀλλ' ἀμπελικῶς; Plut. *Mor.* 472 F τὴν ἄμπελον σῦκα φέρειν οὐκ ἀξιοῦμεν οὐδὲ τὴν ἐλαίαν βότρυς, Anton. 8. 15.

οὔτε ἁλυκὸν γλυκὺ ποιῆσαι ὕδωρ.] For this irregular use of οὔτε see Winer, p. 614, where the editor cites Tischendorf *mihi non dubium est quin fatiscente Graecitate etiam* οὔτε *pro* οὐδέ *sit dictum.* So Apoc. ix. 21 οὐ μετενόησαν ἐκ τῶν φόνων αὐτῶν οὔτε ἐκ τῶν φαρμάκων αὐτῶν οὔτε ἐκ πορνείας αὐτῶν, where οὐ is parallel with οὔτε, not overlapping. In our text it may perhaps be explained by the preceding question being regarded as = οὔτε συκῆ κ.τ.λ. Ἁλυκόν classical, but found elsewhere in the Bible only in phrase ἡ θάλασσα ἡ ἁλυκή, as a name for the Dead Sea (Numb. iii. 12, Deut. iii. 17). The rare phrase ποιῆσαι ὕδωρ is assimilated to π. ἐλαίας above: we find it used of rain Arist. *Vesp.* 261 ὕδωρ ἀναγκαίως ἔχει τὸν θεὸν ποιῆσαι.

Many MSS. and versions read οὕτως οὐδὲ, a smaller number insert μία πηγή and καί after ἁλυκόν. The insertion of οὕτως may have arisen from a dittographia of οὔτε, but the latter insertions were evidently intended to avoid the difficulty of taking ἁλυκόν as a substantive and the subject of δύναται ποιῆσαι. The true relation of the sentences is lost by the insertion οὕτως. The two clauses are not compared with each other, but are both used to illustrate the impossibility of genuine worship proceeding from a heart which naturally vents itself in curses. There is great harshness in the construction μὴ δύναται ποιῆσαι; οὔτε ποιῆσαι. If the government of δύναται is continued, we ought to have ἤ for οὔτε followed by a question; otherwise we should have expected an entirely independent clause, reading ποιήσει for ποιῆσαι.

13. **τίς σοφὸς καὶ ἐπιστήμων ἐν ὑμῖν;**] The interrogative here takes the place of a condition, as in Luke xi. 11 τίνα δὲ ἐξ ὑμῶν τὸν πατέρα αἰτήσει ὁ υἱὸς ἄρτον; μὴ λίθον ἐπιδώσει αὐτῷ; and *ib.* 5–8, where the construction is broken, τίς ἐξ ὑμῶν ἕξει φίλον being changed into a regular conditional form in ver. 8 εἰ καὶ οὐ δώσει διὰ τὸ εἶναι φίλον, διά γε τὴν ἀναίδειαν αὐτοῦ δώσει αὐτῷ, Deut. xx. 5–8 τίς ὁ ἄνθρωπος ὁ οἰκοδομήσας οἰκίαν καινὴν καὶ οὐκ ἐνεκαίνισεν αὐτήν; πορευέσθω...καὶ τίς ὁ ἄνθρωπος ὅστις ἐφύτευσεν ἀμπελῶνα καὶ οὐκ εὐφράνθη ἐξ αὐτοῦ; πορευέσθω κ.τ.λ., Jud. vii. 3 τίς ὁ φοβούμενος καὶ δειλός; ἐπιστραφέτω, Psa. xxxiii. 12 τίς ἐστιν ἄνθρωπος ὁ θέλων ζωήν; παῦσον τὴν γλῶσσάν σου ἀπὸ κακοῦ, *ib.* cvii. 43 τίς σοφός; καὶ φυλάξει ταῦτα καὶ συνήσει τὰ ἐλέη τοῦ Κυρίου, Isa. l. 10 τίς ἐν ὑμῖν ὁ φοβούμενος τὸν Κύριον; ὑπακουσάτω τῆς φωνῆς τοῦ παιδὸς αὐτοῦ, Jer. ix. 12, Hos. xiv. 10, Sir. vi. 33 τίς σοφός; αὐτῷ προσκολλήθητι, other examples in Vorst, p. 211 foll. For a similar use without the interrogative pronoun see n. on ver. 13 κακοπαθεῖ τις ἐν ὑμῖν; προσευχέσθω. Lachmann has no interrogation here, and A. Buttmann (p. 217) argues on the same side, comparing it with other instances in which he thinks τίς is equivalent to an indefinite relative; but the passages cited above are sufficient to settle the question. The abruptness to which Buttmann objects is a marked characteristic of the writer's style. For ἐν ὑμῖν almost equivalent to ὑμῶν cf. below ver. 13, 14, and ἐξ ὑμῶν above ii. 16. Ἐπιστήμων here only in N.T.; it occurs in Deut. i. 13 (of judges) δότε αὐτοῖς ἄνδρας σοφοὺς καὶ ἐπιστήμονας καὶ συνετούς, *ib.* iv. 6 (of Israel) ἴδου λαὸς σοφὸς καὶ ἐπιστήμων, Isa. v. 21 οὐαὶ οἱ συνετοὶ ἐν ἑαυτοῖς καὶ ἐνώπιον αὐτῶν ἐπιστήμονες: used in classical Greek for a skilled or scientific person as opposed to one who has no special knowledge or training. Compare for thought and expression Philo M. 2. p. 421 τίς γὰρ οὐκ ἂν εἴποι ὅτι σοφὸν ἄρα γένος καὶ ἐπιστημονικώτατον μόνον τοῦτ᾽ ἔστιν, ᾧ τὰς θείας παραινέσεις ἐξεγένετο μὴ κενὰς καὶ ἐρήμους ἀπολιπεῖν τῶν οἰκείων πράξεων ἀλλὰ πληρῶσαι τοὺς λόγους ἔργοις ἐπαινετοῖς;

δειξάτω ἐκ τῆς καλῆς ἀναστροφῆς τὰ ἔργα αὐτοῦ.] Cf. above ii. 18. The noun is derived from ἀναστρέφομαι = L. *versor*, as in 1 Pet. i. 17, 2 Pet. ii. 18, Prov. xx. 7, and frequently in Polybius with adverb. It occurs often in both epistles of St. Peter, e.g. i. 15 ἅγιοι ἐν πάσῃ ἀναστροφῇ γενήθητε, i. 18 ἐλυτρώθητε ἐκ τῆς ματαίας ἀναστροφῆς, iii. 2 τὴν ἐν φόβῳ ἁγνὴν ἀναστροφήν, iii. 16 τὴν ἀγαθὴν ἐν Χριστῷ ἀναστροφήν, 2 ep. ii. 7, iii. 11, so in Tobit. iv. 14 and Polyb. iv. 82, 1 κατὰ τὴν λοιπὴν ἀναστροφὴν τεθαυμασμένος, Epict. *Diss.* i. 22, 13 ἐνδέχεται τὴν πρὸς τοὺς κοινωνοὺς ἔχειν οἵαν δεῖ ἀναστροφήν; see Hatch, p. 9. Καλός occurs in this epistle ii. 7, iv. 17, καλῶς, ii. 3, 8, 17: the former is joined with ἀναστ. in 1 Pet. ii. 12. For the general sense cf. Sir. xix. 18 πᾶσα σοφία φόβος Κυρίου, καὶ ἐν πάσῃ σοφίᾳ ποίησις νόμου· καὶ οὐκ ἔστι σοφία πονηρίας ἐπιστήμη κ.τ.λ., Clem. Rom. i. 38 ὁ σοφὸς ἐνδεικνύσθω τὴν σοφίαν αὐτοῦ μὴ ἐν λόγοις ἀλλ' ἐν ἔργοις ἀγαθοῖς. Here the simpler expresion would have been, as De Wette remarks, δειξάτω...τὴν σοφίαν αὐτοῦ, like ii. 18 δείξω ἐκ τῶν ἔργων μου τὴν πίστιν, but it is modified so as to give more emphasis to the two ideas which the writer is here insisting on, viz. deeds *v.* words, gentleness and modesty *v.* arrogance and passion, 'let him show his deeds in meekness of wisdom,' i.e. 'let him give practical proof (of his being wise) from his life and conduct in the meekness which proceeds from and is the true mark of wisdom.'

ἐν πραΰτητι σοφίας.] Cf. i. 21, 1 Pet. iii. 16 (defend the faith) μετὰ πραΰτητος καὶ φόβου, Gal. vi. 1 οἱ πνευματικοὶ καταρτίζετε τὸν τοιοῦτον ἐν πνεύματι πραΰτητος, 1 Cor. iv. 21, 2 Tim. ii. 24 foll. δοῦλον δὲ Κυρίου οὐ δεῖ μάχεσθαι ἀλλ' ἤπιον εἶναι πρὸς πάντας, διδακτικὸν, ἀνεξίκακον, ἐν πραΰτητι παιδεύοντα τοὺς ἀντιδιατιθεμένους, Prov. xi. 2 στόμα ταπεινῶν μελετᾷ σοφίαν, Sirac. iii. 17 ἐν πραΰτητι τὰ ἔργα σου διέξαγε *ib.* iv. 8 ἀποκρίθητι πτωχῷ εἰρηνικὰ ἐν πραΰτητι, also the frequent commendation of the meek in the Psalms, e.g. xxv. 9 ὁδηγήσει πραεῖς ἐν κρίσει, διδάξει πραεῖς ὁδοὺς αὐτοῦ.

14. **ζῆλον.**] 'Jealcusy,' as in Rom. xiii. 13 εὐσχημόνως περιπατῶμεν... μὴ ἔριδι καὶ ζήλῳ, 1 Cor. iii. 3 ὅπου γὰρ ἐν ὑμῖν ζῆλος καὶ ἔρις οὐχὶ σαρκικοί ἐστε; see below iv. 2.

πικρόν.] With allusion to ver. 11. Cf. Eph. iv. 31 πικρία καὶ θυμὸς καὶ ὀργή, Heb. xii. 14, 15 εἰρήνην διώκετε...ἐπισκοποῦντες μή τις ῥίζα πικρίας ἐνοχλῇ.

ἐριθίαν.[1]] 'Party-spirit,' derived from ἔριθος 'a hireling,' especially a woman who spins for hire (Dem. p. 1313. 6, Isa. xxxviii. 12; the idea of *hire* disappears in συνέριθος, *Odys.* vi. 32, Callim. *Epig.* xvii. 3). Probably the word got to be used, like *operae* in Cicero, of partisans hired by political leaders: hence ἐριθεύομαι and its cognates are employed to denote (1) canvassing by hired partisans, and (2) party spirit generally, cf. Arist. *Pol.* v. 3. 9 μεταβάλλουσι δ' αἱ πολιτεῖαι καὶ ἄνευ στάσεως διά τε τᾶς ἐριθείας ὥσπερ ἐν Ἡραίᾳ (ἐξ αἱρετῶν γὰρ διὰ τοῦτο ἐποίησαν κληρωτάς, ὅτι ᾑροῦντο τοὺς ἐριθευομένους) καὶ δι' ὀλιγωρίαν, Polyb. x. 25. 9 (speaking of demagogues) τῆς στρατηγίας ὀρεγόμενοι διὰ ταύτης τῆς ἀρχῆς ἐξεριθεύονται (*cooperatores sibi comparant* Schweigh.) τοὺς νέους καὶ παρασκευάζουσιν εὔνους συναγωνιστὰς εἰς τὸ μέλλον, Philo *Leg. ad Flac.* M. 2. p. 555 τί δὲ ἄμεινον εἰρήνης; εἰρήνη δὲ ἐξ ἡγεμονίας ὀρθῆς φύεται, ἡγεμονία δὲ ἀφιλόνεικος καὶ ἀνερίθευτος ὀρθὴ μόνη, δι' ἧς καὶ τὰ ἄλλα πάντα

[1] WH. read ἐριθίαν with B[1], which however has ἐριθεία in ver. 16. See below κακοπαθίας v. 10, and Tisch. ed. 8, vol. iii. p. 87 foll.

ὀρθοῦται. It is used by St. Paul, Phil. i. 17 οἱ δὲ ἐριθείας τὸν Χριστὸν καταγγέλλουσιν, Rom. ii. 8, Gal. v. 20 ἔρις, ζῆλος, θυμοί, ἐριθεῖαι, διχοστασίαι where Lightfoot translates 'caballings'), and the same list in 2 Cor. xii. 20, except that καταλαλιαί stands for διχοστασίαι, Phil. i. 17 μηδὲν κατ' ἐριθείαν, μηδὲ κατὰ κενοδοξίαν, ἀλλὰ τῇ ταπεινότητι ἀλλήλους ἡγούμενοι ὑπερέχοντας ἑαυτῶν, imitated in Ignat. *Philad.* 8 μηδὲν κατ' ἐριθείαν πράσσειν. It is possible that the later meaning may be coloured in the N.T. by a reminiscence of the earlier meaning: cf. Joh. x., where the spirit of the hireling is contrasted with that of the true shepherd. The verb is used in its original sense of spinning Tobit ii. 11 (mid.) ἡ γυνή μου ἠριθεύετο ἐν τοῖς γυναικείοις καὶ ἀπέστελλε τοῖς κυρίοις, Heliod. i. 5 (act.) αἱ γυναῖκες ἐριθεύουσιν.

μὴ κατακαυχᾶσθε.] This verb was used above (ii. 13) with gen. to denote the triumph of one principle over another, and so in the only other passage where it occurs in N.T., Rom. xi. 17 μὴ κατακαυχῶ τῶν κλάδων. Three other instances of its use are cited, all from the LXX., Zech. x. 12 κατισχύσω αὐτοὺς ἐν Κυρίῳ καὶ ἐν ὀνόματι αὐτοῦ κατακαυχήσονται, and Jer. l. (xxvii.) 11 and 38, where the verb is used absolutely, κατά having only an intensifying force, as in κατακτείνω, κατάδηλος. The question whether it should be thus taken here will be considered in connexion with the following clause.

ψεύδεσθε κατὰ τῆς ἀληθείας.] If you have bitterness you cannot be truly wise, for wisdom is shown by gentleness; your profession therefore is a lie: cf. 1 John i. 6 ἐὰν εἴπωμεν ὅτι κοινωνίαν ἔχομεν μετ' αὐτοῦ καὶ ἐν σκότει περιπατῶμεν, ψευδόμεθα καὶ οὐ ποιοῦμεν τὴν ἀλήθειαν, *ib.* iv. 20, Wisd. vi. 25 φθόνος οὐ κοινωνήσει σοφίᾳ. Some (Wiesinger, Hofmann) take τῆς ἀληθείας to mean the Gospel, as above i. 18, explaining it of false teachers, blind leaders of the blind, who, like those referred to in 1 Cor. i. 18–23, speak contemptuously of the Gospel and misrepresent its doctrines. Perhaps it is simpler to understand it of 'the facts of the case,' as in Mk. v. 13 εἶπεν αὐτῷ πᾶσαν τὴν ἀλήθειαν, for which Bloomfield compares Diod. i. 2 ἔνια κατεψεῦσθαι τῆς ἀληθείας, Jos. *B.J.* prooem. 1 (former historians) καταψεύδονται τῶν πραγμάτων: ('you claim to be enlightened Christians, but enlightenment joined with bitterness and self-seeking comes not from God, but from the devil.') The expression is no doubt pleonastic: it would have been enough to say 'your boast of wisdom is at variance with the truth,' but emphasis is added by the fuller phrase, as in the passage quoted from St. John. If we understand it thus it would seem that κατακαυχᾶσθε must be taken absolutely ('do not boast of wisdom and so lie against the truth') and not with κατὰ τῆς ἀληθείας in the sense of 'triumphing over the truth.' See however Zahn *N.K.* p. 792 *n.*

15. **οὐκ ἔστιν αὕτη ἡ σοφία ἄνωθεν κατερχομένη.**] 'This wisdom is not one that descends from above,' see on ἄνωθέν ἐστιν καταβαῖνον i. 17; and cf. above i. 5, Philo M. 1. p. 571 σοφία ἄνωθεν ὀμβρηθεῖσα ἀπ' οὐρανοῦ, *ib.* p. 524, and on the opposition of θεία καὶ οὐράνιος σοφία to ἐπίγειος σοφία *ib.* p. 51 f. and 1 Cor. i. 19 foll. esp. ii. 6 σοφίαν λαλοῦμεν ἐν τοῖς τελείοις, σοφίαν δὲ οὐ τοῦ αἰῶνος τούτου (= ἐπίγειον)...ἀλλὰ λαλοῦμεν σοφίαν Θεοῦ κ.τ.λ. This false wisdom is described in Sir. xix. 19 foll.

ἐπίγειος.] The first stage in the antithesis to *ἄνωθεν κατερχομένη*, cf. Hermas *Mand.* ix. 11 *ἡ πίστις ἄνωθέν ἐστι παρὰ τοῦ Κυρίου...ἡ δὲ διψυχία ἐπίγειον πνεῦμά ἐστι παρὰ τοῦ διαβόλου* distinctly borrowed from this passage; also John iii. 12 *εἰ τὰ ἐπίγεια εἶπον ὑμῖν καὶ οὐ πιστεύετε, πῶς, ἐὰν εἴπω ὑμῖν τὰ ἐπουράνια, πιστεύσετε;* Phil. iii. 19 *οἱ τὰ ἐπίγεια φρονοῦντες*, *ib.* ii. 10 *ἵνα πᾶν γόνυ κάμψῃ ἐπουρανίων καὶ ἐπιγείων καὶ καταχθονίων*, Plut. *Mor.* 566 D *τὸ ἐπίγειον τῆς ψυχῆς*. Philo (M. 1. p. 49 on Gen. ii. 7 *ἔπλασεν ὁ Θεὸς τὸν ἄνθρωπον χοῦν ἀπὸ τῆς γῆς καὶ ἐνεφύσησεν εἰς τὸ πρόσωπον αὐτοῦ πνοὴν ζωῆς, καὶ ἐγένετο ὁ ἄνθρωπος εἰς ψυχὴν ζῶσαν*) distinguishes two kinds of men, *ὁ μὲν γάρ ἐστιν οὐράνιος ἄνθρωπος, ὁ δὲ γήϊνος ...τὸν μὲν οὐράνιόν φησιν οὐ πεπλάσθαι, κατ' εἰκόνα δὲ τετυπῶσθαι Θεοῦ· τὸ δὲ γήϊνον πλάσμα...ὁ δὲ νοῦς οὗτος γεώδης ἐστὶ τῷ ὄντι καὶ φθαρτός, εἰ μὴ ὁ Θεὸς ἐπέπνευσεν αὐτῷ δύναμιν ἀληθινῆς ζωῆς*, see *ib.* p. 32. St. Paul uses the equivalent *χοϊκός* 1 Cor. xv. 47 foll. The Gnostic Valentinus distinguished between an *ἄνω* and *κάτω σοφία*, and again between the *φύσεις πνευματικαί* akin to the Pleroma, *φύσεις ψυχικαί* containing a mixture of *ὕλη*, and the *φύσεις* which were altogether *ὑλικαί* (Iren. iii. 15), see Neander, vol. ii. pp. 110–145. So Hippolytus v. 6 (p. 134 Duncker) says of the Naassenes, who professed to receive their teaching from St. James, 'they divide the first man into three parts, *νοερόν, ψυχικόν, χοϊκόν*: in like manner they divide all that exists into three classes, *ἀγγελικόν, ψυχικόν* and *χοϊκόν*.' Heracleon *ap.* Orig. xi. 181 (quoted by Stieren on Iren. vol. i. p. 945) speaks of the Holy of Holies as representing the sphere of the *πνευματικοί* and the outer court the *ψυχικοί*, cf. Iren. i. p. 968 'when Jesus said to the Jews *ye are the children of your father the devil*, he speaks to those who are not *φύσει τοὺς διαβόλου υἱούς, τοὺς χοϊκούς, ἀλλὰ πρὸς τοὺς ψυχικούς* who make themselves such by their own fault,' Clem. Al. *Exc. ex Theod.* § 54 'three natures spring from Adam, *πρώτη μὲν ἡ ἄλογος, ἧς ἦν Καΐν, δευτέρα δὲ ἡ λογικὴ καὶ ἡ δικαία, ἧς ἦν Ἄβελ, τρίτη δὲ ἡ πνευματική, ἧς ἦν Σήθ· καὶ ὁ μὲν χοϊκός ἐστι κατ' εἰκόνα, ὁ δὲ ψυχικὸς καθ' ὁμοίωσιν Θεοῦ, ὁ δὲ πνευματικος κατ' ἰδίαν (ἰδέαν?)*,' *ib.* § 56 *πολλοὶ μὲν οἱ ὑλικοί, οὐ πολλοὶ δὲ οἱ ψυχικοί, σπάνιοι δὲ οἱ πνευματικοί· τὸ μὲν οὖν πνευματικὸν φύσει σωζόμενον, τὸ δὲ ψυχικὸν...κατὰ τὴν οἰκείαν αἵρεσιν, τὸ δὲ ὑλικὸν φύσει ἀπόλλυται.*

ψυχική.] On the various meanings attached to the word *ψυχή* see Hatch, pp. 94–130.[1] This use of the adjective is in accordance with the Pauline trichotomy *τὸ πνεῦμα καὶ ἡ ψυχὴ καὶ τὸ σῶμα* (1 Thess. v. 23), cf. 1 Cor. xv. 45 *ἐγένετο ὁ πρῶτος ἄνθρωπος Ἀδὰμ εἰς ψυχὴν ζῶσαν, ὁ ἔσχατος Ἀδὰμ εἰς πνεῦμα ζωοποιοῦν, ἀλλ' οὐ πρῶτον τὸ πνευματικὸν ἀλλὰ τὸ ψυχικόν.* In the LXX. we find it opposed to *σωματικός*, as in Macc. i. 32. In the N.T. *ψυχικός* connotes opposition to the higher principle, cf. Jude 19

[1] The ambiguous meaning of the word *ψυχὴ* in such passages as Lev. xvii. 14 *ψυχὴ πάσης σαρκὸς αἷμα*, and its employment in reference to animals Gen. i. 20, 24, are adduced by Philo and others as proofs of the inferiority of this principle, cf. Philo M. 1, p. 480 *ἐπειδὴ ψυχὴ διχῶς λέγεται, ἥ τε ὅλη καὶ τὸ ἡγεμονικὸν αὐτῆς μέρος, ὃ ψυχῆς ἐστιν, ἔδοξε τῷ νομοθέτῃ διπλῆν εἶναι καὶ τὴν οὐσίαν τῆς ψυχῆς, αἷμα μὲν τὸ τῆς ὅλης, τοῦ δὲ ἡγεμονικωτάτου πνεῦμα θεῖον· φησὶ γοῦν ἄντικρυς ψυχὴ πάσης σαρκὸς αἷμα. εὖ γε τὸ προσνεῖμαι τῷ σαρκὸς ὄχλῳ τὴν αἵματος ἐπιρροὴν οἰκεῖον οἰκείῳ, τοῦ δε νοῦ τὴν οὐσίαν ἀπὸ Θεοῦ ἄνωθεν καταπνευσθεῖσαν ἀνήγαγεν...ὥστε διττὸν εἶναι γένος ἀνθρώπων τὸ μὲν θείῳ πνεύματι καὶ λογισμῷ βιούντων, τὸ δὲ αἵματι καὶ σαρκὸς ἡδονῇ ζώντων.*

ψυχικοὶ, πνεῦμα μὴ ἔχοντες, 1 Cor. ii. 10 foll. esp. 14 ψυχικὸς ἄνθρωπος οὐ δέχεται τὰ τοῦ πνεύματος τοῦ Θεοῦ...ὁ δὲ πνευματικὸς ἀνακρίνει πάντα, *ib.* iii. 1 οὐκ ἠδυνήθην λαλῆσαι ὑμῖν ὡς πνευματικοῖς ἀλλ' ὡς σαρκίνοις, ὡς νηπίοις ἐν Χριστῷ. St. Paul contrasts the σῶμα πνευματικόν with the σῶμα ψυχικόν, 1 Cor. xv. 44. The word was used at a later period in reference to the orthodox by the Montanists who claimed the power of prophecy, Clem. Al. *Strom.* iv. p. 605 P οἱ Φρύγες...τοὺς τῇ νέᾳ προφητείᾳ μὴ προσέχοντας ψυχικοὺς καλοῦσιν: so Tertullian (*Jejun.* 1) gives the name *Psychici* to those who refused to keep the fasts of the Montanists. Hilgenfeld and others who imagine an allusion to St. Paul in ὦ ἄνθρωπε κενέ (ii. 20) regard this as a sarcastic reference to 1 Cor. ii. 10–15; 'your spiritual wisdom is worse than ψυχική, it is δαιμονιώδης.' The distinction drawn by Plato, Aristotle, and the Stoics between the immortal reason, the divine principle in man, and the lower faculties of the soul which perished with the body, certainly coloured the views of some of the Jewish and Christian writers as to the distinction between soul and spirit, which fall in naturally with the wide sense given to the word ψυχή in Aristotle's *De Anima*, and with its use by the Stoics to denote the third grade of existence, the principle of movement in animals, as contrasted with the λογικὴ ψυχή or νοῦς which constituted the fourth or highest grade (see my note on Cic. *N.D.* II. 33). Compare Tatian *ad Gr.* 18 δύο πνευμάτων διαφορὰς ἴσμεν ὧν τὸ μὲν καλεῖται ψυχή, τὸ δὲ μεῖζον μὲν τῆς ψυχῆς Θεοῦ δὲ εἰκὼν καὶ ὁμοίωσις, *ib.* 22 ἡ ψυχὴ μόνη μὲν διαιτωμένη πρὸς τὴν ὕλην νεύει κάτω, συναποθνήσκουσα τῇ σαρκί· συζυγίαν δὲ κεκτημένη τὴν τοῦ θείου πνεύματος οὐκ ἔστιν ἀβοήθητος κ.τ.λ. Justin M. *fr. de Resurr.* § 10 οἶκος τὸ σῶμα ψυχῆς, πνεύματος δὲ ψυχὴ οἶκος (after Plato *Tim.* 30 νοῦν μὲν ἐν ψυχῇ, ψυχὴν δὲ ἐν σώματι συνιστὰς τὸ πᾶν ἐτεκταίνετο), Jos. *A.J.* i. 34 ἔπλασεν ὁ Θεὸς τὸν ἄνθρωπον χοῦν ἀπὸ τῆς γῆς λαβὼν καὶ πνεῦμα ἐνῆκεν αὐτῷ καὶ ψυχήν, Philo *Opif.* M. p. 15 τῷ ἀνθρώπῳ νοῦν ἐξαίρετον ἐδωρεῖτο, ψυχῆς τίνα ψυχήν, καθαπερ κόρην ἐν ὀφθαλμῷ, Nemesius *N.H.* i. τινὲς μὲν, ὧν ἔστι καὶ Πλωτῖνος, ἄλλην εἶναι τὴν ψυχὴν καὶ ἄλλον τὸν νοῦν δογματίσαντες ἐκ τριῶν τὸν ἄνθρωπον συνεστάναι βούλονται σώματος καὶ ψυχῆς καὶ νοῦ, on which Matthiae quotes Irenaeus *Haer.* v. 9. 1 *tria sunt ex quibus perfectus homo constat, carne, anima, spiritu*, and Aug. *de Symbolo, homo habet tres partes, spiritum animum et corpus, itaque homo est imago SS. Trinitatis;* but Augustine in his treatise *de Eccl. Dogmat.* c. 20 blames Didymus for making *spiritus* a distinct principle, Apollinarius having in the meanwhile put forth his theory that the nature of Christ was ἐκ σαρκὸς καὶ ψυχῆς καὶ θεότητος ἀντὶ τοῦ νοῦ...'and so,' continues Matthiae, 'the separation of soul and spirit came to be thought a heresy.'

δαιμονιώδης.] This word is found elsewhere only in the Scholia to Aristoph. *Ran.* 295 and Symmachus, Ps. xc. 6. See above v. 6 φλογιζομένη ὑπὸ τῆς γεέννης, and ii. 19, 1 Tim. iv. 1 (of future apostates) προσέχοντες πνεύμασι πλάνοις καὶ διδασκαλίαις δαιμονίων ἐν ὑποκρίσει ψευδολόγων, Eph. ii. 2 f. those who walk according to the course of this world, κατὰ τὸν ἄρχοντα τῆς ἐξουσίας τοῦ ἀέρος, are described as ποιοῦντες τὰ θελήματα τῆς σακρὸς καὶ τῶν διανοιῶν (apparently corresponding to ἐπίγειος and ψυχική here), John viii. 44 ἐκ τοῦ πατρὸς τοῦ διαβόλου ἐστέ, 1 John ii. 16, *ib.* iii. 8–10, *ib.* iv. 1–6, where τὸ πνεῦμα τῆς ἀληθείας is distinguished from τὸ πνεῦμα τῆς πλάνης. Spitta explains this from the Jewish tradition of the wisdom imparted to the daughters of men by the rebel angels, cf. Jude 6, Enoch xvi. 3, Clem. *Strom.* v. p. 650.

16. **ἀκαταστασία.**] See above ver. 8 and i. 8, 1 Cor. xiv. 33 οὐ γάρ ἐστιν ἀκαταστασίας ὁ Θεὸς ἀλλὰ εἰρήνης, 2 Cor. xii. 20 where it is joined with ζῆλος and ἐριθεῖαι, Prov. xxvi. 28 στόμα ἄστεγον ποιεῖ ἀκαταστασίας, Clem. Rom. i. 3 ἐκ τούτου ζῆλος καὶ φθόνος καὶ ἔρις καὶ στάσις, διωγμὸς καὶ ἀκαταστασία, πόλεμος καὶ αἰχμαλωσία, Epict. *Diss.* iii. 19. 3 οὐδὲν ἄλλο ταραχῆς ἢ ἀκαταστασίας αἴτιόν ἐστιν ἢ δόγμα, Hatch p. 4.

πᾶν φαῦλον πρᾶγμα.] Simply 'every evil thing,' there is no need to take πᾶν = 'eitel' with Hofmann and Erdmann. Compare Epict. *Diss.* iii. 22. 61 ὅπου φθόνοι καὶ ζηλοτυπίαι, ποῦ ἐκεῖ πάροδος εὐδαιμονίας; ὅπου δ' ἂν ᾖ σαπρὰ δόγματα, ἐκεῖ πάντα ταῦτα εἶναι ἀνάγκη.

17. **ἡ δὲ ἄνωθεν σοφία.**] Compare Wisd. vii. 7—30 esp. vv. 25 and 26, *ib.* ix. 10.

πρῶτον μὲν ἁγνή.] First the inner characteristic, purity, then the outer, peaceableness, cf. the blessing in Matt. v. 8, 9. It is the pure who attain to the vision of God which constitutes the highest wisdom. Ps. xix. 9 ὁ φόβος Θεοῦ ἁγνός, Wisd. vii. 24, Matt. v. 8, Acts xv. 9, 2 Cor. vi. 6. 1 Tim. i. 4, Heb. x. 22. We may compare Antoninus viii. 5 συμμνημονεύσας τί τοῦ ἀνθρώπου ἡ φύσις ἀπαιτεῖ, πρᾶξον τοῦτο ἀμεταστρεπτί, καὶ εἰπὲ ὡς δικαιότατον φαίνεταί σοι, μόνον εὐμενῶς καὶ αἰδημόνως καὶ ἀνυποκρίτως.

ἔπειτα εἰρηνική.] The omission of δέ after ἔπειτα is quite classical (Winer p. 721), cf. below iv. 14, John xi. 6: ἔπειτα δέ occurs in Heb. vii. 2. For the association of truth (wisdom) and peace compare Rom. viii. 6 τὸ φρόνημα τοῦ πνεύματος ζωὴ καὶ εἰρήνη, Ps. lxxxv. 10, Prov. iii. 17, Isa. xxxii. 17, *ib.* xxvi. 3 ἀντιλαβόμενος ἀληθείας καὶ φυλάσσων εἰρήνην, Jer. xxxiii. 6, Mal. ii. 6. The word εἰρηνικός is only found elsewhere in N.T. in Heb. xii. 11.

ἐπιεικής.] Aristotle (*Eth.* vi. 11) says τὸν ἐπιεικῆ μάλιστα φαμὲν συγγνωμονικόν, and (*Eth.* v. 14) contrasts ἐπιείκεια 'equity' with strict justice, where Grant quotes the more detailed description given in *Rhet.* i. 13. 17. foll.: 'It is equity to pardon human failings, and to look to the law-giver and not to the law, to the spirit and not to the letter, to the intention and not to the action, to the whole and not to the part, to the character of the actor in the long run and not in the present moment, to remember good rather than evil, and good that one has received rather than good that one has done, to put up with injurious treatment, to wish to settle a matter by words rather than deeds, lastly to prefer arbitration to judgment.' Cope *in loc.* renders it 'merciful consideration.' In Homer the adj. is used in opposition to ἀεικής (= seemly, decorous, fitting). It seems not to be used of persons before Herod. i. 85 (of the son of Croesus) τὰ μὲν ἀλλὰ ἐπιεικής, ἄφωνος δὲ (in other respects a goodly youth). Thucydides (viii. 93) uses it of men who would listen to reason; in Cleon's speech (iii. 90) οἶκτος is joined with ἐπιείκεια (like τὸ ἐπιεικὲς καὶ ξύγγνωμον Plato *Leg.* vi. 757) as one of the things most injurious to a ruling state, cf. *ib.* v. 86. Plato constantly uses it of respectable, well-behaved people, as opposed to those who are rude and violent: in *Rep.* 397 D one who had before been called μέτριος is referred to as ὁ ἐπιεικής, as in Thuc. i. 76 τὸ ἐπιεικές = τὸ μετριάζειν 'moderation'; hence its colloquial use in Plato and Aristotle = σπουδαῖος or ἀγαθός. In the N.T. it always has the more special sense, and is twice joined with ἄμαχος (1 Tim. iii. 3, Tit. iii. 2): in 1 Pet. ii. 18 it is used of a master who is considerate towards his slaves; Acts xxiv. 4 Tertullus begs Felix to hear him with his usual condescension (ἐπιεικείᾳ): the most important passage is 2 Cor. x. 1 παρακαλῶ ὑμᾶς διὰ τῆς πραΰτητος καὶ ἐπιεικείας τοῦ Χριστοῦ, which Matthew Arnold rendered by his phrase of 'sweet reasonableness,' compare Phil. iv. 5, Wisdom ii. 19 ὕβρει καὶ βασάνῳ ἐτάσωμεν αὐτὸν (the just) ἵνα γνῶμεν τὴν ἐπιείκειαν αὐτοῦ καὶ δοκιμάσωμεν τὴν ἀνεξικακίαν αὐτοῦ, *ib.* xii. 18 δεσπόζων ἰσχύος ἐν ἐπιεικείᾳ κρίνεις, Philo M. 2. p. 112 (of God) διὰ τὴν σύμφυτον ἐπιείκειαν καὶ φιλανθρωπίαν. It is the Greek equivalent to the Roman *clementia* (App. *B.C.* ii. 106). The history of the word shows that it is etymologically connected with εἰκός, implying that which is fit and reasonable; but its later meaning was influenced by the idea of a connexion with εἴκω 'to yield,' implying one who does not stand on his rights, but is ready to give way to the wishes of others.

εὐπειθής.] Not found elsewhere in N.T. It is often used of military discipline, as in 4 Macc. 8. 6, Jos. *B.J.* ii. 20. 7. We find it with a gen. Plato *Leg.* i. 632 B εὐπ. τῶν νόμων, with a dat. *ib.* vii. 801 εὐπ. τοῖς νόμοις, with prep. *ib.* vi. 718 C βουλοίμην ἂν αὐτοὺς ὡς εὐπειθεστάτους πρὸς ἀρετὴν εἶναι. In the last passage it should probably be translated 'easy to be persuaded,' as it follows the words 'our exposition of the law' τὰ μὲν πείθουσα, τὰ δὲ μὴ ὑπείκοντα πειθοῖ...βίᾳ κολάζουσα, τὴν πόλιν εὐδαίμονα ἀποτελεῖ. So Philo M. 2. p. 378 διδασκαλίαι εἰσὶ τοὺς μὲν εὐπειθεῖς μαλακώτερον ἀναπείθουσαι, τοὺς δὲ ἀπειθεστέρους ἐμβριθέστερον. The opposite ἀπειθής, ἀπειθεῖν, ἀπείθεια occur several times in N.T. in the sense of 'disobedience.' Musonius (*ap.* Stob. *Ecl.* p. 453, Peerlkamp *Frag.* p. 227), answering the question whether obedience to a father is always right, says that he alone is to be called εὐπειθής who willingly submits to a true fatherly will (ὁ τῷ τὰ προσήκοντα παραινοῦντι κατήκοος ὢν καὶ ἑπόμενος ἑκουσίως, οὗτος εὐπειθής). As ἐπιεικής refers mainly to one in a superior position, so I should understand εὐπειθής to refer to an inferior, and translate 'submissive,' 'docile,' 'tractable,' old English 'buxom,' Lat. *morigera.* The quarrels and rivalries in the Church were due to faults on the side of the latter as well as of the former.

μεστὴ ἐλέους καὶ καρπῶν ἀγαθῶν.] See above vers. 8, ii. 13. An example of such fruits is given in i. 27, while their absence is shown in ii. 15.

ἀδιάκριτος.] Here only in N.T. The meaning of διακρίνομαι above (i. 6, ii. 4) makes it probable that we must understand the adj. here in the sense of 'single-minded,' 'unhesitating' (undivided), as in Heracleon ap. Orig. *Comm. in. Joh.* xiii. 10 (Brooke's Heracl. p. 73) ἐπαινεῖ τὴν Σαμαρεῖτιν ὡσὰν ἐνδειξαμένην τὴν ἀδιάκριτον...πίστιν, μὴ διακριθεῖσαν ἐφ' οἷς ἔλεγεν αὐτῇ, Ignat. *Trall.* 1 ἄμωμον διάνοιαν καὶ ἀδιάκριτον ἐν ὑπομονῇ ἔγνων ὑμᾶς ἔχοντας, *id. Rom. inscr.* πεπληρωμένοις χάριτος Θεοῦ ἀδιακρίτως, *Philad. inscr.* 'Ignatius to the Church' ἡδρασμένῃ ἐν ὁμονοίᾳ Θεοῦ καὶ ἀγαλλιωμένῃ ἐν τῷ πάθει τοῦ Κυρίου ἡμῶν ἀδιακρίτως.[1] It only occurs once in the LXX., Prov. xxv. 1 αὗται αἱ παιδεῖαι Σαλομῶντος αἱ ἀδιάκριτοι, where Delitzsch gives it a secondary passive sense 'the undoubted proverbs,' while Lightfoot, in his excellent n. on Ignat *Eph.* 3 (vol. ii. p. 39), translates it 'miscellaneous,' connecting it with the more common meaning 'undistinguishable': hence it is used for 'confused,' 'vague,' as in Polyb. xv. 12. 9 ἀδιάκριτος φωνή (*promiscuus clamor* Schw.), Epict. *Diss.* i. 16. 12, *ib.* ii. 20. 29 φαντασία μοι ἐγένετο ἐλαίου ἀδιάκριτος ὁμοιοτάτη (*oleo ita simile ut ab eo discerni non posset* Schw.), Test. Patr. p. 641 ἀδιακρίτως πᾶσι σπλαγχνιζόμενοι 'pitying all without distinction,' Greg. Naz. *V. Mos.* p. 232 μάστιξ ἀδ. 'indiscriminate punishment': Lucian *Jup. Trag.* 25 has ἀμφήριστον ἔτι καὶ ἀδιάκριτον καταλιπὼν τὸν λόγον 'leaving the matter undecided,' almost the opposite force to that which it bears here. It occurs also in Clem. Al. pp. 115, 474.

ἀνυπόκριτος.] 'Sincere,' 'without show or pretence,' used of love 1 Pet. i. 22 τὰς ψυχὰς ὑμῶν ἡ γ ν ι κ ό τ ε ς ἐν τῇ ὑ π α κ ο ῇ τῆς ἀ λ η θ ε ί α ς διὰ π ν ε ύ μ α τ ο ς εἰς φ ι λ α δ ε λ φ ί α ν ἀ ν υ π ό κ ρ ι τ ο ν, 2 Cor. vi. 6 ἐν ἁγνότητι, ἐν γνώσει...ἐν πνεύματι ἁγίῳ, ἐν ἀγάπῃ ἀνυποκρίτῳ: of faith 2 Tim. i. 5, 1 Tim. i. 5. It is also found in LXX., Wisd. v. 18, xviii. 16, Clem. Rom. ii. 2, 12 ἐν δυσὶ σώμασιν ἀνυποκρίτως μία ψυχή.

18. **καρπὸς δὲ δικαιοσύνης ἐν εἰρήνῃ σπείρεται.**] Heb. xii. 11 (παιδεία) κ α ρ π ὸ ν ε ἰ ρ η ν ι κ ὸ ν τοῖς δι' αὐτῆς γεγυμνασμένοις ἀποδίδωσι δ ι κ α ι ο σ ύ ν η ς, Phil. i. 11 πεπληρωμένοι καρπὸν δικαιοσύνης τὸν διὰ Ἰ.Χ., Prov. xi. 30 ἐκ καρποῦ δικαιοσύνης φύεται δένδρον ζωῆς, *ib.* iii. 9 and xiii. 2 ἀπὸ καρπῶν δικαιοσύνης, Amos vi. 2 ἐξεστρέψατε καρπὸν δικαιοσύνης εἰς πικρίαν, Hos. x. 12 σπείρατε ἑαυτοῖς εἰς δικαιοσύνην, τρυγήσατε εἰς καρπὸν ζωῆς, Prov. xi. 21 ὁ σπείρων δικαιοσύνην λήψεται μισθὸν πιστόν, *ib.* v. 18, Isa. xxxii. 17 καὶ ἔσται τὰ ἔργα τῆς δικαιοσύνης εἰρήνη (the converse of what is said here), Job iv. 8, Gal. vi. 7. The difficulty of the expression here consists in the prolepsis which regards the seed as already containing in itself the fruit,[2] see Jennings on Psa. xcvii. 11 'light is sown for the righteous,' where the note is 'the affliction entailed by the oppression of the wicked is to the righteous as the seed of light.' Spitta cites Baruch xxxii. 1 *si praeparaveritis corda vestra ut seminetis in eis fructus legis*, 4 Esdr. viii. 6 *des nobis semen cordis et sensui culturam unde fructus fiat.* For the genitive of definition cp. i. 12.

τοῖς ποιοῦσιν εἰρήνην.] The phrase occurs Eph. ii. 15, 2 Macc. i. 4. We have the compound εἰρηνοποιῶ in Col. i. 20 and εἰρηνοποιός Matt. v. 9. I think the dat. here is best explained as dat. comm., not of the agent as in ver. 7. 'A harvest of righteousness' is the issue of the quiet and gentle ministrations of those who aim at reconciling quarrels and being themselves in peace with all men. This is the contrary of i. 20. Spitta understands τοῖς ποιοῦσιν of those who receive the seed, but this would require a preposition such as ἐν: moreover St. James is treating throughout of the teacher not of the hearer.

[1] Dr. Plummer cites Ign. *ad Magn.* xv. ἔρρωσθε ἐν ὁμονοίᾳ Θεοῦ κεκτημένοι ἀδιάκριτον πνεῦμα, Clem. Al. *Paed.* ii. 3, p. 190, ἀδιακρίτῳ πίστει.

[2] Bloomfield compares Antiphanes *Fab. Inc.* iv. 4. M. σπείρειν καρπὸν χάριτος 'sow the fruit of gratitude.' See also Sir. xxiv. 17 τὰ ἄνθη μου καρπὸς δόξης.

IV. 1.—**πόθεν.**] St. James is much given to the use of the interrogative, see ii. 4, 5, 6, 7, 14, 15, 16, 19, 20, 21, 25, iii. 11, 12, 13, iv. 4, 5, 12, 14. For the repetition of πόθεν see iii. 9 ἐν αὐτῇ, i. 19 βραδύς. Notice that the severity of this section, as of that which commences below with v. 13, is marked by the absence of the word ἀδελφοί.

πόλεμοι καὶ μάχαι.] These need not be limited to their narrow sense: the former denotes any lasting resentment, the latter any outburst of passion. Compare Titus iii. 9 μωρὰς δὲ ζητήσεις...καὶ ἔρεις καὶ μάχας νομικὰς περιίστασο, *ib.* v. 2, 2 Tim. ii. 22 f., Gal. v. 15, 2 Cor. vii. 5. The verb μάχομαι is used of chiding or disputing in Gen. xxxi. 36, Neh. xiii. 11, John vi. 52. So in other writers we have πολέμους καὶ στάσεις καὶ μάχας οὐδὲν ἄλλο παρέχει ἢ τὸ σῶμα καὶ αἱ τούτου ἐπιθυμίαι Plato *Phaedo* 66 C (not '*Phaedrus* xv.' as Beyschlag), Cic. *Fin.* i. 13. 43 *cupiditates sunt insatiabiles quae non modo singulos homines sed universas familias evertunt, totam etiam labefactant saepe rem publicam. Ex cupiditatibus odia, discidia, discordiae, seditiones, bella nascuntur...intus etiam in animis inclusae inter se dissident et discordant,* Seneca *Ira* 3. 5 *etiam illa plebeia ira et privata inerme et sine viribus bellum est, ib.* 35 *ista quae appetitis, quia non possunt ad alterum nisi alteri erepta transferri, eadem affectantibus pugnam et jurgia excitant,* Philo M. 2. p. 205 οἱ Ἑλλήνων καὶ βαρβάρων...τραγῳδηθέντες πόλεμοι πάντες ἀπὸ μιᾶς πηγῆς ἐρρύησαν, ἐπιθυμίας ἢ χρημάτων ἢ δόξης ἢ ἡδονῆς (in *Concup.* p. 449 f. he traces out the evil consequences of each species of ἐπιθυμία at length); Epict. *Diss.* iii. 20. 18 πρὸς τὸ παιδάριον πόλεμος, πρὸς τοὺς γείτονας, πρὸς τοὺς σκώψαντας, πρὸς τοὺς καταγελάσαντας, *ib.* i. 22, Test. Patr. p. 538 τὸ πνεῦμα τοῦ φθόνου ἀγριοῖ τὴν ψυχὴν, ὀργὴν καὶ πόλεμον παρέχει καὶ εἰς αἵματα παροξύνει, Clem. Rom. 46 ἵνα τί ἔρεις καὶ θυμοὶ καὶ διχοστασίαι καὶ σχίσματα πόλεμός τε ἐν ὑμῖν;

οὐκ ἐντεῦθεν.] Pleonastic before ἐκ τῶν ἡδονῶν, like αὕτη in i. 27, οὗτος in i. 25, ἄνωθεν in i. 17, serving to bring out what follows into sharper relief.

τῶν ἡδονῶν τῶν στρατευομένων ἐν τοῖς μέλεσιν.] The potential pleasure seated in each member constitutes a hostile force, a foe lying in ambush against which we have continually to be on our guard. Cf. Tit. iii. 3 δουλεύοντες ἐπιθυμίαις καὶ ἡδοναῖς ποικίλαις, 4 Macc. vi. 35 τὸν λογισμὸν τῶν ἡδονῶν κρατεῖν καὶ μηδὲν αὐταῖς ὑπείκειν, *ib.* v. 22 (φιλοσοφία) σωφροσύνην ἐκδιδάσκει ὥστε πασῶν τῶν ἡδονῶν καὶ ἐπιθυμιῶν κρατεῖν, Xen. *Mem.* i. 2. 23 ἐν τῷ αὐτῷ σώματι συμπεφυτευμέναι τῇ ψυχῇ αἱ ἡδοναὶ πείθουσιν αὐτὴν μὴ σωφρονεῖν, *ib.* 5. 6 δουλεύοντα ἡδοναῖς. For the metaphor cf. the parallel passage in 1 Pet. ii. 11 παρακαλῶ ἀπέχεσθαι τῶν σαρκικῶν ἐπιθυμιῶν αἵτινες στρατεύονται κατὰ τῆς ψυχῆς, Rom. vii. 23 βλέπω ἕτερον νόμον ἐν τοῖς μέλεσίν μου ἀντιστρατευόμενον τῷ νόμῳ τοῦ νοός μου, *ib.* vi. 13, Gal. v. 19 f., Philo M. 1. p. 445 εἴ τις βουληθείη τὸν ὄχλον μιᾶς ψυχῆς ὥσπερ κατὰ ἔθνη διανεῖμαι, πολλὰς ἂν εὕροι τάξεις ἀκοσμούσας, ὧν ἡδοναὶ ἢ ἐπιθυμίαι ἢ λῦπαι ἢ φόβοι...ταξιαρχοῦσιν. For ἐν τοῖς μέλεσιν see above iii. 6 and compare Hatch, p. 111, who cites Philo M. 1. p. 511 τὰ σώματος πάθη σαρκὸς ἐκπεφυκότα ἢ προσερρίζωνται, *ib.* p. 692 τὸ ἡμέτερον σῶμα καὶ τὰ ἐν αὐτῷ καὶ δι' αὐτὸ ἐγγινόμενα πάθη, *ib.* M. 2. p. 253 ὅτῳ ἐγκάθηνται καὶ ἐλλοχῶσι πλεονεξίαι καὶ ἐπιθυμίαι τῶν ἀδικιῶν.

2. **ἐπιθυμεῖτε καὶ οὐκ ἔχετε· φονεύετε καὶ ζηλοῦτε, καὶ οὐ δύνασθε ἐπιτυχεῖν. μάχεσθε καὶ πολεμεῖτε.**] This is the reading and punctuation of Westcott and Hort, agreeing in essentials with Alford, Tischendorf and the more recent editors. The R.V. has 'ye lust, and have not: ye kill, and covet (marg. 'are jealous'), and cannot obtain: ye fight and war.' The extraordinary anti-climax 'ye kill and covet' has long exercised the minds of commentators, who have endeavoured to remove it either (1) by weakening the force of φονεύετε, or (2) by strengthening the force of ζηλοῦτε, or (3) by giving a special meaning to the connexion between them.

(1, *a*) 'Kill' means 'hate,' because every one that hateth his brother is a murderer. So Estius, Corn. a Lap., Theile, De Wette, Wiesinger, Beyschlag, Erdmann. (1, *b*) 'Kill' means 'commit moral suicide,' so Oecumenius and Theophylact, φονεύειν φησὶ τοὺς τὴν ἑαυτῶν ψυχὴν ἀποκτιννύντας ταῖς τοιαύταις ἐπιχειρήσεσι.

(2) ζηλοῦτε means 'become ζηλωταί,' *i.e.* assassins; so Macknight and Dean Scott in the *Speaker's Commentary*, referring to Josephus, *B.J.* vii. 8, 1, where the ζηλωταί are said to have been worse than the σικάριοι.

(3) φονεύετε καὶ ζηλοῦτε form a hendiadys, 'ye murderously envy,' *ad necem usque invidetis*. So Pott, Schneckenburger, Gebser, and not much otherwise Bengel, *occiditis per odia et zelum*.

The objections to these expedients are to my mind conclusive. (1) It does not follow, because to show the heinousness of hate it may be represented as virtually equivalent to the murder of which it is the germ, that it is therefore allowable in all cases to substitute the word 'murder' for 'hate.' In the present case it may be safely said that no sane writer, no one who had the slightest feeling for rhetorical effect (and St. James is both eminently sane and eminently rhetorical) could have used φονεύετε in the sense of μισεῖτε before ζηλοῦτε. There is no reason here to lay an exaggerated stress on the idea of hate, if nothing more than hate is intended: not only does it make a mere bathos of ζηλοῦτε, but it weakens the force of the following μάχεσθε καὶ πολεμεῖτε. Others have thought it impossible that those addressed by St. James could be guilty of the actual sin of murder. But in ch. v. 6 we read ἐφονεύσατε τὸν δίκαιον, so 1 Pet. iv. 15 μὴ γάρ τις ὑμῶν πασχέτω ὡς φονεὺς ἢ κλέπτης ἢ κακοποιός, and Didaché iii. 2 μὴ γίνου ὀργίλος...μηδὲ ζηλωτὴς μηδὲ ἐριστικὸς μηδὲ θυμικός· ἐκ γὰρ τούτων ἁπάντων φόνοι γεννῶνται, and I think we should gather from Acts xxi. 20 that some of the assailants of St. Paul at Jerusalem were members of the Christian community. Of (2) it is sufficient to say that there is no evidence of the verb ζηλόω being used in this sense, and nothing to suggest it in the G.T. use of the word ζηλωτής. (3) If ζηλοῦτε preceded φονεύετε, something might be said for the theory of ἓν διὰ δυοῖν: as it is, every one must feel that it is a suggestion of despair.

Lastly, Alford, Bouman, Schegg and others, feeling the unsatisfactory nature of the above-mentioned explanations, have fallen back on the literal rendering. Schegg is the only commentator known to me who makes any attempt to account for the order of the words, which he defends as fellows: 'Die Lust *begehret*, d. h. sie sucht werkthätig zu erreichen, wornach sie gelüstet; die Lust *tötet*, d. h. sie schafft gewaltsam bei seite was ihr hinderlich entgegentritt; die Lust *ringet* um das, was sie zu erlangen im Begriffe ist...Da töten und ringen verschiedene Objekte habet, indem sich töten *gegen*, ringen *auf* etwas richtet, so hat Jakobus psychologisch richtig die Reihen-und-Stufenfolge der Aeusserungen des Gelüstens eingehalten.' It is by no means certain that ζηλοῦτε is to be taken here in the sense, which Schegg assigns to it, of striving after a thing: it is often followed by an accusative of the person. But supposing it to be true that the object of ζηλοῦτε is here a thing, and that of φονεύετε a person, I am unable to see why this makes it psychologically right to put φονεύετε first. Surely it is the resistance to our effort to gain an object which suggests to us the necessity of moving the obstacle out of the way.

I have for many years held the opinion that, assuming the correctness of the text, the only way to interpret it is to place a colon after φονεύετε: and I am glad to find that the same idea has occurred to Dr. J. Chr. K. v. Hofmann, whose commentary appeared in 1876. It is also given as an alternative reading in Westcott and Hort's edition (1881). The easiest way of seeing how the words naturally group themselves is to put them side by side without any stopping: ἐπιθυμεῖτε καὶ οὐκ ἔχετε φονεύετε καὶ ζηλοῦτε καὶ οὐ δύνασθε ἐπιτυχεῖν μάχεσθε καὶ πολεμεῖτε. Can any one doubt that the abrupt collocations of φονεύετε and μάχεσθε are employed to express results of what precedes, and that in the second series ζηλοῦτε καὶ οὐ δύνασθε ἐπιτυχεῖν correspond to ἐπιθυμεῖτε καὶ οὐκ ἔχετε in the first series? Unsatisfied desire leads to murder (as in the case of Naboth); disappointed ambition leads to quarrelling and fighting. Schegg and Beyschlag and Erdmann object to this grouping of the words as harsh and unlike the style of St. James, but abruptness is a marked characteristic with him, see ii. 19 σὺ πιστεύεις ...Θεός· καλῶς ποιεῖς, v. 6 ἐφονεύσατε τὸν δίκαιον· οὐκ ἀντιτάσσεται ὑμῖν. The only difficulty introduced is that the second series (ζηλοῦτε κ.τ.λ.) is joined to the first by καὶ instead of standing independently by its side. Perhaps this may be accounted for by the fact that the figure asyndeton was already employed to mark the change from the antecedents to the consequents. [Dr. Plummer adopts this punctuation.]

Taking it in this way we may compare Epict. *Diss.* ii. 17 θέλω τι καὶ οὐ γίνεται· καὶ τί ἐστιν ἀθλιώτερον ἐμοῦ; τοῦτο καὶ ἡ Μήδεια οὐχ ὑπομείνασα ἦλθεν ἐπὶ τὸ ἀποκτεῖναι τὰ ἴδια τέκνα...ἁπλῶς μὴ θέλε ἢ ἃ ὁ Θεὸς θέλει, καὶ τίς σε κωλύσει, τίς σε ἀναγκάσει; Clem. Rom. i. 3 ἕκαστον βαδίζειν κατὰ τὰς ἐπιθυμίας αὐτοῦ τὰς πονηράς, ζῆλον ἄδικον καὶ ἀσεβῆ ἀνειληφότα, δι' οὗ καὶ θάνατος εἰσῆλθεν εἰς τὸν κόσμον: see Lightfoot on this and the following paragraph, where he cites Clem. Hom. iii. 42 Κάϊν ἑρμηνεύεται ζῆλος, and Iren. iv. 18. 3; also Clem. Rom. i. 4 ὁρᾶτε, ἀδελφοί, ζῆλος καὶ φθόνος ἀδελφοκτονίαν κατειργάσατο, where their effect is traced through a long series of examples: *ib.* 6 ζῆλος καὶ ἔρις πόλεις μεγάλας κατέστρεψεν καὶ ἔθνη μεγάλα ἐξερίζωσεν.

But may it not be that we ought, with Erasmus, followed by Calvin, Beza, Hottinger, Ewald, Stier and Spitta to read φθονεῖτε, supposing this to have been carelessly written φονεῖτε (which indeed we find in the text, though not in the note, of Oecumenius), and corrected into φονεύετε? In 1 Pet. ii. 1 B has the same mistake, φόνους for φθόνους. A similar corruption may have given rise to the reading φθόνοι, φόνοι in Gal. v. 21. where φόνοι is omitted by the best MSS. Conversely in Clem. Hom. ii. 11, φθόνου is wrongly given in the MSS. for φόνου. Certainly the process of thought is thus made easier. Accepting this change of reading, we shall have only the last result, 'ye fight and war,' following the two antecedents, 'ye lust and have not,' 'ye are envious and jealous and cannot obtain': 'we thus see the words ἡδονῶν στρατευομένων fitly associated with πόλεμοι καὶ μάχαι, and these words anticipating μάχεσθε καὶ πολεμεῖτε' Hoskyns-Abrahall in *C.R.* iii. p. 314). Internal unrest (ἡδοναὶ στρατευόμεναι ἐν τοῖς μέλεσιν) in its two stages—desire without possession (of a thing), envy and jealousy which bring us no nearer our aim (of a person)—is followed by outward disturbance (μάχεσθε καὶ πολεμεῖτε). Compare the stages of ἐπιθυμία in i. 14, 15. If it is once recognized that, whatever punctuation we adopt, φονεύετε can only be taken here in its literal sense, it must be allowed that it disturbs the natural order, and strikes, as it were, a false note between the πόλεμοι and μάχαι of ver. 1 and the μάχεσθε and πολεμεῖτε of v. 2.

ἐπιθυμεῖτε καὶ οὐκ ἔχετε.] Both words are used absolutely as in Rom. xiii. 9 (ἐπιθ.), Matt. xxv. 29 τοῦ μὴ ἔχοντος καὶ ὃ ἔχει ἀρθήσεται ἀπ' αὐτοῦ, 2 Cor. viii. 12 καθὸ ἐὰν ἔχῃ εὐπρόσδεκτος, οὐ καθὸ οὐκ ἔχει.

(φθονεῖτε) καὶ ζηλοῦτε.] On the difference between them see Thuc. ii. 64 ταῦτα ὁ μὲν ἀπράγμων μέμψαιτ' ἄν, ὁ δὲ δρᾶν τι βουλόμενος καὶ αὐτὸς ζηλώσει· εἰ δέ τις μὴ κέκτηται φθονήσει, Arist. *Rhet.* ii. 10 and 11 with Cope's notes, Cic. *Tusc.* iv. 17 *invidentiam esse dicunt aegrimoniam susceptam propter alterius res secundas, quae nihil noceant invidenti... aemulatio autem est aegritudo si eo, quod concupierit, alius potiatur, ipse careat*, Trench, *Syn.* p. 100. Both are distinguished from ἐπιθ. as denoting a feeling towards a person rather than a thing. The word ζῆλος with its cognates embraces the two meanings, emulation and jealousy, and it is used also of vehement desire, our 'zeal,' in a good sense. For examples of the former meaning see Acts v. 17 and xiii. 45 ἐπλήσθησαν ζήλου, Rom. xiii. 13, 1 Cor. iii. 3, 2 Cor. xii. 20, Gal. v. 20, and above iii. 14, in all which places the R.V. has 'jealousy': similarly the verb, Acts vii. 9 οἱ πατριάρχαι ζηλώσαντες τὸν Ἰωσὴφ ἀπέδοντο, *ib.* xvii. 5, 1 Cor. xiii. 4, Clem. Rom. ii. 4 μὴ καταλαλεῖν ἀλλήλων, μὴ ζηλοῦν. For ζῆλος in good sense cf. John ii. 17 ὁ ζῆλος τοῦ οἴκου σου καταφάγεταί με 'the zeal (holy jealousy) for thy house will devour me,' Rom. x. 2 ζῆλον Θεοῦ ἔχουσιν, 2 Cor xi. 2. *ib.* vii. 7 τὸν ὑμῶν ζῆλον ὑπὲρ ἐμοῦ, v. 11, Phil. iii. 6 κατὰ ζῆλος διώκων τὴν ἐκκλησίαν; so ζηλωτὴς τοῦ Θεοῦ Acts xxii. 3, τοῦ νόμου *ib.* xxi. 20, καλῶν ἔργων Tit. ii. 14. The verb takes an acc. in the sense of 'seek eagerly,' τὰ χαρίσματα 1 Cor. xii. 31, ζηλῶ ὑμᾶς 2 Cor. xi. 2, Gal. iv. 17, ἐζήλωσα τὸ ἀγαθόν Sir. li. 18, μὴ ζηλοῦτε θάνατον Wisd. i. 12. For the combination of φθόνος and ζῆλος Spitta cites 1 Macc. viii. 16, Test. Sim. 4, Clem. Rom. 3. 4, 5.

ἐπιτυχεῖν.] Used absolutely Gen. xxxiv. 2 (Ἰωσὴφ) ἦν ἀνὴρ ἐπιτυγχάνων ('prosperous'), Epict. *Diss.* ii. 6. 8 ἀλλ' οὐκ ἐπέτυχες, with gen. Heb. xi.

33 ἐπέτυχον ἐπαγγελιῶν, *ib.* vi. 15, with acc. Rom. xi. 7 τοῦτο οὐκ ἐπέτυχεν. It was a *vox technica* of the Stoics, Epict. *Ench.* 2 ὀρέξεως ἐπαγγελία ἐπιτυχία οὗ ὀρέγῃ, ἐκκλίσεως ἐπαγγελία τὸ μὴ περιπεσεῖν ἐκείνῳ ὃ ἐκκλίνεται.

οὐκ ἔχετε.] Repeated like αἰτείτω in i. 5, 6. It is not a further step.

διὰ τὸ μὴ αἰτεῖσθαι ὑμᾶς.] The subject of the infinitive is expressed as in iii. 3, where see n.

3. **αἰτεῖτε καὶ οὐ λαμβάνετε.**] Yet in i. 5 he had said, quoting from the Sermon on the Mount, αἰτείτω καὶ δοθήσεται. But the promise is not unconditional. In the former passage stress is laid on the need for simple faith in the worshippers, here on the right choice of things to pray for.

Why is the active voice used here, and the middle immediately before and afterwards? The latter has a slight additional shade of meaning, which may be illustrated by the distinction (noted by Dobree in Arnold's n. on Thuc. v. 43) between δεινὰ ἐποίουν 'they expressed,' and δεινὰ ἐποιοῦντο 'they felt indignation'; and by Donaldson's distinction between ἰδεῖν 'to see' and ἰδέσθαι 'to behold,' 'see with interest' ('in this particular use of the middle it will generally be found to imply a certain special diligence and earnestness in the action' Winer, p. 318): cf. for this 'dynamic' or 'subjective' middle Krüger *Gr.* § 52. 8 and 10. Sturz in Lex. Xen. s.v. quotes Schol. Aristoph. 156 αἰτοῦμαι τὸ αὐτὸ (τῷ αἰτῶ), ὥσπερ ποιῶ καὶ ποιοῦμαι, πλὴν ὅτι τὸ μὲν αἰτῶ τὸ ἁπλῶς ζητῶ, τὸ δὲ αἰτοῦμαι τὸ μεθ' ἱκεσίας, Phavorin. αἰτοῦμαι τὸ μετὰ παρακλήσεως αἰτῶ καὶ ἱκετεύω. When αἰτεῖτε is thus opposed to αἰτεῖσθε, it implies using the words, without the spirit of prayer. Otherwise, where there is no special reason to emphasize this shade of meaning, the active may be used to include the force of the middle, just as μεταπέμπω is used in the sense of 'send for,' which strictly belongs to μεταπέμπομαι. I add a few examples of the combination of the two voices: 1 John v. 15 ἐὰν οἴδαμεν ὅτι ἀκούει ἡμῶν ὃ ἂν αἰτώμεθα, οἴδαμεν ὅτι ἔχομεν τὰ αἰτήματα ἃ ᾐτήκαμεν παρ' αὐτοῦ, and again αἰτήσει (*act.*) in v. 16, Mark vi. 22–24 αἴτησόν με ὃ ἐὰν θέλῃς...εἶπεν τῇ μητρί, τί αἰτήσωμαι; *ib.* x. 35, 38, John xvi. 24, 26, Justin M. *Trypho* 49 ἡ μήτηρ ὑπέβαλεν αὐτῇ αἰτήσασθαι...καὶ αἰτησάσης ἔπεμψε κ.τ.λ., Hermas *Vis.* iii. 10. 7 τί σὺ αἰτεῖς ἀποκαλύψεις; βλέπε μή τι πολλὰ αἰτούμενος βλάψῃς σου τὴν σάρκα, and just before πᾶσα ἐρώτησις ταπεινοφροσύνης δεῖται· νήστευσον οὖν καὶ λήμψῃ ὃ αἰτεῖς, *ib. Mand.* ix. 4 σὺ οὖν καθάρισόν σου τὴν καρδίαν ἀπὸ πάντων τῶν ματαιωμάτων τοῦ αἰῶνος τούτου...καὶ αἰτοῦ παρὰ τοῦ Κυρίου, καὶ ἀπολήψῃ πάντα...ἐὰν ἀδιστάκτως αἰτήσῃς [here I should prefer to read αἰτήσῃ], *ib.* § 7, Clem. Al. *Strom.* vi. § 63 p. 771 P ὁ ψαλμῳδὸς αἰτεῖ λέγων...καὶ τὸ πολύπειρον τῆς γνώσεως αἰτούμενος ὁ Δαβὶδ γράφει κ.τ.λ.

κακῶς.] 'Wrongly,' as in John xviii. 23 εἰ κακῶς ἐλάλησα. It is explained by the words which follow, and is the opposite to 1 John v. 14 ἐάν τι αἰτώμεθα κ α τ ὰ τ ὸ θ έ λ η μ α α ὐ τ ο ῦ ἀκούει ἡμῶν, cf. Isa. lix. 2, Max. Tyr. 30 ὁ Θεὸς λέγει, εἰ ἀγαθὰ ἐπ' ἀγαθῷ αἰτεῖς, λάμβανε, Theophylact on Luke xviii. 42 ἐπεὶ ἄλλα αἰτοῦντες ἄλλα λαμβάνομεν, πρόδηλον ὅτι οὐ καλῶς οὐδὲ πιστῶς αἰτοῦμεν. This wrong prayer is without submission (v. 7): the petitioner uses it as an instrument of selfishness; he would make religion a help to serving the world, cf. 1 Tim. vi. 4, 5.

ἵνα ἐν ταῖς ἡδοναῖς ὑμῶν δαπανήσητε.[1]] Cf. Luke xv., where *δαπανήσαντος αὐτοῦ πάντα* (v. 14) is explained by *ὁ καταφαγών σου τὸν βίον μετὰ πορνῶν* (v. 30). The object here is understood from *αἰτεῖτε*. In Acts xxi. 24 *δαπ.* is followed by *ἐπί*, in classical writers usually by *εἰς*, but also by *πρός*, *ἀμφί*, or the simple dat.; there is however no occasion to separate *ἐν* from the verb (as Alf.), cf. Thuc. vii. 48. 5 *ἐν περιπολίοις ἀναλίσκοντας*, where Poppo cites Arist. *Eth.* iv. 2. 20 *ἐν τοῖς μικροῖς τῶν δαπανημάτων πολλὰ ἀναλίσκει*, Aristid. *adv. Lept.* p. 62 *τὴν ἐν τοῖς τοιούτοις δαπάνην*, and compares Lat. *consumere in re*. The extreme of this *δαπάνησις* is seen in the *ἐτρυφήσατε* and *ἐσπαταλήσατε* of v. 5. Prayer for this is the opposite to prayer for daily bread, and to Matt. vi. 32, 33 'seek first the kingdom of God, and all these things shall be added unto you, for your Father knoweth ye have need of these things.' Compare the conclusion of Juvenal's tenth Satire.

4. **μοιχαλίδες.**] Recent editors follow A. B. Sin. in omitting *μοιχοὶ καί*, and understand the word in the figurative sense of adulterous souls, in accordance with the language of the O.T., which speaks of Israel as married to Jehovah (Isa. lvii. 3–9, Jer. iii. 20, Ezek. 16 esp. vv. 32, 35, 38, *ib.* ch. 23, Hosea ch. 2), and of the N.T. which speaks of the Church as the Lamb's Wife (2 Cor. xi. 1 2, Eph. v. 22–32, Apoc. xix. 7, *ib.* xxi. 9). It is less usual to find this figure used to express the relation of the individual soul to God, but cf. Psa. lxxiii. 27, Rom. vii. 2–4, Clem. Hom. iii. 28 *ὁπόταν ἡ ψυχὴ ὑφ' ἑτέρων σπαρῇ, τότε, ὡς πορνεύσασα ἢ μοιχευσαμένη, ὑπὸ τοῦ Πνεύματος ἐγκαταλείπεται.* The insertion of *μοιχοί* was natural when *μοιχαλίς* was understood literally, but the context and especially ver. 5 are in favour of the figurative meaning. [Spitta however takes it of literal adultery, though he thinks the feminine is used tropically of both sexes when seduced by evil spirits.] The word, which is unclassical (Lob. *Phryn.* p. 452), is found in LXX. Mal. iii. 5 (where *μοιχούς* is read by some), Rom. vii. 3, 2 Pet. ii. 14 *ὀφθαλμοὶ μεστοὶ μοιχαλίδος*, (Plut.) *Plac. Phil.* i. 7, p. 881 D *ὑπὸ μοιχοῦ καὶ μοιχαλίδος ἐδολοφονεύθη*, and in figurative use Matt. xii. 39, xvi. 4 *γενεὰ πονηρὰ καὶ μοιχαλίς.*

οἴδατε.] See n. on i. 19. The reference is to our Lord's words Matt. vi. 24.

ἡ φιλία τοῦ κόσμου.] The word *φιλία* is defined by Aristotle (*Eth. N.* xiii. 2) *εὔνοιαν μὴ λανθάνουσαν ἐν ἀντιπεπονθόσι φιλίαν εἶναι*, involving the idea of loving, as well as of being loved, cf. John xv. 19 *ὁ κόσμος ἂν τὸ ἴδιον ἐφίλει*, 2 Tim. iv. 10 *Δημᾶς...ἀγαπήσας τὸν νῦν αἰῶνα.* It is not found elsewhere in N.T. but occurs in LXX. (Prov. xxvii. 5). See above i. 27, 2 Pet. i. 4 *ἵνα γένησθε θείας κοινωνοὶ φύσεως ἀποφυγόντες τῆς ἐν κόσμῳ ἐν ἐπιθυμίᾳ φθορᾶς*, Tit. ii. 12 *ἵνα ἀρνησάμενοι τὰς κοσμικὰς ἐπιθυμίας εὐσεβῶς ζήσωμεν.*

ἔχθρα τοῦ Θεοῦ ἐστιν;] Rom. viii. 7 *τὸ φρόνημα τῆς σαρκὸς ἔχθρα εἰς Θεόν...οἱ δὲ ἐν σαρκὶ ὄντες Θεῷ ἀρέσαι οὐ δύνανται*, 1 John ii. 15, Luke vi.

[1] B has the fut. *δαπανήσετε*, as in 1 Pet. iii. 1 *ἵνα κερδηθήσονται*, Gal. ii. 4 *ἵνα καταδουλώσουσιν.*

26, John xii. 43, above ii. 5, Const. Ap. ii. 6 πάντα τὰ τοιαῦτα ἐχθρὰ τοῦ Θεοῦ ὑπάρχει καὶ δαιμόνων φίλα.

ὃς ἐὰν οὖν βουληθῇ φίλος εἶναι τοῦ κόσμου.] For the use of ἐάν instead of ἄν with relatives see Winer, p. 390. It is very common in N.T., especially after a vowel (WH. *app.* p. 173), also in LXX., as 1 Sam. xix. 3 στήσομαι ἐν ἀγρῷ οὗ ἐὰν ᾖς ἐκεῖ...καὶ ὄψομαι ὅ τι ἐὰν ᾖ, Job. xxxvii. 10 οἰακίζει τὸ ὕδωρ ὡς ἐὰν βούληται, Sirac. ii. 7 πᾶν ὃ ἐὰν ἐπαχθῇ σοι δέξαι, *ib.* xiv. 11 καθὼς ἐὰν ἔχῃς εὖ ποίει, *ib.* xv. 16, 17, and in the patristic writings, Clem. Rom. xii. (on Rahab) ὡς ἐὰν ('whenever') οὖν γένηται λαβεῖν αὐτὴν ὑμᾶς διασώσατέ με, and just below ὡς ἐὰν γνῷς παραγινομένους ἡμᾶς, Hermas *Vis.* 3. 13 ὡς ἐάν τινι λυπουμένῳ ἔλθῃ ἀγγελία ἀγαθή τις, εὐθὺς ἐπελάθετο τῶν προτέρων λυπῶν, *ib.* § 8, *ib.* § 2 ὃς ἐὰν πάθῃ, § 3 ὅσοι ἐὰν ἐργάσωνται *ib.* § 1. Numerous examples from classical authors are cited in Viger, p. 516, but they are all corrected (against the MSS.) in the later editions, see Hermann in Vig. p. 833, and Kühner on Xen. *Mem.* iii. 10, 12. It stands in the newly discovered treatise of Aristotle Ἀθ. Πολ. c. 30 τοὺς Ἑλληνοταμίας οἳ ἐὰν διαχειρίζωσι τὰ χρήματα μὴ συμβουλεύειν, *ib.* c. 31 τοῖς νόμοις οἳ ἐὰν τεθῶσιν χρῆσθαι, in Polyb. vii. 9, 5 πρὸς οὕστινας ἡμῖν ἐὰν γένηται φιλία, Anton. 9. 23 ἥτις ἐὰν πρᾶξις μὴ ἔχῃ τὴν ἀναφοράν, Artem. i. 78 οἷα οὖν ἐὰν ᾖ ἡ γυνὴ καὶ ὅπως διακειμένη, οὕτως καὶ ἡ πρᾶξις, Fabricius' text of Sext. Emp. *Hyp.* ii. 163, iii. 37. This use may have arisen from a wish to distinguish between ἄν qualifying a relative, and ἄν qualifying the optative or indicative. As the former frequently introduced a quasi-hypothetical proposition, it was not unnatural to mark it by the addition of a hypothetical particle, particularly as this had already become nearly otiose in such phrases as κἂν εἰ, ὥσπερ ἂν εἰ, while on the other hand ἄν itself was often used as equivalent to ἐάν. Βουληθῇ ('makes it his aim') is important, since a Demetrius may have 'good report of all men as well as of the truth itself,' but no man who makes worldly success his aim can be also a friend of God. Compare Plut. *Mor.* 6 τὸ τοῖς πολλοῖς ἀρέσκειν τοῖς σοφοῖς ἐστιν ἀπαρέσκειν.

καθίσταται.] 'Thereby becomes,' lit. 'is constituted,' see on iii. 6.

5. **ἢ δοκεῖτε.**] The alternatives are, either the friendship of the world is enmity with God, or the Scripture speaks without meaning. Cf. Matt. xxvi. 53 ἢ δοκεῖς ὅτι οὐ δύναμαι; 2 Cor. xi. 7, Rom. vi. 3. For δοκ. see above i. 26.

κενῶς.] Epict. *Diss.* ii. 17. 6 ἢ κενῶς φθεγγόμεθα;

ἡ γραφὴ λέγει.] The same phrase is used Rom. iv. 3, v. 17, x. 11, Gal. iv. 30, 1 Tim. v. 18, cf. above ii. 23, and Westcott *Heb.* p. 474 on modes of citation. For the personification see Lightfoot on Gal. iii. 8. To show the incompatibility of being at the same time friends with the world and friends of God, the writer refers to the mode of speaking common in the O.T. where jealousy is ascribed to God.

No passage in the O.T. exactly corresponds to this. The nearest are Gen. vi. 3–7, Exod. xx. 5 ἐγὼ γάρ εἰμι Κύριος ὁ Θεός σου, Θεός ζηλωτής, expanded in the Song of Moses, Deut. xxxii. (esp. vv. 11, 12, 16, 19, 21 παρεζήλωσάν με ἐπ' οὐ Θεῷ, cf. 1 Cor. x. 22), Exod. xxxiv. 14, 15, Isa. lxiii. 8–16, Zech. viii. 2 ἐζήλωκα τὴν Σιὼν ζῆλον μέγαν καὶ θυμῷ μεγάλῳ ἐζήλωκα αὐτήν. . ἐπιστρέψω ἐπὶ Σιὼν καὶ κατασκηνώσω ἐν μέσῳ Ἱερουσαλήμ. Some commentators (e.g. Ewald) have thought the allusion must be to some lost writing, which Spitta identifies with the apocryphal Eldad and Modad, see below on ver. 5 (3 *d*). Others (Kern, Bouman, Wiesinger, Hofmann) think that the words following ἡ γραφὴ λέγει down to διό are parenthetic, and that St. James is already referring to the quotation from Prov. iii. 34 given in v. 6. But there seems no justification for such a sudden break; and we have other instances of quotations in the N.T. which remind us rather of the general sense of several passages, than of the actual words of any one particular passage in the O.T.: see Alf. on 1 Cor. ii. 9 (which Jerome rightly takes as a paraphrase of Isa. lxiv. 4, while Chrysostom was in doubt whether it was not from some lost book); Eph. v. 14 probably a loose paraphrase from Isa. lx. 1, 2; Rom. xi. 8 made up of Isa. xxix. 10 (Alf., but vi. 10 Jowett) and Deut. xxix. 4; John vii. 38 where Westcott's n. is 'the reference is not to any one isolated passage, but to the general tenor of such passages as Isa. lviii. 11, Zech. xiv. 8 taken in connexion with the original image (Exod. xvii. 6, Num. xx. 11)'; Matt. ii. 23 (which Alf. leaves 'as an unsolved difficulty'); and the differing versions of the same quotation in Heb. viii. 8 f. and x. 16 f. For an account of the various explanations offered here, see Wolf. *Cur. Phil.* v. p. 58 foll., Heisen, p. 883–928, Pott, 329–355, Theile, 215–229.

πρὸς φθόνον ἐπιποθεῖ.] 'Jealously desires,' cf. 1 Pet. ii. 2 (as new-born babes) τὸ λογικὸν ἄδολον γάλα ἐπιποθήσατε, Phil. i. 8 (God is my witness) ὡς ἐπιποθῶ πάντας ὑμᾶς ἐν σπλάγχνοις Χριστοῦ Ἰησοῦ, which Lightfoot translates 'I yearn after,' adding 'the preposition in itself signifies merely direction, but the idea of straining after the object being thereby suggested, it gets to imply eagerness, cf. Diod. xvii. 101 παρόντι μὲν οὐ χρησάμενος, ἀπόντα δὲ ἐπιποθήσας.' He notices the fact that while the simple πόθος, ποθεῖν, &c. are not found in the N.T., the compounds ἐπιποθεῖν, ἐπιποθία, ἐπιπόθησις, ἐπιπόθητος are not uncommon. So in LXX., Psa. xlii. 1 ὃν τρόπον ἐπιποθεῖ ἡ ἔλαφος ἐπὶ τὰς πηγάς, οὕτως ἐπιποθεῖ ἡ ψυχή μου πρὸς σὲ ὁ Θεός, Deut. xxxii. 11 ὡς ἀετὸς ἐπὶ τοὺς νοσσοὺς ἐπεπόθησε ('fluttereth over')[1]; rarely used in a bad sense as Sir. xxv. 20 γυναῖκα ἐν κάλλει μὴ ἐπιποθήσῃς. With the adverbial phrase compare πρὸς ὀργήν, πρὸς βίαν, πρὸς ἡδονήν, and so with δίκην, εὐσέβειαν, ὑπερβολήν, ἀφθονίαν, καιρόν, φύσιν, τύχην, δύναμιν, ὕβριν, ἀχθηδόνα, χάριν, φιλίαν, ἀλήθειαν, φιλονεικίαν. We might perhaps have expected ζῆλος here rather than φθόνος, as we have ζηλωτής and not φθονερός in Exod. xx. 5, but the former always has a bad sense in St. James, and the latter is often used of the feeling towards a rival, see Eur. *Alcest.* 306 μὴ 'πιγήμῃς τοῖσδε μητρυιὰν τέκνοις, ἥτις κακίων οὖσ' ἐμοῦ γυνὴ φθόνῳ τοῖς σοῖσι κἀμοῖς παισὶ χεῖρα προσβαλεῖ, *Iphig. T.* 1268, *Ion* 1025, *frag. inc.* 887 Dind. σὺ μὴ φθόνει (addressed to the mother) 'be not jealous if I love you less than my father,' Plato *Symp.* 213 D, *Phaedr.* 243 C. So, constantly, of divine Nemesis φθόνος θεῶν or θεόθεν (*Alc.* 1135, *Orestes*

[1] [The same Hebrew word is used of the Spirit in Gen. i. 2, where the like rendering would give πνεῦμα θεοῦ ἐπιποθεῖ. This might be applied to men with reference to the Spirit and the water of baptism. C.T.]

974, *Iph. A.* 1097), of which Herodotus writes (vii. 10) φιλέει ὁ θεὸς τὰ ὑπερέχοντα πάντα κολούειν (see below v. 6).

τὸ πνεῦμα ὃ κατῴκισεν ἐν ἡμῖν.] It seems best to take τὸ πνεῦμα as the subject to ἐπιποθεῖ ('the Spirit which he made to dwell in us jealously yearns for the entire devotion of the heart'), cf. Rom. viii. 11 foll. εἰ τὸ πνεῦμα τοῦ ἐγείραντος Ἰησοῦν ἐκ τῶν νεκρῶν οἰκεῖ ἐν ὑμῖν...ἐλάβετε τὸ πνεῦμα υἱοθεσίας, 1 Cor, iii. 16 τὸ πνεῦμα τοῦ Θεοῦ οἰκεῖ ἐν ὑμῖν, Gal. iv. 6, Eph. iv. 30, John vii. 39, xvi. 7, Ezek. xxxvi. 27 τὸ πνεῦμά μου δώσω ἐν ὑμῖν, Isa. lxiii. 11 ποῦ ἐστιν ὁ θεὶς ἐν αὐτοῖς τὸ πνεῦμα τὸ ἅγιον; Psa. li. 11, 12, *De Aleatoribus* 3 nolite contristare spiritum sanctum qui in vobis est et nolite exstinguere lumen quod in vobis effulsit, Hermas *Sim.* 5. 6 § 5 τὸ πνεῦμα τὸ ἅγιον...κατῴκισεν ὁ Θεὸς εἰς σάρκα ἣν ἠβούλετο (Jesus), *ib.* 7, *Mand.* 3. 1 ἀλήθειαν ἀγάπα...ἵνα τὸ πνεῦμα ὃ ὁ Θεὸς κατῴκισεν ἐν τῇ σαρκὶ ταύτῃ ἀληθὲς εὑρεθῇ...καὶ οὕτως δοξασθήσεται ὁ Κύριος ὁ ἔν σοι κατοικῶν, *ib.* 5. 2 ἐὰν μακρόθυμος ἔσῃ, τὸ πνεῦμα τὸ ἅγιον τὸ κατοικοῦν ἔν σοι καθαρὸν ἔσται μὴ ἐπισκοτούμενον ὑπὸ ἑτέρου πονηροῦ πνεύματος...ἐὰν δὲ ὀξυχολία τις προσέλθῃ, εὐθὺς τὸ πνεῦμα τὸ ἅγιον τρυφερὸν ὂν[1] στενοχωρεῖται κ.τ.λ., Test. Jos. x., Benj. vi. If on the other hand we make God or the Scripture the subject and τὸ πνεῦμα the object of ἐπιποθεῖ we may compare Eccl. xii. 12, Isa. xlii. 5, lvii. 16. The object however need not be expressed where it is so easily supplied from the context. If we read κατῴκησεν with the majority of MSS. and versions, the sense will remain practically unaltered: 'the Spirit which has taken up his abode in us jealously yearns, &c.'

The interpretation given above is that of Cajetan, Corn. a Lap. (*putatisne, O Christiani, frustra in Scriptura Deum vocari zelotypum vestri, osorem mundi illique quasi invidentem possessionem cordis vestri?*), Schneckenburger, Kern, Wiesinger, Alford, Hofmann, Ewald, Brückner, Erdmann, Schegg, Beyschlag: with whom agree (so far as πρὸς φθόνον is concerned) Theophylact, Euthymius, Methodius, Oecumenius, Heisen, Gebser, Theile, Winer. It is in my opinion the only interpretation which is alike in harmony with the context and permissible according to the usage of the Greek language; but as some readers may find a difficulty in the word φθόνος, it may be well to give here a brief conspectus of the other explanations which have been proposed.

Bede says on the words '*Ad invidiam concupiscit spiritus qui habitat in vobis?*' *Interrogative per increpationem legendum est, quasi diceret, 'numquid Spiritus gratiae quo significati estis...hoc concupiscit ut invideatis alterutrum? Non utique bonus spiritus invidiae vitium in vobis sed malus operatur.'* He then mentions that others read it without a question in the sense: *adversus invidiam concupiscit, hoc est, invidiae morbum debellari atque a vestris mentibus extirpari desiderat. Alii de spiritu hominis dictum intelligunt, ut sit sensus 'nolite concupiscere, nolite mundi hujus amicitiis adhaerere, quia spiritus mentis vestrae, dum terrena concupiscit, ad invidiam usque concupiscit, dum ea quae ipsi acquirere concupiscitis alios invidetis habere.'*

Cyril *ap.* Theophyl. εἰ φθόνῳ διαβόλου θάνατος εἰσῆλθεν εἰς τὸν κόσμον, καὶ εἰ κατῴκησεν εἰς τὸν ἔσω ὑμῶν ἄνθρωπον ὁ Χριστὸς κατὰ τὰς γραφάς, διὰ

[1] Compare πρὸς φθόνον above.

τοῦτο κατῴκησεν ἵνα τὸν ἐκ τοῦ φθόνου προσγινόμενον θάνατον καταργήσῃ... ὅτι δὲ ἐπιποθήσας ὑμᾶς ὁ Θεὸς κατῴκησεν ἐν ὑμῖν Ἡσαΐας ἐδήλωσεν εἰπών· οὐκ ἄγγελος, οὐ πρέσβυς, ἀλλ' αὐτὸς ὁ Θεὸς ἔσωσεν ἡμᾶς.

Severianus (in Cramer's *Catena*): ἐπιποθεῖ μὲν καὶ ἐφίεται τὸ πνεῦμα τὸ ἐν ἡμῖν τῆς πρὸς Θεὸν οἰκειότητος, τὴν τοῦ κόσμου φιλίαν ἀποστρεφόμενον, αὐτὸς δὲ μείζονα δίδωσι χάριν (τῷ ξένῳ γεγονότι τῆς κοσμικῆς ζωῆς).[1]

Theophylact: οὐ γὰρ κενῶς ἤτοι ματαίως, ἢ πρὸς φθόνον, ἡ γραφὴ τὰ ἀμήχανα ἡμῖν διαγορεύει, ἀλλ' ἐπιποθοῦσα τὴν διὰ τῆς παρακλήσεως αὐτῆς ἐγκατοικιζομένην ἡμῖν χάριν.

Oecumenius has the same, with a fuller explanation: ἢ δοκεῖτε ὅτι κενῶς ἡ γραφὴ λέγει ἢ πρὸς φθόνον; οὐδὲν τούτων· ἀλλ' ἐπιποθεῖ ἤτοι ἐπιζητεῖ τὴν διὰ τῆς παρακλήσεως αὐτῆς ἐγκατοικισθεῖσαν ὑμῖν χάριν.

Euthym. Zig. (also in Cramer's *Catena*): ἢ δοκεῖτε κ.τ.λ. ἀντὶ τοῦ, ἢ νομίζετε ὅτι ματαίως ἡ γραφὴ φθονοῦσα ἡμῖν λέγει...οὐ βασκαίνει, φησίν, ἡ γραφή, τὸ γὰρ πνεῦμα τὸ λαλῆσαν αὐτήν, ὃ καὶ κατῴκισεν[2] ἐν ἡμῖν ὁ Θεὸς καὶ Πατήρ, ἐπιποθεῖ τὴν σωτηρίαν τῶν ἡμετέρων ψυχῶν καὶ μείζονα τῶν κατὰ Θεὸν ἡμῶν πράξεων δίδωσι τὰ χαρίσματα.

Methodius of Patara (in Matthaei's Scholia): ἡ παρὰ τοῦ Θεοῦ ἐνσπαρεῖσα τῇ φύσει νοερὰ δύναμις φθονεῖ τῇ παρὰ τοῦ ἀντικειμένου ὑποβαλλομένῃ καὶ πρὸς ἡδονὰς ὑμᾶς καὶ πάθη κατασυρούσῃ (so Gebser for κατασύρει) καὶ βούλεται μόνα ἡμᾶς τὰ καλὰ ἐνεργεῖν.

The views of later commentators may be more briefly classified in reference (1) to the construction of πρὸς φθόνον, (2) to the meaning of πρὸς φθόνον, (3) to the subject of ἐπιποθεῖ.

(1) It will have been noticed that Theophylact and others put a stop after πρὸς φθόνον, connecting it with λέγει and not with ἐπιποθεῖ, and so we read in A and other MSS. So too Gebser (translating 'Think ye that the Scripture speaks without reason, enviously?') Du Mont and Heumont (*ap.* Wolf. p. 59), Michaelis, Semler, and Spitta. Such a division seems to me to spoil both sentences: the interpretations founded upon it fail to carry on the thought of the preceding verse, and almost all the later commentators are agreed that πρὸς φθόνον can only be taken with ἐπιποθεῖ.

(2) Scarcely less unanimous is the opinion of modern scholars that Theophylact, Oecumenius and Euthymius were right in taking πρὸς φθόνον as equivalent to φθονερῶς. Others have understood πρός to mean 'against,' (*a*) as Cyril above and the second interpreter in Bede, with Luther, Du Mont, Heumont, Bengel, Pott, Stier and Lange in later times. But πρός can only mean 'against' when joined with a word which implies hostility: it cannot have this force when joined with a word which implies strong affection like ἐπιποθεῖ.[3] (*b*) Others again under-

[1] The clause in brackets is supplied by Euth. Zig. [2] So I read for κατῴκησεν.

[3] Resch however thinks this possible. He regards these words as a quotation from a lost Hebrew gospel (p. 256), of which he finds another rendering in Gal. v. 17 τὸ πνεῦμα (ἐπιθυμεῖ) κατὰ τῆς σαρκός. Dr. Taylor notes that in Psa. cxix. 174 the Hebrew word translated 'I have longed' (A.V.) is variously rendered ἐπεπόθησα (LXX.) and ὑπερεπεθύμησα (Symm.). He further notes that in ver. 20, where the LXX. has ἐπεπόθησεν ἡ ψυχή μου τοῦ ἐπιθυμῆσαι τὰ κρίματά σου, the Hebrew construction would be more literally rendered εἰς ἐπιθυμίαν, and that the Hebr. תאב, there translated ἐπιθ. and used in a good sense, as translated by βδελύσσομαι in Amos vi. 8

stand πρός to mean 'towards' or 'with a view to,' as Bede above, 'Does the Spirit desire that you should be envious one of another?' Calvin 'Is the Spirit of God disposed to envy?' so too Bloomfield: Beza and Estius translate '*spiritus humanus ad invidiam proclivis*: Bouman after Wolf and Witsius 'Does the Spirit move you to envy?' As to this interpretation, while it may be granted that ἐπιποθεῖ is occasionally followed by πρὸς in Hellenistic writers (as in Psa. xlii. 1 quoted above), this is only allowable in describing warm affection towards a person, never in speaking of a tendency to a certain state of mind. Still less can ἐπιποθεῖ have the causative force assigned to it by Wolf. (*c*) Others take πρός to mean 'up to,' Lat. *usque*, as the third interpreter in Bede quoted above, and von Soden 'bis zur Eifersucht liebt er den Geist.' Practically this is much the same as the correct interpretation, but the former is without precedent, while the latter is in accordance with analogy, and flows naturally from the ordinary use of πρός to express 'in conformity with.' (*d*) Michaelis, Semler, and Spitta translate 'in reference to envy,' connecting it with λέγει. This would naturally be expressed by περί, and the interpretation is also open to the objections stated under (1).

(3) Bede, Cyril, Methodius and Euthymius rightly regard τὸ πνεῦμα (the Divine Spirit) as the subject of ἐπιποθεῖ. Others make ἡ γραφή the subject, as Theophylact, Oecumenius, and in later times Gebser and Theile (*a*). Others, as Kern and Wiesinger, take God to be the subject understood and τὸ πνεῦμα (the human spirit) the object (*b*). Practically there is not much difference between these interpretations and that which I regard as the right one. Of the two (*b*) has far more claim to consideration than (*a*). A third view (*c*) which makes the human spirit the subject seems to me entirely to destroy the meaning of the passage. (*d*) Spitta with his usual originality makes ὁ φθόνος (understood from πρὸς φθόνον) the subject, and τὸ πνεῦμα, which he takes of the spirit of prophecy, the object. He illustrates this from Test. Sim 3 ὁ φθόνος κυριεύει πάσης τῆς διανοίας τοῦ ἀνθρώπου, and from the story of Eldad and Modad in Num. xi. 24–29, where Moses rebukes Joshua in the words μὴ ζηλοῖς σὺ ἐμέ; καί τις δῴη πάντα τὸν λαὸν κυρίου προφήτας, ὅταν δῷ κύριος τὸ πνεῦμα αὐτοῦ ἐπ' αὐτούς; He further quotes Midrasch Bemidkar r. par. 15, to the effect that the seventy elders were moved with envy against the unauthorized prophets who had received a larger measure of the Spirit than they had themselves, without being elated thereby. This, he thinks, suggests the quotation from Proverbs which follows in ver. 6. He then refers to the words cited from the apocryphal book Eldad and Modad in Hermas *Vis*. ii. 3. and (probably) in Clem. Rom. i. 23 ταλαίπωροι οἱ δίψυχοι, 17 ἐγὼ δέ εἰμι ἀτμὶς ἀπὸ κύθρας, as proving that the book was familiar to the writer of our Epistle. He objects to the interpretation which I have followed

(βδ. πᾶσαν τὴν ὕβριν 'Ιακώβ). He suggests too that in an original Hebrew phrase to the effect 'the Spirit which he made to dwell *in* this flesh' the word translated 'in' (ב) might also be translated 'against,' as where it is used after a verb meaning to envy in Gen. xxx. 1, Numb. 5. 14, Psa. xxxvii. 1, lxxiii. 3. Still this leaves several steps wanting before we could accept Resch's view.

on the ground that we cannot suppose St. James to have spoken of God as acting πρὸς φθόνον, just after he had condemned this feeling in man (reading φθονεῖτε ver. 26). But we have seen that it is a characteristic of the writer to use the same word both in a good and bad sense (πίστις, πειρασμός, σοφία), cf. Comm. on Faith below.

6. **μείζονα δὲ δίδωσιν χάριν.**] More, in consequence of this jealous affection, which shows itself not in the abandonment of the unfaithful spouse, but in further bounteousness; cf. Isa. liv. 7, 8 'for a small moment have I forsaken thee, but with great mercies will I gather thee,' &c., ix. 6, 7, on the effect of the Divine 'jealousy,' Zech. i. 14, viii. 2, where the declaration of God's jealousy of Zion is followed by promises of her future glory. The absolute self-surrender demanded of the Christian is rewarded by richer supplies of divine grace than he could otherwise receive. For the pregnant use of μείζων cf. above i. 12.

διὸ λέγει.] The subject understood is probably God, as above i. 12 ἐπηγγείλατο, and Eph. iv. 8, v. 14, where the same phrase occurs; others take it as ἡ γραφή, cf. above ver. 5.

ὁ Θεὸς ὑπερηφάνοις ἀντιτάσσεται ταπεινοῖς δὲ δίδωσιν χάριν.] Cited in the same form 1 Pet. v. 5. The LXX. (Prov. iii. 34) has Κύριος for Θεός. Clement of Rome (I. 30), who also has Θεός, has probably borrowed the quotation from St. James, as his next sentence reminds us of our epistle, καταλαλιᾶς πόρρω ἑαυτοὺς ποιοῦντες, ἔργοις δικαιούμενοι καὶ οὐ λόγοις.. For ἀντιτ. 'sets himself against' see Acts xviii. 6, Rom. xiii. 2. For ὑπερηφ. 'conspicuous beyond others,' 'outshining them,' and so 'proud, 'haughty,'[1] see Sirac. x. 7 μισητὴ ἔναντι Κυρίου καὶ ἀνθρώπων ὑπερηφανία, *ib.* ver. 12 ἀρχὴ ὑπερηφανίας ἀνθρώπου ἀφισταμένου ἀπὸ τοῦ Κυρίου, καὶ ἀπὸ τοῦ ποιήσαντος αὐτὸν ἀπέστη ἡ καρδία αὐτοῦ, v. 18 οὐκ ἔκτισται ἀνθρώποις ὑπερηφανία, Psalm. Sol. ii. 25, iv. 28, where it is used of defiant wickedness. In St. Peter the quotation simply enforces an exhortation to humility, 'be humble, for grace follows': here we have to suppose ὑπερηφανία ('pride of life,' 1 John i. 16) identified with ἡ φιλία τοῦ κόσμου in v. 4; see the passage just quoted from Sirac. x. 12. The friend of the world is proud because he makes himself his own centre, disowning his dependence upon God, see Trench *Syn.* p. 113 foll., Cheyne on Isaiah ii. 12.

7. **ὑποτάγητε.**] A favourite word with St. Peter.

ἀντίστητε δὲ τῷ διαβόλῳ.] Opposed first to the previous clause, and then the addition of καὶ φεύξεται suggests a new contrast to the clause which follows. Compare the parallel passage in 1 Pet. v. 8, 9, also Eph. vi. 11, 12. The devil is the ἄρχων τοῦ κόσμου τούτου (above ver. 4, John xiv. 30), he inspires hatred and discord (above iii. 15, John viii. 44), the proud fall into his condemnation (above ver. 6, 1 Tim. iii. 6).

καὶ φεύξεται ἀφ' ὑμῶν.] The imperative followed by καὶ is an energetic form of the conditional sentence, see A. Buttmann, p. 196, and compare John ii. 19 λύσατε τὸν ναὸν καὶ ἐγερῶ αὐτόν, also below vv. 8, 10. The promise gives an answer to those who might plead in excuse the power of the tempter, as others pleaded the force of circumstances ordained

[1] It seems to be derived from the adjectival form ὕπερος and φαίνω like ἐλαφηβόλος from ἔλαφος and βάλλω.

by God (above i. 13). Christ's temptation is an example of submission to God's appointment, followed by the flight of the devil. We find a reminiscence of this verse in Hermas *Mand.* xii. 5 οὐ δύναται (ὁ διάβολος) καταδυναστεύειν τῶν δούλων τοῦ Θεοῦ τῶν ἐξ ὅλης καρδίας ἐλπιζόντων ἐπ' αὐτόν. δύναται ὁ διάβολος ἀντιπαλαῖσαι, καταπαλαῖσαι δὲ οὐ δύναται. ἐὰν οὖν ἀντισταθῆτε αὐτῷ, νικηθεὶς φεύξεται foll., *ib.* xii. 2, 4, 6, vii. 2, 3, Testam. Nephth. 8 ἐὰν ἐργάζησθε τὸ καλὸν...ὁ διάβολος φεύξεται ἀφ' ὑμῶν, Test. Iss. 7 ταῦτα ποιήσατε καὶ πᾶν πνεῦμα Βελίαρ φεύξεται, T. Benj. 5. T. Dan. 5.

8. **ἐγγίσατε τῷ Θεῷ καὶ ἐγγίσει ὑμῖν.**] Cf. Test. Dan. 7 προσέχετε ἑαυτοῖς ἀπὸ τοῦ Σατανᾶ καὶ τῶν πνευμάτων αὐτοῦ, ἐγγίζετε δὲ τῷ θεῷ, Psa. cxlv. 18 ἐγγὺς Κύριος πᾶσι τοῖς ἐπικαλουμένοις αὐτὸν ἐν ἀληθείᾳ, Isa. xxix. 13 (quoted in Matt. xv. 8), Hos. xii. 6 ἔγγιζε πρὸς τὸν Θεόν σου διὰ παντός, Deut. iv. 7 ποῖον ἔθνος μέγα ᾧ ἐστιν αὐτῷ Θεὸς ἐγγίζων ὡς Κύριος ὁ Θεὸς ἡμῶν; on which Philo commenting says (M. 1. p. 445) the greatness of a nation consists in τὸ τῷ Θεῷ συνεγγίζειν ἢ ᾧ Θεὸς συνεγγίζει, 2 Chron. xv. 2, Isa. lix. 2, Zech. i. 3, Mal. iii. 7. The phrase was first used of the priestly office Exod. xix. 22, Ezek. xliv. 13, then of all spiritual worship, as in Heb. iv. 16, vii. 19 (where see Alf.).

καθαρίσατε χεῖρας,] In the literal sense this was an ordinary ritual observance, see Mark vii. 3, Exod. xxx. 19–21 (when the priests go into the tabernacle they shall wash their hands and their feet that they die not), *ib.* xl. 30 foll., Lev. xvi. 4; then used of moral purity Psa. xxvi. 6, Job xxii. 30, Isa. i. 16, Jer. iv. 14, 1 Tim. ii. 8, 1 John iii. 3. The same change from ceremonial to moral purity is found in the Lat. *castus*, cf. Cic. *N.D.* i. 3, ii. 71. Purifying before the Passover was general (John xi. 55), see also Acts xxi. 24, xxiv. 16, and Heb. x. 22 (of baptism) προσερχόμεθα ἐρραντισμένοι τὰς καρδίας ἀπὸ συνειδήσεως πονηρᾶς καὶ λελουμένοι τὸ σῶμα ὕδατι καθαρῷ, Matt. xxvii. 4 (of Pilate). Philo M. 2 p. 406 explains χεῖρας in the following words, λόγου μὲν στόμα σύμβολον, καρδία δὲ βουλευμάτων, πράξεων δὲ χεῖρες, *ib.* M. 1. p. 214. Thus it suits with the word ἁμαρτωλός, which is used of open, notorious sinners in the Gospels and in 1 Tim. i. 9 δικαίῳ νόμος οὐ κεῖται, ἀνόμοις δὲ...καὶ ἁμαρτωλοῖς κ.τ.λ., 1 Pet. iv. 18, Jude 15. Καθαρίζω found in Hellenistic writers instead of classical καθαίρω (cf. Westcott *Heb.* p. 346 f.) is less technical than ἁγνίζω which is also unclassical, see Westcott on 1 Joh. iii. 3.

ἁγνίσατε καρδίας δίψυχοι.] This and the preceding clause are combined in Psa. xxiv. 4, lxxiii. 13. The verb ἁγνίζω and the cognate ἁγνισμός are generally used of ceremonial purification, see Exod. xix. 10; but figuratively, as here, in 1 Pet. i. 22 τὰς ψυχὰς ὑμῶν ἡγνικότες ἐν τῇ ὑπακοῇ τῆς ἀληθείας and 1 John iii. 3. For διψ. see above i. 8 and compare Hos. x. 2 ἐμέρισαν καρδίας αὐτῶν: here its full sense comes out as applied to one divided between God and the world, cf. Herm. *Mand.* ix. 7 καθάρισον τὴν καρδίαν σου ἀπὸ τῆς διψυχίας. For the anarthrous καρδίας see Essay on Grammar.

9. **ταλαιπωρήσατε.**] The word, which only occurs here in N.T., is quite classical: it is regularly used of undergoing hardship, cf. Thuc. ii. 101 ἡ στρατιὰ σῖτόν τε οὐκ εἶχεν καὶ ὑπὸ χειμῶνος ἐταλαιπώρει, Jer. iv. 13

οὐαὶ ἡμῖν ὅτι ταλαιπωροῦμεν, v. 20 *τεταλαιπώρηκε πᾶσα ἡ γῆ* ('is spoiled'), Micah ii. 4 *ταλαιπωρίᾳ ἐταλαιπωρήσαμεν* ('we be utterly spoiled'); so *ταλαιπωρία* below v. 1. In Isa. xxxiii. 1 it has a transitive force 'to afflict another.' This is perhaps the only place in which the imperative is used, and I think it is best understood of voluntary abstinence from comforts and luxuries (the *δαπανᾷν* of iv. 3, *τρυφᾷν* of v. 5); so Erasmus, Grotius (*affligite ipsos vosmet jejuniis et aliis corporis σκληραγωγίαις*), Corn. a Lap. and the Romanists generally, cf. Ps. xxxviii. 6 *ἐταλαιπώρησα καὶ κατεκάμφθην*. On the other hand Alf., following Huther as usual, translates 'be wretched in your minds from a sense of your sinfulness'; but if we consider that St. James himself was noted for his asceticism, that St. Paul bids Timothy *κακοπάθησον ὡς καλὸς στρατιώτης Χριστοῦ Ἰησοῦ* (2 Tim. ii. 3, 4, 5) and himself kept his body in subjection (1 Cor. ix. 27); that fasting, sackcloth and ashes were ordinary accompaniments of repentance (Luke x. 13, Dan. ix. 3, Joel i. 13, 14, Jer. iv. 8, Isa. xxii. 12, cf. Ps. xxxv. 13, 14); lastly that our Lord's charge to those who would follow him was to deny themselves and take up their cross, we shall see no difficulty in adhering to the usual meaning of the word.

πενθήσατε καὶ κλαύσατε.] 'Mourn and weep,' coupled in Luke vi. 25 *οὐαὶ ὑμῖν οἱ γελῶντες νῦν, ὅτι πενθήσετε καὶ κλαύσετε*, Mark xvi. 10. This is a call to the godly sorrow spoken of in 2 Cor. vii. 10 and Matt. v. 4.

ὁ γέλως ὑμῶν εἰς πένθος μετατραπήτω.] The verb does not occur elsewhere in the N.T. For the thought cf. Eccles. ii. 2, vii. 2–6, Tobit ii. 6, Sirac. xxi. 20, xxvii. 13, Luke vi. 21, 25; and for the expression 4 Macc. vi. 5 (of resistance to torture) *ὁ δὲ μεγαλόφρων κατ' οὐδένα τρόπον μετετρέπετο*, also the use of the simple verb in Pind. *Isthm.* iii. 16 *τρέψαι ἦτορ πρὸς εὐφροσύναν*, Ap. Rh. iv. 620 *ἐπὶ γηθοσύνας τρέπετο νόος*. Several MSS. have the more usual *μεταστραφήτω* with which we may compare Joel ii. 28 *ὁ ἥλιος μεταστραφήσεται εἰς σκότος*, 1 Macc. ix. 41 *μετεστράφη ὁ γάμος εἰς πένθος καὶ ἡ φωνὴ μουσικῶν εἰς θρῆνον*.

κατήφειαν.] Classical, only found here in the Bible. It describes the condition of one with eyes cast down like the publican in Luke xviii. 13, cf. Philo M. 2. p. 331 *λυπουμένων ὀφθαλμοὶ συννοίας γέμουσι καὶ κατηφείας*.

10. **ταπεινώθητε ἐνώπιον Κυρίου.**] Cf. i. 9, 1 Pet. v. 6 *ταπεινώθητε ὑπὸ τὴν κραταιὰν χεῖρα τοῦ Θεοῦ, ἵνα ὑμᾶς ὑψώσῃ ἐν καιρῷ ἐπισκοπῆς*, Matt. xxiii. 12, Luke xiv. 11, 1 Sam. ii. 7, 8, Job xxii. 28, 29, Prov. xxix. 23, Ezek. xvii. 24, Isa. lvii. 15, Sirac. ii. 17 *οἱ φοβούμενοι Κύριον ἑτοιμάσουσι καρδίας αὐτῶν καὶ ἐνώπιον αὐτοῦ ταπεινώσουσι τὰς ψυχὰς αὐτῶν*. The adv. *ἐνώπιον* is Hellenistic, it has much the same sense as *παρὰ Θεῷ* in i. 27, cf. Luke i. 6 *δίκαιοι ἐν. Θεοῦ*, 1 Cor. i. 29, 2 Cor. i. 2, &c. The adj. *ἐνώπιος* is found in Theocr. xxii. 152. For the use of the passive aorist with middle sense see Winer, p. 327, and compare *πλανηθῇ* in v. 19.

καὶ ὑψώσει ὑμᾶς.] Sums up the preceding promises.

11. **μὴ καταλαλεῖτε ἀλλήλων.**] Returns to the topic of i. 26, ii. 12, iii. 1–10, 14: cf. 1 Pet. ii. 1 *ἀποθέμενοι πάσας καταλαλιάς*, *ib.* ver. 12, iii. 16 2 Cor. xii. 20, Rom. i. 30 *κατάλαλος*, *ib.* xiv. 3–10, 13, Psa. xlix. 20 *κατά τοῦ ἀδελφοῦ σοῦ καταλαλεῖς*, *ib.* ci. 5 *ib.* lxxviii. 19 *κ. Θεοῦ*, Hermas

Mand. ii. 2 πρῶτον μὲν μηδενὸς καταλάλει μηδὲ ἡδέως ἄκουε καταλαλοῦντος ...πονηρὰ ἡ καταλαλιά, ἀκατάστατον δαιμόνιόν ἐστιν, μηδέποτε εἰρηνεῦον, Clem. Rom. ii. 4 μὴ καταλαλεῖν ἀλλήλων, Barn. 20 εὐχερεῖς ἐν καταλαλιᾷ, Test. Gad. 3 (ὁ μισῶν) τῷ κατορθοῦντι φθονεῖ, καταλαλιὰν ἀσπάζεται. Field, *Ot. Norv.*, quotes the definition κατάλαλοι: οἱ διαβολαῖς κατὰ τῶν ἀπόντων ἀδεῶς κεχρημένοι. The word is not used by classical writers. This evil-speaking flows from the pride condemned in v. 16 and is an expression of the hate denounced in vv. 1, 2. It is shown in what follows to imply a usurpation of God's right to judge.

ἀδελφοί.] The three-fold repetition of the word in this sentence is in part required by the different constructions of καταλαλῶ and κρίνω, like the fourfold repetition of νόμος, but it also adds weight to the writer's appeal to their feeling of brotherhood. The appeal is heightened in the third case by the addition of τὸν ἀδ. αὐτοῦ, not simply *a*, but *his*, brother.

κρίνων τὸν αδελφόν.] Compare Matt. vii. 1, Rom. ii. 1, 1 Cor. iv. 5.

καταλαλεῖ νόμου καὶ κρίνει νόμον.] Whoever deliberately breaks a law and does not repent of it, thereby speaks against it and treats it as a bad law, since it is the essence of a law to require obedience, and he who refuses obedience virtually says it ought not to be law. Thus he who speaks against a brother virtually speaks against the law of brotherhood. The law which the writer has in mind is the royal law spoken of in ii. 8, to which reference is made by the word πλησίον in v. 12. The offence against man is also an offence against God, cf. above iii. 9, Matt. xxv. 42–45, 1 John iv. 20, Prov. xvii. 5, Ps. xii. 4, Test. Gad. 4 φυλάξασθε ἀπὸ τοῦ μίσους, ὅτι εἰς αὐτὸν τὸν κύριον ἀνομίαν ποιεῖ· οὐ γὰρ θέλει ἀκούειν λόγων ἐντολῶν αὐτοῦ περὶ ἀγάπης τοῦ πλησίον. The phrase 'speaks against the law' is evidently adapted to the special context, cf. i. 4 τέλειον and τέλειος, v. 11 μαρανθήσεται, vv. 12–14 πειράζω, 15 and 18 ἀπεκύησεν, iv. 1 στρατευομένων after πόλεμοι.

οὐκ εἶ ποιητὴς νόμου.] ποιητὴς λόγου in i. 22, see Rom. ii. 13, 1 Macc. ii. 67. In classical Greek the phrase is used for 'lawgiver,' never for 'doer of the law.' The critical attitude is averse to the dutiful performance of the law. It is only by doing the will of God, so far as it is known to us, that we learn to understand the reasons of it, John vii. 17.

ἀλλὰ κριτής.] Cf. Clem. Hom. xii. 26 foll. 'If you seek to benefit the good only and not the bad, you undertake to perform the office of a judge (κριτοῦ τὸ ἔργον) and not of kindness,' &c., Const. Apost. ii. 36 ἐὰν κρίνῃς τὸν ἀδελφὸν, κριτὴς ἐγένου, μηδενός σε προχειρισαμένου, τοῖς γὰρ ἱερεῦσιν ἐπετράπη κρίνειν μόνοις.

12. **εἷς ἔστιν νομοθέτης καὶ κριτής.**] One who criticises the law is really proposing to enact a better law; but there is only one lawgiver and judge (John v. 22, 1 Cor. iv. 3–5, Taylor *J.F*, p. 83), viz. he who is Lord of life and death, *i.e.* whose sentence takes effect; just as he who exercises the right of sovereignty is the ruler (Matt. xxii. 21). The noun νομοθ έτης does not occur elsewhere in N.T., though both νομοθετέω and νομοθεσία are found. For κριτής see below v. 9.

ὁ δυνάμενος σῶσαι καὶ ἀπολέσαι.] Cf. Deut. xxxii. 39, Psa. lxviii.

20, 1 Sam. ii. 6, 2 Kings v. 7, Matt. x. 28 φοβήθητε μᾶλλον τὸν δυνάμενον καὶ ψυχὴν καὶ σῶμα ἀπολέσαι ἐν γεέννῃ, Luke vi. 9 ἔξεστι τοῖς σάββασιν ψυχὴν σῶσαι ἢ ἀπολέσαι; John xix. 10 ἐξουσίαν ἔχω σταυρῶσαί σε καὶ ἀπολῦσαί σε, Hermas *Sim.* ix. 23. 4 εἰ ὁ Θεὸς καὶ ὁ Κύριος ἡμῶν, ὁ πάντων κυριεύων καὶ ἔχων πάσης τῆς κτίσεως αὐτοῦ τὴν ἐξουσίαν, οὐ μνησικακεῖ ἀλλ' ἵλεως γίνεται, ἄνθρωπος φθαρτὸς ὢν καὶ πλήρης ἁμαρτιῶν ἀνθρώπῳ μνησικακεῖ, ὡς δυνάμενος ἀπολέσαι ἢ σῶσαι αὐτόν; for σῶσαι see i. 21, ii. 14.

σὺ δὲ τίς εἶ;] How weak and incompetent! cf. Rom. xiv. 4 σὺ τίς εἶ ὁ κρίνων ἀλλότριον οἰκέτην; *ib.* ver. 10, Acts xix. 15, John viii. 53 τίνα σεαυτὸν ποιεῖς; see above iii. 5 ἡλίκον.

13. **ἄγε νῦν οἱ λέγοντες.**] The thought of his weakness and ignorance should deter man from judging his fellows and finding fault with the law: it should also prevent him from making confident assertions as to the future. For the interjectional use of ἄγε cf. Jud. xix. 6, 2 Kings iv. 24; for its use with a plural see below v. 1, Hom. *Il.* i. 62 ἀλλ' ἄγε δή τινα μάντιν ἐρείομεν, Xen. *Apol.* 14 ἄγε δὴ ἀκούσατε καὶ ἄλλα, similarly *age* in Latin, of which Servius says (on *Aen.* ii. 707) '*age*' *non est modo verbum imperantis sed adverbium hortantis, adeo ut plerumque* '*age facite*' *dicamus et singularem numerum copulemus plurali.* In like manner we have Matt. xxvi. 65 ἴδε νῦν ἠκούσατε, Arist. *Ach.* 318 εἰπέ μοι τί φειδόμεσθα τῶν λίθων ὦ δημόται; *Pax* 385 εἰπέ μοι τί πάσχετ' ὦνδρες; Plat. *Gorg.* 455 B φέρε δὴ ἴδωμεν, Xen. *Mem.* iii. 4. 7 ἴθι δὴ ἐξετάσωμεν, cf. Sandys on *Lept.* 26. It is usually followed by an imperative or an interrogative, as in *Cyrop.* ii. 1. 6 ἄγε δή, τῆς σῆς δυνάμεως τί φῂς πλῆθος εἶναι; and in the plural as Xen. *Anab.* v. 4. 9 ἄγετε δή, τί ἡμῶν δεήσεσθε; Here it would seem that the following parenthesis has destroyed the construction and changed the question οὐκ οἴδατε ὅτι ἀτμίς ἐστιν ἡ ζωὴ ὑμῶν into the statement οὐκ ἐπίστασθε τὸ τῆς αὔριον κ.τ.λ.

σήμερον ἢ αὔριον.] The reading ἤ of Sin. B. &c. gives a better sense than καί, which occurs in the same phrase Luke xii. 28, xiii. 32, 33; so χθὲς καὶ σήμερον Heb. xiii. 8. For the warning cf. Luke xii. 16 foll., Prov. xxvii. 1 μὴ καυχῶ τὰ εἰς αὔριον, οὐ γὰρ γινώσκεις τί τέξεται ἡ ἐπιοῦσα, Sir. xi. 16, 17, Philo M. 1. p. 132 ὁ γεηπόνος φησί· σπέρματα βαλοῦμαι, φυτεύσω, αὐξήσει τὰ φυτά, καρποὺς ταῦτα οἴσει...εἶτ' ἐξαίφνης φλὸξ ἢ ζάλη ἢ ἐπομβρίαι συνεχεῖς διέφθειραν πάντα· ἔστι δὲ ὅτε...ὁ ταῦτα λογισάμενος οὐκ ὤνατο ἀλλὰ προαπέθανε, Seneca *Ep.* 101 esp. § 4 *quam stultum est aetatem disponere ne crastini quidem dominum*, Sen. *Thyestes* 619 *nemo tam divos habuit faventes crastinum ut possit sibi polliceri*, Soph. *Oed. C.* 566 ἔξοιδ' ἀνὴρ ὤν, χὤτι τῆς ἐς αὔριον οὐδὲν πλέον μοι σοῦ μέτεστιν ἡμέρας. Wetst. quotes many similar passages, among them one from a Jewish story of R. Simeon ben Chal. hearing from the angel of death that his office was to slay those who boasted of the things they were about to do. Edersheim (*Life of Jesus* i. 539) cites a rabbinical proverb 'Care not for the morrow, for ye know not what a day may bring forth. Perhaps ye may not find the morrow.'

πορευσόμεθα εἰς τήνδε τὴν πόλιν.] 'We will go to this city,' pointing it out on the map. So τόδε in Aristotle gets the force of the *particular* as opposed to the *general*. Erdmann and Beyschlag, reading καί above, wrongly translate 'we will journey for two days.' The dispersion of the Jews, which gave them connexions all over the world and let them know at once of any new opening for trade, led to their being constantly on the move. Thus we read of Aquila and Priscilla at Rome and at Corinth (Acts xviii. 1, 2), at Ephesus (*ib.* v. 18), again at Rome (Rom. xvi. 3) and at Ephesus (2 Tim. iv. 19), see above i. 11 ἐν ταῖς πορείαις. [See Zahn, *Weltverkehr und Kirche*, Hanov. 1877. S.]

ποιήσομεν ἐκεῖ ἐνιαυτόν.] Cf. Acts xx. 3 ποιήσας μῆνας τρεῖς, *ib.* xv. 33, xviii. 23, Prov. xiii. 23 δίκαιοι ποιήσουσιν ἐν πλούτῳ ἔτη πολλα. The usage appears to be confined to later Greek, see Shilleto on Dem. *F.L.* p. 392, Vorst, p. 158 foll. There is a similar phrase in Latin, cf. Sen. *Ep.* 66. 4 *quamvis paucissimos una fecerimus dies, tamen multi nobis sermones fuerunt.*

ἐμπορευσόμεθα.] Elsewhere in N.T. only in 2 Pet. ii. 3, where it has a transitive force. In LXX. (Gen. xxxiv. 10) and in profane authors it is intransitive as here.

κερδήσομεν.] Veitch cites examples of this rare form from Anthol. ix. 390, Fragm. Trag. p. 14 Wagner. The Attic is κερδανῶ, with Aor. ἐκέρδανα, Ion. and late Att. κερδήσομαι, Aor. ἐκέρδησα (the latter occurs often in N.T.). R. and P. give ἀποκερδήσω as fut. of the compound. The pass. fut. κερδηθήσομαι occurs in 1 Pet. iii. 2. Dr. Plummer calls attention to the repeated καί separating 'the different items of the plan, which are rehearsed thus one by one with manifest satisfaction.'

14. **οἵτινες οὐκ ἐπίστασθε τὸ τῆς αὔριον.**] 'People that know not (='whereas ye know not,' Lat. *qui non intelligatis*) what belongs to the morrow'; or, reading τά with some MSS., 'the things of the morrow.' The phrase is in apposition with οἱ λέγοντες, as ἀνὴρ δίψυχος with ὁ ἄνθρωπος ἐκεῖνος in i. 7, 8. For the neuter article cf. Matt. xxi. 21 τὸ τῆς συκῆς, 2 Pet. ii. 22 τὸ τῆς παροιμίας, Rom. viii. 5 τὰ τῆς σαρκὸς φρονοῦσιν, xiv. 19 τὰ τῆς εἰρήνης διώκομεν, 2 Cor. ii. 30. For ellipse of ἡμέρας see Winer p. 738.[1]

ἀτμὶς γάρ ἐστε.] Often used for smoke, as in ἀ. καμίνου Gen. xix. 28, ἀ. καπνοῦ Acts ii. 17, ἀ. τ. θυμιάματος Ezek. viii. 11, elsewhere for steam or breath, as in the words attributed to Moses in Clem. Rom. 17 (a quotation, as Lightfoot suggests, from Eldad and Modad) τίς εἰμι ἐγώ; ...ἀτμὶς ἀπὸ κύθρας 'steam from a kettle.' It is found in the versions of Symmachus and Aquila, where the Eng. has 'vanity,' as in Eccl. i. 2,

[1] WH. read here in their text οὐκ ἐπίστασθε τῆς αὔριον ποία ἡ ζωὴ ὑμῶν. ἀτμὶς γάρ ἐστε πρὸς ὀλίγον φαινομένη, agreeing with B except that the latter omits ἡ before ζωή. This seems to me to give a harsh construction for the genitive, and also to weaken the force of the passage. The folly of boasting as to the morrow is naturally exposed by pointing to our ignorance of what will happen on the morrow, and this is itself a consequence of the uncertainty of our life, appearing and disappearing like a shifting mist. The omission of the first step confuses the expression. It was easy for τό or τά to be lost before τῆς, and then γάρ would be dropped in order to supply some sort of construction. Again, the weight of evidence seems to me in favour of retaining ἡ before πρός (which also facilitates the reading of Sin. ποία ἡ ζωὴ ὑμῶν ἡ πρὸς ὀλίγον φαινομένη). The difference in meaning made by the retention of the article is that the tendency to appear and disappear is made a property of the vapour, not a mere accidental circumstance.

ix. 9, xii. 8, Ps. xxxix. 5, lxii. 9, cxliv. 4, Job vii. 16. For the thought see Job vii. 7 μνήσθητι ὅτι πνεῦμά μου ἡ ζωή, Wisd. ii. 4 παραλεύσεται ὁ βίος ἡμῶν ὡς ἴχνη νεφέλης καὶ ὡς ὁμίχλη διασκεδασθήσεται διωχθεῖσα ὑπὸ ἀκτίνων ἡλίου, *ib.* v. 9–14 and passages quoted in Wetstein. The force of γάρ here is to give significance to the preceding ποία. The reading ἐστε is more vigorous than ἐστι, and may be compared with the substitution of ὁ πλούσιος for πλοῦτος in i. 10, where the thought is the same as here.

πρὸς ὀλίγον.] So Heb. xii. 10 οἱ μὲν πρὸς ὀλίγας ἡμέρας ἐπαίδευον, Apoc. xvii. 10 ὀλίγον αὐτὸν δεῖ μεῖναι, 1 Tim. iv. 8 πρὸς ὀλίγον ἐστὶν ὠφέλιμος, Wisd. xvi. 6 πρὸς ὀλίγον ἐταράχθησαν.

ἔπειτα καὶ ἀφανιζομένη.] We might have expected ὕστερον δέ, but the δέ is often omitted after ἔπειτα as in iii. 17, and the καὶ implies 'as it appears, *so also* it disappears': the character of our life is transiency. Elsewhere in N.T. the verb denotes 'to destroy' or 'to disfigure.' It is used of an eclipse in Aristotle and Cleomedes, and generally of the obscuration of the heavenly bodies in Pseudo-Aristotle *de Mundo* vi. 22 πᾶσα κινεῖται ἐνδελεχῶς ἐν κύκλοις ἰδίοις, ποτὲ μὲν ἀφανιζομένη ποτὲ δὲ φαινομένη, μυρίας ἰδέας ἀναφαίνουσά τε καὶ πάλιν ἀποκρύπτουσα ἐκ μιᾶς ἀρχῆς. Aristotle also uses it of the migration of birds (*Hist. An.* vi. 7 ὁ κόκκυξ φαίνεται ἐπ' ὀλίγον χρόνον τοῦ θέρους, τὸν δὲ χειμῶνα ἀφανίζεται).

15. **ἀντὶ τοῦ λέγειν ὑμᾶς.**] Cf. Ps. cviii. 4 ἀντὶ τοῦ ἀγαπᾶν με ἐνδιέβαλλόν με, and above iii. 3 εἰς τὸ πείθεσθαι αὐτοὺς ἡμῖν, where see n. A classical writer would rather have said δέον λέγειν or οἵτινες βέλτιον ἂν εἶπον.

ἐὰν ὁ Κύριος θελήσῃ.] Cf. Acts xviii. 21 τοῦ Θεοῦ θέλοντος, 1 Cor. iv. 19 ἐὰν ὁ Κύριος θελήσῃ, *ib.* xvi. 17 ἐὰν ὁ Κύριος ἐπιτρέπῃ, Heb. vi. 3, Phil. ii. 24 πέποιθα ἐν τῷ Κυρίῳ ὅτι...ἐλεύσομαι, but elsewhere we find St. Paul speaking of his future plans without the use of any such phrase, e.g. Acts xix. 21, Rom. xv. 28, 1 Cor. xvi. 5. A similar phrase was customary with the Greeks and Romans, cf. Arist. *Plut.* 114 οἶμαι γὰρ, οἶμαι, σὺν θεῷ δ' εἰρήσεται, ταύτης ἀπαλλάξειν σε τῆς ὀφθαλμίας, *ib.* 347, 405, 1188 ἢν θεὸς θέλῃ, Xen. *Hipparch.* ix. 8 ταῦτα δὲ πάντα θεῶν συνεθελόντων γένοιτ' ἄν· εἰ δέ τις τοῦτο θαυμάζει ὅτι πολλάκις γέγραπται τὸ σὺν θεῷ πράττειν, εὖ ἴστω ὅτι, ἢν πολλάκις κινδυνεύῃ, ἧττον τοῦτο θαυμάσεται, Plat. *Theaet.* 151, *Laches* 201 ἀλλὰ ποιήσω ὦ Λυσίμαχε ταῦτα καὶ ἥξω παρά σε αὔριον ἢν θεὸς ἐθέλῃ, *Hipp. Maj.* 286 μέλλω ἐπιδεικνύναι εἰς τρίτην ἡμέραν...ὅπως παρέσει καὶ αὐτὸς καὶ ἄλλους ἄξεις. Ἀλλὰ ταῦτ' ἔσται ἂν θεὸς ἐθέλῃ, *Alcib.* I. p. 135 ἐὰν βούλῃ σὺ ὦ Σώκρατες. Οὐ καλῶς λέγεις ὦ Ἀλκιβιάδη. Ἀλλὰ πῶς χρὴ λέγειν; Ὅτι ἐὰν θεὸς ἐθέλῃ, Eur. *Alc.* 783, Minuc. F. 18 '*si Deus dederit;*' *vulgi iste naturalis sermo est*, Senec. *Tranquill.* 13 *tutissimum est de fortuna cogitare et nihil sibi de fide ejus promittere: navigabo nisi si quid inciderit*, &c. Cf. Brisson i. 57. The same language is customary among Jews and Arabs. Ben Sira is quoted to the effect:[1] 'Let no man say he will do anything without prefixing to it "If the Lord will."'

καὶ ζήσομεν καὶ ποιήσομεν.] The boaster forgets that life depends on

[1] Grotius *ap.* Theile *in loc.*

the will of God. The right feeling is, both my life and my actions are determined by Him. To put ζήσομεν or ζήσωμεν into the protasis is to make life independent of God's will, a second factor which needs to be taken into account.

16. **νῦν δέ.**] 'But as the case really stands,' cf. 1 Cor. xiv. 6.

ἐν ταῖς ἀλαζονίαις.[1]] Does not denote the subject of glorying like ἐν τῷ ὕψει i. 9, but the manner in which glorying was shown, 'in your self-confident speeches or imaginations' = ἀλαζονευόμενοι, cf. Clem. Rom. 21 ἀνθρώποις ἐγκαυχωμένοις ἐν ἀλαζονείᾳ τοῦ λόγου αὐτῶν. In N.T. only found here and 1 John ii. 16 ἡ ἀλαζόνεια τοῦ βίου. The adj. is also found twice, each time joined with ὑπερήφανος, see above ver. 6. Aristotle defines it *Eth. N.* iv. 7. 2 δοκεῖ ὁ ἀλαζὼν προσποιητικὸς τῶν ἐνδόξων εἶναι καὶ μὴ ὑπαρχόντων καὶ μειζόνων ἢ ὑπάρχει, see Trench *Syn.* p. 113 foll. Here it implies confidence in one's cleverness, luck, strength, skill, &c., unfounded in so far as the future result is not dependent on them, but not necessarily unfounded in regard to the actual possession of these qualities, cf. Test. Joseph. 17 οὐχ ὕψωσα ἐμαυτὸν ἐν ἀλαζονείᾳ διὰ τὴν κοσμικὴν δόξαν μου, ἀλλ' ἤμην ἐν αὐτοῖς ὡς εἷς τῶν ἐλαχίστων, so Job xxviii. 8 υἱοὶ ἀλαζόνων represents the Heb. 'children of pride' ('lion's whelps' in A.V.). For the plural see above ii. 1 προσωπολημψίαις: Bengel says *arrogantiae exprimuntur in illis verbis, proficiscemur, lucrabimur; gloriatio in praesumptione temporis.*

τοιαύτη.] 'Every *such* boasting,' because there may be a good καύχησις, as in i. 9; cf. 1 Cor. v. 6 οὐ καλὸν τὸ καύχημα ὑμῶν.

17. **εἰδότι οὖν.**] 'So then, if one knows to do good and does it not, there is guilt to him.' The verse contains a general summing up and moral of what has been said before, going back as far as i. 22, ii. 14, iii. 1, 13, iv. 11. B. Weiss explains οὖν by connecting the verse closely with what precedes, as follows: 'if all boasting is bad (even where the speaker may be ignorant or an unbeliever) it is worse still, it is actual sin, for one who knows what is right, to abstain from doing it.' This seems to me very far-fetched. Spitta on the contrary, finding no connexion in the verse as it stands, thinks it must be a familiar quotation and that οὖν has reference to its original context. Instead of εἰδότι καλὸν ποιεῖν...ἁμαρτία ἐστίν, we should rather have expected τὸ εἰδέναι... ἁμαρτία ἐστίν, or ὁ εἰδὼς ἁμαρτίαν ἔχει, as in John ix. 41 εἰ τυφλοὶ ἦτε οὐκ ἂν εἴχετε ἁμαρτίαν, *ib.* xv. 22, 24, 1 John i. 8. For the dative cf. Rom. xiv. 14 οὐδὲν κοινὸν δι' ἑαυτοῦ εἰ μὴ τῷ λογιζομένῳ τι κοινὸν εἶναι, ἐκείνῳ κοινόν, 1 Cor. iv. 3 ἐμοὶ δὲ εἰς ἐλάχιστόν ἐστιν ἵνα ὑφ' ὑμῶν ἀνακριθῶ where see Alf., Clem. Rom. 44 ἁμαρτία οὐ μικρὰ ἡμῖν ἔσται ἐὰν... ἀποβάλωμεν, Hermas *Vis.* iii. 3 τί μοι ὄφελος ταῦτα ἑωρακότι καὶ μὴ γινώσκοντι (where, as here, the infinitive would have been the more usual construction). The phrase ἔσται σοι (or ἔν σοι) ἁμαρτία is common in LXX., e.g. Deut. xv. 9, xxiii. 21, 22, xxiv. 15; also ἁμαρτίαν λαμβάνειν Lev. xix. 17, xxii. 9, xxiv. 15, so Rom. xiv. 20 πᾶν δὲ ὃ οὐκ ἐκ πίστεως ἁμαρτία ἐστί.

For the pleonasm of αὐτῷ cf. John xv. 2 πᾶν κλῆμα μὴ φέρον

[1] So WH. read with B[1]. Similarly they read ἐριθία iii. 16 and κακοπαθίας v. 10.

καρπὸν αἴρει αὐτό, Matt. iv. 16, Apoc. ii. 7 τῷ νικῶντι δώσω αὐτῷ φαγεῖν, esp. after a relative, as Mark vii. 25 γυνὴ ἧς εἶχεν τὸ θυγάτριον αὐτῆς πνεῦμα ἀκάθαρτον, very common in LXX., as Exod. iv. 17 ῥάβδον ἐν ᾗ ποιήσεις ἐν αὐτῇ τὰ σημεῖα, Amos iv. 7 μερὶς ἐφ' ἣν οὐ βρέξω ἐπ' αὐτὴν ξηρανθήσεται, see Winer p. 184, who gives instances from classical Greek. Examples of the infinitive after οἶδα in this sense are found in 2 Pet. ii. 9, Matt. vii. 11. The word καλόν is common with St. James (ii. 7, iii. 13) as with St. Paul (Rom. vii. 18, 19, 21, 2 Cor. xiii. 7, Gal. vi. 9, where the phrase ποιεῖν τὸ καλόν occurs). The anarthrous neuter occurs in the similar phrase πᾶς ποιῶν πονηρόν Mal. ii. 17. For the thought see Luke xii. 47, John ix. 41, xiii. 17, Philo M. 2. p. 518 τῷ μὲν ἀγνοίᾳ τοῦ κρείττονος διαμαρτάνοντι συγγνώμη δίδοται· ὁ δ' ἐξ ἐπιστήμης ἀδικῶν ἀπολογίαν οὐκ ἔχει. The appeal to knowledge here, as above i. 19, is a proof that the writer is addressing Christians.

V. 1.—The persons here addressed are not the same as those addressed in iv. 13. It is no longer the careless worldliness of the bustling trader which is condemned, but the more deadly worldliness of the unjust capitalist or landlord. It is a question whether they are Christians or not. That there were rich members of the Church appears from i. 10, ii. 2, iv. 13 and St. Paul's warnings against the love of riches. On the other hand 'the brethren' in v. 7 seem to be opposed to 'the rich' here; and the prophets, whom St. James imitates, did not confine their threats and warnings to Israel: we have the burden of Moab and Egypt as well as of Israel. If we suppose the words uttered first of all with reference to disbelievers, they will still be applicable to all who in any respect follow in their footsteps.

ἄγε νῦν.] See above iv. 13. For severity towards the rich cf. Luke vi. 24, xviii. 24, 1 Tim. vi. 9, 10, Prov. xi. 28, Amos iii. 10, v. 11, viii. 4 foll., Isa. v. 8, xxxiii. 1, Jer. iv. 8.

ὀλολύζοντες.] Only here in N.T.: it is used in Hom. *Il.* vi. 297 and Herod. iv. 189, of the joyful outcries of women in the worship of Athene; in the LXX. it occurs only as the expression of violent grief, as in Joel i. 5, 13, Isa. xiii. 6 (of Babylon) ὀλολύζετε· ἐγγὺς γὰρ ἡμέρα Κυρίου, *ib.* xiv. 31 ὀλολύξατε πύλαι πόλεων, *ib.* xv. 3 ὀλολύξατε μετὰ κλαυθμοῦ, *ib.* xvi. 7, Jer. iv. 8. So Latin *ululatus*.

ἐπὶ ταῖς ταλαιπωρίαις ταῖς ἐπερχομέναις.] The early Christians were in momentary expectation of the second coming of the Lord, when the world and its lusts would pass away (v. 8): cf. on the ὠδῖνες, the sufferings which precede his appearance, 4 Ezra v. and the prophecies of Dan. xii. 1, Matt. xxiv. partially fulfilled in the siege of Jerusalem, in which some of those here addressed would probably be involved, as many who had come up for the Feast were surprised by the rapid concentration of the Roman armies.

2. **σέσηπε.**] Prophetical perfect as in Isa. xl.2, xliv. 23, xlvi. 1, xlix. 13, lii. 9, liii. 3–10, lx. 1. The verb σ. is only found here in N.T., the active occurs with transitive force Job xl. 7 σῆψον τοὺς ἀσεβεῖς, the pass. *ib.* xxxiii. 21, Psa. xxxvii. 5, Sirac xiv. 19 πᾶν ἔργον σηπόμενον ἐκλείπει. It is questioned whether the expression is intended literally of wealth which, like the manna, will not keep, e.g. of stores accumulated to sell

at a profit; or whether it is abstract and symbolical, all wealth having in itself the character of corruptibility. The terms chosen have reference to the different kinds of wealth, σέσηπε to corn and other products of the earth, σητόβρωτα to rich fabrics, ἴωται to metals; giving examples of corruption arising from an external cause (the moth), or internal, whether deep-seated rottenness or superficial rust. In Matt. vi. 19 another danger, that from thieves, is mentioned. Compare with the whole passage Sirac xiv. 3–19.

ἱμάτια σητόβρωτα.] Rich garments were handed down as heirlooms, cf. Acts xx. 33 'I coveted no man's silver or gold or apparel,' Judges xiv. 12, above ch. ii. 2, Hor. *Ep.* i. 6. 40, Curt. v. 20 *in Persepolin totius Persidis opes congesserunt: aurum argentumque cumulatum erat, vestis ingens modus.* No other instance of the adj. σητ. is cited except Job xiii. 28 παλαιοῦται ὥσπερ ἱμάτιον σητόβρωτον,[1] cf. Sibyll. prooem. 64 (of wooden idols), Isa. li. 8 ὡς γὰρ ἱμάτιον βρωθήσεται ὑπὸ χρόνου καὶ ὡς ἔρια βρωθήσεται ὑπὸ σητός, Sir. xlii. 13 ἀπὸ ἱματίων σὴς ἐκπορεύεται, Hor. *Sat.* ii. 3. 118 *stragula vestis blattarum ac tinearum epulae.* On the σής or *tinea* see Arist. *H.A.* v. 32. 1, Cato *R.R.* 98, Pliny *N.H.* xi. 35 § 117.

3. **ὁ χρυσὸς κατίωται.**] The word is used in Sir. xii. 11 of a mirror dimmed with rust, cf. *ib.* ver. 10 ὡς ὁ χαλκὸς ἰοῦται οὕτως ἡ πονηρία αὐτοῦ, *ib.* xxix. 10 ἀπόλεσον ἀργύριον διὰ φίλον καὶ μὴ ἰωθήτω ὑπὸ τὸν λίθον εἰς ἀπώλειαν, Plut. *Mor.* 164 F ὑπολαμβάνει τὸν πλοῦτον ἀγαθὸν εἶναι μέγιστον· τοῦτο τὸ ψεῦδος ἰὸν ἔχει, νέμεται (cf. below φάγεται) τὴν ψυχήν, ἐξίστησιν, *ib.* 819 E τὴν φιλοχρηματίαν ὥσπερ μεστὸν ἰοῦ νόσημα τῆς ψυχῆς ἀποδυσάμενος ἀπορρῖψον, Hor. *A.P.* 330 *haec animos aerugo et cura peculi cum semel imbuerit, speramus carmina fingi posse?* Epict. *Diss.* 4. 6. 14 (principles not put into practice) ὡς ὁπλάρια ἀποκείμενα κατίωται. The force of κατά is intensive, as in κατεσθίω, καταβρέχω, καταπίμπρημι, κατακαυχῶμαι above iv. 14.

St. James here uses popular language like the author of the apocryphal Epist. Jerem.[2] ver. 11 θεοὺς ἀργυροῦς καὶ θεοὺς χρυσοῦς καὶ ξυλίνους. οὗτοι δὲ οὐ διασώζονται ἀπ' ἰοῦ καὶ βρωμάτων, *ib.* ver. 24 τὸ γὰρ χρυσίον ὃ περίκεινται εἰς κάλλος, ἐὰν μὴ ἐκμάξῃ τὸν ἰόν, οὐ μὴ στίλψωσιν. Strictly speaking it is a property of gold not to rust, Philo M. p. 503 χρυσὸς ἰὸν οὐ παραδέχεται, Theognis 451 εὑρήσεις δέ με πᾶσιν ἐπ' ἔργμασιν ὥσπερ ἄπεφθον χρυσόν, ἐρυθρὸν ἰδεῖν τριβόμενον βασάνῳ, τοῦ χροιῆς καθύπερθε μέλας οὐχ ἅπτεται ἰὸς οὐδ' εὐρώς, αἰεὶ δ' ἄνθος ἔχει καθαρόν, Pindar *fr.* 207 Bergk Διὸς παῖς ὁ χρυσός· κεῖνον οὐ σὴς οὐ κὶς δάπτει. Strabo however speaks (xvi. 2. 42) of a fuliginous vapour rising from the Dead Sea ὑφ' ἧς κατιοῦται καὶ χαλκὸς καὶ ἄργυρος καὶ πᾶν τὸ στιλπνὸν μέχρι καὶ χρυσοῦ, so Diod. ii. 48: Dioscorides v. 91 describes gold rusted by chemicals. Compare Lam. 4. 1 πῶς ἀμαυρωθήσεται χρυσίον;

ὁ ἰὸς αὐτῶν εἰς μαρτύριον ὑμῖν ἔσται.] ἰός (Lat. *virus*), which was used in the sense of poison in iii. 8, and possibly in some of the passages quoted in the preceding note, here stands for rust. The thought is 'You

[1] For a similar formation cf. σκωληκόβρωτος Acts xii. 23.

[2] 'May be assigned with probability to the first century B.C.' Westcott in *D. of B.*

think only of outer riches, your heart is set on treasure here : that treasure is perishing before your eyes : it is a witness of the perishableness of all earthly things, including the body which makes use of it. You yourselves are doomed to a like decay, which will consume that flesh with which you identify yourselves (Job xv. 25, 26, Psa. lxxiii. 7) no less certainly than the funeral pyre of the Gentiles, or that which burns to consume the garbage in the Vale of Hinnom. If you had been willing to lose your lower life, you would have found a higher : the corrupting body would have been nothing to the true self.' Compare Gal. vi. 8 'he that soweth to the flesh shall of the flesh reap corruption,' Isa. li. 8 'the moth shall eat them up like a garment.' Spitta compares Enoch xcvii. 8 foll. 'Woe to you who acquire silver and gold in unrighteousness...they will perish together with their possessions and in shame will their spirits be cast into the furnace of fire,' Sir. xxxiv. 5 ὁ ἀγαπῶν χρυσίον οὐ δικαιωθήσεται καὶ ὁ διώκων διαφθορὰν αὐτὸς πλησθήσεται. May we attach to this general conception a more special application of the figurative rust? It is a witness that you have not used your wealth but selfishly stored it up (cf. Theophr. *Char.* x. τῶν μικρολόγων καὶ τὰς ἀργυροθήκας ἔστιν ἰδεῖν εὐρωτιώσας καὶ κλεῖς ἰωμένας) ; so Calvin *neque Deus aurum destinavit aerugini neque vestes tineis, quin potius haec voluit esse humanae vitae subsidia. Quare ipsa sine usu consumptio testis ipsorum inhumanitatis erit. Auri et argenti putredo quasi materia erit inflammandae irae Domini ut instar ignis eos consumat.* As the rust eats into the metal, so that selfish covetousness, of which it is the sign, shall eat into your materialized soul like a canker, destroying all the finer and more generous qualities.[1] For instances of the phrase εἰς μαρτύριον αὐτοῖς cf. Matt. viii. 4 'show thyself to the priest as a testimony unto them,' x. 18 'ye shall be brought before kings for a witness unto them and the Gentiles,' xxiv. 14, 'the Gospel shall be preached as a witness to all nations,' Luke ix. 5 'shake off the dust of your feet' εἰς μαρτύριον ἐπ' αὐτοὺς 'as a witness against them' (in the parallel passage Mark vi. 11 the dative simply is used), Luke xxi. 13 ἀποβήσεται ὑμῖν εἰς μαρτύριον 'it shall turn to you for a testimony' (in your favour). There is no need to translate ὑμῖν 'against you' ; the rust is a witness first to you and then to all observers. The force of the future ἔσται may be thus expressed : 'when you come to inspect your treasures the rust will be a witness that you have not used them as you ought.'

φάγεται τὰς σάρκας ὑμῶν.] This form of the fut. of ἐσθίω is Hellenistic and is found in Luke xiv. 15 and xvii. 8 διακόνει μοι ἕως φάγω καὶ πίω καὶ μετὰ ταῦτα φάγεσαι καὶ πίεσαι σύ, 2 Kings ix. 36 καταφάγονται αἱ κύνες τὰς σάρκας Ἰεζάβελ, Lev. xxvi. 29 φάγεσθε τὰς σάρκας τῶν υἱῶν, Apoc. xvii. 16 τὰς σάρκας τῆς πόρνης φάγονται, *ib.* xix. 18, 21. The form φαγοῦμαι appears in Gen. iii. 2. Both are condemned by Phrynichus (p. 327 Lob). Cf. σητόβρωτα above, Judith xvi. 17 Κύριος ἐκδικήσει αὐτοὺς ἐν ἡμέρᾳ κρίσεως δοῦναι πῦρ καὶ σκώληκας εἰς σάρκας αὐτῶν, Micah iii. 2, 3, Plut. *Mor.* p. 164 F quoted on κατίωται, Stob. *Serm.* 38.53 ὥσπερ ὁ

[1] Compare Eur. *El.* 387 αἱ δὲ σάρκες αἱ κεναὶ φρενῶν, translated by Keene 'fleshly natures, void of intelligence.'

ἰὸς σιδηρόν, οὕτως ὁ φθόνος τὴν ἔχουσαν αὐτὸν ψυχὴν ἐξαναψήχει, Basil. *hom. de invid.* p. 445 quoted by Suicer *s.v.* φθόνος, Sir. xxxiv. 1 ἀγρυπνία πλούτου ἐκτήκει σάρκας. The pl. σάρκες is used for the fleshy parts of the body both in classical and later writers, e.g. Hom. *Il.* viii. 380 ἦ τις καὶ Τρώων κορέει κύνας ἠδ' οἰωνοὺς δημῷ καὶ σάρκεσσι, Aesch. *Cho.* 280, Theophil. *Ant.* i. 13 νόσῳ περιπεσὼν ἀπώλεσας τὰς σάρκας, and the preceding quotations from the LXX.; while the sing. σάρξ is used for the whole body. Cf. also Menander p. 198 M., Antisth. *ap.* Laert. vi. 5.

ὡς πῦρ.] I think the parallel passages lead us to connect this with what precedes rather than (as WH. and others after Cod. A. and Pesh.) with what follows, cf. Isa. x. 16, 17, xxx. 27 ἡ ὀργὴ τοῦ θυμοῦ ὡς πῦρ ἔδεται, *ib.* xxxiii. 11, Ezek. xv. 7 πῦρ αὐτοὺς καταφάγεται, Jer. v. 14, Ps. xxi. 9, Amos i. 12, 14, v. 6, vii. 4, Heb. x. 27 φοβερά τις ἐκδοχὴ κρίσεως καὶ πυρὸς ζῆλος ἐσθίειν μέλλοντος τοὺς ὑπεναντίους. It is not merely gradual unperceived decay which is to be feared: this is changed into gnawing pain and swift destruction as by fire in the approaching judgment. Cf. Jude 7 πυρὸς αἰωνίου δίκην ὑπέχουσαι, Matt. xxv. 41, Mark ix. 44 ὅπου ὁ σκώληξ αὐτῶν οὐ τελευτᾷ καὶ τὸ πῦρ οὐ σβέννυται.

ἐθησαυρίσατε.] Absolute, as in Luke xii. 21 οὕτως ὁ θησαυρίζων ἑαυτῷ, 2 Cor. xii. 14. In Matt. vi. 19 we have the full phrase μὴ θησαυρίζετε θησαυρούς, cf. Rom. ii. 5 θησαυρίζεις σεαυτῷ ὀργὴν ἐν ἡμέρᾳ ὀργῆς, Prov. i. 18 οἱ φόνου μετέχοντες θησαυρίζουσιν ἑαυτοῖς κακά, Amos iii. 10, Tobit iv. 9, Psalm. Sol. ix. 9. 'The aor. is used as if from the standing-point of the day of judgment, looking back over this life,' Alf. Perhaps it is more correct to say that it refers back to the perfects σέσηπε, κατίωται. The laying up of treasures is anterior to these. The word ἐθησαυρίσατε is pregnant with irony: 'You heap up treasure, but the time for enjoying such treasure has come to an end; it is now only a treasure of wrath in the day of wrath.' For the asyndeton cf. below v. 6.

ἐν ἐσχάταις ἡμέραις.] Cf. Acts ii. 17 ἔσται ἐν ταῖς ἐσχάταις ἡμέραις, 2 Tim. iii. 1 ἐν ἐσχάταις ἡμέραις ἐνστήσονται καιροὶ χαλεποί, Didaché 16. 3 ἐν τ. ἐσχ. ἡμέραις πληθυνθήσονται οἱ ψευδοπροφῆται. The singular ἐν τῇ ἐσχάτῃ ἡμέρᾳ is often used in St. John's Gospel; other forms are ἐν καιρῷ ἐσχάτῳ 1 Pet. i. 5, ἐπ' ἐσχάτων τῶν χρόνων *ib.* v. 20, ἐπ' ἐσχάτων τῶν ἡμερῶν 2 Pet. iii. 3, ἐπ' ἐσχάτου χρόνου Jude 18, cf. Deut. iv. 30, Numb. xxiv. 14, Isa. xli. 23, 4 Esdr. xiii. 18, Vorst p. 109 foll., Westcott on 1 Joh. ii. 18 ἐσχάτη ὥρα. For the general sense see below on ἡμέρᾳ σφαγῆς, and for omission of article Essay on Grammar.

4. **ἰδού.**] For the sing. see above on ἄγε iv. 13.

ὁ μισθὸς τῶν ἐργατῶν.] A reminiscence of the proverb ἄξιος ὁ ἐργάτης τοῦ μισθοῦ αὐτοῦ Luke x. 7, 1 Tim. v. 18. The word is used especially of husbandmen as in Matt. ix. 37.

τῶν ἀμησάντων.] It does not seem that any distinction is to be drawn between this and θερισάντων below. ἀμάω appears to mean originally 'gathering,' 'heaping together,' as of the ant ἴδρις σωρὸν ἀμᾶται Hes. *Opera* 778 , of 'pressing the curds together' ἀμησάμενος *Od.* ix. 247, of preparing a couch εὐνὴν ἐπαμήσατο *Od.* v. 482; hence (in compounds) of heaping up earth round the roots of a plant Xen. *Oecon.* xix. 11

ἐπαμήσαιο δ' ἂν μόνον, ἔφη, τὴν γῆν, ἢ καὶ σάξαις ἂν εὖ μάλα περὶ τὸ φυτόν; *ib.* xvii. 13 ἀντιπροσαμησάμενοι τὴν γῆν τῷ ἐψιλωμένῳ τὰς ῥίζας, of heaping earth on a corpse Herod. viii. 24 τάφρους ὀρυξάμενος ἔθαψε γῆν ἐπαμησάμενος: in its commonest sense of reaping or mowing, getting in the harvest, the active voice is used, as in Homer *Il.* xviii. 551 ἔριθοι ἤμων ὀξείας δρεπάνας ἐν χερσὶν ἔχοντες, *ib.* xxiv. 451 λαχνήεντ' ὄροφον (reeds) λειμωνόθεν ἀμήσαντες, Herod. vi. 28 ἀμ. σῖτον, Arist. *Eq.* 392 ἀμ. θέρος. The word θερίζειν is rather more common for reaping and harvesting, and is given as a synonym of ἀμᾶν by Hesych. Both are used alike of the reaping of corn (ἀμ. in Lev. xxv, 11, Deut. xxiv. 19, Isa. xvii. 5) and the mowing of grass (θερ. in Ps. cxxix. 7). Both are used also in a metaphorical sense of cutting sheer off, as in Hes. *Theog.* 181 (of Cronos mutilating his father) ἤμησε, Soph. *Aj.* 239 (of Ajax) γλῶσσαν ῥίπτει θερίσας.

τὰς χώρας ὑμῶν.] Used here of a field, plot of ground, like χωρίον in Acts i. 18, iv. 34, xxviii. 7, and in classical writers. So we find Luke xxi. 21 οἱ ἐν ταῖς χώραις, *ib.* xii. 16 ἀνθρώπου τινὸς εὐφόρησεν ἡ χώρα, John iv. 35 θεάσασθε τὰς χώρας ὅτι λευκαί εἰσι πρὸς θερισμόν, Evang. Thomae c. 12 ἵνα σπείρῃ σῖτον εἰς τὴν χώραν αὐτῶν. In Amos iii. 9, x. 11 it stands where the A.V. has 'palaces': Josephus (*Ant.* vii. 8. 5) uses it of Joab's field, called μερίς 2 Sam. xiv. 30.

ὁ ἀφυστερημένος ἀφ' ὑμῶν.] 'Which is kept back by you,' 'comes too late *from* you.' The verb is only found here in N.T. In classical writers ὑστερέω and its compounds are intransitive, as also in Sir. xiv. 14 μὴ ἀφυστερήσῃς ἀπὸ ἀγαθῆς ἡμέρας 'be not late for a feast,' Heb. xii. 15 ὑστερῶν ἀπὸ τῆς χάριτος τοῦ Θεοῦ 'falling short of,' Luke xxii. 25 μή τινος ὑστερήσατε; 'did ye come short in anything?', Sir. xxvi. 19 ἀνὴρ πολεμιστὴς ὑστερῶν δι' ἔνδειαν. Of the transitive use we have an example in Neh. ix. 20 τὸ μάννα σου οὐκ ἀφυστέρησας ἀπὸ στόματος αὐτῶν. The passive occurs Diod. xviii. 71 ὑστεροῦντο τῆς χρείας, Eurip. *Iph. A.* 1203 παιδὸς ὑστερήσομαι (?), 2 Cor. xi. 8 'when I was in want (ὑστερηθεὶς) I was not a burden on any man,' Heb. xi. 37 ὑστερούμενοι, θλιβόμενοι, Luke xv. 14, 1 Cor. viii. 8, Phil. iv. 12, Sir. xi. 11 ἔστι σπεύδων καὶ τόσῳ μᾶλλον ὑστερεῖται. Some take ἀπό = ὑπὸ comparing Luke xvii. 25 ἀποδοκιμασθῆναι ἀπὸ τῆς γενεᾶς ταύτης. In both cases I should prefer to explain it as denoting not properly the agent, but the quarter from which the action proceeds. I cannot agree with Huther, Lange and Alford in connecting it with κράζει 'cries from your coffers.' The law required the prompt payment of the workman, Deut. xxiv. 15 αὐθημερὸν ἀποδώσεις τὸν μισθὸν αὐτοῦ· οὐκ ἐπιδύσεται ὁ ἥλιος ἐπ' αὐτῷ, ὅτι πένης ἐστὶ καὶ ἐν αὐτῷ ἔχει τὴν ἐλπίδα καὶ καταβοήσεται κατὰ σοῦ πρὸς Κύριον καὶ ἔσται ἐν σοὶ ἁμαρτία, Levit. xix. 13, Jer. xxii. 13, Mal. iii. 5, Prov. iii. 27, 28, Sir. xxxi. (xxxiv.) 22 ἐκχέων αἷμα ὁ ἀποστερῶν μισθὸν μισθίου, Tobit iv. 14, Hermas *Vis.* iii. 9 βλέπετε ὑμεῖς οἱ γαυρούμενοι ἐν τῷ πλούτῳ ὑμῶν μήποτε στενάξουσιν οἱ ὑστερούμενοι καὶ ὁ στεναγμὸς αὐτῶν ἀναβήσεται πρὸς τὸν Κύριον. Immediately afterwards he speaks of the ἰός received into their heart.

κράζει.] The withholding of wages is one of the four sins which are said to cry to heaven. See Deut. *l.c.*, Gen. iv. 10 thy brother's blood βοᾷ πρός με ἐκ τῆς γῆς, *ib.* xviii. 20 (cry of Sodom), Job. xvi. 18 foll., xxxi. 38, Sirac. xxxii. 17 προσευχὴ ταπεινοῦ νεφέλας διῆλθε...καὶ οὐ μὴ ἀποστῇ ἕως ἐπισκέψηται ὁ ὕψιστος καὶ...ποιήσει κρίσιν. For the oppression of the hireling cf. Job. vii. 2, *ib.* xxiv. 6–12, Sirac. xxxiv. 26.

αἱ βοαί.] Only here in N.T., cf. Exod. ii. 23 ἀνέβη ἡ βοὴ αὐτῶν πρὸς τὸν Θεὸν ἀπὸ τῶν ἔργων, 1 Sam. ix. 16 ἐπέβλεψα ἐπὶ τὴν ταπείνωσιν τοῦ λαοῦ μου, ὅτι ἦλθε βοὴ αὐτῶν πρὸς μέ.

εἰς τὰ ὦτα Κυρίου Σαβαώθ.] From Isa. v. 9 ἠκούσθη γὰρ εἰς τὰ ὦτα Κυρίου Σαβαώθ. The only other passage in N.T. where the form occurs is Rom. ix. 29, a quotation from Isa. i. 9. In the LXX. it is found in 1 Sam. i. 3, 11 'Αδωναῒ Κύριε 'Ελωὶ Σαβαώθ, *ib.* xv. 2, and in Isa. ii. 12, vi. 3 &c. : more often it is translated either by παντοκράτωρ, as in 2 Sam. v. 10, Apoc. iv. 8 compared with Isa. vi. 3, and in Jeremiah and the Minor Prophets, esp. Malachi ; or by δυνάμεων, as in Ps. lix. 5, lxxx. 7, &c., Hermas *Vis.* i. 3 : sometimes it is omitted in the Greek, as frequently in Jeremiah. By later writers it is used as an independent name of God in the nom. or voc. sing. as in Act. Apoc. T. p. 86, Sibyll. i. 316 ὁ μέγας Σαβαώθ. Its immediate reference is to the hosts of heaven, whether angels or the stars over which they preside ; then it is used more generally to express the Divine Omnipotence, cf. Matt. xxvii. 53, Luke vii. 7, 2 Kings vi. 17, Josh. v. 14. See Cheyne's Isaiah, on I. 9. The use of this name is one among many indications serving to show that the epistle is addressed to Jews. Spitta thinks there may be a special reference to the angels as ministers of Divine vengeance, and compares 3 Macc. vi. 17 foll. οἱ 'Ιουδαῖοι μέγα εἰς οὐρανὸν ἀνέκραξαν...τότε ὁ μεγαλόδοξος παντοκράτωρ...ἠνέῳξε τὰς οὐρανίας πύλας, ἐξ ὧν δύο φοβεροειδεῖς ἄγγελοι κατέβησαν.

εἰσελήλυθαν.] In later Greek the regular forms of the imperf., 2nd aor., and perf. were often changed to the type of the 1st aor., as εἶδαν, ἔπεσαν, ἐλάβοσαν, εὕροσαν, εἴχοσαν, cf. Winer, pp. 86–91, and for examples of the perf. John xvii. 7 ἔγνωκαν, *ib.* xvii. 6 τετήρηκαν, Luke ix. 36 ἑώρακαν, Rom. xvi. 7 γέγοναν, Barnabas vii. 3 πεφανέρωκαν. Meisterhans (*Gr. Att. Inscr.* p. 147) cites παρείληφαν from Smyrna 230 B.C., διατετέλεκαν, ἐντέτευχαν, εἴσχηκαν, πεποίηκαν, all B.C. from Laconia.

5. **ἐτρυφήσατε.**] Only here in N.T. The noun occurs 2 Pet. ii. 13 ἡδονὴν ἡγούμενοι τὴν ἐν ἡμέρᾳ τρυφήν, Luke vii. 25. It is used in blame here, as generally in classical authors : in good sense in Isa. lxvi. 11 ἵνα ἐκθηλάσαντες τρυφήσητε ἀπὸ εἰσόδου δόξης αὐτῆς and Neh. ix. 25. Hermas joins it with σπαταλάω in *Sim.* 6. 1 (no doubt a reminiscence of this passage) τὰ πρόβατα ὡσεὶ τρυφῶντα ἦν καὶ λίαν σπαταλῶντα, which is interpreted of those who have given themselves up to the lusts of the world and are afterwards delivered over to the angel of vengeance.

ἐπὶ τῆς γῆς.] In contrast to the judgment in heaven of the Lord of Sabaoth, cf. Matt. vi. 19 μὴ θησαυρίζετε ἐπὶ τῆς γῆς.

ἐσπαταλήσατε.] Found elsewhere in N.T. only in 1 Tim. v. 6 ἡ δὲ σπαταλῶσα ζῶσα τέθνηκεν. It occurs also in Ezek. xvi. 49 ἐσπατάλων αὕτη καὶ αἱ θυγατέρες, Sir. xxi. 15 ἤκουσεν ὁ σπαταλῶν, Barn. x. 3 ὅταν σπαταλῶσιν λανθάνονται τοῦ Κυρίου, Clem. Al. *Paed.* ii. 186 προσεπιθρύπτονται σπαταλῶσαι, *Str.* iii. 7, 59, but is much rarer than τρυφάω and is never found in a good sense. The noun occurs Sir. xxvii. 13 *γέλως αὐτῶν ἐν σπατάλῃ ἁμαρτίας*, and Varro *ap.* Non. p. 46. 12 *spatule eviravit omnes Venerivaga pueros;* the compound verb *κατασπαταλάω* Prov. xxix. 21, Amos vi. 4. The classical word of the same root, *σπαθάω* (fr. *σπάθη*, the batten, used in weaving for the purpose of driving home the threads of the woof), occurs in Dem. *F.L.* p. 354, where Shilleto says that the only example of the literal sense is the play on words in the *Nubes* 55 *ὦ γύναι λίαν σπαθᾷς*, and that elsewhere it only means 'to squander.' In the text however the prominent idea is that of self-indulgence without distinct reference to squandering.

ἐθρέψατε τὰς καρδίας.] No other instance of this phrase is recorded. Oecumenius gives *πιαίνομαι* as the equivalent of *τρέφω*, and this agrees with its use in Hom. *Od.* ix. 246 *ἥμισυ θρέψας γαλακτός* of turning milk into cheese (whence *τροφαλίς* = cheese). It would thus have the same force as *παχύνειν τὴν καρδίαν* Matt. xiii. 15 quoted from Isa. vi. 10, cf. Luke xxi. 34 *προσέχετε μήποτε βαρυνθῶσιν ὑμῶν αἱ καρδίαι ἐν κραιπάλῃ καὶ μερίμναις βιωτικαῖς, καὶ αἰφνίδιος ἐφ' ὑμᾶς ἐπιστῇ ἡ ἡμέρα ἐκείνη*, Acts xiv. 17, Psa. civ. 15.

ἐν ἡμέρᾳ σφαγῆς.] Psa. xliv. 22, Prov. vii. 22 *ὥσπερ βοῦς ἐπὶ σφαγὴν ἄγεται*, Jer. xii. 3 *ἅγνισον αὐτοὺς εἰς ἡμέραν σφαγῆς*, *ib.* xxv. (xxxii.) 34 *ἀλαλάξατε...ὅτι ἐπληρώθησαν αἱ ἡμέραι ὑμῶν εἰς σφαγήν*, Enoch xvi. 1 *ἀπὸ ἡμέρας σφαγῆς*, Philo M. 2. p. 543 *σιτία μοι καὶ ποτὰ καθάπερ τοῖς θρέμμασιν ἐπὶ σφαγὴν δίδοται*, *ib. ap.* Euseb. *P.E.* viii. 14, 26 *τῶν θρεμμάτων τὰ πρὸς ἱερουργίαν πιαινόμενα τῆς πλείστης ἐπιμελείας ἐπὶ τῷ σφαγῆναι τυγχάνει διὰ πολύκρεων εὐωχίαν*, Philemon *ap.* Stob. 51. p. 356, 47 (Meineke, p. 418) *στρατιῶτα κοὐκ ἄνθρωπε καὶ σιτούμενε, ὡς τά γ' ἱερεῖ', ἵν' ὁπόταν ᾖ καιρὸς τυθῇς*, Anthol. i. 37. 2 *πάντες τῷ θανάτῳ τηρούμεθα καὶ τρεφόμεσθα, ὡς ἀγέλη χοίρων σφαζομένων ἀλόγως*, Minucius 37 § 7 (*Deum nescientes*) *ut victimae ad supplicium saginantur, ut hostiae ad poenam coronantur.* For *ἐν ἡμέρᾳ* cf. 1 Pet. ii. 12, Rom. ii. 5. The rich are represented as sinning (1) in getting their wealth by injustice, (2) in spending it merely on their own pleasures. Their folly is shown (1) in laying up their treasures on earth, (2) especially in doing so in the very day of judgment, fattening themselves like sheep unconscious of their doom. Dr. Plummer illustrates from Jos. *B.J.* v. 10. 2, 'Josephus tells us it was all one whether the richer Jews stayed in the city during the siege or tried to escape to the Romans; they were equally destroyed in either case. Every such person was put to death on the pretext that he was preparing to desert, but in reality that the plunderers might get his possessions. . . Those whose bodies showed no signs of privation were tortured to make them reveal the treasures they were supposed to have concealed.' Even more horrible is the description in v. 13. 4.

6. **κατεδικάσατε.**] The word occurs Matt. xii. 7, Wisd. xi. 11, xii. 15, and in the remarkable parallel ii. 20 *θανάτῳ ἀσχήμονι καταδικάσωμεν αὐτόν* (*τὸν δίκαιον*). The middle is used Job xxxiv. 29, Psa. xciii. 21. In classical writers it is followed by a genitive of the person.

ἐφονεύσατε.] See n. on iv. 2, and for the asyndeton Essay on Grammar.

τὸν δίκαιον.] Cf. Wisd. ii. 10–20, esp. *καταδυναστεύσωμεν πένητα δίκαιον*

...ἐνεδρεύσωμεν τὸν δίκαιον ὅτι δύσχρηστος ἡμῖν ἐστιν...ἀλαζονεύεται πατέρα Θεόν...εἰ γάρ ἐστιν ὁ δίκαιος υἱὸς Θεοῦ, ἀντιλήψεται αὐτοῦ κ.τ.λ., a passage regarded by some of the Fathers and by many in later times as prophetic of Christ; by others it has been thought to be a Christian interpolation. We may compare other parts of the same book, *e.g.* iii. 1, iv. 7, as well as Isa. iii. 10 δήσωμεν τὸν δίκαιον ὅτι δύσχρηστος ἡμῖν ἐστίν (from which the passage in Wisdom is borrowed), *ib.* ch. liii., Prov. i. 11, Amos v. 12, Matt. xxiii. 35, xxvii. 19, 24, 1 John ii. 1, iii. 12, Acts iii. 14, vii. 52, xxii. 14, 1 Pet. iii. 18, Luke xxiii. 47. These passages might suggest that we have here a direct reference to the Crucifixion, but in any case ὁ δίκαιος must be regarded as generic and not confined to one individual. Thus the words are applicable to the writer himself, who was known to all the Jews as the Just; cf. the account of his death in Euseb. *H.E*, ii. 23, taken from Hegesippus: διὰ τὴν ὑπερβολὴν τῆς δικαιοσύνης αὐτοῦ ἐκαλεῖτο Δίκαιος καὶ Ὠβλίας, the Jews ran upon him crying out ὢ ὢ καὶ ὁ δίκαιος ἐπλανήθη...λιθάσωμεν τὸν δίκαιον, herein fulfilling the prophecy in Isa. iii. 10 (as Hegesippus says). One of the priests in vain tried to save him with the words παύσασθε, τί ποιεῖτε; εὔχεται ὑπὲρ ὑμῶν ὁ δίκαιος. See below v. 16.

οὐκ ἀντιτάσσεται ὑμῖν.] The subject here is ὁ δίκαιος. A more regular construction would be οὐκ ἀντιτασσόμενον, but the abrupt change to direct statement is a far more graphic way of putting the fact. For the change from aor. to present we may compare the similar passage in Isa. liii. 5–7 ἐτραυματίσθη διὰ τὰς ἁμαρτίας ἡμῶν...καὶ αὐτὸς διὰ τὸ κεκακῶσθαι οὐκ ἀνοίγει τὸ στόμα· ὡς πρόβατον ἐπὶ σφαγὴν ἤχθη, καὶ ὡς ἀμνὸς ...οὐκ ἀνοίγει τὸ στόμα. The present brings the action before our eyes and makes us dwell upon this, as the central point, in contrast with the accompanying circumstances. Others (Hofmann, Erdmann, &c.) take the verb as an impersonal passive, like ἀφεθήσεται below v. 15, meaning 'no opposition is needed,' 'you have your way'; but no instance of this use has been pointed out. It is the middle, not the active, which means to resist, as above iv. 6, and Rom. xiii. 2, Acts xviii. 6, 1 Kings xi. 34, Hos. i. 6. The only example of the passive in the LXX. is Prov. iii. 15, where it means 'shall not be compared with her,' lit. 'set against her.' The clause is made interrogative by WH., as by Benson, understanding ὁ Κύριος (cf. above iv. 6),[1] which was actually substituted for οὐκ by Bentley (ΟΚΣ for ΟΥΚ), but I agree with Herder that this gives a less natural and a less pathetic sense than the reading of the MSS. For the thought see Matt. v. 39, Rom. xii. 19, 1 Pet. ii. 23; and for asyndeton the Essay on Grammar and ii. 13 above.

7 **μακροθυμήσατε οὖν.**] Turning to the oppressed brethren St. James urges patience upon them by the example of 'the just,' and because it is now the last time, the day of slaughter, and their cries have gone up to the Lord of Sabaoth. As γλυκύθυμος means 'sweet-tempered,' ὀξύθυμος 'quick-tempered,' so μακρόθυμος is literally 'long-tempered,' the opposite to our 'short-tempered.' In N.T. we find μακρόθυμος used of God (Rom. ii. 4, 1 Pet. iii. 20), of man (below v. 10 and 2 Cor. vi. 6,

[1] Dr. Abbott would understand ὁ δίκαιος with much the same sense.

also the adv. μακροθύμως Acts xxvi. 3). The verb μακροθυμέω is used of God 2 Pet. iii. 9, of man 1 Cor. xiii. 4. In LXX. we find μακρόθυμος of God Exod. xxxiv. 6, Ps. ciii. 8; of man Prov. xiv. 29, xvi. 32, xix. 11. The word is rare in classical Greek, but μακροθυμία occurs in Menander p. 203 Mein., and μακροθυμέω in Plutarch. On the relation of μακροθυμία to ὑπομονή see Lightfoot on Col. i. 11, and 2 Tim. iii. 11.

ἕως τῆς παρουσίας.] ἕως seems to be first used as a preposition by Arist. *Top.* ii. 2, p. 109*b* ἕως τῶν ἀτόμων,[1] then by Polyb. i. 18. 2 οὐκ ἀντεξῄεσαν πλὴν ἕως ἀκροβολισμοῦ, often in LXX. and N.T. The word παρουσία 'visible presence' is regularly used for the Second Coming, as below v. 8, Matt. xxiv. 3, xxxvii. 39, 1 Thess. ii. 19, iv. 15, &c., 2 Pet. iii. 4. Other expressions are ἀποκάλυψις Ἰησοῦ Χριστοῦ 1 Pet. i. 7, 13; ἐπιφάνεια Tit. ii. 13, 2 Tim. iv. 1; ἡ ἐπιφάνεια τῆς παρουσίας, 2 Thess. ii. 9. Spitta cites Test. Jud. 22 ἕως παρουσίας τοῦ θεοῦ τῆς δικαιοσύνης, Test. Abr. 92. 11 μέχρι τῆς μεγάλης καὶ ἐνδόξου αὐτοῦ παρουσίας, Joel ii. 1 πάρεστιν ἡμέρα κυρίου, ὅτι ἐγγὺς ἡμέρα σκότους.

ἰδού.] As in iii. 4, 5, directs attention to the following illustration.

ὁ γεωργός. For the comparison see Sir. vi. 18 ὡς ὁ ἀροτριῶν καὶ ὁ σπείρων προσέλθε τῇ παιδείᾳ καὶ ἀνάμενε τοὺς ἀγαθοὺς καρποὺς αὐτῆς, Psa. cxxvi. 5, 6, Matt. xiii. 30, *ib.* xxiv. 32, John iv. 35 foll., 1 Cor. iii. 5–9, Gal. vi. 7, 2 Tim. ii. 6, Menander p. 245 Mein. ὁ τῶν γεωργῶν ἡδονὴν ἔχει βίος, ταῖς ἐλπίσιν τἄλγεινὰ παρυμυθούμενος, Tibull. ii. 6. 21 *spes alit agricolas*, &c.

ἐκδέχεται.] Cf. what seems like a reminiscence in 2 Clem. Rom. 20, γυμναζόμεθα τῷ νῦν βίῳ ἵνα τῷ μέλλοντι στεφανωθῶμεν· οὐδεὶς τῶν δικαίων ταχὺν καρπὸν ἔλαβεν ἀλλ' ἐκδέχεται αὐτόν. He goes on to give the reason for this, εἰ γὰρ τὸν μισθὸν τῶν δικαίων ὁ Θεὸς συντόμως ἀπεδίδου, εὐθέως ἐμπορίαν ἠσκοῦμεν καὶ οὐ θεοσέβειαν. The word ἐκδ. is also found Heb. x. 13, xi. 10, 1 Cor. xvi. 11 &c.

τίμιον.] Coupled with αἷμα 1 Pet. i. 19, with ἐπάγγελμα 2 Pet. i. 4. The preciousness of the fruit justifies waiting.

μακροθυμεῖ ἐπ' αὐτῷ.] Same phrase in Luke xviii. 7, Sir. xviii. 10, xxix. 8 ἐπὶ ταπείνῳ μακροθύμησον. See Winer p. 491 on the use of ἐπί with verbs denoting emotion.

ἕως λάβῃ.] The subject is καρπός (cf. above iii. 18) contained in the nearest object αὐτῷ, not (as Luther, Hofmann, Spitta) the husbandman, nor (as Erdmann) the earth. On the omission of ἄν see on ii. 10, and cf. Winer 370, 387, Goodwin § 620.

πρόϊμον.] WH. read πρόϊμον here with B[1], though retaining the ω in πρωινός Apoc. ii. 28, xxii. 16: see their Appendix, p. 152. Xenophon uses it of crops *Oecon.* xvii. 4 πολλοὶ διαφέρονται περὶ τοῦ σπόρου, πότερον ὁ πρώϊμος κράτιστος ἢ ὁ μέσος ἢ ὁ ὀψιμώτατος, and so Hoffmann and Spitta here understand it, as πρώϊμα is used of early figs (Jer. xxiv. 2) and ὄψιμα of wheat and rye (Exod. ix. 32). But the reference is more commonly to rain, as in Deut. xi. 14 δώσει τὸν ὑετὸν τῇ γῇ σου καθ' ὥραν πρώϊμον καὶ ὄψιμον, καὶ εἰσοίσεις τὸν σῖτόν σου, Hos. vi. 4 ἥξει ὁ Κύριος ὡς

[1] The instance quoted from Demosthenes p. 262 is contained in one of the documents of the *De Corona*.

ὑετὸς ἡμῖν πρώϊμος καὶ ὄψιμος (perhaps referred to here), Jer. v. 24, Joel ii. 23, Zech. x. 1. The former rain comes after the sowing, the latter just before the ripening, see *D. of B.* under 'rain.' For the ellipsis of ὑετός see Winer p. 738 foll. and above iii. 11 τὸ γλυκὺ καὶ τὸ πικρόν.

8. **στηρίξατε τὰς καρδίας.**] So Apoc. iii. 2 στήρισον τὰ λοιπὰ ἃ μέλλει ἀποθανεῖν, Luke xxii. 32 στήρισον τοὺς ἀδελφούς σου. This strengthening is more usually ascribed to the Divine working, as in 1 Thess. iii. 13 εἰς τὸ στηρίξαι ὑμῶν τὰς καρδίας, 1 Pet. v. 10, 2 Thess. ii. 17, Ps. li. 12. It is the true cure for διψυχία. The noun στηριγμός occurs in the same sense 2 Pet. iii. 17. As in παίζω and σαλπίζω, the inflexions vary between σ and ξ (Winer p. 110).

ἤγγικεν.] 1 Pet. iv. 7 πάντων τὸ τέλος ἤγγικεν· σωφρονήσατε οὖν, Matt. iii. 2 and often ἤγγικεν ἡ βασιλεία τῶν οὐρανῶν, Luke xxi. 28, Heb. x. 25, Phil. iv. 6 ὁ Κύριος ἐγγύς· μὴ μεριμνᾶτε, 1 Cor. xvi. 22, Barn. xxi. 3 ἐγγὺς ἡ ἡμέρα ἐν ᾗ συναπολεῖται πάντα τῷ πονηρῷ· ἐγγὺς ὁ Κύριος καὶ ὁ μισθὸς αὐτοῦ. For the general belief in the approaching coming of the Lord see 1 Cor. xv. 52, 1 Th. iv. 15, Rom. xiii. 11, 1 John ii. 18; one argument for the lateness of the second epistle of St. Peter is the doubt expressed on this subject (iii. 4) ποῦ ἐστιν ἡ ἐπαγγελία τῆς παρουσίας αὐτοῦ; 'since the fathers fell asleep all things continue as they were.'

9. **μὴ στενάζετε κατ' ἀλλήλων.**] Cf. above iv. 11 μὴ καταλαλεῖτε and the reasons there assigned. The word denotes feeling which is internal and unexpressed, cf. Rom. viii. 23; used of secret prayer Mark vii. 35.

ἵνα μὴ κριθῆτε.] See below v. 12 ἵνα μὴ ὑπὸ κρίσιν πέσητε. It is a repetition of the words in the Sermon on the Mount, Matt. vii. 1, cf. *ib.* v. 23 foll.

πρὸ τῶν θυρῶν ἕστηκεν.] Matt. xxiv. 33 ὅταν ἴδητε πάντα ταῦτα γινώσκετε ὅτι ἐγγύς ἐστιν ἐπὶ θύραις, Apoc. iii. 20 ἰδοὺ ἕστηκα ἐπὶ τὴν θύραν καὶ κρούω, Plut. *Mor.* 128 F ἔνιοι μόλις...πυρετοῦ περὶ θύρας ὄντος ἤδη, θορυβούμενοι στέλλουσιν ἑαυτούς, Justin *Dial.* c. 32 τοῦ βλάσφημα μέλλοντος λαλεῖν ἤδη ἐπὶ θύραις ὄντος, Eus. *H.E.* i. 6. Even to the brethren the Coming is a warning as well as a comfort and encouragement. Winer p. 152 mentions θύραι in his list of anarthrous words.

10. **ὑπόδειγμα.**] John xiii. 15 ὑπόδειγμα ἔδωκα ὑμῖν ἵνα καθὼς ἐγὼ ἐποίησα ὑμῖν καὶ ὑμεῖς ποιῆτε, 2 Pet. ii. 6, Sir. xliv. 16 Ἐνὼχ εὐηρέστησε Κυρίῳ, ὑπόδειγμα μετανοίας ταῖς γενεαῖς. Phrynichus says the correct form is παράδειγμα, we find however in Xen. *de re eq.* ii. 2 ταῦτα ὑποδείγματα ἔσται τῷ πωλοδάμνῃ. Spitta compares 4 Macc. ix. 8 ἡμεῖς διὰ τῆσδε τῆς κακοπαθείας καὶ ὑπομονῆς τὰ τῆς ἀρετῆς ἆθλα οἴσομεν, *ib.* xvii. 23 ἀνεκήρυξεν τοῖς στρατίωταις ὡς ὑπόδειγμα τὴν ἐκείνων ὑπομονήν.

κακοπαθίας.] Only here in N.T., used by Malachi i. 13. For the spelling see W.H. App. p. 153 foll., and compare above ἐριθία iii. 16, ἀλαζονίαις, iv. 16. The verb occurs below v. 13. Both are classical.

τοὺς προφήτας.] How is it that no mention is made of the great example to which St. Peter refers in the words Χριστὸς ἔπαθεν ὑπὲρ ὑμῶν ὑμῖν ὑπολιμπάνων ὑπογραμμόν? Is it that Christ has already been alluded to as the Just, or that St. James wishes to fix their thoughts on Him rather as the Lord of Glory than as the pattern of suffering?

Possibly the Jews of the Dispersion may have been less familiar with the details of our Lord's life, than with the books of the O.T. which were read to them in the synagogue every Sabbath day. The example of the prophets is referred to in other parts of the N.T., as in Matt. v. 12, xxiii. 34, Acts vii. 52, esp. Heb. xi. Noah, Abraham, Jacob, Moses, Isaiah, Jeremiah are preeminent patterns of endurance. Cf. Isa. l. 5 foll., Lam. iii. 27 foll., Heb. vi. 12 *μιμηταὶ τῶν διὰ πίστεως καὶ μακροθυμίας κληρονομούντων τὰς ἐπαγγελίας*. In Heb. xiii. 7 *μνημονεύετε τῶν ἡγουμένων ὑμῶν...ὧν ἀναθεωροῦντες τὴν ἔκβασιν τῆς ἀναστροφῆς μιμεῖσθε τὴν πίστιν*, it is possible that there is allusion to the life and death of St. James himself.

ἐλάλησαν ἐν τῷ ὀνόματι.] Honoured as they were, they still had to bear persecution. Speaking 'in the name' means speaking as representatives of Him who sent them, cf. below v. 14. The simple dative is found Matt. vii. 22, Jer. xliv. (li.) 16 *ὁ λόγος ὃν ἐλάλησας πρὸς ἡμᾶς ὀνόματι Κυριόυ*. This approaches the force of *ἐπὶ τῷ ὀνόματι* (depending on his name, i.e. through his power), which occurs both in N.T., as in Acts iv. 17, 18, and in classical writers, as Dem. *Lept.* 495. 7, Isae. 58. 28 and 85. 3 with Schömann's n. Diodorus xviii. 57 has *γράψας ἐπιστολὴν ἐκ τοῦ τῶν βασιλέων ὀνόματος*.

11. **μακαρίζομεν τοὺς ὑπομείναντας.**] As in i. 12, and Dan. xii. 12, cf. Matt. xxiv. 13 *ὁ δὲ ὑπομείνας εἰς τέλος οὗτος σωθήσεται*, 4 Macc. vii. 22 *εἰδὼς ὅτι τὸ διὰ τὴν ἀρετὴν πάντα πόνον ὑπομένειν μακάριόν ἐστιν*. *Ὑπομονή* is found in connexion with *μακροθυμία* 2 Cor. vi. 4 ff., Col. i. 11, 2 Tim. iii. 10.

Ἰώβ.] Job is not an example of what we should call patience except in his first acceptance of calamity (i. 21, ii. 10). We should rather say that his complaint in ch. iii., his indignation against his friends for their want of faith in him, his agony at the thought that God had forsaken him, were symptoms of an extremely sensitive, vehement, impatient character, which has very little either of Stoic *ἀπάθεια* or of Christian *πραΰτης*, but excites our admiration by its passionate outbursts of exalted feeling. The word means however endurance, and may well be applied to the persistent trust in God shown in ch. xiii. 10, 15, xvi. 19–21, xix. 25 foll. It corresponds to *ἐκαρτέρησε*, used of Moses, Heb. xi. 25. For the reference to Job, cf. Tanchuma 29. 4 *ap.* Schoettgen *H.H.* 1009 foll. *si pauper stat in tentatione et non recalcitrat, ille duplum accipiet in mundo futuro. Ex cujus exemplo hoc addiscis? Exemplo Jobi qui tentatus est in hoc mundo, Deus vero duplum ipsi reddidit.*

ἠκούσατε.] So in the Sermon on the Mount *ἠκούσατε ὅτι ἐρρήθη*. It is properly used of oral instruction in the synagogue. The aor. here must be translated, as in many other instances, by the Eng. perfect.[1]

τὸ τέλος Κυρίου εἴδετε.] 'You are acquainted with the story and have seen in it how God makes all turn out for good.' Alf. reads *ἴδετε* with AB², translating 'see also,' which gives a very uncouth sentence, and would imply that they could have heard the story without seeing

[1] See Dr. Weymouth's interesting Essay on the Rendering into English of the Greek Aorist and Perfect.

the end. On the confusion between ει and ι in the MSS. see note on iii. 3 ἴδε. Ewald understands τέλος as 'das Ziel welches Gott bei Job's Leiden hatte, nämlich seine Liebe zu zeigen,' so Schegg and others, comparing 1 Tim. i. 5 τὸ τέλος τῆς παραγγελίας ἐστὶν ἀγαπή, but it is better understood (as in the Peshitto version *exitum quem ei fecit dominus*) of the end appointed by the Lord, viz. Job's final prosperity and the declaration of his integrity against Satan and the friends, cf. Heb. xiii. 7 ὧν ἀναθεωροῦντες τὴν ἔκβασιν τῆς ἀναστροφῆς μιμεῖσθε τὴν πίστιν and Job xlii. 12 ὁ δὲ Κύριος εὐλόγησε τὰ ἔσχατα Ἰώβ ἢ τὰ ἔμπροσθεν, Ps. 103. 8 οἰκτίρμων καὶ ἐλεήμων ὁ Κύριος, μακρόθυμος καὶ πολυέλεος· οὐκ εἰς τέλος ὀργισθήσεται, 2 Cor. xi. 15 ὧν τὸ τέλος ἔσται κατὰ τὰ ἔργα αὐτῶν, 1 Pet. iv. 17 τί τὸ τέλος τῶν ἀπειθούντων; For the subjective genitive Κυρίου cf. 1 Pet. iii. 14 τὸν φόβον αὐτῶν μὴ φοβήθητε, 2 Cor. xi. 26 κινδύνοις ποταμῶν, λῃστῶν, κ.τ.λ., Test. Gad. p. 685 ὅρον Κυρίου ἐκδέξασθε 'wait the limit appointed by the Lord,' so δικαιοσύνη, εἰρήνη Θεοῦ. Augustine and Bede, with others of the older commentators and Bassett, take Κυρίου of Christ, contrasting what the readers had seen of his sufferings with what they had heard about Job. But this, instead of giving one perfect illustration of the result of suffering rightly borne, gives two imperfect and barely intelligible illustrations. If τέλος is supposed to refer to the Resurrection and Ascension, the main point of the comparison (suffering) is omitted: if it refers to the Crucifixion, the encouragement is wanting. Moreover if Κυρίου is to bear this force here, we should at least have expected the article with it; and the writer in the preceding verse bid them look to the prophets as their examples, not to Christ.

ὅτι.] Epexegetic of τέλος. 'Ye have seen the final result of God's working, (showing) that God is merciful.' Alford, taking it in the sense 'because,' gives a very forced explanation 'look on to the end which God gave Job; and it is well worth your while to do so, *for* you will find that he is very pitiful.'

πολύσπλαχνος.] 'Sympathetic.' Occurs elsewhere only in Hermas *Mand.* iv. 3. 5, *Sim.* v. 7. 4. The equivalent πολυέλεος is found in Psa. ciii. 8, Joel ii. 13. The substantive πολυσπλαγχνία is found in Herm. *Vis.* i. 3. 2, *ib.* ii. 2. 8, iv. 2. 3, *Mand* ix. 2, Justin M. *Tryph* § 55; πολυεύσπλαγχνος Herm. *Sim.* v. 4, πολυευσπλαγχνία in *Sim.* viii. 6. 1, see the n. on *Vis.* i. 3. 2, and cf. εὔσπλαγχνος Eph. iv. 32, 1 Pet. iii. 8, σπλαγχνίζομαι common in the Gospels, both derived from such phrases as σπλάγχνα ἐλέους Luke i. 78, σπλ. οἰκτιρμῶν Col. iii. 12, τὰ σπλάγχνα τῶν ἁγίων ἀναπαύεται Philem. 7, κλείειν τὰ σπλάγχνα 1 John iii. 17, τὰ σπλάγχνα αὐτοῦ περισσοτέρως εἰς ὑμᾶς ἐστιν 2 Cor. vii. 15, αὐτόν, τοῦτ' ἔστι τὰ ἐμὰ σπλάγχνα 'my very heart' Philem. 12, Prov. xii. 10, Isa. lxiii. 15, where Vulg. has *multitudo viscerum tuorum*. The sing. is used in the same sense in Test. Zab. 8 ὁ Θεὸς ἀποστέλλει τό σπλάγχνον αὐτοῦ ἐπὶ τῆς γῆς καὶ ὅπου εὕρῃ σπλάγχνα ἐλέους ἐν αὐτῷ κατοικεῖ, Herm. *Sim.* ix. 24 σπλάγχνον ἔχοντες ἐπὶ πάντα ἄνθρωπον. The word is sometimes used metaphorically by classical writers, as by Eur. *Med.* 220 πρὶν ἀνδρὸς σπλάγχνον ἐκμαθεῖν, but this is of disposition in a wider sense, not specially of compassion. See Vorst, p. 35 foll.

οἰκτίρμων.] 'Compassionate.' Occurs elsewhere in N.T. only in Luke vi. 36, found in LXX. Clem. R. i. 23 and Theocritus.

12. **πρὸ πάντων δὲ μὴ ὀμνύετε.**] This is a reminiscence of our Lord's words (Matt. v. 34) in which, instead of the old rule *οὐκ ἐπιορκήσεις*, he lays down the Christian rule *μὴ ὀμόσαι ὅλως...ἔστω δὲ ὁ λόγος ὑμῶν ναὶ ναί, οὒ οὔ, τὸ δὲ περισσὸν τούτων ἐκ τοῦ πονηροῦ ἐστίν.* The language of the O.T. itself is not by any means uniform on this subject. A Jew might defend the use of oaths by appealing to Deut. vi. 13 (bidding the people swear by the name of God), Psa. lxiii. 11 *ἐπαινεθήσεται πᾶς ὁ ὀμνύων ἐν αὐτῷ*, Isa. lxv. 16, Jer. xii. 16 (though in these passages it is rather the faith in Jehovah symbolized by the oath than the oath itself which is meant); also to the practice of Elijah (1 Kings xvii. 1), Micaiah (*ib.* xxii. 14), and the words ascribed (*ἀνθρωπικώτερον*, as Athanasius says, *ap.* Suic. ii. p. 513) to God himself, Gen. xxii. 16, Psa. cv. 9, Isa. xlv. 23, see particularly Heb. vi. 16 f., vii. 21. On the other hand we read in Sir. xxiii. 7 *παιδείαν στόματος ἀκούσατε τέκνα...ἐν τοῖς χείλεσιν αὐτοῦ καταληφθήσεται ἁμαρτωλός, καὶ λοίδορος καὶ ὑπερήφανος σκανδαλισθήσονται ἐν αὐτοῖς. ὅρκῳ μὴ ἐθίσῃς τὸ στόμα σου καὶ ὀνομασίᾳ τοῦ Θεοῦ μὴ συνεθισθῇς...ἀνὴρ πολύορκος πλησθήσεται ἀνομίας κ.τ.λ.*, Prov. xxx. 9 *ἵνα μὴ πενηθεὶς κλέψω καὶ ὀμόσω τὸ ὄνομα τοῦ Θεοῦ*, which Delitzsch understands of blaspheming against God, cursing him as the cause of his misfortunes, Levit. xxiv. 15 *ἄνθρωπος ὃς ἐὰν καταράσηται Θεὸν ἁμαρτίαν λήμψεται, ὀνομάζων δὲ ὄνομα Κυρίου θανάτῳ θανατούσθω.* This prohibition gave rise to a variety of forms of swearing in which the name of God was not expressed, see Matt. v. 35, 36, xxiii. 16–22, Philo *Spec. Legg.* M. 2. p. 271 'if a man must swear, let him not swear by God, but by the earth, the sun, the moon, the stars, the heaven.' Elsewhere however Philo gives the higher view (M. 2. p. 184) *κάλλιστον δὴ καὶ βιωφελέστατον καὶ ἁρμόττον λογικῇ φύσει τὸ ἀνώμοτον, οὕτως ἀληθεύειν ἐφ' ἑκάστου δεδιδαγμένῃ ὡς τοὺς λόγους ὅρκους εἶναι νομίζεσθαι· δεύτερος δὲ πλοῦς τὸ εὐορκεῖν*, *ib.* p. 271 *οὐ πίστεως ἡ πολυορκία τεκμήριον ἀλλ' ἀπιστίας ἐστὶ παρὰ τοῖς εὖ φρονοῦσιν*, and he goes on to point out the motives, such as hatred, which often lead to swearing. Similarly the Essenes are said to have forbidden all swearing, Joseph. *B.J.* ii. 8. 6 *πᾶν τὸ ῥηθὲν ὑπ' αὐτῶν ἰσχυρότερον ὅρκου, τὸ δὲ ὀμνύειν περιίστανται χεῖρόν τι τῆς ἐπιορκίας ὑπολαμβάνοντες*, so Philo M. 2. p. 458; hence Herod excused their taking the oath of allegiance (Jos. *Ant.* xv. 10. 4). It is difficult to reconcile with this what Josephus says of the oaths they had to take in the course of initiation (*B.J.* ii. 8. 7). So the ancient Greeks, see Pythag. *ap.* Diog. L. viii. 22 *μὴ ὀμνύναι θεοὺς, ἀσκεῖν γὰρ αὐτὸν δεῖν ἀξιόπιστον παρέχειν*, Diod. Sic. x. fr. 16, Epict. *Ench.* 33, cf. Wetst. on Matt. v. 37, and the story told of Xenocrates (Cic. *pro Balb.* 5) *cum jurandi causa ad aras accederet una voce omnes judices ne is juraret reclamasse.*

On the teaching and practice of the Early Christians see *Dict. of Christ. Ant.* under 'Oaths,' Nicod. Evang. p. 532 Thilo (on Pilate's adjuring certain witnesses *ὁρκίζω ὑμᾶς κατὰ τῆς σωτηρίας Καίσαρος*, they answer) *ἡμεῖς νόμον ἔχομεν μὴ ὀμνύειν ὅτι ἁμαρτία ἐστί*, Clem. Al. *Strom.* vii. 8. p. 861 P. esp. § 51 *πεπεισμένος πάντῃ τὸν Θεὸν εἶναι πάντοτε καὶ* αἰδούμενος μὴ ἀληθεύειν, ἀνάξιόν τε αὐτοῦ καὶ ψεύδεσθαι γινώσκων, τῇ συνειδήσει τῇ θείᾳ καὶ τῇ ἑαυτοῦ ἀρκεῖται μόναις...ταύτῃ δὲ οὐδὲ ὄμνυσιν ὅρκον ἀπαιτηθείς, Orig. on Jerem. iv. 2 (where Israel is bidden to swear righteously and truly) says τάχα πρῶτον δεῖ ὀμόσαι ἐν ἀληθείᾳ ...ἵνα μετὰ τοῦτο προκόψας τις ἄξιος γένηται τοῦ μὴ ὀμνύειν ὅλως ἀλλ' ἔχῃ ναὶ μὴ δεόμενον μαρτύρων τοῦ εἶναι τὸ ναί (Lomm. vol. xv. p. 166), Chrysost. *Hom.* viii. *in Act.* (*ap.* Suic. ii. 510) χαλινὸν ἐπιθῶμεν τῇ γλώττῃ· μηδεὶς ὀμνύτω τὸν Θεόν, Photius *Epist.* i. 34 ὁ δὲ εὐσταθὴς καὶ μεγαλόψυχος ἀνὴρ αἰσχυνθήσεται τοὺς λόγους ὅρκῳ πιστοὺς ἀποφαίνειν καὶ τὴν διὰ τῶν οἰκείων τρόπων πίστιν ἀτιμάζειν, Theodoret *Epit. div. decr.* 16. ὁ μὲν παλαιὸς νόμος ἀπαγορεύει τὸ ψεῦδος, ὁ δέ γε νέος καὶ τὸν ὅρκον. Tertullian is inconsistent, denying the lawfulness of oaths in *Idol.* xi. *taceo de perjurio, quando ne jurare quidem liceat,* but allowing it in *Apol.* 33 *sed et juramus sic, ut non per genios Caesarum, ita per salutem eorum.* For a further discussion see Comment below.

St. Augustine has some interesting remarks on this verse (*Serm.* 180). He had always, he says, shrunk from taking it as the subject of a sermon, but as it came in the lesson for the day he felt it his duty to offer some explanation. He sees no harm in oaths if it were not for the danger of committing perjury. They are sometimes required in order to induce belief of an important matter, but as they are certainly too common, it is better to keep on the safe side and avoid them altogether. What especially puzzles him is the *ante omnia.* 'Is swearing worse than stealing or adultery? We must regard it as a hyperbolical phrase used to add weight to the apostolic injunction.' The truer explanation of the πρὸ πάντων is to limit the comparison to what immediately precedes. St. James is not thinking of offences against the moral law generally, but only of those modes of expressing impatience of which he had spoken in the preceding verses μὴ στενάζετε, &c., cf. 1 Pet. iv. 8 πρὸ πάντων τὴν εἰς ἑαυτοὺς ἀγαπὴν ἐκτενῆ ἔχοντες, where this precept is compared with the preceding σωφρονήσατε καὶ νήψατε, not with the first and great commandment, 'Thou shalt love the Lord thy God.' It must be confessed however that we might rather have expected the angry feeling of injustice to have expressed itself in curses than in oaths. The latter seem rather to betoken irreverence and a low tone as to ordinary truthfulness, which would have come more naturally in speaking of the sins of traders in iv. 13, cf. Clem. Al. *Paed.* 3. § 79, p. 299 P. ἐπαίτιος δὲ ὅρκος περὶ πάντων τοῦ πωλουμένου ἀπέστω, and Tert. *Idol.* xi. B. Weiss thinks there is a reference to the asseverations made before the judge of ver. 6. For examples of hasty, irreverent oaths see 1 Sam. xxvi. 16, 2 Kings v. 20. Still the oath supplies a heightened form of expression for almost any feeling, and especially in the case of angry threats, cf. Philo M. 2. p. 271 cited above. For construction of ὀμνύω cf. Hos. iv. 15 μὴ ὀμνύετε Κύριον: the acc. is common also in classical writers. Other constructions are with κατά, εἰς, ἐν. For position of δέ see Index *s.v.*

μήτε τὸν οὐρανὸν μήτε τὴν γῆν.] Both are referred to in Matt. v. 34, 35, where, as also in Matt. xxiii. 16 foll., other common forms of swearing are specified.

ἤτω.] The only examples cited of this form are 1 Cor. xvi. 22 ἤτω ἀνάθεμα, Psa. civ. 31, 1 Macc. x. 31 Ἱερουσαλὴμ ἤτω ἁγία, Aretaeus i. 2. 79, Hippocr. 8. 340 L., Clem. Al. *Strom.* i. 7. p. 339 P. ἤτω τις πιστὸς, ἤτω δυνατός τις γνῶσιν ἐξειπεῖν, ἤτω σοφὸς ἐν διακρίσει λόγων, ἤτω γοργὸς ἐν ἔργοις, quoted from Clem. Rom. 48 with the omission of a final clause ἤτω ἁγνός: in *Strom.* vi. 8. p. 778 the same quotation occurs with ἔστω for ἤτω in the first two clauses. Hermas (*Vis.* iii. 3) has μόνον ἡ καρδία πρὸς τὸν Θεὸν ἤτω, and it occurs in the treatise Ad Diogn. 12 ἤτω σοι καρδία γνῶσις, ζωὴ δὲ λόγος ἀληθής, and in Epiphanius quoted below. It was formerly read in Plato *Rep.* ii. 361 C, but Stallb. now reads ἔστω, Zur. ἴτω. Sterrett *Epigr. J. in As. Mi.* has one instance (no. 31) εἰ δέ τις κακουργήσει, ἤτω ἔνοχος Ἡλίῳ Σελήνῃ, and Prof. W. M. Ramsay (*Zt. f. Vgl. Sprachforschung* 1887, p. 386) cites another from Tiberiopolis in Phrygia κατηραμένος ἤτω αὐτὸς καὶ τὰ τέκνα αὐτοῦ. He also gives several examples of the Phrygian form εἴτου. Dr. E. L. Hicks in a private letter suggests that 'it was a late form adopted through false analogy from βῆθι βήτω, στῆθι στήτω. The resemblance of ὦ βῶ στῶ, ἦν ἔβην ἔστην, ἤμεναι βήμεναι might well lead to this.'

τὸ ναὶ ναὶ καὶ τὸ οὒ οὔ.] 'Let your yea be a yea and your nay a nay' (and nothing more). Edersheim i. 583 quotes a Midrash to the effect that 'the good man's yea is yea, and his nay nay.' I prefer this, which is the ordinary way of taking it, as the simplest and plainest, but Schegg would translate it as a direct quotation from Matt. v. 37 'let yours be the "yea yea", and the "nay nay."' Justin M. while quoting from St. Matt. inserts the article with St. James (*Apol.* i. 16 D) and so Clem. Al. *Str.* v. 100 quotes τὸ τοῦ Κυρίου ῥητόν, ἔστω ὑμῶν τὸ ναὶ ναὶ καὶ οὒ οὔ, *ib.* vii. 67 δικαιοσύνης ἣν ἐπιτομὴ φάναι Ἔστω ὑμῶν τὸ ναὶ ναὶ καὶ οὒ οὔ, and Clem. Hom. xix. 2 τοῖς δὲ νομίζουσιν ὡς αἱ γραφαὶ διδάσκουσιν ὅτι ὁ Θεὸς ὀμνύει ἔφη, ἔστω ὑμῶν τὸ ναὶ ναὶ καὶ τὸ οὒ οὔ. So also Epiphanius *Haer.* i. p. 44 τοῦ Κυρίου λέγοντος Μὴ ὀμνύναι μήτε τὸν οὐρανὸν μήτε τὴν γῆν μήτε ἕτερόν τινα ὅρκον, ἀλλ' ἤτω ὑμῶν τὸ ναὶ ναὶ καὶ τὸ οὒ οὔ. Resch (*Zeitschr. f. kirchl. Wissenschaft u. k. Leben* 1888, pp. 283—288) regards this variety as a proof that we have in them different renderings of the same Aramaic *logion.* Similarly he regards the ὅλως of Matt. and the πρὸ πάντων of James as standing for the same word in the original; and compares τὸ ναί with ὁ Ἀμήν in Apoc. iii. 14. If Stanley and Alford are right in their explanation of 2 Cor. i. 17 (ἢ ἃ βουλεύομαι κατὰ σάρκα βουλεύομαι, ἵνα ᾖ παρ' ἐμοὶ τὸ ναὶ ναί, καὶ τὸ οὒ οὔ;) it has no reference to our Lord's words, and is indeed used in an opposite sense, implying either blamable inconsistency or, as others think, over-confidence and obstinacy.

ἵνα μὴ ὑπὸ κρίσιν πέσητε.] = ἵνα μὴ κρίθητε above v. 9: cf. Sir. xxix. 19 ἁμαρτωλὸς ἐμπεσεῖται εἰς κρίσεις. The judgment would be for the breach of the third commandment.

13. **κακοπαθεῖ τις.**] See on κακοπαθία above v. 10. The verb occurs in N.T. only here and in the Second Epistle to Timothy ii. 3 κακοπάθησον ὡς καλὸς στρατιώτης, ver. 9 κακοπαθῶ μέχρι δεσμῶν, *ib.* iv. 5 νῆφε καὶ κακοπάθησον. For examples of a hypothesis contained in an indicative clause without any hypothetical particle, see above iii. 13 n., 1 Cor. vii.

18 περιτετμημένος τις ἐκλήθη; μὴ ἐπισπάσθω· ἐν ἀκροβυστίᾳ κέκληταί τις; μὴ περιτεμνέσθω, *ib.* ver. 27 δέδεσαι γυναικί; μὴ ζήτει λύσιν. λέλυσαι ἀπὸ γυναικός; μὴ ζήτει γυναῖκα, *ib.* ver. 21 δοῦλος ἐκλήθης; μή σοι μελέτω, Sir. vii. 22–26: also in profane Greek Dem. *Cor.* p. 317. 15 ἀδικεῖ τις ἑκών; ὀργὴ καὶ τιμωρία κατὰ τούτου· ἐξήμαρτέ τις ἄκων; συγγνώμη ἀντὶ τῆς τιμωρίας τούτῳ, id. *Androt.* 601 ἀσθενέστερος εἶ; τοῖς ἄρχουσιν ἐφηγοῦ· φοβῇ καὶ τοῦτο; γράφου, Juv. 3. 100 *rides, maiore cachinno excutitur* with Mayor's n., Roby Gr. § 1553, 1555. In Latin the protasis is usually regarded as a categorical assumption, and so some would take it here, and even in such forms as that in iii. 13, where the sentence begins with the interrogative pronoun. The interrogative is more in accordance with the vivacity which characterizes St. James.

ἐν ὑμῖν.] See above iii. 13 and 1 Cor. xv. 12 λέγουσίν τινες ἐν ὑμῖν.

προσευχέσθω.] Instead of breaking out into oaths.

εὐθυμεῖ.] Classical, found elsewhere in N.T. only in Acts xxvii. 22, 25.

ψαλλέτω.] Properly used of playing on a stringed instrument, as Luc. *Paras.* 17 οὔτε γὰρ αὐλεῖν ἔνι χωρὶς αὐλῶν οὔτε ψάλλειν ἄνευ λύρας. We find it also used of singing with the voice and with the heart, Eph. v. 19, 1 Cor. xiv. 15. The word is only used of sacred music in N.T., but in Sir. ix. 4 of a hired *citharistria*, μετὰ ψαλλούσης μὴ ἐνδελέχιζε.

14. **ἀσθενεῖ.**] 'Sick,' as in Matt. x. 8 and often both in classical and Hellenistic Greek. A special case of κακοπαθία.

τοὺς πρεσβυτέρους τῆς ἐκκλησίας.] The same phrase occurs Acts xx. 17 (of Ephesus). The ecclesiastical constitution of the Jewish churches was developed out of the synagogue, in which, if the place was populous, there was the council of elders (Luke vii. 3) one or more of whom, entitled ἀρχισύναγωγος, like Jairus (Luke viii. 41, 49), was intrusted with the superintendence of the religious meetings,[1] cf. *D. of B.* under 'Bishop' and 'Synagogue,' also *Dict. of Chr. Ant.* pp. 1699 foll. and Rothe *Die Anfänge der christlichen Kirche*, pp. 147 foll. Other references to Christian elders are Acts xi. 30 (the church at Antioch send their contributions to the elders at Jerusalem), *ib.* xxi. 18 (the elders were present during Paul's interview with James), 1 Pet. v. 1 πρεσβυτέρους ἐν ὑμῖν παρακαλῶ ὁ συμπρεσβύτερος. Rauch contests the genuineness of this passage on the ground that the writer elsewhere speaks of διδάσκαλοι and συναγωγή, not as here of πρεσβύτεροι and ἐκκλησία; but ἐκκ. and συν. are convertible terms, not only in early Christian literature (for which see note on ii. 2, Schürer *l.c.* p. 58, Spitta p. 144, 354, and Harnack in *Zt. f. wissensch. Theol.* 1876, p. 104), but in the LXX. A reason for the use of ἐκκ. here may be that it is a general word for the permanent body of the Church, and is appropriately used for the title of its ministers (cf. Matt. xvii. 17 'if thy brother sin against thee'... εἰπὲ τῇ ἐκκλησίᾳ, which has much the same force as 'the elders of the Church' here), while συναγ. refers strictly to the congregation in a

[1] Cf. Schürer *Jewish People* Div. II. vol. 2 § 27, pp. 53—65, § 31, pp. 243—252, Eng. tr. ed, I. We learn from Epiphanius that the Jewish titles were still retained in his time by the Ebionites of Palestine (*Haer.* xxx. 18 πρεσβυτέρους γὰρ οὗτοι ἔχουσι καὶ ἀρχισυναγώγους).

particular building. If James presided over the council at Jerusalem and wrote the letter preserved in the Acts, he cannot have been ignorant of πρεσβύτεροι. We need not of course suppose the word to be used in its later hierarchical sense (see *Dict. of Chr. Ant.* under 'Priest'): Bede *in loc.* understands it simply of age and experience, *tristato praecipiens ut ipse pro se oret et psallat, infirmanti autem vel corpore vel fide mandans ut, qui majorem sustinuit plagam, plurimorum se adjutorio et hoc seniorum curare meminerit; neque ad juniores minusque doctos causam suae imbecillitatis referat, ne forte quid per eos allocutionis aut consilii nocentis accipiat.* It seems better however to regard it as an official title, denoting the leaders of the local Christian society (οἱ προϊστάμενοι 1 Thess. v. 12, οἱ ἡγούμενοι Heb. xiii. 17), who would exercise a general superintendence over the activity of the individual members and over the use to be made of the χαρίσματα. Those who possessed these gifts in the largest measure would doubtless be themselves included in the council of elders (τὸ πρεσβυτέριον 1 Tim. iv. 14). On notification of a case of sickness, the council would, we may suppose, consider whether it was a fit case for the exercise of the χάρισμα, and would depute some of their body to attend to the case and unite in prayer for the sick person (Matt. xviii. 20). Schneckenburger is, I think, right in his view that the writer is not here commending a new remedy, but *remedii semper usitati rectum usum commendare...Noluit tumultario charismatum usu ordinem, jam docendi promiscue pruritu* (iii. 1) *labefactatum, magis turbari.* In Clem. Hom. *Ep. ad Jac.* 12 it is said to be the duty of the deacons, as the eyes of the bishop, to inform the congregation of all cases of sickness, in order that they may visit the sick and give such assistance as the president may think fit. Wetst. quotes from Rabbinical writings showing that it was the custom to send for a rabbi in sickness, and that sometimes as many as four visited the sick at one time. Polycarp (*ad Phil.* 6) mentions visitation of the sick as a duty of the elders ἐπισκεπτόμενοι πάντας ἀσθενεῖς, see Acts xx. 35. On the treatment of the sick and the use of the physician cf. Sir. xxxviii. 1–15 esp. v. 9 ἐν ἀρρωστήματί σου ...εὖξαι Κυρίῳ καὶ αὐτὸς ἰάσεταί σε.

προσευξάσθωσαν ἐπ' αὐτόν.] 'Let them pray (stretching their hands) over him.' Origen (*Hom. in Lev.* ii. 4) comparing the ways of propitiation under the old and new covenants, quotes this verse as follows *si quis autem infirmatur, vocet presbyteros ecclesiae, et imponant ei manus, ungentes eum in nomine Domini. Et oratio fidei salvabit infirmum et, si in peccatis fuerit, remittentur ei.* I do not think this implies any denial of the beneficial effect of oil in bodily sickness (as Dr. Plummer seems to hold in his note on this passage): it is merely that Origen does not care to dwell upon it, as it is unconnected with his particular subject. For the acc. cf. μὴ κλαίετε ἐπ' ἐμέ Luke xxiii. 28, ὀνομάζειν ἐπὶ τοὺς ἔχοντας τὰ πνεύματα τὸ ὄνομα τοῦ Κυρίου Acts xix. 13. It often alternates with the dat. as in Zech. xii. 10 κόψονται ἐπ' αὐτόν, ὡς ἐπ' ἀγαπητῷ, and σπλαγχνίζομαι ἐπ' αὐτόν Matt. xv. 32, Mark viii. 2, ix. 22, but ἐπ' αὐτῇ Luke vii. 13; so πιστεύω with acc. Acts ix. 42, but with dat. Rom. iv. 3, 1 Tim. i. 16: cf. Winer p. 508, 510.

ἀλείψαντες ἐλαίῳ.] Anointing the sick was customary, see *D. of B.* under 'Medicine' and also vol. iii. p. 395, and for instances Isa. i. 6, Luke x. 34. Herod in his last illness was recommended a bath of oil by his physicians (Jos. *B.J.* i. 33. 5). The medicinal properties of oil are also praised by Philo (*Somn.* M. i. 666), Pliny (*N.H.* xxiii. 34-50), and Galen (*Med. Temp.* bk. ii.). The latter calls it ἄριστον ἰαμάτων πάντων τοῖς ἐξηραμμένοις καὶ αὐχμώδεσι σώμασιν. Here the anointing is accompanied by a miraculous healing in answer to prayer, as we are told of the Twelve (Mark vi. 13) ἤλειφον ἐλαίῳ πολλοὺς ἀρρώστους καὶ ἐθεράπευον. Nothing is specified as to the use of oil in the promise recorded by the same Evangelist (xvi. 18) ἐπὶ ἀρρώστους χεῖρας ἐπιθήσουσιν καὶ καλῶς ἕξουσιν, or in Acts xxviii. 8, where St. Paul is said to have healed the father of Publius by prayer and the laying on of hands. In the church of Corinth (1 Cor. xii. 9) gifts of healing (χαρίσματα ἰαμάτων) are mentioned along with the other manifestations of the Spirit. but again nothing is said as to their mode of working. So too Irenaeus (ii. 32. 4) asserts that miraculous powers might still be witnessed in his day, ἄλλοι τοὺς κάμνοντας διὰ τῆς τῶν χειρῶν ἐπιθέσεως ἰῶνται, but is silent as to the use of oil : Augustine in his long list of contemporary miracles (*Civ. D.* xxii. 8) only once mentions the use of oil. On the other hand Tertullian (*ad Scap.* 4) says Septimius Severus was cured with oil by the Christian Proculus; and in the Gospel of Nicodemus (c. 19) Seth, having asked for oil from the tree of life to heal his father Adam, is told that this is impossible, but that hereafter the Christ would come καὶ ἀλείψει αὐτὸν τῷ τοιούτῳ ἐλαίῳ καὶ ἀναστήσεται... καὶ τότε ἀπὸ πάσης νόσου ἰαθήσεται. Irenaeus (i. 21. 5, cf. August. *Haeres.* 16, Epiphan. *Haeres.* xxx. 2) says that the Gnostic sect of the Heracleonites anointed the dying with oil and water to protect them from hostile spirits in the other world. Chrysostom, *Hom.* 3 *in Matt.* (Migne *Patrol. Gr.* vol. 57, col. 384), magnifying the sanctity of Church vessels generally, says, those know how far our lamps surpass all others ὅσοι μετὰ πίστεως καὶ εὐκαίρως ἐλαίῳ χρισάμενοι νοσήματα ἔλυσαν, from which it is inferred that the oil for anointing the sick was taken from the lamps used in church, as is still the custom in the Greek Church, cf. Neale's *Eastern Church, Introd.* pp. 966, 1037, *Dict. of Chr. Ant.* under 'Oil' p. 1453 foll. Cassianus speaking of Abbot Paul says (*Coll.* vii. 26) such virtue proceeded from him, that *cum de oleo quod corpore contigisset unguerentur infirmi, confestim cunctis valetudinibus curarentur.* This may be compared with Chrys. *Hom. in Mart.* (*Patr.* vol. 50. col. 664), where he recommends, as a remedy against drunkenness, the anointing of the body with oil taken from the martyrs' tombs. So the Nestorians mix oil, water and the relics of some saint or, if these are not to be procured, dust from the scene of a martyrdom, and anoint the sick with it (Neale, *l.c.* p. 1036 and cf. Greg. T. *Mir. Mart.* i. 2), On the Oil of the Cross see *Dict. Chr. Ant.* l.c.

From these facts it may be probably inferred that, the anointing with simple oil having ceased to be effective in healing the sick, some endeavoured to add fresh virtue to the oil either by special consecration, or by combining it with the relics of saints, while others, like the followers of Heracleon and the Church of Rome in later times, supposed it to retain a purely spiritual efficacy, thus changing a hypothetical appendage to the injunction (κἂν ἁμαρτίας ᾖ πεποιηκώς) into the essence of the injunction itself. There is, I believe, no recorded instance during the first eight centuries of the anointing of the sick being deferred, as having only a spiritual efficacy, to the point of death, except among the Heracleonites, whose conception of the use of the anointing, as described by Epiphanius *l.c.*, is almost in verbal agreement with the language of a monastic rule for Extreme Unction contained in Martene (*De Antiquis Ecclesiae Ritibus*, vol. 5 p. 241) *ut more militis uncti praeparatus ad certamen aereas possit superare potestates.*

Many stories are told of cures wrought by the Unction for the Sick in *D. of Christian Ant.* pp. 1455 and 2004. In the Greek Church the oil, called εὐχέλαιον, is usually consecrated by seven priests. In the West we find the oil consecrated by laymen and even by women as late as the 6th century. In the 8th century Boniface ordered all presbyters to obtain the oil of the sick from the bishop. It is curious that in the early church it was not necessary for the anointing to be done by a priest: it was frequently performed by the sick man or by his friends.[1] It is not till A.D. 852 that the function of anointing is confined to the priest. The original intention for the healing of the body was forgotten and 'the rite came to be regarded as part of a Christian's immediate preparation for death. Hence in the 12th century it acquired the name of *unctio extrema*. . . . In the 13th century it was placed by schoolmen among the seven rites to which they then limited the application of the term sacrament.' *D. of C. A.*

The effect of this sacrament is thus defined by the Council of Trent (*sessio decima quarta*). After declaring (cap. 1) that it was ordained by Christ (Mark vi. 13) and promulgated in this verse by St. James, the decree continues (cap 2) *res et effectus hujus sacramenti illis verbis explicatur: Et oratio fidei salvabit infirmum et alleviabit eum Dominus; et si in peccatis sit, dimittentur ei. Res etenim haec est gratia Spiritus sancti, cujus Unctio delicta, si quae sint adhuc expianda, ac peccati reliquias abstergit et aegroti animam alleviat et confirmat...et sanitatem corporis interdum, ubi saluti animae expedierit, consequitur.* The dogma is clenched by the following anathemas: Can. I. *Si quis dixerit extremam Unctionem non esse vere et proprie Sacramentum a Christo Domino nostro institutum et a beato Jacobo Apostolo promulgatum, sed ritum tantum acceptum a patribus aut figmentum humanum; anathema sit.* Can. II. *Si quis dixerit sacram infirmorum Unctionem non conferre gratiam nec remittere peccata nec alleviare infirmos, sed jam cessasse, quasi olim fuerit gratia curationum; anathema sit.* Similarly in Canons III. and IV. those are anathematized who think that the Roman rite is opposed to the teaching of St. James and may be safely neglected by Christians, as well as those who think that the Elders mentioned by St. James are other than episcopally ordained priests.

[1] Caesarius of Arles (502 A.D.) during an epidemic recommends a person to anoint both himself and family with blessed oil (*Serm.* 89. 5).

The Roman Catechism adds that it is only to be administered to those who are dangerously ill, that the oil is to be applied to those parts of the body *in quibus potissimum sentiendi vis eminet*, eyes, ears, nose, mouth, hands, feet, *renes etiam veluti voluptatis et libidinis sedes.* Pastors must instruct their people that by this sacrament venial sins are remitted, the soul is freed from the weaknesses contracted by sin, and filled with courage, hope, and joy. If bodily health does not now follow it, this is to be ascribed to the want of faith of those who administer or receive the sacrament. In the form of Visitation for the Sick, in the English Prayer-book of 1549, anointing was allowed if the sick person desired it: 'then shall the priest anoint him on the forehead or breast only, making the sign of the Cross and saying thus' (a prayer for the inward anointing of the soul and for a restoration of bodily health).

As regards the Greek Church Dr. King says (*Rites and Ceremonies of the Greek Church in Russia*, 1772, p. 305) 'though the Greek Church reckons it (the anointing of the sick) in the number of her mysteries, yet it is certain there is nothing throughout the whole office which implies that it should be administered only to persons *periculose aegrotantibus et mortis periculo imminente*, as is prescribed in the Roman Church. On the contrary it may . . . be used in any illness as a pious and charitable work, but not of necessity; and thence I presume the doctors of this church maintain that this mystery is not obligatory or necessary to all persons.'

It is curious that there is no note on this verse in Theophylact, Euth. Zig., or Cramer's *Catena*. Oecumenius on ἀλείψαντες ἐλαίῳ refers simply to the miracles in the Gospels without alluding to any sacramental use of oil in his own day: τοῦτο καὶ τοῦ Κυρίου ἔτι τοῖς ἀνθρώποις συναναστρεφομένου οἱ ἀπόστολοι ἐποίουν ἀλείφοντες τοὺς ἀσθενοῦντας ἐλαίῳ καὶ ἰώμενοι. Bede in like manner speaks only of the use of oil for healing bodily disease: *hoc et apostolos fecisse in Evangelio legimus, et nunc Ecclesiae consuetudo tenet ut infirmi oleo consecrato ungantur a presbyteris et oratione comitante sanentur. Nec solum presbyteris, sed, ut Innocentius papa scribit, etiam omnibus Christianis uti licet eodem oleo in sua aut suorum necessitate ungendo, quod tamen oleum non nisi ab episcopis licet confici. Nam quod ait, 'Oleo in nomine Domini,' significat oleum consecratum in nomine Domini: vel certe quia etiam, cum ungunt infirmum, nomen Domini super eum invocare debent.* Luther's opponent, Cardinal Cajetan, in his comment on this verse denies that it has any reference to the Sacrament of Extreme Unction: *Textus non dicit 'Infirmatur quis ad mortem?' sed absolute 'Infirmatur quis?' et effectum dicit infirmis alleviationem, et de remissione peccatorum non nisi conditionaliter loquitur. . . . Praeter hoc quod Jacobus ad unum aegrum multos presbyteros tum orantes tum ungentes mandat vocari, quod ab extrema unctione alienum est.*

ἐν τῷ ὀνόματι τοῦ Κυρίου.] In v. 10 we had the same phrase used of the prophets only with the omission of the article before K. It is probable however that the words τ. K., which are bracketed by WH., are merely an explanatory gloss, as they are not found in B and are variously given in the other MSS. In that case τὸ ὄνομα will be used here as in 3 John 7)where see Westcott), Acts v. 41 (where αὐτοῦ or some other specifying genitive is added in the inferior MSS.), Lev. xxiv. 11, cf. above ii. 7, and the similar use of ἡ ὁδός in Acts ix. 2, xix. 9, &c.[1] All cures were wrought in the name of Jesus Christ; cf. Mark xvi. 17 ἐν τῷ ὀνόματί μου...ἐπὶ ἀρρώστους χεῖρας ἐπιθήσουσιν, Luke x. 17, John xiv. 13, Acts iii. 6, 16, iv. 10, xvi. 18, xix. 13 (of the exorcists).

15. **ἡ εὐχὴ τῆς πίστεως.**] Prayer proceeding from faith, cf. i. 6.

σώσει τὸν κάμνοντα.] 'Shall restore to health him who is ailing,' cf. Mark v. 23 (lay thy hands upon her) ὅπως σωθῇ καὶ ζήσεται, *ib.* vi. 56, iii. 4, viii. 35, &c.: so in classical writers, Lys. p. 107 Ἀνδοκίδης ἔχει τὰ μήνυτρα σώσας τὴν αὐτοῦ ψυχὴν ἑτέρων διὰ ταῦτα ἀποθανόντων: hence the word σῶστρον was used of a doctor's fee. This is the only passage in the N.T. in which κάμνω is found in this sense, though it is common enough in classical writers, who also use the aor. and perf. participles of the dead. I see no ground for the distinction made by some between ἀσθενῶ and κάμνω.

ἐγερεῖ αὐτὸν ὁ Κύριος.] Cf. Mark i. 31 προσελθὼν ἤγειρεν αὐτήν, Matt. ix. 5, Psa. xli. 8–10. Dean Plumptre compares Acts ix. 34 'J. C. maketh thee whole.' The R.C. interpreters understand it of spiritual comfort.

κἄν.] Not to be taken in its more usual sense 'even if,' as Alford, Huther and B. Weiss. Huther denies that it can ever have the copulative force, but see Mark xvi. 18 κἂν θανάσιμόν τι πίωσιν, Luke xiii. 9 κἂν μὲν ποιήσῃ καρπόν, Demosth. *F.L.* 411 οὗτος ἐκτρέπεταί με νῦν ἁπαντῶν, κἂν ἀναγκασθῇ που συντυχεῖν, ἀπεπήδησεν εὐθέως, Xen. *Anab.* i. 8, 12 Κῦρος ἐβόα ἄγειν τὸ στράτευμα κατὰ μέσον τὸ τῶν πολεμίων ὅτι ἐκεῖ βασιλεὺς εἴη, κἂν τοῦτ', ἔφη, νικῶμεν, πάνθ' ἡμῖν πεποίηται, *ib.* iii. 36, Isaeus p. 66, 4 ὁμοίως ὑπάρχει τὴν αὐτὴν εἶναι μητέρα, κἂν ἐν τῷ πατρῴῳ μένῃ τις οἴκῳ, κἂν ἐκποιηθῇ, and often in the newly discovered *Constitution of Athens*, e.g. § 61 κἄν τινα ἀποχειροτονήσωσιν κρίνουσιν ἐν τῷ δικαστηρίῳ, κἂν μὲν ἁλῷ τιμῶσιν.

ἁμαρτίας ᾖ πεποιηκώς.] We might ask why St. James puts the commission of sin hypothetically after he had distinctly said πολλὰ πταίομεν ἅπαντες. But the clause is probably to be taken as meaning 'if he has committed sins which have given rise to this sickness,' cf. Matt. ix. 2–5 (the healing of the paralytic), John v. 14, *ib.* ix. 2, 1 Cor. xi. 30, Deut. xxviii. 22, 27, Psa. xxxviii., Job xxxiii. 19 foll., Test. Gad. 5 ἐπήγαγέ μοι ὁ Θεὸς νόσον ἥπατος, καὶ εἰ μὴ εὐχαὶ τοῦ πατρός μου ἔφθασαν (I should have died), δι' ὧν γὰρ ἄνθρωπος παρανομεῖ, δι' ἐκείνων καὶ κολάζεται. There is a Jewish saying 'No sick man recovers from sickness till his sins have been forgiven' (Nedarim f. 41*a* cited by Schneckenburger). Lange compares Isa. xxxiii. 24 'The inhabitant shall not say I am sick: the people that dwell therein shall be forgiven their iniquity.'

ἀφεθήσεται αὐτῷ.] Impersonal: 'forgiveness shall be extended to him,' cf. Matt. vii. 2 ἀντιμετρηθήσεται αὐτῷ, *ib.* ver. 7 δοθήσεται, xii. 32 ὃς ἐὰν

[1] Compare Clem. R. ii. 13 ἵνα τὸ ὄνομα μὴ βλασφημῆται, where Lightfoot refers to his note on Ignat. *Eph.* 3, also Taylor, *Jewish Fathers*, p. 81.

εἴπῃ λόγον κατὰ τοῦ υἱοῦ τοῦ ἀνθρώπου ἀφεθήσεται αὐτῷ, xxv. 29, Luke xiv. 14 ἀνταποδοθήσεται, Rom. x. 10 καρδίᾳ πιστεύεται...στόματι ὁμολογεῖται, 1 Pet. iv. 6 εὐηγγελίσθη, Polyc. *Phil.* 2 ἀφίετε καὶ ἀφεθήσεται ὑμῖν, Clem. R. i. 13, Euseb. *H.E.* ii. 9 κατὰ τὴν ὁδὸν ἠξίωσεν ἀφεθῆναι αὐτῷ ὑπὸ τοῦ Ἰακώβου.

16. **ἐξομολογεῖσθε οὖν ἀλλήλοις τὰς ἁμαρτίας.**] Instead of τὰς ἁμαρτίας, read by WH. Ti. Treg. with the best MSS., Alford reads τὰ παραπτώματα, found in K L Pesh., Theophylact, Oecumenius, and Origen *in Proverb.* (Mai *Nov. Bib.* vii. 51) ὁ Ἰάκωβος φησὶν, ἀλλήλοις ἐξαγγέλλετε τὰ παραπτώματα ὑμῶν ὅπως ἰαθῆτε. It may perhaps receive some slight support from the Didache 4. 14 ἐν ἐκκλησίᾳ ἐξομολογήσῃ τὰ παραπτώματά σου καὶ οὐ προσελεύσῃ ἐπὶ προσευχήν σου ἐν συνειδήσει πονηρᾷ, *ib.* xiv. 1 κατὰ κυριακὴν...κλάσατε ἄρτον καὶ εὐχαριστήσατε προεξομολογησάμενοι τὰ παραπτώματα ὑμῶν ὅπως καθαρὰ ἡ θυσία ὑμῶν ᾖ· πᾶς δὲ ἔχων τὴν ἀμφιβολίαν μετὰ τοῦ ἑταίρου αὐτοῦ μὴ συνελθέτω ὑμῖν ἕως οὗ διαλλαγῶσιν, ἵνα μὴ κοινωθῇ ἡ θυσία ὑμῶν, Clem. Ep. ad Jac. 15 ἐξομολογούμενοι τὰ παραπτώματα καὶ τὰ ἐξ ἐπιθυμιῶν ἀτάκτων σωρευθέντα κακά, ἅτινα τῷ ὁμολογῆσαι ὥσπερ ἀπεμέσαντες κουφίζεσθε τῆς νόσου, προσιέμενοι τὴν ἐκ τῆς ἐπιμελείας σωτήριον ὑγίειαν. The latter reading seems to agree better with what appears to be the sense of the passage, if we understand it as referring to our Lord's words reported in Matt. v. 23 foll. and vi. 14 : the sins of the sick man will only be forgiven if he forgives others who have injured him, and if he makes amends for any injuries he may himself have committed. St. James expands the precept out of its narrow application 'let the sick man confess his trespasses to those against whom he has trespassed and let them in turn confess any trespasses which they may have committed against him, and join in prayer for him, in order that he may be healed of his bodily ailment,' into the general rule 'confess your trespasses to each other, and pray for each other at all times, that ye may be healed of all your diseases whether of body or soul.' The use of the word οὖν implies the close connexion of the present with the preceding clause ('since prayer has such power, pray for each other; and, that you may be able to do this better, confess your faults to each other').

If we read ἁμαρτίας it is more natural to understand the confession to refer not to trespass towards man, but to sins towards God (though ἁμαρτάνω is also used of the former, as in Matt. xviii. 15, 21). Such confession (ἐξομολόγησις)[1] was made to John the Baptist (Matt. iii. 6) and by the penitents at Ephesus to Paul (Acts xix. 18), but for long after the apostolic age it seems to have been unusual, except in the case of converts or penitents who were under ecclesiastical censure. For others the words of Augustine held good (*Conf.* x. 3) *quid mihi est cum hominibus ut audiant confessiones meas, quasi ipsi sanaturi sint omnes languores meos*, and the even stronger words of Chrysostom (*Hom. xx. in Gen.* p. 175 (quoted in Bingham xviii. 3, and in *Dict. of Ch. Ant.* under *Exomologesis.* We need not however suppose any reference here

[1] St. John uses the active of the simple verb in place of the more common ἐξομολογοῦμαι, see 1 John i. 9 ἐὰν ὁμολογῶμεν τὰς ἁμαρτίας. In the LXX. ἐξαγορεύω is used in the same sense.

to a formal confession of sin, but merely to such mutual confidences as would give a right direction to the prayers offered by one for the other: so Augustine, commenting on this verse (*Tract.* 58 *in Johan.* quoted by Bingham, l.c.), and Bede *quotidiana leviaque peccata alterutrum coaequalibus confiteamur eorumque quotidiana credamus oratione salvari;* though the latter adds *gravioris leprae immunditiam juxta legem sacerdoti pandamus atque ad ejus arbitrium qualiter et quanto tempore jusserit purificare curemus.* The Greek commentators have no note here. Origen (*Hom. ii. in Ps. xxxvii.*, Lomm. xii. p. 266) points out the use of such confession and at the same time recommends caution in choosing the person to whom confession should be made. He does not limit the selection to presbyters, though they would naturally be thought of, and are generally specified by later writers on the subject.

Some of the Romish controversialists, as Bellarmine, cited by Hooker vi. 5, maintain that St. James in this passage alludes to auricular confession, but Cajetan again speaks the language of common sense: *nec hic est sermo de confessione sacramentali (ut patet ex eo quod dicit 'confitemini invicem'; sacramentalis enim confessio non fit invicem, sed sacerdotibus tantum), sed de confessione qua mutuo fatemur nos peccatores ut oretur pro nobis, et de confessione hinc et inde erratorum pro mutua placatione et reconciliatione.* The practice of auricular confession was not made generally obligatory even by the Church of Rome till the Lateran Council of 1215 under Innocent III., which ordered that every adult person should confess to the priest at least once in the year. In all other Churches it is still optional. Mutual confession was an early custom in monasteries,[1] and the Moravian Societies (which Wesley took as the pattern for the Methodist Classes) used to meet two or three times a week 'to confess their faults one to another and to pray for one another that they might be healed.' The word Exomologesis was borrowed by the Latin Christians, cf. Tertull. *Orat.* 7. For further information see articles on Exomologesis and Penitence in *D.C.A.*

ὅπως ἰαθῆτε.] For the use of *ἴασθαι* in reference to the diseases of the soul cf. Heb. xii. 13, 1 Pet. ii. 24, Matt. xiii. 15, Deut. xxx. 3 *ἰάσεται Κύριος τὰς ἁμαρτίας σου*, 2 Chron. xxx. 20, Isa. vi. 10, lvii. 19, Sir. xxviii. 3, &c., Herm. *Sim.* 9. 23, also the remarkable parallel in Arrian *Anab.* vii. 29 *μόνη γὰρ ἔμοιγε δοκεῖ ἴασις ἁμαρτίας ὁμολογεῖν τε ἁμαρτάνοντα καὶ δῆλον εἶναι ἐπ' αὐτῷ μεταγιγνώσκοντα.* If the word is understood literally of bodily disease (cf. Sir. xxxviii. 9 *τέκνον ἐν ἀρρωστήματί σου μὴ παράβλεπε ἀλλ' εὖξαι κυρίῳ καὶ αὐτὸς ἰάσεταί σε*), as by De Wette, Huther, and Spitta, the connexion of thought is perhaps closer, keeping to the subject of the miraculous cure, which is spoken of in the preceding verse and seems to be referred to in the words which follow, dwelling on the miraculous power of the prayer of Elijah.

πολὺ ἰσχύει δέησις δικαίου.] Compare the saying of R. Jehuda *poenitentia potest aliquid sed preces possunt omnia*, and the promise in Matt. xvii. 20, 21, *ib.* xxi. 21, 22, Mark xi. 22–26, Phil. iv. 13, 1 John v. 14–16, Psa. cxlv. 18, 19, Prov. xv. 29, Sir. xxxii. 7, Clem. R. 21 *μαθέτωσαν τί ταπεινο-*

[1] See examples in Martene *Ant. Eccl. Rit.* iv. p. 38, Athanas. *Vit. Ant.* p. 75.

φροσύνη παρὰ Θεῷ ἰσχύει. For δικαίου cf. v. 6: he is one who by faith fulfils the νόμος ἐλευθερίας. Bp. Wordsworth (*Stud. Bib.* I. 128) and Rönsch (*Das Neue Test. Tertullians*) hold that Tertullian never quotes from St. James; but is there not a reference to this passage in the *De Oratione* c. 28? We find there 1st an allusion to the prayer of Elijah *retro oratio imbrium utilia prohibebat*, and 2nd to the much-availing 'prayer of righteousness': *nunc vero oratio justitiae omnem iram Dei avertit*, and its employment *defunctorum animas de ipso mortis itinere vocare, debiles reformare, aegros remediare . . . Eadem diluit delicta, tentationes repellit*: cf. above ver. 15 and below ver. 20, also i. 5, 6. Spitta strangely understands by δικαίου 'the righteous in heaven' and compares Enoch xxxix. 4 foll. 'the righteous in their dwellings with the angels interceded for the children of men, and righteousness flowed before them as water, and mercy like dew upon the earth,' *ib.* xlvii. 2.

ἐνεργουμένη.] Is this passive or middle? Of the former we have examples 1 Esdr. ii. 19 ἐνεργεῖται τὰ κατὰ τὸν ναόν 'the works of the temple are being pushed on,' Joseph *Ant.* xv. 5. 3 τὸν δὲ πόλεμον ὅτι καὶ θέλει τοῦτον ἐνεργεῖσθαι καὶ δίκαιον οἶδεν, δεδήλωκεν αὐτὸς ὁ Θεός, Arist. *Phys.* ii. 3 *fin.* τὰ ἐνεργοῦντα (πρότερα) πρὸς τὰ ἐνεργούμενα, Polyb. i. 13. 5 ὁ πόλεμος ἐνηργεῖτο, *ib.* ix. 13. 9 δι' ὧν ἐνεργηθήσεται τὸ κριθέν, Barn. i. 7 τὰ καθ' ἕκαστα βλέποντες ἐνεργούμενα 'seeing the several prophecies being accomplished,' Justin *Apol.* i. 12 πεπείσμεθα ἐκ δαιμόνων ταῦτα ἐνεργεῖσθαι, *ib.* 26, *Apol* ii. 7, *Tryph*, 78 εἰπὼν τοὺς τὰ Μίθρα μυστήρια παραδιδόντας...ὑπὸ τοῦ διαβόλου ἐνεργηθῆναι εἰπεῖν, *ib.* (the Magi were carried away) πρὸς πάσας κακὰς πράξεις τὰς ἐνεργουμένας ὑπὸ τοῦ δαιμονίου, *ib.* 79, and 18 τὰ ἐξ ἀνθρώπων καὶ δαιμόνων ἐνεργούμενα εἰς ἡμᾶς, hence the term ἐνεργούμενος used of those possessed (cf. Suicer i. p. 1115), Clem. Al. *Str.* iv. 603 ἀνάγκη ὁμολογεῖν ἢ τὴν κόλασιν μὴ εἶναι ἄδικον...ἢ ἐκ θελήματος Θεοῦ ἐνεργεῖσθαι καὶ τοὺς διωγμούς, *ib.* 615 τὸ αὐτὸ ἔργον διαφορὰν ἴσχει, ἢ διὰ φόβον γενόμενον ἢ δι' ἀγάπην τελεσθὲν, καὶ ἤτοι διὰ πίστεως ἢ καὶ γνωστικῶς ἐνεργούμενον, v. 25, vi. 752 τὰ ἐκ τῆς θείας δυνάμεως διὰ τῶν ἁγίως βεβιωκότων εἰς τὴν ἡμετέραν ἐπιστροφὴν παραδόξως ἐνεργούμενα, vii. 890 εἰκότως ἂν διὰ τοῦ Κυρίου πρὸς τὴν τῶν ἀνθρώπων εὐεργεσίαν ἐνεργούμενος (*Lect. inc.*), Clem. Hom. ix. 12 πολλοί, οὐκ εἰδότες πόθεν ἐνεργοῦνται, ταῖς τῶν δαιμόνων κακαῖς ὑπονοίαις...συντίθενται, Arethas *in Apoc.* v. 6 τὰ σώματα τῶν θνησκόντων τρεῖς ἡμέρας διακαρτερεῖν τῇ φυσικῇ ζωῇ ἐνεργούμενα (i.e. being animated or energized by the mere life of nature). Stephanus cites Polyb. i. 13. 5, ix. 12. 3, 7 and 13. 9, as exx. of the passive, he adds however '*invenitur autem in N.T.* ἐνεργεῖσθαι *significatione etiam activa*,' which the latest editor corrects in the words *immo semper passiva*. So Dr. Hort (in the forthcoming edition of Cl. Al. *Strom.* vii.) writes on p. 852 ἡ ἀκοὴ ἐνεργουμένη, 'passive as always.'

It is denied however by some of the commentators that this use is ever found in the N.T., (Alf.), or at least in the writings of St. Paul (Lightfoot on Gal. v. 6 πίστις δι' ἀγάπης ἐνεργουμένη.) The latter says 'the Spirit of God or the Spirit of Evil' ἐνεργεῖ [cf. 1 Cor. xii. 6 διαιρέσεις ἐνεργημάτων εἰσὶ καὶ ὁ αὐτὸς Θεὸς ὁ ἐνεργῶν τὰ πάντα ἐν πᾶσιν, Gal. ii. 8 ὁ ἐνεργήσας Πέτρῳ...ἐνήργησεν καὶ ἐμοί, Eph. i. 20 κατὰ τὴν ἐνέργειαν ἣν ἐνήργηκεν ἐν Χριστῷ, Phil. ii. 13, Just. *Tryph.* 27, 94, 95, and (of Satan) Eph. ii. 2 τοῦ πνεύματος τοῦ νῦν ἐνεργοῦντος ἐν τοῖς υἱοῖς τῆς ἀπειθείας, Barn. ii. 1 ὁ ἐνεργῶν (=Satan), Justin M. *Apol.* i. 5 οἱ δαίμονες ἐνήργησαν ὡς ἄθεον καὶ ἀσεβῆ ἀποκτεῖναι (τὸν Σωκράτη) καὶ ὁμοίως ἐφ' ἡμῶν τὸ αὐτὸ ἐνεργοῦσιν, *ib.* 26 διὰ τῆς τῶν ἐνεργούντων δαιμόνων τέχνης δυνάμεις ποιήσας μαγικάς, and a little below Μένανδρον ἐνεργηθέντα ὑπὸ τῶν δαιμονίων, *ib.* 23, 54, 62, 63, 64, *Apol.* ii. 8, *Tryph.* 69], 'the human agent or the human mind ἐνεργεῖται (middle).' It is however not quite correct to say that the human agent ἐνεργεῖται; the word in the N.T. is always used of some principle or power at work, whether in the soul or elsewhere, e.g. Rom. vii. 5 ὅτε ἦμεν ἐν τῇ σαρκί, τὰ παθήματα τῶν ἁμαρτιῶν τὰ διὰ τοῦ νόμου ἐνηργεῖτο ἐν τοῖς μέλεσιν ἡμῶν, 2 Cor. i. 6 ὑπὲρ τῆς ὑμῶν παρακλήσεως τῆς ἐνεργουμένης ἐν ὑπομονῇ, *ib.* iv. 12 ὁ θάνατος ἐν ἡμῖν ἐνεργεῖται, Eph. iii. 20 (to Him that can do exceeding abundantly) κατὰ τὴν δύναμιν τὴν ἐνεργουμένην ἐν ἡμῖν, Col. i. 29 ἀγωνιζόμενος κατὰ τὴν ἐνέργειαν αὐτοῦ (*i.e.* Christ) τὴν ἐνεργουμένην ἐν ἐμοὶ ἐν δυνάμει, 1 Thess. ii. 13 (λόγος Θεοῦ) ἐνεργεῖται ἐν ὑμῖν τοῖς πιστεύουσιν, 2 Thess. ii. 7 τὸ μυστήριον ἤδη ἐνεργεῖται τῆς ἀνομίας. Again the active is not exclusively confined in the Hellenistic writers to the immediate action of a good or evil spirit, cf. Prov. xxi. 6 ὁ ἐνεργῶν θησαυρίσματα γλώσσῃ ψευδεῖ μάταια διώκει 'he that getteth treasures by falsehood,' Matt. xiv. 2 αἱ δυνάμεις ἐνεργοῦσιν ἐν αὐτῷ (with which compare ἐνεργουμένην used in Eph. iii. 20, Col. i. 29), Wisd. xv. 11 ἠγνόησε τὸν ἐμπνεύσαντα αὐτῷ ψυχὴν ἐνεργοῦσαν, Prov. xxxi. 12 ἡ γυνὴ ἐνεργεῖ τῷ ἀνδρὶ εἰς ἀγαθὰ πάντα τὸν βίον, cf. Jos. *B. J.* iv. 6 τὰ δοχθέντα τάχιον καὶ τῆς ἐπινοίας ἐνήργουν ('put in practice'), Just. *Tryph.* 7 οἱ ψευδοπροφῆται δυνάμεις τινὰς ἐνεργεῖν τολμῶσι. When we compare such instances of the transitive use of the act. as Gal. iii. 5 ὁ ἐνεργῶν δυνάμεις ἐν ἡμῖν, Phil. ii. 13 ὁ ἐνεργῶν ἐν ὑμῖν τὸ ἐνεργεῖν, Eph. i. 20 ἣν (ἐνέργειαν) ἐνήργησεν ἐν Χριστῷ, and the use of the passive noun ἐνέργημα, it seems more natural to understand ἐνεργεῖσθαι here with a passive force, of prayer *actuated or inspired by the Spirit*, as in Rom. viii. 26 (so Bull '*fervore atque impetu quodam divino acta et incitata*,' Benson 'inspired,' Macknight 'inwrought prayer,' Bassett, 'when energized by the Spirit of God'). In like manner Chrysostom on Rom. vii. 5 οὐκ εἶπεν, ἃ ἐνήργει τὰ μέλη, ἀλλ' ἃ ἐνηργεῖτο ἐν τοῖς μέλεσιν, δεικνὺς ἑτέρωθεν οὖσαν τῆς πονηρίας τὴν ἀρχήν, ἀπὸ τῶν ἐνεργούντων λογισμῶν, οὐκ ἀπὸ τῶν ἐνεργουμένων μελῶν. Cf. Bull '*Examen Censurae* (vol. v. p. 22 foll.) 'ἐνεργεῖσθαι *fere semper id significat quod Latine dicimus agi, agitari, exerceri, effici*': he supports this by Tertullian's renderings of Rom. vii. 5 and Gal. v. 6, and by Chrys. on 2 Cor. i. 6 ἡ σωτηρία ὑμῶν τότε ἐνεργεῖται μειζόνως, τοῦτ' ἐστι δείκνυται, αὔξεται, ἐπιτείνεται, ὅταν ὑπομονὴν ἔχῃ...οὐκ εἶπεν, τῆς ἐνεργούσης, ἀλλὰ τῆς ἐνεργουμένης, δεικνὺς ὅτι ἡ χάρις πολλὰ εἰσέφερεν ἐνεργοῦσα ἐν αὐτοῖς. The passive interpretation being thus supported by the early Greek and Latin commentators, as well as by the constant usage in non-biblical Greek, we are naturally led to ask whether there is any necessity for a different explanation in the nine passages of the N.T. in which the word occurs, viz. eight times in St. Paul and once here. Dr. E. A. Abbott writes to me that, after careful examination of all the Pauline passages, he is convinced that the passive meaning is not only possible but in every case superior to the middle; and Dr. Hort in a private letter takes the same view of our text and of Gal. v. 6 without giving an opinion as to the other examples. Those who attribute the middle sense to St. Paul may illustrate the relations of the active to the middle by the analogy of *τιθέναι* and *τίθεσθαι νόμον*. God acting by his own sovereign will *ἐνεργεῖ*, the principle of good which he engrafts into our nature *ἐνεργεῖται*. But whatever may be our judgment about St. Paul's usage, there is no reason to suppose that St. James would have departed from what appears to have been the uniform custom of all other writers.

I turn now to the explanations offered by previous editors. The old Greek commentators give it a passive sense, Oecumenius and Theophylact interpreting it much as Matthaei's scholiast *συνεργουμένη ὑπὸ τῆς τοῦ δεομένου γνώμης καὶ πράξεως* 'assisted by (actualized by) the intention and the action of the sick man,' and not far otherwise Euthymius and Cramer's *Catena* 'strengthened and heartened by the penitence and obedience of the sick,' which they illustrate by the case of Samuel forbidden to pray for Saul, of Jeremiah forbidden to pray for the Jews. They also give a second interpretation, according to which the just man's prayer is energized by his own life of active godliness (*τὴν δέησιν ἔνεργον καὶ ζῶσαν τοῖς τρόποις τῶν ἐντολῶν ψυχουμένην ...ἰσχυρὰν καὶ πάντα δυναμένην ὁ δίκαιος ἔχει τὴν δέησιν ἐνεργουμένην ταῖς ἐντολαῖς*): cf. Theodoret's note on the next verse *ταῦτα τοῦ θείου πνεύματος ἐνεργοῦντος εἴρηκεν ὁ προφήτης* in the same *Catena*. Michaelis takes it in the way suggested above *preces agitante Spiritu effusae*. De Wette, Hofmann, Huther, Alford take it 'the prayer of a righteous man avails much in its working,' but this gives a very poor force to a word which ought from its position to be emphatic. Erdmann translates 'viel vermag das Gebet des Gerechten indem es sich wirksam erweist,' which appears to me either tautological or unmeaning: prayer is no prayer at all, if it is not real. Bp. Wordsworth seems to strain the force of the preposition (which cannot be other in the verb than in adj. *ἔνεργος*, from which it is derived) when he translates 'working inwardly,' 'inwardly energizing in devotion and love, so as to produce external effects in obedience.' Most commentators take it with Luther 'wenn es ernstlich ist' (so Dean Scott 'when urgent,' he compares Col. iv. 12 *πάντοτε ἀγωνιζόμενος ὑπὲρ ὑμῶν ἐν ταῖς προσευχαῖς*); though some ignore the participial force and make it simply equivalent to *ἐνεργής* (Heb. iv. 12, Philem. 6) or *ἐκτενής* (Luke xxii. 44, Acts xii. 5), as Schneckenburger, Kern, Bouman, Wiesinger. This makes fair sense; but, as we have seen, there is no ground for supposing that *ἐνεργουμένη* may be used in the sense of *ἐνεργὴς οὖσα*. Pallad. *Laus.* 1083 B and Eustath. on *Odyss. δ.* p. 197, 50 are cited for the phrase *προσευχὴ ἐνεργής*. Lange tries to combine the force of the passive and middle, 'die mit der vollen Hingebung an den göttlichen Impuls zugleich gesetzt volle Spannung des betenden Geistes.'

17. **ἄνθρωπος ἦν ὁμοιοπαθὴς ἡμῖν.**] The mention of prayer for the sick in ver. 15 may have suggested the thought of the prophet who raised the son of the widow of Zarephath by his prayer. The classical word

ὁμ. is used by Paul of himself and Barnabas to the people of Lystra, by the Fathers of Christ (e.g. Euseb. *H.E.* i. 2, cf. Heb. iv. 15), in 4 Macc. xii. 13 to show the atrocity of persecution οὐκ ᾐδέσθης ἄνθρωπος ὢν τοὺς ὁμοιοπαθεῖς καὶ ἐκ τῶν αὐτῶν γεγονότας στοιχείων γλωττοτομῆσαι. It was necessary for the writer to insist on the resemblance between us and Elijah because of the exaggerated ideas entertained of the latter at that time (see Sir. xlviii. 1–12) : 'Such potency of prayer is not out of our reach, for Elijah possessed it, though he was partaker of human weakness.' Compare Peter's words to Cornelius, Acts x. 26, and Anton. vi. 19 μή, εἴ τι αὐτῷ σοι δυσκαταπόνητον, τοῦτο ἀνθρώπῳ ἀδύνατον ὑπολαμβάνειν, ἀλλ' εἴ τι ἀνθρώπῳ δυνατὸν καὶ οἰκεῖον, τοῦτο καὶ σεαυτῷ ἐφικτὸν νόμιζε with Gataker's n., also Calvin's n. here, *ideo minus proficimus ex sanctorum exemplo quia ipsos fingimus semideos vel heroas quibus peculiare fuit cum Deo commercium: ita ex eo quod auditi sunt nihil fiduciae concipimus.* For the use of the copulative conjunction (ἦν...καὶ) instead of the participle (ὢν) see Winer 542–544 and above iii. 5 μικρὸν μέλος ἐστὶ καὶ κ.τ.λ.

προσευχῇ προσηύξατο.] For examples of similar reduplication see Luke xxii. 15 ἐπιθυμίᾳ ἐπεθύμησα, John iii. 29 χαρᾷ χαίρει, Acts iv. 17 ἀπειλῇ ἀπειλησώμεθα, *ib.* v. 28 παραγγελίᾳ παρηγγείλαμεν, *ib.* xxiii. 14 ἀναθέματι ἀνεθεματίσαμεν ἑαυτούς, 2 Pet. iii. 3 ἐν ἐμπαιγμονῇ ἐμπαῖκται, Exod. iii. 16 ἐπισκοπῇ ἐπέσκεμμαι, Deut. vii. 26 προσοχθίσματι προσοχθιεῖς καὶ βδελύγματι βδελύξῃ, Jos. xxiv. 10 εὐλογίαις εὐλόγησεν, Isa. xxx. 19 κλαυθμῷ ἔκλαυσεν, Judith vi. 4 ἀπωλείᾳ ἀπολοῦνται, Vorst p. 626, Winer p. 584, Lobeck *Paral.* 523 foll., where analogous instances are cited from classical writers, in some of which the dative is added for precision, as in Dem. 1002. 12 γάμῳ γεγαμηκώς *qui rite confecit nuptias*, but in others has an intensive force, as Plato *Symp.* 195 φεύγειν φυγῇ, compare such phrases as κακὸς κακῶς, and in Lat. *occidione occidere, curriculo currere.* I cannot understand what should lead De Wette, Hofmann, Huther, Erdmann to deny this intensive force which belongs to reduplication in all languages. The last translates 'in einem Gebet betete er,' and says by this is expressed 'nicht der Charakter der Ernstlichkeit und Kräftigkeit, sondern die That des Gebets,' and so, I suppose, Alford '*he prayed with prayer* (made it a special matter of prayer, not *prayed earnestly*. This adoption of the Hebrew idiom merely brings out more forcibly the idea of the verb),' though his meaning is far from clear. A similar intensive phrase is formed by the use of the participle, as in 1 Sam. xxvi. 25 ποιῶν ποιήσεις, δυνάμενος δυνήσῃ, Ps. cxviii. 18 παιδεύων ἐπαίδευσε, Jer. iii. 22 ἐπιστραφῆτε ἐπιστρέφοντες, Lam. i. 2 κλαίουσα ἔκλαυσεν.

τοῦ μὴ βρέξαι.] The genitive of the infinitive is used to express the purpose of an action in classical writers, as in Thuc. i. 4 τὸ λῃστικὸν καθῄρει ἐκ τῆς θαλάσσης τοῦ τὰς προσόδους μᾶλλον ἰέναι αὐτῷ, but the use is much extended in the Hellenistic Greek. Thus it is found not only after verbs immediately expressive of design, as here and in Isa. v. 6 ταῖς νεφέλαις ἐντελοῦμαι τοῦ μὴ βρέξαι εἰς αὐτὸν ὑετόν, and in the Byzantine writers, as Malalas xiv. 357 ᾐτήσατο ἡ Αὔγουστα τὸν βασιλέα τοῦ κατελθεῖν εἰς τοὺς ἁγίους τόπους (cf. Thuc. viii. 40 ἀγγελίαν ἔπεμπον ἐπὶ τὰς ναῦς τοῦ ξυμπαρακομισθῆναι); but it is used also to denote the consequence of an action, as in Acts iii. 12 ὡς πεποιηκόσι τοῦ περιπατεῖν αὐτόν, and even for the simple infinitive, when it stands as subject of the sentence, as in Luke xvii. 1 ἀνενδεκτόν ἐστιν τοῦ τὰ σκάνδαλα μὴ ἐλθεῖν, Acts x. 25 ἐγένετο τοῦ εἰσελθεῖν τὸν Πέτρον, see Winer, p. 408 foll. The verb βρέχει is here used, like ὕει, without a subject, as in Luke xvii. 29: we have the personal use in Matt. v. 45 (ὁ Θεὸς) βρέχει ἐπὶ δικαίους καὶ ἀδίκους.

As regards the facts referred to, we hear nothing of this prayer in the O.T., unless the expression 'before whom I stand' (in 1 Kings xvii. 1) may be interpreted to mean 'stand in prayer' as in Jer. xv. 1, cf. Gen. xviii. 22, xix. 17. The duration of the drought here given is the same as that in Luke iv. 25, which is also found in the Rabbinical tractate Jalkut Simeoni quoted by Schegg after Surenhusius; but in 1 Kings xviii. 1 it is said 'after many days the word of the Lord came to Elijah in the third year saying...I will send rain upon the earth.' We are not told from what point the third year is dated; if it is from the commencement of his sojourn with the widow, as is generally supposed; and if the expression 'end of the days' in 1 Kings xvii. 7 ('it came to pass at the end of the days that the brook dried up') is to be understood, as in other places, of a year or more (see Keil *in loc.* and on xviii. 1, who compares Lev. xxv. 29, 1 Sam. xxvii. 7, Jud. xvii. 10); then the cessation of the drought would take place in the fourth year from its commencement, and Jewish tradition would naturally fix on the middle of the fourth year, as giving the half of the symbolical number, which is so prominent in the prophecies of Daniel and in Apoc. xi. 3–9 (where it is said that the two witnesses 'have power to shut the heaven ἵνα μὴ ὑετὸς βρέχῃ during the days of their prophecy,' i.e. 1260 days = $3\frac{1}{2}$ years). Others suppose the calculation to include the dry season preceding the first failure of the regular periodical rains. It is simply a question as to the origin of a Jewish tradition which undoubtedly existed at the time of the Christian era, and which was probably excogitated by the early rabbinical interpreters. In the fourth book of Esdras (vii. 39) Elijah is cited as an example of intercession *pro his qui pluviam acceperunt et pro mortuo ut viveret.*

ἐπὶ τῆς γῆς.] Merely filling up the idea of ἔβρεξεν as in Gen. vii. 12 ἐγένετο ὁ ὑετὸς ἐπὶ τῆς γῆς, 1 Kings xvii. 7, see above v. 5.

18. **πάλιν προσηύξατο.**] As shown by his attitude (1 Kings xviii. 42), for which cf. Neh. viii. 6.

ὁ οὐρανὸς ὑετὸν ἔδωκεν.] The phrase ὑ. διδ. is used of God in 1 Kings xviii. 1, 1 Sam. xii. 17, Acts xiv. 17 οὐρανόθεν ὑετοὺς διδούς. Josephus (*Ant.* xiv. 2. 1) tells a similar anecdote of Onias (B.C. 64) δίκαιος ἀνὴρ καὶ θεοφιλὴς ὃς ἀνομβρίας ποτὲ οὔσης ηὔξατο τῷ Θεῷ...καὶ ὁ Θεὸς ὗσεν, and Epiphanius (p. 1046) of James himself, ποτὲ ἀβροχίας γενομένης ἐπῆρε τὰς χεῖρας εἰς οὐρανὸν καὶ προσηύξατο καὶ εὐθὺς ὁ οὐρανὸς ἔδωκεν ὑετόν. Clem. Al. (*Strom.* vi. 3, p. 753 P.) cites the legendary story of Aeacus (Paus. ii. 28, p. 179) to the same effect, as being derived from the narrative of the miraculous rain sent in answer to Samuel's prayer

(1 Sam. xii. 17). Compare also the story of the Legio Fulminatrix given by Euseb. *H.E.* v. 5.

ἐβλάστησεν.] The aor. is here transitive as in Gen. i. 11 βλαστησάτω ἡ γῆ βοτάνην, Sir. xxiv. 17 ἐγὼ ὡς ἄμπελος ἐβλάστησα χάριν, more usually intr., as Matt. xiii. 26, Heb. ix. 4. In later Greek the present also is sometimes found in a transitive sense, see Lobeck on *Aj.* l. 869.

19. **ἐάν τις ἐν ὑμῖν πλανηθῇ.**] Returns to the subject of ver. 16. For ἐν ὑμῖν see above v. 13. There seems no reason to give, as Alf., to πλανηθῇ here the passive force which it bears in Apoc. xviii. 23 ἐν τῇ φαρμακείᾳ σου ἐπλανήθησαν πάντα τὰ ἔθνη. The passive aor. is used with a middle force in classical writers, as well as in the LXX. Deut. xxii. 1, Ps. cxix. 176, Ezek. xxxiv. 4, and probably in Luke xxi. 8 and 2 Pet. ii. 15 καταλείποντες εὐθεῖαν ὁδὸν ἐπλανήθησαν. It makes no difference as to the admonition given, whether the wanderer goes astray of his own will, or is led astray by others. See above i. 16 and πλάνη ὁδοῦ just below.

ἀπὸ τῆς ἀληθείας.] See above i. 18, John viii. 32, 1 John i. 6, iii. 18, 19, 3 John 4 (I have no greater joy than to hear that my children) ἐν ἀληθείᾳ περιπατοῦσιν, Wisd. v. 6 ἐπλανήθημεν ἀπὸ ὁδοῦ ἀληθείας, Ps. cxix. 30 ὁδὸν ἀληθείας ἡρετισάμην.

ἐπιστρέψῃ τις.] Found with the same force Mal. ii. 6 πολλοὺς ἐπέστρεψεν ἀπὸ ἀδικίας, Luke i. 16, 17, Acts xxvi. 18, Psa. lxxix. 3, Lam. v. 21, Polyc. *ad Phil.* 6 οἱ πρεσβύτεροι εὔσπλαγχνοι...ἐπιστρέφοντες τὰ ἀποπεπλανημένα, *Apost. Const.* ii. 6 τοὺς πεπλανημένους ἐπιστρέφετε, Plut. *Mor.* 21 (Menander) ἐπέστρεψε καὶ περιέσπασε πρὸς τὸ καλὸν ἡμᾶς, In Matt. xiii. 15 and elsewhere it is used intransitively, much as the passive in 1 Pet. ii. 25 ἦτε γὰρ ὡς πρόβατα πλανώμενοι, ἀλλ' ἐπεστράφητε νῦν ἐπὶ τὸν ποιμένα, καὶ ἐπίσκοπον τῶν ψυχῶν ὑμῶν. The following τις shows that this duty was not confined to the elders. As it belongs to the brethren in common to pray for each other and to hear each other's confessions, so here they are in common exhorted to bring back wanderers to the faith.

20. **γινώσκετε.**] So WH. with Cod B. The majority of the best MSS. have γινωσκέτω, keeping the regular construction. The use of the plural after τις ἐν ὑμῖν may be paralleled by μὴ δῶτε after τις ἐξ ὑμῶν above (ii. 16). On the other hand it is possible that an original γινωσκέτω may have been altered to suit ἀδελφοί μου. Reading γινώσκετε, I should be inclined to treat it as an indicative (as in Matt. xxiv. 32, John xv. 18), calling attention to the well-known fact (like ἴστε in i. 19), probably also to a well-known saying, that conversion involves salvation, rather than introducing it as something of which they had to be informed. Or, if we follow the other interpretation, and consider that we have here an appeal to enlightened self-interest, it may perhaps be thought more worthy of St. James to mention this as a fact in which all are interested, than to insist on it as a motive for the individual who takes in hand to convert his brother.

ὁ ἐπιστρέψας ἁμαρτωλόν.] Why is this repeated? Some say in order to emphasize the fact, but a more obvious reason would be that it belongs to a quotation, and also that it is needed to avoid ambiguity, especially if γινώσκετε is read. Without these words the subject of σώσει would naturally be understood to be 'one of you.'

ἐκ πλάνης ὁδοῦ αὐτοῦ.] Comparing Wisd. xii. 24 τῶν πλάνης ὁδῶν μακρότερον ἐπλανήθησαν *longius aberrabant quam erroris viae ferebant* ('even further than error itself') we might be disposed to make πλάνης depend on ὁδοῦ, translating 'his erring path'; but the usual order of words, when the metaphorical ὁδός is joined with a gen. of quality, is to put ὁδός first, as in Psa. cxix. 29, 30, ὁδόν ἀδικίας ἀπόστησον ἀπ' ἐμοῦ...ὁδόν ἀληθείας ἡρετισάμην, Prov. iv. 24 ὁδ. εἰρήνης, *ib.* viii. 20 ὁδ. δικαιοσύνης, *ib.* v. 6 ὁδ. ζωῆς, *ib.* xii. 19, xv. 25, xvii. 24, Job xxiv. 13, Isa. xxvi. 7, lix. 8. It seems better therefore to translate 'from the error of his way.' In classical prose the article would have been used both before πλάνης and ὁδοῦ. The second article is omitted according to Hellenistic usage because the noun is defined by the genitive of the personal pronoun which follows it (cf. ψυχὴν αὐτοῦ just below, καρδίαν αὐτοῦ, γλῶσσαν αὐτοῦ above i. 26 and Winer, p. 155 foll.), and the first article is omitted by the 'law of correlation' to suit the anarthrous ὁδοῦ, as in Matt. xix. 28 ἐπὶ θρόνου δόξης αὐτοῦ, cf. Winer, p. 175 and A. Buttmann, p. 104. We find the same opposition of πλάνη to ἀλήθεια in 1 John iv. 6 ἐκ τούτου γινώσκομεν τὸ πνεῦμα τῆς ἀληθείας καὶ τὸ πνεῦμα τῆς πλάνης.

σώσει ψυχήν.] After ψυχήν several MSS. and edd. insert αὐτοῦ: if this is the correct reading, it may either be understood of the subject of the verb (=Lat. *suus*, cf. Winer, p. 188 foll., A. Buttmann, p. 97 foll., Meisterhans *Gr. Att. Insch.* p. 122), or, more probably, it repeats the preceding αὐτοῦ, in which case it may have been intentionally inserted to mark that this clause refers to the sinner exclusively, allowing a wider scope to the next clause. In B. however αὐτοῦ comes after θανάτου[1] instead of after ψυχήν, suggesting that it may have arisen from a dittography, and I think the meaning is better without it. The future σώσει is easier to understand if ψυχήν refers to the subject of the verb. 'He who converts a sinner will be himself saved' reads naturally enough, the one action not being either identical or contemporaneous with the other; or again 'He who converts a sinner has thereby saved a soul'; but there is something of incongruity in the words 'He who turns a sinner from the error of his way will save that sinner's soul from death, and will cover a multitude of sins.' The object of the writer is to stimulate and encourage the work of conversion to the utmost, but by the use of the future, instead of the present[2] or past, he puts off the issue of the work to an indefinite distance of time. [Bengel explains it *olim constabit*, it will be seen on the day of judgment that he has saved a soul from death.] Otherwise salvation is regarded and spoken of by the writers of the N.T. sometimes as a fact of the present, sometimes of

[1] So Corbey MS. *salvat animam de morte sua.* The Vulgate has *animam ejus*, but Bede notes *quidam codices habent 'salvabit animam suam'...et re vera qui errantem corrigit sibimet ipsi per hoc vitae caelestis gaudia ampliora conquirit.*

[2] The Pesh. has the present 'covers the multitude of his sins,' so too Corb. and Orig. *Hom. in Lev.* quoted below.

the future. See n. on next clause. For σ. ψ. compare i. 21, and (for the absence of the article) the last note and 1 Pet. iii. 3 ὀφθαλμοὶ Κυρίου ἐπὶ δικαίους καὶ ὦτα αὐτοῦ εἰς δέησιν αὐτῶν. The omission is especially common with the word ψυχή, Heb. x. 39 εἰς περιποίησιν ψυχῆς, 1 Pet. i. 9 κομιζόμενος τὸ τέλος τῆς πίστεως, σωτηρίαν ψυχῶν, 2 Pet. ii. 8 ψυχὴν δικαίαν ἀνόμοις ἔργοις ἐβασάνιζεν. The saving of the soul is attributed to the human instrument in Rom. xi. 14, 1 Cor. vii. 16, 1 Tim. iv. 16, &c.

ἐκ θανάτου.] See above i. 15.

καλύψει πλῆθος ἁμαρτιῶν.] A proverbial expression, which occurs also in 1 Pet. iv. 8 ἀγάπη καλύπτει πλῆθος ἁμαρτιῶν, and which Resch regards as one of the unwritten words of Christ, quoting Clem. Al. *Paed.* iii. 12. p. 306, where it is introduced by φησί, which he understands of Christ; but as the immediately preceding references in Clement are to the O.T. it is more natural to supply Θεός or ἡ γραφή. It is however ascribed to Christ in *Didascalia* ii. 3 λέγει Κύριος ἀγάπη καλύπτει κ.τ.λ. The original is found in Prov. x. 12 (Heb. not LXX.) 'hate stirreth up strife, but love covereth all transgressions,' cf. Psa. lxxxv. 2 ἀφῆκας τὰς ἀνομίας τῷ λαῷ σου, ἐκάλυψας πάσας τὰς ἁμαρτίας αὐτῶν, *ib.* xxxi. 1, 2, Nehem. iv. 5 μὴ καλύψῃς ἐπὶ ἀνομίαν, Ep. ad Diogn. c. 9 τί γὰρ ἄλλο τὰς ἁμαρτίας ἡμῶν ἠδυνήθη καλύψαι ἢ ἐκείνου (Χριστοῦ) δικαιοσύνη; and a saying attributed to Socrates in Stob. *Flor.* xxxvii. 27 ἡ μὲν ἐσθὴς τὴν ἀρρυθμίαν, ἡ δὲ εὔνοια τὴν ἁμαρτίαν περιστέλλει. There can be no doubt about the meaning of the verse in Proverbs, 'love refuses to see faults': are we to attach the same meaning to the quotation in St. Peter, 'Above all things being fervent in your love amongst yourselves, *for* (ὅτι) love covereth a multitude of sins,' where it follows a warning to 'be sober and watch unto prayer'? Here love is recommended *because* it covers (hides) sin. This seems to imply more than the mere shutting the eye of man to sin: it implies that sin, including the sin of him who loves, at least as much as that of him who is loved,[1] is thus cancelled, blotted out even in the sight of God, cf. Luke vii. 47 ἀφέωνται αἱ ἁμαρτίαι αὐτῆς αἱ πολλαί, ὅτι ἠγάπησεν πολύ, and above ii. 13 κατακαυχᾶται ἔλεος κρίσεως. In other Hebrew writings we find love narrowed to ἐλεημοσύνη ('pity' rather than 'almsgiving'), yet with the same promise attached to it, Sir. iii. 28 ἐλεημοσύνη ἐξιλάσεται ἁμαρτίας, Dan. iv. 24 τὰς ἁμαρτίας σου ἐν ἐλεημοσύναις λύτρωσαι καὶ τὰς ἀδικίας ἐν οἰκτιρμοῖς πενήτων, Tobit iv. 10 ἐλεημοσύνη ἐκ θανάτου ῥύεται καὶ οὐκ ἐᾷ εἰσελθεῖν εἰς τὸ σκότος, δῶρον γὰρ ἀγαθόν ἐστιν ἐλεημοσύνη, *ib.* xii. 9 ἐλεημοσύνη ἐκ θανάτου ῥύεται καὶ αὐτὴ ἀποκαθαίρει πᾶσαν ἁμαρτίαν, οἱ ποιοῦντες ἐλεημοσύνην χορτασθήσονται ζωῆς. Or love is narrowed to the keeping of the fifth commandment, as in Sir. iii. 3 ὁ τιμῶν πατέρα ἐξιλάσεται ἁμαρτίας, *ib.* v. 14 ἐλεημοσύνη πατρὸς οὐκ ἐπιλησθήσεται καὶ ἀντὶ ἁμαρτιῶν προσανοικδομηθήσεταί σοι 'pity for a father shall not be forgotten, it shall be imputed to thee for good against thy sins.' Other passages in which almsgiving is referred to as efficacious for the saving of the soul are Didaché iv. 6 ἐὰν ἔχῃς διὰ

[1] [Compare the words of Portia 'it is twice blest, it blesseth him that gives and him that takes.' A.]

τῶν χειρῶν σου δώσεις[1] λύτρωσιν ἁμαρτιῶν σου, Constit. Apost. vii. 12 δός, ἵνα ἐργάσῃ εἰς λύτρωσιν ἁμαρτιῶν σου· ἐλεημοσύναις γὰρ καὶ πίστεσιν ἀποκαθαίρονται ἁμαρτίαι, so Barn. xix. 10. Luke xvi. 9 is naturally understood in the same sense. Similarly Clem. R. ii. 16 καλὸν ἐλεημοσύνη ὡς μετάνοια ἁμαρτίας· κρείσσων νηστεία προσευχῆς, ἐλεημοσύνη δὲ ἀμφοτέρων, then he quotes the verse from St. Peter, and continues ἐλεημοσύνη γὰρ κούφισμα ἁμαρτίας γίνεται, which leaves no doubt as to the way in which he understood it.[2] Bp. Lightfoot in his note says 'in James v. 20 the expression seems still to be used of the sins of others, but in the sense of burying them from the sight of God, wiping them out by the repentance of the sinner.' He however cites Tertull. *Scorp.* 6 as understanding the words to mean 'atones for a multitude of one's own sins': so too Clem. Al. *Quis div. sal.* § 38, p. 956 ἐὰν ταύτην (τὴν ἀγάπην) ἐμβάληταί τις τῇ ψυχῇ, δύναται, κἂν ἐν ἁμαρτήμασιν ᾖ γεγεννημένος κἂν πολλὰ τῶν κεκωλυμένων εἰργασμένος, αὐξήσας τὴν ἀγάπην καὶ μετάνοιαν καθαρὰν λαβών, ἀναμαχέσασθαι τὰ ἐπταισμένα, *ib. Strom.* i. p. 423; in *Strom.* ii. p. 463 ἀγάπη is understood of God's forgiving love. There is a remarkable passage of Origen (*Hom. in Lev.* ii. § 4), in which the different *remissiones peccatorum* in the Gospel are enumerated: (1) baptism, (2) martyrdom, (3) almsgiving (which he supports by Luke xi. 41), (4) forgiveness of others (supported by Matt. vi. 14), (5) converting a sinner, *ita enim dicit scriptura divina, quia qui converti fecerit peccatorem ab errore viae suae salvat animam*[3] *a morte et cooperit multitudinem peccatorum*,[4] (6) love (supported by Luke vii. 47 and 1 Pet. iv. 8); and much in the same way Cassian (*Coll.* xx. 8) enumerating the various ways in which sin may be blotted out, besides simple penitence, mentions the conversion of others by our exhortations.

It appears to me that these passages leave little doubt that Jewish writers generally and some Christian writers thought that one who had brought about the conversion of another had thereby secured his own salvation: if we further consider the use of the future tense (σώσει, καλύψει) touched on in the previous note, and the fact that, if the saving of the soul and the hiding of sins have reference to the sinner, they do not essentially differ from what is already involved in the protasis, which states the conversion of the sinner from the error of his way, it might seem that we ought to interpret the verse as Origen does in the passage just quoted. So Euth. Zig. and Cramer's *Catena* (*in loc.*) τοιοῦτον τὸ ἐν τῷ Ἱερεμίᾳ εἰρημένον, 'καὶ ἐὰν ἐξαγάγῃς τίμιον ἀπὸ ἀναξίου ὡς στόμα μου ἔσῃ.' ἐάν, φησιν, εἷς τῶν ἀπολλυμένων διὰ τὴν κακίαν εὐτελῶν σωθῇ διὰ τῶν σῶν λόγων, ἔντιμος ἔσῃ διὰ τοῦτο παρ' ἐμοί. We may also compare Dan. xii. 3 'they that be wise shall shine as the brightness of the firmament, and they that

[1] Dr. Abbott suggests δὸς εἰς as in the following quotation from Const. Apost.
[2] Compare Taylor, *Jewish Fathers*, p. 27.
[3] So Cod. Sangerm.; libri editi add *ejus*.
[4] This is repeated further on with allusion to the Levitical offering of doves: *Si meditando sicut columba...ab errore suo converteris peccatorem et abjecta nequitia ad simplicitatem eum columbae revocaveris...duos pullos columbarum Domino obtulisti.*

turn many to righteousness as the stars for ever and ever,' the punishment of 'the wicked and slothful servant' Matt. xxv. 26, St. Paul's words in 1 Cor. ix. 16 'woe is me if I preach not the Gospel,' 1 Tim. iv. 16 ἔπεχε σεαυτῷ καὶ τῇ διδασκαλίᾳ· τοῦτο γὰρ ποιῶν καὶ σεαυτὸν σώσεις καὶ τοὺς ἀκούοντάς σου, 1 Cor. iii. 14, 15, Pirké Aboth v. 26, 27, 'whosoever makes the many righteous, sin prevails not over him, and whosoever makes the many to sin, they grant him not the faculty to repent,' Clem. Al. *Str.* vii. p. 863 ὁ γνωστικὸς, ἰδίαν σωτηρίαν ἡγούμενος τὴν τῶν πέλας ὠφέλειαν, ἄγαλμα ἔμψυχον εἰκότως ἂν τοῦ Κυρίου λέγοιτο, Const. Ap. ii. 18 τοὺς ὑπνώδεις καὶ παρειμένους ἐπίστρεφε, ὑποστήριζε, παρακάλει, θεράπευε, ἐπιστάμενος ἡλίκον μισθὸν ἔχεις ταῦτα ἐπιτελῶν, ὥσπερ οὖν καὶ κίνδυνον ἐὰν ἀμελήσῃς τούτων. Spitta cites Sohar p. 47, 17 great is the honour of him who moves a sick man to repent, *ib.* p. 92, 18 great is the reward of him who leads back sinners to the way of the Lord. It may on the other hand be urged that it is at any rate a lower motive than that proposed in Matt. xviii. 15 ἐὰν ἁμαρτήσῃ ὁ ἀδελφός σου, ὕπαγε ἔλεγξον αὐτὸν μεταξὺ σοῦ καὶ αὐτοῦ μόνου· ἐάν σου ἀκούσῃ, ἐκέρδησας τὸν ἀδελφόν σου, and that such phrases as πλῆθος ἁμαρτιῶν and σώσει ψυχὴν ἐκ θανάτου naturally remind us of the preceding ἁμαρτωλός, and of the ἁμαρτία which brings forth death in i. 15, but are unsuitable if used of one whom St. James would be likely to commission to call others to repentance; cf. Luke xxii. 32 σύ ποτε ἐπιστρέψας στήρισον τοὺς ἀδελφούς σου, Psa. l. 16, li. 13, Matt. xv. 14: on the other hand the psalmist who had 'preached righteousness in the great congregation' speaks of his iniquities as more numerous than the hairs of his head (Psa. xl. 9, 12).[1]

It should be remembered however that a proverbial phrase is often used with a certain looseness, and that it is possible to make πλῆθος cover the sins of both parties, as Bede does: *qui peccatorem ab errore convertit, et ejus peccata per hanc conversionem ab aspectu judicis abscondit, et sua quoque in quibuscunque offendit errata ab intuitu ejus qui omnia videt proximum curando contegit;* similarly Bengel and Schneckenburger. Cf. Clem. Rom. ii. 19 (I exhort you to give heed to the things that are written) ἵνα καὶ ἑαυτοὺς σώσητε καὶ τὸν ἀναγινώσκοντα ἐν

[1] Hammond, Hofmann and Schegg following Erasmus and the R.C. commentators generally understand the sins covered to be those of the preacher of righteousness; most modern commentators take them to be the sins of the person converted. Calvin's note deserves to be quoted: *Cibum dare esurienti et sitienti potum videmus quanti Christus aestimet: atqui multo pretiosior est illi animae salus quam corporis vita. Cavendum ergo ne nostra ignavia pereant redemptae a Christo animae, quarum salutem quodam modo in manu nostra ponit Deus. Non quod salutem conferamus ipsi; sed quod Deus ministerio nostro liberat ac servat, quod alioqui videbatur exitio propinquum . . . Alludit potius ad dictum Salomonis quam pro testimonio citat . . . Qui oderunt, libidine sese mutuo infamandi ardent: qui amant, libenter inter se condonant multa; caritas ergo peccata sepelit apud homines. Jacobus hic altius quiddam docet, nempe quod deleantur coram Deo, ac si diceret, Salomon hunc caritatis fructum praedicat, quod tegat peccata: atqui nulla melior tegendi ratio, quam ubi in totum coram Deo abolentur.* Spitta explains the passage from the Jewish idea that all a man's sins were registered in heaven, but that the record might be partially or entirely cancelled by the subsequent performance of good deeds, such as the conversion of a sinner.

ὑμῖν· μισθὸν γὰρ αἰτῶ ὑμᾶς τὸ μετανοῆσαι ἐξ ὅλης καρδίας, σωτηρίαν ἑαυτοῖς καὶ ζωὴν διδόντας, *ib.* 17 (if we are commanded to convert even the heathen, how unpardonable would it be to allow the ruin of a soul which has once known the true God!) συλλάβωμεν οὖν ἑαυτοῖς καὶ τοὺς ἀσθενοῦντας ἀνάγειν ἐπὶ τὸ ἀγαθόν, ὅπως σωθῶμεν ἅπαντες· καὶ ἐπιστρέψωμεν ἀλλήλους καὶ νουθετήσωμεν, *ib.* 15 (he that obeys) καὶ ἑαυτὸν σώσει καὶ ἐμὲ τὸν συμβουλεύσαντα· μισθὸς γὰρ οὐκ ἔστιν μικρὸς πλανωμένην ψυχὴν καὶ ἀπολλυμένην ἀποστρέψαι εἰς τὸ σωθῆναι. In that case we might suppose the phrase σώσει ψυχὴν ἐκ θανάτου to be parenthetical and refer to the converted person, the future being attracted from the main verb. So Zahn (*Skizzen* p. 55) Wer einen verirrten mitchristen bekehrt, damit nicht nur diese Seele vom Tode errettet, sondern damit auch für sein eigenes Seelenheil sorgt, und bei dem Gott viel Vergebung seiner eigenen Sünden finden wird. For a discussion as to what interpretation of the words agrees best with the general teaching of the N.T. and of St. James himself see comment below.

COMMENT

I. 1—15. Paraphrase.

Rejoice when you meet with trials (temptations) of whatever kind, knowing that these are designed to prove your faith and fix in you the habit of patient endurance, with a view to your attainment of the perfect Christian character. To make the right use of trial there is need of wisdom, which must be sought by prayer from Him who gives freely without upbraiding for past neglect or ingratitude. [But prayer, to be effectual, must be the utterance of a fixed purpose which is in no danger of being diverted by changing moods or circumstances. No answer will be given to the prayer of the double-minded and unstable. The true attitude of the Christian is exultation in the glorious truth which has been revealed to him. If poor, he should exult in the new dignity thereby imparted to human nature; if rich, in the fact that he has been taught the emptiness of earthly wealth and station and has learnt to aim at heavenly riches; since the rich man of this world is doomed to pass away like the flower of the field.] Remember however that it is not trial in itself, but the patient endurance of trial to which the blessing is promised. He whose faith has been thus approved shall receive the crown of life promised to all that love God. Let no one say when he is tempted (tried), that God is the author of his temptation, for God, as he is incapable of being tempted, so He tempts none. Each man is tempted by his own lust (impulse), by which he is carried away from right and allured to wrong: lust, when it has conceived, becomes the parent of sin; sin when matured brings forth death.

TRIAL, TEMPTATION—πειρασμός, πειράζεσθαι.

We have here the first attempt at an analysis of Temptation from the Christian point of view. It may be compared with that given by Bishop Butler in his *Analogy*. Speaking of what constitutes our trial both with regard to the present and to a future world, the latter says

(Part I. ch. 4): 'It must be somewhat either in our external circumstances or in our nature. For on the one hand persons may be betrayed into wrong behaviour upon surprise, or overcome upon any other very singular and extraordinary external occasions, who would otherwise have preserved their character of prudence and of virtue: in which cases every one, in speaking of the wrong behaviour of these persons, would impute it to such external circumstances. And on the other hand men who have contracted habits of vice and folly of any kind, or have some particular passions in excess, will seek opportunities, and, as it were, go out of their way to gratify themselves in these respects at the expense of their wisdom and their virtue; led to it, as every one would say, not by external temptations, but by such habits and passions. . . . However, as, when we say, men are misled by external circumstances of temptation, it cannot but be understood, that there is somewhat within themselves to render those circumstances temptations, or to render them susceptible of impressions from them; so, when we say, they are misled by passions, it is always supposed that there are occasions, circumstances, and objects exciting these passions, and affording means for gratifying them. And therefore temptations from within and from without coincide and mutually imply each other.'

Again, speaking of moral improvement by discipline, he says (ch. 5); 'Mankind and perhaps all finite creatures from the very constitution of their nature, before habits of virtue, are deficient and in danger of deviating from what is right, and therefore stand in need of virtuous habits for a security against this danger. For, together with the general principle of moral understanding, we have in our inward frame various affections towards particular external objects. These affections are naturally, and of right, subject to the government of the moral principle as to the occasions on which they may be gratified, as to the times, degrees, and manner, in which the objects of them may be pursued; but then the principle of virtue can neither excite them nor prevent their being excited. On the contrary, they are naturally felt when the objects of them are present to the mind, not only before all consideration whether they can be obtained by lawful means, but after it is found they cannot. For the natural objects of affection continue so; the necessaries, conveniences, and pleasures of life remain naturally desirable, though they cannot be obtained innocently, nay, though they cannot possibly be obtained at all. And when the objects of any affection whatever cannot be obtained without unlawful means, but may be obtained by them; such affection,—though its being excited, and its continuing some time in the mind, be as innocent as it is natural and necessary,—yet cannot but be conceived to have a tendency to incline persons to venture upon such unlawful means; and therefore must be conceived as putting them in some danger of it. . . . This tendency in some one particular propension may be increased by the greater frequency of occasions naturally exciting it, than of occasions exciting others. The least voluntary indulgence in forbidden circumstances, though but in thought, will increase this wrong tendency, and may increase it further till, peculiar conjunctures perhaps conspiring, it becomes effect, and danger of deviating from right ends in actual deviation from it; a danger necessarily arising from the very nature of propension, and which therefore could not have been prevented, though it might have been escaped or got innocently through. . . . It is impossible to say how much even the first full overt act of irregularity might disorder the inward constitution, unsettle the adjustments and alter the proportions which formed it, and in which the uprightness of its make consisted; but repetition of irregularities would produce habits. And thus the constitution would be spoiled, and creatures made upright become corrupt and depraved in their settled character, proportionably to their repeated irregularities in occasional acts. But on the contrary these creatures might have improved and raised themselves to an higher and more secure state of virtue by the contrary behaviour; by steadily following the moral principle supposed to be one part of their nature, and thus withstanding that unavoidable danger of defection, which necessarily arose from propension, the other part of it. For, by thus preserving their integrity for some time, their danger would lessen; since propensions by being inured to submit would do it more easily and of course: and their security against this lessening danger would increase; since the moral principle would gain additional strength by exercise: both which things are implied in the notion of virtuous habits. Thus then vicious indulgence is not only criminal in itself, but also depraves the inward constitution and character. And virtuous self-government is not only right in itself but also improves the inward constitution and character: and may improve it to such a degree that, though we should suppose it impossible for particular affections to be absolutely coincident with the moral principle, and consequently should allow that such creatures, as have been above supposed, would for ever remain defectible, yet their danger of actually deviating from right may be almost infinitely lessened, and they fully fortified against what remains of it.'

Butler then proceeds to argue that 'this world is peculiarly fit to be a state of discipline to such as will set themselves to mend and improve. For the various temptations with which we are surrounded,—our experience of the deceits of wickedness, having been in many instances led wrong ourselves, the great viciousness of the world, the infinite disorders consequent upon it, our being made acquainted with pain and sorrow either from our own feeling of it or from the sight of it in others,—these things, though some of them may indeed produce wrong effects upon our minds, yet when duly reflected upon, have, all of them, a direct tendency to bring us to a settled moderation and reasonableness of temper, the contrary both to thoughtless levity, and also to that unrestrained self-will and violent bent to follow present inclination, which may be observed in undisciplined minds. . . . Allurements to what is wrong, difficulties in the discharge of our duty, our not being able to act an uniform right part without some thought and care, and the opportunities which we have, or imagine we have, of avoiding what we dislike or obtaining what we desire by unlawful means, when we either cannot do it at all, or at least not so easily, by lawful ones,—

these things, i.e. the snares and temptations of vice, are what render the present world peculiarly fit to be a state of discipline to those who will preserve their integrity; because they render being upon our guard, resolution, and the denial of our passions, necessary in order to that end. And the exercise of such particular recollection, intention of mind, and self-government, in the practice of virtue, has from the make of our nature a peculiar tendency to form habits of virtue, as implying not only a real, but also a more continued, and a more intense exercise of the virtuous principle, or a more constant and stronger effort of virtue exerted into act. Thus suppose a person to know himself to be in particular danger for some time of doing anything wrong, which yet he fully resolves not to do; continued recollection and keeping upon his guard, in order to make good his resolution, is a continued exerting of that act of virtue in a high degree, which need have been, and perhaps would have been, only instantaneous and weak, had the temptation been so.'

Butler's distinction between the two factors in temptation, the inner nature and the external circumstances, will help us to understand the contrast apparent in the text between the trial (πειρασμός) in which the Christian is to rejoice, and the temptation (πειράζεσθαι) which must not be ascribed to God, since from Him only good proceeds. The latter is the inner temptation, the former the outer trial, and not even that in its full extent. External circumstances may try us either by suggestions of pain, of which the great example is our Lord's agony in the garden, or by suggestions of pleasure, exemplified in our Lord's temptation in the wilderness, i.e. either by intimidating or by alluring. It is the former, the trial by pain, which St. James has in his mind in the 2nd verse, and by which those to whom he writes were assailed. They were mainly poor and were suffering persecution and oppression from the rich, as we gather from ii. 6, v. 7 foll. They were tempted to murmur against God and to speak evil of men. St. James (below v. 7–11) urges upon them the duty of patience, by showing how necessary it is in common life, by appealing to the example of the prophets, and pointing to the near approach of the judgment day, in which murmuring and impatience would be punished and the blessedness of patient suffering be revealed. Here he bids them rejoice in these trying circumstances, because, if patiently endured, they would confirm their faith and fit them to receive the reward of eternal life promised to all that love God. It is the same motive which is appealed to in the Sermon on the Mount (Matt. v. 4, 10–12) and in 1 Pet. i. 6 foll. Another reason for rejoicing in affliction is given in Heb. xii. 6: it is a mark of God's love towards those whom he chastises. In Acts v. 41 we read that the Apostles, when scourged, rejoiced that they were counted worthy to suffer shame for the name of Christ. St. Peter speaks of the partaking of Christ's sufferings as a ground for rejoicing (1 Pet. iv. 13). St. Paul rejoiced in the thought that he was allowed to supplement the afflictions of Christ for the sake of the Church (Col. i. 24).

The stages of Christian growth according to St. James are as follows:

Trial tests faith; the testing of faith produces endurance; endurance, if it is continued till it attains its end, builds up the perfectly matured Christian character, thoroughly furnished to all good works. For an example of this testing of the faith, patiently endured to the end, we may take the Syro-Phoenician woman. It is manifest what strength of endurance, what unshaken trust in God, she must have gained throngh that one victory. The converse is equally true. Where there has been little trial, there has been little to test and exercise faith, little experience of ourselves, little to instil the habit of submission and resignation, little to lead us away from earth and up to heaven. The old Greek proverb, παθήματα μαθήματα, is adopted by the writer of the epistle to the Hebrews, and applied where, without his sanction we might have hardly ventured to apply it, in the words καίπερ ὢν υἱὸς ἔμαθεν ἀφ' ὧν ἔπαθεν τὴν ὑπακοήν.

But is not St. James' exhortation to rejoice in temptation opposed to the petition 'Lead us not into temptation,' where the same word πειρασμός is used in the same signification of external temptation? In the Lord's Prayer however there is no reason to limit its application to pain-temptation any more than in 1 Tim. vi. 9 (they that will be rich fall into temptation and a snare). In the next place one who is conscious of his own weakness may without inconsistency pray that he may be kept out of temptation; and yet, when he is brought into it through no fault of his own but by God's providential ordering, he may feel such trust in Divine support as to rejoice in an opportunity of proving his faithfulness. St. James speaks to those who are in the midst of trial, and in danger of losing heart in consequence: it was evidently not God's will that they should be kept out of temptation, but that they should turn it to good account; and this is what St. James encourages them to do. Another way of explaining the difficulty is by a comparison of the words in Matt. xxvi. 41 προσεύχεσθε ἵνα μὴ εἰσέλθητε εἰς πειρασμόν. The disciples to whom Jesus addressed these words were already in a situation of extreme trial, and he does not propose to remove them from it: they are all to be sifted. Still they are to pray that they may not enter into temptation, i.e. that they may be so supported by Divine grace as to go through trial without its being able to tempt them. I do not think however that there is any need to limit in this way the meaning of the petition in the Lord's Prayer.

Allowing that St. James is here thinking mainly of trial arising out of affliction, how far may we generalize his 'divers temptations'? Beside pain, sorrow, fear, it will certainly embrace all sorts of perplexities, difficulties, disappointments, anxieties, anything which troubles or annoys us. We are naturally inclined to wish them out of the way, to think of them simply as interfering with the comfort and happiness which we esteem our right. The true way is to regard them as part of our schooling for heaven, helping to form the cross which has to be borne by every Christian. We should strengthen ourselves to bear them by looking away from the pain to the good involved in it, if rightly borne. But may we also rejoice in such tests of faith as are not naturally grievous, in wealth, power, beauty, popularity, prosperity of every kind? Or, yet further, in the external temptations of the world, the flesh and the devil? Might Joseph rejoice in the temptation which came to him in Potiphar's house, as well as in that which came when his brothers sold him to the Midianites? The conquest of pleasure-temptation is not less useful as experience; it is not less strengthening to the character than the conquest over pain: to have gone through such temptation unscathed may be the ground of deepest thankfulness afterwards; but the spiritual joy in resisting temptation of which St. James speaks is not compatible with any lower feeling of pleasure. To have suddenly come into possession of a great fortune is a cause of rejoicing to the natural man: one who has a right sense of the responsibilities and the snares of wealth may shrink from it as a burden, or enter upon it with much anxiety and self-suspicion; but we can hardly conceive of such an inversion of the ordinary view as to allow of a man's rejoicing in wealth as a trial. St. James just below speaks of the poor as rejoicing in his dignity, but the rich in his humiliation as a Christian—both equally difficult and the latter especially painful to the natural man. Onesimus and Philemon may both rejoice in the new relation of brotherhood, which replaces that of slavery and lordship: to the one it may bear the aspect of a levelling up, to the other of a levelling down; but in reality what both rejoice in is the falling into the background of the old transitory distinction in comparison with their common fellowship in the eternal glory.

The call to rejoice is of course not exclusively made to those who are tried. There is a natural joy which is not condemned, but which needs to be associated with the thought of God to guard it from becoming a snare to us (ch. v. 13). 'Rejoice in the Lord always' is a universal precept for all Christians, but one that has to be insisted upon especially in the case of those whose circumstances naturally tempt them to sorrow. It is a bracing appeal to them (like St. Paul's in Eph. vi. 10 foll.) to muster up all their courage, and to look their difficulties in the face, seeing in them a Divine discipline, which they are to accept as sent by Him who knows what is best for them and will not suffer them to be tempted above that they are able. On the other hand there is a false joy springing from a confidence in ourselves and in our circumstances, which shows that we aim at the friendship of the world, and which necessarily separates us from God (ch. iv. 4, 16). This false joy must be exchanged for the sorrow of repentance before the true joy can enter our hearts (iv. 9, 10).

In ver. 12 St. James seems still to have in his eye the rich man who is tried, while he also guards against a possible misunderstanding of the encouragement given in ver. 2. Trial can only be a subject of rejoicing when it is patiently endured. He who gives way to the temptation involved in trial is in no way benefited, but the reverse, unless, as in the case of St. Peter, his discovery of his own weakness leads him to a deeper repentance.

A still more serious error is met in ver. 13. Man throws the blame of his wrong-doing on God, who made him what he is, and placed him in circumstances which it was impossible to contend against. St. James meets this in two ways: (1) by showing that it involves a supposition which contradicts what we know of God, (2) by explaining more fully the nature of internal temptation. (1) (*a*) God is untempable; (*b*) He tempts none. But how are these statements to be reconciled with other passages of Scripture, in which God is said both to be tempted and to tempt? Such are Ex. xvii. 2 'why do ye tempt (πειράζετε) the Lord?' ver. 7 'he called the name of the place Massah (πειρασμόν) because they tempted the Lord, saying, Is the Lord among us or not?' Numbers xiv. 22, Deut. vi. 16 'ye shall not tempt the Lord,' Ps. lxxviii. 18, 41, xcv. 9, Isa. vii. 12, Matt. iv. 7 (where our Lord meets the temptation to cast himself down from the temple by referring to the command in Deut. vi. 16), Acts v. 9 (of Ananias and Sapphira) 'how is it that ye have agreed together to tempt the Spirit of the Lord?' 1 Cor. x. 9 'neither let us tempt Christ as some of them also tempted and were destroyed of serpents' (referring to Numb. xxi. 5 'the people spake against God and against Moses, Wherefore have ye brought us up out of Egypt to die in the wilderness?'), cf. Judith viii. 12 (of the rash oath of Ozias to surrender Bethulia if help did not come within five days) 'who are ye that have tempted God? . . . ye cannot find out the depth of the heart of man, then how can ye search out God or comprehend his purpose? . . . He hath power to defend us when he will. Do not bind the counsels of the Lord our God.' So self-sought martyrdom and the proposal to test the power of prayer by comparing the results in a praying and in a non-praying hospital may in different ways be regarded as tempting God. The distinction is plain between the temptation to sin of which St. James speaks and such cases as these, in which men are said to tempt God, when they make experiments with Him, or take liberties with Him, try how far they may go, so to speak, instead of humbly submitting to what they feel to be His revealed will or His providential ordering; when in the words of Stier they 'anticipate by the word of their own self-will the word of God upon which they should wait.' Man can be tempted because of the propensity to evil in his own nature; God cannot be tempted because He is absolute goodness.

But (*b*) we also read of God tempting man, as where He tested Abraham's obedience by demanding the sacrifice of his son (Gen. xxii. 1), or the Israelites by the forty years' wandering 'to humble thee, and to prove thee (πειράσῃ), to know what was in thine heart,' Deut. viii. 2, or Hezekiah by the Babylonian embassy 2 Chron. xxxii. 31, cf. Judith viii. 25–27. But here again the design of temptation is quite different from that spoken of in the text; it is not temptation with the view of drawing men into sin, but trial with the view of discovering his motives and principles and of gradually building up the perfect Christian character, as stated in the second verse.

(2) What then is the real history of the temptation which allures us to sin? It has its root in man himself, in his appetites, desires and impulses of every sort, suggesting the thought of pleasure to

be obtained (or pain avoided) by the commission of a wrong act. At first the impulse is a blind instinctive movement, involuntary and therefore innocent, but if unchecked it discovers a definite aim, which it seeks to attain by uniting itself with thought and will. Sin originates when we choose to dwell upon the thought of the pleasure suggested, though knowing, or strongly suspecting, that it cannot be lawfully obtained. The desire becomes stronger by indulgence, the thought of sin ceases to shock as it becomes more familiar, until at last that which had been long rehearsed in the imagination is enacted in real life. In most cases the commission of the outward act is followed by something of shame or remorse, which may lead to genuine repentance, but if the sting of conscience is disregarded, the first wrong action is naturally followed by others, which give rise to a sinful habit, and at length conscience is silenced, the will is permanently enslaved, the moral nature is to all appearance dead; and so the soul departs to the other world to receive the reward of the things done in the body. The genesis of temptation is admirably illustrated in the story of Macbeth. In the second scene we have the picture of an innocent and laudable ambition. The interview with the witches shows this ambition perilously sensitive to outward solicitation, and already open to the suggestion of unlawful means for the attainment of the coveted object, a suggestion seconded by his wife's direct instigation, and supported by external circumstances, the nomination of Malcolm as heir to the throne and the visit of Duncan. We have then after many misgivings the final resolve and the execution of the murder: the consequent change from the noble Macbeth, whose nature is full of the milk of human kindness and of whom it is said 'what thou wouldst highly that wouldst thou holily,' to the bloodthirsty tyrant of the later scenes. It is to be noticed that in Macbeth we are always conscious of a background of hellish instigation. This does not appear in the first chapter of St. James, but is recognized afterwards in iii. 6 where the tongue is said to be set on fire of hell, iii. 15 where false wisdom is described as devilish, iv. 7 where we are bidden to submit ourselves to God and resist the devil, 'the tempter' as he is called by St. Paul, who makes use of our natural impulses to bring us to ruin.

Here however a further difficulty arises, for the action of Satan is sometimes said to be permitted by God, as in the temptation of Job; at other times an action is attributed indifferently to Satan and to God, as in the numbering of the people by David, which is said to be instigated by God in 2 Sam. xxiv. 1, by Satan in 1 Chron. xxi. 1; and yet again God seems to be represented as the author of immoral or irreligious conduct in man, as in Ex. ix. 16 'the Lord hardened the heart of Pharaoh.' With regard to the first case the answer is simple: Satan tempts with the design of inducing Job to give up his righteousness and his trust in God: God permits the temptation, because He knows the end will be to prove Job's faith and confirm his righteousness. It is fundamentally the case of those to whom St. James writes. They are in trouble; Satan is allowed to suggest that this trouble is a sign that God neglects them; yet they are to rejoice in this trouble with its attendant temptation, because in this way their faith will be strengthened, and they will learn endurance. In such a case as this it might be said, either that Satan tempted them by Divine appointment, or that God tempted them through Satanic agency. The difference of expression in 2 Sam. xxiv. 1 and 1 Chron. xxi. 1 is due to the idiosyncrasy of the writers, the later writer shrinking from the bold anthropomorphism of the earlier. There is more difficulty in the passage in which God is said to have hardened Pharaoh's heart, especially if we read it with St. Paul's commentary (Rom. ix. 17–24) 'whom he will, he hath mercy on, and whom he will, he hardeneth,' and his silencing of the objector by what looks like an appeal to unlimited power 'Shall the thing formed say to him that formed it Why hast thou made me thus?' It is no doubt in reference to such a passage that we read that the epistles of St. Paul contained 'things hard to be understood which they that are unlearned and unstable wrest to their own destruction.' Perhaps it is most easily explained by regarding it as an abbreviated way of saying that Pharaoh's hardness was the natural consequence of the Divine law which has ordained that prolonged resistance to conscience should result in the searing of the heart, and that this hardness was also part of the providential plan by which Israel was brought out of Egypt and the power of God manifested. It is not meant that Pharaoh was under any compulsion to sin, or that God tempted him to sin. Lastly the argument of St. Paul is more justly regarded as an appeal to man's ignorance than as an assertion of the doctrine that might makes right. Throughout the Bible God's claim to man's obedience is founded on His righteousness. The faith of Abraham rests on this foundation. 'Shall not the Judge of all the earth do right?' In the mind of St. Paul as well as of Moses, no miracle, no sign of power could justify the Israelite or the Christian in accepting a doctrine different from that which he had received from Him whose name is Holy.

Setting aside however the precise language of Scripture, does not experience show cases in which it might be said that man is tempted of God? Take the child of criminal or vicious parents. He inherits a special predisposition to evil, and he is placed in circumstances which encourage and call out that tendency. Here we have to consider (1) the teaching of our Lord with regard to the many stripes and few stripes. Guilt is very different according to the different degrees of light accorded. But (2) every one has received *some* measure of light from above, teaching him that there is a right and a wrong, and further light and strength are given in proportion as the existing light is used. The publicans and sinners were nearer to Christ than the Scribes and Pharisees.

The following scheme may serve to illustrate the teaching of St. James on this subject.

Stages of Temptation.

Pre-Moral Stages	1.	Internal nature with its impulses (ἐπιθυμίαι) which often require some external stimulus (πειρασμός) to rouse them, otherwise remaining dormant.	
	2.	Excitement of particular impulse through external stimulus of present or prospective pleasure or pain.	
Moral Stages	3.	The impulse thus roused is brought under the purview of reason and conscience, and, if unsanctioned by them, constitutes full temptation (πειράζεται).	
	4.	The two ways. Action of will under temptation:	
		(*a*) passively yielding under Satanic influence.	(*b*) actively resisting under Divine influence.
	5.	(*a*) The understanding cooperates with the impulse, suggesting modes of gratifying it, and picturing the pleasure of gratification (συλλαβοῦσα).	(*b*) The will summons up the other powers of the mind and above all seeks aid from God to enable it to resist temptation (ὑπομονή).
	6.	(*a*) The will identifies itself with the impulse and resolves on the steps required to attain the desired object (τίκτει ἁμαρτίαν).	(*b*) The will identifies itself with conscience and refuses all parley with temptation.
	7.	(*a*) Sinful act.	(*b*) Virtuous act.
	8.	(*a*) Habit of vice formed by repetition of vicious action (ἁμαρτία ἀποτελεσθεῖσα).	(*b*) Habit of virtue formed by repetition of virtuous acts (ἡ ὑπομονὴ ἔργον τέλειον ἔχει).
	9.	(*a*) Final result, death (ἀποκυεῖ θάνατον).	(*b*) Final result, crown of life (δοκιμὸς γενόμενος λήμψεται τὸν στέφανον τῆς ζωῆς).

I. 16—18. Paraphrase.

Beware of wrong thoughts as to the character and work of God. All good from the lowest to the highest comes from above, descending from the Source of all lights, with whom (unlike the luminaries of this lower world) there can be neither change from within nor overshadowing from without. God of His own good pleasure implanted in our hearts the germ of His own nature by the preaching of the Gospel, in order that we might be the first-fruits of His new creation.

God the Author of all Good.

To dissipate entirely the idea that temptation comes from God, and that man is therefore not responsible for his sin, St. James here gives the positive side of that characteristic which he had shadowed out on its negative side in ver. 13. God is not merely Himself free from all touch of evil, and therefore incapable of injuring others, He is absolute Goodness, always communicating good to others, and Himself the hidden spring of all good done by others. Nor is it only moral good that comes from Him, though that may be His most perfect gift; but all light, all truth, beauty and happiness, all that at first made the world appear good in the eyes of its Creator, is still His work, His gift. It is vain to look for good from any other quarter, from the lusts of the flesh, or the smiles of the world. Man, however, by his own sin raises up a cloud which hides from him the face of God; and thus he comes to picture to himself a God who is no longer loving, but stern, vindictive, jealous of human happiness. Such an imagination is a delusion of the devil. Even this material sun does not cease to shine behind the cloud which hides it from human view; and God's love, more unchanging than the brightness of the sun, knows no eclipse. In all worlds He is eternally the same, the giver of all good, who cannot do otherwise than will what is best for every one of His creatures. His purpose for us Christians is that we should be the first-fruits, the sample and earnest, of His new creation. Through us He reveals to the world what He would have all men to be. And the means by which He renews in us the divine image, which is the true nature of man, is the declaration of His love, made first through the Son, and then further explained and enforced by those whom the Son has sent to sow the good seed of the kingdom. The teaching of Christ rightly received into the heart constitutes the germ of a new divine life, by which it is the will of God that humanity as a whole should in the end be permeated and transfused.[1]

It shows how liable men are to be deluded by phrases, that Luther, with this passage before him, could imagine the teaching of St. James to be opposed to that of St. Paul. 'By grace are we saved through faith, and that not of yourselves, it is the gift of God' is not a stronger

[1] See Jukes, *Restitution of All Things,* pp. 30–45.

expression of the doctrine of free justification than the words before us, 'of his own will begat he us with the word of truth.'

Regeneration.

It is worth while to compare the different terms used in the Bible to express the change wrought in man's nature by the Divine influence.

(1) It is described as a new birth. This is expressed in the text by the verb ἀποκυέω. St. Peter in his First Epistle (i. 23) employs the verb ἀναγεννάω 'being born again not of corruptible seed, but of incorruptible, through the living and abiding word of God,' cf. *ib.* ii. 2. St. John has either γεννάω ἄνωθεν or the simple γεννάω, as in i. 12, 13, 'As many as received him, to them gave he power to become the sons of God, even to them that believe on his name: which were born, not of blood, nor of the will of the flesh, nor of the will of man, but of God,' *ib.* iii. 3 'except a man be born from above, he cannot see the kingdom of God,' this new birth being further explained by the words in verses 5, 6, 'except a man be born of water and of the Spirit, he cannot enter into the kingdom of God. That which is born of the flesh is flesh; and that which is born of the Spirit is spirit'; similarly 1 ep. iii. 9 'every one who is born of God committeth not sin; for his seed remaineth in him, and he cannot sin, because he is born of God'; *ib.* v. 4 'whatsoever is born of God (πᾶν τὸ γεγεννημένον ἐκ τοῦ Θεοῦ) overcometh the world; and this is the victory that overcometh the world, even our faith,' cf. also ii. 29, iv. 7, v. 1, 18. St. Paul uses the word παλιγγενεσία in Tit. iii. 5 'according to his mercy he saved us by the washing of regeneration and renewing of the Holy Ghost,' and addresses the Galatians as 'my little children of whom I travail in birth until Christ be formed in you' (Gal. iv. 19).

(2) Nearly related to this is the description of the change as that of adoption (υἱοθεσία) or sonship, for which see Rom. viii. 14-17, 'As many as are led by the Spirit of God, they are the sons of God. For ye did not receive a spirit of bondage again to fear, but ye received a spirit of adoption, whereby we cry, Abba, Father . . . The Spirit itself witnesseth with our spirit, that we are the children of God,' cf. Gal. iv. 5, 6, Eph. i. 5.

(3) Or again, that which speaks of a new heart, a new man, a new creation, a new nature, cf. Ezek. xi. 19 'I will put a new spirit within you; and I will take the stony heart out of their flesh, and will give them a heart of flesh.' *Ib.* xxxvi. 25–27, Jer. xxxi. 33, Ps. li. 10, 2 Cor. v. 17 'If any man be in Christ, he is a new creature (καινὴ κτίσις); old things have passed away; behold all things are become new,' Eph. iv. 22 'that ye put off the old man which is being destroyed in accordance with the lusts of deceit, and be renewed in the spirit of your mind; and that ye put on the new man which after God is created in righteousness and holiness of truth,' 2 Pet. i. 4 'in order that through the promises ye may become partakers of the divine nature,' Gal. vi. 15, Eph. ii. 15, Col. iii. 9, 10.

(4) This new nature is further described as a resurrection from

death, and combined with the thought of our being joined with Christ in His crucifixion and resurrection. Thus we read (1 Joh. iii. 14) 'we know that we have passed from death to life, because we love the brethren,' Eph. ii. 4-6 'God, for his great love wherewith he loved us, even when we were dead in sins, quickened us together with Christ, and raised us up together and made us sit together in heavenly places in Christ Jesus,' Col. ii. 12, 13, iii. 1, Rom. vi. 3–11.

(5) At other times it is described as a change from darkness to light, as in Eph. v. 8 'ye were once darkness, but now are ye light in the Lord,' Col. i. 13, 1 Pet. ii. 9, 1 Joh. ii. 8–11.

(6) Or from slavery to freedom, as in Rom. vi. 22 'but now being made free from sin and become servants to God, ye have your fruit unto holiness, and the end everlasting life,' Rom. viii. 2 'the law of the Spirit of life in Christ Jesus made me free from the law of sin and death,' Joh. viii. 32, James i. 25.

(7) Or it is described more simply as conversion or turning, see Matt. xviii. 3 'except ye be converted (ἐὰν μὴ στραφῆτε) and become as little children, ye shall not enter into the kingdom of heaven,' Jas. v. 19.

(8) The most common, however, as well as the most complete description of this change is the receiving of the Holy Spirit, through whom Christ dwells in us and we in Him, see Rom. viii. already quoted, Gal. v. 16–26, Eph. iii. 14 foll., James iv. 5, John xiv.–xvi.

The idea of regeneration was connected by the Jews with their rite of circumcision and also with the admission of proselytes by the ceremony of baptism.[1] It was therefore only natural that when baptism became the sacrament of admission into the Church of Christ it should be regarded as possessing a regenerative power. St. Peter, comparing it with the preservation of Noah in the ark, says 'the like figure whereunto, even baptism, doth now save us' (1 ep. iii. 21). St. Paul speaks of our being saved by the washing of regeneration and renewing of the Holy Ghost (Tit. iii. 5), and says that 'as many as were baptized into Christ did put on Christ' (Gal. iii. 27); that 'ye were buried with Christ in baptism, wherein also ye were raised with him through faith in the power of God who raised him from the dead' (Col. ii. 12). So St. John *l.c.* 'except a man be born of water and the Spirit he cannot enter into the kingdom of God. The love of system led later Church writers to limit the use of the term Regeneration to the special grace conveyed in Baptism, carefully distinguishing it from Justification, Conversion, Sanctification, and so on.[2] In our Baptismal Service water is said to be sanctified to the mystical washing away of sin, and the baptized child is said to be regenerate

[1] See Wetst. on 2 Cor. v. 17, *Dict. of Christ. Ant.* under 'Baptism,' p. 170, Schoettgen, *Hor. Hebr.* I. p. 704, Lightfoot, *H. Heb.* on Matt. iii., John iii., Meuschen, *N. T. ex Talm. illustratum*, p. 286.

[2] See, for an excellent summary of the teaching of the Church of England on this subject, a little tract by Canon Meyrick entitled *Baptism, Regeneration, Conversion*, published by the S.P.C.K.

and grafted into the body of Christ's Church. J. B. Mozley in his treatise on Baptismal Regeneration argues that since regeneration, strictly taken, implies Christian perfection, the assertion here made must be understood hypothetically, as expressing a charitable hope that the person is on the way to perfection. The more common explanation is that all baptized persons are by the fact of their baptism placed in a new state of spiritual capacity. It is important to notice here two things: (1) that the same distinction is made between outward and inward baptism as between outward and inward circumcision. Of the latter St. Paul says, borrowing the figure used in the book of Deuteronomy (xxx. 6), 'he is not a Jew which is one outwardly; neither is that circumcision which is outward in the flesh; but he is a Jew which is one inwardly and circumcision is that of the heart, in the spirit and not in the letter'; and so St. Peter after saying that 'baptism saves us,' adds the caution not 'the putting away of the filth of the flesh, but the answer of a good conscience (συνειδήσεως ἀγαθῆς ἐπερώτημα) towards God'; and St. John, who reports the words 'except a man be born of water and the Spirit, he cannot enter into the kingdom of God,' gives a test by which we may ascertain who is thus born, in the words 'every one that doeth righteousness is born of him' (1 ep. ii. 29), 'whatsoever is born of God doth not commit sin' (*ib.* iii. 9), 'whatsoever is born of God overcometh the world; and this is the victory that overcometh the world, even our faith' (*ib.* v. 4). That baptism was not always a regeneration in this high sense is shown by such instances as that of Simon Magus, who, after he had been baptized by Philip, and received the gifts of the Spirit by the laying on of the hands of Peter, was declared by the latter to 'have neither part nor lot in the matter, but to be still in the gall of bitterness and the bond of iniquity.' (2) We have to remember that the Apostles wrote at a time when adult baptism was the rule, and infant baptism the exception. Baptism was then, as it is now in heathen or Mahometan countries, the confession of the faith of Christ crucified, when it entailed shame, persecution, even death. It was of such confession Christ himself said 'whosoever shall confess me before men, him will I confess also before my Father which is in heaven' (Matt. x. 32); and St. Paul, 'with the heart man believeth unto righteousness; and with the mouth confession is made unto salvation' (Rom. x. 10); with which we may compare the words recorded in Mark xvi. 16 'he that believeth and is baptized shall be saved.' Faith and repentance (or conversion) were the necessary preliminaries to baptism; but baptism, being the outward sign and seal of the inward change, being also the confession of Christ before men, and being accompanied by further gifts of the Spirit, became the summary expression for the new birth which preceded it. It is evident that in these respects infant baptism now is something very different from adult baptism then. Yet these differences do not derogate from the uses of Infant Baptism. We rightly regard the offering of the child to God by the parents in baptism as the first step in the Christian life, the acknowledgment on their part of their duty towards the child as a creature born not for time, but for eternity; and the authoritative declaration on the part of God of His saving will in regard to each child thus brought to Him. In bringing our infants to the font we only carry out the principle laid down by St. Paul (1 Cor. vii. 14) in respect to the children of Christian parents, and obey the word of Christ Himself 'Suffer little children to come unto me.' If all goes on as it should do, we may hope and believe that the child will lead the rest of his life according to that beginning; that there will be a steady onward growth, as in the case of Timothy, without any deliberate falling away, such as to require that entire change of heart and life which we generally understand by the term 'conversion.' In this, which ought surely to be the normal case in a Christian country, the child is brought up to believe that he has not to win God's favour by any special merit of his own, but that he is already redeemed, already grafted into the true Vine, a participator in the gifts of the Spirit, and an heir to all the promised blessings of the Gospel, unless by his own neglect he refuses to avail himself of these privileges. And in such a life as this it does not seem possible to fix on any other moment as the moment of regeneration, except that in which the parents proclaimed their intention to bring up their infant as a member of Christ and a child of God.

It is interesting to observe the acknowledgment of the necessity of a conversion or new birth even among heathen writers. Some found this in the initiation of the mysteries, others in the teaching of philosophy.[1]

The Word of Truth.

As there are some who attribute a magical virtue to the material rite of baptism, so there are others who attribute a magical virtue to sermons. They support their view by citing such texts as the following: 'Faith cometh by hearing, and hearing by the word of God. How shall they hear without a preacher?' (Rom. x. 14, 17); 'God hath manifested his word through preaching' (Tit. i. 3). But we have only to compare the state of things in the early Church with the state of things which now prevails, in order to see how entirely inappropriate such language, literally understood, is to our own time. When St. Paul thus spoke, it is almost certain that there was no

[1] Compare for the conversion of the soul (ψυχῆς περιαγωγή) effected by philosophy, Plato's account of the Cave-dwellers in *Rep.* vii. 514–522, and the Stoic passages quoted by Zeller (vol. iv.[3] p. 255) on the instantaneous change from a state of folly and misery to one of wisdom and happiness, also Seneca, *ep.* 6. § 1 *intellego non emendari me tantum, sed transfigurari...hoc ipsum argumentum est in melius translati animi, quod vitia sua, quae adhuc ignorabat, videt.* For the mysteries compare the words used by the initiated ἔφυγον κακόν, εὗρον ἄμεινον in Dem. *De Corona,* 313, also Apul. *Metam.* xi. 21 *Nam et inferum claustra et salutis tutelam in deae manu posita, ipsamque traditionem ad instar voluntariae mortis et precariae salutis celebrari, quippe cum . . . in ipso finitae lucis limine constitutos . . . numen deae soleat elicere et sua providentia quodam modo renatos ad novae reponere rursus salutis curricula;* and Tertull. *Praescript.* c. 40 *Diabolus ipsas quoque res sacramentorum divinorum in idolorum mysteriis aemulatur.*

written Gospel. It was an oral revelation, passed from mouth to mouth. The words of eternal life spoken by Christ were reported by those who heard him, and these words were spirit and life to all who received them. But even then it made no difference whether they were addressed to many at once in the temple, as by Peter, or to one in a chariot, as by Philip. Nor did it make any difference, when James set the example of preaching by letter, where he could not preach in person, and was followed by Paul and the other Apostles. Preaching is only one out of many Christianizing influences now at work in England. Some go so far as to question whether it would not be for the advantage of all, preachers and hearers alike, if we would give heed to St. James' advice (μὴ πολλοὶ διδάσκαλοι γίνεσθε) and put a stop to four-fifths of the preaching which now goes on. Still there is room for sermons in the adaptation of the Gospel to the varying needs of successive generations, and different classes of men, as well as to the idiosyncrasies of different individuals. And there is need of course for personal influence, especially with the less educated. Next to the influence of believing parents, and in some cases superior to it, is the influence of a schoolmaster like Arnold, of a preacher like Maurice or Keble, in convincing a man of the reality of Christianity.

I. 19—27. Paraphrase.

Since you know that it is God who of his own good pleasure has infused a new life into us by means of the preaching of the Word, listen with eagerness to the Word which comes from Him, remembering that it is not something to talk about or to fight about, but to receive into our heart and to manifest in our actions. Human passion and bitterness are not pleasing to God or productive of the righteousness which God requires, and which He alone can give. Therefore begin by putting away all that unkindness which is so ready to overflow the lips and defile the man; and then open your hearts to receive in meekness the Word sown, which is able to save the soul. Do not however deceive yourselves with the idea that it is enough to be hearers of the Word without carrying it out in action. Such a hearer is like a man who, looking at his face in a mirror, gives one glance, and is gone, and at once forgets what he was like. If we wish to make a right use of the heavenly mirror, the Word which shows us what we are and what we should be, we must not be satisfied with a hasty glance, we must give our minds to it; we must embrace it as the law of our lives and never lose sight of it. Only thus will God's blessing attend our actions. If any one regards himself as a religious man, while he knows not how to bridle his tongue, such a man deceives himself and his religion is of no avail. Such was the religion of the

Pharisees, who devoured widows' houses while for a pretence making long prayers. The religious service which God approves, consists in kindness to all who need our kindness, and in rising superior to worldly motives and solicitations.

Hearing the Word.

The parallel passage in St. Peter shows that the immediate reference here is to the good seed of the Word sown by the preaching of the Apostles. But the rule laid down by St. James need not be confined to this. It is a direction as to the way in which all good thoughts, all higher aspirations, all that raises and purifies our ideal, should be received in the mind. As St. Paul says (Phil. iv. 8), 'whatsoever things are true, whatsoever things are just, whatsoever things are pure, whatsoever things are lovely, these things we are to think upon,' whether we read them in books, or see them in the lives and actions of other men, or have them suggested to us by the teachings of art or nature, or by the voice of conscience, or whatever else may seem to come through the more immediate inspiration of God. In respect to all of these the lesson is the same: 'take heed how ye hear.' Let your hearts and minds be receptive of these higher influences. Hearken for the still small voice, ponder its accents, submit yourselves humbly and lovingly to its guidance. Keep a firm hand on vanity, pride and passion, lest they get the dominion over you, and drive away the Spirit or drown His voice within you. To the same effect are the words of the Psalmist, 'Commune with your own heart upon your bed, and be still,' 'I will hearken what God, the Lord, will say concerning me,' 'Rest in the Lord and wait patiently for Him'; and the words of the youthful Samuel, 'Speak, Lord, for thy servant heareth.' In like manner Wordsworth speaks of the influences of nature.

But pure contemplation is not enough. Man is made for action, as well as for thought and feeling; and if the latter have no influence on his action, they become merely a refined self-indulgence, and tend to dull the moral sense, and harden the heart, until moral renewal becomes all but impossible, because we have destroyed the natural connexion between the emotional stimulus and the response in act. In the well-known words of Bp. Butler: 'Going over the theory of virtue in one's thoughts, talking well, and drawing fine pictures of it; this is so far from necessarily or certainly conducing to form habits of virtue in him who thus employs himself, that it may even harden the mind in a contrary course and render it gradually more insensible, that is, form a habit of insensibility to all moral considerations. For, from our very faculty of habit, passive impressions by being repeated grow weaker.' Few things are more fatal to moral and spiritual growth than the satisfaction derived from a merely aesthetic or sentimental religion.

But, it may be urged, is not a contemplative life a legitimate vocation? Are not some men called to be artists, poets, philosophers, students or teachers, as other men are called to be men of business and action? Is not action itself crippled and wasted from want of knowledge? Is it not one of the most deplorable features of modern life, that there is so much restless activity with so little thought as to the end to be pursued, and the means to be employed for arriving at the end; so much talk and profession, and so little feeling; so much fuss, and so little real enjoyment?

We may allow all this, and yet hold with Bp. Butler and St. James, that it is a disastrous thing for a man to rest satisfied with his own 'passive impressions.' If a poet like Wordsworth devotes himself steadily to the task of raising the standard of thought and feeling among his countrymen, or a jurisprudent, such as Bentham, lives laborious days in order to reform men's ideas of what law should be, and so ultimately to bring about that vast improvement in the statute law of England which has been witnessed in this century, no one could deny that these were in the highest sense men of action. It is true there have been artists and philosophers who were less consciously practical, 'who sang but as the linnets sing,' who wrote or composed in obedience to the inner impulse without any definite idea of benefiting others; whose work nevertheless has been rich in practical results of the greatest importance. Here too, for the work to produce such results, there must have been a high degree of mental activity, and a conscientious effort to render faithfully the impression or the thought by which the writer or artist was possessed. To borrow St. James' figure, no great work of art was ever produced by a mere hasty glance at the mirror of the Divine Word. But St. James is of course speaking primarily of moral and spiritual truth. He does not deny that one who preaches or theorizes on these subjects without practising his own precepts may put forward thoughts which may be good and useful for other men; nor that he may even be a medium, like Balaam, for divine inspiration, though he should be found in the end fighting, like Balaam, for the enemies of God: but what he says is that, to the theorizer himself, moral theory without practice is of no avail, but rather a dangerous snare as fostering the habit of self-deception.

Slow to Speak.

But is it not the duty of a Christian to let his light shine? to preach the Gospel to every creature? Does not the Psalmist say (lxxii. 74), 'my mouth shall speak of thy righteousness all the day,' and St. James himself (v. 20) give a special encouragement to one who 'converts a sinner from the error of his way'? On the other hand, in ch. iii., he warns his readers against being too ready to take upon themselves the office of teacher, and urges on them the necessity of controlling the tongue. Doubtless we are to understand him in the text as deprecating rash and hasty speech on religious subjects, in accordance with the teaching of the wise man, 'God is in heaven and thou on earth; therefore let thy words be few' (Eccl. v. 1, 2). A grave reverence, modesty and humility, careful previous consideration of the subject on which he has to speak, these seem to be the qualities St. James requires in a teacher, in contrast with the flippant familiarity, the readiness to pour out prayers or exhortations on the shortest notice, which are often found so attractive. 'Slow to speak' seems also to imply a long period of testing and preparation for the work of the ministry, in contrast with the plan ascribed to the Salvationists, of taking one who has only just abandoned a life of sin himself, and setting him up to be an evangelist to others. The words 'slow to speak' are applied by Stier to conversation on religious topics as well as to actual preaching. 'How many Christians,' he says, 'hold that God's word is a matter about which people must talk together—God's word which should always speak directly to the heart!... Guard against the so much loved pious conversations, which are often so unprofitable, often no more than mere idle babbling. Do not *talk away* from your hearts the power and blessing of saving truth.' Allowing this to be the general rule, we must not forget that the demoniac was bidden to tell how great things God had done for him; and that however unwilling a man may be to set himself up as *censor morum* or an instructor of others, it is every one's duty to make confession of his own belief and principles when occasion calls for it.

Should we limit the injunction to the sphere of religion, or give it a general application, equivalent to Carlyle's 'Silence is golden'? Let us consider the case of one who was certainly ταχὺς λαλεῖν, the Apostle Peter. His promptness of speech is shown on many occasions, as when he said 'Depart from me, for I am a sinful man, O Lord,' 'Let us make three tabernacles,' 'Thou art the Christ, the son of the living God,' 'This be far from thee, Lord, this shall not be unto thee,' 'Thou shalt never wash my feet,' 'Not my feet only but my hands and my head.' Here we have the immediate, spontaneous, expression of the feelings of the heart, sometimes right, sometimes wrong, but always attractive and interesting. It is this simplicity and openness which draws us so much to the Apostle and makes us place such confidence in his sincerity. So in general, expansiveness and freedom of utterance is both a loveable and useful quality. We do not wish the natural flow to be checked by the constant question 'Is what I am about to say wise? Is it prudent? How will it affect people's estimate of me?' On the other hand what can be more wearisome than a flow of words where there is little of feeling or thought? words which are mere words, or words prompted simply by vanity, or which betray a shallow or coarse or malicious nature? That a talker of this kind should be induced to check the current of his words by asking 'Is this true? Is it likely to pain or injure any one? Can it do good to any one?' is surely much to be desired. But even in the case of natural kindly utterance, some sort of control is desirable. The impulse to hear should balance the impulse to speak. There should be the thought that others too may wish to express themselves, and that the thoughts and experiences of others may be not less interesting and useful than our own to the company at large. There should be the instinctive shrinking from any approach to falsehood, as well as from anything which could give pain or do mischief. There is nothing unnatural or artificial in such control as this, nothing to excite a suspicion of Jesuitism.

But if we have no difficulty in finding cases in which we should all echo the admonition of St. James; if we should allow that for the Jews of his time, as for certain races in our own time, the rule 'slow to speak' might be of very general application; do we not also find cases, especially in England, where a stimulus is needed in the opposite direction? Is there not sometimes a stolid absence of interest both in persons and things, which does away with the chief motive for conversation? or a sluggishness of thought and speech, which amounts almost to dumbness? or a timidity and self-distrust, which make it a painful effort to open oneself to others? In such cases surely the injunction should be: Try to break through the isolation in which you have placed yourself: learn to interest yourself more in others: remember that you too in your own small circle are intended not only to do the will of God, but to be an oracle of God, reflecting back that aspect of the Divine Glory, to manifest which is the reason of your creation. Certainly neither Moses nor Jeremiah were commended for their slowness of speech. In vain the former pleaded 'I am not eloquent, but am slow of speech and of a slow tongue.' 'The anger of the Lord,' we are told, 'was kindled against him' for his unwillingness to carry the Divine message to his countrymen.

Slow to Wrath.

This is not to be understood as enjoining on Christians the habit of Stoic apathy, any more than 'slow to speak' is to be understood as enjoining a Trappist silence. Bp. Butler in his sermons on Resentment has well shown both the use and the abuse of the irascible element in man. One chief means of raising a degraded moral tone is the sight of the indignation produced in persons of a more generous nature by a mean or unkind action. We have many examples of such indignation in the Bible, notably in the language of John the Baptist and of our Lord. What the text means is 'do not give way to the first impulse to anger. Think how often you have had to repent of what you have done or said under the influence of passion: how often you have found that you had misapprehended the facts, or misinterpreted the motives of the supposed offender. Even when there can be no reasonable doubt on these points, in any case do not let yourself be carried away by blind passion; ask yourself how much of your anger arises from the fact that *wrong* is done, and how much from the fact that it is done to *you*, and try to eliminate the latter element; take into account the extenuating circumstances, hereditary predisposition, defective education or whatever it may be. Consider also your own liability to go wrong; and above all consider the royal law, Thou shalt love thy neighbour as thyself. Put yourself into his place, and act towards him as you would wish that another should act towards you under like circumstances: that is, act for what you believe to be the offender's best interests, and in such a way as to arouse his own better feelings.' This warning of St. James against over-hastiness in wrath may be compared with St. Paul's warning against too great persistency in wrath, 'Be ye angry and sin not, let not the sun go down upon your wrath.'

The context however shows that St. James is not thinking so much of the passion of anger in general, as of its indulgence under particular circumstances. He is speaking of the way in which men should receive the Word. 'They should be quick to hear, slow to speak, slow to wrath, seeing that the wrath of man does not work the righteousness of God: therefore they are to receive with meekness the word of salvation.' On a first reading we might be inclined to ask, Who ever supposed that man's wrath could work God's righteousness? Why should St. James have given utterance to a truism like this? But the history of religion proves that there is no more common delusion than this—that the best evidence a man can give of his own orthodoxy is his bitterness towards the heterodoxy of others. The monarch's private vices were atoned for by unsparing persecution of his heretical subjects; to join a crusade against the infidel was regarded as a passport to heaven; to burn a Protestant was an Act of Faith. The *odium theologicum* has passed into a proverb. Nor is it difficult to understand why this should be so. Religion, with its vastly extended horizon and its infinite possibilities as to the future, stimulates in a very high degree the faculties of hope and fear, and in the more anxious and less trustful natures tends to arouse an eager longing for some positive assurance of personal safety. Such an assurance may be either objective or subjective; it may be derived either from the authority of the Church without, or the supposed voice of the Spirit within, testifying that we are children of God. The former assurance may be found in the dogmatic coupling together of Conversion and Final Perseverance as different aspects of the same fact, or in the Viaticum and Extreme Unction of the Church of Rome. The latter assurance may be sought from the presence of what is regarded as an overpowering religious emotion. In the last resort, the former also is subjective, in as much as it depends on the degree of confidence placed in the ecclesiastical authority to which a man has submitted himself: and the fact that this confidence is liable to be shaken by the discovery that others do not acknowledge the same authority, is one main cause of the hatred of heresy, as tending to undermine a man's own faith and destroy his own security. Then this very hatred,—itself, as we have seen, the offspring of doubt and fear.—becomes identified in our thoughts with righteous indignation against sin; and the more fiercely it rages, the stronger is the conviction in the mind of the persecutor, that he is the Jehu appointed to carry out the Divine vengeance against the sinner, and that Paradise is secure to the champion of the truth. Something of the same kind may be observed wherever party spirit (the ἐριθία of the third chapter) runs high;

it is so easy, so comforting to be a good hater, to take for granted that one's own side has a monopoly of intellect and virtue, to accept the party watch-word and join in shouting the party war-cry; so arduous and so humbling to divest oneself of prejudice, to seek the truth for its own sake, to acknowledge the evil in ourselves, and see the good in those who differ from us.

Modes of Self-Deception.

St. James notices in this chapter four ways in which men may delude themselves as regards their religious state in God's sight, and preach peace to themselves when there is no peace. The first is by their fluency in speaking on religious subjects, the second by their religious zeal, the third by their pleasure in hearing sermons or reading religious books, the fourth (see verses 26 and 27) by the punctiliousness of their religious services. Not that any one of these is in itself wrong; they may be all good and right as means of grace; but they are easily capable of becoming a source of self-delusion, because it is so easy to confound the means with the end. Thus under the old dispensation, Isaiah (i. 10–20) was commissioned to declare the utter worthlessness of sacrifices and incense, of sabbaths and holidays, of solemn meetings and many prayers, unless they were accompanied by a moral change, unless the worshippers ceased to do evil, and learnt to do well,—a change exemplified in Isaiah, as in St. James, by kindness shown to the orphan and the widow. In like manner Micah (vi. 6 foll.) contrasts the externalities of a sacrificial worship with that which the Lord requires, justice, mercy, humility. The same contrast is found in the New Testament, as in John iv. 20–24, where Christ himself corrects the Samaritan woman's ideas of the special sanctity attaching to one place above another, in the words 'God is a Spirit, and they that worship him must worship him in spirit and in truth'; and again in Matt. vii. 21–23, where He declares that, to many who have prayed and prophesied and wrought miracles in His name, it shall hereafter be said 'I never knew you; depart from me, ye that work iniquity.' In his next chapter St. James specifies a fifth mode of self-deception, arising from confidence in the orthodoxy of our creed: 'thou believest that there is one God; thou doest well: the devils also believe, and tremble.' To all these various semblances of religion—not necessarily hypocritical semblances, for it is not a seeming to others, but a seeming to self, which is condemned in the εἴ τις δοκεῖ θρησκὸς εἶναι of the 26th verse—he opposes the reality, οὐ γὰρ δοκεῖν ἄριστος ἀλλ' εἶναι θέλω.

II. 1—13. Paraphrase.

An example of the worldly spirit may be seen in your assemblies when a poor man entering is shown to the worst place, and a rich man to the best. How is this regard for worldly distinctions con-

sistent with your belief in Christ, the only glory of believers? Does it not show that you are divided in heart, and allow yourselves to be influenced by lower considerations? In reality the poor have more title to our respect than the rich, since it is among the poor we find those who are rich in faith, and heirs of the kingdom of heaven, while the rich, as a class, maltreat the brethren and blaspheme the name of Christ. If it is from obedience to the royal law of love that we show courtesy to the rich, it is well; but if we do this only from respect of persons, it is a breach of law and defiance of the lawgiver no less than adultery or murder. Remember that both words and actions will be tried by the law of liberty, which regards the motive as well as the deed. If we do not show mercy to others, we shall not receive mercy ourselves. It is mercy only which triumphs over judgment. (See notes on *vv.* 8 and 12 especially.)

Respect of Persons.

It is to be feared that, if St. James were to visit our English churches, he would not find much improvement on the state of things existing in the congregations of which he speaks. While there is perhaps no objection either to the appropriation of sittings, in so far as it assures to regular attendants the right to sit in their accustomed place, or to the exactment of a fixed payment from the well-to-do members of the congregation for the use of their seats; it is surely most contrary to the spirit of the Gospel that all the best seats should be monopolised by the highest bidders. The poor are at any rate not to be at a disadvantage in the House of God. The free and open seats should at least be as good as the paying seats, and it should not be in the power of a seat-holder to prevent any unoccupied sitting from being used.

But the principle here inculcated goes much further than the particular example given. If it is wrong to thrust the poor into bad places in church, it is also wrong to treat them with disrespect in our ordinary intercourse. St. James had before spoken of the change brought about by Christianity in the feelings of the rich and poor themselves: the rich brother was to exult in his humiliation, i.e. in the feeling of common brotherhood which unites all Christians to Christ, and in the special obligation, which lies upon one who is specially favoured, to use his talents and his means for the common good; the poor brother was to exult in his admission to the full rights and privileges of a member of Christ and a child of God. Here he is speaking of the duty of Christians generally towards these two extremes. Apparently he allows of no difference in our behaviour towards them. Our behaviour towards both should be governed by the simple rule laid down by St. Peter, 'honour all men.' This does not mean that we are to show less courtesy than we have hitherto done towards the rich, provided this courtesy proceeds from the right motive; but it means that our courtesy towards the poor should, if anything, be greater than our courtesy towards the rich, partly because they have greater claims upon us—the claims of the widow and orphan were noticed in the previous verse—and partly because it may be more difficult for those who have long been down-trodden to rise to their full dignity as Christians, unless aided by our brotherly sympathy.

There are several questions which suggest themselves here. Does St. James mean that all persons are to be treated exactly in the same way, irrespective of rank, age, sex, colour, creed, nationality, or the special relations by which men are connected one with another? Are all these differences considered to belong not to the man himself, but to the part he plays on the transitory stage of this mortal life? Is it wrong to be influenced by such qualities as beauty, amiability, cleverness, external refinement and good manners? Should our behaviour towards one another be determined only by superiority of moral excellence, as constituting the true essence of the man?

This last distinction must of course in any case put a limit on the injunction to 'honour all men.' We are to honour man as man, but not as coward or liar. It is the godlike, not the bestial or the devilish, in man which deserves our honour. Yet seeing that these elements are bound up in one individual, we must take care that the stern repression which may be the treatment required for the worse elements, does not entirely extinguish or conceal the reverence which should be forthcoming for any manifestation of the higher nature in the man. The reason given in the text for honouring the poor rather than the rich, is that the latter are blasphemers and persecutors, the former the inheritors of the kingdom of heaven. Nor again can we suppose that St. James would disagree with St. Peter's injunction to pay honour to the wife as to the weaker vessel, or that he would fail to recognise the relative duties of parent and child, master and servant, &c. Special honour is due to the king and the magistrate in consideration of the office which they hold. While we give the first place to moral goodness in whatever circumstances it may be found, it is only natural and right to acknowledge with thankfulness God's good gifts of mind or body, provided we are not led by them to condone or to think lightly of the moral defects by which they may be accompanied. We cannot love all alike, nor can we honour all alike, yet still honour and love are due to all who share the image of God (iii. 9).

We come now to the actual case of respect of persons condemned by St. James. Is it right to pay respect to wealth *qua* wealth? It may be right to respect it, in so far as it is the sign and result of honest skill and industry, or if it is used as a stewardship for the good of others; but where it has been accumulated by withholding his fair wages from the workman, and where it is used simply for the purpose of selfish luxury, St. James has no measure in his indignant denunciations (v. 1—6). On the whole we may say that, while he does not altogether deny to the rich a place in the Church, yet he agrees with his Master and with St. Paul in regarding the pursuit of money and the possession of wealth as greatly increasing the difficulty of entering the kingdom of heaven (ii. 6, 7, iv. 13—16). On the other hand a special blessing attaches to the poor.

The question here arises whether, if wealth is thus detrimental and poverty favourable to our highest interests, we should not take steps to diminish the one and increase the other. The writer of our Epistle had himself witnessed the experiment of socialism tried at Jerusalem in the first Pentecostal enthusiasm of the Church. The frequent subscriptions in aid of the Church at Jerusalem, to which St. Paul refers, have been regarded as an indication that the experiment proved a failure from an economical point of view. At all events it does not appear to have been continued for any length of time. Subsequently this view of the comparative advantages of poverty and wealth had great influence on the development of the Mediaeval Church : *privatus illis census erat brevis, commune magnum;* but this did not extend to the secular order of things. Perhaps it may have been reserved to our age, by legislative enactment, as well as by moral and religious suasion, at any rate to limit the two extremes. We cannot doubt that St. James would have approved of what has already been done by the state in England to ameliorate the condition of the poorer part of the community by means of factory bills, free education, free libraries, extended franchise, &c., nor that he would have sympathized with the efforts which are now being made to give the workman a larger share of the profits of labour, and ensure to honest industry a comfortable old age. And as regards the other extreme, it seems natural to assume that he would have approved of a more careful circumscription of the supposed rights of property and also of any measures, consistent with justice, which would tend to check the concentration of wealth in the hands of a few, such as a graduated scale in the income-tax and the death duties. Outside of the action of the state there will still remain plenty of scope for the influence of the Church in drawing classes together, making them realize more the tie of brotherhood, discountenancing wasteful self-indulgence, not less in the smoking and betting and drinking of the poor than in the luxurious living of the rich, compelling all to recognise their responsibility to God for the use of the talents He has entrusted to them, fostering such a tone of public feeling as would make it a disgrace for men to spend their money or energy merely on their own pleasures or interests, and would encourage them to vie with one another in the promotion of art and science and literature, in making the world happier and better and more beautiful than they found it, in a word, in the advancement of God's kingdom upon earth.

One word as to the kind of honour which St. James would have us pay to the poor. It is not of course that we are to flatter them, now that they have become the depositaries of power, with a view of gaining popularity and power ourselves. This would indeed be to act from the 'sinister motives' (*διαλογισμῶν πονηρῶν*) which

St. James ascribes to the flatterers of the rich in his day. Might does not make right now, any more than it did under Roman imperialism or mediaeval feudalism. The true way of honouring the masses, if we like to use that term, is first by taking for granted that they, like the classes above them, are largely made up of reasonable beings, who desire to learn the honest opinions of all who have taken the trouble to form opinions for themselves; secondly, by ourselves doing our best to understand their position, listening with respect to their opinions, and freely pointing out where we believe them to be mistaken; thirdly, by seeking to make them sharers in all the civilizing influences of our time, and as far as possible to raise them to the level of the more favoured classes; in other words, by extending as widely as possible the refinement and culture, the self-respect and self-control, implied in the old name of 'gentleman.' We may hope that in these and other ways much of the bitterness of poverty may be done away with, and that the upward path to competence may be opened to all who are capable of making use of it; but until human nature is entirely regenerated, the ascent of some from the lowest class is likely to be balanced by the descent of others from the upper classes. Nor is this in itself to be regretted, poverty and want being the reformatories provided by nature for the idle and vicious. In time past, it is true, these reformatories have too often acted as incitements to crime rather than to virtue, because the sufferers were left to suffer alone, without guidance for the present or hope for the future. The thought and effort which are now being applied to schemes for the improvement of the condition of the 'submerged tenth' will, we may believe, tend to bring out the good, and neutralize the evil of poverty, while at the same time providing a safe channel for the exercise of Christian charity.

It is however important to remember that the Jewish law, forbidding respect of persons, was directed not less against the partiality which favours the poor, than against that which favours the rich. The caution against the former, which we find in Lev. xix. 15, 'thou shalt not respect the person of the poor,' is certainly as much needed now as it ever was.

Solidarity of Duty and the Law of Liberty.

'He who keeps the law as a whole and fails in one point only is guilty of all.' Such a principle would evidently cause great injustice, if applied in the administration of human law. A child who steals a carrot is not thereby guilty of forgery and murder. If the divine law consisted of rules relating to outward action only, as human law does, the same would be true of it also; but the perfect law of God, as St. James tells us in i. 25 and ii. 12, is a law of liberty. It is fulfilled only when we freely choose what God commands, when His will becomes our will, when we love Him because He loved us; when we love our neighbours as ourselves, because they are children of the same Father, redeemed by the same Saviour, partakers of the same

Spirit with ourselves. If then we systematically neglect any one commandment of God, say, the duty of honouring our parents, it will not atone for this, though we should be most scrupulous in all other respects; the one wilful neglect proves that we were not actuated by a right motive in our obedience to the other commandments: it shows that we were not led by the Spirit of God.

In the 3rd chapter we read 'in many things we all offend' the word (πταίομεν) being the same as that used here, where it is said, that 'he who offends in one point is guilty of all.' How then are any to be saved? This is explained in v. 13 'mercy triumpheth over judgment,' which follows closely on the words 'So speak and so act, as being about to be tried by the law of liberty.' The law of liberty is at once more exacting and more merciful than the law of bondage. It is the former, because it is not satisfied with the outward act: it is the latter, because, where there is real love of good, and real desire and effort to do right, God accepts the will for the deed. To bear in mind therefore that we shall be judged by the law of liberty tends to produce in us a deeper conviction of sin, at the same time that it frees us from anxiety, because we believe that God Himself desires that we may be perfect as He is perfect, and that He will accomplish this perfection in us by the presence of His Holy Spirit in our hearts, if we are willing to receive it.

II. 14—26. Paraphrase.

We have seen that hearing is useless without doing, that the doing which is confined to external forms of worship is equally useless, since the only service which pleases God is that of practical kindness and unselfishness. We have seen further that our faith is of no value if it does not keep us from respect of persons and if it does not manifest itself in love. This may be summed up by saying that faith without works, profession without practice, is worthless, as worthless as a mere verbal philanthropy. Even if such a faith were real, it could not prove its existence; and the uselessness of a bare faith is shown by the fact that even the devils possess such faith. The typical examples of faith given in the Old Testament prove that the faith which justifies must be an active principle. The function of faith is to inspire action, and it is itself perfected by action. An inactive faith is the mere corpse of religion. [See especially notes on vv, 14. 23, 26.]

Faith.

St. James has already told us that trials are sent to test and confirm our faith (i. 3), that without faith prayer is of no avail (i. 6, cf. v. 15, 16), that Christianity consists in faith in the Lord Jesus Christ

(ii. 1), that those who are rich in faith are heirs of the promised kingdom (ii. 5). By this faith he means trust in the loving will of God revealed to us in Christ, and the reception of His word into our souls, as seed into a good soil (i. 17, 18, 21). If we retain our trust in God's all-wise, just and loving Providence, in spite of the trials which He permits, the habit of endurance is strengthened in us and thus we grow up to the full stature of Christian manhood (1. 4). The opposite to faith is worldliness: our faith is shown to be tainted with worldliness if we favour the rich above the poor (i. 27, ii. 2—4). In the verses which we have now to deal with, faith appears in a different light. It is no longer the essence of Christianity, but a mere dead semblance, or empty profession of faith. For the employment of the same word πίστις to denote the two kinds of faith, we may compare the different meanings of πειρασμός and πειράζεσθαι in i. 2, and 13, the former used of a tempting for good, the latter of a tempting for evil; the use of σοφία to express both a heavenly and an earthly wisdom in iii. 15, 17, 1 Cor. i. 17–ii. 16 (and so of πανουργία in Sir. xxi. 12; also the use of ἔρις in Hesiod (*Op.* 11—30) for the emulation which is good, and the quarrelsomeness which is hurtful). This use of the same name for different things is natural enough in the rough and ready speech of men little accustomed to metaphysical analysis or subtle refinements of language, and would be intentionally adopted by those who had to address such hearers. The change of meaning is however prepared for here by the use of the word λέγῃ in ver. 14: not faith in itself, but the profession of faith is declared to be of no avail. The thought of faith is apparently suggested by the statement in ver. 13 that 'love (compassion) is the only thing which can triumph over judgment,' judgment being without mercy to him who has shown no mercy. To this an objection is supposed to be made by the worldly-minded Christian of ver. 1: 'Will not faith also triumph against judgment? What is the good of being an orthodox believer, if I am no better off than a Samaritan or a Gentile or an unbelieving Jew?' St. James replies by the paarble of the talking philanthropist. Just as a profession of philanthropy unaccompanied by kind actions is of no good to the needy, so a profession of faith unaccompanied by righteous actions is of no good to ourselves; both are alike a mere hypocrisy in the sight of God. Such profession is indeed the dead carcase of genuine religion. But in the midst of this diatribe against a dead faith, St. James gives some further particulars of a true faith, such as Abraham's (ver. 22): 'faith cooperated with his works and by works was faith made perfect'; words which are in close agreement with St. Paul's teaching as to 'faith which worketh by love,' and the 'fruits of the Spirit.'

If St. James were not so fully justified by the subsequent history of the Church, we might be inclined to wonder at the scathing words in which he expresses his contempt for those who place their confidence in the orthodoxy of their creed. But it may be questioned whether any form of fetishism has been quite so mischievous, so destructive to all kindly feeling as well as to moral and spiritual and intellectual progress, as the fetish of orthodoxy, i.e. the idea that the assent to a given form of words is both necessary to, and sufficient for salvation, and that heterodoxy is the worst of sins.

We are not to suppose however that St. James would in these words discourage the wish to arrive at a clear intellectual view in religion. The 'word which is able to save the soul' is itself addressed in the first instance to the understanding, though it must penetrate the whole nature before its work can be accomplished. It no less belongs to man, as a rational being to *think clearly*, than it belongs to him, as a moral being, to *act rightly*. 'I will pray with the spirit' says St. Paul, 'but I will pray with the understanding also': and St. Peter, or whoever is the author of the second Epistle which goes under his name, warns us of the danger arising from the misunderstanding of the written word, where he speaks of the hard things contained in St. Paul's epistles, 'which they that are unlearned and ignorant wrest, as they do also the other Scriptures, to their own destruction.' To grasp fully the meaning of each separate statement, as intended by the writer and understood by the original readers, will often tax our powers to the utmost; and we have besides to consider how far each separate statement is to be qualified or limited or balanced by other statements, whether in the same book or in the other Scriptures; and again how far changed circumstances, changed modes of thought and expression, necessitate a change in the form of the doctrine taught;—before we can be sure of what is the actual teaching of the Spirit to the Church in our own day. It is from neglecting these things, from the misunderstanding of forms of speech, or from fixing the mind exclusively on one side of Christian teaching, that erroneous views as to the Sacraments and as to Predestination have become so widely prevalent. It was therefore only natural and right that the Catholic Church should seek to guard against the misinterpretation of revealed truth, first, by drawing up short summaries of the essentials of belief for the use of all her members, and secondly by careful exposition of the teaching of the Bible on particular doctrines, made by the most learned of her sons. St. James is not of course to be regarded as objecting to such formularies or treatises. It is not the creed he finds fault with, but the belief that a man is saved by the correctness of his creed.

Every extreme in religion is sure to give rise to the opposite extreme. If therefore one party exaggerate the importance of a correct statement of Christian truth, and make this correctness consist in a repetition of phrases devised by the Fathers of the fourth or of some later century, rather than in the actual teaching of Christ and his Apostles; if they restrict the freedom of thought by unwarrantable assertions that the Church has already arrived at absolute truth, and that the duty of reason is not to question, but simply to bow down in adoration of a mystery; it was to be expected that another party would spring up, who would not only deny that the Church had any right to put out an authoritative statement of doctrine, but would also deny the possibility of arriving at any conclusion whatever in matters of theology, and even that there was any connexion between doctrine and conduct. Such persons might be disposed to claim the authority of St. James on their side, when he speaks of the profession of a right faith being consistent with devilish wickedness. Nor can we evade this by assuming that the profession is merely verbal. In the supposed case there is real belief, a belief, be it observed, which has a real effect on the believer; but the effect is not that which St. James' opponents claimed for their orthodox faith; not an assurance of a salvation, but the extremity of terror. There can, however, be no doubt of what St. James himself really held in regard to the connexion between thought and action. He spoke in i. 19 of the seminal power of the divine Word received into the mind: he is equally explicit below as to the evil influence of words uttered at the instigation of a wisdom which is earthly, sensual and devilish (iii. 6, 15). But, as is explained in the Parable of the Sower, there are many things which may hinder the word, or the thought, or the doctrine, from producing its natural effect. It may lie altogether on the outside of the mind; it may make a mere momentary impression; it may form strange combination with the already existing growths; as, for instance, the thought of One All-powerful and All-holy, meeting with a will which is obstinately set on evil, is naturally productive of terror. It is only where it finds a good soil, clear of weeds, that the full virtue of the Word is manifested. We need not however assume that the Word is necessarily wasted, where its effect is not immediately perceptible. The use of short formularies, texts or hymns committed to memory, is to store up for the future truths to which the heart may be inaccessible at the moment.

I have in the introduction (pp. lxxxvii. foll) touched on the relation which St. Paul's teaching on the subject of faith bears to that of St. James. We saw there that there was substantial agreement between them, notwithstanding the verbal contradictions which may be found in their Epistles. Both agree that 'in many things we offend all,' that man is saved not by his own merits, but by the goodness and mercy of God. What differences there are may be explained partly by the difference of the errors which they controvert. St. Paul is arguing against a dependence on the scrupulous performance of the Jewish law (what he calls the *ἔργα νόμου*), and against the denial of salvation to the Gentiles unless they conformed in all points to that law. St. James is arguing against a dependence upon Jewish orthodoxy, irrespective of moral conduct (what St. Paul might call *ἔργα πίστεως* or 'faith working by love'). But partly the difference is due to the difference in the character and development of the two men. To the one, whose spiritual experience had been broken by a violent shock, and whose special office it was to open the kingdom of heaven to the Gentiles, the Gospel is the antithesis of the Law; to the other, who had been brought up with Jesus, who had known his disciples from the first, and whose special office it was to make the final offer of salvation to his own countrymen, the Gospel was the consummation of the Law. Again, the one with his deeply speculative nature loves to fix his gaze on the Divine factor in man's salvation, the other with his strong practical bent directs his attention mainly to the human factor;

though each fully allows and even asserts the doctrine complementary to that which may be called peculiarly his own.

III. 1—12. Paraphrase.

Do not be eager to assume the responsibilities of teachers. Hard as it is for man to avoid stumbling in action, it is harder still to avoid it in speech ; so that to guide the tongue aright may be regarded as a test of Christian maturity. As the movements of the horse or the ship are controlled by the little bit in the mouth or rudder in the stern, so the whole activity of man is directed by the use made of the tongue. Like the spark which sets the forest on fire, the tongue, by some little insignificant word, can boast of setting on fire the wheel of mortality, the whole round of this mortal life. In the microcosm of man's nature the tongue represents the unrighteous world, and is used by Satan as his organ. Man has learnt to tame the most savage and venomous of animals, but the tongue is untameable and never at rest, and its venom is the deadliest of all. It is as impossible to combine acceptable worship of God with imprecations on man, God's image, as it is impossible for a fountain to send forth sweet and bitter water at the same orifice, or a tree of one species to bear fruit of another species. (See especially notes on verses 8, 10.)

Use and Abuse of Speech.

The teacher here referred to is of course, in the first instance, the teacher in the congregation. It is the same warning as we read in i. 19 ; the same also is given by St. Paul in 1 Cor. xiv. 26—40. From the latter passage we learn that the Christian assemblies were often scenes of great confusion, in which a number of persons, women as well as men, were trying to make themselves heard at the same time, one with a psalm, one with a revelation, one with a teaching, and so on. St. Paul insists that those who prophesy, or speak with unknown tongues, should speak by two or at the most by three (with which we may compare the μὴ πολλοί of St. James), and that *by course*, so that all things may be done decently and in order. It does not seem that there was any distinct order of teachers : each member of the congregation was at liberty to speak as he was moved by the Holy Spirit, in accordance with the prophecy of Joel, quoted by St. Peter on the day of Pentecost. But even the exercise of the gifts of the Spirit was to be kept under control ; the spirits of the prophets were subject to the prophets : there was to be nothing orgiastic in the Christian service. If there was anything of mere animal excitement, of pushing, or display, or want of consideration for others, this was a sign that the speaker was not exclusively influenced by the Spirit of God (vv. 14, 15). The dangers arising from the over-freedom of the youthful Church have long ago been effectually guarded against in the Church of England by the denial of the right of speech to any but the clergy. But it may perhaps be questioned whether St. James would have consented to purchase immunity from the disorder of which he complains, by investing one of the teachers, not selected for that particular post, as being specially qualified for it, either by the congregation, or by the Apostles, or by the Church at large, but merely nominated by some wealthy person, perhaps one who was an entire stranger to the congregation, and who had never given proof of his qualifications to exercise such an important trust,—whether, I say, St. James would have approved of investing a teacher, so chosen, with exclusive authority over the ritual and the teaching of the congregation, and would further have thought it expedient to enable him, however incompetent or unsuited for the particular post, to disregard the wishes and feelings alike of his ecclesiastical superiors and of the people committed to his charge, by ensuring to him a practically irremovable tenure. And yet, after all our present system does not make St. James' caution inapplicable. We may silence the laity, and still leave too many teachers; since it does not follow that, because a man is ordained and has the charge of a parish, he must therefore be able to preach. A man may be an excellent parish priest without having the qualifications of a prophet and teacher.

We must not, however, suppose that the caution is limited to preaching. It applies to all who set themselves up as instructors of others, whether as schoolmasters, lecturers, politicians, journalists, critics, writers of whatsoever kind, who make themselves responsible, not only for their own actions, but for the seed they sow in the minds of others. As there never was a time when people pressed more eagerly into these professions, so there never was a time when it behoved each man more seriously to ask himself, what kind of vocation he has for the work which he proposes to undertake, and whether he has conscientiously endeavoured to prepare himself for it. As regards education, perhaps the time has now come when it may be possible to require a certificate, both of adequate knowledge and of ability to teach, from others besides the teachers in our elementary schools.

On a first reading, there is to a western mind something odd and exaggerated in St. James' remarks as to the Tongue. The tongue is of course merely the innocent instrument employed by the free will of man. The rhetorical figure by which it stands for the abuse of the faculty of speech, and of which examples have been given in the note, need not however imply a want of earnestness in the speaker, any more than Cranmer's apostrophe to 'this unworthy hand.' In some cases there can be no doubt that temptation comes from 'the pleasures encamped in our members' (below iv. 1). There would be nothing inappropriate, for instance, in ascribing to the palate the evils which arise from gluttony. But there is no physical pleasure in the actual movement of the tongue, and but little in hearing ourselves talk. The pleasures and temptations connected with the use of the tongue as an organ of speech, are entirely psychological; but they constitute an easily recognized department of man's activity, which St. James tickets by this name; and besides, like the pleasures of the palate, they seem to have a separate life of their own, independent of our will, so that we often find it the hardest thing in the world to hold our tongue (ver. 8). The next point which we might be disposed to question is the statement that one who controls the tongue is a perfect man; that, as the movement of the horse is governed by the bit, so the activity of man is governed by his use of the tongue. Perhaps we may find this easier to understand if we go back to the analysis of temptation given in i. 14. Man's own lust is the cause of sin. The angry or impure or impious thought goes on to express itself, first in words, and then in action. Under the Old Dispensation it was wrong action, which was forbidden by the Ten Commandments. St. James, like his Master, bids us stop the evil current at an earlier point. Not only he that kills is in danger of the judgment, but he that says 'Raca' or 'Thou fool.' Evil is to be met and conquered in its initial stage of thought, before the bitter or malicious feeling has had time to vent itself in words. It may be objected that there are cases in which some such vent is needed for the raging passion within, which only becomes more dangerous by the endeavour to stifle it, just as grief when it is unable to find relief in tears. Allowing this to be the case, it need not, in the first place, diminish the value of the general rule that we should accustom ourselves to check the evil impulse in the bud; and, secondly, we have to remember that, in St. James' view, prayer is the natural vent for all the agitations of a Christian (below v. 15). Perhaps however we may conclude from the language used here and above (i 19) that St. James was addressing people more prone than the English to give expression to their feelings in words, people of more fiery and less phlegmatic temper.

We are not of course to suppose that St. James denies or ignores the right uses of the tongue. The very importance he attaches to hearing proves the value he puts on the right kind of speaking, and the description he gives just below of the qualifications of the truly wise teacher is worthy to be compared with St. Paul's panegyric on Charity.

III. 13—18. Paraphrase.

If a man claims to be wise, let him prove his wisdom by his conduct. True wisdom shows itself in modesty, recognizing the immensity of the universe and the narrow limits of man's capacity, and bowing in reverence to God who made both man and the universe. The mixing up of personal feelings, envy, jealousy, ambition and party spirit, with the attempt to teach others, proves the absence of true wisdom. Such a teacher sets up self above truth: his wisdom ceases to be a gift from God: it is charged with other elements derived from the flesh, the world and the devil. It is materialistic, irreligious, hating God and goodness, and is attended by unrest, disquietude and every kind of evil. On the other hand the wisdom which comes from God is first of all pure: it has gained the victory over all the lower impulses of our nature: it is at peace with itself, with God and with man: it is gentle, reasonable, compassionate, single-minded, free from dissimulation, abounding in good fruits. It is by the peaceful activity of such lovers of peace that the seed, which will spring up into a harvest of righteousness, is sown in the hearts of men.

Wisdom.

St. James, following the books of Job and of Proverbs and the sapiential books of the Apocrypha, has already spoken of wisdom as the gift of God, which we are to seek by earnest prayer, and which will enable the Christian to understand the purpose of the trials to which he is exposed, and to make the right use of them (i. 3). In the O. T. the word has a very wide sense, including both science and literature (1 Kings iv. 29—34, Prov. i. 6), but laying most stress on practical wisdom, of which the foundation is said to be the fear of the Lord. Here it is introduced as a sequel to the instructions to teachers, especially religious teachers, and is defined by the moral qualifications which go to the making of a good teacher or student. Freedom from personal objects, single-minded devotion to the pursuit of truth, simplicity, modesty—these qualities are essential to students in whatever department of thought. Gentleness and sympathy, appreciation for the work of others—these qualities are essential to a persuasive teacher. So much we shall all admit; but it may be asked, Is wisdom nothing more than this to St. James? If we test his description of wisdom by applying it to the case of men who are universally esteemed wise, a Thucydides, a Plato, a Shakespeare; or to an Athanasius, or a Pascal, or a Bishop Butler; even to St. Paul or St. John, do we find that it supplies us with anything like an exhaustive analysis of what we know as wisdom in them? It evidently takes no account of the original powers of the mind, or of the strictly intellectual training needed for the full development of those powers. It is as suited to the ordinary Sunday School teacher as to the highest genius. So far, we may regard this exhortation of St. James as illustrating the Christian freedom from exclusiveness. The Gospel addresses itself to the Publican as well as to the Pharisee, to 'this people that knoweth not the law' as well as to the doctor and the scribe. Every one has some mental powers: wisdom consists in the right use of those powers, be they small or great. But there is no reason to suppose that St. James intended to give a complete exposition of his ideas on wisdom in this passage. He is simply dealing with the evils incident to the religious teaching of the time. There were in the Christian assemblies, as we learn from the Pastoral

Epistles and elsewhere, the counterparts of the Jewish rabbis, men fluent and positive and argumentative, who arrogated to themselves the name of wise. St. James says nothing as to the extent of their learning or knowledge; he is content to point out those particular characteristics of heavenly wisdom in which they were manifestly deficient. We cannot argue from this that he would have disapproved of elaborate disquisitions on theological questions such as we read in the Epistle to the Hebrews, or that he would have condemned the pursuit of learning or science for its own sake; but for the present his mind is fixed on practical issues.

IV. 1—17. Paraphrase.

The real source of our quarrelsomeness is the greediness with which each one grasps at pleasure for himself. We are envious, if we see others succeed where we have failed: and we are conscious that our whole life is a failure, as it always must be, when men either omit to pray, or pray only for worldly objects whereby to gratify their selfish impulses. But those who seek the world's favour can never obtain the favour of God. The two are absolutely incompatible. As the Scripture says, 'the Spirit which He has planted in us jealously longs for our love.' It is owing to this jealous affection that He resists the proud and gives grace to the humble. If we submissively accept His chastisement and return to Him, He will return to us, and the tempter, who offers the world to each of us, as he did to Christ, will flee from us also, when he finds we are determined to resist him. This we must do by renouncing all wicked actions and checking all evil thoughts, by learning to take a serious view of life, giving up our thoughtless mirth, practising self-denial and repentance, mourning over sin and humbling ourselves before God. If we thus turn from the world to God, He will raise us up and grant us a share in His kingdom.

Do not think lightly of ill-natured gossip. To speak against a brother or to condemn a brother is really to speak against and condemn the law of God, who has bidden us to love one another, and has given a special warning against this sin in the words, 'Judge not, that ye be not judged.' Shall we venture to set up our opinion against God's law, and claim to do that which has been distinctly forbidden by the sole Lawgiver and Judge? Our duty is not to criticize, but to obey.

A further characteristic of the spirit of worldliness is exhibited in our confident forming of plans for the future, without any thought of the precarious nature of earthly enjoyment, and of our dependence on God for the life of each successive day. All schemes for the future should be accompanied by the proviso 'if God will.'

Do you say that you know all this already? Remember then that it is the knowledge of good, combined with the choice of evil, which constitutes sin.

The World.

The term κόσμος is borrowed from the Greek philosophers who used it to express, first, the divine order apparent in the universe, and then the actual universe and especially the heavenly bodies. In the pantheistic system of the Stoics the κόσμος itself was deified. By the writers of the N. T. it is generally used in a dyslogistic sense. Thus St. James (i. 27) bids his readers 'keep themselves unspotted from the world.' In ii. 5 he speaks of those who were 'poor in the view of the world' as being 'rich in faith.' In iii. 6 he speaks of the tongue as the organ of the unrighteous world in our body. Here he says 'the friendship of the world is enmity with God.' St. John (1 Ep. ii. 15–17) analyses the influence of the world into the 'lust of the flesh, the lust of the eyes and the pride of life.' He tells us further (iii. 1) that the world knew not God and therefore knows not the sons of God; (iii. 13) that the world hateth you; (iv. 5) that false prophets are of the world and the world hears them; (v. 4) 'whatever is begotten of God overcometh the world: and this is the victory which overcometh the world, even our faith'; (v. 19) 'the whole world lieth in wickedness' (or 'in the evil one'); (iii. 17) 'the world's good' is used in the same sense as 'the unrighteous Mammon.' So in his Gospel we read (xiv. 17) that 'the world cannot receive the Comforter'; (xiv. 30) 'the prince of this world cometh and hath nothing in me'; (xv. 19) 'If ye were of the world the world would love its own, but I chose you out of the world, therefore the world hateth you.' So St. Paul 'the world through its wisdom knew not God' (1 Cor. i. 21); 'God chose the base things of the world' (1 Cor. i. 27); and St. Peter 'that ye may become partakers of the divine nature, having escaped the corruption which is in the world through lust' (2 Pet. i. 4). It is evident that in these passages the world is used not for the external universe, but for the world of men, that same world of which we are told that God so loved it, that he sent his Son that the world through him might be saved (Joh. iii. 16, 17); and yet St. James says that one who loves the world thereby becomes an enemy of God. How are we to explain this? What is the exact nature of that world which is so dear to God, and so dangerous to man?

In the simplest sense of the word, the world is each man's natural environment, that into which he enters at birth, and from which he departs in death. It is the immediate present, the seen and temporal, of which our senses bear witness, in contrast to the unseen and eternal; as St. John says 'the world passeth away and the lusts thereof, but he that doeth the will of God abideth for ever.' It supplies the objects of all our appetites, the stimulus to our activities, the occasions of our passions, the subject-matter of our thoughts. This environment is partly inanimate, so far as our senses, thoughts, and appetites are concerned, but far more largely human, in all that has to do with feelings, passions, desires. It is the appointed training-place of the immortal soul. But just as the inanimate world, which was intended to reveal the glory of the eternal Godhead, was itself deified through the folly of man; so the world of humanity, which was intended to be a further revelation of the inner character of God, engrosses our attention until we no longer hear the voice of God speaking in conscience, but take the custom of the world for our law, submit ourselves to its judgment, strive for its prizes, seek its approval,—in a word, worship the world as our God. In speaking of the world we must remember that it is not one, but multiform. Each man's world differs from that of every other man, depending partly on his surroundings and partly on the working of his own mind. The same surroundings may be to one man a channel of divine influence, to another the very embodiment of the worldly spirit. Where the mind of one sees or creates good in all around him, the mind of another may be conscious only of evil; and thus the same set of people may constitute a church to the one, a world to the other. In like manner there will be a broad distinction between man's world and woman's world, the world of youth and the world of age, the world of poverty and the world of wealth. Fashion, politics, religion,—the criminal, the school-boy, the working-man—all have their separate worlds; there is the world of the nun in her convent, of the hermit in his cell. Incalculable mischief has been caused by the imagination that the worldly spirit could be avoided by keeping out of some particular society which men chose to identify with the world. The world is in the heart of man. There may be endless differences in point of refinement between the various forms of the world; but in so far as they all tend to separate us from God and lower our standard of duty, the influence of all is alike baneful. He who makes it his chief aim to gain the favour of his world thereby becomes an enemy of God. And yet all the while each separate soul, included in the aggregate of worlds, is itself the object of God's love, though the worldly influence, which in the Bible often goes by the name of the world, is so hateful to God that, as we have seen, no man can love it without becoming His enemy.

St. James in the text tells us that the cause of quarrelling is our eagerness to get the world's good things, which are palpably limited in quantity, and often derive their chief value in our eyes from their difficulty of attainment. The fact of this limitation inevitably leaves many disappointed of their desire. But even the successful are not satisfied. No sooner is the coveted object attained, than the process of disillusion commences. There is a moment's delight at the victory over our rivals, and again the cloud of disappointment settles over us. We feel that, once more, happiness has eluded our grasp, and we are filled with envy and jealousy of those whom we fancy to be in any respect more fortunate than ourselves, till in the end we find our nearest approach to happiness in striving to prevent or destroy the happiness of others. How is this to be remedied? The Stoics answered: 'By ceasing to desire.' The Christian answer is: 'By desiring to be and to do what God wills, and by desiring others' good rather than our own.'

The Divine Jealousy.

We are familiar with the Greek idea of Nemesis. Excessive prosperity on the part of man even apart from evil-doing, as in the well-known story of the Ring of Polycrates, portended utter ruin, because it provoked the divine jealousy of human happiness. We are familiar also with the ascription of jealousy to the God of the Jews, visiting the iniquity of the fathers upon the children unto the third and fourth generation. This seems to us to belong to the same stage of thought as the *lex talionis* 'an eye for an eye and a tooth for a tooth,' or as the expulsion of Adam out of Eden for fear that he might put forth his hand and eat of the tree of life; or again as the dispersion of mankind over the face of the earth, for fear that they might make themselves too strong by building the tower of Babel. Such conceptions seem to us natural to the anthropomorphism of a rude people and period, when even Moses could urge as a reason for sparing the Israelites the fear that the Egyptians might say, 'because the Lord was not able to bring them into the land which he promised them, he hath brought them out to slay them in the wilderness.' But under the New Dispensation we are perhaps surprised that it should still be possible to make use of a figure which seems derogatory to the Divine Perfection. We think jealousy a defect in human love; how much more in Divine! The phrase itself is no doubt due to the writer's Hebraic tone of thought and speech; but it is at the same time a most forcible expression of a most important truth; and the addition 'He giveth more grace' removes from it all that is unamiable in the idea of jealousy. It is really a parable in which the soul is represented as standing between rival wooers, God and the world. The strongest human passion is boldly taken to represent the Divine longing for the entire possession of the human heart, i.e. for the expulsion of every thought and feeling which interferes with the recovery of the Divine image in man and the attainment of the perfect ideal of humanity. We blame human jealousy, because it is so largely made up of a selfish desire for our own pleasure and honour; so liable to turn into hatred of the object of our passion. The Divine jealousy, as depicted in the N. T., desires nothing but the best good of the beloved object, and hates nothing but that which would injure and degrade it. How is this jealousy concerned in 'resisting the proud, and giving grace to the humble'? Pride here consists in man's claim to be independent of God, to do what he likes and gratify all his natural impulses irrespective of God's will. It is the choice of the temporal in preference to the eternal, of the world in preference to God. This pride is resisted, as was shown in the previous Comment, by the continual failure to obtain the happiness sought for. The Divine jealousy having ordained that the world shall never give satisfaction, he who seeks his happiness there cannot but feel himself continually thwarted in his ambitions, until at last he conceives himself to be the victim of some jealous and hostile power seated upon the throne of the universe. Yet 'He giveth more grace.' Underneath the dark suspicion which blots out heaven from our eyes we are dimly conscious of an appeal to feelings long lost sight of and all but extinct within us. In the Prodigal's heart there begins to arise a loathing, not only for the husks with which he has striven to satisfy the cravings of the immortal soul, but also a loathing for his own folly and sin, a longing for the home which he has forsaken, joined with the sense of his own unworthiness, which makes him fear lest he should have lost it for ever. To one thus humbled grace is given in full measure: the soul, which could never satisfy its thirst from earthly cisterns, finds never-failing supplies of happiness in that inner union with God which is typified by the well of water springing up unto everlasting life.

Accompaniments of Repentance.

Does St. James mean that God's grace and favour are to be won by fasting and self-discipline? Not so; God's loving favour is ours to receive, the moment we believe in it. He means 'be willing to give up what has till now seemed to be the chief interest of your life: give up the pursuit of honours and pleasures: no longer indulge in dreams of conquering your rivals and taking vengeance on your enemies: welcome what may seem the gloom of renunciation: examine yourself to see where you have gone wrong in the past: and set to work to atone, so far as may be, for any wrongs you have done to others. Listen for the voice of God in conscience, and do your duty, as in His sight and relying on His strength, with all the more energy in proportion to its irksomeness and difficulty.' The natural accompaniments of such feelings and resolutions amongst the Jews were weeping and fasting, the rending of clothes and the casting of dust on the head. If these things help the inward change, good: if they are its natural accompaniments, good also: but, if they are used as substitutes for the inner change, or as an anodyne to quiet the conscience and pave the way for the resumption of the former life, then they are nothing better than the vain religion (*θρησκεία μάταιος*) already condemned by St. James.

Judging.

Are we then never to find fault with others? It may be an essential part of our duty, as in the case of a magistrate, appointed for the very purpose of deciding whether the accused is guilty or not guilty; of a parent, who has to train up his children to distinguish between right and wrong; and so in every case where instruction or criticism is required. What St. James means is that we are not to indulge in the habit of fault-finding from the mere love of it, where duty does not call us to it, for the sake of showing off our acuteness and pulling down others by way of exalting ourselves. Even where it is our duty to judge, it should be done under a sense of responsibility, with the consciousness of our own liability to go wrong and a genuine desire for the improvement, not the humiliation, of the person blamed; and further our judgment should be determined by the objective standard of right, not by our private tastes or likings; otherwise we set up ourselves above the law and the lawgiver. There is no fault which brings about its own punishment more certainly than the love of fault-finding. While we become quick to see the mote in a brother's eye, the beam is still growing in our own. The habit of negative criticism is destructive to the creative faculty and to much besides. All human action is more or less blundering; if we choose to concentrate our attention on the blunders, and shut our eyes to the honest aim and the real good effected in spite of the blunders, we lose the stimulus of admiration and emulation; thus deadening within us all that makes life worth living, if it be true, as the poet teaches, that 'we live by admiration, hope, and love.'

Making Plans.

Are we then to live at hap-hazard? not to use our best endeavours to foresee the future and shape our actions in accordance with probabilities? This would be to give up one main use of reason. When our Lord said 'take no thought (R.V. 'be not anxious') for the morrow, for the morrow shall take thought for the things of itself' (Matt. vi. 34), he did not mean to forbid serious consideration of the course to be adopted under given circumstances. He did not mean that it was wrong to make engagements beforehand and to take steps to keep our engagements; that it was wrong for a man to deliberate carefully before choosing a profession or accepting a post which might be offered him; or again, that it was wrong for a statesman to consider carefully what measures he should bring forward in Parliament. His meaning was that we should not worry ourselves with the anticipation of evil: we should make all due preparation for it, and then await it calmly in reliance upon God. As Christ forbade undue anxiety, so St. James here forbids undue confidence. We should bear in mind that we cannot foresee the issues of things; so that what we think desirable now, may turn out hereafter to have been undesirable; and again that the best-laid plans are liable to fail; so that, however good the object, still it may be unattainable by us; that we should therefore not stake our life, as it were, on a single throw of the dice, but join with all our plans for the future the reservation 'if God will,' and the aspiration 'Thy will be done.' Some people, perhaps thinking of Christ's promise of divine assistance to those who should be brought before synagogues and magistrates for his sake (Matt. x. 18), seem to have an idea that forethought and planning are in themselves opposed to faith, and that, in religious matters especially, there is something approaching to impiety in making preparations for the future. It is enough to say in answer to this, that while we are no doubt justified in believing that Christ's grace will be sufficient for us in whatever difficulties, still it is our duty to use all our powers, especially our nobler powers, in God's service; that the powers of imagination, hope, and reason, were given to us especially as guides to action; and that no great and permanent work has ever been effected in which these powers were not fully exercised.

It is probably this passage which has given rise to the common use of the letters D.V., as to which see the note. It is a comparatively trivial example of what may be called the objectification of ideas, which in greater matters has been productive of so much evil in regard to religion. To have acquired the habit of submission and resignation to the Divine Will is all-important for man: but the use of the symbol is a matter of indifference. Where it is used in one place and omitted in another, it would rather seem to imply that, when omitted in writing, it was not present in the mind.

V. 1—11. Paraphrase.

Another form of worldliness is the love of wealth, whether stored by the miser, or squandered by the voluptuary. The decay which threatens unused wealth is itself symbolical of the destruction awaiting its selfish possessor. The cry of the labourer, from whom his just wages are withheld, is not unheard in heaven. As for the voluptuary who, in this final crisis of his country's fortunes, thinks of nothing but personal gratification, he can only be compared to a sheep fattened for slaughter. By the help of an unjust law he may get rid of the unresisting righteous, whose life is a continual witness against him; but let him remember that the Lord is coming to judgment. Let the brethren, on their side, wait patiently and strengthen their hearts to endure for the short period which has still to elapse before the coming of the Lord. Let them take a lesson from the husbandmen who patiently wait for the rains to mature the fruits of the earth, and from the prophets of old who spoke and suffered in the name of the Lord. The story of Job is a striking example of the blessing which awaits patient endurance. It shows us that, however severe may be the trial to which the believer is exposed, God's mercy and lovingkindness will be made manifest in the end. The brethren, however, must remember that the Lord comes not only to take vengeance on His enemies but to judge His people; and must beware of a murmuring, unforgiving spirit.

Sternness of St. James.

What are we to say to the stern denunciation of this passage? Is it not inconsistent with the warning against judging and evil-speaking, given in iv. 11? At any rate it is not inconsistent with the denunciation of the Pharisees by John the Baptist and by our Lord. What would be presumption in an ordinary Christian may be part of the commission of a prophet. It was not presumption in Jonah to declare the approaching downfall of Nineveh: the presumption came in where he expostulated with God for refusing to make good his threats, when they had produced the desired effect. The prophetic announcement of impending evil is not inconsistent with the tenderest sympathy, as is shown by our Lord's lamentation over Jerusalem. Here we can see ample reason for the strongest warning. The rich represented the pride of the world. Their success, their triumphant career of selfish oppression, while it left little hope of the possibility of their own repentance, caused despair in the hearts of the brethren whom they oppressed. It was the truest kindness on the part of the prophet to set before both the fact of imminent judgment revealed to him by the Spirit. To the rich it was the final invitation, the hand-writing on the wall, which, if instantly accepted, might still enable them to seek a share in the humiliation of a Christian (i. 10); to the poor it was the encouragement needed to prevent their falling away. Nor is this prophetic office yet extinct in the Church of Christ. Wherever sin is rampant, wherever oppression and cruelty prevail, where the denunciation of the evil-doer is a dangerous and unpopular service, there the heart of the prophet will still burn within him, till at the last he speaks with his tongue.

V. 12—20. Paraphrase.

Do not make use of oaths of any kind, lest you fall into condemnation. Let all your feelings, whether of joy or sorrow, be controlled and sanctified by laying them before God. In case of sickness send to the elders, and let them pray and anoint the sick person, and the Lord will answer the prayer of faith, and, if his sickness is the consequence of past sin, it shall be forgiven. Confess your offences therefore to one another, and pray for one another, that you may be healed. The story of Elijah on Mt. Carmel shows how great is the power of a good man's prayer prompted by the Spirit of God. If a brother falls into sin, you know that he who brings him back into the right way will be the means both of saving a soul and of hiding a multitude of sins.

Swearing.

From the form of the prohibition, we might suppose that St. James took the same view of the subject as St. Augustine, quoted in the note, and forbade swearing, not so much because it was wrong in itself, as because it was likely to lead to wrong, and therefore to condemnation. He could not have said of murder 'Do not kill lest you fall under condemnation.' At any rate by giving his warning in this form he made it easier for the Jews to accept it. Whatever their practice was, they would certainly allow that there was much careless and irreverent swearing, and that this could not but be displeasing to God. St. James is, however, quoting Christ's own words, and it is therefore probable that he means 'Whatever form of oath you use, it will come under the prohibition of Christ.' Are we to understand from this that every kind of swearing is absolutely forbidden, that the Quakers, for instance, were right in refusing to take an oath in a court of justice? This is not what we should gather from the conduct of St. Paul and of Christ Himself. The former calls God to witness that he is speaking the truth in more than one passage (2 Cor. i. 23, xi. 31, Gal. i. 20, etc.), and our Lord took the oath proposed to Him in the words of the High Priest 'I adjure thee by the living God.' So the angel in the Apocalypse is represented as swearing 'by Him that liveth for ever and ever.' The same rule of interpretation must be applied here as in the case of the other precepts of the Sermon on the Mount. They supply an ideal standard, a goal to be aimed at, but not a code of law to be immediately put into execution, regardless of existing circumstances, and of the manner in which their exact observance would affect our carrying out the two great commandments on which hang all the law and the prophets. Take for instance the precept to turn the other cheek: if this is tried by the principle that we should do to others as we would wish them to do to us, it is evident that the last thing which a sane man could wish for himself or for one whom he loved would be that he should be allowed to strike and insult others with impunity. We have to disregard the letter, in order to keep the spirit of the precept; which is, that a Christian should never act from mere vindictiveness. The law of love requires us to act for the best interest of the offender, i.e. to act in such a way as to induce him to avoid such faults in future. It is only where there is sufficient generosity of character to make a man ashamed of striking one who offers no resistance, that non-resistance becomes the fitting course for a Christian, the right way of obeying the law 'Thou shalt love thy neighbour as thyself.' Yet in proportion as a society becomes Christianized, it becomes more and more possible to practice non-resistance without transgressing the higher law of love, which bids us always act for the best interest of our neighbour. So with swearing: the right state in a Christian community is that all should feel so strongly the obligation of truth, that there should be no occasion for further sanction beyond the simple 'yes' and 'no.' Wherever there is need of more 'it comes of evil.' But often the standard of truthfulness is so low, that it is necessary to appeal to the All-seeing Witness in order to make the affirmant realize what is his duty in respect of the truth. And thus swearing becomes allowable, just as war is allowable in the present imperfect state of things; yet the aim of the Christian should be, as far as possible, to limit the use both of oaths and of war, so as ultimately to get rid of them altogether. See an excellent article, in the *Cont. Rev.* vol. 49, pp. 1–17, by the late Archbishop Magee, on the substitution of a declaration for an oath in admitting members of Parliament. Unhappily in this, as in some other matters, the professed advocates of religion have often taken a lower view than its professed opponents. The earnestness of St. James in this prohibition is probably to be explained by the constant breach of the third commandment caused by the Jewish habit of swearing.

Healing of the Sick by Anointing with Oil and by Prayer.

There can be little doubt that St. James is here describing a miraculous cure following the prayer of faith. To encourage the elders to obey his injunctions, he first insists on the power of prayer, when inspired by the Divine Spirit, and then refers to an example of this power in the person of Elijah, a man, as he reminds them, of like weakness with ourselves. A difficulty arises here: if every sick person could be miraculously healed, how is it that St. Paul did not miraculously heal Timothy and others (1 Tim. v. 23, 2 Tim. iv. 20)? Why was not his own thorn in the flesh removed? We hear occasionally of miraculous cures, but they are plainly exceptional. May not the explanation lie in the word ἐνεργουμένη (ver. 17)? When a miracle was to be wrought the power of the Spirit made itself felt in the prayer which preceded. Elijah himself could not work a miracle at will. He too must wait, like Samson, till the Spirit of the Lord came upon him. One reason why the elders, rather than others, were to be called in, may have been that they were better able to judge what was the will of the Spirit. From v. 16, however, it would appear that the office of prayer and anointing and receiving confessions was not confined to them. It has been already pointed out (pp. cxxiii. foll., clxxvi.) that the assumption here made by St. James, that the anointing of the sick would be attended by a miraculous cure, if performed in the spirit of prayer, is a mark of the very early date of the Epistle.

Are we to consider that the scope of this injunction, which is evidently temporary in form, is limited to the age in which it was written, or is it in any way applicable to our own time? The prayers of the congregation are still requested for the sick in the public services of the Church of England; and to offer such prayers is a natural, we might say, an inevitable outcome of Christian friendship. There are some who disbelieve in anything beyond a subjective answer to prayer. Yet even they must allow that a subjective action on the imagination may produce an objective change in the bodily condition, as has been attested in many cases of faith-healing, both among Protestants and Roman Catholics. But the teaching of St. James and of the writers of the N.T. in genera goes much further than this. Men are to cast every care upon God knowing that He careth for us. If there is a drought, men pray for rain; if there is a bodily infirmity, they pray for its removal; if there is danger or difficulty impending, the example of Christ Himself shows that we are not wrong in asking that 'this cup may be taken away,' provided we add 'nevertheless, not my will, but Thine be done.' In these latter cases, however, we are told that prayer is absurd, or even impious, because it brings us into collision with the laws of nature: and certainly, when we are convinced that a certain sequence regularly follows a certain antecedent by natural law, or, as Christians would say, by God's ordinance,—in such a case it would be not only folly, but the extreme of presumption to ask that God's ordinance might be set aside for our convenience. The husbandman does not pray that the grain which he has sown one day may spring up into the golden crop of corn on the next day, or that it may come to maturity unaided by rain or sunshine. These things he knows to be impossibilities, and he does not ask for them, because he cannot deliberately desire them. But where a change for the better is not, so far as he knows, an impossibility, there he cannot help strongly wishing for the change; and in the mind of a Christian every wish becomes a prayer, because it is joined with the aspiration 'Thy will be done.' If meteorological science is ever so far advanced that the meteorologist can predict the weather with the same certainty as the astronomer predicts an eclipse, prayer for fine weather would become impossible; but wherever desire is possible, there prayer is possible and right. We do not even pray for the recovery of the sick, when the symptoms make it clear that God's will is otherwise: our prayer is then for a peaceful and painless departure.

As the request for the prayers of the Church, so the service for the Visitation of the Sick is founded upon this passage. The parish priest, being notified of the sickness, attends by the bedside, joins in prayer for the sick person, reminds him of his duty to make confession both of his sin to God and of his shortcomings towards other men, assures him of the Divine forgiveness promised to all repenting sinners, administers to him the Sacrament of the Body and Blood of Christ the ever-present Saviour, in whom he realizes his communion with all saints, not only those still on earth, but those who have crossed the dark river before him, and whom he hopes soon to rejoin on the other side.

The Church of Rome claims to keep closer to St. James' injunction by its use of Extreme Unction for the remission of sins and the spiritual comfort of the dying. It is one of the curious phenomena of our time that English Churchmen have been found to regret that our Bishops persist in withholding from the clergy the power to administer this sacrament of comfort[1]; as to which it has been shown in the Notes

[1] See J. H. Blunt's *Theological Dictionary*, p. 772, 'It may be believed, in accordance with the whole stream of Christian belief until recent times, that the spiritual blessing declared to attend the unction of the sick is still given by God: . . . but as modern English bishops do not bless oil for the purpose, this means of grace is at present withheld from their flocks.'

that, as far as we can judge, it was never contemplated by St. James, and that there is no evidence of its use during the first eight centuries by any except an obscure sect of Gnostics. There are others who, while allowing that the belief in spiritual benefit to be derived from Extreme Unction is a mere unauthorized fancy, are still inclined to wink at it, as a means of tranquillizing the mind and preserving it from terrors as unreal and as superstitious as the remedy. If a false theology has fastened on the mind the belief that God's mercy is limited to this life, and that after death He has no further compassion for the sinner who has not repented and believed while on earth, but is henceforth only the Judge and the Avenger, is it not allowable to drive out one error by another? The question is far-reaching, but no lover of truth can hesitate. Even at the last hour let the true Gospel sound in the ears of the dying penitent, still more of the dying saint, who is terrified by suspicions that he has not the right faith or the true conversion. He who has once grasped the idea that Christ is the propitiation for the sins of the whole world; that God's mercies are everlasting over all His creatures; that He will do for each after death exactly what perfect love and perfect wisdom dictate; that Eternal Justice and Eternal Holiness, no less than Eternal Love, are our guarantee against an eternity of evil, will have no need and no wish for a material anointing.

Confession of Sin.

The connexion between suffering and sin was universally believed in, and even exaggerated, when St. James wrote; as is evident from our Lord's words about the Galileans, whose blood Pilate mingled with the sacrifices, and also from the question of the disciples about the man who was born blind. St. Paul asserts that many were punished with sickness and even with death for irreverence in receiving the Eucharist. The Jewish proverb quoted in my note to the effect that 'a man could not recover from sickness till his sins were forgiven' is quite in accordance with our Lord's procedure in healing the sick of the palsy, where the words 'Son, thy sins are forgiven thee' preceded the command 'Rise up and walk'; and both enable us to understand why confession and forgiveness are introduced here in the instructions given for the healing of the sick.

There seems, however, to be a certain want of consecutiveness in the language of St. James. We should have expected the confession of sins to be mentioned before the forgiveness of sins, and even before the prayer for healing, since healing, as we have seen, was regarded as implying forgiveness, whereas is is brought in afterwards as a second thought, though connected with what precedes by the inferential particle *οὖν*. The emphatic *ἀλλήλοις* and *ἀλλήλων* of v. 16 are decisive against the Romish limitation of confession to the priest. Either the Elders mentioned in v. 14 have no special position distinguishing them from the other members of the Church, or, more probably, we are to suppose that the duty of visiting the sick is not confined to them, but falls on the brethren generally. Are we to understand that no one may hear the confession of others unless he at the same time confesses his sins to them? This would seem the most natural meaning of the Greek; but it evidently could not be always carried out. Children ought to confess their faults to father or mother, but it would in most cases be far from expedient that the former should in their turn hear the confession of the latter. On the other hand we can easily conceive cases in which mutual confession is most natural and desirable, since one party is seldom so entirely in the right, as to leave all the regrets and apologies to the other party. If however we are to think of confession here in connexion with healing, it must be the confession of sin against God which is intended: how would this suit the idea of mutual confession? We can understand that confession is made easier to the sinner, if another is ready to join in the expression of sorrow and repentance. We can understand too that an unsympathizing Pharisaic tone is likely to repel any confidences on the part of a penitent. But the idea of mutual confession does not seem altogether appropriate in the case of the sick man, and yet, if the word ἰαθῆτε is taken literally, we seem to be tied down to this case. If on the other hand we give it a metaphorical meaning, we may suppose that the precept is of general application, and that St. James is recommending the habit of mutual confession between friends. It cannot, I think, be doubted that in many respects such mutual confidences might be productive of great good. How much easier it would be to put up with hastiness or coldness on the part of a friend, if we knew that he was himself conscious of his faults and trying to amend them! What a relief it would be to one of a sensitive self-conscious nature to lay his anxieties before another of whose wisdom and sympathy he felt assured! Might it not tend to increase the feeling of Christian fellowship, if those who were exposed to the same difficulties, anxious to conquer the same weaknesses and to practise the same virtues, could break through their isolation and confirm themselves in their good resolutions by the knowledge that they were shared by others? Might it not help to diminish the miseries of life, and to change the course of thoughts which may be tending towards insanity or suicide, if there were more of outspoken sympathy in the world, if people were sure that they might trust their secret feelings to others without fear of being despised or laughed at or shrunk from? The Church of England has wisely refused to follow Rome in requiring regular confession to the priest; yet, where the parish priest is what he should be, wise with the heavenly wisdom described by St. James, none should be better fitted than he by position, training, and experience, to receive such confidences and give the needed comfort and counsel.[1]

On the whole of this section of the Epistle it may be worth while to quote Dr. Arnold's remarks[2]:—

[1] See *Homilies*, p. 479, Oxf. ed.

[2] *Fragment on the Church*, p. 44 foll.

'The object of the passage is to encourage the exercise of those mutual spiritual aids rendered by Christians to each other, which is one of the great objects and privileges of the institution of the Church. The body was to sympathize with its several members. If a man was in trouble, he was to pray; if in joy, to sing hymns: in neither case is the Apostle speaking of private prayer or private singing; but of those of the Christian congregation[1]: there every individual Christian could find the best relief for his sorrows, and the liveliest sympathy in his joy. St. Paul's command "Rejoice with them that do rejoice and weep with them that weep," applies to this same sympathy, which the prayers and hymns of the church services were a constant means of expressing. But if a man were sick and could not go to the congregation, still he was not to lose the benefit of his Christian communion with them; he might then ask them to come to him; and as the whole congregation could not thus be summoned, the elders were to go as its representatives, and their prayers were to take the place of the prayers of the whole church. Care, however, is taken to show that the virtue of their prayers arises not from their being priests, but from their being Christians, and standing in the place of the whole church. For these words immediately follow: "confess therefore to one another your sins, and pray for one another, that ye may be healed: there is much virtue in a just man's prayer, when it is offered earnestly." Now, this most divine system of a living Church, in which all were to aid each other, in which each man might open his heart to his neighbour and receive the help of his prayers, and in which each man's earnest prayer, offered in Christ's name, had so high a promise of blessing annexed to it, has been almost[2] destroyed by that notion of a priesthood, which claiming that men should confess their sins to the clergy, not as to their brethren, but as to God's vicegerents, and confining the promised blessing to the prayers of the clergy as priests, not as Christians, nor as the representives of the whole church, has changed the sympathy of a Christian society into the dominion of a priesthood and the mingled carelessness and superstition of a laity.

'St. John's language agrees with that of St. James: "If any man see his brother sinning a sin which is not unto death, he shall pray, and Christ shall give him life, for those who are not sinning unto death. There is a sin unto death;—it is not for that that I am bidding him to pray." Here the very same blessing which St. James speaks of as following the elders' prayers is said by St. John to follow the prayer of any Christian, a clear proof that the elders were sent for as representatives of the Church, and not as if their prayers possessed a peculiar virtue, because they stood as priests between God and the people.'

[1] I cannot agree with Arnold in confining the exhortation to congregational singing or prayer.

[2] Wrongly printed 'most' in the original. Lond. 1845.

Converting the Sinner.

Is this a new case, or another aspect of the case of the sick man? If the latter, it seems to imply strange sloth and lukewarmness on the part of the Elders, that they should stand in need of exhortation to the performance of a duty, which would not have seemed to be particularly arduous or irksome. The previous verses insist on their power to heal the disease and procure forgiveness by their prayers: v. 20 speaks of the reward. If, as seems more likely, it is a new case, St. James may have added it as an afterthought on finding that his warnings had been chiefly against over-activity, too much vehemence, too much eagerness to teach. In ver. 14 he had begun to speak of our duty towards the sick in body; in ver. 16 he had extended this into a general precept as to mutual help in spiritual matters; in ver. 19 he turns to the case of the backsliders. Even here nothing is said as to the duty of the Church to go out into all the world and preach the Gospel to every creature; nothing is said as to making proselytes from the Gentiles or even from the unbelieving Jews. It is the exhortation of the Bishop, whose aim is the reformation and improvement of the Church, not of the Apostle, whose aim is the extension of the Church by the diffusion of the faith.

In my note I have pointed out that the words of ver. 20, 'he who recalls an erring brother saves (or 'will save') his soul from death and will be the means of blotting out many sins' are capable of two interpretations, according to the reference we give to 'his.' I have mentioned some difficulties which lie in the way of our taking 'his' to refer to the sinner, and have shown that it was not uncommon with Jewish writers to hold forth the prospect of salvation and forgiveness of sins, as an inducement to certain kinds of right conduct, such as alms-giving. I postponed to the present occasion the consideration of the question whether it was possible that St. James should have adopted a similar mode of speaking. We cannot, of course, imagine that he would ever have dreamt of a man's being able to atone for his own sins by his assiduity in calling others to repentance. Such a notion is forbidden, not less by our Lord's words recorded in Matt. vii. 20–22 'Many will say to me in that day, Lord, have we not prophesied in thy name? . . . then will I profess unto them, I never knew you; depart from me, ye that work iniquity,' and by the words of St. Paul in 1 Cor. xiii. 1–3, 'Though I speak with the tongues of men and angels . . . though I have the gift of prophecy . . . though I have all faith . . . though I give my body to be burnt, and have not charity, it profiteth me nothing,' and in ch. ix. 26, 27 'I keep under my body and bring it into subjection, lest having preached to others, I myself should be a castaway,'—than by the words of St. James himself, 'Be not many masters, knowing that we shall receive the greater condemnation,' and by his constant depreciation of mere speaking, unaccompanied by deeds and practice. St. James has told us already how the soul is saved (i. 21–25): not by preaching to others, but by receiving in meekness the ingrafted word, and continuing in the perfect law of liberty. What in fact could be more contemptible in itself and more fatal to any good influence, than for a man to urge upon others a course which he has determined not to follow himself, and expect to be rewarded for *their* faith and works, when he has no faith or works of his own? The passages from the N.T. quoted in the notes do not contemplate the possibility of a preacher of righteousness, who has still to be saved from his sins. It is only in the Apocrypha that we find such unchristian sentiments as 'Almsgiving saves from death and purges away all sins' (Tobit xii. 9). The other quotations are simply encouragements to sincere but sluggish workers, to throw more energy into their work. It is allowable to say 'you have done much evil in the past, try and make up for it by the good you do in the future,' or 'remember that you are appointed by God to be a teacher or an elder: it is not enough for you to keep yourself unspotted in the world: you must bring your influence to bear on others, or you will be found wanting at last': but it is not in accordance with Christian truth to say 'If you make a convert, you will save your own soul.' It appears therefore that we must fall back on the other interpretation understanding 'his' of the sinner. The chief difficulty in this interpretation is that the apodosis seems to add so little to the protasis. 'Conversion' to us already implies 'saving the soul'; but this need not have been so to the first readers of the Epistle. To them the words may have meant 'However many sins the wanderer has been guilty of, still, if he turns, he will be saved from the death he has deserved, and all his sins will be forgiven.' We can imagine that such a promise might have been a great encouragement to those who were dispirited at the state of the backsliders in the church to which they belonged, and doubted whether it was possible to renew them again unto repentance.

INDEX OF GREEK WORDS

(*a*) words not used by any writer previous to St. James.
(*b*) not used in this sense before St. James.
(*c*) not used by any other N.T. writer.
(*d*) not used in the Septuagint (including Apocrypha).
(*e*) post-Aristotelian.
(*Add.*) see Addenda after Preface.

A

B

E

Z

H

Θ

Ι

Π

T

Υ

Φ

X

INDEX OF SUBJECTS

twin brooks series

BOOKS IN THE SERIES

THE ACTS OF THE APOSTLES .... Richard B. Rackham
APOSTOLIC AND POST-APOSTOLIC TIMES (Goppelt) .... Robert A. Guelich, tr.
THE APOSTOLIC FATHERS .... J. B. Lightfoot
THE ATONEMENT OF CHRIST .... Francis Turrettin
THE AUTHORITY OF THE OLD TESTAMENT .... John Bright
BACKGROUNDS TO DISPENSATIONALISM .... Clarence B. Bass
BASIC CHRISTIAN DOCTRINES .... Carl F. H. Henry
THE BASIC IDEAS OF CALVINISM .... H. Henry Meeter
THE CALVINISTIC CONCEPT OF CULTURE .... H. Van Til
CHRISTIAN APPROACH TO PHILOSOPHY .... W. C. Young
CHRISTIAN PERSONAL ETHICS .... Carl F. H. Henry
COMMENTARY ON DANIEL (Jerome) .... Gleason L. Archer, Jr., tr.
THE DAYS OF HIS FLESH .... David Smith
DISCIPLING THE NATIONS .... Richard DeRidder
THE DOCTRINE OF GOD .... Herman Bavinck
EDUCATIONAL IDEALS IN THE ANCIENT WORLD .... Wm. Barclay
THE EPISTLE OF JAMES .... Joseph B. Mayor
EUSEBIUS' ECCLESIASTICAL HISTORY
FUNDAMENTALS OF THE FAITH .... Carl F. H. Henry, ed.
GOD-CENTERED EVANGELISM .... R. B. Kuiper
GENERAL PHILOSOPHY .... D. Elton Trueblood
THE GRACE OF LAW .... Ernest F. Kevan
THE HIGHER CRITICISM OF THE PENTATEUCH .... William Henry Green
THE HISTORY OF CHRISTIAN DOCTRINES .... Louis Berkhof
THE HISTORY OF DOCTRINES .... Reinhold Seeberg
THE HISTORY OF THE JEWISH NATION .... Alfred Edersheim
HISTORY OF PREACHING .... E. C. Dargan
LIGHT FROM THE ANCIENT EAST .... Adolf Deissmann
NOTES ON THE MIRACLES OF OUR LORD .... R. C. Trench
NOTES ON THE PARABLES OF OUR LORD .... R. C. Trench
OUR REASONABLE FAITH (Bavinck) .... Henry Zylstra, tr.
PAUL, APOSTLE OF LIBERTY .... R. N. Longnecker
PHILOSOPHY OF RELIGION .... D. Elton Trueblood
PROPHETS AND THE PROMISE .... W. J. Beecher
REASONS FOR FAITH .... John H. Gerstner
THE REFORMATION .... Hans J. Hillebrand, ed.
REFORMED DOGMATICS (Wollebius, Voetius, Turretin) .... J. Beardslee, ed., tr.
REFORMED DOGMATICS .... Heinrich Heppe
REVELATION AND INSPIRATION .... James Orr
REVELATION AND THE BIBLE .... Carl F. H. Henry
ROMAN SOCIETY AND ROMAN LAW IN THE NEW TESTAMENT .... A. N. Sherwin-White
THE ROOT OF FUNDAMENTALISM .... Ernest R. Sandeen
THE SERVANT-MESSIAH .... T. W. Manson
STORY OF RELIGION IN AMERICA .... Wm. W. Sweet
THE TESTS OF LIFE (third edition) .... Robert Law
THEOLOGY OF THE MAJOR SECTS .... John H. Gerstner
VARIETIES OF CHRISTIAN APOLOGETICS .... B. Ramm
THE VOYAGE AND SHIPWRECK OF ST. PAUL (fourth edition) .... James Smith
THE VIRGIN BIRTH .... J. G. Machen